A DICTIONARY OF
BIBLICAL INTERPRETATION

A
DICTIONARY
OF
BIBLICAL
INTERPRETATION

EDITED BY

R. J. COGGINS

AND

J. L. HOULDEN

SCM PRESS
London

TRINITY PRESS INTERNATIONAL
Philadelphia

First published 1990

SCM Press
26–30 Tottenham Road
London N1 4BZ

Trinity Press International
3725 Chestnut Street
Philadelphia, Pa. 19104

British Library Cataloguing in Publication Data

A dictionary of biblical interpretation.
1. Bible. Interpretation
    I. Coggin, R. J. (Richard James), *1929–*
    II. Houlden, J. L. (James Leslie), *1929–*
    220.6

    ISBN 0–334–00294–X

Library of Congress Cataloguing-in-Publication Data

A Dictionary of Biblical interpretation/edited by R. J. Coggins and
J. L. Houlden.
    p.   cm.
    ISBN 0–334–00294–X
    1. Bible—Dictionaries.   2. Bible—Hermeneutics—Dictionaries.
3. Bible—Criticism, interpretation, etc.—History—Dictionaries,
I. Coggins, R. J., *1929–* .   II. Houlden, J. L. (James Leslie)
BS440.D494   1990
220.3—dc20   *89–28178*

Printed in Great Britain by
Richard Clay Ltd, Bungay, Suffolk

PREFACE

Why *A Dictionary of Biblical Interpretation*, when so many 'Bible dictionaries' are available? Though some information of the kind to be found in those useful works also appears here, our concern has been different, dealing more with the wide range of matters relating to the interpretation of the Bible than its content or the history and cultures surrounding its writings.

The fact that a need has come to be felt for such a dictionary reflects a movement of thought that is partly a shift of interest towards matters of interpretation, but also, and perhaps more significantly, a certain loss of confidence. Where once it was widely assumed that the meaning of the Bible as a whole and in its constituent parts was self-evident to the careful reader, there is now a wider awareness that 'interpretation' is not a task simply additional to the mere 'reading' or 'use' of the Bible, seen as pure and simple in themselves; nor is it something reserved for the few who specialize in it, or perhaps church authorities who pronounce on it; nor yet is it something sinister, the attempt to 'put something over' on readers who would do better without it. No, interpretation is inescapable, inherent in the very act of reading a text, an act which sets up a 'conversation' between text and reader, and perhaps, where a tradition is involved, a multiplicity of conversations stretching back maybe for centuries. This wider awareness has led, among other things, to an explosion of technical terms in this area, and an ever-widening range of methods and techniques. This dictionary sets out to act as an aid to those who wish to enter a territory which may appear something of a maze.

'It is surprising in a dictionary that attempts to be comprehensive to find no article on . . .' If it would be of help to reviewers who feel tempted to lament along these lines, we can say at once that we fully share the regret. Indeed, we could readily supply a list of individuals and themes that we would have wished to include. And our list of regretted exclusions has grown steadily longer as we have reflected upon the material received. We knew before we started that many aspects of interpretation would be involved; neither of us had really appreciated the full extent of the ways in which the Bible has been perceived, or the importance it has had in different areas of religious and cultural life. To have edited this volume has been an education in itself.

That said, some further clarification is called for as to the basis of selection. In a very small number of instances omission is due to the fact that some scholars from whom we were hoping for contributions were unable to provide them, and there is a limit to the time that a whole project can be held up while awaiting a small number of articles. (But we should hasten to add that the overwhelming majority of those whom we approached were most co-operative and prompt in their response, even if only one scholar signified his agreement to take part by actually sending the article he was asked for, virtually by return of post!)

The subjects that have been covered fall into a number of categories: the biblical books; schools, movements and periods in the history of interpretation; technical terms, approaches and methods used in interpretation. All these are topics which are the concerns of the professional biblical scholar, and we hope that there is material here for those whose interests are of that kind. But we hope that the readership of this book will reflect the fact that the interpretation of the Bible has ranged more widely; it soon became clear that we must touch on the fields of literature and painting and music, even if the articles on these topics can only give a glimpse of the riches that are available. We should have liked to go further and have a range of articles on 'the Bible and . . .': politics, and education, and . . . and a whole host of different themes. Space limitations ruled out that kind of ambition.

In all cases where it was appropriate, we have asked contributors to keep in mind the role their topic has played in the history of interpretation, and the way it has itself been interpreted over the years. There are many fascinating and often surprising by-ways in biblical interpretation – old fashions long forgotten and corners of life and culture which the Bible has touched but which rarely figure in the normal view of biblical studies. We have sought to make it possible for readers to be directed to such matters, even if only by brief allusion. Our hope is that, like all the best dictionaries, this work will suck its readers into itself, sending them scurrying to other pages and other works, drawing them into whole new and worthwhile fields of exploration. A dictionary is a point of entry into a world, in this case one that is full of riches, some wildly exotic, others more workaday, but all of significance in relation to our culture in its past or its present.

By and large we have kept articles on individuals to a minimum. Those who have been included are not necessarily the most important, but are often those who fitted into no tidy category, or who were felt to have exercised an influence which was not as widely perceived as it should be. For others, we hope that the admittedly selective index will provide adequate guidance as to where their importance lay. The index of biblical references, similarly, makes no claim to be exhaustive, but should guide its user to those contexts in which a passage of interest has received detailed or significant attention.

Another important way of obtaining additional information, or a different angle on a related topic, is by the asterisks (*) found in virtually every article in the dictionary. These refer to other articles, usually by their specific title; at times we have trusted the reader to exercise judgment, and to work out that, say, 'structure'* invites reference to the article 'Structuralism'. The only exception to this general rule relates to the actual names of biblical books, which have not been asterisked; each of them is the subject of an article, occasionally combined with another related book (e.g. Ezra–Nehemiah; II Peter and Jude). Normally only the first such cross-reference in an article has been asterisked.

There are yet other in-built means of acquiring additional information. Most articles have a short list of further reading bearing on the topic discussed, either appended or embodied in their text. This should serve to amplify points discussed in the article or call attention to other aspects which could not be considered in the available space. Additional reading is of works in English, save in those cases where the only really satisfactory discussion of a topic was judged to be in German or French.

Besides the suggestions for further reading, articles have proposals to 'See also' other articles in the dictionary as a means of acquiring additional or related insights. Not all our contributors agree with one another; and these cross-references will often provide the reader with a different angle on the same subject, or information about a related theme which should be of interest.

One problem area for the editors related to modes of reference. In the Christian tradition the larger part of the Bible has for many centuries been referred to as the 'Old Testament', but this represents a specifically Christian manner of interpretation, and one of our concerns has been to avoid Christian triumphalism and give due weight to Jewish interpretation. In the end we have retained OT and NT, as being the most familiar form of reference, not least because alternatives such as 'Hebrew Bible' are not yet generally established; but we are aware that in years to come this may look like an old-fashioned and perhaps rather patronizing decision. The same is true with dates; we have stuck with BC/AD rather than BCE/CE, for the same reason and with the same qualms as those just described.

It remains only to express our thanks: to those scholars with whom we discussed the initial plan of the book, and who made many constructive suggestions which we were happy to incorporate; to the contributors, of course, for their co-operation, and readiness to explain patiently to obtuse editors the reasons why they felt their theme had to be dealt with in just that way, and why proposals for reducing the length of an article had to be resisted; to Sonia Copeland and others at King's College, London, for administrative and secretarial help; to Margaret Lydamore at the Press, who bore the brunt of our complaints and kept our editorial feet from straying too far out of the prescribed path; and to John Bowden, whose idea the book originally was, and whose enthusiasm and drive have kept us at it. Now it is over to you, the reader.

R. J. COGGINS

J. L. HOULDEN

CONTRIBUTORS

Kenneth T. Aitken, *Lecturer in Hebrew and Semitic Studies, University of Aberdeen.* **Proverbs**

Loveday Alexander, *Lecturer in New Testament, Department of Biblical Studies, University of Sheffield.* **Aretalogy**

Philip S. Alexander, *Senior Lecturer in Jewish Studies, University of Manchester.* **Aqedah; Midrash; Rabbi, Rabbinism; Shekinah**

G. W. Anderson, *Professor Emeritus of Hebrew and Old Testament Studies, University of Edinburgh.* **Scandinavian Old Testament Scholarship**

Graeme Auld, *Senior Lecturer in Old Testament Studies, University of Edinburgh.* **Word of God**

John Baggley, *Team Rector, Bicester Area Team Ministry.* **Icons**

Edward Ball, *Lecturer in Theology, University of Nottingham.*
Covenant; Eye-Witness; Nahum; Smith, W. Robertson; Zephaniah

Margaret Barker, **Pseudonymity**

John Barton, *University Lecturer in Theology, and Fellow of St Cross College, Oxford.* **Authority of Scripture; Canon; Eisegesis; Oracle; Prophets and Prophecy; Verbal Inspiration**

Stephen C. Barton, *Lecturer in New Testament, Department of Theology, University of Durham.* **Community; Ethos; Mystery Cults**

Christina A. Baxter, *Dean, St John's College, Nottingham.* **Barth, K.**

J. Neville Birdsall, *Emeritus Professor of New Testament Studies and Textual Criticism, University of Birmingham.* **Harmony; Manuscripts; Palaeography; Text of the Bible; Textual Criticism (New Testament)**

† Anders Jørgen Bjørndalen, *late Professor, Free Faculty of Theology, University of Norway.* **Allegory**

M. G. Brett, *Lecturer in Old Testament, Lincoln Theological College.* **Intratextuality**

S. P. Brock, *University Lecturer in Aramaic and Syriac and Fellow of Wolfson College, Oxford.* **Syriac Tradition**

George J. Brooke, *Lecturer in Intertestamental Literature, University of Manchester.* **Dead Sea Scrolls; Florilegia; *Pesher***

Raymond E. Brown, SS, *Auburn Distinguished Professor of Biblical Studies, Union Theological Seminary.* **Infancy Narratives**

Richard A. Burridge, *The Lazenby Chaplain, University of Exeter.* **Gospel**

Averil Cameron, *Professor of Late Antique and Byzantine Studies, King's College, London.* **Women in Early Christian Interpretation**

Robert P. Carroll, *Reader in Biblical Studies, University of Glasgow.* **Amos; Authorship; Cognitive Dissonance; Commentary (Old Testament); Duhm, B.; Eschatology; Habakkuk; Ideology; Irony; Jeremiah; Joel; Micah; Obadiah; Torrey, C. C.**

David Catchpole, *St Luke's Foundation Professor of Theological Studies, University of Exeter.* **Beatitudes**

Henry Chadwick, *Master of Peterhouse, Cambridge.* **Augustine**

Ruth Chavasse, *Lecturer in Ecclesiastical History, King's College, London.*
Erasmus

Peter Clarke, *Lecturer in the History and Sociology of Religion, King's College, London.* **New Religious Movements**

R. E. Clements, *Samuel Davidson Professor of Old Testament Studies, King's College, London.* **Abraham; Isaiah; Messiah; Pentateuch, Pentateuchal Criticism**

David J. A. Clines, *Professor of Biblical Studies, University of Sheffield.* **Holistic Interpretation**

R. J. Coggins, *Senior Lecturer in Old Testament Studies, King's College, London.* **American Interpretation (Old Testament); Babylon; Chronicles; David; Euphemism; Ezra-Nehemiah; Holy Book; Israel, History of; Samaritans; Scribes; Word of God; Writings**

Dan Cohn-Sherbok, *Director, Centre for the Study of Religion and Society, University of Kent.* **Liberation Theology**

Mark Corner, *former Lecturer in Religious Studies, University of Newcastle, and freelance writer.* **Fundamentalism**

John M. Court, *Senior Lecturer in Theology and Religious Studies, University of Kent.* **Millenarianism; Revelation of John**

A. H. W. Curtis, *Lecturer in Old Testament Studies, University of Manchester.* **Aetiology; Genesis; Psalms; Theological Geography; Theophany**

Margaret Davies, *Lecturer in the Department of Theology and Religious Studies, University of Bristol.* **Exegesis; Genre; Literary Criticism; Reader-Response Criticism**

Philip R. Davies, *Senior Lecturer in Old Testament, University of Sheffield.* **Apocrypha; Daniel**

John Day, *University Lecturer in Old Testament, and Fellow and Tutor of Lady Margaret Hall, Oxford.* **Creation Narratives**

T. J. Deidun, *Lecturer in New Testament Studies, Heythrop College, University of London.* **Galatians; Romans**

John A. H. Dempster, *Resource Librarian, Strathclyde Regional Council.* **Hastings, J.**

Jennifer Dines, CSA, *Lecturer in Old Testament, Heythrop College, University of London.* **Septuagint**

F. Gerald Downing, *Vice-Principal, The Northern Ordination Course, Manchester.* **Analogy; Apology, Apologetic; Background and Content; Criteria; Cynics; Fact; Hellenism; Hellenistic Writers; Historical-Critical Method; Revelation**

John Drury, *Dean, King's College, Cambridge.* **Luke, Gospel of; Parable; Symbol**

James D. G. Dunn, *Professor of Divinity, University of Durham.* **Christology, New Testament; Diversity; Judaizers**

Alan Dunstan, *Canon Residentiary and Precentor of Gloucester Cathedral.* **Hymnody**

John Eaton, *Reader in Old Testament Studies, University of Birmingham.* **Kingship**

Paul Ellingworth, *Translation Consultant, United Bible Societies, and Honorary Lecturer, University of Aberdeen.* **Translations (Modern)**

Ieuan Ellis, *Fellow, University of Hull.* **English Interpretation; *Essays and Reviews*; Homily; *Lux Mundi***

Grace I. Emmerson, *Visiting Lecturer, Department of Theology, University of Birmingham.* **Esther; Hosea; Jonah; Paronomasia; Syntax; Translation, Problems of**

Philip F. Esler, *Barrister of the New South Wales Supreme Court, and part-time Lecturer in Religious Studies and Divinity, University of Sydney.* **Acts of the Apostles**

C. F. Evans, *Professor Emeritus of New Testament Studies, University of London.* **Resurrection**

G. R. Evans, *University Lecturer in History, and Fellow of Fitzwillian College, Cambridge.* **Mediaeval Interpretation**

Owen E. Evans, *formerly Senior Lecturer in Biblical Studies, University College of North Wales, Bangor.* **Dodd, C. H.; Jeremias, J.**

J. C. Fenton, *Canon of Christ Church, Oxford.* **Resurrection Narratives**

Joseph A. Fitzmyer, SJ, *Professor Emeritus, Catholic University of America.*
  Semitisms
David F. Ford, *Lecturer in Theology, University of Birmingham.*
  Narrative Theology
Birger Gerhardsson, *Professor of Exegetical Theology, Lund University.*
  Oral Tradition (New Testament)
John Goldingay, *Principal, St John's College, Nottingham.*
  Inspiration; Salvation History; Theology (Old Testament)
Friedemann W. Golka, *Professor of Old Testament Theology, University of Olden-
  burg, West Germany.* **German Old Testament Scholarship**
R. P. Gordon, *University Lecturer in Old Testament and Intertestamental Studies,
  and Fellow of St Edmund's College, Cambridge.* **Samuel**
Lester L. Grabbe, *Head of Theology Department, University of Hull.*
  Jewish Background to the New Testament; Josephus
Stuart George Hall, *Professor of Ecclesiastical History, King's College, London.*
  Gnosticism; Marcion; Nag Hammadi; Tertullian
Daniel W. Hardy, *Van Mildert Professor of Divinity, University of Durham, and
  Canon Residentiary, Durham Cathedral.* **Systematic Theology**
C. T. R. Hayward, *Lecturer in Old Testament, University of Birmingham.*
  Aramaisms; Rewritten Bible; Targum
John F. Healey, *Lecturer in Semitic Studies, University of Manchester.* **Ugarit**
Avril Henry, *Reader in English Mediaeval Literature, University of Exeter.*
  Biblia Pauperum
Colin Hickling, *Vicar of Arksey, Doncaster.*
  Corinthian Correspondence; Introduction
W. J. Hollenweger, *Professor of Mission, University of Birmingham.*
  Black Christian Interpretation
Morna D. Hooker, *Lady Margaret Professor Divinity, University of Cambridge.*
  Kingdom of God
Brian Horne, *Lecturer in Christian Doctrine, King's College, London.*
  Dante; Poetry, English
J. L. Houlden, *Professor of Theology, King's College, London.* **Christian Interpreta-
  tion of the Old Testament; Commentary (New Testament); David; Ethics (New
  Testament); Hymns (New Testament); John the Baptist; John, Gospel of; Lec-
  tionary Interpretation (New Testament); Passion Narratives; Peter; Philippians**
Jeremy Hughes, *Kennicott Hebrew Fellow, University of Oxford.*
  Chronology; Genealogies
Alastair G. Hunter, *Lecturer in Hebrew and Old Testament Studies, University of
  Glasgow.* **Canonical Criticism; Other Faiths**
Bernard S. Jackson, *Queen Victoria Professor of Law, University of Liverpool.* **Law**
Werner G. Jeanrond, *Lecturer in Theology, Trinity College, Dublin.* **Hermeneutics**
William Johnstone, *Head of Department of Hebrew and Semitic Languages, Univer-
  sity of Aberdeen.* **Ancient Near Eastern World; Exodus; Moses**
G. Lloyd Jones, *Dean, School of Theology, University College of North Wales,
  Bangor.* **Translations (to the KJV)**
Paul Joyce, *Lecturer in Old Testament Studies, University of Birmingham.* **Ezekiel**
Howard Clark Kee, *William Goodwin Aurelio Professor of Biblical Studies Emeritus,
  Boston University.* **Magic; Miracle in the Biblical World**
Patricia G. Kirkpatrick, *Assistant Professor of Old Testament Studies and Hebrew
  Language, McGill University.* **Legend; Saga**
Michael A. Knibb, *Professor of Old Testament Studies, King's College, London.*
  Pseudepigrapha
L. Kreitzer, *Tutor of New Testament, Regent's Park College, Oxford.*
  Adam; Colossians and Philemon; Ephesians; Thessalonians

W. G. Lambert, *Professor of Assyriology, University of Birmingham.*
Ancient Near Eastern Interpretation; Etymology, Ancient Near Eastern
Sophie Laws, *Part-time Fellow, Regent's College, London.*
James; Peter, First; Peter, Second, and Jude
Judith M. Lieu, *Lecturer in Christian Origins and Early Judaism, King's College, London.* **Johannine Epistles; Pharisees and Scribes**
Barnabas Lindars, SSF, *Rylands Professor of Biblical Criticism and Exegesis, University of Manchester.* **Proof Texts; Son of Man; *Testimonia*; Use of the Old Testament in the New Testament**
Raphael Loewe, *Goldsmid Professor of Hebrew (Emeritus), University College, London.* **Jewish Exegesis**
Andrew Louth, *Reader in Religious Studies, Goldsmith's College, University of London.* **Allegorical Interpretation; Mysticism**
Dieter Lührmann, *Professor of New Testament Studies, University of Marburg.* **Logion; Lohmeyer, E.; Wrede, W.**
Hyam Maccoby, *Lecturer and Fellow of Leo Baeck College, London.* **Antisemitism**
Margaret Y. MacDonald, *Assistant Professor of Theology, St Francis Xavier University, Nova Scotia.* **Early Catholicism**
J. I. H. McDonald, *Lecturer in Christian Ethics and New Testament Studies, University of Edinburgh.* **Hermeneutical Circle; Rhetorical Criticism; Synchronic Exegesis**
A. E. McGrath, *Lecturer at Wycliffe Hall, Oxford.* **Luther; Reformation**
Brian McNeil, *Parish priest, Hamar, Norway. Sensus Plenior*; **Typology**
Ralph P. Martin, *Associate Professor, Biblical Studies Department, University of Sheffield.* **American Interpretation (New Testament)**
Rex Mason, *Senior Tutor, Regent's Park College, Oxford.*
Haggai; Inner-Biblical Exegesis; Malachi; Zechariah
A. D. H. Mayes, *Associate Professor of Hebrew, Trinity College, Dublin.*
Deuteronomistic History; Deuteronomy; Joshua; Judges
S. E. Medcalf, *Reader in English, University of Sussex.* **Comedy**
Deborah F. Middleton, *Lecturer in Religious Studies, University of Lancaster.*
Feminist Interpretation
David K. Miell, *Team Vicar, Walton LEP, Milton Keynes.*
Psychological Interpretation
A. R. Millard, *Rankin Reader in Hebrew and Ancient Semitic Languages, University of Liverpool.*
Writing Materials (Old Testament); Writing and Transmitting Texts
J. Maxwell Miller, *Director, Graduate Studies in Religion, Emory University, Atlanta.* **Archaeology (Old Testament)**
Robert Morgan, *Priest-in-Charge, Sandford-on-Thames, and Fellow of Linacre College, Oxford.* **Biblical Theology; Bultmann, R.; Historicism; History of Religions School; Reimarus, H. S.; *Sachkritik*; Strauss, D. F.; Tendency Criticism; Theology (New Testament); Tübingen School**
Harry Mowvley, *formerly Deputy Principal, Bristol Baptist College.*
Lexicons and Concordances
John Muddiman, *Lecturer in Theology, University of Nottingham.*
Evangelist; Form Criticism; Kerygma
J. Murphy-O'Connor, *Professor of New Testament, Ecole Biblique et Archéologique Française, Jerusalem.* **Archaeology (New Testament)**
R. P. R. Murray, SJ, *Senior Research Fellow, Heythrop College, University of London.* **Jewish Christianity**
Julia Neuberger, *Visiting Fellow, King's Fund Institute.* **Jerusalem**
D. E. Nineham, *formerly Warden of Keeble College, Oxford.* **Cadbury, H. J.; Cultural Relativism; Demythologization; Lightfoot, R. H.; Schweitzer, A.**

R. A. Norris, *Professor of Church History, Union Theological Seminary.*
Antiochene Interpretation
J. L. North, *Barnaby Lecturer in New Testament Studies, University of Hull.*
Vulgate
Richard Parsons, *Vicar of Hendon, Diocese of London.* **Hoskyns, E. C.**
R. A. Piper, *Lecturer in New Testament Language and Literature, University of St Andrews.* **New Hermeneutic; Synopsis; Trajectory**
J. R. Porter, *Professor Emeritus, University of Exeter.* **Calendars; Cultic Interpretation; Folklore; Leviticus; Myth and Ritual; Numbers; Ruth**
Brian G. Powley, *Superintendent Minister, York (South) Methodist Circuit.* **Harnack, A. von; Westcott, Lightfoot and Hort**
Iain W. Provan, *Lecturer in Hebrew and Old Testament Studies, University of Edinburgh.* **Kings; Lamentations**
Bernard M. G. Reardon, *formerly Reader and Head of the Department of Religious Studies, University of Newcastle upon Tyne.* **Catholic Modernism; Liberalism**
D. B. Redford, *Professor, Department of Near Eastern Studies, University of Toronto.* **Egypt**
Christine Rees, *Lecturer in English, King's College, London.* **Metaphysical Poets**
S. C. Reif, *Head of the Oriental Division and Director of the Genizah Research Unit, Cambridge University Library.* **Genizah**
John Riches, *Senior Lecturer, Department of Biblical Studies, University of Glasgow.* **Methodology**
Andrew Rippin, *Associate Professor, Religious Studies, University of Calgary.* **Muslim Interpretation**
B. P. Robinson, *Lecturer in Sacred Scripture, Ushaw College, Durham.* **Anthropomorphism; Tetragrammaton**
Cyril S. Rodd, *Reader in Theology and Religious Studies, Roehampton Institute of Higher Education.* **Computers and the Bible; Ethics (Old Testament); Sociology and Social Anthropology**
J. W. Rogerson, *Professor and Head of the Department of Biblical Studies, University of Sheffield.*
Anthropology; Biblical Criticism; De Wette, W. M. L.; Holy, The; Myth
Charlotte Roueché, *Lecturer in Byzantine Language and Literature, King's College, London.* **Epigraphy**
Christopher Rowland, *University Lecturer in Divinity, and Dean of Jesus College, Cambridge.* **Apocalyptic; Marxist Interpretation; Materialist Interpretation; *Merkabah* Mysticism; Parousia**
Robert B. Salters, *Lecturer in Hebrew and Old Testament, University of St Andrews.* **Masoretic Text; Textual Criticism (Old Testament)**
John F. A. Sawyer, *Head of the Department of Religious Studies, University of Newcastle upon Tyne.*
Etymology; Interpretation, History of; Linguistics; Semantics
C. Schwöbel, *Lecturer in Systematic Theology, King's College, London.* **Calvin**
Ulrich Simon, *Emeritus Professor of Christian Literature, King's College, London.* **Blake, W.; Herder, J. von; Job; Song of Songs**
Janet Martin Soskice, *Lecturer in the Faculty of Theology and Religious Studies, University of Cambridge.* **Figures of Speech; Metaphor**
Graham N. Stanton, *Professor of New Testament Studies, King's College, London.* **Historical Jesus; Matthew, Gospel of; Sermon on the Mount**
Kenneth Stevenson, *Rector of Holy Trinity and St Mary's, Guildford, and Member of the Church of England Liturgical Commission.*
Lectionary; Liturgy, Use of the Bible in; Lord's Prayer
Mark W. G. Stibbe, *Minister, St Helen's Church, Stapleford, Nottingham.* **Semiotics; Structuralism**

Stanley K. Stowers, *Professor of Religious Studies, Brown University, Providence, Rhode Island.* **Epistle**

Roderick Swanston, *Senior Lecturer in History and Analysis, Royal College of Music, and Academic Adviser to the Birkbeck College (London) Centre for Extra-Mural Studies.* **Music, The Bible in**

John Sweet, *University Lecturer in Divinity, and Fellow and Dean of Chapel, Selwyn College, Cambridge.* **Interpretation of the Miraculous**

Robert C. Tannehill, *Professor of New Testament, Methodist Theological School in Ohio.* **Narrative Criticism**

William R. Telford, *Lecturer in Religious Studies, University of Newcastle upon Tune.* **Mark, Gospel of**

Anthony C. Thiselton, *Principal of St John's College, University of Durham.* **Meaning**

Christine Trevett, *Teacher of Biblical Studies, Department of Religious Studies, University of Wales College of Cardiff.* **Apostolic Fathers; Ireanaeus; Papias**

C. M. Tuckett, *Senior Lecturer in New Testament Studies, University of Manchester.* **Messianic Secret; Redaction Criticism; Source Criticism; Synoptic Problem**

Pamela Tudor-Craig, *Art historian and author.* **Art, The Bible in**

Francis Watson, *Lecturer in New Testament Studies, King's College, London.* **Christology, Modern; Coleridge, S. T.; Deism; Enlightenment; Philosophy**

Wilfred G. E. Watson, *Visiting Professor, University of Barcelona.* **Poetry, Hebrew; Philology**

David V. Way, *Tutor in New Testament, Salisbury and Wells Theological College.* **Tradition, History of**

M. P. Weitzman, *Lecturer, Department of Hebrew and Jewish Studies, University College, London.* **Talmud**

R. N. Whybray, *Emeritus Professor of Hebrew and Old Testament Studies, University of Hull.* **Ecclesiastes; Servant Songs; Wisdom Literature**

R. Williamson, *Senior Lecturer in Religious Studies, University of Leeds.* **Hebrews; Philo**

James Welford Woodward, *Chaplain to the Bishop of Oxford.* **Pastoral Care**

Frances Young, *Edward Cadbury Professor of Theology, University of Birmingham.* **Alexandrian Interpretation; Creed; Eusebius; Literal Meaning; Logos; Origen; Patristic Christology; Rhetoric; Soteriology; Spiritual Meaning**

J. A. Ziesler, *Senior Lecturer in Theology, University of Bristol.* **Pastoral Epistles; Paul**

ABBREVIATIONS

AAR	American Academy of Religion
AOAT	Alter Orient und Altes Testament
ASTI	*Annual of the Swedish Theological Institute* (*in Jerusalem*)
ATD	Das Alte Testament Deutsch
AV	Authorized Version of the Bible
BJRL	*Bulletin of the John Rylands Library*
BK	Biblischer Kommentar, Neukirchen
BK.AT	– Altes Testament
BK.NT	– Neues Testament
BWANT	Beiträge zur Wissenschaft vom Alten und Neuen Testament
BZAW	Beihefte zur Zeitschrift für die alttestamentliche Wissenschaft
CB	Coniectanea biblica
CBQ	Catholic Biblical Quarterly
ET	English Translation
ET	*The Expository Times*
EV	English Version
HJ	*Heythrop Journal*
HTR	*Harvard Theological Review*
IBS	*Irish Biblical Studies*
ICC	International Critical Commentary
IDB	*The Interpreters Dictionary of the Bible*
IDB – SV	– Supplementary Volume
IEJ	*The Israel Exploration Journal*
JAOS	*Journal of the American Oriental Society*
JBL	*Journal of Biblical Literature*
JJS	*Journal of Jewish Studies*
JSJ	*Journal for the Study of Judaism*
JSNT	*Journal for the Study of the New Testament*
JSOT	*Journal for the Study of the Old Testament*
JSOT – SS	– Supplement Studies
JSP	*Journal of Social Psychology*
JSS	*Journal of Semitic Studies*
JTS	*Journal of Theological Studies*
KJV	King James Version of the Bible
MAMA	Monumenta Asiae minoris antiqua
NCB	New Century Bible
NEB	New English Bible
OED	Oxford English Dictionary
OTS	Oudtestamentische studien, Leiden
SB	*Studia Biblica*
NT	*Novum Testamentum*
NTS	*New Testament Studies*
PG	Patrologiae Graeca, ed. J. P. Migne
PL	Patrologiae Latina, ed. J. P. Migne
RDK	Reallexikon zur deutschen Kunstgeschichte
RevExp	*Review and Expositor*

RGG	*Die Religion in Geschichte und Gegenwart*
RS	*Religious Studies*
R S V	Revised Standard Version of the Bible
R V	Revised Version of the Bible
SHS	*Speculum Humanae Salvationis*
SJT	*Scottish Journal of Theology*
TDNT	*Theological Dictionary of the New Testament*
TDOT	*Theological Dictionary of the Old Testament*
T U	Texte und Untersuchungen zur Geschichte der altchristlichen Literatur
TWNT	*Theologisches Worterbuch zum Alten Testament*
VT	*Vetus Testamentum*
VT – S	– Supplement
ZAW	*Zeitschrift für die alttestamentliche Wissenschaft*
ZTK	*Zeitschrift für Theologie und Kirche*

Abraham

Abram appears in the book of Genesis as a son of Terah (Gen. 11.26f.) who migrated westwards from Ur of the Chaldeans to go to the land of Canaan, but who settled temporarily in Haran (Gen. 11.31). Subsequently, by divine command (Gen. 12.1), Abram left Haran to go to the land designated by God under the assurance that his descendants would become a great nation, would possess this land, and would become a source of blessing to other families (=clans) of the land (Gen. 12.1–3). His name is later changed to Abraham by divine revelation as a signification of the role he is to fulfil as the exalted ancestor of many nations (Gen. 17.5). The two forms are, however, widely regarded by scholars as dialectical variations of the same name. Its form is typical of a number of similar name formations which consist of a noun, reflecting a divine title, and a verb. The meaning is then 'The father is exalted'.

Abraham is presented in Genesis as the greatest and most prominent of the patriarchal figures of Israel's history. Narratives concerning his adventures and experiences appear in Gen. 12.1–25.8 and his life-span is recorded as 175 years (Gen. 25.7). The promise made by God to Abraham that his descendants would inherit the land of Canaan (Gen. 12.1–4; 15.18–21) is affirmed by a solemn covenant* (Gen. 15.17f., a passage ascribed to JE in literary source criticism*). This promise is thereafter ratified by a further covenant in which Abraham is promised that he will become the father, not of one nation, but of a multitude of nations (Gen. 17.1–8, P). The sign of this (second) covenant is the practice of circumcision upon all male infants on the eighth day after birth (Gen. 17.9–14, P). The initial consequence of this covenant between God (El Shaddai) and Abraham is the birth to Sarai (Sarah), Abraham's wife, of a child, Isaac, when both were past the normal age for childbearing (Gen. 17.17; 18.11).

Several features in the sequence of Abraham narratives in Genesis have lent to it outstanding theological significance and have led to Abraham's gaining a place of central importance in the religious traditions of Judaism, Christianity and Islam (*see* **Muslim Interpretation**). These are:

1. The revelation to Abraham of the nature and mystery of God's identity embodied in his name God Almighty (El Shaddai; cf. footnote in RSV to Gen. 17.1). This has been taken to imply the disclosure to Abraham of the oneness of God and consequently of the doctrine of monotheism.

2. The promise that Abraham's descendants would inherit the land has been important for Jewish tradition, regaining special interest with the rise of modern Zionism in the late nineteenth century.

3. The promise that all nations would be blessed through Abraham has been taken in Christian tradition to be a foretelling of the Gospel of Jesus Christ (cf. Gal. 3.6–9).

4. Abraham has been viewed as a unique example of obedience to God through his willingness, when commanded by God, to sacrifice even his son Isaac (Gen. 22.1–19). This expression of complete trust in God, commonly known as the Aqedah* ('binding' of Isaac, v. 9), has become the source of a rich variety of religious reflection within Jewish, Christian and Muslim tradition, down to the present day.

In seeking to ascertain the historical setting of Abraham's life and work biblical scholarship in the twentieth century has frequently been willing to accept that an authentic kernel of historical memory underlies the traditions regarding Abraham preserved in the OT. At the same time it has generally been unable to achieve any firm consensus regarding his position in Ancient Near Eastern chronology.*

We can note some of the basic approaches adopted. The account in Gen. 14.1–12 of the defeat in battle in the Valley of Siddim by Abraham of a coalition of kings has been examined in the hope of tracing a firmly identifiable royal figure (cf. C. Westermann, *Genesis 12–36*, p. 188). However, no secure identification with a known figure has been attained.

Sir Leonard Woolley's excavations at Ur during the 1920s and 1930s might have been expected to yield further light on Abraham and his world, but no precise evidence regarding Abraham emerged. During the following two decades much attention was given to establishing the cultural setting and customs of the Abraham narratives with a view to demonstrating their historical value (so R. de Vaux, C. H. Gordon, W. F. Albright and H. H. Rowley).

Even this approach has failed to lead to any firm historical conclusions and has yielded to a much greater measure of scepticism being expressed by J. van Seters and T. L. Thompson. Certainly these scholars are correct in recognizing that most of the narrative material concerning Abraham's exploits can only have been composed some centuries after Abraham's death. Yet this does not preclude that an authentic memory of such an ancestral figure had been retained by later generations of Israelites.

Undoubtedly the over-attention to questions of historicity led to considerable scholarly neglect of examination of the narrative themes and intentions of the Abraham stories of Genesis (cf. C. Westermann, *The Promises to the Fathers*, 1980). So also much importance should be attached to such light as the Abraham stories shed on the nature of religion during the age of such patriarchs and prior to the time of Moses (cf. W. McKane, *Studies in the Patriarchal Narratives*, 1979).

In Jewish tradition Abraham has enjoyed great prominence, second only to that of Moses as a pioneer of faith, an exemplar of obedience to God and as a founder of a new religious path. Similarly in Islam his importance has been maintained and no less than 26 suras of the Quran mention him. For Christians also Abraham has served as a representative of piety based on faith and trust, prior to the giving of the law (cf. Rom. 4; Gal. 3; Heb. 11).

See also **Ancient Near Eastern World; Archaeology (Old Testament); Genesis; Pentateuch.**

J. van Seters, *Abraham in History and Tradition*, 1975; T. L. Thompson, *The Historicity of the Patriarchal Narratives. The Quest for the Historical Abraham* (BZAW 133), 1974; R. Martin-Achard, *Actualité d'Abraham*, 1969; R. de Vaux, *The Early History of Israel to the Exodus and Covenant of Sinai*, Vol. 1, 1978, pp. 153–287.

R. E. CLEMENTS

Acts of the Apostles

That Luke should have chosen to continue the Christian story beyond the ascension remains the threshold observation for the interpretation of Acts. No other Christian writer before him, it seems, had conceived that there was more story to tell or that it was of importance to recount the origins and growth of the church. The fact that Luke has taken this step, which plainly represents a drastic alteration of the eschatological outlook of the first generation of Christians, has stimulated scholarly interest in two major respects. First, controversy has raged as to the historical reliability of the narrative, weighed against the possibility that in shaping the information at his disposal the author has suppressed or modified the facts to suit his own purposes. Secondly, questions have arisen in this century as to the theological merits or otherwise of Luke's enterprise, both in its conception and execution, especially in relation to the question of eschatology.*

Acts as history. Comparatively little interest was shown in Acts during the Patristic period. This was probably the result of Acts being rather unhelpful to the early Fathers in mining the N T for material of use in the formulation of creed* and dogma. Irenaeus* constitutes something of an exception to this neglect, since he quoted extensively from Acts to demonstrate the unity of the Apostolic message in his struggle against Gnosticism* (*Adv. haer.* III, 12.1–15).

More interest in Acts was shown in the period following the Reformation,* with Calvin* (1552–54), Hugo Grotius (1646), John Lightfoot (1645) and many others publishing commentaries.*

The antecedents of modern research into Acts lie in the eighteenth century, when under the influence of English Deism* scholars began to carry out historical investigations into the N T. A precursor of this movement and of the study of the political material in Acts came with the publication by C. A. Heumann in 1721 of a tract on the Third Gospel and Acts which argued that they were written as an apology for the Christian religion for the benefit of the Theophilos referred to in Luke 1.3 and Acts 1.1, whom Heumann regarded as a pagan magistrate. Subsequent pioneering essays into the historical investigation of Acts were made by J. D. Michaelis (1750) and by W. M. L. de Wette* (1825), with the latter being one of the earliest commentators to cast doubt upon its historical reliability.

With the writings of F. C. Baur (Professor of Theology at Tübingen,* 1826–1860) from 1831 onwards, research into Acts entered its most fruitful period. Baur was influenced by Hegel's dialectic of history and believed that he detected in the early church an antipathy between Petrine* (Judaic*) and Pauline* Christianity which eventually led to a higher synthesis. He argued that the works of the N T were to be located with respect to their 'tendency', that is, the aim or outlook which motivated their respective authors in the context of this process. For Baur, Acts was an attempt by its author to reconcile Paulinists and Judaists. It was written by a Paulinist to defend Paul's outreach to the Gentiles against Jewish–Christian criticism. Baur was followed by other Tübingers, including A. Schwegler and E. Zeller, both of whom dated Acts to the second century and had a low opinion of its historical reliability.

The 'tendency criticism' * (*Tendenzkritik*) of the Tübingen school stirred up enormous controversy during the remainder of the nineteenth century. An early response came from M. Schneckenburger in 1841, who proposed that Acts did have an apologetic purpose – to present Paul as acceptable to Jewish Christians – but it was nevertheless largely reliable as history. H. A. W. Meyer considered the thesis of the Tübingen school in the second edition of his commentary on Acts in 1854 but largely rejected it, espousing instead the view that although Acts contained unhistorical, even legendary, elements, it was largely reliable. Further opposition to Baur's views came from A. Neander, G. V. Lechler and A. Ritschl (originally a follower of Baur), to name a few.

F. Overbeck's widely influential work on Acts appeared in 1870. He accepted that much of Acts had been shown to be unhistorical, but disagreed with the Tübingen school's assessment of the work's purpose. For Overbeck, Acts was written in the second or third decade of the second century to explain the Gentile Christianity of that time in terms of its past. He also thought it contained a subsidiary purpose in the form of a political apologetic directed towards Roman authorities to assure them that Christianity had been and remained politically innocuous.

In nineteenth-century Britain, the views of Baur and company fell largely on deaf ears, a reception perhaps explained by their radical character, and the fact that they were underpinned by Hegel's philosophy of history (thus triggering the characteristic English suspicion of the explanation of phenomena in terms of systematic bodies of thought). Most British N T commentators had backgrounds in ancient history and classics and these interests flowed into Acts, thus leading to useful research into linguistic, geographical, historical and archaeological * background. J. Smith (in 1848), J. B. Lightfoot (*see* Westcott), W. K. Hobart, and pre-eminently W. M. Ramsay deserve mention in this context. This approach to Acts was later successfully transplanted across the Atlantic where it flowered most fully in the essays in Volume V of the important five-volume work, *The Beginnings of Christianity*, edited by F. J. Foakes Jackson, K. Lake and H. J. Cadbury * (1920–1933).

The British scholars were able to show that Luke was often accurate in his geographical, historical and even nautical details, and this fortified their suspicion of the Tübingers, especially in view of the claim made by the latter that Acts was written well into the second century and reflected the circumstances of that era.

A view gained currency among the British critics (*see* English Interpretation) that if the author of Acts was accurate in some details, namely of historical setting, it was reasonable to suppose he would prove accurate where his accuracy could not be checked, in particular, of course, with respect to the manner in which he had crafted the narrative.* This conclusion, energetically supported in our own time by F. F. Bruce and his followers, such as W. W. Gasque, is of dubious worth. It is falsified, for example, by the phenomenon of the carefully researched historical novel which is still a novel in spite of its author's having got the details of its setting right. Acts is not a novel, but the analogy holds. We are not dispensed from the fundamental task we have inherited from Baur of considering whether and how its author may have recast sources and traditions at his disposal in the light of his own particular purpose, and the consequences of such activity for the historical reliability of the work, simply because he is accurate in many details of historical setting. Accuracy of this type is even less surprising in view of the work's most probably having been composed in the first century and not in the second as the Tübingen critics supposed.

One form of research into Acts – source criticism * – actually had antecedents predating the writings of Baur. Temporarily overshadowed by the *Tendenzkritik* storm, it re-emerged later in the nineteenth century, notably in the works of P. Weiss (1889), P. Feine and F. Spitta (both in 1891), and F. Blass (1894–1896). In the United States, the arguments published by C. C. Torrey * from 1912 onwards for an Aramaic * original underlying Acts 1–15 can be seen as a later development of source criticism. The results of this work were, however, contradictory and unconvincing. Although it failed to delineate any particular sources used by Luke, it did have the beneficial effect of confirming the existence of seams and discontinuities in the narrative.

In 1923 Martin Dibelius wrote the first of a series of articles on Acts which inaugurated a new era of research especially when they were collected and published posthumously in Germany in 1951 (ET 1956). Dibelius' point of departure was the recognition of the necessity for a literary * analysis of the various components of Acts, especially the most important individual stories in the work, to elucidate their individual quality. At the end of the 1923 article Dibelius warned against the premature determination of historical reliability or otherwise of the stories until they had been satisfactorily analysed as to their style. Dibelius' later essays, however, especially on the speeches in Acts, reveal the possibility of style criticism producing results inimical to historical reliability. Thus at times Luke offers abbreviated versions of speeches which can be understood by readers of Acts who know the full story but which would not have been comprehensible to their putative audience. This indicates Lucan composition rather than reliance upon existing sources. The general approach of Dibelius has been appropriated by E. Haenchen in his major (and leading) commentary on Acts which first appeared in 1956 in Germany (ET 1971).

Acts as theology. Recent interest in Acts has largely shifted from the question of its reliability as a source for early church history to that of its status as theology, that is, as a deliberate reinterpretation of earlier traditions by an author desirous of addressing the concerns of his own Christian contemporaries. This change in direction, to be dated to the early 1950s, can be seen to result from a convergence of a number of different factors such as the publication of Dibelius' essays on Acts in 1951, the inauguration at that time of redaction criticism,* which focussed upon the creative individuality of each of the evangelists* as theologians, and a simultaneous outbreak of discussion on where Luke had stood with respect to eschatology.

The last factor has been particularly significant. In his *Theology of the New Testament* (German original 1948; ET 1951), Rudolf Bultmann* argued that Luke had surrendered the original kerygmatic* sense of Jesus and historicized it; that whereas for the eschatological faith both of the early church and of Paul the history of the world had reached its end in Christ, for the author of Acts the history of salvation* continued. The coming of Jesus was a stage, of course crucial, in a process still to be completed at his return.

Philipp Vielhauer's celebrated 1950 essay, 'On the Paulinism of Acts', proceeded by way of something akin to a redaction-critical comparison of Acts and the genuine Pauline correspondence with the aim of isolating Luke's unique theology. On the question of eschatology, Vielhauer's viewpoint was similar to Bultmann's – Luke had replaced the apocalyptic* expectation of earliest Christianity and the christological* expectation of Paul, both of which postulate the end of history, with a redemptive historical pattern of promise and fulfilment. Accordingly, Luke no longer stood within earliest Christianity, but in the nascent early catholic* church. During the 1950s and 1960s Ernst Käsemann strongly supported Bultmann and Vielhauer on this point.

But is Lucan theology really a catastrophic departure from early, and essential, Christianity? To devalue Luke for having made redemption history and not eschatology the centre of his theology, when he was writing at a time when belief in the imminence of the End was justifiably on the wane, seems to offend against common sense. Rather than developing a theology which constituted perhaps the only viable response to the obvious facts of the church's situation, should Luke have buried his head in the sand and attempted to maintain an eschatological fervour when there were forty or fifty years of Christian experience to demonstrate that the End was not nigh? Given that Luke–Acts forms one quarter of the NT, it seems an unfortunate limitation on the biblical resources available for Christian faith and reflection to deny Lucan theology recognition as an authentic expression of canonical Christian thought.

The Bultmann–Vielhauer–Käsemann position has been subjected to heavy criticism from a somewhat different direction by Ulrich Wilckens in his essay 'Interpreting Luke–Acts in a Period of Existentialist Theology' (reprinted in L. E. Keck and J. L. Martyn [eds], *Studies in Luke–Acts*, 1968). Wilckens argues that such criticism is not so much a penetrating insight into early Christian tradition as an expression of the dialectical theology developed by Karl Barth* and others in Germany in the 1920s, which propounded a fundamental chasm between God and humanity (with God being seen as the radical annulment of man) and which maintained that revelation* and history were irreconcilable antitheses. He denies that it is possible to differentiate Paul from Luke on the basis that for the former history was to be understood as 'the perpetually new decision of the individual'. According to Wilckens, for both Paul and Luke salvation has a history. So it is artificial to maintain, in effect, that Paul stands near the centre of the canon, with Luke quite outside it.

The investigation of Acts as theology is also being furthered by research into the literary qualities of the work, both in its own terms (an approach owing much to Dibelius) and in comparison with Hellenistic* literature. C. H. Talbert's *Literary Patterns, Theology Themes and the Genre of Luke–Acts* (1974) contains much of interest, and D. L. Tiede's *Prophecy and History in Luke–Acts* (1980) is a quite penetrating study along these lines. Such studies, by facilitating a more accurate assessment of how Luke shaped his narrative, lead to a deeper understanding of his theological purpose as well. Future interpretation of this type will, however, need to attend more closely to the ever more sophisticated research into the complex relationships between text, author and audience carried on by contemporary literary critics.*

Acts in its social setting. The controversy surrounding Luke's divergence from first generation eschatology originated largely in German biblical circles where the response of the individual to the kerygma was the primary issue of theology. During the last twenty years, however, Lucan scholarship has developed beyond this individual-before-God preoccupation to an interest in the community* for whom Luke was writing, an interest embracing both the inner dynamics of that community and the nature of its interactions – social, political and economic – with the world in which it was located. This new direction in Lucan studies roughly parallels the growing preoccupation among many Christians since the 1960s with broader social issues and perspectives.

Thus, in a series of articles originally published from 1962 to 1971 and collected in *Luke and the People of God* (1972), Jacob Jervell has focussed upon the extent to which Luke wished to present the church as the heir to the promises given to Israel, in response to alienation experienced by Jewish Christians and complaints about Paul. Jervell is concerned, with much support in the text, to show Luke as intent upon securing a direct line of descent from Judaism to the church. He does not, however, appear to regard Jews as having been a significant component in Luke's community, although his results conform well to such a possibility. Continuing interest in this field can be seen in Jack T. Sanders' *The Jews in Luke–Acts* (1987), although I cannot agree with Sanders that the work is powerfully and pervasively 'anti-semitic'.*

A number of commentators, notably P. W. Walaskay ('*And so We Came to Rome*', 1983), have investigated the political theme in Acts, especially the relationship of early Christianity to Rome. Such research has a venerable lineage in Acts scholarship, but has become more promising now that commentators are viewing the political material as directed towards the members of the author's community, not to the outside world.

The recent advent of the social sciences in NT criticism, for example in the writings of G. Theissen, W. A. Meeks and J. H. Elliott, offers much to the study of Acts. The sociology of knowledge – the study of the extent to which ideas have social origins – has recently been utilized, for example, together with well-established techniques such as redaction criticism, in Philip F. Esler's *Community and Gospel in Luke–Acts* (1987), to argue that central aspects of Lucan theology can be explained as a deliberate response to the social, political and economic conditions being experienced by the author's community.

Much remains to be done. As B. J. Malina has argued (in *The New Testament World: Insights from Cultural Anthropology*, 1983, and *Christian Origins and Cultural Anthropology*, 1986), the various NT texts, including Acts, are expressions of a particular culture or cultures very different from our own. Properly interpreting these texts necessitates sharpening our techniques for understanding other cultures and this means attending more closely to the work of ethnographers and anthropologists,* such as Mary Douglas, who have begun to systematize methods of cross- cultural comparison and comprehension.

Interpretation of Acts which fuses to established techniques a more sophisticated literary analysis and an appreciation (sharpened by social-scientific methods) of the cultural, economic and political forces influencing the community for whom it was written is more likely to come close to understanding Lucan theology than the more narrowly focussed scholarship of the recent past. This form of interpretation also offers greater prospects of enabling the Lucan gospel to fertilize contemporary Christian reflection at a time when the problems and challenges we encounter at the social, economic, ecological and political levels have assumed such importance on theological agendas.

See also **Luke, Gospel of; Paul; Sociology and Social Anthropology.**

In addition to titles mentioned in the text see H. J. Cadbury, *The Making of Luke–Acts*, 1927; R. Maddox, *The Purpose of Luke–Acts*, 1982.

PHILIP F. ESLER

Adam

In OT usage, 'Adam' means 'man' in the generic sense, mankind rather than an individual human being. The word is found in the OT more than 500 times, but is rarely used to refer to the first created human being except in the early chapters of Genesis. Even there, it is not easy to know when mankind as a whole is being referred to and when a specific individual, Adam. The present form of the creation stories * originated in a distinctively Israelite context, and it is therefore important to note that the God of Israel, pictured as creator, is understood to be responsible for the creation of the whole human race. Despite frequently stated opposition between Israel and other groups, all are part of the one creation.

A great deal of scholarly attention has been devoted to the significance of the NT passages which refer to Adam and this has had the unfortunate effect of obscuring other types of use in post-biblical Judaism. Already in the Apocrypha* an interest in Adam as an individual human being can be discerned, and this developed in a variety of ways in later Jewish writings. Thus, the roll of famous men in Ecclus. 44–49 ends with the praise of 'Adam (who is) above every living being in the creation' (49.16), though this has sometimes been regarded as a later addition and untypical of the book's overall view, which stresses Adam's ignorance (24.28). But it may be more valuable to see these contrasting presentations as illustrative of the great variety of ways in which the Adam tradition was employed in early Judaism. Levison has stressed that different Jewish writers with very different points of view were able to utilize the Adam traditions to illustrate their own particular thesis; there was no one over-arching presentation to which all had to conform. His argument is that interest in Adam was expressed particularly in wisdom* writings or in apocalypses.* In the former, Adam's dependence upon Wisdom, envisaged as a self-existent being, is stressed (Wisd. 10.1f.); in the latter, speculations are found concerning the pre-existence of Adam, a figure whose earthly existence was a pale reflection of the splendour he had once enjoyed. Philo* held a Platonized version of similar ideas, seeing 'the Man' of Gen. 1 as the heavenly counterpart of the empirical Adam of Gen. 2.

One theme stressed in Jewish writings was the sin of Adam and its effect upon subsequent humanity. II Esdras 3 (which is the beginning of the main part of the book) takes as its starting point the fate of humanity which has been the consequence of Adam's sin: 'Thou didst lay upon him one commandment of thine, but he transgressed it, and immediately thou didst appoint death for him and for his descendants' (II Esdras 3.7). It is clear from such passages as this that the NT usage, though not the only understanding of the Adam tradition, did represent one strand of the presentation of Adam within Judaism.

One other Jewish text should be mentioned: the *Life of Adam and Eve*, part of which is also found in another work, known as the *Apocalypse of Moses*. This comes broadly within the literary form sometimes known as Rewritten Bible,* that is, an elaboration of a biblical text in the interests of an author's particular viewpoint. Here Adam is pictured as explaining to his children the cause and necessity of his own death, within the context of speculation as to a future resurrection.* It is disputed how far this is properly described as a Jewish work; though probably written in Hebrew, it was preserved in Christian circles, which took over this and other pseudepigraphal* writings from their Jewish origin. (It has been suggested that the traditions embodied in this book were among those used by Milton in *Paradise Lost*.) The speculations it embodied are very close to those also found in gnostic* writings and serve as a reminder of the great variety of views which were able to use Adamic traditions for their own distinctive purpose.

Bearing this historical context in mind, we turn to the interpretation of Adam in the NT. There, the use of 'Adam' as a theological theme in relation to Christ provides a place at which the lines of eschatology,* christology* and anthropology (i.e. here, teaching concerning humankind) intersect. The two last areas (anthropology and christology) form the 'twin poles' of the interpretation of the eschatological Adam imagery contained in the NT.

Sections of the Pauline* epistles (I Cor. 15.20–22, 45–49; Rom. 5.12–21 and Phil. 2.1–11) are the most important sources for such 'Adamic' theology, although hints of it can be detected elsewhere in the NT. For instance, Adam may underlie the temptation account in Mark 1.12–13, in which Jesus encounters Satan after the fashion of Adam; and in his genealogy, Luke traces the descent of Jesus back to 'Seth, son of Adam, son of God', thus embedding his immediate sonship of God (3.22) in the human race as God's creation (3.38).

Undoubtedly, the stories of Gen. 1.26–27 and 2.4–4.1 stand as the ultimate source behind much of the 'Adamic' imagery. The Genesis account also provides the impetus for anthropological emphasis. Of the sparse uses of the figure of Adam in OT theology,* Ps. 8 is the only other text to play much of a part in early Christian reflection, I Cor. 15.25f. (cf. Heb. 2.5–9).

Adamic theology is closely related to other christological assertions in the NT, including wisdom and logos* speculations, Son of Man* ideas, questions about pre-existence, etc. Theological interpretation has rightly sought to define more precisely the relationship that Adamic christology has to these other christological declarations, e.g. in the allegedly pre-Pauline hymns* (Phil. 2.6–11; Col. 2.15–20).

The theological interpretations offered for the Adamic imagery contained in Paul's letters are necessarily related to questions about the background of Paul's thought (was the idea for Paul primarily a Jewish one or a Hellenistic* one?). Those who have emphasized Paul's Hellenistic heritage and upbringing have tended to interpret the Adamic imagery in terms of Heavenly Man or Primal Man (*Urmensch*) mythologies.* Such mythologies generally focus on a cosmic, pre-existent being who descends to earth and accomplishes redemption by drawing together all the souls of fallen men, thereby reconstituting humanity and restoring the true image of God, lost through Adam's fall, to mankind. The Heavenly or Primal Man is seen primarily as the one who reverses the effects of Adam's sin. A close connection can thus easily be drawn between Christ as the Second Adam and the parallel gnostic Redeemer mythologies of later writers. This view is especially found within the writings of German interpreters such as Bultmann,* heavily influenced by the History of Religions school.*

Others have emphasized the Jewish heritage and background and have pointed to the place of Adam in apocryphal, pseudepigraphal and rabbinic* literature as a more relevant source of parallels to the Pauline use of the image. Philo's approach to Adam, notably in *Legum Allegoria* and *De Opificio Mundi*, has provided a fruitful basis for comparative analysis of Paul's meaning. Paul is dependent on the type of Adamic speculations we see in Philo: in a passage such as Phil. 2.6–11, Christ is the heavenly Man who came into the world. In any event, the parallels within the large body of Jewish literature are striking and seem to fit the Pauline emphases better than those derived from the purely Hellenistic world.

Scholars have sought to apply this Jewish evidence towards an interpretation of 'Adam' in three particular ways, which are interrelated. The first we may describe as the eschatological* role of Adam. Many interpreters (e.g. W. D. Davies) have noted the link between *Urzeit* (beginning-time) and *Endzeit* (end-time), which underlies the eschatological message of Jewish thought, and the special role of an Adam figure in bringing about the awaited Messianic* Age. We certainly see this echoed within much Jewish literature, including the Essene writings from Qumran (*see* **Dead Sea Scrolls**) (e.g. I Q S 4.23 and C D 3.20). Many have sought to define more precisely how the Danielic 'son of man' figure in 7.13 relates to Adamic theology.

The second way has focussed on the representative role that Adam has as a symbol of the solidarity of the human race. The Hebrew idea of corporate personality is often cited as a foundational idea that is crucial to any interpretation of 'Adam'. The passages in I Cor. 15 are frequently appealed to as expressions of this view, with the 'first-fruits' imagery of vv. 20–23 as an important focal point.

The third way has focussed on the role of Adam as the originator of sin. As we have seen, interpretation centred on Adam as the source of human sinfulness. There are also a few passages which relate the Fall more specifically to Eve than to Adam (Ecclus. 25.24 and I Tim. 2.13–14).

It is in Rom. 5 that many of the tensions involving christology and anthropology are most clearly defined. Nowhere is this more clearly illustrated than in the interpretations of this passage offered by Rudolf Bultmann and Karl Barth.* Bultmann emphasizes the anthropological pole of the Adamic imagery as he focusses on mankind's *existence* as the heart of the image. Barth, on the other hand, emphasizes its christological pole and emphasizes rather its *nature*. The issue thus concerns the perspective from which one understands what it means for mankind (Adam!) to be made in the image of God. Do we begin with Christ and move to interpret mankind as the image of God (Barth)? Or do we begin with mankind and move to interpret Christ as that image (Bultmann)? This close connection between Adamic theology and mankind as made in the image of God rests upon a firm foundation in the N T (II Cor. 4.4 and Col. 1.15), and inevitably has drawn interpreters to consider the larger christological issues involved.

The 'image of God' became a major topic in patristic* discussions about the person and work of Christ and has continued to occupy a place high on the interpretative agenda ever since. Indeed, it could be said that the history of the interpretation of Christ as Second Adam, particularly as it relates to Paul's Letter to the Romans, is a record of attempts at the resolution of that theological tension between christology and anthropology.

The church's early centuries saw the development of other aspects of interpretation of the story of Adam and Eve. These have proved crucial for later Christian understanding and for human self-perceptions in European culture in general, down to the present. It is possible to distinguish two distinct traditions, the former persisting in Eastern Christianity, the latter dominant in the West from the time of Augustine.*

Irenaeus* not only contributed to the working out of Paul's parallelism between Adam and Christ (he also saw Eve as 'recapitulated' in Mary, as part of a total typological* pattern), but also introduced speculation about Adam and Eve themselves. They had been, at the time of the Fall, not adults fully responsible for their actions but children ensnared by the devil from a state of innocence. Some have seen here a quasi-historical way of describing the movement of every human being from childhood to adolescence, with its painful awakenings which are nevertheless essential to growth. This captures, in terms of modern psychological* understanding, something of the hopeful realism which marks Irenaeus' picture.

Other Christian writers of the patristic period also saw Adam in positive terms. While various moral lessons were read from the story of the Fall, and Gnostics imposed diverse allegorical* interpretations, the dominant theological strand in the East (Clement of Alexandria, Origen,* Gregory of Nyssa) took Adam as the symbol* of human dignity and autonomous moral choice. E. Pagels (1988) sees here a vehicle of Christian protest against the hostile weight of Roman government. Man as such was created 'fit to exercise royal rule'. Unfallen, he had been a figure of great splendour, made in God's image, and redeemed, could be again.

By contrast, the second-century Syrian* Tatian and Gnostics of ascetic disposition saw the Fall as the awakening of sexuality, from which redemption brought release, as, later, desert monks, with their stress on fasting, saw the Fall in terms of greed. Later, with far-reaching consequences, Augustine succeeded in substituting for the more optimistic perspective (encountered by him in Pelagius) a view of the human race as morally crippled from conception, by the very fact of procreation by the sexual act. Reading in Latin, he took Rom. 5.12 to say not 'sin came into the world through one man ... in that all men sinned' but 'in whom all men sinned'. Adam was thus the figure of doom whose legacy was only broken through sheer unmerited grace for those to whom it was granted, through the act of Christ. Thus, all human ills were laid at the door of Adam's fateful wrong choice, moral endeavour seemed to be devalued, and the precarious and wholly gracious character of salvation was made plain. Moreover, the world itself was seen less as the natural theatre for human growth in relation to God, than as a deeply flawed and hostile environment awaiting final restoration. All the same, Augustine saw Adam, even unfallen, in realistic rather than idealized terms, as the fount of human society.

While Adam is ostensibly simply the first human being, his story has always been a way of expressing ideas about numerous aspects of the human situation – political, social, psychological and environmental, as well as theological – and a means of exploring humankind's deep perplexities about itself.

See also **Creation Stories; Genesis; Poetry, English.**

C. K. Barrett, *From First Adam to Last*, 1962; Karl Barth, *Christ and Adam: Man and Humanity in Romans 5*, 1956; Rudolf Bultmann, 'Adam and Christ According to Romans 5' in W. Klassen and G. F. Snyder (eds), *Current Issues in New Testament Interpretation*, 1962, pp. 143–65; W. D. Davies, *Paul and Rabbinic Judaism*, 1948; J. D. G. Dunn, *Christology in the Making*, [2] 1989, pp. xvii–xx, 98–128; J. M. Evans, *Paradise Lost and the Genesis Tradition*, 1968; J. R. Levison, *Portraits of Adam in Early Judaism*, 1988; F. Maass, 'Adam' in G. J. Botterweck and H. Ringgren (eds), *Theological Dictionary of the Old Testament*, I, 1977, pp. 75–87; E. Pagels, *Adam, Eve and the Serpent*, 1988; Robin Scroggs, *The Last Adam*, 1966; M. E. Stone (ed.), *Jewish Writings of the Second Temple Period*, 1984.

L. KREITZER

Aetiology

Put at its most simple, aetiology is a study of the cause or origin (Greek *aitia*) of something. The term is often rather loosely used to refer to any story or tradition which has been produced or preserved to explain how some existing phenomenon of nature, condition, custom or institution came into being. Such stories frequently answer the question 'Why?', and can be classified according to a variety of types. Particularly frequent within relatively early traditions are the so-called *etymological** aetiologies (i.e. those which explain why a person or place was so named), although this is something of a misnomer since what is usually involved is a play on words (*see* **Paronomasia**). For example, it is scarcely likely that an Egyptian princess would give Moses* the perfectly good Egyptian name 'Moses' thinking it somehow to be related to a Hebrew verb *māšāh* ('draw out') (Ex. 2.10; cf. e.g. Gen. 3.20; 4.1; 11.9; 16.11, 14; 29.31–30.24; Ex. 15.23)!

Natural or *geological* aetiologies provide the explanation for a variety of natural phenomena, for example the origin of the rainbow (Gen. 9.12ff.), or of a peculiar rock-formation (Gen. 19.26), or the reasons why the snake crawls on its belly and why women suffer pain in child-bearing (Gen. 3.14ff.). *Ethnological* aetiologies explain the relationships between nations or tribes; the rivalry between Esau and Jacob accounts for the enmity between Edom and Israel (cf. especially Gen. 25.23); the relationship between the twelve tribes is accounted for by the tradition that their eponymous ancestors were all sons of Jacob (Gen. 29.31–30.24). *Cultic* aetiologies account for some ritual or ceremony; it is perhaps appropriate to include within this category stories (often involving a theophany*) which explain why a particular place was a holy place and why a sanctuary was located there (sometimes called *sanctuary* aetiologies). In the OT perhaps the clearest example is the story of Passover, providing the answer to the questions posed in Ex. 12.26 ('What do you mean by this service?') and 13.14 ('What does this mean?'). In the NT, the story of the Last Supper provides the answer to similar questions (Matt. 26.26–29; Mark 14.22–25; Luke 22.14–20).

Many stories or traditions combine more than one of these types of aetiology. The story of Jacob's dream (Gen. 28.10ff.) explains both the name Bethel ('house of God') and why Bethel was a holy place to the Israelites (because their God had revealed himself to their ancestor there). Gen. 21.25ff. contains not only two explanations of the name Beersheba ('Well of [the] oath', v. 31; or 'Well of seven', vv. 28–30) but it also explains why this particularly important oasis was an Israelite possession. An even more complex interweaving of aetiological traditions is to be found in Gen. 32.22–32. Jacob's new name 'Israel' is accounted for and explained (vv. 28–29); the place name Penuel/Peniel is explained (vv. 30–31), and it is perhaps to be understood that the name of the river Jabbok is to be linked with the verb 'wrestle' (yē'ābēq) (vv. 22–24); a dietary prohibition is accounted for (v. 32); and it has been suggested that vv. 25 and 31 may explain some feature of cultic practice at the sanctuary.

While some have been prepared to use the term aetiology to describe sizeable sections of biblical material (e.g. that Ex. 1–15 is the aetiological legend explaining the Passover Festival, or even that the whole of the Deuteronomic History* provides the answer to the question 'Why were Israel and then Judah destroyed?'), the term is more often limited to particular traditions or elements within a tradition which explain a cause. Yet it has increasingly been realized that to attempt to assign any tradition which explains a phenomenon to some such literary genre* as 'aetiological legend' is far too imprecise. Similarly, the definition of certain traditions as aetiological on the basis of the presence of particular formulae or features has been shown to be misleading. Childs has analysed the uses of the formula 'until this day' and concluded that it rarely has a truly aetiological function but is usually the writer's personal confirmation of the tradition he has received.

Therefore, rather than designating a whole story or narrative complex as 'aetiological', it is more likely that particular elements which have been incorporated into a narrative should be so designated. The presence of an aetiological element or elements does not render a whole story aetiological. A legend* is only truly aetiological if it owed its origin to an aetiological purpose. Such a conclusion naturally has important implications for the relationship between aetiology and historicity, because there has often been a tendency to assume that the presence of the former ruled out the latter; once a story was defined as 'aetiological', then, by inference, it was assumed that it had been artificially created to answer a question about a cause or origin.

Stories which account for an existing phenomenon can clearly be very different. Rudyard Kipling's *Just So Stories* which provide an answer to questions about how the elephant got its trunk, the whale its throat, or the rhinoceros its skin are clearly very different in character from, for example, the story of Bernadette of Lourdes which accounts for how a particular place came to be regarded as holy. While no one would see the former as anything other than conscious creations to provide an answer to a question, few would doubt that the story of Bernadette does account for the existence of a place of pilgrimage, whether or not they accepted the veracity of the appearances of Mary.

When Gunkel, followed by Mowinckel, applied the insights of form criticism* and categorized certain stories as aetiologies, they were largely dealing with traditions involving a 'mythical concept of causality' (Childs), for example Gen. 3.14; 6.4; 19.26, where the question of historicity would not really be an issue. However, when subsequent studies by such scholars as Alt, Noth, and von Rad identified many of the traditions in Josh. 1–12 as aetiological, the tendency was to conclude that they were therefore of little value for any attempt to reconstruct history. Such a negative evaluation of the historicity of a tradition which contained an aetiological element has been challenged, notably by Bright, who has argued that it is not so much the presence of an aetiological element which is significant, but rather its priority in the formation of the tradition. An aetiological element may well have become secondarily attached to a genuine historical tradition; indeed, Bright claims that within such traditions it can never be proved that an aetiological factor was primary, and that where etymological aetiologies occur they often relate to details of the story rather than being central. The situation may be different with mythical traditions, and where myth* was enacted in the cult it is dangerous to assume that the myths were simply invented to serve as an aetiology of a ritual.

The analysis of an element of tradition as aetiological may well be an important stage in understanding the pre-literary development of the tradition, but it is important to consider that an original aetiological interest may not be uppermost in the mind of the writer when re-using the tradition, or that an element of genuine aetiological interest may be an addendum to a historical tradition. Even the presence of an element of mythical causality within a tradition need not imply that the *whole* tradition lacks any historical basis. Historicity must be judged on other criteria.*

See also **Genesis; Pentateuch.**

J. Bright, *Early Israel in Recent History Writing*, 1956; B. S. Childs, 'A Study of the Formula "Until this Day"', *JBL* LXXXII, 1963, pp. 279–92; id., 'The Etiological Tale Re-

examined', *VT* XXIV, 1974, pp. 387–97; B. O.
Long, *The Problem of Etiological Narrative in
the Old Testament*, 1968.

A. H. W. CURTIS

Alexandrian Interpretation

Under the Ptolemies, Alexandria became a
centre of Greek learning: a famous library
was founded, and scholars, rhetoricians and
philosophers were attracted to the Museion.
This heritage meant that for most of the
period of early Christianity, Alexandria out-
stripped rival centres of learning like Athens,
and it was in Alexandria that the first real
scholarship emerged within Christianity.

Behind Christian scholarship lay two earlier
Alexandrian contributions. First, there was the
production of the Septuagint,* the Greek rendering of the Jewish scriptures; this Christians
took over along with the legend that it was the
inspired work of 70 translators who independently produced identical texts. Secondly, there
was the interpretative work of the Jewish philosopher, Philo,* who wrote in Greek and allegorized his scriptures, though remaining a practising Jew. He adopted the Stoic distinction between 'physical' and 'ethical' allegory, the first
relating texts to truths about God and his
relationship with the world, the second to moral
duties. He also suggested that scripture itself
points to the need for allegory, and that certain
passages cannot be taken literally,* because
they make statements unworthy of God, or
contain inconsistencies or impossibilities.

Christian scholarship in Alexandria built
on these two foundation stones. Among Christians, the first real scholar of the Bible was
Origen.* Adopting the prophetic exegesis of
Christian predecessors, and reacting against
the eccentricities of heretical groups, he built
a more systematic structure on these Jewish
foundations, following the lead of the Christian philosopher Clement.

Prior to Clement and Origen, the predominant strand of Christianity in Alexandria
seems to have been of a Gnostic* character:
the Christian Gnostics, Valentinus and Basilides, were both Alexandrians, and Origen
specifically counters the Gnostic exegesis* of
Heracleon in his commentary* on John. Gnostic exegetes took little interest in prophecy,
treated what scriptures they accepted as allegories of their cosmology, or of their spiritual liberation, and either rejected the OT or
focussed largely on their own understanding
of Genesis. Clement began to redress the balance, producing an intellectual Christianity
which rejected the key Gnostic theme: alienation from the material creation and therefore
from the Creator God.

In resisting Gnosticism while at the same
time appropriating some of its more valuable
insights, Clement was particularly indebted to
the approach of Philo. He spoke of a true
gnōsis (knowledge) to which the intellectual
Christian might aspire. In pointing to this,
Clement adopted spiritualizing interpretations
of the Jewish scriptures, using Philonic allegory. He justified this on the ground that all
religious language is in the form of oracles,
enigmas, mysteries, symbols: * this is true of
Plato's myths, the mystery-religions,* Egyptian hieroglyphics, and so too of the OT. The
truth of scripture comes through a veil and
needs interpretation. But the hidden mysteries
have been unlocked: the key is Christ.

Clement's work can best be described as
scattered thoughts. The work of his successor,
Origen, was more systematic. He applied the
scholarly methods of pagan Alexandria to the
scriptures, recognizing that issues such as the
true text and correct interpretation of this
literature were fundamental to the Christian
cause. Thus he compiled the Hexapla, a compendium of various versions of the scriptures
said to include the Hebrew, a transliteration
of the Hebrew, the Septuagint, and other translations into Greek produced by Jews who
objected to the way certain texts were being
exploited by the Christians in the Septuagint
version. Not only did he take such comparison
seriously, but he also realized the importance
of exposition. He began to produce verse by
verse commentaries* on biblical books. In
this work he was sponsored by a rich man,
Ambrose, who was concerned to see Christian
scholarship develop.

Origen did not confine himself, however, to
basic textual* and philological* questions. Interpretation involved far more than simply
paying attention to the letter, though he
accepted from contemporary Jews the view
that every jot and tittle had significance, since
every jot and tittle was directly inspired by
God. Like Clement before him he exploited
the route pioneered by Philo. Scripture had a
literal meaning* which was not without its
usefulness for the edification of the simple,
but its real importance lay in its moral or
spiritual meaning.* It was as though scripture
had a body, soul and spirit, and ascent to the
higher levels was the principal aim of the
exegete, as it should be also in a person's
moral and spiritual life. Like Philo, Origen
saw the impossibilities and inconsistencies of
scripture as pointing to the need for such
allegorical interpretation;* like Philo he distinguished between moral or ethical meanings,
and meanings reflecting the truth about God
and his relationship with the world.

Where Origen went beyond Philo was in
the sort of spiritual meanings he found in
scripture by means of allegory: these included
not only the cardinal virtues to which good

men aspire, but also specifically Christian virtues like readiness for martyrdom and love for others, even one's enemies; furthermore, longstanding christological* and typological* interpretations of the OT were adopted and developed further in discerning the spiritual world to which the text of scripture pointed. The sacrificial legislation in Leviticus was all about the spiritual sacrifices of Christians, but also about the sacrifice of Christ; the book of Joshua was not just about Joshua's conquest of the Promised Land, but also about the saving work of Jesus (the Greek form of the name Joshua). For Origen, the aim of allegorical exegesis was to reach knowledge of the nature and will of the transcendent God who, out of sheer love, had condescended to reveal himself and his purposes, by accommodating himself to the human level in the 'body' of the text of scripture, and in the person of Jesus Christ.

Origen's systematic account of his method does not seem to correspond very closely with his exegetical practice. In his commentaries, and in the considerable collections of homilies* which are extant, Origen's practice appears muddled: he is often happy to suggest a whole range of possible meanings, without apparently offering any criteria for distinguishing between them. Many get the impression that he operates no system and the whole process is eisegesis.* But the arbitrariness is not without some principles and methods. Like Philo, he exploits etymologies* and symbolic arithmetic, and he often uses scriptural metaphors as a starting point. He assembles many cross-references to justify his suggestions, and makes good use of precedents in the Epistles. Further, he does not altogether reject the literal sense. All of these features provide the material for later developments in the Alexandrian tradition.

Because of a disagreement with his bishop, Origen moved his scholarly operations from Alexandria to Caesarea. A couple of generations later, his mantle fell on Eusebius.* Whether he should really be included in the Alexandrian tradition is perhaps a debatable question, but it is interesting to observe how he inherited not only Origen's library, but also his research interests, his fascination with scholarly investigation into the biblical text, its geographical locations, its apparent historical contradictions, etc., while not in fact showing the same interest in what we might call 'philosophical allegory'. It shows that the tendency to emphasize Origen's allegorism probably distorts the overall picture of his contribution to biblical studies.

It was Didymus the Blind who inherited Origen's exegetical methodology, with its allegorical character. In his own day, Didymus had an immense reputation, further enhanced by the admiration felt for a man of such scholarship who had been blind from the age of four. Jerome referred to him as Didymus the Seeing because of his spiritual perspicacity. Rufinus supposed that he did not need sleep like seeing people, and spent the nights meditating on the scriptures which he knew by heart. He was a contemporary of Athanasius, but remained an ascetic withdrawn from the world throughout the bitter struggles of the Arian controversy and long outlived the principal actors. People came from all over the world to visit him. Rufinus spent eight years with him; many of Jerome's Latin commentaries acknowledge their indebtedness to those of Didymus, though as time went on Jerome became less and less enamoured with allegory, as his hostility to Origen deepened.

Until recently, despite his importance, little of Didymus' work was thought to have survived, probably because of his condemnation along with Origen in the reign of Justinian in the sixth century. But the chance discovery of papyri in a munitions dump at Tura in Egypt during the Second World War has changed the situation dramatically. Gradually the commentaries of Didymus included in this find are being published, and monographs on Didymus' exegesis are beginning to appear. These suggest that the allegorical method was a much more systematic approach to hermeneutics* than has often been suggested. It was not so much an arbitrary 'reading into' the text as a systematic search for its true spiritual reference, based on a coherence of imagery and symbol running throughout the scriptures. The assumption that scripture is a unity is evident in the fact that interpretation often consists of collections of texts with allusive or verbal connections with the text in question, and consistent images like Jerusalem* = church are the basis of allegorical exegesis. Furthermore, Didymus seems to work with a clear methodology: first construing the letter of the text, examining its logic and structure, and enquiring into its 'earthly' or historical reference; then enquiring whether this text has a figurative meaning, and if so what its reference is in the spiritual world.

In fact, what may seem chaotic in Origen develops into an increasingly clear understanding in the later Alexandrians. This understanding is essentially a sacramental view of scripture, as becomes clear in the exegetical work of Cyril of Alexandria. The two levels of meaning relate to two levels of reality, that perceived by the senses and that perceived by the mind. The two co-exist, and the former represents the latter in parables, signs and symbols. Thus the harmony of the created order is a symbol or sign of the wisdom of God, who is transcendent, and the narrative of Genesis represents the drama of fall and redemption, the universal human experience of exile, of spiritual famine, overcome by repentance and return to the Lord. Abraham's* migration and the exodus are paradigms of God's grace bringing conversion. Moses'* writings signify the mystery of Christ in riddles. The words of the prophets belong to their own historical context, yet also refer to the Christ. Parables* have two meanings, the first being obvious, the second requiring exposition which explores the inward, unseen meaning. The two levels of meaning are equally important to Cyril because they relate to his sacramental understanding of a sensible world which is not an illusion, but is nevertheless more than its mere appearance, namely a vehicle of truth and a sign of God.

These two levels of reality find their cohesion in the Word Incarnate, who belongs to both worlds, and yet is one nature of the Word enfleshed. To divide the Christ or accept a docetic understanding of his incarnation undermines this reality. By the time of Cyril, exegesis and dogma have a common undergirding metaphysic. It is not in fact true to suggest that doctrinal debate encouraged greater literalism. No one ever questioned the reference of Proverbs 8.22 to the pre-existent Logos,* despite the embarrassment of a text which on that basis literally favoured Arius. In controversy, exegetical assumptions of a prophetic or allegorical kind were in fact frequently exploited: both sides in the christological controversy agreed that Gen. 49.10–12 referred to Christ and the eucharist. What controversy fostered was not a greater literalism, but a subtle and highly rationalistic debate about meaning:* what exactly did it mean to say 'the Word became flesh' when using human language of something beyond human comprehension? The use of texts in the debate with Antiochenes* shows that an over-simple characterization of the Alexandrian tradition, in terms of allegory contrasted with literalism, fails to do justice to the sophistication of its exegetical and metaphysical thinking.

See also **Allegorical Interpretation; Allegory; Antiochene Interpretation; Literal Meaning; Mediaeval Interpretation; Origen.**

C. Bigg, *The Christian Platonists of Alexandria*, 1913; J. Daniélou, *The Christian Gospel and Hellenic Christianity*, 1964; R. P. C. Hanson, *Allegory and Event*, 1959; A. Kerrigan, *St Cyril of Alexandria. Interpreter of the Old Testament*, 1952.

FRANCES YOUNG

Allegorical Interpretation

Allegory* is a principle of interpretation that treats the text as having a less-than-straight-forward meaning. Thus in the first century BC, one of the earliest theorists of allegory defined it as 'speaking one thing and signifying something other than what is said' (Heraclitus *Homeric Questions*, 5.2). It was readily applied to *inspired* writings, i.e. the writings of the poets, on the grounds that inspiration* preserves the poet from error and ensures that what he says has a meaning that is universal, in contrast to the limited and local significance of ordinary speech. Allegorical interpretation suggests that we seek another meaning than the obvious 'surface' meaning: in contrast to such a 'surface' meaning (the so-called 'literal' meaning*) the allegorical meaning is 'deeper' or 'hidden'. Such an approach to inspired (or sacred) writing was commonplace in the ancient world, and is to be found in the Classical and Hellenistic* tradition, in the Jewish world and in Christianity.

The use of allegory as a method of biblical interpretation has a further justification within Christianity. The earliest Christians were those Jews who believed that Jesus was the Christ, the Messiah,* the 'anointed one' promised by the prophets.* So, in contrast to their fellow Jews, these Christian Jews treasured especially the Prophets, rather than the Law. From evident prophecies of the Messiah, Christians began to treat the whole prophetic corpus as pointing to Jesus (especially the 'Servant Songs'* of Deutero–Isaiah), and ultimately regarded the whole of the scriptures (viz. the 'Old Testament') as prophetic – prophetic of Jesus (this is reflected in the way Christians began to reorganize the 'Old Testament', so that it led up to, and culminated in, the prophetic books). Such a 'prophetic' interpretation of the OT is a form of allegory as it treats the whole Bible as 'speaking one thing (viz. about the religious experience of Israel) and signifying something other than what is said (viz. the fulfilment of all in Jesus)'.

The process of interpreting the scriptures allegorically as foreshadowing Jesus is evident in the NT, in the way the Gospel narratives frequently shape the events of Christ's life so as to see in them fulfilment of OT passages, and more self-consciously in the Fourth Gospel (e.g. John 3.14), Paul (e.g. Gal. 4.21–31, which contains an explicit defence of allegory; cf. I Cor. 9.9f.; Rom. 15.4), and I Peter 3.18–22. The events that foreshadowed Christ are often called 'types': they are patterns that point to the reality fulfilled in Christ. This language is already found in the NT (Rom. 5.14), and is much used in the second century, e.g. in the Epistle of Barnabas, Justin Martyr and Irenaeus.*

With the Christian Platonists of Alexandria,* especially Origen,* we begin to find a more formal treatment of allegory. But al-

ready with Clement there are important developments (some of which manifest the influence of Philo*). The hidden, deeper meaning
discerned by allegory is called 'mystical' * (*mys-
tikos*, hidden, or not to be spoken); the one
who can discern this deeper meaning (whom
Clement calls the 'gnostic') is prepared for it
by his deeper spiritual experience (*see Strom.*
VI, VII, and cf. *The Rich Man's Salvation*,
34–6). Clement envisages several levels of scriptural interpretation: he speaks of the four-fold
character of 'Mosaic philosophy', the first 'historical and properly speaking legislative', the
second concerning those things that belong to
'ethical' matters, the third the 'hierurgical' (or
priestly) which is concerned with 'natural
contemplation' (a deeper understanding of
created reality), and the fourth, the 'theological', which is *epopteia* (the word used in the
mystery religions for the final revelation) –
this last, Clement tells us, is said by Plato to
be a vision of the 'truly great mysteries'
(*Strom.* I.23.176.1f.). The clear foreshadowing
here of the three stages (ethics, natural contemplation, theology) of the spiritual life according to Evagrius, the great fourth-century
theorist of the monastic life, is significant, for
it suggests that the spiritual life entails a
deepening understanding of the scriptures.

Origen echoes much of this. Mostly he
works with a fundamental distinction between
the letter and the spirit (cf. II Cor. 3.6) – the
'historical' meaning of the text and its Christian 'allegorical', mystical interpretation. Contradictions at the historical level alert one to
the realization that this is not the real level on
which the text is meant to be understood:
such contradictions force one to seek an allegorical meaning. Or, as he also puts it, the
scriptures appear contradictory to those not
attuned to the 'music of God', just as some
music sounds out of tune or discordant to
those who are unfamiliar with the principles
of harmony (*Philocalia* 6.2). The deeper meaning is detected by the trained, or sensitive, ear.
Sometimes Origen envisages three levels of
meaning corresponding to the three parts of
the human person: body, soul and spirit
(notably in *On First Principles*, IV.2.4, where
three levels are suggested by Prov. 22.20f.
[LXX], though most of book IV works with
just two levels of meaning). The 'bodily' meaning is the literal, or historical, meaning of the
text, which even the simplest can grasp; the
'soul' meaning the moral lesson that can be
drawn from it for those making progress in
the Christian life; the 'spiritual' meaning the
theological insight only open to the 'perfect'.
Both Clement's and Origen's ways of developing allegory can be seen as extensions of that
interpretation which sees the OT as full of
'types' (*see* **Typology**) of Christ, for the deeper

levels of interpretation are seen as ways of
entering more deeply into the 'mystery' of
Christ (hence they are called 'mystical'), and
that entry is effected as much by faithful
Christian living as by deeper theological interpretation (indeed for Origen the latter requires
the former).

Allegory becomes then one of the tools of
the Christian exegete * and sometimes has a
technical meaning that has little to do directly
with the christocentric perspective that underlies the developed understanding of allegory: e.g. when the use of 'heart' in the
scriptures is said to be an allegory for 'mind'.
But allegory also becomes controversial.
Origen's allegorizing, especially of the account
of creation and fall in Genesis, is regularly
attacked (e.g. by Basil of Caesarea in the
East, by Augustine * in the West); though it is
the results that attract the censure, the method
of allegorizing is criticized simply as yielding
them (neither Basil nor Augustine is averse
from allegory in his own exegesis). In the
Antiochene * school, allegory is attacked as
such, but even so it is allowed that there is a
deeper meaning in the scriptures, which is
discerned *kata theōrian* (by contemplation). In
the West, allegory (*allegoria*) becomes the
usual term for a deeper understanding of scripture which passes beyond the level of fact to
the level of mystery (from *factum* to *mysterium*).

A rather more systematic classification of
allegorical interpretations is developed in the
West in the course of the Middle Ages. Four
levels of interpretation of scripture are
distinguished: literal, allegorical, moral and
anagogical (as in the couplet cited by Nicolas
of Lyra in the form: *Littera gesta docet, quid
credas allegoria,/ Moralis quid agas, quo tendas
anagogia* – the literal sense teaches what
happened, the allegorical what you are to
believe, the moral what to do, anagogy where
you are going), or sometimes in a different
order: literal, moral, allegorical (or tropological), anagogical. Cardinal de Lubac sees a
distinction between the former, more common
and traditional form, and the latter, less usual
one. The latter he sees as a development of
Origen's three-fold distinction, a development
he traces through Ambrose and Jerome, Cas-
ian and Eucherius. It is simply a list or classification. The former, more traditional one, he
sees as a development of the fundamental
distinction between the literal meaning and
the spiritual or mystical meaning, the latter
being distinguished into three: the allegorical
which goes beyond the literal, the moral which
draws practical conclusions from the allegorical meaning, and the anagogical which looks
forward to the goal towards which the practice
of the Christian life is tending. This is not just

a list, but expounds 'an ascesis and a mysticism that can be characterized as christological, ecclesial and sacramental: it is a veritable history of the spiritual life, founded on dogma' (de Lubac, I/1, p. 203). This latter, more traditional and fundamental ordering of the senses of scripture (as these meanings or levels come to be called), de Lubac argues derives from Origen, developing through Augustine and Gregory the Great. Such a four-fold discrimination of the senses of scripture became a valuable method of organizing material in a sermon: many mediaeval sermons work through the four senses of the text, finding in anagogy a suitably rousing conclusion. It also underlies the methods of meditation on passages of scripture that developed during the later Middle Ages and found their classic expression in the *Spiritual Exercises* of St Ignatius Loyola.

Allegorical interpretation became, then, for Christians a way of using the scriptures to express and understand the mystery of Christ within the developing tradition of the church: it was a way of freeing the text of scripture from the confines of its original context of utterance so that it could be a vehicle for the word of Christ to the contemporary church. It is not that the literal historical meaning of the text of scripture is ignored – the church has a history and needs to be faithful to that history – rather it is that the literal meaning does not exhaust for all time the meaning of the scriptures for the church. As the French Catholic poet, Paul Claudel, put it, 'around the imperative and literal sense we learn that there exists a field of figures (one could say: a magnetic field), that is to say of resemblances and analogies oriented in a manner more or less direct and organic towards revealed and confirmed fact' (Claudel, p. 20). It is the 'magnetic field' of the shared faith of the church that orientates the imagery of allegory. Consequently, allegorical interpretation finds it difficult to survive when that shared faith is fractured. Already before the Reformation,* movements for reform had deplored the arbitrary interpretation of the scriptures made possible by allegory, and the humanists criticized what seemed to them a mechanical and scholastic mode of exegesis (though Erasmus* found in the patristic practice of allegory a model to follow). Luther* wanted to found his faith on scripture rather than interpret scripture in the light of the church's tradition, and thus rejected allegory (though he continued to use it in more devotional contexts). In post-Tridentine Catholicism, allegorical interpretation became something justified by ecclesiastical tradition and a symbol of Catholic rejection of Protestantism. Allegorical interpretation continued to be found among those Christians who felt themselves in touch with the tradition of the church: so in England amongst the Caroline divines and notably in the Oxford Movement, when Keble defended allegorical interpretation as part of the 'mysticism' of the Fathers of the church. The Enlightenment,* with its wholesale assault on the notion of tradition, left no room for allegory. Romanticism, as usual, reinforced the Enlightenment in opposing it, so that allegory came to be contrasted with symbol,* the latter being vital and natural, the former dead and artificial.

Allegory can become a form of arbitrary play on words, and will inevitably seem such where there is little sense of tradition as a bearer of meaning which is referred to a sacred text whose value for the religiously committed cannot be specified in advance. (This may occur, for example, when authority is given to the teaching of one who is simply recognized as the greatest of teachers – if that could mean anything – or to a body of wisdom whose only claim to authority is its effectiveness.) But where there is a recovery of such a sense of tradition, allegorical interpretation may again seem a natural hermeneutical method.

See also **Alexandrian Interpretation; Allegory; Christian Interpretation of the Old Testament; Mediaeval Interpretation.**

H. de Lubac, *Histoire et Esprit,* 1950; *Exégèse Médiévale,* 4 vols, 1959–64; P. Claudel, 'Du sens figuré de l'Écriture' in *Oeuvres Complètes,* vol. 21, 1963, pp. 9–90; R. M. Grant, *The Letter and the Spirit,* 1957; Northrop Frye, *The Great Code,* 1982; A. Louth, *Discerning the Mystery,* 1983, ch. 5.

ANDREW LOUTH

Allegory

There are biblical texts which are allegories, and texts parts of which are allegorical. This article is concerned with the question of discovering how such texts may be identified and interpreted.

In essence, an allegory may be said to be constituted by the use of two or more related metaphorical expressions to refer to specific elements of one fact or event. It is important that texts which are actually not allegorical should not be treated as if they were allegorical.

A satisfactory theory of allegory requires a satisfactory theory of metaphor,* though for our present restricted purpose an all-embracing theory is not needed. It is nevertheless important to remember that the context of words used metaphorically will be an extended utterance, whether spoken or written. A metaphor can only function and be grasped as a metaphor in its context within an utterance, not as a single word. It follows that metaphors cannot be entries in a lexicon.* Nevertheless the semantic* function of a metaphor, the very kernel of its metaphoric function, occurs as an admittedly complex element of the lexical semantic meaning of the metaphorically used word in its context. This is not to deny that the utterance within which the metaphor occurs may itself be described as 'metaphorical'. For the purpose of semantic interpretation of metaphors within an allegory it is appropriate to suppose, in common with many linguists, that the meaning of a word can be regarded as a complex of distinct semantic features or components. When a word is being used in a metaphorical utterance, some aspects of the customary lexical meaning of the word are not applicable; they do not correspond to any normal feature of that to which one is referring. This is what I. A. Richards called its 'tenor' (cf. Soskice, 1985, pp. 44ff.). The number of applicable semantic components may nevertheless appear indefinite. That is the so-called 'inexhaustibility of the metaphor'.

A semantic account of the metaphors in an allegory should not only identify the thing or event referred to. That would be enough where the allegory has the function of a riddle; but normally it should also search out semantic components which would be relevant in the internal context of the allegory. The explication of such applicable semantic components, not necessarily many, would serve to elucidate part of the inherent semantic capacity of the allegorical text (Bjørndalen, 1986, pp. 146ff., with reference to Amos 2.9b).

The proposals here set out in brief outline are dependent on the semantic theories of the Dutch linguist Anton Reichling, whose work, published in 1935 and revised in 1967, has never been translated; it is presented and discussed more fully in Bjørndalen, pp. 7–61. An advantage of Reichling's method of distinguishing the different types of usage of words is the provision of a coherent semantic theory whereby to distinguish between metaphorical and non-metaphorical linguistic usage (cf. Soskice). On the other hand, a difficulty arises from the lack of research in the form of semantic analysis of the word-stock of OT Hebrew and Aramaic and NT Greek. But this difficulty must not be exaggerated; it is inevitable that the interpretation of metaphors will to some extent be carried out intuitively (Bjørndalen, pp. 55–8).

Amos 2.9b is an allegory on a small scale, and a brief account can now be given of the metaphors contained within it. The nouns p^eri and *shoresh* are used metaphorically in this verse; RSV translates according to the normal lexical meaning of these words, 'fruit' and 'roots'. But the 'tenors' of the metaphor

are Amorite children, described by reference to their parents. That is to say, within the context of Amos 2.9b the semantic components of these nouns may be classified as: p^eri = +living, +young, +bearer of inherited specific characteristics; *sharoshim* = +living, −young, +giving life, +transferring what is needed to grow up. Taken by itself the sentence Amos 2.9b points to the supremacy of Yahweh and the total extirpation of the Amorites; within the context of Amos 2.6–16 the verse serves as an element of accusation against Israel.

If we now turn to some OT examples of the variety of allegorical texts within the Bible we find that in Hosea 5.1b–2a, verse 1b contains both a metaphor ('judgment') and a short allegory (the 'snare' and 'net'), and 2a probably another short allegory ('the pit') (the Hebrew text of this verse is unclear). That is to say, within this short text the three parts display 'image-shifting' (Murrin, 1969). The interpreter must both pay due attention to the text-unit as a whole and be very sensitive to the diversity of the metaphors.

A short allegory of a different kind may possibly be found in Isa. 14.25a, within the unit Isa. 14.24–27. Here two metaphors stand in synthetic parallelism, the tenor of each being very similar.

An allegory may be combined with or contain one or more similes. Amos 2.9 again offers an example, this time of combining allegory and simile. The first half of the verse contains two similes, the second the allegory we have already considered. They are closely related in the sense that the similes introduce the image to be employed in the allegory, and the allegory uses the same syntactical form as the introduction to the similes ('I destroyed').

An allegory may also contain similes, e.g. in Hos. 5.14f., v. 14a has two similes, in which Yahweh is compared with a lion. In the following allegory, the acts of Yahweh *are* the acts of the lion, acts which form the 'vehicles' of the allegory. In such cases the similes should be seen as parts of the allegory, even though they do not constitute allegorical speech as such (Bjørndalen, pp. 129–31). The similes begin the account, with images which are continued in the allegory itself without image-shifting. In such cases semantic interpretation of the metaphors would be dependent upon the overall content.

If one turns to more extended texts which might be classified as allegorical, two important questions should be posed: Does the text use two or more metaphors related to each other in the sense described above? Does this account comprise the whole or at least the dominant part of the text?

On these criteria Isa. 5.1–6, the song of the vineyard, together with its original commentary, 5.7, can be accepted as an allegory (Bjørndalen pp. 245ff., 338–43). In such a complex allegory there may be words which function as metaphors even though they do not correspond to genuine features in the 'tenor', as part of the specific picture which an allegory may offer of its setting (e.g. Isa. 5.2a). The biblical commentary itself, in 5.7, does not interpret the allegory in the sense set out here; only some of the 'tenors' are alluded to, so that our semantic interpretation would have to build upon the basis provided by the biblical verse. It is not necessarily alien to it.

Another example would be II Sam. 12.1b–4, which anticipates the words of Nathan in vv. 7ff. Here one would have to recognize that an allegory may have one single predominant scopus: 'You are the man!', but it may also use many expressions metaphorically. As with Isa. 5.1–7, the identification of one or more 'tenors' shows the metaphorical character of the narrative. Both in II Samuel and in Isaiah this characteristic had deliberately to be concealed in the original presentation.

One might also point to Ezek. 17.2–10. If this text is an allegory it is so because it contains a series of metaphorically used words in the sense described above. It would show that a biblical allegory may be subject to differing commentaries within the biblical text itself; so here vv. 11–21, 22–24. None of these are semantic interpretations of the allegory, but rather a kind of further utilizing of the allegory by partly re-writing it.

In the NT the explanation of the story of the sower (Mark 4.3–8 and pars.) in 4.14–20 and pars. treats the text partly as an allegory, using some of its 'tenors', but to some extent it builds a new and independent narrative. Matt. 13.49f. treats 13.47f. as a short allegory, whereas Matt. 22.1–13 (the great supper), with its possible metaphorical references to prophets and apostles, is given no explicit commentary.

In allegories an explicit identification of 'tenors' may give a clue to further semantic interpretations of the text. In any case the allegorical character of a text and the semantic interpretation of its metaphors can only properly be established in accordance with the relevant indications from the text itself. The interpretative goal should be to make explicit and understood the implicit semantic resources of the text. The criteria of allegorical speech should be strictly limited to two or more metaphors related to each other in the sense described.

See also **Allegorical Interpretation; Figures of Speech; Literary Criticism; Narrative Criticism; Parables; Reader-Response Criticism.**

A. J. Bjørndalen, *Untersuchungen zur allegorischen Rede der Propheten Amos und Jesaja*, BZAW 165, 1986; G. B. Caird, *The Language and Imagery of the Bible*, 1980; M. Murrin, *The Veil of Allegory*, 1969; M. S. Kjärgaard, *Metaphor and Parable*, 1986; J. M. Soskice, *Metaphor and Religious Language*, 1985.

ANDERS JØRGEN BJØRNDALEN

American Interpretation

1. *Old Testament*. The sheer scale of biblical studies in North America makes any generalization unwise, for exceptions could always be found, but there have perhaps been three areas in which the work of American OT scholars since the Second World War has been of particular significance: archaeology* and its contribution to our understanding of the history of Israel;* the 'biblical theology'* movement; and the application of sociological* insights to biblical study.

In the assessment of the contribution of archaeology the work of W. F. Albright has been of special significance, both in its own right and because of the influence wielded by many of his pupils. Albright himself had spent much time in Palestine in the 1920s and 30s, and was a major influence in bringing order to what had previously been a somewhat haphazard process of archaeological exploration. In the long term, however, he would probably have hoped that his special contribution would be seen in his gift for reconciling a mass of apparently chaotic data and offering reconstructions of the history of whole civilizations: *From the Stone Age to Christianity*, first published 1940, by its very title, is illustrative of his concern to detect a coherent pattern underlying all the available materials. Indeed, much of his writing embodied a distinct philosophical stance which he applied to the interpretation of archaeological and historical evidence. In an OT context this implied a willingness to accept the essential historicity of the biblical account of the people's own past, and the interpretation of the archaeological evidence in terms of the biblical text. Albright himself did not write a large-scale history, but his pupil John Bright, whose *History of Israel* (1959) is still influential, well represented his standpoint. Probably the most widely used introduction to OT study during the last 30 years has been by another follower of Albright, B. W. Anderson, *Understanding the Old Testament* (1957), published in the UK as *The Living World of the Old Testament* (1958).

At a more technical level the tradition typified by Albright continues, with the work of F. M. Cross and D. N. Freedman perhaps two of its most typical exponents, and the renewal of commentary*-writing one of its most characteristic monuments. The tradition of writing commentaries on individual books of the Bible appeared almost to be extinct in the early 1950s, but it was revived, first with the Interpreters' Bible, in 12 volumes (1952–56), and then with the Anchor Bible. This series was launched as an 'interfaith' (Protestant, Catholic and Jewish) attempt to make the Bible available to the general reader, and commentaries on Genesis (E. A. Speiser, 1964) and Jeremiah (Bright, 1965) clearly had this aim in mind; more recent additions to the series have grown to enormous proportions, so that, for example, the Song of Songs, or Haggai/Zechariah 1–8, are given twice the length of those original works.

In some important respects the work of those who first came to notice as pupils of Albright has reached into quite new areas. The work of F. M. Cross may be cited. Not only has his collection entitled *Canaanite Myth and Hebrew Epic* (1973) provided a major resource for the study of the religion of the OT against its contemporary background, his work on the textual tradition has been influential for the evaluation of the Masoretic* text in the light of more detailed examination of the ancient versions and the Dead Sea Scrolls.* This kind of study, pursued by many scholars all over the country, and facilitated by modern technology (*see* **Computers**), would only be possible in a country with the material resources of the USA.

One unfortunate impression occasionally given by Albright and his supporters was that those who did not accept all his conclusions must be regarded as both wrong and misguided, and this sometimes led to the marginalization of other views; C. C. Torrey,* a scholar of genuine but occasionally eccentric insight, would be a case in point. This monopoly of any one school is now much less obvious, and a great variety of views can be found in the areas where 'Albrightians' once reigned supreme: the proposals of G. E. Mendenhall and N. K. Gottwald regarding Israel's establishment in Canaan and the rejection of a nomadic past in the people's history would be one illustration, the scepticism of J. van Seters and T. L. Thompson concerning the historicity of the Genesis traditions another.

The area of biblical theology might seem far removed from that of archaeology, but in practice many of the same scholarly names are found in both areas (e.g. G. E. Wright, Anderson). This is due at least in part to the importance attributed to history: archaeology was seen as a means of establishing a secure historical base, which in turn offered a platform on which to establish a theology of a God whose acts are discerned in historical

events. The origin of the movement, however, has been seen as an attempt to break away from the modernist/fundamentalist dispute which had been so bitter in the inter-war period; was it after all possible to have a responsible theological outlook which took seriously both the Bible's own testimony and the results of critical scholarship?

For a short time, especially in the 1950s, it seemed as if a consensus on these lines could be established, but during the last 25 years, for a variety of reasons, that consensus has broken down. On the one hand, OT theology* has entered a questioning rather than an affirmative phase, well illustrated by the series of books entitled 'Overtures to Biblical Theology' which expressly rejects any claim to be offering firm conclusions; on the other hand, the resurgence of extreme forms of fundamentalism,* which have taken control of many of the leading Protestant churches, has made the emergence of a fresh consensus unlikely. That conclusion is made the more probable by the fact that much writing on religious themes, including the Bible, now comes from those with no confessional commitment; this is especially true of those who approach the Bible with the insights of modern literary criticism.*

It would also be true of many of those who have applied sociological* methods to the study of the Hebrew Bible. As noted above, this has found its best-known illustration in the debate concerning Israel's establishment in Palestine. In place of the OT's own picture, strongly supported by the biblical theology approach, of a violent invasion from outside the borders of the land, attention has come to be focussed on Israel as a society which came into existence only in Palestine, and on the exploration of the nature of that society. This offers a crucial challenge to all those interpretations which regard Israel as unique, unlike any other society of the ancient world and governed by laws different from theirs. The pioneers in this kind of approach have been Mendenhall and Gottwald, and Gottwald has added to his massive study of the settlement process (*The Tribes of Yahweh*, 1979, a work whose acknowledged Marxist* interpretative stance has not endeared it to all readers) an introduction to the whole OT entitled *The Hebrew Bible: a Socio-literary Introduction* (1985). It is clear that the present state of OT study in North America is a predictably diverse one.

R. J. COGGINS

2. *New Testament.* As in the case of OT interpretation, the contribution of American scholarship in the field of NT studies has been both wide-ranging in subject-matter and diverse in viewpoint. This survey, while noting

some earlier work, will concentrate on the particularly fertile period since the Second World War, though even then it is necessary to introduce a measure of selectivity.

(a) *Backgrounds to the scene.* Theological interpretations are necessarily subject to social pressures and a variety of extraneous influences. Over the past forty years, the study of the NT (and much the same is true of the OT) has been influenced and shaped by the following factors:

1. The effects of German scholarship have been felt in a more powerful way than formerly. The links between America and Europe, severed during the war, were re-established, so that by the early 1950s there was movement in both directions. American universities and graduate institutions were able to attract visiting professors from Europe, and in some notable instances to encourage them to stay (e.g. H. Koester and H.-D. Betz from Germany, Krister Stendahl from Sweden). The traffic in the opposite direction made it possible for graduates from American colleges and seminaries to travel for their doctoral research, and so to be exposed to the latest trends in European scholarship. They subsequently returned to their native land to take up teaching posts and to perpetuate and develop what they had learned in the German and Swiss universities in particular (e.g. J. M. Robinson). British-born scholars, such as W. D. Davies, R. H. Fuller, N. Perrin, were soon to swell their ranks.

2. Throughout this period there has been a noteworthy liaison between Protestant interdenominational theological schools and Roman Catholic institutions in a way quite unprecedented. The turning-point was the wartime encyclical of Pope Pius XII, *Divino afflante spiritu,* which encouraged Catholic theologians to embark on the study of biblical questions in a spirit of fresh historical and literary enquiry, with the result that they were drawn more closely to their Protestant counterparts. Several novel consequences have followed. It is now not uncommon for appointments to be made transcending confessional barriers, and for Catholic (and Jewish) scholars to be awarded chairs in traditionally Protestant schools. The writings of both sides are equally respected and valued (R. E. Brown, J. A. Fitzmyer, G. W. MacRae stand alongside such Lutheran names as J. Reumann and K. Stendahl). The dialogue with Jewish scholars is also a hopeful sign in this period, partly due to an encouragement from the Catholic authorities, partly arising out of a fresh awareness of and sensitivity to Jewish backgrounds* to the NT and an admission that too often prejudice and caricature dominated the scene in the past. Thus, the recognition of the Jew-

ishness of Jesus is a common bond uniting scholars of both faiths, (e.g. J. Neusner, S. Sandmel and E. Rivkin on the Jewish side, and E. P. Sanders on the Christian).

3. In the same period, in a country that has taken as axiomatic the separation of church and state, it is interesting to observe that academic research into NT history and religion has moved into secular state colleges and universities, and is no longer confined to denominational seminaries. This widening of interest has led inevitably to an appreciation of biblical study as part of the humanistic tradition (as in British universities) and a slackening of ties with the credal orthodoxy of the mainline churches. Newer disciplines, at home in the universities, have been recruited to assist in scholarly investigation of the NT and its background.

In particular, and building upon the work of the Chicago school (especially Shirley Jackson Case) between the wars, there has been a blossoming of enquiry into the social forces and factors at work in the first-century world in Graeco-Roman society. Apart from the work of the German Gerd Theissen, American scholarship, in the hands of people like W. A. Meeks and H. C. Kee, has taken the lead in this area (*see* **Sociology and Social Anthropology**).

At the same time, American scholars have been to the fore in the development of rhetorical criticism,* aiming to examine patterns of debate and argument in Hellenistic popular philosophy and other literature as a setting of the NT writings (G. A. Kennedy, D. E. Aune); as they have too in the development of literary criticism* of the NT, and especially structuralism* (C. H. Talbert, N. R. Petersen). These recent trends arise directly from the way biblical studies have found a new home on the campus of state universities and in secular departments of religion within the American educational system.

(b) *Situation in the early post-war period.* As a rough generalization (there are always exceptions to be made), the scene at the end of the Second World War may be described like this. While classical liberalism still found some notable champions (e.g. H. J. Cadbury,* John Knox), the main ground was held by three dominant theological powers, each representing a different approach to biblical interpretation, even if the last of the three was found only in embryo.

1. The British influence, seen in C. H. Dodd,* especially with regard to his theory of realized eschatology* in the Gospels and Paul. This concept comported well with the political and social conditions of the time, as America looked ahead to a period of peace and prosperity (until shaken by the cold war, and events in Korea and then Vietnam).

2. The influence of movements of thought variously described under the headings of 'kingdom of God',* 'salvation history',* and (see above, in relation to OT) 'acts of God'. In the 1950s, the work of G. E. Wright, F. V. Filson and others was highly popular, and stress on the central kerygma* gave an appearance of unity to the NT writings. This tendency produced at least one full-scale 'theology of the NT',* that of G. E. Ladd, and may be seen as parallel to trends in Europe (e.g. W. G. Kümmel).

3. Alongside these assured positions, there arrived the disturbing and powerful influence of Bultmann* and an existentialist approach to biblical authority.* Extreme deductions were quickly to follow, leading to the 'death of God' controversy, which produced some negative assessments of Jesus, based on Bultmann's scepticism regarding what may be known of Jesus from the Gospels.* But it was the so-called New Quest for the historical Jesus* that quickly fired the imagination. Led by J. M. Robinson, scholars were quick to pick up whatever gains they could muster from this reaction. Its legacy is seen in two developments that marked the work of Robinson and others in the subsequent decades, the study of Q and of the gnostic documents from Nag Hammadi* (see Trajectory).

(c) *Reactions and developments.* Each of the interpretative starting points referred to has been vigorously challenged in the period that followed. American scholars have played a full part in the redaction-critical* movement which has countered the former sense of the unity of the kerygma expressed in the NT writings and emphasized rather their theological diversity. Also, the recovery of apocalyptic* as the setting of both Jesus and Paul* has made the role of both more situational in the context of their times and less domesticated to our modern period. E. P. Sanders on Paul's problem as a Jew who lived in what he believed to be the new epoch of messianic* fulfilment, and J. C. Beker on the centrality of apocalyptic in Paul's gospel, illustrate how dated is the older liberal realized eschatology approach. Both scholars set a distance between Jesus and Paul on the one hand and their modern readers on the other, and leave us the legacy of how to interpret the NT message for today. The element of historical realism in interpreting the NT had already, earlier this century, been foreshadowed in American scholarship in the work of H. J. Cadbury (especially on Jesus) and Foakes Jackson and Kirsopp Lake (especially on the Acts of the Apostles).

Finally, mention should be made of the attempt to have the NT (and indeed the Bible as a whole) retain its place as the church's book and the witness to God's concern for the world. Canonical criticism,* centring on the work of B. S. Childs, stands at a tangent to the strongly historical tendency of the greater part of the work that has been surveyed, and testifies to an uneasy tension between secular and churchly study of the NT writings and their relevance for the modern reader. This is perhaps a central problem on the future agenda of American interpretation of the NT.

See also **Cadbury, H. J.; English Interpretation.**

RALPH P. MARTIN

E. J. Epp and G. W. MacRae (eds), *The New Testament and its Modern Interpreters*, 1989; D. A. Knight and G. M. Tucker (eds), *The Hebrew Bible and its Modern Interpreters*, 1985.

Amos

Amos, one of the Book of the Twelve (prophets), appears between Joel and Obadiah in the Hebrew Bible and between Hosea and Micah in the Septuagint (LXX).* Modern English Bibles follow the Hebrew rather than the Greek (Christian) order. Amos is a very popular book and prophet in modern biblical studies and is often set as an introductory Hebrew text for undergraduates studying biblical Hebrew. Neither the book nor the prophet can be said to have been significantly important in the history of biblical interpretation. Tobit (2.6) refers to Amos 8.10 (LXX or possibly from memory) as a reflection on how news about a death can ruin a good meal by transforming feasts into mourning. The NT only makes two references to the words of Amos, both of them in the Acts of the Apostles. Stephen's sermon quotes Amos 5.25–27 (Acts 7.42–43 using LXX), and in the debate between the Christian believers of the Pharisees* party and Paul* and Barnabas in Acts 15, James, the leader of the Jerusalem church, cites Amos 9.11–12 (LXX) in vv. 16–18 in order to resolve the debate in favour of the Paul and Barnabas faction. The church Fathers made much use of Amos 4.13 in the controversy with the Arians, who also used it as a proof text* for their position, in the debate about the consubstantiality of the Holy Spirit. Both groups worked with the LXX of 4.13 (cf. Athanasius, *Letters to Serapion on the Holy Spirit*). Jerome's somewhat dismissive phrase *'imperitus sermone, sed non scientia'* in the preface to his commentary* on Amos, suggesting a lack of skill in the sermons of Amos, tended to influence later thinking about Amos as an unlettered rustic. Amos' rusticity became in pious circles a figure of the divine inspiration of untutored souls in contrast to the sophisticated learning of the unregenerate.

Amos, book and prophet, has come to the fore of historical-critical* interpretation of Hebrew prophecy over the past century because, under the influence of Wellhausen and Duhm,* he was seen as the first of the great ethical* monotheists of prophetic religion who transformed the syncretistic religion of Israel into what is fondly thought of as the ethical monotheism of the Hebrew Bible. In this view of the prophet(s), the dependence of the law (torah), as an ethical force, on the prophets, and therefore the historical priority of the prophets over the Pentateuch,* is a domain assumption of scholarship. More recent study of the prophets has made the picture of the relationship between law and prophet a much more complex one, and there is now a tendency abroad to read the prophetic books as dependent, in some sense, on other biblical literature (perhaps as midrash* on and supplementation of the Deuteronomistic history* and other narratives). As the first voice uttering judgment and morality in ancient Israel, it is hardly surprising that Amos should have become popular among educated readers of the Bible. The fierceness and uncompromising integrity of his stand against religion and social oppression have become models of political theology for practitioners of that art in the late twentieth century (see **Liberation Theology; Marxist Interpretation**).

Critical interpretation of Amos focusses on the composition of the book and the social identity of the prophet. The debate between Amos and the priest Amaziah in 7.10–15 has attracted much attention in recent study because it throws into relief the whole question of identifying and authenticating prophets. Amos' denial of being a prophet (cf. Zech. 13.5) helps to deconstruct the placement of the book in the prophetic collection. That the whole debate between priest and 'prophet' appears as a narrative which disrupts the flow of visions material in 7.1–8; 8.1–2 is indicative of editorial framing of the issue and highlights the problem of understanding the composition of the book.

An equally notable element in Amos is the volte-face of 9.11–15, which reverses the absolute word of doom so central to the book of Amos (e.g. 5.2; 7.8; 8.2; 9.1–4). It is a case of, in the justly famous words of Wellhausen, 'Rosen und Lavendel statt Blut und Eisen' ('Roses and lavender instead of blood and iron', Die kleinen Propheten, ³1898, p. 96). This deconstruction of the whole message of doom typical of Amos points to the way the composed elements of the edited volume move beyond the message of Amos to the concerns of a later period. Amos' vision of utter annihilation cannot be the last word to the community, and the later 'eschatologization'* of

the prophets effectively relativizes the doom announced by Amos in favour of a future restoration of the fortunes of Israel (cf. Jer. 30–31).

The exhaustive methodological analysis of Amos by Klaus Koch and companions (Amos: Untersucht mit den Methoden einer strukturalen Formgeschichte, AOAT 30, 1976, 3 vols!) has proved to be remarkably unhelpful, and recent work on Amos has been more influenced by the analysis of Hans-Walter Wolff. He argues for a six-fold formation of the book: A. the words of Amos from Tekoa; B. the literary fixation of the cycles; C. the old school of Amos; D. the Bethel-exposition of the Josianic age; E. the Deuteronomistic redaction; F. the post-exilic eschatology of salvation (Wolff, pp. 106–13). A good example of the influence of Wolff is Robert B. Coote's fine book on Amos which sees in the text three redactions: A. the genuine oracles of Amos against Samaria; B. a seventh-century Judaean redaction against Bethel; C. an exilic redaction of hope. These shaping levels of the book's formation give to Amos an ongoing relevance to issues facing the second temple community and are indicative of the ways in which the prophetic section of the Hebrew Bible was put together in that period. The five-part structure of much of Amos (cf. H. Gese, 'Komposition bei Amos', VT-S 32, 1981, pp. 74–95; usefully discussed in Auld, pp. 46–58) has been considerably expanded by the various redactional* enhancements which constitute the book. In all these developments of the original words of Amos it becomes apparent that, with our inability to distinguish between Amos' words and the words of his followers and editors (Wolff), we must now think of such prophetic books as representing a tradition rather than a prophet.

The heroic figure of Amos, speaking out against social repression and corruption, demanding that justice should flow like a perennial stream, and condemning the wives of the wealthy for their alcoholic insatiability, remains a high point of the mythic reading of prophets. Recently, Hans Barstad has argued that Amos should be read as a religious polemic, as part of an ideological* Kulturkampf, rather than as an essay in ethics (The Religious Polemics of Amos, VT-S 34, 1984). This reading picks up important elements in the book and helps to reduce the striking contrasts between the books of Amos and Hosea (conventionally said to share similar periods and Israelite locations). It also illustrates the fact that a book as small as Amos continues to generate considerable scholarly interest, and its interpretation remains difficult and contentious in spite of the apparent simplicity of the book's relatively short text.

See also **Ethics (Old Testament); Prophets and Prophecy.**

A. G. Auld, *Amos*, 1986; R. B. Coote, *Amos among the Prophets*, 1981; R. S. Cripps, *A Critical and Exegetical Commentary on the Book of Amos*, ² 1955; J. L. Mays, *Amos*, 1969; J. A. Soggin, *The Prophet Amos*, ET 1987; H. W. Wolff, *Joel and Amos*, ET 1977.

ROBERT. P. CARROLL

Analogy

Analogies are perceived or suggested similarities; and in the most basic way, all our action and communication depends on such perceptions and suggestions. It is only on the basis of what many things have in common that we can multiply and refine distinctions. Analogy is the basis of all interpretation and translation.* It is only if we have some points in common with texts that we can begin to discern significant novelties and differences from what we would say or do (*see* **Cultural Relativism**). It is, though, very important to be able to discern the validity and the extent of an analogy. A guinea pig is in many ways like an elephant. The similarity does not extend to giving rides to children or moving logs.

The biblical writings take for granted or propose a vast and motley crowd of analogies, though we often rightly subdivide them into metaphor,* simile, parable,* sign, symbol, and so forth. Family life, body language, kingship, cultus, and so much else are assumed to offer much scope for analogies with one another. There are significant similarities between people and animals, between people and rocks and winds and storm. As well as sharing what may be no more than 'dead metaphors' ('wind' for 'breath'), we ourselves take many of the other analogies for granted: although parenting now may be different from what it was then it cannot be totally different, and so on.

It is important in interpretation to attempt to tell what the writers then thought about the validity and extent of the analogies they deployed. Does talk of feet, legs, hands and arms 'doing things' really imply a belief that they had minds and wills of their own? In what sense(s) is God a rock? There are indications, at least in Isaiah of the exile, and in Ezekiel, that the inadequacies of such analogies are realized (Isa. 40.18f.; Ezek. 1.28). The question whether sufficient analogy remains to warrant any talk at all about God is not fully discussed till Aquinas. But by the first century we have to reckon with the possibility of quite sophisticated approaches to the deployment of analogies, especially in talk of deity (Philo;* Plutarch, *de Iside et Osiride*; Dio, Discourse 12; and Paul* in his unease

with talk of our 'knowing' God – I Cor. 8.1–3; 13.12 – see Revelation*). We cannot assume, one way or the other, whether an analogy is taken to be so extensive as to be intended 'literally'. We have to check if we want to do justice to the text.

To make those checks we need, of course, to test the analogies and 'dis-analogies' that we perceive between our own life and culture, and that of two or three thousand years ago. It can be done only slowly and painstakingly, with no guarantee of success. We may avoid the obvious mistakes of, say, imposing terms like 'middle-class' or 'working-class' on first-century groups, equestrian Romans, self-employed free artisans. But how about a term like 'political'? Jesus in the Gospels* may look very apolitical to Western Christians; to contemporaries the analogy with socially disruptive Cynic* radicals might have seemed much stronger.

See also **Figures of Speech.**

G. B. Caird, *The Language and Imagery of the Bible*, 1980; F. Ferré, *Language, Logic and God*, 1961, ch. 6; G. E. R. Lloyd, *Polarity and Analogy*, 1966, pt II; J. M. Soskice, *Metaphor and Religious Language*, 1985, esp pp. 64–6.

F. GERALD DOWNING

Ancient Near Eastern Interpretation

The Sumerian writing system originated *c.* 3200 BC in southern Iraq, and from the beginning was 'learned' in two senses. First, only scribes* could read and write it, so difficult was it. Secondly, the scribes compiled learned materials for their own use, such as lists of signs and words. This learned material, which started with the beginnings of the writing system, was developed as the system spread to Semitic speakers upstream, reaching Syria in the third millennium, and it became the writing system of Babylonians and Assyrians in the second and first millennia. Formal commentaries on texts were one of the last developments of this learned material, only attested in the first millennium, from both Assyrian and Babylonian sites.

Explanation and interpretation were endemic to this writing system. Its manifold difficulties demanded scholarly aids. The large number of signs in use could not safely be left entirely to human memory, but lists of them had to be classified by some system so that they could be used easily. Then, the writing system used signs for Sumerian roots which did not indicate the pronunciation. So lists of such signs had to gloss each sign with its phonetic value or values. Then, with the spread of the system to Semitic speakers it was necessary to render Sumerian words into a Semitic language, so the tradition became bilingual, and though Sumerian died out as a spoken language by 2000 BC, it continued as the language of learning, and Semitic speakers who wished to be scribes had to master the dead Sumerian with the aid of scholarly manuals. A technical terminology developed within this tradition: for example the tenses corresponding to the Hebrew perfect and imperfect were called 'fast' and 'slow'.

The beginnings of commenting on texts are witnessed in the early second millennium BC when particular words in Sumerian literary texts were given Babylonian translations, often in small script above the Sumerian words. This developed into full translations: Sumero-Babylonian bilinguals. But the needs of interpretation were not fully met in this way. Individual words needed more explaining than a translation provided, and matters of content were not touched upon in translation except indirectly. So the scribes developed the category of formal commentary.* In omen texts some editions interpose sections of comment among the omens, but mostly the commentaries were written on separate clay tablets or waxed writing boards. The problem of the compiler was first to identify the text under comment for users, and secondly to enable the user to locate words being commented upon within that text. The colophon at the end solved the first problem. A typical one read: 'Extracts and explanations (lit. "things of the mouth"), questions of the scholar, on "In the month Tishri" of *Iqqur ipush*'. The last two words indicate an omen series and 'In the month Tishri' was the opening phrase of one section. From this the user could locate the text. Although lines were indeed often counted by cuneiform scribes, line numbers are never used in referring to passages. Instead the line or phrase on part or whole of which it was planned to comment was quoted and the comments followed each such excerpt. Usually only a certain number of lines of any text were commented upon, and this is no doubt why colophons so often speak of commentaries as 'Extracts'. Thus use of text and commentary meant following through from the beginning and matching the lines in the text with those excerpted in the commentary.

The simpler commentaries concern themselves with the meanings of words, the *peshat* of rabbinic* commentators. The word from the text is given first, followed by a synonym, and when only this kind of explanation is offered the material is often arranged in columns, e.g.:

'bind' = seize, 'bind' = defeat

This is explaining an omen apodosis 'that king will be bound' and offers two alternative meanings of the word being explained. Often

these equivalences also occur in the ancient synonym lists. Since the greater number of lexical lists were bilingual, Sumerian with Babylonian translations, the Babylonian commentators also use them to explain Babylonian words. The commentator on the Babylonian *Theodicy* cites the phrase 'You master all wisdom' and then explains: '"You master" means "you embrace" (as proved by): UR (Sumerian) = "catch", UR = "embrace", secondly "master".' The Sumerian UR is given to prove the synonymous character of 'catch', 'embrace' and 'master'. Occasionally a word is referred to the simple form found in the lists, e.g. 'bound' is explained by 'bind'. A more adventuresome commentator may go beyond what the list offered. From the same *Theodicy*, the line 'For the crime which the lion committed the pit awaits him' is commented: 'Pit (Babylonian *hashtu*) = netherworld: to HASH (Sumerian) = destroy.' The original text no doubt refers to the hunter's 'pit' to trap lions, but the commentator, by (to us wrongly) explaining the Babylonian word from a Sumerian root, makes it mean 'netherworld', a possible nuance of the Babylonian word.

Much of this philological matter is on an elementary level and reminiscent of aids in recent Western language teaching for less intelligent learners. These ancient commentators are at times remarkably frank. A very difficult word is not rarely glossed 'I do not know' or 'unclear', or it is passed over while common words are explained.

The more sophisticated commentaries always include some of this simple glossing and parsing, but their greater depth comes either in more advanced philology* or in exposition of content. Some of the philology is etymological, otherwise it consists of more advanced and reliable material. In explaining two entries in a lexical list: 'ZI (Sumerian "rise up") = *nalbubu*, ZI = *shalbubu*' (both Babylonian words meaning roughly 'savage'), the comment is: '"My savage (*nalbubu*) companion defames me (*unaggaranni*);" *nugguru* = "slander"; *shalbubu* = "fierce".' A line is quoted from a Babylonian wisdom text to illustrate the meaning of *nalbubu*, but this contains a further difficult word, which is explained, while *shalbubu* is simply glossed.

Exposition of content can be simple, e.g. the line 'I am Asalluhi who was born in E'unir ...' is explained: 'E'unir is the *ziggurat* of Nippur' (Nippur is in fact a scribal error for Eridu), a comment probably excerpted from a list of temple names. Similar 'factual' material explains another line in the same text: 'I am Asalluhi who surveys the height of the wide heavens', explained in a statement of the height of heaven in Babylonian miles. However, many expositions of content use the text as a peg on which to hang material which to our judgment is not contained or implied in it. This corresponds to the rabbinic $d^e rash$. In this case particular commentaries have different interests. A cultic interest appears in the commentary on the Babylonian *Epic of Creation*. Marduk's mythological killing of Tiamat ('He cut her blood veins and made the north wind bear up [the blood] to give the news', IV 131–132) is explained as referring to a ritual running on the fourth day of a certain month, and the blood is referred to a red garment worn by a participant in this ritual. In VII 91–92, 'Lugal-ab-dubur, the king who scatters (or: scattered!) the works of Tiamat, who uprooted her weapons, whose foundation is sure in front and behind', the text itself is expounding Marduk's names, since *dubur* = 'foundation', but the commentator goes further: '(this refers to) Nabu, (who) [sits] on the dais of destinies in front of Bel on the sixth day, and behind Bel on the eleventh day.' The allusion is to the New Year festival in Babylon in the month Nisan, and while the text under comment refers to Marduk, the commentator saw no problem in referring it to Nabu. Also as written the text contains no allusion to the New Year festival. Some commentaries on omens try to explain why the protasis results in the apodosis, e.g. 'When the exorcist goes to the sick man's house, if he sees a projecting potsherd in the street, that invalid is in a critical state, he (the exorcist) should not approach him.' The connection between potsherd and a fatal illness is established by quoting a literary text, 'He is a potsherd, the man I loved has died,' and by equating 'potsherd' and the loved one through the Sumerian *la* 'potsherd' and the Babylonian *lalû* 'luxury' and so 'loved one'. Other commentaries specialize in astrology, for example 'I am Asalluhi, who dug the canals' is explained: 'canals are the celestial area of Scorpio, who is Tiamat'. Much of this is not yet understood.

There is a whole genre* of Babylonian texts concerned with this kind of thinking, which are often called 'commentaries' by Assyriologists, but which are not commentaries on particular texts. The thought arises from the concept that in the beginning the gods laid down every aspect of human civilization, and so it is right to see connections between nature and culture, e.g. it is proper to note that the 30-day month, regulated by the moon god, is the same figure as that god's mystical number, 30, obtained from putting the major deities of the pantheon in order of importance and assigning them numbers, starting from 60 (a peak of the Sumerian sexagesimal counting) and descending in tens.

Babylonian commenting and interpretation has remarkable similarities to later Jewish and some Hellenistic Greek work. A connection is probable: as one suggestive example, note above the use of 'potsherd' as in the rabbinic *gezērāh shāwāh*, the second of the seven *middôth* of Hillel. This allows, when a key word occurs in two passages, the context of the one passage to be read into the other. Thus 'potsherd' in the omen is interpreted to allude to a person's death because in the other passage it is a metaphor for a dead friend.

See also **Ancient Near Eastern World; Archaeology (Old Testament); Writing and Transmitting Texts; Writing Materials (Old Testament).**

A. Cavigneaux, 'Remarques sur les commentaires à Labat TDP 1', *Journal of Cuneiform Studies* 34, 1982, pp. 231ff.; J. Krecher, 'Kommentare', *Reallexikon der Assyriologie* 6, 1980–83, pp. 188ff.; R. Labat, *Commentaires Assyro-Babyloniens sur les Présages*, 1933; A. Livingstone, *Mystical and Mythological Explanatory Works of Assyrian and Babylonian Scholars*, 1986.

W. G. LAMBERT

Ancient Near Eastern World

This article is concerned with changing perspectives in the interpretation of the OT in the light of changing perceptions of the Ancient Near East.

In 1829 H. H. Milman, later Dean of St Paul's, published a three-volume *History of the Jews* in which he drew a parallel between the desert sheikh and the biblical Abraham:* 'Abraham is the Emir of a pastoral tribe ... in no respect superior to his age or country, excepting in the sublime purity of his religion' (I.23f.). The use of this, to present-day eyes seemingly obvious, analogy was greeted with hostility by Milman's more conservative readers: the inspired record of God's unique saving dealings with his chosen people was, as the title of the work indicated, being explained as far as possible in ordinary historical terms, 'the only safe way of attaining to the highest truth' ([3]1863, I, p. v). The incident illustrates the long-standing debate between 'the defenders of the Bible as revelation and the discoverers of the Bible as history' (B. W. Tuchman), which was soon to be intensified with the rise of Ancient Near Eastern archaeological* research and its epigraphical discoveries.

1. Before the mid-nineteenth century, knowledge of the Ancient Near East was largely confined to information supplied by the Bible itself, post-biblical Jewish writers, especially Josephus,* and classical authors, e.g. Herodotus, supplemented by tales of Jewish and Christian pilgrims and travellers. This relative

lack of precise information made it possible to hold that the OT supplied the earliest record of the origins of the world and of humanity. This presumed antiquity furnished theologians with a subsidiary argument for the authority* of scripture: thus Calvin* writes, 'Great weight is due to the antiquity of scripture ... Whatever fables Greek writers may retail concerning Egyptian theology, no monument of any religion exists which is not long posterior to the age of Moses' (*Institutes*, I.VIII.3); John Wilkins (d. 1672), Bishop of Chester and founder member of the Royal Society, regarded the OT as the oldest literary document in the world, the source of all human language and the origin of the alphabet. Isaac Newton (d. 1727) could express himself similarly.

Even so, the originality, uniqueness and supernatural origin of the OT did not remain uncontested. The possibility that, after all, Egyptian* religion and culture were prior was mooted, e.g. by John Spencer in 1685, a proposal which was to be congenial to the eighteenth-century Deist* view of natural religion and the innate capacity of human reason. Other agents were beginning to disseminate knowledge of the East: merchant venturers and their associates, e.g. Henry Maundrell, Chaplain of the Levant Company (founded 1579) in Aleppo, whose *Journey from Aleppo to Jerusalem* was published posthumously in 1703; military leaders, e.g. Napoleon, who took scholars with him on his expedition to Egypt in 1798; biblical scholars and Christian missionaries – 1841, e.g., saw both the publication of Edward Robinson's *Biblical Researches in Palestine* and the foundation of the Anglican Bishopric in Jerusalem. Meantime, biblical criticism* too had developed apace.

2. Knowledge of the Ancient Near East has grown immeasurably since the mid-nineteenth century through the ever-increasing volume of archaeological discovery. The unlocking of the primary epigraphical sources may be roughly dated to the first decipherments of the bilingual Egyptian Hieroglyphic/Demotic-Greek Rosetta stone by J. F. Champollion in 1822 and the publication of the trilingual Old Persian–Elamite–Babylonian Behistun inscription by H. C. Rawlinson in 1846. Since then, hundreds of thousands of documents from the last three millennia BC, including annalistic, diplomatic, legal, philosophical, mythical, ritual and liturgical texts, have become available. This new knowledge has revealed the relative lateness of OT material, its comparability to Ancient Near Eastern exemplars in form, content and manner of production, and even its possible dependence on them, and has thus undermined subsidiary arguments for the authority of the Bible. Even further, if the biblical material is regarded – as it often has been – as valid only in so far as it is historically reliable, archaeological data assume an important role not only in the critical reconstruction of the historical contexts of the biblical materials but also in the evaluation of these materials themselves. Hardly surprisingly, archaeology has provided fertile soil for controversy.

At one extreme, there have been apologetic attempts to 'prove' the truth of the Bible by showing that archaeological data support the biblical version. A survey in the *Biblical Archaeologist* in 1985 suggests that there are annually published in the American market half-a-million copies of Bible handbooks, 'the conservative perspective' of most of which 'often feeds off a need to authenticate theological positions that are based on the inerrancy of the biblical text. This leads to a selective use of data ... to uphold preconceived ideas of truth.' An example is the citation of J. Garstang's 1930s equation of city walls at Jericho with those destroyed by Joshua, despite their 1950s identification by K. M. Kenyon as Early Bronze. For such conservatives, unlike Milman's opponents, the supporting of the historicity of the biblical Abraham by appeal to desert sheikhs or any other historical data is wholly acceptable – paradoxically enough, for in the process biblical uniqueness is surrendered to comparability.

At the other extreme, there have been excessive claims for the derivativeness of the OT from Ancient Near Eastern originals, e.g. in the Bible–Babel controversy in the early years of the twentieth century or in the use of Ugaritic* to elicit the 'original' meaning of the Hebrew of the canonical text of the Bible in, e.g., the work of M. J. Dahood on Psalms.

A more neutral stance has on the whole been adopted by the learned organizations set up to conduct Ancient Near Eastern research. Thus the Palestine Exploration Fund, founded in 1865, is described in its first *Quarterly Statement* (1869) as 'a Society for the accurate and systematic investigation of the archaeology, topography, geology and physical geography, natural history, manners and customs of the Holy Land'. Some surprise may, however, be aroused by the continuation: not '... for their own sake' but '... for biblical illustration'. It is even more surprising to find among the aims of the Egypt Exploration Society (founded 1882) as defined in 1886, 'illustration of the Old Testament narrative, so far as it has to do with Egypt and the Egyptians'. While it is understandable that such statements were made to secure funding from as wide an interested public as possible, there is here what must now be regarded as unwarranted imperialism on the part of biblical studies, which is expressed also in the application of the term 'biblical archaeology' by, for example, the 'Albright school' to what is properly 'Ancient Near Eastern archaeology'. The vast field of Ancient Near Eastern studies, which stretches in space and time far beyond the compass of the Bible's material references, must be allowed its independence and integrity, without reduction or distortion to fit into the biblical perspective. 'Biblical archaeology' can only concern the selection from that huge area which concerns biblical interpretation.

3. While archaeological discoveries are highly relevant to historical interpretation, their application to the interpretation of the OT has proved to be problematical. Even where apparently neutral annalistic data are available, their meshing with the biblical material is far from straightforward (e.g. the Babylonian and Assyrian king lists with the chronology of the kingdoms of Israel and Judah after the disruption). When it comes to the interpretation of a single event, e.g. the 'fourteenth year' (701?) of Hezekiah (II Kings 18.13ff.), the problems may turn out to be insoluble at the merely historical level. If this is so for one incident, it is much more so for a whole period: thus, the biblical presentation of Israel's establishment in Palestine as a military conquest fits ill with the gradual spread of settlements from Gilead into Manasseh, Ephraim and then Judah suggested by archaeological research in the 1970s and 1980s.

Such problems should not be regarded as some kind of threat to biblical authority which requires that they be minimized or explained away. Rather, they underline the essential character of the biblical material as theological (the debate between T. L. Thompson and the writers in the Millard-Wiseman symposium on the patriarchal narratives is instructive here). The interpreter repeatedly finds that, however far the biblical writers refer to history (and that is a question which is to be calmly addressed and painstakingly established, case by case), they have used it in an entirely flexible manner in order to communicate theological truth. This is true even of some of the latest incidents in the OT, which are closest to the time of editing and therefore most capable of verification, had historical accuracy been the paramount concern (e.g. the chronology of Ezra 4, where events of 80–140 years are treated as one global process of 'The Return from Exile'). The high valuation of critically reconstructed history as the supreme category of OT interpretation is, therefore, misplaced. A Jewish view of the 'midrashic' * quality of the OT is wholly appropriate: 'As creative historiography, the *Midrash* rewrites the past to make manifest the eternal rightness of scriptural paradigms'; it 'exchanges stability of

language and the continuity of history for stability of values and the eternity of truth' (J. Neusner). Against such a perspective, archaeology can be allowed to be a discipline in its own right without insistent pressure from the biblical interpreter to show support, or even relevance, for the biblical record. Most of what the biblical writers intend to communicate is beyond the capacity of archaeology to confirm or refute. The OT must ultimately be interpreted as a theological statement: to that extent, Milman's critics were right.

4. This theological statement is not, however, inert: redactional processes visible internally in the OT show how successive generations of ancient Israel received and reconceived inherited traditions. That is, the OT represents a continual process of hermeneutical transposition of tradition into the terms of new circumstances; thereby tradition itself was augmented. The archaeological rediscovery of the Ancient Near East is of relevance for the appreciation of this hermeneutical achievement. The OT itself recognizes validity in Israel's neighbours' wisdom (e.g. I Kings 4.29ff.); part of the shock of archaeological discovery has been that not only in wisdom * but also in law,* liturgy, myth * and, even, prophecy,* Israel's neighbours too had their analogous materials. It was often in engagement with these current systems that Israel sought to achieve the full articulation of its own faith. The Ancient Near Eastern parallels reveal that Israel's theologians were attempting not only to present the unique in Israel's experience but to relate that unique to general human experience in the accessibility of shared cultural terms. The aim of the interpreter should therefore be not merely to assess how distinctive Israel is over against its Ancient Near Eastern environment (cf. B. Albrektson's controversy with G. E. Wright and others on how far Israel alone among its neighbours thought of history as the theatre of divine activity) but also to trace how Israel recast its understanding of existence in response to the challenge posed by the cultures of its neighbours.

This is an observation of fundamental importance for contemporary hermeneutical practice. In the OT Israel developed its knowledge of God in terms (e.g. 'covenant' *) that were shared by its neighbouring peoples. It is, accordingly, to be entirely faithful to the biblical message when interpreters seek to effect its transposition once again into terms accessible to the culture of their times. There are notable examples of writers in the heyday of the critical movement, for whom indeed biblical criticism provided the necessary artistic stimulus, who have attempted precisely this (cf. E. S. Shaffer). The biblical model of hermeneutics,* both in matter and in manner, forces biblical interpretation into the mainstream of contemporary cultural life and challenges the interpreter to integrate received and reconceived tradition into a valid contemporary comprehensive belief system.

See also **Archaeology (Old Testament)**.

B. Albrektson, *History and the Gods: An Essay on the Idea of Historical Events as Divine Manifestations in the Ancient Near East and Israel*, C B 1, 1967; K. M. Kenyon, *The Bible and Recent Archaeology*, revd edn by P. R. S. Moorey, 1987; P. J. King, *American Archaeology in the Mideast: A History of the American Schools of Oriental Research*, 1983; A. R. Millard, D. J. Wiseman (eds), *Essays on the Patriarchal Narratives*, 1980; Henning Graf Reventlow, *The Authority of the Bible and the Rise of the Modern World*, 1984; E. S. Shaffer, *'Kubla Khan' and* The Fall of Jerusalem: *The Mythological School in Biblical Criticism and Secular Literature 1770–1880*, 1975.

WILLIAM JOHNSTONE

Anthropology

This article deals with anthropology as understood by social anthropologists in Britain and cultural anthropologists in the USA, that is, as the study of the material culture and the beliefs and social organization of pre-industrial societies (*see* **Sociology and Social Anthropology**). Anthropology as the theology of the nature and destiny of humankind is not discussed.

Anthropology did not emerge as a distinct discipline until the nineteenth century, and did not establish methodological precision until the twentieth. Its nineteenth-century pioneers such as J. G. Frazer and E. B. Tyler studied the evolution of societies from simple forms, as evident in ancient and in contemporary so-called primitive societies, to the complex forms of 'civilized' countries. By corresponding with travellers, missionaries and administrators, as well as by combing the classical literatures of antiquity, they assembled a vast amount of comparative material. They were, however, uncritical in the way they used this material. In particular, they did not ask how particular beliefs or practices of a society functioned as parts of a coherent set of symbols* or values. They wrenched beliefs and practices from their contexts, forcing them into grandiose theories about the evolution of culture. In the early twentieth century a strong reaction against their work laid stress on the need for anthropologists to spend long periods living among the peoples they studied, and to see particular items of belief and practice as parts of the total system of the life of a society. This led to the writing of many monographs dealing with individual societies, of which those by E. E. Evans-Pritchard on Zande witchcraft and magic and on Nuer religion have become classics. The effect of this research was to contradict the picture of ancient and primitive societies which had been constructed in the eighteenth and nineteenth centuries, according to which peoples of such societies lived in a mystical, pre-scientific world inhabited by mysterious spiritual forces, and dominated by magic* and superstition. The new picture that was proposed was that of peoples who, while lacking modern scientific knowledge, had considerable skills in understanding and exploiting their environment, and were capable of abstract and logical thought within the terms of their world view.

Since the Second World War, the new movements of structuralism* and cultural materialism have brought additional dimensions. Structuralism, an inter-disciplinary phenomenon introduced to anthropology by the French scholar C. Lévi-Strauss, was an attempt to return to the general theories of culture of the nineteenth century, by regarding phenomena such as kinship systems and myths* as codes which, like language systems, help to shape and structure human behaviour. Cultural materialism* is also an attempt to establish a general theory of culture, with the help of the Marxist* theory that changes to the ecology and economic base of a society ultimately affect its social organization and beliefs.

The use by biblical scholars of models drawn from anthropology has been confined almost entirely to the OT, and has concentrated upon ancient Israelite social structure, myths, sacrifice, magic and religion, and the relation of the individual to the community. Inevitably, biblical scholars have been dependent upon current anthropological theories and have often continued to use out-dated approaches repudiated by anthropologists.

In the late eighteenth century the Göttingen classicist C. G. Heyne used descriptions of North American Indians to interpret ancient Greek society. The picture that emerged was then applied to the opening chapters of Genesis by the Göttingen orientalist J. G. Eichhorn. Adam* and Eve were presented as real people in the childhood of the human race for whom any frightening occurrence in nature such as a thunderstorm was interpreted as a manifestation of divine anger. In this way, supernatural happenings in the OT could be explained as natural occurrences that had been misinterpreted by the pre-scientific and naive Hebrews. This introduced into biblical studies a theory of primitive mentality based on the study of contemporary primitive peoples. With refinements, this theory lasted well into the twentieth century and also influenced the interpretation of the NT, as in D. F. Strauss'* *Life of Jesus* (1835), in which the disciples of Jesus mistook natural occurrences as miracles.*

In the nineteenth century, as it came to be believed that all human societies had evolved socially and religiously along similar paths from simpler to more complex forms, albeit at vastly differing speeds, the OT was fitted into this scheme. The command to Abraham* to sacrifice Isaac (Gen. 22.1–19) was seen as evidence of a society that did not yet recognize individual human rights, while the wars of Joshua were excused on the grounds of the uncivilized customs of those times. The religion of Israel was held to have evolved from animism (belief in spirits) to polytheism, to monotheism, a view that was advocated as late as the 1930s in W. O. E. Oesterley and T. H. Robinson's *Hebrew Religion, Its Origin and Development*. At the close of the nineteenth century, W. R. Smith's* *Lectures on the Religion of the Semites* drew upon the theory that all societies had passed through a phase of totemism, in which groups named themselves after an animal, whose flesh they consumed at sacred meals which established communion with their totem deity. As applied to Israelite religion, Smith maintained that OT sacrifices were originally communion sacrifices which united the people to God. Only much later had sacrifices become the means of propitiating the deity for offences against him. Brilliant as Smith's lectures were, the totemic theory on which they were based was subsequently rejected by anthropologists.

In the early twentieth century, Frazer's theories of the nature of magic and Lévy-Bruhl's researches into primitive mentality were widely drawn upon to produce a picture of the ancient Hebrews which differed only in degree from that current at the end of the eighteenth century. The Hebrews believed that a name or a shadow were in a real sense extensions of a person; they were unable to distinguish clearly, as we do, between an individual and his or her group, and their thinking oscillated between the one and the many as in the phenomenon of 'corporate personality'. They had no conception of nature as a law-governed system of causes and effects, and any happening in the natural world could be a miracle. A variation on this theme was that the Canaanite neighbours of the Israelites lived in a magical-symbolic world, but that God's revelation to Israel through historical events gave them a different view of reality.

This picture of the mental life of the Hebrews was almost completely undermined by the work of anthropologists such as Evans-Pritchard, and more recent work on the OT, initiated in some cases by anthropologists, has followed quite different lines. Mary Douglas in her *Purity and Danger* (1967) examined the prohibitions of unclean animals (Lev. 11.2–23; Deut. 14.3–20) from the standpoint of the Hebrew view of the world. The division of the world in Gen. 1 into heavens, earth and seas implies that the creatures appropriate to each sphere will have certain characteristics. Earth creatures will have four limbs, and creatures that fly will have two wings and two legs. Creatures that do not fit the scheme, e.g. insects with four legs and two wings, are anomalous and forbidden. Within smaller categories of classification, animals which have cloven hooves are expected to eat grass. Pigs, which cleave the hoof but do not feed off grass, are forbidden because they do not conform.

This structural-symbolic approach has also been applied to OT sacrifice. Attention has been focussed not, as in earlier studies, on the presumed psychology of individual Israelites who offered sacrifices, but on sacrifices as part of a social code that divides the world into recognized spheres which preserve a society's stability and order. Thus reality is divided into sacred/profane, life/death, clean/unclean, order/chaos. Within such a scheme, sacrifices perform several functions. They enable some men to change status in order to become priests and belong to the area of the sacred; they repair the damage done when a person violates a boundary, e.g. by touching a corpse or the dangerous and ambiguous substance blood. They restore to the community a person temporarily excluded from it because of contracting a disfiguring illness. There can be no doubt that studies of Israelite sacrifice along these lines have been most illuminating.

However, such studies may seem to imply that societies are static entities in equilibrium, whereas the truth is that they are inherently unstable on account of changing ecological factors from outside, and conflicting ideologies* within. Cultural materialism, eloquently advocated by the American Marvin Harris, regards the 'idealistic' study of symbolic universes as less important than research into how economic change affects societies and their beliefs. He has criticized Douglas' account of why the pig was prohibited in Israel for not going to the heart of the matter, which is that the pig, as a consumer of grains, competes with humans for this source of food. In an area such as ancient Israel, where grain could not be grown abundantly, pig husbandry was not viable, and the pig was prohibited. The insights of cultural materialism have begun to be applied to the OT, most notably by Norman Gottwald in *The Tribes of Yahweh, A Sociology of the Religion of Liberated Israel 1250–1050 BCE* (1979), even to the point where it is claimed that it was the economic and social liberation of Israel that created its faith in Yahweh, and not vice versa.

The difficulty of reading the Bible in the light of general theories of culture is that violence may be done to its content. This is why N. P. Lemche's *Early Israel* (1985) is a model of how to use anthropology. He has read many monographs dealing with specific peoples, in order to discover what possibilities exist regarding types of nomadism, the sedentarization of nomads, their relation with urban centres, their tribal and social structure and their marriage practices. Lemche's aim is not to force the OT into a general scheme, but to broaden our knowledge of social phenomena so that the OT itself may be better understood. The same aim can be seen in recent American studies of prophecy in the light of anthropology, resulting in a reassessment of the phenomenon of ecstasy, and the relation of prophets to their support groups.

During the remainder of the twentieth century we can expect to learn more with the help of anthropology about Israelite social structure and institutions, the effects upon the society of economic and technological change, and how Israelite beliefs were undergirded and expressed through worship, sacrifice and law.*

See also **Community; Materialist Interpretation.**

R. C. Culley and T. W. Overholt (eds), *Semeia* No. 21, *Anthropological Perspectives on Old Testament Prophecy*, 1982; B. Lang (ed.), *Anthropological Approaches to the Old Testament*, 1985; J. W. Rogerson, *Anthropology and the Old Testament*, 1978, reissued 1984; R. R. Wilson, *Sociological Approaches to the Old Testament*, 1984.

J. W. ROGERSON

Anthropomorphism

'Attribution of human form or character' (OED) (Greek *anthrōpos*, man, *morphē*, form). The English term was first used pejoratively with reference to belief in the corporeality of God (those who assert this are styled 'anthropomorphites'), but for the last century and a half it has come to refer to any use of human language about God (or occasionally about subhuman forms of life), whether intended literally or figuratively.

The Bible eschews theriomorphism (speaking of God in animal language), which was commonplace in ancient (including Canaanite) religion, but frequently uses anthropomorphism. To what extent (if at all) some of the anthropomorphic texts reflect a hangover from paganism or, in some cases (e.g. Ex. 24.9f.), from an old Israelite theology in which

men could ascend and see God, rather than a deliberate use of such language for its figurative effect, is uncertain. In many cases, however, it is clear, irrespective of the date of the material – the attempt to date, for example, strands in the Pentateuch* by the frequency of the occurrence of anthropomorphisms has largely been abandoned – that the author is quite consciously speaking in such realistic terms because this best conveys his belief in the personal nature of God. The prohibition of the making of any plastic image of God may have encouraged the construction of such verbal images.

The toning down of biblical anthropomorphisms may have begun within the biblical period (e.g. Isa. 40.28, which after reaffirming the doctrine of creation denies that God has need to rest). It is certainly found in a number of the Greek versions, notably Aquila, Theodotion and (especially) Symmachus (but not, it is now thought, the Septuagint*). In the Targums* YHWH did not 'come down' on Sinai, but revealed himself there; and instead of reading of the anger or repentance of God, we encounter phrases such as that there was wrath or repentance before God. Also, the Word (*memra*'), Glory ('*iqar*), or Presence (*shekhinah*) of YHWH is often substituted for the divine name; this usage is designed, however, not simply to avoid anthropomorphism (a number of anthropomorphisms remain in the Targums) but to define the locus and mode of divine activity.

Many biblical texts stress the elusive, transcendent nature of God. Isa. 40.12–26 states that God cannot be compared to anyone or anything. There are many texts, too, explicitly stating that God is not human – Num. 23.19; I Sam. 15.29; Hos. 11.9 among them. Nevertheless, there were Christians who opted for a literal interpretation of anthropomorphic texts (thus justifying the scorn of pagans such as Julian and Celsus for those who believed in a God who had to rest after creation, or who came down on Sinai). We know of groups of eastern anthropomorphites, such as the followers of Audaeus the Syrian monk from Edessa (*c.* 325) and many of the recluses in Egypt in the fourth century AD. Epiphanius was in 393 denounced by John of Jerusalem as an anthropomorphite (six years later, John himself, in a volte-face, accepted the bodily nature of God). In the West we hear of them among the flock of Ratherius, Bishop of Verona in the tenth century, who took anthropomorphic language literally. Down the centuries, however, few educated Christians have been anthropomorphite (Melito, Tertullian* and Phoebadius attributed 'body' (*sōma*, *corpus*) to God, but by this they meant a specifically spiritual, eternal and immutable materiality; they were not true anthropomorphites). Of God *qua* God, human language could only be used analogically; * but those who think of Christ as the image of the invisible God, the one in whom the fullness of the Godhead dwelt corporeally (Col. 1.15, 19; 2.9; cf. John 1; Phil. 2), can use of him both human and divine language, each in a realistic sense.

Justin (*Dial. cum Tryphone*, 114) says that the rabbis * of his day interpreted texts very literally. He exaggerates the extent of this, but it is, on the face of it, true of many rabbis, most notably of Akiba and his school. Akiba balked at the idea that God is literally visible and corporeal (and indeed it has been suggested that in his later years he largely abandoned his anthropomorphic exegesis * generally), but some rabbis and mystics certainly seem to have spoken of God as having physical extension. Sometimes, indeed, the rabbis added to the biblical stock of anthropomorphisms, as when they spoke of God studying the Torah (*AZ* 3b) or putting on phylacteries (*Ber.* 6a). It seems as if it was frequently those rabbis who were most familiar with pagan writings who stuck to a literal exegesis, fearing perhaps that any figurative interpretation would prove the thin end of the wedge. Perhaps it is not so much (as Justin thought) that they had crude, naive, views of God (after all, they were well aware of texts such as Jer. 23.24 which speak of his omnipresence) as that they thought it unsafe to speculate on what the scriptural expressions meant, and so they contented themselves with repeating them. Kadushin, on the other hand, argues that the rabbis had no views on whether God was corporeal or incorporeal, not being philosophers; they, like the biblical authors, took their stand on experience, not on philosophical concepts. If some, like Akiba's contemporary Ishmael, modified some of the biblical expressions (though they retained talk of God's rejoicing and sometimes of his wrath), this was not because of a belief in the incorporeal nature of God, but in order to do justice to texts speaking of God's otherness.

The Jewish philosophers, on the other hand, have clearly from the start asserted the incorporeal nature of God. Aristobulus, an Alexandrian who wrote around 175–170 BC, explained how anthropomorphic texts should be interpreted figuratively so as to preserve 'the appropriate conception of God': thus, talk of the hands of God represents his power; of his standing, his existence and immutability (8, 10, 2–15). Aristobulus warned against taking talk of God descending to Sinai literally. Philo * continued in the same vein: God being immutable, the activities credited to him, such as creating, were the work of an intermediate

being, the Logos * (similarly mediaeval Jewish mystics referred the anthropomorphic texts to divine emanations such as the *shekhinah* *). Even Judah ha-Levi, who was better disposed than most to the retention of the anthropomorphic expressions authorized by scripture, was quite clear that God is incorporeal. Most explicit of all was Maimonides in his *Guide to the Perplexed* (*c.* 1190). The vehemence of his denunciation of literal understanding of the anthropomorphisms, which may be evidence that it was quite widespread among his contemporaries, finally laid to rest so far as educated Jews were concerned the tendency to read the biblical anthropomorphisms in a realistic sense. Today, the corporeal nature of the biblical God is espoused officially only by the Church of Latter Day Saints, though many individual believers in various religious bodies probably remain 'anthropomorphites' at heart.

W. Eichrodt, *Theology of the Old Testament*, vol 2, 1967, pp. 20–24, 432; *Encyclopaedia Judaica*, vol 3, s.v. 'Anthropomorphism'; M. Kadushin, *The Rabbinic Mind*, [2] 1965, ch VII; A. Marmorstein, *The Old Rabbinic Doctrine of God, II: Essays on Anthropomorphism*, 1937.

B. P. ROBINSON

Antiochene Interpretation

In the setting of early Christian thought, the expression 'school of Antioch' refers to a broad, and hence by no means uniform, tradition of 1. christological * speculation and 2. scriptural exegesis * which was rooted in Syria * and flowered in the late fourth and early fifth centuries in the work of Diodore of Tarsus (d. *c.* 390) and his two pupils, John Chrysostom (*c.* 347–407) and Theodore of Mopsuestia (*c.* 350–428), the latter of whom has been regarded as typifying, or at any rate as epitomizing, the tendencies which distinguish the school. Scholars have pointed to the figures of Paul of Samosata and the martyred Lucian of Antioch as third-century predecessors of this school, though in fact little that is relevant to such a judgment is known about either of them. In any case, the intellectual and ecclesiastical life of Antioch in the fourth century was lively, diverse, and full of conflict. The church in Antioch was a focus of the controversy over the teachings of Arius. In addition, Theodore and Chrysostom were both pupils of the pagan rhetor * Libanius; Antioch was a well-known centre for rabbinical * studies; and Jerome cut his exegetical teeth there at the lectures of Apollinarius of Laodicea. It is not always a simple matter, therefore, to trace with assurance the influences, negative or positive, that contributed to the distinctive style, interests, and teachings of the school of Antioch.

The notoriety of the school derives in the first instance from the dualistic christology which Theodore of Mopsuestia systematized as an antidote to both Arianism and Apollinarianism. As expounded by Theodore's disciple Nestorius, it was repudiated by the councils of Ephesus (431) and Chalcedon (451). This eventually led to the retrospective condemnations of Diodore (by a synod in Constantinople in 499) and Theodore (by the second Council of Constantinople in 553). At least since the time of Theodore's formal condemnation, it has been customary to discern a logical connection, or at least an analogy of intellectual mood, between the exegetical procedures and the christology of these writers; but if there is one, it is tenuous, since Chrysostom contrived to espouse the former while evincing few symptoms of the latter, and Diodore was gladly read by later Syrian Monophysites, to whom the names of Nestorius and Theodore were anathema but from whom we derive significant fragments of Diodore's writings.

One clear consequence of the condemnations of Diodore and Theodore was that their writings, the great majority of which were exegetical (both appear to have commented on nearly every book of the Bible), are not for the most part preserved either in their entirety or in their original language. Most of them are known today in fragmentary form, and often in Syriac (the Nestorian churches regarded Theodore as 'the interpreter' *par excellence*) or in Latin. Chrysostom's work, by contrast, consisted for the most part of sermons, the majority of which treated whole books of the Bible in course, and has been carefully and faithfully transmitted.

Among the accusations brought against Theodore at the second Council of Constantinople some touched on his handling of the scriptures: and notably the charge that he declined to recognize the canonical* authority* of certain biblical books. The charge was not so much wrong as wrongheaded. Where the OT is concerned, it is clear that his canon omitted Ezra–Nehemiah and Chronicles; but this accorded with the normal custom of the Syrian churches. Further he denied that Solomon in writing Proverbs and Ecclesiastes had enjoyed the grace of prophetic inspiration,* and ascribed to him instead (apparently alluding to I Cor. 12.7–11) the gift of wisdom, which he seems to have conceived as another order of inspiration. The Song of Songs Theodore regarded as a straightforward marriage-hymn. He denied either that it is calculated to encourage lewdness or that it treats of the church's, or the individual soul's, union with Christ (two theses that were closely related in the minds of those who sought to give the Song an allegorical interpretation*). Because of the Song's 'domestic' character, he thought, it was just as well that neither Jews nor Christians read it in public; but he plainly accepted it as part of the canon, even as he did the Book of Job, though he deprecated the poetic sections of Job as purely imaginative creations that departed from plain history and ran the risk of injuring the reputation of that righteous sufferer. What Theodore's reflections on these books suggest is not that he sought to truncate the canon as he had received it, but that he assigned differing functions to the various genres* of literature that he found in the scriptures (and perhaps differing orders of inspiration as well) and that his own preference among these genres was for history and prophecy. Where the NT is concerned, it continues to be an open question whether he worked with the same list of books as did Chrysostom (i.e. in effect, that of the Peshitta Syriac version, which omitted II Peter, II and III John, Jude, and Revelation), or whether he worked with the earlier Syrian canon, which had omitted all of the Catholic Epistles. In either case the canon he accepted was not the one that was familiar to the bishops at Constantinople in 553.

At the opening of his *Commentary on John*, Theodore explains the function of a commentator* and how it is distinct from that of a preacher. The commentator's task is to explain the meanings of difficult words and to do so as tersely as is consistent with clarity. Lengthy discourse is justified only when difficult issues present themselves – as, for example, when a false interpretation of some passage has been proposed by 'heretics' (by which Theodore almost certainly means Arians). The preacher, on the other hand, attends to what is clear in a text and may legitimately multiply words, presumably to serve the needs of edification. Theodore in practice follows his own prescription. His commentaries consist for the most part of brisk explicative notes issuing in short paraphrases. When dealing with OT texts, he takes account of other versions and occasionally, at second hand, of the Hebrew text. He notes and refutes contrary interpretations when necessary, sometimes at length. His doctrinal ideas and commitments not infrequently contribute to or govern his exegesis.

In addition, however, Theodore like Diodore takes pains to interpret biblical books as texts to be understood in the light both of their historical setting and of their historical reference. This is especially evident in his treatment of prophetic* writings, among which the Psalms of David* held, for him, a place of honour, since he believed that David first foresaw everything that was to come for Israel. Where prophetic oracles* are concerned, he always tries to establish, where possible, both the circumstances or needs to which they were originally addressed and the historical situation to which, as predictions, they pointed. This policy conforms with his belief that prophecy had two functions: to serve the needs of 'the people who lived at that time', and also to provide 'a certain disclosure of the things that should be manifested at a later time' (P G 66:556C D).

With this concern for the historical setting and reference of a text, Theodore combines the Antiochene school's well-known insistence upon the plain, and in that sense 'literal', meaning* of a text. It was a settled principle with him and his fellow Antiochenes that no text can mean or intimate something 'other' (*allēgorein*) than what it openly says – though, as Chrysostom pointed out, and Diodore and Theodore both recognized, it may convey its plain meaning by way of a figure of speech* (*ek metaphoras*). Hence they firmly repudiated the allegorical method as that was practised by exegetes in the tradition of Origen,* even while acknowledging that the word *allēgoria* had a legitimate sense (as at Gal. 4.24), when it referred to a comparison between past and present events or circumstances. The essential point for Theodore in all this was that every prophetic oracle had to be interpreted as intending to convey a single, self-consistent 'literal' meaning. Hence he could protest against exegetes who 'divide' Zechariah 9.8–10 by applying it partly to Zerubbabel and partly to Christ. He even argued against certain rabbis (who thought differently) that the 'speaker' in each psalm – i.e. the *persona* or role in which the prophet David speaks – must be uniform through the whole of the psalm. Thus Ps. 69, as he sees it, is spoken by David as 'in the person' of the Maccabees, and hence its predictive reference is confined to their circumstances.

One consequence of these principles, to which the second Council of Constantinople hastened to draw attention, was that Theodore found very few passages in the O T that he was prepared to interpret as referring to Christ. Even though he believed that God's sending of the prophets was ultimately for the sake of the Christian dispensation, it was Theodore's conviction that, apart from David himself (in Ps. 2, 8, 45, and 110), none of the prophets spoke directly of Christ. Their immediate vision was confined to the framework defined by the Mosaic dispensation. He did acknowledge, however, apparently on the basis of N T precedent, that the language of some of their pronouncements was applicable to Christ: i.e. that its 'literal' sense *also* suited Christ and his circumstances or his work. Thus he thought that certain events and persons in the O T

furnished imitations or 'types' (*see* **Typology**) of the Christian dispensation: the prophet Jonah 'afforded in his own person a type of the things that would come to pass regarding the Lord Christ' (P G 66:325B). Theodore's teacher Diodore used the word *theōria* to denote the kind of prophetic vision that, in grasping an occurrence in Israel's future history, grasped at the same time, as a kind of overflow, the messianic* reality that it prefigured. His idea seems to have been that such a text has only a single 'sense' (*dianoia*) but is capable of a dual historical application or reference. One clue to the operation of this sort of vision was, for him, a text which, in describing a future event, waxed unduly hyperbolic, so that its language was better suited to Christ than to the event the prophet directly 'saw'. Theodore himself applies this criterion to the case of Zech. 9.8–10. The prophet, he says, is referring to Zerubbabel but speaks so hyperbolically that the words are only found to be fully true 'when they are applied to the Lord Christ'. There is, then, an implicit grasp of the Christian dispensation in a limited number of prophetic and historical texts, but the O T retains a historical function and integrity of its own.

In their handling of the N T, the Antiochene exegetes are of less interest for their method (which remains grammatical and historical at base) than for the doctrinal or moral content of their expositions. Theodore's exegesis of the Fourth Gospel is characteristic in this respect. He saw this Gospel as providing information which the first three evangelists* had omitted and as being more accurate than they about the order of events; but at the same time his interest in it was stimulated by its insistence on the divinity of Christ, which he exploited in refutation of the Arians, and by the problem of the relation between expressions that assert or imply Christ's divinity and those that assert or imply a lowly and human status for him. In this way the Fourth Gospel became a testing-ground for Theodore's doctrine of Christ's 'two natures' – even though his historical sense prevented him from supposing that the figures portrayed in the Gospel held such a doctrine.

Both Chrysostom in an abundance of sermons and Theodore in his commentary on the minor epistles* of St Paul* offer, in vastly different styles, an interpretation of Paul's letters and of his thought. Theodore found the futuristic or eschatological* element in Pauline teaching sympathetic. It fitted admirably into his conception of 'two ages': a present age characterized by mortality, and the future age of the resurrection.* On the other hand, Paul's (and his school's) stress on the partial actualization in present experience of the life of the coming age rendered Theodore uncomfortable, since he envisaged the Christian dispensation in the present age as a type or image of the future age and not as an anticipation of it. In treating the polarity of law and gospel in Paul, both Theodore and Chrysostom stress the gift of the Spirit as the source of people's ability to fulfil the law's demand for a virtuous life, but both are uneasy with Pauline ideas about election and predestination, which seem to them to risk underplaying human agency in the work of salvation. In this, of course, their interpretation is representative of the Greek tradition generally.

See also **Alexandrian Interpretation; Allegorical Interpretation; Jewish Christianity; Patristic Christology; Syriac Tradition.**

R. M. Grant, *The Bible in the Church: A Short History of Interpretation*, 1948; J. L. Kugel and R. A. Greer, *Early Biblical Interpretation*, 1986; L. Pirot, *L'Oeuvre exégétique de Théodore de Mopsueste*, 1913; M. F. Wiles, 'Theodore of Mopsuestia as Representative of the Antiochene School' in P. R. Ackroyd and C. F. Evans (eds), *The Cambridge History of the The Bible*, Vol. 1, 1970.

R. A. NORRIS

Antisemitism

Antisemitic exegesis of the Bible may be defined as any exegesis that puts the Jews into an evil role in sacred history. Denunciation of individual Jews, or even of large numbers of Jews, does not constitute antisemitism. The Hebrew prophets often express such denunciation, but their premise is that the Jews are the people of God, who are failing to fulfil their holy mission, but who will, by repentance, eventually fulfil it. It is only when the Jews are conceived as rejected from the role of God's people, and as playing a negative role in the working-out of God's plan, that denunciation turns into antisemitism.

The most extreme stance, found in some forms of Gnosticism* and in Marcionism,* interprets the OT as essentially an evil text (see, for example, the *Apocalypse of Adam*). Antisemitism, in this standpoint, is closely related to anti-Judaism, since Judaism is regarded as an evil ideology* suitable to an evil people. This view was revived by the extreme wing of the German Christians in Nazi Germany.

Hardly less extreme, however, is the far commoner thesis that the OT, while itself a holy text, gives evidence of the alleged incorrigible evil of the Jewish people. The Jews, in this standpoint, were always an evil people. The prophets whom God sent to them should be regarded as Christians, not as Jews, and the Jews' rejection and murder of these prophets foreshadowed their eventual rejection and murder of Jesus. Important texts for this view are Matt. 23.31–6; John 8.44–7; Acts 7.51–3; and I Thess. 2.15; and also, in the OT itself, Neh. 9.26 and II Chron. 36.16. In this standpoint, antisemitism is not combined with anti-Judaism, the Jews being represented as too evil to appreciate the God-given religion which was eventually to find its true exponents in the Christian church.

The exegetes of the church from the second century onwards frequently employ the above mode of antisemitic exegesis.* Jewish self-criticism, as expressed in the OT, is utilized to depict the Jews as a people which had always been vicious and worthless. Jewish history is depicted as 'a trail of crimes' (see Ruether). Expressions of contrition uttered in the wake of national disaster as part of a programme of regeneration and repentance are taken at face value as showing the utter depravity of the Jews (e.g. *Ep. Barn.* 5,11).

On the basis of such biased exegesis, every specific kind of habitual crime was attributed to the Jews, especially idolatry and sexual vice (e.g. Eusebius,* *D.E.* I,6,17; Aphrahat, *Dem.* 11.1; 15.4; Chrysostom, *Or. c. Jud.* VI,2; Tertullian,* *Adv. Jud.* 1; Irenaeus, *Haer.* IV,14; Justin, *Dial.* 34; Ephrem, *Rhy. C. Jud.* 15). On the basis of Ps. 106.37, the Jews were declared to have been infanticides. Chrysostom even accused them of cannibalism, on the basis of their prophesied behaviour during a long siege (Deut. 25.56). The explicit object of this cataloguing of alleged crimes was to show that the Jews' alleged murder of Jesus was foreshadowed in their whole history.

These charges against the OT Israelites were regularly taken to apply to contemporary Jews too, since their refusal to worship Jesus was regarded as a continuance of their previous depravity (e.g. Origen,* *C. Cel.* II,75; Isidore, *C. Jud.* I,18; Augustine,* *Adv. Jud.* 5 and 7). In particular, as James Parkes has shown, charges of Jewish persecution of Christians were regularly based not on factual evidence but on OT texts bizarrely interpreted to refer to contemporary Jewish–Christian relations. 'The statement of Jewish hostility in general terms is based on theological exegesis and not on historical memory' (*The Conflict of the Church and the Synagogue*). Thus Origen interprets Deut. 32.21 to mean, 'The Jews do not vent their wrath on the Gentiles ... but against the Christians they rage with an insatiable fury.' Yet Origen himself was friendly with Jews, whom he found helpful in his biblical researches. Statements such as Origen's, asserting Jewish hostility and persecution on purely exegetical grounds, have been taken by historians down to the present day as evidence of persecution of the church by the Jews in the second, third and fourth centuries, though a study of the abundant documentary evidence disproves this (Parkes, pp. 121–51).

The doctrine of the depravity of the Jews serves to validate the election of the Christian church in their place as the true Israel. To this end, exegesis of OT prophecy is neatly divided: all prophecies of failure and disaster are allotted to the Jews, and all those of success and prosperity to the church. To emphasize the allegedly foredoomed rejection of the Jews, a technique was introduced of interpreting various OT 'pairs' in this sense: Cain and Abel, Hagar and Sarah, Ishmael and Isaac, Esau and Jacob, Orpah and Ruth – all were taken to symbolize the rejected Jews and the accepted church (e.g. Maximinus, *C. Jud.* I; Tertullian, *Adv. Jud.* 5; Augustine, *Civ. Dei* 15,7; Chrysostom, *Or. c. Jud.* I,7). Of course, models for this kind of exegesis already existed in the NT (see Rom. 9.13 for Esau and Jacob, and Gal. 4.21–31 for Hagar and Sarah).

The total effect of this approach to OT exegesis is to represent the Jews as playing a fated evil role in history. They are expected, even designated, by God to perform the evil deed that in fact functions as a salvation-bringing sacrifice. Although it is often stated by exegetes that God waited patiently for the Jews to repent after each backsliding and only lost all patience after the culminating crime of the murder of Jesus, nevertheless the cumulative effect of exegesis is to represent this outcome as inevitable and as foreseen. Thus the Jews as a whole perform the role assigned to Judas in the Gospels, designated by Jesus to betray him, yet damned for doing so. Such a depiction of the Jews is undoubtedly antisemitic, since it does not merely constitute a form of anti-Judaism but assigns an evil cosmic role to the Jews as a people.

In addition to the exegesis of the OT, the NT texts cited above constantly feature in diabolizing attacks on the Jews, especially John 8.44–47. This text is one of the first cited in Luther's* antisemitic treatise, *The Jews and their Lies*, in which he goes on to say, 'The devil with all his fallen angels has taken possession of this people.'

A less radical thesis dated the reprobation of the Jews only from the time of their failure to accept Jesus as God and Messiah.* On this thesis, the Jews were indeed the people of God up to this time, despite their backslidings. But they lost this role because of their rejection of Jesus, and became an accursed nation, punished by the destruction of their Temple, by exile and by slavery (Aquinas). This thesis, in so far as it validated oppression of the Jews, was full of antisemitic potential, but it could be understood in various forms, ranging from the relatively mild to the most severe.

Its severest form was based on Matt. 27.25, which was taken to mean that the Jews as a people had incurred a self-imposed curse by their conduct in calling for the death of Jesus. This verse, more than any other, became a warrant for charging all Jews with deicide. Modern interpretation sees the verse as an unhistorical addition by Matthew to Mark's narrative, which itself, as regards the alleged choice between Jesus and Barabbas, is replete with unhistorical elements designed to increase the guilt of the Jewish people. But here we touch on the vexed question of how far the antisemitism of the church was not a matter of antisemitic exegesis but a reflection of antisemitic trends in the NT itself.

The mildest form of the less radical thesis, based on Rom. 11.7–12, is that the Jews suffered from 'blindness', mysteriously inflicted by God in order to bring about the salvation of the Gentiles: eventually, this 'blindness' would be lifted. This led to the mediaeval form of toleration of Judaism which regarded the practice of biblical Judaism as licit, but condemned post-biblical Judaism (chiefly the Talmud*) and sought to destroy it. The Jews were to remain in a state of suspended animation until the time came for their conversion to Christianity, shortly before the Second Coming (see Maccoby, pp. 23–38). In so far as the Jews failed to conform to the Christian model for them, and pursued their religious development as if they were still the true Israel with a form of continuity rivalling that of Christianity, they were to be regarded as evil (letter of Pope Gregory IX, Grayzel, p. 241). This attitude may be regarded as a form of anti-Judaism, rather than of antisemitism, but the distinction is hard to maintain in view of the denunciations of the Talmud, the chief canonical work of post-biblical Judaism, as depraved, obscene and blasphemous, and of its followers as perverted and wicked.

The most virulent form of the thesis of the post-Jesus reprobation of the Jews is the doctrine of the Antichrist, based chiefly on exegesis of II Thess. 2.3–12. This doctrine, giving a baleful eschatological* role to the Jews, receives its earliest exegetical expression in the church Fathers (Irenaeus, *Adv. Haer.* V; Hippolytus, *de Antichristo*, and *Comm. on Daniel*; Lactantius, *Div. Inst.* vii, 14ff.). The Pauline* passage was widely interpreted to mean that at the end of days a Jewish Antichrist would arise, who would be regarded by the Jews as the Messiah, and who would lead a powerful Jewish army against the forces of Christianity, led by Christ himself. This scenario fed Christian paranoia, and led to massacres of Jews in the mediaeval millenarian movements, including the Crusades. The same scenario, with its fantasy of a powerful Jewish organization threatening to dominate the world, lies in the background of the modern secularized millenarian movement of Nazism.

Thus exegesis of the Bible has been one of the chief means by which antisemitic notions of the Jews as a congenitally evil people, or as under God's curse, or as the chief obstacle to an eschatological solution, have been transmitted from the ancient to the modern world.

See also **Christian Interpretation of the Old Testament; John, Gospel of.**

Wilhelm Bousset, 'Antichrist' in *Encyclopaedia of Religion and Ethics* ed. John Hastings, 1908, vol. 1, pp. 578–81; Solomon Grayzel, *The Church and the Jews in the Thirteenth Century*, 1966; Hyam Maccoby, *Judaism on Trial: Jewish–Christian Disputations in the Middle Ages*, 1982; James Parkes, *The Conflict of the Church and the Synagogue*, 1934; Rosemary Ruether, *Faith and Fratricide*, 1974; Joshua Trachtenberg, *The Devil and the Jews*, 1966.

HYAM MACCOBY

Apocalyptic

About the time of the rise of Christianity there were produced by unknown Jews texts which purported to offer revelations from God by means of either visions or auditions concerning some of the most intractable problems of human existence, e.g. the reasons for human suffering and the character of God's purposes for the world. The particular concern of these texts to offer divine wisdom by means of revelation is known as apocalyptic or apocalypticism. It represents the form which prophecy* took in the Graeco-Roman period. In its literary form, it shows some marked differences from the earlier prophetic writings and, as one might expect, has included ideas from other streams of Jewish life, particularly the inquiring spirit manifested in the Wisdom Literature* of the OT. In some of the visions, the message is communicated by means of symbolism,* often complex and sometimes rooted in biblical passages. That symbolism not only makes it difficult to discern exactly what historical referent is being alluded to, but also makes the texts themselves susceptible of a variety of other interpretations in different circumstances. The way in which the symbolism of Daniel and Revelation has continued to furnish Jewish and Christian commentators with a mode of discourse on current affairs is testimony enough to the resilience of the imagery and its continued applicability. We find within the Jewish apocalyptic tradition an ongoing use of the imagery in changing circumstances. Thus, the fourth beast mentioned in Dan. 7 comes in Rev. 13 and in IV Ezra 12 to be identified with Rome, whereas almost certainly in the original it had been identified with the Greek regime succeeding Alexander the Great. Equally, this polyvalence has made the apocalyptic literature a happy hunting-ground for many conflicting opinions. Such problems posed by the prophetic element in religion were nothing new for Judaism, for the need to distinguish true from false prophecy had long been an issue (Deut. 13).

In most recent discussion of apocalyptic, a clear distinction is made between apocalyptic and apocalypse. The former refers to a distinct set of ideas or religious outlook with particular well-defined characteristics. The latter is a particular literary type found in ancient Judaism, characterized by its claims to offer visions or other disclosures of divine mysteries concerning a variety of subjects. The literary genre* apocalypse, of which the books of Daniel and Revelation are the two canonical examples, is to be distinguished from apocalyptic, which is usually viewed as a cluster of mainly eschatological ideas which impinged generally on the theology of Judaism, and then of Christianity. Thus passages such as Mark 13, I Thess. 4.16 and the like, are examples of apocalyptic, with their descriptions of the irruption of the Redeemer into history, and, in the case of Mark 13, the cosmic catastrophes which must precede the coming of the heavenly Son of Man.* Thus the word 'apocalyptic' has been used to describe the beliefs concerning the arrival of a new age. It is seen merely as a form of eschatology* which is to be distinguished from the national, this-worldly eschatology of the rabbis.* It possesses the following characteristic features: a contrast between the present age, which is perishable and temporary, and a new age, which is imperishable and eternal; a belief that the new age is of a transcendent kind, which breaks in from beyond through divine intervention and without human activity; an interest in the totality of world history; predestinarian elements, and an imminent expectation of the coming of the new age.

The evidence from the apocalypses themselves, however, indicates that such a dichotomy between a national eschatology found principally in the rabbinic texts, and otherworldly eschatology found principally in the apocalypses cannot easily be substantiated. Therefore, other approaches have been sought to do justice to the apocalypses and their contents.

So, it has been suggested that apocalyptic might be better understood as part of a much wider religious phenomenon in late antiquity; what Hengel has called 'higher wisdom through revelation'.* There are many parallels between the quest for knowledge through revelation in the apocalypses and non-Jewish material. Also, there was a widespread trend in antiquity towards the irrational and the mysterious, so that revelation of what was hidden with God became an indispensable way of giving meaning and purpose to human existence. If we think of apocalyptic in this way, we shall be able to see how the claim of the apocalypses to reveal mysteries about the future, the movements of the stars, the heavenly dwelling of God, angelology, the course of human history, and the mystery of the human plight *all* fall within the category of the mysteries which can only be solved by higher wisdom through revelation.

In the discussion of apocalyptic in the last thirty years or so, there has been a significant difference of opinion about its origins. Links have been suggested with various OT antecedents, notably the prophetic and wisdom literature. The concern with human history and the vindication of Israel's hopes is said to represent the formulation of the prophetic hope in the changed circumstances of another age. Those who take this line, such as Hanson, all stress the close links with prophecy but also point out the subtle change which has taken place in the form of that hope in apocalyptic. This point of view has been very influential, because it has seemed to many that in the apocalyptic literature written round about the beginning of the Christian era, the future hope has been placed on another plane. Its stress from first to last is on the supernatural and other-worldly.

While this view has been most influential, it has not gone unchallenged. It has been suggested that it is the Wisdom tradition of the OT with its interest in understanding the cosmos and the ways of the world which was the real antecedent of apocalyptic. Rather than concentrating on Proverbs and Ecclesiastes, with their practical wisdom applicable to everyday life, our attention is pointed to the activities of certain wise men in antiquity which were not at all dissimilar from the concerns of the writers of the apocalypses. This is 'Mantic wisdom', which includes the interpretation of dreams, oracles, astrology and the ability to divine mysteries concerning future events. There is some trace of the role of such figures in the OT, e.g. in the Joseph stories in Genesis, but particularly in the stories about Daniel, the Jewish seer who interprets the dreams of Nebuchadnezzar and is regarded as a superior sage to all those in the king's court. Dreams, visions, and the like are all typical features of the apocalypses, and it is now recognized that this aspect of the Wisdom tradition may indeed provide an important contribution to our understanding of apocalyptic origins.

Who wrote the apocalypses and why will probably remain a mystery, despite the many attempts to relate the various texts to specific historical circumstances. Such attempts may themselves miss the point of their significance. They are as likely to be manifestations of the bewildered spirit of the age seeking for meaning in the world and in the ancestral tradition as coined for specific crises of faith. Whether or not the apocalypses contain the visions of unknown seers cannot now be decided, as all the apocalypses with the exception of Revelation are written pseudonymously. This makes the task of recovering the actual visionary content all the more difficult. That possibility should not be ruled out, particularly if, as seems likely, some of the visions had their origin in reflection and meditation upon the scriptures which in turn offered an opportunity to see again visions of God and visions of hope once vouchsafed to the prophets in the different circumstances of a later age. Such a view of apocalyptic allows us to see it as part of the story of the mystical tradition in both Judaism (*see* **Merkabah Mysticism**) and Christianity. Such communion with the heavenly world is primarily concerned with understanding the mystery of God's purposes, to facilitate continued adherence to the divine will in circumstances where the reasons for it may have been under pressure. As such, the claim to revelation is a radical, some might say desperate, solution to the problem of religion in the face of the cogency of reason and experience. When human reason reaches the end of its capacity, revelation appears to be the only way to establish the transcendence of God and the ultimate triumph of the divine purposes.

Apocalyptic sets out to reveal things as they really are in the world at large. 'The Apocalypse shreds and rips away that common sense with as much violence as that with which John sees the sky itself removed', as Wayne Meeks has so graphically put it (*The Moral World of the First Christians*, 1987, p. 145). Thus, for example, the Book of Revelation allows no quarter in its rejection of a world order opposed to the justice of God and offers the starkest possible contrast between the regime of the beast and the reign of God on earth. There are no shades of grey here. The reader is left in little doubt that there is only one way left: protest and survive. The characterization of society in the apocalyptic symbolism of Beast and Harlot is a vigorous unmasking and denunciation of the ideology of the powerful, by which they seek to legitimize their position by persecution and economic exploitation. The process of unmasking involves an attempt to delineate the true character of contemporary society and the superhuman forces at work in opposition to God's righteousness in the world. Also, the enormously powerful forces which undergird the oppression and unrighteousness of the world order are shown to be unstable and destined to defeat. In contrast, despite their apparent fragility, the witness of those who follow the way of Jesus is promised ultimate vindication.

In saying this, care needs to be taken not to suppose that use of the apocalyptic tradition has been confined only to the socially and politically marginal, either in the first century or any other period. In the sixteenth and seventeenth centuries, apocalyptic was a source of comfort just as much to those whose place in the political establishment was secure as to those who found in its imagery the source of inspiration for the overthrow of the existing order.

The claim of the apocalypses to offer direct access to the mind of God offers a paradigm for any self-proclaimed agents of God's purposes, the consequences of whose vocation have ranged from the catastrophic to the sublime. What the apocalyptic tradition sanctions is the possibility of continuing to claim revelations from God. It is this after all which forms the heart of the NT belief that a new dispensation in God's saving purposes has come about. Fundamentally important call-visions mark the beginning of the careers of both Jesus of Nazareth (Mark 1.10; Luke 10.18) and Paul* (Gal. 1.12,16), as well as the panoramic eschatological vista of the seer of Patmos. Unless the claim is made that the era of the Spirit who inspires seers and prophets is over (a claim which can hardly be substantiated from the NT), the canonical status of the book of Revelation may be seen to open up the possibility of ever new promptings from the Spirit–Paraclete who will guide God's people into all truth (John 16.13). That is precisely what we find in the Montanist movement and other apocalyptic movements in Christian history. The question inevitably arises of the test which distinguishes the genuine inspiration of the Spirit. If Revelation is anything to go by, the answer is rooted in the conformity of that prophetic witness and the claims made in the vision with the life of the bringer of the Spirit of the messianic age, Jesus of Nazareth. John points out to his readers that it is the Spirit of Jesus which is the spirit of prophecy (Rev. 19.10), and it is surely conformity with that particular apocalyptic visionary which must mark the Christian apocalypse.

Apocalyptic has been regarded as offering an easy answer, through divine intervention, to intractable human problems. The desire for 'higher wisdom through revelation' is then in some sense an answer to the real contradictions of life and to deep pessimism about social circumstances. It offers an answer at the level of ideas to despair of ever being able to make sense of those contradictions. Throughout the history of Judaism and Christianity there are examples of individuals and movements which have claimed to understand the mind of God. Problems arose only when that understanding led to patterns of behaviour which conflicted severely with the conventions of the time. We find that happening in the career of Paul, for example, when his claim to 'a revelation of Jesus Christ' (Gal. 1.12) became the basis of his proclamation of the Law-free gospel to the Gentiles. Revelation can be used to exclude and anathematize opponents and their way of behaviour. Such a use of apocalyptic, which in effect denies the fallibility of the recipient, also removes any possibility of discussion of the subject in hand. Similarly, the claim to revelation and knowledge of the mind of God can result in authoritative interpretations of scripture, e.g. in Dan. 9.23, and in the biblical interpretation at Qumran (see 1QpHab 8). 'Higher wisdom through revelation' can be a disruptive intrusion into well-established patterns of religion, particularly if, as is the case with someone like Fra Dolcino in the aftermath of the disputes over the legacy of St Francis, and with Thomas Münzer in 1524, an apocalyptic conviction is linked with resort to violence. Such dangers have been enough to push this part of the Judaeo-Christian tradition to the periphery. But that is where it has flourished and from where it will continue to threaten the conventional, 'normal' patterns of ecclesiastical behaviour into processes of reassessment in the light of its alternative perspective.

See also **Gnosticism; Mysticism; Pseudonymity; Revelation.**

P. D. Hanson, *Visionaries and their Apocalypses*, 1983; M. Hengel, *Judaism and Hellenism*, 1974; B. McGinn, *Apocalyptic Spirituality*, 1980; C. Patrides and A. Wittreich, *The Apocalypse in English Renaissance Thought and Literature*, 1984; M. Reeves, *Joachim of Fiore and the Prophetic Future*, 1976; C. Rowland, *The Open Heaven*, 1982; id., *Radical Christianity*, 1988; M. Stone, 'Apocalyptic Literature', in Stone (ed.), *Jewish Literature from the Second Temple Period*, 1984.

CHRISTOPHER ROWLAND

Apocrypha

The term denotes those texts found in ancient Greek (Christian) Bibles (*see* **Septuagint**) which are not in the Jewish canon.* These texts, however, were not originally grouped together, but found either among (e.g. I and II Macc.), or as additions to (e.g. Dan. 13–14), or insertions in (e.g. the song of the young men in Dan. 3) the Hebrew (Aramaic) books. The word means 'hidden away', and it is unknown why it came to be used for these writings. Moreover, since early Greek Bibles varied slightly in the number of such books and passages they included, there is no strictly definitive Apocrypha, and certainly no definitive order. However, the contents are generally recognized as comprising the following books: I and II Esdras (respectively III and IV in Roman Catholic Bibles), Tobit, Judith, Additions to Esther, Wisdom of Solomon, Sirach (or Ecclesiasticus), Baruch, the Letter of Jeremiah (these last two sometimes combined), the Prayer of Azariah and Song of the Three Young Men, Susanna, Bel and the Dragon, the Prayer of Manasseh, I and II Maccabees.

History. There are infrequent allusions to, but no quotations from, any of this literature in the NT. However, it was treated at first by the church Fathers as on an equal basis with the books of the Jewish canon, namely as scriptural and inspired. But in translating the OT into Latin (known as the Vulgate*) from Hebrew in the fourth century AD, Jerome naturally followed the Hebrew canon and drew attention, by means of prefaces, to the absence of certain books and passages known from the Greek. Nevertheless, translations of these were provided in the Vulgate, probably some by Jerome, in the positions they occupied in the Greek Bibles, not in a single collection. Even so, there persisted some doubts (even if theoretically expressed) about their status in the Western church; while most mediaeval Latin Bibles contained the apocryphal writings, theologians often drew a distinction between those books also in the Hebrew canon and what were termed the 'ecclesiastical' writings (i.e. as belonging to church but not to the synagogue), and the implication often drawn from this distinction was that the latter were sufficient for edification and instruction, but not for doctrine, except in support of the fully 'scriptural' books. Wycliffe's Bible (*see* **Translations [to the KJV]**), for example, distinguished those books which 'shall be set among Apocrypha, that is, without authority of belief'.

In the wake of the Protestant challenge (see below), the Roman Catholic Council of Trent (1545–1563) affirmed – in the first categorical definition of its canon of scripture – all the books of the Vulgate, with the exception of the Prayer of Manasseh and I and II Esdras, and consequently in the Douay Bible the former appears at the end of the OT, the latter as an appendix after the NT (hence regarded as not fully part of the Bible). Roman Catholic

scholarship frequently uses to denote respectively the books also in the Hebrew canon and the apocryphal books the terms 'canonical' and 'deutero-canonical', the latter in the sense of secondarily canonical (not semi-canonical) – that is, later deemed (by the church) to belong to the canon. By 'apocryphal' Roman Catholics tend to mean what Protestants call 'pseudepigraphical',* namely ancient Jewish and Christian writings never regarded as canonical.

Among the Eastern churches, where the composition of the canon has a more complicated history, there was also uncertainty about the books not attested in the Hebrew scriptures, but the Synod of Jerusalem (1692), which spoke for the Orthodox churches, declared Wisdom, Judith, Tobit, Bel and the Dragon, Susanna, the two books of Maccabees and Sirach to be canonical.

In the West, the doubts about the authority of the apocryphal books for the establishment of doctrine inevitably surfaced in the Reformation.* Among the ecclesiastical doctrines repudiated by Luther* were some that were either mentioned explicitly (such as prayers for the dead, and hence perhaps purgatory, in II Maccabees 12.43–45) or encouraged (such as references to the value of good works, rather than faith, in Tobit and Sirach), in various apocryphal books. It is often suggested that such considerations prompted Luther's dislike of the apocryphal books as a whole. However, it ought to be stressed that the distinction between the books of the Hebrew canon and the apocryphal books was accepted also by many of Luther's opponents. Regarding the religious value of the apocryphal books, Reformers felt free to vary their assessments, most being regarded as useful to Christians, a few as unprofitable. Hence Luther's 1534 translation includes the Apocrypha at the end of the OT, but omits I and II Esdras, because he found in them 'nothing which one could not more easily find in Aesop . . .'. In Calvin's* view also, these books were spiritually and literarily inferior. Certainly, Protestant Bibles have clearly distinguished the Apocrypha from the Hebrew books, and either grouped them together after the prophets and before the NT (apocryphal passages extracted from their former context have thus become 'books' in their own right, e.g. the additions to Esther), or omitted them altogether. Although early editions of the King James (Authorized) version contained the Apocrypha, later editions set what has become the norm among Protestants and omitted it altogether.

Interpretation. There can hardly be said to have been a coherent history of interpretation of the Apocrypha as a whole, precisely because only since the Reformation has it been possible to regard it as a 'whole' in the sense of a literary corpus. Indeed, it is not a coherent corpus in any case. But even of the individual books, one cannot discover a history of interpretation as readily as a history of use. This is partly because, as stated earlier, less doctrinal weight has been attached in both theory and practice to the apocryphal than to the fully canonical books. Their acknowledged value has been, on the whole, as either ethical exhortation or as narrative of exemplary behaviour. Correspondingly, the major uses of the Apocrypha may be divided into the spheres of liturgy and art. Many of the stories, prayers and sayings in the Apocrypha have been interpreted both in Christian and Jewish liturgy* and in sacred and secular art: painting, music, drama and poetry. The popularity of these books in England in the sixteenth and seventeenth centuries is illustrated by the eighty or so references to eleven of the apocryphal books which Shakespeare is calculated to have included in his plays (see below), Samuel Pepys' report of reading *Tobit* during a poor sermon, and Bunyan's discovery of a vital text in Ecclus. 2.10 ('Who ever trusted in the Lord and was confounded?'). The following treatment furnishes examples only of the more evident interpretative issues and trends of certain of the books.

Liturgical and devotional use. The Wisdom of Jesus son of Sirach was originally composed in Hebrew; we have a mediaeval manuscript in this language and fragments found at Masada illustrate its status among Palestinian Jews of the first century A D. It is also perhaps the most important and best-known of these books in the Christian church, as its Latin title 'Ecclesiasticus' ('Church [book]') implies, and especially its section (44.1ff.) known as 'Praise of the Fathers', which begins 'Let us now praise famous men and our fathers that begat us . . .'. 50.20–24, the final exhortation of this section, is also paraphrased within the famous hymn* 'Now thank we all our God'.

Tobit is a moral tale upholding the virtues of almsgiving, fasting and prayer and describing the efforts of the angel Raphael and the demon Asmodeus respectively to aid and thwart human endeavour. Since its main theme is the successful marriage of Tobit's son and his beloved Sarah, the example of this pair figured in, e.g., the marriage service in the Anglican Prayer Book of 1549. In his Latin translation of the advice of Raphael to Tobias before his wedding night (6.17), Jerome actually inserted some additional instructions of his own, including three days of chastity and prayer following the ceremony – possibly by Jerome's time a Christian practice. Tobit has also furnished scenes for several artists, although no one particular episode or

scene has predominated as the dramatic climax, unlike the case of Judith or Susanna (see below).

The Song of the Three Young Men has also found its way into Christian liturgy, being still used in the priest's private thanksgiving after the Roman Catholic Mass. It is also, under the name of the Benedicite, offered as an alternative canticle to the Te Deum in the older Anglican Prayer Books and survives in amended form in the Alternative Service Book of 1980.

Judith recounts the defeat of Nebuchadnezzar's general Holofernes by a Jewish widow, who succeeds, by the use of feminine wiles, in cutting off his head. Unusually for an apocryphal book, this story has been included in Jewish liturgy, that of the festival of Hanukkah, or rededication of the Temple, a festival which also celebrates the military success of the Maccabees. The image of the female warrior recalls Jael (Judg. 4–5) and in turn has been celebrated as a biblical model for Joan of Arc. In the early church Judith was seen as a type of the Virgin, or even of the church; in the Roman Catholic church parts of this book, 13.18–20 and 15.9–10, are read as greetings to the Virgin.

I and II Maccabees tell of the exploits of that family in defeating the Syrians and restoring the Temple. The story forms the basis of the feast of Hanukkah, which is not attested or warranted in the O T, but is referred to in the N T as the 'Feast of the Dedication' (John 10.22). II Maccabees in particular emphasizes the role of martyrdom and its guarantee of resurrection,* especially in the story of a mother and her seven sons, each successively tortured and martyred before her eyes. Much praised by the church Fathers as examples for Christians to follow (not without some protest, since they did not suffer for Christ), the mother in particular was also understood (e.g. by Gregory of Nazianzen) as a prototype of Mary, the Mother of Sorrows. In the Eastern Orthodox Church, where these sons and their mother are still venerated as martyrs, the place of their suffering was transferred to Antioch, where a church was built in their honour. A convent dedicated to the Maccabees also existed in Cologne in the Middle Ages, which claimed, in rivalry with Rome, possession of their relics.

Artistic use. Susanna and Bel and the Dragon are both of a genre unusual in scripture, namely the detective story. In Bel and the Dragon, Daniel unmasks the duplicity of Bel's priests who have been pretending that the god's statue consumes food; later he kills a dragon by feeding it pitch, fat and hair and causing it to explode. Finally, in the lions' den, Daniel is miraculously brought food by

Habakkuk. Metzger has suggested that from the figure of Daniel slaying the dragon has emerged the tale of St George slaying the dragon; though other more plausible origins can be found. The story of Susanna has Daniel vindicating the heroine from being framed by two lechers. Perhaps because of typological* interpretation (Susanna as the church, the two lechers as Judaism and the Gentiles, Daniel as the Lord), Susanna is frequently depicted in early Christian art. Almost certainly Shylock's famous phrase in Shakespeare's *The Merchant of Venice* – 'A Daniel come to judgment' – is an allusion to this story, with the twist that here a woman rescues a man, and from a Jew. His *Twelfth Night* has Sir Toby Belch quoting a ballad called 'the Constancy of Susannah'. The interest of the playwright in this story is further attested by the name of one of his daughters, Susannah. Susanna also furnished the subject of an oratorio by Handel (as did also Judas Maccabaeus, the hero of I and II Maccabees). Susanna has also inspired a number of paintings, usually of one of two episodes: with the accusing elders, or (unsurprisingly) in the bath.

Judith has furnished another popular artistic subject. The theme of the warrior female has, not surprisingly, been a favourite of painters, dramatists and authors throughout history. The story is, for example, mentioned in Chaucer's 'Monkes Tale', and Sir Thomas Arne and Parry each wrote an oratorio on it. Shakespeare called another of his daughters Judith, while Holofernes is the name of the schoolmaster in *Love's Labour's Lost*. On the other hand, Judith holding the head of Holofernes has proved an exceptionally popular subject for artists such as P. van Dyck, Veronese, Tintoretto and Titian.

The Prayer of Manasseh is developed from the tradition in II Chron. 33.11–13 (but not in Kings) that the wicked king Manasseh was taken to Babylon where he prayed and was restored to his throne. Although this story is found in many forms in rabbinic* literature, the actual text of his prayer is found only in Christian writings, the earliest being the *Didaskalia* of the second or third century AD. This work also relates how a flame of fire melted his chains.

See also **Art, The Bible in; Canon; Pseudepigrapha; Septuagint; Vulgate.**

Thomas Carter, *Shakespeare and Holy Scripture, with the Version He Used*, 1905; B. M. Metzger, *An Introduction to the Apocrypha*, 1957; Richard Noble, *Shakespeare's Biblical Knowledge and Use of the Book of Common Prayer*, 1935; Edna Purdie, *The Story of Judith in German and English Literature*, 1927.

PHILIP R. DAVIES

Apology, Apologetic

A defence, reasoned and very likely spirited, of your group's (or just your own) beliefs and practice. In this older, now technical sense, there is no suggestion of excuse or contrition. The defence is made in the face of real or imagined objections or attack. So one might read, 'This apologetic argument seems to be aimed at pagan detractors.' In practice the apologist may himself attack as the best defence (cf. Acts 17.22–31).

It may not always be possible to distinguish between an 'evangelistic' and an 'apologetic' approach to others, and in practice the two may go hand in hand. Both will try to take seriously the hearers' starting point. But apologetic tends to affirm it ('see how much you already agree with us') while evangelistic proclamation tends to challenge ('see how much you need to change!').

Although the ideal audience is thus people outside your own group, and they are the ones you imagine yourself responding to, the main or sole real audience may well be fellow members of your own circle or community. You are encouraging them in the face of hostile propaganda, and doubts and fears experienced within the group. Perhaps you are externalizing uncertainties of your own. There may be little or no genuine likelihood of outsiders ever reading or hearing what you say, even at second hand. But at least you feel you have a good case to make (I Peter 3.15).

It is important for our interpretation of the biblical documents (or any others) to try to be clear what questions are being considered, and whose questions they are. (This is, of course, just one part of building as clear a picture as we may of the background* or context of the material we are studying.) From time to time, then, scholars will argue that a passage is addressing objections from a hostile faction ('Judaizers', perhaps, or 'Gnostics'), or from some complete outsiders.

However, we need to be wary of assuming that most or all of what Paul,* for instance, wrote was in reaction to some hostile stimulus. So, for instance, in Romans the objector whom Paul 'answers' is mostly imaginary; Paul is using the device of the 'diatribe', making up a conversation as a teaching aid. Only at Rom. 3.8 does he seem to quote actual charges that he has heard are being levelled against him. People like Paul may themselves take the initiative in asserting, affirming, or simply celebrating an idea or a feeling for its own sake, quite undefensively. They assume they will be understood, and so it is still important for us as interpreters to know as much as possible of the ideas and habits they and their listeners start with; but their hearers need not have been asking questions, let alone antagonistic ones.

In pre-Christian Jewish scripture there is plentiful evidence for internal factions and external opponents, people who do argue, question and taunt. So Judg. 21.25 could be defending the monarchy, and II Sam. 9–I Kings 2 could be defending Solomon's accession against real or suspected detractors. Much more significant (and much more widely agreed) is the importance for the whole canon of Jewish scriptures of the Assyrian and Babylonian ascendancy, as well as many lesser disasters. Here there are the mocking questions of imagined or real outsiders, and bitter doubts and flat incredulity in the Judaean or wider community. Elijah could mock Baal as a sleeping God: but the same charge could be hurled from outside and voiced from within against Yahweh (Ps. 44; cf. II Kings 18//Isa. 37). Trust in Yahweh's power-and-righteousness is then vindicated by reference to deserved punishment (II Kings 24.3); or to the need to allow the land to enjoy its sabbaths (II Chron. 36.21); and God is in control, but working to a longer term and more complex plan than might have been supposed (Isa. 41.21–24).

It is with the Isaiah of the exile that we begin to find something like a systematic 'apologetic', with recurrent and elaborated themes: the transcendence of God puts human problems into perspective; other deities are no more effective than their idols, by-products of the economic system; victorious leaders will turn out to be doing what Yahweh foretold, administering his punitive and restorative justice; the suffering of his people itself serves Yahweh's purposes, and so on: ideas presented as responses to explicit challenges. Variations on these themes, together with further related ones (e.g. vindication or punishment after death) form an important strand in later apocalyptic,* still answering the questions others pose to the faithful by the misery they inflict. (On this scale, apologetic is close to theodicy, 'justifying the ways of God to humans'.)

The ascendancy of Hellenism* was a spur to further apologetic writing. An inescapable awareness of the multiplicity of traditions and beliefs intensified the effect of conquest, and spokesmen for various subject peoples tried to respond; even the conquerors (Greeks and then Romans) had to face critical questioning, with the Greeks contributing their developed reflective analytical skills. From Jews, in addition to the apocalyptic writings just mentioned (among them note especially the 'Sibylline Oracles'), our main examples of apologetic writings are the Letter of Aristeas, the Wisdom of Solomon, and the writings of Philo* of Alexandria, and of Josephus.* Josephus certainly hoped for a 'real audience' of outsiders; Philo must have done most of his writings to strengthen the resolve of his fellow Jews encountering contemporary Greek learning with its acumen and prestige. These Jewish writers confronted open scepticism, often with a strong moral tone, reacting against myths* telling of all too human deities and their wicked ways and capricious miracles; such tales, it was agreed, must be human inventions, in all likelihood quite recent. If there is deity at all, said the critics, he (or it) must be transcendent and imperturbable, beyond any touchy vindictiveness, graciously encouraging an enhanced flourishing of humankind.

So the standard Jewish apologetic responses included an insistence on the antiquity of the tradition (and Greek learning was seen by such as Philo as in all likelihood derivative from Moses*). Integral to Jewish tradition was a strong moral code, which was determinedly put into practice. The result was an orderly but richly satisfying social and individual life. Jews had no philandering and deceitful deities at loggerheads (so no need there for Stoic allegorizing,* taking the myths as picture-talk for physical reality). However, quaint and curious and seemingly pointless rituals, as well as being very old, could be taken as teaching aids, pointing to deeper realities. As the Stoics said, no deity worth the term could actually need such service. Yet God was concerned and in overall providential control (as the Stoics also insisted), able to provide foreknowledge, able to effect miracles, rewarding and punishing, though impervious to any attempt at magical manipulation of his will. Some of these apologetic answers could be drawn very readily, of course, from existing scriptural tradition.

All of this also provides a tradition of questioning and looking for answers for the early Christians to work with, and for us to bear in mind in our attempts to interpret what they wrote. Convinced though they seem to have been that Jesus had been raised to share God's glory, they could not escape the question, Why should God allow one so important to him to be crucified? (I Cor. 1.23). Lindars painstakingly traces out the 'biblical research' that they seem to have engaged in, pulling together scriptural passages that talk of the suffering of someone devoted to God, in God's service, and especially passages where suffering and humiliation are followed by exaltation. The procedure is similar to the 'pesher'* of some of the Qumran documents (see **Dead Sea Scrolls**): passages are 'interpreted to mean' events in the life and death and resurrection* of Jesus, and of the early Christian communities. It will have seemed the obvious apologetic procedure for Jewish Christians in conversation or dispute with other Jews, or dealing with their own. It will have been much less useful in dealing with pagans' questions, though even they could be impressed by evidence of ancient prophecies fulfilled.

Paul shares much of this apologetic research, for instance in his attempts to explain the refusal of most Jews still to accept the good news (Rom. 9–11). He also takes over standard Jewish 'polemical' apologetic addressed to Gentiles (Rom. 1–2), accepting Stoic pointers to the 'unnatural' mess that humans get themselves into. He is not, of course, addressing outsiders here, and it is not really clear for the most part whether he envisages a 'real' internal faction that holds the views he is arguing against, or whether (apart from 3.8, see above) this is all part of the 'diatribe' device of creating imaginary opponents as a teaching aid. At II Cor. 11.22–3 he seems to be answering a real challenge from opponents within the Christian group. But it is important to understand the extent to which a somewhat paranoid-looking self-defence was a conventional device in contemporary writing: you attack, and defend yourself, before anyone else says a word. Much in Paul may be of these kinds, and not apologetic.

Apologetic proper is, however, an important motif in Luke–Acts, which can be usefully compared with Josephus' very similar (but much lengthier) efforts. Both retell their stories in the way 'enlightened' pagan readers would expect (highlighting moral virtue, piety, courageous poverty, womanly devotion, human repentance and emotion). Both write for their characters speeches which pick out from each group's beliefs (early Christian or Jewish respectively) those elements which pagan writers of the time propose: God is powerful, demanding our virtue in accord with the ancient rules, but then allowing us to flourish, and escape punishment. Both Luke and Josephus will probably have hoped at best to gain a more sympathetic understanding, rather than conversion; both may have done little more than assure their own side that theirs was an entirely respectable religion. But picking out what might make sense to others means neither was putting all his cards on the table, and it is important in our interpretation of Luke–Acts to bear that in mind. The faith of early Christians (as evidenced in Paul's letters) is much richer – and more varied – than those aspects of it which Luke supposed his imaginary outsiders might make sense of.

Acts has sometimes been seen as a more explicitly 'political' apologetic, arguing for legal tolerance from the Roman authorities. We note how often Roman officials are shown to be friendly or at least neutral towards the Christians, and indeed to Jesus in his trial; in the view of Acts it was Jews who killed him. This is more likely to have been just one strand in presenting the Christians as law-abiding, deserving sympathetic respect (perhaps, too, encouraging fellow Christians to live up to that image; compare again Josephus to fellow-Jews). But Luke's account would have carried little legal weight. The stress, though, on respectability, on living up to publicly accepted norms, but better than the pagan public itself, is an important aspect of Christian apologetic around the end of the century (I Peter 2.12; Titus 2.8).

Later, in the second century, a number of Christian writers, of whom Justin Martyr is the best known, wrote explicit 'Apologies', addressed at least nominally to the emperor of the day. Again taking up the work of earlier Jewish writers, they made still more systematic attempts to find common ground in Plato, Socrates and the Stoics, and present Christianity as at least a very good way of life and thought and devotion, but in their view fulfilling all that the most widely admired pagans had been looking for. (The common concern in these writers has led to their being known collectively as 'the Apologists'.) Justin also continued the apologetic dialogue with Jews, on the basis of scripture.

So, if it really is our aim to interpret what was written at the time, we need, among many other factors, to understand the questions that were – or perhaps were – in view in the writing. The issue of apologetics at the time of writing is important. Then in our own attempts to interpret the biblical writings, effective communication demands that we ourselves address our own and others' actual presuppositions – and, if possible, respond to questions that are already being asked. There is always a place for 'good' apologetics in interpretation. The converse is bad communication, and poor apologetics. We also need to be aware that we and others may so want our texts to speak 'relevantly' to us and our listeners that we do not allow what is written to say things we or our hearers cannot agree with, or even – rightly or wrongly – just find tedious, complex, unclear or archaic; or, for that matter, too challenging. To make the text answer our questions on our terms is a powerful 'apologetic' temptation. Some even make a virtue of it.

See also **Historical–Critical Method; Literary Criticism; Rhetoric.**

J. R. Bartlett, *Jews in the Hellenistic World*, 1985; F. G. Downing, *The Past is All we Have*, 1974; id., 'Ethical Pagan Theism and the Speeches in Acts', *NTS* 1981; B. Lindars, *New Testament Apologetic*, 1961; G. Lyons, *Pauline Autobiography*, 1986; J. K. S. Reid, *Christian Apologetics*, 1969.

F. GERALD DOWNING

Apostolic Fathers

The writings of the Apostolic Fathers are diverse in character and span over half a century in date, from Clement of Rome's letter to Corinth (*c*. AD 95, hereafter *Ad Cor*.) to the Roman Hermas' work *The Shepherd*, in its final form perhaps *c*. AD 148. The writers differ in their knowledge and treatment of biblical tradition, but most modern critics conclude that when they were writing, the NT literature was not yet regarded as scripture. It is clear that for these authors, however, the Jewish scriptures were authoritative. They were known in Greek rather than Hebrew.

Clement of Rome referred extensively to the OT, knowing that it was familiar to his readers also. They understood the 'ordinances of the Lord', the 'oracles of God's teaching' and the 'the Holy Scriptures' (2.8; 45.2; 53.1; 62.3; and *passim*). In complete contrast Polycarp of Smyrna confessed his ignorance when writing to the well-versed Philippians. Knowledge of the sacred writings had not been granted him, he said, except an ability to quote Ps. 4.5, though perhaps only via Eph. 4.26 (*Ad Phil.* 12.1). There are few references to the OT in the seven authentic letters of Ignatius of Antioch (*c*. AD 110). Indeed he failed to cite it at all in the Philadelphian letter in which he debated with Judaizers. But he valued it and wrote of the importance of the law of Moses and the prophets, deploring the failure of 'errorists' (probably docetists *and* Judaizers*) to give heed to them (*Magn.* 8–9; *Philad.* 5; *Smyrn.* 5.1). It is not clear whether he has in mind a two-fold canonical division when he writes of law and prophets.

The author of the perhaps Alexandrian Epistle of Barnabas (*c*. AD 125) is different again. Through his *gematria* (= number symbolism) (9.7–9), his allegorical* and typological* exegesis* and his christocentric interpretations (some of a familiar NT kind), he countered Jewish understanding of the covenant* and the scriptures. In the process he denied literal significance to the food laws, circumcision and so on (2–6; 8–13 *passim*). For Barnabas such christocentric interpretation was right *gnōsis* (6.9; 9.8; 10.10; 13.7). Origen* and Clement of Alexandria would argue in much the same way later. Unlike Ignatius (who was not competent in debate regarding things 'written' *Philad.* 8.2) Barnabas confidently, if sometimes over-imaginatively, opposed the claims of Judaism. As is the case in the Didache (1–5), the 'two ways'

material which the Epistle incorporates (18–20) includes ethical teaching derived from the Pentateuch,* Proverbs and Psalms.

These writers introduce OT sayings using 'quotation formulae'. Hence we know that they did regard them as scripture. The formulae vary: Clement, Ignatius and Barnabas like *gegraptai* ('it is written'), though on the one occasion that Hermas uses it he quotes the Apocryphal (and not extant) *Eldad and Modat*. Polycarp's one quotation begins 'as it is said in these scriptures', *Ad Phil.* 12.1, and we find phrases like 'the scripture says', and 'as it was said'.

It is interesting that we do not find such formulae with the use of NT tradition, with two exceptions: in *Barn.* 4.14 and in *Ad Phil.* 12.1. Yet the Apostolic Fathers owe much to the teaching of the NT, even though in recent decades scholars have become more circumspect and unwilling to claim that they 'quoted' certain canonical writings. In the case of Ignatius, for example, whose knowledge of Matthew and John has been widely assumed, we should probably think in terms of his knowing tradition of a type underlying our present Gospels or circulating independently of them. We should not forget the influence of parenesis and liturgy in the communities of these writers, or neglect their witness when considering the Synoptic Problem* and the formation of the Fourth Gospel. What they wrote may sometimes reflect primitive Christian traditions as well as the emphases and cherished teachings of their own localities.

In the time of these Fathers, Paul's* writings were increasingly valued in some circles. Ignatius knew of Peter* and Paul, identified himself with the experience of the latter, who was an 'abortion' and a martyr in Rome (I Cor. 15.8f.; Ign. *Rom.* 4.3; 9.2), and told the Ephesians that Paul had mentioned them 'in every letter' (*Eph.* 12.2). Certainly I Cor. was known to him, perhaps Ephesians and others too. Clement wrote to Corinth citing 'the epistle of the blessed Paul' (47.1f., cf. 24.1; 37.3–5; 41.1; 49.5 and *passim*) and praising its church in the language of Acts 20.35 (2,1 cf. Hermas *Vis.* iii.9.2). Polycarp shared this respect, recalling the truth of the Apostle's teaching and his letters, as well as his labour among the Philippians. He echoed many a Pauline phrase (*Ad Phil.* 3.2; 11.2–3) and had probably made a collection of Paul's writings, as he did of Ignatius' (*Ad Phil.* 13). In contrast the Didache and the *Epistle of Barnabas* are un-Pauline works, and what reminiscences are contained in *The Shepherd* are well integrated and perhaps reliant on common Christian tradition rather than a study of Paul's letters. It is important to note, however, that when our writers use language suggestive of Pauline,

Johannine or other influences, they may be using it in ways quite alien to the canonical writers. Ignatius' treatment of faith and grace provides an example.

The Apostolic Fathers used biblical tradition freely in response to the needs of their readers and in accordance with their own standpoint. Persecution, poverty, judgment, mercy etc. were dealt with using Jesus' Sermon on the Mount (*Ad Cor.* 13.1–3, 'words of the Lord Jesus'; cf. *II Clem.* 6.1; 13.4; *Ad Phil.* 2.3 'the Lord taught'), and sermon material was juxtaposed with OT injunctions in the 'two ways' of the Didache (but not in Barnabas). Clement freely used the 'millstone' saying as a warning to schismatics (46.8) while the Antiochene Ignatius' own prophecy in Philadelphia (*Philad.* 7.1) was prefaced with the statement, 'the Spirit knows whence it comes . . . and tests secret things' (cf. John 3.8; 1 Cor. 2.10). His statement in *Smyrn.* 1.1 that Jesus was baptized 'that all righteousness might be fulfilled by him' is close to the (Antiochene ?) addition in Matt. 3.15, but Ignatius uses it in refuting docetic heretics opposed to the Jesus of history who came in the flesh. Polycarp transmits the teaching of I John 4.2f. and II John 7 (*Ad Phil.* 7.1) for similar reasons, and there is a hint of Luke 24.39 in the non-canonical (or freely adapted) anti-docetic resurrection appearance in Ign. *Smyrn.* 3. Barnabas and Clement have been named by ancient and modern writers as the author of Hebrews. And similarly Polycarp's affinity with some of the teachings of the Pastoral Epistles has suggested to some that he wrote them.

Our writers valued the Jewish and Christian teachings they had received. They refer often to the 'commands' of God or of Jesus Christ, seeing these as guidance for life and for order in the churches. Polycarp, who 'taught everything consistent with the scriptures', according to Irenaeus, insisted that 'the oracles' were not to be abused or perverted, especially not so as to deny the resurrection or judgment (7.1 cf. Irenaeus *Adv. Haer.* 3.3.4 about Marcion*). In this passage false teaching stands opposed to 'the word which was delivered to us' and Polycarp appealed to apostolic tradition and the apostles' examples (6.3; 9; cf. *Ad Cor.* 5.4–7). The apostles were key figures for these writers since the gospel was preached by them and the reliability of the tradition was ensured. Hermas told of their preaching 'The Son of God' (*Sim.* 9.17.1) bringing God's word and withholding nothing (*Sim.* 9.25.2). Their gospel had come from Jesus Christ himself (*Ad Cor.* 42.1f.), and they had been responsible for preaching and appointing officials in the churches (42.3–5 with its distinctive treatment of LXX Isa. 60.17). Ignatius praised those who were of one mind with the apostles (*Eph.* 11.2; *Magn.* 13.1; *Trall* 7.1; cf. *Ad Cor.* 47.4) and with the presbyters who followed them (*Eph.* 11.1; *Magn.* 6.1; *Trall.* 2.2). And like Clement he assumed that the church order he favoured derived from them. He wrote both of 'the Lord' and 'the apostles' giving commands, but we should not assume that he had in mind a division of NT writings into Gospel(s) and Epistles.

The prophets had spoken by grace, Barnabas recorded (1.7; 5.6), while Ignatius made such claims that he could even say in *Magn.* 10.3: 'Christianity did not base its faith on Judaism but Judaism on Christianity.' The prophets were saved, he wrote, because they pointed to Christ, announced the gospel, acted by faith, were inspired by grace. They were indeed proto-Christians and 'disciples in the Spirit' (*Magn.* 8–9; *Philad.* 5.2; 9.2; cf. *Ad Phil.* 6.3; Hermas *Sim.* 9.15.4). Jesus Christ had been 'the door of the Father' for them as for the patriarchs, the apostles and the church. In some of the writings the developing Christian appropriation of the Jewish scriptures becomes very apparent and the distinctions between the old and new dispensations are sometimes eroded (cf. *Philad.* 8). In general, however, the Apostolic Fathers do not stray very far from the spirit of the NT or interpret the OT in ways alien to Christians who had preceded them.

Barnabas tended towards the fantastic (cf. *Ep. to Diognetus* 12), and the Montanist Tertullian* poured scorn on '*The Shepherd*' of the adulterers' for a leniency which was at odds, he thought, with the scriptures (*De Pudicitia* 10.12; 20.2). But when Clement interpreted OT texts allegorically* and christologically,* they were often those treated also by NT writers. Rahab's scarlet thread (Josh. 2.18), which foreshadows redemption through the blood of Christ, is newly interpreted (*Ad Cor.* 12.7), and new too is the appearance in Christian literature of the phoenix as a sign of the resurrection (25). But, as is the case with the later II Clement (2.1–3; 14.2; cf. Gal. 4.27 and Eph. 5.31), other passages in *Ad Cor.* have NT parallels: in Hebrews, James, II Peter and elsewhere.

The Fathers' treatment of 'the gospel' deserves particular mention. Inevitably the question arises whether any of these writers had in mind written gospels. When, for example, Clement wrote of it in 47.2 he was thinking of Paul's work of teaching (cf. NT Phil. 4.15). In 42.1 and 3 he described the preaching of the *kerygma,** just as Barnabas wrote of the gospel's power in the preaching of forgiveness of sins (5.9; 8.3). Neither writer was thinking of a written gospel, and no more was Polycarp when he told of the apostles' evangelizing (*Ad Phil.* 6.3).

The issue is not so clear when we come to the Syrian writers Ignatius and the author of the Didache. The former used 'gospel' and related words eight times in his letters. Good news delivered verbally was intended in *Philad.* 5.2, and in 5.1, those facts about Jesus Christ in which he took refuge. In such a gospel was Christ himself. This deposit of truth preserved those facts: about the coming of the Lord in the flesh, his suffering and resurrection which showed the accomplishment of things promised. 'The gospel', then, was superior to the witness of either law or prophets, good though those were (*Philad.* 9.2; *Smyrn.* 5.1; 7.2). Though much of what Ignatius knew of the Jesus of history can be paralleled in Matthew and (to a lesser extent) in John, it is not evident that he had a written source in mind. The contentious passage of *Philad.* 8.2 best illustrates the uncertainty: 'If I do not find it in the charters (*archeia*), in the gospel I do not believe', some said to him. If *archeia* and gospel are here in *apposition* (and the Greek is unclear) then 'the gospel' (known also as the *archeia*) must be an authoritative written source – for Ignatius responded *gegraptai* ('it is written'). But if, as most scholars argue, the two are in *opposition*, then what Ignatius taught as 'the gospel' was challenged for not according with OT or other written sources. In either case it is acknowledged that Christian teaching must be verifiable in the light of past expectation.

'Gospel' in the Didache appears with quotations from the Lord's Prayer and a passage on mutual reproofs (8.2; 15.1; cf. also 11.2). To a number of scholars it seemed to refer to Matthew's Gospel (cf. 5.2 ff.; 6.5–13; 18.15ff.), for other phrases in the Didache are also reminiscent of it. It need not be dependent on the Gospel as we know it, however. In several places the Didachist wrote of church practices which accord with Gospel provisions (baptism 7.1 cf. Matt. 28.19 and its trinitarian formula; fasting differently from the 'hyprocrites' 8.1 cf. Matt. 6.16; avoidance of blasphemy against the Spirit 11.7 cf. Matt. 12.31). On the other hand, he was showing how the development of such practices was sanctioned by the shrewd application of appropriate texts. It was not exactness of quotation which concerned our writers, even Clement and Barnabas, but rather revelation. Jesus Christ was the revelation of God. Through the Holy Spirit it was he who spoke in the OT (*Ad Cor.* 22.1). Jesus Christ it was also who 'spoke and it came to pass', who was God's Word 'proceeding from silence', and who was at all times the 'one teacher' (Ign. *Eph.* 15; *Magn.* 8.2–9.1).

We owe the Apostolic Fathers a debt. Their writings show us the many ways in which the primitive tradition about Jesus Christ, the apostles, and the church was used and interpreted. It was built upon in changing circumstances and protected from abuse. Clement's spirited use of OT and Christian tradition in countering sedition in Corinth is a model of its kind. Ignatius' language about 'our God' Jesus the Christ, is both reminiscent of the NT and rich in insights from other sources. The ointment on Jesus' head, for example (*Eph.* 17.1 cf. Matt. 26.7; John 12.3), becomes a means to breathing 'immortality' on the church. The star of the nativity shines brightly surrounded by a chorus of other heavenly bodies, so that 'all magic was dissolved' (*Eph.* 19.1; cf. Matt. 2.2–12 but also Gen. 37.9). Their prayers and doxologies tell us much of their understanding of the person of the Lord as well as of the church and the Christian life (*Ad Cor.* 64; 65.2 cf. *II Clem* 20.5; *Barn.* 21.5–9; *Did.* 9–10 on the 'broken bread' of the eucharist and cf. *Ad Cor.* 59.3–61.3). And when Ignatius, conscious of the threat of docetism, writes of 'Jesus Christ . . . conceived by Mary . . . of the seed of David as of the Holy Spirit; born, baptized that . . . he might purify the water' (*Eph.* 18.2), or 'of the family of David . . . God's son . . . born of a virgin, baptized by John . . . nailed to a tree . . . under Pontius Pilate and Herod . . .' (*Smyrn.* 1.1), it is hard to escape the impression that here we are seeing the development of a creed * of sorts.

E. Flesseman-van Leer, *Tradition and Scripture in the Early Church,* 1954; R. P. C. Hanson, *Tradition in the Early Church*, 1962; W. R. Inge et al., *The New Testament in the Apostolic Fathers*, 1905; H. Koester, *Synoptische Überlieferung bei den Apostolischen Vätern*, TU 65, 1957; K. Lake, *The Apostolic Fathers* (2 vols), Loeb Classical Library, 1912; E. Massaux, *Influence de l'Évangile de Saint Matthieu sur la littérature chrétienne avant saint Irénée*, 1950.

CHRISTINE TREVETT

Aqedah

The term *'aqedah* ('binding') or more fully *'aqedat Yishaq* ('binding of Isaac'), derived from Gen. 22.9 ('and Abraham * bound [*vayya'aqod*] Isaac his son'), denotes in rabbinic * literature the whole episode of the offering up of Isaac as recounted in Gen. 22.1–19. Strictly speaking when the rabbis use the term they are not thinking of the simple biblical story, but of a complex of ideas which emerged in rabbinic exegesis of the story. Modern scholarship tends to use the term as shorthand for this complex of rabbinic themes and motifs.

In Targum and midrash. The Aqedah traditions in Targum * and midrash * are rich and diverse, yet underlying them is a coherent body of doctrine comprising a number of key theological insights which have been developed in a variety of ways over a considerable period of time. Taking as a starting point Targum Pseudo-Jonathan (Ps-J) to Gen. 22, the central elements of the tradition may be identified as follows:

1. Contrary to the 'plain' sense of Gen. 22, Isaac was a willing victim, fully aware of what was happening. According to Ps-J (v. 1), he was 37 years old at the time of the story, well able to have resisted his aged father had he so wished. Indeed, the whole episode was initiated by Isaac when, in a quarrel with Ishmael, he expressed his readiness to offer 'all his limbs' to God. The testing of Abraham thus becomes a testing also of Isaac. Abraham's offering of his son becomes Isaac's self-oblation. Both Abraham and Isaac go 'with a perfect heart together' (Ps-J v. 8) to the place of sacrifice. Isaac's willingness and co-operation are a necessary condition for the perfection of his offering. Though he did not die, 'scripture credits Isaac with having died and his ashes as having lain upon the altar' (Midrash ha-Gadol, Gen. 22.19). One tradition states that Isaac's blood was actually spilled upon the altar (Mekhilta de-Rabbi Shim'on ben Yoḥai to Ex. 16.2). Few go this far, but in general it is stressed that Abraham and Isaac did everything they could to ensure that Isaac's offering was unblemished and complied fully with all the laws of sacrifice (cf. Ps-J v. 10). Isaac's willingness to suffer death rather than disobey God opened up the possibility of treating him as a proto-martyr. There are hints of this in Ps-J (note the vision of comfort and approbation which he receives on the point of death in v. 10 – a motif of martyrology). Later martyrs are following in the footsteps of Isaac, and their self-sacrifice, like his, atones for Israel's sin (Babylonian Talmud Gittin 57b).

2. The Aqedah took place on the Temple mount in Jerusalem* (cf. Ps-J vv. 2, 4, 9, 14). The equation of Mount Moriah with the Temple mount is as old as II Chron. 3.1. Indeed, it may be present in the biblical story itself: note the suggestive language of Gen. 22.14, 'Abraham called the name of that place Adonai-jireh; as it is said to this day: On the mount of the Lord [cf. Isa. 2.3] it shall be seen'. This locus for the Aqedah was more, it seems, than a piece of folklore.* It had something to do with legitimating the Jerusalem Temple and its cult.* The Aqedah became the keystone of a powerful sacramental theology of sacrifice. The perpetual offering in the Temple (the Tamid), sacrificed on the very spot of Isaac's self-oblation, was efficacious only because it reminded God of the Aqedah; the Tamid had no value in itself but only as a

re-enactment of the Aqedah (Leviticus Rabba 2.11; the Palestinian Targumim to Lev. 22.27). There was a tendency to extend this concept to other sacrifices such as the Passover lamb (Mekhilta de-Rabbi Ishmael, Pisḥa 7).

3. The Aqedah may be invoked for the benefit of Isaac's posterity. This thought is developed in two distinct ways. One way (followed by Ps-J v. 14) is to stress that the supreme obedience of Abraham and Isaac were works of supererogation which laid up merit for their descendants. This links the Aqedah to the doctrine of the 'merit of the fathers' (zekhut 'avot). The other way is to see the Aqedah as an expiatory sacrifice which atoned for the sins of Isaac's descendants. He offered himself as a representative person: when his posterity invokes the Aqedah, God will reckon it as if they had bound themselves upon the altar before him (Babylonian Talmud,* Rosh ha-Shanah 16a). The Aqedah is sometimes depicted as the central event of the sacred history, on which all other redemptive events (e.g. the exodus, the giving of the Torah on Sinai, and the resurrection of the dead) depend (Genesis Rabba 56.1). Not only has the Aqedah made the resurrection* possible, but in itself – in Isaac's symbolic death and return to life – it is a fitting image of the resurrection (Pirqe de-Rabbi Eliezer 31; cf. Pesiqta de-Rav Kahana, Supplement 1.20).

In the liturgy. The popularity of the Aqedah theology is suggested by the fact that its central ideas are reflected at significant points in the synagogue liturgy. One tradition dates the Aqedah to Passover (Exodus Rabba 15.11). Another claims that the blood of the Passover lamb sprinkled on the lintel and doorposts to protect the firstborn of Israel recalled Isaac's offering on mount Moriah: when God 'saw' the blood (Ex. 12.13) what he saw was 'the blood of the binding of Isaac' (Mekhilta de-Rabbi Ishmael, Pisḥa 7,11). The links with Passover, though old, are not as strong as those with Rosh ha-Shanah. Rosh ha-Shanah is traditionally a festival of judgment, and in this context the atoning merit of the Aqedah is stressed, e.g. the *Musaf* prayer asks God to remember 'the binding with which Abraham our father bound Isaac his son ... how he overbore his compassion to perform your will with a perfect heart. So may your compassion overbear your anger against us.' And one interpretation of the blowing of the shofar on Rosh ha-Shanah is that it is a symbolic, sacramental act which serves, like the sacrifices in the Temple, to remind God of Isaac's perfect offering (Babylonian Talmud Rosh ha-Shanah 16a).

In Jewish art. The Aqedah is a popular theme in Jewish art.* It is depicted in mosaic on the floor of the sixth-century synagogue of

Bet Alfa (at the foot of Mount Gilboa). It is painted on a wall in the Dura-Europos synagogue on the Euphrates (third century AD). It is also represented on amulets – an indication that it was widely seen as a sacred event of unusual protective power. In mediaeval Jewish illuminated manuscripts it is sometimes depicted in strip-cartoon fashion in a series of panels, and sometimes as a composite picture which synthesizes all the elements of the story in a simultaneous presentation. In addition to these narrative pictures, it is possible that the symbol of the shofar alludes to the Aqedah. The shofar is ubiquitous in Jewish art in late antiquity, being found frequently in synagogues, on tombstones, and on small objects. Its use on tombstones is noteworthy. It may be linked to the idea of the eschatological* last trumpet (cf. Amidah, Blessing 10: 'sound the great horn for our freedom'), and so express the hope of resurrection. As noted earlier, the Aqedah is linked in certain traditions with the resurrection. The shofar might also, in some contexts (e.g. Rosh ha-Shanah), symbolize the atoning merit of the Aqedah. The shofar and the ram alternate as symbols of the Aqedah in the margins of fourteenth-century German-Jewish prayerbooks for Rosh ha-Shanah.

In the New Testament. The Aqedah, interpreted as Isaac's perfect self-oblation which atones for the sins of his posterity, has obvious similarities to the NT doctrine of the atoning death of Jesus. The parallels between the Jewish and Christian doctrines seem too exact to be plausibly explained by common use of the sacrificial language and imagery of the OT. Two relationships are possible: either the developed doctrine of the Aqedah is pre-Christian and served as a paradigm for the Christian doctrine; or the developed doctrine of the Aqedah is post-Christian and arose in Judaism as a response to the Christian doctrine. In favour of the latter view is the fact that the notion of the Aqedah as an atoning sacrifice is found only in post-Christian Jewish texts. Moreover, if the Aqedah played a central role in the formation of Christian doctrine one would expect to find more than two explicit references (Heb. 11.17–20; James 2.21) to Gen. 22 in the NT. Neither of these arguments is decisive. The dates at which the Targums and the rabbinic texts reached their present form is not a certain guide as to when the traditions they embody originated: late texts have been shown to contain very early traditions.

From securely dated texts it can be shown that the following elements of the Aqedah are explicitly attested by the first century AD: 1. the identification of mount Moriah with the Temple mount (Jubilees 18.13; see further above); 2. Isaac's willingness (Philo,* de Ab-rahamo 172; Pseudo-Philo, *Liber Antiquitatum Biblicarum* 40:2; Josephus,* *Antiquities* I 222–36); 3. Isaac as a proto-martyr (IV Macc. 13.12; cf. 6.28–9; 17.22); 4. the link between the Aqedah and Passover (Jubilees 17.15–16 + 18.3); 5. Gen. 22 as a symbol of resurrection (Heb. 11.19). Moreover, none of these elements really makes much sense if taken in isolation in a minimalist way. Thus, the link with the Temple mount was surely intended right from the start to validate the sacrifices in the Temple ('aqad' which occurs only in Gen. 22.9, may have been a technical term from the sacrificial cult: cf. Babylonian Talmud Shabbat 54a). But this connection in turn easily generates a number of other ideas, including that of the Aqedah as an atonement. As noted earlier, the various elements of the Aqedah form a remarkably coherent body of doctrine. There can be no question, then, of any wholesale borrowing of ideas from Christianity by the later Jewish sources. Indeed, there is no need to invoke Christian influence at all on these later sources: on the basis of the elements just listed, they were perfectly capable of reaching the full-blown doctrine of the Aqedah without Christian help. The theory of Christian influence on Judaism would posit a historically less likely relationship between the two traditions, for while it is easy to see why early Christianity would have defined its doctrines in terms of the Judaism from which it emerged, it is hard to see why rabbinic Judaism should have borrowed such elements from Christianity. Talmudic sources show a marked lack of interest in Christianity, and such as there is betrays a very low level of knowledge. That the rabbis would have taken over some of the subtler aspects of the Christian doctrine of the atonement would be remarkable. The absence of more explicit references to Gen. 22 in the NT can be explained. The fundamental point is not that the NT writers used Isaac as a type* of Christ, or were concerned with direct exegesis* of Gen. 22, but that certain ideas developed in Judaism with regard to Isaac's offering proved useful to the early Christians in interpreting the death of Jesus. If it could be shown that a developed doctrine of the Aqedah was widespread in first-century Judaism, then there are plenty of passages in the NT for which it would provide a natural and illuminating setting (e.g. Gal. 3.16–17; I Cor. 11.24–25; Rom. 8.32; John 1.29; 3.16).

In the Qur'an (see Muslim Interpretation). Qur'an 37.101–7 offers a terse and cryptic version of the Aqedah, in which the motifs of divine testing, the willingness of the victim, and submission to God are present. Tradition speculated on the identity of the victim, who is simply called 'a wise youth' in the Qu'ran.

Some authorities say he was Isaac, others (by far the more numerous) identify him as Ishmael. Certain Islamic forms of the story contain narrative embellishments which must ultimately derive from Jewish *aggadah*. Noteworthy is the tradition of locating the event at Mecca. The purpose of this seems to be in general to legitimate the Ka'ba as a holy place, and more specifically to give point to the sacrifices offered during the Hajj on the 'Id of Sacrifice, which are said to recall the sacrifice of Ishmael.

The story recorded in Gen. 22 has continued to be fertile ground for the imagination, focussing on the moral and spiritual enigma of the demand of God and the response of Abraham.* Modern examples of reflection on the Aqedah are to be found in Thomas Mann's *Joseph and his Brothers* and Wilfred Owen's poem, 'The Parable of the Old Man and the Young', which Benjamin Britten set to music in his *War Requiem*.

See also **Genesis; Targum.**

N. Calder, 'From Midrash to Scripture: The Sacrifice of Abraham in Early Islamic Tradition', *Le Muséon* 101/2, 1988, pp. 405–32; R. J. Daly, 'The Soteriological Significance of the Sacrifice of Isaac', *Catholic Biblical Quarterly* 39, 1977, pp. 45–75; P. R. Davies and B. D. Chilton, 'The Aqedah: A Revised Tradition History', *Catholic Biblical Quarterly* 40, 1978, pp. 514–46; E. R. Goodenough, *Jewish Symbols in the Greco-Roman Period*, Vol IV, 1953, pp. 172–94; R. Hayward, 'The Present State of Research into the Targumic Account of the Sacrifice of Isaac', *Journal of Jewish Studies* 32, 1981, pp. 127–50; A. J. Saldarini, 'Interpretation of the Aqedah in Rabbinic Literature', *The Biblical Mosaic: Changing Perspectives*, Semeia Studies, 1982, pp. 149–65; S. Spiegel, *The Last Trial*, 1967; G. Vermes, *Scripture and Tradition in Judaism*, 1973, pp. 193–227.

PHILIP S. ALEXANDER

Aramaisms

A term used, often in a rather loose and imprecise way, to signify some actual or supposed influence of Aramaic on biblical and post-biblical Hebrew. It presents three distinct but related difficulties. First, different scholars may use the word with different meanings; second, it is not entirely agreed what constitutes genuine aramaisms; and third, there is debate about how far the presence of aramaisms in a biblical text may legitimately be used to help to date it. That Aramaic and its dialects exerted influence on Hebrew cannot be denied. Israel's landless ancestor is called an Aramaean (Deut. 26.5). Throughout the period of the monarchy, contact with Aramaic

speakers, particularly in the Northern Kingdom, was inevitable (see, e.g. I Kings 19.15–18; 20.1–43; II Kings 5.1–23). Certain features of Northern Hebrew dialect are found also in Aramaic, and have sometimes, as a consequence, been called aramaisms. In the time of Hezekiah, Aramaic seems to have been known at the court of Judah (II Kings 18.26); and its adoption by the Persians as the diplomatic language ensured its widespread use as a *lingua franca* throughout their empire. Parts of the biblical books Ezra and Daniel are composed in it; and many, perhaps most, Palestinian Jews came to use it as their first language in later Second Temple and early Christian times. Indeed, texts from Qumran reveal its vitality and its considerable effect on contemporary Hebrew.

Even so, 'aramaism' is something of a catch-all expression. Some authors refer it to items which, although perfectly at home in Hebrew, are found more often in Aramaic. Such is *'th*, 'he came', used instead of the more usual root *b'*. The former is cognate with Aramaic *'ty*, yet is part of Hebrew lexical stock, but used less frequently than the latter, and distributed differently among the various biblical books. Again, 'aramaism' may designate a Hebrew word whose sense, in a particular context, is properly revealed from Aramaic usage. 'Aramaism' may signify definite choice by the biblical author of an Aramaic word or expression; and finally, it may refer to features of writings like Job and Ecclesiastes which some authorities believe were originally composed in Aramaic and then translated into Hebrew.

The close geographical and linguistic proximity of Aramaic to Hebrew, and the different senses in which scholars speak of aramaisms, require that due caution be observed before any feature of Hebrew be dubbed an aramaism. G. R. Driver stressed how little Hebrew literature from pre-Christian times has survived: were there more, many so-called aramaisms might stand revealed as native Hebrew. Aramaic indeed influenced Hebrew, but Hebrew also influenced Aramaic; and many 'aramaisms', on examination, turn out to be words common to almost all the Semitic languages. Words of Aramaic form, like *stw*, winter, must have been naturalized as Hebrew very early, since no other equivalent word is found in Hebrew. While Aramaic appears as the largest foreign element in Hebrew, more often in poetry than in prose, Driver correctly restricts 'real aramaisms' to conscious borrowings by poets, words relating to trades and professions, and words deriving from Aramaic keeping their original form, mostly in the dialect of the Northern Kingdom. Apart from the last category, 'aramaism' may be seen as 'a philological* convenience rather than demonstrable fact'.

Lists of aramaisms have been compiled, most notably by Kautzsch in 1902 and Wagner in 1966. The latter has some 350 examples, but may be criticized, *inter alia*, for failing to distinguish between words attested in the pre-exilic period and those which entered Hebrew later; for his very wide definition of aramaism; and for inadequacies of methodology.

It is clear, however, that the growth in importance of Aramaic in Second Temple times had a noticeable effect on Hebrew. Aramaisms increase in Late Biblical Hebrew, and are even more evident in Qumranic and rabbinic* Hebrew. In principle, therefore, it may be accepted that frequent occurrence of aramaisms in a particular text may suggest a later rather than earlier date, provided that other elements in the same text are also of undoubtedly late date. Even so, aspects of (e.g.) the Chronicler's language which older scholarship attributed to aramaisms have recently been convincingly explained by Polzin in terms of 'inner-Hebrew' development. Meanwhile, Hurvitz has attempted more clearly to define circumstances in which aramaisms may be used to indicate late dating of individual texts.

See also **Semitisms; Textual Criticism (Old Testament).**

J. Barr, *Comparative Philology and the Text of the Old Testament*, 1968, pp. 121–4; G. R. Driver, 'Hebrew Poetic Diction', *VT*-S 1, 1953, pp. 26–39; A. Hurvitz, 'The Chronological Significance of "Aramaisms" in Biblical Hebrew', *IEJ* 18, 1968, pp. 234–40; R. Polzin, *Late Biblical Hebrew: Toward an Historical Typology of Biblical Hebrew Prose*, 1976; C. Rabin, 'Hebrew'; and E. Y. Kutscher, 'Aramaic' in *Current Trends in Linguistics* ed. T. A. Sebeok, 1970, pp. 304–46, 347–412; M. Wagner, *Die Lexikalischen und Grammatikalischen Aramaismen im Alttestamentlichen Hebräisch*, 1966.

C. T. R. HAYWARD

Archaeology (New Testament)

Archaeology is the scientific study of the material remains of past human life and activities. It is concerned with structures and artefacts of all types, with the exception of written documents whose study has developed into the separate discipline of epigraphy.* It highlights the discoveries made in all excavations which can be dated to the first century AD and which throw light on places or situations mentioned in the NT.

The Gospels. Although the Gospels do not mention where exactly Jesus was born, a pre-

Constantinian tradition represented by the *Protevangelium of James* 18.1, Justin (*Dialogue with Trypho* 78.6), and Origen* (*Against Celsus* 1.51) identifies his birthplace as a cave on the north-western edge of Bethlehem. The venerated cave is part of a larger complex that excavations show to have been in use in both the eighth-sixth centuries BC and at the beginning of the Christian era. Such caves would have served as a stable and/or storage area for a nearby house.

After they had spent a period in Egypt as refugees, a good motive for Joseph's selection of Nazareth as the new residence for himself and his family is provided by the decision of Herod Antipas to reconstruct Sepphoris in 3 BC (Josephus, *Ant.* 18.27). The building programme continued for twenty years and would have provided steady work for an able artisan. Excavations now in progress should eventually give us a vivid picture of the first-century city. Nazareth lay only four miles to the south-south-west, and the Roman road linking Sepphoris with Jerusalem passed through its outskirts. Jesus did not grow up in an isolated village but in a very cosmopolitan environment that cannot fail to have influenced his social attitudes and knowledge of languages. The archaeological exploration of Nazareth has been hampered by existing buildings, but first-century AD house foundations, silos, oil presses, and storage area have been brought to light.

Jesus' 'own city' (Mark 2.1) Capernaum is much better documented. The first-century village was made up of multiple family dwelling units. The walls around and within each unit were built of undressed rounded black basalt stones. Since no mortar was used, such walls could not have supported a second storey, and the roof can only have been of earth laid on palm branches supported by beams. The author of the miracle* story in Mark 2.1–12 knew the conditions of life in Capernaum; it would have been easy for the friends of the paralytic to reach and penetrate the roof (Mark 2.4). In the spaces between the rough basalt stones of the floors of such a house the excavators found coins that helped to date the original construction, and incidentally furnished a graphic illustration of the parable* of the lost drachma (Luke 15.8).

The excavation of one house showed that in the second half of the first century AD the floor and walls of one room had been plastered, a unique phenomenon in Capernaum. Storage jars and lamps had replaced the domestic utensils (cooking pots, bowls, pitchers, and juglets) of the earlier period. A private room had been put to public use, and later inscriptions scratched in the plastered walls indicate that it had become a place of Christian assembly. It is the only known example of a Palestinian house-church. Why this particular room? The most plausible answer is that it was the room believed to have been used by Jesus in the house of Peter (cf. Matt. 8.20).

The houses graphically display the poverty of the inhabitants of Capernaum, which explains why they needed the centurion to build them a synagogue (Luke 7.5), a generous gesture paralleled by that of a pagan priestess who, at the end of the first century AD, erected a synagogue for the Jews of Akmonia in Phrygia (MAMA 6.264). This synagogue has been discovered beneath the late fourth-century one that today dominates the site. Like the surrounding houses it had basalt walls and floor and measured 60 × 79 feet, which makes it significantly bigger than the only other first-century synagogue, that at Gamla. It was here that Jesus preached (Mark 1.21).

A drop in the level of the Sea of Galilee in 1986 brought to light a wooden boat dating from around the beginning of the Common Era which is now exhibited at Kibbutz Ginnosar. With a length of 27 feet and a beam of 8 feet it was the sort of boat used for fishing (Mark 1.19–20), voyages across the lake (Mark 4.35–41), or even as a pulpit (Mark 4.1).

Jericho appears so often in the Gospel narratives because it was on the pilgrimage route from Galilee to Jerusalem. Excavations still in progress have laid bare part of the vast palace of Herod the Great on both sides of the Wadi Qilt, together with its fortress, Kypros, at Tel el-Aqaba and its hippodrome-cum-theatre at Tel es-Samrat. After the dismissal of Archelaus in AD 6 the complex became a town (Luke 19.1) only when the nobility of Jerusalem came down to their winter villas around the palace. This was the only period (December–March) when John the Baptist would have found an audience in the Jordan valley (Mark 1.4–5). The field slaves who worked the date and balsam plantations would not have been permitted to listen to him. Luke's localization of the parable of the pretender (19.12ff.) in Jericho is very apposite, because it was in the palace there that Archelaus intrigued to ensure his succession to the throne of his father, Herod the Great.

The tomb venerated as the grave of Lazarus (John 11.17–18) is in fact in the graveyard of first-century Bethany. The village of the time of Jesus lies 100 yards up the hill to the west, and excavations show that it was inhabited from the sixth century BC to the fourteenth century AD. It was there that Jesus stayed when he came on pilgrimage to Jerusalem because space in the city was at a premium (Mark 11.11–12). It has been calculated that during the feasts the population of Jerusalem tripled from 60,000 to 180,000.

Two reported miracles of Jesus in Jerusalem are given precise locations. Enough has been excavated of the pool of Siloam (John 9.7) to show that it was a 15-yard-square basin surrounded by a portico. The pool at Bethzatha (John 5.2) is now known to have been a pagan healing temple dedicated to Asclepius/ Serapis. It was probably founded by the Roman garrison at the Antonia fortress located some 250 yards to the west. At the time of Jesus the site was outside the city walls, and the essential feature was a series of small rock-cut underground baths. Recognition of this material context gives an entirely new dimension to the miracle story.

According to John 10.23 Jesus and his disciples were walking one winter's day in Solomon's Portico, the eastern boundary of the temple area. Recent studies of the development of the temple area suggest that the line is Solomonic. The oldest masonry is certainly pre-Herodian and there is an ancient gate beneath the Golden Gate, but in the absence of excavations no exact dating is possible.

The upper room in which Jesus ate the last supper (Mark 14.13–16) cannot be identified with any certainty; excavations beneath the Cenacle have proved inconclusive. In order to reach the Kidron valley (John 18.1) Jesus would have had to leave Jerusalem either by the Gennath Gate in the north wall (Josephus, *War* 5.146), which may be that recently discovered in the Jewish Quarter, or more probably by the gate excavated in the southeast corner of the Herodian city. The fact that the Kidron valley had been a graveyard for over 1000 years goes a long way towards explaining Jesus' psychological state in the oldest version of the agony in the garden (Mark 14.32, 33b, 34b). To walk among the tombs even today provokes thoughts of one's mortality.

The traditional site of Gethsemane is probably correct. Behind it is a very ancient rock-cut stairway going to the top of the Mount of Olives where it connects with the ridge running south-east to Bethphage and Bethany. The topography shows that Jesus could very easily have kept ahead of his enemies and escaped into the desert, a factor that made his decision in the garden all the more agonizing.

Jesus was judged by Pilate at the palace of Herod the Great, which Philo* called 'the house of the procurators' (*Leg.* 38). It was situated on the highest point of the Herodian city, thus confirming the name Gabbatha given to it by John 19.13. The base of the great tower Phasael stands to a height of 60 feet, but excavations have revealed only the substructure of the podium on which the palace was built.

Excavations beneath the church of the Holy Sepulchre reveal that the traditional site of the crucifixion and burial of Jesus conforms very closely to the indications given in the Fourth Gospel. Originally a quarry lying just outside the Second Wall (John 19.20), it was transformed into a garden (John 19.41) in the first century BC, and fig, carob, and olive trees as well as cereals were planted there. Golgotha was a corner projecting into the quarry and sloping to the south; the quarrymen had cut around it because it had been cracked by an earthquake and the stone is of very poor quality. Some 30 yards away (John 19.42) a Jewish catacomb was cut into the west wall of the quarry. Although almost completely destroyed by Constantine's engineers, who were interested only in the outermost chamber, enough remains to show that it must be dated in the first century. The catacomb could not have been cut after AD 41 when the site was brought within the Third Wall built by Herod Agrippa.

It is clear from this survey of the archaeological data relevant to the Gospels that one of the sources of the Fourth Gospel gives more detailed accurate information on the topography of Jerusalem than any of the synoptics. Although it may have been given its formal form elsewhere, John is rooted in the soil of Palestine.

The Epistles. The type of systematic survey attempted for the Gospels is not possible for the Epistles, because the Holy Land was a centre of pilgrimage in a way that Christian sites elsewhere in the eastern Mediterranean were not. In consequence, archaeologists who worked in Palestine were interested in anything biblical, whereas those who worked in Italy, Greece, and Asia Minor were classicists, whose interest in anything specifically Christian was minimal. Thus, it is only now that NT scholars are beginning to sift through the archaeological reports on cities such as Antioch, Ephesus, Philippi, Thessalonica and Corinth in order to abstract material that can be dated to the first century, and which may throw light on problems or situations in the Epistles.

This belated interest in archaeological data – by far the greatest single source of new information – was stimulated by the sociological* approach to the NT. Although this approach was pioneered in Germany, the most recent German commentary on the Corinthian correspondence* by F. Lang (1986) typically makes no use of virtually a century of well-published excavations at Corinth. In the English-speaking world the situation is much better. R. Jewett's study of the Thessalonian correspondence (1986) extracts the maximum from the little evidence available,

and in his commentary on II Corinthians (1984) V. P. Furnish makes extremely adroit use of archaeological data to highlight the religious and ethnic diversity of Corinth, and of epigraphic material to explain the administrative structure of the city.

Careful analysis of the reports has permitted a very detailed plan of the centre of Corinth in AD 50, which provides a graphic context for Paul's* encounter with the proconsul L. Junius Gallio (Acts 18.12–17). This event furnishes the principal datable link between Paul's career and world history. The key element is a letter of the emperor Claudius (AD 41–54) inscribed on a broken slab excavated at Delphi. Initially (1905) only four fragments were recognized, but in 1967 Plassart was able to place five other fragments, which significantly changed the tenor of the document, and made the dating of Gallio's term of office in Achaia (AD 51–52) virtually certain. On it depend the dates assigned to all the Pauline letters.

One complex excavated at Corinth throws light on the origin of one of Paul's most distinctive theological concepts, and at the same time clarifies a situation with which he had to deal. The Asclepion just inside the north wall contained a great number of *ex votos*, terracotta replicas of hands and feet, arms and legs, breasts and genitals, eyes and ears. It has been plausibly argued that to Paul these evoked humanity as 'dead', which in turn led him to think of redeemed humanity as a body whose members were 'alive' because they belonged to each other (Rom. 12.5). The Asclepion also contained three dining rooms that could be rented out for private parties. Openings without doors gave on to an open square surrounded by porticos in which the inhabitants of the city took their ease protected by the sea breeze from the pollution caused by the bronze factories in the central area. At once it becomes possible to see what lies behind Paul's question, 'If anyone sees you, a man of knowledge, at table in an idol's temple, might not the conscience of a weak person be led to eat food offered to idols?' (I Cor. 8.10).

Archaeology also provides the simplest explanation for the divisions in the eucharistic assembly which Paul found so distressing (I Cor. 11.17–34). The Pauline churches contained no members from the very top or the very bottom of the Graeco-Roman social scale. The houses in which individuals such as Gaius received the whole community of Corinth (Rom. 16.23), therefore, were nothing like the palaces of the great patrician families. They were probably very similar to the villa excavated at Anaploga in Corinth, which can be dated to the time of Paul. The excavators describe it as 'sumptuous' but its size indicates only moderate wealth. The triclinium (6 × 8 yds) could accommodate 11 people reclining (the normal posture for a meal), whereas perhaps 25 could sit (I Cor. 14.30) in the atrium (5.5 × 6.5 yds). If there were 14 known males in the Corinthian community, the minimum membership of the church must have been between 40 and 50. They could not all have been accommodated in one area, and this immediately provoked a discriminatory division because the heatable triclinium was much more comfortable than the atrium, which was open to the elements. Human nature being what it is, it is very probable that the host ensured that friends of his social class got the best places. Such an unsatisfactory situation provided an obvious incentive for the community to meet in subgroups that would have facilitated the development of factions within the church (I Cor. 1.12).

These examples illustrating how archaeology can directly benefit NT interpretation are but a beginning. When similar work is done on the excavation reports of other Christian centres in the Roman empire our knowledge of the material cultures of the first century will deepen, and new insights into the Epistles will emerge.

See also **Archaeology (Old Testament); Corinthian Correspondence; Epigraphy; Jerusalem; Sociology and Social Anthropology.**

C. Coüasnon, *The Church of the Holy Sepulchre in Jerusalem*, 1974; A. Duprez, *Jésus et les dieux guérisseurs*, 1970; J. Finegan, *The Archaeology of the New Testament*, 1981; J. Murphy-O'Connor, *St Paul's Corinth. Texts and Archaeology*, 1983.

J. MURPHY-O'CONNOR

Archaeology (Old Testament)

Definition. The meaning of the term 'archaeology' has evolved over time and is difficult to define. In ancient literature it refers generally to the recounting of past events. Josephus'* *The Antiquities of the Jews*, for example, was actually entitled *ioudaïkēs archaiologias*. Also in modern popular usage the term may be used in connection with matters of any sort having to do with ancient times. In academic contexts, on the other hand, archaeology refers specifically to research involving the physical remains of past human civilization (and not necessarily the distant past). In accordance with this narrow definition, the work of an archaeologist would be distinguished from that of a geologist (who studies the earth's crust), a palaeontologist (who attempts to trace the evolution of biological forms), a historian (who explores the human past through written records), and so on.

While the more specific 'academic' definition of archaeology is useful, it cannot be maintained rigidly. Artefactual evidence must be studied in physical and historical context. In actual practice, therefore, archaeological research is interdisciplinary; it necessarily involves geology, palaeontology, history, and a host of other related disciplines and subdisciplines. The following discussion, accordingly, without holding rigidly to a narrow definition of archaeology, will focus on explorations in Palestine and research pertaining to the artefactual remains of the people who lived there during biblical times.

Overview. Already in the OT itself, one notices 'archaeological' observations. Having described how the Israelites buried the king of Ai beneath a heap of stones at the entrance of his demolished city, for example, the narrator of Josh. 8–9 assures the reader that the heap of stones 'stands there to this day' (8.29). Other biblical passages mention 'tells' (the Hebrew form is *tel*) and indicate that the writers recognized them to be city ruins (see esp. Deut. 13.16). Still other passages seek to clarify place names. It is explained in Gen. 14.2–3, for example, that Bela is an earlier name for Zoar and that the Valley of Siddim is an earlier name for the Salt Sea (which a modern commentator would explain in turn as an earlier name for the Dead Sea). Elsewhere it is explained that Jebus, which figures in the story of the rape of a Levite's concubine, is actually Jerusalem (Judg. 19.10); that Luz is an earlier name for Bethel (Judg. 1.22); that Ephrath was Bethlehem (Gen. 48.7), and so on.

Geographical detail is characteristic of the OT, and this would have added a sense of immediacy for the ancient Israelites who lived in the land and were familiar with the places mentioned. Unfamiliar place names can have the opposite effect, on the other hand, and in classical times this emerged as a problem even for people living in Palestine. Following the conquests of Alexander the Great and especially during the time of Roman rule, many of the old Semitic place names were displaced by new ones based on Greek and Latin. Fortunately, writers of the day sometimes reported the name changes. Noteworthy in this regard was Eusebius,* Bishop of Caesarea (c. AD 264–340), who produced an aid for Bible study which has come to be known as the *Onomasticon* (literally, 'list of names'). In this work, Eusebius listed over a thousand biblical place names and noted the location of many of them in relation to the main cities and roads of his own day. The *Onomasticon* was regarded as valuable enough for Jerome to annotate and translate it into Latin almost a century later. Mosaics from early Christian churches occasionally show an interest in biblical geography and toponymy. The best example is a mosaic map of biblical Palestine (originally the floor of a sixth-century church) preserved in the modern town of Madaba in southern Transjordan.

Christian pilgrims began to arrive in Jerusalem* already during the second century AD. Later, after restrictions resulting from the Jewish revolts of the first and second centuries were relaxed, they were joined by Jewish pilgrims, and still later by Muslim pilgrims. Although driven by piety rather than scientific or academic concerns, these early travellers deserve to be regarded as the predecessors of modern Palestinian archaeologists. They sought out the actual places where important events had occurred and often recorded what they saw (or were led to believe that they saw). Many of these pilgrims' accounts were collected, translated, and published in the late nineteenth century by the Palestine Pilgrims' Text Society and have proved useful to contemporary archaeologists.

Eventually there began to appear, very rarely at first, travellers who represented a dawning new age of exploration (for example, Leonhard Rauchwolf and Johann Zuallart in the late sixteenth century, Pietro della Valle in the mid-seventeenth century, and Henry Maundrell and Richard Pococke in the eighteenth century). At the very end of the eighteenth century an event occurred which must be regarded as a major turning point in the modern scientific exploration of the Middle East: Napoleon's invasion of Egypt and Palestine in 1798. Napoleon was accompanied by scholars eager to explore and record antiquities. His engineers produced a trigonometrically-based, 1:100,000 scale map of Egypt and the Palestinian coast. Even more important for the future of archaeology, his invasion signalled to other leading nations of the day that a presence in the Middle East was politically and economically advantageous.

Consequently the nineteenth century was a period of increasingly intense foreign involvement in Palestine and, in conjunction with this foreign involvement, increasingly intentional and systematic exploration of the land. The last four decades of the century were especially active in terms of archaeological exploration, with much of the important work conducted under the auspices of the Palestine Exploration Fund (established in London in 1865). Important achievements during the nineteenth century with special relevance for better understanding of the OT include the following: 1. Western Palestine and much of the region east of the Jordan were surveyed and mapped with attention to surface archaeological ruins and local Arabic place names. Especially important was the Survey of Western Palestine conducted by C. R. Conder and

H. H. Kitchener during the 1870s under the auspices of the PEF. 2. Significant strides were made in the study of the historical geography of Palestine, e.g. scholars were able to establish the approximate locations of hundreds of biblical towns and villages whose sites had remained unknown for centuries. Edward Robinson's *Biblical Researches in Palestine and the Adjacent Regions* (1841, 1856) and George Adam Smith's *The Historical Geography of the Holy Land* (1894) contain most of what we know today about biblical toponymy. 3. The excavation of ancient ruins was begun. There emerged a recognition that 'tells' conceal the stratified ruins of ancient cities, and, as the century drew to a close, Flinders Petrie conducted the first excavation of a Palestinian tell (Tell el-Hesy in 1890, under the auspices of the PEF). 4. Thousands of documents from ancient times were recovered by the nineteenth-century explorers and excavators. Although most of these were found in Egypt and Mesopotamia, they had considerable relevance for better understanding of the context from which the OT emerged. Two important inscriptional discoveries in Palestine were the Mesha Inscription (erected by King Mesha of Moab, a contemporary of Ahab and Jehoshaphat; see II Kings 3) and the Siloam Inscription (probably commissioned by King Hezekiah). 5. Finally, nineteenth-century scholars observed and recorded data pertaining to traditional Palestinian life-styles. Although one thinks of this as ethnography rather than archaeology, the two go hand in hand. Observations pertaining to recent Palestinian folk-customs provide clues for interpreting the artefactual record left by earlier inhabitants of the same land.

Beginning with Petrie's work at Tell el-Hesy, attention was turned to the major tells of Palestine. Several of these tells had already been excavated with a wide variety of techniques by the outbreak of World War I. Many more were examined during the post-war years during which time there were also significant advances in excavation and dating techniques. Two key elements in these techniques are stratigraphy and stylistic typology. As indicated above, tells are the stratified ruins of ancient cities; they were formed as the occupational remains from later phases of a city's history were deposited on top of those from earlier phases. All items fashioned by humans have stylistic characteristics, and since styles change in time, it can be assumed that the artefacts found in a particular stratum of a tell reflect the styles which were flourishing during the corresponding phase of the city's history. Palestinian pottery styles have changed gradually through the ages, for example, and archaeologists have been able to reconstruct the sequence of these changes with a reasonable degree of accuracy. Consequently the pottery (even the broken potsherds) found in a particular stratum of a tell enables an archaeologist to date the corresponding phase of the city's history represented by that stratum.

Naturally, biblical scholars went on to correlate the archaeological record as presented by the excavated tells with the biblical account of Israel's history. Already by the late 1920s, however, difficulties had begun to emerge, centred on the ruins of ancient Jericho (Tell es-Sultan). When Ernst Sellin and Carl Watzinger excavated at Tell es-Sultan in 1907–11, they separated three major strata which they identified respectively as the remains of the Canaanite city that Joshua destroyed (according to Josh. 7), those of the Israelite city founded during Ahab's reign (I Kings 16.34), and those of a post-exilic Jewish settlement. By the mid-1920s, however, when pottery dating had reached a degree of sophistication, Watzinger recognized that the Jericho pottery did not support their initial dating of the three city phases. On the contrary, he concluded (and published in 1926) that 'in the time of Joshua Jericho was a heap of ruins on which stood perhaps a few isolated huts'. The implication, of course, was that archaeology disproved the historicity of the biblical account of the conquest of Jericho.

Controversy raged. Many were convinced that Watzinger must have reached a wrong conclusion. Among them was John Garstang, who conducted further excavations at Jericho and made minor soundings at Ai (et-Tell) and Hazor (Tell el-Qadeh), from which he concluded that all three sites were still active cities as late as 1400 BC. This was an acceptable date for the Israelite conquest of Canaan, Garstang contended, compatible with the biblical story as well as the archaeological evidence, and his view gained wide currency during the 1930s. Specialists such as William F. Albright and Père L. H. Vincent were never convinced by Garstang's evaluation of the pottery from these three tells, however, and as more evidence became available from excavations at other tells, it became increasingly obvious that correlating archaeology with the biblical story was more complex than Garstang had supposed.

By the end of the 1930s, two new and competing approaches to the problem had emerged. One of these, championed by W. F. Albright, attempted to produce a correlation between the archaeological record and the biblical narrative by making slight adjustments in the latter where the former seemed to demand it. Albright dated the Israelite conquest of Canaan to the thirteenth century, for example, which conflicts with biblical chrono-

logy, but enabled him to associate the Israelite invasion with a pattern of city destructions which occurred in Palestine at the end of the Late Bronze Age. The other approach, championed by Albrecht Alt and Martin Noth, held the biblical account of the conquest to be a largely literary construct and thus ultimately irreconcilable with the archaeological record. This is not to say that Alt, Noth, and their followers regarded archaeology as irrelevant for the study of biblical history, but they did insist that any attempt to correlate archaeology with the biblical materials should begin with a thorough literary-critical* analysis of the latter. Albright and his followers tended to begin with the archaeological evidence, on the other hand, and to propose 'archaeological solutions' which by-passed the historical uncertainties raised by literary-critical research. Albright's approach, expounded and developed by G. Ernest Wright and others, tended to be favoured among English-speaking scholars. German scholars tended to follow the approach of Alt and Noth.

The on-going debate between the two 'schools' has subsided since the 1960s as a result of new developments in both archaeology and literary-critical research. In Palestinian archaeology, for example, there have been still further developments and increased consensus in excavation techniques, e.g. the so-called Wheeler–Kenyon method, which provides more stratigraphic control. Archaeological projects today usually are designed with more specific goals in mind than before – for instance, to solve particular problems or to fill in specific gaps in our knowledge. Among other things, this has resulted in fewer long-term excavations at big tells, more attention to one-period sites, and surface surveys with attention to the regional patterns. Also archaeological teams are being drawn from an increasingly broader range of disciplines today, more from the sciences than from the humanities. The teams are composed of geologists, botanists, zoologists, hydrologists, and the like, and supported by student volunteers rather than locally hired labourers. Thus a broader variety of data is collected, collected more carefully and, hopefully, more completely understood. Finally, especially among some American archaeologists, there is a noticeable shift of interest away from historical towards anthropological kinds of questions. Less concerned with the political history of ancient times, archaeologists of the new breed want to know what sort of communal configurations existed among the people who lived there and how they utilized or exploited their environment. This shift reflects the influence of 'new archaeology', which emerged among American archaeologists. It also represents a negative professional reaction to methodological abuses; chiefly those perpetrated under the general banner 'biblical archaeology' which often slanted and interpreted archaeological findings arbitrarily in an attempt to correlate them with the biblical record.

Relevance. At least four areas may be identified in which archaeology has contributed to biblical interpretation in the past and can be expected to do so in the future.

1. One of the most important ways is by clarifying the *geography of the land* from which the Bible emerged and by identifying the sites of the hundreds of towns and villages which the Bible mentions. The need to explain some of the biblical place names was recognized already by the biblical narrators themselves, as we have seen, and the impressive results of modern scholarship in this regard become obvious when one compares the best eighteenth-century maps of Palestine with those available today, or compares early Bible maps (the Madaba Mosaic for example) with current Bible atlases. Yet much remains to be learned, and even the most recent Bible atlases should be used with some caution.

It is helpful to distinguish three sorts of evidence which come into consideration for identifying biblical sites: (a) information derived from the Bible itself and other ancient written sources; (b) modern Arabic place names which often preserve the memory of ancient names; and (c) artefactual evidence, especially pottery, which indicates in which period(s) a given archaeological ruin was occupied. Nineteenth-century scholars were limited almost exclusively to the first two kinds of evidence, whereas twentieth-century scholars have depended heavily on the third. All three types of evidence can be misleading, however, so they must be used cautiously and in balance with each other. Ancient written sources may give distorted information as the result of secondary editorial combinations, additions, or changes. Place names are known to have moved from one location to another in time, so that even when the Arabic name of a ruin corresponds to the name of a biblical city, one cannot be certain that the ruin is the exact site of the ancient city. Even the artefactual evidence can be misleading. Any archaeological ruin will preserve only a small percentage of the artefacts from the city's past, and archaeologists usually are able to examine only a small sampling of any given ruin. Indeed the majority of known archaeological ruins in Palestine still have not been excavated at all, which means that archaeologists have access only to their surface remains (often consisting of nothing more than tumbled stones and scattered potsherds). In some cases, therefore, the available artefactual evidence

from a site may not be fully representative of the periods during which it was occupied.

Site identifications are usually made with some degree of uncertainty, therefore, and this has provided a convenient 'escape clause' on occasions when excavations at a previously identified biblical site did not produce expected results. This has been particularly noticeable with the conquest cities, those which, according to the book of Joshua, resisted the Israelite invasion of Canaan. Jericho was only the first of several of these cities whose ruins produced little or no remains from the Late Bronze Age, the supposed conquest period. In each case, it has been suggested that the excavated site was misidentified, and that the real Jericho, Ai, Arad, Heshbon, or Yarmut must have been somewhere else, perhaps nearby.

Furthermore, there is an understandable inclination on the part of those who produce historical atlases to include as many place names as possible on the maps and a corresponding inclination to give questionable site identifications the benefit of the doubt. At the same time, space limitations on maps render it difficult to convey varying degrees of exactness and certainty. The results are maps which convey the false impression that a relatively large number of ancient cities and villages can be located with an equal degree of certainty. Another unfortunate dynamic is that site identifications merely suggested in professional publications sometimes find their way into the secondary literature where they are repeated again and again as if they represented established fact. None of this is to suggest that Bible maps and atlases are totally misleading and of no use. It is simply to emphasize that historical maps by nature are radical oversimplifications of various kinds of primary and hypothetical information for visual presentation and should be used with objectivity and reasonable caution.

2. A second important area has to do with the analysis of the *material culture* of Palestine during ancient times. The information gained helps the interpreter construct a socio-cultural picture of the world from which the biblical text has emerged. The physical layouts of cities, public buildings, private dwellings, etc. are revealed. Examination of public water works and roads from ancient times provides insight into community structures and trade relations. Commercial, military, and religious artefacts – from agricultural implements to weaponry to amulets, liturgical furniture and art – all reveal common elements of everyday life which often illuminate the biblical text. Even such family and personal items as lamps, chairs, cooking utensils, jewellery, and grooming aids give us a 'feel' for life in biblical times which cannot fail to enrich our reading.

Occasionally there are discoveries which clarify certain biblical texts in specific ways. The OT often mentions units of volume and weight, for example, and one of the chief means whereby the modern equivalents have been determined is through archaeological discoveries. Fragments of vessels upon which are inscribed units of volume have been unearthed, also weights inscribed with their values. One notable example of the latter is the discovery of a weight labelled *pîm*. This clarified the meaning of I Sam. 13.21 which, as it is now understood, indicates that a *pîm* was the standard payment required by the Philistines for sharpening certain agricultural implements. Previously, the term was unknown and translators could only guess at the meaning of the verse.

Typically, archaeology provides a more 'democratic' picture of every-day life in ancient times than one gains from written sources, since the latter tend to derive from and focus on leading figures – kings, prophets, and priests – rather than on ordinary people. Both high and low culture come to light in archaeological study. Also, archaeology is sensitive to changes which occur in the material culture of an area over long periods of time, and to recurring patterns which show up in different periods. Were there particular socio-cultural circumstances and developments along the eastern Mediterranean seaboard at the end of the Late Bronze Age, which explain the emergence of the several small monarchies (including Israel and Judah) in the early centuries of the subsequent Iron Age? Will an analysis of recurring settlement patterns in the region provide any clues for understanding the origins of the Israelites? Questions such as these are being explored by archaeologists and biblical scholars alike. One must be careful when considering such issues not to assign ethnic labels to archaeological features without adequate grounds. It is sometimes assumed, for example, that certain early Iron Age features, such as the so-called collared-rim jars and four-room houses, are distinctively Israelite, simply because they turn up in Palestine in the early Iron Age, which we equate in turn with Israel's early tribal period. Yet peoples other than the Israelites were also living in Palestine at that time – Jebusites, Ammonites, and Moabites, for example – and there is every reason to suppose that they used the same kinds of vessels and lived in the same sort of houses.

3. Archaeology has proved to be less useful for dealing with specific issues in *biblical history* than earlier scholars had hoped. Yet it does have some relevance in that regard, which is another area of its contribution to biblical interpretation. In the first place, there are numerous occasions where certain archaeological data can be reasonably associated with an incident reported in the OT (or in some other ancient document) or be called upon in support of a particular historical position; yet the same data may also, sometimes just as reasonably, be interpreted otherwise. Evidence that several Palestinian cities were destroyed near the end of the Late Bronze Age has been associated with the Israelite conquest of Canaan, for example, and then cited as confirming evidence, not only for the historicity of the conquest, but for dating it at that time (thirteenth century BC). Yet these same destructions may be (and have been) attributed instead to widespread peasants' revolts against their Canaanite overlords, or to various other events (including earthquake) which occurred roughly simultaneously.

In short, much archaeological evidence is historically neutral, open to a range of possible interpretations. Correspondingly, many of the examples reported in popular books, articles, and newspaper releases of how archaeology confirms or clarifies biblical history actually have to do with essentially neutral evidence which has been arbitrarily interpreted to fit some aspect of the Bible story (which itself may have been interpreted just as arbitrarily).

Archaeology is not always neutral on historical matters, however. Occasionally correlations can be made which are reasonably firm. It is reported in I Kings 9.15, for example, that Solomon built Hazor, Megiddo, and Gezer. The sites of all three of these cities can be identified with confidence; all three have been excavated; and in each case a city gate and casemate wall was uncovered from approximately the tenth century BC, i.e. Solomon's century. All three fortification systems followed a very similar plan, suggesting that they were part of a single royal building project. The case is not entirely conclusive; for example, there remains some stratigraphical uncertainty at Megiddo. Nevertheless, it seems reasonable to conclude that archaeologists have uncovered Solomonic fortifications at the three cities in question. The strata which include these fortifications provide benchmarks, in turn, for recognizing pre-Solomonic and post-Solomonic phases at the sites and, by comparing the pottery, at other sites in the region.

Samaria (present day Sebaṣṭiyeh) provides another possible benchmark. I Kings 16.24 reports that Omri founded Samaria, and the earliest building phase at Sebaṣṭiyeh can be dated by its pottery to approximately the time of Omri, so it makes sense to attribute the building phase to him. Likewise it makes sense to assign a second building phase at Sebaṣṭiyeh, which seems to have followed soon after the first, to Ahab, Omri's son, also remembered in I Kings as a builder. Lachish provides a third reasonably certain benchmark, assuming that Lachish is correctly identified with Tell ed-Duweir. Stratum III at Tell ed-Duweir would represent the city sacked by Sennacherib in 701 BC, an event described on his palace walls at Nineveh.

Beginning with these benchmarks and constantly comparing the pottery from one site to the next, it is possible to develop still further correlations, each with its own relative degree of certainty, between the archaeological strata and the periods of the Israelite and Judaean monarchies. With few exceptions, such as when written materials turn up in a stratum, these correlations are very loose. Nevertheless, even when all of the necessary qualifications are taken into account, the artefactual record occasionally has a distinctive voice.

Solomon serves again as a good example. The narrators of Kings and Chronicles would have us believe that he was a fantastically wealthy and powerful ruler whose domain extended from the Egyptian frontier to the Euphrates. Yet the relevant passages offer vague and sweeping claims with few details, and most of the details which do emerge actually suggest a rather modest operation. As it turns out, the archaeological evidence also suggests that Solomon's grandeur has been exaggerated. Although the city plans and architectural remains that can be associated with his reign are fairly impressive by local Palestinian standards of the early Iron Age, they are rather ordinary when compared to those of the preceding Bronze Age. They even pale by comparison with those of the following phase of the Iron Age which is possibly to be associated with the Omride dynasty. At Hazor, for example, the fortifications were expanded and strengthened, apparently by the Omrides, beyond those of Solomon's day. Impressive water tunnels were engineered at both Hazor and Megiddo. Solomon's stables at Megiddo, probably not stables after all, turn out now to be Omride. In short, the same artefactual record that suggests that the grandeur of Solomon's reign has been overrated also suggests that the Omride period represented the (still rather modest) 'golden age' of ancient Israel, at least as far as material wealth and engineering accomplishments were concerned.

4. Finally, archaeologists have contributed to biblical interpretation by recovering non-biblical documents from biblical times (and in the case of the Dead Sea Scrolls* by recovering *early manuscripts** of parts of the OT itself). Up to the present, relatively few ancient texts have been discovered in Palestine compared, for example, with the extensive archives found in Egypt,* Syria, and Mesopotamia. To the Mesha and Siloam inscriptions have been added several smaller inscription fragments, numerous seal impressions, and a growing corpus of ostraca. Prior to the 1960s, sherds collected during the course of an excavation were washed clean for examination, and it may well be that the writing was scrubbed from many an ostracon in the process. Since then, however, archaeologists have been dipping the sherds in water and examining them closely for writing before scrubbing. Consequently the recovery rate of ostraca has increased significantly. Fragmentary Aramaic texts discovered at Deir 'Alla in the Jordan Valley feature the prophet Balaam. Strange texts in Hebrew (or 'Canaanite') from Kuntillet 'Ajrud in the Negev refer to (and possibly depict) 'Yahweh and his Asherah'. These are but examples of what we can expect in the future as archaeologists continue to explore. Perhaps it is not too much to hope that royal archives of the Israelite or Judaean kings will turn up some day.

See also **Ancient Near Eastern World; Archaeology (New Testament); Egypt; Israel, History of.**

Joel Drinkard, Gerald Mattingly, and J. Maxwell Miller (eds), *Benchmarks in Time and Culture: An Introduction to Palestinian Archaeology*, 1988; Kathleen Kenyon, *The Bible and Recent Archaeology*, revd edn by P. R. S. Moorey, 1987; H. Darrell Lance, *The Old Testament and the Archaeologist*, 1981; Neil Asher Silberman, *Digging for God and Country,* 1982; George Adam Smith, *The Historical Geography of the Holy Land*, 1894, 1966.

J. MAXWELL MILLER

Aretalogy

The term has come into NT studies relatively recently. Its use derives from the now widely accepted observation that *aretē* ('virtue') in many Hellenistic* texts is used of the marvellous or miraculous* acts of a deity or divine figure (as in I Peter 2.9; cf. Strabo, XVII.1.17). The word *aretalogia* is not itself well attested in ancient texts; slightly better documented is the figure of the *aretalogus*, who appears in Latin texts as a story-teller brought in to entertain at imperial dinner-parties (Suetonius, *Div. Aug.,* 74; Juvenal XV.16).

The term is used by scholars today in two distinct areas:

1. In the study of Hellenistic* religion, an aretalogy is a text in which the powers and virtues of a god or goddess are recited (cf. Ecclus. 36.13). In many such texts, the deity speaks in the first person using an 'I am' (Gk. *egō eimi*) formula. This has suggested a par-

allel with the discourses of the Gospel of John.

2. In NT studies, the word has also come to be used of a narrative recital of the marvellous deeds of a miracle-worker ('divine man', Greek *theios anēr*) or prophet. Thus, as early as 1954, R. L. P. Milburn spoke of an 'aretalogical' element in the apocryphal Acts (*Early Christian Interpretation of History*), and in 1965 Moses Hadas and Morton Smith published a collection of 'aretalogies' under the title *Heroes and Gods*, which included Luke's Gospel alongside Philostratus' *Life of Apollonius of Tyana* as prime examples of the genre.* Despite criticisms, Morton Smith and others have continued to use the term aretalogy both of possible Gospel sources and of possible pre-Christian models for the Gospels.* Others have tried to extend it to include philosophical biography (D. L. Tiede).

Howard C. Kee observes correctly that no ancient author describes such texts as aretalogies ('Aretalogy and Gospel', *JBL* 92, 1973). If the term is helpful, the complaint may be beside the point, though the usage could be misleading, in so far as it implies that an ancient genre-description is in view. But since there is not a clearly defined group of texts to which the name (in this sense) could be attached, it may be better to limit its use to texts (or elements within texts) which recite the *aretai* of a god as 1. above – which also fits better with the little ancient evidence we have for the word. In this sense, many early Christian texts are certainly aretalogical in function and can with profit be studied in the context of ancient religious propaganda, even if we have to look elsewhere for an explanation of their literary form.

E. V. Gallagher, *Divine Man or Magician?*, SBLDS 64, 1982, ch. 1; D. L. Tiede, *The Charismatic Figure as Miracle Worker*, SBLDS, 1972; L. Vidman, *Sylloge Inscriptionum Religionis Isiacae et Serapiacae*, 1969 (texts).

LOVEDAY ALEXANDER

Art, The Bible in

The very specific prohibitions in the second Mosaic commandment where images, not only of the Deity but of all living creatures, are forbidden, stifled Jewish artistic interpretation of the scriptures, though several recent books have demonstrated the importance of the separate Jewish tradition of biblical visualization. It is clear from the books of Kings that Solomon's Temple in Jerusalem was not bereft of imagery (I Kings 7). Indeed, the ancient description of that Temple was a critical source for the Christian iconography of cathedrals. In the early Christian centuries, per-haps under Christian influence, there is some Jewish representational art, notably in the synagogue at Dura Europos. However, Jewish artistic talent, which is demonstrably prodigious, has been channelled towards the abstract arts of music and architecture. In relatively recent centuries, a number of Jewish painters have emerged. Marc Chagall's windows of the Twelve Tribes of Israel in Jerusalem are a landmark not only as a visual masterpiece of the post-war (1939–45) period, but as stamping the modern Zionist movement with a positive attitude to visual expression. The twentieth century apart, the Jewish visual tradition, though not so severely abstract as Muslim art, has seldom gone further than ornrmentation of the textual scroll.

The weight of biblical interpretation in visual terms, of both OT and NT, has therefore been Christian, and immediately raises the question of why Christianity has been prepared for most of its centuries to set aside the second commandment, while holding with dedicated tenacity to the remainder! The answer must lie in the Christian inheritance not only of Judaic monotheism, but of the philosophical and artistic background of Greece, mediated through the Graeco-Roman empire.

The earliest surviving Christian artefact is perhaps the scratched cross behind an altar at Pompeii, which must be of before AD 79. It was made in that provincial Roman town less than fifty years after the crucifixion, for someone perhaps converted by the visit to Rome of Paul or Peter. The Pompeii cross is unequivocal, but there follows an ambivalent area of Christian imagery through the centuries of official persecution. The *locus classicus* of this deliberately evasive epoch is a chamber in the Scarvi under St Peter's in Rome. The underdrawing of a second-century mosaic portrays a fisherman with his net. His purport could be purely Virgilian, or to the initiated he may have stood for Peter, the Great Fisherman. In the vault above, Apollo with a rayed nimbus rides in his horse-drawn chariot. Is he simply Apollo, or does Jesus, the Light of the World, ascend, like Elijah, to heaven?

The art of the catacombs, and of Christian artefacts associated with the centuries before Constantine declared Christianity to be the official religion of his empire in the early fourth century, is of a piece with the mosaic chamber in the Scarvi. Images of Daniel in the lion's den, of Abraham* preparing to sacrifice Isaac, of Jonah and the whale, and of the Good Shepherd, could bear interpretations not specific to Christianity. The Good Shepherd might have been Orpheus. Jonah expelled by the whale could be a river god with a sea-monster. The Cleveland Museum marbles, made probably in the third quarter of the third century in Asia Minor, underline the importance of this particular language. No depiction of Christ giving the keys to Peter and the book to Paul (the *Traditio Legis*), or of the crucifixion, can be confidently attributed to the centuries of persecution. Immediately that was lifted, we find specific images like the ivory of the crucifixion now in the British Museum. It is doubtful whether the crucifixion was avoided in the early centuries because it was too horrific to depict: more probably it was regarded as too overtly Christian. When the crucifixion does emerge, its hallmark is the quiet triumphalism of all early Christian imagery.

The late Roman empire had a taste for thorough visual information: each triumphal arch was decorated with a fuller account of the victories of its emperor than the one before. Christianity inherited an approach too ambitious for the vast extent of the Bible. The system of gathering leaves together to form a codex, as opposed to inscribing a continuous scroll, was devised about the same time as the compilation of the books of the NT and was widely adopted by Christians (*see* **Manuscripts**; **Palaeography**). A scroll must be studied linearly. In a book, visual imagery can be interleaved with the text, mark important divisions, expound turning points of the narrative, or stand in its own right. Christian Bible illustration started in the scroll tradition, attempting a continuous sequence unfolding with the narrative. Our earliest surviving examples are as thorough and as matter of fact as Trajan's Column. Among codices, the Cotton Genesis, illuminated in Alexandria in the fifth century, is embellished with lively little figures in full colour placed in subservient but naturalistic settings. The Vienna Genesis illuminated in Syria, also in the fifth century, runs to over three hundred illustrations, some of apocryphal incidents. On this scale, the whole Bible, or even the Torah plus the Life of Christ, would have been unmanageable. The first full illuminated example of the NT to survive, the Rossano Gospels (Il Duomo di Rossano, Calabria), of the sixth century, represents a further development of the same late antique tradition. Formality is introduced by the use of gold for Christ's garments and for haloes, backgrounds are reduced to necessary props, and the incidents are girded with an undertow of commentaries from the prophets. As St Augustine* declared, 'the New Testament lies hidden in the Old and the Old is fulfilled in the New' – the thesis which underlies mediaeval* biblical scholarship, and gives the key to the biblical illustration of ten centuries.

The artist of the Rossano Gospels inherited the fluency of late antique representational art, and added an intensity of expression. Little faces glow with meaning, gestures under-scoring what is happening are pointed up by enlarged hands, in contrast with small dancing feet. Christ is alone and calm in every scene. This figure, bearded and wearing a toga, is of the same type as the Christ enthroned among his immediate followers in the contemporary apse of Sta Pudenziana in Rome. The fundamental similarity between images of Christ in all Christian traditions and through all subsequent centuries goes back to their common root in the fifth century. Scene after scene in the Rossano Gospels – Christ before Pilate, the Entry into Jerusalem, Christ at Emmaus – was so treated that no representation created since has been more appropriate. The Rossano Gospels, at the threshold of Christian art, stands for the interpretation of the Bible as St Augustine's *City of God* stands for Christian writing. It may reflect lost prototypes in Jerusalem* or Rome. In Sta Maria Maggiore in Rome, built by Pope Sixtus III (423–440), glass mosaics of 27 scenes from the OT survive in the nave, with infancy of Christ scenes over the chancel arch. So extensive a scheme demands more of the NT, but the apse was destroyed in 1288–92. Early Christian cycles in the Roman basilicas are a largely missing link in the history of Christian iconography: the extensive frescoes of OT and NT once covering S. Paulo fuori le Mure (probably made under Pope Leo I, 440–61), are only known through seventeenth- and eighteenth-century copies. There were similar cycles in Old St Peter's.

The brilliance and pace of the Rossano Gospels and its lost relatives could not survive the formalism demanded by the technique of mosaic, a formalism introduced already at Sta Pudenziana, and thence translated to Ravenna and Constantinople. The Ravenna mosaics, notably those of San Vitale of 526–47, fathered Byzantine art. Narrative subject matter was to dwindle, giving way to hieratic images of the virgin and child and apostles and prophets. Separated from the mainstream of Western Christianity by the Adriatic and the *Filioque* Clause in the Nicene Creed, Byzantine art, in Greece and thence into Russia, grafted on to classical roots its own deeply ritualistic language. Byzantine icons* are at first sight intimidating, but so deeply dyed in their own spirituality that the hardened Westerner catches something of the awe of the Virgin Hodegetria, or the distilled tenderness, derived from the Song of Songs, of the Virgin Glykophilousa.

If in the Eastern empire the spontaneity of early Christian art was frozen into Byzantine convention, it quickened to a warm and almost frenetic life through Charlemagne's deliberate and heroic early ninth-century Renaissance in his Western empire.

The manuscripts produced at Charlemagne's court and that of his successors are among the most exciting biblical illustrations of all time. The key is the Utrecht Psalter, made at Hautvilliers in 820–30, where every passage of the psalms is illustrated in lively little shorthand drawings of rivetting stylishness. It probably copied a late antique illustrated Psalter. In the surviving corpus of biblical illustrations, the Utrecht Psalter, with its Canterbury derivatives, stands alone. However, there is one page in the St Florian Gospel Book of c. 834–43, now in Düsseldorf, illustrating a single scene of Christ teaching. This isolated drawing, in much the style of the Utrecht Psalter, could have come from a similar book. The importance of this single page has been underestimated. The subject is not one of the standard topics from the NT which will be so frequently represented throughout the Middle Ages, and argues a very extensive lost cycle of the Life of Christ comparable in thoroughness with the Utrecht Psalter treatment of the Psalms. To compare with it, we can only turn to the 12 silver reliefs on the Golden Altar of Sant' Ambrogio in Milan of c. 850. These, representing the annunciation, the presentation in the Temple, adoration of the Magi, baptism of Christ, marriage at Cana, transfiguration, healing of the man at the pool at Bethesda, throwing out of the money changers, crucifixion, resurrection,* ascension and pentecost, are the fullest cycle of their time.

The ambitious illustrated Bibles of the Carolingian and Ottonian period can be represented by the Moutier-Grandval Bible made at the church of St Martin at Tours, c. 840, with its full narrative cycle of the fall, and by the apocalyptic throne of God (Etimasia) in the Vivian Bible made for the Emperor Charles the Bald, perhaps at St Denis, which has pictures, mostly of OT scenes. These magnificent imperial Bibles of the ninth century rival any produced in Christian history.

The most popular subject in the ivories, which once adorned the liturgical books of the triumphalist ninth to eleventh centuries, is the ascension of Christ, a subject woefully neglected since. The creation of lavishly illustrated Bibles shifted in the tenth century to the English revival associated with St Dunstan. The Benedictional of St Ethelwold made for that Bishop of Winchester during his episcopate, 971–84, still has 28 sumptuous full-page illustrations. The full complement provided an extensive series depicting the heavenly Jerusalem, with pictures marking all the important feasts, concentrating on Christ's infancy and on post-resurrection appearances. The crucifixion is missing, but surviving full-scale figures of the Crucified of the tenth

century – notably the Christ of St Gereon in Cologne Cathedral – are of impressive dignity. They approach the cross in terms of the Dream of the Rood. The English giant roods at Ramsey, Langford, Bitton, Headbourne Worthy and Breamore hint at a similar sense of tragedy subsumed. In the drawing of the later tenth century in a Winchester Psalter, the mourning Mary and John flutter like distressed moths around a luminous Christ.

In the treatment of the crucifixion, as in all biblical illustration, the twelfth century was more formal. The human figure stiffened under the encrusted weight of Byzantine influence, and vitality was overloaded with ceremonial. But the great monastic houses of the twelfth century produced, especially in England, fabulous illuminated books: the Bury Bible, the Lambeth Bible, and above all the Winchester Bible. The glowing palette of these feats of the monastic scriptorium was matched by the pageantry of biblical illustration which at the same time covered all surfaces of twelfth-century churches. The wooden ceiling of Hildersheim, given over to the tree of Jesse; the wooden ceiling of St Savin sur Gartempe, carrying an OT cycle; and the church of San Vincenzo Gallieno are rare survivals of that splendid period. We see the scraped boards of a Romanesque ceiling as a missed opportunity for stone vaulting: the twelfth-century artist saw the panelled ceiling as an unparalleled field for his great cycles of uninterrupted narrative material, usually devoted to biblical topics.

The twelfth century, under the influence of such writers as Honorius of Autun, was the heyday of typology:* the matching of NT and OT persons and scenes. Abbot Suger's great golden cross which once hung in St Denis was embellished with 68 scenes affording parallels for the crucifixion. At St Denis the windows also explored theological patterns, a method of correlating OT and NT already recorded by Bede in the seventh century. He tells us that Benedict Biscop brought back from Rome to Jarrow illustrations of the 'Concordance of the Old and New Testaments'. Among elaborate orchestrations upon the theme – the grandest of them, Nicholas of Verdun's Klosterneuberg altar (its original and larger part of 1181) – offers parallels ante legem (before Moses*) and sub lege. The Klosterneuberg ante legem type for the Adoration of the Magi, which is of course the corresponding scene from the NT (sub gratia), is Abraham bringing gifts to Melchizedek: the sub lege type is the coming of the Queen of Sheba, also with gifts, to Solomon. The ante legem type reflects on the priesthood of Christ, the sub lege type on his wisdom. It follows that, by the twelfth century, biblical illustration had come to emphasize certain areas of both NT and OT, to the neglect of others. The illustration, in the thirteenth century, of 'all the war-like scenes of the Bible' on the walls of the King's Painted Chamber in Westminster Palace, perhaps following those of St Louis' Palace at the Louvre, reflected the exaltation of Christian prowess, the ethos of the Crusades.

But that particular chivalric courtly taste was unusual. Biblical illustration throughout the Middle Ages focussed more commonly on the creation* and fall to Noah's ark, followed by the infancy* and passion* to resurrection cycles, with their types taken from the Old Law. The exception was the book of Psalms which, since it was the staple of Christian and in particular monastic worship, developed its own visual punctuation. The opening words of Ps.1 – *Beatus Vir* – was frequently embellished by an image of King David* making music. Eight images divided the Psalter into daily portions for the weekly diet. This formula was pursued with little alteration till the end of the Middle Ages, though the fifteenth century substituted David in penitence for Jonah emerging from the Whale for the *Salvum me fac* incipit (= opening words of section).

By the thirteenth century the Psalter had, however, been isolated from the rest of the Bible on account of its special liturgical* purpose. The Great Bibles of the twelfth century were then in full monastic use, and the Psalters commissioned in the early thirteenth century, like the Bibles of that date, were of a more convenient private format. Their smaller scale involved contractions in both words and visual interpretation. An early thirteenth-century uterine Bible, for example that of Robert de Bello, of 1224–53, now illustrated the seven days of creation with vignettes down the border, a margin like a miniature lancet window. We may imagine these Bibles in the hand luggage of globe-trotting bishops of a pan-European church, while the relatively stationary abbots remained to consult their equally stationary great Bibles.

The imagery of twelfth- and thirteenth-century Bibles, whatever their scale, concentrated on the *felix culpa*, the fall of man, and its result, the redemption; but imagery in other contexts does sometimes explore the intervening themes of the biblical panorama. The dado reliefs of the portals of Amiens Cathedral offer a number of OT subjects, and so do those of Auxerre. Reims devoted a buttress to apocalyptic* material. The array of biblical quatrefoils at Wells Cathedral spells out the stories of the fall and of Noah in detail, and then telescope the rest of the Old Law. The NT selection at Wells found room for John the Baptist,* as well as Christ, preaching (was the

source pre-Conquest?), but apparently for no miracles at all. A display of gospel material, other than infancy and passion cycles, in the form of small narrative scenes appears on the high altarpieces, probably of 1268, at Westminster Abbey, and of Siena Cathedral, Duccio's Maesta, begun in 1308. At Westminster 3 miraculous scenes – the raising of Tabitha, the healing of the man born blind and the feeding of the five thousand – survive out of 8. The healing of the man born blind (now in the National Gallery) is the subject of one of Duccio's 54 or 58 panels. Apart from his infancy and very full (19 scenes around the crucifixion) passion cycle, Duccio included the calling of Peter and Andrew and the woman of Samaria, the healing of the blind man and the raising of Lazarus – a fair sample of the most important topics in 1300.

One of the most glorious of the thirteenth-century French and especially English Apocalypses is blood brother to the Westminster Retable. In this group of Apocalypses the ancient visions of cataclysm are interpreted in a sophisticated, indeed mincing, visual language. The vials of wrath are opened by angelic hosts with exquisitely arched fingers and tilted wrists.

The winding up of days as envisaged in the Revelation of John occupied a place of peculiar importance in twelfth-century and later iconography. The world had survived the millennium,* which had been attended by prophetic foreboding. Hildegard of Bingen foresaw another deadline in 1200, and thirteenth-century speculation, based on the historical prophecies of Joachim de Fiore, kept apocalyptic imagery in the forefront. Fears were transferred to 1500, arguably the 'time and the half time' of the Book of Revelation. The crack of doom, like the crucifixion, is a mould into which artist and viewer can pour dreads and frustrations as well as pity. The mediaeval doom remains today a haunting image: the busy demons with their toasting forks and the etiolated angels shepherding naked people wearing their insignia of office (crowns, mitres, tonsures) as Manet's Olympia wears her necklace and slippers – these little insignificances are all in the shadow of a gigantic Christus. The scene of Christ sending out the apostles, a topic almost jolly in comparison, on a tympanum at Vézelay, conveys the same awe as a doom, because it is not just the division of humanity into saved and damned that still makes us flinch, but the brooding presence of the just judge.

The drive towards naturalism and accessibility, which marked European art towards 1200, was a setback to doom iconography. The idealized but realistic Christ of the Portail Royale at Chartres, flanked by his stable of evangelists' symbols, carries none of the numinous terror of Autun, of Vézelay and Moissac, of Berzy la Ville, and certainly once of Cluny. The Chartres Christ of *c.* 1140 spoke, nonetheless, for the future. The Last Judgment of the thirteenth century at Amiens, and originally at Notre Dame in Paris, degenerates into a queue of people waiting their turn to be assessed.

Little of the largely intact iconography of the Chartres windows of the years around 1200 is devoted to biblical interpretation. The prophets of the OT are there – most strikingly to provide 'piggy backs' for the evangelists – Jeremiah, Isaiah, Ezekiel and Daniel for Luke, Matthew, Mark and John respectively. There is the tree of Jesse, a window of the infancy, another of the passion, but of the rest two are given to the miracles of the virgin, one to the labours of the months, one to the deeds of Charlemagne and five to individual saints. The thirteenth-century choir screen at Chartres offered another infancy cycle, the great portals a series of patriarchs and saints. However, the thirteenth-century trumeau figures of the Blessing Christ at Chartres, Reims and Amiens are among the most serene in the history of Western Europe. Here is a Christ recognized by his perfection, the Christ of the *Summa* of Aquinas, of belief in a divinely ordaining intelligence. Yet so short is this classic moment that by *c.* 1240, with the arrival in Western Europe from Constantinople of the relics of the Holy Blood and the Crown of Thorns, Christ images begin to appeal by direct reference to his sufferings. St Francis gave us the crib and the stigmatization, reinforcing the emphasis on the humanity and passion of Christ, which was to be of growing importance in popular religion, especially after the Black Death. A lively source of visualization was provided from the later fourteenth century by the mystery plays, which in their turn mounted their chosen scenes (OT to Noah, infancy and passion in detail, and a last judgment) with reference to established visual traditions.

The rare artist who was himself a mystic was uniquely placed to break the circle and mint a new image. The movement known loosely as *Devotio Moderna*, emphasizing the possibility of direct religious experience for any pious person, irrespective of occupation or monastic vows, fathered at least two mystic artists. The earlier, working in the first years of the fifteenth century, was the illuminator known as the Master of Rohan, the only artist who has offered an image of the dead Christ over which his mother faints, while St John turns in reproach to a bewildered and defeated Godhead. Here is an idea of the Father bankrupt of rainbows, a theological concept which has yet to be plumbed. The

other northern artist whose individualism must have sprung from an intense devotional life was Hieronymus Bosch. References to the ecclesiastical scandals of his day were woven into his pictures in a way which we largely miss, though we may deduce attacks on alchemy and on music from his hell scenes. Bosch used the mocking of Christ as a vehicle for his passionate views on the ecclesiastical corruption which was driving Northern Europe to the crisis of the Reformation. An almost pathological emphasis on the suffering Christ was explored with single-minded determination, not only by Bosch but by the slightly younger Altdorfer, Cranach, Grünewald and Dürer.

A more balanced note was struck in Italy, where the 1420s had seen Ghiberti's commission for his second Baptistery Doors in Florence, with 10 of the largest scenes of the OT (large in the panoramic sense), while the cycle of paintings devoted to St Peter in the Brancacci Chapel in the Church of the Carmine gave Masaccio the opportunity for the most dignified and expansive version of the Tribute Money. Fra Angelico could invest his Annunciations with a new simplicity and surprise. Pietro Lorenzetti would have forestalled him there, had not his patron insisted on a more polite convention. All the way from the eighth century (ivory plaque from Syria or Palestine), in Milan, down to Fra Angelico (San Marco, Florence) and Botticelli (Uffizi), the annunciation was portrayed as a narrow door to the incarnation. The focus is not on the winged messenger, but on the girl upon whose *fiat* divinity trembles. The Virgin folds her spirit and the redemption is sown. Hence the placing of this image around door arches or windows – see the Chapter House of Westminster Abbey, *c.* 1253, Prior Crauden's Chapel at Ely, *c.* 1330, Pisanello's S. Fermo Verona, 1423–4; or for the sightless eyes of the great dead to gaze upon (the Duchess of Suffolk at Ewelme in Oxfordshire). Mary, who opened the door to God, can open God's door to us. Where the context allows no actual opening between the two figures, there is usually a visual interval. With Simone Martini's gleaming arabesque of 1333 (Uffizi, Florence), it is the celestial gold ground over which the angel's greeting is pronounced. Fra Angelico (San Marco, *c.* 1440) only provides the grey walls of the cell, which for the monk of interior life may dissolve into the divine vision. Domenico Veneziano's predella of the St Lucy altarpiece (Fitzwilliam Museum, Cambridge) leads our eye into the *hortus conclusus*, with its so-well-bolted door. Botticelli gives a generalized Umbrian landscape over which the hands of Angel and Madonna hover in magnetic communication.

Two great figures of the mid-fifteenth century could portray a compelling figure of Christ: Piero della Francesco and Donatello. As every Byzantine artist who had heaped the waters of Jordan to cover Christ to the waist was aware, the baptism of Christ is a subject as uncompromisingly physical as the passion, and without the narrative pace to carry the observer along. Piero's Baptism (National Gallery, London), with its compositional use of the Golden Mean and its columnar marble tree, has the inevitability of a stalactite or a Brandenburg Concerto. His Resurrection in Borgo San Sepulcro brings the mind to its knees. By the utmost economy of means – the visual props of a village passion play – Piero conveys a Christ who has carried purity inviolate through the jaws of death. The only other attempt to suggest the integrity which could plough Hades and bring out into the light all that history had rolled before him was created in the same decade (1460s), the late Donatello Harrowing of Hell on the pulpit of San Lorenzo in Florence. Donatello there goes beyond the physical perfection he had demonstrated a generation before in his bronze David (Bargello, Florence).

David was more to Florence than the author of the psalms and the chief ancestor and prototype of Christ. As the shepherd boy who defeated Goliath, he was symbol of that belligerent little city. Therefore the great nudes of the Italian Renaissance go by his name. The svelte child of Donatello, drooping in tristesse over the head of his enemy, was followed by Verrocchio's cheeky youth (Bargello), lips curled as he brandishes the dagger which has completed his disdainful task. Michelangelo's gigantic David (Accademia, Florence), pulled from an outsize block of Carrara marble that Agostino de Duccio had already hollowed, was intended for the apex of the pediment of the Duomo. The Florentines thought it too good to be skied and placed it instead in the Piazza della Signoria. The Florentine Council completed the secularization begun by Donatello, whose David had marked the rise of commissions from secular patrons, in his case the Medici for their palace in Florence. Michelangelo's David fingers his sling as he gazes south towards the Goliath of Rome. The last of these great Davids, Bernini's of 1623, is in violent attack, least ecclesiastical of attitudes, and was commissioned for Cardinal Scipione Borghese.

Patronage of biblical art shifted as lay wealth expanded, but subject matter, outside esoteric circles, changed little. The new Italian bourgeoisie wanted pictures for their houses as well as for their churches, but among a smattering of portraits their staple remained a Madonna and Child, now hanging over the prie-dieu as well as above the altar. The Medici thought the subject of Judith wielding a scimitar over the besotted Holofernes appropriate for a garden fountain. Judith was another patron of Florence, so the same sanguinary subject exercised the fastidious Botticelli. The distinction between the canon of sacred scriptures and the secondary but not much later material dubbed Apocrypha * was not a burning issue among Christians before the Reformation.* They were to be printed as part of the Vulgate * Bible, and the striking imagery they provoked ensured their continuing popularity.

The genius of the High Renaissance was worthily employed in the interpretation of biblical subjects. In his unfinished painting for the monks of San Donato a Scopeto, Leonardo da Vinci took up the favourite topic of pageant-loving Florentines, the Adoration of the Magi. It had been treated with popular success as a fashion parade by Gentile da Fabriano in 1423 (Uffizi), and before 1459 by Benozzo Gozzoli to the hilt of splendour in the Chapel of the Medici Palace, and more simply in Cosimo de Medici's special retreat at San Marco. Now in 1481 the alchemy of Leonardo developed the subject as the coming of all men to the crib. His ghostly panel (Uffizi) describes a dream world where all death and all life billow around the Virgin. He left it unfinishable, and the disappointed monks, unaware that they had one of the greatest of all religious icons, went to a polished inferior for a glossy picture. Leonardo meanwhile ignored the detailed demands of new Milanese patrons and resolved his problem in two versions of the Virgin of the Rocks (Louvre and National Gallery, London). Now the multitude of worshippers have left the painting for the floor on which we join them. The virgin addresses us, as we kneel among kings and shepherds. Leonardo's Last Supper, which transforms the Rectory of Sta Maria della Grazie in Milan into the Upper Room at Jerusalem, is perhaps the most famous NT image in the world, and one recently made more visible to us. Calm, inevitable: the composition is built as a symphony. The dual themes of betrayal and consecration, here and nowhere else, find resolution, for Leonardo's Christ dips his right hand into the dish with Judas, while, with his left, he consecrates the Host. The disciples on Judas' side register their dismay, and on the other they worship. Even the dualism male–female was resolved in Leonardo's Christ, for his notes tell us he used two models, one of each sex. (Holman Hunt was to use a female model for the Christ in his Light of the World (1853, Keble College, Oxford), in its day one of the most popular pictures in England.)

The relatively standard scenes around the Sistine Chapel – *sub lege* on the left wall, *sub gratia* on the right – are overwhelmed by Michelangelo's creation cycle upon the vault above it, now also revealed in its brilliancy. Here the cryptic figures of manuscript illustration are expanded to an anthropomorphic imagery that goes as far as the human mind can reach. Michelangelo started at the end of his cycle with the drunkenness of Noah (a subject absurd to us, but still in 1509 carrying the symbolic overload of a type of the mocking of Christ or of the separation of the Gentiles from the Jews). Next to it comes the Flood. It is beyond coincidence that Michelangelo, here and officially, and Leonardo, privately in his sketch books, should have described the overwhelming of our world by deluge. Both knew Uccello's rendering in the Cloister of Sta Maria Novella in Florence, and Uccello derived elements from the ancient mosaics at St Mark's in Venice, which in their turn go back to early Christian sources. And so the nerve-tearing depiction of doomed people struggling in the rising waters goes through all accounts except Leonardo's. In small but dense sketches of gigantic scope, of which Turner's Deluge paintings of three hundred years later are the only, and pale, reflections, Leonardo has dwarfed not just us but our cities to pebbles tossed by a devouring maelstrom.

Many nowadays regard the creation of Adam * on the Sistine ceiling as the climax of art in the service of biblical interpretation. Yet Michelangelo had more in reserve. He plunged ever more deeply into his idea of the Godhead, in his unprecedented development of three stages for the dawn of creation. That Michelangelo was enthralled by the mystery of light and darkness is shown by his subsequent personification of the four times of day as attendants upon the active and contemplative lives in his Medici tombs in Florence. Working backwards on the Sistine ceiling, he expounded first Gen. 1. 6–7 (the separation of the waters above and below the earth); then the creation of the fruitful earth and the creation of sun and moon in a double image (Gen. 1. 11, 14–15). Finally he addressed the opening passages of Genesis in a vision of the Prime Mover from whom all energy spirals. No one (unless it be his admirer William Blake * in imagery of 1795–99) has approached Michelangelo's solemn archetype of power. We may no longer subscribe to the idea of the creator as an old man with a white beard, but before Michelangelo's rendering of Yahweh we still tremble.

The Sistine ceiling alone would establish Michelangelo as the greatest of all visual interpreters of the Bible, quite apart from his studies of the dead Christ variously supported. The note of faultless perfection struck in his 1498 Pietà in St Peter's is almost an inversion of tragedy, out of key with the jagged images of the same subject which were wringing the hearts of Northern Europe. Our first reaction to a mother carrying her dead son over her knees should not be one of admiration. Michelangelo found his way out of this predicament with the help of Dürer's print of the Trinity, circulated from 1511, where the Father holds upright the flaccid body of Christ. Michelangelo's Pietàs were never horizontal again. Since Michelangelo's subject was not a Trinity, we can watch him wrestling with the secondary problem of who might carry the upright displayed body. His painting in the National Gallery and his several life-size sculptures reshuffle the possible combinations of Joseph of Arimathea, Nicodemus, St John and the Marys. In his last days he found his solution and ours – at his final hammer stroke it is the frail mother who bears the impossible burden of her attenuated Son. If Christianity has evolved one visual comment to match the pathos of its theme, it is surely the Rondanini Pietà in Milan. The subject of the Pietà itself is a meditative image distilled from the passion narrative but not there described. It is the fruit of the human psyche deeply scored by the *via crucis*, but not necessarily well-read in the four Gospel narratives.

With the approach of the sixteenth century, the shadow of the Last Judgment lengthened again. In our parish churches it had come indoors to confront the worshipper over the chancel arch. Dürer's cycles of prints of the twin themes of the apocalypse (1498) and the passion of Christ (the Great Passion, 1498–1510, the Little Passion, 1509–11) fuse magnificence of scope with a fever of literal observation. His horsemen of the apocalypse breathe fire from the dilated nostrils of bibulous noses and their horses gallop from the knacker's yard of Nuremberg. Sixty years later Peter Brueghel's Triumph of Death, with its imagery of sub-atomic desolation, has a disturbing topicality (but with no hope, no Christianity). Michelangelo's terrible east wall of the Sistine Chapel, begun in 1536, drew the pith of despair. Rubens' rival Last Judgment of one hundred years later is mere sound and fury.

Why does conviction ebb from visual eschatological matter after the sixteenth century? The verbal threat hung as heavy as ever over Protestant and Catholic alike. The nineteenth century, with its passion for large effects and massed orchestras, saw John Martin's fascination with cataclysmic subjects. He treated the Fields of the Blest like a Three Choirs Festival and his Pit of Hell is a nightscape of the Black Country. The musicians,

Beethoven, Berlioz and Wagner, had the stature to treat such material, and they did, but tangentially. It was left to Elgar, in the *Dream of Gerontius*, to make a direct contribution. Our own century has been marked with too much eschatological behaviour on our part to need threats beyond those of our own making.

The Bible in the vernacular ought to have brought forth a thousand new visual images: yet visual biblical interpretation is not the strong suit of the Protestant north. Prohibitions extending to representations of the deity, of Mary, and of anything stationary enough to be treated as an icon, stultified Christian imagery to the pathetic level of the Bratton Clovelly puppet apostles and prophets, the bathetic Moses and Aarons, to biblical illustrations where political propaganda was laced with Adam and Eve. The pouring of a High Renaissance quart into a late mediaeval pint-pot had already created the havoc of the King's College, Cambridge, stained glass. This visual disaster was spread above all by the prestigious (and, in their way, as splendid as they were out of context pernicious) example of the Raphael Cartoons, sent in 1517 to Brussels to be woven into tapestries. They were rightly admired, but their arrival destroyed the North European art of tapestry design, and threw northern pictorial art quite out of balance. Ostensibly, Raphael's cartoons expounded the Acts of the Apostles, but in reality we are more aware of their purpose as exalting, through St Peter, the papacy, than of their relationship to the text they closely follow. This is the Bible as sectarian propaganda, and the following centuries held plenty of that, sometimes through the baroque trumpets of Rubens, diplomat as well as painter.

Yet the seventeenth century saw two great visual interpreters of the Bible, one from each side of the Catholic/Protestant divide, for the vision follows not the close print of dogma. One of them was the French mystic, Georges de La Tour (1593–1652), who painted his images of Christ in the carpenter's shop, or of the Holy Family, from humble experience consecrated by his own interior riches. His language derived from the Caravaggio who was disgraced for seeking his holy people in the Neapolitan streets. Caravaggio's Supper at Emmaus has dramatic immediacy, but it took the candle of Georges de La Tour to invest the ordinary with the divine.

Rembrandt also explored the theme of the Journey to Emmaus, first treated in the sixth century, and, in one of his versions, that with the Christ in profile, suggested, as no one else could suggest, a believable presence of the divine in a shabby country inn. Rembrandt, like Georges de La Tour, read his Bible, and the Dutch Bible included the apocryphal story of Tobias. On this theme Rembrandt sketched some of his most moving designs, presenting the old parents, the stocky lad, and the protective angel. That folktale was a vehicle for all that Rembrandt knew of poverty, partings and reunion. No doubt he drew the little boy with his own beautiful son, Titus, in mind, though Rembrandt's sketches leave us room to fill in the characters with those we most love ourselves. He survived the death of that only son to paint the prodigal son returning to his father's arms, like Titus perhaps in his last days, with his fair hair shaven. This is one of the numerous parables * of the Gospel that had found no memorable interpretation before Dürer. The Sower (stained glass at Canterbury) was one of the very few parables much illustrated in the Middle Ages.

Rembrandt's Tobit drawings were spun out of himself, unlike his feeble and derivative scenes from the passion painted in 1633–9 at the behest of Prince Frederick Henry of Orange. The distillation of Rembrandt's piety is filtered like the shaft of sunlight across his great engraving of the crucifixion. We have it in various stages, each deeper than the last. Rembrandt belongs to the inner core of artists, with Cimabue, the Master of Rohan, Donatello, Mantegna, Antonello da Messina, Giovanni Bellini, and Michelangelo in his late drawings (expounded by his sonnets), who have themselves stood on the hill of Golgotha, and may report what they witnessed there.

The polite and rational eighteenth century had nothing more to say. What could the delicious frivolity of Tiepolo offer to the Bible? Sebastiano Ricci had a *fête champêtre* for Moses in the bullrushes, and his Resurrection in the apse of Chelsea Hospital depended (as do other eighteenth-century pictures like Bellucci's in St Lawrence, Whitchurch) upon Raphael's unfinished Transfiguration. The visual inheritance of the Renaissance was too complex and too well digested for anything fresh to emerge in these drawing-rooms. Eighteenth-century taste looked back, in a way which infuriated Hogarth, to the Seicento for its standard of great art. Faced with a selection of what the tutors and dealers taught their neophytes to admire – and we may taste this experience in many country houses – we sometimes sympathize with Hogarth. The loot of the Grand Tour was frequently spiced with a genre of paintings impossible before Titian brought total reality to painted flesh – a genre in which the ostensible subject was edifying but the presentation carried a note of the erotic. In this category fall plenty of Salomes with the Head of John the Baptist, numerous Penitent Magdalenes and a sprinkling of Women taken in Adultery, perhaps with the apocryphal Susanna and the Elders as a pendant to David and Bathsheba, or Samson and Delilah. The English Milord could enjoy his seventeenth-century oils publicly as High Art, privately as titillation and vocally as evidence of Catholic depravity, a rare combination of satisfactions.

In 1848 the Pre-Raphaelites declared that they could not look at the Bible through the darkened varnish of uncleaned Renaissance canvases. Their determination to set the Bible into an archaeological and ethnic context gave us Millais' astringent 'Christ in the House of his Parents' that so shocked England. The scene was intended to suggest Palestine in AD10, and if it only conveyed romanticized rural England in 1850, albeit with thoroughly mediaeval symbolic overtones, at least the Pre-Raphaelites had shed a convention which dressed the biblical scenes in generalizations out of Raphael. Millais' painting of 'The Return of the Dove' changed William Morris' life, when he saw it in a picture framer's window in 1857. It is hardly more Mesopotamian than Oxford, but it did represent a new way of looking.

What has happened since? Remarkably little. The two World Wars plunged and re-plunged Europe into a first-hand experience of the Passion of Christ. Some artists, Rouault and Stanley Spencer among them, witnessed both holocausts. Rouault's Miserere prints fuse the two experiences into one, and that darkly biblical. Stanley Spencer blended the patterns of bright floral textiles on plump ladies with a literal rendering of the resurrection in Cookham Churchyard (1923–27). His shock tactics combine the biblical with the common-place, the universal method of mysticism.

In 1968, the Oxford University Press commissioned a series of drawings to illustrate the OT from a galaxy of artists working then, and many of them working still. It was a splendid project well founded and carefully apportioned. Why has it not been followed by a similar illustrated NT? And who in fact has a copy of this illustrated version of the OT – the first fully concerted attempt upon that vast subject since the Biblia Pauperum* in the fifteenth century (if we may set aside the grinding work of Martin Heemskerk and his kind, in the seventeenth century)? After 1945, many artists had attempted to express their new experience of the scope of horror in terms of the Passion of Christ. We have Graham Sutherland's rejected barbed-wire crucifix for Ely cathedral, and his Noli me Tangere (camp follower's version!) at Chichester, as we have his Christ in Majesty at Coventry. Francis Bacon has painted an unrecognizeable triptych of the crucifixion, and the world was more swayed by Salvador Dali's Christ of St

John of the Cross. Thetis Blacker's resplendent Creation banners hang in Winchester Cathedral. Abstract art could do little to interpret the Bible, though expressionism has enlisted the passion of Christ.

But we have a new realism which has gone far already to reclaim beauty as the rightful domain of art. There is much beauty yet to explore in the Bible. The seldom interpreted passage of Christ walking on the waters, for example, was placed by Conrad Witz on Lake Constance in 1456, and became the subject of Tintoretto's masterpiece in Washington (Kress Collection), but has hardly been attempted since. Michelangelo has left just two lyrical drawings of the resurrection. Could our generation, which at the last moment has laboriously discovered the unity of this fragile creation, re-enter the Gardens of Eden and of the resurrection? The sum of biblical illustration is richer and more varied than that of any other sacred scriptures. The gulf between illustration and interpretation, however, is only bridged when artists make this inexhaustible material their own. Where the courage of theologians fails, the visionary is still allowed to tread.

See also **Allegorical Interpretation; Apocrypha; Enlightenment; Icons.**

G. Barraclough (ed), *The Christian World*, 1980; W. Cahn, *Romanesque Bible Illustration*, 1982; J. Dillenberger, *Style and Content in Christian Art*, 1986; E. H. Gombrich, *The Story of Art*, revd edn 1972; A. Grabar, *Christian Iconography*, 1966; J. Harthan, *Books of Hours*, 1977; G. Henderson, *Studies in English Bible Illustration*, 2 vols, 1985; J. Hubert, J. Porcher, W. F. Volbach, *Carolingian Art*, 1970; M. R. Miles, *Image as Insight: Visual Understanding in Western Christianity and Secular Culture*, 1985; L. Reau, *Iconographie de l'Art Chrétien*, Vols II & III, *Iconographie de la Bible*, 1956 & 1957; K. Weitzmann (ed.), *Age of Spirituality: Late Antique and Early Christian Art: A Symposium*, 1986, esp. E. Kitzinger, 'Christian Imagery, Growth and Impact', pp. 141ff.; id., *Late Antique and Early Christian Book Illumination*, 1977.

PAMELA TUDOR-CRAIG

Augustine

Augustine (354–430), the greatest single mind and influence in Christian history, was not a biblical scholar but a systematic thinker and impassioned preacher who read his system out of and into scripture. He knew some Greek, but no Hebrew, and had little or no interest in historical questions. Yet his homilies on the Psalms and on the Gospel and First Epistle of John still convey the intensity and excitement of their author, and are rich in humanity (and social history) as some of his more famous treatises are not. His influence as an exegete has never been greater than when the biblical foundation seems most disputable. His writings abound in citations (about two-thirds of the entire Bible could be reconstructed from his pages).

During his Manichee decade Augustine was repelled from Catholicism by the un-Ciceronian style of the Old Latin Bible, by the polygamy and deceit of OT patriarchs, and by the divergent gospel genealogies. Conversion and baptism (386–7) entailed submission to Christ and his people: 'I would not have believed the gospel had not the authority of the catholic church constrained me to do so' (*C. Epist. Fund.* 6). The church commended scripture as 'the dominical books', a diversity finding unity in Christ and in the love of God and neighbour. Without manifesting the critical interest he shows when dealing with (e.g.) pseudo-Hippocratic texts (*C. Faust.* 33,6), he assumes the traditional authorship of the biblical books. But his concern is exclusively with the Bible's meaning for the contemporary church. Christian extension throughout the known world has fulfilled prophecy.* But in the Bible all history is also prophecy (*Civ. Dei* 16,17). 'When you read, God speaks to you; when you pray, you address God' (*En. Ps.* 85,7). The particular is universalized: Nathanael under the fig-tree represents the human race, fallen (hence Adam and Eve's fig-leaves) but redeemed (*Serm.* 69,4).

God reveals himself both in the rational order and beauty of creation and through scripture (*Trin.* 15,6). Do not so set scripture apart as to think it has a diction all of its own (*C. Faust.* 33,7). Nor is Genesis a source of creation science, a notion which brings discredit on Christians (*Gen. ad litt.* i, 38–9). Like the sacraments, the Bible is provided by God as a means of grace under the conditions of this life (neither Bible nor sacraments will be needed hereafter). The central figure uniting both OT and NT is Christ (*C. Faust.* 12, 7): the humble incarnation is reflected in the style by which scripture is made accessible to all (*Ep.* 137,18). Though much is obscure, on what is necessary to salvation texts are sufficiently clear (*Pecc. Mer.* ii,59; *Doctr.* ii,14) to any goodhearted reader (*Serm.* 137,7). Clear texts explain the obscure (*Pecc. Mer.* iii,7), at least in providing the ground for the rule of faith which is the criterion of acceptable exegesis. Because so much is obscure, many interpretations are current and possible, and indeed valid if orthodox. An interpreter should not contend for his own view, but seek to make his teaching conform to scripture (*Gen. ad litt.* i,37). Obscurities are also providential: we value things more if found after toil (*En. Ps.* 38,2; 138,3).

Apart from scripture, the community has unwritten traditions; e.g. the lectionary usage by which the limits of the NT canon are in process of being agreed (*Doctr.* ii,12); Sunday observance, infant baptism, Lent, Easter, Ascension, Pentecost, Christmas, Epiphany; the 'virtually universal' custom of ending the eucharistic canon with the Lord's Prayer (*Ep.* 149,16) – though as long as there is shared faith and one church, Augustine is indifferent to liturgical variety (*Ep.* 36,22; 54,2; *Civ. Dei* 19,17). Above all the worshipping life of the community is the context in which the Bible is edifyingly interpreted.

To understand the Bible, especially the OT, only literally is to be locked into 'superstition' (*C. Faust.* 18,7). The NT lies hidden in the OT, the OT laid open by the NT (*Civ. Dei* 5,18). Christ is prefigured by Adam* (Eve and Mary represent the church); by Abel's death. Noah's Ark is both the cross, its door being Christ's pierced side, and also the church containing a spiritual élite with many irrational elements. Isaac's sacrifice means the cross, Jacob's ladder Christ as both way and goal. He is persecuted Joseph, battling Joshua. 'Almost all' references to the earthly Jerusalem* refer to the heavenly city. Even Deborah prophesied of Christ 'but so obscurely that exegesis would take too long' (*Civ. Dei* 18,15). Symbolism* also permeates the NT: at Bethlehem the ass represents Gentiles, the ox Jews (*Serm.* 126,11).

Augustine never reproduces Ambrose's principle that scripture has three senses (natural, moral, rational or theological). He is normally content with two – literal-'carnal'-historical and allegorical-mystical-spiritual. One isolated text (*Util. Cred.* 5–8) has a four-fold sense (historical, aetiological, analogical, allegorical), which does not correspond to that which Cassian (*Coll.* 14,8) was to make a standard mediaeval concept. Spiritually interpreted, the OT contains the same faith as the NT. There is 'one faith, different modes' (*En. Ps.* 46,1; *Conf.* 13,35), as Ambrose had taught him. Even OT saints looked for the eternal bliss of the new covenant, not the temporal success promised by the old (*Ep.* 140,5). There could be dispute whether Christ's death had added something new (*C. Faust.* 19,15); Augustine normally thought not.

Heresy arises from bad exegesis* (*Tr. Joh.* 18,1), from a lack of balance and wholeness (*Ep.* 93,23); there is no false doctrine in which error is not mixed with truth (*Quaest. Evang.* 2,40,2). Exegesis is therefore dangerous. But there are clues to correct interpretation in the etymology* of Hebrew names and the mystical meaning of numbers, also in the titles and order of psalms. (Can it be accidental that 46, the years of building Herod's temple, is the numerical value of Adam's name in Greek?) Like most ancient writers, Augustine assumes that even matter-of-fact narratives are polyvalent. Yet allegorized texts settle no doctrinal controversy (*Ep.* 93,24). Paths in the 'forest' of scripture (*Conf.* 11,3) are seen in regular patterns of biblical writers, a principle in which Augustine was anticipated by the Donatist Tyconius' *Book of Rules* (*c.* 370). Augustine's rules are mainly negative and are never systematically presented. A first principle is that nothing unworthy of God can be intended (*C. Adimant.* 7,4). Human language must be inadequate to the mystery of God (*Conf.* 2,10), e.g. his *'fore*knowledge' is really timeless, not just advance information. Even through scripture, revelation* is related to human capacity (*Conf.* 13,18–19). Anthropomorphisms* are figurative: the vision of God will not be with physical eyes (*Ep.* 147). Divine wrath and mercy are not emotional reactions (*C. Adv. Legis* 1,40); a divine question presupposes no ignorance.

Nevertheless, reason is to be submissive before scriptural authority.* Despite reason's objections, the Bible imposes belief in hell (*Civ. Dei* 21). Platonists agreed that no sins go unpunished; but at least for believers divine fire is remedial (I Cor. 3), not so for those who blaspheme against the Spirit by wilful rejection of remission of sins through the church's sacraments (*Serm.* 71,23). Again, reason would suggest that death is a natural biological phenomenon (and that was the view of Ambrose as well as of the Pelagians); but the Bible declares it to be a punishment for sin (*Pecc. Mer.* 1,2). Likewise the Bible establishes against reason's expectations that the will acquires freedom by grace, not vice versa (*Corrept.* 17).

Like Origen,* Augustine finds in absurdities or superfluities or sheer impossibilities a signpost to spiritual intentions (*C. Faust.* 22,96, etc.). But moral precepts are never to be allegorized: except for the sabbath precepts, the Decalogue and OT moral law remain binding for Christians (*C. duas Epist. Pel.* iii,10).

Ambrose had liberated Augustine from his difficulties with the OT by teaching that allegory is lifegiving, literalism pernicious. Augustine came to see that II Cor. 3.6 bore a different sense, namely that moral commandments kill the soul unless the Spirit gives inward power and love of God (*Spir. et Litt.* 8–9); he also saw it to be mistaken to contrast Judaism as a religion of external acts and Christianity as a religion of pure inwardness (ibid. 21). So the meaning is the antithesis of law and gospel as religious principles: 'works do not precede justification' (45). This priority of grace operates as a hermeneutic* principle: words are merely external signs, and they convey their true meaning only as God himself speaks to the heart and mind (*De Magistro*). So even the Bible is first understood by divine illumination. Augustine came to feel that his very personal understanding of predestination was a special gift of God (*Praed. Sanct.* 8). Yet he also regarded it as axiomatic that divine truth is never a private possession and is always one which the people of God will recognize (*Conf.* 13,38). Catholic critics who thought his exegesis of Genesis subjective fantasy or sophisticated Neoplatonism in a pious wrapping (e.g. *Conf.* 12,23–24) caused him much pain. But he also regarded it as a Catholic principle to wish to accept correction (*C. duas Epist. Pel.* ii,5). He dreaded being so suspected of individualist deviation that his orthodox expositions were rejected as distorted (*En. Ps.* 58,1,9). Hence his prayer at the end of *De Trinitate* that God and the church will forgive what is amiss and recognize what is right. In the African churches there were some who felt that he had never really thrown off the rags of his Manichee decade or who were resentful of a theology expressed in such strongly Neoplatonic terms.

Opposition to the Manichees lies in the background of some of his exegesis, especially in the *Confessions*, but also elsewhere. Manichees rejected the idea of original sin; criticized the church's canon* of scripture, and the sacraments of baptism and eucharist; denied that Jesus was born of Mary and crucified; listed contradictions between OT and NT; but accepted most of the Pauline letters and a canon of apocryphal Acts of Peter, Paul, John, Thomas, and Andrew. Augustine would have no apocrypha read in the lectionary (*Ep.* 64), but had room in his library and his own reading for several apocryphal texts, especially the Acts of John (*Tr. Joh.* 124,2 and 7), the Apocalypse of Paul (ibid. 98,8), and the correspondence between Paul and Seneca (*Ep.* 153,14; *Civ. Dei* 6,10,1). The Sibyl, like Balaam or Caiaphas, is also accepted as an extramural prophet (*Ep.* 258,5; *Civ. Dei* 18,23), as also Virgil's fourth Eclogue (*Civ. Dei* 10,27; *in Rom. impf.* 3). One must not think that before the incarnation the only true worshippers of God were Israelites (*Ep.* 102,15). Parallel to Abraham there were philosophers who sought after the Lord (*De gratia et pecc. orig.* 2,33).

Augustine set out his own canon in *De Doctrina Christiana* 2,13. His OT included I–II Esdras, Tobit, Judith, Esther, Wisdom of Solomon, Ecclesiasticus, I–II Maccabees, with the proviso that in debate with rabbis such books could not be cited. Against Gallic critics, he defended the canonicity of Wisdom (*Praed. Sanct.* 27). His NT canon included Hebrews as Pauline, in agreement with the Greek churches, though he was aware that not all in the West upheld it (*Pecc. Mer.* 1,50). He granted that Wisdom and Ecclesiasticus were not written by Solomon (*Civ. Dei* 17,20). Works like the book of Enoch cited in canonical books were not included because they were not inspired (*Civ. Dei* 15,23,4). No one is obliged to believe that Joachim was father of Mary (*C. Faust.* 23,9).

The Manichees argued (*C. Faust.* 32,2) that the NT writings had been corrupted in transmission by interpolation and rewriting in the orthodox interest. The argument made Augustine very sensitive to questions of text. Often he refers to variant readings both in his Latin manuscripts and also between the Latin translations and the Greek codices. *Doctr.* 2,22 declares that the African texts of scripture are inferior to the 'Itala' version; if this is what Augustine wrote (for *Itala, Aquila* has been conjectured and would be good in context), then Augustine thought the Bible text he had encountered at Milan and Rome was more carefully revised and transmitted than that of north Africa. The diffusion of the Vulgate* of Jerome caused some distress to laity accustomed to the language of the Old Latin Bible and, at Oea in Tripolitania, a major row broke out when Jerome's version of Jonah was read. Augustine offended Jerome by remonstrating (*Ep.* 71, and 75 for Jerome's reply). Augustine was also upset when Jerome made his translation of the OT from the Hebrew, not from the Septuagint* (*Ep.* 28), but conceded that both Hebrew and Greek texts were equally inspired. Augustine accepted the story of the Seventy Greek translators miraculously producing the same version, though working independently (*Civ. Dei* 18,43).

With maturity Augustine became more insistent that scripture contains no error (*Ep.* 82,5). Faith could be shaken if the authority of scripture were affirmed only with hesitation (*Doctr.* 1,41). The book represents for him the principle of authority in a revealed religion; therefore its diversities are subordinate to an inner or higher unity – an axiom reflected in the way Augustine can treat one text as a key to the exegesis of a very different text, merely because they have a word in common. Augustine was alarmed by Jerome's notion that at Antioch in Gal. 2.11, Peter and Paul were play acting (*Ep.* 28,3). More difficult, especially for a theologian so influenced by Platonism with its axiom that the historical plane of events in time and space is at best a dim medium for the discernment of eternal truth, was the relation between history and the gospel. Belief in resurrection* was not easy for immature catholics and was a confidence achieved only by the advanced (*Quant. An.*

76). Nevertheless the basic gospel narrative belonged to the credenda: 'there are some things we do not believe unless we understand, others we do not understand unless we believe' (*En. Ps.* 118,18,3).

Pagan critics familiar with Porphyry's *Against the Christians* (a work not directly known to Augustine) attacked the trustworthiness of the Gospels, rejecting all miracles (unless done by magic), and observing that the evangelists tell their stories discordantly. The pagan attacks elicited Augustine's *Harmony of the Evangelists*, in which he denies that the evangelists could have lied or been allowed to suffer lapses of memory (2,29). Two views lie side by side in this work: on the one hand, divergences are explained by observing how natural it is for the same event to be differently described by different people in ways that are complementary, not contradictory (3,13). The pagan critics make the mistake of thinking that God dictates the words (2, 28 and 128), which is not the case. On the other hand, Augustine constantly betrays an anxiety to see the independence of the human authors reduced to a minimum (2.52), and, e.g., sees Matthew's ascription of Zechariah's prophecy to Jeremiah as due to a 'secret providence' (3,30). In this spirit, he writes in *De Civitate Dei* 17,14 that David wrote all the psalms, including those ascribed to other names. This virtually mantic view of inspiration was, paradoxically, that most at home in the Platonic tradition (especially *Ion* 534; *Meno* 99; *Timaeus* 71e). Augustine's discussions of the nature of inspiration* (*Div. Quaest ad Simplic.* 2,1,1 and *Gen. ad litt.* 12) try to bring together the mantic idea of the human mind being ecstatically replaced and the more naturalistic idea of the mind being enhanced and granted charismatic illumination. Augustine's normal explanation of differences (e.g. with the gospel genealogies) is to look to the different theological intentions of the writers: Matthew portrays the lion-like king; Luke the ox portrays the priestly work; John the mystic is the eagle that can gaze into the sun, leaving Mark to paint the man (*Tr. Joh.* 36,5; *Cons. Ev.* 1,9). Augustine's distribution of the four symbols departs from the more influential list of Ambrose (*on Luke*, prologue) for whom Mark is the lion. But he thought Mark an epitomizer of Matthew (*Cons. Ev.* 1,4; more hesitant in 4,11).

Less influential as a biblical commentator* than Jerome, Ambrose, and Ambrosiaster, Augustine exercised a crucial authority for later Western writers, especially by his anti-Donatist insistence on the unity and unicity of the one church, and his anti-Pelagian stress on grace and original sin. In Rom. 5.12 he took 'in quo' to mean that all humanity fell and suffered the penalty of death in Adam (e.g. *Ep.* 157,11). 'God wills *all* to be saved' (I Tim. 2.4) means representatives of every race (*Corrept.* 44). Ex. 3.14 means that God is Being, and so merely to exist is good (*En. Ps.* 121,5–6). He constructed the framework of the late mediaeval and Reformation* debates on justification and the eucharist. In the preface to his Latin works (1545) Luther* records the catalytic effect of reading Augustine 'On the spirit and the letter'. Augustine's hesitant language about the nature of inspiration, despite a tendency towards verbal inspiration, irritated on one side extreme contenders for that view such as Osiander, and on the other side humanist and liberal historians like Richard Simon. Although, in comparison with Ambrose, he is fairly reticent in expounding the Song of Songs to refer to the church, Bernard of Clairvaux's homilies on the book are pervaded with Augustinianisms. It is a measure of the genuine greatness of the man that the fire of his religious mind still burns for modern readers even after the immense shift away from his theology and exegesis associated with the Enlightenment* of the eighteenth century and since. His polemic (*Trin.* 12,9f.) against Ambrosiaster's exegesis of I Cor. 11, denying woman to be in God's image as well as man, did not much diminish the success of Ambrosiaster's opinion in mediaeval times, nor prevent modern writers from mistakenly ascribing to him the view he expressly rejected.

Mediaeval writers echoed Augustine's doctrine that the unworthiness of the minister does not invalidate a sacrament; debated his strong reservations about images in churches (especially Agobard of Lyon); and above all, from Anselm of Lucca (1083) onwards, collected his utterances justifying coercion in the cause of religious truth, at first to underpin the Crusades, later the repression of heresy by the Inquisition. Both sides invoked him during the Investiture Controversy. Otto of Freising (twelfth century) wrote history within the framework of *De Civitate Dei*; but Augustinian theology has never been a fruitful soil for good church history. He provided Anselm with the basis for the ontological argument to the existence of God, and Thomas Aquinas with much of his Five Ways. All subsequent discussion of predestination and free will, on providence and the problem of evil, has worked within his formulations of the central questions. His contention that schismatic baptism is valid (though a means of authentic grace only after reconciliation to the one church) bequeathed a legacy of wide departure from the more negative position of the Greek Orthodox world, and injected into Western search for Christian unity a positive evaluation of separated Christian bodies, thereby making possible, e.g., Vatican II's Decree on Ecumenism (1964).

See also **Allegorical Interpretation; Mediaeval Interpretation; Spiritual Meaning.**

Peter Brown, *Augustine of Hippo*, 1967; M. Comeau, *S. Augustin, exégète du quatrième évangile*, 1930; A. D. R. Polman, *The Word of God according to S. Augustine*, 1961; M. Pontet, *L'exégèse de S. Augustin prédicateur*, 1944; B. Studer, *Zur Theophanie-Exegese Augustins*, Studia Anselmiana 59, 1971.

HENRY CHADWICK

Authority of Scripture

Biblical criticism,* as it has been practised by professional biblical scholars for the last two hundred years, is widely perceived by Christian believers to conflict with belief in the divine authority and inspiration* of the Bible. On the other hand, many (perhaps most) of those engaged in critical study of the Bible are motivated at least in part by a religious commitment, and they do not see their critical conclusions as conflicting with the authority of the scriptures they study. Yet at the same time, some biblical scholars share the belief that criticism has called the authority of the Bible in question, and accordingly have produced various programmes for reintegrating the fruits of criticism with a more traditional view of biblical authority.

The factual details of the history of biblical criticism are common ground for all these positions, but the evaluation of that history is a matter for debate. Biblical criticism, despite some anticipations in church Fathers such as Origen* and in mediaeval Jewish* commentators such as Ibn Ezra, is a child of the Renaissance, the Reformation,* and the Enlightenment.* Both the detailed textual studies of Erasmus,* and the commentaries of Luther* and Calvin,* with their attention to accurate reconstructions of the original text of the NT and their concern for the original, 'historical' sense of scripture, are seen by all as lying at the root of modern biblical studies. But biblical criticism as the systematic posing of questions about the date, authorship,* and historical accuracy of biblical books owes much to English deists* and freethinkers of the seventeenth and eighteenth centuries, such as Thomas Hobbes (1588–1679), and to philosophical thinkers such as Spinoza (1632–77). The modern phase of criticism, however, is predominantly the product of the way these methods of study were appropriated by German scholarship in the nineteenth century. The pioneers in OT study were W. Vatke and W. M. L. de Wette,* in NT study D. F. Strauss* and F. C. Baur. These scholars initiated a movement of intellectual enquiry into the Bible which continues to dominate Protestant biblical studies and which, since the Second World War, has also become central to Catholic and Jewish scholarship.

This brief account is probably not controversial; but there are sharp differences of opinion about the underlying attitudes to the Bible embodied by the spirit of criticism:

1. A dominant interpretation (especially in British and American evaluation of the growth of critical enquiry) has seen in criticism a rationalist and sceptical strain which necessarily has the effect of dethroning the Bible. Criticism, it is said, is the application to the sacred text of various rational procedures and questions which begin from the assumption that the Bible can and should be read (in the famous words of Benjamin Jowett) 'like any other book' (*see Essays and Reviews*). Instead of taking scripture as a divinely-given book which is beyond human reason, critics thus assume that it can be treated, for the purposes of study, as if it were a human creation. Thus it is quite proper to detect inconsistencies and inaccuracies within the biblical text, for the Bible derives (like any other book) from authors with their own prejudices, time-bound assumptions, and limitations. Historical criticism * of the Gospels,* in particular, applies the usual principles of historical enquiry to these sources for the life of Jesus and the early history of the church. This means that it discounts the possibility of miracle* and works with what Ernst Troeltsch called the 'principle of analogy': that there cannot, for the historian, be unique events, since any historical event can be understood only by analogy* with general classes of event known in other times and places. By applying this principle, form critics* (for example) have come to treat the miracle stories in the Gospels as examples of a general type of story found in many cultures. The effect of this is necessarily to reduce the sense that in Jesus the believer is confronted with a unique, divine claim. Thus (it is argued) biblical criticism has the effect, if not the intention, of calling the authority of the Bible into question.

Such a perception of the critical task will see the Enlightenment origins of biblical criticism as extremely significant – as a clue to its essentially rationalistic character – and will point to the early association with deism and with other movements that sat lightly to the divine inspiration of scripture. On the historical fact of the deist origin of much biblical criticism, there is much valuable information in Henning Graf Reventlow's *The Authority of the Bible and the Rise of the Modern World*, 1984; the conclusion that this rationalist origin is also an indication that criticism is hostile in intention to biblical authority may be found in P. Stuhlmacher, *Historical Criticism and Theological Interpretation of Scripture*, 1977.

Once given this perception of the relation between criticism and biblical authority, there are various possible solutions to the difficulty. At the extremes, one may simply abandon the authority of the Bible altogether and rely on a personal reconstruction of the Christian faith (as in some kinds of liberal* Protestantism); or one may argue that the infallible authority of the church should take the place of a now demonstrably fallible Bible (as in Catholic Modernism*). Alternatively one may decide to abandon criticism, on the grounds that it clearly leads to conclusions incompatible with faith. Fundamentalism* has taken this second route, simply turning its back on biblical criticism and arguing that its Enlightenment pedigree proves it to be inherently hostile to the Christian faith.

More moderately, it may be argued that criticism should be allowed its place, but that after the critics have done their (essentially rather destructive) work, there is a place for a more positive, constructive theological task. Sometimes this task is called 'post-critical'. The quest for a post-critical style of biblical study has been the dominant theme in discussions of the Bible in twentieth-century theology since Karl Barth.* Barth was prepared to allow the critics their place, but insisted that serious biblical exposition should be 'post-critical', and should not bracket out the authority and divine inspiration of the scriptural text. In the so-called 'biblical theology* movement' of the 1950s and 1960s Barthian ideas about the unity and distinctiveness of the biblical witness in spite of the conclusions of the critics played a major role in encouraging biblical scholars to synthesize a 'biblical theology' from the biblical text as a finished whole, rather than resting content with what were felt to be the fragmentative conclusions of critical study.

In the last fifteen years, other scholars have attempted similar works of reconstruction. In his book *Essays on Biblical Interpretation*, 1981, Paul Ricoeur speaks of a 'second naiveté' in reading the Bible, in which the exegete does not ignore the results of criticism, but seeks despite them to read the Bible in its simplicity and wholeness. The so-called 'canonical* method' of B. S. Childs similarly seeks to reintegrate the text which the critics have divided and fragmented by asking for the 'canonical intention' of the finished text and then making that (rather than the reconstructions of the critics) the object for exposition. In a rather different way the 'New Hermeneutic'* of the post-War years was an attempt to regain the Bible for the modern church by overcoming the distancing of the text from the reader which, it was believed, biblical criticism had caused through its insistence on reading the text within its original, historical context: this movement may be studied in J. M. Robinson and J. B. Cobb (eds), *New Frontiers in Theology: II, The New Hermeneutic*, 1964.

An alternative way out of the impasse which (according to this first perception of the intellectual roots of criticism) biblical studies find themselves in does not regard biblical criticism as valid but limited (as Barth did), but instead sees it as itself a culturally-determined (*see* **Cultural Relativism**) and in many ways inadequate approach to the interpretation of texts. The reason why it is inappropriate to read the Bible as the critics have done is not, it may be said, anything to do with the Bible's sacred status; no text ought to be read as biblical critics have read the Bible. This is the point of view from which modern literary* theory has been hostile to the reconstructive and historical interests of most biblical critics. Instead, literary theorists have argued, texts should be read as finished wholes without regard to the circumstances, date, and intentions of their authors; 'historical' biblical criticism as traditionally conceived does not provide the interpreter with appropriate tools in any case. 'Literary' readings of the Bible thus now often share the distaste for historical criticism to be found also in canonical critics and in Barth, though the intellectual basis for this distaste is different. But to some extent proponents of these various 'anti-critical' positions have made common cause in recent scholarly writing on the Bible, and the result has been a great burgeoning of interest in the Bible as it stands, and a turning away from the older attempt to get 'behind' the text of scripture. It is widely felt that these newer movements have greater respect for the Bible's authority than the older critical approach had.

2. On the other hand, there is a strong tradition in German theology which sees biblical criticism not as an attack on the authority of scripture, but as a child of the increased respect for scripture which was the result of the Reformation. The case for this may be found in G. Ebeling, 'The Significance of the Critical Historical Method for Church and Theology in Protestantism', *Word and Faith*, 1963, and in A. H. J. Gunneweg, *Understanding the Old Testament*, 1978. It also lies at the root of much of the work of Rudolf Bultmann.* Rather than stressing the Enlightenment roots of biblical criticism, these scholars look back to the importance of Luther and Calvin in asking critical questions about scripture. They see the Reformation

emphasis on the particularity and historical rootedness of the biblical books as legitimating, indeed requiring, the historical-critical procedures which have been developed by modern critics. On this view, the association of early biblical criticism (especially in England) with rationalism is a historical accident; its roots go down into Reformation soil.

In Bultmann, this general perception that biblical criticism flows from the Reformation insistence on minute attention to the Bible as the source of Christian faith is linked to a more specific support for biblical criticism, through an appeal to the principle of justification by faith. Because the Christian is justified by faith in Christ, and not by the historical accuracy of the text of scripture, it belongs to Christian freedom to be able to ask radical historical questions about scripture without any sense that these are somehow forbidden by a theory of scriptural inspiration. To insist on protecting the Bible from historical enquiry thus runs counter to the Reformation emphasis on freedom from 'the law'; biblical critics are not opponents of scriptural authority as the Reformers understood it, but its true heirs. This association of biblical criticism with the 'freedom of the Christian' canvassed by Luther has been strongly argued by James Barr, 'Bibelkritik als theologische Aufklärung', *Glaube und Toleranz: Das theologische Erbe der Aufklärung*, ed. T. Rendtorff, 1982, pp. 30–42. Cf. also Gunneweg, op. cit., p. 55: 'It is in fact possible to regard the "free investigation of the canon" which was proclaimed by Johann Salomo Semler about two hundred and fifty years after Luther's Reformation as a legitimate legacy of the first beginnings and promptings of thought which are to be found in the Reformation ... Historical criticism as applied to the biblical writings took up and continues to take up a basic concern of the Reformation in changed circumstances and with different means. It did this and continues to do it by seeking to lay open the way to an encounter with scripture by questioning and demolishing supposed certainties and assurances, and thus in its own way asserting the *sola scriptura* even in the face of Protestant authorities and traditions in dogma and ministry.'

3. It is possible that neither of the positions outlined so far does justice to the intellectual and spiritual roots of biblical criticism. Two factors in the rise of criticism that are often neglected by the participants in this debate are the pure intellectual curiosity, and the heightened awareness of literary style, that were the fruits of Renaissance learning.

Curiosity about the origins of things, including the origins of literary texts, was an important stimulus to the new learning of

Renaissance Europe. It played its part in sending scholars back to the earliest extant manuscripts of biblical texts and led them to ask questions about the authorship and internal coherence of these texts. Similarly, much nineteenth-century biblical scholarship, especially in Germany, was fuelled by the rise of historical curiosity and the desire to place the history of Israel* and of the early church on the same secure footing of historical enquiry as historians of Greece and Rome were providing for the classical world. Historians such as Julius Wellhausen concerned themselves little with questions of biblical authority, either for or against; they saw the Bible as an invaluable source of historical evidence on which they could draw for the (religiously neutral) task of writing the history of Israel. The quest for academic objectivity in biblical study was not conceived as either a support for or an attack on the authority of scripture. It was part of the integration of biblical and theological studies into the newly-confident humanities (*Geisteswissenschaften*) in nineteenth-century Germany.

But literary perceptions are also important. Much biblical criticism takes its rise from the renewed sensitivity to literary genre* and style which was another fruit of the Renaissance, and which nineteenth-century philology* developed to a fine pitch. Techniques such as source,* form,* and redaction* criticism were conceived as religiously neutral, providing literary categories for understanding the scriptural texts which were independent of questions about their authority or inspiration. It is important to remember that some of the earliest ventures into source analysis of the Pentateuch* were the work of Catholic scholars such as Richard Simon (called 'the father of the criticism of the Old and New Testament' by Lessing for his work *Histoire critique du vieux testament*, 1678). Simon simply reported literary observations on the text of scripture for reasons that had little to do with either Protestant concern for scriptural authority or rationalist doubts about that authority.

The history of Catholic contributions to the development of biblical criticism has yet to be written, but it is probably correct to say that attention to this contribution would undermine the traditional presentation of criticism as either a growing attack on scriptural authority or the gradual perfecting of a Protestant respect for scripture. Many factors which had no immediate bearing on the question of scriptural authority were influential in leading to biblical criticism in the form in which we now know it, and it is misleading to speak as though 'criticism' and 'authority' were either natural opponents or natural allies. In reality, the relation of biblical criticism to both scriptural and ecclesiastical authority is far more oblique than it seems to many people, including many critical scholars themselves. Perceptions of what criticism is about were skewed very early on because of the reactions of those in authority to the beginnings of critical biblical study, and have never really recovered. 'Because the first essays in biblical criticism were interpreted in terms of the issue of authority ... the practice of criticism became polemicized, and more attention was paid to the polemic than to the proper aim of criticism, understanding ... Biblical criticism came to be seen by the world as a glamorous and revolutionary enterprise' (P. J. Lambe, 'Biblical Criticism and Censorship in Ancien Régime France: the Case of Richard Simon', *Harvard Theological Review* 78, 1985, p. 175).

See also **Biblical Criticism; Fundamentalism; German Old Testament Scholarship.**

J. Barr, *The Bible in the Modern World*, 1973; id., *Holy Scripture: Canon, Authority, Criticism*, 1983; B. S. Childs, *Introduction to the Old Testament as Scripture*, 1979; C. H. Dodd, *The Authority of the Bible*, 1928; J. K. S. Reid, *The Authority of Scripture*, 1957.

JOHN BARTON

Authorship

There are no authors, as such or known, of the OT. In the NT some of the letters of Paul* (which follow contemporary Roman epistolary* style) may be an exception to this general rule about the books of the Bible. Each book of the OT is a construct, an amalgam, of multivariate writers and the whole collection (whichever canon* is used) is very much the heterogeneous production of scribal* activity over a long period of time. Hence the OT (and much of the NT) is fundamentally an anonymous work. Its books are not books as we know books from the post-Gutenberg period, but many disparate and different scrolls, no two versions of which are in full agreement with each other, with no original scroll as such to which others may be said to be traceable (*see* **Manuscripts**). Scribal frameworks hold together most of the scrolls but the relation of these frameworks to the contents of the scrolls thereby encapsulated is not known. The processes, canonical or editorial, which produced the OT, are not known either, but Childs has observed, of what he regards as the 'canonical process', that 'a force was unleashed by Israel's religious use of her traditions which exerted an influence on the shaping of the literature as it was selected, collected and ordered. It is clear from the sketch of the process that particular editors, religious groups, and even political parties were involved. But basic to the canonical process is that those responsible for the actual editing of the text did their best to obscure their own identity. Thus the actual process by which the text was reworked lies in almost total obscurity' (p. 78). Thus the anonymity of the Bible is also part of a deliberate policy to distract attention from the authorial identity of the many groups which produced the documents.

The absoluteness of our ignorance of how the Bible came into written existence has prompted some interpreters to turn texts such as Jer. 36 into paradigms of how the prophetic books were produced. A prophet* would dictate his words to a scribal companion acting as his amanuensis who would in turn read out the written document to selected audiences. The rewriting of the scroll (36.32) would introduce differences and additions into the document. A single story such as Jer. 36 cannot serve such a general purpose, and current interpretation of the book of Jeremiah has offered rather different readings of that story in the light of II Kings 22–23. The colophons prefacing the prophetic books have also been read as providing *prima facie* evidence for the authorship of the books (cf. Talmudic* reading of such colophons), but there is no reliable information available which would confirm such an understanding of formal scribal activity. The origins of these scrolls may well have been the oral utterances of various named prophets, but their authorship cannot be shown to be the work of these prophets. On the contrary, the nature of each prophetic scroll, with its developments and transformations of images, language and ideas, militates heavily against the hypothesis of the original speaker being also the writer of the book now associated with his name. For all their association with named prophets the scrolls are essentially anonymous works.

In the earliest period of biblical interpretation (a process incorporated into the biblical text itself), there was a tendency to identify descriptions of texts with authorship: thus the 'law of Moses', associated with Moses* in the narrative, came to mean that Moses had written not only the law but also the books in which the primary story appears. Some warrant for this reading may be seen in the presentation of Deuteronomy as a final sermon by Moses on the plain of Moab, but absolutely no textual or other warrant can justify the attribution of Genesis to him. This is just a traditional belief which came to be a dogma in the Jewish and Christian communities of the common era. Canon being a political strategy with binding power over religious communities (Bruns), such a belief about the authorship of the Pentateuch* became a

'fact' in the interpretation of the Bible until the emergence of modern biblical scholarship. Deuteronomy (to be dated when? very late seventh century? sixth-fifth century?) may be the key pseudepigraph in the Bible for understanding the attribution of books to figures in the past (e.g. the historical books to prophets, many of the Psalms to King David,* Qoheleth, many proverbs and erotica to King Solomon). Hence anonymity tended to give way to pseudonymity* in the Graeco-Roman period. The function of pseudonymity was to acknowledge a writing as belonging to the authoritative tradition associated with past figures and, above all else, to meet the recurring need to actualize (*Vergegenwärtigung*) those traditions for future generations (cf. Meade). Continuity between the present and the past is achieved by pseudepigraphic works.

In late antiquity, when the various Christian and Jewish communities were developing their mainstream structures, scripture was believed to have God for its author. Such divine authorship was mediated through human authors inspired by the deity, using a model of inspiration* drawn from prophetic patterns. Thus the ancient writings came to have a prophetic authority and were often tied to specific authors. Mediaeval* notions of authorship (*auctores*) associated authority with authorship but, because God was the author of scripture, had little interest in the human author's personality or the circumstances of writing. In the thirteenth century there was a shift in focus from the author as simply authority, and interest developed in literary matters such as style (cf. Minnis, pp. 5–6). The Bible remained the great authoritative source with its named authors; authenticity depended on being the production of a named *auctor*, so that apocryphal works (i.e. those of unknown or uncertain authorship) were believed to possess inferior authority. The legacy of this attitude may be seen in post-Reformation* debates about the authorship of individual biblical books, which became one of the distinctive issues in the long battle between traditional church authorities and the emerging historical-critical* treatment of the Bible by scholars. As late as 1880–1, William Robertson Smith* was tried for the heresy (!) of denying the Mosaic authorship of the Pentateuch and removed from his professorial chair in the Free Church Divinity College attached to the University of Aberdeen. Two decades later, George Adam Smith survived a similar heresy trial in Edinburgh. Personality traits apart, the academic community had apparently developed its power bases more securely in the community of faith by the turn of the century.

The heart of modern critical scholarship of

the OT has been the development of pentateuchal studies in terms of the denial of the Mosaic authorship traditionally assigned to the five books. It identified at least four main strands of authorship in the Pentateuch to which it attached the authorial labels J (Yahwist), E (Elohist), D (Deuteronomist), P (Priestly). These characters may have been conceived of as the actual authors of the various strands constituting the Pentateuch, but they were hypothesized writers (fictions doing the work of authors!) and the general theory was known as the Documentary Hypothesis (classically associated with the work of Wellhausen). Many variations have followed this hypothesis in the production of hypotheses without number, but recent pentateuchal studies have abandoned the general theory (cf. Whybray). The authors of the Pentateuch remain firmly anonymous. There is, however, discernible in some recent writing on the Bible a tendency which might be described as a 'back to Wellhausen' attitude. This reinstates the J E D P hypothesis, identifies D as Jeremiah or Baruch (his amanuensis) and makes Ezra the redactor of the Pentateuch (Friedman). This retreat into historicism would make Jeremiah/Baruch also the author(s) of the deuteronomistic history* and challenge the anonymity of the biblical authors. Similar considerations arise with regard to the part played by hypothetical sources (Q, M, L) in the study of the Gospels (*see* **Synoptic Problem**).

The anonymity of the biblical writers chimes in nicely with the 'death of the author' approach to literature of certain post-war French writers (e.g. Barthes). For Barthes 'writing is the destruction of every voice, of every point of origin. Writing is that neutral, composite, oblique space where our subject slips away, the negative where all identity is lost, starting with the very identity of the body writing' (p. 142). Recent structuralist* and post-structuralist readings of the Bible have drawn attention to intertextuality, reading and writerly relations, and the non-referentiality of texts; and the sheer anonymity of the biblical writers wonderfully facilitates such readings. The historicist mode of identifying biblical authors is but the last spasm of a moribund dinosaur.

See also **Ephesians; Pastoral Epistles; Pseudonymity.**

R. Barthes, 'The Death of the Author', *Image-Music-Text*, E T 1977, pp. 142–54; G. L. Bruns, 'Canon and Power in the Hebrew Scriptures', *Critical Inquiry* 10, 1984, pp. 462–80; B. S. Childs, *Introduction to the Old Testament as Scripture*, 1979; R. E. Friedman, *Who Wrote the Bible?*, 1987; D. G. Meade, *Pseudonymity and Canon*, 1986; A. J. Minnis, *Medieval*

Theory of Authorship, ² 1988; R. N. Whybray, *The Making of the Pentateuch*, 1987.

ROBERT P. CARROLL

Babylon

Babylon provides a classic example of the way in which biblical interpretation has operated at different and potentially confusing levels. At one level its importance is clearly historical and archaeological. Knowledge of the whereabouts of Babylon was lost for centuries, but the site – near the great bend of the River Euphrates in modern Iraq – was identified in the nineteenth century, and its significance for OT study has been recognized ever since. The first great period of Babylonian power came under Hammurabi, probably in the eighteenth century BC, and though it is most unlikely that he is mentioned by name in the Bible (attempts to identify him with Amraphel, Gen. 14.1, are now rightly given up) the law code with which he is associated shows important parallels with the laws given to Moses* in the Pentateuch.*

Of even greater importance for OT interpretation was the great collection of texts giving Babylonian accounts of creation and flood, which posed acute problems for those who believed in the uniqueness and the historical reliability of the biblical record (*see* **Creation Narratives**). The issue is one which remains capable of evoking great dispute, as current 'creationist' controversies in North America show. In Germany in the early years of this century there raged an acute 'Babel v. Bibel' controversy fuelled to some extent by anti-Jewish feeling. Many scholars, such as the great Assyriologist Friedrich Delitzsch, claimed that true creative genius in the ancient world was to be found in Babylon ('Babel'), while others upheld the unique authority of the Bible. Here already Babylon has become a symbol:* should the biblical record be accorded unique status, or are other accounts of the human past to be given equal or greater credence?

The Neo-Babylonian empire, the second great period of Babylonian ascendancy, was short-lived (605–539 BC) but of great importance for the OT. The conquest of Judah (597) and sack of Jerusalem and destruction of the Temple (587/6) during the rule of Nebuchadnezzar made a lasting impression on Jewish tradition. (This is true also for the Greek classical tradition, for the 'Hanging Gardens of Babylon' came to be celebrated as one of the seven wonders of the world.) Here too interpretation has been assisted by the discovery of Babylonian texts; the royal Chronicle covering the earlier part of Nebuchadnezzar's reign has been discovered, and it makes specific reference to the capture of Jerusalem in 597.

For Judaism, Babylon came to be regarded as the place of exile, of alienation from one's promised land. The theme is expressed in Ps. 137.1:

> By the waters of Babylon,
> there we sat down and wept.

What may have begun as the taking into exile of the royal family and leading citizens (Jer. 52.28–30 refers to 4,600 exiles) is on the way to being interpreted as the break-up of a whole community, and II Chron. 36.20f. pictures the whole population being exiled and the land left deserted. By the time of Isaiah 40–55 Babylon has become a symbol of the evil oppressor (ch. 47), and the hoped-for return of the people from Babylon is pictured as a new exodus (51.9–11); the downfall of the king of Babylon is pictured in Isa. 14.5–21 (a late addition to the oracles of Isaiah) in mythical* terms appropriate to the downfall of hostile gods.

This symbolic interpretation of Babylon developed in the later biblical period. In Dan. 5, Belshazzar's feast and the writing on the wall are described in terms which makes it clear that they are applicable to any heathen empire which dares to thwart God's purposes. The relevance of this in the NT period for the pretensions of Rome was obvious; and so we find a reference to 'Babylon' in I Peter 5.13 which is most probably a hidden allusion to Rome. This motif is taken further in Revelation, where Babylon is the great whore whose overthrow is gloatingly described in ch. 18. The power of the secular empire is described in great detail so as to make yet more dramatic the impact of its expected overthrow.

In subsequent interpretation 'Babylon' has characteristically been used to symbolize exile and oppression. Exile: as in Abelard's hymn which speaks of our earthly life as 'our long exile on Babylon's strand'; or Petrarch's description of the removal of the papacy to Avignon as the Babylonish captivity of the church, a theme richly employed by Luther.* Oppression: as in the Bob Marley song called 'Babylon System', and in the way in which many black people in the West have come to describe the whole political structure under which they find themselves as 'Babylon'. The biblical symbol is still powerfully evocative.

See also **Ancient Near Eastern World.**

R. J. COGGINS

Background and Context

'There are also many other things which Jesus did; were every one of them to be written, I suppose that the world itself could not contain the books that would be written' (John 21.25). What appears in the bound pages of a modern Bible obviously stems from a vastly greater amount of speaking, writing and other activity going on around. But things do not happen and thoughts do not occur in isolated blocks, ready packaged for selection. When things are done, when words are spoken or written, they are part of a wider mesh of events and ideas and ways of doing things and ways of interpreting what is done and said. If we want to understand, or improve our understanding of, an account of a set of words uttered, or a description of some event, we usually try to discover more of what was said, done and understood. We look for a bigger picture, a longer scene, a more elaborate network of what was going on: the larger whole of which the bit we first focussed on was an integral part, and from which it has been abstracted.

So we try to avoid taking words or phrases out of their immediate context in the writing in front of us. We object to the theatre manager omitting from his poster the first word of the critic's conclusion, 'Not the best way to spend an evening'; and perhaps we object to the preacher taking as starting point 'the kingdom of heaven is like unto a man' (Matt. 13.52) or (in an eighteenth-century sermon on hairstyles) 'top [k]not come down' (Matt. 24.17). The division of the biblical books into chapters and verses is convenient for reference but dangerous for interpretation. So we look at a story in Mark in the sequence in which Mark has it, and appreciate its part in the unfolding of his story, helped by an awareness of what Mark says elsewhere. And we try to understand what Paul* means in Gal. 2.16 by looking first at what he says elsewhere in the letter, and then at what is said in those other letters bearing his name which are most like Galatians in style and vocabulary and in what they most obviously say. Again, even if we conclude that the 'Pastoral Epistles'* (I & II Tim. and Titus), which seem to form a distinct group, were written by Paul, we may accept that we have to interpret them separately in the first place, before comparing and contrasting them with, say, Ephesians and Colossians, or the remainder, the group most widely ascribed to Paul these days.

That then raises another thorny problem: the extent to which the Bible as a whole is the best or even the only context for the proper interpretation of the parts: 'interpreting the Bible by the Bible' (cf. **Canonical Criticism**). We often, for instance, find discussions of 'justification' in Paul prefaced by extended accounts of expressions used in the Hebrew Bible and in the Septuagint,* including many passages to which Paul shows no sign of referring. In this instance the practice may have some validity, for Paul does range widely through Jewish scripture, and consistent patterns there do seem to illuminate what Paul writes. It is much more questionable to run through a modern Bible Concordance looking for words that can be translated 'work' and assume they are all being used the same way by writers who must knowingly or unawares agree with and supplement each other. If we are doing NT interpretation, for instance, we need to be aware of the various ways in which Jews and others at the time interpreted their ancient sacred writings; and we need to try to discover how much a particular writer knew and used particular parts of Jewish scriptures. Paul may well have had difficulty in getting access to a full set of the scrolls of the scriptures. He certainly seems to quote from some parts more than from others, and from memory.

Unless it is clear that particular writers only ever read or listened to existing sacred scripture, we also need to try to ascertain what other writings and what other talk (and non-verbal communication) they engaged with, which may well have had an important influence on them. In practice many interpreters of the Jewish and Christian scriptures have always looked more widely, even if not always very carefully. So most rightly use dictionaries and word-books that are based on painstaking research into words and ideas and practices in the world around. There is nothing in the Jewish or Christian scriptures to suggest that their writers existed in a vacuum (even had they wanted to), and other writings passed down to us or recovered by archaeologists* are widely accepted as part of the context for sacred scripture: Mari, Ugarit,* Tell el-Amarna, Qumran, Nag Hammadi;* as well as Greek and Roman writings from the ancient world, Jewish writings often labelled Apocrypha* and Pseudepigrapha,* and later rabbinic* productions.

That then brings us back to a problem already considered: Where do we stop? Is there a time limit, are there geographical and social limits? The Dead Sea Scrolls* seem to have been in use right into the time of Jesus and the early churches, and there seems to be enough attention to similar issues, sometimes in similar languages, for us to be able to say, 'It is clear that the question of being right before God, or of a strong contrast between "sons of light and sons of darkness" were live issues at the time.' But there is a vigorous dispute at present between those who use later rabbinic material wholesale for NT interpretation, those who use only material ascribed to earlier rabbis (e.g. G. Vermes) and those (e.g. J. Neusner) who say that all the material comes from much later or has been so drastically edited in a different age to express a distinctive view of things as to be almost completely useless for interpreting first-century writings. The same kind of question arises

with the Gnostic* documents from Nag Hammadi (J. M. Robinson; E. Yamauchi).

These questions also arise in using Greek and Roman writings. Clearly the Christian scriptures arose in that world, and most writers cull background material from it. There does seem to be some risk of irrelevance if material is taken from much before the time of Augustus, or much later than Marcus Aurelius (d. 180), for attitudes and practices seem to have changed considerably. It is also sometimes argued that most of our pagan writings from late antiquity came from the pens of aristocrats living in a world of their own, out of touch with the many poor people and the few moderately wealthy ones from among whom the first Christians were drawn. However, a closer look at the first-century world suggests that in oral form aristocratic products moved down through law-courts and theatres and other auditoria, and through household slaves and poor guests at parties, to markets and open shop-fronts; and to a lesser extent, ideas moved back in the other direction. Not only the Cynics,* but also other Hellenistic writers* provide us with essential insights into ideas and attitudes current at the time.

Further, to understand any speaker or writer we need not only to understand the input they may have received, but also the audience or readership they are likely to suppose they are addressing. The audiences for the NT documents we have are all at home in Greek and will all have been exposed to the popular oral Greek culture of the day. From the frequent need to explain Jewish terms and practices referred to in passing, it would seem that the pagan context must for many have been the more important, and we must allow fully for that in our NT interpretation.

All the points made so far might well reinforce the impression that can often be given that the only important background or context is intellectual and verbal, even if we allow for the inclusion of philosophical, literary and political ideas as well as 'religious'. Some of the books with our key words in their titles do just that, and their narrow selectivity should be viewed with great caution.

It is very important to branch out much wider. We need as full a social description of the time as possible, a description of how life was lived, how people related to one another, and their attitudes to life at large. Some of this can be gleaned from remains (documents and inscriptions, pictures, graffiti); some, with more difficulty, from an analysis of housing, town layouts, artefacts and the like. While being able to imagine Peter or Paul in appropriate clothing using likely cooking pots may add to vividness, it is their hopes and fears, likes and dislikes, and their social relationships that really matter if we are to understand them and their thought. An understanding at this level may be much more important than one at the level of abstract theorizing about the gods or the state or the Good.

Along with such social description we may also be helped by various brands of theoretical sociology.* Such theories may help us to look for significant factors among the data from which we try to build up our picture; but may also allow us to attain a deeper understanding of what may have been going on, and how people were reacting. It is, however, important to realize that no theory is well enough established to prove that things must have happened the way the theory imagines, unless there is actual evidence to support the account. We are not in a position to fill in gaps in the evidence with the help of sociology.

All the terms which are important in this area: background, context, environment, setting, 'Sitz-im-Leben' (situation in life), have the recurrent disadvantage in practice of suggesting a sort of stage set, and encouraging us still to view the biblical narratives of sayings and other events as in effect detached, isolated, so that the rest is really only scenery. In fact, all was once integrally knitted together. It is important to stress again that the abstraction of particular sayings and narratives and the attention in narratives to particular aspects of particular sequences of activity is always somebody's choice, and never the only possible choice. Some selection is necessary for us to understand at all; but we will often need to try to put the chosen pieces back into the context from which they have been wrested, so as to understand them better – or at all.

The more isolated and abstracted some document is from the life around, the easier it is to see it as foreign and other. Placing our biblical writings back into more of their original and integral settings does in part allow us to deal with the problems of so-called cultural relativism.* Even if we find few if any direct points of contact between our own views and those in some ancient texts, there may be more, even many more, indirect ones amid the rest of the setting in which they arose.

There is also a critical function involved in a consideration of context. At its simplest, archaeologists may decide that a town referred to in Joshua or Judges as inhabited was entirely derelict or not even built at the time indicated. On the other hand, some findings may confirm a narrative (e.g. the Siloam tunnel, II Kings 20.20). An inscription referring to Gallio's time as proconsul of Achaia may support Acts 18.12. But the logical implication is limited. It does not itself prove

that Luke was right to have Paul and Gallio coincide; and still less does it prove Luke's general trustworthiness as a historian. That his descriptions of legal procedure may fit well with other contemporary accounts does seem to show he knows about standard practice; it does not mean that a standard trial actually took place on a particular occasion. Mark's tale of chaotic and improper treatment of Jesus in his trial may well be closer to the facts than Luke's inherently more 'proper' account. A good fit with what we independently gather about life at the time is necessary if some narrative of events or utterances is to be accepted, but a good fit is not on its own sufficient to establish historical veracity.

This article presupposes a desire to discover one or more levels of past meaning, past reality, in some measure. There are keen readers of the Jewish and Christian scriptures who look only or perhaps also for purely contemporary meaning: How should I understand Matthew, say, as a literary document in circulation today, restricting myself entirely to the narrative world that the Greek text or a modern translation creates for me now? It is not for a contributor to this Dictionary to dissuade from such a venture. It is worth pointing out what difficulties such attempts encounter when trying to gauge what a Pharisee* is from information to be found solely in Matthew. And other questions of context then arise: should it be read in the canon? should it be read in liturgy? how many of these readings and readings of readings is it worth bothering with? how much of 'my' context do I use or impose?

It seems self-evident that it is worth trying to listen to the sorts of things the document may have meant originally, even if we also find other readings also worth undertaking. Issues of context (of reader as well as of writing) will always demand attention.

See also **Archaeology (New Testament, Old Testament); Dead Sea Scrolls; Epigraphy; Gnosticism; Historical-Critical Method.**

C. K. Barrett, *New Testament Background. Selected Documents*, ²1988; F. G. Downing, *Strangely Familiar*, 1986; id., 'Interpretation and the Culture Gap', *S J T* 40, 1987, pp. 161–171; H. Koester, *Introduction to the New Testament*, I, 1982; A. J. Malherbe, *Social Aspects of Early Christianity*, ²1983; J. Stambaugh and D. Balch, *The Social World of the First Christians*, 1987; C. Tuckett, *Reading the New Testament*, 1987, esp ch 2, pp. 136–50.

F. GERALD DOWNING

Barth, K.

Karl Barth (1886–1968) developed a radically different method of biblical interpretation from that of his predecessors. He studied Romans* with his friend Eduard Thurneysen, in preparation for his commentary* which created an immense stir in theological circles (1919, ET 1933 by E. C. Hoskyns*). The stance found therein was programmatic for his later work: it treats the epistle as Word of God* as well as word of man; it is equally concerned with both the hermeneutical* horizons; at the interface of the contemporary world view with the biblical world view, it tries always to adopt the latter. It is more concerned with theological content than with technical discussion of style and shape.

Barth developed great skills as a biblical interpreter, although most of his work was done for dogmatic reasons. Apart from his commentary on Philippians and a book about I Corinthians 15, his exegesis may be chiefly found in the footnotes of the *Church Dogmatics*. Often he expounds small portions which relate to a topic under discussion, but sometimes he takes longer sections, and deals occasionally with whole books. Clearly Barth's double purpose, to establish the meaning of the author and to discover further insights to guide his dogmatic thinking, are not always kept separate; each influences the other in his interpretation.

There is debate among scholars about Barth's attitude to historical criticism. Some consider that he reverted to a pre-critical methodology, but there is evidence that he employed a self-consciously selective procedure which has been called post-critical. For instance, Barth admits that he is not an expert in textual criticism,* but he is always willing to employ it to establish a reliable text. Other critical methods are viewed less favourably because he considers scripture has been 'torn asunder into a thousand shreds ... by unimaginative historico-critical omniscience' (*CD* IV/2, p. 674). Barth's chief criticism of the method is that it is more concerned with recovering the history behind the texts than with understanding the final canonical* form of the texts. This Barth regards as a pointless exercise because revelation* is not to be sought behind or above texts, but in them.

Relying on the work of form critics,* Barth assumes that behind both OT and NT lie oral traditions* whose history may be traced, but he himself stops short of this quest because he considers form criticism should only be employed to illuminate the text as the final redactor left it.

Source criticism* is employed similarly. Barth does not value one source above another; nor does he regard one as more reliable historically or theologically. Each is to be taken seriously for itself, before any theological construction may be made. Barth's method

corresponds well with the more recent redaction criticism,* for he is primarily concerned to discover the author's intended theological meaning, which he is confident it is possible to elucidate. For Barth, oral forms, written sources and redactional comments are equally the word of God.

In the *Church Dogmatics*, Barth's most frequent method of interpretation is continuous exegesis of passages of scripture. Questions of authorship do not feature largely; nor do the background details of geography, sociology,* or even details as to the intended first readers. He discusses the Greek NT with more facility than the Hebrew OT and readily engages with grammatical and syntactical questions. Wherever there is dispute as to the exact meaning of the passage, the immediate context is normative for Barth. Beyond that, he always interprets passages with an eye on the whole canonical context. This does not result in simple harmonization, but in complicated theological relationships which are postulated between contradictory strands of biblical material.

Barth maintains the unity of scripture by understanding it all as related to Jesus Christ: the OT as prophecy, the NT as witness. This never becomes a systematic straitjacket, however, because Barth recognizes that each of the many different literary genres* needs to be handled differently. Straight theological propositions can be used as the basis for deductive theology: concepts are explored because 'it is not the right human thoughts about God which form the content of the Bible, but the right divine thoughts about men' (*The Word of God and the Word of Man*, 1928, p. 43).

Barth's use of biblical themes makes clear that he has a differentiated understanding of biblical unity which enables him to read different parts of scripture as though they were lines of music in harmony. They are taken together, and their variations are noted, never denied. He struggles to create a single theological tune, since he regards it as not only legitimate but imperative to assume that there is a single revelation as there is but one Word of God to his people.

It is in Barth's use of stories that his interpretative method comes to fruition, for he is able to read them imaginatively and realistically whether they purport to be parables,* history, myth* or legend.* Indeed, the whole content of scripture is seen as story. Historical accuracy cannot be established in Barth's view of history, and indeed does not need to be, because Christ 'verifies Scripture simply by the fact that He is its content' (*CD* IV/2, p. 675). These stories are understood in the light of overt theological statements from literature like the Epistles,* because the Gospel* 'hardly says anything about the significance of the event, '(*CD* IV/1, p. 239). Often, Barth interprets stories in a manner which resembles that of structuralists,* though of course he predates them.

Barth does not shy away from employing typological* interpretations of scripture, since he regards repeated characteristic patterns of behaviour by the unchanging God as inherently likely. OT figures and events point forward to Christ, who, as the eternal Word, in any case pre-dates them and is the reality of which they are but shadowy copies. Man, for instance, is in the image of God, because it was always God's purpose to become incarnate. Barth considers that the NT authors did not recognize all the OT types of Christ and freely includes other examples. Barth often employs allegorical interpretation* in relation to parables; one of the clearest examples occurs in his discussion of the Good Samaritan. The man taken by thieves is the questioning lawyer; the Good Samaritan is Jesus. Barth's usual insistence that exegesis must have regard to context is broken here, for these identifications leave him unable to take seriously the command to go and do likewise.

Because Barth takes seriously the whole canon as the interpretative context of any passage, his practice is close to the Roman Catholic use of *sensus plenior*.* The immediate meaning of the OT prophets* leads to a fuller understanding in the light of Christ, which becomes not only their ultimate meaning, but their 'only legitimate sense' (*CD* I/2, pp. 489f.)

At every point, Barth attempted to free his thought from philosophical or anthropological justification and explanation of Christian doctrine, so that he could make not only the content but also the method of his exegesis and doctrine thoroughly biblical.

C. A. Baxter, 'Barth a Truly Biblical Theologian?', *Tyndale Bulletin* 38, 1987, pp. 3–27; G. W. Bromiley, *Introduction to the Theology of Karl Barth*, 1979; Werner G. Jeanrond, 'K. Barth's Hermeneutic' in N. Biggar (ed.), *Reckoning with Barth*, 1988; H. Martin-Rumscheidt, *Revelation and Theology*, 1972; S. Sykes (ed.), *Karl Barth – Studies of his Theological Method*, 1979.

CHRISTINA A. BAXTER

Beatitudes

Forty-four NT sayings, leaving aside questions of literary relatedness, affirm the blessedness of certain persons. Some are single-clause acclamations (e.g. Matt. 11.6; Luke 1.45; 11.27, 28), while others employ the classic OT form in which the person blessed is first defined in respect of attitude or action or experience,

and then the content of the blessing itself is clarified. Such clarification may highlight approved status before God, a close relationship with God, or ultimate eschatological* experience of God. The intention of these sayings is not uniform, some picking up the concern of the 'wisdom'* perspective to affirm* ethical ideals and thus to exhort, while others stand nearer to the prophetic-apocalyptic* concern to provide comfort and encouragement in adverse circumstances. Either implicitly or explicitly, beatitudes in the NT contain some allusion to the person of Jesus and a sense of the present and future implications of commitment to him.

Within the Gospels special prominence is achieved by the collections of beatitudes which initiate the so-called Sermon on the Mount*/Plain in Matt. 5.3–12/Luke 6.20b–23. Structurally these all conform to the classic form, even though some elaboration is evident in the last one, Matt. 5.11f./Luke 6.22f. Their being positioned at the start of an extended speech conforms to the wisdom pattern; their combining to form a collection conforms to a tendency in both wisdom and apocalyptic contexts.

Christian awareness of the beatitudes has tended to be dominated by Matthew's version, in line with the special influence of that Gospel as a whole and, within it, the control of the Sermon on the Mount. In the history of interpretation three main trends can be discerned (Luz). According to the first, the beatitudes are declarations of God's goodness to the needy who depend entirely upon him. According to the second and most recurrent view, the beatitudes represent ethical demands summed up in the call to 'righteousness' or 'perfection' (cf. Matt. 5.48). Response to these demands may be seen either as fulfilment of the conditions for entry to God's kingdom or as the life-style of those who have entered. According to the third view, the beatitudes lay down the principles which inform the life of the Christian community.* These variations of view have not been entirely mutually exclusive, but it is noticeable that they often reflect tendencies either to stress one half of each saying more than the other, or to emphasize one of the quartets (5.3-6, 7-10) at the expense of the other.

It is natural that the analysis of Matthew's collection of beatitudes should take cognizance of the comparative shortness and the use of the third person which is common to all but the last, the shared affirmation that 'theirs is the kingdom of heaven' which allows the first and the eighth to form an *inclusio*, and the concern for righteousness which shows in the fourth and the eighth. This last feature does not establish any division into a pair of quartets, since no distinct homogeneity of subject can be discerned in each group when considered separately. On the other hand, the last short beatitude reads like an admission that the short beatitudes are distinct from the following long one, and that a bridge needs to be built between them, together with a strong hint that the whole collection must be viewed as focussed on the themes of righteousness and the possession of the kingdom of heaven. This focus corresponds with that of Matthew's sermon as a whole (cf. 5.20; 6.1, 33), a fact which not only opens up the topic of the contribution of the beatitudes to Matthew's theology but also helps to answer two central interpretative questions. First, do the beatitudes describe entry requirements or announce eschatological blessings? Secondly, does righteousness stand for a gift of God (conferred in the future eschatological judgment or conveyed, as Paul* would affirm, already to the believer), or does it describe human conduct conforming to the will of God?

On the first, it is doubtful whether Matthew makes any sharp distinction: the synonymous meekness and poverty of spirit of Matt. 5.3, 5 (both being possible renderings of the Hebrew words *anawim* and *aniyyim*) stand alongside humility which is both an entry requirement for (18.3), and a ground of superior status within (18.4), the kingdom. On the second, this distinction might also be regarded as inappropriate in the light of OT and some Qumran usage of the term righteousness both for God's salvific act and for human conformity to a legal norm within the covenant* relationship. Yet Matthew's own usage matches that of other Qumran and Tannaitic material where righteousness stands for what is demanded of man by God, i.e. meticulous human observance of the law as authoritatively interpreted and applied. The notion of a divine gift, arguably introduced under the influence of Paulinizing exegesis, is scarcely compatible with the conviction that there are different varieties of righteousness, one of which is insufficient to guarantee entry to the kingdom (5.20; 6.1). Hence the righteousness envisaged by Matthew's beatitudes stands for human conduct, and the righteousness which counts is the practice of good works (5.16) in conformity to the will of God and dictated by his perfection (5.48) and coming kingship (6.33). For the disciples it is just as firm a present reality (cf. persecution 'on account of righteousness') as is their commitment to Jesus (cf. persecution 'on account of me'), and the two are equal bones of contention with religious opponents. The beatitudes, set in such a context, convey the same message as that affirmed by the righteous sufferer in Wisd. 2.16: 'He calls the last end of the righteous blessed.'

If Matthew's collection of beatitudes integrates with the Sermon on the Mount as a whole and indeed with the overall concerns of Matthean theology, the question of the extent of his creativity and editorial intervention becomes pressing. While it is widely agreed that he may have introduced some small elements, e.g. certain details in which he differs from the Lucan parallel, or that he may have heightened parallelisms with the Psalms (compare Matt. 5.5, 8 with Ps. 37.11; 24.4), one recent proposal (Goulder) is that he is entirely responsible for each and all of the beatitudes. That is, following an ancient Jewish custom of setting out a list of topics and then expounding them in reverse order, Matthew's beatitudes are a midrashic* creation preparing for a presentation of persecution (5.11–16), peacemaking (5.21–26), purity (5.27–37), mercy (5.38–6.4), hunger for righteousness (6.5–18), meekness (6.19–34), mourning (7.1–6) and poverty of spirit (7.7–11). This implies that 'Matthew wrote the beatitudes and Luke rewrote them'. Such a distinctive analysis depends upon tenuous connections of thought (especially persecution in 5.13–16, purity in 5.33–37, and meekness in 6.25–33) and sets aside more obvious combinations within the sermon (e.g. 5.17–20 as a heading for 5.21–48; 5.20 as preamble, and 6.1 as heading, for 6.2–18). It may be doubted whether it successfully overthrows more conventional opinions about the relationship between the two sets of beatitudes in Matthew and in Luke.

Luke's beatitude complex includes an approximately symmetrical set of woes, the origin of which is disputed. As they stand, however, they impose upon poverty a strict socio-economic meaning which extends to hunger and can incorporate sorrow. The disciples, who are present (6.20a) and listening (6.27a), and who designedly epitomize the community of Luke's time, are contrasted with the stereotyped rich who are either absent or, if present and by implication also members of that community, required to abandon prosperity in favour of full Christian commitment. In their poverty, therefore, the disciples represent those who benefit from a social gospel whose contours and colours are illustrated by the programme of the Magnificat (esp. 1.53) and the uniquely Lucan parables* (12.13–21; 14.7–14; 16.1–13, 19–31). Above all, the beatitudes serve to interpret the inaugural sermon which shows Luke's interpretation of Jesus' mission by means of Isa. 61.1f.; 58.6 and his intention to incorporate healings and social rehabilitation equally within the definition of salvation (4.16–30). They unmistakably echo the prophetic tradition. That Luke may have derived such ideas from Matthew is naturally possible but the majority scholarly opinion (which itself incorporates varieties of view on detail) holds otherwise.

The combination of overlap and non-overlap in the two editions of the beatitudes has most often been explained by one or another variant of the Q hypothesis. The currently maintained variants are that Matthew and Luke drew directly upon an identical tradition from Q, or that one or both of them drew upon an already edited version of that tradition, i.e. Q^{Mt} or Q^{Lk}. To this can be added a related spectrum of view about the derivation of the woes from Lucan redaction, from Q^{Lk}, or from Q itself. The resolution of these conflicts of opinion might fairly be expected to respect the following principles, i.e. that a convincing overall history of the tradition is thereby reconstructed; that material consonant with an evangelist's viewpoint may be, but is not compelled to be, his creation; and that whichever hypothesis is most economical will normally be preferable.

Both Matthew and Luke build bridges between the short beatitudes and the concluding long one. Matthew does so not only in 5.10, which picks up the promise of 5.3 and anticipates the concern of 5.11 for the persecuted ones, but also already in 5.9. Within the Gospel tradition 5.9 and Matt. 5.45/Luke 6.35 alone use the term 'son of God' to describe the eschatological heavenly reward for faithful human beings. Since peacemaking and the overcoming of enmity by means of love (5.45) are equivalent, and since the two sayings in question occur so near to one another in the Q sequence, it is likely that one is an anticipation of the other and also a preparation for the beatitude about persecution and conflict in 5.11. Luke correspondingly refers to weeping and laughing in his concluding short beatitude, and OT examples abound to show that the appropriate settings for such actions are those of being crushed by, and then crushing, the opposition of persecutors. In view of the overlap between Matt. 5.4 and Luke 6.24, 25 in the use of the 'mourning + being comforted' pairing, we may conclude that the common source featured such a pairing and consequently that the 'weeping + laughing' combination is Luke's own replacement, that is, his particular way of building a bridge between the short beatitudes and their longer sequel. For this purpose he may well have altered the order to place this saying after the beatitude on the hungry and next to that on the persecuted ones. So Matthew and Luke both felt the need to construct bridge sayings, though they did so in different ways.

The evidence of such creative intervention opens up the possibility that other beatitudes, especially in Matthew, may be attributed to the evangelist. This possibility becomes all the stronger when the beatitudes on the merciful and the pure in heart are related to Matthew's redactional and compositional activity elsewhere. Thus 5.7 is the only beatitude to match exactly the action of human beings and an action of God: this use of the 'measure for measure' principle in connection with mercy is not only in the service of a theme beloved of Matthew (cf. 18.33; 23.23), but also a combination of features of two separate but adjacent sayings in Luke 6.36, 37. This suggests that Matt. 5.7 cannot be older than the stage at which these two distinct sayings were juxtaposed. Similarly 5.8, the beatitude on the pure in heart, doubtless points to Matt. 5.28 and perhaps 7.16–20; 12.33–5/Luke 6.43–5, but probably above all to the far-reaching principle of purity deployed in 15.10, 17–19; the vision of God may, like the status of sonship (5.9; cf. Wisd. 5.5), be another variation on the theme of angelic existence (cf. Matt. 18.10). Finally, the secondariness of the beatitude on the meek is suggested by its doubling of that on the poor in spirit, and its conformity to Matthew's *imitatio Christi* pattern (cf. 11.29; 21.5). Against this background it can hardly be doubted that Matthean redaction, designed to achieve uniformity and consistency, is responsible for 'in spirit' and 'and thirst for righteousness'. All that remains to be decided is whether Matthew or Luke is the person responsible for the discrepancy between second and third-person forms. Opinions are divided, and appeal to what is normal Jewish convention is a reversible argument. The balance of probability perhaps favours Lucan redaction, since he shares with Matthew a concern to integrate the final beatitude with those preceding, but that integration has been achieved more thoroughly when (as in Luke) there is no such discrepancy.

Once the earliest version of the last beatitude on the persecuted ones has been worked out, a smooth tradition-historical sequence can be recovered. The first stage was a trio, but not a list, of beatitudes on the poor, parts of whose miserable experience are sorrow and hunger. Such persons belong to the tradition of the *anawim* of the Psalms, and they are the recipients of a gospel couched in the terms of Isa. 61.1f., 6. The choice of the beatitude form for the articulation of that gospel is made possible by the established tendency to use that form for eschatological proclamation (not this time the wisdom pattern). The second stage was the addition of the beatitude on the persecuted. This was made easy by the fact that poverty includes lack of power in relationships as well as lack of possessions, and therefore the stereotypical poor person is always vulnerable to oppression. While socio-economic circumstances were primary at the first stage of the tradition, the history of the idea of poverty suggests an underlying theme of religious commitment which is then brought to the surface at the second stage. That religious commitment is severely tested in the fires of oppression, an oppression which is countered by a double reflection designed to call forth celebration: first, in typical beatitude style, there is an affirmation of heavenly reward; secondly, in what may be a secondary superimposition, the persecuted ones are identified with the bruised and battered prophets in the Deuteronomic succession (cf. the recurrent use of such a scheme in early Christian apologetic: Matt. 23.34–36/ Luke 11.49–51; Matt. 23.37–39/ Luke 13.34f.; Mark 12.1ff.; Acts 7.51f.; I Thess. 2.14–16).

Matthew, representing one of the alternative third stages, carries this process even further: the beatitudes now (contrary to normal Jewish precedent) form a list, and while religious attitudes do not exclude socio-economic hardship they certainly do not require it. The resurgence of a wisdom motif conforms to his tendency to equate Jesus and the heavenly Sophia. Luke, representing the other alternative third stage, adheres more closely to the second stage (whether or not the woes were contributed by him). The ferocity of the opposition to those who acknowledge the Son of man, reflected in much stronger language in Luke 6.22f. than in that of Matt. 5.11f., may indicate that the lens through which he and his community view the tradition is coloured by the rupture of church and synagogue.

The beatitudes provoke acute theological questions. Although the earliest setting was doubtless one of intense short-term eschatological expectation, do they not have permanent significance by attesting a constant divine attitude to human need and a timeless demand for human remedial action? Although the growth of the tradition serves to highlight certain ideals of piety, which in themselves cannot but be approved, does not the matching tendency to depress the overtly social priorities of the beatitudes have to be viewed critically? And does not the trend towards ecclesiastical domestication have a potentially damaging effect in modifying the criteria on the basis of which that judgment, which continues to be affirmed by the gospel, is put into effect? Such theological questions inevitably arise in connection with the authority of a tradition which is not uniform and static but dynamic and evolving.

See also **Luke, Gospel of; Matthew, Gospel of; Sermon on the Mount.**

Jacques Dupont, *Les Béatitudes*, 1969, 1973; P. Esler, *Community and Gospel in Luke–Acts*, 1987; Michael D. Goulder, *Midrash and Lection in Matthew*, 1974; Robert A. Guelich, *The Sermon on the Mount*, 1982, pp. 62–118; Ulrich Luz, *Das Evangelium nach Matthäus (Mt 1–7)*, 1985; Benno Przybylski, *Righteousness in Matthew and his World of Thought*, 1980; Heinz Schürmann, *Das Lukasevangelium I*, 1969, pp. 325–41.

DAVID CATCHPOLE

Biblia Pauperum

The misleading name *Biblia Pauperum* (Bible of the Poor) was acquired in the eighteenth century. Earlier titles such as 'Concordance of the Old and New Testaments' or 'Selected Chapters of the Bible' are equally unhelpful. It is difficult to name this important mediaeval book, which has several forms.

BP presents a series of picture-groups and short texts based on a highly selective life of Christ, followed by Pentecost and the Coronation of the Virgin. The lost original probably carried 34 such groups; one later version carries 50. Longer treatments close with a Judgment section. Less than a full life of Christ but more than a mere narrative, *BP* shows that *In Vetere Novum lateat, et in Novo Vetus pateat*: 'The New (Law) is hidden in the Old, and the Old appears in the New'. Each NT event (Antitype) is associated with two OT events (Types*). For example, the *Crucifixion* is prefigured by *Abraham's Sacrifice of Isaac* and *Moses Lifts Up the Serpent* (John 3.14; Num. 21.8–9).

The texts vary in style. Each of the three scenes in a group has a rhythmical caption (*titulus*). These can be subtle; for example, one *Temptation of Eve* has *Vipera vim perdit sine vi pariente puella*: 'the serpent loses power, a virgin bearing without labour' (with a pun on *vipera/vi pariente*) anticipating Mary's antidote to Eve's disobedience. Four prophecies (*versus*) function at a deeper level, rooted in patristic* interpretation. Two prose lessons (*lectiones*) describe simpler relationships between types and antitype. Three pictures and nine texts make twelve units in a group. Some later manuscripts have text only. Book-openings are designed as wholes. Early versions carry four groups – 48 units – on each opening. This multiplicity of visual and verbal relationships implies skill and knowledge in the readership.

The simpler relationships are not naive. For example, one of the *lectiones* linking *Crucifixion* and *Moses Lifts Up the Serpent* reads:

According to Num. 21.4–8, when the Lord wanted to free from serpents the people whom the serpents had bitten, he instructed

Moses to make a brass serpent and hang it upon a stake so that whoever looked at it would be rid of serpents. The serpent, hung up and stared at by the people, signifies Christ on the Cross, whom every believing person who wishes to be rid of the serpent (that is, the devil) should gaze upon.

The serpent is both sin and Christ, as implied by the *titulus* for *Moses Lifts Up the Serpent*: 'The hurt are healed when they look at the serpent' refers both to the afflicted Jews and to contemplation of the Cross. One prophecy in the group, 'Can you capture Leviathan with a hook?' (Job 40.20), recalls the tradition in which Satan takes the bait of Christ's body on the 'hook' of the Cross, the fishing line being the long ancestry of Jesus listed in Matt. 1.

The author of *BP* is unknown. Attempts to attribute it to particular religious orders have been inconclusive. The lost original was probably made *c.* 1250. Most versions are Latin, others are Latin and German or German alone; Cornell and Schmidt knew 68 surviving manuscripts in three families, from Austria, Weimar and Bavaria. These vary in layout, number of groups, sequence, details of text and iconography.* The earliest (*c.* 1300) survives incomplete, from the Bavarian family. The earliest complete manuscripts extant are from the Austrian family: one is still in the St Florian monastery where it originated *c.* 1310. *BP* was widely distributed through German and French-speaking Europe. No manuscripts originating in Britain or France are known, although the largest handbook of typology* (not a picture-book) is English: the contemporary *Pictor in Carmine*.

Theories that *BP* was propaganda against Manichaeism are unproven. The persistent idea that it was a preachers' aid is fuelled by the prologue to the *Speculum Humanae Salvationis* (*SHS*), partly derived from *BP*, offering poor preachers unable to afford the whole book a summary to work from. *BP*'s beauty, internal logic, complexity and ownerships suggest use for devotional meditation among clergy and educated laity. Certainly this compendium of traditional imagery itself became, as did *SHS*, a pattern-book. It offers the modern reader a guide to much mediaeval art, including the typological glass at Chartres and elsewhere.

BP was among the earliest books printed; *c.* 1460 it was in blockbook form, with pictures and text in woodcut. Like some manuscripts, the blockbooks present 24 units – two groups – per opening. *BP* was subsequently produced by moveable type. Though typological pictures in books such as Bibles and Psalters were common by the twelfth century, *BP* is the earliest, most popular and longest-surviv-

ing illustrated book wholly employing typology.
See also **Art, The Bible in; Mediaeval Interpretation; Typology.**

Rainer Behrends, Konrad Kratzche and Heinz Mettke (eds), Biblia Pauperum Apocalypsis: *The Weimar MS. Fol. max. 4,* 1978; Henrik Cornell, *Biblia Pauperum,* 1925; Jean Daniélou, *Sacramentum Futuri: études sur les origines de la typologie biblique,* 1950; Avril Henry (ed.), *Biblia Pauperum: A Facsimile and Edition,* 1987; Gerhard Schmidt, *Die* Armenbibeln *des XIV. Jahrhunderts,* Veröffentlichungen des Institutes für österreichische Geschichtsforschung 19, 1959.

AVRIL HENRY

Biblical Criticism

Since the eighteenth century, it has been customary to divide biblical criticism into two branches: lower criticism, dealing with the text of the Bible, and higher criticism, dealing with the origin and compositional growth of the individual books. This division must be regarded as too simplistic, and therefore as unhelpful.

In one sense of the phrase, biblical criticism has been an integral part of scholarship for two thousand years, if by 'criticism' we mean the attempt to study the Bible as rational beings using all the linguistic, archaeological and historical data available. Josephus'* *Antiquities of the Jews* gives an account of OT history in terms dictated by the Graeco-Roman culture of his day. Rabbinic* Jewish scholarship recognized, and harmonized, many of the contradictions and discrepancies in the Hebrew Bible. Origen* sought to establish the correct text of the Hebrew Bible by comparing it with a number of translations into Greek. Eusebius* drew on the traditions of the early church in attempting to establish the provenance and authorship of the Gospels, and he compiled an *Onomasticon* which identified the places named in the Bible. Jerome mastered Hebrew and produced the standard Latin Bible (*see* **Vulgate**) of the church as well as treatises on the translation and interpretation of the Hebrew text which were constantly referred to for many hundreds of years. Augustine* wrestled with the seeming contradictions between the Bible and scientific knowledge, for example, that light was created before the sun (Gen. 1.3, 16), that there were giants before the Flood (Gen. 6.4) and that people lived to be over 900 years old before the Flood (Gen. 5.27).

In spite of this tradition of critical scholarship, which can be chronicled to modern times, it has become customary to divide scholarship into pre-critical and critical periods, with the change from the one to the other occurring somewhere in the eighteenth century. The difference between the two periods is that in the pre-critical period biblical interpretation was subservient to the doctrines of the various churches, whereas, during the critical period, scholars have refused to let religious orthodoxy set limits to the scope or the results of their enquiries.

The distinction between pre-critical and critical periods will be accepted as the basis for this article, although it must be stressed that the distinction is not satisfactory for several reasons. First, the transition to the critical period was not uniform or unanimous. It was in Germany that there emerged, from about the 1760s, a body of professional scholarship whose investigations into the Bible were not limited by doctrinal restraints. However, there was a strong reaction in Germany in the nineteenth century against unfettered criticism, which had considerable influence from 1830 to 1860. In Britain, the path to biblical criticism was prepared by the attacks on the OT by the deists* in the late seventeenth and early eighteenth centuries, without this leading to the establishment of a body of critical scholarship. It was not until the 1870s that British biblical scholars as a group began to accept the results of unfettered critical investigation. The same is true for North America (without the Deist phase), while in Holland, religious diversity from the seventeenth century enabled many individual scholars to make critical contributions. All this was in the area of Protestant biblical scholarship. The Roman Catholic Church remained hostile to biblical criticism until 1943, and Catholic critical scholarship has flourished only since the Second World War.

The second difficulty about the division pre-critical/critical is that it may obscure the fact that some pre-critical scholars were much more open to certain issues than the orthodox defenders of the Bible in the critical period. For example, Calvin,* in his commentary on Genesis, was ready to accept that the account of creation* in Gen. 1 was not meant to accord with scientific discoveries. It was, rather, a description of creation such as could be understood by a normal Israelite. To such an observer, the earth was stationary, and the moon looked larger than the planets. But Calvin accepted that with the aid of a telescope it could be seen that the planets were larger than the moon, which was not, therefore, strictly one of the two great lights (Gen. 1.16). However, Calvin's willingness to allow that Gen. 1 was not meant to be a scientific account of the origin of the world contrasts with the efforts of orthodox defenders of Genesis in Victorian Britain, for whom it was heresy to deny that Gen. 1 could be reconciled with their perception of the science of the day.

Granted the division of biblical criticism into a pre-critical and a critical period, the remainder of the article will describe the transition, its causes, and the problems that it entails.

The rise of biblical criticism. Six topics received prime attention as scholars began to take a critical stance towards the Bible. They were the relation of the OT and NT to each other, the authorship* of the books of the Bible, the morality of parts of the OT, the scope of the laws of Moses,* the difficulty of accepting accounts of miracles,* and the relation between Greek and Jewish Christianity* in the early church.

The main reason for the rise of biblical criticism was the severing of the link between the OT and NT, and the investigation of the former without regard to the latter. As long as the Bible was regarded as a unity, the OT had a theological agenda set by the NT: it recounted, in the Fall (Gen. 3), the condition of mankind (Adam*) which the second Adam (Christ) would redeem. It foresaw in Gen. 3.15 that the offspring of a woman would defeat Satan, and it provided a series of prophecies regarding the coming of a Messiah* who would die an atoning death. It described the establishment of an elect people from the time of Abel and of an elect nation from the time of Abraham,* the purpose of whose election would be fulfilled in Jesus Christ. Christ himself had appeared in veiled form in parts of the OT (cf. I Cor. 10.4) and had spoken in the first person in passages such as Prov. 8.22–30 and Ps. 22 and 109. The high-priestly ministry of Christ and his sacrificial death were anticipated by OT 'types'* in Leviticus and elsewhere. It must be stressed that much of this theological agenda for the OT was seen as clearly present in the NT, and that to sever the link between the two Testaments was a radical and far-reaching step.

The move towards taking this step was occasioned by that shift of perspective during the Enlightenment* in which the world ceased to be seen as a coherent order in which mankind had a clearly defined place. Instead, humanity occupied the centre of the stage, and human reason became the criterion according to which everything was to be judged. From this perspective, the OT was seen to fall far short of what enlightened reason expected of exemplary characters. Abraham had had intercourse with his wife's maid, Jacob had married two sisters, Joshua had exterminated whole populations and Jephthah had sacrificed his only daughter. Worst of all, David,* the supreme example of a king after God's heart and a 'type' of the forthcoming Messiah, had committed adultery and murder and had seen his children indulge in fratricide.

All these features of the narratives had, of course, long been recognized, but they had been justified or excused in various ways. What was new from the seventeenth century onwards was that individual writers no longer excused them, but used them as arguments for regarding the O T as the literature of an ancient oriental people rather than as a divine revelation. The motives of these writers varied. Pierre Bayle (1647–1706), whose article on David in his *Dictionnaire historique et critique* (1692–95) provoked a storm of protest, regarded himself as a Reformed believer; while in Britain, some of the Deist attacks on the O T in the late seventeenth and early eighteenth centuries were apparently veiled attacks upon the Anglican establishment, which had been justified by appeal to the example of reforming kings such as Hezekiah and Josiah. Other attacks were motivated by religious heterodoxy, as in the writings of the Socinians.

These moves did not in themselves establish biblical criticism as an accepted paradigm within an institutionalized body of scholarship. They helped to prize the O T away from the N T, and to stress its historical particularity. At best it became historical background for the N T and was only of value to Christians where its teaching approached that of the spirit of the N T.

While the bond between the two Testaments was being severed, traditional views of the authorship of the biblical books were being questioned. Thomas Hobbes in *Leviathan* (1651) argued that only internal biblical evidence for the authorship of books could be accepted, from which it followed that Genesis to Deuteronomy were written after the time of Moses. Benedict Spinoza, a tolerant Jew living in Holland, maintained in his *Tractatus Theologico-Politicus* (1676) that Ezra had written the Pentateuch* as well as Joshua, Judges, Samuel and Kings, while a French Catholic priest, Richard Simon (1638–1712), suggested that many biblical books received their final form from scribal* schools. This argument about the authorship of biblical books touched upon current beliefs about inspiration.* Especially in Protestant circles, God was believed to have directly inspired known individual writers such as Moses, Samuel, David, Solomon, and the prophets whose names their books bear. To question the traditional views of authorship of books was to question their status as divine revelation.

Another form of attack on the O T which prepared the way for biblical criticism was the questioning of stories of miraculous events. The Deist writer John Toland in his *Hodegus* (1720) interpreted the pillars of cloud and fire in the Israelite camp (Ex. 13.21–2) as an actual fire used by the people. The German Ori-

entalist H. S. Reimarus* went further in an article published posthumously in 1777. He argued that, in its present form, the account of 600,000 males over twenty, together with their families and flocks, leaving Egypt, was absurd. He also maintained that the story of the resurrection* of Jesus was invented by the disciples, who stole his body.

The shift to the acceptance of biblical criticism as a working paradigm for a body of scholarship occurred in Protestant Germany from about 1760. Scholars began freely to investigate the authorship of biblical books, and to divide books such as Genesis into distinct literary sources. During the late eighteenth century, suggestions were made that later became critical orthodoxy, e.g. that Isa. 40–55 was written in the sixth century, and that Zechariah and Daniel were not literary unities. At the beginning of the nineteenth century, W. M. L. de Wette* in his *Beiträge zur Einleitung in das Alte Testament* argued that the history of Israelite religion had in fact been different from that presented in the O T itself, and that Moses had not provided the Israelites with a fully-fledged sacrificial and priestly system. In studies published in 1831 and 1835, F. C. Baur of Tübingen* proposed a radical view of N T history, at the heart of which was a struggle between Jewish and Pauline Christianity, the reconciliation of which resulted in the emergence of the Catholic church in the second century (*see* **Early Catholicism**).

Main problems in biblical criticism. With the severing of the link between the O T and the N T, and with the study of the Bible freed from doctrinal limits, an acute question was raised: according to what principles or agenda is the Bible to be investigated? The answer that critical study is a value-free and objective scientific method is not satisfactory, because no academic discipline, however hard it tries to be objective, can be totally free from the pre-understanding of its practitioners. In actual fact, even in its so-called pre-critical period, biblical scholarship was deeply affected by the prevailing philosophies of the day, such as Neoplatonism, the rediscovery of Aristotle from the tenth century and the philosophical realism and nominalism of the thirteenth and sixteenth centuries. Those who try to disparage biblical criticism on the grounds that it is affected by a particular type of philosophy are either ignorant of the history of biblical scholarship or have not understood it.

The solution is to accept that it is inevitable that the agenda for biblical criticism will be set to some extent by prevailing philosophies and concerns, and to welcome this fact as showing that biblical scholarship is not a moribund discipline, and that the biblical text retains its power to illuminate quite fresh sets of questions when they are posed. Two positions are to be avoided: an attempt to return to a pre-critical mentality with limits set to what it is legitimate to suggest; and a dogmatic trust in the 'assured results of biblical criticism'. Both attitudes reduce the chances of reading the biblical text in new and fresh ways, ways which are legitimate as opposed to perverse interpretations.

If we accept that it is desirable that the agenda for biblical studies should be partly set by contemporary problems, we can see how there has been a meaningful dialogue between the text and the world of its interpreters in the past; and we shall be on our guard against yesterday's questions setting the agenda for today's interpretation. For example, it is perfectly understandable that late nineteenth-century Victorians facing the challenge of Darwinism should have chosen a developmentalist scheme into which to fit their approach to the Bible. S. R. Driver's commentary on Genesis (1904) was said to have saved the faith of his generation by reconciling Genesis with evolutionary thinking. However, there is no doubt that this sort of approach far outlasted its usefulness by becoming accepted as an 'assured result of biblical criticism'.

The past twenty years have seen many of the old 'assured results' radically questioned, although not in every case being overturned. The biggest single change has been the advent of structuralism,* a complex phenomenon common to many academic disciplines, and affecting biblical studies chiefly by encouraging interpreters to study the final form of biblical texts, in contrast to the older concern to trace the growth of texts from their smallest units to their finished form. Other items that have become prominent concerns are the social world of the early Christians, the social organization of early Israel (see **Sociology and Social Anthropology**), and the reading of biblical texts in the light of modern literary* theory, liberation theology* and feminist* concerns. Biblical criticism has probably never been more healthy, more creative and more diversified.

This fact raises two final questions that are of particular concern to committed members of Christian churches. If there are no limits on biblical criticism, what is to stop the method undermining faith altogether, and, are there no criteria for obtaining an authoritative interpretation of the Bible?

What follows can only be an individual attempt to answer these questions, no doubt coloured by the writer's prejudices. Answering the second question first, we can say that there are certain negative norms that must control interpretation. For example, no Hebrew or Greek word should be translated in a way that contradicts all linguistic evidence, and the same is true of larger units of meaning. Again, although texts can have meanings that go beyond what the author consciously intended, it would be illegitimate to interpret a biblical text in a way that flatly contradicted what was generally accepted as the author's intended meaning. At another level, it would be illegitimate to base claims about how we should pattern society today on models drawn from biblical history that are not accurate. Granted the existence of negative norms, biblical interpretation is not an attempt to derive and impose an authorized interpretation. It is a matter of creativity within an area bounded by negative norms.

This is a position which, hopefully, would be accepted by believers and non-believers alike. For believers, factors such as denominational allegiance come into play. Many Roman Catholics will feel that their church's traditional witness to the central claims of Christianity will provide a framework within which they can raise critical questions about the Bible. Anglicans have usually accepted biblical criticism along with a commitment to the incarnation of God in Christ, while the Free Church tradition has accommodated critical scholarship from the standpoint of justification by faith.

There can be no doubt, however, that biblical criticism still presents a problem for many church members, and that the critical method alone cannot meet the needs of a worshipping and witnessing community. The fact that critical scholarship is today self-critical and sensitive to its limitations should indicate that the time has never been more suitable for helping church members to see the value of a method which, whatever its weaknesses, has become the irreplaceable foundation for any serious interpretation of the Bible.

See also **Enlightenment; German Old Testament Scholarship.**

R. Morgan with J. Barton, *Biblical Interpretation*, 1988; J. Rogerson, C. Rowland, B. Lindars, *The Study and Use of the Bible*, 1987.

J. W. ROGERSON

Biblical Theology

This expression, first found in 1629, has its roots in Christian discussion, intensified by the Reformation,* of the relationship of theology to its biblical bases. Since the beginning of the nineteenth century, biblical theology has usually been written by biblical specialists and has accompanied a growing recognition that a linguistic, literary, and historical biblical scholarship can in principle be independent of doctrinal theology and may reach conclusions at variance with the Christian tradition. But the arguments about its character and scope belong within the larger debate about the methods of theology in an intellectual world that reads the Bible critically.

The development of modern biblical scholarship brought about a shift from its original meaning of 'theology that accords with the Bible' to 'the theology contained in the Bible', but both the prescriptive (theology should be biblical) and the more descriptive emphases usually implied some claim to the other. A faith and theology which find their critical norm in the Bible need both.

The phrase, however, is open to criticism, and has been discredited by failures to take seriously the theological diversity and the historical distance of the Bible. Attempts to draw modern theological answers from the Bible directly short-circuit both systematic theology* and biblical scholarship. Only when such inadequate proposals are repudiated can the concept (if not the phrase) be rehabilitated and religious interests in the Bible be given responsible guidance.

All Christian theology claims to accord with the Bible. How it should be biblical, and how biblical it should be, are questions of form as well as of content. The pietist theologians who in the seventeenth and eighteenth centuries used the phrase against Protestant scholasticism were claiming to recover the biblical character of Reformation theology. The same polemical implication, that contemporary theology was insufficiently biblical, and so insufficiently Christian, was present in nineteenth-century 'salvation-history'* theologies, and in more recent outbreaks of 'biblical theology'.

The label has thus often indicated a religiously motivated protest against the abstractions and compromises of academic theology. It has recalled the intellectual discipline to its religious springs. The Bible contains religion, not second-order theology, and a faith understood and theology expressed in biblical terms were expected to be more true to their religious character.

However legitimate this corrective has sometimes been, it cannot absolve a theology that makes truth-claims about reality as a whole from using the rational categories of its day. Theology cannot escape the tension between its claims to know God on a basis of revelation,* and the necessity of using rational categories to express and explicate this truth.

This ancient tension between revelation and reason was in the eighteenth century aggravated by modern rationalism's sense of the difference between tradition and revelation. This required a revolution in theological method and for some 200 years 'biblical theology' has been caught up in that revolution. A

religion that claims to rest on revelation depends on the past, i.e. on tradition, especially its scripture. But however indispensable it may be, if scripture is not itself revelation, its position is changed. Theology is no longer simply biblical interpretation, even if doing theology from the perspective of biblical study can be justified pragmatically by the scriptural status of the Bible. If these texts are to be used in religious ways (e.g. in preaching), some theological reflection which relates their meaning to the interpreter's own religious system is necessary.

Before they were undermined by modern rationalist criticism of the Bible and the new historical sensibility, Lutheran* and Calvinist* orthodoxy claimed to accord with the Bible, despite their Aristotelian form. They did so by producing 'collections' of 'proof-texts'*. These *dicta probantia* were some of the theological statements contained in the Bible, and provided the immediate background for the descriptive use of the phrase 'biblical theology' which became dominant when biblical scholarship was no longer so dependent on its relationship to dogmatics.

This development begins with J. P. Gabler's lecture 'On the proper distinction between biblical and dogmatic theology, and the specific objectives of each' (1787, ET 1980). Gabler insisted that the task of analysing the biblical data was historical in character, and to be clearly distinguished from the philosophical and theological task of articulating Christian belief in the present. Unlike earlier pietists and scholastics, the theologians of the Enlightenment* could no longer naively identify their own modern theology, however true to the biblical witness, with the theology or theologies contained in the Bible.

Gabler made some interesting suggestions about how to move from the latter to the former. These were not pursued, but the historical part of his project provided the agenda for biblical theology in the following century. This was first carried out by G. L. Bauer, who in 1800–2 followed the logic of the historical task by separating Old and New Testaments. Granted this historical distinction, a main problem for subsequent 'biblical theology' has been to explain the unity of the Bible. The difficulty of this task is reflected in the way the phrase has faded out of most critical biblical scholarship.

Despite his theological intentions, Gabler can be seen in restrospect to have pointed to a type of biblical studies not necessarily related to Christian faith and theology. The historical task is in principle independent of that. But the theological contexts in which biblical theologies of the OT and NT were written meant that the descriptive task was in practice still closely aligned to dogmatic theology and ethics.* Theological interests still guided the attempt to understand and communicate the theological content of the sacred writings.

As historical research revealed more sharply the differences between the biblical writers and also the strangeness of their ancient cultures, the tension between the modern interpreters' religious interests and their scholarly methods and results increased. Their use of modern doctrinal categories to analyse and interpret the ancient texts still provided conceptual bridges which helped modern readers find in the Bible vehicles of their own faith and understandings, but by the end of the century these bridges were becoming insecure at both ends. Liberal* theologians preferred psychological descriptions of their faith to empty dogmatic categories, and historians of religion judged these categories more or less inappropriate to the biblical material. Biblical theology was still written by conservative theologians, and used by many clergy, but the cutting edge of biblical scholarship was shifting to historical studies of Israelite, Jewish, and early Christian religion.

A residual idealism and romanticism connected most of this historical scholarship with the authors' own Protestant piety. But these links were shattered for the next generation by the catastrophe of the First World War. A new theology was needed to replace 'culture Protestantism', and a new biblical theology to relate the new theology to Christian study of the Bible. As in the Reformation crisis, it was Christian theological study of the Bible that itself generated a new theology, and so answered both needs simultaneously.

Karl Barth's* theological interpretation of *The Epistle to the Romans* (1919, ² 1921) was biblical theology in both senses, though on a limited front. His subsequent change of direction contained an admission that this prophetic note expressed only part of the biblical witness and was inevitably one-sided, but in certain respects it accorded with the biblical witness and communicated its message through a modern theology that used several biblical categories.

Barth's objection to normal biblical scholarship was that it did not sufficiently engage with the theological content of the Bible. His almost sermonic form of direct address (*Anrede*) embodied a religious claim that the true subject-matter of the Bible is the living God who may confront its hearers. It also contained a methodological suggestion that only a contemporary theology could communicate and mediate this encounter. The idealist synthesis which had previously made historical reconstruction a vehicle for theology was collapsing. Historical study of the Bible was no longer enough.

Barth's alternative approach contributed to the century's most influential synthesis of biblical scholarship and modern theology: Bultmann* combined the two meanings of biblical theology in his interpretations of Paul* and John, even if this limitation precluded his use of a phrase which emphasizes the theological unity of the whole Bible. But Barth's Calvinistic appreciation for the OT covenant,* and the element of biblicism that pervades his work, and his antipathy to liberal Protestantism, also spawned some less satisfactory proposals over the next 40 years, especially in the English-speaking world. These religiously meaningful wanderings labelled 'biblical theology' appear in retrospect to have been in an intellectual wilderness.

In England, Barth's influence was minimal. Hoskyns* translated his interpretation of *Romans* (1933), but even he was more influenced by Kittel and the word studies that led to the *Theological Dictionary* (1933–73). Biblical theologians such as L. S. Thornton and A. G. Hebert, and later A. M. Ramsey and A. Richardson, were doctrinal theologians rather than biblical scholars, and Phythian-Adams wrote more on the OT than the NT. H. H. Rowley followed in the steps of Wheeler Robinson, not Barth. Anglican writers found a theology of the people of God in the whole Bible, and their revival of the distinctively Christian symbols* in an ecclesial environment replaced the worn-out philosophical theology of the 1920s. Even typology* became briefly fashionable in some quarters.

In Scotland, the influence of Barth upon such Calvinist dogmaticians as J. K. S. Reid and T. F. Torrance was a factor, and in North America the banner was carried by such leading OT scholars as G. E. Wright, J. Bright and F. M. Cross, whose chief inspiration was the archaeologist W. F. Albright (*see* **American Interpretation**). American NT scholars were less affected, but Europeans such as C. H. Dodd* and the Mansons, and later O. Cullmann, were highly regarded in the movement. Replacing theology proper with biblical simplicities appealed to a strand of anti-intellectualism in some American religious life. It found support in Barth's sermons, his biblically coloured dogmatics, and his hostility to liberalism and natural theology, not in the philosophical and theological profundity of his *Romans*.

The 'movement', in its 1940s and 1950s form in North America, has been described by B. S. Childs and analysed by J. Barr. Similarities with older religious reactions against academic theology are apparent, in particular the evasion of the necessary engagement of theology with philosophy, and a preference for biblical categories, thought-forms, and slogans such as 'God who acts'. But it also drew selectively upon the previous century's critical scholarship. Some of its linguistic arguments, such as its sharp contrasts between Hebrew and Greek thinking, were flawed, and its attempt to isolate biblical thought from its cultural settings was unpersuasive. Its claims for history as the framework for revelation were bogus because the 'history' appealed to was not real history. Barth's biblicism had had a cutting edge under the emergency of fascism, but was implausible when viewed more critically. In academic circles, this ephemeral movement was by 1960 in a state of terminal decline.

Prior to that biblical theology had been especially popular in ecumenical circles, seeming to promise a basis for inter-Christian *rapprochement* and a revitalization of Christian proclamation. An entirely legitimate attention to the Christian symbol-system was allowed to become a substitute for systematic theology.

Its NT flagship was Cullmann's church-and-Israel-orientated theory of 'salvation-history', not Bultmann's combination of the liberals' tradition of historical scholarship with Barth's early kerygmatic* theology. This neglect of Bultmann's synthesis is intelligible in view of the movement's basic conservatism and the isolation of German theology during and after the Nazi period. But Bultmann's NT theology has proved the century's clearest attempt to combine the two related meanings of biblical theology.

Bultmann's reduction of the enterprise to an interpretation of two biblical witnesses does less than justice to the Christian Bible. But finding its unity in the Word* proclaimed, rather than in its doctrinal content or the history behind the text, proved suggestive to German Lutherans. This combination of modern kerygmatic theology with the new history of traditions* research could even be applied to the OT, as von Rad demonstrated. But the OT contained only pointers to the NT. A Christian biblical theology must find its centre in Jesus Christ crucified and risen, and this cannot be written from the standpoint of historically responsible OT scholarship.

Any unitary theology of the Bible reflecting its modern author's own theology will come into collision with historical knowledge. This can be avoided by accepting the two-stage model advocated by Krister Stendahl (1962), who distinguished the descriptive task of biblical historians from theologians' attempts to apply the biblical witness in their own time. The integrity of biblical scholarship depends on this distinction, and Christian theology has reasons for supporting a historical and exegetical* scholarship based on the grammatical meaning of the texts. A textually indeterminate scripture that could mean anything would mean nothing. But the two-stage model of scholarly exegesis followed by contemporary applications (found in *The Interpreters' Bible*) provides no guidance for moving from historical to theological judgments. The distinction is valid, but it does not solve the methodological* problems of Christians use of the Bible, with which biblical theology is concerned.

This avoidance of conflict between the historian and the believer, necessary as it is for the health of biblical scholarship and so of Christian theology, simply evades the task that the discipline has addressed: that of combining the rational insights of biblical scholarship and the religious interests of Christian theology. This is best done by recognizing that the two sides define the biblical subject-matter differently. Interpreters may draw insight from any quarter, but their own basic aims and interests must determine their frame of reference. If literature is their main interest, they will read the Bible finally as literature; if history, then as a collection of sources. Christian theologians, including those who are biblical specialists, and therefore linguists, historians, and students of literature, assume that the Bible speaks to them of God who is revealed in Jesus the messiah* and known in the Christian church. Their task is to interpret the biblical witnesses on this assumption without doing violence to the historical particularity of this diverse collection of texts. They use whatever rational methods will help them to understand these texts and so serve their religious aim. Such theologically motivated interpretations of individual texts and authors may be described as doing biblical theology, but not as writing *a* unitary biblical theology, much less *the* definitive biblical theology. They can exercise no coercive pressure on systematic theology, but if persuasive they may influence how the Bible is understood in the church, and so help shape Christian faith and theology. Some such experiments may be found in *Biblical Theology Bulletin* [1971–] and the Overtures in Biblical Theology series (1977–). The recent German revival of the genre, by contrast, with its *Jahrbuch für Biblische Theologie* (1986–) shows signs of reverting to the older biblicism.

See also **Theology (New Testament); Theology (Old Testament).**

B. S. Childs, *Biblical Theology in Crisis*, 1970; G. Ebeling, *Word and Faith*, 1963; W. J. Harrington, *The Path of Biblical Theology*, 1979; H.-J. Kraus, *Die Biblische Theologie*, 1970; H. Graf Reventlow, *Problems of Biblical Theology in the Twentieth Century*, 1987; J. D. Smart, *The Past, Present and Future of Biblical Theology*, 1979.

ROBERT MORGAN

Black Christian Interpretation

Black theology. Witvliet sees black theology as a liberation theology* and defines it thus: 'Liberation theology is a criticism of any theology* which in its method strives to be universally applicable and in so doing "forgets" that any reflection is always already part of a particular historical context.' 'Black theology criticizes the theological traditions (of the West) because of their benign neglect of black history and experience.' It 'criticizes the norms of the established schools'. Theology can thus no longer claim *bona fide* scholarship when it constantly overlooks black culture, religion and achievements. It is revealing, says James Cone, 'to note that during my nearly six years of residence at Garrett-Northwestern, not one text written by a black person was ever used as a required reading for a class.'

Black theology is resolutely situational. It takes into account the social and cultural background of the church in which it operates. That is why Karl Barth* started his *Church Dogmatics* with the sentence: 'Theology is a function of the church.' Since black theologians operate in the context of a black church, 'it is not illegitimate to suppose that in Cone's black theology perhaps for the first time in American theology Karl Barth is really accepted and incorporated' (Klauspeter Blaser).

Whether black theology is a true adaptation of Barth or not will probably remain controversial. Cone has much of the evidence on his side. In the case of Bonhoeffer the situation is even clearer. Forty years before any black theology appeared in print he wrote in his reports from America about the deep insights he got from the black Christians and that in his opinion if one wanted to hear the gospel one had to listen to their songs, their prayers, their preaching, and not to the mainline American churches.

Black theology was born in the crucible of suffering. In their spirituals black people expressed their despair and their hope of a coming liberation. One very important ingredient of this black tradition was the 'subterranean stream' of their African heritage. This is not only seen in the vocabulary of Caribbean English but also in the rites of indigenous churches and syncretistic folk religion in the Caribbean, as also in their beliefs in ghosts, ancestors, and the healing powers of their priests, both female and male (Mulrain). Above all it is seen in the oral structure of their liturgies and theologies. An oral theology is a theology which focusses on the parable* not the proposition, on the song not the systematic theology,* on dances and dreams and

not on definitions. For clarifying controversial issues, the common banquet, the eucharist, is more important than the concept. Where the African influence is strong their historiography is oral, their tradition is based on their faithfulness to the ancestors who are believed to be present in their services (*communio sanctorum*).

Until recently these topics were hardly ever treated in theological works by either black or white. They remained the preserve of anthropologists* and historians of culture. That is now changing rapidly. In Europe, however, only the political side of an emerging black theology has been noticed because it is thought that this type of black theology can easily be accommodated into a European Marxist* theology. Nothing is further from the truth. Karl Marx was not a black theologian but a German Hegelian philosopher! Whilst his insights into the interrelation between ideology* and economic/political power will probably continue to be helpful in all theological debate (and as such have still to be fully digested on both sides of the Atlantic) many of his other contributions do not apply to black theology, mainly because he underrated the transformative power of biblical tradition.

African theology. John Mbiti describes Christianity 'as an indigenous, traditional and African religion'. Some might consider this to be an over-statement. Nevertheless in a sense it is perfectly true. A number of the major teachers and fathers of Western Christianity were Africans (Tertullian,* Augustine,* Origen*). They wrote their works in European languages but some scholars suggest that they preached, spoke and thought as well in their respective mother tongues.

Contemporary African theologians are beginning to speak and write in European languages but retain their roots in their respective African cultures and tongues. That is of the utmost importance. They are bi-lingual theologians, at home both in the literary world of the West and in the oral world of Africa.

In the wake of the modern missionary movement the African church was landed with a 'foreign, prefabricated theology which has not grown out of the living Church in Africa' (All Africa Conference of Churches, 1963). Theology in Africa is still mainly done in a 'hothouse'. It is a pale copy of Western theology which can only survive with subsidies and experts from abroad. Many are the complaints of African theologians about the problems of this imported theology.

An African theology must be structurally an oral theology. That does not prevent it from being written since most of the biblical material is written 'oral theology', as form criticism* has amply shown. Furthermore it must take up the issue of the status and value of pre-Christian African traditions. It has to deal with healing (through traditional healers, through prophets of the Independent Churches and in healing liturgies of the mainline churches), with the place of visions and dreams in Christian theology (dreams and visions play an important psycho-hygienic role and are often responsible for conversions of first-generation Christians); and above all it must address itself to the complex issue of dependence on Western capital, know-how and theology.

British black theology. In Britain black theology is less developed. Roswith Gerloff (a German Lutheran), Bongani Mazibuko (a South African Methodist), Patrick Kalilombe (an African Roman Catholic bishop and scholar), John Wilkinson (a British Anglican), Iain MacRobert (a Scottish Protestant), and others have – in cooperation with the Department of Theology at the University of Birmingham – worked for many years at shaping a British black theology. Their methodology* was to start with the tradition of the numerous black Christians: about 900 black congregations in Britain and a very sizeable number of black Christians in Anglican, Methodist and Seventh-Day Adventist churches. The problem is made more difficult than elsewhere for two reasons. 1. Black Christians in Britain have inherited a fundamentalist* ideology; however, underneath the rationalistic borrowed formulation lies hidden a black experience. A white theologian takes the overt meaning of these well-known formulas for the real meaning. When a black person says for example 'I am saved', he or she means salvation for body, soul and mind. That is why for black Christians the societal dimension of the gospel is not disputed. However, the white borrowed American ideology hides and suffocates these insights. 2. In spite of a very large British black constituency, no 'indigenous' black theologian has so far been appointed by any theological institution in Britain. So the dearly-needed scholarly analysis and reformulation of this type of theology is still wanting. A start is being made by a number of black, British-born, post-graduate students at Birmingham University who study the centrality of worship for their theology, the preaching style of black preachers, the place of women in black churches and the African roots of their spirituality. But this is only a drop in the ocean.

The problem of black biblical scholarship. Biblical scholarship must at least fulfil two requirements: a thorough knowledge of biblical languages and backgrounds and an ability to translate the biblical message into the vernacular. As to the first requirement, black

theologians are only recently entering this field of scholarship. As to the second, most black theologians know their vernacular well because they are trained and nurtured in the traditions and cultures of their communities. Unfortunately this type of African scholarship almost never reaches the white community because our biblical scholars generally do not know African languages. So we have to be content with second best, namely its presentation in English (or French, Spanish or Portuguese) by African or Caribbean scholars. 'Language is more than syntax and morphology; it is a vehicle for assuming the weight of a culture. Therefore, this attempt to construct an African theology in the English language is second best, even if it is convenient that it should secure as wide a circulation as possible' (John Pobee).

In the USA, in the English-speaking Caribbean and in Britain black scholars are beginning to operate in and to respect their vernacular English which was until recently considered to be inferior to standard English. But the calypsos, the lyrics of the Rastafarians and above all the spirituals of the American negroes have shown that these are languages, although different from British or American English, which are capable of theological expression. Examples of this are Michael Tippett's masterly use of spirituals in his oratorio *A Child of Our Time* and James Baldwin's use of this tradition in his *Go Tell It On The Mountain*. It is not an inferior form of English, it is simply a different form of English.

John Pobee gives some useful guidelines for an emerging African exegetical tradition. First and foremost he states that biblical criticism* and the historical-critical method* should be taken seriously: 'This method represents the most thorough-going application of a naturalistic historicism to the study of the Bible. It assumes that biblical religion, in both the Old and New Testament, passed through stages of growth and evolution like all ancient religions, and in this evolution was heavily influenced through interaction with its religious environment. This method involves the consistent application of the principle of analogy to biblical religion: the history and development of biblical religion must be analogous to the history and development of other ancient religions.' He adds, however, one point of difference: whereas the *religionsgeschichtliche Methode* (see **History of Religions School**) refuses to be interested in the truth of the Bible or in revelation,* students of African theology should be interested in the truth of the various revelations that confront them in their situation. Further, by taking seriously the non-Jewish sources in the OT and the non-Christian sources in the NT, the biblical texts become case studies for the handling of pre-Christian and non-Christian material. To interpret symbols,* myths,* rites, visions, dreams and stories of one's own pre-Christian tradition is not something that one learns by applying some general principles. One learns it rather in the way one learns to play the violin. One is taught by a real master of the violin. The theologically responsible interpretation of non-Christian material is learned from the masters and models of such interpretation, i.e. the biblical authors. They show us the difference between a theologically responsible and a theologically irresponsible syncretism. A biblically-informed syncretism does not accept pre-Christian traditions because it has learned from the biblical authors how to handle such material responsibly.

Secondly, says John Pobee, black exegesis has to be ecumenical. In Western biblical scholarship the classical denominational differences are receding. This will be even more the case in black exegesis. These denominational differences will be replaced by the legitimate differences between black and white exegesis* – a development which will make clear to black and white that exegesis is, in spite of its academic rigour, co-determined by the questions and the needs of the community in which it operates. Black doctoral candidates in the biblical field have so far received little encouragement to develop their specific exegetical approaches. This might be partly responsible for the lack of specifically black exegetical research.

Finally, such research could become beneficial for Western scholarship. The separation of Western biblical scholarship from the questions and needs of the church has been criticized many a time by concerned scholars in the USA and Europe. White European and American exegetes could learn from their black counterparts that they have to become bilingual if they want to fulfil both requirements of biblical scholarship. They have to master the oral tools they need not only for understanding the pre-literary stages of the biblical texts but also in order effectively to communicate their critical insights to the church at large which badly needs critical information. This has to be done in a form which is understandable and relevant to the theologically largely oral constituencies even of our Western churches. In re-oralizing critical scholarship Hans-Ruedi Weber (a Bible study expert with the WCC) and Theo Vogt (a Swiss Bible study expert working mainly in adult education) have pioneered this type of work which places exegesis again where it belongs, namely in the middle of the Christian community.

See also **Liberation Theology; Other Faiths; Sociology and Social Anthropology.**

Kofi Appiah-Kubi and Sergio Torres (eds), *African Theology en Route. Papers from the Pan-African Conference of Third World Theologians 1977 in Accra, Ghana,* 1979; James Cone, *The Spirituals and the Blues. An Interpretation,* 1972; Kwezi Dickson, *Theology in Africa,* 1984; W. J. Hollenweger (ed.), *Pentecostal Research in Europe: Problems, Promises and People,* 1989; Iain MacRobert, *The Black Roots and White Racism of Early Pentecostalism in the USA,* 1987; John Mbiti, *Bible and Theology in African Christianity,* 1986; George M. Mulrain, *Theology in Folk Culture,* 1984; John Parratt (ed.), *A Reader in African Christian Theology,* 1987; Hans-Ruedi Weber, *Experiments with Bible Study,* 1981; Theo Witvliet, *The Way of the Black Messiah,* 1987.

W. J. HOLLENWEGER

Blake, W.

William Blake (1757–1827) is probably the most original interpreter of the Bible. His genius militates against all predictable and preconceived notions of exegesis. Though one can learn from Blake one cannot imitate him. He offers no systematic or coherent method. Blake is primarily a visionary whose gifts are artistic: acquired scholarship does not touch him, though his knowledge of traditional sources never fails. Dante,* Milton and many other poets and philosophers challenged Blake to contemplate the revealed and revealing truth. He scorned Reason as such, but he is never unreasonable. He has no use for church, sacraments, and priests, yet he is not a revolutionary bent upon destruction. His individualism is not anti-social and his humanitarianism cannot be dismissed as anti-Christian. His *The Everlasting Gospel* takes the reader into the very centre of his unique christology. He is a pioneer of the multi-dimensional understanding of religion, but Jesus remains still at the centre of his questioning: What did Jesus look like? Was he gentle? Was he humble? Was he chaste? Did he teach doubt? Was he born of a pure virgin? Was he unique? According to Blake the forgiveness of sins points to the answer.

Blake's interpretation of the Bible cannot be conveyed in words alone. The enquirer will even prefer to follow the visionary by seeing for himself. Blake's original works can be seen in London in the Tate Gallery, the Victoria and Albert Museum, the British Museum; and in the USA in Boston, New York, Philadelphia, Washington, and Yale. The relevant subjects covered are: God Creating the Universe, the Creation of Adam, Ruth, Christ's Resurrection, A Cycle of the Life of Christ, Life of Moses, Job, The Last Judgment. Numerous art books give a splendid representation of the originals.

Vision is Blake's key to inspiration. Unless you see the scriptural content inwardly and outwardly as a fruit of the imagination there can be no interpretation at all. The poet is not interested in historical minutiae, a reconstruction of the past or a moralizing reductionism. He is not beyond changing the biblical texts to suit his purposes which feed into a complex mythology that is prophetic in its denunciatory power. His eschatology* is balanced by neo-Platonic, Gnostic,* Cabbalistic and heterodox influences. But though Man is fallen, and the human universe approaches disintegration, Blake has visions of man's wholeness and salvation.

The Marriage of Heaven and Hell (1790–93) reflects something of the wild spirit of the times, but it also displays Blake's talent for drawing upon the Bible to express radical philosophy: 'Without Contraries is no progression. Attraction and Repulsion, Reason and Energy, Love and Hate, are necessary to Human existence.' He wants to blend Heaven and Hell and destroy the alleged biblical convention of a sterile monotheism. There is something almost Nietzschean in early Blake with his contempt for those 'who restrain desire' because they are weak. Jesus plays a very odd part in the struggle which is expressed in powerful verse. A sequence of *Memorable Fancy* allows Blake to speak to Isaiah and Ezekiel to probe questions of inspiration and authority. A 'Printing House in Hell' consists of mythological chambers in which angels and devils whir about in fantastic exchanges. Opposing principles – 'grinning and kissing; plucking and devouring' – derive from the Bible, one from Heaven, the other from Hell.

The very long *Jerusalem* is a song in four chapters which retains the passion of biblical inspiration without the crazy outbursts. Blake worked at it between 1804 and 1820; the 100 plates of relief etching are in private collections in England and the USA. This epic has the basic theme of the passage from sleep in this world through eternal death to the awakening of eternal life. Biblical passages of events and portraits of men and women are not interpreted for their own sake, but integrated into a symbolic structure together with mythological material. But, most striking, at least for the British reader, is the personification of Albion and the identification of the homeland with Jerusalem.* Again 'Jesus our Lord', God of Fire and of Love, is central to Salvation, a freeing from the existent bondage, the loss of Wisdom, Art, and Science: 'Nations are destroyed or flourish in proportion as their Poetry, Painting and Music are destroyed or flourish.'

The interpretation of Blake and of his use of the Bible is harder than any interpretation of the Bible itself (although the modern reader is familiar with paradox and cryptic allusions). For example 'Los' entering 'the Door of Death for Albion's sake' denounces 'half friendship' as the 'bitterest enmity', and this eccentric composition is juxtaposed with 'Judgment' and Man's Redemption through Christ. A key to salvation from total despair is found in Los, the poetic principle and emanation from it. Identification is creative interpretation; hence the forty counties of England come under the headings of the tribes of Israel. But identification is more than geographical: all human forms aspire to and attain to the Heaven's gate, 'built in Jerusalem's wall'.

The theme of Jerusalem is better known from the preface to *Milton*: 'And did those feet in ancient time walk upon England's mountains green . . .' Here there is no obscurity. The 'holy Lamb of God' and 'the pleasant pastures' confront the 'dark Satanic mills' with the militant call for the 'bow of burning gold', 'arrows of desire', with the prophetic 'I' universalizing the fight for Jerusalem in the biblical tradition. The *Songs of Innocence* celebrate the Divine Image, whereas the *Songs of Experience* show the 'Two contrary States of the Human Soul' with a simplicity which surpasses most Christian interpretations.

See also **Art, The Bible in**; **Poetry, English.**

Complete Writings of William Blake ed. Geoffrey Keynes, 1974; Jacob Bronowski, *William Blake*, 1972; S. F. Damon, *A Blake Dictionary*, 1965; J. G. Davies, *Theology of William Blake*, 1948; Kathleen Raine, *Blake and Tradition*, 1968; J. Wicksteed, *Commentary*, 1954.

ULRICH SIMON

Bultmann, R.

Rudolf Karl Bultmann (1884–1976) was a pupil of Wilhelm Herrmann in systematic theology,* and of Gunkel, J. Weiss, and Heitmüller (*see* **History of Religions School**). He inherited that school's journal and monograph series, and succeeded Bousset in Giessen (1920) and Heitmüller at Marburg (1921–51), where he became the commanding figure in twentieth-century NT scholarship and hermeneutical* theology.

His first masterpiece was the form-critical* classic, *The History of the Synoptic Tradition* (1921, ET 1963, revd 1968). It followed the history of traditions* approach to the Synoptic* Gospels pioneered by Wrede* and Wellhausen as well as the form criticism of Gunkel and Weiss, and gave Bultmann his reputation for historical scepticism. His critical roots were also plain as he followed Reitzenstein and Bousset in postulating a gnostic* background to the Fourth Gospel (1925) and in a later popular survey *Primitive Christianity* (1949, ET 1956) subtitled 'in the framework of ancient religions'.

In 1922 he attached himself theologically with some reservations to the neo-Reformation or 'dialectical' theology of Barth* and Gogarten, and over the following five years developed his own existentialist form of that kerygmatic* theology. The essays in *Faith and Understanding* I (1933, ET 1969) and *The Beginnings of Dialectical Theology* (1967, ET 1968) show him reaching his final theological position during this period. Unlike his liberal* predecessors, but (in his and Barth's opinion) like St Paul* and Martin Kähler, Bultmann was not much interested in the historical Jesus* 'according to the flesh' (cf. II Cor. 5.16), beyond the 'mere *that*' of his actual existence and crucifixion. The introduction to *Jesus and the Word* (1926, ET 1934) develops Herrmann's proto-existentialist theology with the help of Dilthey's existentialist historiography, and towards the end of this crucial period a younger colleague, the phenomenologist Martin Heidegger, was helping him find a philosophically clarified conceptuality for expressing what the NT teaches about human existence confronted with God.

As a Lutheran preacher and NT teacher in a theological faculty training future clergy to preach, Bultmann aimed to do theology, i.e. articulate his Christian faith responsibly, in and through his interpretation of the NT. Linguistic, literary, and above all historical study provided the necessary scholarly means of understanding texts the normative significance of which could be assumed within the Christian church. But whereas Barth insisted on 'utter loyalty' to the text being interpreted, i.e. uncritical acceptance, Bultmann saw the theological interpreter's duty as also to assess its adequacy to the intended subject-matter, i.e. to the Christian gospel, and if necessary to criticize it (*see* **Sachkritik**). These principles received sharpest expression in his essay on 'The New Testament and Mythology' (1941, ET 1953, revd 1984) which led to the 'demythologizing'* controversy. For Bultmann the central issue was not the concept of myth* or modernity, but the theological necessity of a critical interpretation. For his more serious opponents it was the legitimacy of a reductionist interpretation which in effect eliminated whatever aspects of the Christian tradition did not correspond to the interpreter's own 'pre-understanding' (*Vorverständnis*) of the subject-matter.

Bultmann's view of this theological subject-matter was clearly stated in 'What does it mean to speak of God?' (1925, reprinted in *Faith and Understanding*). For Marburg neo-

Kantians like Herrmann and Bultmann, God cannot be objectified; we can only talk of God in and through our talk of human existence. The cosmological language of myth must therefore be translated into categories describing human existence, most helpfully provided by Heidegger in *Being and Time* (1927, ET 1962), though as a kerygmatic theologian Bultmann insisted that any transfer from the old to the new self-understanding of faith, from inauthentic to authentic existence, occurred in obedient response to the Christian proclamation.

The hermeneutical form in which this modern existentialist theology is presented as a reading or interpretation of the NT is clarified in 'The Problem of a Theological Exegesis of the New Testament' (1925, ET 1968, excerpted in R. Johnson, 1987). It is also summarized in the 'Epilogue' to *The Theology of the New Testament*, Vol. 2 (1953, ET 1955). The theory of interpretation invoked is elaborated in 'The Problem of Hermeneutics' (1950, ET 1955, retranslated Ogden 1985).

In view of its hermeneutical form, Bultmann's own theology is to be found in his actual interpretation of the two NT writers whom he reckons as theologians since they speak of God by speaking of human existence: Paul* and John. His anthropologically-orientated account of Pauline theology was sketched in an encyclopaedia article of 1930 (ET in *Existence and Faith*, 1961) and presented in detail in *The Theology of the New Testament*, Vol. 1 (1948, ET 1952). Because Paul places such weight on his anthropological (flesh, body, mind, conscience, heart, sin, death, world) and his soteriological* concepts, and because 'every assertion about God is simultaneously an assertion about man and vice versa' (p. 191), it is possible to present Pauline theology as a theological anthropology: 'Man prior to the revelation of faith' and 'Man under faith', an analysis of human existence bisected by the Christian proclamation or 'kerygma' which makes possible the new self-understanding. Christology* is cast in the same soteriological mould, because Paul does not speculate about Christ's 'natures' but speaks of him as the one through whom God is working for the salvation of the world and man (ibid.).

The section on John in *TDNT* Vol. 2 (1951, ET 1955) summarizes the theological interpretation already presented in his greatest work, the Meyer commentary* of 1941 (ET 1971). The incarnation is here understood in Kierkegaardian terms of the paradoxical identity of Jesus with God, the historical with the eschatological* event, and faith as a decision when confronted by the word. Jesus reveals nothing about himself except that he is the

Revealer, and the hearer is challenged as an individual to understand himself or herself in a new way, no longer dependent upon the world for security, but entirely on God. The key Johannine concepts are shown to refer to human existence understood in relation to God's eschatological self-revelation in Jesus. 'Theological propositions – even those of the New Testament – can never be the object of faith; they can only be the explication of the understanding which is inherent in faith itself' (pp. 237f.).

This interpretation is fused with some earlier literary and history of religions hypotheses which have proved only very partially persuasive. Of its source-critical theories only the 'signs-source' has found much support, and the hypothesis of a pre-Christian gnostic redeemer myth Christianized by the evangelist, who thus demythologizes or interprets existentially his tradition, is not widely accepted outside Germany. Bultmann further thought that an 'ecclesiastical redactor' had added references to the sacraments and futurist eschatology in order to make the work correspond to general Christian belief, and he also proposed extensive rearrangement of the narrative and discourses to remedy presumed dislocations. The result is a higher degree of consistency than in its canonical form the Gospel possesses.

In these and many other scholarly discussions published in the Meyer commentary on *The Johannine Epistles* (1967, ET 1973), a torso on II Corinthians (1976, ET 1985), 27 articles in Kittel's *TDNT* (including those on truth, knowledge, hope, life, death, faith), and numerous influential articles and reviews, Bultmann maintained and advanced the great nineteenth-century tradition of German critical scholarship into which he had entered by his doctoral dissertation on *Der Stil der paulinischen Predigt und die kynisch-stoische Diatribe* (1910), begun under J. Weiss, and his Habilitationsschrift (or qualifying thesis) suggested by Jülicher, *Die Exegese des Theodor von Mopsuestia* (1912, published 1984). But his chief significance is as the master of NT theology who, after the First World War, combined Barth's theological retrieval of scripture with the climax of the historical movement in Western theology, achieved by the older liberals and especially the history of religions school. The theological construction involved in this is partly visible in his *Theologische Enzyclopädie* (1984), mostly written between 1926 and 1936.

That combination of history of traditions research (including form and some redactional criticism) with a kerygmatic theology which owed much to Luther* was continued by his most influential students, Käsemann, Bornkamm, Conzelmann, Fuchs, and Ebeling,

strongly though they challenged his stance on the historical Jesus, and for two decades after the Second World War Bultmann dominated much German Protestant university theology. But the limitations of doing theology exclusively as scriptural interpretation became evident in the more socially engaged theologies of the 1960s. Weaknesses in Bultmann's own position have also been generally recognized. His interpretation of the NT devalued major witnesses other than Paul and John, especially the synoptic evangelists;* it obscured the centrality of christology for Christianity, underestimated salvation history,* the institutional church, life in Christ, the sacraments, and the future hope. But these criticisms were made and corrections introduced without abandoning his approach to theological interpretation. More fundamental opposition to his project by conservative church leaders led to a minor synodical condemnation in 1949 during the demythologizing controversy, but this has in effect been retracted, and Bultmann is now widely venerated as a teacher of the church. On the other side his project is ignored by biblical scholars who have no theological interests. It is preserved in a diluted form by some evangelical and Roman Catholic theologians, but now requires rethinking in the literary and sociological categories implied by the keyword 'interpretation'.

See also **Form Criticism; Historical Jesus.**

G. Ebeling, *Theology and Proclamation*, 1962, ET 1966; R. Johnson, *Rudolf Bultmann: Interpreting Faith for the Modern Era*, 1987; S. Ogden (tr. and ed.), *New Testament and Mythology and Other Basic Writings*, 1985; W. Schmithals, *An Introduction to the Theology of Rudolf Bultmann*, 1967, ET 1968; A. C. Thiselton, *The Two Horizons*, 1980.

ROBERT MORGAN

Cadbury, H. J.

Henry Joel Cadbury (1883–1974) was an American Quaker who wrote extensively on Quaker history and took an active part in Quaker philanthropic activity. His main life's work, however, was in the field of NT studies (especially Luke–Acts) which he taught, chiefly at Bryn Mawr and at Harvard where he was Hollis Professor of Divinity.

His first major contribution, in 1920, based on his profound linguistic and philological* learning, was to challenge effectively the previously widespread view that the vocabulary of Luke–Acts had a distinctively medical colouring such as might betoken authorship* by a doctor. The same skills underlay his detailed commentary on Luke 1.1–4 (*The Beginnings of Christianity*, vol. ii) which had the important result – though it was not stressed by him – of helping to release the interpretation of

Luke–Acts from the dominance of the idea that it was written by an eye-witness of Paul's* ministry. Combined with an almost encyclopaedic knowledge of the Graeco-Roman world, this sort of learning also enabled him to clarify the meaning of Acts at many points, notably in the commentary in vol. iv of *The Beginnings of Christianity* and in a series of magisterial notes in vol. v. It also made him an invaluable member of the team which produced the RSV translation* of the Bible, a project on which he spent a great deal of time.

He wrote the first account of form criticism* in English and was the first English-speaking scholar to employ the method in the elucidation of the Gospels,* as he did in his *Making of Luke–Acts* in 1927. The book was extremely influential, the more so because Cadbury went beyond the form critics and gave much attention to 'the psychology of authorship', i.e. how Luke as an author selected and edited his material in such a way as to suggest a particular interpretation of the events he recounted. However, at this time, as always, he was on his guard against over-schematization. It seemed to him that in Luke, as little as in Mark, 'is there any thorough-going theological theory that permeates the whole narrative; and many things remain that a single unified theory would hardly have . . . left unexpurgated'. In a series of important articles (never, unfortunately, collected in book form) he pointed to many incidental interests which sometimes led NT writers to include somewhat tangential material in their books. This means that modern scholars must beware of claiming greater architectonic unity for NT books than they in fact exhibit. Some more recent literary and redaction critics would have seemed to him to claim a greater degree of homogeneity in the texts they study than the facts warrant.

The same suspicion of over-tidiness was manifest in two more popular but important and unduly neglected books on Jesus published in 1937 and 1947. Cadbury rejected as anachronistic the idea that Jesus will have worked out an over-all plan for a 'ministry', and he doubted whether 'the kingdom of God'* was ever a single thought-out concept which unified the 'ministry' in the way suggested by R. Otto and C. H. Dodd.* The current use of the term kerygma* he disliked, not only because it involved the misuse of an active noun, but because he felt its use dissembled the great variety of views put forward in the NT, a variety of which he was very much aware long before his time.

The main concern in the books on Jesus, however, was with 'the peril of modernizing' him. In the interest of presenting him as a figure acceptable to the modern world, Cadbury felt, Jesus was often unjustifiably credited with an impossible degree of uniqueness and with other characteristics admired today but not evidenced by the sources. Even in the case of Jesus' teaching, it was how he taught rather than what he taught that Cadbury found interesting. He noted the absence from the Gospel accounts of Jesus' teaching 'of any references . . . to the altruistic motive . . . The deserts or welfare of the other party hardly figure at all.' It is other concerns, notably our own best interests, which are given prominence.

Cadbury was convinced that the evidence is too sparse to permit any full or confident reconstruction of the figure of Jesus; and even had it been otherwise, his lively awareness of the centuries of cultural change separating us from biblical times prevented his believing that we can nowadays adopt biblical patterns of thought as they stand, or establish a first-century teacher as a direct legislator for twentieth-century problems. As will be evident, he was suspicious of movements such as Barth's* which thought to discover one central message (kerygma) in an unjustifiably homogenized NT and then make it authoritative for modern believers. He could understand why the churches were tempted to seek external authority when threatened by secularism and totalitarianism, but he found no difficulty in resisting the temptation himself. He always refrained from justifying his own conduct, e.g. his pacifism, by any literal or legalistic appeal to the words or example of Jesus, feeling, as he used to say, that we may find relevant clues in the Bible but not blueprints. He has in fact been criticized for distinguishing too sharply between fundamental historical data and 'theology', between facts* and interpretation.

If Cadbury made no major contribution to the debate about how the 'relevant clues' are to be interpreted and a modern faith extracted from the Bible, that was for a number of reasons. Apart from the fact that his professional research and his Quaker good works left little time for anything else, he was by temperament something of a bubble-pricker, and his abundant, but slightly wry, sense of humour allowed him to be content with a primarily negative contribution, especially at a time when he felt that many were guilty of what he regarded as loose generalizations and illegitimate short-cuts to modern applications. Yet personally he was anything but negative, and no doubt his stance was a matter of conviction, associated with his Quaker heritage. As a Quaker on the liberal wing of the Society he was inclined to rely on the inner light rather than to look to external authorities; and like Jesus as he reconstructed him, he was content with a religion which linked closely with general human thinking and motivation at their best, and happy to get sufficient light for present action without looking for an all-unifying theological vision. 'He did not ask to see the distant scene; one step enough for him.'

Such figures do not make theological heroes, and Cadbury's work is undoubtedly undervalued and too little known.

See also **American Interpretation; Cultural Relativism.**

M. H. Bacon, Let This Life Speak: The Legacy of Henry Joel Cadbury, 1987 (with full bibliography); Anna Brinton (ed.), Then and Now: Quaker Essays, 1960; see especially the essay by Mary Hoxie Jones; H. J. Cadbury, The Peril of Modernizing Jesus, 1937; Jesus: What Manner of Man?, 1947.

D. E. NINEHAM

Calendars

Modern scholars discuss at length such problems as the existence in Israel of solar and lunar calendars and the relation between them, the origin of the week and the Sabbath, the period when the year began and many other questions; and on several of these matters there is no agreed consensus. Nor is this situation in any way new. The Bible itself witnesses to the existence of various different systems of time-reckoning, reflecting several periods of historical development, and to attempts to order and harmonize them. In particular, the question of the proper calendar came to assume great significance in post-exilic Judaism and led to bitter disputes. The second century BC pseudepigraphical* Book of Jubilees has an exclusively solar calendar and attacks the official lunar one, while its adoption of a similar calendar to that of Jubilees was one reason why the Qumran community broke with the Jerusalem priesthood (see **Dead Sea Scrolls**). Hence the establishment of a definitive calendar was a vital question for the survival of Judaism after AD 70 and detailed attention was devoted to it in rabbinic* legislation, such as the Mishnah and the Talmud.*

The reason why the calendar was viewed as so important was because of its religious significance. Its primary purpose was to specify the occasions on which the great festivals were to be celebrated, and so all the clearly defined calendars in the Bible are cultic* documents. There are a number of these in the OT, and by comparing them it is possible to trace a process of re-interpretation and amplification, corresponding to developments in Israel's religion. It is generally agreed that the basic text

is Ex. 23.14–17, which ordains that all male Israelites are to go on a sacrificial pilgrimage to the sanctuary three times a year. These three occasions clearly mark key points in the agricultural year: the barley harvest, the wheat harvest and the grape harvest, and the fact that the month in which the first occurs has the Canaanite name Abib, 'ripe ear of grain', suggests that they were taken over from the Canaanite population. It is noteworthy that no precise days are laid down for the celebrations, since agricultural operations, because of the vagaries of the climate, could not be precisely fixed. The purpose of all these festivals would be to dedicate the different crops to God by giving him a representative part, thus releasing the remainder for human use.

However, this passage raises two problems of direct relevance to the Hebrew calendar. First, the third feast, Ingathering, is said to take place 'at the going out of the year'. Much debate has centred on whether this phrase denotes the end or the beginning of the year; if the latter, it could be maintained that one aspect of the feast was that of a New Year festival, but in either case it would point to a year commencing in the autumn. But, secondly, it is the feast of unleavened bread which is elsewhere dated in the first month, indicating that the year began in the spring. Scholars are divided as to whether this reflects a later development, when a spring new year was introduced, probably late in the monarchical period, under the influence of the Babylonian calendar; or whether it represents the original Hebrew practice, the autumn new year being the result of post-settlement Canaanite influence, or possibly that there was a double new year observance. What can safely be said is that the lunar month is the basis of Israelite time reckoning, and that the autumn new year festival was standard in pre-exilic times. This usage has continued in Judaism, with rosh hashanah (lit. 'head of the year') being observed in the autumn. Alongside this, the Babylonian calendar, beginning the year in spring, came into use after the exile, when, in addition to the month numbers, the Babylonian month names, e.g. Nisan for Abib, were adopted, a process only completed in rabbinic times.

The remaining festal calendars develop Ex. 23.14–17 in a number of significant ways. There is a decreasing emphasis on the original agricultural connotations of the feasts, and the sacrificial rites are viewed as occasions of homage and thanksgiving to Yahweh. So, the calendar of Deut. 16.1–17 no longer has them celebrated at the local sanctuaries of the farming community but centralizes them at the sole national sanctuary, Jerusalem, and views them as expressions of thanksgiving for the divine bounty. In Lev. 23, the festivals are 'holy assemblies' and are assimilated to the Sabbath, as periods when no work is to be done. Again, in these later texts, the feasts become essentially commemorations of events in Israel's normative sacred history. In Deuteronomy's calendar – it would seem for the first time – the feast of unleavened bread is united with the Passover and its purpose is that the Israelites may remember the day when they came out of Egypt, while in Leviticus the dwelling in booths at the autumn celebration, originally the huts where the harvest labourers dwelt, becomes a similar reminder of Israel's nomadic existence in the wilderness: it may be noted that in Jubilees and at Qumran the feast of weeks is understood as the renewal of the Sinai covenant.* Further, the calendars become increasingly complex as they expand on ever more detailed ceremonial regulations and include celebrations, often long established ones, in addition to the three main traditional feasts. This is seen most strikingly in the elaborate sacrificial directions of the calendar in Num. 28.16–29.39, which includes both the offerings for every day of the year and also, following on from Leviticus, those for the Day of Atonement and other observances in the seventh month.

Other ritual calendar patterns are to be found in the OT, notably the calendar systems culminating in the Sabbath and Jubilee years. The increasing importance of the religious calendar in post-exilic Judaism is also shown by the way in which what are probably ancient rites are added to it and, as with the three traditional feasts, given a new interpretation as commemorations of great interventions of God in history. Such is the case with Purim, of which the book of Esther can be described as the 'festal legend',* and Hanukkah, the institution of which is described in I Macc. 4.36–39. Not only Jubilees, but several other apocryphal* and pseudepigraphical writings, such as II Esdras, the Apocalypse of Baruch and the Secrets of Enoch, are concerned with interpreting the Jewish religious calendar; and its influence has been claimed as a decisive factor in the composition of parts of the NT.

J. Finegan, *Handbook of Biblical Chronology*, 1964, pp. 29–57; T. H. Gaster, *Purim and Hanukkah in Custom and Tradition*, 1950; J. van Goudoever, *Biblical Calendars*, ²1961; R. North, *Sociology of the Biblical Jubilee*, 1954; R. de Vaux, *Ancient Israel: its Life and Institutions*, 1961, pp. 178–94, 468–74.

J. R. PORTER

Calvin

1. *Sola scriptura*. Among the Reformers of the sixteenth century John Calvin (1509–1564)

is unrivalled as the theologian who made a sustained effort to apply the new theological insights of Reformation* theology to the task of biblical exegesis.* In his *Commentaries** he covered almost the complete NT canon and the majority of books of the OT. The exegetical principles employed in carrying out this immense task, as well as his actual practice of interpretation, proved to be highly influential for the development of biblical studies in the post-Reformation era.

It is a common-place of our understanding of church history that the primacy of the Bible as the supreme authority* for faith, doctrine and life is one of the main tenets of the Reformation. One can, however, wonder whether this view of the priority of scripture over all other authorities, usually summarized in the formula *sola scriptura*, is sufficient to characterize the common foundation of the theology of the Reformers as distinct from the theology of their predecessors and the thought of their contemporaries. Thomas Aquinas could be cited as one of the theologians of the scholastic tradition who emphasized that scripture has primary authority for church doctrine, in the sense that the teaching of the church may not affirm anything that is not contained in the Bible and that its authority has to be clearly distinguished from that of the Fathers and the church. On the other hand, it might seem that the Reformers' insistence on using the Bible in its original language for their exegetical work is nothing but the theological version of the general humanist programme of a return to the authentic sources.

The Reformers' view of the Bible is clearly shaped by their theological convictions, which they claim to have gained from the study of the Bible. The Bible is the primary authority in the church because it mediates the Word of God* as the gospel of salvation in Christ. By means of the word of scripture as the message of God's action in Israel and in Christ, which is authenticated as life-giving truth by the Spirit, God calls human beings to faith and constitutes the church as the creature of the divine Word. Therefore the Bible becomes the critical and constructive principle for assessing claims to authority in the church. All other authorities have to be seen as secondary, since their authority is derived from the authority of the Word of God as it is mediated through the word of scripture. In order to give the Bible this central place in the life of the church, it is, first of all, required to study it in its original languages so that the authentic witness to God's action is not in any way distorted. Secondly, it is necessary to make the Bible accessible to all believers so that they can encounter God's promise of grace independent of the alienating claims of an ecclesiastical hierarchy.

The full theological significance of the *sola scriptura* principle can be grasped only if it is taken together with the other two programmatic notions of Reformation theology: *sola fide*, the assertion that faith alone is sufficient for the justification of the sinner without being supported by meritorious moral and religious works; and *solo Christo*, the thesis that Christ alone is the source of salvation, whose efficacy does not depend on the mediation of the church or a specific office in the church. These soteriological* convictions can clarify what distinguishes the Reformers' view of the Bible from that of their scholastic predecessors and their humanist contemporaries. They also help to explain why the sixteenth century became the 'century of the Bible'. At its beginning only a privileged few could use the Bible in the inadequate Latin translation of the Vulgate,* whereas at its end almost every affluent household in Europe could possess a Bible in its own language, based on reliable editions of the original text.

2. *Calvin's theology of scripture.* Although the *sola scriptura* principle points to the common ground in the Reformers' understanding of scripture, this should not disguise the distinctiveness of their respective approaches to the theology of the Word of God and to the practice of biblical interpretation. Calvin's understanding of biblical exegesis is based on Luther's theology of the Word of God and developed against the back-drop of an intimate knowledge of the theory and practice of biblical interpretation of other Reformation theologians. His view of the significance of scripture for the task of theology is presented in the first book of the *Institutes of the Christian Religion*. There is, according to Calvin, a sense of the Divine in human nature, but after the Fall it is so submerged that only the light of scripture can grant certain knowledge of God and ourselves. The ultimate proof of the authority of scripture is that God himself addresses us in the biblical documents (*Inst.* I, 7, 1). But this does not lead Calvin to a simple equation of scripture with the Word of God, which would see the Bible as possessing a supernatural quality that guarantees its character as a sacrosanct depository of divine truths. As the means by which God communicates truth to fallible human minds, the word of scripture can become the Word of God when God authenticates the witness of the biblical authors by the testimony of the Holy Spirit. Just as God is the only reliable witness to himself, so the word of scripture can only find faith in human hearts if it is sealed by the Holy Spirit (*Inst.* I, 7, 4). The Spirit who inspired the biblical writers must also authenticate the biblical message for anyone trying to understand it today. It is God's sovereign grace to use the witness of scripture authenticated by the internal testimony of the Spirit to address human beings (*Inst.* II, 2, 21). With this description of the relationship of the word of scripture and the internal testimony of the Spirit, Calvin rejects both the contemporary Roman doctrine that the authority of the church guarantees the authority of scripture and the view of parts of the enthusiastic left wing of the Reformation that the Spirit mediates truth independently of the word of scripture.

3. *Calvin's exegetical work.* The *Institutes*, the first edition of which (1536) was written in connection with the anti-reform policy of King Francis I of France as a defence of Reformed faith against the accusation of creating public unrest, was in its later editions intended to provide an introduction and guideline to the study of scripture for theological students. In the 'Epistle to the Reader' in the second edition (1539), Calvin declared that in his exegetical writings he would not digress into doctrinal discussions, having treated these issues in the *Institutes*. This is a clear indication that after completing the *Institutes*, Calvin saw his primary literary task as the exposition of scripture. It also highlights Calvin's intention not to overburden the task of biblical interpretation through extensive doctrinal debates, which could lead to a selective treatment of the biblical writings and to the introduction of problems alien to the original intention of the biblical authors.

Between 1539 and 1551, Calvin completed the commentaries on the N T epistles. The commentary on Romans was finished in 1539, I Corinthians 1546, II Corinthians (first published in French) 1547. The other epistles followed in rapid succession. Between 1553 and 1557 Calvin published an exposition of John's Gospel, a commentary in two parts on Acts, and a harmony of the Synoptic Gospels. Around 1550, Calvin began to work on the interpretation of the O T. After he had finished revising the complete edition of the Pauline Epistles in 1557, he devoted his exegetical work entirely to the O T.

When Calvin first came to Geneva in 1536, he had been appointed as a biblical lecturer before he was entrusted with the task of a pastor, and he continued lecturing in Geneva, as well as in Strasbourg during his period of exile 1538–1541, till the end of his life. While the lectures provided useful background material for the N T commentaries, the O T commentaries after 1551 are to a large extent transcripts of lectures. In addition to lectures and sermons, the scriptures were expounded in Geneva in the Congrégations, weekly assemblies where the ministers took turns in interpreting biblical books. After 1549, one can establish connections between the books discussed in these meetings and Calvin's commentaries.

In his exegesis Calvin made extensive use of the scholarly knowledge available at his time, ranging from intimate acquaintance with Greek and Hebrew to geography, history, medicine and philosophy. This approach is part of the legacy of the Humanists, but Calvin has a specific theological justification for it. Since the Spirit of God is the source of all truth, ignoring or refuting the truth when we encounter it amounts to a rejection of the Spirit. Calvin's use of contemporary learning is, however, seldom uncritical. This is documented by his judicious use of the Greek text for his exposition. Up to 1548 he probably used Simon de Colines' edition of the NT of 1534 as his working text. It was then replaced by the 1527 edition of Erasmus' * Novum Testamentum omne. His working texts, however, never had indubitable authority, and Calvin came in many places to diverging decisions which he supported from other contemporary editions.

4. *Principles of biblical interpretation.* Contrary to the Humanists and to other Reformers, Calvin avoided lengthy comments about the principles and methods of biblical interpretation. The main source for his views is the dedicatory letter to Simon Grynée, which is used as the preface to Romans. According to Calvin, the chief virtue of the interpreter is *perspicua brevitas*, clear brevity. This is not just a rejection of the verbosity and prolixity which Calvin saw in the commentaries of some of his contemporaries. Rather, it emphasizes the necessity that the clarity of the exposition must mirror the fundamental clarity of scripture. Calvin remained a firm advocate of the view of the clarity of scripture, which Luther * had defended against Erasmus * of Rotterdam's assumption that the obscure passages of scripture are in need of the clarifying interpretation of the church and of moral philosophy. In this sense the principle of clear brevity is for Calvin the means of gaining access to the mind of the biblical writer (*mens auctoris*), which can only be discovered by investigating the literal* sense (*sensus grammaticus, sensus simplex*, etc.) of scripture. Calvin understood language as the *character mentis*, the imprint of the mind, and therefore it is the supreme means of access to the author's intention. In order to do justice to the mind of the writer, it is not only necessary to investigate the forms of expression as meticulously as possible, but also to pay careful attention to the historical circumstances of a given text (*Inst.* IV, 16, 13) and to the context of a passage (*Inst.* III, 17, 14). Following the guide line of the genuine sense in its

original historical and literary context, Calvin not only reconstructs the cultic setting of certain psalms, but also rejects the christological * interpretation of Gen. 3.15 as being irreconcilable with the original Hebrew.

Calvin already employed many of these exegetical principles in his commentary on Seneca's *De clementia* (1532); but in the context of his theology of revelation * they acquire a new significance. Calvin's concept of revelation is consistently trinitarian. The whole of scripture witnesses to the self-disclosure of the Father through the Son in the Spirit, and this applies to the OT as well as to the NT. Their content is different not in substance, but in form (*Inst.* II. 10, 2). Whereas the OT reveals God the Son in the guise of prophetic * foreshadowing, the NT is the clear manifestation of Christ (*Inst.* II. 9.2). Calvin's exegetical guide-line of trying to penetrate through the language to the mind of the original author functions as an important restriction on a premature christological interpretation of the Hebrew scriptures. The events of the Old Covenant are types for the coming of Christ under the New Covenant. But their typological * meaning depends on their literal meaning, since God has ordained the history of Israel to point to the clear manifestation of Christ who is nevertheless already present in the events of Israel's history. Calvin's commitment to what he understood as the genuine sense in both the OT and the NT could arguably do more justice to the authentic meaning of the Hebrew scriptures than the dialectics of law and gospel employed by contemporary Lutheran theologians. It has, however, been one of the main targets of Lutheran criticism, which is presented in its most radical, but also rather simplistic form in A. Hunnius' *Calvinus Judaizans* (*Calvin the Judaizer, or Judaistic Glosses and Corruptions in expounding Testimonies in Holy Scripture on the Trinity*) (1593).

5. *Calvin and biblical interpretation in the modern era.* With his insistence that discovering the intention of the author is the crucial principle of biblical interpretation and that this requires paying close attention to linguistic expression as well as to historical circumstances and literary context, Calvin was a major influence on the development of modern exegetical scholarship. In Calvin's work these exegetical principles were part of a theological framework where the disclosure of the truth of scripture depends on the internal testimony of the Holy Spirit illuminating the reader, so that he can recognize the truth that is originally constituted through the inspiration of the author and is communicated through his human words. The subtlety of Calvin's approach was partially lost when, at

the turn of the sixteenth to the seventeenth century, a theory of the verbal inerrancy of scripture was developed in Reformed theology (first by Amandus Polanus), which identified God directly as the author of scripture and obscured Calvin's original distinction and relationship between the word of scripture and the Word of God. The Enlightenment* rediscovered Calvin's exegetical principles but divorced them from their theological framework, by replacing the internal testimony of the Holy Spirit with the autonomous judgment of natural reason. In the present situation, where the separation of historical and literary investigation and theological interpretation is increasingly experienced as a crisis of biblical interpretation, Calvin's attempt at integrating both tasks can claim continuing relevance.

See also **Reformation.**

John Murray, *Calvin on Scripture and Divine Sovereignty*, 1979; T. H. L. Parker, *Calvin's New Testament Commentaries*, 1971; id., *Calvin's Old Testament Commentaries*, 1986.

C. SCHWÖBEL

Canon

1. *Introduction.* By the canon of scripture is meant the official list, recognized by the church, of the books of the OT and NT, or in Judaism the list of the books of the Hebrew Bible. Christian communions differ somewhat in their canons of the OT. In the churches of the Reformation,* only the books of the Hebrew Bible are regarded as canonical in the strict sense: OT books extant only in Greek (such as the Wisdom of Solomon or Tobit) are called apocryphal,* and appear in a separate appendix to the Bible; whereas the Orthodox and Catholic churches include these books in their OT, though Catholics refer to them as 'deutero-canonical'. In addition to this, there are a few minor differences between the Greek and Latin forms of the OT, and the Ethiopian tradition also includes the books of Enoch and Jubilees (*see* **Pseudepigrapha**), which are uncanonical for all other Christians. There is now no disagreement about the contents of the NT.

Scholarly study of the origins and development of the canon has not altogether kept pace with the study of the individual biblical books. In the nineteenth century much important work was done at both levels, but in the present century biblical scholars have shown more enthusiasm for studying the growth of individual books (and, indeed, the components out of which they are made) than for investigating the process by which the whole collection came to be regarded as authoritative in Christianity and Judaism. Almost any Intro-

duction* to the OT will show how study of the separate books has pulled ahead of study of the canon, for the latter is usually considered only in a short concluding chapter. Works on NT introduction commonly contain nothing at all on the process of canonization. Increasingly, biblical study has come to mean study of the period within which the biblical books were written, and the history of their reception in the various religious communities that use them has been seen as part of church history or of the history of Judaism. Most major studies of the formation of the Bible as a whole have accordingly been written by church historians. Only in the last decade has an interest in the canonization of scripture come to the forefront of biblical scholarship through such movements as 'canonical criticism',* and even here the interest has been in the theological implications for the church of possessing an officially defined scripture, rather than in the history of its formation.

2. *History.* Neither Christianity nor Judaism has traditionally been aware that the canon had a history. In each Christian communion, for example, a text such as II Tim. 3.16 ('All scripture is inspired by God and profitable for teaching, for reproof, for correction, and for training in righteousness') has been assumed to refer to whichever books that communion recognizes as scripture: the possibility that the author of II Tim. might have had a different 'canon' in mind has simply not been considered. (In fact it is clear that 'scripture' for him can only have meant Jewish scripture, but even so there is no way of telling from this text that he reckoned as scriptural exactly those books that now form the Hebrew Bible.) Where Christians or Jews have been aware that there were disputes in earlier times about which books should be regarded as canonical, these have traditionally been seen as disputes between truth and error, not as part of a creative process by which the identity of scripture was established. Thus at the Reformation the debates between Catholics and Protestants over the status of the 'Apocrypha' were commonly debates about its divine inspiration,* not historical investigations into the process by which it had come to be accepted in the church.

Nevertheless, thoughtful Jews and Christians had long seen that the Bible was a collection of rather disparate books rather than a single work, and had speculated about the means by which it had been assembled. In the fifteenth century the Jewish scholar Elias Levita (1469–1549) suggested that Ezra was responsible for settling the contents of the Hebrew Bible, and both Jews and Christians generally adopted this suggestion. The commonest interpretation of the NT among Christians has always been that it is, directly or indirectly, the writings of 'the apostles', which in turn implies that the books in it selected themselves for inclusion; the idea that anyone compiled it has not generally been an option in Christian thinking. But it was known even before modern scholarship that some of the books in the NT gained acceptance some long time after the death of the apostles, and in particular that the Western church had long debated the apostolic status of Hebrews, and the Eastern church that of Revelation. Thus neither Judaism nor Christianity has traditionally seen the Bible as a book dropped from heaven, or dictated to one person at a single moment. This sense that the Bible is a library of books rather than a single work has never been quite submerged, however strongly some traditions (especially in the Protestant orthodoxy of the post-Reformation period) have stressed its unity and unique divine inspiration. Thus it has been possible for modern scholarship to set about investigating in detail the complex process by which 'the books' (*ta biblia*) became 'the Bible'.

The greatest advances in understanding this process came at the end of the nineteenth century. Modern discussion of the OT canon may be said to begin with the work of H. E. Ryle, *The Canon of the Old Testament*, 1892. The NT canon was the subject of three major works from about the same time: Theodor Zahn, *Geschichte des neutestamentlichen Kanons*, 1888–92; B. F. Westcott, *A General Survey of the History of the Canon of the New Testament*, 1889; and, a little later, A. von Harnack,* *The Origin of the New Testament*, 1925, from the German of 1914. The common ground in all these works was the realization that the Bible was a collection of works which had not for the most part been written in order to be 'scripture', but had gradually acquired authority within Judaism and/or Christianity and had become scripture through favourable reception, dissemination, and eventual collection and 'canonization'.

A breakthrough in study of the OT canon was the suggestion that the three 'divisions' of the Hebrew Bible (Law, Prophets* and Writings*) represented successive stages in its canonization. The Law (Pentateuch*) became fully authoritative as early as the time of Ezra, and the Prophets were closed by the second century BC, while the Writings remained fluid until the end of the first Christian century. The last point was felt to explain the apparent disputes about the status of certain books in the rabbinic academy at Jamnia (Yavneh), reported in the Mishnah (Yadaim 3.5) (*see* **Talmud**). Recent scholarship has rightly doubted whether there was a formal 'council of Jamnia' which ruled on questions of canoni-

city, but has continued to accept that the third division of the Hebrew Bible was as yet unfinished as late as AD 100.

From Ryle onwards, scholars have also attempted to explain the greater compass of the Greek OT as compared with the Hebrew. Until the 1960s, this was usually accounted for by arguing that it represented the canon of Alexandrian Jewry, the shorter Hebrew canon being the Bible of (more conservative) Palestinian Jews. For Protestants this theory had the advantage of making it still relatively easy to defend the Reformers' insistence on excluding the 'apocryphal' or deutero-canonical books from the OT, since it was possible to claim that the 'Palestinian canon' was older and thus more 'original'. A serious challenge to this came in A. C. Sundberg's study *The Old Testament of the Early Church*, 1964, which went further than previous studies in stressing the fluidity of the OT canon in the first century AD. Sundberg suggested that the Writings had remained open until well into the Christian era, and that the shorter Hebrew and longer Greek canons resulted from decisions made as late as the second or third centuries AD by Jews and Christians respectively. The Hebrew canon thus had no greater claim to authenticity than the Greek: scripture for all Jews in the first century was still 'a wide religious literature without definite bounds'. Furthermore, in the early church there was never a Christian canon of the OT which omitted the deutero-canonical books. Not until the work of Jerome and Augustine* in the fourth century did the church begin to wonder whether the shorter Hebrew canon should be adopted, and then on the very assumption that Sundberg was now questioning – the assumption that the Hebrew canon was older and more 'authentic'. Recent studies have sought either to re-establish the traditional consensus (thus S. Leiman, *The Canonization of Hebrew Scripture: The Talmudic and Midrashic Evidence*, 1976, and R. T. Beckwith, *The Old Testament Canon of the New Testament Church*, 1986) or else to extend Sundberg's theory so as to ask whether *any* part of the Bible, apart from the Torah, can be regarded as 'closed' in NT times (see J. Barton, *Oracles of God: Perceptions of Ancient Prophecy in Israel after the Exile*, 1986).

The history of the NT canon is rather less controversial. All modern studies agree that the church was quite slow to recognize any Christian writings as 'scripture' in the same sense as the older Jewish scriptures, and that many books attained canonical status only after lengthy debate. St John's Gospel, for example, was frequently quoted by gnostic* groups in the second century to support their own distinctive doctrines, and so sometimes regarded by Catholic Christians as of doubtful authority. The diversity of the four Gospels,* and the discrepancies especially between the three Synoptics* and John, were widely perceived as a problem, and various more or less artificial devices were needed to ensure that all four would be accepted on equal terms. Thus Irenaeus* in the late second century argued that four distinct witnesses were needed to the gospel, and appealed in support of this to the four beasts of Ezek. 1 (which came to supply the symbolic figures for the evangelists in later Christian iconography*) and to the four points of the compass. The 'Muratorian Fragment', which most scholars believe to come from the end of the second or the beginning of the third century, insists (surely polemically) that John agrees in essentials with the other Gospels, despite its apparent differences. By this time the church was clearly having to cope as best it could with a situation where the Gospels had ceased to be local versions of the gospel story and had all come to be accepted by all Christians, even though they told stories that were at many points mutually incompatible. In a similar way the Pauline* letters were coming to be treated as universal in scope despite their obviously local reference, and various hermeneutical* schemes were tried to reduce their particularity. Thus we find the theory that Paul (like the seer of Revelation) had written to seven churches in order to show symbolically that his message was intended for Christians everywhere – seven being a sacred number signifying completeness.

Such arguments, as many scholars have stressed, indicate how accidental and occasional the growth of a Christian scripture really was. Their very artificiality makes it clear that Christian writers were having to struggle with a scripture which no one had deliberately compiled according to any definite principles. According to the very influential theory of Adolf von Harnack,* the church would never have begun to codify its scriptures at all if the first steps towards a Christian canon had not been taken by the heretic Marcion* in the second century. Marcion held a gnostic system of thought in which Christianity had nothing in common with Judaism, and since this necessarily meant rejecting Jewish scripture, his followers felt the need of a Christian scripture to put in its place. This they found in an expurgated version of the Pauline corpus and the Gospel of Luke (purged of all OT quotations). Faced with the Marcionite challenge, so Harnack maintained, the church had had no option but to produce an alternative 'canon' of Christian writings, and in the process to concede that such writings did indeed have the status of 'scripture'.

Among recent scholars, Hans von Campenhausen (*The Formation of the Christian Bible*, 1972, from the German of 1968) has taken up and modified Harnack's thesis. Others have preferred to argue that Christianity would in any case have felt the need for its own scripture as it moved away from its Jewish roots. Most would probably recognize a variety of factors in the formation of the NT canon; its very untidiness is a pointer to the many stages through which it passed. Recently controversy has centred on the date of the Muratorian list. Many still defend the traditional date, but A. C. Sundberg ('Canon Muratori: A Fourth Century List', *Harvard Theological Review* 66, 1973, pp. 1–41) has argued that it is much later, and thus that the NT canon (like that of the OT, on his interpretation of that) formed more slowly and uncertainly than is usually thought. Certainly the earliest undisputed list containing exactly the present twenty-seven books is in the Festal Letter of Athanasius for 367. But even after this, large segments of the church had quite different ideas. The Syrian* church, for example, continued to use Tatian's *Diatessaron*, a harmony of the Gospels, in preference to the 'four-fold Gospel' of our NT, and ignored the shorter 'Catholic Epistles' such as II and III John and II Peter. An excellent survey of recent discussion can be found in Harry Y. Gamble, *The New Testament Canon: its Making and Meaning*, 1985.

3. *Some issues in the discussion of the canon.* (a) Historical study of the process by which the biblical canon formed has tended to stress two elements: the random or haphazard way that Jews and Christians came to have a scripture, and the importance of tradition in determining which books were eventually accepted.

The first element has caused difficulties for high doctrines of scriptural inspiration, by making it hard to maintain a clear line between 'inspired' and 'non-inspired' works. The factors that led the church or the synagogue to 'canonize' particular works were very diverse, and the inherent quality or value of a book seems to have been only one among a variety of factors. The importance of tradition is also clear: the biblical books are not self-authenticating, and it was their reception over a long period in Judaism or Christianity that resulted in their eventual inclusion in the canon. Especially in the case of the NT, canon studies have highlighted the fact that the earliest Christians managed to transmit and to teach the gospel without any official Christian scriptures different from those of Judaism, and moved only gradually towards codifying their own distinctive literature. Christianity continued to be passed on in many Christian communities, such as the Syrian, through a canon that diverged very widely from that of the mainline Eastern and Western churches.

All this tends to support the Catholic position that the Christian faith is not wholly contained in scripture, but exists before and alongside the scriptural witness to it; and the modern study of the canon has accordingly been perceived by many as tending to undermine the *sola scriptura* principle of Protestant orthodoxy. Put in another way, it may be said that the study of the canon is one important area in which Protestant and Catholic scholars have found themselves united in a way that makes traditional confessional differences hard to sustain. This is part of the ecumenical thrust of modern biblical and historical scholarship.

(b) The word 'canon' (from Greek *kanōn* = rule, standard) itself has perhaps introduced some problems into Christian and Jewish discussion of scripture. The word is not found in its modern sense before the mid-fourth century. Earlier references to the Christian canon use it to mean a standard of faith or life, as the Latin translation *regula fidei* ('rule of faith') makes clear. Judaism has no term equivalent to 'canonical', though in modern Judaism the term has been borrowed from Christian usage. Rabbinic* literature speaks of certain books as 'defiling the hands', a term whose exact meaning is unclear, but which seems to refer to scriptural books considered as physical objects rather than to their content (for example, a translation even of the Pentateuch* does not 'defile the hands'). Again, the term 'canonization' leads a modern reader to look for a conscious decision (perhaps by an ecclesiastical council) which is lacking for all but a few biblical books: for most of the books in the Bible became canonical by long use and widespread acceptance, not by a formal ruling. Only at the margins of the canon did Christians or Jews solemnly resolve disputes about the status of the books. No one ever 'canonized', in this strong sense, the book of Genesis or the Gospel according to Matthew.

Some writers use 'canon' as simply equivalent to 'scripture', but there seems a lot to be said for using the two terms in distinct ways. A community may have scriptures without any sense that they form a closed and defined corpus, and in NT times it now seems clear that scripture did not yet form a closed 'canon' for either Jews or Christians. On the distinction between scripture and canon, see the important discussion by James Barr in *Holy Scripture: Canon, Authority, Criticism*, 1984.

(c) The wide religious literature from which the canonical scriptures of the OT and NT were eventually drawn contained many works that seemed to their first readers just as significant, perhaps even just as divinely inspired, as those that eventually became canonical. Modern scholarship has come to regard such works as important for the historical task of reconstructing the life and religion of Jews and Christians in biblical times. In the day-to-day work of biblical scholarship, it makes little if any practical difference whether a given book is part of canonical scripture; what matters is chiefly its date, provenance, and meaning. Thus in practice biblical scholars need to be familiar with many works from the so-called 'intertestamental' period – not only the Apocrypha, but pseudepigrapha such as I Enoch, Jubilees, or the *Genesis Apocryphon*, and many of the non-biblical texts from Qumran (*see* **Dead Sea Scrolls**) – and with early Christian writings such as the apocryphal gospels, the Didache, and the letters of Ignatius. Modern biblical scholarship is essentially a descriptive discipline, and the religious status attributed to the canonical works cannot be confused with the question of their historical importance. However much the canon continues to matter for faith, therefore, it has become less and less important in professional biblical study. This in turn reinforces the ecumenical convergence of biblical scholars. At least until very recently, it could have been said that the canon had become somewhat marginal in biblical scholarship – a fact which perhaps helps to explain, though it does not justify, the neglect of canon studies noted at the beginning.

(d) On the other hand, the last decade has seen the canon placed back at the centre of biblical studies, largely through the work of J. A. Sanders and B. S. Childs. These scholars in different ways have argued that the exegete should be guided, not by the historically reconstructive style of traditional critical scholarship, but by the religious concerns that led the church to canonize certain of its writings rather than others. This movement, widely known as 'canonical criticism',* is discussed elsewhere; but its importance for canon studies should be noted here. Even from a historical point of view it may be said that the canonizing process is more important than most scholars in the twentieth century have believed. Though it may be an exaggeration to claim that the 'canonical shaping' (Childs) of the biblical materials is the *only* valid subject for biblical interpretation, it cannot be denied that in fixing the biblical books in a certain order and restricting them to the present limited list, Jewish and Christian communities were imposing some hermeneutical constraints upon the texts. 'The canon itself is a locus of meaning' (Gamble, op. cit., p. 79). The arrangement of the Hebrew scriptures into Law, Prophets, and Writings, or of the NT into Gospels, Acts, Epistles,* and Apocalypse had a profound effect on the way all the individual texts came to be read. Though this arrangement was in part accidental, it also included elements of design. While it may reasonably be said that the study of such phenomena belongs to the province of church historians or historians of Judaism rather than to biblical scholars, there is no good reason why biblical scholars should avoid the subject. In any case, the period of the reception of some of the Jewish and Christian scriptures overlaps with that in which others were still being written, so that no absolute separation of the two concerns is possible. Study of the canon may well return to the central place in theological scholarship that it occupied a century ago, and it could prove to be a fruitful unifying interest for biblical scholars, church historians, students of Judaism, systematic theologians, and literary critics.

In addition to works cited in the text see B. S. Childs, *Introduction to the Old Testament as Scripture*, 1979; F. V. Filson, *Which Books Belong in the Bible?*, 1957.

JOHN BARTON

Canonical Criticism

The origins of canonical criticism are to be found in the school of thought known as biblical theology.* The adherents of this school, recognizing that an intolerable gap had opened up between the concerns of academic biblical scholarship and the needs of the churches, sought to use the 'historical' character of the Bible as a mode of interpretation. This gave scholarly respectability to the notion that theology is history, but at the same time tied that notion to a set of scientific disciplines which have since proved antagonistic to the theological enterprise which patronized them. The last twenty years in near eastern history (*see* **Ancient Near Eastern World**) and archaeology* have seen the amassing of evidence which has seriously undermined confidence in the historicity of the Bible – a process which was already well under way by the late 1960s, and which was even then calling in question the belief that God is revealed in history. Out of this situation there emerged, in 1970, a now famous study, *Biblical Theology in Crisis*, by Brevard S. Childs.

Childs identified the crisis as lying first of all in a failure to identify the essential nature of the biblical texts: what does it mean to read the Bible simultaneously from a theological and a critical perspective?

Biblical theologians were agreed that something more important than the actual text lay behind it. For some it was 'the event . . . not the account', and the purpose of exegesis was to recover the event. Again

others spoke of the 'word behind the words', or the 'original meaning' of a passage as normative. The biblical theologians had attempted to modify the liberal insistence that the historical context was the only legitimate perspective for modern objective exegesis. But the result was that no clear alternative had emerged either, regarding the question of context or the subject matter of the interpretation. The confusion was never dispelled as to whether the element of revelation claimed for the Bible lay in the text, in some positivity behind the text, or in a combination of text and event or mode of consciousness (p. 52).

In the later chapters of that book, and in his major work since, Childs has addressed the problem of how to handle scripture within the confessing community; and his method of 'canonical criticism' is by now widely known (and widely criticized!). He has developed the method in relation to both OT and NT, has studied its implications for OT theology,* and has employed his own principles to produce a notable commentary on the Book of Exodus (1974). All of this represents a notable achievement, in some ways a heroic one: few can claim to have created single-handed an entire hermeneutical* system and at the same time to have produced the main body of literature relating to it. But herein lies also one of the serious reservations which have been levelled against Childs' work: it has, by and large, failed to convince either the scholarly guild or the Christian community, each of whose interests the method is designed to reflect in a single methodology.* Only James A. Sanders, whose work both parallels and follows that of Childs, has really taken up the project with enthusiasm. Thus, although their work is of more than marginal significance, it is necessary to say that many questions remain to be answered before it can be further developed. (It is true that many scholars have addressed the issues of the origin and history either of the idea of 'canon'* or of the defining of 'canons' of OT or NT scriptures. While many of their works are likely to be referred to by Childs and Sanders, they should not be regarded as 'canonical critics': their field of enquiry is essentially part of that historical critical* enterprise the critique of which gave rise to Childs' programme.)

Canonical criticism takes as its starting point the nature of scripture as revealed by historical criticism – its puzzles and contradictions, its resistance to any unique interpretation – and asks the question: how does this elusive text live in the communities of faith to which it belongs? It thus aims to be both critical and confessional, in order to reunite the two terms which were so effectively broken apart by nineteenth-century historical criticism. It is clear, therefore, that Childs' agenda is enlivened by the same concern which moved the biblical theology school whose work he so sharply criticized. Anyone who seeks to unite these terms, rather than simply subordinating one to the other, has to face the problem of finding a common factor between them. History, as perceived by the earlier project, proved wanting; in its place Childs offers the notion of canon. What is important about canon is that it offers a kind of internal hermeneutic of scripture. Childs spells this out in a key passage:

> The heart of the canonical process lay in transmitting and ordering the authoritative tradition in a form which was compatible to function as scripture for a generation which had not participated in the original events of revelation. The ordering of the tradition for this new function involved a profoundly hermeneutical activity, the effects of which are now built into the structure of the canonical text (*Introduction to the Old Testament as Scripture*, 1979, p. 60).

There are two clear implications of this view: 1. the fact that a piece of scripture is embedded in a canonical collection is of hermeneutical significance; and 2. scripture itself has already undergone a process of interpretation which contains within it the seeds of further developments. Childs himself had already spelled this out impressively in his commentary on Exodus. Without denying the place of historical criticism – indeed, it would be hard to improve on his treatment of this aspect of the text – he goes on to consider how Exodus relates to other books in the OT, then to the NT, and finally to the thinking of a variety of commentators throughout the Christian period.

Childs' *Exodus* illustrates the difficulty of allowing 'canonical' criticism to take off too freely from the critical launching pad: how do we select interpreters out of the great mass of available material, and how do we avoid bias in our selection? The danger seems to be that the union between criticism and church is illusory – the mere setting of two things alongside each other does not effect their union; it may only serve to highlight their disunity. But if we are to take both terms seriously, it is hard to see how to avoid either the control of interpretation by critical findings (which is where we came in) or the control of critical findings by theological presuppositions (which was precisely what the first critics fought to free the Bible from!).

Quite apart from these reservations, which relate to Childs' claim to have found a way out of the impasse of the dichotomy between church and scholar, there is a serious question over his definition of canon. In so far as the aim is to produce a hermeneutic common to scholars and church alike, it is questionable whether a single definition of 'canon' is available. What is canon for the Protestant churches differs from the Catholic canon, and again from that of the Orthodox. And unless we are to introduce a barrier which would be anathema to many, how can the 'canonical' principle be maintained in the light of the existence of the Jewish canon of the OT, not to mention Jewish scholarly study of the NT? These are not trivial questions – they strike at the very heart of the method, and suggest that it can be accused of misrepresentation on two grounds: it is neither truly canonical (since no single canon can be uniquely defined) nor genuinely critical, in that its rubrics seem to introduce criteria for interpretation which restrict its usefulness to those of a particular religious bent. But it must be recognized that, however flawed his proposals, Childs has at least seen that there are problems and sought solutions. In the remainder of this article we shall look at some of the positive features of the method, and indicate the major studies in the field.

Undoubtedly historical criticism concentrated too much on the minutiae of the text and isolated books from each other, so that canonical criticism's aim of allowing different biblical texts to inform each other is a useful corrective. Given the development of structuralism* and deconstruction in literary criticism,* the renewed interest in the final form of the text, and the growth of rhetorical criticism,* Childs' project is potentially important. It resists the assumption that what historical criticism has to say is all that there is to say, and opens the door to participation by a much wider group of readers in the act of interpretation. There is no theoretical limit to the process – we can read Torah in the light of Ecclesiastes, Ecclesiastes in the light of Job, Job in the light of Deutero-Isaiah, and Deutero-Isaiah in the light of Revelation. Out of this breaking of barriers can come fruitful insights which may in turn illumine the particular texts, and even have implications which historical criticism cannot ignore. And the recognition that these texts are indeed texts with a confessional context is significant: we cannot claim to have exhausted their meaning if we have ignored this aspect. The decision to let canon be the definitive characteristic has plausibility: it relates to that which makes scripture distinctive in the eyes of church, synagogue and mosque. But is the cost too great? For what is gained in the direction of confessional commitment to the texts may be matched by a greater loss of scholarly consensus. Is it possible, in the final analysis, to be a canonical critic without at the same time saying, 'I am a Protestant Christian' or 'I am a Roman Catholic' or 'I am a Jew'? And if not, does Childs' method not belong with typology,* allegory* and the like, rather than in the 'canon' of scholarly approaches to scripture. Although it would be premature to judge the issue, it must be said that the consensus at present is rather against Childs.

The major landmark is undoubtedly Childs' *Introduction to the Old Testament as Scripture*, in which his essential thesis was set out and then applied to the individual books of the OT. The discussion of pp. 30–106 has not really been improved in Childs' later works: its strengths and weaknesses are already evident, and the book as a whole was rather favourably received. Not so, however, in the case of his application of the method to the NT (*The New Testament as Canon: An Introduction*, 1984). Here one senses a rather beleaguered defence of the earlier position with no new arguments and some improbable claims concerning the development of the NT, which prompted a savage review by E. P. Sanders in the *Times Literary Supplement*, 13 December 1985, p. 1431. The themes which are most striking are: an insistence on canon as a force which contributed decisively to the shaping of the NT, the central importance of a confessional stance for canonical criticism, and frequent reference to the process as a dialectical one. The first of these seems to depend on a quite idiosyncratic definition of canon, the second raises again one of the key objections to Childs' proposal, and the third is surely possible without the canonical edifice (see, for example, A. G. Hunter, *Christianity and Other Faiths in Britain*, 1985, ch. 10. pp. 127–47). In his most recent work, *Old Testament Theology in a Canonical Context* (1985), what is perhaps the most natural field for the application of the method is taken up. This is more of a survey than a detailed discussion, with topics opened up rather than dealt with in depth. In some ways this might stand as an appropriate comment on all three of the major studies. Only *Exodus* gets down to the kind of detail which will enable canonical criticism to prove itself; and even there what is most effective is detail of a traditional historical critical kind.

Something should be said, in conclusion, with reference to J. A. Sanders. His early study, *Torah and Canon* (1972), while obviously not strictly a 'canonical critical' exercise, took seriously the effect of 'canonical' processes on the shaping of the final form of the text, and affords an example of a more modest project which, while not making the sort of grand claims that Childs makes, can produce significant results.
See also **Biblical Criticism; Canon.**

R. P. Carroll, 'Canonical Criticism: A Recent Trend in Biblical Studies?', *ET* 92, no. 3, 1980, pp. 73–8; id., 'Childs and Canon', *IBS*, 2, 1980, pp. 211–36; J. A. Sanders, *Canon and Community*, 1984; id., *From Sacred Story to Sacred Text*, 1987.

ALASTAIR G. HUNTER

Catholic Modernism

This term refers to a movement within the Roman Catholic church at the turn of the nineteenth and twentieth centuries, the aim of which was to bring traditional Catholicism into constructive relation with contemporary thought, especially in the fields of history, philosophy and social theory. The term 'modernism' was first applied to it by the ecclesiastical authorities about 1905, and there is a good case for restricting its use in a religious context to the movement in question, although to speak of the latter as though it possessed clear unity of purpose and direction is misleading. It had no organization and not much cohesion, at least at first. Its leading figures – Alfred Loisy (1857–1940), George Tyrrell (1861–1909), Friedrich von Hügel (1852–1925), Lucien Laberthonnière (1860–1932), Edouard Le Roy (1870–1954), Giovanni Semeria (1867–1939) and Salvatore Minocchi (1869–1943) notably – were individual scholars and thinkers working with different interests and presuppositions. But Pius X's encyclical letter *Pascendi dominici gregis* (September 1907) which formally condemned the movement presented a synthetic account of it which the Modernists themselves regarded as unwarranted. At all events the Vatican's assessment was unqualifiedly hostile, and the movement was eventually terminated by the enforcement from 1910 onwards of the anti-Modernist oath on all officeholders in the church, the campaign to extirpate suspected Modernist opinion wherever it might be voiced being rigorously prosecuted. The effect was to impede explorative thinking, especially in biblical study and religious philosophy, for many years to come.

Modernism may properly be seen as the final phase in the 'liberal' Catholic developments that occurred in the Roman church during the nineteenth century. Yet it owed little directly to those preceding it. Rather was it a spontaneous reaction to the intellectual climate produced by the century as a whole, a principal feature of which had been the growth of historical criticism.* Roman Catholic biblical study had been notoriously reluctant to entertain views other than those consecrated by tradition, whereas the Modernists were convinced that in face of historical criticism the apologetic methods of seminary theology were manifestly inadequate. Indeed, the Modernists' own apologetic concern pointed to a new venture in religious philosophy leading, under the influence of positivism and evolutionism, to the propagation of immanentist doctrines irreconcilable with the received Thomism that had lately (*Aeterni Patris*, 1879) been accorded express papal approval.

Not that Loisy himself, in whom the Modernist standpoint found probably its most challenging exponent, ever drew on philosophical theorizing, apart, that is, from the stimulation of his reading – on his own admission – of Edward Caird and J. H. Newman. But in *L'Évangile et l'Église* (²1903; ⁵1929; ET, *The Gospel and the Church*, 1908), his best-known and most original work, he endeavoured to furnish Catholicism with a strikingly new apologetic grounded in a historical criticism no less radical than that associated with German liberal* Protestantism. In fact Modernist biblical exegesis* is virtually identifiable with Loisy's own enterprise as a critical scholar. For, while biblical study was certainly a major interest of von Hügel's, he was not an exegete in the professional sense, and although Semeria and Minocchi in Italy were biblical specialists, their work cannot compare in amplitude and originality with Loisy's. In NT study particularly he achieved a prominence which, despite a growing eccentricity of view in his later, post-Modernist, writings, undoubtedly places him among the outstanding biblical exegetes of modern times. Even in his Catholic days he insisted on a clear distinction being drawn between strictly historical investigation, an autonomous scientific activity, and the theological interpretations expressed in the church's dogma.

As a young man, while studying at the Paris Institut Catholique, he had attended Renan's lectures at the Collège de France, and when later he came himself to teach at the Institut he unhesitatingly adopted the critical method – an audacity (for such it then was) which in 1893 led to his dismissal. Also while at the Institut he had started a monthly review, *L'Enseignement biblique*, through which he hoped to make the substance of his courses available to the clergy at large. *L'Évangile et l'Église* was occasioned by the publication of Adolf Harnack's* *Das Wesen des Christenthums* (1900; ET *What is Christianity?*, 1901), the standpoint of which was firmly liberal Protestant. Loisy countered Harnack's 'ethicizing' interpretation of the gospel by stressing the eschatological* content of Jesus' teaching and pointing out that in any case the gospel as we have it in the NT is discernible

only in the transfiguring light of the apostolic tradition – Catholicism in embryo. So far from its being reducible to a specific 'scriptural' doctrine – the Fatherhood of God, the brotherhood of man – it was a living idea that was to receive increasingly diversified embodiment in the historic church. Such development was, in social and cultural terms, natural and organic. Dogma, hierarchy and cult as Catholic Christianity has evolved them over the ages are changing but legitimate expressions of the gospel's vital impulse. The essence of a religion, therefore, is to be found not in some residual element produced by the analytical methods of academic research but in its continuous and ever-varying experience in time.

Loisy's attempt to resolve the problem of the relations of scripture and tradition in the perspective of historical criticism was not, however, acceptable at Rome, and in 1904 *L'Évangile et l'Église*, along with other of his published works, was placed on the Index as subversive: the fixities of dogma would in the end disappear under the solvents of historical relativism. Following his excommunication in March 1908 Loisy abandoned his stance as a Christian scholar in favour of a broad humanism. Meanwhile the establishment of the papal Biblical Commission in 1902 was to prove to be a brake on critical biblical study for the ensuing half-century, leaving the terrain at best to such conservative exegetes as M.-J. Lagrange. However, it is not unfair to see the issuing of the papal encyclical *Divino Afflante Spiritu* (1943) and the subsequent free flourishing of biblical studies in the Roman Catholic Church as a kind of late vindication of many of the causes for which Modernism stood.

See also **Liberalism.**

J. T. Burtchaell, *Catholic Theories of Biblical Inspiration since 1810*, 1969; G. Daly, *Transcendence and Immanence: a Study in Catholic Modernism and Integralism*, 1980; A. Houtin and F. Sartiaux, *Alfred Loisy, sa vie, son oeuvre*, 1960; E. Poulat, *Histoire, dogme et critique dans la crise moderniste*, ²1979; B. M. G. Reardon, *Roman Catholic Modernism*, 1970; Alec Vidler, *A Variety of Catholic Modernists*, 1970.

BERNARD M. G. REARDON

Christian Interpretation of the Old Testament

If the earliest conceptual task of the Christian community was the articulation of its convictions about Jesus and of the relationship in which he stood to the imminent fulfilment of God's purposes, it was not long before the question of 'Israel' also pressed urgently upon it. Not for some decades (not indeed for considerably longer than that, if we have the whole body of Christians in mind) was this question perceived in terms of the relationship of two religions or even of church and synagogue as two clearly distinct institutions; for most Christians were born Jews or were Gentiles who had some degree of attachment to Judaism. It was perceived rather in terms of the proper qualifications for membership of God's people and of the role of Jesus in the realization of Israel's destiny.

With regard to the former matter, the task of the Christians was one which many Jews had long considered and some had acted upon. The Qumran community (*see* **Dead Sea Scrolls**), for instance, had taken a stand on where God's true Israel was to be found (i.e. in itself and its associates), and numerous Jews had formed opinions about the terms on which Gentiles might be included in the fruits of the new age. But for the Christians it quickly became a matter of special moment and difficulty, largely because of the insistence of Paul * and his fellow-workers in the mission on the incorporation of Gentiles into the church (i.e. the synagogue loyal to Jesus) on a basis of complete equality and without their observing the prized, God-given marks of the Jew: sabbath, circumcision, and dietary laws. This, even more than claims made for Jesus, posed the question of the Christian movement's identity in the early years in relation to Judaism as a whole, and, indeed, to society in general. It had implicit within it already the separation of the two paths of obedience in the people of God. The rapid heightening of claims concerning Jesus, made by more and more Christian groups, soon strengthened the process, so that any chance of the church staying within Judaism as a dissident, reformist group vanished beyond recall.

Not surprisingly, it is then the case that for almost every NT writer, most of them belonging to the later part of the first century, the relationship of church and synagogue, Christianity and Judaism, is an issue of primary importance, a question on which the taking of a view could not be shirked. It is of course a wider question than that of the interpretation of scripture; in an age when novelty in religion was no recommendation, it was part of the business of defining the continuity and the discontinuity to be seen in the coming of Christ. Yet, because of the role of scripture in Israel's consciousness, this latter question was always present. Much of the answering of it was conducted, naturally, by way of the interpretation of specific passages, which were seen to bear on the debate, using established techniques and developing new variants in the process of accommodating Christ, the decisive new factor in the situation. But behind the discussion of particular texts, there stood a series of attempted solutions to the problem as a whole, or, to be less optimistic, a series of ways of perceiving the problem. Each NT writer (and, for that matter, also other early Christian writers) had his own approach, no doubt according to not only his own ideas but also the circumstances facing him. Each may be seen as taking his place on a spectrum, ranging from a frank rejection of much that constituted Jewish identity to the attempt to trace a straight line of continuity from Israel, including the scriptures, to the Christian community. In almost all cases, in fact, the standpoint adopted was one of great complexity, and simple formulations are misleading. Indeed, they have misled subsequent generations, sometimes with catastrophic consequences.

Thus, the modern (and indeed the traditional Christian) reader of the Gospel of Matthew sees in it vitriolic denunciation of the Pharisees * (ch. 23) and willing acceptance by the Jewish people of responsibility for Jesus' execution (27.25). The book seems then to legitimate antisemitic * sentiment, and its interpretations of OT passages validate Jesus and the church at point after point as the fulfillers of God's purposes. But if we assess Matthew from a realistic historical point of view, we reach towards a quite different conclusion. It is true that he shows awareness of church and synagogue as irreparably divided (e.g. 21.43), but it is highly unlikely that he saw this in informed universal terms or with a wide historical perspective. It is much more probable that he judged in the light of local circumstances, where the dispute was still one which, to the observer, must bear most of the signs of internecine conflict. Matthew, holding as he does to Jewish observance as binding on the followers of Jesus, set out to demonstrate that his was the true interpretation of scripture and Jesus its fulfilment. In other words, he was setting out to validate his brand of Judaism as other groups set out to validate theirs. Despite the centrality of Jesus, he maintained more marks of Jewish identity than he renounced.

Similarly Paul, for all his decisive role in precipitating the movement of Christianity out of Judaism, was fervent and ingenious in demonstrating that the ultimate purpose of all he had done and stood for was the realization of a grand vision of 'Israel' where Jews and Gentiles, all children of Adam,* would be at one. From this point of view, once again, negative results came from positive intentions.

However, once the negative results had taken hold, they determined the use of scripture in Christian self-awareness down to the present − with the exception of the limited effects of critical study of the Bible in recent times. Apart from the brief Marcionite presentation of the Christian message in a way that saw the OT as inferior for the purpose of gaining salvation, the church adopted and has maintained the OT as an integral part of its scriptures and read it, despite changing modes of interpretation, as a Christian book. It even obliterated linguistically any consciousness of its being a plurality of books and fused it with the NT by turning the neuter plural *biblia* (= 'books') into a feminine singular (= 'the Book' or 'the Bible'): it is a book to be taken as a single whole.

Determination, doctrinally motivated, to retain the old scriptures compelled the church into this view of them. In pointing out the contradictions of character and behaviour between the deity of the OT and that of the gospel of Jesus, Marcion* had forced upon those who differed from him certain options. For instance, if one was going to hold to belief in the creator God (a belief certainly tenable on independent grounds), it seemed necessary to hold also to the scriptures which revealed this truth, i.e. the OT. Paradoxically, just when the church was becoming institutionally quite separate from Judaism, Marcion had the effect of making many Christians newly tenacious of their Jewish roots, above all with regard to their view of creation and of God's action in history. As far as the second century is concerned, it is not unfair to say that what with hindsight we identify as orthodox Christianity was that part of the Christian movement which remained closest to Judaism in many of its fundamental theological beliefs. In that tenacity, making the OT a Christian book (though largely motivated by the desire to show that it spoke of Jesus at every turn) was a decisive factor.

In effect, Christianity had opted for a 'book-centred' (rather than, for instance, philosophy-centred) way of being religious. From then on, it was both endowed with and saddled with (for it is not without problems for Christian interpretation!) the OT – and compelled to find ways of interpreting it, in all its bulk and variety, in the light of Christian perspectives which, as we are now vividly aware, it was never written to display. Critical innocence meant that, compared with the present day, there was, as we have seen, little awareness of the variety, but the bulk could not be ignored. Seen chiefly as sheer words, it manifested itself as a vast theological jig-saw, to be brought to coherence. It was an invitation to ingenuity, schematization, controversy, and (usually unconscious) drastic selectivity.

It is perhaps futile but also salutary to speculate whether and on what terms Christian belief could have been formed without retaining the OT. It is no doubt the case that,

as a matter of fact, certain beliefs (e.g. about God's relations with the world and with history) came to the fore through the Jewish scriptures; but that is very different from making them dependent theologically on those scriptures in such a way that to accept the beliefs means maintaining the scriptures as authoritative. It is of course true that as a matter of history Jesus stemmed from a Jewish setting and Jewish history and was initially understood in Jewish terms; but that is very different from seeing acceptance of him as theologically bound up with the course of Israel's history, by way of the writings which tell of it.

So uncongenial and, *prima facie*, irrelevant is much of the OT to Christian interpretation (as indeed to any continuing use as a religious authority) that only drastic treatment, again stimulated by determination to retain it as authoritative, sufficed. Fundamentally, it was read in the light of Christian doctrine. Sometimes, this was taken to extremes, as when the early second-century work the *Epistle of Barnabas* (6.11–12) (*see* **Apostolic Fathers**) takes the injunction to Adam in Gen. 1.28 to 'be fruitful and multiply' as a command to spread the gospel. Otherwise, the twin methods of typology* (discerning parallels of symbol* and story between the OT and the NT, e.g. between the crossing of the Red Sea and baptism, or the giving of manna and the eucharist) and allegory* (seeing moral and theological meaning behind statements and stories ostensibly about quite other matters) saved the day. But they have never gone unchallenged and have seemed decreasingly convincing since the sixteenth century. Their practical decline in Christian use and consciousness creates the severest problem for the lively appreciation (as distinct from retention by inertia) of the OT in the church. Some fragments remain, notably in Holy Week liturgies, where stories of the exodus from Egypt (liable to strike the sensitive modern person as portraying a deity of extreme barbarity and partiality) still move the worshipper as a witness to saving continuity with the passion of Jesus, and parallels are drawn between the tree in Eden which brought man's downfall and the 'tree' of Calvary which brought its reversal. Again, one is compelled to ask: are these parallels theologically significant in some way (what do they mean concerning the realities of divine activity?) or simply adventitious illustrations which in theory might have been drawn from anywhere? If the former, what view of God's relation to the world is implicit in them?

It is interesting to note that, perhaps in the light of a turning away from the example of the lives of the saints, Protestant culture (like, indeed, Renaissance humanism before and alongside it) saw a revival of attention to the OT in its own right. Especially in Calvinist* societies like the Netherlands and Scotland, the OT came to be used less as only the precursor of Christ than as the independent source of symbols and moral examples for the enriching and interpreting of personal and national life. In this setting, the Jews, at least of the OT period, acquired positive value as representing a valuable phase of God's guidance for his people in, for example, seventeenth-century Holland or twentieth-century South Africa. It is scarcely too much to say that such societies derived a great part of their imaginative world and self-understanding from the OT. The part played by this element in Victorian England is illustrated in George Eliot's novel, *Adam Bede*.

It is the modern critical study of the OT, both arising from and fostering ever more acute historical sense, which has above all made the whole apparatus of traditional Christian use of the OT problematic. The idea of it as 'a Christian book' is ever harder to maintain – as is, for that matter, the idea of it as a modern Jewish book: both faiths have moved on from the OT as now perceived in its diverse historical settings, as both have made their quite different interpretative accommodation with it. Indeed, despite the various attempts by OT theologians to bring out its unity, it is the diversity of the OT, not just in literary genre* but also in theology, which is now most likely to strike the student.

That is not to say that profound theological ideas in the OT are not of inestimable importance and continuing interest. Along with other styles of thought they are, by whatever tortuous paths, part of the Christian heritage. But whether their importance lies in their being part of the OT (as in some sense authoritative scripture) or is simply intrinsic – and whether it is not better so – is another question. Certainly, they cannot suffice to commend to Christians the whole of the OT. Those approaching these matters from the point of view of relations between Christianity and Judaism in the modern world and in the light of relations between Christianity and other faiths on the wider scale will no doubt find help in disentangling some of the issues which lie at the heart of Christian origins, perhaps above all the assumptions on which the church adopted the OT. They deserve more questioning than they have received recently (the ghost of Marcion is still raised to suppress it!), both with regard to those external issues and for more domestic Christian reasons, such as the use of the OT in liturgy. The decline of allegory made it difficult to see sense in much of that use, though it received a boost from the biblical theology* movement, with its emphasis

on biblical continuities and great themes, as also on 'God's acts in history' (G. E. Wright). That movement had great effect in the liturgical reforms of recent decades. But with the decline in its force, and the strengthening of the sense of the OT as belonging to days long past, the question of its Christian use, not only in theory but also in practice, must surely come once again to the fore.

Though it cannot be said that the question of the OT's precise place (if any) in Christian use has received much serious and candid consideration, it has not been absent from the modern agenda. Harnack* (*Marcion*, 1921, pp. 248–9) wrote: 'The rejection of the OT in the second century was a mistake which the great Church rightly refused to make; the retention of it in the sixteenth century was due to a fatal legacy which the Reformation was not yet able to overcome; but for Protestantism since the nineteenth century to continue to treasure it as a canonical document is the result of a religious and ecclesiastical paralysis.' And Bultmann* (especially in his *Primitive Christianity in its Contemporary Setting*, 1955) depicted Christianity as achieving its true nature only when it had emancipated itself from a religiously degenerate, legalistic Judaism. So easily does a questioning of Christianity's historical dependence on Judaism come to the fringes of antisemitic attitudes.

Of greater interest and significance, however, is Bultmann's understanding of the OT as 'pre-understanding' (*Vorverständnis*) for the NT. Only the NT has the full character of revelation,* but, historically and theologically, the OT provides the essential basis for our being in a position to grasp its message. This both does justice to modern study of the OT (for it makes straightforward historical sense to see OT and NT in continuity in this way) and makes it possible to use the OT theologically in preaching. At first sight, this looks like a variant on traditional interpretation, whereby the OT was read as a Christian book, prefiguring the NT and telling directly of Christ. But, at least in the earliest Christian forms of that approach, the OT had precedence as scripture, with the NT as adjunct; now, for Bultmann, the NT was at the centre, the OT only a preliminary to the gospel (cf. Luther's* perception of it as 'Law' to 'Gospel'). Also, that traditional use was more text-centred, Bultmann's more in terms of theological and existential themes.

More recently, despite the preponderance of historical approaches, various strands in biblical interpretation have (if it were needed) rehabilitated the OT. Both canonical* and literary criticism* have worked with a picture of the biblical story as a single whole, from beginning to end. And students of early Judaism (e.g. E. P. Sanders and G. Vermes) have emphasized both Jesus' Jewishness and the unfairness of a depiction of first-century Judaism such as that discernible in Bultmann (and more so in others). On the other hand, if the cultural distance between ourselves and the OT is the problem, there have been those who point out that the NT suffers from precisely the same difficulties for us, with even more serious consequences for traditional ways of seeing Christianity (e.g. Nineham, 1976).

See also **Antisemitism**; **Cultural Relativism**; **Jewish Exegesis**; **Liturgy, Use of the Bible in.**

B. W. Anderson (ed.), *The Old Testament and Christian Faith*, 1964; James Barr, *Holy Scripture: Canon, Authority, Criticism*, 1983; John Barton, *People of the Book?*, 1988; Northrop Frye, *The Great Code*, 1982; J. Goldingay, *Theological Diversity and the Authority of the Old Testament*, 1987; D. E. Nineham, *The Use and Abuse of the Bible*, 1976; G. E. Wright, *The Old Testament and Theology*, 1969.

J. L. HOULDEN

Christology, Modern

Jesus of Nazareth is the object of two distinct though related disciplines. Modern biblical studies attempt to understand this object in ways appropriate to historical phenomena in general, whereas systematic theology* is primarily concerned with the present significance and meaning of traditional christological statements. The expression 'modern christology' refers to the latter discipline, and in the present context the main emphasis must lie on the use it has made of the methods and results of the former. Not all modern writers on christology treat this as a central issue; for example, Karl Rahner is chiefly interested in the interaction between the christological tradition and modern philosophy, and the main concern of Jürgen Moltmann's *The Crucified God* (1974) is to criticize the traditional understanding of divine impassibility and its christological implications.

It is conventional to regard F. D. E. Schleiermacher (1768–1834) as the founder of modern christology, although a more comprehensive account would also have to consider his eighteenth-century antecedents (*see* **Enlightenment**). Schleiermacher is opposed both to Chalcedonian christology and to the Enlightenment's tendency to present Jesus as a purely human teacher. For him, Jesus is only correctly understood from the standpoint of the Christian experience of redemption, in which believers come to participate in Jesus' own consciousness of God through the gospel picture of him handed down in the church. The Gospel of John is, for Schleiermacher, the clearest

testimony to the human Jesus' perfect relationship with God, and perhaps for that reason he prefers it to the Synoptics as a historical source. He is critical of certain aspects of the synoptic picture of Jesus, pointing for example to the discrepancies between the Matthean and Lucan infancy narratives* and dismissing the temptation story as legendary. Underlying such historical judgments is a theological criterion: 'Nothing concerning him [Christ] can be set up as real doctrine unless it is connected with his redeeming causality and can be traced to the original impression made by his existence.'

Schleiermacher believed that his stress on Jesus' perfect relationship with God helps to resolve the problem of the gospel miracles which so exercised his contemporaries. Although allowance must be made for legendary accretions, Jesus' 'miracles' may be accepted as essentially historical when one sees them as natural effects of the one supreme miracle of his perfect consciousness of God. This theory even leads Schleiermacher to offer a naturalistic explanation of the resurrection:* Jesus did not truly die on the cross, and his God-consciousness enabled him to recover from his ordeal and to appear to his followers. The fundamental historicity of the gospel records is preserved but the theological emphasis now lies on the ministry of Jesus rather than on his death and resurrection.

D. F. Strauss'* *Life of Jesus Critically Examined* (1835) made Schleiermacher's preference for the Gospel of John and his interpretation of the miracle stories seem old-fashioned and idiosyncratic. Strauss asserts that the historian must be entirely free from religious and dogmatic presuppositions, and he criticizes Schleiermacher for allowing theological concerns to answer historical questions. Yet Schleiermacher's stress on the theological centrality of the ministry of Jesus proved capable of being transplanted into a more historically-conscious climate, of which the chief representative in the second half of the nineteenth century was Albrecht Ritschl (1822–89). For Ritschl, Jesus is significant chiefly as the founder of the kingdom of God,* that is, the new ethical community of the church. The kingdom of God is seen here as a present reality destined eventually to incorporate the whole of humanity; that is the message of the parables of the Mustard Seed and of the Leaven. Although this understanding of the kingdom of God eventually proved untenable, Ritschl's insistence that christology must be based on the results of historical research remains important. The kingdom of God becomes the chief criterion for theology because it was fundamental for Jesus' historical ministry, and it is largely on the basis of this criterion that Ritschl criticizes the christological tradition. His work is the first important dogmatic response to contemporary biblical scholarship's preference for the Synoptics as historical sources for the life of Jesus.

The use of a particular understanding of the synoptic Jesus as a dogmatic criterion was also applied within the NT itself. Ritschl's pupil W. Herrmann (1846–1922) argues that the theological value of historical criticism is that it destroys false props for faith, such as a belief in the absolute historical reliability of the Gospels and in various doctrines held by some of the NT authors. Historical criticism helps us to differentiate between what is of primary importance and what is only secondary, and for Herrmann primary importance is attached to 'the inner life of Jesus'. The picture of him we receive within the Christian fellowship creates the impression that 'he was able to remain in that state of soul which we count blessed', and through his mediation we too are brought into communion with God. This certainty is immune from the historian's uncertainties about Jesus' outward life. In many respects Herrmann is closer to Schleiermacher than to Ritschl, but he differs from both in the seriousness with which he takes the problem of historical scepticism.

The assumption that historical criticism must determine the reinterpretation of christological dogma is challenged by M. Kähler (1835–1912). Kähler sets out to defend the thesis that 'the historical Jesus* of modern authors conceals from us the living Christ'. The historians claim to be without presuppositions and to be motivated by purely scientific concerns, but in fact they merely project their own opinions on to their 'historical Jesus'. Only believers, and not historians, will regard the biblical picture of Jesus as trustworthy. For them, the real Christ is the risen Christ of the apostolic preaching – the Christ of the whole Bible, and not merely the Jesus of certain arbitrarily selected and misinterpreted passages in the Synoptics. Like Schleiermacher, Ritschl and Herrmann, Kähler argues that knowledge of the real significance of Jesus is to be found only within the Christian fellowship, but unlike them he uses this point polemically against contemporary historical research. Kähler's plea for the whole biblical Christ was taken up in Britain by P. T. Forsyth (1848–1921), for whom 'the fact on which Christian theology works is the Christ of faith and not of history only, of inspiration and not mere record'.

In general, however, Ritschlian theology was widely regarded as broadly correct at the beginning of the twentieth century. Even J. Weiss, who argued in 1892 for the essentially eschatological* character of Jesus' proclamation of the kingdom of God, had no intention of overthrowing Ritschlian theology as a whole. The emphasis could simply be shifted to other aspects of Jesus' message, such as the divine fatherhood. Alternatively, it was thought possible to distinguish between the eschatological beliefs which Jesus shared with his contemporaries and a view of the kingdom of God which was uniquely his own. A. von Harnack* (1851–1930) argued that it was legitimate for the historian to differentiate in this way between the dispensable husk and the indispensable kernel of Jesus' message. The kingdom of God is in essence not an impending apocalyptic* catastrophe but 'the rule of the holy God in the hearts of individuals'. It is perhaps significant that Harnack allocates the hermeneutical* task of distinguishing husk from kernel to the historian; the notion of a qualitatively different knowledge of Jesus available only within the church has been tacitly set aside.

Karl Barth's* commentary on Romans (²1922) was, among other things, a direct attack on the notion that historical investigation is the only possible foundation for christology. The issue is conveniently summarized in the debate between Harnack and Barth (1923), in which Harnack wrote: 'If the person of Jesus Christ stands at the centre of the gospel, how can the foundation for a reliable and generally accepted knowledge of that person be gained other than through critical-historical investigation?' Barth's reply is that 'the "reliable and generally accepted" knowledge of the person of Christ as the centre of the gospel can only be that of faith awakened by God'. The value of historical critical* study is purely negative, showing us that 'we do not know Christ according to the flesh any more'. Barth is probably thinking primarily of R. Bultmann's* historical scepticism, but he may also have in mind E. Troeltsch's insistence that historical research can never vindicate Christian belief in the unique significance of Jesus.

In the christological discussions in the first part of the *Church Dogmatics* (1932–8), Barth takes issue with many of the historical assumptions underlying the christology of the preceding generation. He criticizes the reconstruction of the development of NT christology in which a purely human figure is gradually transformed into a divine being; this is 'christology historically reconstructed along the lines of Ebionitism'. He does not accept the usual distinction between the Synoptics on the one hand and Paul* and John on the other, arguing that despite all its necessary internal tensions the NT is essentially at one in its testimony to the divine Christ. Unlike many theological conservatives, however, Barth is not gen-

erally concerned to argue for the literal historicity of the gospel texts (his discussion of the
virgin birth is exceptional in this respect).
Their significance is entirely theological; they
bear witness to a historical event – the life,
death and resurrection of the Word (*see*
Logos) become flesh – but the uniqueness of
this event means that the history they recount
is not like the history studied by historians.
Parts of the gospel record which the historian
(perhaps rightly) regards as legendary may
nevertheless function theologically as genuine
testimony to Jesus Christ. Revelation is necessarily hidden within the ambiguous phenomena of 'ordinary history', and the NT authors
were concerned above all to bring this hidden
element to light. It is therefore impossible for
the historian to grasp the truth about Jesus
Christ, known only in the event of faith. Those
who engage in the historical quest are 'chasing
the ghost of a historical Jesus* in the vacuum
behind the New Testament'.

Rudolf Bultmann shares Barth's hostility
towards historical Jesus theology, although
his book on Jesus (1926) might plausibly be
read as an extension rather than a rejection of
that tradition. In general, however, Bultmann's stress on the early Christian preaching
of the cross excludes any real theological interest in what the historical Jesus may or may
not have done and said. The life and fate of
Jesus is simply the historical occasion for the
rise of the kerygma,* seen in characteristically
Lutheran terms as the divine challenge to
natural human self-assertion. Representatives
of the so-called 'new quest of the historical
Jesus' generally accept the broad outlines of
Bultmann's understanding of the kerygma, yet
argue that the kerygma must be grounded in
the preaching and activity of Jesus. Thus, G.
Ebeling argues against Bultmann that 'Jesus
is the criterion of christology'. Ebeling asks
whether faith in Jesus has a basis in Jesus
himself, and argues that 'the faith of the days
after Easter knows itself to be nothing else
but the right understanding of the Jesus of the
days before Easter'. The impossibility of writing an old-fashioned 'life of Jesus' does not
mean that the historical Jesus is completely
hidden from us. In a way that recalls Herrmann, Ebeling devotes particular attention to
Jesus' own faith and his intention of awakening faith in others.

W. Pannenberg's christology marks a decisive break with the tradition of dialectical
theology within which Barth, Bultmann and
Ebeling stand. Dialectical theology distinguishes sharply between the knowledge of
Jesus accessible to the historian and that
which comes only through faith, and it is this
distinction that Pannenberg rejects. In itself,
Jesus' claim to authority (emphasized by the

'new quest') is of doubtful validity. Its validation depends entirely on the resurrection,* in
which the divine verdict on Jesus cancels out
the human one that resulted in his crucifixion.
In developing his case, Pannenberg makes constructive theological use of a number of
themes from contemporary biblical scholarship: Jewish apocalyptic* hopes as the essential background to Jesus' ministry, Jesus' own
eschatological expectations, the importance of
I Cor. 15 in reconstructing the earliest testimony to the resurrection, the centrality of the
resurrection in the development of NT christology, and so on. At one crucial point, however, Pannenberg does depart from current
critical orthodoxy: he believes that historical
investigation vindicates the truth of the early
Christian claim that Jesus has been raised and
that his tomb is therefore empty. Christology
once again rests entirely on historical study.
Pannenberg uses familiar apologetic arguments (the transformation of the disciples, the
authorities' failure to produce a corpse), and
attacks the 'foggy talk of "Easter faith"' with
which 'many authors shamefully evade their
reader's interest in what they think about the
reliability of the Easter tradition'.

Like Bultmann, Paul Tillich expounds christology as the divine answer to the universal
human predicament. The apocalyptic background presupposed in the symbol 'Christ' is
'the state of the estrangement of man and his
world from God'. 'The christological paradox'
is that Jesus is the Christ, i.e. 'the appearance
of the New Being under the conditions of
existence, yet judging and conquering them'.
The theme of the gospel narrative, focussed in
the Caesarea Philippi incident, is that 'he who
is supposed to overcome existential estrangement must participate in it and its self-destructive consequences'. Tillich holds that we
possess only fragmentary and hypothetical
knowledge of the historical Jesus, and that the
attempt to find 'the Jesus behind the symbols
of his reception as the Christ' proved a failure.
Yet theologically this situation is to be
welcomed, since it demonstrates the unity of
the historical fact with the early Christian
reception of it: 'Without the reception of Jesus
as the Christ by the church, he could not have
become the Christ, because he would not have
brought the New Being to anyone.' Like Bultmann, Tillich exploits the positive theological
possibilities of historical scepticism, but with
much more appreciation of the significance of
the gospel narrative.

More recent writing on christology has had
to take into account the contribution of Latin
American liberation theology* to this field.
Jon Sobrino is typical in arguing that christology must be rooted both in contemporary
political realities and in the historical Jesus. A

truly historical christology 'cannot mean reflecting directly on christological dogmas; it
must entail going back over the route that
allowed for the formulation of those dogmas'.
If 'the logical procedure of christology is
nothing else but the proper chronological procedure', the emphasis is placed on the starting
point for the whole process, Jesus' own history
and destiny. The context for this programme
is different from earlier liberal Protestant historical Jesus theology; the latter was motivated by the apologetic need to make the essence of the Christian message clear and credible in a sceptical environment, whereas liberation theology addresses itself to a situation
not of scepticism but of oppression. The Jesus
of liberal* theology tends to be an apolitical
figure whose message is purely religious and
whose crucifixion as a political threat can
only have been a misunderstanding. In contrast, liberation theology emphasizes that the
activity and teaching of the historical Jesus
was political through and through. Jesus was
not an armed revolutionary of a Zealot type,
yet he opposed the political and religious
status quo in word and in deed, seeking to
build a community characterized by a love
and justice consonant with the nature of the
heavenly Father. Caiaphas and Pilate knew
what they were doing when they crucified
him. Despite the greater prominence given to
the political dimension, however, it is tempting
to see this approach to christology as a revival
of the Ritschlian tradition. Seventy years of
Protestant hostility towards this tradition
should not make one overlook its possibilities
for further development.

E. Schillebeeckx's 'experiments in christology' have been influenced by liberation
theology, but are more strongly marked by
interaction with mainly Protestant biblical
scholarship – to such an extent, indeed, that
historical questions tend to take precedence
over strictly theological ones. J. Mackey is
also optimistic about the theological possibilities of historical research. At the heart of
the ministry of the historical Jesus, he believes,
was Jesus' desire to communicate to others
his sense that life is a gift. The 'mythical'
transformation of this historical figure is
assessed positively. S. Ogden, on the other
hand, maintains the Bultmannian insistence
that christology must be based on early Christian testimony to Jesus, not on Jesus himself.
It is, he says, impossible to know whether
Jesus 'had an authentic understanding of his
own existence'; form criticism* rules out in
advance the possibility of a 'new quest of the
historical Jesus'. Common to these and many
other recent writers is the assumption that
biblical scholarship has an essential positive
contribution to make to modern christology.

See also **Christology, New Testament.**

V. A. Harvey, *The Historian and the Believer*,
1967; D. H. Kelsey, *The Uses of Scripture in
Recent Theology*, 1975; G. Lundström, *The
Kingdom of God in the Teaching of Jesus*, ET
1963; A. McGrath, *The Making of Modern
German Christology*, 1986; J. M. Robinson, *A
New Quest of the Historical Jesus*, 1959; W.
Sanday, *The Life of Christ in Recent Research*,
1907; A. Schweitzer, *The Quest of the Histor-
ical Jesus*, ET 1910.

FRANCIS WATSON

Christology, New Testament

The history of interpretation of NT christology
has been marked by the attempt, at best, to
understand the NT texts within the context of
changing and developing philosophical and
dogmatic structures; at worst to use the NT to
support ideas and teachings whose legitimacy
and coherence were effectively unrelated to
the NT.

In the patristic period (*see* **Patristic Christology**) discussion of christology returned again
and again to the key texts, Prov. 8.22; John
1.14; Phil. 2.6–11; Col. 1.15 and Heb. 1.3f.
Initially, when Logos christology formed the
main stream of thought, the principal issue
was whether the Logos* was created. Prov.
8.22 was a favourite Arian verse, and pointed
to the equivalent interpretation of Col. 1.15
('first-born of all creation'). Opposition to the
idea of the Logos as 'created' resulted in a
response to Arianism at these points characteristically dependent more on dogmatic presupposition and less on exegesis* – e.g. *ktizein*
taken in the sense 'appoint' rather than
'create'; Col. 1.15 understood with reference
to Christ's flesh; the *prōtotokos* of Col. 1.15
understood within the distinction between 'begetting' and 'creating' (Grillmeier, pp. 156,
174, 182, 213). In a similar way the virgin
birth narratives (*see* **Infancy Narratives**) were
soon absorbed into a larger doctrine of incarnation and ceased to have independent significance, except as they contributed to a different line of dogmatic development focussing
on Mary.

Still more important was John 1.14, which
might seem to speak straightforwardly of incarnation ('the Logos became flesh'), but with
the sense in which the Logos became flesh
being precisely the issue in dispute (e.g.
Grillmeier, pp. 245, 328). In this debate the
alternatives centred on a Logos-anthropos
(Word-man) christology and a Logos-sarx
(Word-flesh) christology. The former was
typical of the Antiochene* school and
focussed on the human Christ but left the
unity of the divine and human in Christ in
some question. The latter was typical of the

Alexandrian* school and focussed on the pre-existent Logos, leaving Christ's humanity in some unclarity. Thus was formulated in classic terms a tension which has been fundamental to christology from the beginning, reflecting not least the different portrayals of Jesus in Synoptic and Johannine Gospels.

When the focus was more on the issue of relationships within the Godhead, the language of Phil. 2.7 and Heb. 1.3 came to the fore. The problem was what terms like *morphē, charaktēr* and *hypostasis* might mean (Grillmeier, pp. 365, 374). The resolution was provided by giving *hypostasis* a new technical meaning, relating to the distinctiveness of the three divine 'persons' (allowing the new technical formula, one *ousia* and three *hypostases*). The solution, in other words, was not derived exegetically, but could call on Heb. 1.3 for support within a 'language game' where semantic values were in transition (cf. Grillmeier, p. 446).

In short, as the christological and trinitarian debate became more technical, with ever more subtle refinement, it moved further and further from questions of exegesis* as such, and more towards a proof-texting for arguments and positions determined by the different terms and logical constraints of later debates. And so it has continued in greater or less degree since, at least to the extent that the terms of the debates have been determined by the great credal confessions (*see* **Creed**) hammered out in the early centuries.

Something of the same can be said of the other focus in NT christology – on the soteriological* significance of Christ. An early powerful example of exegesis feeding theology was Irenaeus'* development of Paul's Adam* christology in his theory of 'recapitulation'. But for much of the time the theme of atonement was subordinated to what was perceived as the more important issue, the theme of incarnation – as in the classic epigram of Gregory of Nazianzus, 'What has not been assumed cannot be restored' (*Ep.* 101.7). The NT language of sacrifice and ransom in reference to Christ's death was taken seriously, with the usual exegetical assumption being that 'sacrifice' implied a theory of penal satisfaction, and the image of ransom raising the question as to whether a ransom had been paid to the devil. In his classic study, *Christus Victor* (1931), G. Aulen also argued in effect for a more definitive influence of Col. 2.15. But again the momentum and thrust of the discussion usually depended more on dogmatic logic or 'necessary reasons' (Anselm) than on exegesis or exposition of what was taken for granted to be the authoritative scriptural text.

In all this the hermeneutical* technique of allegorizing allowed a wide range of texts to be drawn in without anything approaching an adequate exegetical or hermeneutical control. And while the Reformation* brought a renewed emphasis on exegesis and on the importance of rooting doctrine firmly in the biblical text, in the area of christology the classical categories and paradigms were on the whole too firmly established to allow any real question to arise at the level of exegesis or interpretation.

With the rise of historical and biblical criticism* in the post-Enlightenment* period, however, the philosophical and dogmatic frameworks of interpretation soon came into conflict. The impact was first experienced in the deist* polarization of historical Jesus* and dogmatic Christ, with the clear presumption that the latter was no longer an acceptable hermeneutical option and that the alternative framework of rationalism or idealism or liberal* optimism *ipso facto* provided a sounder interpretation.

The contrast between a historically rediscovered Jesus and a dogmatically determined Christ thus became the modern expression of the older tension between the humanity and divinity of Jesus (cf. the distinction between Logos-anthropos and Logos-sarx). In the modern period it has reappeared in many different forms as a hermeneutical key to the NT texts; e.g., the teacher Jesus and the Hellenized Redeemer, the historical Jesus and the Christ of faith, christology from below and from above, Jesus the Jew and Christ the Lord of the Christian mystery cult, the Jesus of Bible story and the Christ of doctrinal proposition. And it has been a factor in several important developments in biblical criticism: e.g. the emergence of Q as a non-miraculous source outflanking the problem of the miracle-performing Saviour; the questioning of John's Gospel* as being a document of the Christ of faith rather than a source for the historical Jesus; the evolution of form criticism* of Gospels and Epistles as a way of bridging the gap between the historical reality of Christianity's beginnings and the already theologized documents of the NT.

A consistent feature of the past two centuries is the search for parallels, the assumption of the historical-critical method* being that contemporary parallels in idea and idiom can be confidently expected to throw light on the biblical data. In the case of the birth narratives, for example, comparisons have been drawn with talk of demi-gods in Greek myth* and of virgin mothers in Philo.* In dispute is precisely the question of the distinctiveness of the Christian narratives – whether lack of an exact parallel is evidence of a new category provided by revelation* and divine act, or whether a historical context in which similar ideas can be expressed is sufficient evidence of a way of conceptualizing divine interaction with the human sphere within which the thought of a virginal conception is simply a new variant of an older motif, even if the emphasis comes on the word 'new'. Within this larger exegetical debate the influence of Isa. 7.14 in shaping the tradition, and the extent to which all or part of the narratives can be described as 'midrash'* are specific questions still under discussion. The most recent and thorough exegetical study by R. E. Brown underlines the gap which still remains at the end of the day between historical findings and dogmatic affirmation.

In the case of the historical Jesus the hermeneutical problem is equally sharp, though often not perceived to be so. To what extent is the historical method able to allow for a Jesus whose self-consciousness or claims regarding himself transcend categories currently available, or does it inevitably reinforce a polarization between historical Jesus and Christ of faith? The impact of J. Weiss and A. Schweitzer* undermined the Liberal Protestant portrayal of Jesus the moral teacher or social reformer, and left twentieth-century research with a still uncomfortable picture of Jesus the eschatological prophet, predicting the imminent end of history, a stranger and enigma to modern susceptibilities, as well as posing awkward questions to the dogma of Christ's divinity. In more recent years awareness of social unrest in first-century Palestine and of similar structures of oppression in the twentieth century have encouraged a re-expression of the older Jesus-the-revolutionary model in terms of liberation theology. And the continuing revulsion at the horrors of the Holocaust has resulted in a restatement of Jesus-the-Jew, or even Jesus-the-Pharisee. In such cases a christology from below is followed through to coherent and logical conclusion, usually without regard to the gap it leaves between it and the Christ of faith.

The search for parallels to the concept of Christ's saving death has regularly fixed on the myth of the dying and rising god as expressed in the mystery cults of the period. And a 'de-emphasis' on the importance of historical reference, such as has characterized the theology of Karl Barth* and the current resurgence of narrative theology*, provides a larger hermeneutic within which such a historical assessment can be sustained. Otherwise the difficulty of explaining how the mythological expression of the annual cycle of fertility came to be a means of interpreting the death and resurrection of a historical individual has usually proved to be a decisive consideration against such hypotheses. A more plausible analogy/genealogy hypothesis

has been perceived in the martyr theology and the motif of the suffering righteous in intertestamental Judaism which seems to lie behind such formulations as Rom. 5.6–11. With regard to the Gospels one of the chief ongoing debates is whether the model of Suffering Servant* (Isa. 53) or Son of Man* (Dan. 7) provides the more important exegetical key to the central passion statements (particularly Mark 10.45). Outside the Gospels the various disputes focussing on Rom. 3.25 characterize the range of debate – whether and to what extent there is a pre-Pauline formula to be discerned with a different theology of atonement, whether the category of sacrifice was actually promoted by the NT writers in discussing the significance of Jesus' death (this is of interest particularly among German scholars), and whether the language of 'propitiation' or 'expiation', of 'substitution' or 'representation' provides the more appropriate exegesis and interpretation (particularly among English speaking scholars).

Within each phase of biblical criticism* the resurrection narratives* have come under renewed scrutiny: which is the oldest source? how far do parallels of translation to heaven and apotheosis help explain the data? how do form-critical* categories illuminate them? To what extent have the narratives of the empty tomb been determined or redacted in the light of mythological or kerygmatic* considerations or by liturgical practice? The fact that belief in Jesus' resurrection was a central confession of faith from the first has been widely recognized, with I Cor. 15.3–8 providing the decisive evidence. So too the fact that this belief was rooted in resurrection 'appearances'. For those working with a narrowly defined historical method, the most obvious explanations have been in terms of hysterical visions, the conviction that Jesus' message could not die, or cognitive dissonance* (the refusal to accept evident disconfirmation of earlier hopes), though all such explanations labour under the difficulty of explaining the striking differences between the pre-Easter and post-Easter proclamation. For those with a more open model of historical enquiry, however, the interpretative conundrum remains, characterized by the description of the resurrection as 'eschatological event'; how to speak meaningfully within history of an event which by definition transcends or breaks out of history, an event which is utterly unique, without parallel within history, because it marks the end of history and forms a unique interface between this world and the world to come? Where the dividing line between demonstrable history and faith proclamation becomes thus elided, the only solution is to maintain the integrity of the dialogue at both sides of the point of intersection.

On any reckoning the resurrection* is the definitive moment of transition from the historical Jesus to the Christ of faith and inevitably therefore stands at the centre of NT christology as the interpretative key, however that key is formally expressed. This has also been brought home by another major line of research during the same period, that is, into the titles of Jesus – Messiah,* Son of Man, Son of God, Lord, etc. This proved valuable as a descriptive exercise, but unsatisfactory in terms of providing hermeneutical keys for christology. The reason is presumably that the Christ event contributed more to the titles than vice-versa. Titles like Messiah and Son of Man proved incapable of carrying the growing weight of theological significance accorded to Jesus; *kyrios* provided an invaluable transition from pre-Easter ('sir' is its secular sense) to post-Easter (it also means 'Lord'). *Logos* carried the main christological weight into the post-apostolic period, and Son of God proved the most durable title of all. But at each phase it was the burgeoning christology itself which was decisive, either leaving the unadaptable titles behind or steadily transforming the significance of the more adaptable. As labels by which to chart the progress and diverse emphases of earliest christology, titles have continuing interpretative value, but they do not themselves explain that progress or its dynamic.

While such attempts were being made to explain and interpret christology 'from below', the classical creeds continued to provide a framework for those who saw the deficiencies of the historical method as decisive and who continued to interpret the biblical texts in terms of a christology 'from above'. Characteristic here have been the expositions of kenotic christology and Barth's christocentrism. The former, well regarded by many scholars in the late nineteenth and early twentieth centuries, had its putative hermeneutical basis in Phil. 2.7 ('he emptied himself'), though the exegetical toe-hold was tenuous and the debate on the meaning of *kenōsis*, as so often before, depended on dogmatic considerations well removed from the text of Philippians. Barth's theology of the Word, with its disjunction between the word of God* and all human thought, came to hermeneutical expression in his early emphasis on the belief that historical criticism and exegesis are but preparatory to the task of theology and the word of proclamation. Here once again any effective historical control or check on dogma was effectively discounted. More recent attempts to provide a systematic* conceptuality in theology have made greater attempts to root the theological paradigm in the NT, with varying degrees of success: W. Pannenberg, recognizing the cru-

cial interface character of the NT accounts of Jesus' resurrection; J. Moltmann with his more dogmatically oriented focus on the cross; and E. Schillebeeckx trying to work more fully with NT exegesis and scholarship, and finding the resolution in effect in Christian experience.

The most persistent attempt at bridging the christology-from-above/christology-from-below divide has been the quest of the gnostic* redeemer myth, which has dominated much of twentieth-century NT research (particularly under the influence of R. Bultmann*). Its attraction grew partly from the observation of non-Christian features in the developed form of the myth in the later gnostic systems, suggesting the possibility of a pre-Christian form; and partly from the historical method's difficulty in handling the *novum*, the problem of explaining a historical datum which seems to make a 'quantum leap' beyond anything which came before. The presupposition that already before the first century there was a developed myth of a divine figure, who descended from heaven to rescue spiritual entities (fragments of light-souls) trapped within the prison of matter, would certainly explain how Jesus came to be spoken of as a descending/ascending redeemer. The search for the pre-Christian myth has, however, had the character more of a wild-goose chase. The hypothesis that the pre-Christian indications of the myth are fragments of an unattested whole has had to give way before the more credible hypothesis that these elements are building blocks which were later put together to form the developed myth. The dualism of the reconstructed myth fits poorly with the evolution in the Christian texts from a resurrection-centred proclamation to a concept of incarnation (docetism coming later). The key NT texts themselves are better explained as distinctively new evolutions of Hellenistic-Jewish ideas of Wisdom and Adam* provoked by the impact of the whole Christ event.

In fact, in a rather striking way, the interpretation of NT christology has come full circle, with the same texts which provided the biblical subject matter for the debates of early centuries once again at the centre of hermeneutical debate, particularly John 1.14, Phil. 2.6–11, and Col. 1.15–20. As in the early centuries other models have been taken up and tried. An angelomorphic christology can argue for exegetical support in the Son of Man motif of the Gospels and particularly in the visions of the seer of Revelation; but the same factors condemn it to the edges of the main stream of developing christology. A Spirit christology (as in G. W. H. Lampe, *God as Spirit*, 1977) can build strongly on the category of Jesus the prophet and on such texts as I Cor. 15.45, but fails to take adequate account of why the category of prophet proved unsatisfactory to the evangelists and of the dynamic within NT christology. As the evolving christology of the early centuries also bears witness, it was the NT's Adam christology and Wisdom/Logos christology which proved the most productive in drawing out the full significance of the Christ event. This should occasion no surprise since it is precisely the talk of divine image, common to both Adam and Wisdom, which bridges the divide between human and divine and which expresses the revelatory significance which the first Christians evidently experienced in and through Christ: Christ the archetype of man and the window into God.

For the same reason it is the Fourth Gospel which serves as the indispensable bridge between the historical Jesus and the Christ of dogma. For it clearly indicates that stage in Christian reflection, which was still rooted in historical memory of what Jesus did and said (as more clearly expressed in the Synoptic tradition), which (like the earlier NT writers) still saw the primary revelatory and redemptive focus in Christ's death and resurrection as illumined by the interpreter Spirit, and which now saw the need to bring his fuller significance to expression precisely in Gospel format, but using language and categories which would have greatest impact on his contemporaries and readers. To the extent that the Fourth Evangelist was successful in maintaining that three-fold tension, to that extent his Gospel still provides the most important single NT paradigm for expounding the significance of God's revelation in Christ.

See also **Parousia.**

R. E. Brown, *The Birth of the Messiah*, 1977; J. D. G. Dunn, *Christology in the Making*, 1980; E. R. Fairweather, 'The "Kenotic" Christology' in F. W. Beare, *Philippians*, 1959; A. Grillmeier, *Christ in Christian Tradition*, ² 1975; A. J. Hultgren, *Christ and his Benefits: Christology and Redemption in the NT*, 1987; P. Perkins, *Resurrection: New Testament Witness and Contemporary Reflection*, 1984.

                                      JAMES D. G. DUNN

Chronicles

The books of Chronicles have a double importance for biblical interpretation; as well as the way in which they have themselves been interpreted, they provide our earliest (? fourth century BC) major example of interpretation of earlier biblical material. A very substantial part of I and II Chronicles is also to be found in Genesis (the genealogies * at the beginning of I Chronicles) or in Samuel–Kings. It was once supposed that this duplication arose simply from a desire to ensure that nothing had been omitted from the sacred traditions; hence the title of the books in the Greek translation, *ta paralipomena*, 'the things omitted'. More probably the Chronicler was commenting upon the earlier material which was already coming to be revered as sacred, and giving his own explanation of it. Just as a modern commentary * seeks to account for and resolve ambiguities and obscurities in the text being discussed, so this seems to have been part of the Chronicler's purpose. In I Chron. 20.5, for example, the double tradition in the books of Samuel as to who had killed Goliath the Philistine giant is clarified; in I Chron. 21.1 the theological problem posed by God commanding David * to carry out a census and then condemning him for doing so is resolved by attributing the idea of a census to Satan. Elsewhere exegesis is carried out in a less direct fashion; in I Chron. 22 the commissioning of Solomon as David's successor is described in terms reminiscent of Joshua's succession to Moses * in Josh. 1, and in II Chron. 20.15–17 the 'sermon' before the battle uses phrases culled from a variety of other OT texts describing the need for trust in God in times of crisis. It has been maintained that the whole of the work of the Chronicler can be understood as exegesis, but this is probably too limiting.

Among the interpretative concerns of the Chronicler will certainly have been an emphasis on the continuity of the scriptural story, from Adam * (I Chron. 1.1) to the community of his own day; on David * and his line as the true recipients of the divine promises; on the temple at Jerusalem * as the centre of the community (and this emphasis links together the two preceding ones, for the continuity between the first and second temples is stressed, and the role of David in making ready for the temple emphasized); on the way in which history illustrates divine retribution and blessing in accordance with human behaviour. (The modification in II Chron. of the verdict of Kings on Asa and Jehoshaphat, and on Manasseh and Josiah, offers striking illustrations of this understanding of history.)

The last verses of II Chronicles are repeated at the beginning of Ezra, and many scholars have taken this as an indication that Chronicles and Ezra–Nehemiah should be regarded as one work; certainly they share a great concern for the Jerusalem temple as the locus of God's saving activity and its community as the object of his special care, but Chronicles shows a more open attitude to those outside the Jerusalem community than does Ezra–Nehemiah, and it may be that the common origin of the whole collection should not be pressed (Williamson).

Turning to the way in which Chronicles has itself been interpreted, the first impression is that conveyed by the Greek title mentioned above: 'things omitted'. For the most part in both Jewish and Christian tradition Chronicles has received less attention than almost any other part of the Bible. (A revealing example is found in its neglect in Christian lectionaries; in the sixteenth century Cranmer was anxious to ensure that the whole Bible was covered in his Church of England offices of Morning and Evening Prayer – the only significant omission from the annual scheme was Chronicles.)

After a long period of neglect, however, the present century has seen a revival of interest in Chronicles. Where earlier scholars tended to be dismissive, because they regarded the Chronicler as a historian, and as such he could not be relied upon (Pfeiffer), the more recent approach has been to attempt to understand the Chronicler for what he was trying to do rather than to criticize him for failings that may well not have been part of his concern. The point already made, concerning his exegetical interests, is relevant here; similarly it seems legitimate to see part of his purpose as related to the spelling out of the fact and nature of God's continuing beneficence to the community of his own day, despite their outwardly unpromising circumstances. God was still the ultimate ruler, even if they were under the dominion of a foreign political power.

See also **Ezra–Nehemiah; Inner-Biblical Exegesis.**

P. R. Ackroyd, *Studies in the Religious Tradition of the Old Testament*, 1987; R. H. Pfeiffer, *Introduction to the Old Testament*, 1948, pp. 782–812 (for a very negative view of the Chronicler); H. G. M. Williamson, *Israel in the Books of Chronicles*, 1977; id., *1 and 2 Chronicles* (New Century Bible), 1982.

R. J. COGGINS

Chronology

The Bible contains various items of chronological information relating to persons and events from the time of creation to the period of the NT. Part of this information is interrelated to form a continuous chronology which stretches from creation to the time of the Babylonian exile. This is presented in a series of genealogical and regnal notices which are to be found in the books of the Pentateuch* and Former Prophets* (Genesis to Kings). Chronological notices in Genesis specify the total lifespans of Israel's ancestors, and (more importantly) the age of each ancestor at the birth of his successor, from which one can work out the total number of years from creation to the time of Jacob by simply adding together ages

of begetting. Outside Genesis, the chronology is presented in regnal form stating the duration of a king's (or judge's) rule, or periods during which Israel was subject to foreign oppression, or periods of freedom from foreign oppression. On two occasions genealogical* and regnal notices are bypassed with statements specifying a longer chronological period – the duration of Israel's stay in Egypt (Ex. 12.40), or the period from the exodus to the foundation of the temple (I Kings 6.1).

Chronological information outside Genesis to Kings includes Jeremiah's famous reference to a 70-year period of Babylonian domination (Jer. 25.11; 29.10), and Daniel's prophecy of 70 weeks of years (Dan. 9), which was based on the Jeremiah prophecy. There are also various chronological notices and allusions in other prophetic and historical books of the Hebrew Bible, and similar information is to be found in apocryphal* literature and the NT. According to Luke 3.1, John the Baptist began his ministry in the fifteenth year of Tiberius Caesar. In contrast to chronological information in Genesis to Kings, chronological data from other biblical books do not provide a systematic or continuous chronology of long historical periods.

The chronology of Genesis to Kings has a number of internal characteristics that have been fundamental in shaping the later interpretation of biblical chronology. One of these is the fact that this chronology is clearly schematic. According to figures found in the traditional Masoretic text,* the period from the exodus to the foundation of the temple was a round number of 480 years (I Kings 6.1), the duration of Israel's stay in Egypt was 430 years (Ex. 12.40), and genealogical figures for the period from the birth of Abraham* to the entry into Egypt add up to 290 years, giving a round total of 1,200 years from the birth of Abraham to the foundation of the temple. Judaean regnal years from the foundation of the temple to the Babylonian exile also add up to a round figure of 430 years.

The second major feature of this chronology is that it contains a considerable number of internal discrepancies. The 480-year interval between the exodus and the foundation of the temple is not consistent with chronological notices in Judges and Samuel, which give a total of 450 years from the settlement to the death of Eli. If we add 40 years in the wilderness (Num. 32.13) and 44 years for David's reign and the first part of Solomon's reign (I Kings 2.11; 6.1), plus 2(?) years for Saul's reign (I Sam. 13.1) and an unknown figure for Samuel's rule, this takes us well beyond the 480-year total of I Kings 6.1. (According to Josephus,* *Antiquities 6.378*, and Acts 13.21 Saul reigned for 40 years.) The synchronistic chronology of Kings contains a particularly large number of internal discrepancies: reign lengths are frequently incompatible with synchronisms between northern (Israelite) and southern (Judaean) reigns, and Judaean chronology for the period from the revolt of Jehu to the fall of Samaria is 20 years longer than Israelite chronology for the same period.

A third characteristic of this chronology is that it exists in several different versions. The Samaritan* Pentateuch* gives a different set of figures for Pentateuchal chronology, as also does the Greek Septuagint* translation, which moreover frequently disagrees with the Masoretic Text* in its figures for the period from the settlement to the Babylonian exile. Within the Pentateuch, the figures given by the Septuagint total 3,312 or 3,314 years for the period from creation to the birth of Abraham, while the Masoretic figures add up to 1,946 or 1,948 years, and the Samaritan Pentateuch has 2,247 or 2,249 years for the same period (the alternative dates in each case reflect a two-year discrepancy over the date of the birth of Arpachshad, Gen. 11.10).

The existence of three different versions of biblical chronology (not to mention alternative apocryphal and non-biblical versions, such as those of Jubilees and Josephus) is evidence that an intense interest in biblical chronology existed from an early period. This also served to divide later chronological interpretation into three main traditions – a Samaritan tradition based on the Samaritan Pentateuch, a Jewish tradition based on the Masoretic Text, and a Christian tradition based originally on the Septuagint. Within these traditions, three main concerns may be detected: a continuing interest in chronological schematism, a desire to harmonize chronological discrepancies, and a historical interest in integrating biblical chronology with non-biblical chronology to produce a general chronology of world history.

Jewish interest in chronological schematism can be seen in *Seder Olam Rabba*, a rabbinic* tractate which is devoted to the interpretation of biblical chronology, and which concludes with a summary of Jewish chronology for the period from the foundation of the second temple to its destruction in AD 70 (*Seder Olam Rabba 30*). The most striking feature of this summary is that the entire duration of the Persian empire, which actually lasted for over two centuries, is given as only 52 years. The significant point about this figure is that it is clearly schematic: 52 is a round chronological figure, like 7 and 12, because there are 52 weeks in a year (just as there are 7 days in a week and 12 months in a year). More importantly the reduction of the Persian period to 52 years is part of a larger scheme in which the interval between the destruction of the first temple (in 587 BC) and the destruction of the second temple (in AD 70) is calculated to arrive at a round total of 490 years, corresponding to the 70 weeks of years in Daniel 9 (*Seder Olam Rabba 28*). This chronology was later incorporated into the Jewish era of the world, in which years are dated from the world's creation, with year 1 beginning in the Julian year 3761 BC.

Early Christian chronologists displayed similar schematic interests. Most were strongly influenced by the belief that the history of the world would last for six millennia corresponding to the six days of the world's creation, to be followed by a seventh sabbatical millennium paralleling the day in which God rested from his creation (compare the eschatological millennium in Revelation 20.2, which possibly derives from an early formulation of this scheme, and certainly influenced its later development). One result of this analogy between the creation of the world and its subsequent history was that the birth of Christ was normally dated to the sixth millennium of world history, because Adam,* who prefigured Christ, was created on the sixth day of the world's creation. This belief agreed rather well with the chronological data of the Septuagint, and Julius Africanus (*c.* 164 to 240) calculated a period of exactly 5,500 years from creation to the birth of Christ using Septuagint data. Eusebius* (*c.* 260 to 340) later reduced this to 5,199 years, one year short of a schematic total of 5,200 years. One reason for this reduction may have been a desire to 'postpone the millennium', thereby discouraging potentially disruptive expectations of an imminent eschaton.

Eusebius incorporated his chronological calculations into a synchronistic chronicle of world history in which events in the history of different nations were arranged in parallel columns and dated in years from the birth of Abraham. This was afterwards translated into Latin by Jerome, and subsequently gained general acceptance in the West, whereas Eastern Christianity continued to maintain the earlier, longer chronology. Western Christianity later adopted an even shorter chronology based on the Masoretic figures in Jerome's Vulgate* translation of the Bible. According to this chronology, which was worked out by Bede in the early part of the eighth century, Christ was born 3,952 years after the creation of the world. Bede's chronology was almost certainly intended to counteract a popular expectation that the world would end in about AD 800 (6,000 years after its creation according to Eusebian chronology), and one factor in its acceptance may well have been the nonappearance of the expected end.

Harmonistic efforts to explain away apparent discrepancies in biblical chronology are to be found in both Jewish and Christian traditions, with the former influencing the latter. *Seder Olam Rabba* adopts various midrashic* devices for harmonizing these discrepancies. For example, the discrepancy between the chronology of Judges to Samuel and the 480-year figure given in I Kings 6.1 was resolved by the assumption that years of oppression were contained within other chronological periods and could therefore be disregarded for the purposes of overall calculations. This explanation was later adopted by Eusebius, and similar explanations have been taken up by a large number of modern scholars.

Ussher's monumental synthesis of world chronology (*Annales Veteris Testamenti*, 1650), which is included in many editions of the K J V, may be seen as the culmination of previous chronological interpretation. Ussher's date for creation (4004 BC) was not significantly different from Bede's date in chronological terms, and was not in fact original (Thomas Lydiat had arrived at the same date by a different route forty years earlier). But Ussher presented a scheme of world chronology in which almost every apparent discrepancy was harmonized (using co-regencies and interregna), and which was also elegantly schematic. According to Ussher's scheme, Christ was born in 4 BC, exactly four thousand years after the creation of the world, and the temple was completed in 1004 BC, one thousand years before the birth of Christ. Ussher drew attention to this schematism in his preface to the Annals (p. 7), and evidently saw it as confirmation of his belief that human history was ordered according to a divine plan.

Ussher stood at a watershed in the history of the interpretation of biblical chronology. Previously it had been generally accepted that chronological data given by the Bible were historically accurate. However, the later history of interpretation has been one in which this belief was gradually eroded. Scientific theories which were developed during the eighteenth and nineteenth centuries led to the virtual abandonment of any literal belief in the early chronology of Genesis, and historical discoveries of the nineteenth century were to make it increasingly difficult to accept the historical chronology of Kings. In both cases the initial response to these difficulties was to produce new harmonizations for reconciling biblical and scientific or historical data. Scientific harmonizations of the chronology of Genesis are now firmly discredited in all but the most extreme fundamentalist* circles, but historical harmonizations of the chronology of Kings are still widely accepted.

The historical problem is that the chronology of Kings is too long by comparison with Assyrian and Babylonian chronology of the first millennium, which is based on good historical records and is also corroborated by astronomical evidence. The harmonizing response to this problem is to deploy a variety of Ussherian devices including interregna and – more importantly, since we need to shorten the chronology – numerous hypothetical co-regencies. Chronological harmonizations of this type have been championed most notably by E. R. Thiele, but are also to be found in chronological reconstructions by many less conservative biblical scholars.

The main problem with this type of approach is that the alleged co-regencies and interregna are unattested in the biblical text, which regularly associates the start of a king's reign with the death or exile of his predecessor. Other scholars, such as W. F. Albright, have therefore suggested textual corruption as a possible cause of chronological confusion, but the proposed emendations are no less *ad hoc* in character than the co-regencies and interregna proposed by chronological harmonists. A third approach to the chronology of Kings is to assume a series of misunderstandings and mistakes by the author(s) of Kings and/or its later editors.

One crucial weakness of each of these approaches, which are often used in combination, is that they disregard clear evidence of chronological schematism. Julius Wellhausen pointed out a century ago that the total duration of Judaean reigns from the foundation of the temple to the exile (as stated in Kings) adds up to 430 years, and that 50 years to the end of the exile (in 538 BC) brings this to a round total of 480 years that mirrors the 480-year period from the exodus to the foundation of the temple (I Kings 6.1). This gives us a convincing explanation for the discrepancy between the chronology of Kings and historical chronology, which is that the chronology of Kings in its present form is essentially mythical rather than historical. This does not mean that it may not also contain accurate information: I have argued in detail elsewhere that this is in fact the case, and that internal chronological discrepancies and variant data from non-Masoretic traditions offer a way of reconstructing an original pre-schematic chronology. The value of non-Masoretic chronological traditions has also been stressed by other scholars of differing viewpoints.

Biblical chronology is important for two main reasons. It is our main source of information for the historical chronology of Israel and Judah, despite the inherent problems of interpreting this information. And it is also evidence of a mythicizing approach to history in which dates and events were reshaped to fit in with certain religious beliefs. The schematic patterns of biblical chronology and of chronological systems based on biblical chronology are essentially mythical expressions of the belief that human history manifests an underlying divine purpose.

See also **Millenarianism**.

J. Barr, 'Why the world was created in 4004 BC: Archbishop Ussher and Biblical chronology', *BJRL* 67, 1984, pp. 575–608; J. Finegan, *Handbook of Biblical Chronology*, 1964; J. Hughes, *Secrets of the Times, JSOT*-SS, 1989; E. R. Thiele, *The mysterious numbers of the Hebrew kings: a reconstruction of the chronology of the kingdoms of Israel and Judah*, ²1983.

JEREMY HUGHES

Cognitive Dissonance

The theory of cognitive dissonance was developed by Leon Festinger and others in the 1950s. It belongs to that aspect of social psychology known as social cognition research and attempts to account for how beliefs and behaviour change attitudes. It focusses on inconsistency among cognitions and its effects which are said to arouse dissonance. For example, if you believe that the world should have ended years ago there must be some dissonance between this belief and your continued existence today; or, in terms of behaviour, if you believe that you should love your neighbour as yourself but are in fact a religious bigot then some explanation is required as to how you relate practice to belief. All such explanations are responses to dissonance arousal and the theory plots what is essentially the rationalizing activities of humans. The standard responses to dissonance may be summarized as: selective exposure to information (where consistent information is not available), selective attention to it (i.e. looking at consistent information where it is available), selective interpretation (ambiguous information is translated so as to be consistent with the beliefs being defended). In practice these work out as: pick your friends carefully, examine consistent evidence, read only the books which agree with your position, move exclusively in circles of like-minded people, relate all information to your core beliefs and practices. Thus people are biased to select data which reinforce beliefs. In the right circumstances the theory has some explanatory power, though many research programmes have reported only ambiguous evidence in support of it (cf. Fiske & Taylor, pp. 340–68; Carroll, pp. 86–110, 233–5).

Festinger's *When Prophecy Fails* studied a group in the 1950s devoted to the belief that the world would end soon (cf. Alison Lurie's novel *Imaginary Friends*) and developed a number of theoretical points from the group's growth after the failure of their expectations. Part of his comparative data on such groups was derived from traditional Christian beliefs in the second coming of Jesus and the seventeenth-century movement associated with the messianic* claims of Sabbatai Zevi. This application of the theory takes it into the territory of biblical studies. The prophetic traditions of the Hebrew Bible are a fertile source for dissonance theory analysis (cf. Carroll, pp. 111–213). According to Deut. 18.21–22 prophecy* had a predictive aspect, so the survival of failed predictions in the prophetic traditions may allow for the theory's application to prophecy. Here the theory raises many important theoretical and substantive issues in the interpretation of biblical literature and Carroll's analysis of theory and text has by no means exhausted the range of the theory's application to the Bible.

The book of Isaiah affords the most useful material for testing the theory as so much of the book has undergone reinterpretation, some of it in the light of the failure of expectations (cf. Carroll, pp. 130–56; Sweeney, *Isaiah 1–4 and the Post-Exilic Understanding of the Isaianic Tradition*, 1988, p. 196). The use of Isa. 6.9–10 to justify the failure of a mission may well be a resolution of dissonance brought about by that failure and the destruction of the nation. It certainly falsifies the common belief that prophets were preachers of repentance! The use of 6.9–10 in the NT is most instructive (see below). The Isaiah text is open to a number of interpretations and this multiplicity of meanings makes the use of dissonance theory less penetrative. It can only be one among many theoretical explanations and it may not always be the most obvious explanation. But it does raise the question: just how much of theology is dissonance resolution?

The theory is essentially for second-order levels of such literature, i.e. not the original statements themselves but as constituents of beliefs within the later communities which regarded them as authoritative. This means that it is at the level of the reception of texts that the theory has its most useful part to play in biblical studies. Where communities hold to beliefs about the text as predictive, we should expect to find dissonances resolving explanations for the failure of such predictions, or reinterpretative moves proving the fulfilment of prediction (e.g. the messianism of the early churches). Reinterpretative moves may occur also in the texts themselves and it has been argued that the Immanuel material in Isa. 7–9, 11 gives birth to dissonance for Isaiah (Laato, pp. 42–7, 301–26). The traditional understanding of Immanuel as predictive prophecy fits the cognitive dissonance approach perfectly because it reflects all the problems of the reception of texts in later interpretative communities. Isa. 9.2–7 illustrates this point: originally this celebration of the king's accession to the throne was not a prediction but a conventional accession hymn genre.* Received and interpreted by communities without a king but perhaps entertaining messianic hopes it quickly becomes predictive. Failed expectations here would reflect on the interpretative community and not on the text itself! Dissonance theory therefore requires the recognition of the nexus of the text-situation-interpretative community (the so-called 'living tradition') as the object of scrutiny rather than the text *simpliciter*.

The theory has also been applied to NT studies (Gager). The strong sense of mission among the early churches, whereby converts were added to the roll, has all the marks of a dissonance-resolving move. Social support is central to the theory's explanation of dissonance reduction because such support provides social validation of belief (e.g. ten thousand lemmings cannot be wrong! two thousand years of the church must count for something!). The more people who believe something the more likely it is to be true or the less likelihood of it being wrong. Dissonance-arousing experiences must have been a central problem for the early churches. Why did so few Jews believe Jesus was the messiah? Here Isa. 6.9–10 performed wonders for the NT writers because it explained the unbelief of people perfectly (e.g. Matt. 13.14–15; Mark 4.12; Luke 8.10; John 12.40; Acts 28.25–27). The dissonance between the belief that Jesus was the messiah and the Jewish rejection of him is explained by the application of this text. Belief and experience no longer conflict. If Jesus really was the messiah why then was he crucified by the Romans? There is nothing in the prophecies about messiah being killed. A radical hermeneutic of the Septuagint* helped to make inroads on that dissonance and the belief in and preaching of the resurrection* rescued the death of Jesus from crippling dissonance. Paul's letters are full of counter-assertions against treating the crucifixion as a mere death and proclamations of it as part of a grandiose world plan of salvation (cf. his conspiracy theory in II Cor. 4.2–4 to explain the lack of belief in his gospel!). The transformation of the wretched and unjust crucifixion of Jesus into a universal theology of salvation is a classic instance of dissonance resolution. The theory works very well for NT studies in a general way.

There are many aspects of the Bible which would yield to a cognitive dissonance analysis: e.g. the resolution of real social problems by

cultic and eschatological explanations (Habakkuk, Joel, Ps. 73); the failure of the parousia* in the NT. In application to the Bible the theory is open to criticism (Rodd) – all theories are! – but as a heuristic device for reading biblical texts it has a contribution to make. It will add to the many levels at which the text may be interpreted. Mature people can live with dissonance – Keats called this 'negative capability' – but could the communities which produced and then commented on the Bible manage dissonance? If they could, then how did they do it? Consult the theory!

See also **Sociology and Social Anthropology.**

R. P. Carroll, *When Prophecy Failed,* 1979; L. Festinger et al., *When Prophecy Fails,* 1956; L. Festinger, *A Theory of Cognitive Dissonance,* 1957; S. T. Fiske and S. E. Taylor, *Social Cognition,* 1984; J. G. Gager, *Kingdom and Community: The Social World of Early Christianity,* 1975; A. Laato, *Who Is Immanuel? The Rise and the Foundering of Isaiah's Messianic Expectations,* 1988; C. S. Rodd, 'On Applying a Sociological Theory to Biblical Studies', *JSOT* 19, 1981, pp. 95–106.

ROBERT P. CARROLL

Coleridge, S. T.

Samuel Taylor Coleridge (1772–1834) is rightly described by a recent biographer as 'one of the seminal religious thinkers of modern times', and it is surprising that his contribution to theological thought is not more widely recognized. One reason for this may be its disorderly presentation; for one who was in many ways a highly systematic thinker, Coleridge was a remarkably unsystematic writer. Some of his best theological writing occurs in digressions or footnotes during essays on ostensibly non-theological themes, and even in specifically theological contexts his argumentation is often diffuse. Another possible reason for his comparative neglect by modern theologians is the contentious issue of alleged plagiarisms (notably from Schelling in the *Biographia Literaria,* 1817), an issue which the new Princeton edition of his collected works should help to resolve.

In 1798–9 Coleridge visited Germany, returning with a large trunkful of metaphysical works and a good working knowledge of the language. Although he is sometimes said to have been among the first to introduce German biblical criticism* to the English-speaking public, his work on biblical interpretation does not betray any great knowledge or understanding of historical-critical* principles or results. In a typical English reaction to German criticism, he speaks of 'certain biblical philologists of the Teutonic school' as 'men distinguished by learning, but still more characteristically by hardihood in conjecture'. In his *Confessions of an Inquiring Spirit* (published posthumously in 1840), he attacks the notion of biblical inerrancy, yet the results of criticism are alluded to only in passing. His view of the Bible allows room for free critical inquiry, but that is not where his own interest lies.

Coleridge's real significance for biblical interpretation lies in the field of hermeneutics,* where he is able to draw on insights from his work as a literary critic. The theme of *The Statesman's Manual* (1816) is, according to its subtitle, 'the Bible the Best Guide to Political Skill and Foresight'; but in fact he has little directly to say about this rather pedestrian topic, addressing himself mainly to the more general issue of the significance of the Bible for the present. Coleridge is interested in the state of mind necessary for true understanding of the Bible, and he attacks the assumption that its meaning is self-evident: 'The main hindrance to the use of the scriptures ... lies in the notion that you are already acquainted with its contents.' One manifestation of this frame of mind may be detected in language such as, 'It only means so and so': for example, in an imaginary free-thinker's response to Col. I.13–20, 'that by these words (very bold and figurative words it must be confessed, yet still) St Paul *only* meant that the universal and eternal truths of morality and a future state had been re-proclaimed by an inspired teacher and confirmed by miracles'. In this type of theology, the prophets* have a purely antiquarian value, and due allowance must be made for the evangelists'* superstition about evil spirits. Coleridge is implacably opposed to the exegesis of rationalists such as Paley, which will not allow the text to say anything more than the platitudes of 'rational religion'.

Instead, the scriptures are to be seen as 'the living *educts* of the Imagination', understood as the power which unites fluctuating sense-images with the eternal truths of reason. In the Bible, facts and persons have a two-fold significance which is both temporary and perpetual, particular and universal. This does not mean that the biblical symbols* are to be understood as mere metaphors* or allegories* and set in opposition to the 'literal' meaning.* The symbol is characterized by 'the translucence of the Eternal through and in the Temporal', in such a way that the temporal form is inseparable from the eternal content. The presence of the eternal in and with the historical means that the biblical texts can address and answer to our own existential experience of guilt and separation from God.

In the *Confessions of an Inquiring Spirit* (probably written in 1825–6), Coleridge attacks the 'superstitious and unscriptural' view that the Bible as the Word of God* must be infallible. That doctrine ignores the fact that the books were written in different ages and circumstances, in which their authors fully participated; it 'petrifies at once the whole body of the Holy Writ with all its harmonies and symmetrical gradations' – language which suggests that for Coleridge the issue is aesthetic as well as factual. The advocates of inerrancy wrongly believe that what is said of the Bible as a whole (that it is the inspired Word of God) must also be said of every sentence within it. But the value of the Bible is in no way impaired by 'the blessing of Deborah, the cursings of David, or the Grecisms and heavier difficulties in the biographical chapters of the Book of Daniel, or the hydrography and natural philosophy of the Patriarchal ages'. Nor should we resort to the absurd artifices of the harmonizers* when we come across discrepancies in different biblical accounts of the same events.

The proof of divine inspiration* can only be internal: 'In the Bible there is more that *finds* me than I have experienced in all other books put together ... The words of the Bible find me at greater depths of my being.' Those for whom this is true share a common spiritual world: 'You in one place, I in another, all men somewhere, meet [in the Bible] with an assurance that the hopes and fears, the thoughts and yearnings that proceed from, or tend to, a right spirit in us, are not dreams or fleeting singularities, no voices heard in sleep, or spectres which the eye suffers but not perceives.' Here, subjective and objective are united. Subjective experience receives objective confirmation as one discovers it antedated in these writings. Conversely, the objective letter of scripture comes to life only through subjective experience projected on to it.

Thomas McFarland, *Coleridge and the Pantheist Tradition*, 1969; C. Welch, 'Samuel Taylor Coleridge', in Ninian Smart et al. (ed.), *Nineteenth Century Religious Thought in the West*, vol. II, 1985; Basil Willey, *Nineteenth Century Studies*, 1949.

FRANCIS WATSON

Colossians and Philemon

The Epistle to the Colossians has been a major source of theological discussion and debate among Pauline scholars for the last century and a half. Not only has its distinctive theological message been a focal point, notably the exalted christological hymn of 1.15–20, but the question of its literary relationship to other epistles* within the Pauline corpus, particularly Philemon and Ephesians, has also been a subject of much discussion. Closely related is the question whether or not it is a genuine work of the apostle Paul.*

This is a matter which is still a hotly contested issue among NT scholars today. E. T. Mayerhoff in 1838 was the first to call into question the authenticity of the epistle. Since that time the matter has been continually in debate with no clear consensus yet emerging. The theology, vocabulary, grammar and style of the epistle have been scrutinized by many scholars in an attempt to determine precisely the relationship that the epistle has to the undisputed Pauline letters, and to the related letter to the Ephesians. That a literary relationship exists between Colossians and Ephesians is without doubt; but the precise nature of that relationship is highly contentious with virtually all possible permutations being suggested by scholars. For instance, both E. J. Goodspeed and C. L. Mitton have argued that Ephesians was clearly dependent upon Colossians, while F. C. Synge argued precisely the opposite. Both of these interpretations assume Pauline authorship of one or the other of the epistles. E. P. Sanders has argued that the evidence clearly demonstrates a literary dependence of Colossians upon the other, undisputed Pauline letters in such a way that non-Pauline authorship seems indicated. E. Schweizer argued that stylistic features tip the balance against full Pauline authorship but that nevertheless a post-Pauline origin of the letter is unlikely. He suggests that it is an authentic Pauline letter, heavily edited, perhaps by Timothy. More recently, P. T. O'Brien and N. T. Wright have reasserted the traditional view that Colossians is genuinely Pauline and reject any attempt to distance it from the (Pauline?) letter to the Ephesians. A consensus on the question of authorship is unlikely given the present evidence.

One of the most important questions arising out of scholarly study of the epistle concerns the theological controversy to which the letter is said to respond, the so-called 'Colossian heresy' (see especially 2.8–3.4). It appears reasonable to assume that the author of the letter is replying to news brought to him, probably by Epaphras (1.7–8; 4.12–13), concerning the state of the church at Colossae. The precise nature of the controversy is never explicitly stated in the letter and must be deduced from its contents. F. C. Baur in his *Paulus: der Apostel Jesu Christi*, 1845, suggested that it was an expression of second-century Gnosticism,* an interpretation followed by many German scholars influenced by the Tübingen school.* This is now generally recognized to be an extremely problematic (and anachronistic) interpretation. Most scholars agree that the controversy involved some sort of syncretistic Jewish mysticism which expressed itself through the aid of Hellenistic philosophical structure and vocabulary.

A second major focal point has been the eschatological teaching contained in the letter. It appears that the perspective is one of a fully realized eschatology,* with 2.12 and 3.1–4 serving as the critical proof-texts. The fact that within Colossians the 'already/not yet' tension of Paul's eschatology appears clearly resolved in favour of the former has been one of the major arguments for the Deutero-Pauline character of the letter. Much scholarly attention has been directed to establishing the relationship that temporal descriptions of the Christian experience have to spatial descriptions, and Colossians has been in the forefront of such discussions. A. T. Lincoln notes (*Paradise Now and Not Yet*, 1981, p. 131) that in Colossians Paul 'stresses that the salvation Christ brought occurred in history but he draws out the significance of this in relation to the heavenly realm rather than to the fulfilment of God's promises to Israel'.

A third focal area has been that of ecclesiology. The references to Christ as 'the head of the body the church' (1.18) are thought by many to be a phrase so uncharacteristic of the undisputed Pauline letters as to force one to concede non-Pauline authorship of Colossians. Certainly there is a development from Paul's ecclesiology contained in I Cor. 12 or Rom. 12, but whether this curious phrase means or implies a cosmic church (as E. Lohse argues) is a matter of some debate. The issue is further complicated by the fact that the critical words 'the church' are usually taken to be an interpolation added (by Paul or the writer?) to the original hymn.

Without doubt the major contribution that Colossians has made in the history of interpretation lies within the area of christology.* Here the hymn of 1.15–20 has dominated discussion. It is generally recognized that this central passage was originally a (Jewish?) hymn in praise of wisdom which has been reinterpreted christologically. It is thus taken to be pre-Pauline in its basic structure, although Christian interpolations are manifestly evident. The hymn contains many elements which became central for the subsequent doctrinal controversies of the second and third centuries, notably the description of Christ as 'the image of God', 'the firstborn of all creation', 'the head of the body the church' and 'the firstborn from the dead'. Individual verses and phrases became especially critical to christological debates raging in the church. For instance, 1.16 gives one of the clearest examples of a cosmic christology found in the Pauline corpus. Col. 1.15 and 18 were focal points as the question of the two natures of Christ was debated in the period leading up to the Council of Chalcedon, while 1.20 was a critical text in the development of theories of atonement. Almost every Christian commentator turned to Colossians at some point to assert his understanding of the christological basis of the faith. In Irenaeus,* for whom christology was intimately linked to soteriology, the reference to *oikonomian tou theou* in 1.25 played a key role. The christology–soteriology link has been an important aspect of doctrine ever since. It has been seen in a variety of ways, often on the basis of the Colossians hymn as well as other texts, in the attempt to define more precisely the range and scope of the redemption described (is it universal? cosmic? material?). The debate has continued well into this century, the contrasting interpretations of Barth* and Brunner on the subject serving as examples.

As early as Justin Martyr the reference to 'firstborn of all creation' (1.15) was identified with a Jewish theology in which the Logos* was responsible for the creation of the world (cf. John 1.1–3), an idea taken up in various forms by the Alexandrians* including Clement and Origen.* The phrase was also a central debating point in the Arian controversy. Arius interpreted it to mean that the pre-existent Christ was the supreme creature, the pre-eminent created being. Athanasius and, later, Theodore of Mopsuestia (*see* **Antiochene Interpretation**) countered by emphasizing the incarnate state that the pre-existent divine Logos entered – the chief point at issue being the relationship that the pre-existent Logos had with the rest of the created order. The main lines of interpretative tension, concerning pre-existence and incarnation, remain to this day. The doctrine of the divinity of Christ is supported by reference to 1.15, 18, with 2.9 also an important text. At the time of the Reformation*, Calvin*, Luther* and Melanchthon all turned to Colossians as they sought to expound the meaning of Christ for the salvation of the world, moving away from discussion about the nature of Christ (which had dominated for centuries) to a focus on his work.

The Epistle to Philemon has a close literary connection with Colossians, most scholars pointing to linguistic considerations and to the parallel greetings in the two letters as the most important evidence (cf. Philemon 2, 23–24 and Col. 4.10, 12, 14, 17). The personal greetings and references to individuals have given rise to a number of interesting interpretations. The most striking of these relates to the role of Onesimus (Philemon 10 and Col. 4.9). Most scholars accept that in Philemon Paul (whose authorship has scarcely been doubted) is instructing that the runaway slave Onesimus

be freed from his slavery, perhaps so as to serve with him in Christian mission. Ignatius* of Antioch mentions an Onesimus as the bishop of the Ephesian church (Eph. 1.3), a fact which lends support to the interpretation, put forward by E. J. Goodspeed and J. Knox, that Onesimus was indeed freed to that end. Goodspeed suggested that Philemon is in fact the (lost) letter to the Laodiceans mentioned in Col 4.16 and that Philemon himself was the leader of the church there. Knox in *Philemon Among the Letters of Paul* (1935, revd edn 1959) concurs but suggests that the letter 'to Philemon' is actually addressed primarily to Archippus (Philemon 2), who was the owner of the slave Onesimus and who is further encouraged to serve Paul by freeing him in the terms used in Col. 4.17. Paul is thus seen as sending Onesimus back to Archippus via Philemon with both the letters we know as Colossians and Philemon in hand. These suggestions are striking but unprovable and have not been widely adopted. But the personal links between the two letters are often taken as evidence that even if the whole of Colossians is not Pauline, the latter part of it certainly is.

Scholars have suggested three main possibilities as to the place of writing: Ephesus, Caesarea and Rome. The decision about the provenance of the letter has been an integral part of discussion both of Pauline chronology (early or late imprisonment?) and of explanations of the literary connection between the two documents.

The Epistle to Philemon was extremely influential in helping to establish the church's attitude to the institution of slavery up to the collapse of the Roman Empire. Its teaching on the subject was delightfully ambiguous. On the one hand it supported slavery laws aimed at returning runaway slaves to their masters, while on the other hand it proclaimed a new spirit of Christian brotherhood between slave and master but without radically challenging the institution itself. Most recently Philemon has been a focal point in the examination of the social structures of the ancient world, including that of slavery. This is perhaps its most important contribution to modern interpretation as is illustrated by the recent monograph by N. Petersen.

See also **Christology, New Testament; Patristic Christology; Paul.**

F. O. Francis and W. A. Meeks (eds), *Conflict in Colossae*, 1975; Mark Kiley, *Colossians as Pseudepigraphy*, 1986; Eduard Lohse, *Colossians and Philemon*, 1971; Norman Petersen, *Rediscovering Paul*, 1985; J. B. Polhill, 'The Relationship Between Ephesians and Colossians', *RevExp* 70, 1973, pp. 439–50; E. P.

Sanders, 'Literary Dependence in Colossians', *JBL* 85, 1966, pp. 28–45; Eduard Schweizer, *The Letter to the Colossians*, 1976.

L. KREITZER

Comedy

Willingness to recognize comedy in the Bible is arguably the best criterion of one's capacity to read it as one would any other book, rather than as a book limited in its effect by its sacredness. Erich Auerbach effectively began modern treatment of the Bible as literature in his *Mimesis*, 1953, by pointing out a special instance of this. Classical theorists from Aristotle onwards, he argues, tended to divide the representation of reality in literature into two kinds, tragedy and comedy, the former representing the crises of exceptional or ideal individuals in a high style, the latter the common existence of people who are ordinary, or less perfect than ordinary, in a low style; but the Bible knows nothing of such divisions. Its abolition of stylistic division expresses its theme of the dependence of the whole of life on God. However, to recognize this abolition might mean only to recognize a new genre* that has lost some of the special characteristics of tragedy or comedy, and in particular may fall far short of recognizing in the Bible anything comic in the sense of making us laugh. Although the essence of humour is incongruity, and there must be opportunity for humour in the incongruity of presenting creatures confronting their Creator, still the incongruity may evoke solely awe and not humour.

Two Judaeo-Christian traditions, that of mediaeval Christendom and that of Hasidic Judaism (*see* **Jewish Exegesis**), have conspicuously accepted that humour and awe accompany each other in religion: but even they scarcely place it in the biblical text. The English mediaeval mystery play developed the humorous possibilities of figures on the periphery of the biblical story, considered as either ordinary people inadequate to measure up to the supernatural (Noah's wife reluctant to enter the ark, Joseph as cuckold, the shepherds at Christ's birth, Simeon refusing to believe the prophecy of a virgin's conceiving), or over-reaching sinners (Cain, Herod), or people overcome with joy at an unexpected happy ending (Isaac released from sacrifice). But this perhaps never touches the text itself. Of the text, C. S. Lewis reports from his Jewish-born wife, Joy Davidman, 'that no one who knew the Jewish *ethos* from inside would fail to see the fully accepted comic element in Abraham's* dialogue with God (Gen. 18) or in Jonah' (*Letters of C. S. Lewis*, 1966, p. 286). As a general statement, this seems to apply no more to traditional Jewish understanding* than to Christian.

That Gen. 18 was intended to be comic, however, is strongly supported by its structure. Abraham's mistaken belief that he can strike a good bargain with God over Sodom is related immediately after the sole episode of the Hebrew Bible where laughter is frequently mentioned: the laughter of Abraham and Sarah at the message, given by the three who represent God, that they will have a son in their old age – Isaac, whose name puns on *šāḥaq* 'laugh'. The same three announce the destruction of Sodom: the double story presents man comic before God, ending happily in the conception of Isaac, blackly in the sin and punishment of Sodom. There seems to be a parallel with Abraham's dialogue in Gideon's dialogue with God, seeking for a sign (Judg. 6.36–40), possibly even, as G. D. Josipovici suggests in his *The Book of God* (1988, pp. 118–21), a parodic parallel conveying 'a strange discrepancy between words and deeds'. The end, for Gideon, is happy.

A clearer parallel, at any rate in structure, is in Jonah. Jonah first defies God and is driven to obey, then obeys with a result which is not what he expected. The dialogue between Jonah and God beside the gourd that withered, together with the touchingly bathetic ending of the book referring to the cattle of Nineveh, suggests deliberate humour. But there is not, as in the Abraham story, any overt mention of laughter in this story that ends with the salvation, not the destruction, of a city.

On the whole, it must regretfully be said, the more overt the suggestion of laughter in the OT, the more likely the humour is to be that of the laugh over a defeated enemy, the humour of superiority or scorn, and especially to work by representing through this sort of humour the incommensurability of God and man: e.g. Jacob's trickery (Gen. 25.21–31.2), David's* out-witting of Nabal, whose name means fool (I Sam. 25), Haman's hanging on the gallows he had prepared for Mordecai (Esth. 5.14–7.10) and those psalms (2.4; 37.13; 59.8) in which God laughs. Comedy in which delight in the incongruous is connected with a happy ending, with love or with compassion – as probably with Boaz' nervous start when, drunk and in the dark, he finds Ruth at his feet (Ruth 3.8) – requires more readiness to receive it. (See W. F. Stinespring's list of examples of OT humour in *The Interpreter's Dictionary of the Bible*, 1962, 'Humor'.) Sometimes the decision as to what kind of laughter is in question has large interpretative consequences. When God displays the ostrich to Job, is he laughing at his own strength, as like that of the ostrich herself (39.18), or also delighting in her? And in Ps. 104.26, is it Leviathan that plays, or does God play with him? When God in the book of Job displays creation, is he simply forcing Job to realize his folly, or is he also, like his sons, shouting for joy? The name of Job's daughters – Dove, Cinnamon and Box of Eye-paint (42.14) – might suggest humour in the end of the book.

The same sort of tension exists in the Gospels.* It might be argued that one of the most clearly established facts about Jesus is that he found camels funny. They are scarcely mentioned in the whole Bible except *en masse* as items of wealth: but are brought forward by Jesus in two different traditions, first in Mark (10.25, and parallels in Matthew and Luke) as finding it hard to pass through a needle's eye, secondly in Matthew alone (23.24) as being drunk down by legalists who strain out gnats. (A horse would have sufficed if the wit were only satiric rather than humorous.) The first example suggests some indulgence for the rich who are its target, and the second, which goes with satiric but not humorous parallels like whited sepulchres, no indulgence for blind guides.

But the most irresistible case for comedy in the Bible has been made by the actor Alec McCowen in his recitations of Mark, at the sequence which, having involved the disciples twice in forgetting to bring bread, at the feedings of the five thousand and of the four thousand, culminates in their misunderstanding Jesus' advice to beware of the leaven of the Pharisees and of Herod – 'It is because we have no bread' (KJV/AV Mark 6.35 ff; 8.1 ff; 8.14 ff; followed, with some laborious explanation, by Matthew: Luke destroys the sequence). This is the clearly humorous part of Mark's general portrayal of the inadequacy of the disciples, which justifies the picture of humanity already mentioned in the mystery plays. Again, how genial is the humour? Similarly, in Luke's way of expressing the inadequacy of response of the disciples to the resurrection,* where there is certainly comedy in the sense of a story with a happy ending, is Christ's tone one of 'joyous mockery' as Charles Williams describes it in *He Came Down from Heaven* (1950, p. 103), when he says 'O fools and slow of heart to believe ...' (Luke 24.25,KJV/AV)?

The need in interpretation for humour to respond to humour is perhaps expressed by Jesus at the end of the bread-forgetting sequence in Mark, when he alludes to the hard saying of Isaiah (6.9f.), 'having eyes do you not see', etc., more famously used at Mark 4.12 of parables* (Matthew, who alters it there, omits it here). How true this continues to be may be shown by the interpretation of such parables as that of the unjust steward (Luke 16.1–13) which, if it is not humorous, is simply puzzling, but if it is humorous can be interpreted either as by Elton Trueblood in his useful, but possibly rather humourless *The Humour of Christ*, 1965, as a simple condemnation of the steward, because praise of his prudence is 'so preposterous that the sensitive hearer is ... able to see that the clear intent is the exact opposite of the literal statement' (p. 100): or else as, like the humour of the Hasidim, a recognition that true goodness is so extreme and paradoxical that there are lessons to be learnt about it from surprising sources by the partly good. One may compare in Martin Buber's *Tales of the Hasidim*, 1956, the Great Maggid's exposition of the ten principles of service from children and thieves (p. 103), Zev Wolf's praise of gamblers for knowing this much of the service of God, that they should perform it all night (p. 161) and Jacob Yitzhak's love for the sinner who sinned merrily because he was whole-hearted (p. 315); also W. H. Auden's use of them in his essay on Falstaff, 'The Prince's Dog', included in *The Dyer's Hand*, 1963. What C. S. Lewis said in *Reflections on the Psalms*, 1958, is generally true of the recognition of humour in the Bible: 'No net less wide than a man's whole heart, nor less fine of mesh than love, will hold the sacred Fish' (p. 119).

See also **Irony; Literary Criticism.**

In addition to books mentioned, see V. A. Kolve, 'Holy Laughter' in *The Play called Corpus Christi*, 1966.

S. E. MEDCALF

Commentary (New Testament)

A commentary on a biblical book sets out to help the reader with various kinds of explanatory material, so that the text may be better understood. It goes alongside the text, step by step. Not much more can be said by way of general definition, for commentaries have varied greatly over the centuries in the way they have conceived their task and carried it out. The general definition gave the impression that the commentary is a humble servant of the text, seeking to do no more than elucidate difficulties in a neutral and even passive spirit. Readers have often used them under this impression, but they should beware. Like Figaro or Jeeves in relation to their masters, commentaries are generally a great deal more positive, even aggressive, than their official role suggests. They have played a considerable part in furthering the work of interpretation, and in successive periods have been important vehicles for expressing the current modes of interpretation. Sometimes, commentaries have even been standard-bearers of new ways of theological understanding and exegesis.

There is a case for saying that the NT itself

contains writings which are in effect commentaries on earlier writings now found alongside them in the canon,* though their manner of commenting is unlike that which came eventually to be used in the church. Thus, M. D. Goulder has suggested, in *Midrash and Lection in Matthew*, 1974, that the material in the Gospel of Matthew which was not derived from Mark was mostly generated by the author of Matthew as a result of exegetical reflection on Mark rather than from extra traditions available to him. His reworking of Mark is comparable to the Chronicler's treatment of Samuel–Kings, and his methods find partial parallels in Jewish *midrash** (Heb. 'investigation', 'exegesis'*). The theory has met strong challenge, though most scholars agree that both Matthew and Luke have used Mark in such a way as to bring out what they saw as the proper meaning of certain passages, thus demonstrating clearly that every act of interpretation involves adaptation. In so far as their activity comes rightly under the heading of commentary, they illustrate the point made earlier about the apparent passivity of the commentator being an illusion – as also does the writer of Ephesians in his use of other Pauline Epistles, especially Colossians.

So too do the commentators of the Patristic period. The earliest known commentary on a NT book, apart from the partial exceptions just described, is that of the Valentinian Gnostic* Heracleon on the Gospel of John, though his work survives only in quoted fragments. This second-century work evidently offered an interpretation which, even if one envisages possible Gnostic-type elements in the Gospel, forced it into an alien mould.

At the end of the same century came Origen,* the first main-stream Christian scholar to undertake line-by-line commentary on scripture. Critical of Heracleon for imposing his Gnostic interpretation on John, he has himself been seen as viewing the Bible through Platonist spectacles. But the modern reader of, for example, his commentary on the Fourth Gospel is likely to be struck by other features. There is a dearth of what we now think of as helpful information about details of the text, and in fact the text seems often some way removed from Origen's mind. It reads like a stream of scriptural consciousness, referring to passages minimally or (to our minds) oddly related to the one under discussion, and viewing it all in the light of a comprehensive picture of Christian faith and knowledge. The key lies in Origen's belief in the unity of scripture as testimony to God's single and wide-ranging revelation.* It is in fact what we should call a theological and spiritual meditation on the Gospel, and it bears the same character as expository sermons of the period. In works like Augustine's* expositions of Genesis and his *Enarrationes in Psalmos*, typical allegorical* interpretation predominates, as generally in elucidation of the OT in particular, though like others he also included explanatory material of a more straightforward kind.

In mediaeval times, commentaries on biblical books often became the repository of knowledge and lore of little direct relevance to the text, as if the lack of more suitable genres of literature led authors of, perhaps, a scientific turn of mind to include information which was of interest to them. They were stimulated by a broad conviction that the Bible was the source of every kind of truth. In relation to their primary purpose, commentaries had by this time acquired a characteristic that has persisted to the present day: referring back to previous (in effect, patristic) authorities, before going on to express new ideas. In this respect, the sense of building on a venerated past as represented by great and saintly teachers, commentaries were at one with theology as a whole. The work of the thirteenth-century Bishop of Lincoln, Robert Grosseteste, exemplifies both these features. Commentators of this period varied a good deal in their interest in matters of technical elucidation of exegetical problems, and in their willingness to investigate linguistic aspects. Hugh of St Victor (twelfth century), for example, one of an important school of French exegetes, learnt some Hebrew and consulted Jewish scholars.

The Middle Ages also saw the development of interest in the 'letter' or literal sense (*see* **Literal Meaning**) of scripture, in the sense of bringing out vividly the pictorial aspect of stories. Once more, this was part of a wider process, the growth of lively preaching on the Gospels, especially by the new orders of friars, and the promotion of methods of meditation which involved the devout imagining of biblical scenes.

If commentaries had always served theological and spiritual purposes in accordance with the needs of successive periods, they proved in the period of Reform in the sixteenth century to be a major instrument of change. Two factors came to the fore. First, the development of new possibilities of studying the Bible in the original languages (notably as a result of the publication of Erasmus'* Greek NT in 1516), enabling scholars to be aware of a new range of technical issues relating to the evidence for the text itself and its meaning. Secondly, the arising in the work of Luther* of a new concentration on the authority of 'scripture alone'. The key moves in his own thinking had come about to a large extent in the process of his preparation of lectures on the Psalms and Galatians. These two factors have largely characterized the work and importance of commentators down to the present. The former points to the vast scholarly labour of many kinds which has come more and more to mark the study of the Bible. The latter has figured chiefly in Lutheran and Reformed circles, where commentaries, above all on the writings of Paul, have continued to express a major theological message. By far the most influential example of such a commentary is that of Karl Barth* on Romans, 1919, with its attack on liberal theology and its propounding of dialectical theology, but that of E. Hoskyns* and F. N. Davey on the Gospel of John, 1940, is often put in the same category.

In the critical period, though commentaries have naturally continued to express the theological as well as the academic standpoints of their authors, a certain consensus on what should be expected of a commentary has come about. Chiefly, it is a matter of an introduction* dealing with historical, literary and other issues in relation to the writing in question, followed by a passage by passage and word by word discussion of points of difficulty or interest, together with an attempt to bring out the author's intended sense. We have already remarked on the illusory element in what looks at first glance like objectivity: point of view and the exercise of judgment are inevitable features of the work of commentary writing. Nevertheless, the areas where these features operate change from time to time. With the growth of ecumenism, it is no longer as easy as formerly to tell Catholic from Protestant commentaries. Once more, the ethos of the times makes itself felt. So, naturally, do new movements in scholarship. For example, D. E. Nineham's commentary on the Gospel of Mark, 1963, reflected form criticism* in a more thoroughgoing way than its predecessors.

The subject of movements in scholarship, however, raises the issue of the continuing role of the commentary. Over many years, it has had an unrivalled place among the instruments of biblical study, as is amply testified by the great range of commentary series on the market and the constant appearance of new ones: plainly, many people believe that the way to learn about the Bible is to follow through the text with the aid of a commentary. Yet so wide and diverse is the range of methods now brought to the study of the biblical books, and perhaps especially the Gospels, that it is hard to unify them in a presentable way in relation to a text followed loyally, one section after another. Nowadays, the tangle of issues is so complex that it is virtually impossible to encompass them satisfactorily in the discussion of passages seriatim. Indeed,

to work in commentary form may be to be misled.

Thus, an appreciation of the theological outlook of a Gospel writer (see **Evangelist**) is better presented in terms of an overview of the Gospel as a whole, as is an attempt to uncover the social and historical circumstances of its writing. Following the path with eyes glued to the ground immediately ahead is not the only way to see the countryside through which one is walking. While some modern commentaries, notably E. Haenchen on Acts, 1971, have managed to combine stimulating clarity of overall approach with presentation of detail, others simply clog the mind and leave the reader who is interested in anything more than small matters wondering where to turn.

There may, however, be a future for a new kind of commentary, limited to a single method of approach – perhaps that of 'narrative' or of structuralism. Here a following through of the text from a specific point of view may contribute to understanding without attempting to monopolize the mind.

Theologically more significant would be commentary along lines laid down in the hermeneutical* work of Paul Ricoeur (e.g. in his *Essays on Biblical Interpretation*, 1981). This would alter radically the focus in which critical study is seen. He discounts the claims of historical method as 'romanticist' and false, in so far as it reckons to yield an entry into the writer's mind and life. Instead, there is to be direct encounter with the revelatory text, which, once written, he sees as freed from its original historical context and intention. It constitutes its own witness to 'the Word'. There is a sense in which this marks a return to pre-critical ways of working with a text – a text rather than, as so often now, in effect the people behind it. It is an approach which abandons the uncommitted neutrality of the historian and reintroduces faith into the process of apprehending the text. In this respect, he is the heir of Barth and Bultmann* in their exegetical work. The Christian interpreter is foolish to come to the NT as if with one hand tied behind his back.

Only time will tell whether innocence can be recovered and whether historically-minded commentators will be content with a new role or even to disappear altogether. So far the signs are that, whatever new approaches may be arising, they must be accepted and somehow worked with, however hard and uncertain a task they often give to the theological user of the text.

There is, then, a case to be made against the commentary. It takes an unusually good commentator to transcend the section-by-section approach to which the task for the most part commits him (or her). He is almost bound to give the impression that a text may be 'understood' by discovering the lexical meaning of its words and the bearing of its historical references. His form impels him towards gross hermeneutical oversimplification. A text is more than the sum of its details, its thought more than the individual steps in its argument. It is false optimism to expect a commentary to reveal all that a text has to give. Even with the matter included by convention in introductions, a commentary too often fails to convey much sense of the thrust of a writing as a whole or to give the reader a coherent picture of the mind disclosed by it.

It is partly that too much has been expected of the commentary, partly that the conventions which have come to govern the genre are, perhaps necessarily, too narrow. The case against the commentary has a theological aspect, related to the place of the Bible in Christian theology; an academic aspect, concerned with both the many-sided question of the proper elucidation of texts and the best way of presenting scholarly work on them; and a practical aspect, concerned with the needs of those who wish to read the texts. Dissatisfaction is more often felt (as boredom, bafflement, or disappointment) than expressed.

There is also a case to be made on the other side. The commentary remains a useful way of assembling and presenting a mass of sheer information about a text. To follow a commentary from cover to cover remains an unrivalled discipline, enabling the reader to immerse himself or herself in the argument of a text, usually without undue distraction from the commentator. There is a sense in which the good commentator lets the text speak for itself. The commentator minimizes the obtrusion of the scholar and maximizes the presence of the biblical writer. The commentator is, despite all necessary qualifications, the servant of the text in a way and to a degree that, for example, the writer of a monograph is not.

This has a special value at the present stage of biblical scholarship, especially in relation to the Gospels and Acts. Redaction criticism* and the general interest in the evangelists as theological writers of considerable subtlety and distinctiveness have led to the production of numerous works attempting to identify their theological ideas. Some of them are open to the criticism of concentrating too much on certain features of a Gospel, in order to achieve a coherent picture, to the neglect of other features which may be hard to reconcile with what is presented as the dominant conception. Admirable and creative though this approach to the Gospels is, it suffers from this

defect – and there is no form of writing so calculated to remedy it as the commentary, forcing attention on the text, item by item, giving to each its due weight. The commentary allows no escape into generalities or analyses which gloss over difficulties and inconveniences.

Whether the commentator's craft is on the wane and whether it should be are debatable questions which deserve more discussion than they have received. Teachers and preachers could derive advantage from a more critical attitude to that approach to the Bible which the commentary represents. But no doubt it will survive, continuing to modify itself imperceptibly from one style to another, and fulfilling certain indispensable roles, but not perhaps hogging the centre of the stage quite as much as in the past. In the history of Christian theology, NT commentators, from Origen to Augustine, Luther to Barth, have used their work to make major contributions to the movement of Christian thought. Is the commentary likely to play that part again?

See also **Hermeneutics; Introduction; Meaning.**

See the following articles in *The Cambridge History of the Bible*: 'The Bible in the Early Church', Vol. I, 1970; 'The Exposition and Exegesis of Scripture', Vol. 2, 1969; 'Biblical Scholarship: Editions and Commentaries' and 'Aids to the Study of the Bible: Commentaries', Vol. 3, 1963. And J. L. Houlden, 'The New Testament Commentary Scene' in *King's Theological Review*, IV, 1981, pp. 45– 53; W. G. Kümmel, *The New Testament: the History of the Investigation of its Problems*, 1973; B. Smalley, *The Study of the Bible in the Middle Ages*, 1952, 1983; R. W. Southern, *Robert Grosseteste*, 1986.

J. L. HOULDEN

Commentary (Old Testament)

The roots of OT commentary are to be found in the Hebrew Bible itself. They are constituted by the multiplicity of inner-biblical* exegeses to be found throughout the text and the dynamic relations between *traditum* and *traditio* within the books of the Bible (cf. Fishbane, pp. 1–19). These processes represent the continuity between statements of the past and the ever-growing need of (religious) communities in the present to remake that past in their own image by transforming the traditions through comment, development and alteration. A good example of this development is Dan. 9.2,24–27, where the 'seventy years' of Jer. 25.12; 29.10 become 'seventy *weeks* of years' and are transformed into a programmatic future of the people and the holy city. New or changing hermeneutic* frameworks change the meaning or significance of texts and commentaries are required to indicate, embody or codify such changing meanings. The earliest commentaries on biblical books which appear in extra-biblical form are the Qumran *pesher**-type commentaries (e.g. on Habakkuk) and they illustrate perfectly the updating of the text constitutive of such commentaries (*see* **Dead Sea Scrolls**). The N T equally demonstrates such an updating process and the changes introduced by changing hermeneutic perspectives. Rabbinic* commentaries and the Aramaic paraphrases (targums*) also function as explanatory and updating accounts of the biblical texts.

The flourishing of the commentary genre* in the early Christian churches belongs to the period of late Roman literary activity. These commentaries on the Greek (*see* **Septuagint**) and later the Latin (*see* **Vulgate**) versions of the Hebrew Bible continue Jewish modes of commenting on the sacred text, but, using different hermeneutical principles, produced very different kinds of commentary. Continuity and update remained important features of such commentaries, but the allegorizing mode (typical earlier of Philo's* Greek philosophical approach to Hebrew scriptures) was required in order to bypass the plain sense of much of Torah and to allow the Bible to be read as a Christian textbook. With the development in Jewish and Christian communities of the belief in their various scriptures as divinely inspired books, the text came to have many concealed meanings, as well as constituting the totality of all revealed knowledge hidden in the text (cf. Bruns). Commentary became necessary as an oral or written explication of the text and as an uncovering of its hidden meanings. Allegory and typology* helped to reveal the concealed truths of the text and the framing hermeneutic of the various communities supplied the key to the understanding of scripture. Often the sheer difficulty of the original text (in whatever receptor language) made commentary necessary and the obscurity of scripture meant that a 'need for interpretation' (*Deutungsbedürftigkeit*, to use Auerbach's famous phrase from his seminal essay on biblical interpretation, 'Odysseus' Scar', in *Mimesis*) was built into the text. Also because language is naturally resistant to yielding up its meaning and the writing of speech involves an estrangement of language, there is always a need to unriddle writing (Bruns, p. 20). The divine word (*see* **Word of God**) spoken by prophets and holy men inspired by the divine spirit or, in Christian circles, that word embodied in Jesus Christ (*see* **Logos**) constantly required interpretation, and so when written down it generated a massive and complex tradition of commentary writing. (The precise status of scripture in the early Christian communities is far from clear, but by the fourth-fifth century at the latest most of the Christian churches had acquired scriptures of their own as commentary on the Jewish books and as scripture in its own right.)

The complex and multivariate genre of commentary served the causes of church and synagogue until the rise of the modern age when the development of the independent academy added yet a third level of service to that of understanding and propaganda. This academic evolution continued the (secular) approach to the study of the classics but also applied it to the interpretation of the Bible and created the historical-critical* study of the sacred books. So was added a more complex dimension to the production of biblical commentaries which, with time, was to produce a source of commentary writing independent of church and synagogue. The Protestant Reformation* of the sixteenth century had necessitated the production of new styles of commentary writing, in order to combat the magisterial interpretation of the Bible hallowed by centuries of scholastic learning (in fact modern hermeneutics owes its origins to this oppositional mode of biblical interpretation). Indeed the production of so many commentaries in the sixteenth century moved Montaigne to dismiss commentaries as increasing doubt and ignorance: 'There is more trouble in interpreting interpretations than in interpreting the things themselves, and there are more books on books than on any other subject. We do nothing but write comments on one another. The whole world is swarming with commentaries; of authors there is a great dearth' ('On experience', *Essays*, Book 3, ch. 13). Since then matters have not improved.

The modern commentary is very much the product of the academic world, though the sheer diversification and multiplicity of commentaries is also a tribute to the efficiency of the Gutenberg revolution in book-production. Outstanding series of commentaries have rendered every book of the Bible accessible to modern understanding at whatever level is thought desirable (e.g. academic, philological, literary, theological, ecclesiastical, devotional, propagandist, etc). The great devotional commentaries of the past (e.g. Matthew Henry, J. C. Ryle, the Puritan writers) remain as time-conditioned expository works treasured by minority groups within various ecclesiastical traditions, and theologically constructed commentaries (e.g. *The Epistle to the Romans* by Karl Barth,* 1919) have, from time to time, generated their own momentum and shaped thinking for a generation among acolytes and interested parties. Between these levels of production most series of commentaries achieve their expected goals and perform in conformity to their house style. The different types may be classified loosely by the formats used in the series (e.g. the ICC is a highly philological* series, whereas the OTL is more interpretative and theological, and the NCB uses a verse-by-verse, phrase-by-phrase approach), or by their approaches to the Bible whereby the commentator consciously writes from his own viewpoint (e.g. Barth) or by their treatment of the text as speaking to the present (the classical form of commentary) or by their use of several different levels simultaneously and more than one methodology.*

The multiplicity of different commentary series represents a wide-ranging set of choices of approach, treatment and purpose for different interpretative communities and guilds. It also highlights what some would see as 'a crisis' in the biblical commentary genre (cf. Froehlich, 'Bibelkommentare – zur Krise einer Gattung', ZTK 84, 1987, pp. 465–92). The long history of commentary production and the many different series proliferating at the moment raise questions about what a commentary is or should be, for whom it may be intended, what format it should take, and what methodological procedures it should follow. A commentary is primarily a textbook (Froehlich) and therefore has its Sitz im Leben in the academy. But biblical commentaries are janus-like in that they must also face the ecclesiastical or synagogal communities and so also have an important Sitz im Leben in the religious guilds. Many scholars are practising Christians or Jews and do not find it easy to ignore commitment either to scholarship or to religious belief when producing commentaries. Academy and ecclesia (synagogue) are not always in agreement, often (as the cases of David Strauss* or Robertson Smith* demonstrate only too well) they are at loggerheads because their domain assumptions, procedures, methodologies and purposes differ considerably. Theologians inevitably demand that biblical commentaries should serve the needs and purposes of the churches (e.g. Anderson, Childs), while recognizing that academic standards also must be maintained. The 'faith' element in theological commentary is fundamental to the theologian (Childs), yet academics who produce commentaries on the Bible may well not share a common faith with other commentators or belong to a faith guild in the first place. This fracture within the commentary-producing community has begun to raise questions about the nature of commentary writing and will undoubtedly lead to further important discussions about the diverging paths of academy and ecclesia/synagogue in the future (cf. the unease expressed by Brueggemann on 'thin interpretation' in Interpretation 42, 1988, pp. 268–80).

Discussions about the nature of commentary writing do exist (cf. Hobbs), but there is an evident need for a fuller debate between practitioners of the art and the various communities which use the commentary genre. What is required is a metacommentary of the production of commentaries which will take into account the ethics of reading, the sociology of scholarship and of the guilds which are keepers of the texts. The term 'metacommentary' is Frederic Jameson's and relates to the hermeneutic enterprise: 'All thinking about interpretation must sink itself in the strangeness, the unnaturalness, of the hermeneutic situation; or to put it another way, every individual interpretation must include an interpretation of its own existence, must show its own credentials and justify itself: every commentary must be at the same time a metacommentary' (Jameson, p. 5; my emphasis). From the prologue to Ben Sira to the introduction to the latest commentary the materials for a metacommentary are available but need to be brought together in a more systematic way. The rewritten* Bible (cf. Vermes) is the aim of all commentary and interpretation, and the processes of rewriting the Bible today have become too multivariate as well as too multitudinous for the commentary writer to be able to take stock of the whole field. It is a crisis of conspicuous production and consumption, as well as a critical moment in the writing of commentaries.

See also **Commentary (New Testament).**

B. W. Anderson, 'The Problem and Promise of Commentary', Interpretation 36, 1982, pp. 341–55; G. L. Bruns, 'Secrecy and Understanding', Inventions: Writing, Textuality, and Understanding in Literary History, 1982, pp. 17–43; B. S. Childs, 'Interpretation in Faith', Interpretation 18, 1964, pp. 432–49; M. Fishbane, Biblical Interpretation in Ancient Israel, 1985; E. C. Hobbs (ed.), The Commentary Hermeneutically Considered, 1978; F. Jameson, 'Metacommentary', The Ideologies of Theory: Essays 1971–1986, vol. 1, Situations of Theory, 1988, pp. 3–16; G. Vermes, Scripture and Tradition in Judaism, 1961.

ROBERT P. CARROLL

Community

In recent study of the NT, there has been an explosion of interest in ideas of community. The roots of this interest are complex and various. In Roman Catholic scholarship, Vatican II has had a major impact on the study of ecclesiology and its foundation in the Bible and the Fathers. A number of R. E. Brown's recent books (e.g. The Community of the

Beloved Disciple, 1979) reflect this impact, as well as showing the complete convergence of methodologies for historical-critical* study which has occurred between Catholic and Protestant exegetes.

In Liberal* Protestantism, Rudolf Bultmann's* interpretation, which tended to reduce NT theology* to individualistic categories compatible with existentialist philosophy, has been subjected to extensive criticism. This, in turn, has made possible a renewed focus on the social, communal and political dimensions of early Christian beliefs and practices. In Germany, the writings of G. Theissen (e.g. *The Social Setting of Pauline Christianity*, 1982), W. Schottroff and W. Stegemann are instances of this development.

The ethos of the 1950s and 1960s, a period of rapid economic development, political protest and social experimentation in the West played a part also. At the academic level, the social sciences (*see* **Sociology and Social Anthropology**) came into prominence in a new way; while at the social level, there was a widespread quest for alternative life-styles and patterns of community. Much writing since then about community in early Christianity is indebted, to some extent, to these kinds of developments (e.g. R. Banks, *Paul's Idea of Community*, 1979; and, for a general account of the social context of modern theology, R. Gill, *Theology and Sociology: a Reader*, 1987).

Another factor is the impact of the charismatic movement, spread throughout a very wide range of Christian churches and denominations. The custom of this movement to appeal to the charismatic element in Christian origins as a warrant for change in Christian understanding today has influenced a number of accounts of community and the Spirit in the NT (e.g. J. D. G. Dunn, *Jesus and the Spirit*, 1975). Even very specific topics have attracted extensive study: glossalalia being a case in point (e.g. the 535 pp. guide to research by W. E. Mills, *Speaking in Tongues*, 1986).

Modern fashions in christology and ecclesiology have been influential, not least in the ongoing process of Bible translation. A good example is the curiously literal interpretation given to Paul's idea of the church as the 'body of Christ' in the frequent paraphrasing in the NEB (e.g. Col. 1.1–2, 28; Phil. 3.8–9; Eph. 1.13). Commenting upon this, E. A. Judge has argued that such an interpretation has been read into a metaphor* of Christian community the plain sense of which is associational.

Contemporary movements of liberation* have been yet another force behind the study of community in the NT. Feminist* scholars have traced the roots of women's oppression in church and society today to the patriarchal-ization of authority in the early church. At the same time, they have also discovered egalitarian strands and symbols of women's liberation in the NT texts. A similar critical ambivalence marks the response of those who come to the Bible from the viewpoint of political theology, and again, the focus on ideas of community is central.

Developments in relations between Jews and Christians today have provided particular stimulus for investigating relations between communities of Jews and Christians in the first century. Here, a central issue has been how these groups defined their respective identities. Put theologically, how did they answer the question, Who are the people of God? The work of scholars like E. P. Sanders and Jacob Neusner is important in this regard.

Two trends in recent NT historiography are worth mentioning. One is the development of a more genuine social history approach, which tries to relate early Christian beliefs to the material and social concerns of particular groups of believers (e.g. S. Scott Bartchy, *First Century Slavery and the Interpretation of I Cor 7.21*, 1973, on slaves; R. F. Hock, *The Social Context of Paul's Ministry*, 1980, on manual labourers; F. W. Danker, *Benefactor*, 1982, on patrons and clients; D. L. Balch, *Let Wives be Submissive*, 1981, on women and households). The other is the use of methods and models from the social sciences to describe more precisely the dynamics of community formation and boundary management in early Christianity (e.g. W. Meeks, *The First Urban Christians*, 1983; S. C. Barton, *NTS*, 32, 1986).

A selective overview of discussions relating to particular texts will show first, at the historical level, that community formation and maintenance were all-pervasive concerns in early Christianity; secondly, at the theological and phenomenological levels, that Martin Buber's characterization in *Two Types of Faith* (1951), of Christianity as a religion of the individual (over against Judaism as a religion of community) cannot be sustained.

The Gospel of Matthew shows much evidence of the editing of the traditions about Jesus to meet the needs of a community in transition in the period after the destruction of the temple in AD 70. To distinguish his community from developments in Pharisaic* Judaism, the evangelist identifies an alternative source of authority, Jesus the Son of God; presents an alternative and more rigorous interpretation of the law as the basis for a common life under God (Matt. 5–7); and gives a strategy of mission to Gentiles as the basis for a reconstituted people of God (Matt. 10; 28. 16–20). To deal, on the other hand, with problems of community maintenance, the evangelist creates a kind of 'community rule'

(Matt. 18); urges an ideal of the community as a non-hierarchical brotherhood (Matt. 23.8–10); places heavy emphasis upon the love commandment (Matt. 5.43–48); and threatens judgment upon hypocrites (Matt. 23–25).

Although redaction criticism* of the Gospel of Mark went some way towards the identification of the Marcan community, much greater precision was attained when this approach was combined with sociological analysis in H. C. Kee, *Community of the New Age* (1977). Kee argues that Mark's audience was a missionary sect whose ethos* was markedly at odds with dominant social mores and whose world-view is apocalyptic.* Membership is voluntaristic and inclusive, and the nurture of insiders has a strongly esoteric quality. The novel, counter-cultural aspect of Mark's understanding of social relations is seen in the prominence he gives to women (and children) as models of bold faith and sacrificial service. Feminist scholarship has brought this latter point to the fore. Yet another approach, which focusses on the mythological and parabolic dimensions of Mark, shows how the narrative functions both to establish a new world and to subvert the old. The locus of the holy is related to being 'on the road' with Jesus rather than in the temple at Jerusalem.

Until recently, Luke-Acts has been read primarily as a source for reconstructing the history of the early church and, in particular, of the primitive Christian community in Jerusalem. The focus of attention here has been the 'enthusiastic' ethos of the community and its various expressions of *koinōnia*, such as the practice of goods in common and the regular gatherings for meals in members' houses. Philip Esler's *Community and Gospel in Luke-Acts: The Social and Political Motivations of Lucan Theology* (1987) breaks new ground by trying to give a sociological profile of the community of Luke's own day. He argues that Luke-Acts is best interpreted as written to provide legitimation for a Christian group whose relations with both the Jewish synagogue community and the wider Gentile society were fraught with the inevitable tensions and pressures arising from the Christian group's sectarian character. So, for example, the reason for Luke's interest in table fellowship is to legitimate Jew-Gentile commensality in his community and to maintain Jew-Gentile cohesion in the face of strong opposition from Jews and Jewish Christians who see the practice as a threat to the identity of the Jewish *ethnos*, i.e. the national/religious community.

The Fourth Gospel and the Johannine Epistles represent a distinctive trajectory* in earliest Christianity, and one explanation for this distinctiveness has to do with the character and history of the Johannine community.

By reading the Fourth Gospel as a kind of window on to the community, the picture that has emerged is of a community radically estranged from the wider society, the society of the synagogue, and even the society of other Christian groups. An introverted 'us and them' ethos seems dominant. Just as the Jesus of the Gospel is a stranger to the world and even to his own people, so too is the Johannine community. The highly polemical portrayal of 'the Jews' is an interpretation of the time of Jesus in the light of subsequent experiences of expulsion from the synagogue. The reinterpretation of the sacraments and the shift of attention away from the twelve apostles are hints of a community at odds with the Jerusalem church. Striking, instead, is the concern with the intensification of individual members' faith and knowledge and the emphasis on the need for love within the brotherhood. The epistles are evidence, perhaps, of the fissile, unstable character of the Johannine community.

The study of community in the NT has reached its greatest precision in relation to the letters of Paul.* This is because, to a degree more obvious than in the case of the Gospels, Paul's writings are occasional pieces directed to particular groups in particular places. Close study of the letters has made it possible to reconstruct the character of the groups founded by the apostle, the social level of their members, relations within the groups and between them, their beliefs and practices, their disciplinary procedures and attitudes to outsiders, and their struggle to establish boundaries and a sense of identity over against various alternative groups and patterns of association. Some scholars have proceeded by focussing on Paul's relations with his churches (e.g. J. H. Schütz, *Paul and the Anatomy of Apostolic Authority*, 1975; and B. Holmberg, *Paul and Power*, 1978). Important here is the question of power and its interpretation by Paul in his dealings with both the Jerusalem church and his own communities. Others have attempted to delineate the most important aspects of Paul's understanding of community. Here, the emphasis has fallen upon Paul's doctrine of freedom and new creation 'in Christ' and upon the local, believing community as the locus for shared experience of the eschatological Spirit. Hence, Paul's conception of authority and ministry in the community is essentially charismatic, with a strong recognition of the mutual interdependence of members and an ideal of unity as the outworking of the diversity of members' contributions.

Yet another focus for scholars has been the social setting of Paul's groups. E. A. Judge (*The Social Pattern of Christian Groups in the First Century*, 1960) broke new ground in showing that early Christian ideas of social obligation need to be interpreted in relation to the particular social institutions which they presuppose: the city-state, the household, and the unofficial association. More recent work has taken the study of these three kinds of institution much further (see J. Stambaugh and D. Balch, *The Social World of the First Christians*, 1986). The urban ethos of Paul's groups has been explored by G. Theissen (1982) and W. A. Meeks (1983). The significance of the household as providing their setting and constituency, their role relations and dominant authority patterns, as well as potential sources of conflict, has been investigated by scholars such as N. R. Petersen (*Rediscovering Paul*, 1985), J. Koenig (*NT Hospitality*, 1985) and S. C. Barton (1986). Comparison with Graeco-Roman voluntary associations is still at a fairly preliminary stage, but advances have been made by, for example, R. L. Wilken (*The Christians as the Romans Saw Them*, 1984).

Influenced by the feminist movement, many attempts have been made to interpret and explain the rather confusing evidence about the role of women in the churches of Paul. It is accepted widely that, whereas Paul was a social radical in his insistence on the removal of boundaries separating Jew and Gentile in the people of God, his position on the roles and status of women (and slaves) in the Christian gatherings was more conservative and pragmatic, in spite of his wholehearted endorsement of the baptismal formula referred to in Gal. 3.27–28. Major contributions to this question have come from, among others, K. Stendahl (*The Bible and the Role of Women*, 1966), E. S. Fiorenza (1983) and M. Hayter (*The New Eve in Christ*, 1987).

The novel, experimental and charismatic ethos of Paul's groups made them prone to conflict. Such conflict has been a further area of investigation. Some have emphasized the doctrinal elements in the conflicts (e.g. W. Schmithals' hypothesis about Paul's gnostic* opponents). Others have drawn attention to the sociological factors and have tried to correlate the sociological and the doctrinal (e.g. G. Theissen, 1982; and R. K. Jewett, *The Thessalonian Correspondence*, 1986). Increasing recognition is being given to the pastoral aspects of Paul's self-understanding as apostle and to his theology as pastoral theology (e.g. A. Malherbe, *Paul as Pastor*, 1987).

Until recently, the study of I Peter has focussed on the extent of the epistle's indebtedness to a (hypothetical) early Christian baptismal liturgy. Two new studies, however, have brought communal concerns to the fore. D. L. Balch's book, *Let Wives Be Submissive: The Domestic Code in I Peter* (1981), argues that the rules in I Peter about social obligations

generally and the ordering of household relations in particular represent an assimilation of group norms to the norms of the wider society. In some tension with this interpretation, although once again concentrating upon the household as the locus of early Christian community, is J. H. Elliott's *A Home for the Homeless: A Sociological Exegesis of I Peter* (1982). Elliott argues that the addressees of the epistle are marginalized 'resident aliens' (*paroikoi*) of Asia Minor whose conversion has increased the antagonism of the native residents towards them. They constitute, therefore, a 'conversionist sect' in tension with the society-at-large. The strategy of the letter is to confirm the believers in their social and religious separation from outsiders and to emphasize their incorporation into an alternative family, the 'household of God' (cf. I Peter 2.5; 4.17).

The interpretation of the ideas about community in the Pastoral Epistles* has been dominated by the debate over Early Catholicism* (*Frühkatholizismus*) in the NT, a debate which goes back at least to F. C. Baur and the Tübingen school* in the mid-nineteenth century and whose most vigorous prosecutor this century has been E. Käsemann. The Pastorals, along with Luke-Acts and other late NT texts, have been seen as literary expressions of certain developments in second-generation Christianity: the fading of the parousia* hope, the tendency towards increasing institutionalization, and the crystallization of Christian beliefs into set forms in order to guard against 'enthusiasm' and heresy (see J. D. G. Dunn, *Unity and Diversity in the New Testament* 1977, ch. XIV). Certainly, it is commonly accepted that the ideas about authority and community in the Pastorals constitute a substantial modification of the more Pauline ideal of participatory, charismatic community in the direction of hierarchy and patriarchy in matters of governance, and orthodoxy and tradition in matters of belief. As yet, thoroughgoing sociological analysis of the developments in community reflected in the Pastorals is in its infancy (see D. C. Verner, *The Household of God*, 1981). A useful beginning is J. G. Gager's *Kingdom and Community* (1975), which includes a discussion of charismatic authority and its routinization in order to show that 'a good deal of nonsense has been written about the decline of primitive Christianity into "early Catholicism"' (p. 67).

A convergence of a number of trends in biblical interpretation and theology has brought a renewed interest in the book of Revelation and the situation of its addressees. Following the tradition of historical geography and social history, as exemplified at the turn of the century by the work of Sir

William Ramsay, is C. J. Hemer's book, *The Letters to the Seven Churches of Asia in their Local Setting* (1986). This study draws upon a mass of literary, archaeological* and epigraphic* data in order to throw light upon local conditions likely to have affected the Christian groups in Asia Minor.

The sociological trend has been important also. With respect to the interpretation of biblical, Jewish and Christian apocalyptic generally, the social sciences have been employed to help clarify what kinds of groups develop an apocalyptic world-view and millennialist hopes and under what kinds of conditions (e.g. N. Cohn, *The Pursuit of the Millennium*, 1957; J. G. Gager, 1975). Typically, apocalyptic literature represents the response of an alienated, marginalized and persecuted group in a society undergoing rapid cultural change. The apocalyptic vision offers a new conception of reality and an alternative (i.e. countercultural) symbolic universe in terms of which the alienated group can sustain its life. Among studies of the Johannine Apocalypse from this point of view, J. G. Gager (1975) discusses the 'therapeutic' function of the myth of the millennium for the persecuted community; A. Y. Collins (*HTR*, 79, 1986, pp. 308–20) shows how the language of vilification of enemies plays an important role in the self-definition of the community; and D. E. Aune (*Biblical Research*, 26, 1981, pp. 16–32) focusses on the social location of the seer and the reasons for his advocacy of a strict policy of nonconformity and opposition to the influence of the dominant, alien culture.

Emphasis on apocalyptic as the protest literature of the socially and politically marginalized has corresponded with the concerns and interests of liberation theology.* From the liberationist perspective, the ideas about community and society in Revelation are still relevant today: especially the unmasking of the ideology* of the powerful; a vision of the future which serves as a powerful critique of the present; and the call to prophetic protest and to a common life which does not accommodate to the perverse values of the society-at-large (*see* C. Rowland, *Radical Christianity*, 1988).

See also **Anthropology; Ethos; Psychological Interpretation; Sociology and Social Anthropology.**

R. E. Brown, *The Churches the Apostles Left Behind*, 1984; G. Forkman, *The Limits of the Religious Community*, 1972; P. D. Hanson, *The People Called: The Growth of Community in the Bible*, 1986; G. Lohfink, *Jesus and Community*, 1985; D. Rensberger, *Johannine Faith and Liberating Community*, 1988.

STEPHEN C. BARTON

Computers and the Bible

Computers can assist biblical scholars in four main ways:

1. As word processors with Greek and oriental fonts which can now include cuneiform and Egyptian hieroglyphs, and which make available the normal facilities of editing a text that are found in English word processing; 2. to aid the learning of the languages through learning routines and grammatical analysis of texts; 3. to expedite the work of those producing Bibles in new languages overseas through machine translation or machine-assisted translation, building on the extensive work which has been done in modern languages in Europe, Canada, the USA, Japan, and elsewhere, including Israel; 4. to carry out statistical and other studies on the text. The first three touch only indirectly on interpretation and will not be considered further beyond commenting that word processing has reached a fairly advanced stage, computer-assisted learning of the biblical languages is being developed very slowly, and tremendous difficulties are being experienced in machine translation even in the case of those European languages where substantial sums of money are available for the research.

The main capability of computers is their large storage and retrieval capacity, their accuracy, and their fast operating speeds, but these are coupled with an almost total lack of intelligence. This means that they can count, search for particular morphemes, words, or phrases within a text, calculate frequencies of the occurrence of these grammatical forms, compare sections of text, and perform statistical tests on the data they have amassed, and therefore conduct stylistic and linguistic analysis. But their low levels of intelligence mean that they will only do what they are instructed to do and, even more irritatingly, will do exactly what they are told. The quality of the results of computer analysis depends therefore upon the questions which the researcher asks, and his or her own decision as to what analyses of the data are to be made. Computer science has now reached the point where the limits are set more by the lack of imagination on the part of the biblical scholar than by the inability to carry out the processing of the data by the computer, although some problems such as machine translation are to some extent waiting for the 'fifth generation' of parallel architecture machines before significant progress is made. Since scholars are mainly interested in the output they tend to rely upon the most common programming languages, but it has been argued that greater attention to the languages, for example modern AI languages such as Prolog which are more suitable for computational linguistics, might lead to more effective use of the computer by linguists.

At the simplest and in many ways most useful level, computers can produce concordances and statistical word lists. A slightly more developed stage is to detect differences of style. One of the earliest applications of computers to NT research was an analysis of the Pauline letters to determine which were written by Paul* himself. At the time most NT scholars were highly sceptical of the use of computers outside the sciences and critical, almost scathing, reviews of the work were made, despite the fact that the four great Pauline letters and Philemon were pronounced to have been written by the same author and distinguished from the others attributed to Paul. Since then far more satisfactory methods of analysis have been developed, but the most frequent use of computers beyond the compilation of concordances has remained within the field of traditional 'literary criticism',* examining questions of sources and authorship, often with only minor advances beyond word counts which are then subjected to statistical tests. It must still be remembered that all the computer is doing is to run a test which has been devised by the human researcher and has carried out very rapidly a series of operations which would take a tediously long time if attempted manually although they could have been performed in that way. The use of the computer neither improves nor reduces the quality of the research as such, and it is no more 'objective' than any other method of analysis, but because it can work so rapidly it makes possible analyses which could not be attempted without its aid because of the time that would be taken to carry them through.

Computers could be used in textual criticism* and the comparison of manuscripts provided suitable data bases were produced, and those undertaking research in grammar enabled to carry out linguistic analysis as well as examining the frequency of particular grammatical forms. For the NT, GRAMCORD (short for 'GRAMmatical concORDance package program'), produced by Paraclete Software, runs on a mainframe or PC with hard disk, and is extremely flexible.

Fundamental to all computer assisted research is the possession of an adequate data base. Unfortunately scholars have tended to work independently and have devised a variety of methods for representing the Greek or Hebrew text, adding means for indicating morphological data. Even if agreement on encoding the text were obtained, decisions would still have to be made concerning which text is to be used. At present there appears to be duplication of effort, but some of this is due to the very different interests of individuals and research teams. The machine-readable text produced in one centre tends to be linked with a particular piece of research rather than being open to a variety of uses. Moreover, since so many different machines and computer languages are employed, compatibility between data bases and research programs is beset with obstacles.

The data base may contain more than one version, so that, for example, the Hebrew may be aligned with the Septuagint* or the Peshitta. Data bases are currently available for the Hebrew OT, the Septuagint, and the NT, and are being developed for other versions. Optical scanning is now at a stage which makes it practical for the reading of manuscripts (it has been successfully used with mediaeval texts). This will remove much of the labour of typing in the texts, although ambiguities in the grammar and syntax of natural languages will probably always require a considerable amount of human interpretation and encoding of data.

Currently a 'Computer Assisted Research Group' works within the Society of Biblical Literature in North America, and among other institutes may be mentioned the Belgian based 'Centre; Informatique et Bible'. Biblical scholars, however, cannot work in isolation. What is essential if progress is to be made is closer collaboration between biblical specialists and others using computers in the humanities in such areas as linguistics, machine translation, and artificial intelligence.

No bibliography is attached to this article because the extremely rapid development of the field would make any readings very quickly out of date.

CYRIL S. RODD

Corinthian Correspondence

Paul* reached Corinth, after leaving Athens (Acts 18.1), in the spring of 50 (Barrett). His last contact with the city, as far as our knowledge goes, was the visit almost certainly implied in Acts 20.2, which we can date in about 54. During these four years Paul remained in close touch, both by visits and by letter, with the exuberant young Christian community he had founded. Of his visits we know only what he tells us himself, which is less than we should like to know. The letters, however, survive, at least in large part. Possibly there were only two, identical with the present First and Second Epistles (henceforth I, II). It is more likely that there were more than two. A relatively small body of opinion finds more than one original letter, or letter-fragment, in I. Considerably more scholars see the hand of a redactor in II. The latter's last four chapters are widely thought to have originated as a separate document. The two chapters dealing with the raising of funds for the Jerusalem church (8 and 9), and some part of chapters 1 to 7, are also variously thought to have once had a discrete existence (6.14 to 7.1 is rather generally agreed to be a distinct fragment and perhaps not by Paul). Composed as they were, however, almost without exception within such a remarkably short span of time, the letters or letter-fragments we now have as I and II are of immense interest and value no matter what their original form and order may have been.

The value of the Corinthian correspondence to the interpreter of the NT is at least three-fold. It was engendered by its author's first-hand knowledge, and access to first-hand reports, of what was happening in a newly-founded urban Christian church near the original homeland of Hellenistic* culture during the third decade of the Christian movement. It thus forms an archive of incalculable importance for the historian of that movement's organization, leadership and practices. Here it is almost exclusively I that has attracted attention. More particularly, the correspondence as a whole furnishes the student of the apostle Paul with data of greater richness, from some points of view, than any other letter from his hand. Thirdly, both I and II are rich in theological interpretation in more than one respect.

The Corinthian Christian community* itself was described in the earliest introduction to I as composed of 'Achaeans' (Greeks – that is, Gentiles) who had been 'in many respects corrupted by false prophets, some deceived by the wordy rhetoric of philosophy, others by sects of the Jewish Law'. The first note is of interest, since Acts 18.4, borne out by the evident identity of the Crispus of I.1.14 with the synagogue president of Acts 18.8, clearly implies that the community had mixed racial and religious origins. However, the Marcionite* author of the second-century prologue in question had his own reasons, clearly, for presenting the converts Paul had made as originally non-Jewish; it must be added that the evidence of I itself (notably 12.2) supports this Marcionite's view.

The two groups of 'false prophets' received little further attention from interpreters of the Corinthian correspondence until the nineteenth century. Attempts to define more precisely the 'sects of the Jewish Law' seem to have begun with F. C. Baur. There was, he claimed, only one such 'sect', and its leader was the apostle Peter as the main representative of a Judaizing, Law-observant Christianity in fundamental opposition to the Christianity of Paul. This epoch-making theory of Baur was first enunciated in an article of 1831, arising from study of the Corinthian correspondence and taking the form of an essay on the 'Christ-party' of I.1.12. Baur saw this group (now usually seen as not a distinct group at Corinth at all) as closely related to the 'party' of Peter, and the manifestation in Corinth of the more widespread movement with which Baur was concerned.

It is, however, in II that the question of the identity of Paul's opponents has inevitably and persistently been raised. Baur's influence has been such that some relation between the opponents in II and Peter has often been detected, though it is not now thought that the opponents had been authorized by Peter himself to claim his patronage, if indeed they did so at all. The more urgent question has been whether Paul's Jewish–Christian successors (see **Jewish Christianity**) in the mission to Corinth were connected with affairs in Jerusalem, or whether they were Christians who had been adherents of a strongly Hellenized form of non-Palestinian Judaism. Some features of Paul's polemic in II support the latter view, though it is possible that Paul himself had little contact with his opponents and may not even have met them. He may have been almost as uncertain about their origin and stance as we are.

The second group of 'false prophets' identified by the Marcionite prologue had been 'deceived by the wordy rhetoric of philosophy'. Here the second-century author sounds strangely modern: it is only fairly recently that the educational standards of some, at least, of the Corinthians have been highlighted (rhetoric* and philosophy played a major part in ancient Hellenistic education). However, as soon as it began to be appreciated (at least as early as Lüdemann's study of Paul's anthropology in 1872) that Hellenistic culture constituted an intellectual milieu in strong contrast with that of relatively uneducated Palestinian Jews, the significance of the Hellenistic background of the membership of the Corinthian church was bound to prompt speculation. The exponents of the 'history-of-religions school'* were quick to interpret both the behaviour and ideas of the Corinthians and Paul's response in terms of the dualism characteristic of Hellenistic thought. From this it was a short step to identifying the Corinthian Christians as Gnostics,* as was done for the first time by W. Lütgert in 1908, though the most influential statement of this interpretation of some puzzling features of the behaviour and slogans (e.g. 'All things are lawful', I.6.12) of the Corinthian Christians remains that by W. Schmithals in 1956.

This approach to the interpretation of (mainly if not exclusively) I falls under the condemnation of *obscurum per obscurius*. We know little about what might have prompted men and women in Corinth to shout 'a curse on Jesus' (I.12.3) or, if married, to deny one another conjugal rights (I.7.5); but we know nothing at all about any gnosticism before the middle of the second century. Recent writing has therefore used cautious language ('proto-gnostic', 'pre-gnostic').

Even so, it has to be admitted as striking that the Corinthians exhibited in their sexual behaviour just those opposites of asceticism and libertinism (for the latter, see I.6.15–20) that we find as antithetical expressions of dual-istic contempt for the body in second-century gnosticism. Certainly this, in itself, does not entitle anyone to go very much further than Barrett. It is a discussable question, he thinks, 'how far [popular] philosophy and [popular] piety had combined in the right proportions and the right context to produce gnosticism'. And yet, on any showing, to that question the answer must be given 'far enough, at any rate, to engender the will to flout, in act, certain moral conventions received by other Christ-ians'. The presence in Corinth of something like the acorn of the next century's oak can hardly be denied.

Was that acorn itself, however, really some-thing that fell from the intellectual and religi-ous environment of the Corinthians? Or could it be the fruit of specifically and indeed in-tensely Christian experience, and interpreta-tion of that experience, both on Paul's part and on that of his converts? J. C. Hurd claimed that the latter was the case. 'Enthus-iasm', a passionate appropriation in both belief and conduct of the certainty that Christ would very soon come again, governed Paul's initial evangelism in Corinth. The same en-thusiasm pervaded the resultant conversion of the Corinthians. There was indeed an inter-vention from outside in the history of Corin-thian Christianity. But it was a Christian intervention. The Jerusalem church prom-ulgated rules (Acts 15.29 – the so-called 'Apos-tolic Decree' which Paul found himself obliged to accept, but which shocked the en-thusiastic Corinthian Christians, afire as they were with the freedom of the Spirit as they awaited the End. Thereafter, Paul, newly con-strained by this unwelcome but ineluctable ruling, found himself at loggerheads with spir-itual children who were doing no more than be most willingly obedient to their father's original encouragements. Through meticu-lous, yet bold, analysis of I, Hurd reconstructs a detailed exchange of letters between Paul and Corinth of which I itself is the final stage. The standing, as historical report, of Acts 15 remains the crucial foundation of this reading of I. For those unpersuaded that the 'Apos-tolic Decree' was what Acts claims it to have been, Hurd's reconstruction as he states it

cannot convince. But his insistence that I re-cords a dialogue with intelligent as well as conscientious readers remains valuable. His portrait of a Paul who adjusts his original convictions under the pressure of pastoral con-cern is persuasive. His contention that we can explain I without recourse to the hypothesis of gnostic influence must be carefully heeded. Above all, perhaps, we must endorse his vindi-cation of the integrity and commitment of the Corinthian Christians, and to some extent, at least, of their morals.

Since Hurd's book, interest in the Corin-thian community has taken a different turn. Light has been cast on the profile of its mem-bership by sociological research. If the society of a Hellenistic city of the prominence of Corinth (recent though its re-foundation as a Roman city had been) formed a pyramid, it is likely that sections both near the summit and on the ground were represented in the Corin-thian church. Erastus (Rom. 16.23, thought to have been written in Corinth) may have enjoyed one of the four most senior offices in the city. Failing that, he was at least a man of substantial social prominence. The heads of households named in I were also probably persons of consequence. On the other hand, there were slaves (I.7.21) and indigent people (I.11.22) in this community. Some, perhaps most, of these lower-ranking members were either owned by, or in a well-defined rela-tionship of dependence on, their richer fellow-Christians. Many, indeed, had no doubt received baptism at their master's or patron's behest: some of the moral problems at Corinth are perhaps to be accounted for through con-version under a kind of duress. The contiguity, cheek by jowl in the same room, of persons of dramatically different status may cast light on what Paul says about the 'strong' and the 'weak' (I.8.7ff.; cf. Rom. 14.1ff., Theissen). Those accustomed to the free exercise of their power of choice may have applied it in religi-ous as well as purely domestic matters, while the literally unemancipated were that in other senses also.

Of the illumination shed by the Corinthian correspondence on the interpretation of Paul as thinker and pastor little need be said here. It is perhaps curious that a man of uncertain social status (though possibly taken for a Cynic-style philosopher; thus Hock) should have been appealed to in Corinth, and in I have answered this appeal, as one exercising an undoubted right to decide on the points raised. It is less surprising, though the shock to Paul himself is palpable throughout most of II, that between the despatch of the con-tents of the two letters as we now have them 'a person or persons unknown' should have succeeded in poisoning the attitude of the

Corinthians towards Paul. II.10.10 shows that rhetorical competence – so central to the Hellenistic educational ideals, and important, therefore, in social evaluation – was a yardstick by which Paul had been measured to his detriment. Further, his successors in the mission to Corinth had been astute. They had persuaded his former friends and followers to classify him with the sophists of the ancient market-place who preached for reward (II.4.2, 5). They had invoked cultural motives no less persuasive than the doubt they cast on his status as an apostle, to distance Paul's converts from their mentor. From the vigour and deep conviction with which Paul in II vindicates his right to their allegiance and love we learn much about Paul the man and Paul the pastor, as well as about his interpretation of what apostleship means.

The Corinthian correspondence also exhibits Paul at his most diverse in methods of interpretation of the OT. At I.9.9 he dismisses out of hand the literal meaning in order to wrest an allegorical* sense from the text. Elsewhere he can apply the OT text quite straightforwardly (e.g. II.9.9). At I.10.1–11 and II.3.6b–18 extended OT passages are interpreted in terms of the salvation brought by Christ in a way we can remotely put in parallel with the pesher* procedure at Qumran. At I.15.45ff. we may perhaps see Paul engaging in a polemical way with Alexandrian* exegesis of Gen. 1.27 with 2.7. For Philo* and perhaps for his antecedents two men were created, first the archetypal celestial man and only afterwards the empirical man of flesh and blood. Paul, with his eye on the future coming of Jesus, the true Man from heaven, reverses the order. Possibly we are overhearing, at this point, a scholarly discussion between Paul and his colleague Apollos ('by civic origin an Alexandrian', Acts 18.24).

Scholarly interpretation of a more specifically Jewish kind is to be observed at I.7.12 and 9.15, this time dealing not with the OT but with a tradition of the teaching of Jesus. Using the known right of the rabbis* to interpret an injunction for a practical situation in such a way as, in effect, to negate the original command, Paul in both cases reverses the teaching in question. Liturgical anxieties too, as well as doctrinal and ethical ones, prompt him to adopt the role of interpreter. The religious practice of his readers is corrected by pointing out its true significance, through appeal, in the case of glossolalia and the eucharist, to Isaiah and Jesus respectively.

On a broader scale, Paul in both epistles enters into the process of interpreting Christian affirmation. Some of the Corinthians seem to have initiated a fully realized interpretation of the primitive eschatology: we already enjoy the exhilarating blessings promised for the Last Day. (Indeed, they may have learned this from Paul himself, II.5.17, where 'new creation' is an eschatological concept found to be taking place now; cf. also II.6.2b.) Paul corrects this at various points and most notably in I.15.51–8. The structure of time postulated in the Jewish apocalyptic* works and taken over in some of the earliest Christian affirmations (above all in the prayer *Maranatha*, I.16.22) is not to be collapsed into the present moment of the Christian's life.

It is, however, in the 'crucicentric' interpretation of his own work that we find Paul at his most profound in the Corinthian correspondence. In I.1.18–2.5 it is principally the content (though also the manner) of the Christian preaching that is identified as a message concerning the cross. At II.4.7–18, 6.4–10, 12.9f. and 13.4, it is the manner of Paul's preaching that in some way embodies the 'powerlessness' exhibited in the suffering and death of Jesus. Paul as Christian and as pastor interprets not only the OT and the gospel but also his own experience.

C. K. Barrett, *A Commentary on the First/Second Epistle to the Corinthians*, 1968, 1973; id., *Essays on Paul*, 1982; H. Conzelmann, *I Corinthians*, 1975; R. Hock, *The Social Context of Paul's Ministry*, 1980; J. C. Hurd, *The Origin of I Corinthians*, 1965; R. P. Martin, *2 Corinthians*, 1986; W. A. Meeks, *The First Urban Christians*, 1983; G. Theissen, *The Social Setting of Pauline Christianity*, 1982.

COLIN HICKLING

Covenant

Historically, the word has been used as a prime designation for the relationship established by God with humanity and the world, and for the orders of life, theologically understood, so formed ('dispensations'), either in broad and general terms, or more often with reference to specific human groups and to relationships understood to subsist in particular modes or phases. Its customary usage, to denote the two literary collections which form the Christian scriptures, the Old and New Testaments (with Latin *testamentum* indeed understood not as 'last will' but as the equivalent of Greek *diathēkē* which it commonly renders in the Vulgate,* potentially open to misunderstanding in interpretation: cf. H. von Campenhausen, *The Formation of the Christian Bible*, ET 1972, pp. 267f.), originates with patristic writers around AD 200, and is derivative from the usage which saw these collections as bearing witness respectively to the old and new orders of salvation, itself ultimately rooted in NT use of the 'old–new' contrast (especially II Cor. 3.6, 14;

but against seeing the Pauline usage as determinative of the literary titles, cf. W. C. van Unnik, *Sparsa Collecta* II, 1980, pp. 157–71).

Since titles may themselves be understood to express particular hermeneutical* frameworks and tasks, it should be noted that the broad designations '(scriptures of) the old and new covenants' have served both to express a unifying view of the respective collections by relating the totality of each to a fundamental divine–human reality, and to denote the two collections, and that theological content, in their relationship ('covenant') as well as their distinctness ('old', 'new'). Vital theological convictions are thus being indicated, but the labels themselves offer only a very broad interpretative framework (A. H. J. Gunneweg, *Understanding the Old Testament*, ET 1978, pp. 36f.) and entail for Christian theology a hermeneutical task which has continued from its earliest days, with the employment of a wide variety of different models to express the continuity and the discontinuity, often emphasizing one rather than the other, and frequently within the context of the terrible social embodiment of Christian claims to superiority over Judaism with its 'superseded' covenant (*see* **Antisemitism**).

In spite of this formally significant use of the term 'covenant', the notion itself has not always played a major constructive role in theology and biblical interpretation. It seems that 'since the phrases "old covenant" and "new covenant" did not acquire a literary application until the late second century, well after the collection of Christian scriptures had begun to take shape, it is clear that in its origins the collection had nothing to do with the biblical covenant idea' (H. Y. Gamble, *The New Testament Canon*, 1985, p. 22). Covenant does not figure as a very fertile theological concept among the Fathers; but Irenaeus* does begin to develop a theology of covenant, stressing against his opponents both the unity and the differentiation of old and new, and speaking also of a succession of four covenants (Adam,* Noah, Moses,* Christ) within a 'history of salvation'. In later times, theological constructions in which covenant has played a major role have featured chiefly within the Reformed tradition, and generally with greater stress on the continuity and unity between old and new: this is true in differing ways for Calvin* (e.g. *Institutes*, Bk II, chs x–xi), for the covenant theology of H. Bullinger (1504–75: see Gunneweg, pp. 57–9), for the later 'federal theology' associated principally with J. Cocceius (1603–89: see Gunneweg, pp. 63–5), which began to focus more on the sequential nature of the covenants with a theological periodization of salvation history,* and for English Puritanism. In each case, OT interpretation operating within such frameworks played a vital role in affording patterns for the organization of the godly society of the new covenant people. More recently covenant, understood as fellowship between God and humanity, broken by sin and restored in Christ, has figured importantly in the theology of Karl Barth* (*Church Dogmatics* IV/1, ET 1956, pp. 22ff.) and, e.g., in H. Berkhof, *Christian Faith*, ET 1979. It seems likely that Barth's work in particular may with other factors have stimulated twentieth-century interest in the place of covenant ideas in biblical theology* and interpretation.

This is because the shift, characteristic of much nineteenth-century scholarship, from systematic*–dogmatic presentations of 'biblical theology' to historicist-descriptive accounts of the course of Israelite religion, often led to a devaluing or neglect of the role of covenant in that religion, irrespective of its role in the finished texts themselves, since these were used primarily as sources for reconstructing the living religious history behind them. So while H. Schultz, attempting to blend systematic and historical approaches, could still see covenant as the principal expression of the personal and moral relationship between Israel and Yahweh, anchored in the very beginnings of Israel's history at Sinai (and before), in relation to which the law and saving ordinances were to be interpreted (*Old Testament Theology* II ET 1892, pp. 1ff.), critical historians commonly saw covenant as a late feature – and perhaps a deleterious one, depending on what judgments were employed in evaluating the history. For J. Wellhausen, the original natural bond which joined Yahweh and Israel was only at a late stage replaced by the idea of a morally-conditioned 'covenant', whereby in the seventh-century Deuteronomy and later literature the prophetic* preaching of God's righteous judgment on Israel, which was seen to find fulfilment in a series of massive national disasters, gave rise to the belief in a contractual relationship predicated on Israel's obedience to the law (*Prolegomena . . .*, ET 1885, pp. 417–19, 468f., 473f.).

Covenant is here a late and injurious growth which led to the post-exilic stultifying of the true spirit of free communion with God supposedly characteristic of Israel's earlier days. This position was worked out in fuller detail by R. Kraetzschmar (1896); for such views, 'covenant' could hardly play a central part in constructive biblical interpretation. But, very strikingly, W. Eichrodt's great and influential work (1933–9), which marked the modern resurgence of OT theology,* made covenant its major organizing principle: Eichrodt saw the concept of the relationship between Israel and Yahweh, inaugurated by God's free historical activity in making Israel his people and going back to Moses, as determinative for the whole of the people's existence and for the OT itself, whether or not the actual term 'covenant' (Heb. *berît*) always appears (*Theology of the Old Testament* I, ET 1961, pp. 13f., 17f., 36ff.). It is no principle drawn from without, therefore, and forcibly imposed on the OT material by some dogmatic scheme, but a consciousness basic to the structure of Israel's faith in its varied expressions and by means of which a coherent account may be given of an essentially unified Israelite world of faith, while still seeking to do justice to its historical character. Many of Eichrodt's emphases were to be influential in the later 'biblical theology movement': covenant as expressing divine initiative and action, the link with the exodus,* the stress on event rather than on human religious ideas, and the historical rather than the myth-orientated dynamic of Israel's faith.

From another angle, too, the roughly contemporary works of A. Alt and M. Noth, which argued for the origins of Israel in its distinctive sense as a tribal confederation, constituted by covenant with Yahweh and regulated by divinely-given law from the start, appeared to underline not only the centrality of the covenant in Israel's life, but also its nature as institution rather than primarily as idea; regular festivals of covenant renewal, which involved theophany* and the proclamation of God's law, were held to be instrumental in shaping major elements of the pentateuchal* tradition, the older Sinai narrative in Ex. 19ff. and the form of Deuteronomy (G. von Rad; differently, A. Weiser). In so far as a cultic* matrix was presupposed, it could also be argued that such a covenant festival, (later?) celebrated in the Jerusalem* temple and reflected in (e.g.) Ps. 50, was the interpretative key to many psalms (cf. A. Weiser, *The Psalms*, ET 1962, pp. 23–52, 391–9; but see later discussion in H.-J. Kraus, *Theology of the Psalms*, ET 1986, pp. 54–9). There are fairly obvious theological undercurrents in much of the emphasis on Israel's covenantal origin: Israel in what is taken to be its 'normative' sense is formed not 'after the flesh' but 'after the spirit'.

Arguments that covenant is expressive of social and political relations, already put forward in other ways by (especially) M. Weber and J. Pedersen, were taken further by the contention of G. E. Mendenhall (1954; see *The Biblical Archaeologist Reader* III, ed. E. F. Campbell, D. N. Freedman, 1970, pp. 25–53) and others that Israel (and perhaps already Moses himself) had drawn on the form of ancient international (notably Hittite) vassal treaties, with their characteristically recurring structural elements and by which the overlord bound his vassal king to abide by stipulations, probably in gratitude for the suzerain's benevolence, in order to express the nature of its relationship with Yahweh forged by his action in the exodus events. Though caution was urged (e.g. by D. J. McCarthy, *Treaty and Covenant*, ²1978), on historical as well as form-critical* grounds, particularly as far as the Sinai narrative was concerned, the hypothesis of such a borrowing was widely accepted, and generated a great many attempts to interpret features of the OT material in the light of what came to be regarded as a very deep permeation and, indeed, essential shaping of Israel's covenant theology by treaty forms and ideology. This was supposedly demonstrated not only for individual motifs but also for broader elements of form (e.g. the 'covenant lawsuit'); and the existence of a developed, cultically expressed covenant theology often seen in such terms was taken to be the essential presupposition of the preaching of the great prophets* – thus reversing Wellhausen's view (cf. R. E. Clements, *Prophecy and Covenant*, 1965). Most strikingly, Deuteronomy itself came to be understood as a quite direct reflection of the ancient treaty form for Israelite theological purposes (McCarthy), though with some dispute as to the precise implications of this postulated borrowing (of later Assyrian forms contemporary with the literary origin of Deuteronomy itself?) for understanding the genesis and significance (theological and political) of the book (cf. e.g. M. Weinfeld, *Deuteronomy and the Deuteronomic School*, 1972).

In the last two decades there has, however, been a very marked decline in appeal to borrowed treaty forms as the key to explaining the origins and meaning of OT covenant theology. It is very far from clear that this appeal can give a plausible explanation of 'covenantal' features in the prophetic books (cf. Clements, *Prophecy and Tradition*, 1975, ch. 2); attempts to correlate the structure and individual elements within Ex. 19ff. with treaty-forms are unconvincing; and even if Deuteronomy has been 'influenced' in some degree by a treaty pattern, it is doubtful how far this is the case and what its implications are, both for tracing the historical and religious dynamics of the book's origin and for its theological interpretation.

On the other hand, it has long been noticed that it is in Deuteronomy and the books closely associated with it (the 'deuteronomistic history'* and Jeremiah) that the term 'covenant' appears most frequently and consciously to denote Yahweh's relationship with Israel as graciously instituted at Horeb: Deuteronomy in its finished form presents itself as a covenant document. We must, however, note at this juncture the variety of covenants (of different types) of which the OT as a whole speaks, particularly those with Noah (Gen. 9), with Abraham * (Gen. 15 and 17), with David * (II Sam. 23.5; cf. II Sam. 7), as well as those future 'new' and 'eternal' covenants promised in prophetic collections related to the disaster of the exile (e.g. Isa. 55.3; Jer. 31.31–34; 32.36–41; Ezek. 37.26; also Hos. 2.18ff.?). In source-critical * and traditio–historical * terms, these varied traditions have diverse though sometimes interwoven roots, and the variety urges caution in assuming that we can simply use 'covenant' or '*the* covenant' as a broad theological cipher, adopting without more ado that traditional unifying view expressed by the label 'Old Testament'. Furthermore, there has been much recent discussion of the terminological and semantic issues associated with the word *bᵉrît*: is it appropriately rendered by 'covenant', which may (though need not) in English express a bilateral relationship? E. Kutsch (*Verheissung und Gesetz*, 1973) has argued strongly that the word denotes rather 'obligation' imposed either on oneself (as a promise) or on another party, and that this is its fundamental and primary sense in the OT, crucial to its theological interpretation. This set of issues remains under discussion (on the etymological and wider semantic questions see J. Barr, in *Beiträge zur Alttestamentlichen Theologie* ed. H. Donner et al., 1977, pp. 23–38).

Now L. Perlitt in particular has detailed the claim that the centrality of covenant in Deuteronomic theology is best accounted for by regarding it as essentially created within that theology and as having no real antecedents in earlier tradition (*Bundestheologie im Alten Testament*, 1969), so that references to 'covenant' in the Sinai narratives (as Ex. 19.5; 24.3–8) or in earlier prophets (as Hos. 8.1) must be regarded as evidence of wider Deuteronomistic reshaping of that material. Though many scholars have continued to argue for some use of a divine *bᵉrît* idea earlier and as perhaps contributing to the deuteronomic concept, Perlitt's view that it is in the seventh-century Deuteronomy that covenant becomes a central theological idea has been increasingly influential. In part a return to Wellhausen's position, it has led to further questioning of the historical roots of the Sinai traditions in Ex. 19ff. themselves (most radically by J. van Seters, in *Canon, Theology, and Old Testament Interpretation* ed. G. M. Tucker et al., 1988, pp. 111–30). E. W. Nicholson (1986) has broadly endorsed Perlitt's views, while finding some antecedents for the *bᵉrît* concept in Hosea and Ex. 24.3–8; and he has argued that through its use in Deuteronomy it functions as a highly potent idea or symbol * capable of transforming and shaping the life of Israelite society, orientating it towards a radically desacralized world-order in which Yahweh's gracious and righteous will alone constitutes the basis and goal of Israel's life.

Furthermore, it now appears likely to many scholars that the 'covenant image' of the prophets belongs more to the redactional moulding of much prophetic material and its linkage with the unifying Deuteronomistic picture of prophecy than to the prophets' relating to an already-existing and quite precisely contoured covenant theology (and institutions; see Clements, *Prophecy and Tradition*, ch. 4). It seems at least clear that it is to the Deuteronomists that we must look for the primary, creative theological use of the *bᵉrît* concept, which became the dominant impulse in the formation of the OT as a covenant literature, and in which the Horeb covenant appears as the major tradition to which other covenants are related (cf. Clements, *Old Testament Theology*, 1978, pp. 96–103, 118–20).

In spite of the overall title, covenant ideas play a comparatively restricted role in the NT. The word *diathēkē*, used in the Septuagint * as the normal rendering of *bᵉrît* (on the semantic * aspects cf. W. Horbury in *VT*, XXXVI, 1986, pp. 37–51) appears 33 times, of which 17 occur in Hebrews (cf. H. Braun, *An die Hebräer*, 1984, pp. 217f.), with its central theological and hermeneutical emphasis on the new covenant, better than the old, of which Christ is the mediator and which is understood to be that promised in Jer. 31 (quoted in Heb. 8.8–12; 10.16f.); *diathēkē* appears to be used in 9.16f. (as indeed already in Philo *) in a dual and punning way, between its ordinary secular Greek sense of 'will' and that of 'covenant' (cf. Luke 22.29). Paul * deploys differently the contrast between old and new in II Cor. 3 and in Gal. 3.15–18 (with dispute as to whether the sense 'will' is demanded in v. 15); 4.24: the covenant theme is brought into close relationship with that of 'eschatological * promise' (*epaggelia*; cf. also Eph. 2.12) and the covenant as promise to Abraham is given theological priority over the order related to the law – the nature or scope of the priority Paul sees remains under discussion. In Rom. 11.27 a quotation of Jer. 31.33 is understood to refer to the eschatological salvation of Israel, while in Rom. 9.4 Paul speaks of 'the covenants' as belonging to the Jews (the precise referent is uncertain). Elsewhere, Paul's eucharistic tradition includes Jesus' word 'this cup is the new covenant in my blood' (I Cor. 11.25; cf. E. Käsemann, *Essays on New Testament Themes*, ET 1964, pp. 127ff.), which seems to bear some relation to the longer text at Luke 22.19b–20, but differs markedly from the

Marcan wording (14.24, cf. Matt. 26.27f.). Though the association of blood and (new) covenant seems to draw on Ex. 24.8; Jer. 31.31 (and Zech. 9.11?), the textual and exegetical issues, including the question of relationship between the different sayings, and their historical origins, are very thorny; but interpretation should try to do justice to the particular significance of the sayings in connection with the total theological structures of the respective Gospels* in which they occur.

Apart from the Lucan reference to the covenant as God's promise to Abraham (Luke 1.72; Acts 3.25; cf. 'the covenant of circumcision', 7.8), this is the virtual sum of NT usage: it is not large, and covenant ideas do not explicitly figure very prominently. 'The natural assumption is that the term "covenant", though widely current in contemporary sectarian and reformist movements, was not felt particularly congenial by the early Christians and was used by them therefore only in rather limited applications' (J. Barr). On the other hand, while the specific theme of the 'new covenant' was prominent at Qumran (see **Dead Sea Scrolls**), Second Temple Judaism in its most prominent Palestinian forms itself cannot be comprehended apart from its commitment to the covenant (cf. C. Rowland, *Christian Origins*, 1985, pp. 25–8), understood as a gracious divine initiative to which detailed obedience to the Torah was the appropriate response. The emphasis placed by E. P. Sanders (*Paul and Palestinian Judaism*, 1977, pp. 84ff., 101ff., 419ff.) on this 'covenantal nomism' as central to Jewish experience, in contrast to the conventional stereotypes of Jewish 'legalism', has not only stimulated major exegetical reconsideration of the work of Paul, and of Jesus himself, but has also made contact with the growing unease among OT scholars with views which see Second Temple Judaism as fossilized legalism which had lost the springs of living religion.

In regard to theological interpretation, such views have operated as one way of highlighting the Christian religious distinction between 'old' and 'new' covenants, for the terms have been seen as expressing not simply the historical, but also the theological continuities and discontinuities between Judaism and Christianity. Biblical interpretation can hardly avoid a continuing struggle with those issues, for they go to the very heart of the nature of Christian faith. Eichrodt's focus on covenant as a 'centre', a prime conceptual reality by means of which the theological content of the OT material may be brought together in a coherent whole (cf. H. Graf Reventlow, *Problems of Old Testament Theology*, ET 1985, pp. 49–51, 125ff.; R. Smend, *Die Mitte des Alten Testaments*, 1970, esp. pp. 44ff.), could be taken not only as such an organizing principle, but also as a theological norm, indicating the vital and irreducible core of the OT which could function in Christian theological interpretation. However, even if the concept of a 'centre' is reckoned to be a valuable one, it could still be asked whether covenant is the most appropriate choice; and if we understand the subject-matter of the texts as the theological reality to which witness is borne, how can such a 'centre' actually help in an interpretation of those texts which can take seriously both the historical shaping of the texts in all its stages up to the final redaction, and the finished literary form itself?

That covenant should be understood not in idealist terms, but as social* reality belonging to Israel's origins as a liberated* society, 'the bonding of decentralized social groups in a larger society of equals committed to co-operation without authoritarian leadership and a way of symbolizing the locus of sovereignty in such a society of equals' (N. K. Gottwald, *The Tribes of Yahweh*, 1979, p. 692), indicates one significant direction in which contemporary interpretation is moving, though it may lay itself open to charges of reductionism (B. S. Childs, *Old Testament Theology in a Canonical Context*, 1985, pp. 24f., 176f.). Much recent study, as noted, has come to see 'covenant' in Israel's life less as related to specific institutional-political expressions, and more as a powerful idea or symbol, not to be hypostatized, yet with vitality to shape a people's life and identity. We may thus see the OT as a 'covenant literature', made such by the dynamic theological reinterpretation which is bound up with the centrality of the Horeb covenant and to the formation of the literary whole (Clements). Even so, precisely how the different covenant traditions are to be related to each other in contemporary interpretation remains at issue. What does it mean that the Noah, Abraham, and Sinai-Horeb covenants are now linked in one sequential narrative complex? Should $b^e rît$ in Gen. 9 or 15 or 17, or in Ex. 19ff. be understood in the sense(s) it bears in Deuteronomy, taken as the interpretative key to the Pentateuch-Torah? And if a 'covenant-unifying tendency' is apparent in Deuteronomy, with everything now related to the centrality of Horeb, what of the promised 'new covenant' of (some) prophecy?

We should perhaps avoid taking $b^e rît$ as a univocal expression in the OT (cf. G. von Rad, *Old Testament Theology* I, ET 1962, pp. 130, 133) and see its meaning and significance rather in relation to the specific and varied contexts and linguistic networks to which it belongs, but including the wider (redactional) narrative and other continuities in which the term appears. Decisions will have to be taken as to where priorities in interpretation – and in theological judgment – lie. But this is only to reaffirm that biblical interpretation cannot escape concern with the interrelations of the motifs of covenant, law, and promise in either Old or New Testament.

This theme of covenant has indeed played a major part in the self-understanding of many political groups who have seen themselves as God's covenant people; examples from Cromwellian England, the Netherlands establishing independence from Spanish rule, or nationalist South Africa (cf. J. A. Michener's epic novel, *The Covenant*, 1980) come readily to mind. Similarly it plays a determinative role in the liturgical* language of many Christian traditions (cf. the annual Methodist 'covenant service').

See also: **Biblical Theology; Christian Interpretation of the Old Testament; Theology (Old Testament); Use of the Old Testament in the New Testament.**

G. Quell, J. Behm, '*diatithēmi, diathēkē*', *TDNT* II, ET 1964, pp. 104–34; D. R. Hillers, *Covenant. The History of a Biblical Idea*, 1969; D. J. McCarthy, *Old Testament Covenant. A Survey of Current Opinions*, 1972; M. Weinfeld, '*bᵉrît*', *TDOT* II, ET 1975, pp. 253–79; E. Kutsch, 'Bund', *Theologische Realenzyklopädie* VII, 1981, pp. 397–410; E. W. Nicholson, *God and His People. Covenant and Theology in the Old Testament*, 1986.

EDWARD BALL

Creation Narratives

There are two accounts of creation in Genesis, the first in Gen. 1.1–2.4a, commonly attributed to the Priestly source (P), and the latter, which merges into the story of 'the fall', in Gen. 2.4b–3.24, generally attributed to the Yahwist source (J).

The Priestly account is generally dated to the sixth or possibly fifth century BC, and is characterized by a sober and repetitive style, and tends to emphasize the majestic transcendence of God, who is referred to in the Hebrew as *ᵉlōhīm* (EVV God). God brings the world into being by divine fiat and his creative work (consisting of eight actions) is spread over six days, as follows: 1. light, 2. the firmament and separation of the waters, 3. (a) earth and sea, and (b) vegetation, 4. the heavenly luminaries, 5. sea creatures and birds, and 6. (a) land animals, and (b) man. The symmetry between days 1–3 and 4–6 will be apparent. God rested on the seventh day, and this constituted a kind of aetiology* of the Sabbath.

Before the development of modern geology and evolutionary theory, it was normal for Christians and Jews to understand the account in Gen. 1 as a literal description of the creation of the world. Many of the most bitter religious disputes in the nineteenth century turned on this issue: was it possible to remain a believer if the literal meaning* of this chapter was not accepted? Edmund Gosse's memoir, *Father and Son*, describing how his immensely learned father tried to resolve the problem by suggesting that God had deliberately created the fossils, illustrates how families could be divided by the issue. More recent conservative apologetic* has discussed at length the question whether the 'days' must necessarily be understood literally, and how the problem of the existence of light before the creation of the sun could be resolved. The recent resurgence of 'creationism' in North America has served as a vivid reminder that this issue is still a live one (*See* **Verbal Inspiration**).

Among apologists who would not wish to be regarded as fundamentalist* it is common to emphasize that Gen. 1 expresses theological truths rather than being a scientific account. However, it should be pointed out that whilst the assertion that God is the creator of the world is no doubt the primary thing here, this is expressed in terms of primitive science, cf. the references to the cosmic waters above the heavens and below the earth and the solid firmament of heaven.

Does Gen. 1 contain a doctrine of *creatio ex nihilo* (cf. II Macc. 7.28)? If, with some scholars, we render vv. 1f. as a subordinate clause, 'When God began to create the heavens and the earth, the earth being without form and void . . .', we would not have *creatio ex nihilo*. However, on balance we should probably translate v. 1 as 'In the beginning God created the heavens and the earth', since this short sentence seems more characteristic of the style of P in Gen. 1, as well as having the support of all the ancient versions (cf. John 1.1). One could conceivably then understand the chaos described in v. 2 as being the result of God's creative activity in v. 1, and we would have *creatio ex nihilo*. It is, however, more likely that v. 1 represents a summary statement of God's creative activity in the chapter as a whole ('the heavens and the earth' most naturally denoting the completed universe), in which case the question whether we have *creatio ex nihilo* is left open.

The P account centres on the creation of the world (unlike J), but man nevertheless has a special place: he forms, as it were, the apex of a pyramid, whereas in J he is the centre of a circle. Man (unlike the animals) is said to be made in the image of God (1.26, 28). Traditionally, Christian theology took this to refer to man's spiritual nature, but the word image (*ṣelem*) makes it difficult to exclude a physical element (cf. Gen. 5.3). Probably both spiritual and physical kinship are included, since the Hebrews saw man not in terms of body-soul dualism but as a psycho-physical totality. As a result of man's special status before God, he is empowered as God's steward to have lordship over the world, though this is not intended in any harsh sense (1.26ff., cf. Ps. 8.5ff., EVV 4ff.).

It is clear that the P creation narrative has developed from earlier traditions. Most commonly compared has been the so-called Babylonian creation epic, *Enuma elish*, a work recited at the Babylonian new year (Akitu) festival. Part of *Enuma elish* recounts Marduk's defeat of the female sea monster Tiamat and his subsequent creation of heaven and earth, apparently each from one half of her. In 1895 H. Gunkel, in his book *Schöpfung und Chaos in Urzeit und Endzeit*, argued that a number of poetic allusions in the OT to Yahweh's conflict with a dragon or dragons and the sea at the time of creation (cf. Pss. 74.12–17, 89.10–15 [EVV 9–14], Job 26.12f., 38.8–11, etc.) were an Israelite appropriation of the Babylonian Marduk-Tiamat myth; he also maintained that Gen. 1 itself represents a demythologization of this myth. Appeal was made to the use of the word *tᵉhōm* 'sea, deep' to describe the watery chaos in Gen. 1.2, which is cognate with the name of the sea monster Tiamat.

However, as a result of the discovery of the Canaanite mythological texts from Ugarit* in Syria, it is now clear that the OT's allusions to Yahweh's conflict with dragon(s) and the sea represent the appropriation of a Canaanite rather than a Babylonian myth (though the two myths may be ultimately related). In addition to a detailed account of Baal's victory over Yam (Sea), we have brief allusions in the Ugaritic texts to Baal's defeat of the seven-headed sea monster Leviathan, also known as the 'dragon' and 'the twisting serpent' (terms all found in the OT), and this latter conflict may have been associated by the Canaanites with the creation of the world, as in the OT. Unfortunately, we do not possess an actual Canaanite creation text, though from his epithets it is clear that El was the creator god. Anyway, the OT allusions to dragon and sea conflict have a Canaanite rather than a Babylonian origin; even the use of *tᵉhōm* in Gen. 1.2 does not prove dependence on *Enuma elish*, since although the word is philologically related to Tiamat, its form indicates that it is not simply borrowed from the Babylonian word. The case for the dependence of Genesis on specifically Babylonian traditions is much stronger

in the case of the flood story, where striking parallels with the account of Utnapishtim in the Gilgamesh epic (tablet 11) have been noted. An earlier version of the Mesopotamian flood tradition is found in the Atra-hasis epic, where it is set in a primaeval context following on not so long after the creation of man, as in Genesis.

As for the more immediate background of Gen. 1, one source may be Ps. 104, a psalm alluding to various aspects of creation in the same order as they appear in Gen. 1, suggesting that some relation exists between them. That it is Ps. 104 which is earlier than Gen. 1, rather than *vice versa*, is supported by the fact that the psalm is more mythological:* in Ps. 104.7 we actually have an allusion to the divine conflict with the sea, whereas in Gen. 1.6ff. God's control of the waters is simply a job of work; and in Ps. 104.26 we hear of God's creation of Leviathan, whereas Gen. 1.21 speaks in demythologized terms of 'great sea monsters'. Moreover, Gen. 1.24 employs an unusual form of the word for 'beasts' (*ḥayᵉtō*), attested elsewhere only in poetry, including Ps. 104.11, 20, suggesting that a poetic source underlies Gen. 1, perhaps Ps. 104. Interestingly, Ps. 104.6 uses the word *tᵉhōm* to denote the chaos waters. Also Ps. 104.3 refers to Yahweh's riding on the wings of the wind prior to his defeat of the chaos waters, which supports the view that the *rūaḥ* of God hovering (birdlike) over the waters in Gen. 1.2 refers to the wind rather than the Spirit of God. Finally with regard to Ps. 104, it should be pointed out that this psalm shows evidence of dependence on Pharaoh Akhenaten's hymn to the sun-god Aton, which may thus be claimed to be one of the sources ultimately lying behind Gen. 1.

Further evidence of a mythical background behind Gen. 1 comes in 1.26, 'Let *us* make man', which probably alludes to God's consulting his heavenly court; cf. Job 38.7, where 'all the sons of God shouted for joy' at the time of creation, though admittedly we do not read that God consulted them.

The Yahwist source, traditionally and probably rightly dated to the tenth or ninth century BC, is so-called because it characteristically uses *Yahweh* (EVV Lord) as the name for God. However, uniquely in Gen. 2.4b–3.24 we find *Yahweh ᵉlōhīm* (EVV Lord God) employed; *ᵉlōhīm* (God) was probably added by a later redactor to make clear the identity of the deity with that referred to in Gen. 1.

In contrast to the P creation account, the J version centres on man. There is, however, in Gen. 2.4b ff. a fragment of an account of the creation of the world (called 'the earth and the heavens' in contrast to P's 'the heavens and the earth'). In J the vegetation, animals and woman are made subsequent to man, and this reflects a different order of creation from that found in P. Moreover, in contrast to the transcendent deity of P, Yahweh is depicted in anthropomorphic* terms, e.g. making man like a potter (2.7), planting a garden in Eden (2.8), and walking in the garden in the cool of the day (3.8).

The J creation account is centred on the garden of Eden. Eden probably means 'delight' or 'luxury'. The common view that it derives from Akkadian *edinu* 'steppe, plain' (itself a loan-word from Sumerian *edin*) is open to linguistic objections as well as being semantically inappropriate. Eden is set at the source of the rivers Tigris, Euphrates, Pishon and Gihon (2.10–14). The last two rivers cannot be identified with certainty, but the first two are well-known Mesopotamian rivers, thus suggesting a location for Eden either in the Persian Gulf or in Armenia. The Sumerians actually located their Paradise (Dilmun) in the Persian gulf, but Eden is perhaps more likely to be in Armenia. Ezek. 28.14, 16 locates the garden of Eden on 'the mountain of God', and Armenia is highly mountainous (cf. Gen. 8.4, where Noah's ark lands on one of the mountains of Ararat, i.e. Armenia). Possibly there is a reflection here of the dwelling place of the supreme Canaanite god El (equated in the OT with Yahweh), which was located according to the Ugaritic texts on a mountain 'at the source of the rivers', and in the Hittite-Canaanite Elkunirša myth is situated precisely at the source of the river Euphrates.

The trees in the garden of Eden are singled out for special mention, the tree of the knowledge of good and evil and the tree of life. The former, the eating of whose fruit leads to man's 'fall', clearly conveyed divine wisdom (3.6, 22), probably omniscience, 'good and evil' constituting the totality of reality (cf. II Sam. 14.17, 20). The views that moral discernment or sexual knowledge are intended seem less likely. The other tree, the tree of life, is clearly regarded as conveying immortality, and although it is mentioned in 2.9, it is not alluded to again until the end of the story in 3.22, 24, when man is driven away from the garden to prevent him eating of it and living for ever. The magic plant bestowing immortality in the Mesopotamian Gilgamesh epic has been compared: Gilgamesh, having sought out Utnapishtim, the hero of the Mesopotamian flood story, obtains the magic plant but while he is bathing a serpent snatches it and rejuvenates itself. Thus expression is given to the belief in the futility of man's quest for immortality. This futility also finds expression in another Mesopotamian text, the myth of Adapa, of whom we read, 'To him he (*sc.* Ea) had given wisdom; eternal life he had not given him', an interesting parallel to Gen. 2–3 in view of the nature of the two trees.

The serpent which tempts man in Gen. 3 does not denote Satan, belief in whom emerged only in the post-exilic period, though this equation is found later, as in the apocryphal* Wisdom of Solomon 2.24. Following man's disobedience, we find in Gen. 3.14ff. a series of aetiologies explaining not only why the serpent goes on its belly, but also women's labour pains and subordination to men, and man's toil. It is disputed whether death is also construed as a punishment for man's sin in the original story (cf. Gen. 3.19), as in Rom. 5.12 and subsequent Christian theology, or whether man is considered mortal from the beginning, as Gen. 3.22 possibly implies.

In Ezek. 28.12–19, part of an oracle against the king of Tyre, we find a variant version of the story of the garden of Eden: the king of Tyre is spoken of as if he was in Eden, and he is cast out by a cherub because of his hubris (cf. Eden, casting out of the man, and cherubim guarding the garden in Gen. 2–3).

In the Septuagint* translation the term *paradeisos* is applied to the garden of Eden, a word derived from a Persian word for a park. By means of the principle according to which the last things will correspond to the first things (new heaven and earth, etc.), Paradise eventually became a term for heaven (cf. Luke 23.43).

Belief in Yahweh as creator pervades the OT and is not confined to Gen. 1–3. It is particularly prominent in the Psalms and Deutero-Isaiah and is the fundamental presupposition underlying Israel's wisdom literature* (Proverbs, Job, Ecclesiastes). Although not as central to the OT as the cluster of beliefs relating to Yahweh's special relationship with Israel, it is an important concept to which renewed attention has been paid in recent years. In addition, whatever one's views as to the proper understanding of the early chapters of Genesis, it is important to remember the rich legacy that they have bequeathed to us in art* and poetry* and music.*

See also **Ancient Near Eastern Interpretation; Ancient Near Eastern World; Genesis.**

Commentaries on Genesis 1–3, including G. von Rad, *Genesis*, ² 1963 and C. Westermann, *Genesis 1–11*, 1984; B. W. Anderson (ed.), *Creation in the Old Testament*, 1984; F. Blanquart and L. Derousseaux (eds), *La Création dans l'Orient Ancien*, 1987; S. G. F. Brandon, *Creation Legends of the Ancient Near East*, 1963; J. Day, *God's Conflict with the Dragon and the Sea*, 1985, ch. 1; A. Heidel, *The Babylo-*

nian Genesis, [2] 1951; J. B. Pritchard (ed.), *Ancient Near Eastern Texts Relating to the Old Testament,* [3] 1969; H. N. Wallace, *The Eden Narrative,* 1985; C. Westermann, *Creation,* 1971.

JOHN DAY

Creed

Creeds, in the sense of fixed formulae to be memorized, did not emerge earlier than the late third century, and the context in which they emerged was the training of catechumens in the faith before being received by baptism. They were in the first place confessions of faith rather than tests of orthodoxy, though by the early fourth century the credal form was being adopted for statements of doctrine agreed by official church councils, and suspected heretics were being asked to subscribe to such definitions of the faith.

It is clear that these definitions were taken to be summaries of scriptural teaching: it is significant, for example, that the Fathers at Nicaea were embarrassed by the need to adopt non-scriptural terminology to achieve their ends. Finally convinced that Arius' understanding of the nature of the Logos,* the Word or Son of God, was not orthodox, they had to find a way of excluding him, despite the fact that he was happy to accept any phrases culled from scripture and claim that they could and should be interpreted in line with his understanding. With reluctance the non-scriptural term *homoousios* (of one substance) was adopted. By contrast at Constantinople, the new clauses concerning the divinity of the Spirit refrained from using *homoousios* and built up a statement out of II Cor. 3.17 ff. and 3.6, together with John 6.63 and 15.26. The same creed quotes Luke 1.33 against the view taught by Marcellus of Ancyra that Christ's kingdom is not eternal, despite its basis in I Cor. 15.28. Creeds and scripture were mutually dependent, the one interpreting the other, and endeavouring to reconcile apparent contradictions.

This interdependence is seen the more clearly if we attend to a certain important precursor of the creeds. At the turn of the second and third centuries, Irenaeus* and Tertullian* were appealing to what they called the Canon of Truth, or the Rule of Faith. Clearly this was not a reference to a fixed formula: Irenaeus spells out his Canon of Truth in more than one place, and in quite different wording; Tertullian uses another form still. Yet in important respects they go over the same ground as became the norm in the later fixed credal formulae, and anticipated many of the familiar credal phrases.

To take Irenaeus as the prime example, it is clear that he quotes this summary of Christian belief in order to confute the false understanding of scripture current among the Gnostic* heretics. Gnostics were claiming that the Creator God (or Demiurge) of the Jewish scriptures was a fallen being, and not the transcendent spiritual Father revealed in Jesus Christ. Irenaeus did not have the benefit of a fully formed 'Bible', but he had received a tradition which regarded the Jewish scriptures as prophecy, which used the Law and the Prophets and some other Jewish writings as authoritative, and which also accepted some Christian writings, in particular four Gospels and some Epistles. These books were to be interpreted in line with the tradition that the God of the Jews was also the Father of the Lord Jesus Christ, and through his Holy Spirit the same God inspired the prophecies. Irenaeus' argument for the unity of God and the unity of scripture depends upon the Canon of Truth, the traditional summary outline which explains what the scriptures are all about. This is both the yardstick by which the scriptures were to be interpreted, and itself dependent upon the scriptures in being no more than an 'overarching view' of their content. This anticipates the assumed relationship between scriptures and the later fixed credal formulae.

After the victory of the Nicene faith (though, as we saw, in a slightly different formula) at the Council of Constantinople in 381, doctrinal controversy took the form of debate about the proper interpretation of the creed. At the Council of Chalcedon the Fathers refused to attempt a new creed, but appended a definition explaining the one already agreed. In the course of the preceding debates, creed and scripture had been measured against one another. Thus Cyril maintains that as in Phil. 2, so in the creed, there is one subject – the Logos who is in the form of God who then takes the form of a servant. His opponents sought to distinguish the Godhead and the manhood not only in interpreting key texts of scripture, but also in their exposition of the christological clause of the creed. For both sides, scripture and creed maintained their interdependence.

The creed eventually established itself not only within the rites of Christian initiation, but also within the eucharist. It belongs to worship as confession, that is, affirmation of God in his being and his activity. But its use as 'test of orthodoxy' tended to affect the way such formulae were viewed, especially in the West where the so-called Apostles' Creed enjoyed authority alongside the Nicene Creed. At the Reformation,* the historic creeds were accepted alongside the scriptures, but also articles of belief were drawn up in an atmosphere of heat and controversy, and subscription to particular articles or confessions was demanded for political reasons. The creeds were increasingly regarded as similar in their nature and function, and 'freethinkers' began to question their validity and use.

So suspicion of creeds became a feature of 'nonconformity', and the recitation of the creed within worship disappeared where fixed liturgical forms were rejected. Quakerism in particular has a quite fundamental opposition to the attempt to define the faith in such formulaic terms. The result of these developments is that the close interrelationship between creed and scripture has tended to break down. Indeed some, like the Unitarians, believed that in rejecting the creeds they were being faithful to scripture, since they found no doctrine of the Trinity or of Christ's divinity therein.

Confessional formulae, however, have always been a feature of Christianity, and already in the NT it is possible to trace the use of summaries and formulaic phrases to confess the faith in worship and preaching and in the face of persecution (e.g. I Cor. 15.3ff.: I Tim. 3.16). An essential process of discerning the main thrust of scripture, which at first presented itself as a somewhat indeterminate and diverse collection of sacred books, contributed to the development of larger scale summaries in a basically binitarian or trinitarian shape, to be used both to instruct new adherents and to determine what was and was not the correct interpretation of scripture. Out of this process the creeds emerged.

See also **Patristic Christology.**

J. N. D. Kelly, *Early Christian Creeds*, 1960.

FRANCES YOUNG

Criteria

Criteria are standards for testing and for coming to a judgment on an issue. We may be fully aware of the standards we ourselves use, and may always make them clear to others. But even the most self-critical writers in fact operate with criteria that they themselves take for granted and we need to be on the look-out for them. Protestant writers have tended to see the prophets as the authentic voice of Israel, priests and the cultus as agents of external corruption. Even more blatantly, what someone approves in the Jesus tradition or the letters of Paul may be described as Jewish-Palestinian and genuine; what a writer finds unacceptable may be ascribed to the influence of mystery cults or of Gnosticism,* a move to 'early Catholicism'* – and spurious. Factors derived from later (e.g. Reformation) times may affect judgments about Christian origins.

It is easy, of course, to use such stringent tests, such sceptical criteria, that no historical reconstruction of a particular period or movement or life is possible. In a strong sense of 'know', there may be very little that we do 'know' about the distant or even the quite recent past. But questions still remain: where does the evidence in question belong? and by what criteria do we allocate it to a particular time and place and people rather than to other(s)? In a recent critical assessment of current OT scholarship, Garbini argues that much OT material is much later than most scholars accept: but then himself begins to use arguments like 'it cannot be coincidental that . . .' (p. 85), which sound very like others' assertions earlier dismissed. We certainly are not told why 'it' cannot be a coincidence, i.e. how he knows. In practice our criteria can only help us to assess which are more or less likely among suggested hypothetical accounts and explanations.

Most of us share with most historians assumptions about natural regularities. Although we may differ in our attitudes to reports of miracles,* at least where none is mentioned we assume none occurred. This assumption is an important implicit criterion. And although we may on the other hand agree that there are no 'laws' of individual or social behaviour, we accept as criteria the many common generalizations about human beings on which explanatory historical narratives are generally based. But we need to notice that these generalizations differ. Garbini (p. 132) assumes that pre-Davidic Israelites 'must' have had kings of a kind – without reference to e.g. N. Gottwald, *The Tribes of Yahweh*, 1979, who argues from the assumption that people could get on very well without kings.

In biblical studies the term 'criterion' itself tends mostly to be used in discussing tests for deciding whether sayings or stories attributed, say, to Jesus or to Jeremiah are to be taken as genuine, or whether they should instead be ascribed to other contemporaries or to subsequent oral or editorial tradition. What does not stand the test is then (at best) given full consideration under another heading – or (reprehensibly) left quietly on one side and not discussed at all. The criteria that are explicitly used for this sorting process are obviously important and themselves warrant careful assessment.

Writers who discuss their standard tests often confine themselves to four such 'criteria', though, unfortunately, there is no widespread agreement on what to call them (and many more do seem to be deployed without being discussed). The four criteria are: Dissimilarity; Authentic Context; Multiple Attestation; and Coherence. (The first of these in particular gets a number of titles, e.g. Dual Irreducibility, Dual Exclusion, Discontinuity.)

For example, we might take the story in

Mark 1.9–11 of John* baptizing Jesus. Working through our criteria in reverse order, we might argue that this fits well with other scattered references to John, and with Mark 10.38–39; they hang together: 'coherence'. Next, we note that similar stories occur in the other three Gospels (and there is a reference in Acts 10.38); and while Matthew and Luke seem to depend on Mark's story, large parts of their accounts are independent; and the account in the Fourth Gospel is mostly quite distinct. So we appear to have a number of apparently separate witnesses: 'multiple attestation'. Then we may go on to remind ourselves that the Jewish historian Josephus* has an account of John and his baptizing, as well as notes of other disturbances in the wilderness; and many of these strands in the Gospel accounts seem to match concerns we find expressed in the near-contemporary Dead Sea Scrolls.* There seems to be a good match: 'authentic context'. And finally, despite the appearance of a version of the story in all four Gospels, and despite the good match with the background, and despite the way the heavenly voice (in the synoptics) or the Baptist (in the Fourth Gospel) announce Jesus' divine sonship, the episode itself stands out quite strikingly: this is a very humble Jesus, coming to the Baptist, to one who (in the Synoptic Gospels) offers a baptism of repentance. Matthew and the Fourth Evangelist seem to display some embarrassment: in Matthew the Baptist only agrees when Jesus makes his own righteousness explicit, and insists; in the Fourth Gospel Jesus never actually gets baptized at all. The coming to the Baptist and (in Matt., Mark and Luke) the acceptance of baptism contrasts with the evangelists' usual insistence on Jesus' high status, it is 'dissimilar' from ('discontinuous with') their usual tendencies, and so is not likely to have been made up by them (or their churches before they wrote). And there seems to be no sign of it having been normal Jewish or pagan practice for a charismatic leader to begin by accepting such a baptism: it is not the kind of common tale early Christians might be thought to have felt others would expect to find; there is nothing 'similar' from which it might have been copied. (It cannot be 'reduced' to a product from such other sources, they are 'excluded', to use some of the other terms noted above.)

So far, then, by all four criteria, by all four tests for deciding this kind of issue, the story that Jesus accepted John's baptism of repentance seems to many critical historians to come out well.

As a number of other critics have pointed out, however, there are some very real problems with these and other popularly accepted

criteria, and especially with the first two, 'dissimilarity' and 'context'. The first problem is that these seem to be based on contradictory presuppositions. If an account of an utterance or of some other event does fit well in its narrated context (say, Galilee at the time of Jesus) it can only do so by precisely not being 'dissimilar' from what we know of Galilee at the time. 'Authentic' by one criterion, it is automatically excluded by the other. Still, if we find Jesus saying something distinctive about issues we know were live at the time, in an appropriate setting, then both criteria can work without cancelling each other out.

But that leaves us with further logical and practical problems, for both of these criteria are forms of argument from silence, which must always be suspect. If we had more evidence about first-century Judaism – or, for that matter, about contemporary east Mediterranean 'paganism' – we might find much more of our NT material closely paralleled elsewhere. That would afford a much clearer match with 'context', of course; but the 'dissimilarity' would have dwindled as markedly. On the other hand, more information might put things we now think we know into clearer focus, and the distinctiveness of the Gospel material might be enhanced. These criteria do not seem to afford on their own a proper basis for deciding what should or should not be considered as authentic or significant by anyone engaged in interpreting the teaching of Jesus, or of an early Christian community, or an evangelist. (That they may still be of limited use is suggested below.)

The other two criteria also have weaknesses: 'multiple attestation' depends on debatable decisions about whether and how one evangelist, say, used another, or how 'Deuteronomic' the book of Jeremiah is, about how independent the witnesses can be shown to be. And 'coherence' is, of course, a particularly subjective issue. Matthew presumably thought the vindictiveness of ch. 23 cohered with the manifold forgivingness of ch. 18; we may be unable to harmonize them.

It is also important to realize that any large-scale use of the criterion of dissimilarity in determining, say, what material relates to Jesus is bound to produce a very distinctive figure, one who contrasts strongly both with the varied Judaism of his day, and with his later followers. In fact this may often represent the theological conclusion the author had intended, even an unexamined presupposition of the kind already noted above. In that case it is not just the quantity, but rather the interpretation of the material judged 'authentic' that has been largely pre-determined. It has been decided in advance that Jesus had little or nothing (or little or nothing of importance) in common with fellow Jews, or later Christians with him; and while that interpretation may be argued, it ought surely not to be imposed by the historian's sleight of hand.

Nonetheless, it may be seen that these criteria have a proper use within the construction of a historian's total picture, in which he or she presents these dissimilarities and innovations, those congruences and continuities, such-and-such an account of the data and of the 'witnesses'; and this kind of coherence with, perhaps, that amount of room for strain or even paradox. But the criteria are then – rightly – part of the total hypothesis, not an objective basis where everyone else's craft founders and only mine can safely anchor.

See also **Cultural Relativism; Historical Jesus.**

R. S. Barbour, *Traditio-Historical Criticism of the Gospels*, 1972; D. R. Catchpole, 'Tradition History' in I. H. Marshall, *New Testament Interpretation*, 1979, pp. 174–8; F. G. Downing, *The Church and Jesus*, 1968, esp. ch. VI, pp. 93–131; G. Garbini, *History and Ideology in Ancient Israel*, 1988; *JSOT*, 39, 1987, pp. 3–63; J. Z. Smith, *Map is not Territory*, 1978; C. Tuckett, *Reading the New Testament*, 1987, pp. 104–9.

F. GERALD DOWNING

Cultic Interpretation

Cultic interpretation implies that large parts of the OT material are properly to be understood either as texts actually produced for, and used in, Israel's liturgical worship or as more or less direct reflections of such texts. This understanding is closely linked with the recognition of the centrality of the cult and its effective power in the religious life of the nation, particularly as this was developed in the work of the 'Myth and Ritual'* school and by Scandinavian* scholars.

It is perhaps in connection with the psalms* that the cultic view has been most striking, influential and convincing, and here the pioneering studies of H. Gunkel provided the initial impetus for future developments. Gunkel's form-critical* analysis of the Psalter was accompanied by two further significant insights. First, he set out to discover the 'setting in life' of each of the psalm groups he discovered, that is, the occasion for which it was produced and on which it was used, and the setting was a real occasion of worship. Secondly, he showed that the contents of the Psalter, at least in their original form, did not just constitute 'the hymn-book of the Second Temple', but were part of the pre-exilic cult and thus provided important indications of its character. It is true that Gunkel considered that some psalms in a particular category have, in their existing state, been freed from their cultic associations, but it was still possible to uncover their original setting and significance. Thus, his 'hymn' and 'liturgy' categories were originally sung in choral worship, the 'communal laments' formed part of a public liturgical ceremony, including fasting and sacrificial offerings, the 'royal psalms' accompanied actual celebrations of regular occasions in the life of the pre-exilic monarchy (see **Kingship**), and the 'individual thanksgivings' were uttered in connection with a worshipper's sacrifice, though, perhaps rather curiously, he held that the 'individual laments', so frequent in the Psalter, had lost their former setting and were only reflections of an earlier cultic reality. Even more significant for future developments, his approach led him to reveal the presence of a number of recurring festivals in the Israelite calendar* not attested elsewhere in the OT. Hence, Ps. 24 showed the existence of an annual festival when the Ark was carried into its shrine in the Temple and Ps. 132 an annual celebration of the establishment of the dynasty and the royal sanctuary of Zion.

A much more thoroughgoing cultic understanding of the psalms, which has largely determined all future studies in this area, was carried out by S. Mowinckel in a series of works which extended Gunkel's approach considerably further. In particular, Mowinckel claimed that Gunkel was unduly influenced by the individualistic and evolutionary presuppositions of the scholarship of his time and had failed to see the central and creative role of the cult in early societies, which more recent work in anthropology* and Ancient Near Eastern* civilization had begun to disclose. Thus, on the one hand, the 'individual laments' were not, as Gunkel envisaged, expressions of personal piety, only distantly related to the cult, but formal compositions of the Temple personnel used to accompany a purificatory ritual on behalf of a wide range of worshippers. On the other hand, it was from the psalms, viewed as directly cultic texts, that Mowinckel primarily drew his evidence for the existence of a great Jerusalem* autumnal festival, centring on the re-enactment of creation* and the proclamation of Yahweh as universal king. He brought together a large number of psalms as forming part of the liturgy of this festival, mainly the categories of 'enthronement songs' and 'songs of Zion', which Gunkel had isolated but interpreted eschatologically* and as influenced by the the canonical prophets,* but also a considerable number of Gunkel's hymns and liturgies. The discovery of such a festival and the elements of its worship was undoubtedly the most important result of Mowinckel's cultic approach to the psalm material.

Mowinckel's position in this matter has been widely accepted, although it has never been without its critics, such as N. H. Snaith and others. Subsequent scholars have revised and developed his work, along various lines which seek to bring out particular aspects of the New Year ceremony in the light of an understanding of the psalms they employ as directly cultic texts. The 'Myth and Ritual' school and Scandinavian scholars have called attention to the presence of myth* as the verbal part of a corresponding ritual in many of these psalms and stressed their resemblance to comparable Ancient Near Eastern texts and celebrations, highlighting in particular the royal psalms as evidencing the central place of the king in the New Year festival. This kind of approach is seen very clearly in the work of I. Engnell, who viewed virtually all the psalms as embedded wholly in the cult and interpreted the 'individual laments' in their present form as a 'democratization' of texts which originally gave expression to the ritual humiliation of the king at the New Year. British scholars, such as A. R. Johnson and J. H. Eaton, while taking much the same attitude to the character of the psalms, are more cautious in interpreting them in the light of possible Ancient Near Eastern parallels and emphasize rather their place in a pattern of distinctively Israelite worship.

In line with this emphasis, there has been an increasing tendency to speak of the autumn festival as an 'enthronement festival', in which Yahweh was enthroned on Zion – or in which his kingship was celebrated there – rather than as a New Year festival, a term which could suggest Ancient Near Eastern connotations. The 'enthronement songs', 'the songs of Zion', the psalms referring to a procession and laying up of the Ark, together with others, would find their setting on this national occasion. Somewhat differently, it has been suggested, first by A. Weiser but followed by several others, that the festival in question is best thought of as a 'covenant* renewal festival', thus stressing its essentially Israelite nature, the core of which was a theophany of Yahweh over the Ark to confront the nation and summon it to renew the covenant allegiance to him. A large number of psalms, where Yahweh speaks in the first person and which contain references to the covenant and its law, are to be understood as the liturgy accompanying the dramatic theophany.

Another area in which a cultic interpretation has been influential is that of the prophetical* books. This is the result of the recognition of the existence of 'cultic prophets', who were active in Temple worship and to whom are to be attributed those passages in the psalms which resemble the canonical prophets and such psalm elements as the oracular pronouncement of 'the certainty of a hearing', characteristic of the individual laments. Against this background, a number of scholars, especially, though not exclusively, in Scandinavia, have proposed that a number of the shorter prophetical writings are in fact liturgies, unitary compositions composed for public worship on specific occasions. The books of Joel, Zephaniah, Nahum and Habakkuk in particular would be examples of such direct cultic poetry. More widely, it would now be generally recognized that even those prophetical books which cannot be linked so intimately with actual worship were much influenced by the cult, that they often adopt and adapt its rituals, concepts and language patterns and on occasion quote specific liturgical texts.

The various points at issue may be illustrated by the book of Amos. It has been suggested that Amos himself was a cultic prophet and that all the oracles in his book were uttered in a cultic setting. This opinion has not gained wide acceptance, but many who reject it would still see considerable parts of the book as based on liturgical practices. Thus, Amos 1.3–2.16 may follow the pattern of a ritual cursing of enemies, such as is attested in Egyptian* sources, while Amos 3.1–4.13 could be basically an adaptation of the liturgy of the 'covenant-renewal' festival, especially the element in it of the covenant lawsuit between Yahweh and his people: this element is found in other prophetical writings, for example, Isa. 1, and would plausibly reflect a common cultic background. Lastly, it is generally held that Amos 4.13, 5.8–9 and 9.5–6 are fragments of an actual hymn employed in worship, perhaps, because of the creation theme in them, on the occasion of the New Year or Enthronement festival.

Indeed, it is the great autumnal celebration, with its themes of creation, conflict with chaos, and Yahweh's victory and proclamation as king, which has often been regarded as the most pervasive cultic influence on the prophetic writings. In particular, this has brought a new understanding of the nature of Deutero-Isaiah. Engnell claimed that the whole was an imitation of the cultic poetry of the New Year festival, with the servant* reproducing the royal ritual pattern of suffering, death and resurrection.* Such a view depends on Engnell's own reconstruction of the festival but, even if this is rejected, there can be little question but that the whole of Deutero-Isaiah has the character of cultic psalmody and that it exemplifies throughout the concepts and language of the 'enthronement psalms' in particular.

The recognition of the great significance of

the cult for the entire societal life of pre-exilic Israel in twentieth-century OT study also led scholars to see the extent to which important national events found expression and understanding in acts of worship: one may think of celebrations at the sanctuary of a victorious battle or rites of penitence and fasting in the face of some crisis. From this it was a short step to ask whether certain narratives in the OT are to be viewed not so much as historical accounts or aetiological* tales but rather as compositions originally produced for a cultic ceremony or as reflecting such a ceremony. A considerable number of narratives has been analysed from this standpoint but three typical examples may perhaps be mentioned. First, a pioneering study was that of J. Pedersen on Ex. 1–15. He argued that the whole complex of traditions in these chapters has acquired its existing form through the cult, in which the events described are experienced anew by being recited at the Passover ceremony and are depicted in ancient cultic terminology: the defeat of Pharaoh reflected Yahweh's defeat of the primaeval chaos 'sea', a theme, as already noted, central to the autumnal festival. Secondly, a similar connection with the Passover celebration was proposed by H.-J. Kraus for Josh. 2–6, in which he finds a festival at the shrine of Gilgal that took place in connection with Passover and Unleavened Bread, centred on the crossing of the Jordan by the Ark as a re-enactment of the Exodus crossing of the sea. Subsequent studies have developed Kraus' position by showing how much the details in these chapters are influenced by the same ancient cultic themes to which Pedersen pointed in Ex. 1–15. Thirdly, much the same features have been observed in the 'history of the Ark' in I Sam. 4–6 and II Sam. 6, beginning with A. Bentzen's article 'The Cultic Use of the Story of the Ark in Samuel'. Building on his work, scholars have emphasized the intimate connection between II Sam. 6 and Ps. 132, which, as has been seen, has long been recognized as a liturgical text, so that II Sam. 6 may be considered as a historicization in a narrative of the accompanying festival ritual.

Many other areas of the OT have been subjected to a cultic interpretation: again, it is possible to refer only to a few examples. P. Humbert suggested that Gen. 1, with its hymnic form, was a text recited at the New Year celebration, much as the Creation Epic was on the similar occasion in Babylon, the seven-day pattern of creation mirroring the duration of the festival; and S. H. Hooke argued that many sections of the Pentateuch,* for example the Cain and Abel story, were originally shaped by cultic and liturgical considerations. The antithesis 'weeping/laughter',

terms which frequently occur in cultic contexts in the OT, was seen by F. F. Hvidberg as a pattern adopted from the Canaanite cult. Again, the juxtaposition of blessings and curses in such passages as Deut. 28 and Lev. 26 is to be accounted for by an actual proclamation of blessing and curse in Israel's public worship. Entire books of the third section of the Hebrew canon have been given a cultic understanding. Some scholars have claimed that the Song of Songs depicts the 'sacred marriage' and is a collection of songs to be sung when it was celebrated, while, for S. Terrien, the book of Job is a drama based on the ritual and myth of, again, the New Year festival.

It need hardly be said that many of these and similar theories are highly contentious and the subject of much debate: indeed, many scholars are suspicious of the kind of approach to the Bible represented by cultic interpretation, even if they do not wholly reject it. No doubt, in particular cases, exaggerated claims have been made and debatable evidence over-pressed. Nevertheless, the fact that so much attention has been paid to it in OT studies in this century indicates its fascination for scholars and its continuing value as an interpretative tool.

See also **Myth and Ritual; Psalms.**

Gunkel's major work on the psalms is unavailable in English, though see his large-scale dictionary article, translated as *The Psalms*, 1967. A good exposition of his views by A. R. Johnson is in H. H. Rowley (ed.), *The Old Testament and Modern Study*, 1951, pp. 162–81. See also I. Engnell, *Critical Essays on the Old Testament*, 1970, chs 5 and 6; A. R. Johnson, *The Cultic Prophet in Ancient Israel*, [2]1962; H.-J. Kraus, *Worship in Israel*, 1966, esp. pp. 152ff.; S. Mowinckel, *The Psalms in Israel's Worship*, 2 vols, 1962; J. Pedersen, *Israel*, III–IV, 1947, pp. 728–37.

J. R. PORTER

Cultural Relativism

Cultural relativism is the name for an approach to interpretation which takes very seriously the differences between cultures. Cultural relativists insist that virtually every expression of belief or opinion is relative to a particular cultural context. An example will make clear something of what that means. If a doctor says that a patient is suffering from a vitamin deficiency, the statement, straightforward though it may seem, is quite specific to our cultural situation. Vitamins were not identified till the early years of this century, and the word itself was coined only in 1912, so interpretation of any medical condition in such terms was impossible before that time.

Scientific and technological change is taking place so rapidly today that before long diagnosis in terms of vitamin deficiency will almost certainly have been superseded by more specific and sophisticated forms of diagnosis, though in the nature of the case we cannot tell what they will be. It will then become clear that our particular way of interpreting this medical condition was peculiar to our time and place.

Not only so: it was not accidental that vitamins were identified when they were. Whatever chance factors may have been involved, the identification could not have taken place unless certain conditions had been fulfilled – for example, until the science of chemistry had reached a certain stage of development, and the scientific techniques employed in the discovery had become available; and those possibilities in turn depended on developments and discoveries in other fields.

So it becomes clear that this particular medical diagnosis is tied up with an appropriate state of affairs in many different areas of our culture, and would be impossible in the context of any other state of affairs. This insight can be generalized: cultures are coherent systems, and the way things are understood in one area of experience is all of a piece with the way they are understood in other areas in the same culture. This generalization can be advanced the more confidently because the reasons for it are increasingly understood. Differences between cultures are due, in large part at least, to differences in the things that are taken for granted in them, to differences in basic presuppositons. T. E. Hulme (1883–1917) put the point succinctly: 'there are certain doctrines which for a particular period seem not doctrines, but inevitable categories of the human mind. Men do not look on them merely as correct opinion, for they have become so much part of the mind and lie so far back that they are never really conscious of them at all. They do not see them, but other things *through* them ... It is these abstract things at the centre, these *doctrines* felt as *facts*, which are the source of all the other more material characteristics of a period.' Similarly, R. G. Collingwood spoke (in 1940) of every civilization's being dominated by some 'constellation of absolute presuppositions' which determine the types of question all its members ask and the types of answers they find satisfying. It follows that when the 'doctrines felt as facts' change, the perspective is changed and so is the way in which everything is understood. Once a culture is firmly established, the same set of presuppositions controls the understanding of things in every area of life, and it is for that reason that understanding in one area cannot deviate significantly

from that in others. Moreover, since our absolute presuppositions lie too far back for us to be aware of them, it is impossible consciously to emancipate oneself from one's culture and deliberately interpret things in ways fundamentally incompatible with it.

That is not to say, however, that cultures are monolithic and completely dictate their members' beliefs and attitudes. Admittedly, certain types of interpretation will be completely ruled out in a culture; for example, diagnosis in terms of vitamins was impossible in the eighteenth century; and today, in the context of modern scientific medicine, it is impossible to interpret illness along the lines of the four humours theory of the body prevalent in the sixteenth century; but there are many areas where differences of opinion and interpretation are entirely compatible with integrity and good sense. For example, there are many today who believe in the effectiveness of exorcism and the objective existence of angels; others do not, but there is nothing in the culture to *compel* the adoption of one view of the matter rather than the other.

Religious beliefs are not exempt from the consequences of this state of affairs. That needs to be emphasized because it is sometimes suggested that they are – for example on the grounds that God does not change; but even if it is true that God does not change, ideas and beliefs about him (or her!) do; and they are what directly concern us in this context. Nor will it do to argue that sacred texts are unaffected by cultural change because they are inspired vehicles of revelation.* Even if we were to take the most rigid view of inspiration* and hold that God was directly responsible for every word of the Bible, it would still be true that if he was to make himself understood by the ancient Jews, not only had he to address them in ancient Hebrew, and not, for example, in sixteenth-century French, but he had to express himself in cultural terms familiar to them, and not, say, in those of the Italian Renaissance.

The question thus arises how far and by what means it is possible for members of one culture to understand and appropriate ideas or beliefs from another culture. For present purposes it may be useful to make a rough and ready distinction between 'understanding' and 'appropriating', and to discuss them separately.

So far as understanding is concerned, a lot will clearly depend on how different the two cultures in question are. It will, for example, be much easier for a modern Western interpreter to understand eighteenth-century European culture than to understand, say, the culture of the Aztecs or that of primitive China. In the case of widely differing cultures, the process of understanding makes great demands on interpreters. First, they must have an intimate knowledge of the history, customs and practices of the culture they seek to understand, of the meaning of the words and phrases in its language and of the various forces which influenced it; then they must have a very considerable amount of empathy and sensitivity, for they have to synthesize all they have learned and to transcend their own cultural formation sufficiently to reconstruct what it would have been like to live within that synthesis. They have, as the Germans say, to 'feel their way into' it (*Einfühlung*) in their imaginations. At best the process can never lead to more than an approximation. Not even the most learned and sympathetic Egyptologist, for example, will claim to have discovered what exactly it was like to be an Egyptian of the eleventh dynasty.

The importance of this for biblical interpretation will be obvious, because all the cultures of the biblical period were widely different from ours. The full extent of the difference is apt to be masked for us because of the way the Bible has been constantly and progressively reinterpreted between ancient and modern times, so that it comes to us ready-framed with a whole range of interpretations, some of them quite modern, which make it seem less alien than it really is. In fact it is alien enough to tax the abilities of even the most learned and sensitive modern interpreters; and at many points consensus about its meaning is far from having been reached. For example, what exactly members of the biblical cultures understood themselves to be doing when they carried out the rites described by the Hebrew and Greek words usually translated 'sacrifice' is far from clear; so is the meaning they attached to the terms somewhat misleadingly translated in English versions as 'Son of Man'* and 'kingdom of God';* and what would it have been like to live expecting the end of the world at any moment, as New Testament Christians did?

However, a considerable degree of understanding of the biblical text has been achieved, and one of the results is to make clear that in many cases the original meaning was very different from what it was taken to be by later interpreters, including those on whose interpretations traditional Christian orthodoxy has been based.

One particular aspect of this matter calls for fuller discussion, namely the application to the Bible of historical-critical method,* one of the characteristic products of modern Western culture. The impact of this has been the greater because of a key feature of the Bible itself. Unlike many sacred texts, the Bible is not exclusively, or even mainly, taken up with abstract doctrinal and ethical teaching. A great deal of space is devoted to accounts of a number of historical events, which are of very various kinds and dates, but which the Bible interprets as so many items in a single coherent line of divine action through which the salvation of mankind was accomplished.

The extent of the problem created by the application of historical-critical method to these accounts is still a matter of debate; that is because in many cases the historical verdict turns on the judgment of alleged supernatural occurrences, about the possibility of which differences of opinion are possible, as we have seen. At the present time there are sharply divergent views about whether the evidence is such as to justify acceptance of the Virgin Birth (*see* **Infancy Narratives**), for example, or the bodily resurrection* of Jesus. On any showing, however, many of the biblical events are unhistorical in whole or part. Differences in the ability or the intention of responsible people to report the past accurately are among the things which mark off modern culture from the majority of earlier cultures most signally. In days when there were few historical records and few opportunities for consulting such as there were, accounts of the past tended to be vehicles for edification quite as much as ways of reporting exactly what had happened. Given the conventions then prevailing, no intention to deceive was involved; a scholar of such complete integrity as Origen* could report without any sign of disapproval that the evangelists had on occasion 'preserved the true spiritual meaning in what at the corporeal level might be called a falsehood'. More often, no doubt, the biblical writers simply repeated in good faith sources which had undergone edificatory elaboration at earlier stages.

Scholars have adopted different strategies for dealing with these inaccurate accounts. Some have concentrated on an attempt to reconstruct the genuine historical facts behind the biblical accounts and to put them forward as a basis for a modern religious faith (cf. most notably the nineteenth-century efforts to substitute the Jesus of History for the Christ of Faith as the subject of modern Christian allegiance). Others, more sceptical about the possibility of such reconstructions on the basis of the evidence we have, and aware that the conclusions of historical research can never be more than provisional (the *provisionality* of their conclusions is fully accepted – indeed emphasized – by all modern historians, especially where events of the distant past are concerned), have concentrated on the religious faith which comes to expression in the stories, recognizing that in historically naïve societies, traditional accounts of the past are often a way of expressing faith. In the view of these scholars the task of the interpreter is to understand and explicate the faith expressed in these stories, whatever their historical value.

When studied intensively, with the help of all the techniques, archaeological, text-critical, philological and so on, that modern culture makes available, these beliefs reveal themselves in most cases as belonging essentially to cultures very different from our own. For example, underlying them at many points is the doctrine, then 'felt as a fact' throughout most of the Mediterranean area, that 'without the shedding of blood there can be no remission of sins'. To most people in the modern West this seems not only not self-evidently true, but not true at all.

Such expressions of belief, it is suggested, can be adopted in our culture only if they are put through the sieve, as it were, of some such question as that posed by Leonard Hodgson: 'What must the truth be now if people who thought as they did put it like that?'

However, not only is such a question easier to ask than to answer, but, as posed, it might seem to imply the assumption that there will be some modern equivalent for every biblical belief, an assumption which has only to be stated to be seen to need questioning.

The question of the extent to which biblical beliefs can be appropriated today, while it has been rather neglected in Great Britain until recently, has attracted a good deal of attention in France, Germany and elsewhere. It has been pointed out that the ways in which a question such as Hodgson's is answered will depend on the body of beliefs, assumptions and expectations (*Vorverständnis*) with which it is approached; which raises the question what the appropriate *Vorverständnis* for the interpretation of the Bible is. There is clearly some risk of circularity here, but *see* **Demythologization.**

Brief mention must be made of another approach, namely that of Karl Barth,* which, if it could be accepted, would solve the whole cultural-relativist problem so far as it concerns biblical interpretation. According to Barth, the only *Vorverständnis* appropriate to the Bible is one which recognizes it as being, or containing, the Word of God,* which came directly down from above and enters into no correlation at all with human cultures; it has no point of contact (*Anknüpfungspunkt*) with them. Accordingly, those who approach the Bible humbly, as the Word of God, and are content to accept that there are innumerable inadequacies and unjustifiably arrogant claims in their cultures, will find that God speaks to their condition through the Bible, whatever their cultural background may be. It is difficult to know whether this is an attempt to solve the cultural-relativist problem or

whether it simply sidesteps it. In view of what was said above, it is hard to attach a meaning to the assertion that the Bible does not correlate with human culture, unless it means that God miraculously transposes the language of the Bible into a vehicle for his unconditional offer and demand. In practice Barthians seem driven both to deny many well-founded insights of contemporary culture and to absolutize what appear to be culturally-conditioned categories in the Bible, and indeed the Christian tradition.

Some recent biblical interpreters, who approach the text from the side of literary criticism,* also appear relatively untroubled by the problem under discussion. A literary-critical movement which arose after the First World War (the so-called New Critics) rejected 'archaeological, quasi-scientific and documentary' study of literature, i.e. study based on the belief that sound interpretation must always start from the author's original meaning and intention. Dubbing this the 'intentionalist fallacy', these critics regard the text itself as the proper object of study; it should be confronted in its immediacy to see what meaning it may yield to a particular reader, when studied as a whole.

In relation to the Bible, this approach has taken various forms, many of them marked by emphasis on the biblical canon and on the need to treat each book or passage as an integral part of the biblical whole, indeed as a part which must be understood in the light of its particular position in the canon. Psalms 1 and 150, for example, must be interpreted not as independent items, but as respectively the opening and closing sections of the Psalter (*see* **Canonical Criticism**).

It is perhaps too soon to evaluate this approach with any confidence, if indeed it can fairly be described as a single approach. In the hands of judicious practitioners it has often enriched understanding of the text by detecting hitherto unnoticed interconnections, meanings and motifs. On the other hand, it is questionable whether the Bible – or indeed many of its constituent parts – are books in the literary sense implied, and the approach is apt to share the dubious assumption of the New Critics that there is no essential difference between now and then, the spirit of man being one and continuous. Moreover, with its firm relegation of authorial intention, this approach, in many of its forms, quite consciously rejects any possibility of distinguishing 'correct' from 'incorrect' interpretations, with obvious implications for any attempt to find in the Bible authoritative answers to questions of faith and morals.

The study of hermeneutics* along these lines has been taken up by many biblical exegetes, including a number of evangelical scholars. They tend to insist on the importance of the right initial *Vorverständnis*, while accepting that that initial *Vorverständnis* will, and should, get modified as reading continues (*see* **Hermeneutical Circle**). However, unless the choice of *Vorverständnis* rests on something other than the individual interpreter's personal predilections, circularity, in a vicious sense, seems unavoidable.

It will be noticed that all these proposed solutions of the problem presuppose some element of sameness and continuity between cultures. Hans Jonas, for example, a colleague and admirer of Bultmann,* talks of 'an unchangeable fundamental structure of the human spirit as such', and Structuralists* would agree, though their structure, and the evidence for it, are different. Some element of continuity there must be, for us to be able to penetrate the minds of other cultures at all, but the nature and extent of it are still the subject of vigorous debate. Sir Isaiah Berlin, for example, dismisses as 'fallacious' any 'belief in a fixed, ultimate, unchanging human nature', and C. M. Radding, in *A World Made by Men*, 1985, has recently argued that the very modes of cognition vary from culture to culture.

Perhaps the most judicious statement of the case at present is that of Lionel Trilling: 'to suppose that we can think like men of another time is as much of an illusion as to suppose that we can think in a wholly different way'. That being so, it will be clear that, if we accept traditional assumptions, the problem which cultural change raises for biblical interpretation is real enough. However, no way of solving it compatible with those assumptions has been found, and it may well be that the attempt to use the Bible as a source of authoritative solutions to contemporary problems, after the manner of Article VI of the Church of England, will have to be given up in favour of a more open-ended and open-textured procedure for arriving at religious truth, according to which contemporary faith and experience will play a larger part than they have done hitherto.

See also **Christian Interpretation of the Old Testament; Commentary (New Testament); Criteria; Interpretation, History of.**

L. Dewart, *The Future of Belief*, 1967; Van A. Harvey, *The Historian and the Believer*, 1966; G. D. Kaufman, *Relativism, Knowledge and Faith*, 1960; D. E. Nineham, *The Use and Abuse of the Bible*, 1976; J. H. Newman, *Essay on the Development of Christian Doctrine*, 1845 and later eds; D. L. Sills (ed.), *International Encyclopedia of the Social Sciences*, vol. 3, 1968, pp. 543–7, art. by D. Bidney; E. Troeltsch, *The Absoluteness of Christianity*, 1901, ET 1971; G. Tyrrell, *Christianity at the Crossroads*, 1909.

D. E. NINEHAM

Cynics

'Dogged' ('canine') individualists tracing their views and life-style back to Diogenes of Sinope (late fourth century BC). In the first century AD we get the impression that they could be met at every street corner, alley-way and temple approach, haranguing the crowds that passed. They could usually be distinguished by their unkempt appearance: threadbare doubled cloak, a staff perhaps, a satchel for food, most likely barefoot. They tried to encourage others to share their simple and 'natural' life, and exposed the artificiality, pretence and lack of freedom in conventional society concerned with wealth and status. Theirs was 'more a way of life than a philosophy'. They tried to spread it by wit and parable, by cheek ('frank-speaking', *parrhēsia*) and ostentatious misbehaviour. A provincial aristocrat like Dio of Prusa (AD 40–120) might adopt the Cynic style, and Nero's minister Seneca had a Cynic, Demetrius, as a sort of 'domestic chaplain'; but many were ordinary free working people. Their radicalism was seen as a challenge by those in authority; for some it extended as far as insisting 'there's no reason for a woman to be any worse than a man'.

There is no mention of Cynics in the biblical documents, Jewish or Christian (although Philo* and Josephus* and the later rabbis are all aware of them). The earliest explicit evidence for any link between Cynics and Christians stems from the mid-second century (Justin Martyr, Lucian of Samosata). In biblical interpretation in the middle of the twentieth century the Cynics have been largely ignored as irrelevant, despite the arguments of earlier writers (Dill, Dudley). More recently it has been suggested that the early Christians following the 'mission charge' of Jesus (Mark 6.7–13; Luke 9.1–5; 10.3–11) were trying to distinguish themselves from this disturbing element. Since the mid-1980s, however, the Cynics have been receiving much more attention from NT historians, as it is realized that at least some early Christians would not only have looked like a kind of Cynic (and there were many varieties of dress and approach), but that their repetition of the tradition of Jesus' teaching as we have it in the Synoptic Gospels would very often have made them sound like Cynics too (Downing). And although Paul* does not much echo their general teaching, he very often discusses the style of his approach in the terms they used (Malherbe, 1987): for instance, 'gentle as a nurse' (I Thess. 2.7).

As with any other aspect of the cultural

context of early Christianity and contemporary Judaism, differences can be as significant as similarities, and there are important strands of early Christian belief (in the Gospels and in Paul) for which there is little or no Cynic parallel: healing, eschatology,* and especially a human now exalted as Lord. Indeed, Diogenes in the old traditions often appears very sceptical about divine activity, though a man like Dio could appear much more devout.

The similarities, however, are considerable, and they may give us a strong lead in our attempt to interpret how the early Christian use of the tradition of Jesus' teaching is likely to have been understood. Understanding an audience and the kind of 'feed-back' it would offer to people addressing it is essential in any interpretation of the message, especially a message delivered orally (*see* **Background and Context**). And if our interpretation of the gospel tradition in the early church can be made clearer and more sure in this way, we may also have a better basis for our interpretation of the intention of Jesus himself.

Jesus and John* before him are presented as reprimanding and challenging their hearers, showing scant respect for people in authority and their so-called benefits. Race, birth, social position, wealth, are all irrelevant. What matters is the way you live your life, the 'fruit' you yield. God is to be trusted in the natural world around; the birds and beasts find food without having to store it up, and so will you (Matt. 6.25–33 and Luke 12.22–31 compared with Musonius Rufus 15, Epictetus I 9.7, and Dio 10.15–16; many more instances in Downing). Wealth and social prestige are distractions from being your real self. In relation to other people you are expected to be patient and forgiving (however much you excoriate their wrong-doing). You are in fact very likely to suffer, for people are not going to enjoy being disturbed. But you must live up to the standard you proclaim, if you are to stand any chance of being taken seriously. The call to the new life-style takes precedence over all the claims of family and convention. All this and much more can be found in the tradition of Jesus' teaching and in our sources for popular Cynicism, and often in very similar words and images (Downing).

This insight is very important for our interpretation of the tradition in its early days. It shows at the very least that the teaching was meant to be taken seriously, the hard demands were meant to be acted on. The disruptive social consequences would have been obvious to all who listened; they are not a sign that the teaching was not meant to be taken literally. They would have been seen at the time as politically charged, and dangerous.

Once this point is accepted (and the debate is only just under way again at the time of writing) then it may be appropriate to consider that Jesus may himself have worked out his message in response, at least in part, to Cynic tradition. If our other evidence is trustworthy, Cynics are very unlikely to have missed disturbing at least the towns of Galilee and the Decapolis. Herod Antipas' new capital, Sepphoris, was a very Greek town with Jewish inhabitants, only a few miles from Nazareth. The similarities we now find between Jesus' teaching and that of Cynic contemporaries could be put down to coincidence, or to later Christian creative writing: but the similarities are too extensive for simple coincidence to be likely, and it is hard to imagine circumstances in which followers of Jesus would have ascribed wholesale Cynic motifs in particular to a leader who had had quite other intentions.

'Why not consider the beasts and the birds, and see how much more painlessly they live than humans do, how much more pleasantly and healthily ... they have one enormous advantage ... they are free of property ...' (Dio of Prusa, *Discourse* 10.16).

See also **Sociology and Social Anthropology.**

F. G. Downing, *The Christ and the Cynics*, 1988; D. B. Dudley, *A History of Cynicism*, 1937/1967; A. J. Malherbe, *IDB Supp.*, 1976, pp. 201–3; id., *The Cynic Epistles*, 1977; id., *Social Aspects of Early Christianity*, 1984; id., *Paul and the Thessalonians*, 1987; J. Stambaugh and D. Balch, *The Social World of the First Christians*, 1986.

F. GERALD DOWNING

Daniel

Daniel falls into two parts, stories (chs 1–6) and visions (chs 7–12), which have been to some extent interpreted differently. Popular interest has been drawn rather to the stories, such as the Fiery Furnace (ch. 3), Belshazzar's Feast (ch. 5), or the Lions' Den (ch. 6), while scholarly or dogmatic interest has largely concentrated on the visions. Since the stories have been retold as examples of fortitude and religious fidelity rather than made subject to explicit interpretation, the visions (but including ch. 2) will occupy more attention here.

The visions convey predictions of events from the beginning of the Babylonian exile until the culmination of history. There are two basic lines of interpretation which can be traced. One understands the sequence of events to culminate in the so-called 'Maccabean period', and, mostly, holds the book to have been written then, and hence not to be genuinely predictive. The second line of interpretation, which may be called 'actualizing', accepts the book as genuinely and infallibly predictive, and thus perceives in it references to recent and still future events.

The major elements in Daniel's 'prediction' are 1. a scheme of four world kingdoms (chs 2 and 7), 2. a chronology of 490 years from the beginning of the 'exile' till the end of history (ch. 9), 3. the figures of the 'son of man'* and the 'holy ones' who belong in the final kingdom which will supersede the fourth earthly one (ch. 7).

1. Ancient interpretation

The 'Maccabean' interpretation. The earliest interpretation of Daniel, when the book was composed (*c.* 166 BC) and shortly after, recognized the four kingdoms of Dan. 2 and 7 as Babylon, Persia, Media and Greece, and the final monarch of the fourth kingdom (a 'little horn' in chs 7 and 8, the 'king of the north' in chs 11–12) as the Seleucid Antiochus IV ('Epiphanes'), who in 167 abrogated the daily Temple sacrifice and set up a non-Jewish altar there (referred to as a 'desolating sacrilege'). Chs 11–12 trace his career until its end; but the manner of his death and the resurrection and judgment which were to follow did not transpire. The 'holy ones' are the nation of Israel, or a righteous group within it; the 'son of man' symbolizes the 'holy ones', but may have quickly come to be understood as their angelic patron Michael.

This interpretation of Daniel's predictions is probably reflected in I Macc. (written *c.* 100 BC), if the phrase 'desolating sacrilege' ('abomination of desolation') in 1.54 is an allusion to Daniel (8.13; 9.27; 11.31). It also represents the tradition of the Syrian* church, attested by Aphrahat, Ephrem and Ishodad, on which Porphyry the anti-Christian philosopher drew.

Porphyry (*c.* AD 270–320), whose views on Daniel are preserved only in the commentary of Jerome, attacked the Western Christian interpretation of Daniel (see below), holding that the book was (as he put it) a 'forgery', written after the events it describes, namely after the Maccabean victory over Antiochus. Many of Porphyry's conclusions and arguments have been accepted by modern critical orthodoxy, which accepts the Maccabean interpretation.

Actualizing interpretations. The apparent non-arrival of the glorious end predicted in Dan. 12 and the advent in the Near East of yet another kingdom, Rome (mid-first century BC), prompted another phase of interpretation which stretched Daniel's historical scheme to incorporate these developments. In the War Scroll from Qumran (*see* **Dead Sea Scrolls**), which alludes freely to Daniel, the final battle of the 'children of light' is waged against the Kittim, who are not, as in the OT including Daniel, the Greeks, but the Romans. The de-

struction of the Temple in AD 70 suggested a different application of Daniel's 'desolating sacrilege'; in Matt. 24.15 this prediction of 'Daniel the prophet' is applied to the future, on the lips of Jesus, though the evangelist's own comment ('let the reader understand'), found already in Mark 13.14, suggests that the fall of the Temple has already come to pass.

Both IV Ezra (II Esdras) and Josephus* (*Antiquities* 10.186ff.), at the end of the first century AD, also see the fourth kingdom as Rome and apply Daniel's predicted 'desolation' to AD 70. However, Josephus, writing under Roman patronage for a non-Jewish audience, is extremely discreet over the implication that Rome, as the fourth kingdom, would be overthrown according to Dan. 2 and 7.

The book of Revelation draws on Daniel deeply but also quite creatively. To simplify, one may say that emphasis lies on the identification of the 'son of man', the 'holy ones/saints', the 'little horn' and the fourth 'beast' of Dan. 7. Whether or not the term 'son of man' in the Gospels is to be understood in the light of Daniel, the connection is clear in Revelation (e.g. 1. 13–14), while the 'holy ones' are the church and the 'beast' or 'little horn' (now conflated) is a Roman emperor, either Nero or Domitian. In such an interpretation, the final kingdom which, according to Dan. 2 and 7, supplants the fourth kingdom, is the kingdom of Christ, inaugurated by his resurrection and represented by the church which is suffering the tribulations hinted at in Dan. 12.1.

In the second century, another disaster befell Jerusalem when Hadrian built on its ruins a new Roman city, Aelia Capitolina. Jerome refers to a Jewish interpretation of Dan. 9 which reflects these more recent events, and indeed adopts it himself. Again according to Jerome, there was a Jewish interpretation linked to the proposal of Julian the Apostate (361–363) to rebuild the Temple.

Traditional Western Christian interpretation of Daniel continued to view Daniel as a prophet; while in the Jewish Bible the book belongs with the Writings,* in the Christian OT it stands at the head of the Minor Prophets. The church also used the Greek version which contained additions to the Hebrew/Aramaic: the song of Azariah and of the three youths in the furnace, and the stories of Bel and the Dragon and Susanna, found in the Apocrypha.* The reference in 9.26 to the 'cutting off' of 'an anointed one (messiah*)' was applied to Jesus, while the 'king of the north' of ch. 11 (also the 'horn' and/or the 'beast' of ch. 7) is the Antichrist, whose coming will bring woes but then salvation for the chosen.

In the Reformation,* it was the theme of earthly versus heavenly sovereignty, which runs throughout Daniel, that attracted especial attention. In his *Commentaries on Daniel*, Calvin* defended French Protestants against royal power by appealing to the lesson from Daniel that 'earthly princes lay aside all their power when they rise up against God'.

Jewish interpretation. After the calamities of AD 70 and 135, brought about by Jewish political aspirations, the book of Daniel was largely ignored, and Daniel projected as a wise man, not a prophet. His personal example, not his prediction, was stressed. The two stories of Daniel in the Apocrypha, Susanna and Bel and the Dragon, also stress his deductive powers, which respectively rescue an innocent girl from the clutches of evil men and demonstrate the foolishness of idolatry. A number of post-Talmudic commentators wrote on the book, including Saadia, the Qara'ite Ali ibn Jephet, Rashi, Ibn Ezra, Isaac Abrabanel and Joseph ibn Yahya. A mediaeval composition inspired by the book, called the *Ma'asey Daniel* ('The Deeds of Daniel'), was even used in contemporary political polemics. But Jewish interpretations were free of any messianic elements. Nevertheless, the stories of Daniel, reflecting the dilemmas of the Jewish people in a threatened minority under non-Jewish kings, were particularly appropriate for the plight of mediaeval Jews.

2. Modern interpretation

The rationalism of the seventeenth century led, over the next two hundred years, to doubts about the traditionally held authenticity of Daniel's predictions and, ultimately, to a revival of the arguments of Porphyry in favour of the Maccabean date of authorship. Accordingly, in the nineteenth century the battle was joined, with conservative reaction on the part of Hengstenberg and Keil in Germany, Wilson in the United States and, in England, Pusey, for whom the issue was represented as critical to Christian faith. For Pusey, as for many conservative Christians, the authority of the book could not admit of any manner of fiction: it was 'either divine or an imposture'. But S. R. Driver's thorough advocacy of the Maccabean view helped to set the balance of scholarly opinion in its favour.

During this century, actualizing interpretation has nevertheless continued among fundamentalists* – e.g. Jehovah's Witnesses – and the most famous individual effort to interpret recent world history in the light of Daniel is H. Lindsay's *The Late Great Planet Earth*, 1970. Interest in apocalyptic since the 1940s has provoked a revival of scholarship on Daniel, with increasing attention to its ideology and social background. The stories are now generally ascribed to the Persian period, and seen to offer a more harmonious resolution of the conflict between human and divine sovereignty than the visions. While a host of critical questions remains disputed, there are signs that, as with other biblical books, Daniel is being increasingly studied as a literary product in its own right and not at the mercy of debates over historicity or the nature of apocalyptic.

See also **Apocalyptic; Millenarianism; Revelation of John.**

G. L. Archer, Jr, *Jerome's Commentary on Daniel*, 1958; G. K. Beale, *The Use of Daniel in Jewish Apocalyptic Literature and in the Revelation of St John*, 1984; J. Braverman, *Jerome's Commentary on Daniel* (CBQ Monograph Series 7), 1978; J. T. McNeill (ed), *On God and Political Duty*, [2] 1956, pp. 101f. (for Calvin on Daniel); J. A. Montgomery, *Daniel* (ICC), 1927, pp. 105–9.

PHILIP R. DAVIES

Dante

Between the years 1300 and 1321 Dante Alighieri (1265–1321) composed his best-known work and one of the greatest literary achievements of the Middle Ages, the *Divine Comedy* (*Divina Commedia*). Written in Italian, this poem is the story of the author's own imaginary journey in mid-life, 'nel mezzo del cammin di nostra vita', through *Hell* (*Inferno*), *Purgatory* (*Purgatorio*) and *Heaven* (*Paradiso*) to the vision of God the Holy Trinity. What immediately strikes the modern reader is the wealth of allusion to the Bible (the Latin Vulgate*) and classical mythology. Without some knowledge of these sources, especially the former, much of the meaning of the poem will remain obscure. There are 96 clear, unambiguous biblical references in the poem's 100 cantos and over 70 direct quotations. 50 allusions occur in *Purgatory*, 32 in *Paradise* and only 13 in *Hell*. This fact itself is significant: hell and heaven are places of finality; the damned are fixed for ever in their separation from the love of God, the blessed spirits in heaven have arrived at that state of joy which cannot be altered. Only the souls of those who are being purged are in a state of movement; they progress towards beatitude. Meditation on the Word of God* in scripture will not affect the condition of those in hell or in heaven; it simply serves to remind them of what they have lost or achieved. But the souls in purgatory have the words of the Bible often on their lips; such reverent meditation upon the revelation of God enables their repentance to be more profound, their acceptance of the pains of purgation more eager, and their movement towards release from the mountain of purgatory all the more swift.

It is clear from Dante's other works that he

was well versed in the various methods of mediaeval* scriptural interpretation, but when he came to the *Comedy* the literal meaning* of the text is what he most frequently presents to us. 'Spiritual' meanings* do appear from time to time, but they are used only sparingly. In this concentration on literal sense, he was probably showing the influence of the new Franciscan attitudes to biblical interpretation. We know that Dante (although initially taught by the Dominicans) was deeply affected by Franciscan sentiment, and we can see from the way he uses scripture that his concern was primarily with the direct evocation of religious feeling. It is not surprising therefore that when biblical material is introduced it is most frequently done simply and directly. But before that is illustrated, we should note uses of the Bible which are less simple.

First there is the 'hidden' allusion: a fleeting reference to a biblical text in which the words of the Vulgate are only faintly echoed, though we may suppose that the author expected the reader to catch the echo and thereby have his response to the verse of the poem enhanced. An example of this technique can be found in the opening words which recall Isa. 38.10: '. . . *in dimidio dierum meorum vadam ad portas inferi*'. Recognizing these allusions is a difficult matter for those who read the poem only in translation for so subtle are some of the references that only knowledge of both mediaeval Italian and the Latin original will enable one to detect them.

A more elaborate kind of biblical allusion occurs in the last few cantos of *Purgatory*. Here the understanding of the text relies upon the reader's ability to recognize not only the biblical references (Genesis, Isaiah, Song of Songs) but also the allegorical* use to which Dante puts them. The moment has come (in the story) for the departure of Dante's guide Virgil and the arrival of his new guide Beatrice. Virgil cannot enter heaven: Beatrice's place is with the blessed in heaven: in an earthly paradise their lives can touch. This is the place of the meeting of philosophy and theology; the point at which Reason, having brought human nature as far as it can by natural power, has to pass over into Faith. Here Grace enters to perfect Nature, but Nature already purified and in a state of innocence. The achievement of this earthly paradise is the achievement of Eden. Beatrice's entrance is heralded by the thrice-repeated cry: 'Veni sponsa de Libano' (Song of Songs 4. 8). Dante and Beatrice 'become' Adam* and Eve, and, at a further allegorical level, mankind and Christ.

Before entering this earthly paradise Dante (and Virgil) has climbed the mountain of Purgatory. After the initial terraces there are seven cornices or ledges to be negotiated, cornices upon which the capital sins are purged: Pride, Envy, Anger, Sloth, Avarice, Gluttony and Lust. At each cornice one of the Beatitudes* is referred to. At the cornice of the proud: Matt. 5.3: 'When we were turning our steps there, "*Beati pauperes spiritu*" was sung in such tones as no word would tell' (Canto XII, 109–111). At the cornice of the envious: Matt. 5.7: 'When we had reached the blessed angel he said with a glad voice: "enter here" . . . "*Beati misericordes*" was sung behind us and "Rejoice thou that overcomest"' (Canto XXV, 34–39). At the cornice of the wrathful, Matt. 5.9, and so on. Furthermore, at each cornice the penitent souls are being cleansed. Only two of these prayers are non-biblical. The gluttonous recite Ps. 51.15, '*Labia me Domine*'; the avaricious recite Ps. 119.25, '*Adhaesit pavimento anima mea*'. Perhaps the most remarkable of all the prayers is that which is given to those on the very first cornice – at the root of all sin, Pride. It is the Paternoster; with the clauses interlaced with brief meditations 'directed towards the virtue of humility' (D. L. Sayers). In addition to all this, carved into the face of the rock at intervals are biblical scenes life-like in their beauty.

We may deduce from all this that Dante's thought, his vision of the world, humanity, sin and redemption, is rooted in the Bible: though of course his method of reading and interpretation, his selection of texts and the use to which he puts them are not the same as ours. He refers only once to Paul's Letters (*Hell*, II, 13), a fact which may strike us as strange. The Book of Revelation appears, but no other book from the NT, apart from the Gospels. His attention is focussed throughout on the Psalms and the Gospels. The reason for this is two-fold. First, these are the parts of the Bible that figured most prominently in the liturgy* of the mediaeval church. Secondly, his selection of texts shows his indebtedness to the Franciscan spirit: a devotion to those parts of the Bible that appealed most strongly – simply and directly – to the religious sensibility. His imagination is pictorial; actual physical scenes are continually being brought before our eyes. Even in *Heaven*, the most philosophical of all the *cantichi*, we are meant to envisage the eagle, the cross and the rose. We must also deduce that the culture in and for which Dante was writing was profoundly biblical. It is the ease and naturalness with which the many bibilical allusions are introduced that convinces us of this fact. Since the seventeenth century, there have been no modern parallels.

See also **Allegorical Interpretation; Mediaeval Interpretation.**

William Anderson, *Dante the Maker*, 1980; A. C. Charity, *Events and their Afterlife*, 1966; Kenelm Foster, *The Two Dantes*, 1977; Beryl Smalley, *The Study of the Bible in the Middle Ages*, 1952.

BRIAN HORNE

David

Every individual figure of any importance within the biblical tradition has been the subject of interpretation as far back as we are able to trace; and this is certainly true of David. Though a setting within the history of Israel* can be asserted with fair confidence, the nature and scope of his historical achievement are much more difficult to assess, and from an early date it appears as if his life was the subject of legendary* embellishment.

That he originated from the family of Jesse of Bethlehem there is no reason to doubt; the more extended genealogy offered in Ruth 4.18–22 must be treated with greater caution. His struggle against Saul is described in I Sam. 16–31 in terms of the underdog resisting the overmighty ruler; but it would not be difficult to construct an alternative scenario according to which it was David's guerrilla band which did much to prevent Saul binding Israel together into an effective state. In the ancient world as in the modern, the line between the terrorist and the freedom fighter is not an easy one to trace.

After Saul's death David became king, first of Judah and then of Israel also, apparently by a kind of dual monarchy (II Sam. 5.1–5); the forty-year period of his rule appears to be an approximation to signify a complete generation, and precise dating is therefore impossible; the tenth century BC is the approximate period. The biblical account of his reign reaches a climax in II Sam. 7, with the description of God's covenant* with him and his line; thereafter he is pictured in a state of increasing decline, unable to control his own family and the victim of a series of plots and intrigues. This account, sometimes known as the Succession Narrative, found in II Sam. 9–20; I Kings 1–2, offers one of the most vivid narrative sequences to be found anywhere in the Bible; the extent of its historicity has been much debated.

Within the OT the reputation of David came to be elaborated in three distinct ways. First, he came to be regarded as the ideal warrior. In a culture where God himself could be regarded as a warrior (Ex. 15.3), such a tradition was highly complimentary; it is epitomized in the story of Goliath, the Philistine giant, said to have been killed by Elhanan (II Sam. 21.19), but for whose death subsequent tradition has given David all the credit (I Sam. 17).

Secondly, David came to be regarded as the founder of the musical traditions of Israel's worship, and in particular the psalms. He is mentioned in Amos 6.5, in a somewhat unflattering context, as one who 'invented instruments of music'. This type of tradition is developed further, so that 73 individual psalms are described as 'of David'; the preposition 'of' has certainly come to be regarded as implying authorship,* though it seems unlikely that that was its original intention. The links with the accounts of his life in Samuel are taken further in the headings to a number of psalms, associating their contents with events in his story. (These introductions have been omitted from some modern translations,* notably the NEB.) Though it is unlikely that Davidic authorship of any individual psalm could be established, the link is an appropriate one, for the psalms seem to have been the vehicle of the royal Jerusalem* cult,* of which the king* was in a real sense the chief minister.

This leads to the third way in which the David tradition was developed within the OT itself: the picture of David as the true founder of the Jerusalem cult. This is developed most fully in Chronicles. The tradition that the temple was established in the time of Solomon, David's son, was too strong to be changed, but in I Chronicles David is pictured as completing all the preparations for the temple, down to the last detail of building materials and the organization of the worship; indeed the Chronicler has so organized his presentation as to make David the real originator of the people's worship, despite the contradiction of the earlier narrative in II Sam. 24 that this involved.

David was a king; yet monarchy in Israel came to a disastrous end, and the Deuteronomistic history* put the blame for this on the kings. But David, despite his own blemishes, was regarded as a glorious exception to this catalogue of failure, and the few who escaped the almost universal condemnation were judged as having followed the steps of their 'father' David (II Kings 18.3; 22.2). So, after kingship had been overthrown, hope survived that God would raise up a future king from the line of David (Isa. 11.1; Ezek. 34.23f; Micah 5.2).

David thus became an appropriate focus for messianic* hope, yet the evidence for such a figure being prominent in Jewish hopes at the turn of the eras is meagre; basically, one or two references in the Dead Sea Scrolls* (4QFlor and 4QTest), and a more extensive example in Pss. of Solomon 17.

It is therefore all the more interesting and

perhaps surprising that earliest Christianity, and possibly Jesus himself, gave to the symbol* of 'Davidic messiah' considerable prominence among the galaxy of titles used to express and illuminate the significance of Jesus. However, there may also have been, at the earliest stage, some opposition to this identification. Though as it is now placed the episode at Mark 12.35–37 must surely be intended to say that *though* Jesus is descended from David he is nevertheless superior to him, the original meaning may have been that Jesus was messiah *despite* not being of that stock.

If non-Davidic descent was ever an obstacle to the making of messianic claims on behalf of Jesus it was soon overcome. In Romans Paul speaks of Jesus as 'descended from David according to the flesh' (1.3), a unique expression which may be part of a pre- or non-Pauline formula. Mark first exploited the Davidic theme in relation to Jesus (2.23–28; 10.46–52; 11.1–10; 12.35–37), and Matthew and Luke took it up with enthusiasm, especially in the genealogies* (Matt. 1.1, 6; Luke 3.31), and, for Luke, the infancy narratives* (1.27–32, 69; 2.4, 11). John alludes to the same theme (7.42), with typical irony,* in relation to Bethlehem. The genealogies must surely be seen as theological rather than historical statements.

Why should the significance of Jesus have been expounded in Davidic terms? In almost all the ways in which the Gospels portray him he was so un-Messianic and so un-Davidic. It has seemed to some that precisely the element of paradox required to see such an unregal and unwarlike figure as Jesus in Davidic terms points to Jesus himself having originated the claim, in a spirit of heavy theological irony. He would upturn existing concepts and associations, and his 'kingship' would be the very opposite of worldly empire (cf. Luke 22.24–27). One might compare St Francis, in his total poverty, seeing himself as proprietor of all nature.

Others, however, have seen in this strand an indication that Jesus did in fact entertain firmly political aspirations, albeit of an eschatological* or apocalyptic* kind: in effect, he identified himself with such a figure as that depicted in Ps. Sol. 17, soon to be vindicated by God's intervention (see **Reimarus, H. S.; Schweitzer, A.**). The journey to Jerusalem, the formal entry, and the incident in the temple all suggest this, and it is supported by other features in the Gospel narrative. But such a role was tragically denied to him, and his followers were led (by the processes of cognitive dissonance*) to present him as wholly pacific. On this reading it would be puzzling that the Davidic strand was not suppressed, rather than being defiantly sublimated;

possibly the so-called 'messianic secret'* might relate to this interpretative transition.

One scenario would relate the issue less to christology* than to Jesus' message. He, in the role of prophet, preached the rule of God, and it was only subsequently that the messenger came to be identified with the message. Part of that process was a growing sense of Jesus himself as 'king', perhaps as God's vice-gerent before the final end (e.g. I Cor. 15.22–28; Matt. 16.28). The idea of Jesus as the Davidic messiah may then have arisen in connection with this identification of Jesus in kingly terms.

In subsequent interpretation the David tradition has been used in a variety of ways. During the period when it was axiomatic that states would be ruled by kings, David was constantly set up as the model of kingship. At least from the time of Charlemagne to that of Louis XVI of France, kings were bidden by their clerical entourage to model their rule on that of David. In literature the relations between David and Goliath, David and Jonathan, and David and Bathsheba, have provided the inspiration for writings of every kind, and similarly in art,* the first and last of these themes have been a constant source of inspiration, while the second has been taken up, with doubtful scholarship, by 'gay rights' campaigners. Strangely, 'the sweet psalmist' has influenced composers of music less than one might have expected. But the use of the David theme does not end there; David is pictured in I Samuel as a shepherd, the best-loved of all psalms (Ps. 23) has come to be attributed to him, and so the whole pastoral* tradition is associated with him. On a more political level, the contrast between David and his ill-starred predecessor Saul has provided a model for moralists down the ages. What an irony it was, therefore, that the badge which Jews were forced to wear as a mark of their humiliation in Nazi Germany should be known as 'the star of David'.

See also **Messiah; Samuel.**

R.-J. Frontain and J. Wojcik, *The David Myth in Western Literature*, 1980; D. M. Gunn, *The Story of King David*, 1978.

R. J. COGGINS and J. L. HOULDEN

De Wette, W. M. L.

Wilhelm Martin Leberecht de Wette (1780–1849) was born in Ulla near Weimar, studied theology and philosophy in Jena, and held teaching posts in Jena and Heidelberg before moving to the newly-founded University of Berlin in 1810. In 1819 he was dismissed from Berlin on political grounds and moved to Basel in 1821, where he remained until his death.

De Wette is popularly best known for his doctoral dissertation of 1804, in which he argued that Deuteronomy* was written, probably in the seventh century, by a different author from Genesis–Numbers. However, his most important and influential works in the field of biblical studies (he also wrote on ethics, dogmatics and the study of religion) were his *Beiträge zur Einleitung in das Alte Testament* (1806–7), his Psalms commentary* and his introductions* to the OT and NT.

The *Beiträge* were a major step forward in biblical criticism* in that they proposed a reconstruction of the history of Israelite religion that was at variance with the picture in the OT. De Wette showed first of all that the books of Chronicles were dependent upon Samuel and Kings, and that their picture of a priestly and levitical religion which had been in place since the time of David* was unhistorical. If Chronicles was disregarded, it was then possible to accept the picture of Israelite religion implicit in Samuel and Kings and the patriarchal narratives of Gen. 12–50 (which de Wette regarded as having been composed during the monarchy). These books suggested that before and during the early monarchy, there was no centralized priesthood with a prerogative to offer sacrifice. This could be done by heads of families, prophets* or kings.* Only towards the end of the monarchy did the priesthood begin to extend its power, as was apparent in the demand for centralization of worship and sacrifice in Deut., which was associated with Josiah's reform in 622–1. According to de Wette, Moses* bequeathed to Israel the Decalogue and the ark and Tent of Meeting. He did not institute a fully-fledged system of sacrifices and priesthood as claimed in Exodus, Leviticus and Numbers. Already implicit in the *Beiträge* was the position to be advocated so brilliantly by Wellhausen in 1878 and 1883, a fact acknowledged by Wellhausen himself, with the difference that de Wette believes that Deuteronomy was later than the priestly regulations in Exodus, Leviticus and Numbers, whereas it was fundamental to Wellhausen's position that these priestly regulations were post-exilic.

De Wette's *Psalms* commentary of 1811 was part of an abortive series planned by de Wette and J. C. W. Augusti to accompany their new translation of the Bible. It broke new ground in that it dismissed the historical interpretation of the psalms as too speculative, and proposed instead a literary-aesthetic approach. This involved classifying the psalms according to their literary* types, of which de Wette identified hymns (including thanksgivings of individuals and the nation for God's deliverance), psalms of Zion and the temple (including Pss. 15, 24 and 132), royal psalms

(including Pss. 2, 20–1, 45, 72 and 110) and individual and communal laments. In this way, de Wette anticipated the form-critical* classification of the psalms pioneered a century later by H. Gunkel. On the other hand, de Wette was unenthusiastic about the attempts to reconstruct the cultic* background to the psalms, which had become a feature of OT scholarship in the late eighteenth century. These were too hypothetical and shifted attention from the literary qualities of the psalms.

De Wette's OT introduction appeared in seven editions from 1817 to 1852, and established itself as the standard work of its type until it was superseded by Bleek's Introduction in 1860. Translated by the American Theodore Parker in 1844, it also assisted the rise of critical scholarship in North America. Because the subsequent revisions softened the radicalism of the first edition, the work was sensitive to the conservative reactions to biblical criticism in Germany from 1830. It remained, however, the clearest guide to critical scholarship of its day, and its lucid but concise formulations assured its wide use.

During his Basel period, de Wette worked mainly on the NT, his introduction appearing in 1825. This was notable for denying that Paul* was the author of Ephesians and II Thessalonians. He advocated the view of his teacher J. J. Griesbach that Matthew was the earliest Gospel, and that Luke was dependent upon it. John was a late Gospel, influenced by Gnostic* thought, and reflecting the struggle between the early church and the synagogue.

De Wette was a man ahead of his time, many of whose insights were too advanced to be accepted or established by the scholarly opinion of his day, but who has been subsequently vindicated in many respects.

See also **German Old Testament Scholarship; Pentateuch, Pentateuchal Criticism; Psalms.**

J. W. Rogerson, *Old Testament Criticism in the Nineteenth Century; England and Germany*, 1984.

J. W. ROGERSON

Dead Sea Scrolls

The term covers the literary discoveries mostly made between 1947 and 1960 from seven sites close to the Dead Sea: Qumran, Wadi Murabba'at, Naḥal Ḥever, Naḥal Ṣe'elim, Naḥal Mahras, Khirbet Mird, and Masada. The first part of this article discusses the interpretation of the Bible in the scrolls from Qumran; the second part describes the wider significance of all the discoveries for the modern interpretation of the Bible.

1. *The interpretation of the Bible at Qumran.*
  (a) *The nature and status of the biblical*

text. From the number of copies of some biblical books and from the way they are used in quotations in some non-biblical texts, it is clear that the Qumran community and its forebears understood that certain books were authoritative. All the books of the Pentateuch* are well represented (15 MSS. of Gen., 15 of Ex., 9 of Lev., 6 of Num., 25 of Deut.), as are the Former and Latter Prophets.* All the Writings* except Esther are also present. Some works not now in the biblical canon were also deemed authoritative: for the author of the Damascus Document (CD 16.3–4), the Book of Jubilees was authoritative, as was probably a Testament of Levi (CD 4.15). It is likely too that the writings of Enoch (11 MSS) in some form were authoritative for some members of the community (cf. Jude 14–15).

No single biblical MS from the Qumran caves corresponds in every detail with previously known texts or versions of the Bible, though most show affinities with one or more of the known witnesses. This variety of textual witnesses was acknowledged by the Qumran community: e.g. Hab. 2.16 is written in 1QpHab 11.8–11 with a Hebrew (*hr^cl*) that matches what also occurs in the LXX ('stagger'), but in the commentary there is clear knowledge of the MT Hab 2.16 (*h^crl*; 'be uncircumcised'). Also, some scribes* undertook a major interpretative rewriting of the biblical books in order that these authoritative texts should remain significant. In a broader sense these MS are also biblical; they include the rewritten versions of the Pentateuch (as yet unpublished) and the Temple Scroll (11QT) which is a harmonized and supplemented edition of Ex., Lev., Num., and Deut., presented as an authoritative divine speech to Moses.*

In addition to Hebrew and Greek biblical texts, some Aramaic* versions of biblical books have also been discovered in the Qumran caves. Akin to the known targums,* these works include the free rendering of Genesis (1QapGen; with many details that make the text more coherent and intelligible in a fashion close to the tradition represented in Jubilees), the targum to Lev. (4QtgLev), and the targums to Job (4QtgJob, 11QtgJob). It is known that in some circles Job was as important as the Pentateuch.

(b) *Interpretation within the biblical text.* Before the content and orthography of the Hebrew Bible were fixed at the end of the first century AD, within the scribal traditions of handing on the authoritative texts there were moves towards standardization. In some MSS this emerges as consistent spelling, in others in the way they are carefully corrected, and in some there is deliberate harmonization between similar passages. This activity was not practised by the Qumran scribes alone; it can also be seen in biblical scrolls that were not copied at Qumran, but brought there later. Much of this deliberate adjustment of the received text is interpretation: e.g. in 11Qpaleo-Lev Frg. I.1–2, an extract from Lev. 20.24 on the possession of the land is inserted into Lev. 18.27 which discusses sexual offences similar to those of Lev. 20; that this assimilation is interpretative is supported by 11QT 66.11–17 which contains a similar assimilation of Lev. 18 and 20, and by 4QpPs^a 2.8–10, which links the possession of the land described in Ps. 37.11 with deliverance from the snares of Belial which include sexual offences (CD 4.15; 5.8–9).

Also, when biblical texts are cited before receiving commentary, they are occasionally altered to fit the commentary all the better. Thus 'enemies' of Ps. 37.20 is adjusted to 'lovers' (4QpPs^a 3.5a), so that the commentator can then identify them with 'the elect'. This is not a scribal error in the commentary, for no MS of Ps. 37.20 contains this reading; 'enemies' is also suitable for the parallelism within this verse of the original psalm. Since only one Hebrew letter need be changed to bring about the new reading, this alteration amounts to an early form of '*al tiqre*', a rabbinic* interpretative technique in which one letter in the original word is 'not read', but another letter is substituted for it.

(c) *Explicit interpretation.* Many MSS of the Qumran community contain explicit biblical interpretation. This is basically of two types, in both of which there is usually attention to the original context of the passage quoted as well as the use of exegetical devices: e.g. the explanation of one text by another through catchwords, the use of paronomasia* (word-play). On the one hand, there is exegesis that makes the biblical text relevant and contemporary. To this category belong the commentaries or *pesharim** which alternate between biblical quotation and commentary introduced with a technical formula. On the other hand, biblical passages are used to support contemporary belief and practice, which in legal matters is usually derived from biblical passages in the first place. The use of biblical texts in the rules (1QS, 1QSa, 1QM, CD) belongs in this category: e.g. Ex. 23.7 and Isa. 2.22 are used in 1QS 5.15–17 to justify rulings concerning the disciplining of community members; the study of the Law in the wilderness is justified by the quotation of Isa. 40.3 (1QS 8.14). Also, the simple listing of authoritative passages with no commentary in 4QTest offers support to the community's understanding of who would be the protagonists in the eschatological* age.

The number of explicit quotations in the

non-biblical scrolls together with the number of copies of each biblical book allows the tentative observation that amongst the books of the Pentateuch the Qumran community had a preference for Deuteronomy, amongst the Prophets a preference for Isaiah, amongst the Writings a preference for the Psalms. A similar set of preferences can be seen amongst the NT authors.

(d) *Implicit interpretation.* Even in the commentaries and rules biblical concepts and phraseology have implicitly influenced the authors, but implicit biblical interpretation is particularly a feature of poetic and liturgical texts. In the hymn in 1QH 4, Isa. 53 is deliberately used to reinforce the poetic device of inclusion: in the initial lament the author describes how he is despised and not esteemed, banished from the land (1QH 4.8; cf. Isa. 53.3,8); and in the closing section, recalling God's compassion, he resolves to face the scourge (1QH 4.36; cf. Isa. 53.4,8). The use of Isa. 53 in this hymn shows how the author identified with the servant of Isaiah in his own spiritual and physical struggles; some of his vocabulary nearly amounts to quotation, some is the careful use of synonym. 1QS contains several liturgical sections; the adaptation of Num. 6.24–26 in 1QS 2.2–4 makes the blessing specific to the Qumran community.

2. Interpretation of the Bible as a result of the Dead Sea discoveries

(a) *The text of the Bible.* The discoveries from the Dead Sea have had most effect on OT textual criticism.* The variety of texts has given a vast amount of information (much still to be published and analysed) about the history of the biblical text in the Second Temple period. Some MSS (e.g. 1QIsa^b) are close to what was known already in the Masoretic* text (MT), some (e.g. 4QpaleoExod^m, 4QNum^b) are close to what was known already in the Samaritan Pentateuch, some (e.g. 4QJer^b) have many readings close to the *Vorlagen* of the Septuagint* (LXX). Most of the biblical MS from Qumran have a mixture of affinities with previously known texts and versions and so may more fairly be classified as independent witnesses to the text of the Hebrew Bible.

Various theories have been proposed to account for all this textual diversity. Some scholars have suggested a chronological development, with the Samaritan type as the earliest, which was gradually revised towards an evolving standard text. It was from this that the MT emerged. F. M. Cross attracted much support in the 1960s and 70s for his adaptation of W. F. Albright's ideas. Cross argued that there were not three deliberate recensions, but text-types resulting from natural developments occurring in various places in isolation: the Babylonian type was the forerunner of the MT, the LXX was translated from the Egyptian type, and the Palestinian, which was most expansionist, was the forerunner of the Samaritan Pentateuch. By the first century AD, all three types were to be found at Qumran. In response to Cross, some scholars have appealed for a tighter use of terminology and the application of a methodology akin to that used by NT text critics for establishing text-types and families; others have rejected Cross' assumption of an *Urtext* and argued that there was a variety of textual traditions from the earliest times. Notably, S. Talmon proposed that three types survived because each was adopted by one of the three religious groups to survive, Jews (MT), Samaritans,* and Christians (LXX). More recently E. Tov has proposed that each MS. should be studied on its own merits and not just in relation to the three text-types already known; for Tov, although the Samaritan Pentateuch has some text-typical features, the MT and LXX can only be textual witnesses, not norms for text-types.

This textual diversity has shown that far from there being a simple development of texts from one single prototype, the history of textual transmission is immensely complicated. The quotations in 4QTest show the complexity well: the first is from Ex. 20.21 in the proto-Samaritan tradition (Deut. 5.28–29 + 18.18–19 MT), the second is Num. 24.15–17 with many minor differences from the MT, the third is Deut. 33.8–11 which contains a variant found only in the Old Latin, the fourth a quotation from the so-called Psalms of Joshua (perhaps considered at Qumran of equal authority to the Pentateuch) which includes a version of Josh. 6.26 akin to that of the *Vorlage* of the LXX.

Also, to begin with, scholars trained in traditional methods of text criticism were tempted to consider all variants as the result of scribal mistakes or sectarian polemic. But a text like 4QpaleoExod^m with its many affinities with a proto-Samaritan version of Exodus shows that the Samaritan Pentateuch, often considered as a sectarian recension, contains some readings superior to the MT and that it was probably only sectarian in two minor ways: in its insistence on referring to Mt Gerizim in its tenth commandment (Sam. Ex. 20.17), and in its narrow reading of Ex. 20.24 as 'In *the* place where I *have caused* my name to be remembered'. Even in those two places the text has been handled with scrupulous care, not arbitrary adjustment.

The MSS from the Dead Sea have caused a positive re-evaluation of the LXX and influenced its study in three striking ways. First, both the Hebrew texts which attest readings in agreement with the LXX and the Greek texts themselves show that the history of the translation* into Greek of each biblical book, and even of sections of each book, must be discussed by itself; it is no longer possible to pose an overall theory for the origin and transmission of the Greek text. Secondly, for some books the Greek text had been considered closer to free paraphrase than translation; but in some cases the Dead Sea Scrolls offer us Hebrew texts (e.g. for Samuel, Jeremiah) no longer extant elsewhere which justify the Greek rendering. Thirdly, the Scroll of the Minor Prophets in Greek from Naḥal Ḥever and other Dead Sea biblical texts have required scholars to re-assess the recensional development of the Greek text, particularly whether or not the Old Greek was ever revised towards a Hebrew text before the revision of Theodotion.

Before the discovery of the Dead Sea Scrolls the principal evidence for a variety of texts in the late Second Temple period was the biblical quotations in the NT. However, since they were all in Greek, the variety was usually explained in relation to developments in the Greek recensions. The scrolls now provide examples of Hebrew texts that match the *Vorlagen* of some of the NT quotations: e.g. Amos 9.11 as quoted in 4QFlor 1.12 matches its quotation in Acts 15.16, and 4QExodᵃ 1.3 reads 'seventy-five' with the LXX Ex. 1.5 and Acts 7.14.

(b) *Biblical scholarship.* The Qumran scrolls have provided some evidence in support of some of the theories of OT scholars. The texts of the Pentateuch and its subsequent rewritings vindicate to some extent scholarly understandings concerning the compositional history of the Pentateuch itself. The marginal marks in 1QIsaᵃ show that its copiers knew that a new section (though, of course, not necessarily the work of another author) began at 40.1. The presentation of Deut. 32 in 4QDeutᵐ in half-lines as poetry vindicates those modern translations that set out passages as poetry.

(c) *Revival of interest in Apocrypha* and pseudepigrapha.* The scrolls have helped stimulate this. For the Apocrypha 2QSir, 11QPsᵃ 21.11–22.1 and MasSir provide material to be compared with the Cairo texts as well as the Greek version of Ben Sira, and 7QEpJer Gr provides the oldest fragment of the Greek Letter of Jeremiah. Four Aramaic and one Hebrew Ms. of Tobit have yet to be published. In addition 4QPrNab, 4QPsDan arᵃ⁻ᶜ, and 4QPsDan Aᵃ provide further information on how Daniel traditions developed (cf. Three Ch., Sus., Bel.).

For the pseudepigrapha already known,

parts of seven MSS of the Book of Jubilees have so far been published (six more from Cave 4 are reported); these show that the text of Jubilees has been reliably transmitted in translation. The eleven MSS of Enoch traditions fall into two categories: fragments from seven MSS correspond to parts of the first, fourth and fifth sections of Ethiopic Enoch, fragments from four MSS are copies of a very detailed astronomical book. No fragments of the Parables (I Enoch 37–71) have been found at Qumran. As yet the Dead Sea finds have not been taken fully into account in pseudepigrapha research; they are usually grouped apart from those texts known already. But such treatment is a distortion of the significance of this literature which includes examples of nearly every genre of pseudepigrapha (testaments, apocalypses, wisdom* texts, rewritten* biblical works, prayers and liturgical texts). Although preserved in the Qumran caves, most of these works were not composed at Qumran and are not narrowly Essene,

(d) *Re-evaluation of the history of Palestinian Judaism.* As a result of the Dead Sea Scrolls the history and nature of Judaism in the Second Temple period has had to be reworked. The setting for the final stages of the writing of some of the OT books, the first few centuries of their transmission, and the setting for early Christianity have all been reconsidered. The principal element emerging in the new picture is one of religious pluriformity in Palestinian Judaism which is variously handled in differing political situations.

This pluriformity is reflected in various attitudes to the Law which the scrolls contain. These reflect the debates within Judaism on the content and function of the Law: the way it should be expressed in the cult, the extent to which it should be associated with myth and with visionary interpretation, the extent to which it should be applied, and the manner of its application. At Qumran the Essene community seems to have argued usually for the universal application of the Law in a strict sense: only the community members could live up to its demands.

(e) *Influence on the interpretation of the NT.* Despite the suggestions of J. O'Callaghan for 7Q3–18, no copies of the NT books have been found at Qumran. However, because many of the scrolls are Jewish texts contemporary with the NT, the Dead Sea Scrolls have influenced the interpretation of the NT against its Jewish background in several ways, though they cannot be used to refute any of the claims of the NT authors. Primarily the scrolls help explain the diverse use of biblical texts by the NT authors. There are parallels between NT proof-texting,* e.g.

in the passion narratives and in Matt. 1–2, and the Qumran *pesharim*.

The scrolls have also illuminated the interpretation of NT eschatology, especially messianism. The Qumran community considered itself to be living in the 'latter days' in anticipation of God's final intervention. In the literature which the Qumran community had in common with other groups, there are texts on angels and demons, on divine judgment, and on the relationship between the moral order and the natural world (cf. e.g. Mark 13.24–27; Rom. 1.20). In the Qumran Essene texts there is generally an expectation of three eschatological figures, a prophet, and the messiahs of Aaron and Israel (1QS 9.11). These figures are variously present also in the NT, either with John the Baptist* filling the role of the prophet and Jesus that of the Davidic messiah,* or with Jesus filling all three roles (e.g. John 1.21; 6.14–15; 19.21).

Some elements in early Christian organization are also better understood through comparison with Qumran parallels. The common ownership of property is a feature of both (1QS 6.17–25; Acts 4.32–5.11). The office of *episkopos*, 'bishop' (I Tim 3.1–7), may be equivalent to the *mebaqqer*, 'overseer' (1QS 6.11–12), of the community. Twelve is a prominent symbol for both groups (1QS 8.1; 1QM 2.1; 4QOrd 2–4,3–4; 4QpIsa^d 1.4; Matt. 19.28; Rev. 21.14; etc.). The use of a different calendar* at Qumran has been applied to the difficult question of the date of the Passover, suggesting that Jesus celebrated the Passover (Mark 14.12–16) according to the solar calendar, but that his crucifixion was dated in relation to the day of preparation (Mark 15.42; John 19.31) of the luni-solar calendar.

(f) *Influence on understanding of the formation of the canon.** The scrolls have provided new information on the development of the Hebrew canon. The Temple Scroll suggests that there was a scribal school that considered it possible to present as authoritative a major rewriting of the Pentateuch. 4QSam^a provides a text of Samuel akin to that of MT I Chron.; either I Chron. influenced the transmission of Sam. or the author of I Chron. used a text like that of 4QSam^a which differed from that which the rabbis later decided to make authoritative. 11QPs^a and the many copies of Pss at Qumran have yet to be fully appreciated in relation to the development of the content and order of the Psalter. Esther, which it seems the Qumran community probably did not regard as authoritative, was later endorsed by the rabbis, whilst other works that they did acknowledge were later excluded.

See also **Jewish Background to the New Testament; Jewish Exegesis; Manuscripts.**

F. M. Cross and S. Talmon (eds), *Qumran and the History of the Biblical Text*, 1975; J. A. Fitzmyer, *The Dead Sea Scrolls: Major Publications and Tools for Study*, ²1977; M. A. Knibb, *The Qumran Community*, 1987; E. Tov, 'Hebrew Biblical Manuscripts from the Judaean Desert: Their Contribution to Textual Criticism' in *JJS* 39, 1988, pp. 5–37; G. Vermes, *Jesus and the World of Judaism*, 1983; id., *The Dead Sea Scrolls in English*, ³1987.

GEORGE J. BROOKE

Deism

Leslie Stephen, the nineteenth-century historian of eighteenth-century English religious thought, sees the essence of deism as a radical reinterpretation of the 'Vincentian Canon': *quod semper, quod ubique, quod ab omnibus creditum est* (true faith is that which is universally and always believed). If God is truly just and good, he must make himself and his will known to all people at all times in the same way. In his treatise, *de Religione Gentilium* (1645), Lord Herbert of Cherbury summarizes the articles of this universal natural revelation as follows: belief in one supreme God, who ought to be worshipped, above all by the practice of virtue; the efficacy of repentance (without any atoning sacrifice) to gain forgiveness of sins; and the existence of rewards and punishments in a future state. Belief in a natural religion, discoverable by reason alone, was in fact common ground between the deists and most of their more orthodox opponents. The difference between them is that the deists are prepared to use this religion of reason as a basis from which to criticize the Bible and traditional Christian beliefs, whereas their opponents' aim is to defend Bible and tradition. In individual cases, however, this dividing-line can be difficult to draw.

In their discussion of general issues of biblical interpretation – for example, the place of reason, or the possibility of miracles* – the deists belong within the broader intellectual framework of the Enlightenment.* Several of them, however, made notable contributions to the development of a historical and critical approach to the study of the Bible. Their motivation is more critical than historical – indeed, their whole philosophy of religion is essentially ahistorical – yet because they approach the Bible critically, they often notice problems which more conventional interpretation had ignored or suppressed.

Anthony Collins wrote his *Discourse of the Grounds and Reasons of the Christian Religion* (1724) in response to an earlier work by W. Whiston (1722), which had discussed the discrepancies between citations of the OT in the

NT and the Hebrew (Masoretic*) and Septuagint* texts. Collins claims that the truth of Christianity stands or falls with the literal fulfilment of OT prophecy, and, taking five key proof texts* from the Gospel of Matthew as examples, argues that prophecy* is understood only in a 'mystical'* or 'allegorical'* sense, without any evidential value. Thus, the literal,* historical meaning of Isa. 7.14 is that the promised child is the prophet's own son. NT authors who apply OT prophecies to their own times do so only as an accommodation to the prejudices of their contemporaries. The implications are that there is no basis for Christian belief, and that the OT requires to be studied historically without reference to the NT.

Between 1727 and 1730 Thomas Woolston published six *Discourses on the Miracles of our Saviour*. He sees himself as complementing Collins' work on prophecy by attacking the second pillar of conventional apologetic, the miracles which were said to confirm the divine origin of Jesus' mission. Woolston's method is to laugh this argument out of court. Jesus' cursing of the fig-tree is a sign of petulance, as foolish as throwing the chairs about because dinner is not ready on time. It is regrettable that Jesus did not pass on to his disciples his power to turn water into wine along with authority to remit sins. The resurrection* is a monstrous imposture carried out by the disciples, who stole the body the day before it was due to rise. The miracle stories are simply ludicrous, and even the Fathers conceded this by interpreting them allegorically. Historically, Woolston's importance is that he shifted discussion of miracles from the general level to the gospel texts.

For Thomas Morgan, the central problem of the Bible was the immorality and superstition to be found in the OT. Paul* is the hero of his book, *The Moral Philosopher* (1737). In his opposition to the Jewish law and Jewish Christianity* (that is, the religion of clericalism and belief without evidence), Paul was 'the great Free-thinker of his age, the bold and brave defender of reason against authority'. He criticized not only the Jewish misuse of the law as a means of earning salvation, but the law itself, even though this brought him into conflict with the other apostles. He alone saw Jesus not as the Jewish Messiah* but as 'the common saviour of the World, without distinction between Jew and Gentile'. The book of Revelation, with its blind hatred towards those of other beliefs, is a product of the Jewish Christianity Paul opposed, and it is a tragedy that Catholic Christianity adopted the Jewish position, leaving the Gnostics* and Marcion* as the sole representatives of Pauline freedom. The anticipations of F. C.

Baur are striking, but Morgan's real interest is in the contemporary controversy between 'free-thinkers' and the Anglican church.

In *The True Gospel of Jesus Christ Asserted* (1738), Thomas Chubb distinguishes the gospel preached by Jesus from the gospel of the early church. The gospel Jesus preached was not a historical account of matters of fact, such as we find in the creeds.* The credibility of these facts depends on our assessment of the evidence, but this has nothing to do with the message Jesus preached to the poor. Nor should his gospel be confused with the private opinions of any of the NT authors. St John may have believed that the Word was with God, and the Word was God (*see* **Logos**), but the simplicity of Christ's own teaching is far removed from the abstruseness of such doctrines. In the modern jargon, Chubb had discovered the problem of 'the Jesus of history and the Christ of faith', of how 'the proclaimer became the proclaimed'.

Ideas such as these were drawn together and restated by Hermann Samuel Reimarus* who was heavily dependent on the English deists, many of whose works were available in German translation. Jesus, he argues, taught nothing contrary to Jewish belief; he did not understand himself as Son of God in the orthodox Christian sense, and it was not his purpose to found a new religion. It was the disciples who, after his death, fraudulently introduced new dogmatic elements into their preaching, notably the atonement and the resurrection. The fraud is exposed by careful study of the resurrection narratives,* which are full of contradictions. This argument illustrates both the limitations and the insights of deist biblical interpretation. The explanation of every departure from the purity of natural religion in terms of 'fraud' shows an almost complete lack of historical sense; yet genuine problems in the biblical texts are sometimes clearly perceived.

See also **Biblical Criticism; Christian Interpretation of the Old Testament; Enlightenment; Historical Jesus.**

H. Frei, *The Eclipse of Biblical Narrative*, 1974; W. G. Kümmel, *The New Testament. The History of the Investigation of its Problems*, ET 1972; H. Reventlow, *The Authority of the Bible and the Rise of the Modern World*, ET 1984.

FRANCIS WATSON

Demythologization

The English translation of the German word *Entmythologisierung* coined by Hans Jonas and used by Rudolf Bultmann* to describe an essential feature of his programme for interpreting the NT. Although the term refers only to one feature of this method, it can hardly be understood without some knowledge of his approach as a whole.

Bultmann's starting point was the fact that any set of religious beliefs has to be expressed in terms of some cultural context, some particular way of understanding reality (*see* **Cultural Relativism**). If, for example, the message of the NT was to be intelligible at the time of writing, it had not only to be formulated in Hellenistic Greek, the only language most of the readers – or authors – understood; it had to be stated in terms which meshed in with the sort of world-view familiar to most of them. Thus the world is conceived in the NT as a flat disc, with heaven as a place above and hell a place beneath: the existence and activity of angels, demons and other supernatural creatures are presupposed, and it is taken for granted that the course of history and of individual lives is constantly redirected, and human minds and attitudes changed, by miraculous interventions on the part of God or the Devil.

When a world-view is superseded, as the NT world-view has been superseded, especially in the last two hundred years or so, any religious belief stated in terms of it ceases to be intelligible, or at any rate acceptable with integrity, by those whose thought is governed by new ways of understanding things.

Does that mean that the teaching in question has simply to be abandoned as untenable? Bultmann thought not. True religion, he believed, is never basically a matter of metaphysical systems and doctrines; it consists essentially of a relationship with a supernatural Thou by whom men and women are confronted, and who can be recognized and known in personal confrontation, but never objectively described in neutral and impersonal statements. Thus NT texts, for example, which might appear to be insisting on a certain philosophical or metaphysical account of Christ, almost always turn out in fact to be ways of claiming that in him we are confronted with the ultimate demand of God and the choice and judgment that go with it.

Once that is understood, it becomes clear what the task of biblical interpretation is: to set out in terms intelligible and acceptable today the nature of the divine-human relationship to which the NT bears witness, to make clear that it is still a live option and to show how it is to be appropriated. Bultmann used the word myth* to bring out the obsoleteness of the first-century world-view. Such a usage is more readily intelligible in German than in English, and in the light of it part of what the interpreter has to do is to release the essential message from its 'mythical' framework, i.e. to demythologize it. The process is less negative than that might at first suggest; for a little reflection will show that a set of beliefs can be demythologized only by being reformulated in terms which are not mythical to the addressees. At this point misunderstanding can easily arise as a result of Bultmann's loose and confused way of using 'myth' and its cognates. He sometimes uses the word to make the point that it is never possible to talk of the supernatural in literal, non-symbolic, language. In that sense all language about God in every age is bound to be mythical. Even in the other sense discussed above, however, the word is ambiguous. As culture changes, the outlook of an earlier age will always seem mythical to people who come later; to people living a thousand years hence, for example, *our* way of putting things will no doubt seem to be mythology, and we can, if we wish, speak of transmythologization (i.e. from biblical mythology into ours) rather than demythologization; but Bultmann, though aware of this point does not stress it because we who live now can sense it only in a rather abstract way; there is a practically important sense in which for us the first-century world-view is myth and ours is not. Our ways of speaking about the supernatural mesh in – or certainly should mesh in – with the rest of what we know about reality, in a way that first-century ideas do not.

The vital question then is: in what terms must the NT gospel be set out if comprehension and acceptance of it are to be possible for people with a modern Western outlook? At this point another aspect of Bultmann's thought is relevant. He pointed out that incapsulation in an outworn world-view is not the only stumbling-block the NT gospel presents to people today. There is also the fact that the NT claims to meet needs the modern reader is often unaware of having. This is a particular instance of an important general truth: no document can speak to us unless we approach it with an appropriate 'pre-understanding' (*Vorverständnis*). It is not just that we shall be unable, for example, to understand a document written in Greek unless we already understand the Greek language; more generally, we shall not be able to understand a treatise on philosophy or psychology, let us say, unless we have at least some preliminary awareness of the problems it sets out to solve. So far as this situation arises in connection with the NT, part of the interpreter's task is to discover the forms in which the needs met by the gospel are felt in our culture. To discover that is to discover the appropriate *Vorverständnis* for understanding the Bible today.

Bultmann was deeply influenced by the earlier writings of the philosopher Martin Heidegger, who was one of his professorial colleagues at Marburg from 1922 to 1928. In his book *Being and Time* (1927, ET 1962), Heidegger offered what seemed to Bultmann an almost definitive analysis of the character and problematic of existence as a human being, all the more significant because it was not produced by a believer or with any religious *arrière pensée*. According to Heidegger's analysis, though human beings are *in* the world, they are not *of* it – they transcend it in their consciousness of it and of themselves as separate from it. We all have our own individual and unique being, and to be ourselves – to be 'authentic', as Heidegger would say – we must preserve this separateness and individuality, and not become lost or immersed in the world, as if we were simply objects passively controlled by its forces and pressures. However, people do get so immersed; they lose their identity and their responsibility for their own destinies, and become puppets controlled by the pressures of collective humanity; they become desperate for security, but rely for it on the resources available in this world, which they know to be finite and uncertain, and of which, therefore, they seek more than their fair share. This may be expressed by saying that they yield to the dominion of this world. Such a condition Heidegger described as 'fallenness', and he regarded it as inevitable, once self-responsibility has been abdicated.

Bultmann argued that if people can be enabled to see in this analysis the truth about their condition, they will also be able to see that the NT is speaking of matters vitally relevant to their situation and needs. They will be for the first time in a position really to hear the word of God.*

How is this word mediated through the NT? Not, according to Bultmann, through the figure of the historical Jesus or his *ipsissima verba*. For Bultmann was doubtful, to say the least, about the possibility of our recovering more than the barest minimum about the historical Jesus; but that did not trouble him because he believed it is in any case wrong to attempt to establish faith on any supposedly 'objective' basis. Through the Christ-figure put forward in the NT, and particularly through the account of the cross, God offers us what is in Heidegger's terminology a 'repeatable (*wiederholbar*) possibility', namely the possibility of total authenticity, of a life lived entirely out of God's future and God's resources. Our response to this offer Bultmann described in eschatological* terms. If we respond positively, that will mean the end of our previous existence, with its attempt to achieve meaning and security on the basis of this world. 'When anyone is united to Christ, he is a new creature: the old life is over; a new

life has already begun' (II Cor. 5.17). Moreover, the manifestation of this new possibility through the NT is in a special sense the work of God, and it faces us with an ultimate either-or, before which we can appeal to no higher considerations. We must decide which way of life to choose; our choice involves our whole being and we are totally judged by the way we decide. It is important to be clear that Bultmann recognized – indeed emphasized – the need for an act of sheer faith such as is likely to seem a scandal to the wisdom of this world. It was only the unnecessary scandal presented by the incapsulation of the faith in an outmoded framework that he sought to remove.

In Bultmann's view, the only key event in the NT accounts of Jesus which can be regarded as an objective historical event is the crucifixion, with its clear indication that life comes only from complete reliance on God's resources. The other key events, for example the virgin birth (*see* **Infancy Narratives**) or the resurrection,* are 'existential-historical' – i.e. events which have no objective historical status but are ways of expressing and bringing out the meaning of the cross. For instance, the virgin birth emphasizes that the cross was the fruit of God's initiative, the resurrection that the way of the cross is the true way, etc.

Criticisms of Bultmann's programme have been of very different kinds, and are apt to cancel one another out. From one side the complaint has been of too sweeping and indiscriminate a relegation of virtually the entire NT world-view to the realm of the mythical. Critics point out, to take just one example, that some believers today who go along with modern astronomy in their view of the world and the heavens still regard angels and demons as anything but mythical. Certainly, as we have seen, Bultmann is somewhat summary and confused in his handling of the category of the mythical, but readers can easily decide for themselves what elements of the New Testament framework should be regarded as myth, and adjust the application of Bultmann's method acordingly. From the opposite side comes the complaint that Bultmann's use of myth is not broad enough. He seems (rightly) to reject as mythical all attempts to objectify the supernatural, and all claims that God breaks through the closed connection of worldly events. Why then does he not reject all conceptions of God as a genuinely independent reality and of his breaking through to human beings by way of confrontation? God acting by way of confrontation is still God acting, and the idea is vulnerable to Bultmann's own critique. Altogether, Bultmann's somewhat airy dismissal of the metaphysical problems raised by religion is seen by many as a weakness of the whole tradition in which he stands.

Another criticism has been that Bultmann virtually swallows whole one particular analysis of the human condition, thus making acceptance of Heidegger's views the prerequisite for understanding the gospel.

When these and other criticisms have been allowed for, it remains that Bultmann isolated with great clarity a key problem – probably in fact the key problem – for biblical interpretation today. As for his solution, it can at least be argued, as he himself did, that something very like it is to be found in the NT itself. In Paul,* in the words attributed to Jesus, and elsewhere in the NT, the response which is sought to the saving event is by way of faith, obedience and imitation rather than by way of any particular formulation of the meaning of what has happened. 'Jesus is Lord' is essentially the expression of practical response; it is later, and many would say less profound, strata of the NT that insist on 'patterns of sound words' (cf., e.g., II Tim. 1.13; I Tim. 1.10; II Tim. 4.3; Titus 1.9,13).

The term 'demythologization' is sometimes used more broadly, to cover any proposal for reformulating biblical truth in terms intelligible today. Whatever use may be made of it, it should be remembered that it was Bultmann who first gave it currency in connection with biblical interpretation, that he did so with an essentially positive intent, and that the programme in which he incorporated the idea was the advantage of suggesting a quite specific (Heideggerian) language in which the formulation of biblical truth can be effected. Whatever may be thought of that particular language, unless some specific interpretative framework is adopted, the question how biblical truth is to be formulated today can become so open-ended as to be virtually unanswerable.

See also **Bultmann, R.; Myth.**

H. W. Bartsch (ed.), *Kerygma and Myth* (2 vols) 1953, 1962 (esp. vol. i, pp. 1–44); R. Bultmann, *Theology of the New Testament* (2 vols), 1952, 1955; id., *Jesus Christ and Mythology*, 1960; R. Johnson, *The Origins of Demythologizing*, 1974; J. Macquarrie, *An Existentialist Theology*, 1955; id., *The Scope of Demythologizing*, 1960; L. Malevez, *The Christian Message and Myth*, 1958.

D. E. NINEHAM

Deuteronomistic History

The deuteronomistic history, comprising the books of Deuteronomy, Joshua, Judges, Samuel and Kings, is a postulate of the literary and historical criticism of the OT. It was first described by Noth, who showed these books

to be a composition independent of the Pentateuchal* documents and to constitute the first continuous history of Israel using a variety of older independent traditions. Four characteristics indicated the unity of the work: its consistent language; the regular appearance, at critical points in the history, of summarizing speeches or narratives; its consistent chronology; its coherent theology. The work was written during the exile and aimed to account for the destructive conclusion in which Israel's history issued.

Critics of Noth's view have highlighted a number of inherent weaknesses: there is no coherent attitude expressed towards the monarchic institution; it is unlikely that an exilic author would have written for his contemporaries a work of the nature described by Noth; it is difficult to determine precisely what the theme of the work is. As a result, there has been a widespread move away from Noth's view of a single author of a single work towards a more complex picture of successive editors at work in different periods of time and with different purposes. Two chief trends have developed.

Smend, with Dietrich and Veijola, has proposed a view of the deuteronomistic history according to which it has gone through three stages of redaction. In Joshua the work of the deuteronomistic historian (DtrH), for whom Israel's conquest of the land was complete and successful, has been supplemented by a 'nomistic' deuteronomistic editor (DtrN), especially in Josh. 23, but also in parts of Josh. 1 and 13, for whom the conquest has been successful 'to this day', while its complete success is conditional on obedience to the law. In the account of the monarchic period a third deuteronomistic hand, coming between DtrH and DtrN and reflecting prophetic interests (DtrP), may be traced. All three redactors belong closely together, the later using the language of the earlier. Chronologically also the three stages are not far separated: the work of the historian records the release of King Jehoiachin from prison in exile while the following two stages of editing were completed by the early post-exilic period.

The second trend may be traced back to von Rad, but comes to full expression in the work of Cross and Nelson. Von Rad noted that the deuteronomistic history not only relates the judgment of the law but also contains a messianic motif which comes to expression in the positive evaluation of David as the standard by which his successors are judged. The tension between them has prompted Cross to argue that there are in fact two themes in the deuteronomistic history: the sin of Jeroboam and his successors, coming to a climax in the account of the fall of the northern kingdom in II Kings 17; the promise of grace to David, which reaches its climax in the story of Josiah's reform in II Kings 22–23. By relating Josiah's destruction of the remnants of the cult of Jeroboam and his attempt to restore the kingdom of David, this story brings together both themes in a work of propaganda issued to support Josiah's religious and political policies: he is the new David in whom is to be found true faithfulness to Yahweh.

Thus, the deuteronomistic history was originally a pre-exilic composition concluding with the account of the reign and reform of Josiah. Its extension, to incorporate reference to the destruction of Jerusalem and the exile, is the work of a second deuteronomistic editor who has here, and in his additions throughout all the books of the history, turned that history into an explanation of Judah's ultimate experience of catastrophe. Nelson has shown how the different forms of regnal formulae, by which each king in Israel and Judah is introduced, give literary support to this view: the formulae used for the last four Judaean kings, who followed Josiah, come from an editorial hand later than that which composed the formulae for the earlier kings.

Such attempts to describe the history of redaction of the whole deuteronomistic history encounter considerable difficulties. The criteria by which redactional layers are to be distinguished are still uncertain, and, while at some stage the work was put together as a whole, the view that a given stage of redaction is to be traced throughout (most of) the constituent books of the deuteronomistic history may not take adequate account of the probable complexities of the process. Significant stages of redaction, embracing limited parts of the work, probably both preceded and followed its appearance as a single entity. The working out of the redactional development of subsections of the deuteronomistic history has still to be completed before a satisfactory comprehensive picture can evolve.

Major contributions towards this have been made by a number of studies. Seitz has determined two significant stages in the growth of Deuteronomy, characterized by two series of superscriptions, the earlier of which marked the provision of the deuteronomic law with a parenetic introduction, and the later the incorporation of the deuteronomic law into the deuteronomistic history. Richter has mapped out the history of the growth of Judges by a study of the formulae which brought the independent stories into a collection and of the introductory passages which brought together deliverers and judges into an account of the period of the judges. For Kings, Weippert has distinguished three groups of judgment for-mulae, relating to progressively more extensive sections of the books, so providing an outline of their history of development. On the other hand, Lohfink has identified a distinctive form of expression in Deut. 1–Josh. 22, through which the deuteronomist describes the conquest as Yahweh's dispossession of the older inhabitants of the land in favour of Israel. This may suggest that Deut. 1–Josh. 22 once had independent existence, and only at a later stage was combined with other materials to yield the whole work extending from Deuteronomy to II Kings.

Against these trends in the redactional study of the deuteronomistic history, Hoffmann has argued that the work is a unity and should be studied traditio-historically rather than as the final deposit of a redactional history. He implies by this that the deuteronomist was an original, creative author, making use mainly of oral tradition. His intention was to write a history of Israel * as a history of cultic reforms and reformers. The detail of these accounts is not a reflection of historical recording, but is part of the literary presentation: the detail is the deuteronomistic way of giving historical verisimilitude to his account.

Van Seters has a similar understanding of the literary creativity of the deuteronomist, arguing that he is Israel's first historian whose work, after the removal of its (extensive) later additions, has a uniform style and outlook. Its purpose, however, is conceived of by van Seters in broader terms than those expressed by Hoffmann: it is concerned with articulating the people's sense of identity through an account of its history. In its purpose and its technique, the use of different literary genres * such as the king list, the royal inscription, the chronicle, and the incorporation of popular stories, the work of the deuteronomist is comparable with that of Herodotus.

Polzin's analysis of the first part of the deuteronomistic history deliberately renounces all questions of historical development of the material and the possible presence of later additions, in an attempt to interpret the text as it now stands, its various tensions being used to elucidate the overall thrust of the work. Polzin makes a basic distinction between the voice of the narrator and that of whom the narrator speaks. The latter predominates in Deuteronomy (voice of God/Moses *) and the former in the remainder of the deuteronomistic history. Nevertheless, even in Deuteronomy the narrator contrives to present his own voice as authoritative to a degree equal to the voice of Moses, and thus lays the foundation for claiming his own understanding of the law and his application of it both to the history of Israel and to his own contemporaries as authoritative. The validity of this style of reading the text is very much a matter for further discussion; its deliberate renunciation of the traditional critical methods may be held to remove the basis for the very identification of the deuteronomistic history (which has been marked out by such methods) as a text to be treated in this way.

See also **Deuteronomy; Israel, History of.**

F. M. Cross, *Canaanite Myth and Hebrew Epic*, 1973; A. D. H. Mayes, *The Story of Israel between Settlement and Exile*, 1983; M. Noth, *The Deuteronomistic History*, ET 1981; R. Polzin, *Moses and the Deuteronomist. A Literary Study of the Deuteronomic History*, 1980; J. van Seters, *In Search of History*, 1983.

A. D. H. MAYES

Deuteronomy

The interpretation of Deuteronomy reaches back to its origins. Perhaps originally conceived of as 'the law of Moses', * analogous in form and purpose to other Ancient Near Eastern law-codes, it soon came to be understood as the law of a covenant * relationship between God and Israel established by Moses in the plains of Moab. This covenant-making, understood as a second event in relation to the first covenant made at Sinai, is alluded to in the very name 'Deuteronomy'. This title is derived from the Septuagint * (LXX) and is based on an ungrammatical rendering of Deut. 17.18. That verse commands that the king should have 'a copy of this law'; the LXX, however, translates the phrase as 'this second (or, repeated) law', and so interprets the whole book in relation to the first event of lawgiving at Sinai.

In the NT (Acts 3.22; Heb. 1.6) Deut. 18.15ff.; 32.43 (LXX) are quoted with messianic * significance. It may be that they formed part of a collection of proof texts * on specific topics; such collections, incorporating passages from Deuteronomy, are known from Qumran (*see* **Dead Sea Scrolls**). In the actual methods of exegesis also the NT use of Deuteronomy conforms with established Jewish practice. The literal understanding of the text is exemplified in Matt. 4.4; 22.37 etc.; the midrashic * use of the text, in which a variety of passages is brought to bear on an argument, is apparent in Rom. 10.18–21 etc.; and the allegorical interpretation * of Deut. 25.4 appears in I Cor. 9.9f. In addition, it has been proposed that Luke 9.51–18.14 reflects a Deuteronomic order of topics.

That Moses was the author of Deuteronomy, along with the rest of the Pentateuch, * was generally accepted in ancient tradition, though some difficulty was felt with regard to the record of Moses' death at the end of Deuteronomy: some rabbis attributed the account to Joshua, others to Moses himself writing at God's dictation. Mediaeval commentators, such as Ibn Ezra, accepted Mosaic authorship, but seem to have considered that some passages were added after the death of Moses.

The lack of scholarly agreement on most issues related to the study of Deuteronomy means that a brief account of its critical interpretation must select, perhaps arbitrarily, which views to represent. Within three broad and interrelated categories, covering historical, redactional and literary approaches, something of the variety of current interpretations may be described.

1. The argument of de Wette * in the early nineteenth century that the book of the law found in the Temple in Jerusalem, on which Josiah based his reform (II Kings 22–23), was Deuteronomy, or part of it, has been central to the *historical approach*. That theory is still widely maintained, though usually with two modifications: first, much of the present Deuteronomy, especially its historical and parenetic sections, would not have formed part of the lawbook of Josiah, but were added later; secondly, the reform of Josiah had a strong political motive, and was probably well under way before the appearance of the lawbook which then acted as a further impulse. Of those, however, who have rejected the theory, some have dated Deuteronomy to a much earlier time, arguing that the centralization law of Deut. 12 should be given a different interpretation or that it is a later addition to the book. Others have suggested that the laws are generally idealistic, and that the collection constitutes a speculative reform programme to be ascribed to the post-exilic Jerusalem priesthood.

In some recent study the story of Josiah's reform has become problematic. Noth's argument that the deuteronomistic historian incorporated an existing official record of the reform (II Kings 22.3–23.3) together with material derived from the 'chronicles of the kings of Judah' (II Kings 23.4–20) was largely supported by Lohfink's analysis which suggested that the story of the finding of the lawbook was a single unit deriving from the time of Josiah and structured on the form of a covenant renewal ceremony. Spieckermann's rather different analysis, which distinguished a basic text which had gone through three stages of deuteronomistic editing, and had been further supplemented by late or post-deuteronomistic additions, at least shared the conclusion that the account of the finding of the lawbook in the temple and the making of a covenant were pre-deuteronomistic.

On the other hand, recent analyses of II Kings 22–23 by Dietrich, Würthwein and others, has cast doubt on the pre-deuteronom-istic origins of just those aspects of the story of Josiah's reform. The detailed account of the reform measures, in II Kings 23.4–20, contains no reference to the finding of a law-book on the basis of which the reforms were implemented. It is only later deuteronomistic editing, to be understood within the theologi-cal framework of the whole deuteronomistic history, which has introduced the references to the lawbook and covenant making. The story cannot, therefore, provide support for a historical linking of Deuteronomy with the time of Josiah.

2. The *redactional* * *approach* to Deuter-onomy, which replaced older documentary analyses, goes back to Noth, who argued that Deuteronomy is the first part of the deuter-onomistic history,* and that in it the deuter-onomistic historian has incorporated the al-ready existing deuteronomic law. In Deut. 1–3(4); 31–34 the deuteronomist has provided a historical framework for the law, and has continued his historical account in the follow-ing books of his history. In a quite compatible approach, Seitz has noted that Deuteronomy contains two series of superscriptions which mark two stages in the history of the growth of Deuteronomy: one group (1.1; 4.44; 28.69 [EVV 29.1]; 32.1) covers a larger extent of material than the other, and, since it has close parallels elsewhere in the deuteronomistic his-tory, may be held to derive from the time that the deuteronomic law was incorporated into that history; the other, earlier series of superscriptions (4.45; 6.1; 12.1) marks the stage at which the existing deuteronomic law, characterized by the connection of older law collections with the centralization laws, was provided with a parenetic introduction in Deut. 5–11.

A further development of this redactional approach claims that deuteronomistic editing in Deuteronomy was carried out in two stages rather than one. Deut. 4.1–40 is a literary unit which both depends upon and yet is not an original continuation of Deut. 1–3. It is an insertion through which a later deuteronom-istic editor (who has contributed also to Deut. 6–11; 26–32) has imbued Deuteronomy with specifically covenant or treaty thought-forms and vocabulary. Thus, in Deuteronomy, as elsewhere in the deuteronomistic history, a distinction can be drawn between the work of a deuteronomistic historian and the editing of a later 'nomistic' deuteronomist.

3. Aspects of the *literary analysis* of Deut-eronomy are rooted in von Rad's observa-tion that Deuteronomy has a structure consist-ing of four sections: a historical and parenetic introduction (Deut. 1–11); the presentation of the law (12–26.15); the sealing of the covenant

(26.16–19); the blessings and curses (27ff.). This can be recognized as the form of a cultic ceremony of covenant making, and Deuter-onomy can be seen as the end result of a complex process of growth, rooted in a regu-larly repeated ceremony of this nature. This theory of Deuteronomy's structure seemed then to have been broadly confirmed by subse-quent study of Ancient Near Eastern treaty texts and their influence on OT covenant forms, especially the form of Deuteronomy.

The formal structure of Deuteronomy and some of its distinctive vocabulary (love, know, walk after, fear, obey the voice of, serve) are strongly reminiscent of treaty forms and vocab-ulary, but the precise definition of the rela-tionship between them remains uncertain. Deut-eronomy is not a treaty document and some of its contents do not relate easily to the treaty form. Moreover, it seems likely that it is with Deuteronomy in its later stages that the treaty relationship exists, since it is with the later deuteronomistic editor that covenant thought and language come to the fore.

Stylistic analysis approaches the text synch-ronically, rather than historically, and is con-cerned with describing its rhetorical-stylistic techniques. This does not necessarily imply the literary unity of the text being studied (though the unity of Deut. 4.1–40 has been shown by the stylistic study of Braulik), for, as Lohfink's treatment of Deut. 5–11 indicates, the result of such study may be a very complex picture of the origin of the text. It is a highly controlled form of analysis, one aspect of which is par-ticularly noteworthy: the interchange of second person singular and second person plural forms of address, widely used as a criterion of source division or as a means of distinguishing the original Deuteronomy from its deuteronomistic framework, should rather be given a stylistic interpretation. Every change in number is a new form of address. Whether or not the stylistic explanation will be adequate for every occasion of change of address is yet to be seen. Even if it may come to be shown, however, that in certain deuteronomic texts or at a certain stage in the development of a text, a particular number was characteristic, this phenomenon can no longer be used as a reli-able independent criterion of source analysis or distinction between stages of redaction.

Two literary approaches to the law, of a rather different nature, should be particularly mentioned. Carmichael has argued that the laws of Deuteronomy are not a direct practical response to conditions of life and worship in Israel's past, but are new literary constructions derived from the scrutiny of Israel's historical records, and the purpose of the lawgiver is to be defined as that of explaining the legal and ethical implications of the narratives.

Connections between the laws and the historical traditions undoubtedly exist, but the exclusive application of this approach tends to produce a tangle of uncontrolled and sometimes fanciful relationships. More credible is the argument of Kaufmann and Braulik that the deuteronomic law is the deliberate arrangement of existing laws in an order based on the order of the demands of the Decalogue. This influence of the Decalogue has long been suspected, but the method by which it has been exercised on the arrangement of the laws is only now becoming clear, in part as a result of the study of non-biblical law codes. In legal corpora generally the following principles of arrangement apply: laws, possibly of diverse origins, are grouped together according to their general topic; within each topical unit the laws are arranged according to clear principles of priority; the individual laws and larger subsections of each topical unit are arranged on the basis of the concatenation of ideas, keywords and phrases, and similar motifs. As far as Deuteronomy is concerned, it may be established, in addition, that the topical units are ordered according to corresponding commandments of the decalogue. This approach combines a credible type of literary explanation with enough flexibility to allow for the further investigation of the pre-deuteronomic history of individual elements in the law.

Polzin's compositional analysis, which is interested in the text only as it now stands, aims to show how, by blurring the distinction between the voice of Moses and the voice of God, the deuteronomist exalts the authority of Moses. The deuteronomist then also breaks down the difference between himself and Moses, between his audience and that of Moses, by fusing their temporal perspectives through the repeated use of 'this day' and also by being the only voice, besides that of Moses, which quotes the words of God directly. The distinction between his teaching authority and that of Moses is gradually obliterated, so that the authority of his account of Israel's history and his application to it of the deuteronomic law become firmly established. The discontinuity between this reading of Deuteronomy and other approaches, even those which share its literary concerns, should not be ignored. The nature of any fruitful interaction between them has yet to be determined.

See also **Deuteronomistic History; Law; Moses; Pentateuch.**

R. Alter and F. Kermode, *The Literary Guide to the Bible*, 1987; C. F. Evans in D. E. Nineham (ed.) *Studies in the Gospels*, 1955; A. D. H Mayes, *Deuteronomy* (New Century Bible), 1979; id., *The Story of Israel between Settlement and Exile*, 1983; E. W. Nicholson,

Deuteronomy and Tradition, 1967; M. Weinfeld, *Deuteronomy and the Deuteronomic School*, 1972.

A. D. H. MAYES

Diversity

The issue of diversity in the Bible as a factor in biblical interpretation has only emerged in the modern period. Prior to that it was hidden from view by the dogmatic assumption that the biblical texts should be subject to a uniform interpretation. The Christian interpretation of the OT* was the only admissible one. The apostolic faith, or the rule of faith, effectively determined the contents of the NT canon* and so also the understanding of the canonical writings. Attempts to justify different interpretations from within the canon, as in the case of the Montanists and mediaeval millenarian* movements, were by the same criterion ruled to be heretical. The various splits in Eastern Christianity, between East and West, and within Western Christianity (the Reformation*), resulted simply in different dogmatic paradigms, with paradigms which diverged from one's own dismissed as heretical. The diversity lay not in the text, which each party and faction assumed still to provide a single homogeneous expression of the one orthodox faith, but in the paradigm of doctrine adopted. Luther* might be willing to recognize different levels of canonical authority in the NT writings, but the universal assumption that the unclear should be interpreted in the light of the clear, with allegorizing* as a further aid in dealing with difficult passages, meant that the unity of the biblical writings remained a fundamental assumption of hermeneutics.*

With the Enlightenment,* however, came the recognition of historical distance and difference between present and past and of the need both to question assumptions regarding the past and to locate the biblical texts more fully within the context of that past. In biblical interpretation this came to expression particularly in the distinctions between dogmatic theology and biblical theology* (J. S. Semler) and between the historical Jesus* and the dogmatic Christ (the Deists,* including H. S. Reimarus*). Alongside descriptive categories like law and prophets came the new evaluative category of myth.* In the nineteenth century various distinctions became increasingly important in the study of the NT – between the Synoptics and John's Gospel in their value as sources for the life of Jesus, between Jewish Christianity* and Pauline* Christianity (F. C. Baur), and between the simple moralizing of Jesus and the Hellenizing religion of Paul (Liberal Protestants: *see* **Harnack, A. von**). Nevertheless, the unity of the scriptures, interpreted in the light of Christ, and of the apostolic faith, continued to be strongly maintained by most students of the Bible and to be taken for granted within the Christian churches.

The twentieth century has been marked by an increasing awareness of the complexity of the historical picture and of the character of the biblical writings. In the case of the OT, the work of J. Wellhausen in particular posed the issue of different kinds of religion lying behind the OT documents, and the increased interest in Jewish wisdom literature* brought with it an awareness of a Jewish religious thought much more open to foreign influence than had previously been appreciated. In turn the contribution of R. Bultmann* and the continuing Christian recoil from the Holocaust, with its increasing respect for Judaism in its own right, have brought to sharper focus the tension between OT and NT within the Christian Bible. The 'history of religions' school* widened the spectrum contained in the NT still further, by setting Jesus firmly in the context of Jewish apocalyptic* and Paul within the context of syncretistic Hellenism,* and by underlining the fragmentary nature of the information contained within the texts.

More recently, W. Bauer posed the question of whether there had ever been a single form of Christianity, an orthodoxy from which other forms diverged, and whether the true picture was not of diverse forms of Christianity from the first, with one faction gradually succeeding in suppressing the others. His thesis focussed on the second century, but had obvious implications for the first century and for the NT documents themselves. These implications have been picked up and pushed further and back into the NT writings particularly by H. Koester, with the claim that gnosticizing* or syncretistic Christianity is as old as Jewish or Pauline Christianity. At the same time the Dead Sea Scrolls* have had a similar effect on the understanding of first-century Judaism. The assumption of an orthodox Judaism (rabbinic Judaism, assumed to be the normative form of Judaism in the period before AD 70) has been increasingly abandoned, and the new realization of the diversity of the Jewish matrix of Christianity has further fed the appreciation of the diversity of both Jewish and Christian scriptures.

Few today would be prepared to argue for a complete centrifugal diversity of the biblical writings, without any centripetal force holding them together. In the case of the OT the most obvious unifying factor is the sense that Israel has been chosen by the one God, with covenant* and law as the clearest expressions of that bond. In the NT it is the faith-conviction that God has brought his revelatory and redemptive purpose to its climax in Jesus, particularly in his death and resurrection. That Jesus fulfils Jewish hope and God's original purpose in choosing Israel is the glue which holds OT and NT together in one Bible. Nor is there much dispute about the fact of diverse genres and contexts in which the common faith came to expression – in different types of writing, in more Hellenized and less Hellenized documents, in Jewish Christian and Gentile Christian forms.

But the issue and dispute about diversity remains. 1. How broad is the unifying strand which unites these writings? For example, with reference to the NT, was there already, virtually from the beginning, a fuller understanding and expression of (apostolic) faith, a *lex orandi* which forms a norm of orthodoxy, so that the diversity becomes relatively less significant? 2. How and at what points did diversity become unacceptable? Is there not running through the biblical writings a clear statement that various kinds of conduct and belief put the participants beyond the pale? 3. To what extent did the different contexts and diverse circumstances in which Jewish praxis and Christian faith came to expression in the biblical documents merely shape a uniform and unchanging core? And to what extent does the diversity enter into the core itself? Is the diversity as fundamental as the unity? However these questions are to be resolved, the important factor which diversity points up is the historical particularity of the experience of God's word. And the fact of such diversity within the one canon provides the dynamic which keeps historic faith and modern meaning in positive and creative interaction. As Paul recognized, 'the body' remains a powerful paradigm of unity sustained in and by diversity.

See also **Cultural Relativism.**

W. Bauer, *Orthodoxy and Heresy in Earliest Christianity*, 1972; J. D. G. Dunn, *Unity and Diversity in the New Testament*, ²1990; J. Goldingay, *Theological Diversity and the Authority of the Old Testament*, 1987; H. Koester, Introduction to the New Testament, Vol. 2, *History and Literature of Early Christianity*, 1982; C. F. D. Moule, *The Birth of the New Testament*, ³1981.

JAMES D. G. DUNN

Dodd, C. H.

Charles Harold Dodd (1884–1973) has been described as 'the greatest and most influential British New Testament scholar of the twentieth century' and as one in whom 'the international world of scholarship recognized ... one of its most creative and influential minds'. It was Dodd who coined the term 'realized eschatology'* and brought into the forefront of all discussion of NT theology the term 'kerygma'.* Both terms have been for over 50 years part of the current coin of NT scholarship.

Dodd's classical training enabled him to bring to the study of the NT a mastery of textual and linguistic detail, seen at its best in his major commentaries on Romans (1932) and the Johannine Epistles (1946) as well as in *The Bible and the Greeks* (1935). His gift of lucid and non-technical exposition, based on profound and authoritative scholarship, is seen at its best in both the first and last of his books: *The Meaning of Paul for Today* (first published in 1920, reissued 1958) and *The Founder of Christianity*, 1970.

In an early book, *The Authority of the Bible*, 1928, Dodd set forth his understanding of the unified witness of the Bible to Christian faith. Later, in *According to the Scriptures*, 1952, he shed new light on the question of the fulfilment of the OT in the NT; discarding the theory of a primitive 'book of testimonies', he argued for the early development of a method of biblical study in which key passages from the Prophets and Psalms were selected, being understood as wholes even when only individual verses or phrases were actually quoted, which came to form 'the substructure of all Christian theology'.

This theory is closely related to Dodd's insistence, first enunciated in *The Apostolic Preaching and its Developments*, 1936, that underlying the NT as a whole there was a proclamation of the gospel, common to all the apostles, which declared that God had fulfilled the promises of the OT in the coming, life, death, resurrection* and ascension of Jesus Christ and the gift of the Holy Spirit, and called upon men and women to respond in repentance and faith to that divine saving action. This understanding of the kerygmatic unity of the NT has proved influential, even though it is generally recognized in the light of subsequent research that Dodd overstressed the unity of the NT documents at the expense of their diversity* of emphasis and sought to delineate too precisely the pattern of the primitive kerygma.

The same tendency to carry too far a brilliantly original thesis is also recognized in the case of the second of the seminal works which Dodd published in the mid-thirties, namely *The Parables of the Kingdom*, 1935. There can be little doubt that he went too far in seeking to force all Jesus' sayings about the kingdom of God* into the mould of 'realized eschatology' and to eliminate the futurist element; indeed Dodd himself in *The Coming of Christ*, 1951, subsequently modified his theory to some extent. Nevertheless, the insistence that the parables* were uttered in an actual situation in the life of Jesus and were concerned with a situation of conflict brought about by his own appearance opened a new era in the study of the parables.

In *Gospel and Law*, 1951, Dodd expounded the relation of the kerygma to the didache, the latter embodying the ethical ideal, both corporate and individual, which is implicit in the former. Another feature of his reconstruction of the kerygma is his belief that it included some reference, however brief, to the historical facts of the life of Jesus. The written Gospels were in fact statements of the kerygma in which this historical element was extended and developed. In a famous article, 'The Framework of the Gospel Narrative', reprinted in *New Testament Studies*, 1953, Dodd even claimed, *contra* K. L. Schmidt and the German Form Critics,* that the primitive church transmitted, along with isolated units of tradition, 'an outline of the Ministry of Jesus, with some regard at least to its topographical and chronological setting', and that this can be discerned in the outline of Mark's Gospel. The same conviction that the Gospels can yield to responsible critical study genuine historical knowledge about Jesus finds expression in *History and the Gospel*, 1938, and also significantly in the portrait of Jesus which was to be Dodd's swan-song and which he dared to entitle *The Founder of Christianity*.

Moreover, in this portrait he made judicious use not only of the Synoptics but also of the Fourth Gospel. The justification for this is found in the second of Dodd's monumental works on John's Gospel, *Historical Tradition in the Fourth Gospel*, 1963, in which he presents an impressive body of evidence for the conclusion that behind the Gospel there 'lies an ancient oral tradition independent of the other Gospels, and meriting serious consideration as a contribution to our knowledge of the historical facts concerning Jesus Christ'. *The Interpretation of the Fourth Gospel*, 1953, had exemplified in their full maturity Dodd's mastery of all aspects of the Judaic* and Hellenistic* backgrounds of NT thought, his magisterial expertise in textual and linguistic studies and his unrivalled gift of lucid exposition. These major works of his later years have led many to the view that, in the words of his obituary in *The Times*, 'Dodd was greatest as a Johannine scholar.' The truth is rather that he was equally at home in every part of the NT – with the exception of the Book of Revelation!

See also **English Interpretation; Historical Jesus; John, Gospel of.**

W. D. Davies and D. Daube (eds), *The Background of the New Testament and its Eschatology*, 1956; F. W. Dillistone, *C. H. Dodd, Interpreter of the New Testament*, 1977; W. E.

Powell (ed.), *C. H. Dodd 1884–1973: The Centenary Lectures*, 1985; J. A. T. Robinson, 'C. H. Dodd' in A. W. Hastings and E. Hastings (eds), *Theologians of Our Time*, 1966, pp. 40–46.

OWEN E. EVANS

Duhm, B.

Bernhard Duhm was born on 10 October 1847 in Bingum, East Friesland, and died in Basel after a traffic accident on 1 September 1928. He studied in Göttingen under Ewald, Lagarde and Ritschl, becoming a Privatdozent there in 1873 and an *ausserordentlicher* Professor in 1877. In 1889 he became Professor at Basel where he succeeded Rudolf Smend and there he remained until his death. When he died the whole town mourned him.

His most important publications were: *Die Theologie der Propheten als Grundlage für die innere Entwicklungsgeschichte der israelitischen Religion* (1875), a work which made the prophets the creative geniuses in the development of ancient Israelite religion rather than the more traditional view which attributed that role to Moses* and the Torah. His later work *Israels Propheten* (1916, [2] 1922) modified that approach by allowing a prior place to Moses and following the, by then, critical orthodoxy approach to the order of things in the Hebrew Bible. His two great and most influential commentaries,* a form he favoured, were *Das Buch Jesaja* (1892, [5] 1968 with a biographical preface by Walter Baumgartner) and *Das Buch Jeremia* (1901). He also published commentaries on Job (1897) and Psalms (1899, [2] 1922). His rectorial speech of 1896 'Die Entstehung des Alten Testaments' (published 1897) gives the flavour of his piety and learning.

Duhm was essentially a one theme man: the prophet* as a religious genius working with genuine visions and ecstasy. The prophets were men 'consecrated to God' (*Gottgeweihte*) who argued against the cultic and magical practices of their own time in favour of what can only be called a form of moral idealism. The ethical idealism of these prophets was their true contribution to the formation of Israelite religion. His discussion of Micah 6.1–8 under the heading 'true worship' (*Theologie*, pp. 183–8), with its focus on 'doing justice' (cf. Amos 3.10), allowed him to see in Micah's teaching a mediation between destruction and hope which for the first time mooted a possibility eventually developed in the Christian doctrine of reconciliation. Thus for Duhm the prophets were essentially theologians and as such had an apologetic* value for his understanding of Christianity. If modern scholarship on the prophets has moved far from this position now, Duhm's stress on morality has been highly influential in the reading of the prophets over the past century.

In three areas Duhm may be said to have set the agenda for twentieth-century biblical studies: 1. the prophets as poets and religious geniuses; 2. Isaiah studies; 3. Jeremiah studies. In very many modern studies of the prophets there has been a tendency to stress their insight into the nature of things and this approach is essentially a reworking of Duhm's emphasis. The prophet as poet provides a way of reading the material text, but as a religious genius the prophet has become for many readers a heroic model of a very protestant figure, true to God and hammering out a (political) theology against fierce opposition from false religious positions. It is part of that religious idealism which Bible readers are always prone to and, though harmless, is so often a misprision of the text.

Duhm's work on Isaiah and Jeremiah set the questions for research this century. His division of Isaiah into three parts remains a fixed point of modern biblical studies, though his emphasis on primary (authentic) and secondary (inauthentic) sources in the prophetic books is rapidly losing its force today. He separated out the so-called 'Servant Songs'* from Isa. 40–55 (42.1–4; 49.1–6; 50.4–9; 52.13–53.12), assigning them to the margins of the scrolls and to spaces between the larger sections (cf. *Jesaja*, [5] 1968, p. 311). Hence the status and meaning of these songs are central concerns of all modern discussions of Isa. 40–55, though there have been recent attempts to bid farewell to this approach to the poems (Mettinger). If scholars would not insist so much on reading Isa. 40–55 as the product of an individual prophet towards the end of the Babylonian exile it might be easier to argue for their integration into those chapters! Duhm's stress on the prophet as poet comes over very strongly in his treatment of Second Isaiah. His division of Jeremiah into the poems of Jeremiah and the rest of the book (its bulk!) as the work of others has been very influential in the modern study of Jeremiah. It remains a good starting point in any discussion of that book. More recent discussions about the nature of biblical poetry and the whole question of the 'historical Jeremiah' have moved the arguments on considerably since Duhm's time. But his commentary remains one of the finest on Jeremiah, full of insight and shrewd observation finely expressed (sadly never translated into English).

Baumgartner describes Duhm as 'a brilliant lone wolf' (*ein genialer Einzelgänger*), combining two of his most striking features – the brilliance of his thought and his tendency to go his own way. Of such is the kingdom of heaven! Also, it may be whispered, of such is the republic of scholarship in whose realms Bernhard Duhm still shines as one of its brightest stars.

See also **German Old Testament Scholarship; Isaiah; Jeremiah; Prophets and Prophecy.**

R. E. Clements, *A Century of Old Testament Study*, revd edn 1983, pp. 61–6; H.-J. Kraus, *Geschichte der historisch-kritischen Erforschung des AT von der Reformation bis zur Gegenwart*, ²1969, pp. 275–83; T. N. D. Mettinger, *A Farewell to the Servant Songs*, 1983.

ROBERT P. CARROLL

Early Catholicism

The concept draws its origins from the tendencies of both Roman Catholic and Protestant scholars to claim the early church, in particular the NT church, for their own denominations. Traditionally, it has been employed by Protestant scholars to point to the transformation of the early church into an institution exhibiting various 'Catholic' characteristics. Such characteristics have often been judged negatively.

There is no agreed definition of Early Catholicism. However, the notion is used to describe a church which exhibits at least some of the following characteristics: 1. hierarchical in contrast to charismatic ministry; 2. clear distinction between sound doctrine and false teaching; 3. stress on ethics; 4. depiction of the church as the instrument of salvation; 5. reference to apostolic succession and transmitted authority; 6. emphasis on sacraments; and, 7. appeal to a tradition bearing a deposit of faith.

Likewise, there is a lack of consensus with respect to which writings might fairly be called Early Catholic. Some scholars reserve the label for writings outside the NT canon,* beginning with the letters of Ignatius of Antioch which reveal a reverence for the monarchical episcopate, or I Clement, with its reference to succession in the ministry. Still others find evidence of Early Catholicism in one or more of the following NT writings of late date: Luke–Acts, I and II Tim., Titus, Eph., Jude and II Peter.

In tracing the history of Early Catholicism as a category of NT interpretation, one may distinguish between evidence of the idea in studies of the early church (using varying terminology) and the actual delineation of the equivalent German term *Frühkatholizismus* which has emerged as the most common description of the phenomenon in the programmatic debates of German scholars. As far back as the last century, evidence of the concept can be found in the work of both F. C. Baur and A. Ritschl. Later, it figured prominently in the debate on church order between R. Sohm and A. von Harnack,* a debate

which plays a central role in R. Bultmann's* discussion of 'The Development Toward the Ancient Church' in his *Theology of the New Testament*.

It appears to have been E. Troeltsch who was responsible for the actual term *Frühkatholizismus* and for the description of its constitutive elements in his classic work of 1911, which later appeared in English as *The Social Teaching of the Christian Churches*. In 1935 the theological implications of the development were discussed by A. Ehrhard in his *Urkirche und Frühkatholizismus*. In the last half of this century the significance of *Frühkatholizismus* has been of interest to such NT scholars as P. Vielhauer, W. Marxsen and especially E. Käsemann.

In an effort to provide an explanation for the development of Early Catholicism, Käsemann points to the disappearance of imminent expectation combined with the threat of gnostic* 'enthusiasm'. While understanding the development as based on historical necessity, Käsemann acknowledges his regret that the church did not remain true to Paul's conception of the nature of the church and let justification by faith give way to ethics as a dominant concern. What he finds especially objectionable is the use of the fiction of authority transmitted from the apostles: Paul, whose ideas on ministry would undoubtedly be in opposition to those found in Early Catholicism, is made to establish the new orders himself (e.g. Acts 14.23; Titus 1.5). He is made to convey a principle of tradition and legitimacy which effectively binds the Spirit to office and absolutizes the church.

The spirited reaction to Käsemann's work (especially from Roman Catholic scholars) includes acknowledgment of the valuable insight gained into the diversity,* even divergence, among the documents of the NT canon. Of equal significance has been the analysis of the relationship between the writings that bear traces of Early Catholicism and the changing historical situations of the period from the end of the first century to the middle of the second century. Reluctance has been expressed, however, to understand these writings as representative of a single movement when none of them reveals the totality of characteristics which were part of the 'Great Church' of the latter half of the second century. It is argued that it might be best to understand the documents as disclosing varying, but converging, Early Catholic solutions to crises in community life. These solutions were amplified and adopted by the later church.

Critics have also noted a tendency among those who discuss the development of Early Catholicism to exaggerate the distance between the earliest church and emerging Catholicism. This might be related to the fact that even such diverse commentators on the phenomenon as Bultmann, Conzelmann, and Käsemann are shaped by the perspective of dialectical theology which insists that history does not necessarily mean progress. For Käsemann, who explicitly states that the core of the Christian faith is expressed in Paul's teaching, the Early Catholic stage of history cannot be given absolute validity. Established offices appear as the corruption of an earlier time when charisma formed the basis of all ministry. Recently, however, scholars relying on insights from the social sciences* for their historical research have claimed that leadership in Paul's churches is not a purely charismatic phenomenon, but involves a complexity of social factors and is far from excluding the element of personal authority. In addition, the development of the early church has been analysed under the guidance of such sociological concepts as 'institutionalization' and the 'routinization of charisma' which assist in providing a vision of the relationship between stages of history.

Perhaps to avoid the hazards of denominational bias in N T interpretation, there has been an effort in recent decades to consider the Early Catholic writings more on their own terms, rather than always by way of comparison with a more favourable earlier period. No longer content with broad explanations for the phenomenon, scholars are calling for a thorough consideration of the complexity of problems facing individual communities, including the death of the earliest authorities, growth, and increased tensions with the outside world. Yet, earlier discussions of *Frühkatholizismus*, especially by E. Käsemann, continue to challenge scholars to reflect upon the theological and historical questions raised by evidence in the N T of a transformation of church communities that followed the disappearance of the apostles.

See also **Acts of the Apostles; Apostolic Fathers; Paul.**

D. J. Harrington, 'E. Käsemann on the Church in the New Testament', *Heythrop Journal 12*, 1971, pp. 246–57, 365–76; id., 'The "Early Catholic" Writings of the New Testament: The Church Adjusting to World-History', *The Word in the World* ed. R. J. Clifford and G. W. MacRae, 1973; B. Holmberg, *Paul and Power*, 1978; E. Käsemann, *Essays on New Testament Themes*, 1964; id., *New Testament Questions of Today*, 1969; W. Marxsen, *Der 'Frühkatholizismus' im Neuen Testament*, 1958; K. H. Neufeld, '"Frükatholizismus" – Idee und Begriff', *Zeitschrift für Katholische Theologie* 94, 1972, pp. 1–28.

MARGARET Y. MACDONALD

Ecclesiastes

The evaluation of this book has been a matter of controversy from the very first. According to the Mishnah* it was very highly esteemed by some early Jewish authorities (including Rabbi Aqiba) but regarded by others with suspicion. It was eventually admitted into the canon* (according to tradition, at the Council of Jamnia, *c.* AD 90), probably because its author, 'Qoheleth', was believed, on the basis of the statement in 1.1 that he was 'the son of David, king in Jerusalem', to be none other than Solomon; nevertheless, doubts about its merit continued to be voiced by some rabbinical writers on various grounds, notably that it abounds in inconsistencies and that it contains passages contrary to Jewish orthodox beliefs. These criticisms have been repeated frequently during the course of the history of its interpretation.

But once the canonical status of the book had come to be generally accepted, Jewish and Christian interpreters alike attempted by various means to make it appear both consistent and orthodox. Christian exegetes such as Jerome, for example, interpreted its frequent reflections on the futility of human existence as intended to persuade the reader to reject the vanities of this world and embrace the monastic life.

The view that Ecclesiastes was not written by Solomon but comes from a much later stage in the development of Jewish thought was first put forward by Martin Luther,* who attributed it to Ben Sirach. Subsequently a similar conclusion was reached on linguistic grounds: Grotius (1644) pointed out that its language marks it out as one of the latest of the OT books. This argument is now universally accepted. During the last hundred years a consensus of opinion has emerged which places the book in the Hellenistic* period, but before the Maccabaean Revolt. This consensus has put its interpretation on an entirely new basis: it is now clear that Qoheleth's teaching must be interpreted in the light of the intellectual equipment which, as a learned Jew of the Hellenistic period, he may be presumed to have possessed. This equipment was two-fold: it comprised, on the one hand, familiarity with the entire Jewish religious tradition as enshrined in the OT in virtually its final form, and, on the other, at least a partial acquaintance with Greek thought and culture. The question of the extent to which his teaching was influenced – whether positively or negatively – by each of these two intellectual traditions now became one of great importance for the understanding of his thought.

Most recent scholars maintain that there is

no evidence of a direct dependence on Greek philosophy, and that the most which can be affirmed is that Qoheleth's thoughts sometimes run parallel with those of Greek writers, a circumstance which is hardly surprising when the general intellectual atmosphere of the age in which he lived is taken into account. That his distinctive methods of argument, unique in the Old Testament, and his questioning of traditional beliefs owe something to the spirit of the times is not disputed; but it is now more and more emphasized that he was principally an interpreter – though an extremely radical one – of the biblical tradition, especially but not exclusively of that part of it which is represented by the so-called 'wisdom literature'.* It has also been maintained that he was familiar, no doubt indirectly, with the more extensive wisdom literature of the Ancient Near East.

Evidence of Greek influence on Qoheleth was also adduced on the grounds that the extremely unusual, and in some ways unique, Hebrew in which the book is written is partly accounted for by his acquaintance with the Greek language. Recent investigation has, however, proved conclusively that although the influence of other Semitic languages – certainly Aramaic and possibly Phoenician – can be detected in Qoheleth's use of Hebrew, no Graecisms are to be found in the book, and that there is in fact no evidence at all that he was familiar with Greek.

That there are inconsistencies of thought in the book is undoubtedly the case, though recent study of Qoheleth's methods of argument has shown that there are fewer of these than had previously been supposed: it now appears that he sometimes quoted an opinion contrary to his own and then proceeded to argue against it, a fact not recognized by earlier interpreters since these quotations of his opponents' views are not specifically indicated in the text.

Other contradictions, however, cannot be explained in this way. Some commentators, notably C. Siegfried (1898), accounted for them by postulating a series of editors who attempted to render the book more orthodox by 'correcting' it with substantial additions of their own. It is now recognized that such a procedure, carried out on the massive scale which such a theory would entail, would have been pointless and self-defeating. Although it is possible that 'orthodox' glosses may have been added to the text here and there, it is now generally recognized that whatever genuine inconsistencies of thought there may be in the book – some of these may be deliberate paradoxes on the author's part – are inconsistencies which were present in the mind of the sole author, Qoheleth himself. This

view becomes the more probable if, as many modern interpreters believe, the book is not a unitary treatise but a collection of separate *pensées* or notes made by him at different times, perhaps in connection with his public lectures (cf. 12.9), and assembled by an editor or editors who deliberately refrained from modifying the material in order to impose upon it an artificial unity.

Various attempts have been made to discover in the book a coherent philosophy or system of thought; but these have been frustrated by its literary disjointedness, which makes it difficult to discover where the main emphases lie. Is Qoheleth best described as a pessimist, a realist, or even, in spite of appearances, an optimist? Did he totally reject the conventional belief that righteousness leads to happiness and wickedness to disaster, or did he merely wish to point out that there are exceptions to the rule? Did he regard God as a remote deity unconcerned with human affairs, or as the beneficent giver of all good gifts? On these and other fundamental questions the book is susceptible of quite different interpretations, and there is at the present time no consensus of opinion about its basic message. It remains, as it has always been, an enigma which continues to fascinate its would-be interpreters.

J. L. Crenshaw, *Ecclesiastes. A Commentary*, 1987; R. Gordis, *Koheleth – The Man and His World*, 1968; M. Hengel, *Judaism and Hellenism*, 1974; G. von Rad, *Wisdom in Israel*, 1972; R. N. Whybray, *Ecclesiastes*, 1989.

R. N. WHYBRAY

Egypt

Ironically, although Ancient Egypt of all the great powers of the day was Israel's closest neighbour, its influence on the Hebrew community was minimal. Israel was part and parcel of the Western Semitic speaking world, and its roots are buried deep in the coast and hinterlands of the Levant. Ugarit,* Mari, even Boghaz-Keui, offer much more profitable fields of research than Memphis. Not surprisingly, therefore, although Egyptology since the Second World War has experienced significant advances, little of this has had any profound bearing on biblical studies.

In the field of language, the forty-five years since the end of the Second World War have been dominated in Egyptology by much landmark work. Of prime importance are the linguistic studies of H. J. Polotsky, which set in motion much scholarly endeavour directed mainly towards polishing and refining the master's basic ideas. While this made next to no impact on biblical studies, of more relevance are the advances in orthography and lexicography. In particular, refinement in the understanding of syllabic orthography and detailed study of Canaanite loanwords in Late Egyptian have contributed greatly to Western Semitic toponymy and Hebrew lexicography.

On the other hand, claims have been made for the dependence of the technical vocabulary of Hebrew on Egyptian which do not uniformly inspire confidence. Formerly A. S. Yahuda and at present M. Gorg have sought to find Egyptian *Vorlagen* for many Hebrew words within the spheres of architecture and the cult, but, while some derivations may well be correct, a significant number strike one as highly ingenious.

Egyptian archaeology* has had a far greater impact on biblical studies. Although modern scientific method in excavation came late to Egypt, the resumption of work after the Second World War produced results which were of considerable importance to biblical scholarship. Montet's work at Tanis seeded debate, albeit wrong-headed at the time, over the location of Pi-Ramesses, regarded as one of the 'store cities' of Ex. 1.11, and, indirectly, the nature, period and duration of the Israelite sojourn (Van Seters, 1966). Bietak's excavations at Tell ed-Dab'a, begun in the mid-1960s, and continued after the interruption of the Egypto-Israeli War, cast a flood of light on the Hyksos occupation, as did Holladay's work at Tell el-Maskhuta. Of particular importance is Oren's survey of the north Sinai route between the Delta and Gaza. Here almost all periods of occupation were represented by some site or other, and the distribution and nature of the New Kingdom fortresses was most instructive. In fact, prolonged investigation, in the main by Israeli archaeologists, has shed a flood of light on the reciprocal impact of Palestine and Egypt during the empire period of the Late Bronze Age.

Egyptological research bearing particularly on history and archaeology has impinged on OT historical studies in two areas: the period of the exodus* and conquest, and the united monarchy. With respect to the former, the end of an era in research methods and foci may be discerned falling at about the middle of the present century. This era had been characterized by a somewhat naive acceptance of sources at face-value coupled with a failure to assess the evidence as to its origin and reliability. The result was the reduction of all data to a common level, any or all being grist for a wide variety of mills. Scholars expended substantial effort on questions which they had neglected to prove were valid questions at all: under what dynasty did Joseph rise to power in Egypt? Who was the Pharaoh of the Oppression? The Pharaoh of the Exodus? Can we identify the princess who drew Moses* out

of the river? Where did the Israelites make their exit from Egypt, via the Wadi Tumilat, or a more northerly point? One can appreciate the pointlessness of such questions if one poses similar queries with respect to Egyptian 'leper' stories of the fourth to first centuries: under which Pharaoh in fact did the Jews (*sic*) contract leprosy, King Hor (Manetho), or Bocchoris (Lysimachus)? How many lepers were there, two hundred and fifty thousand (Chaeremon) or one hundred thousand (Apion)? In which quarry did Osariph organize them? And so on. The prior necessity of evaluating sources had not been met.

Perhaps it was the plethora of theories on the exodus, none convincing, but each capable of being defended to some degree, that pointed up the futility of this approach. Beginning in the 1950s, further attempts to solve this problem along traditional lines are conspicuous by their absence, as scholars tried different tacks.

There was a tendency to sidestep the conundrum of the exodus, and concentrate more on the conquest and settlement. But here the embarrassment to the traditional conservative position was acute. As more and more sites named in the Conquest narrative as having been sacked by the invading Israelites yielded to archaeological investigation, it became apparent that few of them had been in existence in the Late Bronze Age. The list includes Kadesh-barnea, Hormah, Hesban, Jericho, Ai, and Gibeon, none of them showing occupation before the Iron Age, and certainly uninhabited in the fourteenth and thirteenth centuries. A literal reading of the Joshua conquest seemed ill-advised. A reappraisal of the Egyptian empire in Western Asia led increasingly to socio-economic models to explain the phenomenon called the 'Conquest'. In one view the appearance of early Israel in Canaan constituted a social revolution in which large segments of the peasantry and the lower classes withdrew from the formal system of Canaanite city-states. It was a 'peasants' revolt', not an invasion of Palestine from without. A good deal of inspiration was derived from the phenomenon of the *'Apiru*, a class of landless renegades found everywhere in the Middle East during the Second Millennium, who had fled urban society and existed on their wits and their banditry along the fringes of the settled communities (Loretz, 1989). If an exodus had to be brought into the picture, it was as a catalyst and the numbers were passed off as small (ibid., pp. 107–8).

The *'Apiru* in Palestine during the Late Bronze Age are simply organized bandits, in actual fact a tiny fraction of the overall population, according to the Amenhotep II list of prisoners of war. They function most effectively in precisely those regions (e.g. Canaan, Phoenicia) where the Egyptian conquests had terminated the native 'Great Kingships' and *ipso facto* effective policing power. All that was left were the village headmen who of themselves had no power to provide protection against robbers. These headmen, the *hazanuti* or mayors, were lackeys of Egypt milked by the imperial authority, and at odds with the populace; and it is a wild exaggeration to term these poor farmers 'an agrarian elite'.

The 'Peasants' Revolt' theory minimizes or ignores the role of ingressing elements (nomads or semi-nomads) in the demography of Palestine in the Late Bronze II period; yet such there certainly were. Over sixty years ago the perspicacious work of Alt apprised our forebears in the discipline of the possibility that the 'conquest' consisted initially of an infiltration of nomadic clans in search of summer pasturage. The later studies of Helck and especially Giveon collected material and focussed attention on the phenomenon of the transhumants (Egyptian *s3sw* from a root *s3s* meaning 'to wander') within ancient Canaan.

Study of toponym lists from the reign of Amenhotep III showed a concentration of the Shasu tribes between the Beqa'a and the Wady Hasa; and the appellative of one of the tribes, viz. the tetragrammaton,* excited some at least of the scholarly investigators into drawing the correct conclusions (Astour, 1979).

If, thanks to a balanced view of the evidence, the *s3sw* appear a much more fruitful field for scholarly cultivation in the search for the components and mechanisms of the conquest, what becomes of the exodus? Thankfully, of late, it has receded to its appropriate position in the study of OT themes, viz. a tangential but powerful adjunct to the historical mainstream.

Continued research and excavation have, in the past two decades, conspired to point to a seventh-to-sixth century BC date as the time of origin for most of the background detail in the exodus narrative. This is true especially of the topographical information regarding Goshen and the route of the exodus. While the excavations of Bietak at Tell ed-Dab'a have given the lie to the old identification of Sa'n el-Hagar (Tanis) with Pi-Ramesses, there are no sure examples of the writing of the latter with the elision of Pi- (Redford, 1987, pp. 138–9); and the likelihood is that the name in its occurrence in the Joseph and exodus stories (Gen. 47.11; Ex. 1.11; 12.37) owes more to the later, legendary renown of the nineteenth-century king than to a contemporary place name. Excavations at Tel el-Maskhuta, convincingly identified with Pithom, renewed in 1976, have proved that (apart from a Hyksos settlement) the site was occupied only

from *c.* 600 BC onwards. Migdol (Ex. 14.2) is certainly the place of the same name known from the sixth century as a border fortification where Judaean mercenaries were installed (Jer. 44), and which has now been convincingly identified with a Saite site on the eastern Delta. Ba'al Zaphon, modern Ras Kasrun, is no older than the Saite period (Redford, 1987, p. 144), while Etham and Pi-hahirot find acceptable *Vorlagen* in Saite and Ptolemaic texts (ibid., p. 142). Goshen itself continues to defy interpretation, although one can now point to the presence of Qedarite elements in the West Delta in Persian times and to the currency of the dynastic PN *Gashmu* (ibid., p. 140).

Elsewhere in the exodus narrative 'Egyptian colouring' has been difficult to elicit and never free from controversy. The birth-narrative of Moses owes more to West Asian forms than to Egyptian (Redford, 1967); and the plagues are arguably too general in their form and geographical appropriateness to be confined to a Nilotic locale. Smearing blood on the doorposts has been viewed in the light of ancient Egyptians' use of the colour red for apotropaic purposes, but this too fails to convince. Nonetheless, it has been maintained that the slaying of the eldest son has strong parallels in Egyptian mythology, and that *Pesah* derives from Egyptian *p3sh* 'the sacrifice'. Similarly, it can be shown that the phenomenon of moving back the waters so that the dry bottom appears derives from a folkloristic motif represented in Egyptian literature of the Middle Kingdom and Ptolemaic times. The 'magicians' (Ex. 7.11,22; 8.7,18,19) have good Egyptian credentials, although the form of the name and their 'tale-role' approximate forms common in Demotic and late literature.

From Egypt itself, of course, no evidence is forthcoming. The total silence of New Kingdom sources on anything like the biblical event must be taken into account and accommodated; and to pass the whole off as the escape of some inconsequential pastoral clan from the eastern Delta is to trivialize the tradition. The exodus narrative is an interloper in the account of Israel's history:* the origin stories of the individual communities which went into the make-up of 'Israel' in the guise of tribes, know nothing of it. The Judaean traditions make Judah settle down in the territory to which eponymously he lent his name (Gen. 38); Manasseh is half-Aramaean (I Chron. 7.14); Ephraim the eponym of the tribe is settled already in the Shephelah and lives out his life there (I Chron. 7.21–22), not born and living out his life in Egypt (Gen. 38); the sons of Gad are found in Bashan, not Egypt (I Chron. 7.21–22). Nowhere in the great corpus of genealogical* information in the Chronicles is the exodus to be found.

The evidence does not give much solace to those holding a traditional view that the exodus narrative reached its present form in stages, passing through accretional steps of redaction and embellishment. The language often puts one in mind of a noisome botanical growth. Some literature does originate in this curious manner, but in the present piece (as we have it) there is only one major element which predates the seventh to sixth centuries. That is the basic theme that 'Israel' had at one time descended to Egypt, had suffered bondage there, and had eventually been expelled with signs and wonders! The narrative as a whole dates from late in Israel's history, when Saite redevelopment of the eastern Delta provided the only details the author, lacking any traditions of substance from an earlier age, had to draw on. If one must pinpoint an historical event underlying the exodus, the Hyksos expulsion presents itself as the most likely; and this view has long had a currency among Egyptologists (Gardiner, 1922; Redford, 1987).

The futility of attempting to construe the exodus and Sinai material as reasoned history has led numerous scholars nowadays to stress the mythological* themes which inform the traditions, and to deny historiographical intent (cf. Ahlstrom, 1986). The sporadic attempts still being made to read exodus as history are highly ingenious and unconvincing.

The second period expected to be illuminated by Egyptian evidence is the United Monarchy, but here so little corroborative material is forthcoming that biblical scholars seem almost to be straining at gnats. Their treatment of the age of Saul, David and Solomon degenerates into little more than a paraphrase of the biblical text, interlarded with arcane interpretations and often written with rhetorical flourish.

But while Egyptology can say little about the history of the United Kingdoms, a case has been made for the impact of Egyptian wisdom, at this time, on Israel (cf. Williams, 1981). In fact, studies in Egyptian wisdom literature* have proved the most promising source for comparative material for the biblical scholar. The need in a new monarchic state, with pretensions to sophistication, for scribal* training and 'belles lettres' has often been invoked to sustain the assumption that the age of Solomon constituted the 'Hebrew Enlightenment'. That biblical literature does owe something to Egypt – cf. Pss. 1, 104, Prov. 26, Song of Songs, etc. – is long since proved; but the argument that it is linked with Solomon's reign is wholly *a priori*. These examples of direct dependence could as easily reflect the susceptibility of all of Canaan to cultural influ-ence from Egypt over much longer periods of time.

See also **Ancient Near Eastern World; Exodus.**

G. W. Ahlström, *Who were the Israelites?*, 1986; A. Alt, 'The Settlement of the Israelites in Palestine' in *Essays in Old Testament History and Religion*, 1966, pp. 133–69; M. C. Astour, 'Yahweh in Egyptian Topographic Lists' in *Festschrift Elmar Edel*, 1979, pp. 17–34; A. H. Gardiner, 'The Geography of the Exodus', *Recueil Champollion*, 1922, pp. 203–15; O. Loretz, *Habiru/Hebräer*, 1989; D. B. Redford, 'The Literary Motif of the Exposed Child', *Numen* 14, 1967, pp. 209–28; id., 'An Egyptological Perspective on the Exodus Narrative' in *Egypt, Israel, Sinai*, 1987, pp. 137–62; id., *Egypt and the Holy Land in Antiquity*, forthcoming; J. van Seters, *The Hyksos: a New Investigation*, 1966; R. J. Williams, 'The Sages of Ancient Egypt in the Light of Recent Scholarship', *JAOS* 101, 1981, pp. 1–19.

D. B. REDFORD

Eisegesis

A modern coinage, by analogy with exegesis,* to denote the practice of reading one's own ideas into (Greek *eis*) rather than out of (Greek *ex*) the text of scripture. The earliest instance of the word recorded in the *OED* Supplement, from P. Schaff, *Through Bible Lands*, 1878, illustrates the meaning perfectly when it refers to 'the eisegetical manner of those allegorical and typological exegetes who make the scriptures responsible for their own pious thoughts and fancies'. The term is thus commonly used to refer to the practice of 'pre-critical' commentators on the Bible, who were anxious to find the doctrinal system to which they already adhered propounded in scripture, and who therefore resorted to various devices such as allegory,* typology,* or other kinds of strained exegesis in order to show that scripture supported their position. As Benjamin Jowett put it in his famous essay 'On the Interpretation of Scripture' (*Essays and Reviews*,* 1860, p. 368), for such interpreters scripture becomes 'the weathercock on the church tower, which is turned hither and thither by every wind of doctrine'.

To say that in pre-critical times interpreters practised eisegesis is not necessarily to accuse them of bad faith; they may have genuinely believed that the text meant what they proposed, but with hindsight we can see that what they regarded as exegesis was in fact eisegesis. But in modern theological controversy the charge of eisegesis is usually taken (and often meant) as an accusation of intellectual dishonesty. The interpreter, it is implied, knows full well that the text does not really mean what he claims.

More radical modern biblical critics, however, have sometimes suggested that there is in reality no exegesis that is not eisegesis, for interpreters can only find in texts what they are looking for. The question of 'objectivity' in interpretation has been a major area of debate in hermeneutics,* some scholars insisting that a text has a fixed and inherent meaning which it is the task of the exegete to identify, others retorting that texts have no determinate meaning independent of the stance of the interpreter. Clearly for this second group the very term eisegesis betrays a mistaken understanding of how interpretation should operate. Perhaps for this reason, it has never become a term deliberately adopted by any school of interpretation as a description of its own work, but has remained (like fundamentalism*) a word used almost exclusively by those hostile to the approach it identifies.

Quite apart from these debates about the nature of interpretation, it may be doubted whether eisegesis is a good or helpful coinage. It evidently rests on an etymological explanation of its twin, exegesis, as implying that interpretation consists of drawing out (ex + hēgesthai) the meaning from a text. This explanation of the term exegesis, however, is false: the object of the verb exēgesthai is originally not the text, but the reader for whose benefit interpretation is being carried out. The exegete is (from an etymological point of view) one who leads the reader out (like a guide introducing a tourist to the beauties of a landscape), and explains the text to him. In classical Greek an exēgētēs was either an interpreter of oracles, or a person who showed visitors round a holy place and explained the significance of its rites to them. The term exegesis is thus originally neutral as to different interpretative theories and procedures: it is not tied to the theory that interpreters have the task of drawing meaning 'out of' a text. The idea that meaning is a separable entity which can be extracted from a text is probably too crude a notion of the interpretative act in any case, and it is a pity that students of the Bible have come to think that the term exegesis commits them to such an idea. It is possible to believe that texts have an objective or determinate meaning without seeing exegesis as a kind of juice-extraction process; and accordingly it is possible to disapprove of the phenomenon usually called eisegesis without thinking this term the best device for signalling one's disapproval.

JOHN BARTON

English Interpretation

The radical origins of English interpretation can be found in Thomas Hobbes' discussion of biblical authority in *The Leviathan* (1651) and his conjecture that Moses* was not the author of the entire Pentateuch,* while Judges, I and II Samuel and I and II Kings were written after the captivity in Babylon. Hobbes also pointed out the historical gap between the NT books and their adoption into the canon. John Locke in *The Reasonableness of Christianity* (1695) held that the obvious sense of scripture was the true one and the 'plain and direct' meaning of words and phrases, rather than abstruse principles, should be sought; revelation should conform to the light of reason. Deists* like Collins, Toland and Woolston took up these ideas and maintained that much of the OT was allegorical,* NT miracles* were often spurious, and (Toland) there should be no 'different rule to be followed in the interpretation of scripture from what is common to all other books'.

The hostile reaction to these thinkers underlay the conservative nature of English interpretation for the next century. An exception to this was Robert Lowth's *De Sacra Poesi Hebraeorum* (1758) which treated the psalms and other OT literature as poetry;* his new translation of Isaiah followed in 1778. Herbert Marsh produced some pioneering work on the origins and composition of the Gospels, as an English response to Griesbach and Michaelis, and he translated the latter's introduction to the NT of 1750. His own lectures on the *Criticism and Interpretation of the Bible* (1809) held that scripture 'must be examined by the same laws of criticism which are applied to other writings of antiquity'.

A different approach is evident in E. B. Pusey's *Lectures on Types and Prophecies of the Old Testament*, delivered in 1836. The Tractarians' 'Romanticism', their sense of history and interest in symbolism provided a new impetus in theology, and Pusey was critical of 'orthodoxy' with its crude understanding of prophecy as merely predictive of single events. He saw a better model in patristic* exegesis which realized the typological* character of the whole OT and the organic and inter-related nature of Christian belief. These suggestive ideas were also found in Isaac Williams' *Devotional Commentaries on the Gospel Narrative* (1842–9). However, Pusey's lectures remained unpublished, and he himself became a symbol of reaction, as his commentary on Daniel (1864) demonstrated. H. L. Mansel's important defence of traditionalism, *The Limits of Religious Thought* (1858), grounded the theory of regulative truth, in a highly conservative view of the Bible.

The Broad Church challenge to orthodoxy was announced in *Essays and Reviews** in 1860, particularly in Jowett's essay on the interpretation of scripture. H. B. Wilson, editor of the book, accepted F. C. Baur's late second-century date for the Fourth Gospel and other positions of the Tübingen school.* By 1867 Wilson was also advocating Holtzmann's theory of the priority of Mark and the 'two document' hypothesis (*see* **Synoptic Problem**). At Cambridge the partnership of Westcott,* Lightfoot and Hort followed a more mediating line, in the footsteps of S. T. Coleridge* and F. D. Maurice. Coleridge saw in Idealist theology an answer to the rationalism of Locke and the English empiricists, which had influenced the belief of Paley and others that Christianity must be 'proved' and that an essentially external defence of faith, focussed on the Gospel miracles, was the ideal. Such 'evidential Christianity' was outdated, he argued, and an altogether more interior view of scripture was necessary. Coleridge's own special distinction between the (interior) 'reason' and the (external) 'understanding' can be seen in Thomas Arnold's statement that the 'understanding has its proper work to do with respect to the Bible, because the Bible consists of human writings and contains a human history'. This history was an educative process, and thus Arnold gave a positive place to the OT revelation; cf. his essay *On the Right Interpretation and Understanding of the Scriptures* (1832).

For Maurice revelation was organic and progressive; the Bible contained specific examples of God's work in all human history, it was a 'lesson book', and its real inspiration lay in this and not in some miraculous inerrancy of the sacred writers. Maurice's Johannine and Platonic cast of mind, his strong social interests, and his emphasis on the subjective as well as objective aspect of revelation, were reflected in the exegesis of the Cambridge school, while the textual scholarship of Westcott and Hort was confirmed in their edition of the Greek NT in 1881 which became the basis of many commentaries from then on.

English writers were slow at first to engage in the 'quest for the historical Jesus', though translations of Strauss'* *Das Leben Jesu* (1835) and Renan's *La Vie de Jésus* (1863) were quickly available. J. R. Seeley's *Ecce Homo* was published in 1865 and R. D. Hanson's *Jesus of History* in 1869, but the more orthodox *Life of Christ* by F. W. Farrar (1874) was the most popular, appearing in many languages and editions and uniting Renan's psychological and imaginative insights with an acceptance of the miraculous and supernatural elements. Farrar's greatest service to liberal scholarship was his weighty *History of Interpretation*, published in 1886. The decade between 1880 and 1890 saw a great advance in biblical studies, and Farrar's

book was the historical defence for it. Patristic mediaeval,* and even Reformation,* exegesis, he claimed, had intervened between the reader and scripture, but true interpretation could only be based on the 'literal,* grammatical, historical and contextual' sense. The interpreter must establish a sympathetic attraction between writer and reader which would bridge the passage of the centuries. Farrar also contended that modern critical interests could be combined with a reverential approach to scripture; and this became the hallmark of much British theology for the next fifty years. Thus, S. R. Driver, Pusey's successor as Regius Professor of Hebrew, was able to reverse the conservative bias of OT teaching at Oxford, and advocate the Graf-Wellhausen theory, while retaining the confidence of the religious establishment.

A Scottish parallel can be found in the influential books of William Robertson Smith,* *The Old Testament in the Jewish Church* (1881) and *The Prophets of Israel* (1882), which were written from the same standpoint, visualizing the OT as a history of grace and the prophets as witnesses to God's justice and mercy in the development of the people of Israel, rather than as teachers of propositional doctrines. A wider perception of 'salvation history' was also marked in the *Theology of the Old Testament* by A. B. Davidson (1904) which stressed the importance of OT religion in its own right, and not merely as a 'designed shadow or adumbration of the new dispensation'. *Lux Mundi,* * in 1889, brought the High Church party into line with these new 'positive' liberal trends. This was also the period of new translations* (e.g. the RV in 1884), more adequate lexicons* and concordances, and new periodicals like *The Expository Times* (1889) (*see* **Hastings, J.**). The *International Critical Commentary* was launched in 1895 with Driver's study of Deuteronomy.

A generation later the work of B. H. Streeter led the field in source criticism* of the NT. His *Studies in the Synoptic Problem* appeared in 1911, and his major volume, *The Four Gospels* (1924), set the seal on the previous ninety years' research on the synoptic question since Lachmann. Besides elaborating the 'four-document' hypothesis, Streeter postulated the existence of 'Proto-Luke', and he also sought an early Caesarean text of the Gospels. E. C. Hoskyns'* interpretation of Gospel origins showed the influence of Weiss and Schweitzer* and their portrayal of the enigmatic figure of the eschatological Jesus. *The Riddle of the New Testament* (1931), which he wrote in collaboration with F. N. Davey, was also much indebted to the 'biblical theology'* method of Kittel's *Theologisches*

Wörterbuch. The post-liberal mood of these years ensured a wide and continuing readership for the *Riddle*, both at home and abroad. Hoskyns translated the second edition of Barth's* commentary on Romans in 1933, and his posthumous commentary on the Fourth Gospel appeared in 1940. The partnership of Kirsopp Lake and F. J. Foakes-Jackson, in *The Beginnings of Christianity, The Acts of the Apostles* (1920–33), should also be noticed.

Form criticism* made an early appearance in J. M. Creed's commentary on Luke in 1930, but its more pronounced use was in R. H. Lightfoot's* *History and Interpretation in the Gospels*, in 1935, in which he followed Dibelius' rather than Bultmann's classifications. His *Locality and Doctrine in the Gospels* (1938), owing much to the German E. Lohmeyer,* was a further development in tracing the theological motivations which shaped the evangelists' material and what Mark's 'geography', in particular, implied. The more cautious British reponse to *Formgeschichte* was exemplified in Vincent Taylor's *The Formation of the Gospel Tradition* in 1933; it was, he said, 'a tool with limited powers!' Taylor's impressive commentary on Mark appeared in 1952. This rejected the 'Ur-Markus' theory and analysed the material according to Taylor's own form-critical classification, that of pronouncement stories, miracle stories, stories about Jesus, Marcan constructions, summary statements, and sayings and parables. Another scholar who began his career in the inter-war years was T. W. Manson who, in books like *The Teaching of Jesus* (1931), proposed what was held to be a distinctively 'British' interpretation of the suffering Son of Man,* that Jesus' understanding of the title was corporate, was derived from Dan. 7 and was embodied in his own person as he went to the cross. Most important of all was C. H. Dodd,* whose 25 books spanned half a century. Dodd gave a new direction to NT studies with his *The Apostolic Preaching and Its Developments* (1936), while his *Parables of the Kingdom* (1935) initiated a lively debate both here and on the continent.

Post-war British scholarship in the person of Alan Richardson continued to affirm biblical theology, as can be seen in the *Theological Wordbook of the Bible* (1950), which he edited, and his *Introduction to the Theology of the New Testament*, published in 1958. Richardson, along with other British writers, was critical of the extremes of Bultmann's* 'demythologizing'* theories, and the full impact of this movement was not felt until later. G. D. Kilpatrick's *The Origins of the Gospel According to St Matthew* (1946) was a fresh approach in which the evangelist's liturgical and community setting (the Gospel as a revision of an early Christian lectionary) was elucidated. Another new and individual voice was that of Austin Farrer who, in *A Study in St Mark* (1951) and *St Matthew and St Mark* (1954), explored the themes which gave a literary unity to the gospels and which, he believed, made the supposition of a 'Q' source unnecessary. Farrer's work was in one sense a delayed response to Lightfoot, and its object was to 'follow out the symbolical and interpretative element in the Gospel to its furthest point'. He rejected the idea of Mark as a compiler but saw the Gospel as a living whole built round a skeleton of numerical symbolism associated with the healings of Jesus. Matthew expanded the Marcan symbolical pattern, as did Luke. No historical facts were, however, falsified in this literary activity.

A British contribution to Qumran studies was H. H. Rowley's *The Zadokite Fragments and the Dead Sea Scrolls* (1952), one of more than 20 books which Rowley wrote on the OT and related subjects, beginning with his *The Aramaic of the Old Testament* in 1929 and important studies on the book of Daniel in 1935. Rowley's range of international contacts, his eleven years' editorship of the Society for OT Study Book List, and his initiation of the *Journal of Semitic Studies* in 1956, helped to enlarge the horizons of OT scholarship in this country.

Catholic biblical research in Britain, evidenced in earlier works like B. C. Butler's *The Originality of St Matthew* (1951), took advantage of the new climate following the Second Vatican Council, and such studies as W. J. Harrington's *The Path of Biblical Theology* (1973) and John McHugh's *The Mother of Jesus in the New Testament* (1975) were the result. The Jerusalem Bible appeared in 1966 and quickly established itself as an impressive translation into the vernacular. It was followed in 1985 by a thoroughly revised version, The New Jerusalem Bible.

Recent developments in biblical studies, such as the post-Bultmannian 'new quest', redaction criticism,* new theories of hermeneutics,* and structuralist* interpretation of biblical myth,* have engaged British scholars. Many of the assumptions of a generation ago, concerning the 'Word Book' approach to the Bible, the theological interpretation of the OT, and the continuity between the cultural outlook of biblical society and our own, are in a state of flux: the books of James Barr (*The Semantics of Biblical Language*, 1961, *Old and New in Interpretation*, 1966, and *The Bible in the Modern World*, 1973), D. E. Nineham (*The Use and Abuse of the Bible*, 1976), and R. E. Clements (*Old Testament Theology. A Fresh Approach*, 1978) are instances of this tendency. Long-held critical positions have also been put aside in J. A. T. Robinson's *Redating the New Testament* (1976), placing the Gospels and other writings before AD 70, and *The Priority of John* (1985).

Such developments may mean that the character of English interpretation is changing: it has been fairly consistent since the acceptance of 'higher' criticism in the 1880s, avoiding dramatic swings of fashion, cautiously assimilating continental (and, more recently, American*) currents of thought, and maintaining a connection with religious practice, i.e. there has until recently been no tradition in Britain of biblical scholarship standing outside the churches and consciously pursuing a life of its own. A change may be apparent in another way in the challenge to higher criticism itself, as manifested in 'narrative theology'* and theories such as 'canonical criticism'* which question the basis of diachronic linguistics and the belief that the historical questions concerning a literary text are the most important ones.

S. Neill and T. Wright, *The Interpretation of the New Testament 1861–1961*, [2]1988; J. Rogerson, *Old Testament Criticism in the Nineteenth Century. England and Germany*, 1984.

IEUAN ELLIS

Enlightenment

The older tendency was to speak of the *Aufklärung* as a German intellectual movement of the second half of the eighteenth century, associated with such figures as Herder,* Lessing and Kant. The equivalent French term, *Illumination*, was also in use in English language texts. More recently it has become customary to speak of 'the Enlightenment' in a more comprehensive sense as a European movement whose origins can be traced back at least to the mid-seventeenth century; 'the Enlightenment' has become virtually synonymous with 'the Age of Reason'. If the term is extended in this way, one should not expect to find a single, coherent intellectual movement with clearly defined goals. Even the catchword, 'Reason', can mean quite different things: for example, demonstrating the existence and attributes of God by quasi-mathematical proofs, examining the historical evidence for the NT miracles, or assessing Christian doctrine by the criterion of general moral principles. The common denominator is the sense that fundamental Christian beliefs have become problematic and that all our intellectual resources are required to investigate whether and in what sense they are true. If, in the age of the Reformation,* the central question was which of the rival forms of Christian beliefs was the true one, for the Enlightenment the question

was how and whether the articles hitherto accepted by all Christians could be shown to be true.

During this period the foundations were laid for the historical-critical* study of the Bible, developed in the German universities during the latter part of the eighteenth century and dominant ever since. Five main aspects of the biblical interpretation carried on in this period have proved of lasting significance.

1. The Reformation had drawn a sharp distinction between scripture and tradition, the original biblical texts and subsequent developments in the life of the church. The Enlightenment accentuated this distinction; its stress on 'reason' is often not directed against scripture as such but against the way it has been used or misused within the church. The metaphor of 'enlightenment' presupposes that the past is identified with almost unrelieved darkness; it is an era of ignorance, fanaticism and superstition, from which we are now emerging for the first time, able at last to see clearly the objects around us – including scripture.

John Toland may serve as a spokesman for this outlook. In the preface to his book, *Christianity not Mysterious* (1696), he points out that although public opinion welcomes improvements in the arts and sciences, it deplores them in religion. Yet improvements are necessary if reason is to prevail. The gospel must be clearly distinguished from ecclesiastical doctrines, in which scripture is tortured to force it to defend particular systems. In this respect there is no difference between infallible popery and infallible Protestantism; the one is characterized by unscriptural ceremonies, the other by unfathomable doctrines, and in both reason and liberty are suppressed. The reason why unintelligible beliefs ('mysteries') are still asserted is that reason is distrusted and our predecessors blindly venerated. Thus we are told that 'we must adore what we cannot comprehend' (Toland may have the doctrine of the Trinity in mind at this point). Yet the church fathers who formulated these mysteries were violent, credulous and ignorant, and their only privilege over us is priority of birth. From the second century onwards, Fathers, priests and philosophers corrupted pure Christian truth by introducing mysteries, and the exposure of this 'priestcraft' is the fundamental principle of the Reformation.

Toland argues for the priority of reason in interpreting scripture. Where it appears to contradict reason, we are not to assent to it but to suspend judgment; understanding its historical background more clearly may well help to resolve the issue. Toland's respect for the Bible seems to be genuine, and his hostility is directed solely towards what he sees as its misuse in church tradition. Scripture is essentially simple and intelligible, and it should not be used as the foundation for elaborate superstructures of mysterious dogmas. Once reason is recognized as the hermeneutical key, the whole previous history of interpretation is swept away and we are for the first time in a position where real understanding is possible. We see here in embryonic form the prospect of a biblical scholarship priding itself on its historical awareness, its objectivity, and its freedom from the bondage of dogma.

2. Characteristic of the Enlightenment is an implicitly or explicitly Socinian christology in which the traditional doctrine of the divinity of Christ is ignored or denied; it is in this tendency that the origins of the so-called 'quest of the historical Jesus' * are to be found. John Locke's *The Reasonableness of Christianity* (1695) was influential in this respect. Locke starts from the question of what it is essential to believe in order to be a Christian, and he finds his answer not in the creeds * but in the earliest Christian preaching: we must believe that Jesus is the messiah,* whose divine mission is authenticated by miracles and the fulfilment of prophecy.* Locke claims that he opposes those who 'made Jesus Christ nothing but the restorer and preacher of pure natural religion', but the difference between this view and his own is not very great. The sole content of Jesus' messianic mission is his proclamation of the will of God, the universal moral law which can also be known independently by the light of nature.

Locke's position is based on an implied antithesis between simple, biblical belief in Jesus as the messiah and later christological and trinitarian dogma. During the eighteenth century, a corresponding antithesis was increasingly found within the NT itself. Thomas Chubb, in *The True Gospel of Jesus Christ Asserted* (1738), contrasts the gospel preached by Jesus Christ not only with Johannine incarnational christology (*see* **Christology, New Testament**) but also with the alleged historical facts such as the resurrection * which the apostolic preaching made central. The gospel preached by Jesus Christ to the poor was a gospel of pure natural religion and morality, and it is this that we must believe. The Protestant doctrine of the primitive Christian fall from the purity of the gospel is now applied to the NT itself.

This solution to the problem of the NT was especially popular in Germany. The distinction between the gospel of Jesus and the gospel of the apostles is fundamental to Reimarus' theory of Christian origins, but it is also presented in more sympathetic form in two monographs by J. G. Herder, on the synoptic and the Johannine portrayal of Jesus respectively (1796–7). The Gospels,* according to

Herder, are not biographies but documents of Christian faith in Jesus as the messiah. The Gospel of John is the least biographical, but we find in the first three Gospels remarkable agreement in the sayings material despite the divergences in the narrative. It is here that we find the gospel preached by Jesus himself, at the heart of which was the fatherhood of God and the brotherhood of man. Jesus' work was to bring in the kingdom * of God, an order which would be worthy of God and humanity, and one way in which we in our time can further that cause is by turning the religion about Jesus back into the religion of Jesus.

Similar views are to be found in Kant's *Religion within the Limits of Reason Alone* (1793), though in the context of a very pronounced emphasis on the autonomy of morality. Kant distinguishes between Christianity as natural religion and Christianity as learned religion: the former was taught by 'the Teacher of the Gospel', and is found in its purest form in the Sermon on the Mount,* while in the latter Jewish elements such as belief in historical facts were introduced by the founders of the Christian communities. Kant, however, does not ascribe fundamental significance to any history, even the historical Jesus. Writing a history of religion is impossible, for pure morality has no public status. Historical or pseudo-historical narratives must be interpreted morally without regard for the author's intention, since the function of the Bible is to make us better rather than to give us information about the contingencies of history.

3. The Enlightenment is much exercised to find in the Bible 'evidences' of the truth of Christianity, and at the heart of this issue was the question of the biblical miracles. In book 4 of his *Essay concerning Human Understanding* (1690) Locke discusses the whole question of the grounds of assent to a historical testimony. One should take into account factors such as the number, skill and integrity of the witnesses, the author's intention (where the testimony is from a book), and the internal consistency of the narrative. Particular difficulties arise, however, when the testimony contradicts our common experience of the ordinary course of nature. No general rules can be laid down for assessing such testimonies, except that arguments for and against must all be duly considered. With his usual caution, Locke tries to exclude the biblical miracle stories from this process of investigation; but it was clear to many of his readers that these stories could claim no exemption from his principles.

Rational investigation along these lines was undertaken by conservative apologists as well as their opponents. One well-known example is Thomas Sherlock's *Tryal of the Witnesses* (1730), in which the apostles are put on trial for allegedly fabricating the story that Jesus had risen from the dead. After due consideration of the evidence for and against, the foreman of the jury returns a verdict of 'not guilty'. This work was a response to Thomas Woolston's *Six Discourses on the Miracles of our Saviour* (1727–30), which had poured scorn on many of the NT miracle stories on the grounds of their internal inconsistencies and improbabilities. Sherlock's reply concentrated on the single, central miracle of the resurrection, and the implication is that if a genuine miracle is established here, the other lesser miracles will fall into place.

Hume's famous 'Essay on Miracles' (1748) was written in response to this kind of apologetic. His starting-point is the problem, noted by Locke, of assessing a testimony which contradicts our usual experience. Our experience uniformly contradicts the possibility of a dead man coming back to life, and uniform experience is proof; for it is always more probable that witnesses should be lying or mistaken than that an event contradicting our uniform experience should have occurred. The conclusion is that 'no testimony is sufficient to establish a miracle unless the testimony be of such a kind that its falsehood would be more miraculous than the fact which it endeavours to establish'. Needless to say, no such testimony is to be found. We may take the miracles in the Pentateuch* as an example: which hypothesis is more extraordinary, their falsehood or their actual occurrence?

The evidential use of miracles was also attacked by Lessing. In the controversy he initiated by publishing excerpts from Reimarus' *Schutzschrift* (1774–8), Lessing opposed orthodox theologians' attempts to defend revelation by historical means. In this way, he argued, eternity is made to hang on a spider's thread; historical exposition inflicts greater wounds on religion even than scholasticism. The only evidence and proof we should look for is our present, inward knowledge of God through Christ – the demonstration of the Spirit and of power. Lessing influenced Coleridge's* attack on the 'evidential school', represented above all by William Paley's *Evidences of Christianity* (1794).

4. A sometimes crude but nevertheless significant way of understanding the Bible was to expose it to ridicule. Pierre Bayle's *Dictionnaire historique et critique* (1696) is one of the sources of this tradition, the best-known exponents of which are Voltaire and Tom Paine. The article on David* proved particularly contentious; Bayle asserts that 'the profound respect which we owe to this great king and prophet should not prevent us from expressing our disapproval of the occasions on which he went astray'. He also has some caustic things to say about the story of the fall (Gen. 3). Considering the fact that the destiny of the whole of humanity was at stake, 'it must be admitted that the two creatures to whom God had confided the salvation of mankind could not have looked after it worse ... they put up less resistance than a child when someone is trying to take away its doll'. God cannot be absolved from responsibility on the grounds that he had bestowed free-will on his creatures: 'No good mother who has given her daughters permission to go to a ball would not withdraw her consent if she were to know for certain that they would lose their virginity there, and any mother who did know that for certain, and let them go after exhorting them to be good, and threatening them with punishment if they failed to return home virgins, would be justly convicted of loving neither her daughters nor chastity.'

Thomas Woolston was an English precursor to Voltaire and Paine. The best way, he tells us, of convincing people that the gospel miracle stories are untrue is to treat them 'ludicrously'. We read (John 5) that when an angel troubled the waters at the pool of Bethesda, the first person into the water was healed; Woolston subjects this account to a barrage of irreverent questions. Did the angel descend to wash himself? Did he come head first, feet first, or breast first like a goose? Those who were most mobile and who therefore needed healing least were the ones who received it; why did the city authorities not organize things better, as they would surely have done in London? Was it fitting that hundreds of people should tumble into the water for the diversion of the mob, with only one being healed and the rest emerging like drowned rats? The only conclusion can be that the letter of the NT 'lies abominably'.

Woolston's irreverence greatly distressed the nineteenth-century historian of the period, Leslie Stephen, an agnostic for whom the 'melancholy, long, withdrawing roar' of the 'sea of faith' was a matter for intense regret. Yet Woolston and others who held the Bible up to ridicule are historically important as an indication of a widespread general mood. Readers of such works were presented with the prospect of a time in which the Bible would lose its cultural dominance. Laughing at it sprang from the same sense of unease that led to the more 'serious' demand that it should be subjected to objective rational investigation.

5. Rational investigation of the Bible meant historical investigation. Locke attempted to put this principle into practice in his posthumous *Paraphrases and Notes on the Epistles of St Paul* (1705–7). The main reason for the

obscurity of the Pauline letters is, he tells us, our ignorance of the historical circumstances that gave rise to them. We must pay attention not just to the parts – the usual flaw in detailed commentaries – but to the whole, attempting to reconstruct the apostle's purpose in his historical setting. Thus, Paul's* purpose in writing to the Romans is not to provide a compendium of (Protestant) dogma, but to define the position of Jews and Gentiles within the church; the letter can only be understood if that is constantly borne in mind.

However, it was in the German* scholarship of the latter half of the eighteenth century that the methodological and hermeneutical issues raised by historical interpretation were most fully discussed. In his *Treatise on the Free Investigation of the Canon* (1771–5), J. S. Semler distinguishes between scripture and the Word of God,* arguing that no reader who believes in the divine love will be able to accept the inspiration* of every part of the Bible. There are no historical grounds for the traditional assumption that the Bible is homogeneous, and the canon* came into existence only as the result of clerical discussions about what should be included in public reading. For Semler, the importance of this historicizing of the question of the canon is that it makes possible an interpretation of the texts in which historical understanding, as opposed to edification, is primary.

The increasing autonomy accorded to historical interpretation also led to its separation from dogmatic theology. In his inaugural lecture at Altdorf in 1787, J. P. Gabler summarizes the distinction as follows: 'Biblical theology bears a historical character in that it hangs on what the sacred writers thought about divine things; dogmatic theology, on the other hand, bears a didactic character in that it teaches what every theologian through use of his reason philosophizes about divine things in accordance with his understanding, with the circumstances of the time, the age, the place, the school, and similar matters of this sort.' Thus the former remains essentially unchanging, whereas the latter changes constantly, as a cursory glance at church history will confirm. The task of biblical theology,* as distinct from dogmatic theology, is to separate out those parts of scripture valid only for their own times from those which are permanently valid. In carrying out this task, it is important to draw out the distinctive characteristics of the individual biblical authors, asking only about their views on divine matters, without recourse to the doctrine of inspiration.

By the end of the eighteenth century, the ideal of a rational, historical interpretation of the Bible was firmly established (at least in

Germany), and many of the main characteristics of nineteenth- and twentieth-century historical criticism are already discernible. The Enlightenment's biblical interpretation is important not only because it anticipates some of the problems that have preoccupied more recent biblical studies, but above all because it laid the foundations on which modern biblical studies still rest. In order to understand the superficially obvious and self-evident principles of the discipline, it is necessary to trace them back to their Enlightenment roots.

See also **Christology, Modern; Deism; Miraculous, Interpretation of the.**

The Cambridge History of the Bible (vol. 3), 1963; H. Frei, *The Eclipse of Biblical Narrative*, 1974; W. G. Kümmel, *The New Testament. The History of the Investigation of its Problems*, ET 1972; A. McGrath, *The Making of Modern German Christology*, 1986; H. Reventlow, *The Authority of the Bible and the Rise of the Modern World*, ET 1984; John Rogerson, Christopher Rowland, Barnabas Lindars, *The Study and Use of the Bible*, 1988.

FRANCIS WATSON

Ephesians

The Epistle to the Ephesians, like its closely-related companion within the Pauline corpus, Colossians, has had, at certain periods, an importance in the history of interpretation disproportionate to its size.

The fact that the letter, while replete with Pauline expressions, does not conform to the literary style of the rest of the Pauline corpus, uses terms such as *ekklēsia*, *mustērion* and *oikonomia* with different meanings from those found elsewhere, and does not give much pastoral information about the destination church or contain personal greetings (the reference to Tychicus in 6.21 is the solitary example in Ephesians and it has a virtually exact parallel in Col. 4.7), has caused many scholars to question its authenticity as a letter of the apostle Paul.* Erasmus* in 1519 was the first to suggest that it was probably from a hand other than Paul's, although the case against Pauline authorship was not seriously argued until the work of the British Unitarian scholar, E. Evanson, in 1792, and then of De Wette* in his *Lehrbuch der historisch-kritischen Einleitung in die kanonischen Bücher des Neuen Testaments*, 1826.

Nevertheless, the letter is very well attested, and plainly seen as Pauline, in the work of early church writers by a number of quotations and allusions, and many based their theological interpretations upon it. It exerted a decisive influence, for example, on Irenaeus'* doctrine of recapitulation through the curious verb *anakephalaioō* in 1.10.

It has been argued that Ephesians was in origin an encyclical letter to the churches in Asia Minor. The fact that many of the oldest and best manuscripts omit the reference to 'in Ephesus' in 1.1 has lent support to this suggestion, as has its dearth of personal or local references. Marcion* actually took it to be the lost letter to the Laodiceans mentioned in Col. 4.16, an interpretation which still finds some adherents today. Ephesians does bear a marked literary relationship to Colossians. E. J. Goodspeed (*The Meaning of Ephesians*, 1933) suggested that it was a covering letter to the Pauline corpus itself, a summary written by Onesimus, who collected the letters, to honour his master Paul, and that this accounts for the differences in literary style, tone and senses of words between it and the undisputed letters, combined with the constant reminiscences of passages in most of them, but Colossians above all.

Most scholars accept that Colossians is chronologically prior to Ephesians and that Ephesians develops many of the theological ideas of Colossians, taking them a step further towards early catholicism.* This development is most clearly seen in the areas of ecclesiology, angelology and eschatology. E. Schweizer goes so far as to say that 'the most important impact that Colossians has had is the fact that the Epistle to the Ephesians came to be written' (*The Letter to the Colossians*, 1982, p. 245). It appears clear that the author of Ephesians was dependent upon an existing Pauline corpus as the numerous parallels to the vocabulary and ideas of the other nine Pauline letters demonstrate. Thus, the trend in scholarly circles is to reject Pauline authorship in favour of a Deutero-Pauline author, but there is by no means a consensus on the matter.

In any case, even the most conservative of interpreters (such as D. Guthrie, *New Testament Introduction*, 1970) have acknowledged that Ephesians reads like a summary of the great themes of the Christian faith and concede that it contains little that ties it to a specific congregation and setting. This strikes many as stretching belief in the genuineness of the letter beyond the bounds of credibility, given the firm NT tradition that Paul spent a significant period of his ministry in Ephesus (Acts 19) and was presumably familiar with the Christians there. Written to such an audience the letter would surely seem distant and impersonal. On the basis of a careful comparison of Ephesians and Acts, R. P. Martin has suggested that Luke himself was the author.

The theology and christological message of Ephesians are essentially Pauline in terms of titles and descriptions used, but often their general sense is not. For instance, Paul's understanding of the 'foolishness' of the cross found in I Cor. is superseded by a triumphalist presentation of the cosmic role of Christ. This dimension of christology* in Ephesians has provided one of the most fruitful areas of theological interpretation in the letter, that of the inter-relationship between christology and ecclesiology. The description of the church as a cosmic, universalized body well on the way towards institutionalization has been noted by Catholic and Protestant scholars alike and has led to attempts to locate the letter in a late first-century context.

The eschatological teaching in the letter is expressed in strongly 'realized' terms, cf. 1.20–23 and 2.5–7. There is little to temper this emphasis with elements of a futurist eschatology.* In this respect, Ephesians goes beyond its sister-epistle Colossians in its declaration about Christian existence as being 'in the heavenlies' (1.3, 10, 20–23; 2.6; 3.9–10; 4.9–10; 6.10), an expression which occurs nowhere else in the Pauline corpus (but note Col. 3.1).

The liturgical content of the letter, such as the 'hymn' in Jewish 'blessing' form in 1.3–14, has been the subject of considerable agreement, with many scholars agreeing that much of the material is baptismal in reference. Kirby has sought to assess the possibility that the letter was originally a baptismal homily.

Some scholars, notably E. Käsemann and H. Schlier have argued that Ephesians contains clear signs of being influenced by gnostic* ideas and language. Some have gone so far as to suggest that it presupposes a gnostic 'redeemer myth' in its composition. Similarly, K. G. Kuhn pointed to the numerous linguistic and theological similarities between the letter and some of the Dead Sea Scrolls* and argued that Ephesians was a product of the Essene community in Qumran. Both suggestions are unlikely and merely reflect the fact that Ephesians makes use of thought forms prevalent in the ancient world of the time.

See also **Colossians and Philemon; Pseudonymity.**

Marcus Barth, *Ephesians*, 1974; J. C. Kirby, *Ephesians, Baptism and Pentecost*, 1968; K. G. Kuhn, 'Der Epheserbrief im Lichte der Qumrantexte', *NTS* 7, 1960–61, pp. 334–46; Andrew T. Lincoln, *Paradise Now and Not Yet*, 1981; Ralph P. Martin, *New Testament Foundations*, Vol. 2, 1978, pp. 223–38; C. L. Mitton, *Ephesians*, 1976; J. A. Robinson, *St Paul's Epistle to the Ephesians*, ² 1928.

                                                               L. KREITZER

Epigraphy

Recent decades have seen an explosion in both the discovery and the analysis of inscriptions, which survive in various materials, but chiefly on stone surfaces of many kinds – on public and private buildings, statues and statue bases, paving and tombstones – all over the Graeco-Roman world. The documents which were formally inscribed include laws, official letters, dedications of buildings or of offerings and honours for individuals. Private inscriptions include prayers and graffiti, but the largest single category is on tombstones. The discovery, decipherment and study of inscriptions is referred to as epigraphy.

Because these documents are direct survivals from antiquity, they offer a major source of evidence which can supplement that obtained from literary sources. But they are also limited in the kinds of information which they supply. For example, a very large number of inscriptions is concerned with the activities of prominent persons and imperial officials; texts survive which refer to Pontius Pilate, Herod Antipas and other prominent figures in the N T narratives, and it is from an inscription at Delphi that we know the date of the proconsulship of Gallio (Acts 18.12). But the purpose of such inscriptions, which was to honour the men concerned, means that they only convey very formal information.

A less direct use of inscribed texts, which is perhaps more important for the understanding of the world of the N T, is in interpreting the social context in which Christianity originated and developed. Thus, inscriptions in Greek found in Palestine have brought home the prominence of that language and so of Hellenistic * culture in first-century Judaism, even in its heartland. A notable example is the so-called 'Theodotos inscription' from the Jerusalem of the first century A D, recording the building of a synagogue by Theodotos, 'priest and head of the synagogue', whose father and grandfather are similarly described and who founded the establishment. Readers of the Gospels * are reminded immediately of Jairus in Mark 5.22. A similar point is made by the large number of Greek inscriptions on Palestinian ossuary jars (holding the bones of the dead) from the period.

Inscriptions are even more important in understanding the world of the early missionary journeys. It was Sir William Ramsay, in the late nineteenth century, who, in a series of heroic journeys in Asia Minor and a flood of publications, showed how the evidence of inscriptions for the civic life of the first century A D supported and supplemented the account given in the Acts of the Apostles and the writings of Paul.* An inscription from Thessalonica, now on display at the British Museum, confirms the accuracy of the description of local officials there as 'politarchs' (Acts 17.6–8). Such references do more than just confirm the accuracy of the terminology. Paul,

writing from Corinth, refers to a certain Erastus as '*oikonomos* of the city' (Rom. 16.23); this is given particular interest by the existence of an inscription on a pavement at Corinth which reads 'Erastus laid this pavement at his own expense in return for the aedileship' (i.e. another office in the city hierarchy). This reading of the damaged inscription is, it has to be said, not beyond challenge, but if the two men are one and the same we are helped in the process of revising the traditional interpretation of I Cor. 1.26ff. which led to a perception of the early Christians as of low social status. Not all were from that level of society; on the contrary, at least from the time of Paul's mission in cities of the Greek world, some were reasonably affluent, and Paul's words, it seems, are to be read ironically. G. Theissen (*The Social Setting of Pauline Christianity*, 1982) has given a full exposition of Paul's attitudes in I Corinthians on this basis, using a wide range of evidence.

By far the majority of all inscriptions of the early Christian period are Gentile and pagan; but a valuable number survive from the Jewish world, particularly from the Diaspora communities of Asia Minor. The discovery of inscriptions referring to women as chief officers of synagogues in certain cities in Asia Minor puts Paul's and Luke's favourable references to women's role in early church life into context (*see* **Women in Early Christian Interpretation**). References to so-called 'God-fearers' attached to synagogues in Aphrodisias confirm what has long been suspected but always uncertain – that this was a relatively formal term for Gentiles who linked themselves to synagogues, attracted by the life and teaching of Judaism (cf. Acts 10.22; 13.16,26).

Finally, an inscription giving the rules of a private cult-group or 'club' in Philadelphia in Asia Minor (dating from a period somewhat earlier than the origins of Christianity) refers to the group as a 'household' (cf. I Tim. 3.5; I Peter 4.17), shows that it was open to 'men and women, free people and slaves' (cf. Gal. 3.28), and lays down strict moral rules for its members (I Cor. 5.11). Readers of the N T, often conditioned to think of pagan life as licentious and of the early churches as in an institutional vacuum, should be aware of such parallels.

Epigraphy is therefore essential to our understanding of the language, institutions and preoccupations of the society within which early Christianity developed. It reveals the extent to which Christianity was shaped by its origins, and highlights its genuinely unique features, above all, its centring on the person of Jesus. As that society is revealed more clearly by the study of its inscriptions, it becomes easier to perceive and avoid the perils of anachronism, by which we judge Christianity in the light of later developments, in effect viewing the first days from the point of view of an encapsulated tradition and its future. We can illustrate this aspect by noticing that the RSV and many other versions translate *episkopos* ('overseer') in I Tim. 3.2 (though not in Acts 20.28!) by 'bishop' and *diakonos* ('servant') in Rom. 16.1 by 'deaconess'. It is unlikely that, at the time, writer or reader 'heard' these terms as bearing such a technical and ecclesiastical sense. Similarly, it is unclear whether the use of the word *ekklēsia* for the Christian congregation itself carried any special religious overtones ('church'), perhaps because of Septuagintal* use for 'the congregation of Israel', or was so colourless that we should simply render it 'meeting' or 'assembly'.

In these ways, epigraphy carries us from the forming of a more accurate picture of early Christian life into modes of theological perception. It may even challenge traditional ways of looking at aspects of Christian belief. It certainly affects matters relating to Christian institutions and the meaning of words used in the NT.

Illuminating as it is as a tool in the study of the NT, it is not without its dangers. There is always a tendency to generalize from what are after all the accidents of discovery and to make comparisons where there are none to be made. Knowledge of the ancient world is, despite the thousands of discoveries, patchy, partial and spasmodic. The outbreak of 'scroll mania' following the discovery of the Dead Sea Scrolls* (i.e. seeing links with the NT at every turn) has led scholars to be more cautious in other comparable cases.

See also **Archaeology (New Testament); Sociology and Social Anthropology.**

B. J. Brooten, *Women Leaders in the Ancient Synagogue*, 1982; R. L. Fox, *Pagans and Christians*, 1989; P. N. Harrison, *Paulines and Pastorals*, 1964, pp. 100–105 (on Erastus); G. H. R. Horsley (ed.), *New Documents Illustrating Early Christianity*, successive volumes from 1981, reproducing and discussing new discoveries bearing on NT passages and vocabulary; E. M. Meyers and J. F. Strange, *Archaeology, the Rabbis and Early Christianity*, 1981; J. Murphy-O'Connor, *St Paul's Corinth*, 1983.

CHARLOTTE ROUECHÉ

Epistle

Twenty-two of the NT writings either take the form of letters or include letters (cf. Rev. 2–3). Interpreters have recognized this fact throughout history but only in recent times have they emphasized that NT letters are Graeco-Roman letters. Commentators in the ancient and Byzantine church sometimes recognized that NT writers had employed common Graeco-Roman letter types, epistolary styles and conventions. The humanist scholars of the Renaissance (*see* **Erasmus**) and Reformation* periods also made similar observations. For the most part, however, the letters were read in theological ways as parts of scripture so that they tended to be dehistoricized and departicularized. In other words, until recent times, their status as scripture tended to submerge their status as letters.

The Reformation accentuated a Western tradition of interpretation already developed in Augustine* which viewed the NT letters as documents of theological conflict. This tradition culminated in F. C. Baur, who systematically subsumed all early Christian religion, life, and literature under the model of ideological* conflict. The letters of Paul* and the Pauline school were all read as apologetic and polemical letters. This reduction of letters to one epistolary genre viewed in terms of theological content, caused the 'properly epistolary features' (prescript and postscript) and parenesis to be marginalized as the framework to the theological body of the letter.

Modern scholarship on the subject of letters has been dominated by two intellectual currents: critical historical and literary approaches, and European romanticism. Although Baur employed anachronistic rather than Graeco-Roman genre categories for letter types, he did correctly stress the occasionality of early Christian letters. In the latter part of the nineteenth century and up until the First World War, several scholars using historical-critical methods* began to compare early Christian letters with a broad range of ancient letters, works on rhetoric,* and popular philosophical literature. That movement was largely checked until very recent times by the dominance of romanticism in conjunction with the discovery of the papyri from Egypt. More than anyone else, Adolf Deissmann was responsible for this shift. The papyri provided thousands of common everyday letters and documents for comparison with the NT letters. Previously, scholars had only letters surviving through literary transmission.

Deissmann's conclusions have dominated NT scholarship until quite recently. For him the papyri showed three things. First, the letters of Paul were writings of the lower classes and Paul was a champion of slaves and the lowest classes of free men. Second, the peculiarities of NT Greek are not a result of semitic influences but of the common vernacular or koinē speech. Third, while some NT letters like II Peter and Hebrews are literary letters or 'epistles', the letters of Paul are real letters.

Thus the key Romantic distinction between literature and real life came to dominate NT scholarship on letters. According to Deissmann, letters are private, unliterary, purely occasional, unconventional, and artless. They are direct unmediated expressions of the author's personality. This view lent itself to psychological and existentialist interpretations of Paul's letters. The later NT letters by contrast were literary epistles. They are public, conventional, artful, cold, and impersonal. This distinction between the real letters of Paul and the literary epistles of later Christianity corresponds to the myth of a genuine charismatic Christianity followed by a degenerating institutional Christianity.

Although Deissmann's distinctions were at once criticized for being too sharp, they have continued to control the field. Thus two claims have dominated work on the Pauline letters in this century. Many have argued that Paul's letters are representatives of the Hellenistic letter tradition seen in the typical papyrus letter. Paul's letters until very recently have been compared almost exclusively to the papyri. Letters preserved through literary transmission have been mostly ignored. Here the focus of much illuminating work has been on Paul as a Christian modifier of Hellenistic formulas and phraseology (e.g. address, thanksgiving, farewell) from the prescript and postscript of letters. Others have continued to emphasize that Paul's letters are unique and incomparable. This claim has often been associated with the romantic notion that earliest Christian literature in general is unique because it is eschatological. Some scholars have also seen similarities between Paul's apostolic letters and the letters of Hellenistic kings. In the light of comparison with a full range of ancient letter types, however, these proposed similarities have appeared to be rather farfetched attempts to invest Paul with an unrealistic authority and institutional role.

Recent scholarship has sharply criticized the old generic conceptions of NT letters – apologetic, polemical, theological treatise, apostolic pronouncement, pure expressions of personality or existential self-understanding – as anachronistic. Some of this criticism grew out of the approach generally known as 'the form criticism of letters' where NT epistolary texts were given formal and functional comparison with a broad range of Jewish and other Graeco-Roman 'forms', e.g. lists of virtues and vices, modes of scriptural interpretation, household codes, hardship lists.

There has also been an increasing understanding of and appeal to ancient rhetoric, although there is not yet a consensus about the level and type to which the NT letters belong. Finally, NT letters have now been studied in the light of ancient epistolary theory, handbooks on how to write letters, and well-established letter types. Most of the NT letters have been shown to be Christianized forms of ancient hortatory types of letters, e.g., I Thess., parenesis; I Cor., admonition and advice; Gal., rebuke and advice. Formally and functionally, they are closest to the hortatory letters of ancient moralists and philosophers. These findings have far-reaching implications for the understanding of the authors' purposes, relationships to their audiences, and modes of communication. Paul now appears not so much a theological polemicist as a builder of Gentile Christian communities. The conventions and rhetorical methods of the hortatory tradition are well known, and shed much light on the interpretation of particular letters. The Pastoral Epistles, for example, very closely resemble pseudonymous philosophical letters which present an ideal teacher as a model for imitation. Attempts to identify those being attacked in the Pastoral Epistles are beside the point. Many of the perennial problems of reading Philippians as a unitary work simply disappear when the interpreter understands how it employs conventions from the letter of friendship. Similar examples could be given about virtually every letter in the NT. Thus, the knowledge of Graeco-Roman epistolary types and epistolary theory has brought a major advance in the understanding of NT letters.

See also **Genre**.

W. Doty, *Letters in Primitive Christianity*, 1973; S. K. Stowers, *Letter Writing in Greco-Roman Antiquity*, 1986; J. L. White, *Light From Ancient Letters*, 1986.

STANLEY K . STOWERS

Erasmus

The biblical studies of Desiderius Erasmus (*c.* 1469–1536) marked a watershed in the development of NT studies for four reasons. First he brought new objectives to biblical interpretation; these were the restoration of scripture, and with it the restoration of theology, in marked contrast with the aims of the schoolmen; he advocated a knowledge and propagation of that pure 'philosophy of Christ', which 'is not drawn from any source more abundantly than from the evangelical books and from the Apostolic Letters', and the renewal of society in 'true piety' through these studies. Secondly, he broke with the mediaeval* fourfold interpretation of scripture: the literal,* allegorical,* tropological and anagogical; he discarded scholastic commentaries on the Bible, and though he had a knowledge of mediaeval scholarship it was never his starting point. Thirdly, Erasmus dominated the biblical humanism of the early sixteenth century which employed the tools and techniques of the Italian humanists of the fifteenth century in linguistic research into the texts of scripture and the Fathers of the church. He never deviated from the humanist precept to return *ad fontes*; the search for the correct text and its translation had to precede the interpretation of scripture. Finally, he was the first to publish a Greek and a revised Latin version of the NT alongside the Vulgate.* Erasmus took upon himself to make an improved Latin translation without mandate from church or council (Fifth Lateran, 1512–1517), with the Greek text to verify his revisions, adding *Annotations* '. . . in order that firstly they should enlighten the reader as to what has been changed and why, and secondly that they should explain everything which seems complicated, unclear or difficult' (*Dedication to Leo X*). Erasmus was, in all probability, pressurized by his printer, Froben of Basel, to hasten publication in 1516, and his Greek text relied on comparatively recent and sometimes defective MSS. The Complutensian Polyglot Bible, although printed, was not published until 1522.

Erasmus considered Latin the language of educated Christendom and therefore continued to think of the NT as a Latin book; in this respect, his biblical studies foreshadowed the Latin translations of Sebastian Castellio (1551) and Theodore Beza (1565–1598). The *Paraclesis*, his preface to the 1516 *Novum Instrumentum*, made famous his willingness to support vernacular translations of the Bible.

The increase in Pauline studies throughout Europe reflected the sixteenth century concern with doctrines of salvation, from Italian humanists and reformers such as Gasparo Contarini (1493–1542) to Jacques Lefèvre d'Étaples (1455–1536), who published commentaries on the Latin text of the Pauline Epistles in 1512. Later he and Erasmus disputed the translation and interpretation of Heb. 2.9. As Erasmus prepared his *Novum Instrumentum*, Luther* was lecturing on Romans (1515–1516). Erasmus heard Colet (1466?–1519) lecturing on the Pauline Epistles when he first came to England in 1499. As early as 1501, Erasmus was himself working on Paul's Epistle to the Romans (work now lost); in the *Enchiridion* (1503) he emphasized spiritual and allegorical exegesis, before he came to value more highly the philological approach to interpretation which he defended in his preface to Valla's *Adnotationes in Novum Testamentum* (1505). Lorenzo Valla (*c.* 1406–1457), in revealing weaknesses in the text of the Vulgate, opened up the prospect of new exegesis.

Important influences on Erasmus' biblical studies were Florentine Neoplatonism (to which Colet probably introduced him), and the work of the church Fathers, especially of Jerome and Origen.* Erasmus discussed his approach to scripture and its interpretation in letters, *apologiae*, prefaces and dedications to further editions of the *Novum Testamentum* (1519, 1522, 1527, 1535) and in the *Ratio verae theologiae* (1518), *De libero arbitrio* (1524), *Hyperaspistes* (1526, 1527), and *Ecclesiastes, sive de ratione concionandi* (1523, pub. 1535). Parallel with his work on successive editions of the NT, he published *Paraphrases of the New Testament* (1517–1524, with collected editions in 1524, 1532, 1534). Their reception was enthusiastic compared with the controversial reception of his *Annotations*.

Erasmus maintained that the tools of exegesis should be a knowledge of the three languages, Latin, Greek and Hebrew, together with training in the disciplines of the *studia humanitatis*, especially grammar and rhetoric. Erasmus did not master Hebrew and therefore restricted his biblical studies accordingly. The first step in the elucidation of scripture was to ensure that the grammar was correct; where problems of interpretation remained, he advised collation with works of the Fathers, but the centrality of Christ in scripture should never be lost.

Erasmus' two-fold hermeneutic,* literal and spiritual, reflected the Neoplatonic contrast of body and soul, which influenced his understanding of scripture. The literal, grammatical and historical sense was closely related to the spiritual, which was both allegorical and tropological or moral; the allegorical sense should not prove dogma. He did not agree with Luther on the clarity of scripture: 'For there are some secret places in Holy Scriptures into which God has not wished us to penetrate more deeply and, if we try to do so, then the deeper we go, the darker and darker it becomes, by which means we are led to acknowledge the unsearchable majesty of the divine wisdom, and the weakness of the human mind.' This passage from *De libero arbitrio* is set in a deeply Platonic context. In moral interpretation, Erasmus emphasized a complete transformation, where 'studies are transmuted into morals', because 'in this kind of philosophy, life means more than debate, inspiration is preferable to erudition, transformation is a more important matter than intellectual comprehension. Only a few can be learned, but all can be Christian, all can be devout, and all can be theologians' (*Paraclesis*) – a passage which prefigures Luther's teaching on the priesthood of all believers.

Erasmus, through his efforts to restore scripture, was forced into the controversies of that 'age of reform'. He may often have been close to Luther in his understanding of scripture, but he did not reach the latter's position on justification. He became involved in the eucharistic controversy of the 1520s, but in the case of the sacraments he accepted the authority of the church. His biblical studies spelt reform, but he refused to use them to divide the Christendom of which he remained a devoted citizen; his work looked to the future and to the foundation of N T philological scholarship.

See also: **Luther; Reformation.**

Collected Works of Erasmus, 1969–;: Vol. 42, R. D. Sider (ed.), *Paraphrases on Romans and Galatians*, 1984; J. H. Bentley, *Humanists and Holy Writ*, 1983; J. P. Payne, *Erasmus: his Theology of the Sacraments*, 1970; A. Rabil Jr, *Erasmus and the New Testament: the Mind of a Christian Humanist*, 1972; E. Rummel, *Erasmus' Annotations on the New Testament*, 1986.

RUTH CHAVASSE

Eschatology

In the study of the Hebrew Bible eschatology has been one of the most systematically misleading concepts used by interpreters of the text. The traditional and classical definition of eschatology, the study of the last things, relates to 'the four last things: death, judgment, heaven, and hell' and belongs to the systematic exposition of Christian dogmatics as imposed on the Bible. In the sense of 'the four last things' there is no eschatology in the Hebrew Bible. Indeed it is arguable that there is no '-logy' in that book because it lacks any systematic, coherent or consistent representation of a doctrinal or dogmatic nature. Composed of multivariate metaphors,* images and figures, often inconsistent, contrary, and contradictory, the different books constituting the Hebrew Bible provide impressionistic and paradoxical elements lacking a unifying structure. Only when rearranged by a systematic thinker or theologian into a suitable pattern can the book be made to yield the appearance of a unified textbook on a particular subject. Such rearrangements may be seen in the production of the post-conciliar churches' understandings of the Bible and occasionally in the readings of Torah by orthodox Jewish communities. So a separation must be made between the biblical text (of whatever canon) and its reception in various religious communities of the Common Era. A reading of all the biblical and extra-biblical texts bearing on thoughts and images of the future will demonstrate the multiplicity of discrete and disparate viewpoints entertained in the circles

which produced or maintained these writings. Moore in his classical study of the 'Hereafter' in early Jewish thought characterized the treatment of the subject in the sources he studied as displaying 'misplaced ingenuity', 'exegetical whimsicality', 'eccentricity of opinion', and 'contortions of exegesis' (cf. pp. 355, 380, 381). But these are judgments which reflect the hopelessness of trying to produce from the biblical texts a consistent and systematic picture of the future. The ingenuity is determined by the paucity of information rather than a chicanery of exegesis,* though the search for a comprehensive account of the future was part of the prevailing beliefs about the type of literature contained in the canon.

The sharp contrast between the text and the ideologies* of the communities using it must be retained in considering the differences between Jewish and Christian understandings of the future, though it should not be supposed that either approach belonged to a monolithic community. In the early centuries of the Common Era there were many Judaisms (cf. Neusner), just as there were very many different Christian churches (cf. J. Herrin, *The Formation of Christendom*, 1987). For Jews the central feature of 'eschatology' concerned the land of Israel (*see* **Jerusalem**). In Christian thought this aspect of Jewish belief and expectation had little or no eschatological significance. The messiahs* of the various Judaisms clearly represented a different kind of messianic belief from whatever may have been characteristic of Christian messianism of that period (though messianism was never a necessary element of Jewish thought). Indeed it is difficult to say wherein Christian thinking about Jesus of Nazareth as the messiah fits into any known Jewish notion of messiah, other than in the use of the term 'messiah' (*christos*). Common beliefs about the afterlife, resurrection* and divine judgment may have been shared by Jews and Christians, but the use of 'common' here is perhaps an optimistic judgment on a wide variety of images and beliefs about the future. Even the notion of messiah was not a particularly significant one in the development of the churches.

If eschatological readings of the biblical text have been very much reader-response* programmes, reading into that text current and contemporary belief systems in conjunction with prevailing socio-political factors, the study of eschatology may be read backwards and forwards in relation to the various canons of scripture and the development of eschatological and apocalyptic* possibilities in the subsequent centuries (cf. McGinn, *Visions of the End: Apocalyptic Traditions in the Middle Ages*, 1979). In the development of the classical Christian eschatology (i.e. the four last things), images and metaphors from the Bible were married to myths* and legends* from extra-biblical sources (some perhaps hinted at in various canons of scripture) to produce what may with reason be called the Gothic vision of heaven and hell. In this phantasm of the afterlife, God and the Devil were dualistic forces locked in combat over man's soul, a combat already won by God in terms of the Christus Victor myth. The development of the Devil, very much the work of Origen* and Augustine,* owed something to the patristic exposition of the Bible but much more to ancient myths going back to the figure of Humbaba-Huwawa-Hibibi-Ḥaby in ancient Near Eastern legends (cf. Forsyth, *The Old Enemy*, 1987). Much of this development was peculiar to Christian thought. as orthodox forms of Judaism had no place for a devil, original sin or other aspects of an infernal mythology (ironically and tragically Jews formed part of the demonology of many Christian communities). In the late mediaeval* period the apocalyptic visions (much more dominant in Christian belief than in Jewish) became part of the driving forces behind major social upheavals as expectations of the end of the world and the second coming of Jesus disrupted European society (cf. Cohn, *The Pursuit of the Millennium*, ³1970). The Puritan refinement of hell as a place of infinitely painful torture was simply the final stage of the development of the late mediaeval Christian teaching about the afterlife of the damned (cf. Dante's* *Inferno*). Although the rise of rationalism and the emergence of the scientific revolution helped to dowse the fires of hell, eternal damnation remained part of dogmatic Christian belief (cf. Rahner, 'The hermeneutics of eschatological assertions', *Theological Investigations* 4, 1966, pp. 323–46; cf. 'Hell', *New Blackfriars* 69, 1988, pp. 467–503). Its counterpart, the blissful life of the redeemed in heaven, flourished until at least the Victorian age. In the twentieth century, catastrophes such as the 1914–18 War, the Shoah, and the many millions killed in ideological* wars have tended to reduce Christian eschatology to the deer park of esoterical sects and denominations. After the failure of the Sabbetai Sevi movement among Jews of the seventeenth century (cf. Scholem, *Sabbatai Sevi: The Mystical Messiah 1626–1676*, 1973), the development of messianism among Jews tended towards the quietistic forms of Hasidic expectations in the shtetls of Russia and Poland. Since the Shoah and the creation of the state of Israel, the diversity (and lack) of futuristic beliefs among Jews has fragmented any serious Jewish eschatology.

A comprehensive treatment of Christian and Jewish eschatology would fill many volumes. Tracing the roots of such developments is a different and more difficult task. The Bible has contributed to the growth of such eschatologies and apocalypses but is by no means the sole source of them. Among scholars there is a tendency to read the biblical text as a thoroughgoing eschatological book using the categories of later theological systems, though it has to be recognized that there are traces of an eschatologizing hermeneutic* in the editing of the prophetic* books and the production of the Christian Bible. This principle can also be seen in the interpretation of the Hebrew/Greek Bible in the Qumran community (*see* **Dead Sea Scrolls**), in the Targums,* and in the NT. It is especially apparent in the formation of the collection of the minor prophets (e.g. Amos 9.11-15; Hab.; Zech. 9–14; Mal. 4.5–6) and may represent an eschatological glossing or transformation of the texts in conformity with the hermeneutic processes of the editing and canonizing communities. Here eschatology simply means 'the future', immediate or near (i.e. 'the latter days', 'in that day', 'the days are coming'). If different texts are taken together a future schema of things may be dimly discerned, but the hermeneutic moves involved in the grouping together of discrete and disparate texts are not easily justified. Alternative pictures of the future may be drawn from a different selection of texts, and it is difficult to resist the conclusion that there is a high degree of arbitrariness involved in any such selection process. In some statements the nations go up to Jerusalem and there learn the divine *torah* (Isa. 2.2–4; Micah 4.1–4; cf. Zech. 14. 16–21), in others no strangers shall ever enter the city again (Joel 3 [4].17). The sectarianism which is one of the dominant features of the final form of the book of Isaiah survives the divine creation of the new heavens and the new earth to the extent that the book ends on a sectarian note (66.24)! Thus the confused eschatological pictures of post-biblical Jewish writings faithfully reflect the confusions of the images of the future in the prophetic texts.

Eschatology, modified to mean expectations for the immediate or not-too-distant future, in the Hebrew Bible may be summarized as: the future will be the past with the kinks ironed out. Its substance is determined by Israel's past. Everything will be renewed in the future: new heavens and new earth, new heart, new spirit, new covenant* (Isa. 65–66; Jer. 30–31; Ezek. 34–39). This cosmic renewal in effect constitutes a divine *J'adoube*! The brevity of such a summary does not do justice to the variations and oppositions between different expectations contained in the prophetic collections, but it indicates the general drift of the imagery. Some traditions focus on Zion the city (Gowan makes this the central and unifying feature of biblical eschatology), others have a more arcadian and pastoralist emphasis (e.g. Hos. 2.14–23; Jer. 31.2–20). These differences reflect distinctive origins, traditions and emphases which scholarly-constructed synthetic eschatologies tend to flatten out into undifferentiated comprehensive accounts of the future.

A different approach to OT eschatology is taken by scholars who emphasize the importance of comparative mythology and the neighbouring cultures of Israel. They see the biblical images as fragments of a much larger set of beliefs centred on myth and royal ideology (*see* **Kingship**) (e.g. Gressmann, *Der Messias*, 1929; Mowinckel, 1959). Here eschatology is mythology recapitulated. In support of this approach may be cited the expansionary development of eschatology in apocalyptic sources and in the post-biblical Christian and Jewish communities. (The writers and editors of the Hebrew Bible have exercised strong censoring controls on the amount and range of pagan imagery and belief permitted in their scrolls.) Elements characteristic of common Ancient Near Eastern* beliefs may be found in the royal psalms and the ideology of kingship, though deuteronomistic editing and censoring may have distorted much of what now appears in the Bible (cf. Barker). A liturgy such as Isa. 33 may reflect a larger background of a 'cosmic covenant' and the importance of Ugaritic literature cannot be gainsaid for the understanding of such texts. Some texts bespeak aspects of the marriage between heaven and earth, God and people (Hos. 2.14–23; Isa. 62.1–15), which are redolent of ancient mythology. Reading biblical texts against the larger background of common ancient myth may entail reinterpreting them in ways quite different from their conventional understanding. A notable example of this kind of reinterpretation would be current rethinking of the role of belief in an afterlife in the Hebrew Bible. The conventional view of the matter is that there was no belief in an afterlife before the second century BC when the apocalyptic work of Daniel appeared (cf. 12.1–3), and references to resurrection elsewhere (e.g. Isa. 26.19) were metaphors of national resurgence (cf. Ezek. 37.1–14). Now a number of scholars have argued for a greater degree of influence from Canaanite thought on Hebrew thinking about the underworld (Dahood's Anchor Bible Commentary on the Psalms will eventually become the classical formulation of this approach), and others have claimed that from the time of the exile belief in resurrection began to emerge among the Israelites.

A fundamentally important feature of biblical eschatology is apocalyptic thought, though most of the apocalypses do not appear in the Bible. Only Daniel (to some extent) and the Book of Revelation would be regarded as having any claim to being apocalypses, though some scholars have tended to discern apocalypses in Isa. 24–27; Joel; Zech. 9–14. Hanson has argued at length that the origins of apocalyptic are to be found in late prophecy (from Isa. 56–66 onwards) when there was a resurgence of mythological thought which transformed prophecy from contemplation of the historical to sectarian fantasies about a transcendental future. A sharp distinction should certainly be made between prophetic and apocalyptic eschatology, but tracing the origins of apocalyptic to prophecy does appear to be a misprision of the evidence. Eschatology may have been an element in the production of apocalypses, but the visionary experience and access to divine secrets (via revelation by various media) as well as the study of scripture were the central elements of the apocalypses.

Eschatology in the NT is an equally difficult subject and for many of the same reasons. As with every aspect of biblical studies questions of interpretation are paramount. A plethora of attitudes and expectations about the future appears in the Gospels and the writings of Paul* and these fragments of hope cannot be turned into a consistent eschatology. NT scholars argue about whether the eschatology of Jesus and the earliest Christian communities was individual, historical, apocalyptic, realized or inaugurated (cf. Caird, pp 243–71), but the texts are inchoate and variable and so cannot be used to demonstrate a fully worked-out view of the future. Like the writings of the Hebrew Bible and the numerous apocalypses, there was no uniformity of expectation among Christian communities, and not until the time of Augustine did a coherent eschatology make its appearance. Images of the future drawn from scripture and imagination provided diverse expectations in different communities and often the expectation was generated by exposition of a particular motif (e.g. sabbatical eschatology: cf. Buchanan, *The Consequences of the Covenant*, 1970, pp. 9–18; on messianism, cf. Becker; Neusner).

The patchwork quilts of various discrete eschatologies have been woven into seamless robes by biblical theologians working from the direction of dogmatic or systematic* theologies. Thus von Rad relates the eschatological message of the prophets to 'an entirely new action in history on the part of Jahweh' (*Old Testament Theology* 2, 1965, p. 116) and simplifies the eschatological phenomenon to 'the extremely revolutionary fact that the prophets saw Jahweh approaching Israel with a new action which made the old saving institutions increasingly invalid since from then on life or death for Israel was determined by this future event' (p. 118). The idealistic nature of this assessment is typical of theologizing interpretations of biblical texts and ignores how subsequent communities actually developed their social structures. Eschatology here is a series of abstractions from the text informed by the commentator's own theological holdings which provide, at best, an anachronistic reading of that text. To remove the texts from social and cultic processes may be the essence of theologizing with them, but it really does not provide us with any idea of how such beliefs functioned in their time. The piecemeal nature of the prophetic collections militates against a systematic presentation of the images of future hopes, and the development of messianism in the Roman period provided various communities with new hermeneutic approaches to the images and incorporated them into a further series of developing notions and fantasies about the future. Charting all these diversifications of ancient myths, many of which had actual social and political consequences in their time, is perhaps the best way to attempt to define what is meant by that many splendoured thing called 'eschatology'.

See also **Kingdom of God; Parousia.**

M. Barker, *The Older Testament: The Survival of Themes from the Ancient Royal Cult in Sectarian Judaism and Early Christianity,* 1987; J. Becker, *Messianic Expectation in the Old Testament,* 1980; G. B. Caird, *The Language and Imagery of the Bible,* 1980; J. J. Collins, *The Apocalyptic Imagination,* 1984; D. E. Gowan, *Eschatology in the Old Testament,* 1986; P. D. Hanson, *The Dawn of Apocalyptic,* ²1979; G. F. Moore, *Judaism in the First Centuries of the Christian Era. The Age of the Tannaim,* 1927, vol. II, part VII; S. Mowinckel, *He That Cometh,* 1959; J. Neusner, *Ancient Judaism and Modern Category-Formation: 'Judaism,' 'Midrash,' 'Messianism,' and Canon in the Past Quarter-Century,* 1986; C. Rowland, *The Open Heaven: A Study of Apocalyptic in Judaism and Early Christianity,* 1982.

ROBERT P. CARROLL

Essays and Reviews

One of the most controversial religious books of the nineteenth century, *Essays and Reviews* was published in March 1860 under the editorship of H. B. Wilson. Its seven contributors were all associated with the universities of Oxford and Cambridge; two (Baden Powell and Benjamin Jowett) were professors, Wilson was a former professor. The book went into many editions and sold over 40,000 copies. Regarded as the manifesto of the radical wing of the Broad Church party, it was attacked by both High Churchmen and Evangelicals, and more than 400 books and articles were written in reply. In 1864 it was formally condemned by the authorities of the Church of England.

Essays and Reviews challenged traditional views of both the inspiration and authority of the Bible. Frederick Temple, in an essay obviously indebted to Lessing's *The Education of the Human Race,* attempted to clarify the nature of scriptural authority if the Bible belonged to a past stage in man's religious evolution. His solution was that the Bible was not a law book but a historical record which modern man was best able to appreciate. 'When conscience and the Bible appear to differ, the pious Christian immediately concludes that he has not really understood the Bible.' Rowland Williams, in an essay on 'Bunsen's Biblical Researches', introduced a wider public to a prolific German author, a pupil of Schleiermacher, and a leading exponent of higher criticism. Baron Bunsen did not believe that the Pentateuch* was written by Moses,* or that David* was the author of the whole Psalter, and he considered that the book of Daniel was a late work, written after the events it was alleged to predict. Much Christian interpretation of the OT was, therefore, misplaced, and it should not be seen as a series of messianic* predictions. 'The Bible is an expression of devout reason, and therefore is to be read with reason in freedom.' There was no 'chronological element in revelation', and no predictive element in prophecy.* Powell, who wrote on the 'Evidences of Christianity', held that Christianity 'as a real religion must be viewed apart from connexion with physical things'; belief in divine intervention in setting aside the laws of nature was mistaken, and the historicity of the Gospel miracles* must thus be questioned. Wilson believed that the future of Christianity in Britain lay in a comprehensive national church, embracing all people of good will, and forsaking all claims to absolute knowledge. The Bible which would serve this national religion must be interpreted 'ideally' and not as a statement of literal fact. Here as elsewhere in *Essays and Reviews* extreme views (e.g. Baur's late date for the Fourth Gospel) were used in support of a wider idea of revelation.* 'On the Mosaic Cosmogony', by C. W. Goodwin, held that it was impossible to reconcile Genesis and geology, and the Mosaic account of creation was a 'human utterance' given from a pre-scientific viewpoint which was now of cultural interest only.

The longest and most important essay, by Jowett, dealt specifically with the interpretation of scripture. Jowett claimed that historical criticism now enabled modern man to arrive at the true understanding of the Bible: the accretions of centuries of interpretation which had become confused with the original meaning could be swept away. Inspiration could be judged only by examining the writers and their context, and this must take into account the 'well ascertained facts of history and science'. The synoptic evangelists were not three independent witnesses of the gospel history, and a common oral tradition underlay their accounts. Such conclusions inevitably affected the authority of scripture, which should now be seen in its possession of universal truth – that ideal perfectly exemplified in the teachings of Jesus. Jowett's most notorious statement, 'Interpret the scripture like any other book', summed up the effect of the essay: the sacred hermeneutic* of scripture must defer to the secular. The Bible was not written in a manner different from other ancient documents: it used human language, and the texts were transmitted like any others; the common rules of hermeneutics must therefore apply to the OT and NT. However, the recognition of the interpretative phenomenon did not affect the basis of faith, which lay beyond the province of criticism and could not be harmed by it.

The essayists thus reversed many orthodox assumptions about the unity and integrity of scripture. The Bible was not the *locus* of revelation but a confirmation of it, and the principle of private judgment, rather than deference to traditional authority, provided the key to its interpretation.

The book's main importance was its shock value in dispersing the ignorance about biblical criticism which obtained at the time. Jowett held that this had been deliberately fostered by the two main religious parties, and English theology lagged far behind the level of scholarship found on the continent. The names of German critics are, for that reason, frequently cited in *Essays and Reviews*. The book marked a turning point, and though conservative attitudes were hardened as a result of the campaign against the writers, a period of liberalization was bound to follow. *Essays and Reviews* created a climate which made possible within twenty years the publication of the works of S. R. Driver, W. Robertson Smith,* and T. K. Cheyne, all of whom accepted the broad critical positions found in the book. The negative and extreme tone of *Essays and Reviews* was, however, avoided, and in this and other respects the book occupies an isolated position in the development of English theology. It did not really belong to the liberal tradition fostered by Coleridge,* Arnold, and Maurice. Westcott,* Lightfoot, and Hort, as representing the Cambridge school, were critical of it. Its sudden appearance in 1860, without plan or collective re-

sponsibility, suggested that it was merely an opportunist publication.

The weaknesses of the book are exemplified in Jowett's essay. Though regarded as radical and far-reaching in its time, the essay does not contain a blueprint for a school of historical criticism. Jowett's interest was in the Bible as literature, to allow the text to speak freely to the reader, once the detritus of past centuries of interpretation had been removed. He does not seem to have doubted that the text would speak, however large the passage of time between writer and reader. The equipment necessary for this task was that of a poet as well as a critic, 'demanding much more than mere learning, a degree of original power and intensity of mind'. This appears to have been an imaginative exercise rather than one of historical reconstruction, using the tools of critical scholarship.

See also **English Interpretation.**

I. Ellis, *Seven Against Christ. A Study of 'Essays and Reviews'*, 1980; P. B. Hinchliff, *Benjamin Jowett and the Christian Religion*, 1987; B. M. G. Reardon, *From Coleridge to Gore*, 1971.

IEUAN ELLIS

Esther

The interpretation of Esther, a problem for many centuries, is still a lively subject. Although long a popular book in Judaism for its association with the Purim festival, until the third century AD there were doubts in some rabbinical circles whether it rightly had a place among the books which 'defile the hands', that is, the holy books (Megillah 7a), and possibly more than an accident of history accounts for its absence from the Qumran discoveries. In Christian circles a negative view of its value is not confined to early times. Luther's* famous criticism of it as an alien work of Judaizing tendency and pagan impropriety finds an echo in the twentieth century among those who consider its canonical status unjustified (L. B. Paton, *Esther*, 1908; O. Eissfeldt, *The Old Testament: An Introduction*, 1978).

What kind of book is this which makes no reference to God either explicitly or by allusion (4.14 is unlikely to be such), in which prayer has no place and fasting is the only remotely religious activity? Surprising, too, in a book concerned with the survival of a Jewish community, is its apparent lack of interest in specifically Jewish observances such as dietary laws. In all these respects the book stands in marked contrast with Daniel. For Esther at Ahasuerus' court there appears no tension or conflict of loyalties. These strange features of the Hebrew story are highlighted when compared with the Greek versions (Septuagint* and Lucian) for here the 'deficiencies' are supplied not only by the six major additions contained in the Apocrypha* but also by numerous variants in the canonical parts. There are many references to God, prayer is prominent (13.8–18; 14.1–19), and Esther herself is outspoken in her revulsion against her position at the Persian court (14.15–19). The story is now overtly religious. Moreover the whole perspective of the Greek tale is changed. Through the first and last of the additions (particularly 11.5–11; 10.4–12) the court intrigue of the Hebrew version takes on an eschatological perspective as a cosmic struggle between Jews and all Gentile nations, Haman appropriately becoming the apocalyptic 'Gogite' (cf. Ezek. 38–9). The Jewish tone is not lessened. Indeed the story becomes more strongly anti-Gentile. The Greek additions are, however, undoubtedly secondary, and to suggest, as some have done, that the references to God have not been added to the Greek but excised from the Hebrew lest in the boisterous revelry of Purim they might accidentally be profaned is pure speculation. In fact these so-called deficiencies of the Hebrew version may themselves point us to the story's genre as a wisdom tale. This would account too for the lack of reference to two central concerns of the OT in general, namely Israel's land and history, the latter made good in the Greek version by reference to the patriarchs (13.15; 14.5) and the exodus (13.16). The book of Esther may be understood as an illustration of applied wisdom, the wisdom of Proverbs in action (Talmon). Like wisdom literature* in general it is anthropocentric, and underlying causes are not its concern. The difficulty of adequately defining wisdom influence, however, has made this interesting view less than generally convincing.

It is now widely acknowledged that, despite chronological and other difficulties, the story has a historical basis, and fairly represents the situation in the Persian empire in the time of Xerxes, hence its not infrequent characterization as a 'historical novel', or, emphasizing still more strongly the historical element, a 'novelistic history' (Clines). It must not be interpreted in isolation, but is to be read in the light of Israel's traditions, especially the Joseph and Exodus stories, the latter perhaps serving as its model. In their light who else but God could work such dramatic reversal, the very theme by which the book is ordered? 'God, as a character of the story, becomes more conspicuous the more he is absent' (Clines). His power and intervention in his people's affairs are axiomatic. They do not need spelling out. God *will* deliver, whoever may be his instrument (4.14). It is, therefore, more than simply a story of human cunning.

Yet is it not an objectionable tale of vengeance and slaughter? There are elements of this in ch. 9 particularly (the original tale may well have ended with ch. 8), but the overwhelming emphasis falls on the right of the Jewish community to defend itself. If the edict of 8.11, initiated by Mordecai, seems harsh, two points need to be made in clarification: 1. The previous edict decreeing the annihilation of the Jews cannot be revoked, only neutralized by this second edict; 2. Here, too, the emphasis is on defence. It is doubtful whether slaughter of women and children is envisaged (contrast NEB), for, whereas in 3.13 the phrase 'children and women' is clearly part of the object of the verb 'to annihilate', in 8.11 it is, as its position makes clear, the object of the participle 'attacking'; 'them, their children and women, with their goods as booty' is cited from Haman's edict and should be in quotation marks (Gordis, *JBL* 95, 1976). In this mainly defensive reaction to threatened genocide lies in part the religious significance of the book. The Purim festival perpetuates for the Jews not bitterness but the joy of deliverance and the ground of future hope (Gordis). The inclusion of this book within the canon of scripture confronts Christians with the reality of Israel and with the essential Jewishness of the roots of our faith.

D. J. Clines, *Ezra, Nehemiah, Esther* (New Century Bible), 1984; R. Gordis, *Megillat Esther*, 1972; C. A. Moore, *Daniel, Esther, and Jeremiah: the Additions*, 1977; id., *Studies in the Book of Esther*, 1982; S. Talmon, 'Wisdom in the Book of Esther', *VT* 13, 1963, pp. 419–55.

GRACE I. EMMERSON

Ethics (New Testament)

The interpretation of the ethical material in the NT has for the most part marched in step with the general interpretation of the NT in its various phases. But long before the NT as a canonical body of writings was available to the church, those writings already, in the process of their composition and early use, played an important part in the development of Christian ethics and also serve as vital evidence for that development.

They show that while some basic elements in early Christian ethics derive from the widespread current wisdom of the Graeco-Roman world, much of it shared by Jews and pagan teachers alike (e.g. lists of virtues and vices, Rom. 1.29ff., and catalogues of duties in the household, Col. 3.18ff.), its most distinctive features reflect either the strong eschatological perspective of earliest Christianity (e.g. Paul on marriage, I Cor. 7) or the career of Christ, seen as implying certain moral norms for

Christians (e.g. the stress on humility, a quality not otherwise highly regarded, Phil. 2.6–11; or generous self-giving, II Cor. 8.9). Most notable of all is the widely testified emphasis on love, whether for God (Mark 12.30, quoting the Jewish *shema*) or neighbour (Luke 10.25–37) or enemy (Matt. 5.44) or one's fellow-Christians (John 13.34). While this feature is by no means unparalleled in the Judaism of the time (*see* **Jewish Background to the New Testament**), the range of the love-command and the prominence accorded to it are notable in the tradition of Jesus' teaching, and indeed elsewhere in early Christianity, e.g. I Cor. 13 and Gal. 5.6.

This matter draws attention to the major interpretative achievement of early Christianity: its pluriform attempt to come to terms with the Jewish Law.* In so far as this was a matter of interpretation rather than rejection, it may be seen (at least to begin with, until the church became more independent of Judaism around the end of the first century) as part and parcel of the continuous process of interpretation of the Law within Judaism itself, in this case stimulated and necessitated both by the teaching of Jesus and by the church's belief in him as messiah* or exalted Lord. Early Christian groups ranged from the fairly conservative (Matthew, e.g. 5.17–19) to the fairly radical (aspects of Paul,* especially those matters, such as circumcision, sabbath and food laws, which threatened to divide Jews from Gentiles within the Christian group) in their re-interpretation of the Jewish Law, though as far as its strictly ethical (as distinct from liturgical and ceremonial) provisions were concerned, the church mostly took them over (e.g. Rom. 13.9). The earliest systematic reflection on how Christians should interpret the Law is in the *Letter to Flora* by the second-century Gnostic* Ptolemaeus.

Already in the later writings of the NT itself, a sense of Christian law begins to be manifested (e.g. I Tim. 1.8–10), necessitated by the requirements of good order in the increasingly Gentile Christian congregations and stimulated by decline in practical belief in the world's imminent end. It is this rule-providing role which soon became normative in the use and interpretation of the NT received as canonical. It helps to account for the special popularity of the Gospel of Matthew, which is particularly rich in teaching given by Jesus. Alongside the OT (interpreted with varying degrees of subtlety and according to diverse theories of its place in Christianity), the NT came to be used as a reservoir of texts for the illumination and resolution of ethical problems and the provision of moral guidance. An example of the discussion of ethical problems simply by way of the assembling and

balancing of texts may be seen, in relation to the question of the owning of property, in Umberto Eco's novel, *The Name of the Rose*, 1983, pp. 341ff. In the public life of the church, especially in the mediaeval Western church, the dominant idiom was legal, and the Bible was treated, in effect, as a source-book of legal instructions. It is instructive to note that a matter such as Henry VIII's petition to the papacy to divorce Katharine of Aragon was argued out less in terms of the NT teaching on the subject than of the OT texts which could be held to deal more specifically with the case (marriage to a deceased brother's widow). Meanwhile, at a more popular level, the Ten Commandments were from the later Middle Ages given prominence in the basic instruction of the laity (alongside the Lord's Prayer and the Apostles' Creed), a role they retained in Reformation catechisms. It speaks loudly for the verbal authority given to scripture as a whole and for the need felt for detailed moral instruction that it was this OT formula that fulfilled this central role and not the two-fold command to love God and neighbour found in Jesus' teaching (Mark 12.28–34). In the Church of England, the Decalogue was even put up at the east end of churches and recited in the communion service, and only in the abortive Prayer Book of 1928 was it replaced by the two-fold command to love.

Through most of the pre-critical period (and indeed since), ethical material in the NT has found a place not only, where appropriate, in forming canon law and in basic Christian instruction in school and parish, but also in the work of spiritual formation. From the thirteenth century in particular, in the Western church, there was a systematic effort to encourage the practice of the sacrament of penance and of spiritual direction, often at a rudimentary level, but also along lines which led to profound contemplative experience and reflection. In this area, part pastoral, part ethical, part spiritual, stories and sayings from the Gospels played their part as examples, and the teaching on love (fortified by the use of the Song of Songs from the OT) found its full outlet, especially in monastic life. The sense, already implicit in the NT but neglected in some of the more practical aspects of Christian institutional life, that belief, moral growth and spiritual formation belong inescapably together, here found renewed expression.

It was only in the eighteenth century that Christian ethics came to be identified as a distinct subject of study, alongside the other academic disciplines of Christian theology which achieved discrete existence at that period, especially in the Protestant universities of Germany. In this context, NT ethics could gradually come into focus as a topic meriting attention, but in practice it has most commonly been studied in relation to more central questions of NT scholarship (e.g. as part of the enquiry into the historical Jesus) or in its specialized aspects (e.g. C. Spicq's massive work on *Agapé dans le Nouveau Testament*, 1958–9). There is realism in the former approach, in that for the NT writers themselves 'ethics' was not an independent subject but part and parcel of their total outlook. There is value, too, in the latter approach for the sake of establishing clarity about the numerous facets of ethical language and ethical concern in early Christianity and its environment.

In addition, ethical matters have come to the fore in a variety of ways in the context of the successive styles of enquiry to which the NT has been subjected in the era of critical scholarship. Thus, for example, form criticism* resulted in the identification of certain modes of ethical expression in the early church. It has been held that there were collections of the sayings of Jesus, perhaps linked by theme or even by catch-word, which first circulated orally and were eventually incorporated into one or other of the Gospels. Such collections lie behind longer units like the so-called Sermon on the Mount* (Matt. 5–7) and can be seen in such passages as Matt. 6.19–34, centring on the theme of anxiety, or Luke 16.8b–13, centring on the theme of property and the word *mammōn*. Or one can identify brief statements of the duties of various groups within the household ('household codes'), and compare them with similar statements in Jewish and Hellenistic* sources (e.g. Col. 3.18–4.1).

Redaction criticism* shifted attention from the units which may have lain behind the Gospels to the ideas and processes which gave rise to each Gospel as an independent work, and ethical matters came to be discussed so far as they were relevant. Not surprisingly, they have figured largely in work on the Gospel of Matthew, notably in the fundamental study of that Gospel's redaction, G. Bornkamm, G. Barth and H. J. Held, *Tradition and Interpretation in Matthew*, 1960, much of it relating to Matthew's teaching on the Law.

More recent studies of both Gospels and other NT writings have focussed on their social background and viewed them from a sociological* point of view. Much of this work has inevitably considered ethical subjects, such as the roles of the sexes and of slaves, in the setting of Jewish or Graeco-Roman society.

It is not surprising that a varied range of questions occupies those who write on NT ethics. Some of the chief ones are:

1. Paul's ethics: how far does his teaching derive from the Jewish and Hellenistic ethos of his upbringing, and how far does it relate to central aspects of his theology, such as christology (Phil. 2.6–11) or eschatology (on marriage, I Cor. 7, and work, II Thess. 3.6ff.)? How far is he moved by nicely-judged pastoral considerations (again on marriage questions, I Cor. 7), and how far by a sense of God-given authority (e.g. I Cor. 3.17)? And what is the role of ethics in the business of salvation as seen now in the light of Christ?

2. Jesus' ethics: what was the attitude of Jesus to the Jewish Law – to accept and endorse it, to intensify it, or to demote it from its central position in the light of his own mission and the coming of the kingdom* of God? This means in effect both a discussion of historical probabilities and an assessment of diverging evidence in the Gospels, with Matthew indicating that Jesus accepted and intensified the Law for his followers, and Mark (almost certainly writing before him) indicating a policy of supersession, even a pushing of the Law to the margins. What is involved is the complex issue of how much in the Gospels goes back to Jesus and how much is conditioned by later tradition and in particular the outlook of the Christian communities which wrote them, each differing in its attitude to the matter in hand. The deeper question relates to Jesus' linking his proclamation concerning God, his nature and his demands, to specific moral matters: wealth, marriage, the status of women, and political authority. Most problematic of all, perhaps, is the understanding of the command to love, which is thrust into prominence: in what sense is this determinative?

3. Hermeneutical* matters: these arise in two ways. Anyone writing a comprehensive study of NT ethics (and there has been something of a spate of such works in recent years) faces decisions on how to arrange the material. Despite the immense complexities and uncertainties in arriving at knowledge of what is attributable to Jesus and what comes from the churches, almost all begin boldly with chapters on the ethical teaching of Jesus, then move on to the early church, Paul, and other NT writings. This programme is open to grave objection and can readily be a source of confusion and misinformation. Drawing upon NT studies as a whole, we are bound to recognize the powerful role of the evangelists in the portrayals of Jesus in the different Gospels – and the considerable variations between those portrayals. On the other hand, Paul, directly available in his letters, gives our earliest and most vivid evidence. Jesus' ethical (and other) teaching has to be more tentatively arrived at, *by way of* the various portrayals given in the Gospels, which belong to the later first century and were written in the light of concerns dominant at that time.

The other hermeneutical question, felt by most writers on NT ethics, concerns the relevance and usefulness of NT rulings or counsels today. It may be that doctrinally determined convictions about their continuing direct authority, above all if they come from Jesus himself, affect the strong investment of attention in a primary treatment of Jesus' ethics, almost regardless of the difficulties. Students should recognize that in making judgments about present-day applications of NT ethics, writers are inevitably conditioned by their more general doctrinal standpoint – about the role of scripture in Christian judgment, about the location of authority in Christianity, about matters of Christian identity. These may themselves be affected by non-theological factors, such as the degree to which a writer has allowed for sociological factors in determining the decisions of Christian institutions in every period or has come to feel the force of the relativism of moral judgments in relation to their specific contexts.

See also **Cynics; Ethics (Old Testament).**

John Bowden, *Jesus: The Unanswered Questions*, 1988, ch. 7; J. L. Houlden, *Ethics and the New Testament*, 1973; R. N. Longenecker, *New Testament Social Ethics for Today*, 1984; Wayne Meeks, *The Moral World of the First Christians*, 1986; J. T. Sanders, *Ethics in the New Testament*, 1975; Allen Verhey, *The Great Reversal: Ethics and the New Testament*, 1984.

J. L. HOULDEN

Ethics (Old Testament)

The study of OT ethics has to face all the problems involved in writing an OT theology: the literature preserved in the canon comes from a long period of history; it consists of several different genres; most, if not all, of the books have been subject to a long process of editing. To attempt a theology or ethics of the OT is likely to mean, therefore, that a unity is imposed upon the variegated deposit of material, although most scholars are aware of the historical dimension and attempt to reflect it in the way they set out the evidence.

More recently it has been realized that there are not only differences across history but also within a particular period. On the whole the OT contains 'official' religion. Popular religious and moral practice may have been very different. By reading between the lines and using archaeological evidence from Palestine, some have made a few tentative steps in presenting the beliefs of the ordinary Israelite, but it is unlikely that more than an impressionistic picture will be possible.

All these difficulties bar the way to the presentation of OT ethics, but there are further problems in addition. Sociology* has made scholars sensitive to the different levels at which moral norms operate. At the very least the actual practice needs to be distinguished from the moral norms which are accepted by the different groups within society and from the 'official' norms set out, for example, in law* codes. The relation between these three levels in OT times is obscure. Why, for example, in both Israel and Mesopotamia, was reference so seldom made to the law codes in prophetic utterance and judicial decision?

Moreover, because the OT is not a treatise on moral theology, the basis of OT ethics is not immediately apparent. The dominance of the laws and the prophetic 'Thus said Yahweh' might suggest that the OT ethic is grounded on obedience to the commands of God, and this is certainly true of the completed canon, even if the wisdom* writings fit in somewhat uneasily. Older scholars were convinced that this was so. But John Barton has argued that two forms of 'natural law' are to be found in the OT: norms which all men are expected to recognize and accept as right and proper, and an ethical system which is built into the nature of things. He suggests that there are therefore three types of implicit moral philosophy underlying the OT writings: obedience to God's revealed will, 'natural law', and the imitation of God.

It is only in the modern critical period that 'Ethics' has separated out as a distinct discipline within biblical studies. This does not mean that the moral teaching of the OT was disregarded. The Bible was treated as a source of divine law, and texts selected across both Testaments were used to support ethical judgments, an approach which is still found when politicians quote Gen. 9.6 in support of capital punishment, or conservative churchmen oppose the ordination of women to the priesthood on the basis of the character of the OT priesthood, the early chapters of Genesis, and quotations from Paul. It has been well documented with regard to the debate over slavery in North America in the nineteenth century. Even within the period of critical scholarship expositions of ethics were largely descriptive, usually following the reconstruction of the development of Israelite religion popularized by Wellhausen. Under the influence of the Biblical Theology* movement, ethics tended to be subsumed under theology and was presented in too unified a way. It was only when scholars alert to sociology, social anthropology and philosophical ethics began to examine the OT that presentations of a genuine OT *ethics* began to be made. In the last decade the questions outlined in the first part of this article have come to the fore. The impossibility of writing an 'Old Testament Ethics' is now generally accepted, although conservatives continue to attempt synthetic expositions. For these reasons it seems unprofitable to try to present a historical survey, and for the rest of this article I shall pick up a number of limited issues that have been discussed in recent journal literature as illustrating the problems.

A lively debate has centred on the significance of the OT evidence. Anthony Phillips interpreted the Decalogue as 'Israel's Criminal Law'. From legal and narrative material he argued that Israel distinguished between crimes and torts, and he connected the apodeictic laws of the Decalogue with Noth's amphictyony and Mendenhall's theory of suzerainty treaties (though he later retracted this, asserting that his theory does not depend upon those particular views of the origins of the covenant and the law). To safeguard the covenant* and avoid divine punishment upon the community, the decalogue set out the crimes for which the penalty was death. Phillips' initial study was wide-ranging, and two issues were picked up by Henry McKeating in discussions of adultery and homicide. First, he pointed out that there is not a single account of an adulterer or an adulteress actually being put to death in any of the historical books, and that alternative penalties for adultery are found in the prophets and the wisdom writings. From this he argued that the Decalogue was rather a list of actions that were displeasing to God and that Israelite ethics cannot be read off from the laws. What needs to be considered is the status of the laws in ancient Israel. Secondly, he considered the sanctions that are applied to the breach of any moral system, and from the example of adultery showed that legal punishment is only one of a whole battery of sanctions, moral, prudential, and social, so that in Proverbs the adulterer is warned to beware of the anger of the aggrieved husband and that he will suffer loss of prestige in the community.

In the subsequent discussion Phillips claimed that the disagreement revolved around the question of whether the OT law was distinctive or was characteristic of ancient Near Eastern laws. This does not seem to be the key issue, however, and what comes out of this particular debate is the level at which the ethics is being considered and the way the evidence is obtained. Here John Barton has made a valuable contribution. Drawing on the methods of Kenneth Dover's study of popular morality in classical Greece, he proposed that what needs to be examined is what the prophets and other speakers in ancient Israel judged that their hearers would accept as morally right, and he worked this out in relation to Amos' prophecies against the nations. This is a valuable insight, although it is doubtful how fully it can be

carried through; it may depend upon a greater degree of knowledge concerning the original setting and purpose of the OT writings than is actually available to us.

Despite extensive recent use of the narratives in OT ethics, the law, the prophets, and the wisdom literature remain the main centres of interest.

Apart from detailed studies of individual laws, such as 'Thou shalt not steal', attention has been given to the 'motive clauses' (e.g. Ex. 20.12b). These appear to increase in frequency with the lateness of the codes in which they are found. They have been classified as explanatory (an appeal to common sense), ethical (a direct appeal to the conscience), religious (with reference to the cult and to theological premises), and in relation to salvation history, and it has been argued that these clauses distinguished the OT laws from other codes in the ancient Near East. More recently, a more elaborate analysis has been made and motive clauses have been identified outside Israel. Nevertheless, the type of clause found in the OT still appears to be distinctive. Certainly, the large number of motive clauses in the OT makes these laws characteristically hortatory.

Motive clauses are common in the book of Proverbs also, and the form and thrust of these clauses have suggested to some scholars that the ethos of wisdom is based on the created order, although this may fall short of a full natural theology. Since the *Sitz im Leben* of wisdom is still so hotly contested, we are far from a rounded exposition of the ethic of the wisdom writings.

Among the many studies of prophecy, two issues may be singled out: the basis of prophetic ethics and its central content. A striking feature of Amos, Isaiah and Micah is their failure to use the word 'covenant', and Wellhausen saw this as evidence for the late introduction of the concept, a view to which several modern scholars have returned. Those who place the covenant earlier, such as Eichrodt, explain the absence of the term in these prophets as due to the mechanical way in which it was popularly regarded, so that the prophets had to go behind it to ideas of election and deliverance. Some would set the origin of the idea at the time of Hosea and the Deuteronomists. Allied to this question is the relation of the prophets to the law. The rarity of direct quotation from the law codes and even from the Decalogue led one scholar to interpret Jer. 7.9 as evidence for the gradual crystallizing of ethical prescriptions during the lifetime of Jeremiah. The debate concerning the origin of the ethics of the prophets continues. Two distinct traditions have been discerned, one (in Amos, Micah and Isaiah) based on a general concept of humaneness and righteousness, the other (in Hosea) viewing Israel as committing apostasy by rejecting the covenant and the law of Sinai. The two traditions come together in Jeremiah.

Turning to the content of the prophetic message, a central issue is whether the prophets were social reformers or something else. It has been argued that the social context of the eighth-century prophets was economic development, with the dispossession of the peasants by the wealthy being achieved with the support of the monarchy and through the use of the law courts, leading to a widening gulf between rich and poor. The basic economic problem was land ownership, the political issue the corruption of justice. The prophets were not ethicists or social reformers but announced the certainty of divine judgment. Certainly, there is a striking contrast between the words of the prophets which are largely addressed to social wrongs, and the Decalogue which can be interpreted in an individualistic way.

Several scholars have picked up the position of the poor. As long ago as 1967 Norman Porteous traced out the variations in the OT teaching about the poor, showing that poverty was felt to be a real problem in many narratives, in the laws and in the prophets, but that the wisdom writers viewed it as culpable and indicative of idleness. More recently the vocabulary used by the prophets and in Proverbs has been compared and a contrast in the understanding of poverty between these two groups has been drawn; despite their benign regard for the poor, the wise men are a ruling and wealthy élite without any awareness that the urban population was becoming rich by exploiting the poor. But does 'poor' mean poverty-stricken in the OT? Several scholars have pointed to the way the psalmists, like their counterparts in other cultures of the ancient Near East, use 'poor' in the religious sense of 'pious' and 'devoted to God'.

As is to be expected, there has grown up a considerable literature on the position of women in the OT, and nowhere does the stance of the writer affect the interpretation more obviously. The older scholars tended to give little space to the subject, and when they did it was mainly in the context of marriage. Recent feminist writers adopt two rival approaches, either rejecting the OT entirely as 'patriarchal' or arguing that correctly understood it gives a secure place to women. A dominant question, in view of the current debate in the churches on the ordination of women, is why women in OT times could be active in every sphere apart from the priesthood. Many different reasons have been proposed: women were too weak physically to handle the sacrifices, or too busy in the home where their true priesthood was exercised, or

had such low status in society that it would have been impossible for them to exert authority, or their exclusion was part of a wider attack on fertility religion, or their periodic ritual uncleanness rendered them unfit to approach holy things.

One final question may be noted. It is often suggested that the OT contains a 'distinctive' ethic, with the implication that it is 'higher' than that found among other peoples of the ancient Near East. At Ugarit,* however, to judge the cause of the widow and to banish those who oppress the poor was the duty of the king, and it has been pointed out that verses from Proverbs may be exchanged with passages from the wisdom writings of Egypt and Babylon without any noticeable drop in moral quality. The reverse of this is that such customs as 'the ban', the total destruction of captured cities such as Jericho, which is so offensive to us, were practised outside Israel. Moreover, the pervasiveness of the demand for purity, which is found in much of the legal material in the OT, and accounts for the intermingling of ritual and ethical laws, is common to many simple societies. Attempts to find distinctive features include noting the prevalence of apodeictic laws, the hortatory nature of the legislation, the social ethics of the prophets, the influence of the theological concepts of salvation history and covenant, and the unique combination of individual and social morality. All such suggestions go part of the way but are not fully convincing. Certainly it is impossible to speak of a 'unique' ethics in the OT. Yet the social equality of all male Israelites and the precedence of persons over property rights seem to mark off Israel from such societies as that of Babylon, and while figures similar to the Israelite prophets appear elsewhere in the ancient world, nowhere has such a succession of men who fearlessly declare God's will and announce his punishment of social wrong been found.

See also **Ancient Near Eastern World; Ethics (New Testament); Law.**

J. Barton, 'Approaches to Ethics in the Old Testament' in J. Rogerson (ed.), *Beginning Old Testament Study*, 1983; W. Eichrodt, *Theology of the Old Testament*, 2 vols, 1961, 1967; H. McKeating, 'Sanctions against adultery in ancient Israelite society, with some reflections on methodology in the study of Old Testament ethics', *JSOT* 11, 1979, pp. 57–72; C. J. H. Wright, *Living as the People of God*, 1983.

CYRIL S. RODD

Ethos

A basic axiom of the historical-critical method* of interpreting the Bible is that the meaning of the text cannot be grasped fully without some knowledge of its historical and social setting. In recent study of the NT, in particular, greater precision in historical criticism has been gained by the adoption of analytical concepts provided by the social sciences. 'Ethos' is one such concept, especially in the form in which it has been defined and elaborated by the American anthropologist, Clifford Geertz:

> In recent anthropological discussion, the moral (and aesthetic) aspects of a given culture, the evaluative elements, have commonly been summed up in the term 'ethos', while the cognitive, existential aspects have been designated by the term 'world view'. A people's ethos is the tone, character, and quality of their life, its moral and aesthetic style and mood; it is the underlying attitude toward themselves and their world that life reflects. Their world view is their picture of the way things in sheer actuality are, their concept of nature, of self, of society. It contains their most comprehensive ideas of order (*The Interpretation of Cultures*, 1973, pp. 126f.).

Study of the ethos of early Christianity helps the interpreter to understand better the connections between what Christians believed, the ways they behaved and what it felt like to belong. It brings to the fore the communal dimension, and places what is said to or about individuals in the context of what is assumed as customary for the group. The doctrinal teaching and ethical instruction contained in the texts of the NT are treated no longer as abstractions to be interpreted irrespective of the concrete cultural and social milieux of which they are an expression. Instead, in a more holistic* way, an ethological approach attempts to relate early Christian theology and morality to the actual life-styles of particular groups of believers in the first century. As Leander Keck (1980, p. 29) points out in his essay on NT ethics,* questions about what is to be done are inseparable from the question, Who is the doer and what are his or her communities?*

It is not possible to give a unitary account of the ethos of the first Christians. A broad comparison of the mission of Jesus and the mission of Paul makes this plain. One was rural and Galilean, the other urban and cosmopolitan. Whereas Jesus spoke parables* in Aramaic (*see* **Semitisms**), Paul* gave *paraenisis* (exhortation) in Greek. Whereas the Jesus movement was mendicant, ministered to the poor and warned of the dangers of riches, Paul worked to support himself and received benefactions from wealthy patrons. If the aim of Jesus was to renew an old community, Israel, the aim of Paul was to create a new

community, of Jews and Gentiles together. The shift from Jesus to Paul is represented in the change of message and medium: from Jesus' prophet-style announcement to Israel of the imminent 'kingdom of God'* by means of parable* and miracle,* to Paul's preaching (and writing) to Jews and Gentiles of Jesus as universal *Kyrios* (lord) and to the worship of Jesus in small, emotion-charged house groups.

But if a unitary account is not possible, important beginnings have been made in describing the ethos of the various groups which lie behind the NT texts and their sources. This work proceeds in a number of ways. First, there is a comparative aspect. The ethos of the first Christians is thrown into relief by analogy with that of contemporary non-Christian groups like the Qumran Covenanters (*see* **Dead Sea Scrolls**), the Pharisees,* the mystery cults,* and philosophical schools such as the Stoics and Cynics.* Recently, Gerd Theissen (*The First Followers of Jesus*, 1978) and F. G. Downing (*Jesus and the Threat of Freedom*, 1987) have used analogies between the Jesus tradition and traditions depicting the values and life-style of the Cynics to argue for the existence of a quite radical, counter-cultural strand in early Christianity: that of itinerant preachers who, following Jesus' own example, abandoned their families and occupations and rejected customary observances in order to preach repentance at a time of deep socio-economic and political crisis in Palestine. Such a reconstruction, it is argued, provides the most plausible ethos for those first followers whose life-style found expression and legitimation in the Q tradition.

A second way of giving definition to the ethos of the early Christians is to focus on the management of group boundaries. Wayne Meeks (1979) has shown that the ethos of Pauline Christianity is best described as that of an 'open sect', in some respects accommodating to the norms and structures of the macrosociety, in other respects hostile and exclusivist, with an insistence on moral purity within the churches and the importance of maintaining autonomy in the ordering of their internal affairs. In an earlier study, C. K. Barrett (*NTS*, 11, 1964–65, pp. 138-53) drew attention to the diverse attitudes in the Christian sources to 'meat offered to idols', the relative tolerance of Paul (e.g. I Cor. 8.4ff.) contrasting markedly with the absolute intolerance of the Seer of the Apocalypse (e.g. Rev. 2.14, 20). Such degrees of tolerance are an important indicator of differences of ethos between one Christian group and another and of varying degrees of pessimism with respect to 'the world'.

The ethos of the Christian groups was affected strongly by the response of outsiders.

This is a third important area of investigation. Study of the often fraught relations between Christians and Jews in the first and early second centuries is particularly relevant here. For instance, the ethos of moral rigour and total commitment to doing the will of God characteristic of the Gospel of Matthew reflects, in part, mutually hostile relations with Pharisaic Judaism in the period after AD 70. Matthean anti-Judaism (*see* **Antisemitism**) is interpreted by scholars today as a highly polemical response, reinforced by an apocalyptic* world-view, to experiences of persecution and rejection at the hands of the believers' own compatriots and kinsfolk. Similarly, as J. L. Martyn (*History and Theology in the Fourth Gospel*, 1979) has shown, the rather introverted ethos of Johannine Christianity reflects experiences of expulsion from the synagogue communities of the Jews. Ironically, the excluded become themselves exclusive, although in terms which make possible a common life of considerable novelty, based upon belief in Jesus rather than blood-ties and observance of Torah, and open therefore to Samaritans* and Greeks, as well as to Jews.

If relations with various forms of Judaism affected the ethos of early Christianity, so did relations with the native inhabitants of the cities and with the Roman imperial authorities. D. L. Balch (*Let Wives be Submissive*, 1981) has argued, for example, that the conservative, subordinationist ethos of the household code of I Peter represents an attempt to take the sting out of outsiders' accusations that conversion to Christ and membership of a Christian group were subversive of relations at the civic and domestic levels. Such accusations were brought frequently against members of oriental cult groups and other forms of voluntary association. The stress in early Christian writings on the control of charismatic ministries, the maintenance of moral rigour and social decorum, and the reinforcement of the patriarchal household order (suitably 'Christianized'), is due largely to a strong and understandable concern to avoid unnecessary conflict with fellow-citizens and political authorities.

Study of the rhetoric,* rituals and dominant symbols* of the Christian groups is a fourth facet of the description of what it felt like to belong. As early as 1933, A. D. Nock commented that the usages of Greek vocabulary in the NT 'are the product of an enclosed world living its own life, a ghetto culturally and linguistically if not geographically'. A strikingly similar conclusion was reached by Meeks (*JBL*, 91, 1972, pp. 44-72) in his study of the distinctive imagery and language patterns of the Fourth Gospel. According to Meeks, the Fourth Gospel makes most sense, not as a missionary tract, but as the expression of a group whose ethos is isolationist and sectarian. Just as Jesus is a stranger to, and estranged from, the world, so too is the Johannine community.

Finally, although by no means exhaustively, an indirect contribution to the study of the ethos of the first Christians has been the repeated confirmation that the texts of the NT bear witness to a wide range of diversity in the beliefs, values and practices of the groups to which they are addressed. Such diversity is a basic clue to something fundamental about early Christian life-style: it was argumentative, passionate, self-critical, innovative and charismatic, with a relative absence of formal, centralized structures of authority. This picture has been reinforced by studies which have shown the importance of eschatology* in early Christian thought, the prominence given to experiences of, and beliefs about, the Spirit, and the elements of disconcerting novelty in the social relations of church members. Feminist* scholarship has contributed on this latter point, in particular, highlighting the tensions reflected in the sources between an ethos which encouraged innovation in gender relations and the dominant, patriarchal ethos which sought conservatively to subordinate women and to maintain the traditional polity of the household.

See also **Anthropology: Community; Sociology and Social Anthropology.**

S. C. Barton, 'Paul, Religion and Society' in J. Obelkevich et al. (eds) *Disciplines of Faith: Religion, Patriarchy and Politics*, 1987, pp. 167–77; L. E. Keck, 'On the Ethos of Early Christians', *Journal of the American Academy of Religion*, XLII, 1974, pp. 435–52; id., 'Ethos and Ethics in the New Testament' in J. Gaffney (ed.), *Essays in Morality and Ethics*, 1980, pp. 29–49; W. A. Meeks, *The First Urban Christians*, 1983; id., *The Moral World of the First Christians*, 1986; id., '"Since then you would need to go out of the world": Group boundaries in Pauline Christianity', in T. Ryan (ed.), *Critical History and Biblical Faith*, 1979; J. H. Schütz, 'Ethos of Early Christianity', *IDB*–S V, 1976, pp. 289–94.

STEPHEN C. BARTON

Etymology

Etymology has played an important role in biblical interpretation, especially the interpretation of the Hebrew Bible, since ancient times. The most obvious examples are the etymologies given in the Bible itself for proper names such as Eve (Gen. 3.20), Moses (Ex. 2.10), and Jesus (Matt.1.21). Rare or difficult words frequently prompted etymological discussion in rabbinic and patristic commentaries. The encyclopaedic *Etymologiae* of Isidore of Seville (*c.* 560–636) was an important work cited by numerous mediaeval scholars. The Jewish scholars Saadiya (892–942), translator of the Hebrew Bible into Arabic and author of a Hebrew-Arabic dictionary, and David Kimchi (1160–1235), author of a Hebrew grammar and a dictionary entitled *The Book of Roots*, marked further developments in the etymological approach to Hebrew, in particular the isolation of the 'root' of each word and comparison with other Semitic languages.

The publication of Bishop Walton's *Biblia Sacra Polyglotta* (1654–7), with Castell's *Lexicon Heptaglotton* (1669) soon after, provided an additional impetus to comparative philology.* By the end of the eighteenth century Hebraists and other biblical scholars generally believed that etymological data were of primary importance for our understanding of the Bible, a belief which was further strengthened in the nineteenth and twentieth centuries by the publication of grammars and dictionaries of newly-discovered or deciphered languages, notably Babylonian and Ugaritic. Biblical Hebrew dictionaries, unlike most other dictionaries, gave pride of place to etymology. Studies of words like *'ibri* 'Hebrew', *qadosh* 'holy', *qahal* 'assembly', *'emet* 'truth', *dabar* 'word' and the like similarly assumed that their etymology would reveal their 'true meaning' or 'literal meaning'. For the same reason, theological colleges and seminaries encouraged students of the Hebrew Bible to study more than one Semitic language. It was not until the publication of James Barr's *Semantics of Biblical Language* in 1961 that these assumptions were seriously questioned.

The etymology of a word may or may not affect its meaning in a particular context. Some English words (e.g. 'girl') have no etymology at all. Others have an etymology which, however fascinating, is of historical interest only and quite irrelevant to its actual usage today (e.g. 'syringe' from Greek *surinx*, 'panpipes'). Others might have a popular etymology, quite unrelated to the linguistic facts, but which makes good sense: 'decadent', for example, might be understood to mean 'lasting for only a decade'! The assumption that etymologies are always helpful is unwarranted and misleading. The primary evidence for the meaning of a word always comes from within the context in which it is used.

The extraordinary preoccupation with etymological data in modern biblical studies was due mainly to the fact that in the Semitic languages, including Hebrew, the 'root' of most words is easier to investigate than it is, for example, in modern European languages. The Semitic language group is relatively close-

knit. It is a branch of the Hamito-Semitic family of languages which include ancient Egyptian, Coptic and many modern African languages (Berber, Hausa, Tigre, etc.), and itself has three branches comprising East Semitic (Accadian, Babylonian, Assyrian), West Semitic (Ugaritic,* Hebrew, Aramaic, Punic, Arabic, etc.) and South Semitic (South Arabian, Ethiopic, etc.). One striking feature of these languages is their basis in a common word-structure, which consists of three (less often one, two or four) consonants. Thus the root S L M is common to Arabic *salām* 'peace', *islām* 'submission' and *muslim* 'one who submits'. Proto-Semitic forms, from which later Semitic words have developed, can often be reconstructed with a fair degree of plausibility. Sound laws control how each Proto-Semitic sound appears in the various Semitic languages in which it occurs, and many Hebrew grammars contain a simple table of correspondences: Arabic *s* = Aramaic *sh* = Hebrew *sh*, Arabic *ā* = Aramaic *ā* = Hebrew *ō*; and thus Arabic *salām* = Aramaic *shelām* = Hebrew *shālōm*. The consonantal script in which Hebrew, Aramaic, Ugaritic, Arabic and other Semitic languages are written also makes a word's root peculiarly conspicuous and facilitates comparison with other languages.

Another reason for the prominence given to etymology in the study of the Bible is that Christian interpreters often worked within a non-Hebrew, and indeed frequently anti-Jewish, context with the result that their knowledge of Hebrew tended to be rather academic and restricted to biblical Hebrew. Instead of devoting the same meticulous attention to actual Hebrew usage, in the vast post-biblical Jewish literature, as they would to Greek or Latin or English sources, biblical scholars confronted by a difficult or intriguing Hebrew word would go to dictionaries of Arabic, Babylonian, Ugaritic, Ethiopic or another Semitic language. Distrust of the Jewish sources as 'late' and therefore less reliable than Ugaritic or reconstructed Proto-Semitic, although they are in fact historically closer to biblical Hebrew and in the same language, led to further 'etymologizing'.

The abuse of etymology and comparative philology has had a number of harmful effects on biblical interpretation. In the first place, there is the totally erroneous assumption that 'root-meanings' or 'what words originally meant' can be studied with a greater degree of objectivity and precision than other meanings. This has led to the neglect of other more delicate semantic techniques, devised to identify the precise nuances of a word in its context and in relation to its closest synonyms. Studies of *'ibri*, 'Hebrew', for example, which are dominated by the etymological discussion of its relation to Akkadian *ḫabiru*, a word with pejorative overtones, have difficulty with passages like Gen. 14.13; Jonah 1.9; II Cor. 11.22; and Phil. 3.5.

Another error in some biblical 'etymologizing' is due to the unthinking assumption that all the comparative Semitic data are equally relevant: an Arabic meaning is as useful as a Ugaritic one. For example, written Arabic appears to be the most conservative of all the Semitic languages in its phonology and grammar, but this does not necessarily apply to meaning. Thus although Arabic sources are all post-biblical, they may be a more valuable source for reconstructing 'original' Semitic sounds and forms (e.g. case-endings which no longer exist in Hebrew) than Ethiopic, but far less useful in reconstructing 'original' meanings than the very much more ancient Ugaritic sources.

Etymology is an exact science. Unfortunately, for reasons mentioned above, biblical commentaries and theological writings in general contain statements and theories on 'root-meanings' that are not only irrelevant but unreliable, based on dubious etymologies and an inadequate knowledge of the relevant languages. Barr cites innumerable examples: e.g. the meaning of *dabar*, 'word' explained by an etymology relating it to *debir*, 'the inner sanctuary of the Temple'; *qahal*, 'assembly', derived from the same root as *qol*, 'voice' (*Semantics*, pp. 107–205). In particular, Kittel's influential *Theological Dictionary of the New Testament* and other theological dictionaries of the Bible where such etymological data are given prominence, have had a profound effect on modern theology.

The quest for original meanings, parallel to the archaeologists' quest for 'what actually happened', does violence to the history of religious tradition. If the Bible was merely an ancient text like the Gilgamesh Epic or the Code of Hammurabi, then no account would have to be taken of the long and complicated process of its transmission down to the present day, and the one goal of the interpreter would be to discover the original meaning of the text. As things are, the biblical text does not come to us directly from the Ancient Near East, and cannot be totally separated from the religious beliefs, practices and institutions of the communities that have preserved it. The NEB contains many cases where a meaning based on modern etymological theories, many of them attributable to G. R. Driver (see Barr, *Comparative Philology*, pp. 320–37) and unknown to earlier generations, is preferred to a traditional interpretation (e.g. Judg. 1.14; Ps. 137.5; Isa. 53.3). A reconstructed 'original' may be the oldest meaning, but that does not guarantee its truth or appropriateness in its present context. Nevertheless the value of etymological data

properly used, as an aid to understanding the Bible, should not be overlooked. It seems likely that the consonantal root of a Hebrew word does carry meaning. A group of words containing the root *'-mn*, for example, appears to have a semantic element in common, something like 'firmness'. This does not mean that the 'fundamental' or 'original' meaning of Hebrew words for 'truth', 'faith', 'believe' etc., which contain this root, is 'firmness'. But it does suggest, at a subtler level of semantic* description, that 'firmness' is among the associations and nuances of these words as opposed to synonyms derived from a different root. The etymology of the word *raḥamim*, 'love', 'compassion' is another example. It is derived from the same root as the word *reḥem*, 'womb' and, without suggesting that a speaker consciously connects these terms every time he uses one of them, it is likely that the distinctive meaning of *raḥamim*, as opposed to other terms for love in Hebrew, is best explained (at least in some contexts) by reference to the caring love of a mother for her child (cf. Isa. 49.13–15). Careful study of how words are actually used in context will prove whether, after all, their 'root-meaning' is significant.

Popular etymologies may also be important as evidence for how words are actually understood, however far removed they may be from historical fact. Some biblical examples were given at the beginning of this article. Modern examples would include the widespread belief that Hebrew *hoshia'*, 'save', 'help' is derived from an Arabic word meaning 'to give room to', and that 'salvation' consequently has some suggestion of 'spaciousness' in its meaning. The etymology, invented by the eighteenth-century philologist A. Schultens, is almost certainly wrong, but the idea is attractive, and associates *hoshia'* with words like *hirḥib*, 'to give room to' (Ps. 4.1) and *merḥab*, 'space', 'freedom' (Ps. 18.20; 118.5), in some modern writings on salvation.

See also **Etymology, Ancient Near Eastern; Masoretic Text; Philology; Textual Criticism (Old Testament).**

J. Barr, *The Semantics of Biblical Language*, 1961; id., *Comparative Philology and the Text of the Old Testament*, 1968; S. Moscati (ed.), *An Introduction to the Comparative Grammar of the Semitic Languages*, 1964; J. F. A. Sawyer, 'Root-meanings in Hebrew' *JSS* 12, 1967, pp. 37–50.

JOHN F. A. SAWYER

Etymology, Ancient Near Eastern

Modern philology* was of course unknown in the Ancient Near East. The existence of the tri-consonantal Semitic root was first grasped only in the Middle Ages. The distinction between the language groups such as Semitic and Indo-European was similarly not perceived, and the difference between cognates (words of similar meaning and form due to a common origin) and loan words was also blurred. Words were related according to their superficial phonetic resemblances and apparent relationships of meaning. Thus Babylonian scholars could propose a Sumerian etymology for a Semitic Babylonian word, and Jewish scholars could connect a Hebrew or Aramaic word with a similar sounding Greek one.

There existed, however, a fascination for words and meanings beyond what was needed for everyday communication, from which systems of philology and etymology* were developed. Two reasons may account for this. First, it was probably held that human speech had been given by the creator or creators in the beginning, so that it would in some sense communicate the divine mind. This is nowhere stated expressly, but God's diversifying of human speech according to Gen. 11.1–9, and his promise of supplying ultimately 'refined speech' on 'the peoples' lips' (or, as many emend, 'my people's lips', Zeph. 3.9) clearly states God's control in this matter, which suggests that he gave language in the beginning. A passage in a Sumerian myth is generally understood to state that in the beginning the whole human race praised the god Enlil in one language, but then the god Enki brought about the different languages as known in historical times. This too seems to imply divine control over language from the start.

The ancient concept of 'name' is the second reason for the ancient fascination with language. It was not, as to us, an identification tag, but rather a hypostasis of the person or thing. 'Who is your name?' (rather than 'What?'), in Judg. 13.17, is paralleled by the Old Babylonian Gilgamesh X. iv, 5ff. 'Who is your name?', with the reply, 'Gilgamesh my name am I'. In Gen. 2.18–20 God made animals and birds and brought them to Adam to be named. The name given decreed the creature's character: 'eagle' made the bird in question a particular bird of prey. Similarly, at human births the name given either reflected the circumstances of the birth or fixed the child's destiny. Note Nabal 'Fool' (I Sam. 25.25), Cain (root *qyn*) as 'obtained' (root *qny*) from God (Gen. 4.1). The philology is often wrong to us. The Semitic *qayin*, 'blacksmith', is unrelated to *qny*, 'obtain'. Samuel ('Name, i.e. offspring, of God') was because the child came as a result of the mother's 'asking' God, despite the fact that the name Samuel cannot be related to the root 'ask', *š'l* (I Sam. 1.20). Such explanations are often

spoken of as folk etymology or word play in the modern world, but this may trivialize what was serious to the ancients. To understand their thought we must take these matters seriously.

In ancient Mesopotamia 'to be called a name' is to exist. The first line of the Babylonian Epic of Creation, 'When above heavens were not named, below earth was not called a name' means simply 'Before heavens and earth existed'. Similarly, 'people, as many as are called a name' means 'all the people'. Most personal names had meaning and were clearly chosen with care (the first king called 'Sargon' = 'legitimate king' was a usurper). Word play is not recorded in such matters, though it may have been common among ordinary people; note in a popular saying a word play on *mešrû*, 'wealth', and *mešlu*, 'half' (*BWL*, 219 5).

Scribes,* however, had their own learned etymological science based on Sumerian, which has many monosyllabic roots with many homophones among them. It was used on gods' names in an etymological theology, and on Babylonian words generally as a technique of philology. Names and words were divided into syllables, and these syllables were then explained from Sumerian roots. Some of these interpretations were entirely correct: many divine names are Sumerian and in origin were epithets, so that the simple meaning was entirely acceptable to the ancients. But Babylonian scholars often produced several contradictory meanings of one name. Thus Marduk had a name Shazu, derived from an earlier form Shazi of unknown origin and meaning. It was mostly written with the signs *sha*, 'heart', and *zu*, 'know', so with a little exegesis it was explained 'who knows the heart (= mind) of the gods'. But in addition the Sumerian root *su(d)*, 'distant', 'remote', was also used to give the sense as 'profound mind', an epithet derived from Marduk's traditional skill in exorcism and found in the name by (to us) bogus philology. Thirdly, Marduk had a common Babylonian epithet *rēmēnû*, 'merciful', from *rēmu*, 'pity', which, like its Hebrew cognate *rehem*, also means 'womb'. The Sumerian *sha*, 'heart' is also 'middle' and 'womb', and *shazu* as a professional title is 'midwife' ('knower of the womb'). This was reinterpreted by the Babylonian scholars as 'knower of pity' and so Marduk's traditional mercy was found to be adumbrated in his name Shazu. Similarly Ekishnugal, the name of the temple of the moon god in Ur, was explained 1. 'guardian of all the peoples' (*gal* = guard; *kish* = all; *nu* = people), and 2. 'light of the great heavens' (*nu* = light; *gish* = heavens; *gal* = great). Semitic words were submitted to the same process. The adjective *shalbabu*, 'wise', from the root *lbb* as in *libbu*, 'heart' and 'mind', is explained from the Sumerian *sal* = 'wide' and *ba* = 'make', breadth of mind being a Sumero-Babylonian concept of wisdom. Plain and to us straightforward explanations of Semitic Babylonian words occur only rarely. Marduk's name Ashāru, from the root *'šr*, 'muster', is expounded: 'Ashāru, who, in accordance with his name, mustered the divine destinies' (*Epic of Creation* VII, 122).

The learned ancient Mesopotamian etymology, based on Sumerian roots, seems to be the source of the rabbinic (*see* **Jewish Exegesis**) hermeneutical technique *nôṭrîqôn*, by which Hebrew or Aramaic words are broken down either into several smaller words (which is rarely possible) or into individual letters, which are then taken as the initial letters of a succession of words. The technique is not really appropriate to Hebrew and Aramaic, but arose naturally in a world where Sumerian, with its abundant monosyllabic and homophonous roots, was the subject of academic study. Such study was alive in the earlier Hellenistic* world and could have been absorbed by learned Jews in Babylonia.

See also **Aetiology; Ancient Near Eastern Interpretation.**

J. Bottéro, 'Les Noms de Marduk' in M. de Jong Ellis (ed.), *Essays on the Ancient Near East in Memory of Jacob Joel Finkelstein*, 1977, pp. 5–28.

W. G. LAMBERT

Euphemism

The substitution of more acceptable words for those thought likely to cause offence; in particular, where blasphemy or obscenity might be involved. As such, euphemism has played a minor but significant part in biblical interpretation.

1. A recurrent issue for religious believers in many traditions is the appropriate way of speaking of God so as both to retain appropriate reverence and to express confidence in his accessibility. (Current debate whether God should be addressed in liturgical prayers as 'you' or by the now more formal 'thou' illustrates the issue.) In many parts of the OT God is addressed in a remarkably direct and uninhibited fashion, as in the urgent requests that he awaken from sleep (Ps. 44.23–26; cf. 78.65f.), but it is also possible to detect increasing inhibition in speaking too directly to or about God. Thus in Deuteronomy the 'name of the Lord' is referred to, and in Ezekiel his 'glory', where we might have expected direct reference to God himself. In this respect it is instructive to compare the directness of the report of Isaiah's vision ('I saw the Lord', Isa. 6.1) with the later and much less direct language of Ezekiel which refers to 'the appearance of the likeness of the glory of the Lord' (Ezek. 1.28).

The best-known example of this shaping of religious language by considerations of reverence is to be found in the fact that in the later OT period the divine name, Yahweh, passed almost completely out of use, so that a tradition preserved in the Mishnah (*see* **Talmud**) tells us that it might only be pronounced by the High Priest when he went into the Most Holy Place on the Day of Atonement each year. One section of the psalter (Pss. 42–83) appears to have been edited so as to replace the divine name by the more general *elohim*, meaning 'God', presumably on grounds of reverence. In the Masoretic text* of the Hebrew Bible the consonants of the divine name are provided with the vowels of a different word, so that its proper pronunciation remains uncertain; the form 'Yahweh' is a reconstruction based on modern scholarly study. The Jerusalem Bible is the only established modern translation* to use that form consistently, and the convention of replacing the divine name by other forms (e.g. G*d, the Holy One, Adonai) is still widespread in Judaism (*see* **Tetragrammaton**).

One remarkable feature of this reverence which affects the usage of the OT itself in the sense that certain words cannot be used in connection with the divinity. When Job's wife urges him to 'Curse God and die', the Hebrew actually says 'Bless God'; and this usage still survives in contemporary English in such expressions as 'I'm blessed if I know', where the real meaning is 'May I be cursed if . . .'

2. Obscenity, or the fear of it, also poses problems in biblical language. At times this seems to be little more than excessive delicacy, as when RSV renders the direct Greek of John 11.39 as 'there will be an odour'. But the more general problem, particularly of sexual references, has been widely felt. The Song of Songs, for example, uses extremely direct sexual language, and part of the reason for its interpretation in both Jewish and Christian traditions in non-physical terms has been this unease with the directness of its language. (The use of similarly direct sexual language in Ezekiel may well be one of the underlying reasons for the restrictions imposed in Judaism upon the reading of that book by those of tender age.)

Even in the OT itself there are examples of a resort to euphemism to avoid directly sexual language. Thus in Isa. 6.2 the description of the seraphim speaks of two wings to cover their 'feet', where this is a euphemism for the sexual organs (cf. also I Sam. 24.3, where the Hebrew 'cover his feet' is rendered 'relieve himself' in RSV). The Hebrew word *yad*, literally 'hand', can also be used euphemistically of the male sexual organ. Thus in Isa. 57.8 the Hebrew is literally 'you have looked at a hand', but in the context of the condemnation of alien religious and sexual cults, a reference to the sexual organ is almost certain. In such passages the theme of power, associated both with the hand and with sexuality, may well be present. Another, less certain, example is the use of the Hebrew verb 'to know' for sexual intercourse (e.g. Gen. 4.1); this may be a euphemism, but it may be a part of the normal semantic * field associated with that verb.

If so far we have been concerned with passages where modern translations have avoided too explicit a use of sexual or obscene language, it is also noteworthy that in the case of the NEB such a sense has often been claimed for the original and introduced into the translation where most students would question it; the NEB rendering of Judg. 1.14 is a notorious case in point.

See also **Figures of Speech; Song of Songs.**

TDOT V, pp. 399–403 (on 'hand'); M. H. Pope, *The Song of Songs*, 1977; E. Ullendorff, 'The Bawdy Bible', in *Studia Aethiopica et Semitica*, 1987, pp. 236–67.

R. J. COGGINS

Eusebius

Eusebius of Caesarea is best known as the first historian of the church. Without his great compilation, much would have remained unknown to us, both information and indeed documents. To take but one example, which is in fact relevant to biblical interpretation, he preserved in the *Ecclesiastical History* our earliest evidence concerning the writing of the Gospels by quoting paragraphs from Papias.* It is true that his comments tend to obscure rather than illuminate the interpretation of those extracts, but at least the extracts exist through his scholarship.

Eusebius was fundamentally a scholar. From his teacher and spiritual father, Pamphilus, he inherited Origen's * library in Caesarea, and most of his works are great compendia of quotations from a wide-ranging collection of books. His principal interest was apologetic: besides the *History*, which is apologetic in its aim, he produced the *Praeparatio Evangelica*, showing how the world was prepared for the Christian gospel in the work of pagan philosophers and thinkers; and the *Demonstratio Evangelica*, collecting and explaining proofs of the gospel from the Jewish scriptures. Valuable extracts from many lost writings are preserved by Eusebius' pen, including almost all we know of the literature of Hellenistic Judaism.

Eusebius' scholarship also embraced biblical study, as befitted a disciple of a disciple of Origen. When Constantine founded fifty new churches in Constantinople, it was to Eusebius that he turned for 50 copies of the scriptures. Clearly the legacy of the Hexapla was still alive. Eusebius' text-critical work consisted in extracting from it the Septuagint * column, and putting alternative readings into the margin. He also introduced into manuscripts of the Gospels the system known as the Eusebian canons, a way of indicating the parallels. Each Gospel is divided into numbered sections: then tables are provided which put each section by number into the appropriate 'canon': I contains items found in all four Gospels, II contains sections in what we call the Synoptics, III those in Matthew, Luke and John, IV in Matthew, Mark and John, V in Matthew and Luke only, etc., until X lists the passages peculiar to each Gospel. The system passed over into Syriac and Latin manuscripts as well as Greek; Jerome adopted it for the Vulgate.* It will be found in printed editions of the Greek Testament.

No doubt this analytical work alerted Eusebius more particularly than most to the difficulties presented by discrepancies between the Gospels, though it was not something that had gone unremarked before. He produced a work called *Gospel Questions and Solutions*, addressed to Stephanus, which apparently tackled the problem of the infancy narratives * in two books; this was followed by another addressed to Marinus which dealt with the resurrection narratives.* The full text of both has been lost, only fragments surviving; an epitome (or summary) appears to give some idea of its content. There clearly was some biblical criticism in the ancient church.

Eusebius lived in Palestine, and took advantage of that location. The *Onomasticon* is a gazetteer of biblical sites arranged in alphabetical order. Jerome translated it into Latin. It remains an important document for the topography of the Holy Land. In the work Eusebius refers to three earlier parts which are now lost, providing a plan of Jerusalem and its Temple, with quotations describing various locations, a topography of ancient Judaea with the inheritances of the twelve tribes, and interpretations of Hebrew terminology. Eusebius was primarily a great compiler of information. He inherited the critical approach of Origen, while taking biblical history very seriously. One suspects that the scholarly side of Origen also took it seriously, despite his propensity for allegorical interpretation. *

Given his scholarly bent, his interest in history, his critical streak, and his Origenist heritage, what was Eusebius' exegetical work like? We possess little to go on; despite his reputation as a student of the Bible, extant material is sparse. However, the commentators who produced the *Catenae* preserved substantial fragments of a *Commentary on the Psalms* and a *Commentary on Isaiah*; the discovery of an almost complete copy of the latter was reported in 1934, and the text has since been published. We can also glean something of Eusebius' exegetical method from the *Demonstratio Evangelica*.

Eusebius often refers to versions other than the Septuagint, and indeed to the Hebrew. His interest in the OT, as in so much else, is both scholarly and apologetic. He insists that the meaning of prophetic texts lies in their fulfilment in later historical events. He takes this to be what the prophecy is literally about. He uses allegory to interpret numbers, animals and natural phenomena, as most of his contemporaries did, but on the whole he is fairly reserved in his use of allegory, avoiding the kind most often associated with Origen. He is simply not interested in 'spiritual' or 'mystical' insights. His interest is in prophecy, and the exegetical distinctions he makes relate to that interest. There are direct and veiled predictions; veiled predictions are like riddles that have to be solved, and the process of solving involves the kind of allegorical correspondences noted above. This may seem as arbitrary as Origen's spiritualizing, but it has a different kind of result. It keeps Eusebius' approach to scripture more closely grounded in the unfolding events of history. Eusebius' theology could be summed up as a doctrine of God's providential guidance of the historical process, evidenced in the fulfilment of prophecy, and culminating in the events of his own time.

J. Quasten, *Patrology*, vol. III, 1970; Frances Young, *From Nicaea to Chalcedon*, 1983.

FRANCES YOUNG

Evangelist

The word derives from the Greek for 'one who brings good news'. It is, like 'apostle', virtually a linguistic invention of early Christianity (only one secular instance of the word survives from antiquity, in a late inscription, *CIG* XII.1.675). It is employed in two distinct ways: to designate 1. someone who fulfils a certain ministerial office or function in the church; and 2. the writers of the canonical Gospels.

1. In the NT, the term always occurs in the former sense, and appears only three times, in the later, deutero-Pauline writings. In Eph. 4.11, for example, ministerial gifts are listed as follows: 'some to be apostles, some prophets, some evangelists, some pastors and teachers'.

In NT usage, therefore, 'evangelist' may be defined as a 'missionary successor to the apostles'. The currency of the term in this sense was short-lived, limited to the immediate sub-apostolic period (AD 70–110). It was destined soon to disappear, as residential officers (bishops, presbyters, deacons) began to take precedence over itinerant, missionary ones.

In later church order, 'evangelist' crops up now and again, e.g. as a synonym for a liturgical deacon (*Apostolic Church Order* 19), and, in some Protestant denominations, as the title for a local, usually lay, missioner. In common usage, it is a honorific, functional term, referring to an evangelical preacher with an international reputation who conducts revivalist and missionary rallies on a large scale.

2. From the end of the second century onwards, a new specialized meaning of the term emerges, which is more directly relevant to the business of biblical interpretation. Just as 'the gospel' began to be understood as a literary category, referring to written accounts of Jesus' life, so also 'evangelist' became a term denoting specifically the authors of the four canonical Gospels (Hippolytus, *On Antichrist* 56; Tertullian, *Against Praxeas* 21,23). Since, according to church tradition, the evangelists were identified as themselves apostles (Matthew and John) or apostolic assistants (Mark and Luke), this use of the term became temporally restricted to the first generation. The original evangelists were understood to possess unique gifts of historical veracity and doctrinal truth. From their identification with one or other of the four living creatures around God's throne (Rev. 4.7; cf. Irenaeus, *Against Heresies* III, 11.8), there flowed a rich vein of allegorical and iconographic symbolism,* which reinforced belief in the profound insight, diversity and complementarity of the four-fold gospel.

In modern biblical interpretation, the word continues to have this second, specialized sense, but with a different range of nuances which mirror changing emphases in gospel criticism and varying estimates of the role and contribution of the gospel writers.

The study of the language, dating and sources of the Gospels in the nineteenth century gradually called into question the traditional view of the identity of their authors (first in the case of Matthew; subsequently of the others) and reference to 'the evangelist', therefore, in works of modern scholarship is often no more than a convenient way of sidestepping the issue of authorship.

*Source criticism** thinks of an evangelist typically as a literary editor of earlier texts: his contribution is confined to fitting texts together into continuous narrative, modifying their style to suit his own, comparing what they offer with other, oral sources of information and choosing between variants or incorporating more than one version of any saying or incident. The Lucan Prologue (Luke 1.1–4) provides explicit justification for this profile of an evangelist. On the majority view of Synoptic inter-relationships, 'Matthew' can be understood as a very similar kind of editor. Some scholars still want to make an exception for 'Mark', seeing this Gospel as a direct transcript of eye-witness testimony, but most others argue that here also the editing of earlier sources (cycles of miracle stories, sayings collections and a pre-formed passion narrative) can be detected. Nor is the Fourth Gospel entirely a separate case; for whether its author was working on the Synoptic Gospels, or on special sources of his own (a 'signs' collection, revelation discourses, etc.), he can also be seen as an editor, albeit of a freer kind. On the source-critical view, therefore, an evangelist is properly so named only in virtue of the subject matter of his work; as far as his particular intention or method is concerned, he is simply an editor. In this approach, attention is focussed chiefly on the reconstruction of the Evangelists' sources and ultimately of the historical events of Jesus' ministry.

*Form criticism,** emphasizing the decisive effects of the transmission process on gospel material before it was committed to writing, thinks of an evangelist typically as a collector and preserver of oral tradition. 'Mark' and 'Matthew' especially are only in the slightest degree the authors of their Gospels; they are, rather, anonymous servants of the church's communal memory. And since personal reminiscences had been filtered out of that memory and were no longer accessible to them, and their material belonged to one continuous, all-enveloping stream of tradition, the Gospel writers were in no position to exercise full editorial control over it. They shared with the material they preserved a basically propagandist ('kerygmatic'*) purpose, and they can, therefore, be called evangelists, in the functional sense of ministers and preachers of the Word. But just as the fragmented character of the tradition made any attempt at biographical reconstruction impossible, so also the weight and authority of the tradition prevented any attempt to impose upon it a consistent theological view. In so far as the author of Luke–Acts exhibits a degree of historical intention, even though he inevitably lacked the necessary historical resources, he is less typically an evangelist than the other Synoptists. The author of the Fourth Gospel manages to achieve theological consistency in his work, but only at the expense of departing radically from the tradition.

These minimalist accounts of the evangelists as literary editors or scribes of the tradition are supplemented and in part corrected by the method known as *redaction criticism.** By focussing attention on the aspects of a Gospel for which its author is directly responsible, i.e. decisions about the inclusion, omission and ordering of material, rephrasings, summaries, explanatory comments and so forth, and by assembling these data together, it may be possible to discern a consistent redactional viewpoint. The evangelists were, it is claimed, self-confident enough to resist at certain points the pressure of their sources and/or of the communal memory. By sometimes quite slight but deliberate and subtle alterations of the inherited material, they adapted it to suit their own contemporary circumstances and theological views. Thus, for example, each of the Synoptists implies different priorities in Christian discipleship, 'Mark' emphasizing the vocation to suffering, 'Matthew' the summons to ethical righteousness, and 'Luke' the experience of the Spirit. Much more detailed reconstructions of the peculiarities of the individual evangelists have been proposed, some of them highly controversial. But the general effect of this approach has been to rehabilitate the Synoptic evangelists as creative authors, to renew interest in the overall purpose and resulting genres of their work, to introduce often quite sharp distinctions between the Synoptists, but conversely, by recognizing them to be theologians, to close the apparent gap between them and the Fourth Evangelist.

The focus of redaction criticism on the final form of the text, along with growing doubts in recent scholarship about the findings of source and form criticism, has led to a number of new literary approaches to the Gospels which may loosely be designated *narrative criticism.** This method in effect abandons the attempt to distinguish between inherited tradition and an Evangelist's own contribution, and works instead on the assumption that he is equally and fully responsible for everything he writes. An evangelist, on this view, is an artist who uses narrative techniques (plot, characterization, irony, etc.) to tell a story which creates its own story-world and has its own integrity, quite apart from any reference it might have to events in the real world. If redaction criticism closes the gap between the Synoptics and 'John' as theologians, narrative criticism does the same for them as literary artists.

These various critical methods produce, therefore, different general estimates of an evangelist, whether as editor of sources, preserver of tradition, interpretative redactor or literary narrator. In addition, the peculiar features of individual Gospels may lead to particular understandings of their authors, such as 'Matthew' the catechist and rabbi or

'Matthew' the scribal school, 'Luke' the historian or apologist, and 'John' the prophet or mystic. When the discussion is widened to include the authors of the so-called apocryphal gospels, some of which, like the Gospel of the Hebrews and the Gospel of Peter, are generically similar to the NT texts, the phenomenon of an evangelist becomes even more varied. But in spite of this diversity, a unifying common denominator may be observed: an evangelist seeks to promote faith through the medium of a life of Christ. This type of religious biography is widely held to be unique to Christianity, in that the life of its subject is no mere illustration of a belief system in action, it actually constitutes the substance of that belief. Thus, the precedence given to the work of the evangelists in the NT canon, and in the liturgy and doctrine of the church, arises from the distinctive Christian belief in the incarnation.

See also **Gospel**; **John, Gospel of**; **Luke, Gospel of**; **Mark, Gospel of**; **Matthew, Gospel of**.

TDNT 2, pp. 736–7; *IDB* 2, p. 181; E. Best, *Mark, the Gospel as Story*, 1983; M. Dibelius, *From Tradition to Gospel*, 1934; H. Leclerq, 'Evangelistes, symboles des' in *Dictionnaire d'Archéologie Chrétienne*, 5, 1922, pp. 845–52; J. Massie, 'Evangelist', *Hastings Dictionary of the Bible* 2, pp. 797–7; N. Petersen, *Literary Criticism for NT Critics*, 1978; J. Rohde, *Rediscovering the Teaching of the Evangelists*, 1968.

JOHN MUDDIMAN

Exegesis

Most English words for interpretation have Latin roots: 'interpretation' itself, but also 'explanation', 'explication', 'exposition' and 'commentary'.* Only two words have Greek roots. The first, 'hermeneutics',* means, in Greek, either 'translation' or 'interpretation', and was used in both senses in classical, biblical and patristic texts. In English, however, it refers to the 'science of interpretation', and is distinguished from the second English word derived from Greek, 'exegesis', the subject of this article. In classical Greek, *exegesis* has two meanings: 1. 'statement, narrative', and 2. 'explanation, interpretation, commentary'. At Athens in classical times, an exegete was someone who interpreted oracles, the religious and ceremonial laws, and the heavenly signs. Exegetes also acted as local guides at temples, recounting traditional tales. In the Greek OT, only the first of the two meanings is found (the word does not occur in the NT), but in patristic texts, it is also used for 'commentary' or 'the exposition of scripture'.

In English, 'exegesis' indicates either an 'explanatory gloss', for example, 'the second sentence is an exegesis of the first', or a more extended exposition, especially of scripture or a scriptural passage. Murray's Oxford Dictionary cites examples since the seventeenth century. The word suggests a close reading of scriptural texts, explicating terms and sentences, and is often contrasted with 'eisegesis',* a derogatory expression, which insinuates that the interpreter has imposed his own pious thoughts and fancies upon the text. Allegorical* and typological* interpretations are often labelled 'eisegesis'.

One of the places in which to find examples of biblical exegesis is in a verse-by-verse commentary.* All critical commentaries include exegesis, although many also discuss other interpretative issues, like form, genre,* or significance for the modern reader. Some even separate exegesis from the running commentary, and place it in the 'notes', since it deals with matters of translation and the explanation of technical detail. The art of exegesis lies in elucidating expressions in their appropriate historical context. It attempts to establish the most original reading of the text and to explain variants (*see* **Textual Criticism**); it draws on present knowledge about the histories of languages and cultures to explore the nuance of particular words and phrases; and it makes use of archaeological* evidence to help locate sites and establish chronologies.* In other words, it explores three determinations of meaning: intra-textual,* extra-textual, and inter-textual. Intra-textual meaning is determined by the exact wording of the text, and by the immediate literary context of words and sentences. It answers questions like: What is the original reading? Does this word or phrase occur elsewhere in this text with a similar or different meaning? What is the grammatical structure of this sentence and what is its relationship to what precedes and follows? Extra-textual meaning is determined by the historical, cultural and geographical context in which the text was produced, which it presupposes, and to which it refers. Inter-textual meaning is determined by the references or allusions one text makes to another, as in the Gospels' use of passages from their scripture. These matters must be decided before an adequate translation can be made from the Hebrew, Aramaic, or Greek. Some of these issues will be illustrated in the examples which follow. The first explores both the grammatical functions of words and sentences, and their historical and geographical context. The second attempts to determine both the original wording of the text and its appropriate translation into English.

1. On the oracle in Amos 9.7: 'Are you not like Cushites to me, O Israelites? A saying of

Yahweh. Did I not bring up Israel from the land of Egypt, and the Philistines from Caphtor, and Aram from Kir?', J. L. Mays provides the following exegesis: 'The opening questions are rhetorical; they are in fact assertions made by Yahweh in an assault upon the theology of the addressees. Both questions take up the theme of "Israel and Yahweh", but their intention is to bring to light a dimension of that relationship with which Israel does not reckon. Precisely why Amos chose the Cushites for comparison with Israel must unfortunately remain somewhat obscure. Cush was the Old Testament name for the territory of Ethiopia and Nubia, but Cushites are seldom mentioned. An isolated tradition in Num. 12.1 reports that Moses' Egyptian wife was a Cushite, and that Aaron and Miriam opposed him because of her. Cushites appear as servants and eunuchs in Israel occasionally (II Sam. 18.21; Jer. 38.7). Jeremiah's proverb about the Cushites' colour is at least a play on their strangeness (Jer. 13.23). On the evidence one can say no more than that the Cushites were a distant, different folk whom Israelites knew mostly as slaves. "You are to me," says Yahweh, "as these Cushites are to you." What the comparison does is to humiliate Israel completely with respect to Yahweh, to reduce them to the role in Yahweh's order of things which the Cushites played in their own society. The relation of Israel to Yahweh creates no privileges, no special status which qualifies his sovereignty; it is rather one which manifests that sovereignty in radical fashion.

In the second question the exodus from Egypt is listed along with the migration of the Philistines and Arameans, and therefore put on the same footing. The reference is a clue to Amos' surprisingly full knowledge of the general historical traditions of the region, even more striking than the material used in the oracles against the nations (1.3–2.3). The migrations of the Philistines from the Aegean area (Caphtor = Crete) and of the Arameans from Kir (a Mesopotamian locale; cf. 1.5) had occurred early in the twelfth century, not long after Israel was settled in the hill country of Palestine. The Philistines and Arameans had been the classic foes of Israel; and yet their history, says Yahweh, was none the less his work than the Israelites' move from Egypt. Putting the matter in this way brings into focus the pivotal utterance in the text: "Did I not bring Israel up from the land of Egypt . . .?" This basic datum of Yahweh's historical relationship with Israel is neither denied or robbed of emphasis by its expansion to include the Philistines and Aram. What is denied and shattered is a theology based on that datum' (*Amos*, 1969, pp. 157–8).

The example shows, incidentally, that the reconstruction of the history of Israel and Judah is based on the exegesis of biblical and non-biblical texts. Although the discovery of non-literary artefacts can supplement knowledge gained from the texts themselves, exegesis is fundamental. Then the reconstruction can be used to make sense of oracles like Amos 9.7, which, in turn, help to confirm the reconstruction. Nor is the enterprise entirely circular, because one text can illuminate another.

2. The International Critical Commentary defines its aim as bringing together all the relevant aids to exegesis: linguistic, textual, archaeological, historical, literary and theological. Hence, the commentary on the *Epistle to the Romans* by C. E. B. Cranfield (new series, 1975, 2 vols, pp. 425–8) contains the following exegesis of *panta sunergei* as part of an exposition of Romans 8.28, which the RSV translates: 'We know that in everything God works for good with those who love him.'

'The question how *panta sunergei* should be construed is complicated by a variation in the textual tradition. While the majority of witnesses attest the shorter reading, P^{46} B A sa sy^{pal} arm attest the addition of *ho theos* after *sunergei*. Some support for the longer reading is also to be found in Origen, though not in his commentary on Romans as translated by Rufinus, in which the shorter reading is followed without question. At least 8 possibilities have to be considered:

(i) to accept the longer reading and explain *panta* as an accusative of respect ("in all things", "in all respects") (see the RSV);

(ii) to accept the longer reading and explain *sunergei* as transitive and *panta* as its object (so, for example, Sanday and Headlam translate: "Causes all things to work" while RV margin gives "worketh all things with them");

(iii) to accept the shorter reading and supply *ho theos*, explaining *panta* as in (i);

(iv) to accept the shorter reading and supply *ho theos*, explaining *sunergei* and *panta* as in (ii);

(v) to accept the shorter reading and take *panta* as the subject of *sunergei*;

(vi) to accept the shorter reading and understand the subject of *sunergei* to be the same as the subject of the last verb of v 27, namely, *to pneuma*, explaining *panta* as in (i);

(vii) as in (vi), but explaining *sunergei* and *panta* as in (ii);

(viii) to accept the shorter reading with the emendation of *panta* to *pneuma* or *to pneuma*.'

The commentary goes on to discuss each of the alternatives in detail, and to conclude that (v) is 'almost certainly right'. The verse is therefore translated: 'We know that all things prove advantageous for their true good to those who love God.'

In this way, exegesis serves as the basis for further reflection, whether within or outside commentaries. The recent debate among Pauline scholars, for example, about Paul's relation to the Law and Judaism, which was opened by the publication of E. P. Sanders' *Paul and Palestinian Judaism* (1977), involves the exact definition of terms within their appropriate historical contexts. Ignorance of the relevant language, history, culture and geography can lead to invalid or uncertain exegesis, which in turn can foster misinterpretations.

Exegesis, though necessary, is only the first stage in the interpretation of a text.

See also **Criteria; Interpretation, History of; Meaning.**

R. Quirk, *Words at Work: Lectures on Textual Structure*, 1986.

MARGARET DAVIES

Exodus

1. *The Book of Exodus as historical source.* Taken at face value, Exodus presents a unilinear narrative of consecutive incidents. All Israel, the heirs of the promises to the Patriarchs, had become slaves in Egypt. In answer to their cry God commissioned Moses to deliver them. After ten plagues, culminating in the death of all the firstborn in Egypt, the Pharaoh was finally constrained to let Israel go. The Israelites were delivered from the pursuing Egyptians by the miraculous parting of the Red Sea. They were led through the wilderness, sustained by divine gifts of water, manna and quails and protected from their enemies, to Mt Sinai, where God made a covenant* with them and revealed his law. The specification of the tabernacle, where God's presence dwells in the midst of his people, was given. Despite all these provisions for the maintenance of the relationship, Israel apostatized in the incident of the golden calf. Nonetheless, the covenant was remade on the former terms. Exodus ends with the construction of the tabernacle and the descent of the glory of God.

But how far can Exodus be properly termed 'historiography', in the conventional sense of a work based on primary sources which traces the network of causation between events at a mundane level? This question became particularly acute with the widespread acceptance since the last third of the nineteenth century of the reconstruction of the literary history of the Pentateuch* in terms of the 'New Documentary Hypothesis' associated especially with K. H. Graf and J. Wellhausen. If, as on that theory, Exodus represents a compilation of four literary documents, J, E, D and P, dated between, say, the mid-ninth and the mid-fifth century BC, i.e. some 600 to 1,000

years later than the date of the exodus given in I Kings 6.1, it cannot be a primary, but at best a secondary, historical source, which is more likely to reflect the interpretation of the periods within which it was written than faithfully to portray the original event.

Since then, two major lines of research have sought to circumvent the historical agnosticism generated by this hypothesis.

(a) The recovery through archaeology* of the Ancient Near Eastern environment of the Late Bronze Age (*c.* 1560–1200 BC), at some point during which most scholars would date the exodus.

Particularly significant was the discovery in 1887 at El-Amarna in Upper Egypt of diplomatic correspondence between the Pharaohs Amenophis III and IV and, among others, Canaanite subject kings, dating from the late fifteenth to early fourteenth centuries. This correspondence disclosed the strength of the Egyptian Empire in Canaan and included reference to 'ḫabiru', whom scholars still plausibly relate to, but do not identify with, 'Hebrews'.

The Amarna letters are written in Babylonian. The discovery and decipherment of other Babylonian texts, e.g., the publication of a version of the Flood in 1872 and in 1902 of the law-code of Hammurabi (*c.* 1700 BC), prompted a high evaluation of Babylonian civilization and its impact on the culture of Canaan at the time of Israel's origins.

Since then, the discovery and editing of innumerable texts from Egypt (e.g. the Merneptah stele of the third quarter of the thirteenth century, which mentions 'Israel') and Western Asia, as well as the deductions of field archaeologists at hundreds of sites throughout the region, have enabled an account of the history to be attempted on the basis of primary sources. Results from the point of view of reconstructing the detail of Israel's early history are, however, disappointingly meagre.

What is reasonably clear is that many of the incidents recorded in Exodus can be plausibly fitted into patterns of activity evidenced for Semites in the period, though at no precisely definable points. Descent, sojourn and exodus have numerous parallels in the Egypt of the second millennium; the notion of covenant bears some resemblance to Ancient Near Eastern treaties already evidenced in the Late Bronze Age. No reference has been found to Moses* or any of Israel's forebears. Biblical scholars are divided about even the basic question of chronology.* Given that the three Pharaohs in Exodus are anonymous, the strongest historical link with the period remains the reference in Ex. 1.11 to store-cities, Pithom and Raamses. The latter seems to point unambiguously to the period of the nineteenth

('Ramesside') Dynasty (end of the fourteenth to thirteenth centuries). The isolated reference, however, seems hardly adequate to defend more than a generalized knowledge of New Kingdom Egyptian history on the part of an ancient Israelite, who could as well be resident in Canaan as in Egypt (cf. general Palestinian knowledge of Egyptian conditions in, e.g. Isa. 19; Ezek. 29–32).

(b) The discovery of Ancient Near Eastern narrative and legal texts of the third–second millennia BC has encouraged comparisons with the Pentateuchal materials and a reappraisal of their possible antiquity: the documents identified by the New Documentary Hypothesis may not have reached their definitive written form until the first millennium, but they may contain much older written and oral traditions. The 'Book of the Covenant' (Ex. 20.22–23.33), with its parallels to e.g. the Hammurabi law-code, is a clear example. The method for studying older traditions embedded in literary documents is commonly termed 'form criticism'* and owes its rise particularly to the work of H. Gunkel in the years around 1900. The approach may be illustrated from the work of M. Noth.

In Noth's view, the content of the Pentateuch may be analysed into five 'themes', each with its history of transmission. One of these, 'exodus', may be traced back to the 'bedrock' of a historical event, the destruction of the Egyptians in the Sea (Ex. 15.21b). While not all Israel can have been involved ('Israel' as an entity only came into being in Canaan), the tradition is so widely shared that many clan elements, later to become part of Israel, must have participated in it. The tradition was first formulated orally by reciters within the liturgy of the central sanctuary of the tribal league. It was embellished with stock narrative motifs like sojourn, conscription, plagues and flight. It was further developed orally by popular narrators by the addition of semi-nomadic wilderness traditions showing knowledge of the watering-places and caravan routes between Egypt and Canaan. Similarly there was a southern tribal tradition of making and renewing covenant associated with Sinai. The pentateuchal documents, J, E, JE, D and P, represent the adoption of these traditions, with many narrative links such as genealogies and itineraries, into literary works of sustained theological reflection, attributable to 'authors'.

One may well feel that there is a high degree of speculativeness about such historical reconstructions. Noth concedes, 'We must deduce it (the growth of the exodus "theme") happened this way even without being able to give evidence in detail'; his contention for the existence of a pre-monarchical 'all-Israel' central sanctuary has been heavily criticized since

the 1960s. The assumptions that have been made about the character of Exodus as a historical source are equally debatable (cf. Ex. 15.21b, Noth's 'oldest testimony'!). What is certain historically is that Egypt was in the Late Bronze Age an imperial power, which with varying degrees of success dominated the land of Canaan. The revolution in military technology, which is marked in archaeological terminology by the change from 'Bronze Age' to 'Iron Age', coincided with, and no doubt contributed to, the eclipse of Egyptian power, which was also marked by the invasion of the Sea Peoples from the west and the gradual settlement of Semitic semi-nomads, including Israel, from the east. The exact degree of cause and consequence among these factors is for the Ancient Near Eastern historian to debate.

For the biblical interpreter a cautious conclusion would be that the undoubted fact of release from the Egyptian yoke is interpreted theologically in Exodus: the individual elements of the narrative may or may not be 'traditions'; some at least could be literary inventions of writers seeking to present theological truth within a relatively coherent narrative (e.g. Ex. 16). The resources available to these writers included materials of many kinds: general historical knowledge about the broad course of events provided the framework within which other historical and folk lore,* legend* (e.g. Ex. 2), religious practice (e.g. Ex. 12f.) and legal traditions (Ex. 20ff.) have been exploited to present a story which is a verisimilitude of life in the times of Israel's putative origins. Within such a perspective, standard rationalistic attempts to change the Red Sea into the 'Reed Sea' or to reduce the number of Israelites participating in the exodus from the two or three million implied by Ex. 12.37f. because of embarrassment at historical impossibilities are entirely beside the point. For the biblical writers, all Israelites were slaves in Egypt, all were delivered and Egypt's power was definitively neutralized at its frontier. All that is historically true, if by 'Egypt' one means not only metropolitan Egypt of the Nile Valley but the West Asiatic empire as well. But for the biblical writers 'this was the Lord's doing and it was marvellous in their eyes' and was for them merely the starting-point for the significance of the exodus.

2. *The book of Exodus as theological statement.* The inconclusiveness of the historical discussions forces the interpreter once more to raise the question of the nature of the material. The elements of the miraculous and divine (Ex. 15.21b!) should already indicate that the exodus narrative is a work not primarily of historiography but of theology. The

adventitious events of history can be only approximately appropriate to portray the ideals of the relationship between Yahweh and his people. The narrative is, therefore, highly selective in its choice of historical data: the purpose is to illuminate the data chosen only in so far as they illuminate the faith which determines the choice. Even those historical data used are refashioned in order that the intractable mass of events can portray what ought theologically to have happened within the relationship – and, by implication, should still happen. Further, elements other than history, chiefly religious institutions (e.g. passover, covenant) and law, are primary and pervasive and are, thus, no less apt than reconstruction of historical events to express the continuing relationship; it is only under the impetus of the narrative that they are given an event quality which is only marginally characteristic of them.

If, then, the primary quality of the exodus narrative is theological, one should in the first instance seek to identify the purpose of the theologians responsible for it. In view of the distance of the narrative from the original events and the complexity of the materials brought together to expound the exodus as a theological theme, to try to reconstruct the theological outlook of those involved in the period of the historical exodus itself, interesting and potentially valuable though that may be, will remain a very speculative enterprise. Rather, the narrative demands to be appreciated in its painstakingly gathered and summated form. It is highly likely that the material has grown through two overall theological editions.

(a) The earlier of these is to be associated with Deuteronomy and the deuteronomistic presentation of the history of Israel which emanated from the exile. This is to be seen particularly clearly in the Sinai pericope in Ex. 19–40, where the originally secular, inter-human, concept 'covenant' is used theologically to express the relationship between God and Israel, as most typically by the deuteronomistic school. As in Deuteronomy, the Ten Commandments, beginning with the self-disclosure of Yahweh as a God who rescues his people and restores them to their status of freedom (the fundamental affirmation of the OT), function as the supreme enunciation of the terms of the covenant, spoken directly by God himself in the hearing of the people, of which the remainder of the law is the detailed exposition. This edition, written in the exile, is marked by theological pathos: the God, who has thus shown himself to his people as liberator and has performed all things necessary for their status as his freemen, has been rejected by them. The apostasy of the golden calf (31.18–32.35) corresponds to the deuteronomistic presentation of the apostasy of Jeroboam (I Kings 12.28) and stands emblematically for the history of the Israelite monarchy (II Kings 17.7ff.). The people suffer inevitable alienation. Nevertheless, God in his forgiving mercy remakes the covenant on the same terms as before (34). As the Ten Commandments represent an ideal state, wherein each head of household is a prosperous farmer within a community of those of equal status, so the deuteronomistic edition of Exodus is, like Deuteronomy itself, part of an eschatological statement of restoration portrayed in the idealized terms of 'settlement in the land flowing with milk and honey'.

(b) The complementary presentation in the P-writer's edition must equally be seen within his overall design of the final form of the Pentateuch. The general theme is focussed in the concept 'holiness': the immanent presence of the transcendent God of creation is represented by his glory dwelling in the tabernacle in the midst of his people (the climax in Ex. 40); Levitus (P) expounds the rites of the cult, its personnel and those who may participate in it, culminating in the 'Holiness Code' for the generality of the people (Lev. 17–26). Thus legislation on, e.g., festivals (Ex. 12f.) and sabbath (Ex. 16), the careful specification of hierarchy at Sinai (Ex. 19; 24), the detailed specification of the tabernacle and its furnishings, with the prescriptions for the consecration of the priesthood (Ex. 25.1–31.17), and the consequent construction of the tabernacle in meticulous execution of this heavenly blueprint so that it represents in microcosm the dwelling-place of God in macrocosm (Ex. 35–40), all correspond to this overall theme of the P-writer. The fact that the P-writer also presents his ideal within the context of the wilderness, especially when that concept is used typologically of exile by Ezek. 20, may suggest that his interpretation also is intended to be taken eschatologically.

3. *The exodus as theological resource.* Already within the OT the exodus functions, using the terminology of R. Smend, as 'aetiology'* and 'paradigm'. The latter is especially characteristic also of NT and subsequent usage.

As 'aetiology', the exodus contributes to the explanation for Israel's origin and continuing existence as the people of God ('*because* Yahweh delivered our fathers, *therefore* we are his people'). It similarly functions as theological shorthand to provide the justification for all manner of practices, though, in all probability, none of them has in origin anything to do with it (Passover, e.g., was probably an ancient nomads' rite, Unleavened Bread a farmers'; covenant is a commonplace of Ancient Near Eastern life, law a gradually developing corpus): but Israel is enjoined to observe its rites and festivals and to keep the law because they were once 'slaves in Egypt'. Much other legislation is similarly justified by reference to the exodus, e.g., naturally, that dealing with the Israelite slave (Deut. 15.15), or the prohibition of maltreating the helpless (Deut. 24.18, 22) or the foreigner (Ex. 22.21[EVV]); less obviously, just weights and measures (Lev. 19.36), circumcision (Josh. 5), sabbath (Deut. 5.15), feast of weeks (Deut. 16.12) and feast of tabernacles (Lev. 23.43).

As 'paradigm', the exodus provides a pattern for the continuing experience of God's people ('*as* Yahweh delivered our fathers, *so* he delivers us').

(a) In the OT. The Pentateuch itself, as a double edition of multiple materials dealing with Israel's origins and development, already represents a process of reflection on the exodus, which spans the whole period of the OT. Outside the Pentateuch the exodus functions in at least four ways:

(i) As pattern of Israel's guilt. Israel's spurning of the God who has revealed himself in exodus and prepared everything for her welfare in covenant is the root cause of all the dislocations of her history, pre-eminently the exile. The exodus functions here negatively as the aetiology of Israel's judgment (see above). This usage seems to be particularly typical of the Deuteronomists, e.g. the Deuteronomistic History in the great prospective and retrospective editorial comments (e.g. Judg. 2.12ff.; II Kings 17.7ff.) and in the speeches which, Thucydidean-like, are placed in the mouths of the chief personages (e.g. Judg. 6.7ff.; II Kings 21.10ff.).

(ii) The exodus functions positively as paradigm of release into liberty. Cf. the parallels in the narrative of the crossing of the Jordan into the Promised Land to that of the Red Sea (Josh 3.7ff.; cf. Ex. 14.10ff.). It becomes the ground for hope or appeal for those who perceive themselves to be in a situation of slavery (e.g. Hag. 2.5; Dan 9.15). This is especially typical of Pss., whether the Hymn and Thanksgiving (e.g. 78) or the Lamentation (e.g. 74; cf. Isa. 63.7–64.12).

(iii) As springboard for creative hermeneutics,* particularly in Isa. 40–55, where there is an explicit exhortation to look for a still greater act of liberation than that once experienced in the exodus (e.g. 43.18). This greater act is predicated on the fundamental theological premisses on which the exodus itself stands: the name of God (e.g. 43.15); creation theology (e.g. 42.5–9); the cosmic dimension, indicated by the use of mythological language – the exodus is a replay of the primal battle (e.g. 51.9f.; cf. Ps. 74.14).

(iv) As ground for eschatological expectation. E.g. new exodus (e.g. Isa. 11.11–16); Zion as new Sinai (e.g. Isa. 2.1–5; 60–62); new covenant (e.g. Jer. 31.31–34).

(b) In the NT, the use of exodus material may be regarded as analogous to that in the OT.

(i) It may be used directly as warning, e.g. I Cor. 10.1–13.

(ii) As part of the scriptures presupposed by the NT, Exodus vocabulary may be used more or less unconsciously as the natural mode of expression of those who identify themselves with the tradition of the OT: thus, e.g., 'treasured possession' (Ex. 19.5; Titus 2.14), 'kingdom of priests, holy nation' (Ex. 19.6; I Peter 2.9), 'sweet savour' (Ex. 29.18; Eph. 5.2). Such usage already affirms validity and paradigmatic quality. Material may be more deliberately cited and applied as directly valid, e.g. the commandments (Matt. 19.18f.; James 2.11).

(iii) It provides a stock of vocabulary to portray the new series of acts of God associated with Jesus, already in such all-pervasive terms as 'ransom', 'redemption', 'salvation' (e.g. I Cor. 6.20; I Peter 1.18f.). In particular, Jesus is the paschal lamb (Ex. 12.3ff.; I Cor. 5.7f.); and the new covenant is sealed in blood (I Cor. 11.25; cf. Ex. 24.8).

The creative hermeneutics of the NT is chiefly evidenced by the use of the 'how much more' argument (cf. the rabbinic *qal waḥomer*). Thus the commandments are 'fulfilled' (Matt. 5.21,27,38). There is a relation of correspondence between prototype and more glorious realization, e.g. manna (John 6.31), cloud and crossing of Sea (I Cor. 10), covenant (II Cor. 3) and, especially, in the elaborate series in Hebrews concerning exodus, Sinai, wilderness, entry, tabernacle/temple and its personnel and rites. The correspondence between microcosm and macrocosm already implicit in Ex. 25.40 is explicit in Heb. 8.5.

(iv) Exodus provides a reservoir of eschatological vocabulary, especially in Revelation: the whole is predicated on the name of God (e.g. 1.4); there are many other details, e.g. the plagues (e.g. 8.7ff.), the accompaniments of theophany (e.g. 8.5), the engraved names (21.12), the book of life (3.5), the song of Moses (15.3). Cf. Heb. 12.18ff., where Sinai is again replaced by Zion.

(c) In subsequent thought, pre-eminently, in the modern period, in liberation theology, but already in the Netherlands of the sixteenth century and later, in the legitimating mythology of many a nationalist movement in rebellion against foreign oppression. Features characteristic of liberation theology, such as 'bias towards the poor', 'raising of consciousness' and the creative 'completing of the hermeneutical circle'* in praxis which imparts genuinely new insight, find a ready echo and justification in the biblical material. But the exodus is not to be exclusively appropriated by any one group; its message is for all God's people. In the search for apposite application it must be not unimportant to keep in mind the observations made above about the nature of the biblical material. The zeal of Yahweh is directed towards liberating all his people and towards providing them with the relationship with himself and with one another as the means by which the freedom of those who are God's slaves can be attained and maintained. Under the constraints of the unilinear narrative this liberation is portrayed in terms of deliverance from the oppression of the Egyptians. But that is merely the signal instance which exemplifies the underlying principle. Martin Luther King has caught that principle accurately when he writes, 'The meaning of this story is not to be found in the drowning of Egyptian soldiers ... Rather, this story symbolizes the death of evil and of human oppression and unjust exploitation.' It is, therefore, an under-interpretation of the exodus to look for an oppressor and an oppressed and to understand its liberation merely in terms of social revolution, though there may be contexts in which that is the overriding imperative. As Israel's writers were well aware, history is never so clear-cut into two parties absolutely differentiated into right and wrong, but is full of ambiguities on both, or, rather, on all, sides. The eschatological dimension adds a further, sobering, element: in the wilderness of this world no more than an approximation to the ideal society, portrayed illustratively in idyllic terms in the Decalogue, is possible for stubborn and rebellious mortals. The summons to the community, individually and corporately, is to identify the ^{ʿa}nawim, the humiliated, deprived of full status, among whom all humanity is to a greater or lesser degree to be found, to unmask the forces of all kinds, not just social and political, but personal and individual, leading to that deprivation and to proclaim and vindicate liberty in the name of the God of the exodus.

See also **Ancient Near Eastern World; Moses; Pentateuch, Pentateuchal Criticism.**

B. S. Childs, *Exodus*, 1974; J. H. Hayes and J. M. Miller, *Israelite and Judaean History*, 1977; B. Van Iersel and A. Weiler (eds), *The Exodus – A Lasting Paradigm*, Concilium 189, 1987; M. Noth, *A History of Pentateuchal Traditions*, 1972; R. de Vaux, *The Early History of Israel* I, 1978; R. N. Whybray, *The Pentateuch: A Methodological Study*, *JSOT-SS* 53, 1987.

WILLIAM JOHNSTONE

Eye-Witness

Since historical narrative must depend ultimately on eye-witness testimony, study of the eye-witness character or otherwise of biblical narrative has commonly formed an important element in discussion of the relationship of the texts to history, especially in considerations of their meaning, function, and value. We may here distinguish several principal kinds of material:

1. Passages in first-person narrative form, which appear to attest participation in or observation by the narrator of the events recounted, as with the 'memoirs' of Ezra (Ezra 7.27–9.15) and Nehemiah (Neh. 1.1–7.5; 12.31–13.31) and the 'we-passages' in Acts 16.10–17; 20.5–15; 21.1–18; 27.1–28.6. It should not easily be assumed, however, that we here have access to straightforward 'objective' historical description. Although it is commonly accepted that we possess Nehemiah's own vividly dramatic account, with less unanimity about the Ezra material, yet the discernment of a perhaps complex composition-history and the presence of apologetic and theological factors at the least counsel caution. Even where the text offers a broadly coherent and plausible history-like account, the first-person narrative should not be taken over uncritically for historical construction; and if we pay greater attention to the literary-theological form of the text itself, then we must do justice to the redactional ordering of the material. This in itself reflects a major shift from chronological-historical description, however valuable to the historian the sources may be in themselves. Similarly with the 'we'-sections in Acts: these vivid accounts, in which the first-person pronouns are traditionally understood as affirming the author's participation in the events narrated, but are claimed by others to be a stylistic trait adopted for literary reasons (so e.g. E. Haenchen), need to be seen first in terms of the total narrative structure, and not as fuel for historical apologetic.

2. Passages referring directly to an author's or editor's dependence on oral or written eye-witness testimony either in general terms (as with Luke 1.1–4) or for specific happenings (as John 19.34f.), or to his own eye-witness authority (as I John 1.1–4; John 1.14). Here too, such claims must be viewed in relation to the character and purpose of the works to which they belong. Luke's statement must be examined both with regard to the sources he has actually used and with reference to the form and nature of the prologue. The prologue itself must be compared with similar passages in older Greek and contemporary Hellenistic historians (with their comments on and their own practice in the use of eye-witness testimony) and perhaps in other works by writers from the ancient world, and also

examined in terms of its specific claims. These need to be assessed in connection with the characteristically Lucan picture of the distinctive apostleship of the Twelve, their role as witnesses (*martures*) of both the resurrection and the earthly ministry of Jesus (Acts 1.21f., cf. Luke 6.13), the nature of their appointment and equipment for that task (Luke 24), and the theological purpose of that total picture. To a disputed degree, especially when Luke–Acts is set alongside Paul's claim to apostolic seeing of the risen Lord (I Cor. 9.1., cf. 15.8f), we should detect here an objectivizing tendency in the picture of a limited and specifically authorized apostolate and the establishing of a chain of accredited eye-witness testimony to Jesus (cf. II Peter 1.16–18?). The theological evaluation of such concepts in relation to different interpreters' understandings of the Gospel is highly significant.

Traditional views of the apostolic authorship and authority of John's Gospel have depended heavily on the apparently direct indications of eye-witness testimony (esp. 19.34f.; 21.24; 1.14; cf. I John 1.1–4) taken in conjunction, most notably by nineteenth-century British scholars (*see* **English Interpretation**), with internal traits held to suggest such an origin: narrative vividness, exact and minute details of time, place, and action, the 'naturalness' of the characterization and portrayal of events, which could not 'but have come from direct experience' (B. F. Westcott,* *The Gospel according to St John*, 1881, pp. xviii–xxi; so J. B. Lightfoot, W. Sanday and many others down to L. Morris, *Studies in the Fourth Gospel*, 1969). Crucial theological issues were held to be at stake here, given the centrality of the Johannine-based incarnation in Anglican theology and the apologetic identifying of theological and historical truth. Not only are appeals to vividness and detail highly questionable. The function of Johannine eye-witness should be seen in connection with the probably complex history and sociology of the Johannine community. Most importantly we must suggest that these statements are theological and may not legitimately be mixed with material supposed on other grounds to be historical, and the one type used to support the other chiefly to argue that the Gospel thus provides us with 'raw' historical data. They should rather be interpreted (cf. also John 15.27; I John 4.14) strictly within the literary–theological network created by such broader interconnected motifs as 'witness', 'seeing', and 'glory' – otherwise the hermeneutical issues are likely to be badly warped. The eye-witness issue thus encapsulates, not only for John, but in mutually differing ways for the other Gospels too, fundamental questions about the nature and bearers of the primary witness to Jesus and the relationship between the past of Jesus and the continuing present of his followers.

3. Material which, though itself making no direct or indirect claim to eye-witness origin, has frequently been held to possess it. Obvious examples are Mark's Gospel, held by many in ancient and modern times to be connected with the preaching and eye-witness memory of Peter, on the basis of both external patristic testimony (of uncertain value) and the character of the content itself, with stress once more laid on narrative 'freshness' and vivid detail as evidence for near eye-witness origin and consequent historicity (so e.g. V. Taylor); and the King David* story in (at least) II Sam. 9–20 + I Kings 1–2, identified since the nineteenth century as a distinct source and, because of its apparent historical plausibility and graphic style, widely thought to be near contemporary with the events it was believed to describe with astonishingly modern skill. But just as important recent work indicates the need for caution in thus interpreting the David narrative, given both the extreme ambiguity of the criteria for eye-witness origin and the highly-wrought literary character of the text, so too the argument for Mark's close dependence on near eye-witness material must be questioned on similar grounds, given also different views of Mark suggested by form,* redaction,* and literary* criticism. To allow a historical hypothesis of eye-witness origin for Mark to exercise a dominating influence in interpretation runs the risk of subverting the implications of the Gospel itself regarding the disciples' incomprehension, and the theological nature of the connection between Jesus and the Gospel's addressees.

'Eye-witness' arguments have been used both in conjunction with dogmatic views of the reliability of scripture and, since the rise of historical criticism,* as the bases for supposed 'purely historical' judgments about the actuality of events and (sometimes) their interpretation. Thus, for example, much nineteenth-century British work, still imbued with a pre-Kantian empiricist view of perception, believed that for the eye-witness there arises a direct correspondence between perception and the nature and truth of the events; and the shorter the gap between event and written 'record', the less the possibility of distortion and decay of the testimony. The criteria for identification of first-hand witness become important: characteristically there were deployed both wider arguments about the historical credibility and psychological realism of the material, and aesthetic criteria – simplicity, freshness, verisimilitude, lifelike detail. Where such testimony was identified, it was accepted as conveying objective access to 'the facts'.

Yet we have not only to question the criteria,* but also to introduce criticism arising from the philosophy and psychology of perception (e.g. G. L. Wells, E. F. Loftus, *Eye-witness Testimony*, 1984); such testimony does not provide straightforward access to reality, and it is hermeneutically naive to suppose that its presence in or behind a text readily solves issues of meaning and truth. Postulated identification and role always operate within the context of broader patterns of understanding and faith, subject to continuing critical reflection. Eye-witness claims are subordinate to the literary-theological structures of the texts themselves, including where relevant the literary effect and purpose of first-person narration (cf. R. Scholes, R. Kellogg, *The Nature of Narrative*, 1966, ch. 7; F. Kermode, *The Genesis of Secrecy*, 1979, ch. 5). The topic thus exemplifies acutely the still crucial question of the relation of the distinct but not separate historical and theological tasks within biblical interpretation.

See also **Evangelist; Fact; Narrative Criticism.**

W. Michaelis, *'autoptēs, epoptēs, epopteuō'*, *TDNT* V, ET 1968, pp. 373–5; D. E. Nineham, *Explorations in Theology 1*, 1977, pp. 24–60; A. A. Trites, *The New Testament Concept of Witness*, 1977.

EDWARD BALL

Ezekiel

Ezekiel, the son of Buzi, was a Jerusalem priest apparently deported to Babylonia in *c.* 597 BC, together with the young king Jehoiachin and other leading citizens of defeated Judah. He experienced a call to prophesy* in Babylonia in *c.* 593 BC. The biblical book which bears his name (48 chapters in length) is one of the three major prophetic books, along with Isaiah and Jeremiah.

The text of the book itself bears marks of interpretation and elaboration, though it is more difficult to distinguish with confidence between primary and secondary material than is the case in most other prophetic books. It seems that the disciples of the prophet and their descendants, perhaps even a 'school of Ezekiel' (Zimmerli), were responsible for this process of elaboration. The range of scholarly opinion is broad, from Greenberg (who denies all elaboration) to Garscha (who allows only about thirty verses to the original prophet); most regard the bulk of the book as coming from Ezekiel himself, subsequent addition being generally of a 'hopeful' kind (e.g. 16.59–63; 17.22–24; 20.40–44).

Fishbane has explored the use and reinterpretation of earlier biblical texts by the authors of Ezekiel. In its turn, the book of Ezekiel

exercised a significant influence on the later writings of the Hebrew Bible. This is perhaps most evident within the books of Daniel (e.g. Dan. 7), Joel (esp. Joel 2–3) and Zechariah (e.g. Zech. 14); more generally, the book of Ezekiel had a pervasive effect on the development of apocalyptic,* both within and beyond the canon.* However, awareness of Ezekiel was not limited to this tradition; in the Apocryphal Wisdom of Jesus ben Sirach (Ecclesiasticus) we find explicit reference to the prophet (Ecclus. 49.8).

Though by no means one of the most frequently cited OT books, Ezekiel has left its mark on the NT. The image of the Good Shepherd (John 10) owes much to Ezek. 34, and the book of Revelation reflects the symbolism of Ezekiel at numerous points (e.g. the four living creatures of Rev. 4). Less widely recognized are the broader theological influences to which Ezekiel contributed. The emergence of a theology of 'grace' among the exilic prophets (cf. the giving of a 'new heart' and a 'new spirit' in Ezek. 36) is not without its importance to Paul's interpretation of the Christian gospel. Moreover, the development of the hope of resurrection* within post-exilic Judaism owes something at least to Ezekiel's expression of the hope of national restoration in the striking vision of the valley of dry bones (Ezek. 37), later vividly illustrated by the synagogue paintings at Dura Europos in Mesopotamia (*c.* third century AD).

Turning to post-biblical Judaism, the *Exagoge* of 'Ezekiel the Tragedian' (*c.* second century BC) is a drama which recounts the story of the exodus from Egypt; the name of the author may only be coincidental. However, the *Apocryphon of Ezekiel* (first century BC to first century AD), though extant only in fragments, seems to stand in closer relation to the biblical Ezekiel and may possibly have its origin as a midrash* on the canonical book. *The Lives of the Prophets* (*c.* first century AD) includes a section on Ezekiel, in which the legend that he was killed in Babylonia by the ruler of Israel is recorded. It is likely that all three of these works are Jewish in origin, though they have been preserved (for the most part) only in Christian sources.

Of particular importance is the tradition of Merkabah* ('chariot') mysticism – an influential if controversial phenomenon within post-biblical Judaism, associated particularly with Johanan ben Zakkai. Meditation on the vision of the moving throne of Yahweh in Ezek. 1 was practised, sometimes even leading to the experience of ecstasy. Allusions to such mysticism are found in a range of rabbinic tractates (including *Hagigah* and *Megillah*) and in the Targum* of Ezekiel. This and other features associated with the book (such as its alleged contradictions of Mosaic Law and also the explicit sexual language of Ezek. 23 and other passages) led some to regard Ezekiel with suspicion, and there were even doubts about its inclusion in the Hebrew canon of scripture.

Though not among the most popular books in Christian tradition, Ezekiel plays a recurrent role in both patristic and scholastic literature, as Neuss has shown at length. In later times, the prophet's radical theocentricity was admired by Calvin,* who produced a commentary on Ezek. 1–20. Ezekiel gained favour among some liberal critics of the nineteenth century on account of its supposed individualism, but such a reading of the book has since been contested.

The place of Ezekiel in modern literature is not insignificant. William Blake's* indebtedness to the book was considerable, as is seen in *The Marriage of Heaven and Hell*, where the prophets Isaiah and Ezekiel dine with the author. Blake also produced illustrations of several scenes from Ezekiel. The play *Juno and the Paycock* by the Irish writer Sean O'Casey ends with an anguished plea that Ireland's 'hearts o' stone' be replaced with 'hearts o' flesh' (cf. Ezek. 11.19; 36.26).

Perhaps one of the most bizarre legacies of Ezekiel is found in the legend of the last of the British giants, Gog and Magog, whose statues stand in London's Guildhall; these figures appear to derive their names, by an obscure route, from the Gog of Magog who makes war on the people of Israel in Ezek. 38–39. In popular culture the influence of the book remains extensive, from sayings such as 'wheels within wheels' (cf. 1.18) and 'like mother, like daughter' (16.44) to Negro spirituals, such as 'Dem Bones' (cf. 37).

K. W. Carley, *Ezekiel among the Prophets*, 1975; M. Fishbane, *Biblical Interpretation in Ancient Israel*, 1985; I. Gruenwald, *Apocalyptic and Merkabah Mysticism*, 1979; S. H. Levey, *The Targum of Ezekiel*, The Aramaic Bible 13, 1987; W. Zimmerli, *Ezekiel*, 2 vols, 1979, 1983.

PAUL JOYCE

Ezra–Nehemiah

The books of Ezra and Nehemiah are found together in the third part of the canon of the Hebrew Bible, the Kethubim (Writings),* and have always been closely associated; indeed, they were reckoned as one book until the Middle Ages. Their relation with Chronicles is also close; many scholars regard Chronicles–Ezra–Nehemiah as having originally been one continuous presentation of the people's history, but this view has been challenged (Williamson) and needs further examination. Certainly the relation between Chronicles and

Ezra–Nehemiah is a close one, symbolized by the identity of the end of Chronicles with the beginning of Ezra.

Nothing is known of either Ezra or Nehemiah as individuals save through the books that bear their names; the first-person material in Neh. 1–5 sometimes described as his 'memoir' is more likely to reflect a literary convention for setting out what the subject of a narrative would be likely to have said. Interpretation must therefore focus primarily upon the books. There it is noteworthy that their role is presented quite separately (the references which bring them together at Neh. 8.9 and 12.26,36 are almost certainly secondary) yet each fulfils a strikingly similar role. Each is the loyal servant of a Persian king Artaxerxes, sent to carry out the royal will in the province of Judah; each has the task of restoring the community; each has a particular concern for the purification of the religious loyalists from the stigma of mixed marriages (Ezra 10; Neh. 13); each is presented as having been the recipient of divine favour to enable him to carry out his task in the face of opposition.

The traditions relating to Ezra and Nehemiah both soon became the subject of interpretation within Judaism, though to a striking extent they were the subject of separate treatment. The apocryphal book I Esdras reaches its climax with the description of Ezra's work, and breaks off just at the point where in the biblical record Nehemiah would have been introduced. In other books of the Apocrypha,* by contrast, Nehemiah is mentioned but not Ezra. Thus in II Macc 1.18 Nehemiah is pictured as the one who had restored the temple, and (2.13) played a large part in gathering together the community's sacred writings; and in Ecclesiasticus Nehemiah but not Ezra is included among the 'famous men' (49.13).

In general, however, Ezra has been regarded as the more significant, and his role has been interpreted in two quite distinct ways. On the one hand a series of apocalyptic* writings was attributed to him; as is customary with that genre they are pseudonymous,* and it is not at all clear why Ezra should have been regarded as their author. The best known of these writings is found in the Apocrypha as II Esdras. (Esdras is the Greek form of Ezra; the book is also known as IV Ezra.) But in Judaism Ezra also came to be revered for the formative part he had played in shaping the community; by gathering together the holy books of the fathers; by introducing the square script, originally used for Aramaic, in which Hebrew is still written today; and by founding the 'great synagogue', the body wherein holy traditions were handed down to the later rabbis. Whether there is a historical basis for any of these attributions must remain very doubtful.

Ezra and Nehemiah were not prominent in early Christian interpretation, though it is quite likely that chs 1–2, 15–16 of II Esdras were Christian additions to that book, suggesting that Ezra was highly regarded by some early Christians, who claimed him as one of their spiritual ancestors. Among modern scholars a great deal of attention (perhaps a disproportionate amount) has been paid to the issue of their chronological order. Each is said to have worked during the reign of a Persian king Artaxerxes, and the traditional view has been that Ezra preceded Nehemiah. There are, however, some aspects of their work which could be more easily explained if Nehemiah's mission had been the earlier, and so it has been widely suggested that he served Artaxerxes I and came to Jerusalem in 445 whereas Ezra's mission took place under Artaxerxes II in 398 (Rowley). More recently, however, the general scholarly tendency has been to revert to the traditional order, partly because of our ignorance of the overall history of the period, and to pay more attention to the significance of the way in which their work is presented.

More important than these attempts at historical reconstruction is the significance of Ezra in particular in the establishment of Judaism, particularly through his role in bringing the book of the Law* to the Jerusalem community. (It may be a part of the process which has drawn the two leaders together that this achievement of Ezra is actually described in the book of Nehemiah, ch. 8.) Again, it is probably vain to speculate as to the precise identity of the book of the Law; the importance of the account lies rather in the assertion of the importance of the Torah for the true community. Neh. 7.73–8.8 has been described as an 'ideal scene', presenting the community as loyal to the law of Moses; the reference to interpretation in verse 8 has been understood as the forerunner of the later Targums.* Whatever the historical value of such interpretation, it presents an idea which was to be crucial in the later self-understanding of Judaism.

See also **Chronicles.**

P. R. Ackroyd, *I & II Chronicles, Ezra, Nehemiah*, 1973; K. Koch, 'Ezra and the Origins of Judaism', *JSS* 19, pp. 173–97, 1974; H. H. Rowley, 'The Chronological Order of Ezra and Nehemiah' in *The Servant of the Lord*, pp. 137–68, ²1968; H. G. M. Williamson, *Ezra, Nehemiah* 1985; id., *Ezra and Nehemiah*, 1987.

R. J. COGGINS

Fact

A more difficult word in use than might seem likely at first glance. In an important sense, in history and in the interpretation of past writings we never have 'the facts' themselves, the deeds, the events, the things said-and-done, the *facta*. What we have is 'statements of fact', for which 'fact' is conventional (and very useful) short-hand. 'What are the facts?' is a request for written or verbal statements – which can never be entirely neutral. It is always one set of words (or words and figures) rather than various others that is chosen, it is always some aspect or aspects of a situation that is or are stated, rather than others. We meet a traffic accident (but perhaps it was no accident, someone engineered it); we want 'the facts'. We are told, 'the road was greasy', 'the child ran out at the last moment', 'the driver was drunk', 'a wasp distracted me', 'the brakes were in bad repair'. Any one of these statements or any combination of them may be selected as our interpretation of a complex event. Yet we may still quite properly ask, 'Is that a fact?', asking if it can be shown to be a true statement of fact, asking, too, whether others may be more relevant. So though every statement of fact is already interpretative, it does not mean that 'just anything goes'. We always have the right to ask for more support, better warrants both for the statement and for its selection as relevant. We can do this in Bible study as much as in court.

The foregoing argument is opposed to writers, such as C. Becker, B. Croce, and Alan Richardson, who so stress the element of interpretation in the historian's choice and wording of his or her facts as to seem to suggest that all is totally and undifferentiably subjective.

On the other hand, it has to be admitted that historians are in a more difficult position with their facts than are at least some natural scientists, such as atomic physicists, who deal in large numbers of very similar events, in series that can be readily extended. In those circumstances it is much easier to obtain agreed statements of fact among colleagues and even among interested non-specialists. The facts seem to do more than warrant a particular interpretation, they demand it. Historians are more like geologists and palaeontologists dealing with particular unrepeated strata or genera. Even agreed statements of fact may allow for very different overall interpretation.

E. P. Sanders has argued for a particular restriction of our usage of the term 'fact'. Because sayings are so obviously recorded to make some particular point, they are too liable to distortion to count as good evidence. Only narratives of events are at all likely to provide us with 'facts'. Jesus, in this instance, has to be interpreted primarily or solely on the basis of critically assessed stories about things that happened. But Sanders seems to ignore the way in which all actions (events that are not accidents) are by definition 'intentional', meaningful, suffused with interpretation in the doing and again in the telling. There is no quick or easy way through events to 'hard facts', free of others' or our own interpreting.

There is no cause for historians, including interpreters of the Jewish and Christian scriptures, to despair. Our work may even so be 'factually accurate', while still avoiding being 'dully factual'. There may be a very considerable range of interesting statements that are widely accepted to be 'factually true' by people with very different beliefs and commitments. There was a ruler, it may be agreed, whose name is conventionally transliterated as David, who reigned in Jerusalem around 3,000 years ago; there was a Galilean we call Jesus who was officially sentenced to crucifixion and executed around 1,950 years ago; it may be an agreed statement of fact that Jesus' followers believed that this death was intended by God, and that God had raised Jesus from the tomb to power and glory. It may be agreed that there is good evidence to support these assertions, that such things happened, or such things were believed.

On the other hand, there is no chance of establishing among our contemporaries at large that what Jesus' followers seem to have believed about God's intentions and Jesus' resurrection * to glory are themselves factual. The death may be agreed to be 'fact'; but not that God intended it. That Jesus' resurrection was believed may be agreed as 'fact'; but not that it happened. Many who concern themselves with the issues cannot accept such assertions as even potentially factual, not simply because they do not find the evidence here persuasive, but rather because what is being said is too far from ordinary experience for any standard assessment of factuality to apply.

For some, only the sorts of statements that deal with massive regularities are allowed to count as 'factual', and nothing that even seems to run counter to such observed regularities can be given credence. Even if we are reluctant to accept a dogmatic 'positivism' of this kind, we cannot afford to ignore the critical implications for historians of commonly observed and accepted regularities, for unless such regularities can be widely assumed, the historian is lost. He has to work on the assumption that inky marks on paper retain much of their original shape over time; that entirely fresh documents indistinguishable from old ones do not 'spontaneously' appear; that armies have maximum marching speeds and minimum water requirements, and so on. Once he starts relaxing his hold on such regularities at some point, there seems to be no firm ground for retaining them at others. If we allow that a particular narrated miraculous divine intervention 'in fact' happened – then why only

this one? What if much more that seems implausible is really to be seen as miracle? Any admission of 'miracle' as 'fact' risks evacuating the term 'fact' of its meaning and value: all starts to slide into fairy story.

Widespread agreement can turn out to have been mistaken (as in the history of the natural sciences, for instance). But interpretation based in statements of fact whose evidential warrants are widely agreed is the most likely of all to be valid. For the present, the theological interpretation, the traditional Christian evaluation which is then given to those more or less widely agreed conclusions must remain something extra: faith related to these 'facts' but not factually demonstrable.

See also **Ideology.**

J. L. Austin, 'Unfair to Facts' in *Philosophical Papers*, 1961, pp. 102–122; F. G. Downing, *The Church and Jesus*, 1968, pp. 132–178; id., *Jesus and the Threat of Freedom*, 1987, pp. 150–155; V. A. Harvey, *The Historian and the Believer*, 1966, pp. 204–245; A. MacIntyre, *After Virtue*, 1981, pp. 76–83; E. P. Sanders, *Jesus and Judaism*, 1985.

F. GERALD DOWNING

Feminist Interpretation

Modern feminist interpretation of the Bible came into existence in the nineteenth century with the appearance of *The Woman's Bible*, published between 1895 and 1898, which was the end result of the pioneering work of Elizabeth Cady Stanton. Living in a society where women were regarded as unequal and subordinate to their male counterparts according to the law of the land, she believed that the key to legislative reform lay in the way in which the Bible was interpreted, since the Bible formed the bedrock to Western law. She believed that the new higher criticism of the Bible which was flourishing in liberal academic circles provided support for her work. The authority of the Bible's teaching on women could be brought into question at a time when academics were debating its status as the infallible Word of God. *

Feminist interpretation of the Bible offers an alternative assessment of the biblical evidence as seen through the eyes and experience of women readers and theologians. From the time of Elizabeth Cady Stanton, and in the light of the extensive work done in the area during the last twenty years, many feminist theologians have sought to prove that the attitude of hostility towards and the low estimation of women tend to have their roots in the history of biblical interpretation rather than in the biblical text itself. This tendency is encapsulated within the biblical canon * itself in the work of the author of I Timothy. He interpreted the Genesis creation narrative* to the detriment of Eve, and subsequent church Fathers took up and developed his interpretation. They blamed the first woman for the estrangement between God and humanity so that Eve and her daughters became the source and sign of original sin. Biblical material concerning women was either marginalized or interpreted in this context.

Attempts at solving the problems facing women as they approach the Bible form the bulk of literature produced by feminist theologians. The varied types of solution offered show that feminist theology is a broad term, encompassing many differing feminist theologies. The two main branches can be termed 'radical' and 'reformist'. In essence the former tends to reject the Bible and Christianity in favour of an alternative, essentially feminine religious experience. The latter, whilst rejecting most Christian tradition about women, sees the Bible as the means of reconstructing a positive Christian theology for women. These two 'camps' have their origin in the North American feminist movement of the 1960s. Most British Christian feminists would place themselves within one of the two.

There is a third dimension to feminist theology that does not appear in a recognizable form in the United States. There, conservative Christianity has singled out feminism as one of the major causes of all the problems in Western society. The women who belong to that tradition see feminism as an enemy to their faith and their status. It would be highly unlikely that they would recognize anything positive in feminist theology. Yet precisely this is what has happened in conservative Christianity in Britain, and in these circles this third dimension can be discerned. In the spirit of the women who campaigned for the emancipation of slaves and the humane treatment of prostitutes, a form of feminist theology has appeared in the work of such Christians as Elaine Storkey (*What's Right with Feminism*, 1985) and Mary Evans (*Woman in the Bible*, 1983), both of whom could be described as belonging to the Conservative Evangelical tradition. Their biblical interpretation adheres closely to the position of Conservative Evangelicalism where the Bible holds the central position of authority. Nothing within the biblical text can be rejected, but it is to be explained in the light of the role of women in late twentieth-century society. In contrast to both reformist and radical examples, this dimension appears more as Christian apologetics for the twentieth century than as feminist theology. Yet, set alongside biblical interpretation on the question of women produced by other Conservative Evangelical writers their work could be perceived as extremely radical.

For example, Elaine Storkey takes the concept of a husband's 'headship' over his wife outlined by Paul in Eph. 5.21ff., and interprets it in non-authoritative terms which describe the husband instead as a source of life. She draws attention to the picture of a reciprocal and balanced relationship drawn by the Apostle, and disposes of the feudalistic model of marriage occasionally found in the writings of the church Fathers as well as some evangelical commentators. Likewise, Mary Evans produces a fascinating interpretation of Gen. 1–3 where she highlights the positive role of Eve who, for example, is described as Adam's* 'helper', the same noun which is used elsewhere in the Bible to describe God in relation to Israel. It is also noted that whereas Christian theology has always stressed that Christ as the second Adam has overthrown God's judgment on the original Adam, Eve's punishment, to be ruled over by her husband, is left untouched and would seem to remain outside the reach of Christ's salvific work.

The most famous example of a radical feminist theologian is Mary Daly. In her first book, written as a member of the Roman Catholic Church, *The Church and the Second Sex* (1968), she began to examine the oppression of women by the church as understood by Simone de Beauvoir in her classic study *The Second Sex*. Although at this time Daly is critical of the church, she sees in the Second Vatican Council the sign of hope for the liberation of women and she is critical of de Beauvoir's disillusionment with the church.

As time went on Daly became increasingly radical, losing patience with the crawling pace of ecclesiastical reform, and she began to move outside the boundaries of the Catholic Church to express her changing theology. In 1973 her second book was published, *Beyond God the Father*, in which she outlines the case against the Bible and Christianity. Her attack is levelled at all forms of Christianity, but Roman Catholicism in particular. She takes a central theme such as Mariolatry and shows how a seemingly positive feminist aspect of Catholicism has been manipulated by male theologians until it has become a means of subjugation for ordinary women.

Mary Daly feels that Christianity, in fact the whole Judaeo-Christian tradition, is a male structure designed by men for men so that: *when god is male the male is god*. To change, for example, the language of the Bible from exclusive male terminology for God to inclusive language incorporating both male and female would be superficial packaging with the core symbolism remaining patriarchal. Instead she calls for a 'castration of language and images that perpetuate the structures of a sexist world'. She calls not for a cosmetic change from 'he' to 'she', but a much deeper transformation in our comprehension of God from that of noun to verb, as the Being in which we participate. On this view, radical feminism must reject the Judaeo-Christian tradition in favour of an exclusively female articulation of female religious experience. Biblical Yahwism is recognized as simply one ancient Israelite male cult, and radical feminists attempt to reconstruct its ancient female counterparts. These female cults are based on a matriarchal rather than patriarchal structure. Because most of those involved in this movement have arrived at their present theology after a journey through Christianity, this religious experience is called 'post-Christian feminism'. For Daly the key to this new religious experience is 'sisterhood' which forms the 'antichurch', both being the product of female consciousness-raising. Daly has become increasingly radical in her subsequent publications: *Gyn/Ecology; The Metaphysics of Radical Feminism* (1978), and *Pure Lust* (1984). In these she attacks not only Christianity but Christian feminists. She describes them as 'robotized tokens' who play into the hands of phallocentric male supremacists. Only lesbian radical feminists can rise above the normal experience of male patriarchy. Mary Daly has completely broken away from Christianity and Christian feminism. Christian feminists are regarded as traitors who have compromised with the enemy: men. Although her name is perhaps the best-known in the context of religion and feminism, Mary Daly only represents a minority of feminist theologians. She is the individual most closely associated with post-Christian feminism in America. In Britain, Daphne Hampson is its chief exponent.

The major difference between radical and reformist feminism is that whereas the former, on looking at the Bible and the Judaeo-Christian tradition from a feminist stance, can see the only solution to be its rejection, the latter decides to stay with the tradition. Although the term 'radical' is reserved for those feminists who have moved away from the Judaeo-Christian tradition, it would be misleading to assume that the term cannot suitably apply to the reformists. The ideas and concepts that have resulted from their biblical interpretation constitute some of the most radical exegesis of modern biblical criticism. It can challenge conventional biblical translation, and even question the canonical status of certain passages. The best-known reformist biblical scholars are Rosemary Radford Ruether, Phyllis Trible, and Elisabeth Schüssler Fiorenza. All are professors working in North America. Although these scholars apply various and differing methodologies to the biblical text, they share a common approach in that they all attempt to go directly to the text, rather than through the history of interpretation, both ancient and modern. Having read the text through their feminist eyes they turn then to the accepted interpretation and criticize that in the light of what they have read. This method explains their label: as with the scholars of the sixteenth-century Reformation,* the Bible becomes the standard by which religious belief and practice are judged.

This contemporary practice of going directly to the text and believing that, when read correctly or decoded, it contains all the answers to the exegete's questions, puts the work of feminist theologians alongside the most recent developments in literary criticism* of the Bible. Phyllis Trible employs the method of rhetorical criticism* when examining key biblical texts for women. She describes this method as both scholarly and intuitive, and it produces ingenious interpretation. In her book *God and the Rhetoric of Sexuality*, (1978), she applies this methodology to the story of Eve in Genesis and discovers, not the divine sanctioning of the subjugation of women, but rather a story of the equality of the sexes as being both complementary and co-operative, and sharing in both sin and punishment. Her work is a fine example of exegesis of the Hebrew text. For example, she translates *adam* as 'earth-creature', formed out of *adamah*, 'earth', rather than 'man'. Man and woman are not created until Gen. 2.22–23, when the two are called *ish* and *isha* respectively. As a consequence of this interpretation it is made clear that the species called *adam* in Gen. 1.26–27, created in the divine image, included both male and female.

Rosemary Radford Ruether has taken on the task of answering the criticisms of Christian feminism articulated by Mary Daly. Her main criticism of Daly's theology is its exclusive nature. It is not harnessed to any form of human liberation save that of feminism. No man can share in this liberation, however oppressed or starving he may be. He remains the enemy by virtue of his gender alone. In contrast to Daly, Ruether sees feminism as part of a general movement of liberation for all, both male and female, who are subjected to oppression. In this theology we can recognize Ruether's continued commitment to Christianity, or more particularly, her commitment to biblical religion found in the books of the prophets and the Synoptic Gospels. In terms of biblical interpretation, Ruether is most memorable for her work on the figure Mary of Nazareth. In her books *Mary, the Feminine Face of the Church* (1979), and *Sexism and God Talk* (1983), Ruether reclaims the biblical account of this important individual from the patriarchal mythology of Christian tradition which had transformed her into a passive victim who had no say in her own destiny. By examining the account of Mary found in the opening chapters of Luke's Gospel from a feminist perspective, Ruether discovers a different character. Mary is presented by Luke as a discipleship model for all humankind, one who has faith comparable to Abraham's and courage which reflects that of Christ in the giving of herself for the fulfilment of God's salvation plan. She is a woman who is in charge not only of her own destiny, but also the destiny of the whole of humanity. In saying 'yes' to God Mary was not playing the passive victim, but rather in her strength she was exercising her autonomy. Her words in the Magnificat anticipate the theme of social justice taken up by Jesus at the beginning of his ministry when, according to Luke, he reads from Isa. 61. Ruether points out that in speaking the words of the Magnificat Mary fuses together feminist theology and liberation theology.

Like Ruether, Elisabeth Schüssler Fiorenza rediscovers the centrality of women to the Christian gospel. The title of her book, *In Memory of Her* (1983), is taken from Mark 14.3–9, where, to the consternation of the disciples, an anonymous woman anoints Jesus' head with precious ointment. Jesus' defence of the woman stands in judgment against today's marginalization of women by the major Christian traditions. Fiorenza applies modern criticism to the NT, using in particular the sociological* approach, to discover that female subordination was not part of the original gospel, but rather the result of the church's eventual compromise with Graeco-Roman society.

See also **Liberation Theology; Women in Early Christian Interpretation**.

Ann Loades, *Searching for Lost Coins: Explorations in Christianity and Feminism*, 1987; Letty M. Russell, *Feminist Interpretation of the Bible*, 1985; Phyllis Trible, *Texts of Terror: Literary Feminist Readings of Biblical Narratives*, 1984.

DEBORAH F. MIDDLETON

Figures of Speech

In the broadest sense, modes of expression which are out of the ordinary. Hebrew and Christian scriptures are full of self-consciously figurative language, but our analysis and classifications of figures of speech *per se* is very much a classical legacy, mediated by the rhetorical tradition. To some extent the traditional distinctions are still employed today, although, as we shall see, modern linguistics would question the ancient rationale for them.

Classical rhetoric* made a distinction between figures and tropes (or 'turnings'). Tropes were held to be substitutions or transferences of word for word. The most important of these was metaphor.* Other common tropes are metonymy, simile, synecdoche, and hyperbole.

By contrast, figures of speech, or schemata, were held to be matters of composition involving more than one word. These result from the manipulation of sound or arrangement of words in the context, for example the repetition of a word or phrase for rhetorical effect, anaphora. A further distinction was made between figures of speech and figures of thought, the former being aspects of grammar and the latter aspects of argumentation. An example of a figure of thought here would be prolepsis, where the speaker introduces objections into his argument only in order to answer them himself. Prolepsis is a Pauline favourite, 'Are we to continue in sin that grace may abound? By no means!' (Rom. 6.1; see also 6.15 and 7.7).

Modern writers are sceptical of the separation of thought and language which the distinction between figure of speech and figure of thought implies. It is also now widely recognized that tropes are not simply the manipulation of individual words but depend, as do the other figures, on wider features of context for their interpretation. As a result, modern linguistic theory considers the distinction between trope, figure of speech and figure of thought somewhat arbitrary, if not otiose. In scholarly as well as common speech 'figures of speech' has come to refer to the whole range of what were formerly called tropes and figures.

If there is a kernel of truth to the traditional groupings it is that they give some indication as to whether the oddity associated with a figure was primarily semantic, syntactic or pragmatic. A metaphor has no characteristic syntactic form. Simile, on the other hand, while semantically very like metaphor, is distinguished syntactically by 'like' and 'as' structures, thus, 'one whose rash words are like sword thrusts' (Prov. 12.18). Yet simile, like metaphor, must be identified semantically, otherwise one would have no means of distinguishing simile from straightforward predications.

Pragmatic features taking into account wider context and audience are of the essence of figures such as rhetorical question; for example, 'If God is for us, who is against us?' (Rom. 8.31). Paul's question, although displaying a characteristic form, can be seen as rhetorical only in the context of his wider argument.

It can readily be imagined that the possibilities of discriminating different figures of speech are virtually limitless; any innovation in style or use might qualify. Quintilian already in his own time (AD 40–95) wearied of the multiplicity of classifications. Indeed the same sentence can even deploy more than one figure, for example, 'If their tent-cord is plucked up within them, do they not die, and that without wisdom?' has both metaphor and rhetorical question (Job 4.21).

Questioning of the basis for the traditional classifications should not lead us to dismiss the importance to religious and biblical language of the study of these stylistic elements. Indeed, modern philosophy of language and semantics, in pointing out the inextricability of thought and language, of meaning and its expression, gives us more reason to pay serious consideration to them. Stylistic considerations are not a matter of ornamental excess; what one says is decisively affected by how one says it. For example, consider Paul's* development of the christological metaphor of 'second Adam'.* In Rom. 5, Paul employs a series of parallelisms, e.g., 'as by one man's disobedience many were made sinners, so by one man's obedience many will be made righteous' (5.19). The parallelism is a powerful rhetorical device, but it is integral to Paul's meaning. The basis of a good many historical disputes in theology is difference as to whether, and in what sense, a particular figure of speech should be definitive of Christian belief.

Setting aside debatable claims that Semitic peoples show particular predilection for certain figures of speech (for instance, hyperbole), it is certainly possible to say that ancient writers, like modern ones, often show a preference for certain figures and argumentative styles. These stylistic elements are important features of text and argument and deserve the interpreter's close attention.

Some figures of speech are:

aggregation, strengthening an enumeration of parts: 'Their idols are silver and gold,/ the work of men's hands./ They have mouths, but do not speak;/ eyes, but do not see./ They have ears, but do not hear;/ noses, but do not smell' (Ps. 115.4–6).

anaphora, the repetition, either of syllables within a word, or, more characteristically, of the first words in two successive sentences or phrases: the repetition of 'blessed' in the Beatitudes (Luke 6.20ff.).

antithesis, the aligned use of two sharply contrasting phrases: 'I have baptized you with water, but he will baptize you with the Holy Spirit' (Mark 1.8).

hyperbole, exaggerated statement: 'You blind guides, straining out a gnat and swallowing a camel!' (Matt. 23.24).

metaphor, the figure by which we speak of one thing in terms which are seen as suggestive of another: 'Thou didst bring a vine out of Egypt; thou didst drive out the nations and plant it' (Ps. 80.8).

metonymy, the use of a term with close association or symbolic connection with that under discussion: 'The Lord brought us out of Egypt with a mighty hand and an outstretched arm', where 'mighty hand' is associated with power (Deut. 26.8). This verse also involves the metaphorical prediction of a human form to God.

oxymoron, asserting a seeming contradiction: 'You blind guides' (Matt. 23.24) and 'Has not God made foolish the wisdom of the world?' (I Cor. 1.20).

simile, a figure which suggests comparison and has a characteristic 'like' or 'as' structure: 'My brethren are treacherous as a torrent-bed' (Job 6.15).

synecdoche, the use of a part for the whole, or vice versa; closely associated with metonymy: 'Yet it was I who taught Ephraim to walk, I took them up in my arms' (Hos. 11.3). Ephraim refers to the Northern Kingdom.

See also **Allegory; Literary Criticism; Metaphor; Rhetorical Criticism.**

G. B. Caird, *The Language and Imagery of the Bible*, 1980; George A. Kennedy, *Classical Rhetoric and its Christian and Secular Tradition from Ancient to Modern Times*, 1980; id., *New Testament Interpretation through Rhetorical Criticism*, 1984; Ch. Perelman and L. Olbrechts-Tyteca, *The New Rhetoric: A Treatise on Argumentation*, 1969; Janet Martin Soskice, *Metaphor and Religious Language*, 1985.

JANET MARTIN SOSKICE

Florilegia

Florilegium is the Latin-based equivalent of the Greek-based word 'anthology', meaning literally 'a collection or selection of flowers'. Florilegia are collections of selected passages from the writings of previous authors. For Christian literature the label is technically applied to such collections from the late fourth century AD onwards. These collections have various antecedents and are of various kinds.

Non-Christian florilegia are traceable to the third century BC or even earlier. Poetic selections were used for instruction, for pleasure, and for philosophical argument; the poetic saying of Aratus in Acts 17.28 is vaguely attributed to 'some of your poets' and may derive from a florilegium. Collections of poetic oracles were also made; the quotation from Epimenides the Cretan in Titus 1.12 may come from such a work. Prose passages were collected for aesthetic purposes, but chiefly to provide guides to the moral life. These were often lists of pithy maxims from diverse sources and are known especially amongst Epicureans; since in I Cor. 15.32 Paul seems to use Isa. 22.13 to argue against an Epicurean stance, he could be citing the widely known extract from Menander in 15.33 on the basis of some such florilegium. John Stobaeus (fourth-fifth centuries AD) is regarded as the greatest non-Christian anthologist; his four books include prose and poetic extracts from classical authors including Neoplatonic and Hermetic writings and probably influenced the writing of John of Damascus (c. AD 675–749), as well as the Laurentian Florilegium (fourteenth century) which contains both pagan and Christian texts.

Early florilegia by Christian authors imitate those of the classical tradition. Clement of Alexandria (c. 150–215) (see **Alexandrian Interpretation**) in the *Stromateis* lists apt quotations from classical authors, extracts which recur in the works of John Stobaeus. Origen* (c. 185–254) mistrusted poetic maxims but used selections from the school tradition. Gregory of Nazianzus (329–89) seems to have preferred the poets. Didymus (c. 313–98) in his work *On the Trinity* has selections of quotations which are also used by John Stobaeus.

The first anthologies which were Christian both in authorship and in content were based on biblical texts. Like their non-Christian counterparts they were often designed to be guides to the moral life, but many were also compiled in the context of the debate with Judaism. The oldest collection is that of Cyprian, Bishop of Carthage (d. 258), who compiled three books of *Testimonia* (*Ad Quirinium*). The first two are mostly extracts from the OT presented as typological* proof-texts justifying the existence of the church: texts are selected to show how the church is the heir of God's promises to his people, how the old covenant* is abolished, and to prove the divinity of Christ and the supernatural character of his birth, crucifixion, resurrection and coming again. The third book is mostly NT extracts grouped thematically for Christian living: almsgiving, abstention from oaths, rejection of usury and mixed marriages, martyrdom, purity of speech, honouring of parents, prayer, etc. Apart from the superscriptions, the texts are given without commentary.

It is unlikely that Cyprian was the first to write a testimonium. Because combinations of the same OT passages are used more than once in the NT, some scholars argue that even the first generation of Christians had testimony* books, lists of proof-texts* for apologetic use. The best evidence for such a theory is the combination of Isa. 28.16; Ps. 118.22; Isa. 8.14, cited variously in Matt. 21.42; Rom. 9.33; I Peter 2.6–8; and in the *Epistle of Bar-*

nabas 6.2–4. Amongst the Dead Sea Scrolls* is also a list of texts without commentary (4QTest), probably compiled to demonstrate who would be the protagonists in the messianic age: Ex. 20.21 (Sam.); Num. 24.15–17; Deut 33.8–11; and an extract from the so-called Psalms of Joshua (4Q*379* 22.2.7–14). Another Qumran text (4QFlor) contains the quotation and interpretation of II Sam. 7 and Pss. 1 and 2, a combination of OT texts also to be found in Acts 13.33–37 and Heb. 1.5.

Between these texts and Cyprian, there is no clear evidence for the existence of collections of proof-texts, although the Epistle of Barnabas groups together several anti-temple and messianic texts, as do Justin, Irenaeus* and Clement of Alexandria. From the fourth century AD come two sheets of papyrus (P.Ryl. 460) inscribed with Isa. 42.3–4; 66.18–19; 52.15; 53.1–3, 6–7, 11–12; Gen. 26.13–14; II Chron. 1.12; and Deut. 29.8, 11, all texts that could be construed messianically or in relation to the history of the church.

The florilegia from the late fourth to the fifteenth century have been variously classified. Sometimes prose florilegia are distinguished from poetic ones, sometimes those in Greek from those in Latin; more commonly they are listed according to their purpose as dogmatic, ethical, spiritual (ascetic) or legal. Many dogmatic and legal florilegia contain little or no use of the Bible at all: e.g. the *Philokalia* of Basil the Great and Gregory of Nazianzus consists solely of extracts from the writings of Origen. Yet, extracts from the Bible occur in some examples of all the different kinds of florilegia.

Sometimes, as in Cyprian's *Testimonia*, biblical extracts form the sole content of the florilegium, so that the only way to perceive the way the Bible has been used in the collection is to analyse the method behind the editor's selection. For example, the compiler of the fifth-century *Testimonia de Patre et Filio et Spiritu Sancto* forms a collection of the biblical sources for the doctrine of the Trinity; within the work the passages are simply listed in the canonical order of the biblical books.

More common are the florilegia which mix quotations from the Bible with extracts from the Fathers or from non-Christian literature. With the rediscovery of classical authors in the West, these were particularly common in Western Christianity from the twelfth to the fifteenth centuries. Sometimes this kind of mixed florilegium uses the biblical text to control its subject matter. Related to this kind of florilegium are the *Catenae* (chains) which seem to originate with Procopius of Gaza in the early sixth century. In the *catenae*, biblical texts are systematically interpreted through the listing of choice comments from previous interpreters. So, for example, Thomas Aquinas' *Catena Aurea* on the four Gospels follows the text of the Gospel section by section and offers elucidation of the principal verses by using OT texts, other NT texts, and quotations from the Fathers; the whole is a typological demonstration of how the Gospels fulfil the OT. In this way, in some cases, the florilegia are difficult to distinguish from biblical commentaries.* Indeed, to some extent they are the Christian version of the increasingly influential traditions of biblical exegesis within Judaism which resulted in the widespread writing and use of *midrashim,** commentaries which combine scriptural elucidations with sayings from the authorities of earlier Tannaitic and Amoraic times. Sometimes the authoritative biblical interpretations of the Fathers are grouped under questions and answers of master and disciple as in Wicbold's eighth-century *Liber quaestionum super librum Genesis.*

Some of the ethical florilegia are also akin to Jewish writing. The seventh-century *Testimonia Divinae Scripturae*, addressed to Christians in Carthage, begins with a short treatise on the Trinity and then lists long extracts from Proverbs and Ecclesiasticus as the basis of Christian behaviour. The ethical florilegia are thus a continuation in the Christian tradition of the wisdom* literature of the OT; just as the philosophers are used in the pagan ethical florilegia from the second century BC onwards, so in these texts the OT is not simply fulfilled in Christianity, it is of direct application to Christian life. The way in which straight scriptural quotation is often introduced by a Prologue reflects the form of Ecclesiasticus itself. Another seventh-century ethical florilegium, *Fl. Frisingense*, organizes scriptural and patristic quotations thematically, but the scriptural texts are generally presented to be taken literally. Although mediaeval* ethical florilegia sometimes present texts because of their allegorical* significance, they also continue to preserve the literal meaning, even though little attention is paid to the original context or setting of the passages concerned. In this way, ethical florilegia also mirror the continuous interest in *halakah* and the restatement of the plain meaning of scripture in much contemporary mediaeval Judaism.

The best-known of the spiritual and ethical florilegia is John of Damascus' *Sacra Parallela* (eighth century); in three books (on God, man, and virtues and vices), biblical and patristic extracts are presented systematically: alphabetically in the first two books, in contrasting pairs in the third. The popularity of some of the spiritual florilegia should not be underestimated. For example, over 360 copies (from the ninth to the sixteenth centuries) still survive of the eighth-century *Liber scintillarum*, a work of 81 chapters of short scriptural extracts combined with patristic quotations designed for private devotional use. In the spiritual florilegia, passages of the Bible are presented sometimes literally or historically, sometimes with attention to the moral element (as in the fourth chapter of Benedict's *Rule*), but more often allegorically in order to illustrate something more profound.

Florilegia have continued to be compiled for different purposes right up to the present day. For example, Lopez de Mesa (1544–1615) compiled a florilegium of biblical and patristic texts to enable Jesuit missionaries in Mexico to travel light. Oliver Cromwell had the *Souldier's Pocket Bible* produced during the English Civil War for a similar reason. There are currently very many devotional florilegia in print throughout the world; one of the continuing reasons for the production of florilegia is to enable ease of access to texts, including the Bible, which might otherwise appear complex and alien. Florilegia inevitably distort their sources and for the Bible often suggest a coherence of thought or a harmonization of events that is not present in the Bible as a whole; Cyprian himself, in the preface to *Testimonia*, argued that extracts were no substitute for reading complete works.

For present-day research, the florilegia enable us to see the extent of ancient libraries, both how large some must have been for collections to be made and also how small others were, using florilegia as a substitute for an extensive collection of texts. The florilegia also show the influence of particular biblical books and patristic theologians. They often furnish us with extracts of texts that have long since been lost in their original form, or, where a text is extant elsewhere, they sometimes preserve a form of the text which can contribute towards the reconstruction of the history of the texts of the Bible and the Fathers. They also illuminate the way in which differing viewpoints were juxtaposed, and so they reveal the nature and extent of some doctrinal debates.

See also **Proof Texts;** *Testimonia.*

C. H. Dodd, *According to the Scriptures*, 1952; M. A. Fahey, *Cyprian and the Bible*, 1971; J. A. Fitzmyer, '4Q Testimonia and the New Testament', *Essays on the Semitic Background of the New Testament*, 1971, pp. 59–89; J. R. Harris, *Testimonies* I–II, 1916–20; H. M. Rochais et al., 'Florilèges spirituels', *Dictionnaire de spiritualité* 5, coll. 435–512.

GEORGE J. BROOKE

Folklore

It is not easy to define what precisely is meant by folklore, since different practitioners understand it in different ways and the study of the subject has become ever more complex, especially in the twentieth century when it has been increasingly shaped by such developments as social psychology, sociology* and structural* linguistics.* The influence of folklore studies on biblical scholarship has largely been determined by the extent to which scholars, especially OT scholars, have applied to the Bible the methods and conclusions of folklorists of a given period, methods and conclusions which have often been superseded in more recent folklore work. However, it may perhaps be said that, as far as biblical studies are concerned, two generally accepted aspects of folklore have been particularly significant. On the one hand, folklore is the investigation of popular customs and customary behaviour, and their meaning for the society in which they are at home. On the other hand, it studies the popular verbal expressions of such a society, by classifying them into various categories, such as myths,* legends,* folktales, riddles and proverbs, with a special interest in the origin and development of the material in oral tradition.*

A well-known example of the former concern is represented by J. G. Frazer's *Folklore in the Old Testament* (3 vols, 1918), which also illustrates the outlook of folklorists representative of a particular epoch. Frazer took for granted the dominant evolutionary approach of the later nineteenth century and saw folklore study as revealing the survivals, in a more complex society, of ideas and customs characteristic of the primitive stage of a universal human development. Hence, many apparently strange happenings in the OT, for example the majority of the episodes in the story of Jacob, could be seen, not as actual events, but as reflections of folk beliefs and practices to be found all over the world, especially among so-called 'primitive' peoples. In this way, a whole substratum in Israel's evolution could be rediscovered.

Frazer's methods and assumptions have been widely criticized. His comparative method did not allow for differences of culture and time or for the fact that an apparently similar custom in two societies might have a very different significance in each. Above all, Frazer's concept of the 'primitive', even supposing early Israel could be thus categorized, was wholly negative, a state of 'savagery and superstition'. More recent studies of early peoples have produced a much more positive evaluation of their belief-systems, which is reflected in T. H. Gaster's up-dating of Frazer's work, where Gaster makes clear that the folkloristic elements in the OT retain a validity for people in all ages, even down to the present.

The second pre-occupation of folklore studies, its interest in literary* genres,* was brought to bear on the OT by H. Gunkel, whose work has been the foundation on which most succeeding scholars have built. Gunkel began with the patriarchal narratives, which he described as 'legends' in their existing form, though they derive from even more ancient popular folk-tales. These narratives are to be distinguished from history writing and they do not recount historical events, although they may well throw light on the character of Israelite society at a particular time. So, for example, to take the Jacob cycle again, Gunkel argued that its original components had been two independent folk-tales; one, involving Jacob and Esau, was a folk story about a shepherd and a hunter, the other, dealing with Jacob and Laban, told of a contest between an older and a younger shepherd. The tales could be isolated because they all displayed much the same distinctive literary form, marking them off as individual units, such as brevity of the narrative,* differentiation between chief and subordinate personages, the way in which thought is expressed only in action, and many other features. They were products of the 'collective people' and would originally have been transmitted in a family setting, but later they acquired a more artistic shape when they came to be recited by a class of peripatetic professional story-tellers, and still later they were woven together as the extended cycles that now comprise Genesis. Hence Gunkel saw his work as marking a step forward in that it showed that the contents of Genesis must have existed first in oral tradition and were for long orally transmitted. It was the recognition of the contents as basically folk tradition which led to this conclusion, because folklorists had collected their material from the lips of actual story-tellers. Later, Gunkel extended his investigations to the study of the folk-tale in the OT in general. Here, his conclusions had much in common with those of Frazer: OT folk-tales reveal both a 'primitive' mentality, with a religious outlook very different from the developed faith of later Israel, and the presence of regularly recurring motifs which occur among many other peoples – though it must be pointed out that Gunkel's literary sensitivity caused him to place a much higher value on this kind of material than had Frazer.

Gunkel's work has both acted as a springboard for further developments by other scholars along the lines he adumbrated and has also provoked questions about the validity of his opinions in the light of modern folklore research, which has moved on considerably since his day. In the first place, his emphasis on the place of oral tradition in the OT stimulated some biblical scholars to a more thorough examination of this phenomenon and to claim for it a much greater importance in the growth of the OT than he had done, although it needs to be observed that many of these scholars were not greatly concerned with the particular contribution of folklore as such. Scandinavian* scholars, such as H. S. Nyberg, I. Engnell and E. Nielsen especially, have argued that much more of the OT than had hitherto been realized consists of traditions which were oral in origin and had been transmitted orally over a long period and only committed to writing at a comparatively late date. Further, in ways similar to Gunkel, they claimed that oral tradition could be confidently distinguished from written material by certain literary criteria* and also that oral traditions generally reliably preserve their original form, being accurately passed on by the trained memories of successive transmitters.

Such conclusions have been criticized from various standpoints: here we shall only mention some which arise from the progress of modern folklore research. Folklorists have devoted much attention to the way in which tales are in fact transmitted, by studying the techniques employed by story-tellers in various societies, and have emphasized the importance of the actual performance of such story-telling. They have observed that the oral narrator does not work with a fixed pattern which he has learned by heart, but rather he makes a creative use of traditional motifs and expressions to produce a tale to meet the needs and expectations of his audience, which may not be the same on all occasions. Any consideration of the nature of oral material in the Bible and the process of its transmission needs to take account of such flexibility.

Secondly, several recent studies have noted the complex interaction between oral and written traditions and their transmission in societies where both are known, as would appear to be the case with ancient Israel, and the danger of drawing too sharp a distinction between them in the way that OT scholarship has often done. The criteria adduced for distinctively oral material still largely reflect the 'epic laws' of the folklorist A. Olrik, set out in an article of 1909 (ET in A. Dundes, ed., *The Study of Folklore*, 1965). But while Olrik's laws remain illuminating for the particular category of folk-tale, though not necessarily for all folklore material, they can now be seen to be equally applicable to both oral and written texts, for the latter may display much

the same characteristics as the former. Hence the presence of clearly oral material in the OT, for example in Genesis, which biblical scholars have frequently taken for granted, must now be considered a much more open question.

A more fruitful contribution of folklore studies to the understanding of the Bible may perhaps be found in their interest in identifying the motifs and genres which characterize folklore material. A central concern of folklore study is the classification of motifs common to all folk literature, and a work like Gaster's shows how many of these are present in the OT. But the contemporary interest in structuralism has directed folklorists more specifically towards how such stereotyped elements function to create a regular pattern and movement in many tales. V. Propp's *The Morphology of the Folktale* has been especially influential. Propp held that popular tales all display a limited number of stock characters and stock functions which they perform. His methodology* has been used to elucidate the character of a number of OT narratives, without the necessity of considering whether or not they are oral or written texts. What is interesting is that Propp's analysis can be applied to quite extensive OT narratives and this raises the question whether these have been made up of small, independent units in the way that, since Gunkel, has often been supposed: for example, the whole Jacob narrative has been viewed in terms of Propp's roles and functions, giving a very different view of its composition from that of Gunkel. In the same way, we may briefly observe that the approach of what is known as 'structuralism', which is not dissimilar, though not identical, to that of Propp, has influenced both folklorists and biblical scholars in their assessment of story material. Not only has a structuralist interpretation been proposed for a number of OT narratives, such as the material about Saul and David,* but considerable sections of the NT, such as the accounts of Jesus' passion,* have been subjected to a similar analysis.

With regard to genre studies, an essential concern of folklore investigation, Gunkel had described a number of these in the OT in his dictionary article 'Sagen und Legenden' of 1931. Since his time, OT scholars have devoted much attention to the precise understanding of such categories and the terms used to indicate them: thus, considerable discussion has centred on whether the German *Sage* is better rendered in English as 'saga'* or as 'legend'. Classifications from folklore narrative research, such as tale, legend, saga, fable, etc., have been almost universally adopted in OT scholarship and the understandings of them by one or more folklorists have been employed in exegesis.* A single instance may be given by way of illustration, the influence of the theories of A. Jolles on C. Westermann and K. Koch. Jolles claimed that *Sage* should not properly be understood as designating a story of heroic deeds or state events but that it has its origin in the family and the family's interest. This has led both Westermann and Koch to distinguish between two types of saga, and to see the patriarchal narratives as rooted in the family and telling of family matters, in contradistinction to traditions, such as those of Saul and David, which are heroic saga. The classification of genres and their significance has undoubtedly shed light on a great deal of OT material, but the folklorist may still want to ask questions about its real value in that area. Genre classifications are debatable and confused even in their primary context of folk-narrative research, and the problem is intensified when they are imported into the context of a somewhat different discipline. This is perhaps the main problem in the immediate future for the significance of folklore for biblical studies.

G. W. Coats (ed.), *Saga, Legend, Tale, Novella, Fable: Narrative Forms in Old Testament Literature*, 1985; T. H. Gaster, *Myth, Legend and Custom in the Old Testament*, 1969; H. Gunkel, *The Legends of Genesis*, 1901, ² 1964; id., *The Folktale in the Old Testament*, 1917, ET 1987; P. G. Kirkpatrick, *The Old Testament and Folklore Study*, 1988; P. J. Milne, *Vladimir Propp and the Study of Structure in Hebrew Biblical Narrative*, 1988.

J. R. PORTER

Form Criticism

The normal English translation of the German term *Formgeschichte* (literally, form history), coined in 1919 by Martin Dibelius to describe his analysis of the popular oral tradition* underlying the written Gospels. He was influenced by a similar approach to parts of the OT, pioneered by Hermann Gunkel around 1900, for which he had proposed the more general term *Gattungsforschung*, or genre* analysis. Because biblical form criticism has been developed from these beginnings in slightly different directions, two definitions are required, if confusion is to be avoided. 1. Narrowly and more commonly, form criticism is an aspect of tradition* history; it is concerned with the classification of the typical structures of oral tradition, their relation to social setting (*see* **Sociology and Social Anthropology**), and the changes which they undergo over time. 2. Broadly defined, form criticism is that aspect of the study of the biblical writings which is concerned with the form or genre of whole works and of their constituent parts, whether or not these works or their components ever existed orally.

Late nineteenth-century biblical research had been preoccupied with the detection of sources.* The Graf–Wellhausen hypothesis and the Marcan and 'Q' hypotheses had revised scholarly views of the composition of the Pentateuch* and the Synoptics.* But the sources, like the books into which they were eventually incorporated, were still treated as the unique products of individual authors, and their relation to the corporate development of religious faith and practice remained unclear. Moreover, source-critical method could offer no guidance in tracing the tradition back behind the sources to its basis in historical reality. Form criticism supplemented source criticism in both these respects. It offered a scientific method, which broke through the limitations of philological and literary study of the texts, to answer current questions about religious development and about the transmission of historical memory. It did this by drawing attention to the typical features of texts, that is the communally shared conventions of genre which supply the context for any act of written or spoken communication. It thereby enabled the literature to be related to society, and the texts to be related to history, opening a new window on to the lived experience of those communities, ancient Israel and the early church, from and for which the biblical literature was produced.

Form criticism and oral tradition. Form is the means by which oral tradition achieves stability and continuity; it may be viewed as equivalent to the art of writing for literature. In oral poetry, the rules of structure, metre, stress, rhyme, stock epithets, etc. facilitate the processes of memorization and reproduction. In prose tradition also, particularly in story-telling, the accepted rules of narration in a culture provide the framework for any particular performance. Form criticism in the primary sense begins from this insight and attempts to differentiate the limited number of formal oral types (e.g. hymns, curses, laments, proverbs, laws, tales, myths* and legends*) with their various sub-types, and to define more closely the rules that each type tends to follow. It explains the origin and preservation of such forms with reference to the social 'setting in life' (German, *Sitz im Leben*) in which each predominantly functions (e.g. worship, education, entertainment, politics and the law), and it tries to trace an evolutionary development from primitive to more complex examples of a type, thus allowing historical judgments to be passed concerning their antiquity.

The beginnings of the method are to be found in nineteenth-century classical and folklore* studies, but its critical refinement is one of the great achievements of biblical scholarship. Gunkel was particularly successful in applying this method to the psalms, no longer to be understood as the outpourings of a solitary poetic genius but as reflecting the varied liturgical traditions of a worshipping community.* He also investigated the literary pre-history of the legends of Genesis and discovered in them the oral folk tradition of ancient Israel. Following his lead, scholars have attempted to classify the different oral forms in the OT, to reconstruct their social settings and trace their evolution. In the legal material (see Law), for example, the distinction between casuistic and apodictic forms has been explained by reference to their different life-settings in the law courts and the cultic assembly respectively. Similarly, in the earlier prophets,* patterns like the messenger formula or the oracle of woe are understood as religious adaptations of the forms of royal diplomacy and mourning rites.

Despite the obvious difference in time scale and social spread between ancient Israelite tradition and the early church's memory of Jesus, the Gospels contain similar features which invite form-critical analysis. K. L. Schmidt concluded from his study of the framework of the history of Jesus (1919) that the Synoptics, aside from their passion narratives,* were composed from small, independently circulating units of oral tradition (pericopae). Reliable historical data for reconstructing a biography of Jesus cannot, therefore, be deduced from the present ordering of the accounts of his ministry. M. Dibelius and R. Bultmann* classified these units into a limited number of recurring types and deduced their social function for the early Christian community (especially in preaching and teaching). Working independently of each other, they invented different terms to describe the forms; Dibelius preferred to identify them according to their presumed function, e.g. paradigms and exhortations, while Bultmann's terms reflect comparison with similar forms in other ancient literature, e.g. apophthegms and logia.* While the terminology varied, the overall conclusions were remarkably similar. They concluded that not only the original chronology, but also much of the historical particularity of the Jesus tradition had been smoothed away as the oral tradition was conformed to the post-Easter proclamation, or kerygma,* of the early church. On the positive side, the method offered rare insight into the life of the church, prior to the period of the Pauline epistles. Oral tradition analysis of the Synoptics was all but completed in the work of these pioneers and has advanced only in minor details since. Oral forms have been discovered

elsewhere in the NT, e.g. fragments of the parable* tradition embedded in the Fourth Gospel (e.g. John 5.19–20) and confessional formulae and hymns in the letters (e.g. Rom. 1.3–4; Phil. 2.6–11).

Although the basic insight, that oral folk tradition is the major component of several biblical works and is at least one factor in most of them, has been widely accepted by scholars, reservations about the method have increasingly been registered, principally the following.

First, form criticism underestimates the role of the authors in the composition of the biblical literature. Since the presumed oral tradition is now only available via its final literary crystallization, it may have been subtly but significantly changed as it was written down. It is possible that the presence of popular speech-forms in a text could in certain cases be a sign of literary sophistication, or even ironic imitation of folk tradition. Gunkel made this point about the psalms, but it was ignored in the later form critical researches of Mowinckel. And in the NT, form critics have simply assumed that the synoptic writers are not authors in the proper sense, but anonymous scribes and editors of community tradition. Since about 1950, redaction criticism* has been developed as a partial corrective to the minimal understanding of authorship* implied by source and form criticism. There remain, however, unresolved tensions between the three techniques that make up the classic tradition* historical method. Thus, different versions of the same story or saying may be interpreted as evidence either of variants arising in oral tradition, or of separate documentary sources or of conscious redactional alteration. Not infrequently, competing and mutually exclusive explanations are offered of the same limited data. So, more recently, narrative criticism* and similar approaches have been introduced, which respond to the difficulty in a radical way, by ignoring tradition history altogether in the practice of biblical interpretation.

Second, form criticism can be accused of abstract idealization and logical circularity. It is open to doubt whether the short, 'pure' forms reconstructed by form critics ever actually existed, for the surviving textual material is often complex and 'mixed'. The division of a passage like Mark 2.1–12 into two parts, a miracle* story and a pronouncement story, does not mean that they need ever have circulated independently. To reconstruct the life-setting from the form and then to explain the form by appeal to its life-setting is to argue in a circle, and to ignore the possibility that a particular form may be transmitted in a variety of different settings, to none of which it is entirely subordinate. For example, miracle stories might have been used, as they sometimes are in the written Gospels, as preaching illustrations or ethical examples, so that in terms of their function they should be placed in the same category as paradigms, or exhortations. In other words, the relation between the forms of oral tradition and their social function or life-setting is much more complicated than the method is willing to acknowledge.

Lastly, form criticism tends to exaggerate the extent to which communities adapt and even generate tradition to suit their immediate needs, and to discount the conservative aspects of oral tradition, the controlling influence of eye-witness* testimony in the formation of historical narrative, and the possibility that certain types of material, poetic and legal especially, were fixed by deliberate memorization on the part of official tradents. Having delivered biblical exegesis from the positivism and individualism of earlier scholarship, it was as though form criticism ran the risk of the opposite errors, namely historical scepticism and sociological determinism. In NT interpretation, the work of R. Bultmann* was particularly influential here. His combination of form criticism with neo-orthodox fideism and a Christian existentialism effectively excluded concern with Jesus from the agenda of biblical interpretation for a whole generation of critical German scholarship. For, apart from the parables and a few eschatological sayings, the Jesus tradition was irrecoverable behind the formative faith and preaching of the community. It was only as partial exceptions to form-critical principles were acknowledged, implicitly, for example in the criterion* of dissimilarity, that the question of the historical Jesus* could be reopened by Bultmann's followers.

Despite these reservations, form criticism is an indispensable tool of biblical interpretation. When popular oral tradition is preserved or closely reflected in the biblical literature, recognition of the fact may serve to moderate our expectations of the text and therefore perhaps our sense of disappointment at its lack of theological sophistication: conversely, it may well also increase our excitement at being in touch with a living faith, free of self-conscious theorizing.

Form criticism and genre analysis. In English the borrowed French word genre* indicates some large-scale literary or aesthetic category, such as drama or landscape painting. The German equivalent used in form criticism, *Gattung,* covers, in addition to this, smaller-scale structural features of a work of literature and oral forms of communication. This semantic difference is the cause of the confusion which the second, broader definition of form

criticism given above attempts to avoid. It was Gunkel's express intention to use the form-critical method to furnish a complete literary history of the OT, and not just a folkloric study of those books which happen to have an oral prehistory. Consequently, in OT studies particularly, the term form criticism is frequently understood in the broader sense.

Recognition of the genre of a piece of writing is of primary importance for its interpretation. The history of exegesis of the early chapters of Genesis demonstrates, for instance, the disastrous consequences of mistaking poetic mythological narrative for doctrinal or historical prose. But genre is a complex phenomenon, indicated not merely by the presence of distinguishing formulae in a particular text, but also by its content, and by the less evident characteristics of its mood and intention. For example, a historical novel may be cast in the form of a fictional correspondence and still retain its membership of the genre (cf. the apocryphal letters of Paul and Seneca as a possible example from antiquity). Similarly, certain books of the Bible are framed in a form which their content, mood and intention belie. Thus, Deuteronomy is only superficially classified as a law-code; and the book of Job, despite its opening and closure, lacks the other indicators of conventional wisdom literature.* Hebrews and I John are similar to the letters of Paul* except in the absence of certain formal epistolary features (*see* **Epistle**); whereas the Revelation of John, which begins in an epistolary way, is generically very different. Form alone, therefore, cannot determine genre, and form criticism has to be applied in conjunction with other literary critical* considerations.

The NT Gospels* pose a special problem of overall genre. The form-critical analysis of the oral tradition on which they depend led to the judgment that they are not to be classified as biographies. But this is more a judgment upon the nature of their contents than of their form, since they bear many similarities to the genre of *Lives* in Hellenism, and Luke's Gospel at any rate clearly expresses its intention to be biography (Luke 1.1–4). Nevertheless, the difficulty of proving that such Hellenistic models could have influenced the earliest Gospel, Mark, has led to a variety of other suggestions; for example, Mark as a whole, and not just ch. 13, as apocalyptic,* and Mark, more like the Fourth Gospel, as a christological treatise clothed in narrative form.

Form criticism is not only interested in the genre of complete books, fundamental though that is for their interpretation; it is also concerned with smaller formal structures within them. So, for example, we can identify in Amos certain standard patterns, like the oracles against the nations (1.3–2.6), but consideration of what follows them in the context of the whole book makes it clear that they are not being employed in their natural sense: the prophet's intention is to warn Israel, not to lambast her enemies (2.6ff.). Similarly, Paul's letter to the Romans begins (1.18–32) with a Jewish onslaught against pagan corruption, in a conventional moralistic style; its intention, however, is an ironic reversal of its form (see 2.1ff). The formal analysis of passages like these helps the interpreter to detect the real intention of the writer and so to avoid misplacing the emphasis.

In the above examples, the forms employed, the prophetic oracle and the Cynic* diatribe, are basically oral; but the texts which they have influenced are literary creations. However, it would be wrong to assume that oral tradition always uses form in a straightforward natural way, and that artistic or ironic modifications of form are a mark of literary self-consciousness. For the distinction between oral and written is far less clear with the biblical material than it is for us today. Amos and Paul would have 'composed' orally and their works were 'published' orally. The books of the Bible are mostly scripts intended for oral recitation in community, and not the private property of individuals to be perused at leisure. Form criticism is in this respect more in tune with the nature of the biblical writings than the excessively literary approaches which have become popular in recent times.

The concept of life-setting is still important, when form criticism is understood in our second sense; but it has to be understood broadly. All literature, not just units of oral tradition, has some kind of life-setting. This can be a recurring institutional context: it is, for example, possible that Deuteronomy was designed for recital at a covenant* renewal ceremony; Mark's Gospel may have had its setting in the Easter liturgy. A given work may, on the other hand, arise uniquely at a particular occasion, from some creative impulse or intellectual concern. But it is the strength of form criticism to insist that texts cannot be isolated from life. Language itself is a social construct, and every piece of oral tradition or written composition, every ordinary fragment of communication or heavily stylized literary creation draws from and contributes to a socio-cultural matrix which is revealed in its form. This characteristic emphasis of form criticism qualifies it as the precursor of the modern disciplines of socio-linguistics and the sociology of literature, and distinguishes it from the text immanent method of the 'new criticism'.

See also **Gospel; Oral Tradition; Tradition, History of.**

R. Bultmann, *The History of the Synoptic Tradition*, 1921, ET 1963; M. Dibelius, *From Tradition to Gospel*, 1934; B. Gerhardsson, *Memory and Manuscript*, 1964; H. Gunkel, *The Legends of Genesis*, 1901; E. Güttgemanns, *Candid Questions Concerning Gospel Form Criticism*, 1979; K. Koch, *The Growth of the Biblical Tradition*, 1969; E. V. McKnight, *What is Form Criticism?* 1969; G. N. Stanton, 'Form Criticism Revisited', in M. Hooker and C. Hickling (eds), *What about the New Testament?*, 1975; S. H. Travis, 'Form Criticism', in I. H. Marshall (ed.), *New Testament Interpretation*, 1977; G. M. Tucker, *Form Criticism of the Old Testament*, 1971.

JOHN MUDDIMAN

Fundamentalism

The word originated from a series of tracts written between 1909 and 1915, *The Fundamentals*, which were designed as a re-statement of central Christian doctrines. Their authors wrote from a conservative Protestant perspective, although it should not be forgotten that this was a time of retrenchment in the Catholic church, most notably as seen in Pope Pius X's encyclical *Pascendi domini gregis* of 1907. The twentieth century opened with movements of reaction in both Protestant and Catholic circles against liberalism* and modernism, and cross-fertilization between the two should not be overlooked.

Despite this relatively recent origin of fundamentalism as a specific movement, its claim is to restore the true faith, combining what it believes to be the doctrines of the Protestant Reformers with the informal, enthusiastic organization of the early church. Like the charismatic movement, which claims to return to the Spirit-filled Christian communities established immediately after Pentecost, fundamentalism views itself as 'new' only in so far as it represents a new effort to restore traditional Christianity. Partly for this reason, many British fundamentalist Christians prefer to be called 'evangelicals', that is to say a movement intending to re-state the central *evangelium* or Christian gospel for today.

The question of biblical authority* and inspiration* formed only part of the wide range of doctrines dealt with by *The Fundamentals*. Despite this, fundamentalism as a movement has come to be associated in particular with a certain view of the Bible. This view is sometimes characterized as one of interpreting the text literally, but the critical point for the fundamentalist is more that of scripture's absolute inerrancy. If a literal interpretation of the Bible is likely to suggest error, then the fundamentalist will jettison the literal interpretation.

Thus fundamentalist commentaries * prefer on the whole to interpret the days of creation * in Gen. 1 as 'geological ages' or long eras of time, rather than as literal periods of twenty-four hours. Since the chapter refers to the 'morning and evening' of the days of creation, abandoning the literal understanding has its difficulties, but it is believed to be indispensable in order to maintain a correspondence to scientific fact.

The tendency to judge the truth of the Bible in terms of its correspondence to scientifically established data is an important characteristic of fundamentalism, because this determines the way in which it understands inerrancy. Some biblical interpreters would happily concede that the creation story is a 'myth' * but nevertheless deny that this makes it appropriate to call it wrong or in error. Since it does not intend to be scientifically accurate information about the origins of the universe, it should not be judged in these terms. Fundamentalist interpreters, on the other hand, tend to draw their understanding of truth only from the canons of scientific empiricism. Critics see this as evidence of an old-fashioned, nineteenth-century approach to problems of truth and knowledge. It is also seen as an explanation of the tendency for fundamentalism to have a greater appeal to the 'Anglo-Saxon' culture of Britain and America than to that of continental Europe. Fundamentalists are seen by their critics to approach the Bible seeking the sort of narrow accuracy that is characteristic of a certain attitude to truth (rather like Gradgrind and the horse in Dickens' *Hard Times*!).

Certainly fundamentalist interpretation tends to concentrate upon those parts of the Bible the truth or falsity of which it sees to be dependent upon 'simple matters of fact'. Passages of theological or spiritual reflection, like the 'farewell discourses' of John 13–17, tend to be ignored in favour of passages which the fundamentalist takes to be straightforward historical narrative, such as the miracle stories. Ironically, the concern for scientific accuracy often displaces the very miracle which it is designed to support. Thus fundamentalist commentaries frequently interpret Jesus' walking on the water or stilling the storm by reference to the phenomena of sandbanks and sudden squalls in the area of the Sea of Galilee. Scientific evidence to support the star of Bethlehem is discovered in astronomical charts suggesting a rare conjunction of planets in the sky at the time. By so doing, the fundamentalist endeavours to establish that the text is an accurate scientific record: but the price of such an approach is that it abolishes the miracle in the very process of demonstrating its authenticity.

Indeed, despite its overt hostility to 'liberalism' it could be claimed that fundamentalism shares with its opponent a reductionist, scientific mentality, and that in some ways both come from the same stable. One uses science to reject the Christian faith as traditionally perceived, the other uses it to prove it; neither is sufficiently aware of problems concerning the nature and limitations of its particular scientific approach.

Fundamentalists claim close ties with the Protestant Reformers.* They see themselves as re-stating the Christian commitment to scriptural authority in the face of modern biblical criticism. Where the sixteenth-century Reformers had to wrest the Bible from an ecclesiastical tyranny, their twentieth-century counterparts have to wrest the Bible from a tyranny of scholars. Instead of an ecclesiastical élite determining the meaning of scripture, the problem nowadays is seen as an academic élite. An access to the Bible once denied to the ordinary Christian by the church is now denied by the biblical critics. Detached scholars in universities appear as the modern equivalent of mediaeval allegorists * robbing scripture of its simple truth. From the point of view of its critics, such an attitude displays well both the populism and the anti-intellectualism of many fundamentalists. At the same time, it has to be pointed out that many of those who clearly identify themselves at some point along the spectrum of fundamentalist and 'evangelical' thinking have been accepted by academics generally as profound and reputable scholars in their own right.

In reality, the claim to bear the mantle of the Protestant Reformers is a difficult one for fundamentalists to sustain. Luther * and Calvin * were prepared to criticize parts of the Bible in a way that contemporary fundamentalists would not. Luther's rejection of the Letter to James as 'a right strawy epistle' and willingness to see it removed from the canon, or Calvin's questioning of the authorship of II Peter, could not be reconciled with a modern fundamentalist view of biblical inerrancy. Where the Protestant Reformers sought to distinguish between the words of the text and the Word of God * which those words mediate to the reader, the fundamentalist tends to identify the two. Rather than (to use an analogy of Luther's) the biblical text 'containing' the Word of God as a casket might contain a precious jewel, scripture is said to *be* the Word of God. A more proper heir to the Protestant Reformers in respect of maintaining this distinction between Word and words would be the school of neo-orthodoxy rather than fundamentalism. This distinction may seem pedantic, but it is in fact crucial. It allows the interpreter to claim that an infallible message is being conveyed through a fallible medium (the text itself), whereas the fundamentalist insists that without an infallible medium the message itself cannot be relied upon. As a result, questioning the infallibility of the text becomes for the fundamentalist equivalent to questioning the infallibility of God. Failure to accept that every detail in scripture is correct is equated with failure to trust God.

Where notions of inerrancy are concerned it is crucial to identify what exactly is being deemed inerrant. Is it the text or is it the interpretation of the text? The emphasis of the fundamentalist tends to be upon the inerrancy of the text. But establishing an infallible Bible is of little use if it is not 'correctly' understood.

Fundamentalism draws upon the doctrine of the Holy Spirit in this context, claiming that the Spirit will act as the divine means through which a right understanding of the text can be created within the mind of the reader. However, this hardly provides an answer to the problem. How does the Holy Spirit operate in the mind of the believer, and why does it permit the very different interpretations of the Bible that arise within fundamentalist circles themselves? It is significant – and at least partly an explanation of their many divisions – that problems of hermeneutics* are all but ignored by fundamentalists. Their emphasis is upon establishing the absolute truth of the Bible which they then assume to be self-evident to any reader approaching the text two thousand years later. Partly because of their tendency to select certain passages which are believed to be 'straightforward historical narrative', fundamentalists give the impression that the only problem is to 'accept' the Bible rather than to understand and apply it in one's own time.

The hermeneutical vacuum in which a fundamentalist approach to the Bible leaves us is another aspect of the culture in which it tends to thrive, that of naive empiricism. Fundamentalist interpretation thinks of the reader in a passive way, 'receiving' truths from scripture and having no active role of his or her own in understanding and processing those truths. The presumption is that 'facts'* can simply be amassed without any prior involvement of the interpreter. It has to be said that such an approach is not absent in the academic world of biblical exegesis generally. Naive empiricism is as much the hallmark of the liberal as of the fundamentalist, a further example of the way in which these two mutually antagonistic schools of thought tend to reflect each other. Both have a naive confidence in the power of the Bible to speak for itself to the modern reader. Neither considers the *Sitz im Leben* of the reader to have any significance for the process of understanding.

Both talk in terms of 'the meaning' or 'the truth' of a passage as if these were capable of being fixed for all time. They may disagree over what 'the truth' is, but they share an equal confidence in the possibility of snatching it from each other's hands. Neither seems to have considered the profound implications of contemporary hermeneutics, or even of Kantian epistemology. Neither seems to recognize with Gadamer that there are two horizons to be considered in the work of interpretation, that of the reader as well as that of the writer.

For this reason, many of the points made by fundamentalist criticism can be by-passed without needing to be refuted. For suppose it is conceded that every word of the Bible is infallible. There is no reason why this should give us any confidence in our reading of it. Unless we can be sure that we can gain an infallible understanding of this infallible text, its inerrancy fails to offer us the confidence we need. It is our supposed inerrancy, rather than that of the text, which causes the difficulties. This intrusion of ourselves as readers of scripture into the work of understanding is the real problem for fundamentalism, one which overshadows the well-worn arguments about the authority of the text.

One of the most interesting developments in fundamentalism over the last few years has been the nature of its involvement in political controversy. It is common to associate fundamentalists with right-wing politics, and to give as an example of this the so-called 'Moral Majority' in the United States. Care has to be taken here, since nearly two-fifths of the members of this grouping are Catholics, and the image of the movement is too often identified with that of one of its aggressive leaders, the evangelist Jerry Falwell. More significantly, the last few years have seen the emergence of a number of left-wing fundamentalists, of whom the most notable is probably Jim Wallis, associated with the Sojourners who live and work in poor areas of Washington DC. The phenomenon of radical fundamentalism challenges the image of the fundamentalist as a political reactionary, despite the close association of well-known evangelists like Falwell and, in previous years, Billy Graham with Republican Presidents like Nixon and Reagan. In Great Britain, too, the stereotype of 'conservative evangelicals' as apolitical or even outright advocates of right-wing politics has been challenged by those who have argued that radical traditions such as those associated in the last century with William Wilberforce and the evangelical revival are the true ancestors of contemporary evangelicalism.

The obvious divisions on political and social issues within fundamentalist ranks reflect an interesting aspect of selectivity in biblical interpretation. The 'radical' fundamentalist emphasizes passages like Acts 2.44–5 in order to commend a society in which an equality of wealth between individuals exists. Others point to Jesus' teachings on non-violence in the Sermon on the Mount* or his refusal to resist arrest in the Garden of Gethsemane in order to argue that Christians must be pacifists. Such approaches arguably mirror those of politically conservative evangelicals who argue on the basis of passages like Rom. 13.1 ('Every person must submit to the supreme authorities') that Christians must not challenge the political *status quo* in their countries.

Very different conclusions are reached by the two groups concerning the Christian's attitude towards the state. Such conflicts of interpretation exist between parties who share a common conviction that scripture is infallible and the supreme authority for Christian belief. Their differences illustrate once again that an authoritative text without an authoritative method of interpretation (as provided by the tradition of the church and its *magisterium* in Roman Catholicism, for instance) produces a variety of understandings. Confidence in the Holy Spirit as the divine guide to knowledge of scripture is hardly borne out by the many different directions in which that guide has patently led the faithful!

It can be argued that this is a problem faced by Protestantism as a whole since the Reformation. However, traditional Protestant churches have always attempted to set out the main principles of scripture in the form of creeds,* and these have in turn operated as practical guides to interpretation of the text. The Augsburg Confession in Lutheranism, the Westminster Confession in the Church of Scotland, even the Thirty-nine Articles within Anglicanism – all have served not only as a summary of Christian belief but also (in the tradition of the early church) as a 'rule of faith', a guide to the main teachings of the church as derived from scripture. Fundamentalism lacks this feature, although it has of course a 'hidden tradition' of interpretation based upon the views of its own leaders. This, however, has been challenged by the 'radical' fundamentalism of the last few years. Consequently, the problem of understanding the meaning of the text in the modern world is bound to be faced by fundamentalists if the movement is not to fragment.

A further development makes this imperative. Within or on the borders of the fundamentalist movements are the so-called 'millenarian'* believers, who see in certain biblical texts clear prophecies of the circumstances in which Christ will return to earth and the present world-order be brought to an end. Millenarianism illustrates that biblical literalism can be applied as much to putative future events like the end of the world as to supposed past events like the ejection of Adam and Eve from the Garden of Eden or the Flood.

In recent years, millenarianism has revived in the United States, and a scenario of the imminent parousia has been built up around political developments such as the creation of the state of Israel, the Common Market, the rise to world power of the Soviet Union and China, and the development of nuclear weapons. Writers like the retired riverboat captain Hal Lindsey have popularized the idea that God will employ nuclear weapons as an instrument of the divine will to bring the present order to a close. Such ideas have been much less influential in Britain, but they still pose a problem for 'mainstream' fundamentalism. The millenarian movements, like the radical fundamentalists, are committed to the absolute authority and inerrancy of the biblical text. But their interpretation of it is at variance with that which most fundamentalists or evangelicals would regard as sound. The vacuum created by failure to consider problems of exegesis has spawned an anarchy of interpretation within fundamentalism. It is difficult to see how this fissiparous tendency in the movement can be overcome without the development of a fundamentalist hermeneutics, but this in turn must challenge the ideological resistance to problems of hermeneutics within fundamentalism itself.

Fundamentalism has been challenged in a number of ways. It has been condemned as politically reactionary. It has been considered a product of psychological infantilism offering an impossible certainty of conviction to the believer (a condition for which in the United States there is now an organization, 'Fundamentalists Anonymous', to help those who have become 'dependent' upon its simple solutions and rigid, hierarchical structure). Such criticisms often fail to do justice to the variety of opinion within the broad spectrum of fundamentalist thinking. However, it is difficult to avoid the conclusion that this very breadth reflects a weakness that is common to all its forms. That is the failure to recognize what the early Protestant Reformers recognized about the Bible, that it was (to use a favourite phrase of Luther's) a wax nose, capable of being moulded in a number of ways by people who were in no disagreement as to its absolute authority. Fundamentalism may not be the heir to the Protestant Reformation as such, but it is certainly the *reductio ad absurdum* of one of its basic claims: *Scriptura sui ipsius interpres* – scripture interprets itself.

See also **Hermeneutics; Inspiration; Verbal Inspiration.**

J. Barr, *Fundamentalism*, 1977; id, *Escaping from Fundamentalism*, 1985; G. M. Marsden, *Fundamentalism and American Culture*, 1980; R. J. Neuhaus and M. Cromartie, (eds), *Piety and Politics*, 1987; J. I. Packer, *'Fundamentalism' and the Word of God*, 1981; J. Wallis, *The Call to Conversion*, 1981.

MARK CORNER

Galatians

The chief phases of interpretation have been: the second century; the patristic era; the Reformation;* and the age of historical criticism.* The question of the relationship between the Jerusalem apostles and Paul's Judaizing* opponents has been central to controversy over the epistle. The most innovative and influential interpreters have been Marcion,* Luther* and F. C. Baur.

Second century. Marcion (*fl.* 130?), the first theologian to make systematic use of Paul's epistles, apparently appealed above all to Galatians to support his teaching that the gospel was completely opposed to the OT and that Paul had been commissioned by Christ as sole guarantor of the true gospel in place of the Twelve, who had corrupted Jesus' revelation through their partial relapse into Judaism. Galatians could supply abundant grist to Marcion's mill, for it records some of Paul's sharpest strictures on the law, his claim to a direct commission from Christ, his defence of one, unalterable gospel against 'false brethren' who conspired to denature it, and his clash with Peter at Antioch. To sustain his interpretation of the epistle, however, Marcion was compelled to excise from it any indication of continuity between the gospel and the OT or of concord between Paul and the apostles (apparently 1.18–24; 2.6–9a; 3.6–9, 15–25; 3.27–4.2; 4.21–26 [retained but revised], 27–30). Marcion's appeal to the authority of the epistles concentrated the minds of orthodox churchmen, forcing them to come to terms with Paul's theology.

Of the use made of the epistles in second-century gnostic* circles the briefest mention must suffice. Contrary to recent claims that the Gnostics were the first people to make constructive use of Paul's epistles, the evidence such as it is suggests that they used them in a highly selective and predatory manner, exploiting single verses (and often single words) to support preconceived ideas. Colossians and Ephesians naturally provided the richest pickings. Galatians apparently supplied such gems as 3.19f. (applied to creation rather than to the giving of the law); 4.22ff., 26; and 6.14, which they found specially congenial.

More intriguing is the use made of Gala-

tians in the anti-Paul invective of the *Kerygmata Petrou*, a writing of uncertain date and provenance (*c.* AD 200, Syria?), used as a source by the pseudo-Clementines. In it Peter is made to conduct a vicious attack upon Paul (under the guise of Simon the magician), 'the man who is my enemy', denying his apostleship and castigating him for opposing him and teaching the abolition of the law. Of particular interest are his recriminations over Paul's effrontery at Antioch and the debate between them on whether a visionary experience can match instruction by the historical Jesus as a qualification for apostleship (*Homilies* XVII, 13–19). That the author has Galatians in mind is clear from verbal allusions to its text. Very significant is the manner in which the writing combines anti-Paul polemic with a gnostic doctrine of pairs or syzygies in which the Peter/Paul antithesis is ranged alongside such dualities as heaven/earth, day/night, male/female prophecy (*Homilies* II, 15–17). The *Kerygmata Petrou* reveals the form which opposition to Paul took in a particular second-century Jewish-Christian* milieu of pronounced gnostic tendencies. It is a matter of debate whether its anti-Paul polemic has any historical links with opposition to Paul in his own lifetime; we cannot exclude the possibility that it conveys echoes of the opposite camp's reaction to the conflict reported in Galatians. The author is no fairer than Marcion had been to Paul's account of his dealings with the apostles: in both cases Gal. 1.18 and 2.6–9 are ignored. Both interpretations, however, have the merit of calling attention to the jagged edges of Galatians which appear to have been too easily smoothed down in the mainstream tradition and which were to be completely removed by patristic exegetes.

Patristic era. Of the extant commentaries the most notable are those of Chrysostom and Theodore in the East and Ambrosiaster, Pelagius, Jerome and Augustine* in the West. Origen* greatly influenced the tradition; of his commentary little remains, but Jerome says that he followed it. Two theological tendencies exhibited by these commentaries are illustrated here. They show to what extent opposition to Marcion influenced patristic exegesis and at the same time exemplify the exegetical orthodoxy against which Luther was to react in his interpretation of the epistle.

1. The commentators seized every opportunity of showing that the gospel stood in continuity with OT revelation, and this not in spite of the law (as in Galatians) but very largely because of it. The gospel is a new law and the old law was a gospel: they differ only in degree. Thus, for example: almost all the commentators thought that the 'mediator' of the law in Gal. 3.19f. was Christ. Origen and

Jerome judged that the 'weak and beggarly elements' (Gal. 4.9) also had their 'splendour', which was dimmed only by comparison with the brighter light of Christ. Vital to this interpretation is the separation of the law's 'ceremonial' and moral requirements: only the former (dismissed by the commentators as 'Jewish superstition') were disapproved of by Paul. The commentators were less concerned to analyse Paul's critique than to deflect it from that part of the Law which they needed to protect as the bond of continuity between the old and the new.

2. Marcion had driven a wedge between Paul and the Twelve. The commentators did their utmost to unite them. What was at stake was the church's awareness of itself as heir to a unified apostolic doctrine. Ambrosiaster's description of Paul as Peter's *unianimus co-apostolus* speaks volumes. Marcion had held that the apostles had favoured the counter-mission to Paul 'to the point of corrupting the gospel'. Chrysostom insisted that the apostles had only 'permitted' law observance, and Jerome that they had only 'pretended' to take it seriously out of regard for the weaker brethren. The Antioch incident (Gal. 2.11ff.), a windfall to all manner of foes, greatly exercised all ecclesiastical writers. Cephas was not Peter at all, but a namesake (Clement of Alexandria); or Peter and Paul had orchestrated the scene for the purpose of edifying in turn Jewish and Gentile Christians (Origen). This theory dominated exegesis for more than a century. It was championed by both Chrysostom and Jerome. The dispute between Jerome and Augustine on this issue is famous in the annals of history. For Augustine the Holy Spirit would have had nothing to do with such a ruse: Peter was truly 'reprehensible', but his humility redeemed him. Aquinas later explained that Peter's sin was only venial.

Reformation. Luther's work on Galatians (1515–1538) spans his youth and maturity. He was understandably enamoured of its 'doctrine of righteousness'. But the novelty of the epistle's contribution to his theology lay not in its 'doctrine of righteousness' (which added nothing substantial to what he had learnt from Romans), but in the implications of this doctrine for the relationship between gospel and church as reflected in Gal. 1–2.

For Luther these chapters (and especially 1.1, 8; 2.11ff.) were the cutting edge of the epistle. They played a central role in the crucial years of his theological development leading up to his break with Rome. Already in his Romans commentary he had rejected the traditional apologetic interpretation of Gal. 2.11ff.: Peter's sin 'was certainly a *mortal* sin, for it was against the gospel and the salvation of the soul' (on Rom. 6.10). Still in his Catholic period (1516–17), he concluded ominously from Gal. 2.6 that 'a person's external quality is of no relevance for the preaching of the gospel'. Thereafter his interpretation of Gal. 1–2 became programmatic in his revolt against papal authority: exegesis and living conflict coalesced. Any Christian with greater insight is above the pope as Paul was above Peter at Antioch (1518). When the pope errs it is the Christian's duty to oppose him openly (1518). At Antioch Peter gave scandal in the matter of 'faith and eternal damnation' (1519). Peter was guilty of heresy (1519). Here was the point of no return for Luther. Fourteen years after the break with Rome Luther was as trenchant as ever: Peter's conduct was nothing less than 'a denial of Christ, contempt of his blood, a scoffing of the holy Spirit. Better that Peter go to hell than that we deny Christ.'

Historical criticism. While Galatians continued to be cherished in Protestant tradition, Luther's reading of chs 1–2 was soon put aside in favour of the doctrine of the authority of scripture (Peter too was a canonical author!). There was a revival of the apologetic interpretation of these chapters, which was helped as it always had been by Acts' portrait of apostolic harmony. It was F. C. Baur, like a latter-day Marcion, who disturbed these untroubled waters. In pursuit of a thoroughgoing historical explanation of the church's origins, Baur inferred (1831) from the Corinthian and Galatian epistles (especially I Cor. 1.11f. and Gal. 2.11ff.) that earliest Christianity was split between Petrine (Jewish) and Pauline (Gentile) factions. (He at first exonerated Peter from direct involvement in the conflict, but later changed his mind.) From the resolution of the conflict by a process of give and take there emerged the Catholic church. A crucial confirmation of this reconstruction was supplied by the pseudo-Clementines, which Baur thought reflected a second-century survival of Petrine Christianity.

Having pivoted his reconstruction on Galatians Baur proceeded to evaluate other NT writings according to their thematic proximity to this epistle. By 1845 he had concluded that besides Galatians only I and II Corinthians and Romans were authentic. All other NT writings reflected the post-apostolic tendency to neutralize the earlier conflict and were therefore inauthentic. Acts in particular, with its merging of Paul into Peter and vice-versa, was entirely unreliable.

Opposition to Baur's reconstruction began in his own day and continued to influence Galatians studies well into our century (e.g. Munck, 1954!). The chief objection to it was that it failed to recognize the complexity of both Jewish and Gentile Christianity in the first centuries. This criticism went hand in hand with a rehabilitation of Acts and a more nuanced appraisal of the kind of Jewish Christianity reflected in the pseudo-Clementines. The debate was virtually confined to Germany; in England J. B. Lightfoot took up the traditionalist cause in his classic commentary on Galatians (1865).

In spite of the general rejection of Baur's findings, his critical aims and especially his conviction that exegesis depends absolutely on historical reconstruction have powerfully affected all modern exegesis, sometimes subserving but now more often challenging traditional 'dogmatic' treatments. The question of the location of the Galatian churches ('north Galatia', the original Galatian territory in central Anatolia, or 'south Galatia', the later Roman province of Galatia which extended much further south) is not now as earnestly debated as it was in the nineteenth century (many scholars consider it unresolvable), though it is not without its importance for chronological and historical reconstruction, particularly in regard to the data of Acts and those of Gal. 1–2.

The question of the identity of the agitators in Galatia continues to be of fundamental concern to interpreters. The traditional view that they were Jewish Christian hard-liners from Jerusalem remains the majority one. Its supporters, like Baur's early critics, have generally been anxious to distinguish their position from the more moderate one espoused by the apostles (though James' approval of a law-free Gentile mission has frequently been questioned). The traditional view has not gone unchallenged. It does not take into account the whole of Galatians, notably the 'ethical' section, which is thought to be aimed at libertines. This observation has prompted various new suggestions: Paul was combatting two groups, the one Judaizing and the other libertine (Lütgert, 1919; Ropes, 1929), or one group of Jewish syncretists (Crownfield, 1945), or a group of Gentile Judaizers (Munck, 1954). Schmithals (1956, 1965) has proposed Jewish or Jewish-Christian Gnostics, while Wegenast (1961), Georgi (1965) and Koester (1971) have been content to return to a position closer to Crownfield's. A consensus seems impossible since everything depends on deciphering countless tantalizing clues in the text, to say nothing of the basic question, which is how far 'mirror-reading' of Paul's epistles can safely be taken.

Some idea of the diversity of overall treatments of the epistle can be got from the following range of studies: Schlier's influential commentary (1949, [13]1965), the writing of which curiously prompted its author to transfer his allegiance from Luther to the pope; Lönning's plea (1970) for a return to the full-blooded

Lutheran use of chs 1–2; Mussner's commentary (1974) with its fine feel for Catholic-Lutheran and Christian-Jewish dialogue; Betz's commentary (1979), which combines a traditional Lutheran interpretation with a sustained reading of the epistle in the light of ancient rhetoric* and letter-writing; the attempts of Drane (1975) and Hübner (1978) to explain 'tensions' between Galatians and other epistles of Paul by theories of development or revision in Paul's thought; O'Neill's attempt (1972) to make sense of Galatians by expunging from the text whatever he considered should not be there; and the work of E. P. Sanders (1977, 1983) and H. Räisänen (1983), who have reacted vigorously against the Lutheran view which sees Paul's antagonism to the law as a matter of profound theological principle and have sought rather to relate it more pragmatically to what was undoubtedly his real concern – the Gentile mission to which he felt himself called.

See also **Acts of the Apostles; Jewish Christianity; Paul.**

R. J. Hoffmann, *Marcion, On the Restitution of Christianity*, 1984; George Howard, *Paul: Crisis in Galatia*, 1979; W. G. Kümmel, *The New Testament: The History of the Investigation of its Problems*, 1973; J. B. Lightfoot, *St Paul's Epistle to the Galatians*, reissued 1969; G. Strecker, 'The Kerygmata Petrou' in E. Hennecke (ed.), *The New Testament Apocrypha*, Vol. 2, 1965, pp.102–127; M. F. Wiles, *The Divine Apostle*, 1967.

                                                    T. J. DEIDUN

Genealogies

Biblical genealogies have seldom been regarded as interesting reading, but the fact that the Bible contains several quite extensive sections of genealogical material shows that genealogical claims were considered significant by the original biblical writers. Major blocks of genealogical matter are to be found in Gen. 4, 5, 10, 11, 25, 36, 46; I Chron. 1–9; Ezra 2; Neh. 7. 11; Matt. 1 and Luke 3. Some of the genealogical material in Genesis also contains chronological information which forms part of a systematic chronology* of world history.

Early biblical interpreters showed considerable interest in this chronological material, and also attempted to provide solutions to various inconsistencies in the genealogical record. The fourth-century rabbi Mar Zutra is quoted in the Babylonian Talmud* as saying, 'Between Azel and Azel (I Chron. 8.38–9.44) they were loaded with four hundred camels of exegetical interpretations' (b. Pesah 62b). Christian exegetes were more interested in harmonizing the genealogies of Christ than in the genealogical difficulties of Chronicles. The Gospels of Matthew and Luke both trace Jesus' descent from Abraham* (Luke's genealogy also goes back to Adam*), but the two genealogies diverge widely from the time of David,* with only four names in common for this period: David, Shealtiel, Zerubbabel, and Joseph.

Attempts to harmonize this discrepancy are now of purely historical interest. Tatian (c. 160) resolved the problem by omitting the genealogies from his gospel harmony (the Diatessaron). Later, Africanus (c. 164–240) suggested that the problem could be overcome by assuming a levirate marriage (Deut. 25.5–6), whereby Joseph's legal father (Jacob or Heli) was distinct from his actual father (Heli or Jacob). Africanus' theory required the further supposition that Jacob and Heli were half-brothers, since it was necessary that they should have different fathers. And one must also logically assume a second levirate marriage involving half-brothers to account for the presence of Shealtiel and Zerubbabel in both lists, or else suppose that there were two individuals with the unusual name of Zerubbabel, both descended from David, and both having fathers called Shealtiel – another rare name – in the same period of Judaean history. Despite these improbabilities Africanus' theory was widely accepted for many centuries.

An alternative solution, which goes back to patristic times, but gained widespread acceptance at the time of the Reformation, was to suppose that Luke's genealogy traced Jesus' descent through Mary and not Joseph. This required a forced interpretation of Luke 3.23, and also failed to explain the presence of Shealtiel and Zerubbabel in both genealogies.

Harmonistic* approaches to the problems of biblical genealogies were largely swept away with the advent of modern critical scholarship in the nineteenth century, and Wellhausen was scornful of any attempt to derive historical evidence from the genealogies of Genesis and Chronicles. It was also noted, by Stade and others, that some of the OT genealogies appear to draw relations between ethnic groups rather than individual persons, and that the device of naming eponymous ancestors is sometimes dropped with the inclusion of simple gentilics or plural nouns. Scholars also noted a distinction between linear genealogies (tracing a single line of descent from an ancestor to a descendant) and branching or segmented genealogies (tracing several lines of descent).

Within the last century, two main approaches to the question of biblical genealogies have emerged. These may be categorized loosely as 'literary' and 'comparative', and are complementary rather than exclusive: the literary approach considers biblical genealogies within their literary (and pre-literary) context, whereas the comparative approach studies biblical genealogies in the light of classical or Ancient Near Eastern evidence or in comparison with modern anthropological data.

The literary approach to biblical genealogies may be seen in a wide-ranging study by M. D. Johnson, which presents a detailed discussion of biblical genealogies in general, and of the gospel genealogies in particular. Johnson argues that the OT genealogies have a variety of functions and purposes, and are effectively a genre of historical writing, but that later Judaism narrowed these functions to two main concerns: national purity of descent and messianic speculation. The second of these concerns provides a context for studying the meaning and purpose of the gospel genealogies. M. D. Goulder (Midrash and Lection in Matthew, 1974) has drawn attention to the number symbolism* in Matt. 1.1–17 (6 × 7 generations signify 'days' and point to Jesus' coming as a 'sabbath' of fulfilment) and to the role of the four women in the list.

Two other scholars who have contributed to the literary study of biblical genealogies are G. von Rad and M. Noth. The former inferred the existence of a 'Toledot' book from Gen. 5.1 ('Toledot' is Hebrew for 'generations'), and argued that this document provided the Priestly writer of the Pentateuch* with most of his genealogical material. However, other scholars have argued that the Toledot book was a more restricted document underlying Gen. 5 and 11, or that 'the Book of Generations' is simply a title to Gen. 5. Noth's contribution was to argue that genealogical lists were sometimes forged for the purpose of connecting blocks of tradition which he regarded as originally unrelated, such as the Abraham and Jacob traditions. A recent contribution by S. Tengström notes that the Priestly stratum of the Pentateuch presents linear genealogies in narrative form ('X begat Y') but uses list form (sons of X: Y, Z . . .') for segmented genealogies (the distinction between narrative and non-narrative genealogies was also noted by earlier scholars).

The comparative approach to biblical genealogies finds a recent exponent in R. R. Wilson. Anthropological* evidence was extensively used by biblical scholars of the nineteenth century, but this evidence came to be discredited among anthropologists because it was collected by untrained and unreliable observers, and was treated in isolation from its original social context. However, Wilson has recognized that these deficiencies can be remedied by using evidence from twentieth-century anthropologists and comparing this with evidence from Ancient Near Eastern texts. The main conclusion which emerges from this study is that Ancient Near Eastern genealogies and modern oral genealogies are not normally intended as historical records, but are created and transmitted for social, political, or religious purposes. In consequence, genealogies are frequently altered to conform with changing social or political or religious circumstances, and incompatible genealogies are sometimes transmitted and accepted as 'correct' in different cultural contexts. This is clearly relevant to the study of biblical genealogies. For example, Aram is listed as a son of Shem – a distant ancestor of Abraham – in Gen. 10.22, but is portrayed as the grandson of Nahor – brother of Abraham – in Gen. 22.20ff. In the light of Wilson's study, the most probable explanation of this discrepancy is that the author of Gen. 10.22 envisaged a more distant degree of ethnic relatedness between Israelites and Aramaeans than the author of Gen. 22.20ff., and this in turn could be dependent on changing political relations between Israel/Judah and the Aramean states. Biblical scholars normally ascribed Gen. 10.22 to a 'Priestly' writer who lived at a later date than the 'Yahwistic' author of Gen. 22.20ff.

See also **Chronicles; Chronology.**

M. D. Johnson, *The Purpose of the Biblical Genealogies*, 1988; D. E. Nineham, 'The Genealogy in St Matthew's Gospel' in *Explorations in Theology 1*, 1977, pp. 166–87; R. R. Wilson, *Genealogy and History in the Biblical World*, 1977; id., 'Between "Azel" and "Azel": interpreting the Biblical genealogies', *Biblical Archaeologist* 42, 1979, pp. 11–22.

JEREMY HUGHES

Genesis

The English title of the book comes from the Latin transliteration of the word by which it was known to the Greek-speaking Jews of Alexandria. Their title was taken from the Septuagint* translation of Gen. 2.4a which may be rendered 'This is the book of the origin (*geneseōs* – a genitive form whose nominative is *genesis*) of heaven and earth . . .' The most widely used Hebrew title is in fact the first word of the book, *bᵉrēʾšît*, traditionally translated 'In the beginning', a rendering which has been challenged but which has recently been defended by Westermann. Within the Jewish tradition, other titles have been used, such as 'The Book of the Creation of the World', 'The Book of the Upright' (thinking particularly of the patriarchal narratives), or 'The First Book'. The KJV/AV gives as the full title 'The First Book of Moses called Genesis', and the RV has 'The First Book of Moses commonly called Genesis', both reflecting the tradition of Mosaic* authorship.*

That the stories preserved in the book of Genesis were a fruitful source for those of later generations who wished to pass on teaching to their readers is shown from the variety of relatively early adaptations of and interpretations of the Genesis material (*see* **Rewritten Bible**). The Book of Jubilees purports to be a secret revelation passed on by angels to Moses on Mount Sinai, but is in fact based on Genesis and the beginning of Exodus, and was written (originally in Hebrew, then translated into Greek, and thence into Ethiopic) in the second century BC, probably during or just after the Seleucid persecution. Although sometimes the biblical book is quoted directly, it is more often embellished and elaborated with additional material, in particular legal, reflecting the book's halakhic interest. Jubilees is also noteworthy for its advocacy of the solar calendar,* by which it dates biblical events, and which is presented as fundamental to the ordering of the universe. Abraham* is presented as the epitome of wisdom, faith and endurance.

A work which has become known as the Genesis Apocryphon was among the first group of scrolls discovered at Qumran (*see* **Dead Sea Scrolls**). The scroll is badly preserved and only five of the twenty-two extant columns can be reconstructed with reasonable certainty. It represents an expanded paraphrase in Aramaic of the Genesis story from Lamech to Abraham with a number of additions to make particular points. For example, in columns nineteen and twenty, the story of Abraham and Sarah in Egypt is expanded to stress how God protected Sarah and demonstrated his power over Pharaoh and his household with 'scourges and afflictions'. The work does not appear to have the halakhic interest of Jubilees (on which it may depend, though it is possible that an earlier version precedes Jubilees), or the Testaments of the Twelve Patriarchs.

This latter work comprises twelve distinct units, each of which depicts one of the sons of Jacob making his testament to his own sons prior to his death. The patriarchs recount episodes from their own lives which illustrate various virtues or vices, and their sons are encouraged either to follow the good or avoid the bad example of their fathers. In the form in which it survives the work is from Christian circles, though its origins are probably Jewish.

An interpretation of part of the Joseph story is provided by a work written in Greek, perhaps addressed to Gentile readers in Egypt at about the turn of the era, entitled *Joseph and Aseneth*. It deals with the problem that despite the clear evidence in Genesis that the patriarchs were expected to take wives from among their own kindred, Joseph is recorded as having married the daughter of an Egyptian priest. The difficulty is addressed in part by stressing the conversion of Aseneth (the priest's daughter) from pagan worship and presenting her as a proselyte, and in part by recounting a tradition that she was the daughter of Shechem and Dinah and not in fact a foreigner. The main purpose of the writer is to urge that eternal life is only to be achieved through the worship of the God of Israel.

As examples of the ongoing interpretation of the Book of Genesis in Jewish circles, attention can be drawn to such works as the Targum* Onkelos, dating from the second century AD, largely a literal rendering of the original, though some sections are paraphrased and there is a strong tendency to avoid anthropomorphism;* Genesis Rabbah is a haggadic midrash* on Genesis which originated in Palestine perhaps in the fourth century, and provides a chapter by chapter, verse by verse exposition, usually involving the linking of a verse from elsewhere in scripture with that being expounded. Based to a large extent on Genesis Rabbah is the later Genesis Rabbati, usually ascribed to Moses ha-Darshan of Narbonne in the eleventh century, one of whose features is its quotations from the Testaments of the Twelve Patriarchs and other apocryphal and pseudepigraphical* writings. It was at about this time that other important mediaeval Jewish commentaries* were being produced, such as those of Rashi (eleventh century) and Ibn Ezra (twelfth century) (see **Jewish Exegesis**).

It is clear that the NT writers knew and used the traditions of Genesis. The story of Cain and Abel is alluded to on a number of occasions and it appears that Cain had come to be regarded almost as the archetypal villain, and Abel the epitome of righteousness (cf. Matt. 23.35; Luke 11.51; Heb. 11.4; 12.24; I John 3.12; Jude 11). Paul* needs to interpret the traditions of the promises to the forefathers of Israel in such a way as to show that the heirs to the promises are not 'the children of the flesh' but 'the children of the promise' (Rom. 9.6–13). The writer of the Fourth Gospel, in his prologue, re-interprets the account of creation* by 'word' at the beginning of Genesis in the light of his understanding of Jesus as the Word made flesh (John 1.1–18).

Noteworthy among the early Christian commentators on Genesis for the style of his interpretation was Origen,* who wrote his Homilies on Genesis in the third century. By way of illustration of his approach, it may be noted that in his discussion of the creation of the great lights in his first Homily, he likens the relationship of the sun, moon, and sky to that of Christ, the church, and humanity; just as the moon receives its light from the sun so that it can enlighten the night, so the church receives its light from Christ, the light of the world, and in turn enlightens those who are in the 'night of ignorance'. The 'stars' are such great figures of the past as the patriarchs, Moses, David,* and the major prophets.* In his second Homily, on Noah's Ark, Origen sets out to establish a literal* (secundum litteram) explanation as a foundation from which to climb to a spiritual* explanation which is mystical* and allegorical* (adscendere ad spiritualis intelligentiae mysticum et allegoricum sensum). Thus the idea that the occupants of the Ark lived in different rooms is linked to the thought of Isa. 26.20, and then a comparison is drawn between those saved in the Ark and the people saved in the church. The small number of those in the Ark in close relationship with Noah is compared to those close to Jesus, capable of sharing his word and receiving his wisdom. Below them in the Ark are the animals and beasts which have no reason, the most savage being at the very bottom. These are likened to those who are simple and innocent, and those whose violence and savagery has not been softened by faith. After climbing through the various stages, one reaches Noah himself, whose name is said to mean 'rest' or 'just', and who is in fact Jesus, because it was not the ancient Noah who fitted the words of Lamech, his father (Gen. 5.29), but Jesus, who gave rest to the people and delivered the earth from the curse.

It is no surprise that the allegorical type of interpretation should have been criticized by later commentators. Luther* was particularly critical of Augustine's* allegorical approach to the six days of creation, and commented in his preface to the first chapter of Genesis that 'What he (i.e. Moses) wants to teach us is nothing about allegorical creatures, or an allegorical world, but something about real creatures and about a visible world, which we can see, feel and handle.' Calvin* defended the historicity of Genesis in the Argument at the beginning of his commentary, noting that Moses does not '. . . put forward divinations of his own, but is the instrument of the Holy Spirit for the publication of those things which it was of importance for all men to know', and stressing that Moses' task was to commit to writing for the first time facts which had been handed down from generation to generation. The material is thought to be directly relevant to the story of Christianity and the life of the individual Christian, for in the Dedication of his commentary he speaks of Genesis demonstrating how 'God, after the destructive fall of man, adopted to himself a church', and indicates how much it would benefit its readers 'if they would learn prudently to apply to their own use the example of the ancient church, as it is described by Moses'. Luther is a little more cautious, warning that it might be misleading to regard the patriarchs as an example in all they did and therefore to imitate all their acts; there is, for example, no need to copy Noah in the building of altars!

These indications of the thought of the Reformation* period underline an attitude to Genesis which prevailed until the nineteenth century. The book had been written by Moses, was basically factual and historical, could be read for religious and ethical guidance by Christians as well as Jews and, for Christians especially, the story of the Fall was of particular significance. But then such views were assailed on two fronts; the factual basis of the earlier chapters in particular was challenged by modern scientific thinking about the origins of the universe and the evolution of the animal kingdom; and the critical approach to the literature of the Bible gave rise to serious questions about the historicity of Genesis.

The early stages of awareness of some of these questions gave rise to theories which in retrospect seem bizarre but were nevertheless the first stirrings of independent historical criticism.* Notable among them is the work of Isaac La Peyrère which enjoyed widespread fame (and notoriety) in the second half of the seventeenth century. Of French Protestant origin, La Peyrère solved the problem raised by the two creation stories in Genesis by holding that they told of two distinct creations, the first of mankind as a whole, the second that of the Jews. There was thus a race of 'pre-Adamites' whose existence solved a whole bevy of puzzles: the provenance of Cain's wife, the origin of the inhabitants of distant and separate parts of the globe like America and Greenland, and the over-long world history believed in by the Chinese and other peoples whose 'knowledge' was not formed and confined by the Bible.

The modern interpretation of Genesis cannot be considered in isolation from the wider issues of pentateuchal criticism and of the types of literature of which the Pentateuch* is composed, although only the briefest of mentions can be given to these topics here. Various hypotheses have been put forward to account for the literary growth of the Pentateuch. The 'fragmentary hypothesis' argued that the Pentateuch was compiled by an editor from a number of fragments which had previously been unconnected. An alternative approach, sometimes known as the 'supplementary hypothesis', envisaged a single basic document supplemented by various fragments. The view which has come to predominate in pentateuchal criticism is the 'documentary hypothesis' which suggested that it was produced as a result of the gradual compilation of a number of independent documents, and did not reach its final form until well after the Exile. In its classical form, the documentary hypothesis envisaged four documents, of which only three are relevant to Genesis, viz. the J or Yahwistic source (which uses the divine name Yahweh), the E or Elohistic source (which refers to God as *elōhîm), and the P or Priestly source (from its interest in the priesthood and matters of ritual). (The fourth source, D or Deuteronomic, corresponds largely to the Book of Deuteronomy.) Many modifications have been suggested to the basic hypothesis, including additional sources or different layers within the main sources, and, perhaps most notably, a tendency to think less of written documents but rather of circles of tradition. Recent studies of the Pentateuch in the light of ancient historiography have raised questions about the relative antiquity of the various sources, and the possibility that a single author in the sixth century BC may have written the Pentateuch using material available to him at the time and some of his own invention.

Brief mention must also be made of discussions of the different types of literary material in the Pentateuch, and in Genesis in particular. In part this interest arose from the application of the form-critical* approach, with its attempt to analyse the various units of tradition and establish their original context and function, and thus to discover something of the pre-history of the strands of narrative. Recently there has been an increasing interest in seeking to identify the principal narrative* genres* employed in the Hebrew Bible. Coats has listed the main genres as: saga,* tale, novella, legend,* history, report, fable, aetiology,* myth.* He notes that the first major unit of narrative in the OT corresponds to the book of Genesis, which he describes, with regard to the genre of the narrative, as a 'cycle of sagas' (a primaeval saga and two family sagas). He argues that the primaeval saga does not serve merely as an introduction to the Pentateuch, but is a key element within the patriarchal theme with which Genesis is concerned.

The views of Coats just noted provide a link between the wider pentateuchal issues and the interpretation of Genesis specifically. The term 'saga' has come to be widely used in referring to the narrative material, although this designation has been challenged, and the smaller units of tradition have been assigned to a variety of types, e.g. cosmological myths, anthropological* myths, cult* legends, aetiological legends. The material in chs 1–11 has often been seen to be different in character from that in chs 12–50, and the book has therefore often been regarded as virtually two distinct units, the Primaeval History and the Patriarchal History. Certainly different approaches to the interpretation of these sections can be discerned.

With regard to the interpretation of chs 1–11, the material was basically accepted as factual and historical until about the mid-nineteenth century, with the Christian tradition placing particular emphasis on chs 1–3, in which the account of Creation was followed by that of the Fall from which ultimately Christ came to bring salvation. When natural science and literary criticism * challenged traditional beliefs, it came increasingly to be realized that questions such as that of the historicity of the material were not really relevant, and interest switched to such issues as the original function of the various units of tradition, whether it was possible to reconstruct a theology of each of the sources, and, above all, the religious significance of the material. The understanding of God's dealings with Israel as 'salvation history' * could see creation as the first of God's saving acts on behalf of his people.

While few would wish to argue for any significant amount of historicity in chs 1–11, the situation is rather different with chs 12–50. Again, traditionally these were regarded as historical recollections of such actual people as Abraham, Isaac, Jacob and Joseph. But once the literary critics had shown that the traditions were not committed to writing until centuries after the events they purported to describe, questions began to be asked whether such material could be of any value in reconstructing a history of events in the first half of the second millennium B C, and it was suggested that the stories were back-projections which in fact reflected beliefs and practices of the time of writing. Various interpretations of the patriarchal stories followed, including the view that the patriarchs were originally gods and the stories had their origin in ancient myths, or that the stories should be understood as tribal history in which the 'individuals' were eponyms of tribes. Another suggestion was that the stories were legends which perhaps contained an underlying kernel of historicity, but which had been substantially embellished in the process of oral * transmission. A reaction to the prevalent scepticism about the historicity of the patriarchs came as a result of the increasing archaeological * activity in the Middle East; since, it was argued, the patriarchal stories seem to have preserved accurately a picture of the customs and life-style of the early second millennium, why could they not have preserved accurate reminiscences of individuals from that period? However, it has subsequently been suggested that some of those who have used archaeology as the basis of such claims have tended to stress the similarities of custom and overlook not only the differences, but also the possibility that such customs were current at a later period. The debate about the historicity of the patriarchs continues, but again there is increasing stress on the religious significance of the stories, for example in the working out of the theme of promise and fulfilment. Von Rad comments that 'the patriarchal narratives deal more with God than with men', and suggests that the human beings are not important in themselves but as the objects of divine planning and action.

Although chs 1–11 and 12–50 have been considered separately, it is necessary to return briefly to the question whether they do form distinct units or whether Genesis should be considered as a unity. Recently Westermann has defended the former view, arguing that chs 1–11 deal with certain universal truths about human existence which are not linked to any specific period of time or people, and so should not be subordinated to the patriarchal stories; there is theological significance for the whole of the O T in prefixing the primaeval story to the history, for the God who rescued Israel from Egypt and whom Israel encountered throughout its history was at the same time the creator of heaven and earth and human beings.

The necessity to understand Genesis as a unity has been argued notably by Childs, who believes that consideration must be given to the overall canonical * shape of the book, and he follows a number of earlier scholars in seeing the structure as based on the repeated use of formulae incorporating the Hebrew word *tôlᵉdôt*, 'generations' or 'descendants' (2.4; 5.1; 6.9; 10.1; 11.10; 11.27; 25.12; 25.19; 36.1; 36.9; 37.2). There has been much discussion of these formulae, including whether they begin or end each section of the text: it has even been suggested that the formulae represent the colophons which marked the end of each of the eleven tablets whose contents have been linked to produce an account of the primaeval and patriarchal periods! Childs believes that the purpose of the formulae is to give the book a unified structure and to make clear the nature of the unity, 'to describe both creation and world history in the light of the divine will for a chosen people'. The canonical shape of the book 'serves the community of faith and practice as a truthful witness to God's activity on its behalf in creation and blessing, judgment and forgiveness, redemption and promise'. It is not necessarily to agree with all the details of such an approach to claim that consideration of Genesis in such a light may be more rewarding for the modern interpreter than delving into the minutiae of some of the more extreme examples of literary criticism.

See also **Abraham; Adam; Creation Narratives Pentateuch, Pentateuchal Criticism.**

Brevard S. Childs, *Introduction to the Old Testament as Scripture* (ch. on 'Genesis'), 1979; George W. Coats, *Genesis, with an Introduction to Narrative Literature*, 1983; Gerhard von Rad, *Genesis*, revd edn 1972; R. K. Harrison, *Introduction to the Old Testament* (ch. on 'The Book of Genesis'), 1969; Claus Westermann, *Genesis 1–11*, 1984; *Genesis 12–36*, 1985; *Genesis 37–50*, 1986.

A. H. W. CURTIS

Genizah

The Semitic root *gnz*, from which the noun *genizah* is formed, means 'hide', 'cover', 'bury' and is probably Persian in origin. Its earliest occurrence in Jewish literature is in the late books of the OT where it refers to the storage of valuable items (I Chron. 28.11; Esth. 3.9, RSV 'treasuries'). By the early rabbinic period the noun is used to describe the removal from circulation of some sacred item which is, for one of a number of reasons, no longer to be used. As Jewish religious law developed it became customary for communities to consign to a *beth genizah*, or simply *genizah*, i.e. a storage place, written texts that were either damaged, worn, obsolete or heretical but could not be destroyed for fear of transgressing the third commandment. This was understood to proscribe the obliteration of the name of God and was extended by some Jews to the protection of a variety of Hebrew and Jewish literature, all of which might lay some claim to a degree of sacredness.

The contents of a synagogue's *genizah* were in some cases removed to caves or buried in the ground to disintegrate naturally while in others they were amassed in a store-room over many generations. While damp or humid conditions and the vicissitudes of Jewish life usually ensured their decomposition or dispersal, the relatively stable history of the Ben Ezra synagogue in the dry climate of mediaeval Cairo (Fusṭaṭ) led to the unique survival there of some 200,000 fragmentary texts, many of them dating from about a thousand years ago, written in various languages mainly on vellum and paper but also on papyrus and cloth. This 'Cairo Genizah', as it has come to be known by scholars, began to be exploited by researchers late in the nineteenth century when unscrupulous synagogal officials took to selling items from its valuable contents to dealers and visitors. As a result of such transactions, famous libraries in St Petersburg (now Leningrad), Paris, London, Oxford, Cambridge, New York and Philadelphia ultimately each acquired thousands of fragments and smaller institutions also took their share, but it was Solomon Schechter, Reader in Talmudic Literature at the University of Cambridge, who persuaded the chief rabbi of Cairo to allow him to remove 140,000 items, almost three-quarters of all known fragments, to Cambridge University Library in 1897.

It is beyond dispute that these Genizah fragments represent the most important discovery of new source material for every aspect of scientific Hebrew and Jewish studies ranging from the early mediaeval period until the age of emancipation. As they have been deciphered and identified, especially as a result of the work of the Cambridge Genizah Unit, previous ignorance has been dispelled by information and earlier theories have been drastically modified. Among the fields of study that have most benefitted from these developments has been the history of the OT's transmission and interpretation. Although there are some variants to be found in the Genizah remnants of scrolls and codices (themselves significant for the history of scribal* techniques), the consonantal text was substantially as it is today and it is rather in the area of vocalization that major discoveries have been made. It emerges that three major systems, two emanating from the Holy Land and one from Babylon, were in vogue a thousand years ago and that it took two or three centuries for the Tiberian system of Ben Asher to become what is now regarded as standard.

Whether inspired by the Syriac* Christian example, by Muslim* concern for the accuracy of the Qur'an or by an internal feud with the Karaite Jews who preferred the biblical to the rabbinic tradition, such attention to the accurate recording of the vocalized text had its effect on exegesis. The schools of Masoretes (literally, 'transmitters' or perhaps 'counters') who surrounded the text with vowel points, cantillation signs and explanatory notes inevitably recorded thereby their own understanding of its meaning, or the understanding that they had inherited from generations of readers (*see* **Masoretic Text**). Their methodical approach also encouraged the development of those Hebrew philological* studies that provided the basis for literal interpretation of the OT in later mediaeval and modern times. The interest in making sense of the Hebrew text was of course mainly inspired by its regular recitation before the congregation in the synagogue.

The material from the Cairo Genizah confirms that there were annual Babylonian and triennial Palestinian lectionaries* for both pentateuchal and prophetic readings but that they existed in such variety that it is impossible to identify any one order that may be traced back to early Christian centuries. Not only Hebrew lectionaries used by the Jews but also Palestinian Syriac versions of Christian scripture have been discovered, and the range of biblical translations to be found in the Genizah exemplifies the wide variety of languages represented there. In the pre-Islamic centuries the dominant language of the diaspora Jews was Greek, and seventh-century fragments have been found of the Greek translation prepared for them by Aquila some 500 years before. Whether or not this Aquila is, as has been suggested, identical with Onqelos, the author of the main and literal synagogal targum,* is not clarified by the Genizah texts, but they do have much to add to our knowledge of the development of that popular genre of Aramaic translation.

Various known and unknown compilations of targumic material have been identified, some of them lengthy elaborations of the text, some poetic versions of the narratives and some incorporating halakhic (that is, Jewish legal) interpretations of verses that run counter to what is found in the Talmud.* Because of the ancient nature of the custom of translating the Hebrew Bible into Aramaic it was not abandoned when Arabic replaced Aramaic and Greek as the Jewish vernacular but was incorporated with an Arabic rendering into a trilingual version. Such a rendering, which was written in Hebrew characters and recorded the popular Arabic dialect of the Jewish communities, apparently also existed in a variety of forms, until the version of the tenth-century ga'on (= leading teacher) Saadya ben Joseph, like the targum of Onqelos, became the standard one. It was not unusual for Jews to write their vernacular in Hebrew characters and the Genizah has preserved Judaeo-Greek, Judaeo-Persian, Judaeo-Spanish and Judaeo-German texts, a number of which are relevant to the history of biblical interpretation. Even stranger than these linguistic phenomena are surviving folios of Karaite Bibles that demonstrate how some of that Jewish sect recorded the text of the Hebrew Bible in Arabic characters, perhaps as a means of retaining an independent religious identity.

Scholarly understanding of the historical development of midrashim,* or rabbinic commentaries, throughout the millennium following the destruction of the Temple in AD 70. also owes much to Genizah research. Hitherto, the earliest manuscripts were mediaeval, from the initial periods of Ashkenazi Jewry in the West, while now there are hundred of fragments written in the East at a much earlier date and representing an older textual tradition. Furthermore, new midrashim, anthologies and commentaries have been discovered, both halakhic (legal) and aggadic (non-legal) in nature, and have reconstructed a picture of colourful and heterogeneous Jewish exegesis of the OT. As such a variegated approach gave way to the more linguistic and philological commentaries of the tenth to the twelfth centuries, so the written evidence from the Genizah also records the influence of the centralized Babylonian authorities in effecting the change and thereby thwarting some of the Karaite efforts to discredit rabbinic interpretation as lacking the serious, literal dimension.

Since the Cairo Genizah also preserved a wealth of documents relating to everyday life in a mediaeval Mediterranean society, there are also fragments of children's exercises in biblical Hebrew, illuminated biblical texts, musical notations for the liturgical use of verses, and correspondence that relates to the study of Hebrew scriptures by male and female, young and old, expert and beginner. It should not be forgotten that the Hebrew text of Ben Sira (Ecclesiasticus), the two major manuscripts of the Damascus Document or Zadokite Fragment (= CD) and various versions of *Toledoth Yeshu*, recording early Jewish folklore about Jesus, have likewise been recovered from the Genizah source.

See also **Jewish Interpretation.**

Encyclopaedia Judaica, 1972, 7, cols 404–7; 16, cols 1333–42; S. D. Goitein, *A Mediterranean Society: The Jewish Communities of the Arab World as Portrayed in the Documents of the Cairo Geniza*, 1–4, 1968–83; M. L. Klein, *Genizah Manuscripts of Palestinian Targum to the Pentateuch*, 1–2, 1986; S. C. Reif, *A Guide to the Taylor-Schechter Genizah Collection*, 1973, 1979; id., *Published Material from the Cambridge Genizah Collections: A Bibliography 1896–1980*, 1988.

S. C. REIF

Genre

A kind of literature or literary species; for example, tragedy, comedy,* novel, biography, romance, history, essay or letter. Each genre makes use of a particular style in its treatment of specific subjects and motifs within a structure whose unity gives meaning to its parts. For example, tragedy arouses fear and pity by using elevated language to depict important actions which carry disastrous consequences for the main character because of a conflict of values; biography provides a history of a person's life. Recognition of the genre, therefore, brings with it expectations about content, style and structure, in the service of a coherent meaning. Mistaking the genre, for example mistaking a novel for history, can lead to complete misunderstanding. Genres are not static entities, however, and texts belonging to the same genre exhibit family resemblances rather than identical traits. Broad definitions are helpful in approaching a new text, but every instance needs to be placed within the history of the genre, with its changing emphases and shifting boundaries.

There is a wide range of genres in biblical literature, which exhibits both continuities and discontinuities with contemporary literature from the Ancient Near East* and the Graeco-Roman world (*see* **Hellenism; Hellenistic Writers**). For example, myth* and history in Genesis have much in common with some forms of Canaanite and Babylonian myth and history, yet Genesis is distinguished from them by its depiction of a single, all-powerful, all-knowing God, whose purpose gives meaning to human activity and form to the narrative. Although biblical history is quite unlike post-Enlightenment history writing in the West, it is still history, with many varieties: myth, legend,* saga,* tribal or national history; histories of kings, priests and prophets with biographical elements. All share one characteristic: the omniscient narrator gives information about the eternal purposes of God and the secrets of men's hearts. The Gospels* and the Acts of the Apostles vary in their combinations of elements from biography, history, apocalyptic* and wisdom,* but each shares with OT histories both the perspective of the omniscient narrator and the theological form.

All four Gospels are deeply indebted to scriptural stories of prophets, especially Moses in Exodus–Deuteronomy, and Elijah and Elisha in I and II Kings, for their arrangement of material (narratives interspersed with teaching and miracles), for their general form (rejection by the people and vindication by God), and for their motifs, vocabulary and style. It would be true to say that, although Jesus is presented as messiah,* his role is that of a persecuted prophet. But the synoptics modify this genre in two significant directions. First, Daniel's view of history, from the perspective of resurrection* and Last Judgment, generates features like the apocalyptic* discourse (Matt. 24–25 and parallels) and the account of the resurrection, although the appearance stories also owe much to OT theophanies.* Secondly, the belief in demons who corrupt people and make them ill, shared by some Jews, Greeks and Romans in the first century, gives us Jesus the exorcist. The Fourth Gospel, by contrast, has no exorcisms, although it mentions Satan, and exhibits more influence from wisdom literature and Deuteronomy, while not completely abandoning a future eschatology,* at least in the Gospel's present form. In spite of the variations, however, these four Gospels belong to the same genre. They are theodicies, vindicating God's purpose by telling the story of Jesus. To readers of Hellenistic biographies, themselves very diverse in type, they would seem surprising because of Jesus' provincial and politically suspect career, because of their theological and anthropological presuppositions, and because of their eschatological expectations, but they would not be so alien as to be completely incomprehensible.

Similarly, biblical wisdom literature* is in some respects like contemporary non-Israelite kinds, whether in the form of collections of proverbs or of extended dramas, but, again, its theology makes it distinctive. The same can be said of biblical poetry in hymns, proverbs, and prophetic* oracles,* with their spectrum of parallel patterns; or of biblical law codes.

Of particular concern to recent interpreters of the Bible has been the definition of historical and biographical genres, the distinctions between prophecy, apocalyptic and wisdom, and the varieties of letters (*see* **Epistle**).

Some of the NT letters are directed to particular problems in individual churches, and evidence personal contact between the sender and receivers. This is true of Galatians, I and II Corinthians, Philippians and I and II Thessalonians. On the other hand, the letter to the Colossians is also directed to the church of the Laodiceans (4.16) and may be taken as less particular and more representative. The letters to the Romans, Ephesians and Hebrews, or the letter of James, should be placed further along the scale from particular to general, since, although they must be interpreted within historical contexts of the first-century church, they encompass the concerns of many individual congregations. Romans and Hebrews, like Ecclesiastes in the OT, each presents an exposition of a thesis. Ephesians, like I and II Peter and Jude, is a manifesto. The letters of James and I John have more in common with epigrammatic wisdom literature like Ecclesiasticus. Similarly, letters addressed to individuals rather than groups are of more than one sort: the personal letter of Paul* to Philemon about a slave; the letters to Timothy and Titus as representative pastors, or that to 'the beloved Gaius' (III John) as the representative of the favoured group in the community. II John, to 'the elect lady', could be addressed either to an individual or, more probably, to the church.

We are in possession of a great many letters from the Hellenistic and Roman periods which help to provide the literary context for these Christian versions. Like contemporary letters to friends, Paul's letters to particular churches function to maintain contact between the absent apostle and the congregations, and the opening and closing of each letter use similar formulas, but with significant differences. Paul writes as a superior to inferiors, yet, while expressing his authority, the letters encourage responsibility in the recipients by calling them 'saints' and 'brothers'. Moreover, they develop the usual greetings and good wishes by introducing prayers for God's grace.

The main body of the NT letters, however, unlike correspondence between friends, includes instructions akin to those sent by philosophers to pupils, but again with a distinctive Christian colouring. The more formal and less personal letters, like Romans or Hebrews, contain rhetorical* arguments in the manner of public preachers, but in a less elevated style than in the letters of Seneca, which were designed for an educated public and posterity. The collection into a corpus of letters, originally occasioned by individual circumstances, modifies the genre, giving to all of them a representative character. Defining the genre helps the reader to understand the force of the statements each letter contains.

The genre of apocalyptic literature continues to exercise fascination. A group of scholars recently accepted the following working definition: 'apocalypse' is a genre of revelatory literature with a narrative framework, in which a revelation is mediated by an other-worldly being to a human recipient, disclosing a transcendent reality which is both temporal, in so far as it envisages eschatological salvation, and spatial, in so far as it involves another supernatural world. This definition seeks to distinguish the form and content of 'apocalypse' from prophetic, wisdom and other kinds of revelatory literature. Some characteristics, like pseudonymity* and autobiographical form, are common but not ubiquitous. The function served by an apocalypse is: to interpret present reality and earthly circumstances in the light of the supernatural world and of the future, and to influence both the behaviour and the understanding of the readers by means of divine authority. The suggestion that it offers compensation to the deprived has been criticized but not replaced.

Genres are defined to facilitate appreciation of the text as a whole, placing the parts within a comprehensive and meaningful unity which serves a general purpose. This activity, therefore, is similar to but different from that of form criticism*. Form criticism deals with short passages, separates them from their literary context, defines the form of each to discover its purpose, and relates it to the social context in which the individual form functioned; for example, cult legend or prophetic woe saying. Genre definition deals with larger units, like the book of Genesis, or even the history from Genesis to II Kings, highlights the repetition of motifs and themes, balances juxtaposed features, and relates the whole complex to broader social functions like that of providing a national and religious identity during the Babylonian exile.

D. Aune, *The New Testament in its Literary Environment,* 1987; G. W. Coats (ed.), *Saga, Legend, Tale, Novella, Fable,* 1985; A. Y. Collins (ed.), *Early Christian Apocalypticism: Genre and Social Setting,* Semeia 36, 1986; A. Fowler, *Kinds of Literature,* 1982; C. H. Talbert, *What is a Gospel?* 1977; id., (ed.), *Luke–Acts,* 1984.

MARGARET DAVIES

German Old Testament Scholarship

During the last two centuries OT scholarship in Germany has been dominated by one man, Julius Wellhausen. While the nineteenth century can be regarded as a gradual build-up towards Wellhausen's source-criticism of the Pentateuch,* the twentieth is characterized by the reception and rejection of and – in its latter half – by a return to Wellhausen.

It is virtually impossible to do justice to all of Wellhausen's predecessors, but three names at least need to be mentioned: Reuss and Graf as his forerunners and Kuenen as his companion in arms. Eduard Reuss (1804–91) taught at the Protestant seminary at Strasbourg/Alsace and became a member of Strasbourg's theology faculty when the university was founded in 1872. He was the teacher of Karl Heinrich Graf (1815–69) with whom he carried on a regular correspondence until the latter's early death. It was Reuss who introduced Graf to the work of Richard Simon, the 'father of historico-critical research'. By putting a late date on the OT's cultic laws, Reuss gained a new picture of the history of Israel. The OT prophets are older than the 'Law' and both predate the psalms.

It was Graf who publicized his teacher's ideas (*Die sogenannte Grundschrift des Pentateuch,* 1869). According to Graf, neither the book of Deuteronomy nor Judges–Kings presuppose the laws and narratives of the so-called Priestly Code. Hence P has to be regarded as the latest source of the Pentateuch 'new documentary hypothesis'.

The Dutchman Abraham Kuenen (1828–91) was a practical person who helped much to publicize and defend the views of Reuss, Graf, and Wellhausen. As a good historian Kuenen was aware of the preliminary nature of all historical research. He was interested in the OT purely for historical reasons. Behind its documents Kuenen tried to discover what he regarded as the 'real history'. Kuenen's alignment with the Wellhausen camp is sometimes referred to as the Dutch–German school.

Julius Wellhausen (= W.) (1844–1918) was born in Hameln (Hamelin, North Germany). In 1862 he began his studies at the university of Göttingen. He became a pupil of the OT scholar Heinrich Ewald, but this relationship gradually came to an end during the years 1866–70. In 1870 W. gained his doctorate in theology and two years later was appointed to an OT chair at the university of Greifswald on the shores of the Baltic sea. It was here that he met the classicist Wilamowitz. The two scholars, finding themselves without a true equal in their own faculties, became life-long friends.

Greifswald also saw in 1878 W.'s first concept of his 'history of Israel', based on the studies of Reuss and Graf. But as ecclesiastical opposition grew to W.'s work, he resigned his chair in the theology faculty and took on two appointments in Semitic studies at Halle/Saale (1882) and Marburg (1885). At Marburg he came into contact with the NT scholar A. Jülicher to whom he confessed: 'I have become fed up with the OT.'

In 1892 W. returned to home territory by being called to a chair at the university of Göttingen. From about 1900 onwards he began to concentrate more and more on the NT. W. died on 7 January 1918. Apart from his historical work, W.'s philological* studies were concerned with Hebrew and Semitic lexicography. He never wrote any commentaries on the OT.

W. established the famous four-document hypothesis which is named after him in his hexateuchal studies (*Die Composition des Hexateuchs*, a first draft as early as 1866 and a more mature version in 1877). He divided Genesis – Joshua into four parallel documents dating from the ninth century BC to post-exilic times: J (Yahwist), E (Elohist), D (Deuteronomy) and P (Priestly Code). While *Literarkritik* (source criticism*) was used before and after W., its peculiar form as the four-document hypothesis was his very own contribution, based on important studies by Reuss and Graf. It would only be fair to refer to it as the Reuss–Graf–Wellhausen hypothesis (rather than naming Kuenen who was the propagandist and defender of the idea, but not so much its creative spirit).

Why was W. so interested in *Literarkritik*? It was on the basis of datable 'documents' that he was able to construct a history of Israel's religious development. As opposed to some modern works on *Literarkritik*, W.'s *Composition des Hexateuchs* was not an end in itself, but the foundation of two major historical studies, the (*Prolegomena zur*) *Geschichte Israels*, 1878, and his *Israelitische und jüdische Geschichte*, 1894.

Working from the post-exilic date which had been established for the legal and priestly passages of the 'Hexateuch' (P) by Reuss, Graf, and Kuenen, W. asked the question: Is the 'Law' to be regarded as the basis of ancient Israel or as the foundation of post-exilic Judaism? W. then proceeded to show that as a result of Israel's necessary inner development the 'Law' can only be placed in the late period, that of the beginnings of post-exilic Judaism.

W. views Israel's history as consisting of three epochs which correspond to his source analysis (J E – D – P). Taking the cult as an example, W. regards the early period (J E) as the time when Israel's religion emerged like the fresh water of a well. During this 'natural' period of Israel's religion the patriarchs would sacrifice to their God when and wherever the spirit moved them, and sanctuaries would be erected all over the country as a spontaneous expression of Israel's worship.

Already the next epoch (D) meets with W.'s disapproval as Deuteronomy requires the centralization of worship, a severe restriction on the spontaneity of worship so dear to W. Matters appear to him to have deteriorated even further during the third epoch (P) when cultic and ritual legislation have killed off any natural and spontaneous form of worship. Thus W. reaches an entirely negative view (*Denaturierung*) of post-exilic Judaism which hardly does it justice, though it ought not to be forgotten that he allocates more space to the Second Temple congregation in his *Israelitische und jüdische Geschichte* than most scholars.

The charge of anti-Judaism (*see* **Antisemitism**) is never far off when W.'s views on the Second Temple period are under discussion. But even more frequently has W. been accused of Hegelianism, e.g. by Hans-Joachim Kraus, *Geschichte der historisch-kritischen Erforschung des Alten Testaments*, 1956, [2]1969, pp. 255–74. This attack has in turn produced a spirited defence by Lothar Perlitt, *Vatke und Wellhausen*, BZAW 94, 1965, pp. 153–243. Obviously the roots of W.'s views on postexilic Judaism need investigating.

When W. divides Israelite and Jewish history into three epochs (J E – D – P), we are reminded of Hegel's view of the self-realization of absolute spirit in three stages: thesis – antithesis – synthesis. But as Hegel regards the third stage as the absolute climax of such a development, nothing could be further away from W.'s analysis of Second Temple theology. W. Vatke, a self-confessed Hegelian, has a much more positive view of post-exilic Judaism than W. (cf. Perlitt).

What then are the roots of W.'s position? Ironically, a four-source hypothesis might serve as the best explanation: 1. With Herder* and the Romantic movement, W. regards the early period in the history of any people as a true expression of that nation's spirit. He prefers the fresh spring water of the old days to the 'cisterns of the epigones' (*Prolegomena*, p. 409). Only in ancient Israel does W. hope to find the unadulterated spirit of that people. Rather than appealing to Hegel and Schleiermacher, W. acknowledges his indebtedness to Herder and Goethe on the one hand and to French linguistics on the other.

2. In the Lutheran* tradition of the dialectic of 'Law and Gospel' W. takes a negative view of the 'Law' and hence of post-exilic Judaism. The use of the term 'Law'* itself in preference to the Torah in which the psalmists delight is indicative of W.'s attitude. It is hardly possible to come to an adequate view of the significance of the Torah in Judaism from the starting-point of the Lutheran 'Law and Gospel' dialectic.

3. W. is also a child of his time in his failure to recognize any merit in the post-exilic cult. Nineteenth-century Protestantism was totally blind to the significance of cultic actions. The influence of the Enlightenment* and of its rationalism had reduced religion to a purely intellectual pursuit. While Pietistic revivals emphasized the 'spontaneity' of religion, both failed to make any sense of the symbolism of the cult.

4. Typical of his time is also W.'s political attitude. Like Karl Budde (cf. F. Crüsemann, *Der Widerstand gegen das Königtum*, 1978), W. regards the monarchy (*see* **Kingship**) as the most acceptable and superior form of political order (Budde: monarchy = order; period of the Judges = anarchy and chaos). According to W., the monarchy is the basis of all forms of order, and on its soil all further Israelite institutions have developed. It was intellectually fruitful, as can be seen from the appearance of the oldest Israelite literature at that time. Nature and agriculture were replaced by the state, the nation, and history as the major concerns of religion (*Geschichte Israels*, vol I, 1878, pp. 429f.). Post-exilic Jewry was bound to appear as decadent from such a position, and even the emergence of the Hasmonaean dynasty does not seem to have mellowed W.'s judgment.

Such are the roots of W.'s negative view of post-exilic Judaism. The charge of Hegelianism has to be considered untenable. But we do agree with Kraus's assessment that W.'s historical conscientiousness has done the utmost to reconstruct through critical analysis the 'true history' from its sources.

W.'s *Literarkritik* was applied to the prophets by Bernhard Duhm* (born 1847 in Bingum, East Frisia). Duhm was strongly influenced by the Romantic understanding of personality, hence his view of the prophets as great, ethically autonomous, religious personalities. In order to get back to these personalities Duhm used Wellhausen's *Literarkritik*, dividing the prophetic material into 'genuine' and 'non-genuine'. With this unfortunate distinction he held back the necessary understanding of the later traditions for decades.

Three others of Wellhausen's comrades in arms deserve at least a mention by name: Rudolf Smend Sr, Karl Budde, and Bernhard Stade. Stade founded in 1881 the *Zeitschrift für die alttestamentliche Wissenschaft* (*ZAW*) which even today still publishes articles on *Literarkritik* in the spirit of Wellhausen.

At the beginning of the twentieth century archaeological discoveries in Mesopotamia sparked off the *Babel-Bible controversy*. Friedrich Delitzsch in a Berlin public lecture on 13 January 1902 entitled 'Babel and Bible', asked the question: Can the Bible still be considered divine revelation if the Babylonian accounts of the origin of the world and of the great flood turn out to be older than the biblical ones? Clearly his own answer was in the negative. This devaluation of the OT by Delitzsch was gratefully taken up thirty years later by the Nazis and their theological fellow-travellers. Nearly all the famous German Assyriologists succumbed to extreme ideologies.

The second half of the nineteenth and the early twentieth centuries was also the time of the *Religionsgeschichtliche Schule* (History of Religions school*). Biblical exegesis was extended to become a history of ideas primarily through the use of oriental sources. H. Gunkel's *Schöpfung und Chaos* (1894) and H. Gressmann's *Der Messias* (1929) were the main works of this school. Gunkel and his colleagues were trying to discover *das Eigentümliche*, the very special character of Israelite religion, by finding out how this religion was transformed in the process of time. Gunkel's term *Eigentümlichkeit* derives from the Romantics' idea of individuality (in the line from Spinoza to Herder).

This leads us to Hermann Gunkel (1862–1932) himself, the father of form criticism,* who was born in Springe near Hanover. Gunkel began to teach in 1888 at Göttingen university, moving to Halle/Saale in 1889 and to a personal chair at Berlin in 1894. He succeeded two colleagues in established chairs, Stade at Giessen in 1907 and Cornill at Halle in 1920. Gunkel retired in 1927 and died five years later.

Gunkel was strongly inspired by Herder. He contended against Wellhausen's *Literarkritik* that most problems of an OT text were older than the written version and were due to developments at the stage of oral tradition. Trying to cope with such problems only at the stage of writing would ultimately lead to the invention of more and more 'documents' (Smend Sr: J1 + J2; Eissfeldt: J + L = lay source; Fohrer: J + N = nomadic source). *Literarkritik* was finally going to self-destruct, and its demise warrants no chronicler.

Gunkel sought to overcome Wellhausen's source-critical and purely historical method through the concept of an Israelite history of literature (*Die israelitische Literatur*, 1925, reprinted Darmstadt 1963). He defined the history of Israel's literature as the history of her literary genres* (*Reden und Aufsätze*, 1913, p. 31). Each literary genre has its original setting (*Sitz im Leben*) in a clearly defined place in the life of the people of Israel. If we want to understand these genres (*Gattungen*) we have to ask: Who is the speaker? Who are the audience? What kind of atmosphere dominates the situation? What effect is intended? What Herder had perceived purely intuitively, Gunkel now tried to discover with proper scholarly methods.

Gunkel's *magnum opus* was clearly his Genesis commentary, which appeared in several editions from the turn of the century ([5]1922 = [7]1966; ET of the introduction, *The Legends of Genesis*, 1964). Gunkel states his thesis in the first paragraph: 'Genesis is a collection of sagas'. He notices that the saga* as a poetic narrative is much more suited than prose narrative to represent religious ideas. Investigating the various types of sagas Gunkel finds myths* which he defines as stories of the gods. He was also the first scholar to define aetiologies* (explanations of the origin of certain peoples, customs, names, sanctuaries etc.). He introduced this term from medicine into biblical research (F. W. Golka, 'Zur Erforschung der Ätiologien im Alten Testament', *VT* XX, 1970, pp. 90–98). As the sagas combine into saga clusters, Gunkel becomes interested in the history of the transmission of these traditions (*Überlieferungsgeschichte*) (*see* **Tradition, History of**).

In his commentary on the Psalms Gunkel defines various genres by using the following criteria: 1. Psalms belonging to the same category must be connected with the same part of the cult. 2. They must have common sentiments. 3. Their individual sections have to show the same form of language. Thus he finds the following genres: hymns, songs of YHWH's enthronement, individual and collective laments/songs of thanksgiving, royal psalms, songs of pilgrimage, wisdom* psalms etc. This research serves Gunkel's interest in the history of Israelite piety.

While Gunkel's contribution to the study of the prophets is perhaps less impressive than his work on Genesis and the Psalms, he

devoted a great deal of energy to hermeneutical* issues. His position could be labelled as 'liberal': 1. Exegesis must not be subservient to ecclesiastical practice. 2. All dogmatic premises must be eliminated. 3. The OT is not a source-book of theological doctrines. 4. The *heilsgeschichtliche* interpretation of the OT is inappropriate. And Gunkel also makes two positive assertions: 1. The nucleus of OT religion is piety. 2. All exegesis needs to be related to history, in particular the history of religion. For Gunkel theology clearly equals *Religionsgeschichte*. Such a position turned out to be a weak one when it came to the Nazis' assault on the church and the OT in particular.

The struggle of the Confessing Church against the Nazi state and its ecclesiastical sympathizers (1933–45), in which the role of the OT played a major part, has been chronicled by Carsten Nicolaisen, *Die Auseinandersetzung um das Alte Testament im Kirchenkampf 1933–45*, unpublished dissertation, Hamburg 1966. The Nazi attack on the OT stemmed from three roots: 1. racial antisemitism, 2. the rejection of the OT by Assyriologists and even biblical scholars (Babel-Bible controversy), and 3. the culture-critical conviction that the end of Christianity had come (F. Nietzsche). Alfred Rosenberg in his *Myth of the Twentieth Century* demanded the abolition of the OT as a religious book: 1. The OT's 'tout and cattle trader stories' must be replaced by pure Nordic sagas and fairy-tales. 2. A racially inferior people such as Israel must no longer be the subject of general admiration. 3. Israel's God is a tyrannical demon who has sprung from confused Jewish religious thinking.

The real scandal broke out on 13 November 1933 at a public meeting in Berlin's 'Sports Palace' (*Sportpalastkundgebung*) where 20,000 people and the whole leadership of the 'German Christians' (Nazi sympathizers) passed a resolution demanding the abolition of the OT. This was too much even for Hitler's own *Reichsbischof* who condemned the resolution.

But German Lutheran* Christianity was theologically ill-equipped to fight for the OT. While Calvin* had emphasized the unity of the Old and New Testaments, Luther differentiated much more between the two as Law and Gospel; though Luther, as opposed to Wellhausen, would also have found 'gospel' in the OT. The Confessing Church at its Barmen Synod (29–31 May 1934) was bailed out by a Calvinist. Following a proposal by Karl Barth,* the Barmen Declaration reasserted the unity of the two Testaments on the basis of a christological interpretation of the OT.

Barth's christological interpretation of the OT no doubt secured the survival of the church in this struggle with the Nazis. But at the same time, because of Barth's christocentrism, the seeds were sown for a new Christian anti-Judaism. Does a christological interpretation of the OT not ultimately deny the Jews the right to their own Bible?

How insecure German theological understanding of the OT had become was apparent from the controversy over the direction of a new series of commentaries, the *Altes Testament Deutsch* (ATD). Was the christological interpretation (Barth, W. Vischer) to triumph or would the religio-historical view (Sellin, Baumgärtel, Hempel) hold its own? Herntrich and von Rad on the one hand and Weiser on the other finally arrived at a compromise in 1936. Neither view was to be allowed a free rein. It was not a question of either/or, but the dialectical tension between both positions had to be endured.

Scholars who were associated with the ATD commentary included Gerhard von Rad and Martin Noth. Both took up issues of Pentateuchal criticism raised by H. Gunkel, von Rad in the field of form criticism and Noth in the area of tradition-history. While Gunkel applied the form-critical method to the smallest possible unit, von Rad was interested in the literary genre of the entire 'Hexateuch' (*Das formgeschichtliche Problem des Hexateuchs*, BWANT IV, 1938, ET 1966): 1. The 'Hexateuch' contains a number of statements of faith summed up in a 'Creed' (Deut. 26.5ff.). 2. The 'Hexateuch' represents an accumulation of different materials which have reached their final shape under the influence of this 'Creed'. 3. The entire 'Hexateuch' has to be considered as a literary genre and the question of its *Sitz im Leben* has to be answered.

Von Rad differentiates between exodus* and Sinai traditions. Both have different settings in the Israelite cult. Eventually these traditions became detached from the cult and were incorporated by the Yahwist into his great *heilsgeschichtliche* structure. This explains, according to von Rad, the origin of the 'Hexateuch'. Von Rad criticizes Gunkel's fixation on the earliest stages of the tradition. This has led Gunkel to neglect hermeneutically the final stage of the composition in which the individual elements have now found their places.

Martin Noth, *A History of Pentateuchal Traditions*, 1948 (ET 1972), aims to investigate the *pre*-literary history of Pentateuchal traditions, not just earlier literary stages. He postulates a common basic source (*Grundlage*) for J and E, though not much has been left of E by the Pentateuchal redactor. Noth analyses the

'themes' of the Pentateuch in greater detail, compared to von Rad's two main traditions of Exodus and Sinai. But he is less confident than von Rad about our ability to determine a cultic *Sitz im Leben* for these traditions.

Following his teacher, Albrecht Alt, Noth develops a view of Israel as an *amphictyony* (*The Laws in the Pentateuch*, 1940, ET 1966). This sacral confederation of the tribes becomes an institution for Alt and Noth to which they relate many elements of the OT. Noth regards e.g. the lesser judges as the spokesmen of apodictic law, which Alt had discovered.

Pentateuchal research in the line of Gunkel/von Rad/Noth continues in Germany with the work of two Heidelberg scholars, Claus Westermann and Rolf Rendtorff, the former favouring Gunkel's form-critical, the latter his traditio-historical approach. Westermann is best known for his Genesis commentary (*BK* I, 3 vols, 1966–82, ET by John Scullion 1984–87), which is based on his programmatic essay, 'Arten der Erzählung in der Genesis' (1964). This essay is accessible to English readers in *The Promises to the Fathers*, ET 1980.

As with Gunkel, the question of sources is of no interest to Westermann. While the phantom of an 'Elohist' is altogether dispensed with (cf. *Genesis*, vol II. on ch. 20), J and P play no significant part. When Westermann investigates the form of the narratives of promise, such an investigation cuts by definition across the boundaries of 'documents' and includes all promises. He rejects the attempt by the American Albright school to regard the narratives of Genesis as direct evidence of historical events as well as the tendency of the German Alt/Noth school, which is concerned purely with the transmission of such narratives in later Israel and which regards the question whether these narratives might have something to say about the Patriarchal age itself as almost impossible to answer. Claus Westermann, as the son of the Berlin Africanist Dietrich Westermann, finds such positions unhelpful and would rather ask whether the Genesis narratives which originated at a pre-literary stage do not allow us here and there a glimpse of prehistorical times. This is the purpose of Westermann's investigation of the 'promises to the fathers'.

To begin with, the expositor has to realize that all patriarchal narratives are family narratives. The underlying form of community is of prime importance for our understanding of these stories. Westermann is able to show that the promises of a son, which guarantees the future of the community, of land, the goal of nomadic migration, and of God's protection during such migration, go back to the patriarchal age and religion. The promise of multiplication, however, is no longer part of family narrative but presupposes the horizon of the nation. The same is true of the promise of blessing, as blessing originally cannot be promised but is passed on through the laying-on of hands.

From the results gained by his study of the narratives of promise Westermann proceeds to a detailed analysis of the primaeval history and the Abraham and Jacob–Esau stories. From this analysis it is obvious that 'documents' have lost their significance, but that pentateuchal criticism has to start from an investigation of the narratives and the structures of society which they reflect. This form-critical approach Westermann also applies to the Psalter (*The Praise of God in the Psalms*, 1966) and to prophecy (*Basic Forms of Prophetic Speech*, 1967).

Rolf Rendtorff re-opened the debate on pentateuchal criticism with his book, *Das überlieferungsgeschichtliche Problem des Pentateuch* BZAW 147, 1977 (for an English summary cf. his 'The "Yahwist" as Theologian? The Dilemma of Pentateuchal Criticism', *JSOT* 3, 1977, pp. 2–9). Rendtorff views the present state of pentateuchal criticism as follows: 1. There is a Priestly layer in the Pentateuch but scholars disagree as to what might be its specific purpose and as to which texts might form its basis. 2. In addition to P there is either one further source or several further sources or layers; but scholars disagree concerning their number, their limits, and their relationship to one another. This whole construction is only kept together by the fact that all these scholars come from a tradition of research for which the documentary hypothesis is sacrosanct. So even when individual arguments fail, the overall assumption is never subjected to close scrutiny.

J and P are no continuous sources for Rendtorff; E, of course, never existed anyway. Rendtorff recommends that scholars should go back to the drawing-board and attempt to prove the existence of connections (*Querverweise*) between J texts in the primaeval history, the patriarchal and exodus traditions etc. It then becomes obvious that each cycle of traditions has its own prehistory. As the various complexes of traditions hardly ever refer to each other, the idea of continuous sources becomes questionable. When Rendtorff judges that the assumption of sources no longer makes any helpful contribution to the study of the Pentateuch, he is not attacking *Literarkritik* as such, but only the dogmatic assumption of four sources.

The greater part of the texts of the Pentateuch, according to Rendtorff, had already grown together into larger units before they were joined together to the present Pen-

tateuch. This second stage Rendtorff attributes to a deuteronomic redaction, the first and only redaction to be concerned with the Pentateuch as a whole. Thus the idea of continuous sources has to be abandoned for the study of the Pentateuch. Even a late post-exilic dating of J (H. H. Schmid, *Der sogenannte Jahwist*, 1976) still means 'chasing a phantom' (Rendtorff, p. 150).

Thus criticism of Wellhausen initiated by Gunkel with his form-critical and traditio-historical approaches reaches its climax in the works of Westermann and Rendtorff. Their results have received international approval, particularly in the Anglo-Saxon world and in Israel. Yet in Germany outside Heidelberg Westermann and Rendtorff appear to be totally isolated, and the spirit of Wellhausen is raising its head again. Source-critical studies are legion, and whereas Wellhausen would have left us at least with half-verses, analysis has become even more refined.

I select just one example of this newest source-critical cum redactio-critical approach, Ludwig Schmidt, *'De deo', Studien zur Literarkritik und Theologie . . .*, BZAW 143, 1976, where the author manages to find in the 48 verses of the book of Jonah both a basic source (*Grundschicht*) and a redaction (*Bearbeitung*). Schmidt's source division is particularly original, as he finds 'Elohim' in the *Grundschicht* and 'YHWH' in the *Bearbeitung*. Alas, Jonah 4.10 does not fit Schmidt's theory. He therefore assumes that the redaction has changed an original 'Elohim' into 'YHWH'. Needless to say Schmidt has no textual evidence on his side, not one single manuscript, but proceeds purely on the basis of a circular argument.

Both versions, however, contain 'narrated doctrine', both are close to 'wisdom circles', and both have been written by 'enlightened Jews', a term Schmidt does not hesitate to borrow from Emanuel Hirsch, a theologian whose views on the Jews, enlightened or otherwise, were at least somewhat dubious during the Third Reich. Schmidt's basic source speaks of God as the creator (universalism), while the redaction emphasizes YHWH's status as the only true God and the fact that he is gracious and merciful.

Anybody trained in systematic theology might perhaps suspect that the former (creation) is the basis of the latter (uniqueness, mercy). And this is indeed the way Deutero–Isaiah argues with the doubting exiles: the creator is also the redeemer (Isa. 40.12–31). Further evidence is provided by the post-exilic hymns or 'descriptive Psalms of Praise' (Westermann) with their two-fold division: God's greatness/majesty – his mercy/kindness. So why two versions? Obviously the idea of a text as a literary unity has become unthinkable for scholars still spellbound by the documentary hypothesis.

Why German scholarship has taken this retrograde step back to Wellhausen and turned its back on the achievements of Gunkel and his followers is hard to say. There seems to be a certain isolationism in German OT studies. Non-German literature is not widely read. The American sociological* approach to the history of Israel (Mendenhall, Gottwald) is not seriously considered, with the notable exception of B. Lang among the younger generation. Literary criticism* in the Anglo-American sense of the word is not discussed by German scholars, and a book like Robert Alter's *The Art of Biblical Narrative* (1981) would be virtually unknown to students. Wisdom research in Germany is still based on unproven and outdated theories ('schools', 'class of wise men', 'royal court') and their refutations have been virtually ignored.

See also **American Interpretation; Scandinavian Old Testament Scholarship.**

In addition to books cited see R. E. Clements, *A Century of Old Testament Study*, ²1983; J. W. Rogerson, *Old Testament Criticism in the Nineteenth Century*, 1984; R. N. Whybray, *The Making of the Pentateuch*, 1987.

FRIEDEMANN W. GOLKA

Gnosticism

A 'gnostic' (*gnōstikos*) is one who claims, affects or aspires to 'gnosis' = knowledge. In scripture it is usually a divine or spiritual gift (Jer. 31.34; Phil. 3.8–9), but claims to knowledge may be vicious (I Cor. 8.1–3; I Tim. 6.20). From the later second century onwards (Irenaeus),* 'gnostic' is used to label certain groups who claim divine knowledge, and 'Gnosticism' traditionally refers to the heresy or pattern of heresy such groups represent. Some mainstream Christians (like Origen* and his follower Evagrius Ponticus [d. 399]) continued to use 'gnostic' to define the highest spiritual insight.

In modern times the History of Religions school* (Richard Reitzenstein 1861–1931; Wilhelm Bousset 1865–1920) applied the terms to a religious movement or system older than Christianity, based on Iranian and Hellenistic* ideas. The shape of this Gnosis emerged clearly in Manichaeism, the religion founded in Persia by Mani (AD *c.* 215–275), but its workings were observed in and behind the NT.

If such a religion existed before Christ, a great many texts from the NT can be seen reflecting it. Gnostics claim knowledge, so any attacks on false claims to knowledge are anti-gnostic. The contrast of light and darkness, frequent in John and Paul,* and statements implying that the world is in the power of an evil god or demon (II Cor. 4.3–4; I John 5.19), are gnostic. So is the contrast of flesh and spirit. Gnostic asceticism is alleged to be attacked (Col. 2.20–23; I Tim. 4.3; 5.23). Because Manicheans and gnostics rejected the world, their Revealer could have only a spiritual consistency, and his flesh was unreal or a temporary disguise. So assertions about the flesh of Christ (John 1.14; I John 4.1–3) are anti-gnostic. Similarly, belief in a future resurrection* of the body is repulsive to gnostic dualism, and is interpreted in terms of present spiritual experience ('realized eschatology'*). This reinterpretation is both asserted (Rom. 6.3–6; John 11.24–26) and resisted (I Cor. 15.12–19 etc.; John 5.26–29; II Tim. 2.18). The idea of a heavenly being who descends to earth with a message of truth, light or liberation is fundamentally gnostic (Matt. 11.25–27; John 3.11–13), and the original version of John's Gospel and the teachings source ('Q') in Matthew and Luke have been claimed as essentially such revelatory texts. More broadly gnostic is the idea of Christ as a pre-existent divine being who comes to earth (II Cor. 8.9; Phil. 2.5–7) to gather into his body the elect (John 11.51–52; I Cor. 12.13), who deceives and defeats the evil powers (I Cor. 2.7–8; Col. 2.14–15), who vivifies believers with his Spirit in rites of initiation (John 3.5) and communion (John 6.56–57), and with eternal knowledge of God (John 17.3). Such interpretations, finding gnosticism in the NT itself, prevailed for much of this century, chiefly in the school of Rudolf Bultmann,* notable exponents on the Pauline side being Walter Schmithals, and of the Johannine writings Ernst Käsemann.

But while such interpretations make sense provided there was already a gnostic religion with which the NT texts could be compared, and with which early Christianity could be seen as interacting in this mixed way, the original History of Religions school derived the outline of gnostic belief from a third-century AD religion (Manichaeism), and then used the NT to prove that it already existed. That such a religion existed before Christ lacks concrete evidence, though it proved fruitful in NT exegesis, and formed the launching-pad for Bultmann's great exercise in reinterpreting the NT message in personal existentialist terms ('demythologizing'*). Repeated efforts have been made to find evidence. First, hope lay in the ancient writings of the Mandaeans, a baptizing sect which still survives in Iraq and claims to originate with John the Baptist.* Their teaching in some respects resembles gnostic ideas. Bultmann used these texts to interpret John's Gospel, and they figure large in vol. 2 of Foerster's *Gnosis*. But the Mandaean books have suffered much re-editing after the rise of Christianity and in opposition to it, and cannot be relied upon as pre-Christian. Secondly, it was hoped to find gnostic features in the Dead Sea Scrolls,* and some elements are there: asceticism, the conflict of light and darkness, apocalyptic* revelation, ritual washings and cultic meals. But the crucial features, the viciousness of creation and the heavenly revealer-redeemer, are absent. Attention turned thirdly to the codices from Nag Hammadi.* Some of these showed evidence of gnostic texts adapted to a Christian framework (*Apocryphon of John*), or interpreted biblical history with a revealer/redeemer but no apparent knowledge of Jesus or the church (*Apocalypse of Adam*). But even if the claim of non-Christian or Christianized Gnosis is correct, it is difficult to claim on the basis of texts written in manuscripts of the fourth century AD that they are certainly pre-Christian. While some interpreters of Gnosticism stay with the pre-Christian theory (Foerster, Rudolph), there has been a widespread revolt against it even in Germany (for diverse opinions see A. H. B. Logan and A. J. M. Wedderburn [eds], *The New Testament and Gnosis*, 1983). It is generally thought better to see the NT texts as forming the basis for gnostic interpretation in the second century and after, rather than as reflecting an existing gnostic religion. That does not exclude the possibility that some Christians even in the NT period understood their faith in ways later identified as gnostic; this applies especially to those attacked in later books like the Pastoral Epistles.

The name 'Gnostic' first applied to various groups who interpreted the creation story* on special principles. Leaving aside Marcion,* a miscellaneous group (Layton's 'classical Gnosticism') included Ophites and Sethians and the Barbelognostics represented by the popular *Apocryphon of John*. Their myth* begins with an ultimate Father from whom a number of spiritual beings (aeons = 'ages, realms, worlds') emanate. One of these is Wisdom (*Sophia*), who tried to act independently of her partner Thought (*Ennoia*), and unintentionally produced a mis-shapen being called Ialdabaoth. This monstrosity stole some of her power, and became the creator of the spiritual powers who rule this world (archons), and, with their help, of the physical universe and of Adam* and Eve. The Genesis creation story is then retold, with Wisdom (otherwise the Holy Spirit) trying to rescue, by infusing spirit-life and knowledge, the unfortunate creatures of her son. The temptation in Gen. 3 becomes an attempt to impart true knowledge to those imprisoned in ignorance by their evil or clumsy creator. Cain and Abel are begotten

by Ialdabaoth's powers, but Adam begets Seth, who receives some pure spirit, and is the ancestor of the pure. Adam and Eve and most of their descendants are shut up in oblivion of their true origin. The well-known features of OT history are generally reinterpreted: when Ialdabaoth tires of the world and attempts to destroy it, Noah and the pure people escape by hiding in a cloud of light ('not, as Moses* said, in an ark'). There is almost complete preoccupation with Genesis, and with the mythical background of heavenly pre-history. Certainly the revealer (Christ as the incarnation of the heavenly Seth, or some other figure), by imparting this information about the beginning of all, enables the hearer to recognize his own spiritual origin and come to conversion and knowledge. In concentrating on Genesis, the Gnostics were like other Christians, for whom it was the chief tool of evangelism in the pagan world. The source of the gnostic myth itself is uncertain. It is syncretistic, combining elements of Greek philosophy, eastern religions, and Jewish speculations about Wisdom and the pre-existent Law.* The large number of names for spiritual beings, Eleleth, Oroiael, Daueithei, etc., have a Hebrew or Aramaic ring, but the effect could be artificial.

Valentinus was an intelligent and fluent Alexandrian who worked in Rome and flourished 140–160. He elaborated a Christian gnosis on Platonist philosophical lines. We are quite well-informed about Valentinianism, but his numerous followers developed his system in various ways. His aeons, 30 in all, which constitute the 'fullness' or 'entirety' (*plērōma*), have Greek names with biblical sources: Deep, Silence, Word, Mind, Man, Church, Love. Wisdom (*Sophia*) transgressed out of desire to know the Original Father (Deep), which led to the separating of an inferior Wisdom with the Hebrew name Achamoth, distinct from Sophia, shut out of the Fullness by a Limit called the Cross. This fall is itself a spiritualized version of the sin of Eve. Achamoth is saved from her passions by a Saviour (Jesus) sent from the Fullness. She generates the Creator (Demiurge), whose intentions are good, and improves his creation with spiritual nature. Flesh must perish, and with it carnally minded people. But some are purely spiritual, and ultimately are taken back to the Fullness with Achamoth. Between are the 'psychics', who (like Achamoth) are saved by repentance, and may at least reach her inferior heaven (the 'Ogdoad'). The knowledge which enables this process came to earth with Jesus. Valentinus is said to have composed a *Gospel of Truth*, but it is not likely to be the book of that name from Nag Hammadi. The threefold division of humanity is widespread in

Gnosticism. The system was promoted by one Ptolemaeus, who taught that the Law of Moses came from the Creator, and was neither evil nor perfectly good, but necessary and just. He sustains the whole system by repeated reference to the NT: for instance, Paul wrote of the aeons (Eph. 3.21); the first twelve aeons are implied in the twelve years of Jesus (Luke 2.42); the first two letters of Jesus' name (*iota* and *ēta*, I H) represent the number of the remaining aeons (10 + 8), and the saying about the iota and tittle of Matt. 5.18 alludes to the group of ten. Such spiritual exegesis of the NT is repeatedly illustrated by the Valentinian scholar Heracleon, whose commentary* on John's Gospel is the earliest on a NT book: the descent of Jesus to Capernaum at John 2.12 is his descent into the material world, to start a new dispensation; the great feast of 2.13 is the passion of the Saviour.

Another school was founded by Basilides. His complicated creation myth has a non-existent God producing a three-fold sonship, which separates into a super-celestial realm, an Ogdoad with its Great Ruler, and a Hebdomad where the Ruler of this world presides. Neither ruler knows there is a god above him, and in this world part of the superior sonship is mixed in for the benefit of the inferior. With the gospel, the Rulers successively learn the truth from above, and they transmit it downwards to the physical world. In the passion of Jesus Christ the 'distinction of kinds' begins. He descended from the superior realm, through the Ogdoad and Hebdomad, and has portions from each. Each portion has its place, and following him the sonships are restored to where they belong, and each realm and ruler becomes oblivious to all the rest. Basilides' system is constantly sustained by biblical texts, from OT and NT, taken out of context and allegorized.* He accepts the NT history, but sets it in his wide framework of philosophical myth. The law came from the Ruler of the Hebdomad, and is reliable if so understood. A psalm-book, a gospel, and twenty-four books of gospel exegesis are attributed to Basilides.

Besides leading theologians and many lesser writers, other Christian groups adopted views or documents of gnostic character. Notably the Christians of the Edessa region in Syria, where St Thomas was venerated, produced apocrypha like the *Gospel of Thomas* and *Thomas the Contender* from Nag Hammadi, and the *Acts of (Judas) Thomas*. The last describes his missionary journeys, featuring baptismal and eucharistic ceremonies of unusual character (oil predominates at baptism, water at eucharist), an emphasis on virginity, and a *Hymn of the Pearl* which recounts the whole gnostic spirituality in the story of the lost son pursuing the precious pearl, but needing to be roused from slumber by the call from the far country of his origin.

Orthodox critics (Irenaeus, Origen) were to claim that gnostics distorted particular texts by ignoring the total pattern of the Bible. But the orthodox themselves constantly imposed contemporary meanings on ancient texts, ignorant of and uninterested in their original purport, and the gnostics had a framework (sometimes a canon) of their own as an exegetical tool just as their critics did. The decisive move was dislodging God the Creator and law-giver from the ultimate position, and postulating a (better) 'God beyond God'. Whether or not that was first done by the Pauline extremist Marcion, Paul's ambiguous attitude to the law as both good and evil perhaps supplied the leverage. In the end it could not be Christian; even for Paul it is decisive that 'Christ died for our sins according to the scriptures' (I Cor. 15.3).

See also **Marcion; Patristic Christology**.

Werner Foerster, *Gnosis. A Selection of Gnostic Texts*, 2 vols, 1972/1974; Bentley Layton, *The Gnostic Scriptures. A new translation with annotations and introductions*, 1987; Elaine Pagels, *The Johannine Gospel in Gnostic Exegesis*, 1973; id., *The Gnostic Paul: Gnostic Exegesis of the Pauline Letters*, 1975; Kurt Rudolph, *Gnosis*, 1977; W. Schneemelcher (ed.), *New Testament Apocrypha*, 1963/1965.

STUART GEORGE HALL

Gospel

The study of the word within the writings of the early church shows a clear linear development from an original meaning of 'the good news concerning, or as preached by, Jesus' to 'the written documents describing his preaching, ministry, passion* and resurrection'.* The noun *euangelion* ('good news', 'gospel') has religious, salvific connotations in secular Greek from Homer onwards, especially within the imperial cult in proclamations and inscriptions. Within the OT, however, the noun has no such meaning, although the verb *euangelizesthai* is used with a theological sense, e.g. Isa. 52.7; 61.1 (LXX).

The theological use of the word becomes both common and vital with Paul.* The gospel is the whole of the good news about Jesus Christ and that which God has done in and through his death and resurrection (I Cor. 15.1ff.). Although Paul is clear that there is only one gospel (Gal. 1.6–7), at the same time the word can be used to describe the content of his own preaching, 'my gospel' (Rom. 2.16). This link between the gospel and preaching is made clear in the Gospels, where *euangelion* often occurs in Mark and Matthew connected with 'preach' (*kērussein*, Mark 1.14; 13.10; 14.9; Matt. 4.23; 9.35 [*see* **Kerygma**]); also, the verb *euangelizesthai* is used echoing Isaiah (Matt. 11.5/Luke 7.22; Luke 4.18). For Luke, this is the characteristic activity of Jesus and his disciples (e.g. 9.6; 20.1; Acts 8.25; 14.7). Mark probably intended a similar meaning when he began his account of Jesus with the words, 'The beginning of the gospel of Jesus Christ' (Mark 1.1).

However, this linking of the content of the early Christian preaching with narrative about Jesus' ministry, death and resurrection was to bring about a change in the word's use. In the NT, *euangelion* is always singular and applied to the content of Christian belief; the same is mostly true of the Apostolic Fathers.* The use of the word, especially in the plural, to refer to the actual written documents first emerges clearly in Justin Martyr (mid-second century AD) and increases through the works of the Ante-Nicene Fathers until by the time of Eusebius* this becomes the dominant meaning, applied both to the four canonical examples and to apocryphal and gnostic* gospels. Thus, while for *biblical theology*ated the question of 'gospel' concerns the content of early Christian preaching, for *biblical interpretation* the key issue is: what sort of text or book is 'a gospel'? In other words, we must engage in a search for the genre* of the Gospels.

If the study of the word 'gospel' shows a linear development, the study of the genre of the Gospels appears at first sight to be essentially circular. Initially, parallels were sought within biographical literature, only for such comparisons to be denied explicitly throughout the middle of this century; however, biographical answers have come back into vogue in recent years. Justin Martyr provides the first recorded example of such a view with his description of the Gospels as 'memoirs' (*apomnēmoneumata*) of the apostles (e.g. I *Apology* 66). This description echoes the title of Xenophon's work on Socrates, the *Memorabilia*, and suggests that the Gospels belong within the sphere of historical and biographical writings. The Gospels were interpreted in a similar manner right up to the turn of this century.

The nineteenth-century 'lives' of Jesus used the Gospels as biographical sources in their portrayal of Jesus. Ernest Rénan relied on them for his *Vie de Jésus* (1863), likening them in his introduction to 'legendary biographies' such as those of the saints, heroes or philosophers. A similar approach was adopted by C. W. Votaw in *American Journal of Theology* 19 (1915) where he suggested that they are like 'popular biographies', designed more to acquaint the reader generally with the subject than to provide critical or historical analysis. Thus, he compared the Gospels with works on Apollonius of Tyana (*c.* AD 10–97), Epictetus (*c.* AD 50–130) and especially those by Plato and Xenophon on Socrates (469–399 BC).

The development of form-critical* approaches to the Gospels in the 1920s changed all this. The focus of attention was turned away from the evangelists* themselves and their finished products to the pre-literary oral* transmission of the individual units of the Gospels, or *pericopae*. Crucial to this approach was the idea that the Gospels were folk literature, not to be compared with classical literary works; and the Gospel writers were seen as popular storytellers or mere stenographers responsible solely for writing down the oral material as it came to them from the tradition. Thus any questions about the 'writtenness' of the Gospels, such as their genre or the authors' intentions, were simply not possible. So Rudolf Bultmann* concluded that there are no parallels or analogies to the Gospels within contemporary literature; they have none of the features one might expect from a biography, such as description of Jesus' human personality, psychological development or character. In fact, according to Bultmann, they are unique from a literary point of view, *sui generis*; and this became the consensus view of critical scholarship for the next fifty years.

There are, however, major problems with such an approach to the interpretation of the Gospels. The sharp distinction of 'folk literature' from other literary products is problematic; the concentration on the individual units meant that the significance of the Gospels as wholes was ignored (*see* **Holistic Interpretation**); and the stress on the oral tradition led to the almost total eclipse of the evangelists as authors. Further, there are severe difficulties from the point of view of literary* theory with the suggestion that any work is *sui generis*; how can anyone produce something totally unique, and how can anyone else then make sense of it?

Thus the critique of form criticism which went on in the 1960s, and the rise of redaction criticism,* led to a reopening of literary questions about the Gospels. Redaction criticism stressed the importance of seeing the four Gospel writers as individuals, each with his own creative theological purposes. Given this view of the evangelists, questions about their creative literary intentions, including the question of genre, could not be far behind. In the last twenty years or so, many different attempts have been made to solve the problem of the genre of the Gospels, though to date none has won total, or even widespread, support.

M. Hadas and M. Smith suggested that the Gospels were a form of aretalogy,* defined as an ancient type of biography portraying the career of an impressive teacher or miracle* worker, often called a 'divine man'. J. M. Robinson and H. Koester had similar ideas, though, here at least, their concept of the gospel 'trajectory'* was an attempt to get away from rigid and static notions of the gospel genre: it underwent development even within the NT period. Unfortunately, the lack of any real examples of aretalogy together with difficulties over the description of the 'divine men' rendered this attempt unsuccessful.

Others sought to find parallels between the Gospels and Jewish literature, within either the OT or the rabbinic* corpus. Michael Goulder put forward the suggestion that the Gospels were lectionaries,* designed to be read in sections in worship through the year, and composed according to the principles of Midrash.* This too has been less than compelling, and research into rabbinic literature only demonstrates the absence of anything like the Gospels as whole books, even though there are parallels for individual units of tradition.

Attempts to place the Gospels within the web of contemporary Graeco-Roman literature have been made chiefly in America over recent years. Practically every Graeco-Roman genre has been proposed for the Gospels at some stage, but the most common approach has been to re-examine the genre of biography – and so the wheel has come full circle with the same works now being proposed as parallels as were suggested a century ago. C. H. Talbert has investigated various classical parallels as well as providing a thorough critique of Bultmann's *sui generis* idea. Philip Shuler proposed the genre of 'encomium or laudatory biography', and then attempted to fit Matthew into it; though whether the genre actually exists is debatable. By far the best attempt to locate the Gospels in their literary environment is that of David Aune, who sees them as a sub-type of Graeco-Roman biography, except for Luke–Acts which is 'general history' because of its two-volume nature.

The picture is thus one of an apparent circle, as the Gospels are being once again considered by a number of scholars as some form of biography. Of course, it is not really the case that we are back where we were a century ago. All that has been considered along the way must be borne in mind, such as the benefits of form criticism, even if conclusions like the *sui generis* idea are now seen as erroneous. The sheer breadth and diversity of recent suggestions for the genre of the Gospels, together with the lack of any consensus, implies that the techniques of biblical interpretation will not solve this problem on their own. Many of the proposals are severely flawed in their understanding of one or both of two areas, namely critical literary theory of genres and the development of first-century literature.

Accordingly, a new methodology must be sought through the medium of inter-disciplinary study of gospel criticism, genre theory and literary development. When this is done, it can be seen that the understanding of genre used by many NT critics is inadequate. Notions of unique, *sui generis* works springing fully fledged from an oral tradition are not feasible, but neither are the rigid, static genres defined by one or two generic features, as proposed by scholars like Schuler. Comprehensive study of genre, including insights from structuralists* and other modern theorists, shows that genre is a dynamic and flexible set of expectations which form a kind of contract or code between author and reader; thus proper appreciation of a work's genre is necessary for valid interpretation of it to take place. In order to ascertain the genre of the Gospels, it will be necessary to examine them in the light of the whole range of generic features and compare the results of this with a similar examination of other examples of the proposed genre.

Equally, literature contemporary with the Gospels must be further examined for possible analogies. Since genre is identified by both form and content, it will be important that a wide variety of features (such as structure, size, subject, purpose, etc.) is compared, in order to avoid the facile parallelomania which arises all too easily from identifying one or two points of contact between the Gospels and some other works. Ancient biography is a broad and flexible form of literature with various recognizable examples surviving, even if it is difficult to define the genre precisely. It is a sensible place to start looking for the genre of the Gospels, if only because of the enormous impact the figure of Jesus has upon the Gospels. Close analysis shows the way he dominates the action and content, as well as the structure of their actual language. If it can be shown that similar features occur regularly in a wide range of ancient *Lives*, then this would go some way towards establishing the biographical genre of the Gospels, with all that this would entail for their interpretation.

David Aune, *The New Testament in its Literary Environment*, 1987; P. L. Shuler, *A Genre for the Gospels*, 1982; C. H. Talbert, *What is a Gospel?*, 1977.

RICHARD A. BURRIDGE

Habakkuk

Habakkuk is one of the most puzzling books in the OT. It is a complexly edited book whose structure of laments, oracle * and vision, collection of woe oracles, and a formal prayer with performance rubrics is titled 'oracle' (*maśā'*), a form frequently used for oracles against foreign nations. The prophet * to whom this congeries of forms is attributed is uncertainly named, as Habakkuk in the Masoretic text,* but Ambakoum in the Septuagint.* The complex redactional ploys in the book have rendered it almost incoherent as a book and it has a long history of discrete interpretative analysis in the modern period (cf. Jöcken).

Nothing is known about Habakkuk the prophet: he appears in the 'Bel and the Dragon' (*see* **Apocrypha**) episode in the additions to Daniel, and *The Lives of the Prophets* (12.1) makes him a Simeonite. The earliest interpretation of the book appears in the Qumran community where a *pesher* * commentary on the text has been found (*see* **Dead Sea Scrolls**). It is essentially a midrashic * reading of Habakkuk in the light of the community's times and experiences, but is also an invaluable guide to how texts were read in the late Second Temple period (cf. Brownlee). The line in 2.4b, 'the righteous one shall live by his (LXX my) faith-(fulness)', is famous because of its use by Paul in Rom. 1.17; Gal. 3.11 (cf. Heb. 10.38) in the context of his teaching concerning justification. It also appears in the Babylonian Talmud * as the final reduction of the 613 precepts of Moses * to the one principle of faith (*Makkoth* 24a).

Nothing in the text permits an accurate dating of either the book or of any of its parts. Many modern exegetes favour a dating between 626 and 587 because of the reference to the Chaldaeans (*kaśdîm*) in 1.6 and the lack of any sense of Jerusalem's destruction in 587. This interpretation of *kaśdîm* is one of the central interpretative problems in the modern study of Habakkuk. If the *kaśdîm* are the Babylonians then the original enemy would be the Assyrians (cf. Isa. 10.5–19), but the complex editing of the book makes this a less likely solution than many commentators imagine. Duhm * emended it to *kittîm*, an inspired anticipation of the Qumran interpretation of the meaning of *kaśdîm*, and related the allusion to the campaign of Alexander the Great after the battle of Issus in 333. Independently of him C. C. Torrey * also argued for the prophecy of Habakkuk as a meditation on the conquests of Alexander and emended *kaśdîm* to *kittîm* accordingly. The use of *kaśdîm* in the text would therefore reflect an archaizing technique and suggests a midrashic * use of conventional biblical phrases which points to a late date for Habakkuk. Neither Duhm nor Torrey has been followed by many scholars, though even

Childs (p. 453) allows the possibility of 'a literary layer of post-exilic material'.

The diversity and complexity of analysis of Habakkuk demonstrates the puzzling aspects of the text as now constituted. Its internal tensions defeat coherent exegesis and the theological overview of Childs has the virtue of imposing on the text a meaning hardly derived from a reading of the text. Habakkuk is an excellent book for demonstrating the extreme problems of all conventional analyses of prophetic texts. As a ragbag of traditional elements held together by vision and prayer Habakkuk illustrates the way prophetic books have been put together in an apparently slapdash fashion. Only the situational and transformational analysis of a Qumran community can give coherent meaning to the text!

See also **Prophets and Prophecy.**

W. H. Brownlee, *The Midrash Pesher of Habakkuk*, 1979; B. S. Childs, *Introduction to the Old Testament as Scripture*, 1979, pp. 447–56; B. Duhm, *Das Buch Habakuk*, 1906; G. Fohrer, *Introduction to the Old Testament*, 1970, pp. 451–6; P. Jöcken, *Das Buch Habakuk*, 1977; C. C. Torrey, 'The Prophecy of Habakkuk' in *Jewish Studies in Memory of George A. Kohut*, 1935, pp. 565–82.

ROBERT P. CARROLL

Haggai

The post-exilic prophets (Haggai, Zechariah, Malachi) have not always been highly regarded. Their emphasis on the temple and its ritual worship has been contrasted unfavourably with the ethical teaching and attacks on outward ritualism delivered by the pre-exilic prophets. A characteristic verdict is that of W. Neil writing of the oracles of Haggai: '. . . they represent a sad decline from the ethical vigour and conviction of those pre-exilic prophets. Haggai's chief concern is the re-establishment of the cultus, the shell rather than the kernel' (*IDB*, 1962, Vol 2, pp. 510f.). Perhaps such a view, expressed also in relative critical neglect of these prophets, owed much to the views of J. Wellhausen who in 1878 wrote of the development of post-exilic Judaism, 'It no longer has its roots in childlike impulse, it is a dead work . . .'

Nearer our own time a growing recognition of the value of the cult * as a lively and valid expression of religious devotion and the close ties of at least some of the pre-exilic prophets to the cult has led to a re-evaluation of the work of the post-exilic prophets. A pioneer in this has been P. R. Ackroyd (*Exile and Restoration*, 1968) and a contemporary bibliography now shows a number of significant commentaries on these books.

It has long been recognized that the material

in the book is of two kinds, the oracles of Haggai and third-person description of his preaching and the response it evoked, the so-called 'editorial framework' (1.1, 3, 12, 13a, 15; 2.1, 2, 4f., 10, 20). In 1896 Klostermann suggested that the book of Haggai together with Zech. 1–8 represented an account of the building of the temple edited by Zechariah, a view which has surfaced again in slightly different form in the commentary by C. L. and E. M. Meyers (1987), who maintain that 'Haggai and the first eight chapters of the canonical book of Zechariah belong together as a composite work' (p. xliv), and the rather different view of D. L. Petersen (1984) that the book of Haggai belongs to the genre of a 'chronicle' or 'history narrative' much like some sections of the book of Jeremiah. In 1967 W. A. M. Beuken examined the 'editorial framework' and concluded that it emerged from circles similar to those from which Chronicles came. His work was supplemented by R. A. Mason (summarized in his commentary, 1977, pp. 8–10). While Mason believed the final form of the book was nearer to the time of Haggai, both agreed that it represented an attempt to show that the prophet's hopes for the future were already finding a valid if as yet only partial fulfilment in the emergence of the post-exilic temple theocracy presided over by the priestly line, through whom the blessing of the presence of God in the temple was mediated to the people. A very different view of the book is that of P. D. Hanson (*The Dawn of Apocalyptic*, 1975), who saw Haggai and Zechariah as standing in the 'theocratic' line of Ezekiel more concerned with the re-establishment of Zadokite priestly power than the 'otherworldly' hopes of Second Isaiah and later 'apocalyptic'* visionaries.

Varied as all these interpretations are, they all suggest a much livelier and more positive assessment of Haggai's contribution to the religious life and experience of his time than was customary in the earlier works referred to at the beginning of this article.

See also **Prophets and Prophecy; Zechariah.**

J. Baldwin, *Haggai, Zechariah, Malachi*, 1972; R. J. Coggins, *Haggai, Zechariah, Malachi*, 1987; R. A. Mason, *The Books of Haggai, Zechariah and Malachi*, 1977.

REX MASON

Harmony

The three Synoptic Gospels are interrelated (*see* **Synoptic Problem**). Whichever of the conflicting current hypotheses we accept as the best interpretation of the fact, it is clear that in certain details they differ even in the description of events and the wording of sayings which they have in common. This might be due to differences of information of source, or to differences of theology or redactional* tendency. The Fourth Gospel may or may not have been composed with knowledge of one or more of the Synoptics: debate goes this way and that, but whichever view is right, we have the same options of explanation, which are not mutually exclusive.

The resultant situation is one of divergent testimony, sometimes in great matters such as the duration of the ministry of Jesus, and the placing within it of a crucial event such as the cleansing of the temple. Sometimes events are similar but not identical, such as the anointings of Jesus in the various Gospels. Sometimes the same event is differently described, as the healing of the centurion's servant in Matthew and Luke.

Our approach to these phenomena is analytical, whether we incline to seek historical fact* or theological interpretation in the Gospels. But the unsophisticated even of our day will seek another resolution of the implicit problems, namely in assuming the unity of the tradition and consequently harmonizing discrepancies. In this they are in line with antiquity. It would appear that some, if not all, Gospels circulated separately immediately after their composition, but very soon we can discern from quotation and allusion that more than one is known to a particular author. By the end of the second century, the concept of 'the four-fold gospel' is a theological commonplace to the extent that Irenaeus* of Lyons, in a well-known passage (*Against the Heresies*, 3.11, 7 & 8), compares this necessary four-foldness with the four-foldness of earth, with its 'corners' and 'winds', and the four-foldness of heaven, where four creatures bear up the divine throne. God breathes upon his church from four quarters, which are the Gospels.

It would seem that we have an earlier witness to this concept in the specific harmonization of the Gospels into a unified literary whole by Tatian. This activity was mentioned by Eusebius* (*Ecc. Hist.* 4,30,6), who says that the title *Dia Tessarōn* was given to the finished product. Victor of Capua, in his preface to the harmonized form of the Gospels in the sixth-century Latin MS. Codex Fuldensis, uses Eusebius' reference, but gives the title *Dia Pente* to the finished work. These two terms Diatessaron (by means of four) and Diapente (by means of five) are technical terms of Greek musical theory, and either can indicate the perfect harmony. If the term Diapente was original, it may have a further indication, namely that Tatian was using not only the four Gospels but a fifth source. There are in fact some slight traces in the literary remains of his work of what we should term apocryphal material, the most striking being probably the shining of a light upon the Jordan following Jesus' baptism. Eusebius seems not to have seen a copy, and very little has survived in Greek. We have a fragment from the third century, from the border fortress of Dura Europos on the Euphrates. Our chief evidence is from Eastern sources, especially the commentary upon the Concordant Gospel (= Diatessaron) by the fourth century Ephrem the Syrian, and an Arabic translation, made from Syriac* in the eleventh century. There are many other traces in Eastern Christian sources. In the West, there are a number of Gospel harmonies, which share many common features with the Eastern witnesses, but differ in other respects. It is a matter of debate whether we should take these as direct evidence for Tatian's work: some scholars work directly from them, others proceed with great caution.

Using the Prologue, Tatian begins with John, and follows John rather than the Synoptics when confronted with choices between explicit historical-chronological statements. But in a matter such as the cleansing of the temple, he follows the synoptics. He follows in general the order of Matthew for the ministry, but it is John's passion narrative* that he adopts where there are differences. The Dura Europos fragment is from the end of the account, treating the action of Joseph of Arimathea in burying Jesus: it shows a very careful interweaving of the detail of distinct accounts. In the main body of the gospel story he neglects Luke, and there is no trace of the Lucan prologue, which suggests that the neglect was deliberate. In R. M. Grant's judgment, Tatian proceeded as a historian who 'relied on the tradition of the priority of the apostolic Matthew to the sub-apostolic Mark and Luke, and ... treated John as an apostolic writer who arranged his Gospel for symbolic purposes ... He was concerned not with what the evangelists may have meant but with what they reported.'

The popular piety of the Middle Ages in the West (see Mediaeval Interpretation) and the Eastern churches nourished itself on the Life of Jesus, and many of the gospel harmonies owed a great deal to the Diatessaron, either directly or indirectly. The earliest periods of the printed book also saw a number of Gospel harmonies produced, although it is not clear whether these were related to their mediaeval forerunners. A number of modern Lives of Jesus and dramatic adaptations of the gospel story, such as Dorothy L. Sayers' radio play series The Man Born to be King, are strongly harmonistic.

As an aspect of unsophisticated Christian culture, the production and use of harmonies seems to derive from three sources. It represents an answer to the problem of the fourfoldness of the tradition, with its resultant conflicts, without recourse to academic subtlety (at least without resort to the complexity of learned presentation). It holds up a single Jesus, drawing on all the aspects of the four Gospels' presentation, generally depicting him both as an object of devotion and a model for imitation. The inclusion of elements not from the canonical Gospels fills in the gaps about childhood, early maturity and later motivation, and generally seeks to give a picture of the man Jesus. While not much favoured, or even studied, in circles of academic biblical scholarship, the harmony will almost certainly continue to survive.

See also **Inspiration.**

R. M. Grant, *The Earliest Lives of Jesus*, 1961; C. H. Kraeling, *A Greek Fragment of Tatian's Diatessaron from Dura* (Studies and Documents III), 1935.

J. NEVILLE BIRDSALL

Harnack, A. von

Adolf von Harnack (1851–1930), a disciple of Ritschl, was the leading exponent of liberal Protestantism at the turn of the century (*see* **Liberalism**). He taught at Leipzig, Giessen and Marburg before being called to Berlin in 1888. His views brought him into regular conflict with the church. The call to Berlin, for example, was opposed by the supreme council of the Evangelical Church, but it was upheld by Bismarck's cabinet and the Emperor. Despite ecclesiastical hostility Harnack exerted an immense influence. He was a prolific author, notably in the field of early church history and the development of doctrine. He was the personification of *Kulturprotestantismus*. His fame was not confined to academic circles, and when he retired from his Berlin professorship in 1921 he could have become the German ambassador to Washington.

The liberal Protestants saw in the new science, history, the opportunity to establish the Christian faith on a firm foundation. Their famous 'quest of the historical Jesus'* was prompted by the wish to discover Jesus 'as he really was', before the faith of the church transformed him into the 'biblical Christ'. The presupposition of liberal Protestantism was that, if only the real Jesus could be recovered, he would certainly prove to be full of meaning and value for the present. But this assumption supplied a motive other than disinterested historical enquiry, and it is not surprising that between the lines of the liberal accounts of Jesus the religious viewpoint of their authors can be discerned. Their overriding desire was to speak to their age.

Harnack shared fully this apologetic concern. His *magnum opus* was his *History of Dogma*, in which he argued that dogma was 'a work of the Greek spirit on the ground of the gospel'. The original gospel was corrupted by the appropriation of alien metaphysical concepts from the church's Hellenistic* environment. The same theme was taken up in *Das Wesen des Christentums*, a course of public lectures delivered in the winter of 1899–1900, translated into English as *What is Christianity?* It is often said that according to Harnack the essential teaching of Jesus is about the fatherhood of God as the basis for the brotherhood of man, but so bare a summary is seriously misleading. The teaching of Jesus is in fact summarized under three heads: the kingdom of God* and its coming; God the Father and the infinite value of the human soul; and the higher righteousness and the command of love. Harnack does not maintain that the kingdom is brought about by human effort. 'The kingdom of God comes by coming to the individual, by entering into his soul and laying hold of it. True, the kingdom of God is the rule of God; but it is the rule of the holy God in the hearts of individuals; it is God himself in his power.' As for the relation of Jesus himself to the gospel, 'he desired no other belief in his person and no other attachment to it than is contained in the keeping of his commandments'. 'The gospel, as Jesus proclaimed it, has to do with the Father only and not with the Son.' The uniqueness of Jesus is not an ontological uniqueness. A key text for Harnack is Matt. 11.27. 'Jesus is convinced that he knows God in a way in which no one ever knew him before', and it is his vocation to reveal and communicate this knowledge to others. Jesus' own place in the gospel is as 'its personal realization and its strength'.

In his NT criticism Harnack adopted conservative positions. In *Luke the Physician* and *The Acts of the Apostles*, for example, he argued for the traditional authorship and the general accuracy of Luke-Acts. But he believed that the time had come for Protestantism to reject the OT as a canonical document. In a study of Marcion* he stated that its retention in the sixteenth century was a fate which the Reformation* had not been able to avert; its conservation any longer was 'the result of a religious and ecclesiastical paralysis' (*see* **Christian Interpretation of the Old Testament**).

Towards the end of his life Harnack joined in public debate with Karl Barth.* In 1920 they were the platform speakers at a student conference, when Harnack found Barth's address incomprehensible. In 1923 he posed 'fifteen questions to the despisers of scientific theology' in the pages of *Christliche Welt*. A correspondence ensued. The fundamental differ-

ence between them concerned their evaluation of man's cultural and ethical achievement. For Barth, 'the gospel has as much and as little to do with barbarism as with culture'; for Harnack, this is 'a radical denial of every valuable understanding of God within the history of man's thought and ethics'. According to Barth, God is utterly other than man and only he can reveal himself, and 'the task of theology is at one with the task of preaching'; according to Harnack, if 'historical knowledge and critical reflection' are disdained, the gospel is in danger of being 'given over into the hands of devotional preachers who freely create their own understanding of the Bible and who set up their own dominion'.

The theological pendulum swung against liberal Protestantism. Its doctrine of man came to seem too optimistic, its doctrine of God insufficiently radical. And its picture of the Jesus of history, which it believed had been secured by historical criticism,* was increasingly attacked by means of the same historical criticism. Nevertheless, it is probably still the case, as Rudolf Bultmann* wrote in his introduction to a new edition of *What of Christianity?*, that 'the popular understanding of the Christian faith ... accords in some measure with the portrait drawn by Harnack, even if it does not achieve his earnestness and subtlety'. Whatever criticisms we may wish to make, we should recognize that Christianity as Harnack presents it belongs to the tradition of inwardness: it is 'eternal life in the midst of time, by the strength and under the eyes of God'.

G. W. Glick, *The Reality of Christianity: A Study of Adolf von Harnack as Historian and Theologian*, 1967; V. A. Harvey, *The Historian and the Believer*, 1967; W. Pauck, *Harnack and Troeltsch: Two Historical Theologians*, 1968; B. M. G. Reardon, *Liberal Protestantism*, 1968; H. M. Rumscheidt, *Revelation and Theology: An Analysis of the Barth–Harnack Correspondence of 1923*, 1972.

BRIAN G. POWLEY

Hastings, J.

James Hastings was born in 1852, just nine years after the inception of the Free Church of Scotland to which his parents belonged. After attending Aberdeen Old Grammar School and university, he studied at the city's Free Church College from 1877. Brought up in a traditional Free Church background, he thus received his theological education at precisely the time when the church was embroiled in the impeachment of Robertson Smith* over his espousal of continental critical methodology. It was Hastings' contention that Christianity had nothing to fear from judicious scholarship, and that confidence would be restored if the work of the scholars were fully understood. Consequently, it became his objective to mediate the outcomes of moderate scholarship to churchmen and laity alike. This objective he pursued both personally through his pastoral ministry (at Kinneff, Dundee and St Cyrus), and, as he saw it, vicariously, through the ministries of those enlightened by the publications he edited, among them *The Expository Times* (1889–), the *Dictionary of the Bible* (1898–1904), and the *Encyclopaedia of Religion and Ethics* (1908–1921). It was therefore appropriate that, in 1913, he was awarded the Dyke Acland medal for his work in popularizing biblical research.

An evangelical commitment to the continuing relevance of the Bible pervaded his thinking. While eschewing speculative 'advanced' criticism, he held with Robertson Nicoll that 'all true criticism [was] preparing the Bible for a renewed reign', and, it was said, aimed in his editorial work to give the pulpit a greater power by enriching it with knowledge-encouraging preaching which, while taking full cognizance of recent research, remained essentially orthodox. 'The old methods,' he remarked, 'have passed away, but the doctrines of grace have been left on a surer foundation than ever.' He was concerned that a common perception among educated people that the core facts* of the gospel were in dispute even among the clergy was leading them to regard the Christian message as irrelevant, and contended that, if such scepticism were to be overcome, the church must affirm that biblical scholarship was establishing, not undermining, the essential facts of Christianity.

Similarly, the chief motivation for the *Encyclopaedia* was his belief that the study of comparative religion had hitherto been monopolized by those antagonistic towards Christianity: he aimed to demonstrate that such study enriched rather than diminished the Christian faith. He considered that, to be complete, the examination of any doctrine must take into account the various 'manifestations of that doctrine in the religious life of the world'. These manifestations, far from being 'versions' or 'perversions' of the Christian doctrine were, he claimed, 'parts of the complete doctrine', which could be traced until they attained what he called a 'purification' or 'new birth' in the transcendent Christianity. Such study would result in a vision of Christ altogether 'larger, fuller'.

By the time Hastings died in 1922, his views were widely accepted in the UK and America, and his obituarists were unanimous in according him a not inconsiderable proportion of the credit for this acceptance.

John A. H. Dempster, '"Incomparable Encyclopaedist": The Life and Work of Dr James Hastings', *ET*, Vol. 100, pp. 4–8 October 1988. E. R. Micklem, 'James Hastings', *Dictionary of National Biography 1922–30*, 1937, pp. 409f.;

JOHN A. H. DEMPSTER

Hebrews

Hebrews lacks an epistolary opening, though it does contain an epistolary style final chapter (*see* **Epistle**). The author himself describes it as a *logos paraklēseōs*, 'a word of exhortation' (or 'encouragement') (13.20). Probably written not long before AD 70, it contains no reference, amid all the allusions to the Levitical cultus, to the Jerusalem Temple. It is an early example of a Christian thinker's theology, within which christology* plays a crucial part, constructed upon the only scriptures Christianity possessed at that time, the OT. Of the author of this Christian interpretation and application of the OT we know neither the name nor the place where he wrote. As for his readers, it is almost certain that they were Jewish Christians on the brink of lapsing into their original Jewish beliefs (*see* **Jewish Christianity**).

It was to dissuade them from doing this that the unknown author attempted to build a Christian theology, and especially a christology, upon the OT. For the OT was regarded by him and his readers as God's word,* by nature prophetic and reaching its culmination in the Word which God spoke to mankind in a Son (1.1). Such a climax was to be expected, for, in the author's view, the OT prefigured a consummation beyond itself. The opening words, which have a Johannine ring, contain a description of the Son as the agent of creation, as the reflection of the divine glory, and as the one who 'bears the very stamp of his nature'. They also credit him with making 'purification of sins'. Then, possibly because too much reverence was being shown by his readers to angels, the author embarks upon a lengthy comparison between the angels and Jesus. Ps. 2.7 and II Sam. 7.14 are interpreted to mean that no angel, and indeed no other being, is a son in the same sense that Christ is (cf. 4.14). Using a series of quotations, mainly from the Psalms, the author seeks to establish the superiority of the Son, now risen, ascended, and seated at God's right hand, waiting for the subjection to him of all his enemies. In one verse (1.8), the Son through whom God had earlier been said to have spoken his final word ('in these last days'), is presented as the one addressed in the words 'Thy throne, O God, is for ever and ever' (Ps. 45.6). This and other features of the descriptions of the Son used by the author of Hebrews to set forth his christology may indicate that he was interpreting OT language as implying a Logos* christology (cf. 2.2, where even the law is said to be the 'message' [*logos*] delivered by angels), though the word Logos is never directly applied to the Son, unless it is in 5.12–13.

Not only is the Son shown to be superior to angels, he is also shown, on the basis of Ps. 110.4, applied to him in, e.g., 5.6 to be superior to the Jewish Levitical priests and high priests. He is the supreme 'mediator' (9.15) of Jeremiah's new covenant;* he is the 'forerunner' (6.20) who has gone ahead into the heavenly Jerusalem* and is now 'exalted above the heavens' (7.26; cf. 9.12 and 9.24). He is (9.24) in 'heaven itself'. He is the perfect high priest ('made perfect for ever', 7.28), and has offered the perfect sacrifice. 10.4 declares emphatically that no animal sacrifice can remove sin. What the author argues, in 10.5ff., using Ps. 40.6–8, is that Christ came into the world to achieve within an authentic human life, 'a body', perfect obedience to the will of God. What had been said to be impossible by means of animal sacrifices, has been achieved, according to the author, by Christ's bodily sacrifice of himself. The single sacrifice (see 10.12; 9.2ff.; 9.11ff.; and 9.26ff.) offered was himself, his martyrdom on the cross, described in an OT fashion as 'his own blood' (9.12). The 'purification of sins' referred to in 1.1 had been accomplished and he also inaugurated the new covenant forecast in Jer. 31.31f., cf., 8.8–12. So, the author argues that the priestly ministry of Jesus was superior to the Levitical ministry and the covenant he mediated was superior to anything it had to offer. He has finally put sin away, he now exercises his ministry for us in God's immediate presence (see 9.24), and he will return one day 'to save those who are eagerly waiting for him' (7.28). As a priest for ever, after the order of Melchizedek (Ps. 110.4; cf. 5.6), he is a permanent high priest, who 'continues for ever' (7.24), always able to save (7.25). The author bases his interpretation in part on the fact that in the light of Ps. 110 (cf. 7.3), Melchizedek was made, like the eternal Son of God, an eternal priest.

What Hebrews says about faith is also an extension of an OT theme into the author's Christian theology. The definition of faith in 11.1 is based upon his knowledge of Abraham* and the other Jewish patriarchs, together with the ancient heroes and martyrs. Linked with this interpretation of faith is an understanding of the life of the believer as a pilgrimage towards the heavenly Jerusalem, like Abraham's journey (11.8; cf. the description of the life of faith in 11.13). It should not, however, be overlooked that one of the transmutations of OT ideas that the author executes is involved in his belief that, though

a pilgrim, the believer has, in part, reached the goal (12.22). A Jewish notion is transformed by the interpretation of it in terms of the author's realized eschatology.*

The Letter to the Hebrews represents a sophisticated and successful attempt by an early and learned Christian theologian to explain the significance of Jesus in terms both of his continuity with Judaism and also of the consummation of major elements in Judaism, especially its priesthood and sacrificial system, in his life, death, and resurrection. The author is one of the earliest Christian OT exegetes. For him Christianity is not so much a new religion outside the Jewish fold as the culmination and completion of Judaism's history, hopes and faith.

One of the important contributions to the history of biblical interpretation made by Hebrews has to do with the differences of opinion which occurred in the early church about its apostolicity. Eastern Christianity accepted the epistle as apostolic (Pauline) earlier than the Western church, but later the West as a whole accepted this view. At the Reformation,* Luther* and Calvin* both questioned it so that, although it was a tiny step, the door was opening to a new era of critical scholarship in which traditional views were questioned and sometimes rejected.

The Fathers in general made much use of Hebrews, and variously contributed to its interpretation. Chrysostom was the first, in a series of homilies, to undertake a systematic exegesis of the epistle. His exegesis uses Johannine language of the incarnation of the Logos. On 4.15 he comments that the word 'likeness' was used because Christ's likeness was to our human flesh, but not to human sin – he assumed our flesh but not our sinfulness. Attention was drawn by him to the epistle's stress on Christ's unimpaired and real humanity, but he also tended to regard the divine in Christ as overruling the human and at times overlooked his temptations and sufferings.

Origen* expressed the doubts felt in the early church about the authorship of Hebrews in his famous statement, 'who wrote the epistle, God alone knows the truth'. In a passage on Christ as a priest after the order of Melchizedek, he makes the important point that it is only to God that man prays, 'but not apart from the high priest'. A particularly interesting passage in Origen occurs in the *Dialogue with Heraclides*, where he quotes 2.9 in the form 'apart from God' (Christ's death thus shows that God alone has immortality). Elsewhere, however, when the other reading ('us') suits his argument, he cites the commoner variant 'by the grace of God'. He cites a number of passages, including Ps. 45.7 (in 1.9), to demonstrate that Christ had no sense of sin, though he did have a rational soul (with its power to choose between good and evil). That soul was 'anointed' by God, and so *christos*.

Origen combines the description of the Son as the 'invisible image' (Col. 1.15) with the words of 1.3, 'the brightness of his glory and the express image of his person', and he devotes a whole section to discussing how there can be, as 1.3 implies, 'another figure of that person besides the person of God himself'. He describes the Son as the Logos and deals with 1.3a by using the analogy of a gigantic statue filling the universe, so large that no one could see it, and another one identical to it in appearance but on a smaller scale. So even though the brightness of God is something that man cannot look upon, men are able to look upon it in Christ. In his *Contra Celsum* he claims that in view of 1.3 he who has seen the Son has seen 'in him who is the image of God, God himself'.

There is a hint that, like Chrysostom, Origen regarded the christology of Hebrews as a Logos christology. The words of his quotation from the *Acts of Paul* in *De Principiis* I.2.3 appear to be suggested by the words of 4.12, and, together with John 1.1, affirm that the Word had no beginning since the Father has always been a Father. Elsewhere Origen uses 1.3 to assert the eternity of the Son – the Son is the splendour of the everlasting light which could never exist without splendour. Tertullian * employs texts from Hebrews in the construction of his christology, in his criticism of Marcion,* and in his critique of the claims of Judaism. For him the two-edged sword in 4.12 is Christ, 'the Divine Word of God'. In *De pudicitia* he bases on 6.1ff. the view that there is no second repentance for 'the adulterer and fornicator'. He concludes that Barnabas was the author of Hebrews, and he attacks the heresy of Theodotus who said that Christ was born of the Holy Spirit and the Virgin, but was inferior to Melchizedek.

Cyril of Alexandria placed great emphasis on the divinity of Christ and attributed his priesthood to his humanity, but, he said, only his possession of divinity enabled him to make expiation of sins. Ambrosiaster omitted Hebrews from his Pauline commentaries, but this did not stop him from alluding to it. In his comments on I Tim. 1.3 he draws an analogy between the chain of faith which linked Timothy, his mother and his grandmother and the view stated in Hebrews that Levi was still 'in the loins' of his ancestor when Melchizedek greeted him.

Jerome saw the importance for the author of Hebrews of the psalter which, in its entirety, he says, 'sings in prophecy of our Lord'. Christ for him had spoken previously by the prophets, but spoke, in his earthly life, in person. Great stress is placed on the theme of the heavenly pilgrimage of the believer – 'the saints in this present world are but pilgrims on earth', hastening with all the soul's ardour to Paradise.

The Reformation produced two great commentators on Hebrews, the leading Reformers themselves. One of Luther's contributions to the interpretation of Hebrews, which he regarded as giving chiefly a thorough scriptural exposition of the High Priesthood of Christ, was his inspired suggestion that Apollos, described in Acts 18 as a man 'learned in the scriptures', was the author. But just as he described James as 'a strawy epistle', so he detected in Hebrews the same kind of theological straw and hay (cf. I Cor. 3.12). Nevertheless, the author had gained much from the apostles and was a learned OT scholar, though Luther compares the teaching of Hebrews unfavourably with that of Paul,* lacking as it does the doctrine of justification by grace apart from works through faith.

Calvin noted the lack of good commentaries on Hebrews, which he described as 'altogether divine', and proceeded to supply one. On the authorship question, he states that he could find no reason to attribute it to Paul. His commentary consists of detailed, verse by verse exegesis, in the style of a modern commentary (and is still useful to the student).

The end of the nineteenth century saw the appearance, in 1889, of one of the still great commentaries, that by B. F. Westcott.* It sees the 'ruling thought' of Hebrews as Christ's high priesthood. It presents Christ as able to perform that task perfectly because he was perfectly Son of Man and Son of God. Christ, Westcott argues, was a 'natural priest', seeking to create harmony, and a 'theocratic priest', mediating between man and God. Christ had fulfilled the Aaronic priesthood through the offering of his life and his entry into God's presence where he also fulfilled the royal high priesthood of Melchizedek, a type of 'a universal priesthood'. As such a high priest, he represents men to God and God to men, offering the believer's prayers to God and guaranteeing access to him. In an interesting comment, which reveals his personal stance, Westcott notes that the 'modern conception' of Christ pleading his passion in heaven and offering his blood there is not present in Hebrews.

Alexander Nairne, in his *The Epistle of Priesthood* (1913), like several other writers, concentrates on the subject of Christ's priesthood. Nairne interprets the incarnation as the perfect sacrament of the divine and therefore Christ's priesthood as that of one who partook of flesh and blood in order, as a priest, to bring men to God. Great stress is placed on the expressions of the idea of access to God which punctuate the epistle. Christ's priesthood is described as a 'natural priesthood', eternal and based on a world-wide ancestry. The main image of the epistle is said to be a Christ perfected 'for the purpose of continual onward process'. The sacrifice of Christ is repeated, but only in the sense that in each believer when he offers himself to God in Christ and in the worship offered in the eucharist the sacrifice avails again.

Among many other twentieth-century commentaries is that by Ernst Käsemann, ET *The Wandering People of God*, 1984. It is a work of special importance. The author argues that behind Hebrews is an underlying gnostic* mysticism* and the concept of a heavenly pilgrimage of the Christian community. The epistle's eschatological goal is for Käsemann a reality located in the future, for 'man possesses the Gospel here on earth only as promise'. G. W. Buchanan's commentary (in the Anchor Bible) puts forward the view that Hebrews was written to a monastic community in Jerusalem. The method of scriptural exegesis that most influenced the author was that of the rabbis,* and Buchanan draws heavily on this in his own exegesis. An unusual conclusion reached, in the exegesis of 7.27, is that Jesus was not wholly sinless but had to offer a sacrifice for his own sins as well as for those of the people. The humanity of Jesus, according to the view put forward in this commentary, involved his proneness to sin, his temptations, and his own experience of sinfulness.

Robert Jewett has devoted his work on Hebrews, *Letter to Pilgrims* (1981), exclusively to seeking to show that its leading concepts are Gnostic in character; in particular, that of the spiritual pilgrimage of the believer towards a beatific vision of the heavenly realities.

An important work in French, the massive commentary by C. Spicq, sets out to demonstrate that in respect of language, thought and scriptural exegesis, the influence of Philo* on Hebrews was overwhelming. This view has been contested by, among others, R. Williamson, *Philo and the Epistle to the Hebrews* (1970).

Pauline Giles' work, *Jesus the High Priest* (1984), compares the priesthood concept as found in John and Hebrews, concluding that verbal parallels are few, but there is a shared common tradition, a common christology, and a similar interest in the ascended Christ.

Modern theologians, in debates about the historical Jesus and the humanity of Jesus, have made constant use of Hebrews because of its emphasis on the genuinely human nature and experience of Jesus. John Knox, who in his *The Humanity and Divinity of Christ* (1967) says that its christology is 'pure kenoticism', relies almost entirely on Hebrews for evidence of the humanness of Jesus. Wherever the question of Jesus' humanity has been discussed, references to Hebrews are frequent. Its interpretation as containing a Logos christology, and perhaps a Johannine-style affirmation of the incarnation of the Logos, has recently appeared in, for example, the work of J. D. G. Dunn, who sees a Logos christology in Hebrews in some ways similar to that in Philo, but claims a stronger influence for 'wisdom' thought and finds no full-blown doctrine of Christ's pre-existence in 1.1–3.

F. F. Bruce, *The Epistle to the Hebrews*, 1964; J. H. Davies, *A Letter to the Hebrews*, 1967; D. Guthrie, *Hebrews*, 1983; W. Manson, *The Epistle to the Hebrews*, 1951.

R. WILLIAMSON

Hellenism

The term is used widely, though not entirely uniformly, of the period from Alexander the Great onward, when Greek language, culture and commerce became dominant all round the eastern Mediterranean, together with long established settlements in Sicily and southern Italy, and further west. This influence was even extended in Roman times, with wealthy Romans, at least, expected to be bi-lingual (even if Cicero and others also provided Latin expositions of Greek thought). The extent to which local non-Greek traditions from their side entered and shaped the Greek tradition is debated; but certainly the cults of other peoples and their attitudes were taken up and disseminated, and a significant number of eminent intellectuals came from Greek cities well away from the Greek mainland, for instance from Syria, including the Decapolis.

For the period of Roman expansion, and at least from the end of the Republic, 27 BC, most writers talk of 'the Graeco-Roman world', while perhaps retaining 'Hellenism' for the articulated culture.

Hellenistic culture was very diverse. Its common basis, its scripture almost, was provided by Homer, supplemented by Hesiod. Basic literacy among townsfolk, women included, was presupposed (even if native Egyptians used professional letter-writers). The more highly literate would be expected to admire Socrates and know something of Plato, and at least to have some awareness of more recent philosophical 'schools' (Stoic, Epicurean, Peripatetic [Aristotelian], Cynic,* Pythagorean, and Sceptic) and perhaps be committed to one. They would go to the theatre for the classic tragedies, especially those of Euripides, as well as often bawdy comedies and mimes. Popular culture was largely oral, in market-place, theatre, court, public assembly, lecture-hall and private house, and a great deal was shared.

It is difficult to discuss its ethos in just one paragraph, especially when there was so much variety. Though life was still very corporate, the pluralism of the time allowed for doubt, agnosticism, choice, and some real possibilities for individualism. Most philosophies stressed personal integrity and personal development. Some were pious, providentialist, politically conformist, and monotheistic in tendency; others, sceptical and socially disruptive. None of the easy generalizations that still appear is warranted. Some people were perhaps pessimistic about the physical, seeing their intellectual spirit 'imprisoned' in the body. Most appreciated that all information is assimilated through the senses; humans are bodily, and glad to be. Some may have seen no sense in history; but others saw a rational providence in control of the nations. Many people may have been mildly or energetically hedonist and by some standards 'immoral', especially sexually (though Epicureans, for instance, went for very intellectual and aesthetic pleasures); but others espoused an ethic of virtue, and a severe critique of popular religion that Jews could readily acknowledge. There was great intellectual curiosity, some of it of a rather abstract kind; but much (e.g. in architecture and other civil engineering, and in medicine) was much more empiricist.

An understanding of this 'Hellenism' in its variety and in the extent of its influence has a considerable effect on the interpretation of any biblical or other material that arose in its context. A great many Jews in the period designated lived away from Judaea and Galilee, were involved in the Greek world, spoke Greek, and often lacked any knowledge of Hebrew or Aramaic. At least some of the questions that concerned them were questions raised among Greeks; some of the Greek responses to their own questions also proved persuasive. Our evidence stems mainly from Alexandria. The grandson of Jesus ben Sirach around 130 BC found it necessary to translate his grandfather's Hebrew wisdom into Greek, and had the requisite skill. Two centuries later the learned Philo* of Alexandria shows no sign of understanding Hebrew, and is entirely dependent on the now highly venerated Septuagint* (LXX) translation of Hebrew scriptures into Greek. As ben Sirach's grandson notes, and as is evident, the normal sense of words in another language has a strong though not necessarily dominant influence in any transla-

tion* (context still affords powerful controls). The Wisdom of Solomon, usually taken to have been composed in Alexandria around 100 BC, shows what a ready welcome Stoic thought could receive; and Philo, later, made a much more thorough attempt to assimilate Greek philosophy and wider culture, and find ways to make Jewish tradition available in Greek terms that seemed to him admirably suited to the task. The very conservatively Jewish author of IV Maccabees (perhaps from Syrian Antioch) is also steeped in Stoic philosophy. Where Jewish writings clearly come from Alexandria,* or from elsewhere in the Greek-speaking world outside Galilee and Judaea, it is accepted that some awareness of Greek culture is going to be needed by any interpreter.

There continues to be much less agreement on the extent of Hellenistic influence in Judaea and Galilee, and therefore, on the extent to which a knowledge of Hellenistic culture should be used in interpreting documents and traditions stemming from those areas. (A decision on this affects the use of the so-called 'criterion* of dissimilarity': does an apparent Hellenistic motif in words ascribed to Jesus necessarily betray a later origin?)

It is important to note that exegetical work from c. 1920–1970 very often takes a clear distinction between Jewish and Greek culture for granted. A massive example is afforded by G. Kittel, though the work he edited (*Theological Dictionary of the New Testament*) is often also a very good starting point for understanding aspects of Hellenistic thought (although there is a marked preference in it for classical Greek sources, rather than for material from the Graeco-Roman period). Considerable play is made with supposed structural differences between Greek and Hebrew ways of thinking as supposedly demanded by the respective languages: the Greek as 'static', the Hebrew as 'dynamic'. Many weaknesses in this case were pointed out by J. Barr; and now any writer wanting to make any such contrast should do so in terms of a careful exegesis of what is actually said by the various Greek and Hebrew authors used.

Yet even if interpretation is not predetermined by a Greek-Hebrew divide, it is still important to try to decide whether Jewish cultural life in Galilee and Judaea went on largely in isolation from the Greek world around, or whether there was penetration at discernible levels or sectors, and, if so, how strong it was.

M. Hengel has shown how soon in the period standard Hellenistic governmental practice was adopted in Judaea, with its ethos and language. The Maccabean literature suggests a mass popular opposition to a later imposition, a century-and-a-half after Alexander; but Josephus* and other sources (including archaeologists'* findings, e.g. the Zeno papyri) suggest than much more Hellenization had already taken place, and the revolt was a late reaction to an attempt by Antiochus IV to make explicit what many had by then tacitly accepted.

The use of Greek in Jerusalem and Galilee in the first and second centuries AD is demonstrated by many inscriptions, notably on burial urns; fragments of the LXX and other Greek manuscripts have been found even at Qumran (see Dead Sea Scrolls), among them an infirmarian's notes using the standard insights of Greek medicine (4QTherapeia). M. Hengel (1974, I, p. 105) is not alone in wondering whether we must not allow for considerable bilingualism in Galilee and Judaea in the first century, needed by all for official business, and needed by, for example, people from Nazareth going to market or just for sightseeing to Herod Antipas' new city of Sepphoris, seven miles away, or to any of the nearer independent Greek cities of the Decapolis. Some of these cities produced eminent philosophers during our period. At least one of them, Oenomaus of Gadara, is thought by some to have been well thought of by rabbis of his day for his trenchant criticisms of (pagan) religion. Certainly a number of Greek 'loan-words' appear in the later rabbinic writings (sanhedrin-sunedrion; ephikouros: Epicurean; prozbol-pros-boulēn; and so on). Other influences, Stoic, Cynic, Platonic, have been detected.

Nonetheless, in the rabbinic* sources there is not a great deal of obviously Hellenistic thought, so that it is possible still to argue that the influence was only occasional and superficial, leaving the Judaism of Galilee and Judaea quite distinctive (G. Vermes). A contrary case emerges from the voluminous studies of J. Neusner, who insists that from the compilation and writing of the Mishnah (see Talmud) onwards something quite new was being created, a quite fresh Judaism in the mind and in daily discipline; one from which most traces of the past, including past encounters with Graeco-Roman culture, were bound to disappear.

The importance of Hellenism, or of later Graeco-Roman culture, for Jesus remains difficult to determine given the state of the evidence. Students of the NT, however, need to take fully into account the fact that all of its documents were written in Greek for people whose normal language that was: they are the context, the audience whose response will have had a formative effect on any communication addressed to them. Most NT quotations from Jewish scripture are from a recognizable LXX

version; very few show signs of being translated independently from Hebrew. Many of the NT writings assume that their hearers need to have Jewish customs explained to them; they have grown up in the 'pagan' Graeco-Roman world.

And when the synoptic* tradition of Jesus' teaching is compared closely with other popular ethical and religious communication of the day in the Graeco-Roman world around, especially with those who saw themselves as Cynics, a very considerable overlap of motifs, attitudes, imagery and even language emerges (Downing). Study of this material has only recommenced recently, but it may turn out to be important for the interpretation of the Jesus tradition.

'Hellenistic influence' on Paul* has been much more readily accepted. At present there is less readiness than formerly to find him much affected by the ethos and practice of the mystery cults, but much careful comparison is being made between Paul and other writing of the time, in letters, philosophical discourses, and legal arguments. Much more attention is being paid to 'genre'* (Gattung), to rhetorical* matters of form and style, both on the small and on the large scale. Considerable attention was paid to such concerns at the time Paul wrote, and awareness of what the form and style of a document, or a part of it, conveyed in the Graeco-Roman world is important for the proper interpretation of the 'content'. Form and matter are closely connected (D. E. Aune).

Whether or not Gnosticism* (or generalized 'gnostic tendencies') is an important part of ongoing Hellenism within the first-century Graeco-Roman world is another hotly disputed matter. It must be said that there is nothing in any of our contemporary Greek or Roman authors to suggest any awareness of gnostic cults as such, even though the psycho-social tendencies which seem to underlie them in the second century are certainly present.

Quite apart from any direct influence on biblical writers, Hellenism had a powerful effect on the early Fathers on scholars throughout the Middle Ages (see Mediaeval Interpretation), on both Renaissance and Protestant and Catholic Reform,* and on the Enlightenment,* and down to the present day. So too, as we have seen, it has powerfully influenced traditions of biblical interpretation. An awareness of some of its more dominant forms is a necessary tool for any thoroughgoing interpretation.

See also Hellenistic Writers; Jewish Background to the New Testament.

D. E. Aune, *The New Testament in its Literary*

Environment, 1987; C. K. Barrett, *New Testament Background, Selected Documents*, 1957/1988; M. L. Clarke, *Education in the Ancient World*, 1971; F. G. Downing, *Strangely Familiar*, 1985; E. Hatch, *The Influence of Greek Ideas on Christianity*, 1890, reissued 1957; M. Hengel, *Judaism and Hellenism*, 1974; id., *Jews, Greeks and Barbarians*, 1980; H. Koester, *Introduction to the New Testament, I: History, Culture and Religion in the Hellenistic Age*, 1982; A. D. Nock, *Essays on Religion in the Ancient World*, 1972.

F. GERALD DOWNING

Hellenistic Writers

As noted in the previous entry, authors styled 'Hellenistic' have tended to be paraded simply to provide a contrast with Jewish and early Christian writers. The latter were pictured as Palestinian and plebeian, practical and concrete, the former as theoretical and abstract Greek and Roman aristocrats.

However, with a wider acceptance of the pervasiveness of Hellenism in the eastern Mediterranean, more painstaking comparisons are now being made, and similarities as well as differences noted. So now it is seen as important to allow that the Apocryphal* and pseudepigraphical* Jewish writings from this period, whether written originally in Hebrew, Aramaic or Greek, are often in appreciable measure 'Hellenistic' in character as well as date (Bartlett, Charlesworth). The extent to which translating the still growing 'canon' of Jewish sacred scriptures into Greek (the Septuagint*) necessarily 'Hellenized' what was originally Hebraic may be debated; it certainly facilitated a Hellenizing interpretation of those writings (Philo*). Sometimes the influence of Hellenism is to be seen in the inclusion of the latest Greek science (I Enoch), sometimes Stoic metaphysics (Wisdom of Solomon); sometimes an entire genre is adopted (e.g. the religious romance, *Joseph and Asenath*); sometimes a genre* with a great many incidental references to Hellenistic commonplaces (the Jewish 'Sibylline Oracles'). The blend can be so thorough that scholars have been left debating in at least one instance (the so-called *Letters of Heraclitus*: Malherbe) whether they are dealing with a Jewish or a pagan writer.

We do not, as it happens, have very much early non-Jewish Hellenistic writing left to us (apart from later summaries and excerpts, and some interesting everyday papyrus remains from Egypt) (*see* **Palaeography**).

The scene changes when we reach the first centuries BC and AD, from which we have a much greater wealth of comparative material (largely preserved by later Christians who clearly saw it as part of their heritage). Most

of it is very literary, and most of the authors were wealthy aristocrats. It has been argued that this material, this *Hochliteratur*, cannot be relevant to our attempts to interpret the writings of poor Christians. However, the oral and public nature of contemporary culture needs always to be recognized: in law-courts, public assemblies, theatres, markets, games and homes, this material was declaimed and discussed among a wide range of men and women.

The number and range of discernible major forms is considerable. There are histories, antiquities and biographies. There are romances, with more or less explicit erotic content, but also religious, social and ethical themes. There are formal and family letters, literary epistles,* business and other occasional letters; and transcripts of speeches for various occasions, serious, genially entertaining, bitingly sarcastic (and often still very funny). There are philosophical treatises. There are poems and plays of many kinds. There are descriptions of other countries, and collections of beliefs and practices from many fields. There are technical treatises on medicine and architecture. Not all of these are directly relevant to the interpretation of the NT. All help us understand better life around the time of their writing, and increase the possibilities of checking whether we are genuinely understanding or are facing quite alien ways of thinking.

Among writers most often quoted the following may usefully be picked out:

Epictetus was a freed slave, roughly contemporary with Paul,* and taught in Rome (save when he was exiled). He was in touch with aristocrats and with ordinary people. He used a Greek style close to that of Paul, and they both shared the 'diatribe' device, a teaching aid involving the imaginary presence of a not very intelligent opponent. Epictetus was a Stoic with marked Cynic* leanings, and was like Jesus in the tradition at least in his opposition to wealth and self-delusion, often using similar metaphors. He was a pupil of Musonius Rufus, a warm and attractive figure, whose teaching on marriage, and on trusting God for our physical well-being also mirrors concerns of Jesus. Another of Musonius' pupils was (or so it seems) Dio Chrysostom of Prusa, a man of wide-ranging concerns, well travelled, in touch (he claimed) with all kinds of people. As did many others with Stoic or Cynic convictions, he suffered exile under Domitian, and journeyed round the eastern empire and beyond as a ragged Cynic philosopher, but often doing menial jobs to support himself, rather than beg. Some of his ethical and theological views seem particularly close to ideas in the NT (Mussies). The Cynic Epistles (Malherbe) are a further important source for expressions of this kind of viewpoint, frequently closely paralleling concerns and attitudes of early Christians.

Also important for NT studies, but representing by and large rather different views, is Plutarch, writing around the end of the first century AD, a widely read eclectic Platonist. He is noteworthy especially for his *Parallel Lives*, with their narrative presentation of views of character, ethics, politics and religion; but also for his interpretation of cultic myths (*On Isis and Osiris*), where we are assured that we start to get to know God through a glass, darkly, but more is to come; for his very critical views on popular religion (*On Superstition*); and for an essay wrongly attributed to him, on education (Betz). Though he, too, sometimes quotes Cynics with approval, he is much readier than they to accept and admire authority, and Roman authority at that.

Representing yet another and more sceptical stance, but also widely in touch with the general public, is Lucian of Samosata, writing in the first half of the second century AD. His ironic pictures of contemporary life include some of our earliest pagan references to Christians, as well as both sympathetic and hostile portraits of Cynics.

Others especially worth considering, for their own interest, as well as for the use made of them by today's NT scholars, are Cicero, eclectic writer of the previous century, popularizer in Latin of Greek thinking, much used by others in the next century; Seneca, eclectic and splendidly hypocritical moralist, the similarity of whose concerns to some of those of Christians led an early Christian to write an imaginary correspondence between him and Paul; Quintilian, often now used with Cicero in analysing Paul's letters, categorizing speeches and writing as legal (forensic), persuasive (epideictic), or more practical (deliberative); and Pliny the Younger, Tacitus and Suetonius, the latter providing our other earliest 'outsider' reactions to the new Christian movement.

Though many of these writers express attitudes (mostly hostile) to Jews, and help us understand the situation of Jews and then of Christians in the early empire, they offer us little help in interpreting canonical Jewish scripture. The only Jewish writers from the first century who attempted explicitly to respond to Hellenistic culture and whose works at all extensively survive for us are Philo and Josephus.*

In addition to the bibliography for the previous entry, see J. R. Bartlett, *Jews in the Hellenistic World*, 1985; H. D. Betz (ed.), *Plutarch's Ethical Writing and early Christian Literature*, 1978; A. J. Malherbe, *The Cynic Epistles*, 1977; G. Mussies, *Dio Chrysostom and the New Testament*, 1972; G. W. E. Nickelsburg, *Jewish Literature between the Bible and the Mishnah*, 1981; M. Whittaker, *Jews and Christians, Graeco-Roman Views*, 1984. Most of the non-canonical Jewish texts are available in translation in J. H. Charlesworth (ed.), *The Old Testament Pseudepigrapha*, 2 vols 1983–5.

F. GERALD DOWNING

Herder, J. von

The exegetical genius of Johann Gottfried von Herder (1744–1803) can never be divorced from his life and the polemical tensions which belonged to his age. He reacted against the pietism of his childhood without ever wholly shedding a pietistic feeling. He explored the depth and futility of the Enlightenment* and abjured the rationalism of Kant without denouncing Reason and philosophical activity. He pioneered the place of popular songs and of poetry as a basis for theological claims without condoning a merely literary understanding of religion. His enthusiastic discovery of Shakespeare and the work of Lowth did not lead to the reduction of Christ to myth* or fable. Herder opposed the remnants of feudalism and engaged in the typical prerevolutionary sweep of protest as expressed in the spirit of 'Storm and Stress', and yet accepted gladly the privileged position of a court preacher and superintendent at Weimar until his death. There is hardly a topical concern and controversy which fail to find an echo in his writings and speeches. As an educator and critic he is constantly striving to put humanity at the centre of an eternal destiny. But his humanism rings with a biblical diapason despite Platonic tunes, such as the affirmation of the immortality of the soul, and even the influence of Spinoza in his famous dialogue, 'God'.

It would therefore be idle to look for a Herder hermeneutic in a single key. A good example of his preaching has come down to us in his inaugural sermon in Weimar in 1776. He relies upon the prayers of the congregation, cites Luther,* and regards his office as a major pillar in established power. The light of the gospel is both spiritual and secular, for the good of all. His text is nothing less than the whole of Matt. 22.1–14. He is not interested in the historical background to this parable of the marriage feast. The words are celestial images now to be planted in human society. The kingdom* of God has its roots in the OT and this prophetic expectation is fulfilled in Christ and now in the whole world. Nature in its diverse manifestations and also human endeavours witness to this joyful presence which can only be lost through false cares. But the sublimation of human instincts prepares the people for the grace which stills human greed and violence. Herder emphasizes that the past, e.g. the fate of the Jews, is not our affair for the marriage is 'ours'. Christendom, however, being far from perfect, must be cleansed from idolatry and arrogance; the heavenly vocation must be obeyed so that virtue may prevail for the good of those who rule and those who are ruled. This type of sermon must have been preached countless times since Herder's day. Karl Barth* judges his great success as ambiguous if only because he makes human experience the pivot of Christian existence: 'the fiery dawn of a new age . . . may after all have been perhaps only the transient glow of a Bengal light.'

Yet Herder anticipates an interpretation which has proved lasting. The Bible is by human beings for humans, beyond the limits of dogmatics, rationalism, historicism. The gulf which separates us from the past can be traversed by our creative empathy with authors and peoples. In the 32 volumes of his collected works the presence of biblical allusions covers the pages always with the aim of giving a happy and uplifting 'higher unity' to a miserable and morally degraded society. Humanity is endangered unless ruled by God.

Of all the books commented upon, the work on the Song of Songs (1778) shows the strength and weakness of this 'epoch-making' author (a Socialist epithet given in the DDR). Mystical speculations are discarded; Herder has no time for the typological identifications of the King, the Shepherd, and the Maiden. The Song is for him a collection of oriental love lyrics, but this secular estimate by no means lessens the religious significance: the particular implies the universal, and the passion of the lovers, the poetical imagery, the analogies, the air of spring and flowers, the physical properties of beauty, point indeed to the human destiny of perfection. Yet this erotic dance is not pagan but the completion of chaste fidelity, sealed in marital mutuality and beyond death. This is an enthusiastic rendering based upon a scholarly analysis; it is meant to articulate a messianic,* even Christian, union not only of individuals but also of church, state, and humanity.

Karl Barth, *Protestant Theology in the Nineteenth Century*, 1972, Part I, Ch. 8; R. T. Clark, *Herder: His Life and Thought*, 1969; J. K. Fugate, *The Psychological Basis of Herder's Aesthetics*, 1966.

ULRICH SIMON

Hermeneutical Circle

'Every interpretation moves of necessity in a circle' (Bultmann,* *Essays*, p. 247; the idea is found in Schleiermacher and Dilthey: cf. Painter, pp. 56–66). At first sight, to be invited to go round in circles is not an attractive proposition. Since, however, the circle tends to operate at several levels, it is not inappropriate to think of it as a spiral.

1. The primary circle is concerned with the composition of the work. The interpreter has to relate the parts to the whole, and the whole to the parts (Bultmann, *Essays*, p. 236; Eagleton, pp. 74, 77). Thus, in Mark 12.28ff. the scribe asks Jesus about the pre-eminent commandment (the part) of the Law (the whole). To discern the relationship of part to whole in this way presupposes the interpreter's sensitivity to both (cf. 12.32ff.).

2. The interpreter is not unlike the translator confronting a text which seems at first strange and remote but which commands interest and attention. To 'get inside' the text involves drawing upon one's own experience of historical existence and thus setting in motion the hermeneutical circle: 'to translate means to make understandable, and this in turn presupposes an understanding' (Bultmann, *Existence and Faith*, p. 292). The presuppositions in question, however, are to be distinguished from prejudices, which would distort the text. To draw on stored historical experience is to find a way of asking questions of the text. 'There cannot be any such thing as presuppositionless exegesis' (ibid., p. 290).

3. The interpreter is thus involved in the issues which the text raises. Interpretation is a dynamic process which presupposes the reader's openness to 'the claim which confronts one in the work' and a willingness to be 'called forth out of oneself' towards a new fulfilment of one's being. Reading, therefore, serves to 'disconfirm' our habits of perception (Iser), as the lawyer in Luke 10.25ff. discovered. He had to come to terms with the text of the parable, with its challenge to his prior understanding and praxis (10.36f.), and to face up to the nature of his presuppositions and prejudices. Thus in reading, 'our initial speculations generate a frame of reference with which to interpret what comes next, but what comes next may retrospectively transform our original understanding, highlighting some features of it and backgrounding others' (Eagleton, p. 77). The essential factor is to recognize the possibility of transformation. If one slips into the view that one only gets out what one puts in, the circle has become a vicious one (Eagleton, p. 80).

4. Ricoeur relates the hermeneutical circle directly to faith, in a formula reminiscent of Anselm: 'to understand, it is necessary to believe; to believe, it is necessary to understand'

(*Essays*, p. 58). There is, however, a progressive as well as a circular pattern in faith development. To believe is 'to listen to the call', but to hear the call involves interpreting the message (*Essays*, p. 15). For Ricoeur, revelation occurs through all that the text says and in what it effects in us as we 'hear' the text. Thus, as we respond to the faith-witness which the NT enshrines, we are implicated in the world which opens out 'in front of' the text and become witnesses to and doers of the word.

5. Ricoeur's work suggests that a circular pattern operates through the process of biblical interpretation as a whole. In his Preface to Ricoeur, Mudge writes: 'And so we come full circle: from our initial naïve fascination with texts in which testimony is preserved in *poesis*, through the critical disciplines which help us overcome idolatry and dogmatism, to the post-critical moment when we ourselves begin to testify . . .' (*Essays*, p. 27). In relation to academic study, this model serves to indicate that no single discipline is an end in itself but a contributor to the wider process of interpretation. In relation to praxis, the model can be used to demonstrate how biblical interpretation relates to practical disciplines such as homiletics, education and ethics.

See also **Hermeneutics; Meaning**.

R. Bultmann, 'The Problem of Hermeneutics' in *Essays, Philosophical and Theological*, 1955; id., 'Is Exegesis Without Presuppositions Possible?' in *Existence and Faith*, 1961; T. Eagleton, *Literary Theory: An Introduction*, 1983; W. Iser, *The Act of Reading*, 1980; J. Painter, *Theology as Hermeneutics*, 1987; P. Ricoeur, *Essays on Biblical Interpretation*, 1981.

J. I. H. McDONALD

Hermeneutics

1. *The beginnings of modern hermeneutics.* Hermeneutics means theory of interpretation. Accordingly all past and present reflections on methods of biblical interpretation are hermeneutical by nature. From the earliest Jewish and Christian interpretations of the Bible until the beginning of the nineteenth century, the history of hermeneutics was largely identical with the methodological discussion and development of biblical exegesis. However, especially under the influence of Friedrich Schleiermacher (1768–1834) hermeneutics entered a new stage in its career. He distinguished sharply between the principles of general hermeneutics and the concerns of a particular hermeneutics, such as for instance biblical hermeneutics. Hermeneutics in general was now characterized as the art of understanding any written text; and biblical interpretation, Schleiermacher insisted, must not contradict these general hermeneutical principles. Schleiermacher stressed the equal importance of two necessary and related moves in every act of text understanding: grammatical interpretation (i.e. the reader's recognition of the linguistic convention and the stylistic particularity of the text) and psychological or technical interpretation (i.e. the appropriation of the overall meaning of the text by the reader).

As a result of Schleiermacher's influence, hermeneutical thinking has since been developed on two levels: 1. hermeneutics as a general philosophical discipline, and 2. hermeneutics as a sub-discipline of those disciplines among the humanities which have a particular hermeneutical concern, e.g. biblical and theological or legal studies. However, each level of hermeneutical development has influenced the other. In particular, the fruitful tension between philosophical and biblical hermeneutics has either given rise to or at least promoted the discussion of such important topics as the nature of text, the act of reading, the authority of particular readings of a text, the social character of all interpretation, and the relationship between theory and praxis.

2. *The development of modern hermeneutics.* Schleiermacher's approach to general hermeneutics attempted to overcome the stalemate in biblical interpretation caused both by Protestant Orthodoxy, which affirmed the literal inerrancy of scripture (*see* **Inspiration**) and therefore sought a pure and objective literal exegesis, and by the Roman Catholic practice of subjecting biblical interpretation to certain unchangeable dogmatic assertions. Allegorical interpretation* was ruled out by Schleiermacher, and belief in the inspiration of a biblical text was no longer allowed to exempt such a text from radical interpretive scrutiny. He demanded that the principles of human understanding be applied to all texts; no extra-textual authority was therefore admissible. Schleiermacher's most influential follower in the hermeneutical sphere, Wilhelm Dilthey (1833–1911), went so far as to declare hermeneutics *the* foundational discipline of all human sciences. He stressed the epistemological concerns of hermeneutics now that the humanities had to cope with a growing historical consciousness, and thus he widened the scope of philosophical hermeneutics even further. While Schleiermacher's hermeneutics was concerned with understanding human utterances, the aim of Dilthey's hermeneutics was now the understanding of all human experience. Next, the phenomenological movement beginning with Edmund Husserl (1859–1938) led hermeneutical reflection on the one hand

to a more detailed consideration of how meaning* is produced in language, thus retrieving a major concern of Schleiermacher's thought; on the other hand, through Martin Heidegger's (1889–1976) early investigations into the existential conditions of the human search for authentic meaning, it re-emphasized the foundational nature of hermeneutics for all philosophical thinking. In particular, Heidegger's analyses of the 'hermeneutical circle'* and of the role of presuppositions in every act of understanding (cf. his *Being and Time*, 1927) encouraged a new interest in the hermeneutical principles which govern every act of text interpretation. Heidegger's hermeneutical thinking has had a strong impact both on contemporary philosophers such as Hans-Georg Gadamer and Paul Ricoeur, and on theologians such as Rudolf Bultmann,* Gerhard Ebeling and David Tracy. Thus, Heidegger has played as significant a role for the development of modern hermeneutics as Schleiermacher did before him.

Gadamer's approach to philosophical hermeneutics is guided by his attempt to clarify the way in which truth manifests itself in the act of understanding. Thus he is not interested in outlining a detailed programme for text interpretation; instead he wishes to examine the structure of all understanding. Understanding never constitutes a purely objective or subjective human relationship with a given 'object'; rather it participates itself in the being of that which is understood, i.e. it participates in the history of the effects of a text (or work of art). The process of understanding is initially fuelled by our prejudices: we always have some kind of initial grasp of the whole which must, however, be progressively challenged by the more detailed act of understanding. The term 'hermeneutical circle' refers to this circular nature of understanding. For Gadamer, the goal of understanding is both the fusion of horizons, for instance the fusion between the horizons of the reader and of a given text, and the act of entering the tradition of which the text in question is representative. Gadamer's anxiety to emphasize the involvement of the interpreter in the object which is to be understood and his resulting mistrust of all objectivist pretensions made him blind, however, to the need for methodological correctives in the act of understanding. Jürgen Habermas and Paul Ricoeur pointed to this problem: Habermas analysed events of systematically distorted communication in which no truth is likely to be disclosed, while Ricoeur, who unlike Gadamer was interested particularly in text interpretation, corrected and amended Gadamer's hermeneutical programme by insisting on a methodological dimension in all acts of interpretation. Ricoeur

agrees with Gadamer that our understanding is initially moved by our prejudices or guesses as to what the overall meaning of a text may be. But this initial understanding must be validated by thorough explanatory procedures which then may lead us towards a more critical understanding. For Ricoeur, method is not an enemy of understanding, but a necessary helpmate. Therefore he could welcome the contribution of structuralist* text analysis, though he warned against the imposition of structuralist ideologies* on the act of understanding.

More recent hermeneutical discussions have been concerned with the textuality of texts, i.e. the nature of a text (cf. text-linguistics), and with the act of reading (*see* **Reader-Response Criticism**): is it mainly the text which directs the act of reading or is it more the reader (or the community of readers) which determines the meaning of a text? Thus, the phenomenological movement's concern with the production of meaning continues to dominate the hermeneutical discussion today, although now much closer attention is paid to questions of text genre* and text style (cf. literary criticism* and theories of style).

3. *Modern hermeneutics and biblical interpretation.* The distinction between a general philosophical hermeneutics and particular hermeneutical inquiries such as biblical interpretation has proved to be very valuable for both hermeneutical enterprises, as is evident from the recent development of biblical interpretation. The discussion of general hermeneutical principles has helped biblical interpretation better to assess its own hermeneutical possibilities and limitations. As a result, both the preliminary nature and the pluralism of biblical interpretation could be understood as unavoidable hermeneutical conditions. These insights exposed the hope for one absolute and authoritative reading of scripture as uncritical and called into question many Christian doctrines which were proclaimed to be based on inerrant biblical interpretation. However, while the fuller social and ecclesial consequences of hermeneutical reflections are only beginning to be appreciated in Christian communities, the academic study of the biblical texts has long been influenced by developments in philosophical hermeneutics. In the nineteenth century, biblical interpreters following Lessing and Schleiermacher had already been responding positively to the new understanding of history and to the rapidly growing awareness of the development of literary forms (cf. the history of the historical-critical method*). In the twentieth century so far two stages in the reception of philosophical hermeneutics by biblical interpreters may be distinguished:

1. Bultmann's response to Heidegger's existential hermeneutics transformed the self-understanding of biblical interpretation significantly, though not without attracting protests particularly from Karl Barth* and his followers. Both Barth and Bultmann agreed that biblical interpretation ought to be more than the purely historical and philological* analysis of biblical texts; both scholars emphasized the faith response provoked by these texts as the primary concern of biblical interpretation. Yet while Barth considered reflection on the philosophical presuppositions of biblical interpretation as an illegitimate imposition on these texts, Bultmann and those scholars who followed him by propagating 'The New Hermeneutic'* (among them Gerhard Ebeling, Ernst Fuchs, Robert Funk and James M. Robinson) saw this reflection as the necessary foundation for any modern and responsible biblical exegesis.

Bultmann accepted Heidegger's analysis of the hermeneutical circle and stressed the resulting insight that exegesis without presuppositions was impossible. Moreover, he followed Heidegger's existentialist concerns and language by demanding that the act of biblical understanding ought to become an act of eschatological decision for authentic Christian life. His particular programme of demythologization* aimed at translating into a modern horizon those biblical passages which reflected the world-view of a past era and which therefore were of themselves no longer able to challenge the self understanding of the modern reader. Thus, he did not suggest we ignore the mythological parts of the Bible, but urged us to interpret them. Nevertheless, at times Bultmann's existential interpretation of the Bible led to a reductionist view of biblical texts, especially when these were seen merely as occasions for the transformation of only individual readers rather than groups and no longer as also referring back to the originating events of Christian faith.

2. Gadamer and Ricoeur are currently influencing biblical scholars, especially in Europe and North America, by drawing their attention to the need to interpret the biblical texts as works rather than as accumulations of individual sentences. Moreover, by emphasizing the truth-disclosing potential of classical texts, both philosophers point to the transformative quality of the interpretation of such texts. Reading biblical texts then cannot be considered a neutral activity; rather, it participates in the effective history of these texts. As a result, biblical interpretation can come into its own only when it tries critically to relate to what these texts talk about, i.e. to their theological reference. According to Ricoeur, philological, historical, literary-

critical and other ways of explicating the texts will add to our understanding, yet never replace it. Thus, it appears that modern hermeneutics emphasizes anew the demand for a proper biblical theology.

Related to the reception of Ricoeur's hermeneutics, biblical scholarship is presently much engaged in the debate on questions of textual genres and styles and their role in the process of reading, and has already made many important contributions to this discussion. A discussion of the ethics of reading is only beginning, both in philosophical hermeneutics and in biblical interpretation. However, it is likely to emphasize further the need for biblical scholars to participate in the present hermeneutical discussion.

See also **Exegesis; Meaning.**

Werner G. Jeanrond, *Text and Interpretation as Categories of Theological Thinking*, 1988; Kurt Mueller-Vollmer (ed.), *The Hermeneutics Reader: Texts of the German Tradition from the Enlightenment to the Present*, 1985; Paul Ricoeur, *Essays on Biblical Interpretation*, 1980; James M. Robinson and John B. Cobb (eds), *The New Hermeneutic*, 1964; Anthony C. Thiselton, *The Two Horizons*, 1980; David Tracy, *Plurality and Ambiguity*, 1987.

WERNER G. JEANROND

Historical-Critical Method

This method has been in use in some fashion since before the time of Christ, at least in courts of law examining witnesses and documentary evidence (see Quintilian, *Institutes*). In the Graeco-Roman world, where most people concerned with the writing of history had had a legal training or at least experience of the courts, it was natural to extend the critical assessment of others' testimony to an appraisal of the efforts of historians. It was available to literate Jews such as Josephus,* and to Christians, and was used especially by Antiochene* theologians, with those from Alexandria* less welcoming. But even readers who did attempt to appreciate historical aspects of the 'literal'* sense might still spend more time on the moral lessons, the spiritual allegory,* and the hints of heaven; for most, these were the more highly prized senses of scripture.

A concern for a historical strand within the literal sense of scripture was always a possibility where people went to law over charters and deeds, as well as where the classical heritage was preserved, directly or indirectly, through the early Fathers. A renewed interest of this kind can be found in Aquinas, but even more influentially when it became a basis for the use of scripture in the Papal Chancery. Allegorical senses could be multiplied endlessly; lawyers wanted something more precise. The early fifteenth-century canon lawyer, Lorenzo Valla, who showed the *Donation of Constantine* to be a forgery, also wrote critical *Notes on the New Testament* which influenced Erasmus* and Ximenes.

More general religious controversy encouraged a wider search for original (and so historical) meaning. Mediaeval 'spiritualism' as well as the Renaissance and the Reformation* sat lightly with or actively opposed the outward ceremonies of the church, already typified in the rites of Judaism. Thus much of the OT could be seen as 'merely' an historical phase in God's pedagogy (Reventlow). What the NT documents could be shown to have originally and positively meant or implied was discussed by Colet and Reuchlin, but became a matter of life and death with Luther* and Calvin.* Reventlow and others suggest that a key part in the growth of historical-critical study of the Bible was played by English deists* of the seventeenth century; but also that it was only when biblical interpretation became politically less sensitive in the eighteenth century (no longer providing constitutional title-deeds), that historical criticism was free and able to flourish. In this period, its thorough application to the biblical texts is usually attributed to German (or Swiss-German) writers, such as Semler, Michaelis, Reimarus and Lessing, who treated scripture 'like any other book' which purports to make factual historical assertions.

The procedures and their logic remain very much akin, as already suggested, to what goes on in and before a trial at law. Documents are scrutinized to check whether they are what they purport to be, emanating from the authors claimed for them, un-tampered with; if they seem to be copies, the quality of the copying must be ascertained. Witnesses are examined for the coherence of their account, and for its match with others' testimony. Word-for-word replication suggests collusion, complete disparity leaves all in doubt. If a witness starts to use a vocabulary or style that is out of character, the judge begins to suspect prior prompting, or, perhaps, hearsay evidence at second or third hand, or some flight of literary fancy. All will need to be assured that the witness is using words, phrases and sentences in line with general usage; odd local or technical jargon will need to be explained. Counsel will dig deep to discern or disprove possible ulterior motives, social, financial, personal and psychological, that may be inspiring the form a piece of testimony is taking. In addition to all this, general plausibility is also an important factor: does what is claimed tally with common experience? So we may reach a range of agreed statements of fact.*

The construction of a case on the basis of the agreed statements of fact, the historical interpretation offered, is discussed elsewhere in this volume. Suffice it to note here that evidence and interpretation intertwine. Evidence has to be interpreted, has to be understood as evidence. The historian has to have something (or some things) in mind, some idea of what one is looking for. There is no 'pure objectivity' at any point. But historical-critical method allows us to attempt to reach commonly accepted truth, at least at some levels, in some areas. The historian displays the basis for an explanation and others can test not only the logic and power of the explanation, but the validity of its factual evidential base.

The use of such methods in biblical interpretation may be opposed for various reasons. They may seem disrespectful to a sacred text, or they may raise doubts about cherished beliefs. To some, they may seem quite irrelevant, for it is, of course, entirely possible to approach parts or all of the Jewish and Christian scriptures purely as works of literary imagination and construction. What emerges from such 'readings' may be entertained very seriously and gratefully; and questions of history do not need to arise at all. This latter approach would constitute yet another 'sense' beside the three non-literal senses of the mediaeval theologians, but it may have much in common with them in its teasing out of a non-historical 'spirituality' for the reader to engage with. It is, however, quite possible to enjoy a literary critic's* appraisal of the Gospel of Mark or the book of Jeremiah in a present-day reading without abandoning a concern for either in its historical context (including its historical literary context, probably quite different from a modern critic's version). And one may well want to go further and ask Mark, for instance, more searching questions, not just about his story of Jesus and the world, but about the views of those who told the stories before he wrote them down, and about the light they may throw on the Jesus to whom they are attributed.

J. Barr, *The Bible in the Modern World*, 1973; M. Bloch, *The Historian's Craft*, 1954; R. E. Brown, *The Critical Meaning of the Bible*, 1986; S. Neill and T. Wright, *The Interpretation of the New Testament 1861–1961*, ²1988; D. E. Nineham (ed.), *The Church's Use of the Bible, Past and Present*, 1963; H. Graf Reventlow, *The Authority of the Bible and the Rise of the Modern World*, 1984; C. Tuckett, *Reading the New Testament*, 1987.

F. GERALD DOWNING

Historical Jesus

The term refers to the life and teaching of

Jesus as reconstructed by historical methods. Our knowledge of the first-century Jewish context in which Jesus lived and taught is partial (*see* **Jewish Background to the New Testament**) and the traditions about Jesus which have survived are limited and difficult to interpret. Hence 'the historical Jesus' will only ever be a partial picture of 'Jesus as he was'.

Since modern historical methods were developed only towards the end of the seventeenth century, historical reconstruction of the life, teaching and intention of Jesus is a modern phenomenon. The sharp distinction between the 'Jesus of history' and the 'Christ of faith' which Reimarus* drew in 1767 was largely unknown in earlier centuries. Two basic presuppositions kept close questioning of the Gospels off the theological agenda. In spite of the discrepancies in details in the Gospels, they were considered to have been written under divine inspiration,* hence their general historicity was not in doubt. Since Jesus was the divine Logos,* only non-believers could doubt that he performed the miracles* recorded in the Gospels.

However, some of the roots of the modern quest for the historical Jesus are very deep: a general interest in the life of Jesus and in the problems raised by Gospels did not begin in 1767. Several of the issues which have been prominent in modern quests for the historical Jesus were well known in the early church.

There was a general interest in the story of Jesus in the first century. Alongside his theological and catechetical aims, Mark intended to set out a coherent account of the ministry and downfall of Jesus: he was concerned with both the story and the significance of Jesus. Similarly, Matthew and Luke (and perhaps even John) modified some of the traditions at their disposal *partly* in the light of their own particular convictions about the story of Jesus.

The problems raised by discrepancies in the Gospels were recognized early in the second century. The Gospel of the Ebionites harmonized traditions from Matthew, Mark and Luke and 'revised' some of them in accordance with the Ebionites' 'heretical' views. In his *Dialogue with Trypho* (*c.* AD 160), Justin Martyr may well have drawn on a harmony* of the Synoptic Gospels (*see* **Synoptic Problem**). About AD 170 Tatian produced a harmony of all four Gospels on the basis of careful reflection on the variations and discrepancies within the Gospels. Tatian's *Diatessaron* was translated into many languages and used widely well into mediaeval times. The impulse towards the production and use of harmonies came not so much from an awareness of the evangelists' differing theological emphases as from a desire to avoid the embarrassment caused by the variations in the details of the four accounts of the life and teaching of Jesus.

In the second century, 'orthodox' Christians were forced to reflect on the origin and reliability of the Gospels they accepted as authoritative by the appearance of numerous apocryphal gospels, and by 'heretics' such as Marcion,* Montanus and various Gnostic leaders who produced their own versions of some gospel traditions. Jewish opponents such as Trypho (whom Justin Martyr quotes extensively in his *Dialogue*) and the anonymous Jew cited by the pagan Celsus (both of whom Origen* quotes in his *Contra Celsum, c.* AD 248) distinguish between the 'real' Jesus and later Christian claims.

In one particularly interesting passage (I:41–2), Origen records that Celsus' Jew said to Jesus, 'When you were bathing near John, you say that you saw what appeared to be a bird fly towards you out of the air. What trustworthy witness saw this apparition, or who heard a voice from heaven adopting you as son of God? There is no proof except for your word and the evidence which you may produce of one of the men who were punished with you.' Origen is forced to reflect on the nature of historical evidence: 'an attempt to substantiate almost any story as historical fact,* even if it is true, and to produce complete certainty about it, is one of the most difficult tasks and in some cases is impossible.' Origen mounts a careful reply, using 'historical' arguments, including an appeal to 'neutral' evidence provided by the Jewish historian Josephus.* The historical criticism of his opponent forces Origen to reflect on the nature of historical evidence and to use historical criticism himself.

Even when he is not responding to opponents, Origen frequently draws attention to historical problems in the Gospels. Some difficulties, he explains, are due to the way in which the text has been transmitted; some have to be resolved by a spiritual or allegorical* reading of the text.

Origen's main concern, however, was not with what he sometimes calls contemptuously 'mere history'; the true meaning of the Gospels lies 'beyond the history'. Origen partially anticipates the sharp distinction Reimarus* drew in 1767 between the historical elements in the Gospels and orthodox Christian theological claims about the significance of the life of Jesus. In his commentary* on John, Origen notes that 'people marvel at Jesus when they look into the history about him, but they no longer believe when the deeper meaning is disclosed to them; indeed they suppose it to be false'. Whereas Origen wants to wean his readers away from the 'history' of Jesus to the 'deeper meaning' of the Gospels, Reimarus hopes that by 'looking into the history about Jesus' his readers will abandon any 'deeper meaning' in favour of rational or natural religion.

In spite of the importance the sixteenth-century Reformers * attached to scripture, they did not grapple seriously with the discrepancies in the Gospels. Luther * commented on the different chronology of the cleansing of the temple in the Synoptic Gospels and in John: 'The Gospels follow no order in recording the acts and miracles of Jesus, and the matter is not, after all, of much importance.' Calvin * often made astute comments on problems in the Gospels; occasionally he even made his own conjectures, but, like Luther, he played down the importance of the difficulties. The Lutheran theologian Osiander insisted that if an event is recorded more than once in the Gospels, it happened more than once. So in his harmony of the Gospels, the daughter of Jairus was raised from the dead several times and Jesus cleansed the temple twice!

The year 1778 is usually said to mark the beginning of 'the quest for the historical Jesus', a quest which, in spite of interruptions and changes of direction, continues to this day. In 1778 G. E. Lessing published anonymously a seventh extract from a longer work H. Reimarus had completed in 1767, just a year before his death. At this point the censor caught up with Lessing and he was forbidden to publish further extracts. The seventh fragment was entitled 'On the Intentions of Jesus and His Disciples'. On the basis of a close historical analysis of the biblical traditions, Reimarus set out a non-supernatural account of Christian origins which distinguished sharply between what he took to be the real (or historical) Jesus and the later evaluations of his significance made by his followers. This distinction between the 'Jesus of history' and the 'Christ of faith' has been prominent in all modern study of the Gospels.

Important though Reimarus' work undoubtedly was, its significance in the history of modern study of the Gospels has often been overestimated. Lessing's secretive publication of Reimarus' work caught the imagination of later writers. The prominence given to Reimarus by Albert Schweitzer * undoubtedly enhanced his reputation as a great pioneer. Schweitzer's influential survey of lives of Jesus, *Von Reimarus zu Wrede*, 1906 (ET *The Quest of the Historical Jesus*, 1910) began with a bold claim about the significance of Reimarus' work: 'Before Reimarus, no one had attempted to form a historical conception of the life of Jesus . . . there had been nothing to prepare the world for a work of such power as that of Reimarus.'

This is an exaggeration. Schweitzer fails to note that Reimarus was strongly influenced by several predecessors, especially the English Deists.* Like the Deists, Reimarus believed in God, but not in revelation,* miracles * or other supernatural interventions. In *The Reasonableness of Christianity* (1695), John Locke had distinguished between the simple faith propounded in the Gospels and the 'other truths' found in the Epistles.* In the first half of the eighteenth century, several other Deists handled the text of the Gospels freely in their attacks on traditional Christianity. And well before Reimarus wrote, the first steps in textual criticism * and in inquiry into the origins of the Gospels had been taken.

The publication of D. F. Strauss'* *Life of Jesus* in 1835 was a major milestone in the modern quest for the historical Jesus. Strauss' book led to an immediate furore. He was dismissed from his post in Tübingen * and 'refuted' in numerous publications. Unlike Reimarus, Strauss did not see himself as an opponent of Christianity: his *Life of Jesus* was intended to pave the way for his own theological reconstruction of Christian belief.

In three respects Strauss anticipated later developments. He was one of the first scholars to undermine confidence in the historical value of the Fourth Gospel. By depicting Jesus as an apocalyptic * enthusiast he recognized that a carefully reconstructed portrait of Jesus would not necessarily be congenial to modern men. He partially anticipated later form criticism * in his insistence that many of the individual traditions about Jesus were 'mythical' *, i.e. expressions in story-like form of religious ideas.

In 1847 F. C. Baur (one of Strauss' former teachers) also denied that the Fourth Gospel contained any historical traditions. Unlike Strauss, Baur concentrated on the use the evangelists * made of the gospel traditions. The four evangelists all had their own individual theological emphases, or tendencies. A century later redaction * critics refined this important insight.

Strauss and Baur both accepted Matthean priority, the dominant solution of the Synoptic Problem * in their day. In almost all other respects the questions they raised (though not all their answers) are still prominent today in serious discussion of the historical Jesus. In their responses to Strauss which were published in 1838, C. H. Weisse and C. G. Wilke argued independently for the priority of Mark. H. J. Holtzmann's lucid and thorough exposition (1863) of the 'two-source' solution of the Synoptic Problem won wide acceptance. On this view, Matthew and Luke both drew on two sources, Mark and Q, which were considered to be a sound basis for historical reconstruction.

In the final decades of the nineteenth century, many writers believed not only that a 'scientific' life of Jesus could be written, but also that it could form the basis for Christian theology. Numerous lives of Jesus were written, some of which were little more than romantic fantasies. Those by E. Renan and F. W. Farrar enjoyed particular popularity. Quite often psychological* explanations of the motives and intentions of Jesus were provided. Gaps in our knowledge were often filled out with imaginative reconstructions. For example, Luke 2.40–52, the only passage in the Gospels which tells us anything about the childhood of Jesus, was often filled out with guesswork about 'the hidden years of Jesus'.

The first two decades of the twentieth century brought a dramatic change in direction in study of the historical Jesus. Albert Schweitzer concluded his *Quest for the Historical Jesus* (1906) with William Wrede's* claim (1901) that Mark's Gospel was shaped to a considerable extent by the theological convictions of the early church (especially concerning the messiahship of Jesus) (*see* **Messianic Secret**). Schweitzer's own portrait of Jesus as a fanatical apocalyptic prophet who tried to force God to usher in his kingdom was in stark contrast to the portraits set out in the popular lives of Jesus. Questing after the historical Jesus seemed to lead either to the theology of the early church or to an uncongenial Jesus.

In 1919 K. L. Schmidt showed that Mark could not be read as a chronologically accurate account of the life of Jesus. Behind the Gospels are originally independent units of tradition which were later linked together loosely, often on the basis of their subject matter. M. Dibelius (1919) and R. Bultmann* (1921) analysed the traditions behind the Gospels according to their 'form' (hence the term 'form criticism'*). The various 'forms' of the traditions were related to the needs of the early church – to missionary preaching, to catechetical instruction, to debate with opponents, or to worship. The first followers of Jesus only retained traditions which were relevant to their life and faith.

Although some form critics believed that it was possible to reconstruct the earliest 'form' of the traditions, they were not interested in setting out a historical reconstruction either of the story of the life of Jesus or of his original teaching. They claimed that historical and biographical reminiscence was of no interest at all in the early church. Jesus was worshipped as 'Lord' and his parousia* was expected soon. Jesus was not a 'hero' (as most of the nineteenth-century lives assumed) whose actions and attitudes were to be imitated.

Many form critics appealed to the words of Martin Kähler written in 1896: 'Just as the light of the sun is reflected in every drop of the bedewed meadow, so the full person of the Lord meets the reader of the gospels in each little story.' In other words, each individual tradition is itself 'gospel' or proclamation. On this view the gospel traditions tell us more about the post-Easter proclamation of the early church than about the historical Jesus.

The contrast with the nineteenth-century 'quest' could hardly be more marked. For many nineteenth-century scholars a reconstructed biographical account of the life and personality of Jesus was part of the very essence of Christianity. For the form critics, the historical Jesus was of no particular interest: for them (as for the followers of Jesus who transmitted the gospel traditions), the 'proclaimed Christ' of the Easter message was all-important. The Gospels may tell us a few things about the life and teaching of Jesus, but this is, as it were, incidental or even contrary to their original intention.

At first sight Bultmann's *Jesus* (1926) seems to hark back to the nineteenth century, for it contains a 150-page exposition of the teaching of Jesus. In their Preface to the 1958 English edition, the translators were so wedded to the traditional approach to the historical Jesus that in referring to Bultmann's book as 'a strictly historical presentation of the teaching of Jesus in the setting of the thought of his own time', they completely misunderstood his intention. Bultmann, however, took pains to emphasize that he was not concerned to provide a 'strictly historical presentation', but a 'continuous dialogue with history'. He insisted that in every word which the historian says about history he is saying at the same time something about himself. The words of Jesus 'meet us with the question of how we are to interpret our own existence. That we be ourselves deeply disturbed by the problem of our own life is therefore the indispensable condition of our inquiry.' Bultmann was interested only in those parts of the synoptic tradition which confront us with the question of how we are to interpret our own existence. He was even prepared to utilize passages which he believed (on historical grounds) belonged to a later stratum of the tradition. Whereas most studies of the historical Jesus in modern times have tried to keep theology at arm's length from historical investigation, Bultmann deliberately united historical and theological interpretation.

In 1953 Bultmann's most distinguished pupil, Ernst Käsemann, challenged his teacher's repeated insistence that reports of the past life of Jesus were of neither interest nor use to the early church – or to the church in the twentieth century. His lecture entitled

'The Problem of the Historical Jesus' sparked off what came to be called the 'new quest' for the historical Jesus. Käsemann insisted that 'there are still pieces in the synoptic tradition which the historian has to acknowledge as authentic if he wishes to remain a historian at all'; he then discussed some of the traditions he considered to be authentic. His concern, he wrote, was 'to show that, out of the obscurity of the life story of Jesus, certain characteristic traits in his preaching stand out in relatively sharp relief, and that primitive Christianity united its own message with these'.

Scholars associated with the 'new quest' explored the extent of continuity between the historical Jesus and the Christ of early Christian proclamation. They rightly sensed that if the Christian gospel centres on the crucified and risen Jesus as the decisive revelation of God, then Christian theology must be at least interested in what can be known about Jesus by historical inquiry. Bultmann had always been exceedingly wary of any attempt to prove or even to bolster faith by historical claims about Jesus. But several of his former pupils insisted that their new-found interest in the historical Jesus was by no means a return to nineteenth-century attempts to ground Christian faith in a reconstruction of the life and teaching of Jesus.

Alongside the theological concerns of Bultmann and of the 'new quest', some of the historical questions prominent in the nineteenth-century quest have continued to be debated regularly in the twentieth century. Biographies of Jesus certainly went out of fashion with the ending of the 'old quest', but many scholars have continued to offer historical reconstructions of the life and teaching of Jesus. Some have worked with the tacit assumption that the historical Jesus must always be central in Christianity; others have shown little or no interest in the theological implications of historical research.

The following may be noted as examples of the varied continuing interest in the historical Jesus. 1. Reimarus' claim that Jesus had deliberately roused political aspirations has been discussed repeatedly. In 1967 S. G. F. Brandon expounded the theory fully, arguing that Jesus and his disciples sympathized with the Zealots' attempts to incite rebellion against the occupying Roman forces. Brandon drew on Martin Hengel's magisterial study of the Zealots (1961; ET 1989), though Hengel himself has been a firm opponent of Brandon's views. 2. In his extensive writings on the teaching of Jesus, J. Jeremias* drew on his unrivalled knowledge of first-century Judaism. He believed that the main lines of the preaching of the early church were already present in the teaching of Jesus. 3. Several scholars (including Jeremias) have followed up M. Black's attempt (1946) to reconstruct the original Aramaic* of some of the sayings of Jesus. Progress has been disappointing, partly because so little Galilean Aramaic which can be dated with confidence to the first century has survived. Our knowledge of first-century Judaism, however, has increased dramatically over the past four decades (*see* **Jewish Background to the New Testament**). This in turn has stimulated several attempts (notably by G. Vermes in his *Jesus the Jew*, 1973) to set the actions and teaching of Jesus in the context of first-century Judaism.

In the past decade, several major studies of the historical Jesus have appeared. They may turn out to mark the beginning of a 'third quest' for the historical Jesus. Two authors (B. F. Meyer, *The Aims of Jesus*, 1979, and A. E. Harvey, *Jesus and the Constraints of History*, 1982) do discuss the implications of their historical work for christology,* but on the whole theological questions are less prominent than in the 'new quest'. The recent studies all pursue historical questions much more rigorously than was the case in most of the nineteenth-century 'lives' of Jesus. Several focus particularly on the overall intentions of Jesus – the very issue first raised by Reimarus. J. Riches (*Jesus and the Transformation of Judaism*, 1980), M. J. Borg (*Conflict, Holiness and Politics in the Teachings of Jesus*, 1984) and E. P. Sanders (*Jesus and Judaism*, 1985) have explored the relationship of Jesus to first-century Judaism; their work will undoubtedly stimulate further research.

There is now general agreement that Jesus was a prophet-teacher who had healing gifts and whose teaching methods were (in part) unconventional. Jesus certainly did not intend to found a new religion. He did not repudiate scripture, though on occasion he emphasized some scriptural principles at the expense of others. With a few rare exceptions, he did not call in question the law of Moses. Jesus believed that he had been sent by God as a prophet* to declare authoritatively the will of God for his people.

The key to the story of Jesus is its ending. Jesus went up to Jerusalem for the last time in order to confront the religio-political establishment with his claim that the kingdom of God was at hand. On the basis of his convictions about the presence, power and will of God, Jesus called for a re-ordering of Israel's priorities. In that sense, he sought the renewal of Judaism.

A sketch along these lines would be accepted by most historians today, and a sociological* approach has sharpened the picture by characterizing Jesus as a 'charismatic leader' (cf. M. Hengel's book of that title,

1981). The details will continue to be debated. It is likely that our increasing knowledge of first-century Judaism will enable some modest advances to be made, though it is unlikely that additional direct sources will ever be found. It will always remain difficult for the historian to establish which traditions in the Gospels go back to Jesus of Nazareth.

Some recent writers have claimed that Christian theology today would do well to remain content with the continuing religious value of the 'stories' set out by the four evangelists. They argue that in comparison with the riches available within the Gospels as we now have them, digging behind them will never produce more than a few nuggets of fools' gold.

Most scholars, however, believe that a continuing quest for the historical Jesus is inevitable and necessary. Christian believers will want to ask about the basis on which their faith stands. If they are wise, they will welcome the sharp questions of the uncommitted scholar who shares their interest in Jesus of Nazareth. The continuing fascination of Jesus for men and women of many cultural and religious backgrounds will encourage rigorous scrutiny of the first-century sources. Even though the results of historical inquiry will always be limited and provisional, they will be of interest to Christian and non-Christian alike. And that keen interest will in turn fuel further historical investigation.

See also **Gospel**.

G. Bornkamm, *Jesus of Nazareth*, 1960; John Bowden, *Jesus: The Unanswered Questions*, 1988; L. E. Keck, *A Future for the Historical Jesus*, 1971; R. Morgan with J. Barton, *Biblical Interpretation*, 1988; J. M. Robinson, *A New Quest of the Historical Jesus*, 1959; G. N. Stanton, *The Gospels and Jesus*, 1989.

GRAHAM N. STANTON

Historicism

This word, found first in English around 1920, corresponds to the German *Historismus* (occasionally also translated 'historism'). The concept is tangled, containing a variety of sometimes contradictory meanings, but its nodal point lies in the prestige of historical study in nineteenth-century German culture. Its philosophical threads stem from the Enlightenment's* (Vico, 1725; Herder,* 1774) and especially Hegel's secularization of the Christian vision of a unified human history. The belief that history holds the keys to human existence and self-understanding originates here. But it was the success of the new critical methods pioneered by Ranke and Niebuhr which gave the historical discipline such prestige that it could plausibly bid to take over other disciplines, imposing genetic explanations and

evaluations outside their proper sphere. In 1884 C. Menger criticized Schmoller for making economic theory too dependent on economic history, and this objection to disciplinary imperialism is one strand giving the concept, like its parallel *Psychologismus*, the negative flavour it has in the dialectical theology of Barth,* Gogarten, Brunner and Bultmann.*

The historical *a priorism* of Hegel, reflected by Marx,* was rejected by most historians around 1850. Popper's attack on historical determinism (*The Poverty of Historicism*, 1957) has thus confused matters by giving prominence to a quite secondary meaning of the word: belief in laws of historical development and the possibility of prediction, on analogy with the natural sciences. But unlike early social scientists, most German historians (e.g. Burckhardt and even Hegel's pupil Droysen) emphasized the concrete, unique and individual in history, drawing on Goethe and Humboldt ('On the Historian's Task', 1821 ET 1967) rather than Hegel for their theory, and persuading some philosophers (Dilthey, Windelband, Rickert) to see in the *Geisteswissenschaften*, or historical sciences, a way of looking at the world radically distinct from the natural sciences. The decline of philosophical idealism, whose quasi-theological overarching framework had given a larger meaning to detailed historical research, and the determination of the historians to investigate the past in its own terms, without allowing present-day attitudes to influence their judgments, sharpened the relativism inherent in all historical consciousness and led some to the philosophical opinion that all social and cultural phenomena, all categories, truths, and values, are historically conditioned and relative to their context (*see* **Cultural Relativism**). This value relativism, with which the word is primarily associated, suited the historians' ideal of objectivity. In that positivistic climate even the best research tended to become a mere accumulation of historical knowledge, offering no guidance for life and indeed undermining any attempt to establish cultural values. The debilitating effects of this were brilliantly exposed by Nietzsche (without using the word *Historismus*) in *On the Uses and Disadvantages of History for Life* (1874, new ET R. J. Hollingdale, 1983).

Though found in Schlegel (1797) and especially in Feuerbach's polemics against relativism (1830s), the word only became common in the first third of the present century, when many wrote of the cultural 'crisis' brought by the historicizing of Western thought. In Dilthey's view this amounted to an 'anarchy of values'. No one saw the difficulties posed for the Western tradition by the inevitable historicizing of our thinking more clearly than the theologian

Ernst Troeltsch. He hoped 'to overcome history with history' by finding some metaphysical justification for deriving norms from religious and intellectual history. But German idealism had worn too thin to provide generally accepted norms, and a more radical recourse to the tradition, re-investing some of it with the authority it had lost under the relativizing impact of critical investigation, was espoused by Barth.

Biblical scholarship and church history had long been caught up in the relentless pursuit of historical knowledge, though the ideal of freedom from extraneous norms was (as in the Enlightenment) turned mainly against pre-judgments deriving from the dogmatic tradition, and only rarely against contemporary religious value-judgments. Barth tried to break the stranglehold on biblical theology* exercised by a historical research paradigm that could no longer accommodate the Christian conviction that the Bible is intended to mediate divine revelation.* Without denying historical and philological research their proper place, Barth brought to the text a neo-Reformation* understanding of revelation which did not depend on that research. As developed by Bultmann, this anti-historicist kerygmatic* theology has been thought to do insufficient justice to the historical components in Christian faith. The seventy years since Barth's commentary on *The Epistle to the Romans* (1919) have confirmed the futility of evading the questions posed to Christian theology by modern historical study. But they have also justified Barth's wisdom in denying this a controlling interest.

Theology is not alone in disputing the claim that historical research can dictate our view of reality as a whole, and that a boundless relativism is inescapable. These metaphysical claims have been generally abandoned and the English word is now used in the more modest, epistemological sense of 'the belief that an adequate understanding of the nature of anything and an adequate assessment of its value are to be gained by considering it in terms of the place it occupied and the role it played within a process of development' (M. Mandelbaum). Modern theological study can listen and give due weight to such claims without absolutizing them. The suggestion that historical study alone can provide an adequte understanding of religion is as absurd as an attempt to deny its legitimate place. What the place of history in theology actually is remains a question to which contemporary theologians give different answers. But the quest for an objectivity that denies the interpreters' own interests and values now appears a form of self-deception, and even self-destructive. Christian theologians' interest in the ques-

tion of God in history points them back to the idealist combination of historical research and theory, not to the positivist denial of theory in the name of a false objectivity. The commitment of Marx and Hegel, duly disciplined by the historian's passion for truth, has more in common with theology than the intellectual poverty and social impotence of the late nineteenth-century historicism which still guides much biblical scholarship.

See also **New Testament Theology.**

V. A. Harvey, *The Historian and the Believer*, 1966; G. G. Iggers, 'Historicism' in *Dictionary of the History of Ideas*, Vol. I, 1973–4; M. Mandelbaum, 'Historicism' in *Dictionary of Philosophy*, Vol. IV, 1967; F. Meinecke, *Historism*, ET 1972; A. Richardson, *History Sacred and Profane*, 1964; H. Schnädelbach, *Philosophy in Germany 1831–1933*, 1984.

                                    ROBERT MORGAN

History of Religions School

The label *religionsgeschichtliche Schule* was attached by 1903 to a small group of younger biblical scholars qualifying in Göttingen around 1890. Initially attracted there by the reputation of Ritschl, but learning more from Duhm* and Lagarde, they were united in rejecting Ritschl's biblical theology* and insisting on a more rigorous application of historical critical methods to early Christianity. In particular they insisted on taking full account of its religious matrix, i.e. contemporary Judaism (*see* **Jewish Background to the New Testament**). Later on, when others of the group were finding parallels between early Christianity and the mystery religions, the hermetic literature, and Gnosticism,* the label became associated with hypotheses about Hellenistic* and oriental influences. Bousset and Heitmüller gave grounds for this extension, but the original view of the 'school' was that any pagan influences on the NT had been mediated through inter-testamental Judaism (*see* **Pseudepigrapha**). This emphasis on the Jewish context finally became commonplace following the discoveries at Qumran (*see* **Dead Sea Scrolls**).

What is now commonplace was once strongly contested, even by the greatest liberal historians, Wellhausen (*see* **German Old Testament Scholarship**) and Harnack,* and several of the original group found difficulty in obtaining professorial posts. It was not strictly a 'school' with a 'head'. It included from the outset A. Eichhorn and his friend W. Wrede* and the two key figures Gunkel and Bousset. On the periphery were Ritschl's son-in-law J. Weiss and Bousset's friend Troeltsch who was later seen as their systematic theologian. W. Heitmüller arrived later but became another key figure, and W. Bornemann, H. Hackmann and A. Rahlfs were also associated with the group. Gunkel's later pupil H. Weinel and his friend H. Gressmann, like P. Wernle in Basel, were quick to share the approach, but were not part of the group.

The first book marking the new concern with context was Gunkel's *The Influence of the Holy Spirit: The popular view of the Spirit in the apostolic age and the teaching of the apostle Paul* (1888, ET 1979). J. Weiss, *Jesus' Proclamation of the Kingdom of God* (1892, ET 1971) is also typical in exploring the Jewish apocalyptic* background, though Bousset by contrast insisted on the distinctiveness of Jesus. The profile of the group became clearer in 1895 with Gunkel's *Schöpfung und Chaos in Urzeit und Endzeit*, on Gen. 1 and Rev. 12, and Bousset's *Antichrist*, followed in 1896 by a commentary on the Book of Revelation. Programmatic statements followed, from Wrede in 1897 (ET 1973) and Gunkel in 1903 (ET in *The Monist*, 1903): Wrede banished the remnants of a dogmatic approach from 'New Testament theology'* (so-called), calling instead for 'a history of early Christian religion and theology', and Gunkel in *The Religiohistorical Interpretation of the New Testament* opened his monograph series with the provocative claim that, judged purely historically, early Christianity was 'a syncretistic religion'. In the same year Bousset published *Die Religion des Judentums in neutestamentlichen Zeitalter* (1903), but then followed the classicist R. Reitzenstein (*Poimandres* 1904) into Hellenistic and oriental fields with *Hauptprobleme der Gnosis* (1907). W. Heitmüller's *Im Namen Jesu* (1902) and later writings explored the Hellenistic antecedents of baptism and Lord's supper in Paul* (1903) and early Christianity (1911). His most provocative conclusion, in 1917, was that Paul was the father of Roman Catholic sacramentalism rather than of the Reformation.* He also detected a layer of pre-Pauline Hellenistic Christianity in the NT tradition. This became important for the school's greatest synthesis, Bousset's *Kyrios Christos* (1913, ET 1970), and for *The Theology of the New Testament*, Vol. 1 (1948, ET 1952) of its greatest pupil, Rudolf Bultmann.*

Gunkel's transfer to OT teaching in 1889 proved significant because there he discovered that history of religions research must also involve history of traditions* investigation of pre-canonical* layers in the biblical material. His classic commentaries on Genesis (1901) and selected Psalms (1904) pioneered form criticism,* involving both a comparative and a history of traditions dimension. In NT studies the latter task was advanced above all by Wrede, and form criticism by J. Weiss.

Such highly technical scholarship, requiring a wide knowledge of comparative material and a sense of how folk lore* develops, made historical study of the Bible a more specialist concern than it had been before. But these scholars wanted to share the results of their research with a wider audience, confident that historical study would deepen the understanding of religion, and encourage participation. They were liberal theologians, seeking to persuade the church to welcome new knowledge and at the same time addressing the wider culture. The monograph series FRLANT (still published by Vandenhoeck and Ruprecht) and review journal *Theologische Rundschau* (edited from 1898 by Bousset and Heitmüller) were therefore complemented by a series of 'generally comprehensible' semi-popular short books (*Religionsgeschichtliche Volksbücher*), a collection of short commentaries* on the NT (*Die Schriften des neuen Testaments* ed. J. Weiss, 1906–7), and the encyclopaedia, *Die Religion in Geschichte und Gegenwart*, 1909–14, largely the achievement of Gunkel.

The judgment that the so-called 'history of religions school' represents a high-point in the historical movement within Christian theology places it in the succession of F. C. Baur and the great liberal historians who absorbed his critical historical approach while rejecting his philosophical theology. It also places them where they placed themselves, in the history of theology, even though today they are celebrated more by those who understand biblical research in exclusively historical terms for freeing the discipline from doctrinal entanglements. It is the quality of their historical research that accounts for their influence on subsequent biblical scholarship, but the attempt of some of them (Bousset, Troeltsch, Gunkel) to connect a Schleiermacherian type of theology with their literary, historical, and sociological research has again attracted attention, following the demise of the Barthian* reaction against liberal Protestantism.

See also **Liberalism.**

W. G. Kümmel, *The New Testament. The History of the Investigation of its Problems*, 1973; G. Lüdemann and M. Schröder, *Die Religionsgeschichtliche Schule in Göttingen*, 1987; B. Moeller (ed.), *Theologie in Göttingen*, 1987; R. Morgan with J. Barton, *Biblical Interpretation*, 1988.

ROBERT MORGAN

Holistic Interpretation

An approach to the interpretation of a biblical text that concentrates on the work as a whole. The term 'holistic', which is not commonly employed by those who really do holistic interpretation, may be used as a convenient label for a number of quite different interpretational strategies which have in common their opposition to what they see as the fragmentation of the work by other scholarly approaches.

Holistic interpretation may in fact be defined best by contrast to disciplines like form criticism* and source criticism;* whereas these are concerned ultimately with the units out of which the completed work has been composed, and therefore proceed by taking the completed work apart, any holistic approach studies the work as it exists, in its full extent, asking the questions appropriate to the whole rather than to its parts. To some extent, of course, all interpretation is inevitably holistic, for everyone seeks to interpret units, which is to say wholes; the difference between a holistic and a non-holistic approach lies in the size of the wholes. Holistic interpretation works with 'the final form of the text', itself a problematic phrase, i.e. the total work in more or less the shape in which it has come down to us, without consideration of its pre-history as a text. It is a 'synchronic* interpretation' rather than a 'diachronic' one.

As a literary* approach to written texts, holistic interpretation makes use of the normal analytic tools of literature criticism; it focusses on plot, point of view, characterization, narrators,* implied readers, rhetoric,* structure, and so on. As a type of interpretation, it concerns itself with meaning,* and so works with concepts like theme, tendency,* ideology* and theology.

Before considering the possible historical origins of the approach, it would be appropriate to present some examples of it in operation.

In the case of the book of Job, the scholarly orthodoxy has been that the present book, the final form of the text, is a compound of a prose narrative and a poetic dialogue; the original extent of the dialogue has in the course of time been expanded by the addition of the speeches of the fourth friend Elihu (chs 32–37) and other material like the poem on Wisdom in ch. 28. A typical non-holistic interpretation of the book has been, in accord with this reconstruction of the process of the book's growth, an interpretation of what is regarded as the 'original core' of the book, ignoring or marginalizing the speeches of Elihu and privileging the poetic portions over the prose narratives. The book has thus been seen as essentially the conflict of a man with his God over the matter of his innocence and his undeserved suffering. If, however, the book as a whole is the object of interpretation, it is hard to avoid including in even the briefest statement of its theme a quite different element, namely the withholding from the suffering human of the knowledge which would transform his understanding of his suffering. Job is in that case not merely engaged in a struggle to clear his

name, but is involved in a totally unnecessary conflict, since the prologue to the book has already made clear that in God's eyes Job is indeed a thoroughly innocent man. Again, in a non-holistic interpretation, the concluding prose narrative in which Job has his fortune restored can be set on one side as a secondary addition which is of little consequence for the meaning of the book as a whole. But a holistic interpretation will reckon with the fact that in the epilogue the principle of exact retribution, with which the book elsewhere seems to be in conflict, is implicitly affirmed. So adopting a holistic approach to the book determines how a fundamental question about the book's meaning will be answered: does the book affirm or deny that prosperity is the result of piety?

If we take the case of the Gospels,* it is obvious that a major scholarly concentration in the past has been upon identifying the elements in them that can be safely assigned to the historical Jesus,* and, by contrast, those that have to be set to the account of the early church. This quest for historical reconstruction inevitably means a fragmentation of the Gospels themselves as literary works, since they are being studied not for what they themselves are saying, but for what light they may shed on something beyond themselves. As against this historically-motivated approach, a holistic approach will ask of the Gospel of Luke, for example, what portrait of Jesus and other characters the book develops, what its chief story-line is, how the individual narratives within the story contribute to the overall direction of the book and how their meaning is determined by their location at a particular point in the flow of the narrative.

To take an example: according to the usual critical analyses, the infancy narratives* in Luke were traditions or even texts drawn by the evangelist* from a source available to him; it was only to be expected, therefore, that they would not be fully in harmony with the outlook and concerns of the evangelist himself. In a holistic reading, however, it will be asked how these narratives function in the story as it now is, and no explanation of their contents in terms of their historical origins will serve as an answer to that question. Thus, when Zechariah speaks of the raising up of a horn of salvation 'that we should be saved from our enemies, and from the hand of all who hate us' (1.69, 71), a holistic approach will insist on asking whether or to what extent this expectation at the birth of Jesus is shown in the later pages of the Gospel to have been fulfilled. It might indeed have to be argued that, despite the prophetic character of Zechariah's words, this is an expectation that is not actually realized in the Gospel, and that

that very fact is something the Gospel is asserting. In other words, on this approach the tension between the birth narratives and the rest of the Gospel is not to be accounted for as an accident in the editing of disparate sources (even if in historical reality that was the case) but is to be reckoned with as a significant part of the total statement the Gospel is making.

A final example of a holistic interpretation, in this case one that has as yet not been seriously attempted, is provided by the biblical books Genesis to II Kings. By all literary standards, these books constitute a whole, being a coherent narrative organized on a simple chronological* principle with a clear beginning and end. But because the historical origins of Genesis to Deuteronomy (or, to Numbers, or, to Joshua; *see* **Pentateuch**; **Deuteronomistic History**) differs from that of the remainder of its contents, this work is hardly ever acknowledged as a single whole. Studies of its plot, theme, characterization, or meaning are almost entirely lacking, for no other reason than that strictly historical or genetic questions have dominated scholarship.

How is the holistic approach to biblical texts to be situated within biblical criticism and interpretational theory generally? Holistic interpretations first became prominent in the 1970s, and it is inconceivable that a method whose introduction to the field can be dated so precisely did not have historical antecedents or did not arise under the influence of contemporary trends of thought. But it is important to recognize that holistic interpretation was not consciously developed from a theoretical base established within biblical criticism or in general literary theory. In this respect it differs from structuralism* or deconstruction, for example, where what took place was an application of a previously worked out theoretical position to the biblical texts. In the case of holistic criticism, it seems that literary theory has been drawn upon somewhat piecemeal as an authorization for procedures that holistic interpreters had already been deploying upon the biblical texts. This sequence of events is probably the explanation why it is so hard to find any systematic theoretical account of holistic interpretation.

It seems clear that the primary motivation for many holistic readings has been an instinctual or commonsensical dissatisfaction with the net results of historical-critical scholarship. Even if the historical-critical* method had been leading to greater assurance about the validity of its results, it could always have been protested that it systematically regarded the text as a window through which to scrutinize something other than the text, namely historical actuality. But a wave of uncertainty, from the late 1960s onward, about all kinds of historical-critical conclusions, concerning the Pentateuchal sources, the historical Jesus, and many other issues, led some scholars to ask whether there was some other more rewarding object of enquiry within the field.

Among the general intellectual trends to which holistic interpretation felt an affinity may be mentioned literature criticism and structural linguistics.* Literature criticism by the 1950s and 1960s had largely retreated from the earlier scholarly concerns about authorship,* date, and influences to more strictly literary interests, whether in stylistics, the emphasis on 'the work in itself' (New Criticism), questions of value and influence (F. R. Leavis), or the beginnings of literary theory, including narratology (Greimas, Genette, Bremond). In linguistics, the dominance of de Saussure's structural linguistics authorized concentration on the synchronic aspects of language, i.e. of language viewed as an integrated system, rather than upon the history of the language. Chomsky's generative linguistics further emphasized the functioning system, not historical development.

Within biblical criticism, the movements from which holistic interpretation has drawn moral support if not actual methodological ideas include redaction criticism,* structuralist exegesis and canonical criticism.* Redaction criticism, with its hey-day in the 1960s, shares many of the same impulses as holistic interpretation, and indeed in some respects may be viewed as a branch of it. Its concern is the total intention of the biblical author, especially as it is evidenced in the use made of pre-existing materials. Classically in gospel criticism, the evangelist's theology and purpose have been reconstructed by concentrating on the evangelist as author. Most redaction critics are, however, more historically oriented than holistic interpreters: the horizon of their enquiry is the authors' intentions in their own time, not the significance of the work in its own right. Since the 1970s, structuralist exegesis, i.e. the application of structuralist theory to the interpretation of texts, has been, when applied to works as a whole, a form of holistic interpretation, since it enquires after the deep structures that bind the work together (or, in some cases, create unresolvable tension); but it does not always take the work as a whole as its object. Canonical criticism, likewise originating in the 1970s, asks about the significance of a biblical work, both in the course of its development over time and as a final end-product, to the religious community that produced and preserved it. It is alert to the differing meanings the work will have had in differing historical circumstances in the course of its composition and beyond, in the course of its reading by various communities – matters which are not germane to holistic interpretation as such – but it is a form of holistic interpretation in striving for comprehension of the work as a whole.

Some misconceptions about holistic interpretation should be corrected. It is not necessarily inimical to historical-critical enquiry; it simply brackets out of its programme almost all historical questions because it is considering the literary work as a closed but functioning system. It does not endeavour at all costs to show that biblical books are unified narratives, without tensions or contradictions; rather, it takes as its starting point the assumption that what now appears as a single work, such as the book of Job, should be the primary object of study. It does not ascribe to the 'final form of the text' any special status other than that it is in most cases the only extant form of the text, and it is prepared in principle to concern itself with any reasonably 'whole' form of the text that may be reconstructed, whether with or without secondary additions, scribal errors, etc.

Can holistic interpretation, with a programme now more or less twenty years old, remain a justifiable approach in the post-structuralist world of contemporary literary theory? Arguably it can. Deconstruction, in setting out to show how texts can undermine the assumptions they affirm, does not dispute the importance of the question of meaning in the work as a whole, though it argues that texts do not convey univocal meanings. And in denying the existence of 'transcendental signifieds', i.e. entities beyond the world of the text which the text endeavours to represent, it does no more than erect a philosophical platform for a position to which holistic interpretation is already sympathetic on purely pragmatic grounds.

Reader response* criticism, which locates meaning in readers rather than in texts, rightly focusses attention on the role of the interpreter to a degree lacking in some holistic interpretations. It further impinges on holistic interpretation in that the more the reader's experience of texts is taken into account in the act of interpretation, the more important synthetic and holistic perspectives usually become, for readers crave coherence, no matter how much the facts are against them. Materialist* and feminist* criticisms, of course, often resist a concentration upon the literary work, demanding interpretations that devolve from the historical circumstances of the work's composition and that impinge upon the historical situation of the interpreter. That is to say, they insist upon questions that holistic interpretation has programmatically bracketed out, and that they are entitled to do. Holistic

interpreters are thereby reminded that their approach is not the only legitimate approach to the biblical texts.

See also **Narrative Criticism.**

––––––

J. Barton, *Reading the Old Testament*, 1984, pp. 127–9; D. J. A. Clines, *The Theme of the Pentateuch*, *JSOT*-SS, 1978; D. Rhoads and D. Michie, *Mark as Story*, 1982; S. Rimmon-Kenan, *Narrative Fiction*, 1983; M. Weiss, *The Bible from Within*, 1984.

DAVID J. A. CLINES

Holy, The

Underlying the English word 'holy' is the idea of property or possession, so that in a religious sense, something that is 'holy' belongs to deity (for a different view see OED entry 'holy'). Thus understood, the holy is in opposition to the secular and is part of a scheme of classification of reality into distinctive categories, with important consequences for social organization and activity. It is widely used in the OT in this sense.

However, for much of the twentieth century a quite different view of the holy has dominated the study of religion, that expressed in Rudolf Otto's *The Idea of the Holy* (1917, ET 1923). As a young lecturer in Göttingen, Otto became a follower of the philosophy of J. F. Fries (1773–1843) as reformulated by Leonard Nelson, and believed that religion was basically a non-rational category of human experience which is grasped by intuitive feeling. Thus, far from seeing the holy as a distinctive sphere belonging to the divine, which could only be approached by humans with great caution, Otto regarded the holy as a common feature of human experience which was the basis of religion. In its most 'primitive' moments it produced feelings of terror and awe, and made people aware of their creatureliness in the presence of the 'wholly other'. Otto had experienced such feelings in a synagogue in Morocco as the 'holy, holy, holy' song of the seraphim (Isa. 6.3) was chanted.

Otto found in the Bible a number of instances of encounter with the 'numinous', as he called the holy in its most basic form. Isaiah professed himself to be utterly lost when he heard in his vision the hymn of the seraphim (Isa. 6.5), and Peter* professed his unworthiness to be in the presence of Jesus following the miracle of the great catch of fish (Luke 5.8). Otto traced how, beginning from primitive feelings of awe, the holy had been directed into ethics, so that ultimately to be holy was to live a holy life.

In the OT, the holy is best thought of as that which belongs to God, and which can be approached only with caution. In Ex. 19.12

the people and their animals must not touch the border of Mt Sinai, on pain of death. In Lev. 8–9, an elaborate ritual is prescribed which transfers priests from the realm of the everyday to that of the holy, so that they can mediate between God and the people. In Joshua, when God gives victory to Israel, a city and its spoil become the property of God, and they must be destroyed utterly and not used for secular purposes (see Josh. 6.17–19 where the silver and gold are sacred [Hebrew 'holy'] to God and are to go into the treasury of the Lord). Blood, which is used in the sphere of the holy to make atonement (Lev. 17.11), is consequently dangerous in everyday life. Even the discharge of blood at the normal menstrual periods of a woman has to be dealt with ritually by the woman and those with whom she comes into contact (Lev. 15.19–30).

These and similar ordinances imply a separation between the holy and the everyday. However, the idea of the holy is extended to the people of Israel and the land of Israel. Because both are the possession of God they too are holy. This holiness is to be respected in a variety of ways: by the correct observance by the people of the boundary between the holy and the everyday, by the avoidance of religious and social customs of neighbouring peoples, by the execution of criminals, by the observance of the sabbatical years and by the impartial administration of justice and the maintenance of a fair and just social order.

But the OT also affirms that God *is* holy, not simply that the holy is what belongs to God alone. In some passages it is the awesome and frightening aspect of God's being that is meant. Thus Josh. 14.19 says: 'You cannot serve the Lord; for he is a holy God; he is a jealous God ... If you forsake the Lord and serve foreign gods, then he will turn and do you harm.' In Isaiah, God is holy in the sense that he expects justice to be done, and punishes the people when it is neglected (Isa. 5.24–25). In Isa. 40–66 the holiness of God is his intention, as the incomparable One and the creator, to redeem his people, as in Isa. 43.14–15: 'Thus says the Lord, your Redeemer, the Holy One of Israel: "For your sake I will send to Babylon and break down all the bars ... I am the Lord, your Holy One, the Creator of Israel, your King." ' In Ezek. 36.20–24, the holiness of God is his intention to vindicate his name in the eyes of the nations, after it had been profaned by Israel's disloyalty and by the harsh treatment of the Israelites and their land at the hand of others.

It is impossible to trace a development of the idea of the holy in the OT. Rather, we have a cluster of related ideas, and 'primitive' feelings of awe and wonder both persist and are worked out in terms of the universal moral and social claims of the incomparable One and the need to approach with caution the areas of life that properly belong to him.

In the NT the holy is seen in some new ways. Jesus is presented as abolishing distinctions between the clean and the unclean (Mark 7.19), and by describing his death as occurring 'outside the camp' (Heb. 13.11–12): there is a deliberate blurring of the distinction between the holy place where sacrifice was offered and the place where the remains of sacrificial animals were disposed of. Holiness becomes an action of God in justifying those who have faith in Jesus Christ (I Cor. 6.11), and those who belong to him are called 'holy ones'. Yet arguably there is no fundamental difference between this understanding of holy and that in the OT. In both cases, God acts in order to make a people belong to him. In the NT this action is seen as having universal application and consequently entailing the ending of the social mechanisms that served to delineate one people from among the other nations.

See also **Anthropology; Magic.**

N. Soderblom, 'Holiness', *Encyclopedia of Religion and Ethics*, vol. 6, 1913; G. Lanczkowski, D. Kellermann, M. Lattke, 'Heiligkeit', *Theologische Realenzyklopädie*, vol. 14, 1985.

J. W. ROGERSON

Holy Book

It is customary to speak of Judaism, Christianity and Islam as 'religions of the book', in view of the great veneration they have traditionally given to the Tenakh (Hebrew OT), Bible and Qur'an respectively. What is not always borne in mind is that religion does not automatically involve giving a special status to holy writings. If religion is 'the practice of sacred rites' (*Concise Oxford Dictionary*), it need not require a holy book to approach God or the gods. Most religions will, no doubt, have acquired sacred texts, but these have often been concerned with the proper performance of the different cults; they were not themselves regarded as divine words, but were rather important means of guiding worshippers so that they could approach the divine presence properly. The paganism of the classical world would provide many examples of this usage.

That religion meant cult is still true for Israel in much of the period described in the OT. When the prophets or the books of Kings attack false religious practice, what is being condemned is wrongly directed cult. Though no doubt such collections as the Decalogue (Ex. 20.1–17) were revered in written form, there is no agreement when it originated. The first claim for obedience to a written scroll is found in the account of Josiah's reform (II

Kings 22), and from then on Judaism paid great regard to the sacred traditions which had been handed down, allegedly from the time of Moses.* The Torah (*see* **Pentateuch**), many of whose detailed prescriptions must originally have functioned as a guide to religious practice, came itself to be the object of religious devotion. The exile, with its disruptive effect on the national cult, may have furthered the belief that God's words to the people were best preserved in written form, and it is widely held that many older traditions reached their definitive form at the time of the exile; but of this we have no unambiguous evidence.

Christianity was thus unique among the great religions of the world as being born with a book already in its cradle. The NT provides ample evidence of the tension which this provoked. To some extent this arose in terms of the question whether Christians were still bound by the requirements of their scripture, that is, the Law and the Prophets; in the Gospels, Sabbath observance features most prominently, whereas in the Pauline Epistles, circumcision is a great point at issue. But there was a more basic concern: if the Christian body believed itself to be guided by the Holy Spirit, how was that conviction to be reconciled with the belief that God's word was written down already in the scripture? The variety of means used to interpret the OT gives some indication of the tensions that were experienced.

The NT is written in Greek, but it incorporates within itself many quotations from and allusions to, the OT, originally composed in Hebrew. We know nothing in detail of any particular problems that were raised by this rendering of the holy book into another language; perhaps the fact that parts at least of the OT had already been translated into Greek may have made the process seem a natural one. Certainly many (though not all) of the OT quotations in the NT seem to be based on the Septuagint* translation.

But at a slightly later period the issue of whether the holy book might legitimately be translated out of the holy language in which it had been handed down became an extremely sensitive one. In Judaism hostility towards the Greek translations became extremely virulent, but this is perhaps attributable to the use made of Greek forms of the Hebrew Bible by the Christian church. Later still, some of the hostility towards vernacular translations* found in Western Europe in the Middle Ages must surely have been based on the fear that the holy text had been given by God to his holy church in its received form and must not be tampered with. The holy book was regarded as a sacred object in itself, to be revered but not necessarily to be understood. (It is an attitude which is certainly not extinct, as witness the hostility evoked in Greece by translations into modern Greek, and the opposition in Britain to translations which interfere with what has been described as the 'sacred English original' of the KJV/AV.)

The difficulty of how appropriately to handle a sacred text is one which has continued to occupy Jews and Christians, not least in the post-Enlightenment* age when it has seemed increasingly difficult to maintain that a collection of ancient texts could supply answers to all of a modern person's religious needs. More generally, and especially in the West, academic study of religious history has inevitably seemed to devalue the status of holy books. Detailed critical analysis of any historical process must inevitably de-mystify it, and much of the sanctity of the holy book lies in the aura of mystery which it induces: in church the solemn carrying of the Gospel-book in procession, with lights and incense; in pious homes the setting of the Bible apart on a special shelf by itself.

One of the most interesting questions for the historian of religion must be the extent to which Islam (*see* **Muslim Interpretation**) is able to resist the critical questioning of its holy book, the Qur'an, of the kind that has now become so widespread in many traditions of Judaism and Christianity. In those traditions new claims for the importance of the sacred text in its final received form have been made by the proponents of canonical criticism;* the issue of the 'holy book' is still a live one.

See also **Authority of Scripture.**

___

F. F. Bruce and E. G. Rupp (eds), *Holy Book and Holy Tradition*, 1968; C. F. Evans, *Is 'Holy Scripture' Christian?*, 1971.

R. J. COGGINS

Homily

The early Christians took over the practice of the scripture homily from their Jewish forebears. Justin Martyr, in his description of Christian worship in his first Apology, mentions that there were readings from the prophets and 'the memoirs of the apostles', and at the conclusion of these the president of the brethren 'exhorts us to the imitation of these good examples, in speech' (I *Apology* 67). Tertullian* in *De Anima* also speaks of addresses during Christian services. The so-called II Clement (*c.* 150), often regarded as the first surviving Christian sermon, in the post-NT period, calls on the hearers to 'pay attention to that which is written, so that you may save both yourselves and him who is the reader among you' (II Clement 19.1). The first specific example of a homily on scripture

is from Clement of Alexandria on the text of
Mark 10.17–31. To the question, 'Can the
rich man be saved?', Clement's answer, based
on the exposition of scripture, is clearly 'yes'.
For Clement's pupil, Origen,* the exposition
of the Bible in the context of the liturgy* was
of supreme importance, for scripture was the
spiritual essence of the universe. As the Spirit
had caused scripture to be written in the first
place, so now he guided its interpretation for
those who heard the word. Origen is significant in a number of ways. Thus, he holds that
the homily is more than mere speech, so he
distinguishes between the *logos* (*sermo*), the
address based on the models of classical ora-
tions, and the *homilia* (*tractatus*), the preaching of the word closely following the biblical
text. Again, the exposition of scripture in the
liturgy is for him evidently different from exegesis in a doctrinal treatise; the aim of the
scripture homily is practical, a means of uplift-
ig the faithful, and always seeking the application of the message in their lives. This last
point is fundamental: Origen's homily on Gen.
10.5 shows why the address is never simply a
bare commentary on the biblical passage: 'It
is not a time to comment but to edify the
church of God, and to move inert and nonchal-
ant hearers by the example of the saints and
mystical explanations.'

Origen laid down clear hermeneutical* principles to guide preaching from scripture, based
on his threefold division of meaning: the literal
or verbal sense, the moral, and the mystical or
spiritual. Origen's own practice was apparently to follow the passage verse by verse,
expounding it grammatically as well as historically, and then to lead his hearers to the
more profound spiritual meaning. The latter
usually involved allegorization* of the biblical
passage. Thus, in the story of Noah the ark is
a type of the church, and its spiritual meaning
for the individual is to encourage him to prepare for his conversion, which also is an ark.
The 42 stages in the journey of the children of
Israel typify the soul's passage to paradise. He
sees the ceremonial and ritual law of Israel as
matters to be explained mystically,* while
there are elaborate symbolical meanings for
the prophecies* concerning Jerusalem and
Israel. For Origen the whole of the OT spoke
of Christ.

Origen's principles may be seen operating
in the Cappadocian Fathers of the fourth century. For Basil the Great, scripture was 'the
means of nourishing the spiritual life of the
faithful', and his sermons on the *Hexaemeron*
(the six days of creation), the Psalms, and the
Gospels, reflect this. Gregory of Nyssa also
produced homilies on the *Hexaemeron*, Ecclesiastes, the Song of Songs, the Lord's
Prayer,* and the Beatitudes.* Gregory's use

of allegory was restrained and conditioned by
the spiritual needs of his congregation. Nonetheless, the historical facts in the Bible are
not provided simply for information but to
lead men to virtuous life (Homily on *The
Titles of the Psalms*). The Antiochene* school,
reflecting more Aristotelian interests and a
somewhat greater fidelity to the literal text,
produced another kind of preacher with a
different style of exegesis in the pulpit, most
notably John Chrysostom, the 'golden
mouthed', who was the greatest preacher of
the Greek church. Chrysostom's range
covered catechetical and liturgical subjects,
while his homilies on the Bible became models
for preaching both in East and West; they
include sermons on Genesis, the Psalms, Matthew, John, the Acts, and the Pauline epistles.
In the West, Jerome is said to have become
less allegorical in his preaching as he became
older, while Ambrose inspired Augustine*
with his rhetorical gifts as well as his expositions of the *Hexaemeron*, the Psalms, and the
Gospel of Luke. Augustine himself constantly
expounded scripture in a preaching career
which lasted for thirty years and frequently
included two sermons daily on Sundays. His
De Doctrina Christiana describes the effect
which his preaching had on his hearers as
they were confronted with scripture. The
fourth book speaks of the nature of homiletics: the ideal of the homily is 'to teach, to
please, to move'. The preacher must search
for the proper understanding of the text and
pay attention to the literal meaning, though
Augustine in practice seems to have made
much use of allegorical and mystical interpretations, as his homilies on the Sermon on the
Mount, the Fourth Gospel, and the epistles to
the Romans and Galatians suggest.

In the Middle Ages (*see* **Mediaeval Interpretation**) there were many varieties of expository preaching. Mystical interpretation
reached new heights in the sermons of Bernard
of Clairvaux, while popular expositions of the
gospel were found in Franciscan preachers.
The scholastic period produced an elaboration
of homiletic theory, and the sermons of
Thomas Aquinas and Bonaventure show how
the rules of logic and dialectic were best
employed. Allegorization continued to be the
staple of the homily. Origen's three-fold sense
evolved into the four-fold sense, i.e. the literal,* allegorical, moral, and spiritual. The
water-pots of Cana were the six ages of the
world, but they also stood for man's spiritual
constitution. Jerusalem* was not only the historical earthly city, but allegorically the
church, morally the individual believer, and
spiritually the heavenly Jerusalem or Zion.
The sermons collected in the famous *Hortulus
Reginae* of Meffreth of Meissen (*c.* 1447) con-

tain various examples of allegorical interpretation; and they also indicate that scripture could be explained by reference to classical and philosophical authors. These sometimes present a curious juxtaposition, but the practice is defended on the grounds that Paul had made a similar use of quotations in his epistles. The dangers in allegorization of the extreme kind were recognized. Nicholas of Lyra in the fourteenth century published his *Postilla Litteralis* which alerted preachers to the necessary distinction between the literal and mystical understanding of the Bible, and his work had a wide circulation. On the eve of the Reformation,* the *Circa modum Praedicandi* produced at the eleventh session of the Fifth Lateran Council (December 1516) complained of the poor quality of expository preaching and sought a more faithful rendering of the text. The Reformers' return to a literal sense in framing the homily is obviously anticipated in Wycliffe's sermons, though they did not abandon the other senses entirely. Wycliffe held that preaching should be direct and simple in method and restricted to the exposition of scripture. The spiritual meanings must be secondary: 'the literal witt is the sweetest, wisest, and most precious' (*Sermo* XII). His homily on John 3.1, the visit of Nicodemus to Christ, is a good illustration of his principles in action. The visit is placed in the context of the Gospel and Christ's ministry, and John's intention to expound in it the doctrine of the Trinity (facilitated by the Vulgate form of the passage) is drawn out, without any artificiality.

Manuals of preaching in the mediaeval era throw some further light on the manner of exposition following the gospel in the mass. The German priest Conrad (*c.* 1200) describes the homily as follows: the biblical passage is introduced in a brief explanation, then each verse is commented on and its relation to the whole explained, and finally there is a brief exordium. His sermons cover both Epistle and Gospel for the entire year. The anonymous 'Schwarzwald preacher' of about the same period follows the same pattern. Alain of Lille's *De arte praedicatoria*, also *c.* 1200, describes the serious nature of the homily, and the need to compare scripture with scripture in the elucidation of the text. The *Quo ordine sermo fieri debeat*, written by Guibert of Nogent (d. 1124), deals with the four-fold interpretation of the Bible and the moral teaching in the homily.

The sixteenth-century Reformation, both Protestant and Catholic, restored expository preaching to a position of prominence. The Reformation raised again the question implied originally in Origen's work. What is the relation of the text and exposition of it? How does the text determine preaching, and how does preaching bring out the true meaning of the text? A creative movement like the Reformation insisted on a close relation between the two; for Luther* the deeper understanding of the Bible was the work of the preacher and not simply the scholar in his study. 'I take pains to treat a verse, to stick to it . . .' The preacher must be *bonus textualis*. Preaching from the vernacular became the first priority, and Luther's translation* of the German Bible was employed in his own sermons to obvious effect. The typical homily preached by Luther reveals a close attention to the passage, a christocentric application, even if the book under consideration is from the OT, and a direct reference to the hearer's situation in the sight of God. The language is often colloquial and the use of the imagination striking. Luther resorted to allegorical and typological* methods as well as the occasional scholastic definition, though without the artificiality and remoteness of the doctors. The Weimar edition of his works contains more than 2,000 sermons by Luther, the great majority (since he kept close to the lectionary) being on the Gospel and Epistle for the day. By contrast the Reformed tradition, associated with Zwingli and Calvin*, aimed at systematic exposition of the entire scripture. Hence, Calvin's treatment of the OT included 200 sermons on Deuteronomy, many others on the prophets, Job, I Samuel etc., and, in the NT, a series on the Gospels and Epistles (100 on Timothy and Titus) which are remarkable for their range and variety. Calvin's hermeneutical tenets, as enunciated in the *Institutes*, were applied consistently in his preaching. The Holy Spirit brings the scripture to life and guides the preacher's interpretation, while the proclamation of the word as the centre of worship makes the Bible the judge of congregation and community. Calvin's background in trilingual humanism (Latin, Greek, and Hebrew) ensured that his sermons paid close attention to the original meaning of the text and, while he used typology, he avoided allegory and also insisted on the direct relevance of OT norms in the conduct of both church and state. Calvin's appeal is always to the will and to the moral imperative of the gospel.

The Catholic Reformation expressed the need for a return to scriptural preaching in the *Decretum super lectione et praedicatione* of the Council of Trent, and the statement in the twenty-fourth session entitled *De Reformatione*. Seminaries for the training of priests so that they might better expound the Bible were one result of this emphasis. Two great Catholic preachers of this era who showed the ideal in action were Charles Borromeo and Joseph Bellarmine. Reformation in preaching was also the object of the 'little method' of Francis de Sales (1604), while a century later Fénelon's *Dialogues* (1717) maintained that pulpit eloquence was a matter of uniting simplicity and practicality with a full knowledge of the Bible.

In the Church of England, the first *Book of Homilies* (1547) consisted of twelve sermons which were meant to be read in default of a homily by priest or curate, and they also served as a guide for the construction of sermons. Each homily is built on a clear plan in which the biblical passage is explained and placed in its setting, and its application in the life of the believer and the community is drawn out. There is no show of learning, and dogmatic and ethical content is straightforward; the average length is about twenty minutes; cf. also the second *Book of Homilies* (1563) which contains a fine example in Homily 16, 'Of the Gifts of the Holy Ghost'. William Perkins' *The Arte of Prophecying* (1613) represented the Puritan ideal of preaching as grounded in the exposition and application of the vernacular scripture, though the polemical content is marked. In the following two centuries, in the preaching of Andrewes, Tillotson, and Jeremy Taylor, in England, and Bossuet and Bourdaloue, in France, pulpit oratory reached new heights, often far removed from the 'homilia' ideal of Origen. Inevitably, there was a reaction, as may be seen in Spener's insistence on an exact and extended exegesis of the text, avoiding speculation and showy effect. The advice was taken to heart in the preaching of the Pietist movement in Germany. In England, under the influence of this movement, John Wesley and George Whitefield enjoined 'scriptural holiness' in their sermons. Of the 40,000 sermons preached by Wesley a number have been preserved. His homily on Justification by Faith (*Standard Sermons*, V, 1739) is a typical example of his style in which exegesis of the relevant scripture passages leads by stages to a searching examination of the hearer's conscience and an appeal for newness of life; cf. also the sermon on Christian Perfection (*Standard Sermons*, XXXV, 1741) or the thirteen homilies on the Sermon on the Mount (XVI–XXVIII).

Expository preaching in the modern period has been decisively affected by the far-reaching changes in religious understanding in the nineteenth century, particularly the rise of biblical criticism* and the 'secular hermeneutic' of scripture that accompanied it. Notable instances of classical expository preaching which denote a conservative reaction to 'higher' criticism include in the nineteenth century the Baptist C. H. Spurgeon and the Anglican H. P. Liddon and in the twentieth century the

Evangelical D. M. Lloyd Jones. However, a line of thinkers beginning with F. D. E. Schleiermacher (1768–1834) have attempted to adjust the scripture homily to the new outlook. Schleiermacher brought a fresh interest to the question of the relation of scripture and preaching which was such a feature of the Reformation. Himself a great preacher, he countered the challenge of biblical criticism with his theory of religious experience. The hearer is not simply a vacuum to be energized by the word, and the Bible confirms rather than engenders revelation.* Schleiermacher also held that the meaning of a text transcended its immediate historical setting and had a fresh value in each new generation, even with due acceptance of the critical method.

In the twentieth century, the 'demythologizing'* programme of Rudolf Bultmann* has stressed this 'existential' truth of scripture which, however, does not depend on a continuity between the preached word and the historical Jesus;* cf. Bultmann's sermons, *This World and the Beyond* (ET 1960), which show how fundamental proclamation is to his theology. This centrality of the proclaimed word is even more true for Karl Barth,* who represents another reaction to Schleiermacher: clearly, expository preaching no longer depends on a Bible which is literally inerrant, nonetheless the Word of God* which stands in judgment on man's hubris – and all religious experience – speaks through, and only through, scripture. Barth's volumes of sermons, show his ability to discern in the text the elements of divine transcendence, the otherness of God but also his 'humanity', which are so marked in Barth's theology. For him the homily is always doctrinal and always related to the Christ of whom the entire OT and NT revelation speaks.

The scripture homily today involves a compromise between time-honoured beliefs in the unity of the Bible, its historical accuracy and christological interpretation, and a cautious acceptance of historical criticism and those studies which bear on the problem of interpreting the concepts and vocabularies of past cultures. Expository preaching has been affected by changing patterns of worship in the Western churches and by the decline in religious allegiance generally, but the second Vatican Council emphasized the importance of the homily (using the tools of modern study) in the liturgy as did the liturgical movement in other churches. In liberation theology* (*see also* **Marxist Interpretation**), the 'critical' aspects of the homily, the judgment of the word on the human political and social condition, and the demand for justice and human dignity, have been especially prominent.

Y. Brilioth, *Landmarks in the History of Preaching*, 1950; F. E. Crowe, *Theology of the Christian Word. A Study in History*, 1978; E. C. Dargan, *A History of Preaching*, reissued 1954; B. Reicke, 'Synopsis of Early Christian Preaching' in A. J. Fridrichsen (ed.), *The Root of the Vine*, 1953.

IEUAN ELLIS

Hosea

An adequate interpretation of the book of Hosea must take account of its complex history, for its origins lie in the northern kingdom shortly before it fell to Assyria in 721 BC, but the history of its transmission belongs to Judah (1.1), as does that of the entire Hebrew canon.* Transmission is itself creative; in reapplying the message to fresh situations it adds a new dimension to an older word. It is, therefore, not only the many textual and exegetical problems of the book which complicate its interpretation but the possibility that different theologies may undergird it.

Three main areas are of particular concern for the book's interpretation: the significance of the prophet's personal life, the relation of words of judgment to those of salvation, and the possibility that Judaean influence has radically reshaped the prophet's message. The prophet's marital experience is given prominence in the first section of the book, an indication of its importance in relation to his message. It is commonly assumed that it was this which taught Hosea both the obduracy of human sin and the magnitude of divine love, but the presentation of the events in chs 1 and 3 suggests otherwise. His marriage to Gomer and his reclaiming of the unnamed adulterous woman are alike presented as symbolic actions, that is to say, not the means of revelation to the prophet, but the means of his proclamation to the nation. Such, too, is the function of the symbolic names as is evident from elsewhere in the OT. They are not necessarily more indicative of the status of the children so named than are *Ichabod* (I Sam. 4.21) and *Shear-jashub* (Isa. 7.3). The whole is a proclamation of Yahweh's judgment and love.

Hosea, with Jeremiah, has been the most frequent subject of psychological* interpretation among Old Testament prophets, and many attempts have been made to reconstruct his life story. This is not merely an impossible task in the absence of sufficient evidence; more seriously it is a misuse of the material. The proclamation is central, not the prophet. Whether the narrative speaks of one woman or two is not made clear. The former is more likely by analogy with God's relationship to Israel, but ultimately there can be no certainty,

a problem compounded by the ambiguity of the phrase 'woman of harlotry' (*'ēshet zenū-nīm*; 1.2). Was Gomer a prostitute (*zōnāh*), or representative of her contemporaries who were involved in fertility rites (Wolff)? This, too, is why the prophet's story ends abruptly in 3.3. Of the success or failure of his efforts there is no hint. The focus is on his obligation to love in demonstration of Yahweh's love, loving not the penitent but the persistently sinful nation ('even while they turn to other gods', 3.1).

This is fundamental to the question of the relationship of judgment and salvation within the book. The nation is beyond hope of reform (5.4,6; 7.1f.). There is a note of finality in the words of judgment, embracing not only the nation's present but its future also in the destruction of the coming generation (9.11ff., 16). But is Hosea simply a prophet of doom 'turned by the Judaean editors into the most forgiving spokesman of divine love' (Stinespring)? The book's most valuable insight would lie then in the secondary Judaean material. Others have attempted to relate the judgment and salvation oracles chronologically, generally attributing the latter to a later period of the prophet's ministry when despair of the nation's future may have yielded to hope as he realized the extent of divine love. The tentative nature of this argument is clear, depending as it does on an attempted reconstruction of Hosea's life story.

The allegory* of ch. 2 is instructive. Not divorce proceedings but rather a soliloquy (Andersen and Freedman), it moves through longing for repentance to the finality of total rupture (v. 13). But then comes the divine 'therefore' (v. 14). Because the nation has forgotten him, Yahweh will cause her to remember, and that not by judgment but by his saving action (Clines). Here is a fundamental aspect of Hosea's message. The divine initiative in salvation springs not from the nation's penitence but from Yahweh's compassion on the hopelessness of her sin, and is itself the prelude to her transformation.

In the present arrangement of the material, however, a different note occasionally sounds: the initiative for restoration lies with the nation and her repentance is the prerequisite for Yahweh's intervention in salvation. This is particularly evident in the secondary juxtaposition of call to repentance (14.1–3) and promise of salvation (14.4ff.) and in the arrangement of fragmentary sayings in 2.16–23 where Israel's repudiation of Baal worship and her knowledge of Yahweh appear as the precondition of the restoration envisaged in 2.18 and 2.21ff. respectively.

Of the surprisingly large number of references to Judah in this book of northern origin some, it is reasonable to suppose, originated in Judah. An undoubted example occurs in 12.2 where the following etymologies of Jacob (Gen. 25.26) and Israel (Gen. 32.28) make it clear that Judah is not part of the original text. That it is a later addition is likely, too, in those references which are not integrated into their context (e.g. 5.5; 6.4,11; 10.11). Here the criticism of Judah's life and worship is extensive. In contrast, the issue in 5.8–14, where literary unity and historical background in the Syro-Ephraimite war of 733 BC suggest Hosean origin, is specifically that of the disunity and mutual hostility of the one people of God. The Judaean editors, far from adding consoling words for Judah, with a seriousness equal to Hosea's confronted their own people with the prophetic word, with Israel's fate a challenge and a warning. There can, therefore, be no simple attribution to Hosea or to Judaean influence on the basis of a critical or favourable attitude to Judah respectively, nor should the reference to the Davidic* king (3.5) too readily be described as secondary. The hope of cultic and political restoration corresponds chiastically to the political and cultic deprivation of 3.4. The Davidic kingship, with its principle of dynastic succession, may well have represented the stability and possibility of unity to which Hosea was committed.

More than in any other eighth-century prophet, it is possible to see in Hosea a developing interpretation of the people's earlier traditions incorporated into his message: the story of Jacob (ch.12), and of the exodus (ch.11). It is commonly held that Hosea's influence may be seen in Deuteronomy and in Jeremiah, who shares with him the view of the wilderness wandering as a honeymoon period and takes up themes which had earlier been characteristic of the northern kingdom.

In the NT, Jesus is twice (Matt. 9.13; 12.7) presented as replying to his critics by requiring them to reflect upon Hos. 6.6, and the book is directly referred to on a number of other occasions (cf. Luke 23.30; Rom. 9.25f.; I Cor. 15.55; I Peter 2.10). Perhaps more revealing for the way in which the NT writers handled scripture is the use of Hos. 11.1, describing Israel's deliverance from Egypt, as pointing to Jesus' flight to Egypt in his infancy* (Matt. 2.15), and of Hos. 6.2, with its obscure reference to 'the third day', as prefiguring Jesus' resurrection* on the third day (I Cor. 15.4).

F. I. Andersen and D. N. Freedman, *Hosea*, 1980; D. J. A. Clines, 'Hosea 2: Structure and Interpretation', *Studia Biblica* 1978 I, *JSOT–SS* 11, 1979; G. I. Emmerson, *Hosea. An Israelite Prophet in Judean Perspective*, JSOT Supplements 28, 1984; W. F. Stinespring, 'A

Problem of Theological Ethics in Hosea' in J. L. Crenshaw and J. T. Willis (eds), *Essays in Old Testament Ethics*, 1974; H. W. Wolff, *Hosea*, 1974.

GRACE I. EMMERSON

Hoskyns, E. C.

The biblical work of Edwyn Clement Hoskyns (1884–1937) began in the 1920s when the Liberal* Catholic movement of which he was a member was gaining importance in the Church of England. Using the tools of critical scholarship it produced a theology; supernatural in character, orthodox in tone, and creative in expression, it was to dominate biblical, especially NT studies, for the next two decades. *Essays Catholic and Critical*, published in 1926, was representative of the movement, containing articles in the biblical field by W. L. Knox, A. E. J. Rawlinson, K. E. Kirk and E. G. Selwyn, as well as Hoskyns' own contribution, 'The Christ of the Synoptic Gospels', which concluded that 'the characteristic features of Catholic piety have their origin in Our Lord's interpretation of His own person'. This is very much the keystone of the movement's theology.

Hoskyns arrived at this conclusion by rejecting the Liberal Protestant interpretation of Christian origins given by Harnack,* whose lectures he heard as a student in Berlin. He was initially influenced by Harnack's Catholic Modernist* opponent, Alfred Loisy, but came to see the danger of submerging Jesus within the Catholic Church to which he had given rise. In 'The Christ of the Synoptic Gospels', Catholic Modernism is given barely a paragraph and Loisy is relegated to a footnote. Hoskyns was also influenced by A. Schweitzer's* emphasis on the transcendental, eschatological* nature of Jesus' teaching about himself and the kingdom,* and these themes formed the basis of discussions between English and German theologians, their papers being published in *Mysterium Christi* (1930).

Hoskyns' first major book (in collaboration with F. N. Davey), *The Riddle of the New Testament* (1931), illustrated to the intelligent non-expert how the analytical processes of the NT critic worked to produce the conclusion that Christian origins in their varied forms coincided with what Jesus himself proclaimed and claimed for himself.

In 1923 Hoskyns was commissioned to write a commentary* on the Fourth Gospel which was not completed at his death in 1937. Work on this was interrupted by his translation of Barth's* *Römerbrief* (published in 1933), which had the effect of encouraging Hoskyns to revise his commentary. The style was sharpened and, together with the influence of Schlatter's *Der Evangelist Johannes* (1930), his reading of Barth pushed Hoskyns' interpretation of John further towards a Jewish* and rabbinic* background and towards placing it firmly within the biblical and early Christian tradition.

The posthumous *Crucifixion–Resurrection* (1981) takes forward theologically the theme of *The Riddle*. The fragments from which the work is composed show how the death and resurrection of Jesus form the central pivot on which NT theology and ethics rest.

Hoskyns' biblical interpretation is very much a 'child of its time', representing an emerging English school of Catholic critical thought, which originated with Gore, but covered a wider canvas by being influenced in varying degrees by Loisy, Schweitzer, Barth and Schlatter. It was also a reaction against 'liberal' and 'modernist' interpretations of the material. Its interest lies in its somewhat *sui generis* character.

See also **English Interpretation; Liberalism.**

Biographical introduction by G. S. Wakefield to *Crucifixion–Resurrection*, 1981; R. E. Parsons, *Sir Edwyn Hoskyns as a Biblical Theologian*, 1985.

RICHARD PARSONS

Hymnody

The Bible is the most important source of Christian hymnody, not only because of its authority* in the Christian church, but because it contains so much hymn material. Of this, the psalms are the most obvious instance, but some other biblical songs and poems have found their way into modern as well as ancient liturgy.

One form of Christian hymnody has therefore been the metrical paraphrase of the psalms and other parts of scripture. (In this article it will be convenient to confine the word 'hymn' to the metrical form in which it is commonly understood.) From the time of the Reformation,* metrical psalms were an adjunct to Anglican worship, and they were to become an integral part of the services of the Church of Scotland and of early English Dissent. The Old Version of Sternhold and Hopkins and the New Version of Tate and Brady were commonly bound up with the Book of Common Prayer and used in conjunction with its services. To the psalms were added similar metrical versions of other parts of scripture (e.g. Magnificat) regularly used in public worship. The paraphrasing of the psalms in metre was an exercise that attracted many writers, among them such literary figures as George Herbert (*see* **Metaphysical Poets**), John Milton and Joseph Addison, although their writings were not originally designed for congregational singing. The tradition of the fairly strict paraphrase has not died out. Among contemporary writers, Timothy Dudley-Smith has produced a well-known metrical version of the NEB text of the Magnificat (*Hymns Ancient and Modern New Standard*, 1983, 422; hereafter AMNS) and Ian Pitt-Watson has used the same translation for a metrical version of Ps. 139 (*Hymns and Psalms*, 1983, 543; hereafter HAP). Brian Foley and Erik Routley are among those whose metrical versions of psalms appear in contemporary hymn books. There are, moreover, off-shoots of Presbyterianism that still decline to sing anything in worship that is not strictly scriptural. But more often it is the thought of the psalm rather than its precise language that inspires the modern hymn-writer.

The beginning of this last process may be traced to Isaac Watts (1674–1748), who in a lengthy and pungent preface justified the title of his work: *The psalms of David imitated in the language of the New Testament, and applied to the Christian state and worship*. Watts saw no reason why Christians should sing the psalms as if they were still living under the OT dispensation; his aim was, he declared, to make David* 'speak the common sense of a Christian'. So his version of Ps. 72, instead of looking for the coming of a messianic* king, opens:

Jesus shall reign, where'er the sun
doth his successive journeys run

and may be compared with the more conservative paraphrase of James Montgomery (AMNS 142). Some of the psalms remain close to the original, and probably Ps. 90 ('Our God, our help in ages past') could be sung by Jews as well as Christians. An example of Watts' milder Christianizing of the psalms may be found in his use of Ps. 19:

Nor shall Thy spreading gospel rest
Till through the world Thy truth has run;
Till Christ has all the nations blest,
That see the light or feel the sun.

(AMNS 168: the hymn in its entirety interprets both of the apparently divergent parts of the psalm.)

From early days, Watts had been critical of the praise offered in the Independent churches of which he was a member, and some years before his great work on the psalms, he had published *Hymns and Spiritual Songs* in three books, of which one has the title 'collected from the Holy Scriptures'. Here the same principles are applied; a paraphrase of Isa. 52.7–10 is conflated with Matt. 13.16–17 and entitled 'the Blessedness of Gospel Times'. But most of the hymns here are meditations on a single verse of scripture. The most

famous ('When I survey the wondrous cross')
occurs in the hymns 'prepared for the Lord's
Supper', and has the heading 'Crucifixion to
the World by the Cross of Christ Gal. 6.14'.
In view of this, it is surprising that many
hymn books have omitted the fourth verse:

His dying crimson, like a robe
Spreads o'er his body on the tree,
Then am I dead to all the globe
And all the globe is dead to me.

It is even more surprising that Watts should
have countenanced its possible omission by
putting this verse in brackets.

Watts believed that the whole Bible must be
interpreted in the light of Christ, and that
when passages from it were used in Christian
hymnody, they must bear witness to that light.
This is also true of the hymns of Charles
Wesley and of those of his brother, John.
What seems to be a paraphrase of Isa. 35
turns out to be a celebration of the Christian
gospel. A hymn entitled 'David and Goliath'
soon identifies the latter as 'my own besetting
sin' and the hymn ends:

Faith in Jesu's conqu'ring name
Slings the sin-destroying stone,
Points the Word's unerring aim,
And brings the monster down.

But the vast majority of Wesley's hymns are
not in any way paraphrases. His use of the
Bible was more daring and innovative. His
hymns are a mosaic or tapestry of texts. The
editors of the sumptuous reprint of the 1780
*Collection of Hymns for the Use of the People
called Methodists* (1983) have placed in the
margin the scriptural references to the hymns;
they have confined themselves to those allusions that are unmistakable and indisputable,
but an appendix gives examples of how some
hymns might be annotated if every possible
reference were included. Here are the obvious
allusions in one of the most used of Wesley's
hymns:

O thou who camest from above
                              John 3.31
The pure celestial fire t'impart,
                              Luke 12.49
Kindle a flame of sacred love
                              I Chron. 21.26
On the mean altar of my heart!

There let it for thy glory burn
With inextinguishable blaze,
                              Lev. 6.13
And trembling to its source return
In humble love, and fervent praise.

Jesu, confirm my heart's desire
                              Rom. 10.1
To work, and speak, and think for thee;

Still let me guard the holy fire,
And still stir up thy gift in me;
                              II Tim. 1.6

Ready for all thy perfect will,
                              Rom. 12.2
My acts of faith and love repeat,
                              I Thess. 1.3
Till death thy endless mercies seal,
                              Eph. 4.30
And make the sacrifice complete.
                              *Phil. 2.17;
                              II Tim. 4.6*

The example illustrates two features of
Wesley's use of the Bible. First, he digs out
some obscure texts – in this case one from
Leviticus as a main inspiration for the hymn.
Such examples abound, in the following case
using Gen. 27.37:

Pronounce the glad word,
And bid us be free;
Ah! hast thou not, Lord,
A blessing for me?

All scripture is, in fact, grist to his mill; he
called the 1780 collection 'A little body of
experimental and practical divinity'; and it
has been claimed that if all copies of the Bible
were lost, a skilful man might extract much of
it from these hymns.

Secondly, Wesley does not confine himself
to the King James Version. For the psalms,
he often prefers Coverdale (*see* **Translations
[to the K J V]**). In John Wesley's *Notes on the
New Testament*, his own translation constantly
differs from the KJV, and there are scores of
instances in which he anticipates the Revised
Version which was to appear more than a
century later. Such amendments of the KJV
are reflected in the hymns. John sometimes
corrected those of Charles, and although
Charles Wesley is unquestionably the author
of the vast majority of the hymns that bear
this surname, scholars continue to debate the
precise contribution made by his brother.

When hymns are used, as they were by
Wesley, to expound doctrine, it is not long
before they become didactic in character –
preaching to those who sing them or, at least,
inviting them to take to heart that which they
sing. The *Olney Hymns* were published in
three books, and a facsimile was printed in
1979 to celebrate the bicentenary of the first
publication. The first book has hymns on
select texts of scripture, and these are set out
in biblical order. I Kings 10.1–9 is entitled
'Queen of Sheba' and leads us on to 'one
greater than Solomon'. The next hymn, on I
Kings 17.6, begins:

Elijah's example declares,
Whatever distress may betide;

The saints may commit all their cares,
To him who will surely provide.

The famous 'Amazing grace' is based on I Chron. 17.16–17 and entitled 'Faith's review and expectation'.

The didactic use of scripture in hymnody has survived and indeed sometimes flourished in this century. At one level, it is found in Sydney Carter's song 'When I needed a neighbour' (AMNS 433), at another in the verses for Passiontide by the contemporary hymnwriter, Fred Pratt Green:

To mock your reign, O dearest Lord,
they made a crown of thorns;
set you with taunts along that road
from which no man returns (AMNS 517).

The ancient office hymns similarly used scripture in order to teach the significance of the Christian Year. Sometimes a story is retold in order to underline the occasion of celebration. Sometimes, a group of stories is brought together, as in, 'Why, impious Herod, shouldst thou fear?' (English Hymnal, 1933, 38), where the themes of Herodian persecution, the wise men from the East, the baptism of Jesus, and the changing of water into wine at Cana are brought together in a hymn for the Epiphany season. Sometimes, the hymn seeks to suggest dispositions in the worshipper which should arise from what has been recalled. 'The glory of these forty days', after recalling the fasts of Moses,* Elijah, Daniel and John the Baptist,* continues:

Then grant us, Lord, like them to be
Full oft in fast and prayer with thee:
Our spirits strengthen with thy grace,
And give us joy to see thy face.

An interesting example from the point of view of exegesis of the Bible concerns the Passiontide hymn from the seventh century, Vexilla Regis ('The royal banners forward go'). The line 'God ... hath reigned in triumph from the tree' (regnavit a ligno Deus) reflects a very early Christian corruption of Ps. 96.10, already established in the second century. In his Dialogue with Trypho (ch. 73), Justin alleges against his Jewish opponent that the Jews have falsely erased from the text of the psalm the key words 'from the tree' which had been fulfilled in the crucifixion of Christ! The emended text was a key influence in the development of a way of interpreting Christ's death that was dominant for centuries, expressed in art* and devotion as well as in this important hymn (and already adumbrated in the theology of the Gospel of John): Jesus' death was an act of kingly triumph.

Once people were prepared to admit that hymns need not be strict paraphrases of scripture, the floodgates were opened to those which were simply allusive to the Bible. Hymns of the various revival movements are sometimes based on a single phrase of scripture. In Sankey's collections, a hymn called 'Beulah Land' has the text 'A land of corn and wine – Deut. 33.28', and this text provides the opening line. But the chorus:

O Beulah land, sweet Beulah land,
As on thy highest mount I stand,
I look away across the sea,
Where mansions are prepared for me,
And view the shining glory shore:
My heaven, my home for evermore!

seems to owe rather more to The Pilgrim's Progress than to Isa. 62.4. From the same collection, and indeed in many hymn books, is the children's hymn 'When he cometh', which is a sort of meditation on Mal. 3.17. From American spirituals comes a short hymn of encouragement which has achieved some popularity in Britain, too. The chorus runs:

There is a balm in Gilead
To make the wounded whole,
There is a balm in Gilead
To heal the sin-sick soul.

Jeremiah's question (8.22) is therefore turned into affirmation.

For different and more modern examples of allusive hymns, we turn to two twentieth-century examples. The first, Erik Routley's 'There in God's garden stands the tree of wisdom', is a translation of an Hungarian hymn in which the tree of life (Rev. 22.2) inspires meditation on the healing cross (AMNS 514). The second, 'Lord God, your love has called us here', by Brian Wren, is an attempt to provide an alternative to (not a substitute for) Wesley's 'And can it be' (HAP 216). Although the latter has but one clear quotation from the letter to the Romans, its theology is pretty squarely based on that letter (AMNS 489).

This article has been concerned with hymns which derive in some way from the scriptures, but brief notice must be taken of those which have had the scriptures thrust upon them. It was the custom of Hymns Ancient and Modern until 1950 to place a text above every hymn, and this was followed by most other Anglican and many Free Church hymn books of the period. The texts were selected by the editors presumably to indicate that the hymn was scriptural in content and perhaps to give some idea of its general theme. Sometimes the author's original text was ignored: the standard edition of Hymns Ancient and Modern puts 'what things were gain to me, those I counted loss for Christ' over 'When I survey', instead of the text on which Watts had based it. The custom was dropped in Hymns Ancient and Modern Revised and very few post-war hymn books have retained it. The *New Standard* version of the same book uses a few texts and headings – sometimes for historical reasons, sometimes to indicate to worshippers what they are about to sing.

A recent attempt has been made in the English-speaking world to create a hymn book arranged according to the canonical* order of the books of the Bible. *Rejoice in the Lord* (1985) is the hymn book of the Reformed Church in America, and had Erik Routley as its musical editor. Its subtitle is 'a hymn companion to the scriptures', and its preface runs: 'The hymns begin where the Bible begins – with God's act of creation, and they conclude where the Bible concludes – with the great vision of God's eternal city.' Between these two are God's care for Israel and his mighty acts in Christ. Some reviewers have pointed out that despite this great aim, there remains – perhaps inevitably – some arbitrariness in the arrangement of the hymns.

The modern liturgical movement has meant that contemporary hymn books have recovered or sought a number of hymns on the scriptures themselves – hymns on 'the excellency and variety of scripture' – to use the title which Isaac Watts gave to one part of Ps. 119. Such hymns are often short, and used in some traditions between the readings at the eucharist.

We began with the claim that the Bible is the most important source of Christian hymnody. In conclusion, it can be claimed that the hymns which survive from one generation to another are, in the main, those which are based upon the Bible or are strongly scriptural in content. Such hymns are less subject than others to fashion and fad. A congregation affirming the world mission of the church cannot now sing 'From Greenland's icy mountains'. despite the poetic content of the hymn; but it can still sing:

Jesus shall reign where'er the sun
doth his successive journeys run;
his kingdom stretch from shore to shore,
till moons shall wax and wane no more.

See also **Hymns (New Testament); Liturgy, Use of the Bible in; Metaphysical Poets; Music, The Bible in; Poetry, English.**

ALAN DUNSTAN

Hymns (New Testament)

The early Christians inherited the OT psalms, using them where appropriate, like the other scriptures, to make theological points, and as religious songs. Mark (and Matthew) refers to the disciples' singing of hymns after the Last Supper, the liturgically fitting reference being to Pss. 113–118. Acts 16.25 uses the same word (*humneō* = 'sing a hymn') with reference

to Paul and Silas. In relation to plainly liturgical occasions, Paul also speaks of the singing of such songs as an ingredient in worship in I Cor. 14.15,26. The words here are *psallō*, *psalmos*, which may be general in their meaning and not refer specifically to 'the Psalms'. Col. 3.16 (paralleled in the probably dependent Eph. 5.19) refers to the thankful and mutually admonitory use of *psalmoi*, *humnoi* and *ōdai pneumatikai* (= 'spiritual songs'), which are more likely to be rough synonyms than technically distinct categories.

The upshot is that it is probable that from very early days, Christians were composing and using their own religious songs and singing was playing a part in their worship. We have no knowledge of the character of the music they used, but can we know what the words were? The worship vividly described by Paul in I Cor. 14 seems to have been ecstatic rather than sober, and one may wonder whether songs were more likely to have been produced for the moment rather than with a view to preservation and repetition.

However, it is widely held that, within texts of quite different kinds, there are embedded early Christian hymns which enable us to see something of early Christian practice in this matter. Some have seen this as in no way surprising in that, in their view, a great deal of the NT literature either reflects the practice of worship or was written with use in worship in mind. We should note that the identification of hymns in the NT writings derives from certain kinds of modern interpretative interest or awareness. First, the form-critical* principle, that the elements in the NT are to be categorized according to literary form and genre,* and that this analysis enables one to gain a picture of the use of the various passages in early Christian life. The latter aspect is not difficult to decide in the present case. Secondly, concern to distinguish contexts of thought. If a given passage is, in origin, likely to be independent of its present context, then it may tell us about the ideas of Christians other than the writer of the book as a whole and need not be seen in the context of the rest of his thought. It will give us an independent point of entry into the thought-setting of early Christianity. Thirdly, general interest in the behaviour and institutions of early Christian groups.

Instances of early Christian hymns in the NT are discerned with varying degrees of confidence. The following are the most significant candidates:

1. Phil. 2.5–11. The poetic and rhythmic character of this passage was pointed out as long ago as 1899 by Johannes Weiss, and its identification as a christological hymn has been vigorously advocated, especially by E.

Lohmeyer* (*Kurios Jesus*, 1928) and R. P. Martin, though it is still not universally accepted. Other matters are also unclear, despite the minute analysis which the passage has received. If it is poetic, then what kind of poetry is it? Resistant to analysis in terms of Greek metre, it may be written along the looser lines of Hebrew poetry* (though in either case, division into sections is open to a variety of possibilities, and a later infiltration of words and phrases is often supposed). If semitic in form, then perhaps it is semitic in thought; but then, it may instead be proto-gnostic* in overall concept. And what does the cultural background indicate about authorship: did Paul compose it or inherit it? If the latter, we learn much about early Christian creativity and theological audacity.

2. Col. 1.15–20. Many of the same issues arise as in relation to the Philippians passage, though dependence on Jewish wisdom* theology is more confidently claimed.

3. Minor Pauline passages, such as Phil. 3.20f., Eph. 5.14, and I Tim. 3.16 are put forward as 'hymnic'. This raises acutely the question of genre. Modern classifications of material help the analyst, but may be wholly anachronistic as far as the first century is concerned. It may be equally accurate (and inaccurate), for example, to classify Eph. 5.14 as 'baptismal liturgy' and I Tim. 3.16 as 'creed'.*

4. With less confidence and equal difficulty about genre, the Prologue to the Gospel of John (John 1.1–14 or 1–18) and I Cor. 13 ('the hymn to love') are frequently classified as 'hymns'. Both these attributions raise a further problem: how plausible is it that these passages are (or have lying behind them) independent compositions? In each case, there are features which distinguish the passage from the context and even the author of the work as a whole, but there are also features which bind it very closely to its present setting.

5. The Lucan 'canticles'. Luke 1–2 (*see* Infancy Narratives) contain three passages (1.46–55; 1.68–79; 2.29–32) which the church has recognized as hymns (and another, 2.14, which it made the basis for a hymn) from early times: the Magnificat, the Benedictus, and the Nunc Dimittis. The same problem arises as in 4: are they already existing songs (J. A. T. Robinson thought that the Benedictus was originally a hymn about John the Baptist) or Lucan compositions? There is certainly a case for seeing them as highly expressive of Lucan theology.

6. Hymns in the Revelation of John. In passages like 4.11; 5.9f.; 7.15–17; and 15.3f., we have liturgical pieces, with, in some cases, the formal description, *ōdē* ('song'). They are depicted as expressions of the worship of heaven, but are they in fact the worship of

earth? Are they expressive of the theology of the writer of the Revelation – that the earthly church participates in the worship of heaven, with the two sides of the community essentially at one? It is interesting that, generally, these songs have not come to liturgical prominence in the church – with one notable exception, 4.8, itself dependent on the hymn that Isaiah heard being used in heaven, Isa. 6.3. This came into the very heart of the liturgy of the eucharist as the Sanctus.

Though some scholars consider them Jewish, what is probably our most extensive collection of early Christian hymns is not to be found in the NT at all, but in the *Odes of Solomon*, probably going back to the first or second century. Similarly, one of our most vivid glimpses of early Christian hymn-singing is also from a non-scriptural source, the famous letter of Pliny the Younger to Trajan (*Letters*, 10.96), describing the activities of the Christians of Bithynia in the early years of the second century.

See also **Colossans; Philippians.**

J. H. Charlesworth, *The Odes of Solomon*, 1973; R. P. Martin, *Carmen Christi*, 1967; J. T. Sanders, *The New Testament Christological Hymns*, 1971; M. H. Shepherd, *The Paschal Liturgy and the Apocalypse*, 1960; L. L. Thompson, 'Cult and Eschatology in the Apocalypse of John', *Journal of Religion*, vol. 49, 1969, pp. 330–50.

J. L. HOULDEN

Icons

Icons form an integral part of the life, spirituality and worship of Orthodox Christians, and are prominent in Orthodox churches and homes; the word 'icon' refers primarily to painted wood panel images, but can also include the wall paintings and mosaics of Orthodox churches; for Orthodox Christians the word 'icon' is also related (Greek *eikōn* = image) to the biblical themes of man's creation* in the image of God (Gen. 1.26–27), of Christ as the image of the invisible God (Col. 1.15), and of our humanity being restored to its true image and likeness in Jesus Christ (II Cor. 3.17–18).

Icons are not in themselves interpretations of the Bible; rather, they express the holy tradition of the church, and the renewed humanity which we share in Christ and in the communion of saints. For Orthodox Christians, the holy tradition is expressed in many ways – in the Bible, the creeds,* the councils of the Church, the liturgy,* the writings of the Fathers (*see* **Patristic Christology**), and in icons.

The subject matter of icons is not exclusively biblical. Some of the best-known icons (like the figures of the Mother of God holding the incarnate Son, and the Christ Pantocrator) express truths that are to be found in the Bible and in the doctrinal teaching of the church, but they are not strictly illustrations or interpretations of the Bible. Many saints represented in icons are from the post-biblical period. Many of the 'church feasts' icons and icons relating to the life of the Virgin Mary derive from material found in the apocryphal gospels (e.g. her presentation in the temple by her parents Joachim and Anna, and her dormition).

Biblical material used in icons is interpreted in the light of the Orthodox understanding of the holy tradition. In most icons of a biblical subject we need to remember several specific factors: the event or person represented; the doctrinal teaching conveyed through the icon; the liturgical context of the icon in the cycle of the church's feasts, and the icon's powerful visual focus which complements the verbal texts of the liturgy; the acceptance of multiple meanings beyond the strictly historical – hence the importance of the tradition of allegorical* interpretation commonly accepted by most of the early Fathers of the church. Certain themes can be taken to illustrate this varied tradition of interpretation.

Icons of the Holy Trinity are based on the story of the hospitality of Abraham* in Gen. 18.1–8. Using a tradition of allegorical interpretation going back to the second century, this episode is seen as a revelation of the Holy Trinity under the form of the three angelic visitors whom Abraham received, a revelation that is completed and fulfilled in the incarnation and at Pentecost. The figures of Abraham and Sarah, the house, the oak of Mamre, and the preparations for the meal are included in icons before the fifteenth century, along with the three angelic figures. About 1425 the great Russian icon painter and disciple of St Sergius, Andrei Rublev, painted an icon of the Holy Trinity for the Holy Trinity Cathedral in the monastery at Zagorsk founded by St Sergius; this icon became the source of a modified tradition of icons of the Trinity; many of the details in the earlier tradition are omitted and Rublev concentrates attention on the three angelic beings seated around a table in the centre of which is a chalice holding the head of a sacrificial victim. Through posture, gesture, colour and geometrical design this icon sets before us the mystery of the Holy Trinity. A biblical incident is used as a starting point, but the icon embodies the church's understanding of the trinitarian nature of the Godhead and invites us to enter on the way that leads to 'theosis' or 'deification', i.e. full union with the Godhead.

Icons of the nativity bring together biblical and other material from the church's tradition (see **Infancy Narratives**). The wise men (Matt.

2.1ff) and the shepherds (Luke 2.8ff) are placed beneath the heavenly host of angels, and flank the recumbent figure of the Mother of God who lies beneath the entrance to a cave; in the cave lies the incarnate Son in a small sarcophagus watched over by an ox and an ass; in the lower levels of the icon midwives wash the infant Jesus, and Joseph is tempted to disbelief by the devil disguised as a shepherd (cf. apocryphal gospels of pseudo-Matthew and pseudo-James). The icons aid the church's celebration of the incarnation; hence, the ray of Divine Light penetrates the darkness of the cave where the incarnate Son has entered the dark world of mortality and sin; his incarnation is welcomed by wise men and shepherds, and by the ox and ass (cf. Isa. 1.3); the presence of the midwives fulfilling their duties stresses the truly incarnate nature of the self-emptying Word of God. The Word becomes flesh, and we behold his glory; the icon expresses the doctrine of John 1.14 (see **Logos**).

Icons of the transfiguration show how various elements in an incident and its interpretation can be brought together visually. The white-robed figure of Christ is on the mountain top with the mandorla behind him signifying the divine realm to which he belongs and which he manifests; on either side of Christ are Moses* and Elijah, signifying that their ministry has been fulfilled by Christ the new law-giver and prophet; Peter, James and John are dazed and unable to bear the brightness of this vision of the divine glory of the incarnate Lord; the colours in the icon and the liturgical texts for the feast make it clear that this event is eschatological* in character, anticipating the glory of both the resurrection* and the second coming.

Icons of the raising of Lazarus vividly present the gospel narrative and its significance. The kneeling figures of Mary and Martha plead with Christ for his help; a servant removes the stone from the entrance to the tomb; groups of disciples and of Jews help to balance each half of the icon, but the major focus of attention is the relationship of Christ and Lazarus: Christ the life-giver calls forth Lazarus from the realm of the dead; the white, bound figure of Lazarus stands out against the darkness of the cave (reminiscent of the cave in nativity icons, etc). The feast of the raising of Lazarus is on the Saturday before Palm Sunday, prefacing the events of Holy Week and Easter; the raising of Lazarus prompts the Jews to kill Jesus (John 11.47–53), and thus leads directly to the great life-giving triumph of the crucifixion and the resurrection. The icons resonate with all the subtlety and symbolism that are present both in the Gospel of John and elsewhere in the later liturgical and spiritual tradition of the church, using and interpreting the Gospel.

The interpretation of biblical material in icons is presented to the eye through a visual language that has developed over many centuries; it is not a language of academic biblical criticism but a language of theology and spirituality which has evolved within the church, to mediate God's continuing self-disclosure in Jesus Christ and his church.

See also **Art, The Bible in;** *Biblia Pauperum.*

John Baggley, *Doors of Perception*, 1987; Vladimir Lossky, *In the Image and Likeness of God*, 1975; Leonid Ouspensky, *Theology of the Icon*, 1978; Leonid Ouspensky and Vladimir Lossky, *The Meaning of Icons*, 1982; Gervase Matthew, *Byzantine Aesthetics*, 1963; Timothy Ware, *The Orthodox Church*, 1963.

JOHN BAGGLEY

Ideology

The term originated in the period of the French Revolution and was created by Antoine Destutt de Tracy to describe a philosophical discipline which would provide the foundation of all the sciences (Barth, p. 1). Napoleon Bonaparte's hatred of ideology and ideologues gave the term a bad name in the nineteenth century and since then it has always had connotations of invective and accusation. The work of Karl Marx and Friedrich Engels (*The German Ideology*, 1846) developed, at great length, the analysis of ideology as a negative quality, reflecting the distortion created by it in the class struggle and causing 'false consciousness' in the perception of social reality by those living under the dominant ideology. Since Marx, ideology has tended to mean the processes of the production of meanings and ideas within any given social formation, reflecting elements of praxis and legitimation, deformation and distortion. As a term for a system of ideas providing a framework for perceiving social reality and generating practical concerns, ideology is not necessarily a pejorative term – it may describe the ideas informing any world-view which moves people to action or it may even be confined to a set of ideas peculiar to one person (e.g. the ideology of Lenin as distinct from that of Bolsheviks, the ideology of Calvin* in contrast to that of Calvinists, cf. Plamenatz, pp. 15–17). Where there are ideas there is ideology. The influence of Marx has seriously muddied the water for discussions of ideology by contrasting ideology with truth or science, so that ideology in Marxist and 'marxisant' terminology is a decidedly pejorative word. Mannheim's major study of the term contrasts it with utopia (another weasel word!), and this dichotomy between the two has been influential in recent theologico-political debate. Ricoeur's magisterial treatment of the subject covers all the important thinkers on ideology (Marx, Althusser, Mannheim, Weber, Habermas, Geertz) and offers an account of religion as occupying a dialectical position between ideology and utopia.

The definitional and discursive treatments of ideology are such that it would take a book-length disquisition to provide an adequate background to the subject of the Bible and ideology. Defining ideology as 'the confusion of linguistic with natural reality' (P. de Man, *The Resistance to Theory*, 1986, p. 11) would render all biblical language open to the hermeneutics of suspicion in order to dismantle its ideological distortions of social reality. On the other hand, defining ideology as idolatry (cf. Turner, *Marxism and Christianity*, 1983, p. 227) would expose those religions based on aspects of the Bible as idolatrous connivers in evil. If ideology is a field, a whole anonymous way of thinking (cf. Ricoeur, p. 118), then the ideological aspects of the Bible are what determined the writers' consciousness without their control, and ideological analysis of the text becomes a difficult task. Better to work with less loaded notions of ideology and scrutinize the text for its ideological holdings as expressed by language and ideas. The extent to which these may be said to have distorted the writers' approaches to (social) reality (i.e. ideology as producing false consciousness) cannot be determined by the modern reader because there is (as yet) no access to the social world of the Bible outside the text (developments in archaeology* and cultural materialist* readings of the world of the Bible may amend this lack). Against this background of many complex issues of definition, treatment and interpretation, the little there is of ideological analysis of the Bible may be treated with the respect due to any inchoate account of work in progress.

The interpretation of the Bible as an ideological system or set of ideological systems (the different canons* describe discrete ideological matrices and nexus) is quite a recent development of biblical studies because in the past it was more normal to study the religious ideas or theological concepts of the Bible. Using the term 'ideology' instead of 'theology' or 'religion' draws attention to the social and political aspects of biblical thought, which are often ignored, glossed over or denied in conventional scholarship. These aspects are stressed by N. K. Gottwald *The Tribes of Yahweh*, 1979, an impressive ideological analysis of biblical religion.

An equally impressive, though very different in approach and execution, treatment of the Bible as ideological literature is M. Sternberg's *The Poetics of Biblical Narrative*, 1985. It deals with the text *qua* text and analyses the narrative* and literary* aspects of the Bible as a book. Sternberg treats the Hebrew Bible as ideologically singular: that is, the world view projected and the rhetoric* used to project it belong together; representation cannot be dissociated from evaluation (p. 37). Here the biblical (or to be precise, the biblical writers') world of ideas (i.e. their ideology) is detectable from the modes of narrative presentation, though ambiguity and complexity can render the biblical text difficult to read. Sternberg's poetics is a triumph of close readings which refuses to 'disambiguate' the text, though critics with rather different ideological axes to grind have been less than persuaded by his arguments. Between these two markers of politics and poetics, ideological study of the Hebrew Bible is likely to develop over the next few decades.

A study of biblical literature as ideological production, in which the poetics of discourse and narrative is scrutinized for meaning and signification, can offer an alternative approach to the Bible from that of the more conventional historical-critical* method (cf. Polzin, *Moses and the Deuteronomist*, 1980, pp. 12–24). It focusses on the text as literary construction rather than on implied or hypothesized sources, backgrounds or editings. Close readings of the text seek in it the ideological voice(s) detectable by literary analysis and grasp the meaning of the text in relation to such basic ideological stances (cf. Polzin). This may entail limiting the scrutiny to such large expanses of text as the primary narrative in Genesis–Numbers (the Priestly perspective of ritualized ideology?) or the work of the Deuteronomists in Deuteronomy, Joshua–Kings, where the search for ideological control is more likely to be fruitful than in the shorter books of the Bible. On the other hand, the four collections of prophetic* material (Isaiah, Jeremiah, Ezekiel, and the Twelve) would yield significant finds if studied from the viewpoint of the ideological scrutiny (e.g. city and sect, community and ideology, purity and cult, eschatology* represent the ideological signatures of these four collections).

Long ago (1929), Mannheim suggested that the notion of 'false consciousness' is of religious origin and 'appears as a problem whenever the genuineness of a prophet's inspiration or vision is questioned either by his people or by himself' (p. 62; cf. I John 4.1). Much of the Hebrew Bible's presentation of prophecy is dominated by the biblical equivalent of 'false consciousness' (cf. Jer. 23.9–40; 27–29; Ezek. 13–14.11). Some of this polemic is against specific prophets on behalf of a particular prophet (Jer. 27–29), but a good deal

of it is simply 'against the prophets' (Ezek. 13; Micah 3.5–7; Jer. 23.9–40). Conflicting ideologies of prophecy* may be behind some of this material, with an anti-prophet ideology informing other discrete traditions. The central ideology of Deuteronomism concerns the divine word, often as mediated by prophets (esp. in the Deuteronomistic History*). But even Deuteronomy had to regulate for the behaviour of prophets, knowing a fulfilment of prophecy which represented false consciousness (13.1–5) and a fulfilment which could determine the authenticity of prophets (18.15–22). The presentation of Moses* as the prophet *par excellence* (Deut. 34.10–12) is indicative of the deuteronomistic ideology of prophecy, but inflected in a certain direction which facilitated other ideological movements intent on differentiating between the epoch of Moses and that of the prophets (Blenkinsopp, *Prophecy and Canon*, 1977, pp. 80–95; cf. Rivkin, *The Shaping of Jewish History*, 1971, pp. 3–41). It is also possible to see the prophets as ideologues, berating the community and inducing in it a self-hatred which reflected an ideology hostile to foreign culture (*Kulturkampf*) and at loggerheads with indigenous Hebrew culture, and prophecy as the ancient equivalent of modern ideology in the pejorative sense (Feuer, *Ideology and the Ideologists*, 1975, pp. 197–202).

The general production of the Hebrew Bible has been analysed as an ideological construction of conflicting parties by Morton Smith (*Palestinian Parties and Politics that Shaped the Old Testament*, 1971) and, more recently, has been explored by Giovanni Garbini (*History and Ideology in Ancient Israel*, ET 1988). Neither scholar's work has been received well by the guild of biblical scholars. This reception in itself has ideological factors which reflects the guild's tendency to follow an American-Israeli reading of the Bible in a historicist* manner or a cleaving to the older historical-critical holdings as fixed dogmas (the guild is not monolithic, so there are notable exceptions to this generalized observation). Although Smith and Garbini are in no sense similar in outlook, method or thought, they both have made serious and telling criticisms of the biblical material and much scholarship which tends to parrot the biblical ideology. They focus on a number of issues which will be central concerns of biblical studies for decades to come.

Part of the importance of the work of Smith and Garbini is that they also raise questions about the guild which studies the text. The scrutiny of the Bible for ideology (*Ideologiekritik*) is in its infancy but any study of ideology is a complex matter and involves many levels of investigation. One of the most important figures in this developing field is Ferdinand Deist, whose writings on *Ideologiekritik* have made an initial foray into the field. The importance of his approach is in its focus on the ideology (ideas system) of the critical method and presuppositions used in interpreting the text and their influence on the results of exegesis.* As a methodological* analysis of interpretation, *Ideologiekritik* uncovers another layer of textual reading but one which focusses on the exegete more than on the text. By asking questions about the epistemological bases of the interpretive method, Deist makes the enterprise more sophisticated and alerts the guild to the need for an ideological scrutiny of itself.

At this stage of the argument, ideology relates to a number of complex issues in textual interpretation (cf. Jameson). Ideologies of the text, ideologies of the holding communities (e.g. synagogue, church), and ideologies of the teaching guilds (i.e. the authorized interpreters) all become necessary subjects of the *Ideologiekritik* enterprise. Here the ethics of reading and the sociology of scholarship as well as the reception of texts and the modes of their production are all part of the ideological scrutiny required of alert scholars. Methods of appropriating texts may reveal or conceal ideological factors which should be part of the debate about the meaning and function of texts. Non-hermeneutic circularity and relativization are the perils of this kind of analysis, but failure to allow for ideological distortion in texts or among their patrons can easily engender 'false consciousness'. At this point the guild of scholars may find itself having to recognize the political nature of its activities and grasp the implications of much recent scrutiny of ideology in allied fields of study.

The pejorative view of ideology treats it as the equivalent of 'original sin' in literature and politics, but a more dialectical view of the matter is available. Ideas play a necessary part in the human enterprise of imaginative productions and interpretations, but they always have the potential for becoming 'ideology' in the bad sense of generating distortion and false consciousness. *Ideologiekritik* as a methodological principle keeps the exegete aware of these possibilities and protects the exegesis from servitude to special interests. Or to put it in words, paraphrased by modernization from the great ideological book and the ultimate Ideologue itself, addressed to Cain, 'ideology is couching at the door; its desire is for you, but you must master it'.

See also **Israel, History of; Methodology.**

H. Barth, *Truth and Ideology,* ²1976; F. Jameson, *The Ideologies of Theory: Essays 1971–1986*, vol. 1, *Situations of Theory*, 1988; K. Mannheim, *Ideology and Utopia: An Introduction to the Sociology of Knowledge*, reissued 1960; J. Plamenatz, *Ideology*, 1970; P. Ricoeur, *Lectures on Ideology and Utopia*, 1986.

ROBERT P. CARROLL

Infancy Narratives

Material about Jesus' conception, birth and youth, strikingly never echoed elsewhere in the NT, is found in very different narratives in Matt. 1–2 and Luke 1–2. In part these narratives can themselves be looked upon as interpretations of elements in the early preaching and ministry stories about Jesus, elucidating his theological and family background before he came on the scene to be baptized by John; e.g. by explaining in what sense he was Son of David* (because he was born at Bethlehem and because Joseph had Davidic descent); by showing that he was Son of God even before the baptismal announcement (in that his first recorded words spoke of the Temple as his Father's house and in that he was conceived by the Holy Spirit without a human father); by throwing light on the Joseph whose son he was called (attributing to Joseph features of his OT namesake who also received revelation in dreams and went to Egypt); by resolving the ministry issue (Mark 3.31–35) of the relative importance of Jesus' natural family *v.* his family of disciples who heard the word* of God and did it (showing his mother as a disciple who hears the word of God from an angel and says it should be done); and by having Jesus embody the whole history of Israel (starting the story of his origin with Abraham* begetting Isaac or with the parents of John the Baptist* who are carbon copies of Abraham and Sarah). Because of their interpretative role, some scholars classify the infancy narratives as *midrashim,** even though they do not interpret texts. Their midrashic style should not disguise the likelihood that they contain ancient tradition, perhaps popular rather than kerygmatic.*

Once written, Matt. 1–2 and Luke 1–2 became the subject of extraordinary expansive interpretation, more so than other gospel passages, perhaps because they and the passion narratives* were the only truly sequential stories. The expansion imaginatively smoothed out difficulties that had been created and filled in what was left unmentioned. Ignatius, knowing either these narratives or the traditions on which they drew, implicitly reconciles Johannine pre-existence christology* with Matthean-Lucan conception christology, so that the Word (*see* **Logos**) takes flesh in the womb of the Virgin Mary (*Eph.* 7.2; *Smyrn.* 1.1; *Magn.* 8.2; also Justin, *Apol.* 1.21, 33) – the approach adopted by the larger church ever since. By mid-second century the

Protevangelium of James and Justin show luxuriant growth in interpretation. The latter's *Dialogue with Trypho* (78.1, 9) traces the magi to Arabia; they have turned from superstitious sin to the adoration of the true God. A cave near Bethlehem becomes the birthplace in *Dial.* 78.5 and *Prot. Jas.* 18.1. The *Protevangelium* devotes much attention to Mary: her parents were Joachim and Anne (1.1; 2.1); she was presented at the Temple and reared there; in national competition she was betrothed to Joseph, an old man with children from a previous marriage (9.2), thus explaining the appearance of 'brothers' of Jesus in the canonical Gospels. Indeed, even the birth of Jesus is miraculously virginal, for the child appears suddenly and Mary's physical organs remain intact (18–20).

Continuing this expansive interpretation, Irenaeus* (*Adv. Haer.* 3.9.2) reflects on the symbolism* of the magi's gifts, while for Tertullian* (*Adv. Marcion* 3.13) they are almost kings. Zoroastrian and thus Persian background is attributed to them by Clement of Alexandria (*Strom.* 1.15), leading to the standard iconography* with Phrygian caps which when depicted in the Constantinian basilica at Bethlehem, reportedly touched the hearts of the Persian soldiers who ravaged Palestine in 614, causing them to spare the church. The sixth-century mosaic of St Apollinaris (Nuovo) in Ravenna, together with a later superscription, fixes the identity of the magi for the West: the white-haired Melchior; the young Caspar; the black-skinned Balthasar. Cologne preserves not only the tradition that the three met once more to celebrate Christmas Mass in Armenia in AD 54, but also the relics of the magi which travelled more widely than the original owners. Understandably, Egyptian Christians are fascinated with the flight to Egypt and fill in legends about the holy family's stay there, preserved in Arabic infancy gospels. The Lucan narrative lends itself less to imagination, but Mary and her child become one of the most common art* motifs, majestically depicted with the decor of a Byzantine empress in the East, more humanly and sentimentally in the West, eventually producing the ubiquitous Madonna. In a chain stretching from catacomb art of *c.* 200 to Menotti's *Amahl and the Night Visitors*, art and legend* are more influential interpreters of the infancy narratives than are theologians and commentators. When for midnight Mass at Greccio in 1223 Francis of Assisi set up a Christmas creche or crib, harmonizing Matthean magi, Lucan shepherds, the apocryphal cave, and animals from Isa. 1.3 (which had long been seen to comment poignantly on Jesus' rejection), he had more enduring effect on how ordinary Christians would read, hear, and interpret the narratives than all the biblical commentaries* put together.

Often in head-on collision with such Christian imagination, critical scholarship of the last two centuries has debunked and devalued the narratives. They were seen to be irreconcilable with material in the post-baptismal sections of the Gospels (where Jesus is an unknown), with each other (Matthew's flight to Egypt *v.* Luke's peaceful return to Nazareth), and with our knowledge of history (no astronomically detectable star rising in the East and coming to rest over Bethlehem; no one universal census under Augustus; Quirinius' census a decade after the death of Herod the Great). The silence of the rest of the NT raised doubts about the virginal conception, with some dismissing it as a crassly physical misunderstanding of Jesus' divine sonship and others finding it irreconcilable with the more profound pre-existence christology.* Frequently, the narratives were explained as fictional creations from pagan legends of gods mating with women or as midrashic embellishments of the story of the baby Moses* and the wicked pharaoh, and the Septuagint* of Isa. 7.14. Most frequently an alternative of natural engendering by Joseph was offered; but some recent feminist writing has posed Mary as the victim of rape, with Jesus being illegitimately conceived. (Illegitimacy was already part of anti-Christian Jewish polemic *c.* 180 [Origen,* *Adv. Celsum* 1.28, 32, 69] but there through Mary's adultery.) H. Conzelmann, in his influential *The Theology of St Luke*, 1960, dismissed the infancy narrative as not fitting his analysis of Lucan thought.

More recently this writer and others have attempted a middle road of interpretation, i.e., acknowledging the many historical difficulties in the narratives, but taking seriously the essential points on which Matthew and Luke agree (virginal conception, birth at Bethlehem, Davidic descent) as representing early Christian tradition antedating both. They have seen the narratives proclaiming authentic gospel christology (Jesus as Son of David and Son of God, comparable to Rom. 1.3–4) and with their OT flavour serving as a bridge between the Law* and Prophets* and the post-baptismal ministry that constituted the gospel proper.

*See also **Biblia Pauperum**; Luke, Gospel of; Matthew, Gospel of.*

R. E. Brown, *The Birth of the Messiah*, 1977 (supplement *CBQ* 48 [1986] pp. 468–83, 660–80); H. Hendrickx, *Infancy Narratives*, ²1984.

RAYMOND E. BROWN, SS

Inner-Biblical Exegesis

A term which has entered mainly OT studies

comparatively recently to indicate a method of biblical interpretation which has been receiving increasing attention, e.g. M. Fishbane's major study *Biblical Interpretation in Ancient Israel*, 1985. As its name implies, the method concerns itself with indications of the re-use, re-interpretation and re-application of earlier scriptural material within the OT itself. (There might be logic in applying the term also to the Synoptic Gospels, but this appears not to have taken place as yet.) There are many possible methods of such exegesis but some of the main ways which can be detected are 1. the appearance of glosses; 2. the way biblical material has been arranged in its present form; 3. direct quotation; and 4. the re-use of earlier scriptural themes and traditions.

'Gloss' is the name given to statements or verses which appear to have been added secondarily to the text. Since scholars often disagree over the criteria* by which a particular verse may be identified as a gloss, something of a subjective note is injected into the method from the beginning. Nevertheless there is often wide agreement, and it has been instructive to see how attitudes towards glosses have changed. In the nineteenth century, scholars often spoke of a 'mere gloss' and in their commentaries* sought to strip them away in order to get back to the 'authentic' words of the original. Conservative scholars often denied there were any glosses. Both groups would thus see little value in additions to the 'inspired' text. This attitude has changed. In 1957 a Jewish scholar, J. Weingreen, argued that 'rabbinic*-type' glosses which emerged early in Judaism were to be found even within the OT itself (the article appeared later in his book *From Bible to Mishna*, 1976). In 1956 P. R. Ackroyd published an article entitled 'Some Interpretative Glosses in the Book of Haggai', in which he argued for a conscious theological motive in glosses in the Hebrew text (2.5; 2.17) and the Greek text (2.9, 14). Ackroyd has been a pioneer in the whole study of inner-biblical exegesis as a recent collection of his essays, *Studies in the Religious Tradition of the Old Testament*, 1987, shows on almost every page.

One example of the purpose which can be served by a gloss is seen in Amos 2.4f. The book begins with a series of oracles against foreign nations for which God will judge them. They depict fairly red-blooded war crimes but lead up to the climax of charges against Israel which is seen as no better in God's sight than its pagan neighbours. The climax is weakened, however, by a very 'Deuteronomistic'* condemnation of Judah, whose 'crimes' are described in bland and conventional language. Usually this has been regarded as a gloss. Contemporary scholarship asks of it, 'What is the function it serves?' It is clear that the book has been finally edited in the southern kingdom of Judah and so this verse probably represents an attempt of later preachers to relate Amos' words to their contemporaries. They expound Amos' message with an exegesis which applies it to a later situation and so gives it new relevance.

Arrangement of material can also be a form of early exegesis. An example is offered by I Sam. 8–10. At least two accounts of the origin of the monarchy are found here side by side, one extremely critical (I Sam. 8.10–18) and one very favourable (9.15–21) (*see* **Kingship**). By placing these different views of monarchy together, the editor appears to be making the theological point that monarchy, like all human institutions, is ambivalent. Used aright it can be an instrument of God for the good of his people. Abused, it can be a source of tyranny and corruption. The Hebrew monarchy illustrated both faces during its history.

An example of exegesis by direct quotation can be found in Dan. 9.1f., 24–27. Jeremiah's prediction that the Babylonian exile would last seventy years is quoted and 'expounded'. It is said that he actually meant 'seventy weeks of years'. Not only is this meant to extend the judgment of 'exile' down to the book's own time (second century BC) but it makes use of a theological motif from II Chron. 36 to do so. The Chronicler there linked the 'seventy years' of exile to the legal idea that land polluted by the sin of its inhabitants needed to 'enjoy its sabbaths', that is, to lie fallow for its seven year periods of rest in order to recover (II Chron. 36.21, cf. Lev. 26.34). That, according to the Chronicler, was the theological purpose of the exile and the writer of the book of Daniel takes up the idea to explain why the people have had to endure an 'exile' period of judgment ever since.

The use of theological themes or motifs is sometimes harder to identify. Yet allusions can be indicated subtly in a number of ways. The Chronicler presents David* as the great founder of the temple and its worship (I Chron. 22–29). While Solomon builds it, David passes on the 'plan' (Heb. *tabnîth*) and encourages all the people to make contributions (I Chron. 28.11; 29.1–9). This is strongly reminiscent of the Priestly writer's account of Moses'* part in the construction of the tabernacle. He also received a 'plan' from God (Ex. 25.9) and encouraged the people to offer gifts for its building (Ex. 36.3). The Chronicler appears to be suggesting that David was a 'second Moses' and that the temple era which he inaugurated was like a new exodus stage in God's dealing with his people, much as the author of Isa. 40–55 saw the return from exile in Babylon as a 'second exodus' eclipsing the first in splendour (e.g. Isa. 43.16–21).

There are dangers in this kind of biblical interpretation, the chief of them being that of subjectivity. Some can see allusions and citations where others cannot. It is not always easy to know, when two passages coincide, who is borrowing from whom or whether both have a common source or whether the resemblance is purely coincidental. Knowing as little as we do about the process by which scripture was written down and when, and what sources were available to different people in different centres, it is hazardous to try to specify the process by which one writer could 'cite' another. Nevertheless the value of the approach is that it delivers us from an over-rigid view of the OT as a purely literary production. We can recognize something at least of the process by which communities preserved, passed on, re-used and re-expounded earlier scripture in relating it to their own circumstances. In place of the remote 'scribes'* of earlier scholarship we may catch something of the heart-beat of the communities* of faith using 'scripture' much as present-day communities do still today.

See also **Authorship**; **Interpretation, History of**; **Rewritten Bible**.

In addition to titles mentioned, see D. A. Carson and H. G. M. Williamson (eds), *It is Written: Scripture Citing Scripture*, 1988.

REX MASON

Inspiration

Various models or metaphors* have been used to describe the status or significance of the Bible as a whole. These include revelation* (the Bible as the unveiling of otherwise hidden truths), authority* (the Bible as the declaring of information or command which demands assent), canon* (the Bible as a measure of belief and behaviour), and inspiration (the Bible as having its origin in God himself).

Talk in terms of the inspiration of scripture was common in the biblical and patristic periods, though the actual terms inspiration/inspired occur on only a few occasions in English versions. The classic passage is II Tim. 3.16–17, which declares that 'all scripture is inspired by God and profitable for teaching, for reproof, for correction, and for training in righteousness . . .' (RSV). The reference is presumably to the Jewish scriptures in whatever form they were known to the author and his church. NEB translates 'every inspired scripture has its use . . .', but this hardly implies the view that there is such a thing as an uninspired scripture. Contemporary Jewish thinking may have regarded some material as scriptural and normative without being inspired (so S. Z. Leiman, *The Canonization of Hebrew Scripture*, 1976), but it would not have seen any of scripture as uninspired and useless.

II Tim. 3.16 is exceptional not only for its use of the Greek word *theopneustos*, 'God-breathed' (NIV), but also for its attribution of inspiration to the text rather than to its author* (both the Greek word itself and its application to the text itself recur in the patristic period with reference to writings eventually included in the NT, beginning with Clement of Alexandria, *Stromata* vii 16 [vii 101, 103]). It thus contrasts with the further classic passage II Peter 1.20–21, '. . . no prophecy ever came by the impulse of man, but men moved by the Holy Spirit spoke from God'. With this expression one may compare the references in more mainstream NT documents to the Holy Spirit's being involved in the uttering of words preserved in the scriptures. Thus in Mark 12.36 Jesus refers to David* declaring 'in the Holy Spirit' (RSV 'inspired by the Holy Spirit'); cf. Acts 1.16; 4.25.

It is characteristic of such passages that inspiration is a hermeneutical* category. The Spirit's involvement is alluded to because it underlies the text's meaning and demand for a later audience. Behind the human author is a divine initiative and activity which give his words a reference beyond that known to him. Further, this inspiring Spirit is the Spirit of Christ (cf. passages such as I Cor. 12.3 which link the Spirit and testimony to Christ); thus belief in the inspiration of scripture justifies the conviction that passages which make no overt reference to Christ refer to him covertly. In the present century, too, K. Barth* (*Church Dogmatics* i, 2; ET 1956) emphasizes the christocentric aspect to inspiration.

In the context of contemporary emphasis on a historical approach to exegesis, it is unlikely that a stress on the inspiration of a work will offer a convincing rationale for these approaches to interpretation which allow for the discovery in the text of meanings that the author would not recognize. We may, however, see it as drawing attention to the depth dimension to the text which underlies the contemporary interpreter's expectation of discovering something there that 'speaks' beyond its original context. It may also point to the assumption that the Spirit who is involved in the origin of scripture is also involved in relating the text to our present. Even if it is inappropriate to see the inspiration of scripture as signifying that it is inspiring and life-giving, it is important to note that it is the Spirit who makes a proper understanding of scripture possible.

During the patristic and mediaeval* periods, belief in the inspiration of scripture was an uncontroversial part of the church's formal beliefs. Whatever its genre* (narrative, psalmody, letter, etc.) or background and origin, it constituted a static source-book for Christian doctrine. Theologians such as Origen* and Chrysostom were aware that often scripture does not seem to be conveying information with exactitude, and to explain this fact they formulated an understanding of the Holy Spirit's 'condescension' or 'accommodation' to the scripture's human authors. This motif was taken up in the Reformation* period by John Calvin,* who also developed the notion of the Spirit's involvement with the hearers, as well as with the authors of scripture, in the doctrine of the Spirit's illumination, or of the Spirit's inner witness regarding scripture's being the word* of God (e.g. *Institutes* i, 7). This development took place in the context of debate between Protestant and Roman churches and between mainstream Protestantism and more radical groups (e.g. *Institutes* i, 9; iv, 8); against both of these, Calvin made the inspiration of scripture the basis for its unique status over against post-scriptural tradition and the teaching authority of the church, and against latter-day Montanism.

It is doubtful whether the Bible itself, however, sees the Spirit's involvement with its writers as phenomenologically distinctive; the distinction between the Bible and other sources of truth is better made on the basis of other models referred to at the outset. It is in any case doubtful whether it is wise to attempt in this way to relate the models to each other, e.g. by understanding God as inspiring people so that they can receive his 'revelation' which then has 'authority' and can function as 'canon'. As models they are independent of each other and each potentially offers a total account of the phenomena of scripture from a different perspective.

In the wake of the Renaissance and the Enlightenment,* the Bible came to be studied 'like any other book', and this raised a number of questions regarding its inspiration. First, inspiration came to be a way of speaking of the origin of secular works of art, whose creators may well feel that something was 'given' to them. Writers such as J. G. Herder* (*The Spirit of Hebrew Poetry*, 1782–3) applied the artistic notion of inspiration to scriptural works: their inspiration is that of great religious teachers and poets through whom God speaks as he speaks through other works of art. Secondly, the nineteenth century saw the development of critical approaches to the origins and nature of the books, which exposed the utter humanness of the process whereby they came into being and made it more difficult to affirm that they manifested the inerrant truth which the doctrine of inspiration im-

plicitly or explicitly claimed for them. Attempts to restate the doctrine of inspiration by writers who accept the approaches of biblical criticism, such as W. Sanday (*Inspiration*, 1893) and Charles Gore (in *Lux Mundi**), and by writers who reject them, such as B. B. Warfield (e.g. *The Inspiration and Authority of Scripture*, reprinted 1951), need to be seen as responses to this situation. It is henceforth a commonplace of conservative works that acknowledging scripture's inspiration logically entails acknowledging its absolute historical truth or inerrancy, an inference not drawn in the early or Reformation periods when the concern with inspiration had other interests. A third result of the impact of biblical criticism was the awareness that many biblical books did not come into existence as the work of inspired individuals but as the result of a process involving a variety of traditionists, sources, and redactors. This suggested that inspiration needed to be seen as more of a community than an individual matter, in keeping with the biblical stress on the work of the Spirit in the corporate life of the people of God.

But a further result of the impact of biblical criticism has been that in the present century, mainstream theological attempts to consider the significance of scripture have paid more attention to the other models noted above than to inspiration. Conservative works such as those of J. I. Packer (*'Fundamentalism' and the Word of God*, 1958) rightly see themselves as restating Warfield's position in the context of the questions which came into prominence in the nineteenth century, especially concerning the relationship of the inspiration of scripture to its human origin.

Over the centuries writers have hinted at a number of ways of understanding the nature of the inspiration of the scriptures and the relationship of this inspiration to human authorship, but these questions have been the subject of little sustained attention, except in Aquinas. Often writers have confined themselves to denying what they saw as potentially misleading inferences regarding the matter. The biblical language of speaking 'in the Spirit' (Mark 12.36) or being 'moved by the Holy Spirit' so that one 'spoke from God' (II Peter 1.21) suggests an inspiration which took the form of possession by the Spirit, God using human beings as instruments in a way which did not involve their minds even as receptors of a divine message (cf. Acts 1.16; 4.25; and some OT descriptions of prophetic experience, such as Ezekiel's). But it is compatible with inspiration taking the form of the dictation of messages by God, which may be the understanding suggested by the familiar 'thus says Yahweh' of the prophets* and by some of their own accounts of their experience (e.g. Isa. 6); here the human mind is engaged (cf. I Peter 1.10–12) and the message apparently emerges when the person involved is in a psychologically normal – if heightened – state. Most modern writers are inclined to reject these first two understandings and to stress the way the prophets' own personalities are reflected in their words, which might seem to be excluded by these understandings; they stress how God works through his providential shaping of the human personalities, who then write what they want to write but which happens to be what God wants written. W. J. Abraham (*The Divine Inspiration of Holy Scripture*, 1981) begins by considering the way in which one human being may inspire another to do something; he thus sees inspiration as a matter of God influencing human beings by who he is and what he has done, their writing then being entirely their own work.

One difficulty which underlies this discussion is that the inspiration model best fits the prophetic material in scripture, since the prophets refer explicitly to divine involvement in making them speak and giving them their material. The meaning of inspiration must change when extended to narrative, prayers, dialogue involving human speakers as well as divine, God sometimes contradicting the human speaker (Jer. 15) and human authors contradicting themselves (I Cor. 1.14–16); further, our understanding of inspiration needs to be able to embrace the fact that different levels of insight are expressed in different parts of scripture. It seems best to allow for the possibility that each of the different understandings of inspiration may apply to some of the material in scripture; which of them is appropriate will vary from work to work and from text to text.

See also **Authority; Fundamentalism; Verbal Inspiration.**

In addition to works cited, see P. J. Achtemeier, *The Inspiration of Scripture*, 1980; L. Alonso Schökel, *The Inspired Word*, 1967; G. C. Berkouwer, *Holy Scripture*, 1975; K. R. Trembath, *Evangelical Theories of Biblical Inspiration*, 1988; B. Vawter, *Biblical Inspiration*, 1972.

JOHN GOLDINGAY

Interpretation, History of

The view that the history of interpretation is an integral part of biblical studies, and should not be left entirely to theologians or church historians, is now widely held. For over two centuries it has been almost universally assumed that the only legitimate goal for biblical research was what the original text was and what it originally meant. Anything later,

Jewish or Christian, ancient, mediaeval or modern, represented a decline from that ideal, and was not worthy of scholarly investigation, or not at any rate by biblical experts. A true biblical scholar was someone who, like a classicist or an ancient historian, knew a number of ancient languages and was familiar with the cultures of the Ancient Near East:* Babylonian, Egyptian,* Canaanite, Hellenistic,* Roman and so on. Scholarship of this type resulted in something of a rift between the study of the Bible and the rest of theology and religious studies. Fortunately the situation has changed, and the history of interpretation increasingly takes its place alongside textual criticism,* biblical archaeology,* form criticism* and the rest as a discipline in its own right.

The Bible is not just an Ancient Near Eastern text like the law-code of Hammurabi or the Dead Sea Scrolls.* It is read aloud in the liturgy* of countless religious communities all over the world, and is preached upon and acted upon as a contemporary text. Experts on the Bible cannot simply ignore this fact. There is something wrong with a commentary* on Isa. 1.3 that does not even mention the fact that it is the scriptural basis for the ox and the ass in traditional nativity scenes (*see* **Infancy Narratives**), or a discussion of 7.14 that concentrates on proving that the Hebrew text does not use the word for 'virgin' when this is one of the main proof texts for the doctrine of the virgin birth. It is a simple historical fact that the traditional Christian interpretation of these verses has been vastly more influential in the history of Western civilization than the Hebrew original. In a course on Judaism or Jewish history, priority would naturally be given to the Hebrew, but in the context of biblical studies, which in most academic institutions includes the NT, then what Christians believe the text means is as important as what it originally meant in ancient Israel, if not more so.

The text is alive. The seeds that were sown in ancient Israel have never stopped growing. To some, the result is an overgrown garden, badly in need of weeding or pruning: they have had their way for several centuries. To others, the history of interpretation is something of great importance, both as an insight into the history of religious thought and, in its own right, as a subject for critical scholarship. Some texts have been horribly misused. Some interpretations are more beautiful or more effective or more convincing than others. Some speak more eloquently to one generation than to another. But it is unscientific to ignore them or dismiss them without first giving them a fair hearing as an integral part of studying the Bible.

1. One major recent development in biblical studies which affects the role of the history of interpretation is a new interest in the text as it stands. In canonical criticism,* rhetorical criticism* and structuralism,* the text comes first, and the highly technical, often controversial and inconclusive discussion of sources,* literary form, redaction,* authorship* and the like comes second. Questions about the meaning of the text come before questions about who wrote it and when, and what were his sources; and for that kind of question, the centuries of Jewish and Christian exegetical tradition are a treasure-house of useful insights. Early Jewish and Christian interpreters examined every word, every image in scripture, often with a greater degree of semantic* sophistication than many modern commentators, asking searching questions, looking for subtleties, and sometimes recognizing nuances or associations missed by modern interpreters. What Jerome or Rashi makes of the text is frequently not only interesting and important in its own right, but as valuable for understanding the text as much of the ancient archaeological and philological* data cited in our commentaries. It is remarkable how often modern literary analysis of the biblical text matches ancient and mediaeval* interpretations, especially in Jewish studies, since Jewish scholars (*see* **Jewish Exegesis**) tend to be better acquainted with their rabbinic* and mediaeval sources than Christians are with theirs.

There are other unmistakable signs of a shift of emphasis in biblical studies from the quest for original meanings to scholarly interest in later interpretations. What happened to the eighth-century prophets' words in exilic and post-exilic literature and how the history of Israel* is retold in Chronicles are popular subjects for serious research. New editions and critical commentaries on the OT apocrypha* and pseudepigrapha* and on the NT apocrypha are being published. The sectarian literature from Qumran, Nag Hammadi,* the Cairo Genizah* and elsewhere has tended to stir up more general interest, outside the world of archaeology, than the discoveries at Ugarit,* Ebla and the like, and this is increasingly reflected in the world of OT and NT scholars. The publication of critical editions of the text of the Septuagint,* the Peshitta (*see* **Syriac Tradition**), the Vulgate* and the Targumim,* as well as some of the ancient and mediaeval exegetical literature in Greek, Syriac, Latin, Aramaic and Hebrew, is another indication of a shift in the allocation of resources. The ancient versions are now more than ever being studied as literature in their own right, as evidence for Hellenistic Jewish thought (LXX), for example, or the history of Eastern Christianity and the origins of Islam

(Peshitta), rather than merely as witnesses to the Hebrew text.

Another area in which the history of interpretation is proving its importance is biblical semantics. Post-biblical Hebrew is historically and culturally closer to biblical Hebrew than are, say, Ugaritic or Arabic, although traditionally biblical philologists have made more use of other semitic languages than of the vast resources available in Mishnaic (*see* **Talmud**) and mediaeval Hebrew. Jewish interpretations are especially helpful for the understanding of the Hebrew text of the OT. Being for the most part in Hebrew, they avoid the distortions of translation into another language. There is a degree of continuity from the earliest stages in the process down to the most recent, which is not possible outside the Jewish tradition.

In this respect it is important to distinguish between Jewish and Christian interpretation. Christian interpretations have a different value. They are almost without exception not in Hebrew, and the vast majority of them, in Western Christianity at any rate, are based on the Latin Vulgate. Their contribution to biblical interpretation is therefore not so much at the level of helping us to understand what the original text is about, as in showing us how an ancient text can speak to every generation. This distinction between the history of Jewish and Christian interpretation is not a watertight one, since clearly one of the chief aims of Jewish midrashic* commentaries was also to make an ancient text relevant to the present day, while Christian interpreters, with or without a knowledge of Hebrew, not infrequently throw light on the original meaning. The methods used were often the same too. But the two Bibles, Jewish and Christian, Hebrew and Greek (or Latin or Syriac or English), parted company at an early date, and the two branches of the discipline reflect that divergence.

Another factor in the new status afforded to the history of interpretation comes from the modern literary critics'* concept of 'reader response'.* Given an autonomous text like the Bible, the original meaning of which we can only guess at, attention inevitably moves from the intention of the author to the perception of the reader or listener. What is known of the reader's circumstances or what it is in the text that could possibly yield such an interpretation, are treated scientifically and carefully analysed. This is in marked contrast to traditional biblical scholarship, which dismisses such data as irrelevant or misleading because they do not help us to get back to the original meaning of the text. Since, however, the Bible is nothing without readers and listeners, some scholarly attention to the history of their responses would seem to be called for.

2. The history of interpretation begins within the Bible itself. There are examples of the homiletical exegesis of texts from the Pentateuch* and elsewhere in the prophets* (e.g. Isa. 58.1–12; cf. Lev. 16; 23.24–32), historiographical writings (e.g. II Chron. 20.1–20: cf. Isa. 7.4, 7) and the Psalms (e.g. Ps. 51: cf. II Sam. 12; Ps. 90: cf. Ex. 32). These already make use of similar methods to those employed by later rabbinic exegetes. Early Jewish interpretations of the Bible in Hebrew and Aramaic, as represented by the Dead Sea Scrolls, the Targums, the Talmuds* and the midrashic literature, reflect religious and political developments up to the rise of Islam. Of the great mediaeval Jewish commentators, Rashi (1040–96) is the most influential in subsequent Jewish and Christian tradition. Like his two successors, the much travelled Abraham Ibn Ezra (d. 1167) and David Kimchi (1160–1235), he combined literal interpretation with a respect for rabbinic tradition, and sought to refute christological interpretations (e.g. Isa. 7.14). Ibn Ezra is the most original of the three, and even questions the Isaianic authorship of some of the Babylonian prophecies in 40–66 (40.1). Rabbinic Bibles still print Targum, Rashi, Ibn Ezra and Kimhi alongside the biblical text.

The earliest Greek version of the Bible (the Septuagint) contains significant references to the Jewish community in Egypt (e.g. Isa. 10.24; 19.25), and Greek words for 'law', 'word', 'wisdom', 'knowledge' and the like, which introduce Hellenistic* theology and prepare the path from Hebrew scripture to subsequent Christian and gnostic* developments. The choice of Greek *parthenos*, 'virgin', for *'almah*, 'young woman' (Isa. 7.14) is the best known and most influential example of this. Jerome's Latin translation had a similar effect on the history of biblical interpretation in Western Christendom. For example, the influential writings of Isidore of Seville (*c.* 560–636) are largely dependent on Jerome.

The history of interpretation nicely echoes the history of the church. Patristic interpreters sought to find scriptural authority* for every detail of their christology* (e.g. the begottenness of the Word in Prov. 8.22, 30 (cf. KJV), the mystery of the incarnation in Isa. 53.8 (KJV), and the Trinity in Isa. 6.3; 42.1). The whole life of Christ could be found in the Book of Isaiah, from the annunciation (7.14) and nativity (1.3; 9.6; 60.6) to the healing miracles (35.5–6; 53.4), the passion (53.7–9; 63.1–6), the resurrection* (52.13; 53.11) and the sending out of the disciples into all the world (66.19).

For the mediaeval church the Bible spoke a different language. First, under the influence of the cult of the Virgin Mary, verses like Isa. 45.8 and 53.2 and Jer. 31.22 took on a new meaning related to the miracle of the virgin birth. The ancestry of Jesus also held a particular fascination for the mediaeval commentators, living as they did in a society where kings and knights set great store by their lineage, and in this context Isa. 11.1 acquired special significance. The entrance to many European cathedrals is flanked by the ancestors of the messiah,* each symbolically clutching a branch of the 'Tree of Jesse', and elaborate 'Jesse windows', based on 11.1 and Matt. 1.1–17, are among the most popular motifs in mediaeval Christian stained-glass windows.

The Reformation* heralded a shift from the church's traditional interpretation of scripture, mostly in Latin, to the quest for what the original text meant. Despite frequent anti-Jewish interpretations (e.g. on Isa. 2.22; 4.3), Luther* made considerable use of Hebrew, the Jewish sources, Jerome, Nicholas of Lyra and other Hebraists, and branded some traditional Christian interpretations as 'childish errors'. The seventeenth century witnessed a widening gap between theology and the scientific study of the Bible. Hugo Grotius (1583–1645), for example, also rejected the traditional christological interpretation of many passages (e.g. Isa. 11.1–2; 42.1; 53) in favour of philological exegesis. Questions of literary unity, structure, composition, purpose and even reader response became increasingly important for biblical commentators, and finally questions of date and authorship ushered in the age of modern critical scholarship. For two centuries commentators saw their task as primarily one of reconstructing what actually happened and recovering the *ipsissima verba* of the biblical writers, making full use of all the newly discovered archaeological finds from the Middle East. Exegesis was to a large extent left to preachers (*see* **Homily**).

The history of how biblical texts have been interpreted in music* and literature is also illuminating and informative, and need not be left by biblical scholars entirely to musicologists and literary critics. The mediaeval selection and interpretation of texts for liturgical* use (e.g. Isa. 11.1; 22.22; 45.8; 63.3 for Advent) reflects the theology of the time, and can be more interesting than their original, often obscure meaning. Handel's *Messiah*, Brahms' *German Requiem* and Julia Ward Howe's *Battle Hymn of the Republic* reward careful study both in their own right and as witnesses to the meaning of the biblical texts they interpret. The same applies to Milton's handling of the creation* story in *Paradise Lost*, Wilfred Owen's interpretation of Gen. 22 in his 'Parable of the Old Man and the Young', and Thomas Mann's *Joseph and his Brothers*.

In twentieth-century Europe antisemitism,* rooted in Christian interpretations of the

Bible, reached its climax in the Nazi holocaust. Regimes in South Africa, Israel and elsewhere quote biblical authority for oppressive policies. On the other hand, human rights activists, freedom fighters and Third World 'base communities' have found their inspiration in the Bible too. For them, passages about liberation from poverty, disease and oppression in Exodus, Job, Isaiah and elsewhere, are given new force by the bias of liberation theology * (see also **Materialist Interpretation**). Isaiah has become the prophet of justice and peace, rather than the prophet of the nativity and the passion. Christian feminists * have found new significance in the few biblical passages where the feminine nature of God is described (e.g. Deut. 32.11, 18; Isa. 42.14; 49.15), and in the role of women as leaders (e.g. Deborah, Mary) and suffering servants (e.g. Jephthah's daughter).

3. As a branch of biblical studies, alongside textual criticism, archaeology, comparative philology and the rest, the history of interpretation has its own problematic and methodology. There is first of all the problem of the sheer quantity and diversity of the material. Confronted by 2,000 years of homilies, commentaries, theological treatises, political speeches, paintings (see **Art, The Bible in**), sculptures, hymns,* oratorios, poems * and novels in many different languages and from many different historical contexts, where are the historians of interpretation to begin?

There have been few attempts at systematic histories of interpretation. L. Diestel, *Geschichte des Alten Testaments in der christlichen Kirche* (1869), is the outstanding exception. J. Pelikan, *Jesus through the Centuries* (1985), shows how biblical stories react to social and political developments in the history of the church. The interpretation of Isa. 53 has been the subject of several historical studies, notably Neubauer and Driver, *The Fifty-third Chapter of Isaiah According to the Jewish Interpreters* (1877). B. S. Childs' *Exodus* (1974) illustrates the value of systematically including later rabbinic and Christian interpretations in a critical commentary. There is clearly a need for every commentary to incorporate this dimension of exegesis in one form or another. Access to the primary sources is becoming less difficult as more and more of them are being translated into modern European languages. Many important studies by theologians and others who use the Bible, from the early church Fathers down to Rosemary Radford Ruether and Gustavo Gutiérrez, are published with full indices of biblical references. The same applies to standard reference works like the *Cambridge History of the Bible* (1963–70). The task is not an easy one, but it is immensely enriching, and above all it will help to relate the critical study of the Bible to the life of the people who use it.

What criteria * can be used to evaluate one interpretation over against another? Amid many conflicting interpretations of one text, which is the 'correct' or 'true' one? It must first of all be said that there is no theoretical or theological justification for the view that the original meaning of the text is always the correct one or the most valuable. In the first place, there is the problem of whether 'original meaning' refers to the meaning of original separate literary units (e.g. Gen. 1.1–2.4a without 2.4b–3.24; Amos without 1.1f., 9.11–15, etc.; Ps. 127 without its heading; Ecclesiasticus without its editorial framework) or of the text as it stands. The final (or 'canonical') form of the text is itself one stage in the history of interpretation. Moreover, the manuscripts * in which the final form of the text is preserved are the result of centuries of scribal activity, and are themselves further stages in the history of interpretation. The problem of defining the 'original meaning' of a word or speech or book, and of discovering what it was, is thus highly complex. The *ipsissima verba* of the Yahwist or the prophets or Jesus, however successfully divorced from their literary context by modern scholarship, cannot claim canonical status. It is no more acceptable to cite the interpretations and theories of nineteenth- and twentieth-century scholars as though they are outside the history of interpretation. They too reflect the bias of their cultural * environment, as recent studies of Christian scholarship under the Nazis, for example, clearly show.

Given the highly complex history of the Bible in Christian and Jewish tradition, and the rich diversity of interpretations recorded for almost every passage, it would be a gross oversimplification to maintain that any one stage in the process is always and unequivocally the best or most important, for every passage and for every purpose. Historians will place special emphasis on the meaning of the text as it can be reconstructed for whatever period they are interested in. Philologists will measure interpretations, in Latin or Aramaic or English or German, according to their relationship to a reconstructed original Hebrew or Greek text. Theologians will evaluate them critically, not primarily against the criteria of chronological priority or closeness to the 'original', but in their own right, as witnesses to what Jews and Christians believe. If biblical scholarship is more than history and philology, it must take account of the context of the Bible, not only the original *Sitz im Leben* of separate literary units, but also its continuing 'contextualization' in the religious communities that have preserved it and for whom it makes sense.

See also **Biblical Criticism; Christian Interpretation of the Old Testament; Hermeneutics; Inner-Biblical Exegesis; Meaning.**

M. Fishbane, *Biblical Interpretation in Ancient Israel*, 1985; C. Klein, *Anti-Judaism in Christian Theology*, 1978; J. Rogerson, C. Rowland and B. Lindars, *The Study and Use of the Bible*, 1988; B. Smalley, *Study of the Bible in the Middle Ages*, 1983, pp. 112–95.

JOHN F. A. SAWYER

Intratextuality

The term was introduced into theological vocabulary by George Lindbeck in his influential book *The Nature of Doctrine* (1984). The newness of the term itself should not, however, obscure the fact that it brings together older ideas. For the sake of clarity we may distinguish between two aspects of intratextuality, one social* scientific and the other literary.*

The social scientific aspect. The idea of intratextuality draws upon a family of social scientific approaches which hold that experiences and events are only understood with reference to a framework of categories and values developed within a particular culture. This 'interpretative' tradition of social science seeks to explicate these categories and values within their own native framework rather than reinterpret them within technical scientific frameworks. This contrasts, for example, with the cultural materialist* tradition of social science which attempts to account for native categories through an analysis of environmental, technological, and economic factors. It would not trouble a materialist that the natives do not explain their own culture in these terms.

Within the interpretative tradition, religions are conceived of as socially embodied interpretative schemes, with both cognitive and behavioural dimensions, that structure human understandings of God, the self and the world. These interpretative schemes, exemplified especially in a community's sacred narratives, decisively shape the perceptions of individuals. On this view, a religion is a kind of cultural and linguistic system; it is a symbolic* framework – a web of meaningful signs, actions, and institutions – which both constrains and enables human life.

Lindbeck associates the idea of intratextuality with this 'cultural-linguistic' conception of religion which stands in the interpretative tradition of social science. He suggests that the primary task of doctrinal theology is to reflect upon the 'grammar' of the Christian symbolic system which is encoded in canonical texts. In this sense, theologians are reflective informants who interpret their own tradition using the native categories of holy writ. These categories explain external realities rather than external realities explaining scripture. Reality is only understood *through* the lens of the text. However, in emphasizing the textuality of the Christian symbolic system Lindbeck moves considerably beyond the claims of social scientists. The metaphor* of 'culture as text' enjoys a wide currency in the interpretative tradition of social science but no one imagines that cultures are nothing but texts. The metaphor simply indicates that the social scientist is interested in interpreting cultural 'meanings' as they would be understood by a native. But Lindbeck's argument does actually emphasize texts as such.

The literary aspect. Lindbeck opposes his cultural-linguistic model of religion to two other 'extratextual' models, both of which locate the primary realities of religion outside any particular interpretative scheme. In the case of the first, so-called 'cognitivist' model, religion is essentially a set of informative propositions about objective religious referents, whether these are historical events or metaphysical realities. The focus on the referents themselves virtually dispenses with the symbolic framework through which they are understood. In the case of the 'experiential-expressive' model, a religion is thought to be a set of non-informative and non-discursive symbols which express a deeper layer of subjective or existential feeling. In this latter model, religious language is essentially an inadequate vehicle for truths which lie deep in the human spirit. Lindbeck argues, on the other hand, that the particular language of a religious tradition is far more significant than this second model would suggest.

While these two models are abstractions, they can at least throw some light on the kinds of views which are rejected by intratextualists. Extratextual models imply that biblical language either reflects objective truths or expresses a deeper subjectivity. In either case, the primary data or referents of religion can be represented in many different ways. Scripture is thereby readily translatable into extra-scriptural categories. Against this, intratextual theologians argue that the 'meaning' of a religious text is inseparable from the particular language within which it is formed. Intratextual theology describes reality by means of a privileged interpretative framework, which, in the case of Christianity, is provided by scripture. Lindbeck rejects the idea that a referent can in itself provide the means for revising scriptural categories; there is no such thing as self-interpreting reality. Reality is only understood within (possibly competing) interpretative frameworks.

Implications for biblical studies. In evaluating the contribution of intratextuality to biblical studies we should distinguish between the constituent elements of Lindbeck's proposals. On the one hand, it is possible to construe his cultural-linguistic model of religion as simply an endorsement of interpretive social science. At least one biblical scholar, Wayne Meeks, takes the cultural-linguistic model to be a fitting rationale for his own style of social history. Meeks rightly points out, however, that Lindbeck's understanding of scripture actually precludes a cultural-linguistic approach to historical reconstruction. Social historians cannot give a special privilege to canonical* texts, whereas Lindbeck insists that theology should be not just metaphorically but literally intratextual; it should be bound to the symbols and descriptions encoded in holy writ – and this apparently indicates an exclusive dependence on the final form of scripture. The theological meaning of Jesus Christ, for example, arises out of the descriptions of his identity in the gospel texts themselves, rather than out of inquiries into the historicity of events in his life, his existential significance, or his metaphysical status.

In this respect, intratextual readings are quite literally text-centred. Intratextualists do not seek to reconstruct the symbolic system of ancient authors; they seek, rather, to grasp the meanings of the texts in themselves. Lindbeck is careful to point out, however, that this very opposition between immanent textual meaning and historical-critical* reconstruction was unavailable before the rise of modern biblical criticism.* Intratextuality is not a return to 'pre-critical' ideas; it is 'post-critical' or 'post-modern'. In actual exegetical practice, the idea of intratextuality is probably best embodied in the canonical approach to biblical studies developed by Brevard Childs, as well as in the theological writings of Hans Frei and Ronald Thiemann.

See also **Canonical Criticism.**

H. Frei, *The Eclipse of Biblical Narrative*, 1974; C. Geertz, *The Interpretation of Cultures*, 1973; R. M. Keesing, 'Anthropology as Interpretive Quest', *Current Anthropology* 28, 1987, pp. 161–76; W. Meeks, 'A Hermeneutics of Social Embodiment', *HTR* 79, 1986, pp. 176–86; R. Thiemann, *Revelation and Theology*, 1985.

M. G. BRETT

Introduction

The word has a technical sense well established in German biblical scholarship but not altogether current elsewhere. In this sense, it is virtually synonymous with biblical criticism* as that discipline, or group of disciplines, has been practised between the Enlightenment* and the decades following the Second World War. In brief, introduction envisages the student of the literature contained in the biblical canon* (to which it is exclusively restricted) as a historian of Jewish or Christian origins. Its aim is to assemble information of every kind that is calculated to facilitate such a reader's appreciation of the text before him in its original historical and religious context. It hopes to enable him to 'think dead men's thoughts after them'. Thus introduction has at times deliberately sought to present the text to its reader as a historical document possessing no special religious or faith-derived privilege.

The discipline so vigorously pursued from the mid-eighteenth century to the present was not without antecedents in less critically-orientated times. In a rudimentary sense, indeed, it is as old as the provision, perhaps in the fourth or third century BC, of the superscriptions prefaced to some of the psalms in the Masoretic text* of the Hebrew Bible and in the Septuagint* (the major Greek translation). These superscriptions (e.g. to Pss. 3, 18, 51) claim to inform the reader of the situation in the life of David* in which he composed them. Similarly, it has been claimed that I Chron. 29.29f., if the reference is indeed to I and II Samuel, was intended to function as introduction to those books.

Probably, however, we are entitled to regard introduction as a Christian innovation. As early as the second half of the second century AD the ten Pauline epistles accepted as genuine by Marcion* – that is, all those bearing Paul's name except the Pastoral Epistles* – were furnished with prologues composed in support of Marcion's teaching. At about the same time the four canonical Gospels received prologues intended in precisely the opposite sense; they were written to controvert the position of Marcion. With whatever ulterior doctrinal purpose they were drawn up, the form of these prologues was the provision of basic historical information about the works concerned. Only slightly later than these prologues – if the date c. 200 may still be accepted – a document was put together which survives with the loss of its opening section and is known as the Muratorian Fragment or the Muratorian Canon. It is possible that this document assembles what were at first discrete prologues to each of the books regarded by the author as universally accepted for reading in church (he also names some works over which doubt had been expressed in certain quarters). Very limited factual information is given in most cases, and sometimes this has an apparently polemic purpose. Nevertheless, the Muratorian Fragment is in a somewhat rudimentary sense the first introduction to the NT.

After the second century, the best-known

example of biblical introduction is provided by the prologues composed by Jerome, often drawing on the work of earlier Jewish scholars, for groups of books or individual books in his Latin translation of the Bible (*see* **Vulgate**). These prologues, and later those of other authors, form part of the text of many manuscripts of the standard Latin Bible. Shortly after Jerome's death in 420, a Greek writer, Adrianos, working independently of Jerome, wrote a treatise on biblical hermeneutics* to which he gave the title 'Introduction [*Eisagōgē*] to the Divine Scriptures'. This, while very different in character and aims from the prologues of the second century and later, was the first work to bear the title 'introduction'. The word, in its Greek form, also appears in the titles of some broadly similar books in the Middle Ages and the Reformation* period.

Jerome's prologues offered a model which was followed when the Bible began to be translated* into various vernaculars, both in England and on the continent. Luther's* prefaces are the best-known examples. Introduction in its modern sense, however, did not begin to be provided until the birth of biblical criticism – as it may be claimed – with some seminal pages in Hobbes' *Leviathan* (1651), followed by the works on the OT (1678) and the NT (1693) of R. Simon, a Roman Catholic who sought, in part, to recruit the new science for polemical ends. But it was nearly a century before the work of J. S. Semler prepared the way for the first full-scale exemplars of biblical introduction. In 1780–83 J. G. Eichhorn published a three-volume *Introduction to the Old Testament*, to be followed from 1804 to 1827 by five volumes devoted to the NT. J. D. Michaelis' massively influential *Introduction to the Divine Scriptures of the New Covenant*, originally published in 1750, appeared in a fourth and greatly expanded edition as two volumes in 1788. Both works had far-reaching effects. The prominence given by Eichhorn to history of the canon and to textual criticism* is continued in most subsequent introductions to both Testaments; Michaelis, while adopting an idiosyncratic view of the canonicity of certain books, represents in voluminous detail the application of historical investigation to the individual books of the NT, in explicit independence of the question of their inspiration* (which, indeed, Michaelis did not deny); and this, too, set an example followed in most subsequent introductions to the NT.

The later history of OT introduction exhibits some pruning of the agenda. At first, authors aiming to achieve the purpose already sketched felt obliged to draw on a wide range of information. Grammar and lexicography,* geography, archaeology,* historical records

from areas adjacent to Israel, and history of religion might all be regarded as appearing of necessity in books intended to supply the historian with all he might need in reading the literature of ancient Israel. As these fields became increasingly specialist disciplines in their own right, it became less necessary and indeed less practicable to include them in a general introduction to the OT. As, however, commentaries on individual books began to be published, their own introductions naturally devoted space to the findings of these disciplines where appropriate.

For the NT the most influential figure during the middle of the nineteenth century was F. C. Baur. His bold reconstruction of early Christian history as a conflict between Petrine (Jewish-Christian) and Pauline (law-free) movements was epoch-making. He contributed to the development of NT introduction by an important article published in 1850. Preoccupied with the ever-recurrent question of authority,* he insisted that introduction is a 'theological science'. Its task is to address the books of the NT not simply through what they tell us of themselves but above all in terms of what has made them canonical. Canonical criticism* has recently taken up this concern again with some vigour. However, the tendency to equate study of the books with the writing of a history of early Christianity continued undiminished.

If the leading figures in biblical research during the nineteenth century were to be found in the Protestant university faculties of Germany, others were not altogether silent. Despite its apologetic aims, the introduction by the Roman Catholic scholar J. L. Hug (1808) is important. And in 1818 a Prebendary of St Paul's, T. H. Horne, published an *Introduction to the Critical Study and Knowledge of the Holy Scriptures* which went through several editions and is a solid work in four volumes. Horne commends two English predecessors as well as a number of continental introductions. His own book seems to have suffered neglect, perhaps because of its conservative stance. Despite the fact that S. Davidson's three-volume OT introduction (1848–51) originated as an edition of Horne's work, S. R. Driver (1891) for the OT and J. Moffatt (1911) for the NT ignore Horne altogether. However, it is these last-named contributions that first exhibit English-language scholarship taking its place in the field of biblical introduction (B. W. Bacon's book of 1900 is too short to place beside them).

During the present century the volume of scholarly publication in languages other than German and from other than German Protestant sources has steadily increased, with Holland, the Scandinavian* countries, Britain and

North America adding to the flow. Not until the emancipation of Roman Catholic biblical scholarship by Pius XII's encyclical *Divino Afflante Spiritu* (1943) was there any significant contribution from Roman Catholics (though three introductions to the NT were published by German Roman Catholic writers during the first half of the century). From 1943 onwards, however, this relative silence has been broken by works in French as well as German.

The geographical and confessional expansion of biblical study has been accompanied by an important change in the nature of introduction. Despite Baur's plea, until quite recently the agenda of introduction has excluded the place of the biblical writings in the formation of doctrine. Neither the Scottish Presbyterian Moffatt, just mentioned, nor the Roman Catholic A. Wikenhauser in his volume of 1953 (for which the imprimatur was not given until the posthumous fourth edition of 1961) assigns any space to theology. It has been otherwise with commentaries* on individual books of both Testaments. Commentators have, more perhaps than the authors of introductions, eroded the long-lasting and sometimes self-conscious exclusion from introduction of all that might address the reader as a religious person and not merely as a historian.

There have been other developments in biblical study during the years following the Second World War, and these, too, have been reflected in introductions, once again more extensively in those prefaced to commentaries than in those dealing with either testament as a whole. One radical shift has indeed been contained within old wineskins with a consistency that is perhaps surprising. From the publication of Gunkel's work on Genesis (1895) onwards, the contents of an increasing proportion of the OT have been perceived as essentially oral* rather than literary material. Its history lies in the minds and mouths of communities; fixation in writing was relatively late and secondary. K. L. Schmidt, M. Dibelius and R. Bultmann* brought the Synoptic Gospels into the same category; their successors showed that these do not exhaust the quantity of NT text that must also be so regarded.

Yet from its outset the science of introduction had been explicitly devoted to the text of the Bible as literature, that is, as a written deposit. The role of form criticism* and tradition-history* has indeed been included in the agenda of introduction, forming – for example – the substantial first part of O. Eissfeldt's *The Old Testament: An Introduction* (1934). But, in NT introduction, it was not until N. Perrin's work of 1974, subtitled 'Proclamation and Parenesis, Myth and History', that

we find an English-language introduction organized on the basis of the assumption that oral tradition and the categories into which it can be divided should dictate the arrangement of a handbook of this sort. By providing at the outset of his book chapters on the cultural and historical background of the Christian movement and the outline of its early history, Perrin focusses attention on the community in which oral forms emerged rather than on the texts it ultimately produced.

Initiatives in biblical study since about 1960 will prove harder to incorporate within the framework of introduction as traditionally understood, if indeed they can be so incorporated at all. The reading of the text 'for its own sake' in narrative* theology renders introduction otiose. So does the quest for structure* in the motifs detectable in a text regardless of its original provenance and even of its relation to a supposed autograph. The reader who accepts the guidance of these new disciplines in biblical study has no need of historical or text-critical information, still less of information about the history of the canon; he has, indeed, no need of antecedent information at all. He meets the text with his mind *tabula rasa*. If the disciplines in question prove to be those of the future, introduction is a branch of biblical study which, with several others, will prove to have exhausted its usefulness.

But it is likely that historians, whether of Christian or Jewish origins or, indeed, of some unusually well-documented areas within Hellenistic* culture, will be always with us. Readers will still be at hand for whom it is important to know as much as possible about the provenance and background of a text under review. The value of introduction will vary from one part of the canon to another. Already, indeed, the character of the material judged appropriate in the opening pages of a commentary on Judges is likely to be somewhat different from the equivalent material in a commentary on Galatians. Introduction is more likely to become increasingly diversified than to suffer atrophy.

See also **Commentary; Interpretation, History of.**

W. G. Kümmel, *The New Testament. The History of the Investigation of its Problems*, 1973; J. W. Rogerson, *Old Testament Criticism in the Nineteenth Century*, 1984.

COLIN HICKLING

Irenaeus

Irenaeus of Lyons (Lugdunum), presbyter (*fl.* 175–195), succeeded the martyred bishop Pothinus at the request of the local Christians. He had probably studied in Rome, and in Smyrna had been a pupil of Polycarp. That martyr's teachings had been formative in his childhood (Eusebius *HE* 5.20, 5–8). He stands in the shadow of the Apostolic Fathers* but also resembles the Apologists. Irenaeus could be conciliatory (*HE* 5.26, 11) but he confronted head on the errors of Valentinian Gnosticism,* of Marcion* and others. His work, originally in Greek, *Against Heresies* (*Adversus Haereses*), is extant in parts and an early, close Latin translation was made, as well as Armenian and Syriac versions. Its purpose was *The Detection and Overthrow of Falsely Named Knowledge* (*Gnōsis*). The *Demonstration* (*Epideixis*) *of the Apostolic Preaching*, apologetic with some exposition of Christian theology, offered christological proofs from the OT. Other writings, quoted from or mentioned by Eusebius* and others, included *On the* (*Valentinian*) *Ogdoad; Concerning Knowledge* (*Peri Epistēmēs*) and *On Schism*.

For Irenaeus both the OT and more recent Christian writings were sacred. However, heretical teachers falsified God's oracles (*AH* 1 *Praef*). Scripture itself would refute heresy, though his opponents had scant respect for either scripture or tradition. They used both oral and written material for their own ends, he argued, forcing unnatural meanings from biblical names and expressions, supporting their typology* and numerological speculations from details in the Gospel stories, and so on. Distortion, fantasy and blasphemy resulted. Marcion had mutilated the scriptures openly.

In response Irenaeus avoided fanciful interpretations, 'philosophy' or appeals to superior intelligence. The scriptures, he maintained, were plainly intelligible and unambiguous. He offered no parallel Christian *gnōsis* (cf. Clement of Alexandria). Knowledge of Jesus Christ, truly and fully incarnate, who showed forth God's love, was accessible as was the apostolic teaching. There was no secrecy, no 'perfect knowledge' for some and no need for the subtleties of interpretation beloved by Gnostics. Such things led to impiety. Obscurities in one passage of scripture could be clarified by reference to other passages and there was order, consistency and construction (*hupothesis*) in it. Scripture was harmonious but heretics obscured such harmony by seizing selectively on the language of the Fourth Gospel (e.g. the *Logos** title) or differing Hebrew names for God (2.35,3).

Above all Irenaeus had to uphold Christian monotheism. In opposition to those who identified the creator with an inferior Demiurge, he insisted at length that in the OT as in Christian teachings the truth about the one God was revealed. Moses,* the prophets and all four Gospels revealed it. Jesus Christ had spoken through Moses and the Spirit had inspired the prophets to tell of him. In Jesus Christ was the perfection of the law. Salvation history was seen as a process of education (*paideia*), with Father and Son working in unity for revelation* and redemption: from covenant* to covenant through incarnation to the ultimate restoration of the intended God-humankind relationship. Whether from Moses,* the prophets, Jesus, or the apostles who preached and 'dictated' sayings (epistles?), scripture and tradition were one in their witness to one God.

He argued his case using a wealth of biblical references and may have had some knowledge of Hebrew as well as of the Septuagint* (LXX). He described the origins of the LXX, defending its version of Isa. 7.14 against those of Aquila and Theodotion. Very often, however, his quotations do not match the Received Text.

In *Adversus Haereses* we see the beginnings of the allegorizing* of the NT (e.g. in the Prodigal Son and Good Samaritan stories); an example of inconclusive speculation on the number of the Beast in Rev. 13.14ff.; and pneumatology and eschatology* retaining their significance in second-century thought. Irenaeus needed to argue for the ultimate preservation of flesh as well as soul, and the nature of the future blessings described reminds us of the hope of Papias.* Irenaeus also records the tradition (allegedly from John and others) that Jesus' ministry had lasted more than ten years.

His witness to the developing Christian canon* is important. He cherished four Gospels (challenging the likes of the Ebionites and those who misused Luke). The lion, calf, etc., signs for the evangelists are explained, and the authors and origins of the Gospels mentioned. He knew Paul's* letters well enough to comment on his 'transposition' of words. But Paul suffered both disparagement and over-esteem in Irenaeus' day. The Pauline Adam*–Christ comparison as developed by Irenaeus is an example of his view of 're-capitulation', with Eve and Mary also introduced into his scheme.

The teachings of the Gnostics were at odds with a right understanding of incarnation, baptism, redemption, etc. With copious use of scripture Irenaeus refuted them, for theirs was a system which 'neither the prophets announced nor the Lord taught nor the Apostles delivered' (1.8,1).

See also **Gnosticism.**

J. Daniélou, *Gospel Message and Hellenistic Culture*, 1973; E. Flesseman van Leer, *Scripture and Tradition in the Early Church*, 1954; R. P. C. Hanson, *Tradition in the Early Church*, 1962; P. Perkins, 'Ordering the Cosmos: Irenaeus and the Gnostics' in W.

Hedrick, R. Hodgson (eds), *Nag Hammadi,
Gnosticism and Early Christianity*, 1986; A.
Roberts and J. Donaldson (eds), *The Ante-
Nicene Fathers*, Vol. 1, 1885.

CHRISTINE TREVETT

Irony

'A mode of speech of which the meaning is
contrary to the words' (Dr Johnson). As such,
irony in texts has always called for subtlety of
reading and acuity of hearing. Thus irony is
often in the ear of the beholder! Irony is part
of literary discourse, but there have been remarkably few full-scale studies of irony in the
Bible (Good is a notable exception). Definitional problems and the high level of abstraction from the text required for the analysis
may account for the lack of comprehensive
treatment. The practical approach of definition by examples (cf. Caird, pp. 51, 104–5,
134) can lead to the multiplication of illustrations beyond necessity. There is throughout
the OT an ironizing distance between a narrator and the narrated tale which often deconstructs the narrative and militates against
its use as propaganda (cf. the story of David *
as king). Even the deity is represented as a
master of irony, displaying a gift for it as well
as being both its engineer and its beneficiary
(Sternberg, pp. 155–6). Yet the risk of irony is
that it will be taken seriously (e.g. the Book of
Jonah) and the irony missed! Biblical irony is
to be found at the level of the words of texts
(illocutionary), but also in the attitudes of the
narrators (perlocutionary) and in the general
ironizing distancing evident in the presentations of narratives. The ideological * singularity of the Bible (cf. Sternberg, p. 37) may
account for the substantial amount of irony
in the book.

Good analyses six different examples of
ironic presentation in the OT: Jonah as the
absurdity of God; Saul as the tragedy of greatness; Genesis as the irony of Israel; Isaiah as
faith on the brink; Qoheleth as the limits of
wisdom; and Job as the irony of reconciliation. The capacity of these texts for irony
analysis is considerable, especially in broad
terms. Good considers Abraham * as the irony
of promise, Jacob as the irony of brotherhood
and Joseph as the irony of providence. Other
ironic perspectives are easily discerned:
Abraham pimping out his wife Sarah among
the foreign monarchs (Egypt, Canaan), enriching himself greatly while failing to beget
progeny. Joseph saves his family only to make
them the forebears of slaves and saves Egypt
only to have it devastated by those slaves!

In the book of Judges, irony abounds as
the Israelite clans are presented on the edge of
triumph over the Canaanites, only to disintegrate into warring factions and end in savage

brutality and rapine (cf. Klein). The story of
Deborah and Barak's defeat of the Canaanites
under Sisera is filled with irony, as the women
dominate the battle and the men are dis-
comfited (Barak) or murdered (Sisera) in prose-
poetry tellings of the tale (cf. Bal). Samson
is a further study in irony as he is unravelled
by foreign women but destroys the Philistines.
Such stories are typical of the delicious irony
with which the OT portrays men as the outwit-
ted victims of women's ruses – out of the
weak comes forth strength!

If the story of Saul is 'a masterpiece of
structure, dramatic order and suspense, and
tragic irony' (Good, p. 80), the presentation
of King David is hardly less ironic. Thus the
ageing David, so long represented as the
leader of men and follower of women, is
shown towards the close of his life as clutching
the comely young Abishag to him for warmth.
In the three Hebrew words represented by the
phrase 'but the king knew her not' (I Kings
1.4) reams are written and a life deconstructed.
That is the essence of biblical irony: lapidary,
subtle, and tantalizing in its implications. The
naked irony of Michal's rejoinder to her husband David ('How the king of Israel honoured
himself today . . .' II Sam. 6.20) is palpable
and typical of the way women punctuate the
story of David and ironize the tale of the king
(cf. David's treatment of Uriah the Hittite in
the matter of Bathsheba).

Irony among the prophets * tends to be
confined to their words and interrogations of
kings or people. But where there are narratives
about prophets, ironic distance can be
observed. The incident of Balaam's ass, while
more lampoon than irony, is treated in the
Midrash Rabbah on Num. 22 for its ironic
features. Elijah on Carmel lampooning the
prophets of Baal with irony and invective,
with subsequent butchering of the prophets, is
paralleled by Elijah on Horeb pleading for his
own death. The noise and spectacle of Elijah
on Carmel are ironically mimicked in the story
of Elijah on Horeb where the theophany is
not in the noise but in 'a still small voice' of
divine presence. The story of Jonah is equally
a study in the ironic presentation of a foolish
prophet-like character, though readers often
miss the irony and assume a paradigmatic
story of repentance, divine love of the nations
or some other theological dirigible impervious
to such Swiftian irony. Gottwald reads canonical prophecy in terms of comedy * and tragedy
and sees the role of irony as saving 'prophecy
from its frequent melodramatic tone' (Gottwald, p. 93). Here irony may be the reader's
means of saving prophecy from charges of
rhetoric and melodrama rather than being a
device of presentation.

Job and Qoheleth are two of the most dominant pieces of ironic writing in the Bible. Dicing with Job's fate, God finally batters him into submission with the question, redolent of irony, 'Will you even put me in the wrong? Will you condemn me that you may be justified?' (40.8). The whole book leaves the reader pondering the ironies of life made greater by the undergirding irony of a deity not necessarily well disposed towards his creatures. Qoheleth is the great Hebrew ironist (Fisch, pp. 158–78, 193–5) for whom everything is 'vanity', even wisdom and vanity itself! Examples of irony abound in the book (e.g. 9.11). Everything is fleeting and insubstantial, yet the book could not end in a more ironic way than it does with the command 'Fear God and keep his commandments' (12.13). Here is the ironic dismissal of the writer's perpetual ironizing of life. If Qoheleth's irony ironizes the world it also lacks synthesis and so he negates the negation and arrives at a positivity (Fisch, p. 175). In the emptiedness of empty life there is responsibility, remembering, pleasure and the givenness of life!

With Qoheleth biblical irony reaches its zenith, yet loses its soul. Perhaps it is as Kierkegaard observed: 'Humour contains a much deeper scepticism than irony, for here it is not finitude but sinfulness that everything rests upon. Humour also contains a much deeper positivity than irony . . .' (*The Concept of Irony*, ET 1966, p. 341). Is Qoheleth's irony a mask for humour?

While the NT lacks the mature reflective literary approach of irony so characteristic of the Hebrew Bible, elements of irony may be detected in the parables* of Jesus, the different presentations of Jesus *vis-à-vis* the authorities of his time in the Gospels, and in the book of Revelation's counter-proclamations against the might of Rome ('Babylon') in favour of the persecuted followers of Jesus. The parables of Jesus force the hearer to grasp the irony of their transvaluation of all values and to intuit their meaning. The secret of the kingdom* is told in order to be kept from those outside the charmed circle of disciples (Mark 4.10–12). In the kerygmatic* proclamation of the early churches, this ironic approach to teaching was mostly lost or discarded in favour of myth* and, later on, dogma, when the parable teacher (Cupitt's iconoclast) became the object of dogmatic teaching (the churches's icon). Here irony governs the presentation of Jesus and turns the ironist into an object for popular consumption. Irony enters the soul of the churches!

See also **Comedy; Figures of Speech.**

M. Bal, *Murder and Difference*, 1988; G. B. Caird, *The Language and Imagery of the Bible*, 1980; D. J. Enright, *The Alluring Problem: An Essay on Irony*, 1986; H. Fisch, *Poetry with a Purpose*, 1988; E. Good, *Irony in the Old Testament*, ²1981; N. K. Gottwald, 'Tragedy and Comedy in the Latter Prophets', *Semeia* 32, 1984, pp. 83–96; L. R. Klein, *The Triumph of Irony in the Book of Judges*, 1988; M. Sternberg, *The Poetics of Biblical Narrative*, 1985.

ROBERT P. CARROLL

Isaiah

With its 66 chapters, the book of Isaiah is one of the longest of all the biblical writings and it may certainly be regarded as the most complex of the many literary compositions of the OT. The book itself contains an abundance of indications that it has been formed as the product of a long series of progressively made additions and of various attempts at editorial shaping. In one sense it can be classified as a prophetic collection, since it contains prophecies originating from as early as the eighth century BC to as late as the fifth, and possibly fourth, century. It is more than an anthology of prophecies, however, since most of the later material in it has been added, not simply to augment the earlier prophecies, but in order to show how these should be re-interpreted and re-applied to the new situations which had arisen for Israel since their original declaration.

Structure and contents. The book falls fairly readily into two main parts, with chs 1–35 representing the earliest section, often loosely referred to as 'First' Isaiah, although this is rather misleading, and chs 40–66 forming the second part ('Second' Isaiah). The first part is based upon the prophecies of Isaiah, where the superscription in 1.1 shows him to have been a prophet active in Judah and Jerusalem from *c.* 737 until *c.* 700 BC. The second part contains prophecies all of which date from a time after 550 BC and extending for at least a century later.

In between the two parts we find a section (chs 36–39) which consists largely of narratives in which the prophet Isaiah appears as a prominent political spokesman. This section is a slightly expanded version of a series of reports also to be found in II Kings 18.13–20.21. It is usually taken that the latter location is the more original and that an editor has incorporated them into the book of Isaiah for completeness. However, such a conclusion has not passed unchallenged, and it is evident that these narratives serve very effectively to form a bridge between the two major divisions of the book.

We can discern within the book of Isaiah firm signs of a careful, and theologically motivated, work of editing. This has set the contents into broad units. The structure and contents of these, however, do not correspond directly with the relative ages of the material, nor necessarily with the original intentions of their origin.

Date and composition. Various superscriptions appear in the book (1.1; 2.1; 13.1), and the psalm of 12.1–6 has undoubtedly been composed to mark the end of the major unit of 1–12. There are certain broad indications that some loose chronological ordering has meant that later material has often been added at the end of the collection so that it appears last. This is only a very partial guide, however, since a wide scholarly consensus regards the latest section of the entire book as chs 24–27, which display a thoroughgoing apocalyptic character. This observation warns against the often made assumption that the present collection can simply be treated as comprising two books (chs 1–39. 40–66). There is a major division after ch. 39, so that the two parts may be loosely characterized as an 'Assyrian' and a 'Babylonian' part, but this only provides a limited basis for assessment. The inclusion of the 'Babylon' prophecies of 13.1–14.23 has contributed fundamentally towards promoting the inclusion of further prophecies relating to Israel's exile to Babylon in chs 40–55.

When we come to enquire about the manner and purpose of this complex composition, various theories have been put foward. Two major Jewish scholars (*see* **Jewish Exegesis**), Ibn Ezra in the thirteenth century and B. Spinoza in the seventeenth century, recognized that chs 40–66 possessed a sixth-century BC Babylonian background. Most commentators, however, both Jewish and Christian, simply assumed that the book was based upon a single authorship from Isaiah of Jerusalem in the eighth century BC without submitting this to further question. Such a theory became increasingly untenable with the careful analytic researches which began with the work of J. C. Doederlein and others in Germany in the late eighteenth century. Such analyses, which reached a high-point with the major commentary by B. Duhm* in 1892, noted the disparate dates of the separate units, but offered little by way of explanation for their collection into a single book. Duhm argued that three major units are to be found in chs 1–39, 40–55 and 56–66, which are more or less self-contained (loosely defined as 'First', 'Second' and 'Third' Isaiah).

In 1926, the Norwegian scholar S. Mowinckel proposed that the book in its entirety should be regarded as the work of Isaiah's disciples who could be assumed to have been active, mainly in Jerusalem, for a period of at least three centuries. The theory, however, produced no clear evidence for the existence

of such a school of prophetic disciples other than the book itself. More specifically, it does nothing to account for the major shifts in theological emphasis that appear in the book (e.g. concerning the Temple in 66.1–2).

In spite of some attempts to re-establish the claim that all of the book originated in the eighth century BC with Isaiah of Jerusalem (O. T. Allis, E. J. Young, J. N. Oswalt), the contrary evidence is too overwhelming for this to be considered. J. D. W. Watts has sought to interpret the book as the 'vision' of Isaiah of Jerusalem, composed in the second half of the fifth century BC, but based upon an otherwise undated corpus of tradition originating with the prophet in the eighth century.

In company with the other three major collections of prophecy which constitute the Latter Prophets of the OT, it is arguable that a form of literary and thematic unity binds together the book of Isaiah. This recognizes that a modest nucleus of prophecies from Isaiah of Jerusalem is to be found at the heart of the book. A central theme of this was the impact upon Israel and Judah of the armies of Assyria (cf. 5.26–30; 8.5–8). The reasons for this invasion, its many consequences, and how eventually Babylon replaced Assyria as the threatening power (cf. 13.1–14.23), then led to an extensive development. In this, new prophecies were added, earlier ones reinterpreted, and many metaphors* and word-images extended in new directions. Out of this process, in a complex sequence of chain-like additions and revisions, the present book was given shape. A major step was undoubtedly provided by the incorporation of chs 40ff. into 1–35. Even after this, however, further expansions were made to the earlier part, notably by the inclusion of chs 24–27. The whole process was not complete until the late fifth, or more likely the fourth century BC.

Of great importance is the recognition that the literary structure of the book has pursued two main purposes. The first of these is to offer a progressive 'up-dating' of the message of Isaiah in the light of the political developments that subsequently took place. These primarily concern Assyrian imperial control over Judah and its subsequent replacement by that of Babylon, and eventually Persia. The second goal has been to integrate Isaiah's teaching into the mainstream of Israel's life, and this particularly focussed on the future of the Davidic* kingship* (see further below under 'Central Themes').

Central themes. Subsequent to Isaiah's death, his prophecies remained the subject of profound reflection and re-examination. He had forewarned of the coming of the Assyrian menace (5.26–29; 8.7) and the reasons for this (5.8–23), so such prophecies were regarded as holding the key to understanding when such a threat would cease. It is understandable therefore that, when Assyrian control over Judah began to collapse during Josiah's reign (639–609 BC), this should have been linked to Isaiah's prophecies (10.5–15, 33–34; 14.24–25). Many scholars believe that this was the age when the promise of renewed greatness attaching to the Davidic dynasty was incorporated into the prophecies (9.2–7). Subsequently, a renewed threat to Judah came from Babylon, and this too came to be associated with Isaiah's prophesying (13.1–8), the threat from Babylon replacing that of Assyria. This threat in turn called forth the addition of prophecies concerning the downfall of Babylon (13.17–22; 14.4–23) and eventually the incorporation into the Isaiah scroll of an extended collection of prophecies relating to the fall of Babylon and Judah's return from exile there (40–55). At what stage in the formation of the book this occurred is not wholly clear, since chs 40–55 appear at one time to have formed a separate collection. It is possible that chs 56–62 were combined with 40–55 before the final addition of chs 24–27, 34–35 and 63–66 brought the compilation of the book to completion.

A primary theme of the book is that of the threat of oppression from a foreign (Mesopotamian) power. This has lent a strongly political colour to the entire book, and the foreign oppressor is viewed as the destroyer of Israel, leaving only a remnant of the former nation to survive. The expectation of the eventual return of the many exiles of Israel to their homeland becomes a dominant feature of the hope contained in the book (11.12–16; 27.12–13; 34.16–17; 35.1–10).

In this hope, the Davidic kingship is given a significant role to play (9.2–7; 11.1–5; 32.1–8), although in 55.3–6 this is subjected to a major reinterpretation. Similarly Mount Zion comes increasingly into the forefront of the divine purpose, as the idea of a nation Israel recedes (14.32; 62.1–12). Throughout the book, however, the idea of a divine plan and purpose embracing all nations repeatedly reappears, with contrasting emphases on judgment upon the sinners of these nations and hope for their eventual participation in Yahweh's plan of redemption (especially 19.16–25; 60.1–22).

Viewed as a collection of prophecies dealing with Israel's destiny among the nations, the book of Isaiah remains one of the most wideranging and theologically stimulating of the entire OT. Although often uneven in its insights, it presents a dramatic and comprehensive series of affirmations that the movement of history and the rise and fall of all nations lies in the hands of one God.

History of interpretation. Early Christian exegesis* of the book of Isaiah was largely dominated by the interpretation of the royal prophecies of 9.2–7 and 11.1–5 as long-range foretellings of the birth of the messiah.* The Immanuel prophecy of 7.10–14 was linked with these, giving this also a royal messianic significance and making it a most important witness to the belief in the virgin birth of Jesus of Nazareth (cf. Matt. 1.23). Once 53.1–12, declaring the sufferings destined for God's 'Servant',* was further linked with these messianic prophecies and itself interpreted messianically, the book of Isaiah came to be one of the foremost writings of the OT for the early Christian church; e.g. Justin and Irenaeus* gave extended interpretations of 53.1–12. Jewish exegesis, contrastingly, was deeply concerned to refute these Christian claims to the christological* meaning of the book of Isaiah.

A more perceptively historical basis of interpretation was established in the Middle Ages by the major commentaries on the book by the Jewish scholars Ibn Ezra (1090–1164) and David Kimchi (1160–1235). Not until the eighteenth century, with the major commentary on the book by Bishop Robert Lowth (1778), was a more critical literary approach initiated among Christian scholars. This was carried a whole step further with the brilliant philological and linguistic insights of W. Gesenius in his commentary of 1829. Modern critical studies, exploring fully the prolonged literary history that led to the formation of the book, can most readily be said to have begun with the pioneering work of B. Duhm* published in 1892. This initially led to too great an emphasis upon the separate units of the book, with little attempt to explain their being brought together in a unity. More recently the work of S. Mowinckel, J. Vermeylen and others has sought to trace the unifying features of the book.

See also **Prophets and Prophecy; Servant Songs.**

R. E. Clements, *Isaiah 1–39*, 1980; O. Kaiser, *Isaiah 1–12*, ² 1983; id., *Isaiah 13–39*, 1974; C. R. Seitz (ed.), *Reading and Preaching the Book of Isaiah*, 1988; J. D. W. Watts, *Isaiah 1–33, 34–66*, 2 vols, 1985, 1987; C. Westermann, *Isaiah 40–66*, 1969; R. N. Whybray, *Isaiah 40–66*, 1975.

R. E. CLEMENTS

Israel, History of

The claim made on behalf of both Judaism and Christianity that they are 'historical religions' has meant that through much of their development great interest has been taken in the historical accounts in the OT. The dates found in many editions of the KJV/AV, based on the chronology* worked out by Archbishop Ussher in the seventeenth century, are one illustration of this concern.

Since the Enlightenment,* however, the development of new models of historical study has led to increased interest in the OT among professional historians, since the books Genesis–II Kings provide one of the most extensive historical surveys to have been handed down from the ancient world. A strong convention has developed that study of the OT should begin with a survey of Israel's history. In recent years, however, there has been increasing disagreement as to what can really be known of that history. Are the writings that purport to record history in fact properly understood if they are treated as 'history books'?

At one extreme those who maintain the inerrancy of the biblical text commonly regard its historical reliability as one of the crucial tests of that inerrancy, and they therefore continue, for example, to regard Gen. 1 as quite literally the beginning of history. There may be differences of view as to whether the 'days' in Gen. 1 are to be understood literally, but such events as the universal flood or the extended life-spans of the patriarchs, and anything else which seems to be at odds with a scientific world-view, are maintained as an essential part of the story.

Alongside this there have been many presentations of the history of Israel which would not wish to be regarded as fundamentalist,* but have nevertheless presented that history largely as a paraphrase of the biblical text from Gen. 12 on. In particular, archaeological* finds are utilized when they appear to support the biblical story; when discrepancies arise, the hope is commonly expressed that future discoveries will provide a resolution of the 'problem'. That is to say, the essential reliability of the account of the patriarchs in Genesis, or of the conquest of the land under Joshua, is assumed, and other sources of information are approached in the light of that assumption. The work of W. F. Albright and his many pupils in the USA has characteristically followed this approach; the standard history by J. Bright is perhaps the best known example of it.

A complication was introduced by the notion of *Heilsgeschichte*, 'salvation history',* much emphasized in the work of G. von Rad and others. Certain events were held to be of especial importance as demonstrating the acts of God in history, with the exodus as the paradigm example of such an understanding. Theologically such an approach proved valuable, and it was indeed characteristic of the 'Biblical Theology'* movement, but at the historical level it has proved much more difficult to sustain. Are the 'mighty acts' of God

susceptible to the normal criteria* of historical investigation? To what extent are they the products of the community* of faith? Questions such as this have not been satisfactorily resolved, and this approach has to a great extent fallen out of favour.

But there are wider problems in the presentation of Israel's history. Thus, in the book of Exodus, the community is regularly described as 'the Israelites' (the 'children of Israel' in the picturesque language of older translations). But it would be very widely held that the term Israel is quite inappropriate outside Palestine, and that the description of the Exodus-group as 'Israelite' is a theological back-projection from the perspective of a later time. Once concerns of ideology* have been recognized, however, all kinds of additional problems emerge, for it is now generally acknowledged that the Deuteronomistic History* (Joshua–II Kings) is as much an ideological as a historical presentation. Is it therefore legitimate to use it as the basis for an attempt to reconstruct the people's history? This applies with particular force to the earlier period of history, for which no external cross-checks are available to link Israel's story with that of other nations. But it is also clearly relevant to the choice of personalities and events to be described: it is essentially a story of kings rather than ordinary men and women; its concerns are overwhelmingly religious, as if the people of ancient Israel were interested in nothing else; and every action is subject to specific moral judgment based on Deuteronomistic standards.

Issues of this kind have led in recent years to increasing doubt whether the history of Israel can legitimately be regarded as sufficiently surely established for its use in the traditional way. And this doubt arises from a variety of factors. The approaches of Ramsey, Garbini, and Lemche, for example, differ markedly from one another: Ramsey is concerned with the lack of 'fit' between the biblical texts and the archaeological* evidence, Garbini with the ideological character of Israel's understanding of its own past, Lemche with a sociological* approach to Israel's history. Yet, despite this difference of approach, they all reach very similar conclusions concerning the possibility of our being able to know the history of Israel. Even the accounts of David,* often considered as *terra firma* by those sceptical of the earlier biblical books, are full of legendary* elaborations which raise acute problems for the historian. Ironically, when we do meet a biblical character in a non-biblical text (Ahab, in the annals of the Assyrian king Shalmaneser III, *c.* 853 BC), the event referred to, the battle of Qarqar, is not mentioned in the OT. Only with the later, eighth-century, Assyrian threat does some measure of correlation become possible between biblical and non-biblical material. It is, of course, this possibility of cross-checking one's data which is at the very heart of the historian's task.

It must therefore appear as if the days of the primarily historical introduction* to OT study (an approach which goes back at least as far as Josephus*) may well be numbered. Since many of the prophetic* collections have also been studied using the same method, with, for example, the eighth-century prophets grouped together and interpreted in the light of their presumed historical setting, the changes involved will be considerable. What kind of model may emerge to replace the historical one cannot yet be determined with confidence.

See also **Biblical Criticism.**

J. Bright, *Early Israel in Recent History Writing*, 1956; G. Garbini, *History and Ideology in Ancient Israel*, 1988; N. P. Lemche, *Ancient Israel*, 1988; G. W. Ramsey, *The Quest for the Historical Israel*, 1981; J. A. Soggin, *A History of Israel*, 1984 (esp. pp. 1–40, on the methodological problems involved in writing a history of Israel).

R. J. COGGINS

James

The epistle of James is the first of the 'Catholic' or 'General' epistles* in the NT: placed in this category because of its address to the widely-defined audience of 'the twelve tribes in the Dispersion' (1.1). It first found acceptance in the canon* of the Eastern church, where Origen* was the first to quote it with explicit attribution. Eusebius* classed it among the 'disputed' books of the NT, since he was aware that it was not universally known or used in the church. Athanasius, however, placed it unhesitatingly in the canon list of his Festal Letter of AD 367. The epistle appears to have been known to the second-century Roman author of *The Shepherd of Hermas*, but it was not until the latter part of the fourth century that it was established in the use of the Western church. Hilary, Augustine* and Jerome all quote it, and it appears in the lists affirmed by the councils of Hippo (393) and Carthage (397). The church in Syria apparently continued to be ignorant of it until its inclusion in the Syriac* Peshitta translation *c.* AD 412.

The early authors unanimously identified the James of the opening address as 'the Lord's brother' of Gal. 1.19, the leader of the church in Jerusalem (Acts 15.13; 21.18). Jerome, who was troubled by the question of the relationship between Jesus and James, identified this James as 'the son of Alphaeus' (Mark 3.18), and as Jesus' cousin, and this

has been widely accepted in Catholic tradition. If the traditional authorship is accepted, the epistle would have been written in Palestine before AD 70. There are, however, no clear references in the text to a geographical setting or to known external events, and scholars who think that the epistle is pseudonymous* have variously located it in Syria or Rome, while the similarity of its interests to the Apostolic Fathers,* I Clement, Hermas and the Didache, has led some to date it late in the first century.

The general nature of the epistle's contents may explain its neglect in the period of the formation of the canon, and indeed beyond. It has been read for practical ethical* guidance rather than to establish doctrine or moral principles. Some passages have, however, had a particular importance. The instruction for anointing the sick by the elders of the church (5.14–15) has served as a proof-text for the sacrament of Unction of the Sick and of the Dying (Extreme Unction). The ruling against oaths (5.12) was appealed to, with Matt. 5.33–37, by some Protestant groups, especially the Quakers, in support of their refusal to take oaths in court; and this is discussed in Article 39 of the Articles of Religion in the Anglican Book of Common Prayer.

The authority of the epistle and its status in the canon were vigorously disputed by Martin Luther.* He found its argument that 'a man is justified by works and not by faith alone' (2.24), and that 'faith by itself, if it has no works, is dead' (2.17), diametrically opposed to Paul's* doctrine of justification. In his 1522 Preface to the NT he stigmatized James as 'an epistle of straw'; denied it apostolic authority, since it is the work of an apostle to preach Christ, as Paul does; and relegated it to the end of his translation.

Subsequent discussion of the epistle, apart from seeking to reconcile Paul and James, has centred on its character and the evidence it provides of earliest Christianity. In the mid-nineteenth century, F. C. Baur interpreted the history of the early church in terms of a conflict between the original Jewish Christianity* of Jerusalem and the Gentile Christianity of Paul, and subsequent attempts at reconciliation leading to the 'synthesis' of early Catholicism.* He saw the epistle of James as an attempt at rapprochement from the Jewish Christian side. The identification of James as 'Jewish Christian' was carried to an extreme by L. Massebieau and F. Spitta (1895, 1896), who both argued that the epistle was originally a Jewish document brought into Christian use by the simple addition of 'Jesus Christ' at 1.1 and 2.1. A more elaborate reconstruction of a Jewish original for James was made by A. Meyer (1930), who analysed it as the 'Testament of Jacob' to his twelve sons, on the analogy of the *Testaments of the Twelve Patriarchs*.

With the source-critical analysis of the Synoptic Gospels, it could be seen that passages in James have parallels in material common to Matthew and Luke, so-called Q; and when Q was thought to represent one of the earliest strata of the gospel tradition it could be argued that James also represents an early stage in Christian development, close to the original teaching of Jesus, maybe as that was preserved in the first Palestinian Christian communities. On the other hand, there are also close parallels with material peculiar to Matthew's Gospel, so that James might belong to a later stage in the history of tradition and to the church of the Matthaean redactor.

After source criticism,* form-critical* study of the Gospels concentrated on classifying the individual units of material in the Gospel sources. M. Dibelius (1921) applied the same method of analysis to James, and described the document as 'parenesis': a text composed of a mass of individual admonitions of general ethical character, assembled without any necessary logical sequence or overall interpretation. J. H. Ropes (1916) classified the epistle as a 'treatise', and argued its resemblance in content and style to the diatribe, or to popular philosophy of the Hellenistic* world.

The debate on whether James is early or late and Jewish- or Gentile-Christian continues in modern commentaries. Since the publication of the Dead Sea Scrolls,* especially the *Manual of Discipline*, further parallels have been adduced to argue its Jewish character and Palestinian origin. In any event, the epistle witnesses to the variety of early Christianity: a type of Christian faith which claimed Jesus as Lord and waited for his coming but was unconcerned with speculative christology;* which attached great importance to ethical conduct and to prayer; and which had a strong sense of community* and mutual responsibility. This sense of community was expressed in part in a violent hostility to the rich, seen as its enemies (1.9–11; 2.1–7; 5.1–6), and this element in the epistle gave it a place in Karl Kautsky's Marxist* interpretation of early Christianity and has more recently given it some currency in liberation theology.*

Peter H. Davids, *The Epistle of James: A Commentary on the Greek Text*, 1982; Martin Dibelius, *James*, 1976; Sophie Laws, *A Commentary on the Epistle of James*, 1980.

SOPHIE LAWS

Jeremiah

Jeremiah is the longest of the prophetic*

books and is different from the other books in the prophetic collection in appearing to contain material on the life and thoughts of the prophet as well as the more usual poems and speeches. In the history of piety, the figure of Jeremiah has been a constant model of mystical* spirituality. More negatively, the gloomy spirit of depression which permeates the book associated with him has given rise to the word 'jeremiad' – a long mournful lamentation or complaint (a reputation assisted by the traditional attribution of the book of Lamentations to Jeremiah; cf. LXX Lam. 1.1). The representation of Jeremiah as having been active during the period of the fall of Jerusalem* to the Babylonians (*c.* 587 BC) made him particularly significant for some of the literature produced after the Roman destruction of Jerusalem (AD 70). Thus the book and its central character have somewhat paradigmatic qualities which influenced much of the long history of the interpretation of Jeremiah. If the figure of Jeremiah remains, to some extent, a popular typological character in that history today, it must be said that the modern interpretation of the book of Jeremiah has moved far away from such biographical concerns. Both aspects, however, book and prophet, constitute the twin foci of Jeremiah studies and involve complex hermeneutical* issues which undermine any simple resolutions of interpretative problems.

The history of the interpretation of Jeremiah begins in the Hebrew Bible itself, with references to certain *topoi* of the book in II Chron. 36.21; Dan. 9.2 (the 'seventy years' of Jer. 25.11–12; 29.10). The 'new covenant'* of 31.31–34 does not figure largely in the Qumran community literature (*see* **Dead Sea Scrolls**), but is important in NT material on the 'last supper' (I Cor. 11.25; Mark 14.25; Matt. 26.28; Luke 22.20) and is cited at length in Heb. 8.8–13; 10.15–18. Here the words of the prophet are used to argue the claims of the nascent Christian communities to be the fulfilment of ancient expectations. In the pseudepigraphal* *Paraleipomena of Jeremiah*, Jeremiah is made a witness to the Christian kerygma* and his resuscitation during stoning echoes the death and resurrection* of Jesus, thus making him a *figura* of the Christ. There is, however, no single account of the death of Jeremiah – no death notice appears at all in the canonical book of Jeremiah! – but a bifurcation of traditions about how he died: naturally (e.g. Syriac Baruch; Jewish conclusion to *Paraleipomena Jer.*; Seder Olam 26); or was stoned (e.g. *Vita Jeremiae*; Midrash Num. 30.15; Christian conclusion to *Paraleipomena Jer.*; most of the church Fathers). The allusion to stoning in Heb. 11.37 may well be to Jeremiah, though the generality of the reference might just signify martyrs of the churches.

The destruction of the Temple in AD 70 is echoed in the literature which emphasizes Jeremiah's role in the safeguarding of the sacred cult objects when the national shrine was desecrated. In II Macc. 2.4–8 the legend of Jeremiah's hiding of the altars, ark and tent appears, and elements of this legend occur in the *Paraleipomena Jer.* where he hides the sacred vessels in the earth so that they may avoid destruction. In some legends he assigns the key of the temple to the heavens until such time as the people are restored to their own land. These stories are in striking contrast to the tales in the biblical book where Jeremiah's interest in Temple matters is fairly limited (cf. Jer. 27–28 on the *topos* of the sacred vessels; also Dan. 1.2; 5.2–9), but they reflect deep anxieties about the sacred place after the Roman conquest of Jerusalem destroyed it. Rembrandt's famous painting, 'Jeremiah lamenting the destruction of Jerusalem', admirably captures some of these motifs in its depiction of the ageing prophet in a mountain cave (cf. II Macc. 2.4–5) mourning the burning city (seen peripherally at the edge of the painting) while guarding the sacred vessels, curtains and – nice Protestant touch this! – the Bible (Rijksmuseum, Amsterdam).

An important *topos* developed from the book of Jeremiah is the strange companionship of Jeremiah and Baruch. It is an inchoate relationship in the biblical text (cf. 32.12–13, 16; 36.4–32; 43.2–3, 6; 45.1–2), but is highly developed in the pseudepigraphal* literature (Baruch is entirely absent from the NT corpus). As Jeremiah's confidant and companion in some of the literature, he is an extension of the biblical figure of Baruch; but in some stories, he displaces Jeremiah in importance and makes the great speeches attributed elsewhere to Jeremiah (e.g. Syriac Baruch). Also in this latter role he is a producer of apocalypses.* There is great scope for intertextual* studies on this pair of companions in relation to the biblical narratives and the pseudepigraphal literature. Such studies would produce valuable information on the structures of storytelling in the Bible and related literature (*see* **Narrative Theology**).

Apart from the many quotations from and allusions to the book of Jeremiah in the NT (e.g. Matt. 16.14; Luke 19.46), the book is also alluded to in various church Fathers (esp. in Justin and the homilies* of Origen*). But because Jeremiah was such a gloomy individual and his book so devoted to destruction, early Christian writers did not find his work as cheerful or as edifying as that of Isaiah (a valuable survey of the uses of Jeremiah in early Christian and Jewish sources is C. Wolff, *Jeremia im Frühjudentum und Urchristentum*, 1976). In mediaeval* times his gloominess is

his trademark and, though formally represented with the other prophets in and on cathedrals (e.g. on the outside of Chartres), his representation is easily recognized by its depiction of age and sadness (e.g. Rembrandt; the Sistine Chapel).

In modern times the interpretation of Jeremiah has continued to be along autobiographical and pietistic lines (the four-and-a-half volumes of John Calvin's* commentary on Jeremiah anticipate much of the piety and theology typical of the subsequent centuries of writing on both book and character). The lyrical poetry of the book of Jeremiah has attracted the poets – perhaps Gerard Manley Hopkins' Sonnet 74, 'Thou art indeed just, Lord, if I contend . . .' (based on Jer. 12.1ff.), is the best example. English poetry* has many fine examples of Jeremiah-influenced poems and so have many other languages, especially Rilke's magnificent 'Jeremiah' poem in German. Franz Werfel's novel, *Hearken unto the Voice* (1937), is devoted to the story of Jeremiah, and Stefan Zweig's *Jeremiah: A drama in nine scenes* (1929) focusses on the conflict between Jeremiah and the priest Pashhur and the prophet Hananiah. In Israeli education, the figure of Jeremiah has attracted attention because the social context of his work was a time of war, and since the founding of the State of Israel warfare and threatening neighbours have been Israel's lot. The controversial nature of Jeremiah's apparent collaboration with the enemies of Jerusalem and his encouragement of treason among the people are features of his story which allow for argument and debate among Israeli schoolchildren (cf. J. Schoneveld, *The Bible in Israeli Education*, 1976). A less satisfactory use of Jeremiah in relation to modern war appears in L. E. Binns, *Jeremiah: A Prophet for a Time of War* (1941), where the unsuitability of Jeremiah for Binns' purposes never quite catches the writer's attention. Jeremiah, book and character, continues to attract modern readers and political theologues as a model of ministry or action in contemporary religion and politics, though the elegiac tone of the biblical lyrics suggests a good deal of misreading going on here.

The modern historical-critical* interpretation of the book of Jeremiah has been shaped by the work of Bernhard Duhm* (*Das Buch Jeremia*, 1901) and Sigmund Mowinckel (*Zur Komposition des Buches Jeremia*, 1914; *Prophecy and Tradition*, 1946), building on the critical approach to scripture of the previous centuries of European scholarship. Here the focus has been on determining the origins of the poetic and prosaic moieties of the book and the assigning of different sections to different sources or streams of tradition. The similarity of much of the language, style and theology of parts of Jeremiah to those of Deuteronomy and the Deuteronomistic History* has led to the development of a theory of a deuteronomistic edition of the book. On the other hand, some scholars have argued for an identification of this kind of language with that used by the historical Jeremiah.

These two views of the prose of Jeremiah have tended to define the polarized positions on the interpretation of the book since the Second World War. They also characterize one of the central issues in recent Jeremiah studies: the extent to which the material in the book can or cannot be identified with the historical Jeremiah. The older synthesis of the interpretation of the book as the product of the prophet Jeremiah, with some additional material from deuteronomistic sources, best typified by John Skinner's classic work *Prophecy and Religion: Studies in the Life of Jeremiah* (1922) combining learning and piety, has now disappeared and the academic study of Jeremiah has fragmented into competing hypotheses about the book and radically different strategies of reading it. Some approaches emphasize the connections between the book (as we now have it) and the original prophet Jeremiah, while others question the extent of such connections or challenge the conventions of reading biblical texts implied by such an historicist* approach to literature.

Most of the twentieth century's scholarship on Jeremiah has been German (e.g. commentaries* by Cornill, 1905; Volz, 1922; Rudolph, 1947, ³1968; Weiser, 1952, ⁸1981), with a few exceptions (e.g. A. Condamin, *Le Livre de Jérémie*, ³1936; Hyatt in *The Interpreter's Bible* 5, 1956; John Bright's Anchor Bible volume on *Jeremiah*, 1965). But the tide has now turned and the most interesting and solid work on Jeremiah is being produced by English-language biblical scholars. McKane's magisterial half-commentary (limited to Jer. 1–25) (1986) is an exhaustive philological* analysis of the text and its versions in the light of the history of the book's interpretation. He advances a theory of corpus building which accounts for the repetitive and untidy nature of chs 1–25 and takes the argument about the composition of the book a stage further than previous commentators. This theory will focus attention on the social location of the development of the book and holds promise for future research. Carroll's much shorter but completed commentary develops some of the issues raised by his earlier study, *From Chaos to Covenant* (1981; see also his J S O T Guide, *Jeremiah*, 1989), but in a more radical way questions the way scholars have read biblical books and uses an *Ideologiekritik* (*see* **Ideology**) approach to the substance of the

text. Opposition to this approach will be stronger among scholars because it offends against the inertia of the academic and theological guilds which governs how texts are conventionally read! The questions raised about the nature of prophetic books and the literariness of the figure of the prophet Jeremiah will generate controversy about the production of ancient texts, the ethics of reading, and the sociology of scholarship. Such questions and controversies could prove to be a salutary radicalizing of reading texts in the light of the necessity of theory and the scrutinizing of conventional assumptions, but are more likely to polarize the guilds into theological defences of traditional beliefs about texts and a pietization of scholarship.

The production of monographs on Jeremiah in English (from the Sheffield School of Biblical Scholars' printing presses) and German continues apace. This Indian summer of Jeremiah studies (it will be charted by Herrmann's massive B K A T on *Jeremia* which began to see the light of day in 1986) holds much promise for the future and must inevitably change the face of such studies in the next century. On the other hand, the figure of Jeremiah discerned by the traditional reading of the book will continue to appeal to the lyrically minded and will encourage the politically active to engage in local politics in a prophetic way. How academic and activist readings of the text should be reconciled (if at all!) will also become a focus for Jeremiah studies. The long history of the book's interpretation looks like having as long a future.

In addition to titles mentioned, see L. G. Perdue and B. W. Kovacs, *A Prophet to the Nations*, 1984.

ROBERT P. CARROLL

Jeremias, J.

Joachim Jeremias (1900–80), one of the most distinguished biblical scholars of the twentieth century, for the greater part of his career held the chair of N T in the University of Göttingen. His major works have been translated from the original German into English and French, thus gaining for him world-wide renown and influence, especially in the area of the interpretation of the ministry and teaching of Jesus in the light of its Jewish background.*

Jeremias knew Palestine intimately, having spent part of his boyhood there, and brought to his study of the N T an expert knowledge of Hebrew and Aramaic and an authoritative understanding of rabbinic* Judaism. His first book, originally published in 1923, became a standard work in its field and passed through a succession of revised editions before being translated into English under the title *Jeru-*

salem in the Time of Jesus: An Investigation into Economic and Social Conditions during the New Testament Period, ET 1969. He made several notable contributions to Kittel's *TWNT*, some of which proved of great importance for subsequent exegesis, particularly the articles on 'lamb', 'stone' and 'cornerstone', and the article on 'Servant* of God' in which he collaborated with his OT colleague, W. Zimmerli, and which was published in an English translation as *The Servant of God*, 1957. Another important work, a translation of which appeared in 1958, is *Jesus' Promise to the Nations*, in which Jeremias argues that Jesus' own mission was confined to Israel but that he also foresaw a world mission to be fulfilled when the Gentile nations would be gathered round Jerusalem, where the last judgment of Israel and the nations would take place. Of far-reaching influence also were two short books in which Jeremias argues persuasively that infant baptism was already practised in the NT period: *Infant Baptism in the First Four Centuries*, 1960, and *The Origins of Infant Baptism: A further study in reply to Kurt Aland*, 1963.

Important as all these works are, however, the name of Jeremias is probably associated primarily with his seminal studies of two aspects of the teaching of Jesus – the eucharistic words and the parables* – and with his comprehensive treatment of the proclamation of Jesus in *New Testament Theology*, 1971. Characteristically, the author revised and added new material in successive editions of the former studies, which reached their final forms (in English) in *The Eucharistic Words of Jesus*, 1966, and *The Parables of Jesus*, 1972. In marked contrast to the prevailing tendency of contemporary German NT scholarship, and with an approach more akin to that of such British contemporaries as C. H. Dodd,* T. W. Manson and V. Taylor, Jeremias was convinced that careful and responsible application of source-critical* and form-critical* principles could yield positive and constructive results in the discovery of the *ipsissima vox* of the historical Jesus* and the understanding of his mind and purpose. 'In the synoptic tradition,' he wrote in his *Theology*, 'it is the inauthenticity, and not the authenticity, of the sayings of Jesus that must be demonstrated.'

Arguing cogently for the identification of the Last Supper with the Passover Meal and for the originality of the Longer Text in Luke 22.19f., Jeremias seeks to recover the original words of institution spoken by Jesus in Hebrew (or Aramaic) (*see* **Semitisms**), which he claims to be the essential foundation of all historical and theological interpretation of the death of Christ. Jesus viewed his own impending crucifixion as the vicarious and sacrificial

death of the Servant of the Lord of Isa. 53, a view which Jeremias claims to be fully consistent with the results of his own exhaustive study (with W. Zimmerli – see above) of that concept.

Again, Jeremias' detailed examination of the language, style and contents of the parables leads him to the confidence that, after all secondary accretions and embellishments have been removed, it is possible to recover the original parable and the situation in which Jesus told it. This leads to the conclusion that in all his parables Jesus compels his hearers to come to a decision about his person and mission: 'The hour of fulfilment is come . . . For he has been manifested whose veiled kingliness shines through every word and through every parable – the Saviour.' It is in this context that Jeremias offers (with the approval of Dodd himself, as he claims in a footnote) the expression *sich realisierende Eschatologie* (or 'eschatology* that is in process of realization') as an improvement on C. H. Dodd's 'realized eschatology'. In his *Theology*, Jeremias applies the same approach and method to the entire synoptic account of the work and words of Jesus, and provides what almost amounts to 'a life of Jesus from call to crucifixion and resurrection'.

In a small volume containing four lectures delivered in English in America, *The Central Message of the New Testament*, 1965, the general reader may find distilled many of the fundamental insights of Jeremias' contribution to NT interpretation and Christian theology.

Matthew Black, 'Joachim Jeremias' in A. W. Hastings and E. Hastings (eds), *Theologians of Our Time*, 1966, pp. 123–31.

OWEN E. EVANS

Jerusalem

In the Torah (Pentateuch*), Jerusalem is not mentioned at all by name, except arguably as Salem (Gen. 14.18) in connection with Melchizedek. Later interpretation, however, both Jewish and Christian, suggests that the book discovered by workmen whilst repairing the Jerusalem Temple walls in the reign of King Josiah (approx 640–609 BC) was a version of the book of Deuteronomy. That certainly ties in well with what we know of Josiah's reforms, in ridding the country of pagan practices and in generally cleaning up and restoring the Temple to its former glory. It also matches up well – some would say too well – with the constantly reiterated phrase in Deuteronomy itself, about the centralization of worship within the place where 'God shall choose to cause his name to dwell there'.

It is equally possible, and often argued in the light of critical interpretation of the

Hebrew Bible in general and the Pentateuch in particular, that this proves that it is Jerusalem that was meant, and suggests that Deuteronomy itself is a very late book, written in or around the time of Josiah (i.e. long after its purported Mosaic time), possibly with strong political motives on the part of the priests or the Levites, who could see some advantage in centralizing worship in Jerusalem and regaining some of their old authority. Whichever is the case, it is hard to believe that the constant reiteration of 'the place where God shall choose to cause his name to dwell there' does not suggest Jerusalem in some way.

But the real emphasis on Jerusalem, unmistakable in every way, comes with King David.* David unified the country after lengthy battles with his erstwhile father-in-law Saul and proclaimed Jerusalem the capital. Though he did not build the Temple there, his son Solomon did, and it is the Davidic line which has given such richness to the traditions surrounding the city. For Jerusalem was the city of David, forerunner of the messiah* in Jewish tradition. In Christian tradition, Jesus had to be linked into the Davidic line to satisfy the strength of that strand of thought, and it was from Jerusalem, according to Muslim* tradition, that Mohammad ascended to heaven. It is a city which has enormous importance in the literature of three of the world's great religions, both within and outside the Bible.

For no examination of Jerusalem as interpreted in and from biblical literature can conceivably ignore Jewish post-biblical literature, or the historical material of Christian and Muslim tradition. That is perhaps particularly important around the period of the Crusades with its emphasis on freeing the Holy City from the infidels. There is no method of looking at Jerusalem without understanding its role as the 'Holy City', and the pull that it has had on the adherents of all three religions, each group of whom has wanted the city in its possession, for the sake of its holy places, and its strong historical link with themselves. Thus Jews have always built their synagogues with the Ark, in which the scrolls of the Torah are kept and over which the eternal lamp burns, orientated towards Jerusalem. Christian churches have the same orientation, whilst Muslims, though they pray facing Mecca, nevertheless regard the Dome of the Rock as one of their holiest sites.

Where then does this intensity, this passionate desire to possess the place, this relationship with a small geographical area, come from? It does not lie in the splendour of the site of the city itself, for, as has often been remarked, Jerusalem seems a curious choice for a city that was to be so dominant in world thought,

with its poor access, poor water supply, and few natural riches in resources. Nor does it stand on the most ancient trade routes, or provide the key to one of the areas prized by the ancient warring civilizations. So its history lies far more in its significance religiously, as a modest hill-fortress became the city of David, Solomon, the prophets, Jesus, and Mohammad.

For there is a promise of eternity in the concept of Jerusalem. When Nathan the prophet promises an eternal dynasty to David (II Sam. 7), it is in conjunction with the idea of the building of the Temple in Jerusalem. The idea that David's line will rule forever, that the messiah will be of the Davidic line, and that God will, in some way, dwell in Jerusalem rather than elsewhere, is crucial to Jerusalem's religious significance. That, of course, already exists within the Hebrew Bible itself, in the promises of David's status as origin of the messiah ('And there shall come forth a shoot out of the stock of Jesse . . .' Isa. 11.1). It continues in the NT, with its emphasis on Jesus' origins as involving Jerusalem and the number of Jesus' miracles* and sermons actually given in Jerusalem. And in the poetic books of the Hebrew Bible, the other quality of Jerusalem in later literature has its origins, that of its great beauty. The imagery is hyperbolic – 'beautiful in elevation, the joy of all the earth' (Ps. 48.3), or 'the perfection of beauty, the joy of all the earth' (Lam. 2.15). This is continued in the concept of the ideal Jerusalem, found in later Jewish thought, where, after the ingathering of the exiles, Jerusalem will be full of precious stones and pearls and all Israel will come and take their stones from there (*Pirke de-Rav Kahana* 137a), or, from *Midrash Rabba*, itself an anthology of rabbinic* legend related to the Hebrew Bible, comes the tradition that God will build (rebuild) Jerusalem out of sapphires 'and the stones will shine like the sun, and the nations will come and look upon the glory of Israel' (*Exodus Rabba* 15.21).

But none of this really makes sense without the idea of destruction and rebuilding. Part of that concept comes within the Hebrew Bible itself. The prophets* sing of the impending destruction. Biblical scholars have argued endlessly about the extent to which prophetic writings are in fact the product of a later period when it was already known that the city was at least partially if not wholly destroyed. This is a difficult subject historically. In 701 BC Jerusalem was apparently saved at the last moment from Sennacherib's hordes, in accordance with Isaiah's prophecies that the mighty Assyrian conqueror will not succeed in vanquishing Jerusalem, which is assured of divine protection both because of the honour of God's own name, and because it is David's city. The fact (if it is really a fact) that the city was not destroyed may have led to the idea that Jerusalem was immovably great and indestructible, a view which was bound to lead to the 'pride before a fall' view of Jeremiah and Ezekiel. But the psalmists took on the idea of Jerusalem's invincibility, and described God as its eternal protector and made the city the 'city of God', a description which runs through Jewish and Christian literature of the later periods.

Jeremiah and Ezekiel were firm in their negation of the idea of Jerusalem's semi-magical resistance against all odds. Jeremiah preached that Jerusalem's safety was contingent upon her people actually following God's ways. If they forsook God's ways, they would see Jerusalem fall victim to the destruction all the other small cities suffered at the hands of conquerors. Here lies the beginning of the destruction motif. Jerusalem has become '. . . rebellious and defiled, the oppressing city' (Zeph. 3.1), and Ezekiel continues with an attack on Jerusalem's inhabitants which describes them as even worse than Samaria and Sodom in wickedness. Jerusalem became a desolate city. The motif of destruction was fully formed. The psalmist wrote of the Babylonian exile: 'By the waters of Babylon we sat and wept . . . How shall we sing the Lord's song in a strange land? If I forget thee, O Jerusalem, let my right hand forget her cunning. If I do not remember thee, let my tongue cleave to the roof of my mouth; if I prefer not Jerusalem above my chief joy' (Ps. 137).

In contrast with this comes the vision of the restored Jerusalem. Jeremiah is realistic; his vision is of a rebuilt city much like the old one, with a clear demarcation of an enlarged area the city would cover. But Ezekiel goes into another dimension. Jerusalem is not mentioned by name. It is 'a city in the south . . . up on a very high mountain' which he describes, and it is simply a background for the Temple, a city entirely sanctified to God, the place where God will dwell (an allusion to Deuteronomy), with the name: 'the Lord is there'. It is the other prophets who give the restored Jerusalem its spiritual and religious significance. Zechariah argued that Jerusalem's sanctity will be recognized by all the nations, whilst both Isaiah and Micah see the 'mountain of the House of the Lord' (identified with Jerusalem) as the source of justice and peace for all nations. 'For out of Zion shall go forth the law, and the word of the Lord from Jerusalem' (Isa. 2.3). This is the passionate universalism of the Jerusalem image, picked up at various times in Jewish and Christian tradition. It runs hand in hand with the fervent love of Jerusalem and Zion to be found in Isaiah and repeated in the Psalms and elsewhere in both biblical and later literature.

But this was the vision of the real Jerusalem. There is no feeling that they were searching for an ideal. This was reality, often perceived as truly historical. No wonder then that the Christian description of Jewish textual interpretation in its plainest meaning, the *peshat*, was the *sensus judaicus*. Everything was literal. The destruction happened. So did the restoration described in Ezra and Nehemiah. Then came the final destruction by the Romans. Despite all this, they hoped for a real and physical restoration. They hoped to go there, to be part of the rebuilding, because it really was the 'city of God'. Unlike its role in Christian interpretation, the celestial Jerusalem played a relatively minor role until quite late in Jewish history. For Jews there was no point in worrying about some ideal Jerusalem when there was a real city, neglected, with its western Temple wall still standing but uncherished. Therefore it was no amazing romanticism that made the legal code of Judaism regard Jerusalem as special. It was special, historically speaking, and not to acknowledge that would have been a denial of a central theme of the religion. Thus in the Talmud,* despite its date being long after the destruction of Jerusalem, a special holiness still pervaded the city. If a person prays, he or she has to turn towards Jerusalem. The obligation of making a pilgrimage to Jerusalem remained even after its destruction, and anyone who sees the destruction of the city has to say: 'Zion has become a wilderness, Jerusalem a desolation' (Isa. 64.9), a practical interpretation of the verse. Theoretically, people had to mourn the destruction of Jerusalem every day, and *aides-mémoire* of its destruction were to be incorporated into everyday life. For instance, it was stated that 'A man may whitewash his house, but he should leave a small area unfinished in remembrance of Jerusalem; a man may prepare a full meal, but he should leave out an item of the menu in remembrance of Jerusalem; a woman might put on all her ornaments, but she should leave off one or two in remembrance of Jerusalem' (*Tosefta Sotah* 15; 12–14; *Baba Bathra* 60b).

The destruction figured large in the people's thinking about Jerusalem. But there had been promises of the restoration, when Jerusalem would become a special, splendid city, source of all good values for the world. Why then was it destroyed? According to the aggadic literature (the non-legal, interpretational material of the rabbinic literature usually referred to as midrash*) there are many reasons. It was because the people practised idolatry and bloodshed, in accord with prophetic condemnations. In the period of the Second Temple, according to Yochanan ben Torta, they did study the Torah, they were observant of all of Jewish law, and every kind of good manners was found amongst them, 'but they loved money and hated one another without cause' (Jerusalem Talmud, Yoma 1.1, 38c). Other interpretations include the fact that relationships between human beings had deteriorated to a great extent, or that the relationship between human beings and God had become appalling, with desecrations of the sabbaths and festivals, and omissions of the reading of the daily prayers. Although all this can be very loosely based on what is to be found in the prophetic writings, ostensibly relating to the destruction of the First Temple, it is quite clear that it had become far more generalized, being used equally as a way of explaining the destruction of the Second Temple, and, indeed, as a way to explain that the city of Jerusalem itself was not in Jewish hands.

But what then will bring about the restoration of the city? Samuel bar Nachmani said that Jerusalem would not be rebuilt until the exiles were all gathered in. God will rebuild Jerusalem and never destroy it. Jerusalem will be far bigger than it had been. It would be extended on all sides and there would be room for all the exiles. 'The Holy One, blessed be He, will in days to come add to Jerusalem more than a thousand gardens and a thousand towers' (*Baba Bathra* 75b). And the commonest view of all, sometimes linked with the idea of the coming of the Messiah, was that quoted by Simeon bar Gamaliel, that 'all nations and all kingdoms will in time to come gather together in the midst of Jerusalem' (*Avoth de-Rabbi Nathan*, 35, 106).

This idea has to be linked with the concept of a celestial Jerusalem. There was a strong view, based on Isaiah's vision of the heavenly temple in ch. 6, that there was in fact a heavenly Jerusalem. There is a classic exposition of this idea, which has great importance for Christian thinking as well as Jewish. It starts off with the verse in Hosea (11.9): 'The Holy One is in the midst of thee, and I will not enter into the city.' To this Rabbi Yochanan said: 'The Holy One, blessed be He, declared: "I shall not enter the heavenly Jerusalem until I can enter the earthly Jerusalem."' Is there, then, a heavenly Jerusalem? Yes, for it is written: "Jerusalem, thou art builded as a city that is compact together"' (Ta'anit 5a). Or there is the other delightful interpretation that the heavenly Temple was created before the world was made (based again on Isa. 6). The heavenly Jerusalem was 'fashioned out of a great love for the earthly Jerusalem' (*Tanhuma*, Pekudei, 1). This is based on the variety of biblical passages extolling the beauty both physical and spiritual of the earthly Jerusalem.

So beautiful was it that a celestial and perfect image of it had to be created in the heavens.

But it is, of course, far from being so simple. For the creation of the idea of the celestial Jerusalem meant that ultimately it was possible to argue that the celestial Jerusalem and Temple became varieties of the same thing. They became idealized, spiritualized. They were the sources of all good, far superior to anything the earthly versions had to offer. This was largely accepted by Christian thinking, as it rejected the idea of the physical restoration of the city of Jerusalem and the Temple. John's vision in Revelation is that of a spiritual 'new Jerusalem', an image which persisted in Christian thought and particularly its hymnody,* as far as William Blake's* 'Jerusalem', and even arguably into our present day. It is the view of the apocalyptic* books, to be found in Enoch (90.28–9) and IV Ezra (7.26). But in the early rabbinic period this view was entirely rejected within the aggadic literature, with its constant assertion that the earthly Jerusalem would rise till it reached the throne of the divine majesty (*Pirkei de-Rav Kahana* 143b and *passim*). It was much later, in the literature written in Muslim countries and arguably under Muslim influence, that the idea reappeared of a heavenly Jerusalem coming down and appearing on earth fully built and perfect, a view far nearer that of the Christians in their picture of the celestial Jerusalem. In Christian thought, the Jerusalem image has been nowhere more powerful than by means of Augustine's* *City of God*, seminal for European political theory, and rooted in Ps. 87.3: 'Glorious things are spoken of you, O city of God'.

Mainstream Jewish interpretation was much more about the real city, dwelling at length both in liturgy and commentary on its decline and ruin. In the poetry of the mediaeval Spanish Jews the message of longing becomes ever more intense, with the desire to return increasingly apparent. Judah Halevi is the classic example of this genre of poetry, earning the title of 'the singer of Zion'. Jerusalem is 'beautiful of elevation, the joy of the world, the capital of the great king'. He himself did set out to return to Israel: 'My heart is in the east . . .'; and that longing and mourning over the destruction of the city was typical of the period.

Whilst a few mediaeval Jews made the journey from Spain or North Africa to the Holy Land, a common motif throughout Jewish literature was that of the desirability of the return, based on the prophetic books. The classic example is perhaps that in the Passover liturgy, the *haggadah*, in which the cry goes up: 'Next year in Jerusalem'. Next year in Jerusalem is both figurative and actual. The desire is for the restoration of the city to its true glory, for the establishment of the messianic city. But at the same time the Passover story is about the journey from slavery to freedom, from Egypt to the promised land. There is a kind of irony in the parallelism between the good journey from Egypt to Israel and the bad journey from Jerusalem to the diaspora, from freedom to bondage. But the main interpretation is of the journey from slavery as perceived as the lot of Jews in the West (even when, historically, the conditions were not bad), to freedom in Jerusalem. Part of it is the celestial Jerusalem, the city of God and the city of the messiah's coming. That is where the ingathering of the exiles will take place, and that is where the prophetic forecasts will be fulfilled. It is not literally next year in Jerusalem, but metaphorically so. And the return must always be prayed for, every day.

Jerusalem is central to Jewish thinking and prayer. From its centrality, both Christianity and Islam have derived a Jerusalem theology and made it central to their thinking. The difference is that for Jews, most of the time, in most places, it has been a physical and geographical reality, however distant it seemed. It encompassed other ideas, other values, and a universalistic message. But in fact it was the real city that was longed for – 'Next year in (the real) Jerusalem', a cry which has its roots in the exodus story, and in the prophetic promises of return.

See also **Jewish Exegesis.**

D. R. Ap-Thomas, 'Jerusalem' in D. Winton Thomas, *Archaeology and Old Testament Study*, 1967; S. W. Baron, *Social and Religious History of the Jews*, 1937; Israel Exploration Society, *Jerusalem Through the Ages*, 1968; S. Runciman, *History of the Crusades*, 1951–54; C. Thubron, *Jerusalem*, 1969.

JULIA NEUBERGER

Jewish Background to the New Testament

Through much of history Christian writers and commentators have been hostile to Jews and Judaism (*see* **Antisemitism**). Nevertheless, even from the early period of the church Fathers, Jewish belief and practice have been drawn on at times for interpretation. Origen* and especially Jerome realized the value of Hebrew for a correct understanding of the Bible. But it was only at the Renaissance that Christian scholars in any number came to have a knowledge of Hebrew and direct access to Jewish writings in the original or in Latin translation. Works such as John Lightfoot's *Horae Hebraicae et Talmudicae* (1658–78) with its illumination of the NT from rabbinic* litera-

ture have appeared sporadically since the Reformation.* More usually, however, Jesus has been compared with the OT prophets rather than with his contemporaries, so that it can certainly be said that a serious concern with the 'Jewish background to the NT' is a recent phenomenon.

A major stimulus for the current interest has been discoveries of new sources of information. One of the most exciting of these was the Dead Sea Scrolls,* but other sources long known (though sometimes neglected) have received a revival of interest: the Apocrypha* and Pseudepigrapha,* the Targums,* the Septuagint,* Philo,* and Josephus.* Also important are a variety of inscriptions and papyri which throw light on ancient Judaism.

1. *Sources of information*

Dead Sea Scrolls. The discovery of the Qumran scrolls in 1947 produced a flurry of interest and activity which has not slowed. Along with concern for the OT text and related topics has been the question of what light the scrolls might throw on the NT. Although some scholars drew parallels between the Teacher of Righteousness and Jesus, a direct connection between Qumran and Jesus has generally been rejected. More widely accepted is the idea that John the Baptist* may once have been an Essene (assuming Qumran is to be connected with the Essenes, which most scholars accept), and most would agree that some converts to Christianity may have been former Essenes. However, the scrolls are usually seen as a more general reservoir of data for ideas shared by much of Judaism of the time.

Apocrypha and pseudepigrapha. This is basically a designation of all the non-rabbinic Jewish literature apart from Qumran and the individual writers in Greek such as Philo and Josephus. The writings in this group are of a variety of literary genres* and from a wide period of time. Many of these works have been known since antiquity and all but a few for the past century or more. The difficulty is that most do not survive in their original Hebrew or Aramaic texts but in translation, sometimes two or three times removed from the original (a few were of course composed originally in Greek). Because of the need to master exotic languages such as Old Slavonic or Ethiopic and for other reasons, these were neglected from the turn of the century until the last couple of decades. Now, though, a great deal is being done in the study of these important relics of ancient Judaism.

Philo and Josephus. The subject matter of these two writers is very different in many ways, but both belonged to the first century AD and both wrote in Greek. Philo composed commentaries on the Pentateuch,* mainly the book of Genesis, which emphasized allegorical* interpretation. Josephus was a historian, but the paraphrase of biblical history in his *Antiquities* serves as a commentary at many points. Both writers were influenced by Greek literary theory and rhetorical* style.

Targums and rabbinic literature. The Targums are Aramaic translations of most of the OT. Some are very periphrastic with a considerable amount of interpretative material. Although the precise origin of the Targums is disputed, it is generally agreed that they are rabbinic in their present form. Rabbinic literature includes legal collections, such as the Mishnah and Talmuds,* and commentaries* (midrashim*) on various sections of the OT. There is a major methodological problem with the use of the Targums and rabbinic literature to illustrate the NT. This is the fact that this literature in its present form is often much later – sometimes centuries later – than the NT. Does a passage in the Targums or a rabbinic writing demonstrate an understanding current in first-century Judaism or only an interpretation which developed later?

2. Topics in the current debate

Jesus. As a Jew living in Palestine, Jesus (*see* **Historical Jesus**) is naturally to be understood in the light of the Judaism of his own time and place, and many different points about his life and teachings could be discussed. However, interest has centred upon certain topics, including his original sayings, messianism* and the 'son of man',* and the model of the rabbi.

Sayings of Jesus. It is clear from certain passages (e.g. Mark 7.34; 15.34) and from the general linguistic situation of Palestine that Jesus spoke Aramaic as his first language. Therefore, a great deal of interest has focussed on trying to reconstruct the original Aramaic form of his sayings from the Gospels (*see* **Semitisms**). Apart from the important question of whether it is legitimate to take the Gospel material as verbatim quotation, the major debate has been the precise form of Aramaic which Jesus would have spoken. Some (e.g. Matthew Black, *An Aramaic Approach to the Gospels and Acts*, 1967) have freely drawn on the language of the Targums and even of the Old Syriac* translation of the Gospels in the task of reconstruction. Others (especially J. A. Fitzmyer, *A Wandering Aramean*, 1979, pp. 1–27) have argued strongly that this is a later phase of the language and that the closest equivalent to the Aramaic of Jesus' time is to be found in the Qumran literature.

Messianism and the 'son of man'. Although it is generally accepted that Jesus did not claim to be the messiah, the early church nevertheless understood him in this role. But what sort of messiah? It is now clear that there was not one single view of messiahship in Judaism but rather a variety. Thus, some Qumran texts speak of messiahs of Israel and Aaron (*CD* 12.23; 19.10–11), as well as of a prophet who seems to be a third 'messianic' figure alongside them (1 QS 9.11). An important question is whether any section of Judaism held to a 'suffering messiah'; most discussions have concluded there is no evidence that such was found until much later, and the image of Jesus as a suffering messiah was a uniquely Christian development.

In the Synoptic* Gospels Jesus is often presented as referring to himself as the 'son of man'. In both Hebrew and Aramaic, 'son of man' is normally only an idiomatic expression meaning 'man' or 'human being' or even 'someone'. It has even been argued that 'son of man' in Aramaic can be a synonym for 'I' and that this is the sole significance of Jesus' usage (so G. Vermes, *Jesus the Jew*, 1973, pp. 163–8, opposed by J. A. Fitzmyer, *A Wandering Aramean*, pp. 152f.). On the other hand, the 'one like a son of man' in Dan. 7 is often interpreted as representing a heavenly being, while the term 'son of man' in the Parables of Enoch (I Enoch 46–48, 62–63) refers to a heavenly messianic figure. Could Jesus have been obliquely claiming (or at least interpreted by the Gospel writers as claiming) messiahship by use of the ambivalent term 'son of man'?

There are two problems with the view that it is used as a messianic title in the Gospels. One concerns the significance of the term in Dan. 7, since many scholars have claimed that 'the one like a son of man' is only a symbol for the people of God. Others have argued that, while this figure does include the people of God in representation, the specific reference is to the archangel Michael. The other problem involves the dating of the Parables of Enoch. Since these are not found among the Enoch fragments at Qumran, some have wanted to date this section of Enoch to the post-70 period. But several recent scholars maintain the older view that, though later than the other sections of Enoch, the Parables are still pre-70. The important thing is to realize that the debate still continues without any clear consensus as to the significance of the phrase 'son of man' in the Gospels (contrast, for example, the following recent works: B. Lindars, *Jesus Son of Man*, 1983; S. Kim, '*The "Son of Man"' as the Son of God*, 1983).

Jesus as rabbi. Jesus has often been compared to the figure of the rabbi or sage well known from rabbinic literature. It has even been argued that Jesus taught his disciples to memorize his sayings, as was thought to be customary among rabbis and their students (B. Gerhardsson, *Memory and Manuscript*, 1964, opposed by M. Smith, *JBL* 82, 1963, pp. 169–76). All theories which compare Jesus with the rabbis or the Pharisees* must take account of a major problem of scholarly method: the question whether and how far the later rabbinic literature may legitimately be used to reconstruct the pre-70 situation. Recent work, especially by Jacob Neusner and his students, has attempted to stratify the rabbinic traditions and make determinations about what is probably early and what late (see especially J. Neusner, *From Politics to Piety*, 1973). It has become clear that even the earliest phase of rabbinic literature (the Tannaitic literature, primarily the Mishnah, Tosephta, and the Tannaitic midrashim) still reflects primarily the developments and concerns of the second century even though sometimes drawing on pre-70 traditions. While much that has been done is controversial and much remains to be done, scholars can no longer simply retroject the society reflected in the Mishnah or Talmuds into pre-70 Palestine. Although the term 'rabbi' was probably used in the time of Jesus, the figure of the rabbinic sage seems likely to be a much later development and to assimilate Jesus to it is at the very least methodologically suspect. (Perhaps a better parallel for Jesus would be such charismatic figures as the itinerant healer or miracle*-worker for which we have some information; see Vermes, *Jesus the Jew*, pp. 58–82.)

The same applies to the Pharisees and other opponents of Jesus among the contemporary Jewish sects (A. J. Saldarini, *Pharisees, Scribes and Sadducees in Palestinian Society*, 1988). We probably know most about the Pharisees, but even here their beliefs, organization, and position in society are debatable. As for other groups such as the Sadducees, we have only a handful of statements and these usually constitute a neutral witness at best, but more often openly hostile testimony. The source closest to the time is Josephus, but many feel his testimony is biased not only by his concern to describe the sects in a way appealing to Graeco-Roman readers but also by his own affiliation with the Pharisees. To what extent his testimony should be accepted and filled out with data from rabbinic literature is still an important scholarly problem (see further Neusner, *From Politics to Piety*).

Old Testament quotations. A great deal of scholarly literature has been written about the quotations of the OT in the NT (see the survey by M. Miller in *JSJ* 2, 1971–72, pp. 29–82). The majority of quotations in the NT are from the Septuagint (LXX), the basic Greek translation of the OT. In some cases this represents a fairly literal rendering of the traditional Hebrew or Masoretic text* (MT). At other times, however, the LXX itself represents an interpretative rendering, either because of the translator's understanding or because of a Hebrew text different from the MT. An example is found at Acts 15.16–18. The LXX of Amos 9.11–12 is quoted here, but the rather different understanding comes from a slightly different reading of the Hebrew text of Amos.

Many quotations differ to a lesser or greater extent from the LXX. The question is whether these are merely paraphrases incorporating early Christian interpretation of various passages or whether they are exact quotations of variant traditions or interpretations among the Jews of the time. For instance, could some of them be quotations from the Targums? The question is whether the Targums existed already at this time. We know that some OT books were already translated into Aramaic because portions have been found at Qumran. On the other hand, these are usually quite literal, whereas the rabbinic Targums often have a much more periphrastic translation.

Old Testament exegesis. A final question concerns the way in which NT writers interpreted the OT. Their exegesis* may take its point of origin from a quotation in which the Greek differs significantly from the Hebrew of the MT. NT writers naturally see the OT through their understanding of Jesus, and often this is sufficient to explain their particular interpretation. But many times the exegesis of a particular passage shows close agreement with either the technique or the content of an interpretation known from Jewish literature. For example, I Cor. 10.4 speaks of the 'rock which followed' the Israelites in the desert. We know that there was a Jewish tradition which said that the rock from which water came when Moses struck it (Ex. 17.1–7) actually moved around with the Israelites in their travels and continued to provide them with water (Pseudo–Philo, *Biblical Antiquities* 10.7; 11.15). Paul* draws on this tradition to provide a type of Christ.

Some of the commentaries at Qumran give a so-called *pesher** form of exegesis. That is, a verse or passage is quoted, followed by a formula, such as 'its meaning (*pesher*) is', and then an interpretation which relates it to some aspect of the Qumran community or history. Some scholars have pointed out that there is a parallel in that NT writers often quote OT passages and then interpret them in the light of the life of Jesus or the history of the Christian church. The comparison is legitimate even if there is no direct influence from the Qumran community, for there is a similar mental stance; on the other hand, one must be cautious about referring to the NT interpretation as a form of *pesher* exegesis.

There are a few instances of allegory in the NT, such as Gal. 4.22–31. Here the major parallel is Philo of Alexandria whose exegesis is generally of an allegorical nature.

One should note that the term midrash is sometimes used of interpretative passages in the NT. Although the Hebrew term midrash is probably roughly equivalent to 'commentary', it grew out of the particular commentaries found in rabbinic literature. Some recent writers have objected to the use of the term as a generic designation for exegesis of OT passages in the NT. This is especially problematic in that the rabbinic midrashim have a content and flavour widely different from that of the NT even if individual parallels can sometimes be found. (P. S. Alexander in *Synoptic Studies* ed. C. M. Tuckett, 1984).

Two important points need to be kept in mind as one tries to understand the NT in its historical setting. One concerns the question of whether the NT is best explained as having a 'Jewish background' or is better understood from a 'Hellenistic'* or other background. Although a thorough discussion is beyond the scope of this article, the short answer is that the two ideas are not mutually exclusive. Much of our knowledge of early Judaism comes from sources in Greek. Also, Judaism was very much affected by Hellenization, especially in the Diaspora (see M. Hengel, *Jews, Greeks and Barbarians*, 1980). The best comparative material for any particular NT passage is not something which one can pronounce on in advance. Sometimes a passage can be clarified from Jewish literature or practices, sometimes from a non-Jewish Greek or Roman writing, sometimes from Gnostic* literature, or sometimes from some other source of information. Each argument or proposal must be looked at on its own merits and weighed against alternative explanations.

A second point is perhaps the most central of the whole article: Judaism before AD 70 was a pluralistic phenomenon. There were all sorts of different groups, factions, sects, and ideologies.* It is now beginning to be widely recognized that there was no 'orthodox' Judaism of the time, apart from the central temple cult and a few key practices such as circumcision. This means not only that many different sorts of Jews were converted to Christianity in the initial phases of the church, but also that the early church itself began as a movement within Judaism and only later saw itself as something separate. The Judaism of Jesus' day was not a monolithic religion but a complex variegated entity the precise nature of which is still being intently studied and explored.

See also **Dead Sea Scrolls; Jewish Christianity; Jewish Exegesis; Use of the Old Testament in the New Testament.**

In addition to works cited, see: J. A. Fitzmyer, *Essays on the Semitic Background of the New Testament*, 1971; W. S. LaSor, *The Dead Sea Scrolls and the New Testament*, 1972; B. Lindars, *New Testament Apologetic*, 1961; E. P. Sanders, *Jesus and Judaism*, 1985.

LESTER L. GRABBE

Jewish Christianity

The study of early Christian Bible interpretation must include consideration of the period when many Christians still saw themselves as Jews, and explained their Christian faith by interpreting the scriptures using Jewish methods though for a new purpose. Evidently the NT writers fall within this period and category, whereas from the next century writers are increasingly identified by Gentile origin and culture, and use methods of interpretation which reveal other influences besides Jewish tradition. It seems reasonable, therefore, to describe the earlier period (whatever its limits, for these varied in different areas) and its methods of biblical interpretation as 'Jewish Christian'. Unfortunately this term compounds the variable character of both its components and no general agreement has yet been reached either on how to define the term sociologically* and doctrinally, or on what are the limits of its applicability to Bible interpretation. It is necessary, therefore, first to outline the problem of defining 'Jewish Christian' and then to propose a system of criteria,* before attempting to summarize the characteristics and methods of Jewish Christian Bible interpretation.

Early Jewish Christian groups (especially Ebionites, Nazoraeans and Elkesaites) are named and described by several patristic writers and finally quite extensively by Epiphanius, with frequent mention of continued observance of the Jewish law and adoptionist christology; but the patristic evidence gives us more problems than clear lines for historical reconstruction. We are told more about legal observance and christology than about Bible interpretation as such. As for writings which identify themselves as coming from Jewish Christian groups, the most extensive evidence, after the NT, is constituted by the Pseudo-Clementines, the core of which may go back to the second century; but their apologetic arguments are rarely purely biblical, and their sectarian (Ebionite?) tendency makes them more a particular example than a basis for generalizations.

Prior to the problems of the material evidence is that of the diversity of Judaism already before the rise of Christianity, with the probability that this diversity was carried over into early Jewish Christianity. Though Mishnaic (*see* **Talmud**) rabbinism* stands in the tradition of the Pharisees,* there was no 'normative Judaism' before the end of the Second Temple in AD 70. Among the heirs of ancient Israel there were the Jerusalem 'establishment', who controlled the Temple, together with those who looked to the Temple as their religious focus; among those who rejected that 'establishment' we can identify the Samaritans* and the Qumran sectaries (*see* **Dead Sea Scrolls**). The latter also inherited an older quarrel over issues such as the calendar, which motivated I Enoch and Jubilees – works which came to be regarded as 'scripture' by some Christians though rejected by the rabbis. Among and beyond these groups and movements, various forms of messianic* expectation, as also of popular superstition, were widely current in a population which included both admirers of the Pharisees and more alienated sections, well described as 'lost sheep of the house of Israel'. In this variety, however, it is a mistake to see Hellenistic* Judaism as constituting a type or movement. All existing types could easily be represented both in Palestine and in the Diaspora, and then among converts to the Christian movement. Several distinct strands of Jewish heredity are distinguishable within the NT itself, as also in second-century Christian documents, including those stemming from various kinds of Gnosticism;* some of these reveal many elements of Jewish origin. Any attempt to define Jewish Christianity while forgetting the diversity of pre-rabbinic Judaism will be vitiated from the start.

Whatever kind of Jewish heredity is discernible in an early Christian group, the Jewish characteristics are likely to be subject to degrees of intensity. Consequently a typology of Jewish Christianity cannot be a static map, but is rather a complex of 'Jewish' elements, each of which is exemplified by cases which can be located along a spectrum from maximum to minimum, but always within a form of belief which sees Jesus as the Messiah and in a special relationship to God. Such a method is already suggested by Justin's critique of Jewish Christian positions (*Dial.* 46–47), from a 'maximum' insistence on full observance of the law, with social exclusiveness, to a tolerant acceptance of Gentile Christians. Among past attempts to define Jewish Christianity, some are unsatisfactory because of too rigid criteria based on Jewish observance,

while others, by concentrating on forms of thought and expression, produce a vague and too widely applicable definition. This is true of the most ambitious attempt to characterize Jewish Christianity, that by Jean Daniélou. If used critically, his *History of Early Christian Doctrine* is most valuable for its rich and stimulating survey; but his criteria for declaring themes Jewish Christian are subjective and misleading. He neglects the NT, relies too much on the problematic category of 'apocalyptic',* and classifies under Hellenistic and Latin Christianity some elements which are as 'Jewish Christian' as anything in the volume dedicated to the latter. Daniélou's thematic approach needs to be checked by seeking more objective criteria for identifying groups and tendencies.

A 'spectrum' method applied to early Christian writers might work with such criteria as the following, all of them subject to variable degrees, so that significant evidence for individuals or movements can be located at points on one or (usually) more spectrums: 1. Jewishness by birth or upbringing; 2. sense of identification with the Jewish heritage (often expressed by some degree of observance of the law), and 3. use of styles and methods of argument common in Jewish writings. Three further criteria establish spectrums of other kinds: 4. as a dimension of criteria 1. and 2., we should also look for indications of roots in different kinds of Judaism. Here it would, of course, be anachronistic to seek a criterion in terms of 'normative Judaism', but a spectrum might be constructed in function of inherited attitudes to the Jerusalem temple and the parties which accepted it, ranging from favourable to disaffected or actually hostile. 5. Theological evaluation of Jesus: here the criterion could be relationship to Jewish monotheism, the spectrum ranging from simpler to more complex solutions, from 'low' or adoptionist christologies* at one end (as are ascribed to the Ebionites) to the 'high' christologies of Phil. 2.5–11 and the Fourth Gospel at the other (thus the Nazoraeans are said to have believed in the virgin birth). The range of the spectrum, however, is not due to increasing Hellenization; the whole range is Jewish Christian, the 'higher' end owing more to ideas inherited probably from Apocalyptist circles in sectarian Judaism (and therefore relatable to spectrum 4). 6. Attitudes to Pauline and Gentile Christianity. The NT is the monument of mutual acceptance by Jewish and Gentile Christians, symbolized by Acts 15. Paul,* who seems to have maintained Jewish observance in a flexible way, fought to hold together what he saw as the essentials of the Jewish heritage and its extension to Gentile converts.

In relationship to Bible interpretation, criterion 3. is clearly primary, and might even seem sufficient to indicate Jewish Christian character; but 'Jewish' styles and methods remained traditional after the definitive estrangement of the church from Judaism, so that they are found in church writers who respond negatively to all the other criteria. In the summary offered below, styles and methods are classified from their instances in writings, from the NT to the traditions represented by Aphrahat, which locate themselves on one or more of our Jewish Christian spectrums. Though Aphrahat may be of Gentile origin and his writings are dated 336–45, their highly traditional nature justifies regarding them as containing the outstanding extant compendium of Jewish Christian biblical interpretation. Aphrahat represents a Christianity which must have separated itself from the Jewish community with which he remains in dialogue; J. Neusner has recognized in the latter the convert Jews of Adiabene, maintaining a simple, biblical faith in isolation from the Babylonian rabbis,* yet not sectarian.

Christian literature of the first three centuries has left us no continuous commentary on any biblical book to compare with the examples of interpretation which, especially by being found at Qumran, are proved to have existed already in the Jewish world, such as the Targum* of Job or the sectarian *pesharim** on prophets and psalms. NT writers constantly claim to know and give the 'true meaning' of a scriptural text or figure, in ways like that practised at Qumran, and they similarly weave unconnected texts into chains of *testimonia*;* but until Origen* Christian writers, Jewish or Gentile, rather *exploit* the Bible for their own purposes than attempt continuous exposition. Nor do we find Christian 're-writing' * of biblical narratives as in the 'Genesis Apocryphon', or claims to produce a new edition of Mosaic revelation as in Jubilees or the 'Temple Scroll'. Christians, of course, claimed new revelation,* mediated both by Jesus and by others through a renewed gift of prophecy, expressed in new messages and also in re-interpretation of biblical texts with reference to Christ and the life of the church; but the focus is on the new context. Like all kinds of Jews, Jewish Christians read their Bible as a collection of divine oracles, which when decoded could give messages for later times. But whereas the Pharisees and their rabbinic descendants made the Pentateuch the focal centre and claimed that their oral *torah* had the same divine authority, Christians viewed all the scriptures through a prophetic perspective and claimed to know the true meaning by the guidance of the Holy Spirit. Nevertheless some of the most frequent modes of biblical exposition among Jewish Christians (followed

by others) remain entirely Jewish in both theme and style, viewing the period of the first covenant * positively in its own right, and even not always referring explicitly to Christ.

1. Series of exemplary figures from Bible history. These are found especially (a) in contexts of exhortation or warning and (b) in prayers reminding God of occasions when he heard prayer in the past. The latter style is related to (c) 'aretalogies' * or recitals of divine saving acts; the converse of these might be called (d) 'anti-aretalogies', i.e. recitals of acts of the evil one, probably originating in exorcism rituals. Pre-Christian examples of (a) are Ben Sira 44–49 (the 'men of *hesed*'), Wis. 10 (both an aretalogy of Wisdom and a sequence of exemplary figures, identified only by allusion), and IV Macc. 16.20–21. Formally close to this are Heb. 11 (the heroes of faith) and the exemplary sequences in I Clement 9–12 and 16–18. This form remains frequent, always with far more biblical than Christian examples, till the tradition of this (and other types) is summed up in the liturgical section of the *Apostolic Constitutions* (between VII,37 and VIII,12) and most extensively of all by Aphrahat. Type (b), a sequence of those who prayed and were heard, is found in III Macc. 6 and in Mishnah *Ta'anit* 2,4, and then in many early Christian examples, not only verbal but also iconographical,* in catacomb frescoes, on sarcophagi and in plastic art, e.g. the Podgoritza bowl. A background in Jewish and Jewish–Christian exorcism is probable both for some of these prayers, for examples of type (d) occurring in apocryphal early Christian literature (e.g. *Acts of Judas Thomas* 32) and again in Aphrahat's handling of various themes of sin. All these examples of scriptural exposition, not by detailed commentary but by thematic summary, show Jewish Christianity, followed by much of subsequent tradition (except for the Marcionites, who rejected the scriptures and the God they revealed), growing from its Jewish roots, often with no expression of breach or tension. Only when the exemplary series takes the form of a catalogue of accusations leading up to the rejection of Christ does its rhetoric* become hostile. Anti-Jewish polemic is served rather by other uses of scripture, especially 'testimonia' (see below).

2. Christian *torah*. Though Jewish Christians of Pharisaic character seem to have been responsible for (e.g.) the Gospel of Matthew and the Epistle of James, there exists no body of Jewish Christian halakhah of rabbinic type. Individual examples, argued in quasi-rabbinic style, occur in the gospel accounts of Jesus' controversies, but here and elsewhere they are sporadic and unsystematic. Pentateuchal laws may be made to yield entirely non-legal senses

by allegorization,* as in the Epistle of Barnabas 7–10. The collections of instructions for behaviour which develop from the NT epistles through the *Didache* and the *Didascalia* to the *Apostolic Constitutions* (all revealing Jewish Christian characteristics) may frequently appeal to scripture, but are in a different key from rabbinic *halakhah*. Even when Jewish observances are simply accepted as normal (e.g. those governing marital intercourse, discussed by 'Peter'* in Ps.-Clem. *Hom.* XI.28,30), Jesus is appealed to for the right balance, as against 'the Pharisees and scribes among us'. The Jewish Christian Elchesai seems to have taught elaborate rules for ablutions and food, but with a curious admixture of spiritualism and magic, even farther from rabbinic Judaism (or other Jewish Christians).

3. A rebirth of prophecy. This claim is explicit in the NT (especially in Luke–Acts but also in Paul) and remains strong in early Christianity at least till its last primitive exponent, Montanus. For Ignatius (*see* **Apostolic Fathers**) Jesus is 'our archives'; his death and resurrection* take the place of the scriptures (*Philad.* 8). Not only is Jesus the mediator of new revelation, but the Holy Spirit gives his disciples prophetic power to interpret all scripture in terms of Christ (cf. I Cor. 10.11; I Peter 1.10–12). This is taught by Christ himself in Luke 4 and 24, and vividly exemplified in Acts 2, where Peter declares that Joel's vision of the outpouring of the Spirit of prophecy has just been fulfilled, and then confidently interprets two psalms as being 'really about' Jesus – a new use of the *pesher* method.

The major Jewish Christian work claiming to be inspired prophecy is the Book of Revelation. It is a Jewish messianic apocalypse which may preserve hints of sectarian animus (cf. 1.9 and 3.9; ch. 11 is hostile to Jerusalem, and the vision in ch. 17 might originally have belonged to a similar context). The book's relationship to scripture is dependent but not simply interpretative. Much of its material is inspired by Ezekiel, Zechariah, Daniel and probably the Enoch tradition, but even the most dependent passages are no literary pastiche; rather they must have long matured in the seer's memory and imagination. No passage is simply a commentary on scripture texts, yet by alluding to famous themes the author implicitly interprets them for his new prophetic purpose. His millenarianism* reflects the apocalyptic developments of biblical prophecy; it was shared by some Jewish Christians but viewed with disfavour by many in the Gentile churches.

4. Finding Christ in the scriptures. The view of the Bible as a body of divine oracles* or 'mysteries' became general in second-temple Judaism. Closely analogous to the Qumran form of this view is the Christian form, in which the key to all mysteries is Christ. Though some prophecies are more obviously and explicitly messianic, the former scriptures as a whole are regarded as prophetic with reference to Christ and his new dispensation; almost any text can be interpreted in this way, whether it is formally predictive or is in a narrative, legal, sapiential or hymnic genre.* This reinterpretation of texts was facilitated by the practice of detaching them from their contexts and collecting them as *testimonia* or proof texts,* arranged thematically, a technique attested already at Qumran. The practice is implied by some NT passages; several sequences are traditional by the second century, and from the third there are formal collections.

(a) Passages are interpreted as explicitly speaking of Christ, by use of one or other of the already established messianic models – royal, prophetic, or priestly. The *royal*, Davidic model is dominant in early Christianity, triumphalist readings being modified by widespread use of texts relatable to the passion, especially Isa. 53 and Ps. 22. Psalms or other passages belonging to the royal temple liturgy are read as prophecies of Christ. The *prophetic* model (known at Qumran, and the main form of Samaritan messianism) is applied to Jesus especially by Luke and is implicit in the Fourth Gospel; it is most fully expounded in the Pseudo-Clementines (*Hom.* II, 6ff.; III, 11–19), but in a peculiar form, tracing the 'true prophet' from Adam.* A *priestly* model (also figuring in Qumran expectation) could be applied to Jesus either by relating him to the Aaronic priesthood or by claiming a 'higher' title for him. Hebrews rejects the former way but stresses the latter, by means of Melchizedek, but without developing the royal or angelic associations of this figure (as they are now illuminated by Qumran texts); yet, despite Heb. 7.13–14, some Jewish Christians ascribed the Aaronic priesthood to Jesus, either by descent (Irenaeus,* *frag.* 17) or, as we find in Syriac tradition, through ordination by John* at his baptism. (b) The reference of prophetic texts is transferred from their original subjects to Christ (e.g. Hos. 11.1, on Israel brought from Egypt, is referred to Jesus in Matt. 2.15); any psalm can be read as being about (or a prayer of) Christ in his life, passion or glorified state. (c) Theophanies are interpreted as earlier appearances of Christ, not only by post-apostolic writers but already in the NT (e.g. John 12.37–41). The theme of Christ's pre-existence, whether as Wisdom or as some being of angelic nature (the author of Hebrews starts by urging the inadequacy of such a theory) was prepared for in sectarian Judaism, and need not be ascribed to influences either late or non-Jewish. (d) Persons, events, institutions or objects may be regarded either as important in their own time and concrete existence (in this most Christians except Marcionites agreed with Jews) or symbolically, as 'types'* of Christ, the cross, the church etc.; this is frequent from the NT on, in both Jewish and Gentile Christian writings. The presupposition is that the same Holy Spirit guided the events, the former writers and the Christian interpreters. To modern critical theory typology may seem as illegitimate as allegory, but it is fair to distinguish between modes of reading which arise by response to a text's intrinsic potentiality to generate metaphor* and symbol* (e.g. the paradise, flood and Babel stories) and an allegorizing technique which artificially imposes interpretations with no basis in the text. Artificial allegory is found already in the Epistle of Barnabas and continues in Jewish Christian writers, not necessarily under the influence of Philo,* whose main impact was on non-Jewish Alexandrian church Fathers. (e) Passages could be helped to deliver what the new readers were convinced was their full and true meaning by means of interpretative glosses and expansions. This was already Jewish practice in targums. (The existing Targums* are hard to date, and claims for early dating have often been rash; but vernacular paraphrases of scripture must have developed well before the common era, and at least the Targum of Job is pre-Christian.) Jewish Christian glosses of this type may account for alleged citations such as Matt. 2.23 and 27.9–10, several in 'Barnabas' and I Clement, and those defended by Justin in *Dial.* 71–74, including the famous 'from the cross' added to 'the Lord has reigned' in (LXX) Ps. 95.10. Further, the elaboration of targumic interpretations by haggadic midrash,* together with the composition of para-biblical, supplementary works in genres such as the testament or the visionary ascent narrative, are typical of Jews and Jewish Christians alike. The perspective of 'oracles of God' precluded any development of a critical distinction between canonical prophecy and apocalyptic literature claiming venerable authority. The survival of most of the latter is due to Jewish Christians, who valued this legacy coming largely from more or less 'disaffected' Jewish circles.

It has been emphasized that the NT is the primary monument of primitive Jewish Christianity; its authors reveal hints of different backgrounds in Judaism and various degrees of Hellenistic culture. Besides the Gospels* which came to be canonical, we hear of Gospels of the Nazoraeans, the Hebrews and the Ebionites. It is not clear how many distinct works these refer to: probably two, but perhaps forms of one (Matthaean?) tradition, in Hebrew or more probably in Aramaic. Citations from these Gospels in Origen* and Jerome suggest a more 'targumic' character in comparison with our Greek Gospels. The oldest parts of the Pseudo-Clementines contain some early Gospel interpretation which has been judged Ebionite, but this has been interwoven with other material into a less sectarian synthesis. The collection of 'secret sayings of Jesus' called the *Gospel of Thomas* may contain primitive material, but as arranged it is an interpretation of Jesus' teaching with encratite and somewhat gnosticizing tendencies, suggesting an origin in Jewish Christian ascetical circles in Syria. (A similar background, but more definitely gnostic, is suggested by the *Gospel of Philip*.)

5. The relationship of the church to its Jewish roots, the former covenant* and contemporary Jews is a major theme of early Christian Bible interpretation and apologetic. Here too there is a spectrum of attitudes. Paul in Rom. 9–11 insists that God's promises cannot fail, but that his plan will embrace Jews and Christians together, and 'Barnabas' criticizes some Christians who say that 'our covenant is still theirs' (*Ep. Barn.* 4). At the other end is the claim that the Jews by rejecting Jesus as the Christ have lost to the church their status as God's people. This is already the interpretation attached to Jesus' parable of the wicked tenants (Matt. 21.33–40) and, though this theme sounds most harshly in Gentile Christian writers, it must be Jewish Christian in origin. Its roots are in biblical prophecy, especially as interpreted by circles disaffected towards those holding power in Jerusalem; such a voice sounds in Stephen's speech in Acts 7, and the charge that the Jews killed Christ may well have first been brought from within the Jewish family and only later adopted, with a different understanding, by Gentile Christians. The thesis that the church has become the 'New Israel' is a classic theme of anti-Jewish *testimonia*, but it can still be expressed in a less hostile way and in a more 'midrashic' idiom, as when Aphrahat weaves an allegorization of the vineyard poem in Isa. 5 (including some details paralleled in the targum) with the parable of the tenants and an account of the passion cast in vineyard metaphors. Aphrahat supports his frequent presentations of the 'New Israel' thesis with more *testimonia* than any other patristic writer, and with surveys of biblical history either consecutively (as in *Dem.* 23) or by comparison-series of biblical examples; yet his comparative courtesy as a controversialist shows that he is not addressing the Jews as an unrelated stranger but that, like the *Didascalia* before him, he still reflects a Jewish Christian sense of solidarity with Judaism.

At least some characteristics of Jewish Christianity and its styles of exegesis have survived longest in the churches of the Near East, especially those of Syriac and Ethiopic tradition.
See also **Jewish Background to the New Testament; Judaizers.**

J. Barton, *Oracles of God*, 1986; J. Daniélou, *A History of Early Christian Doctrine*, ET 1964–77, esp. vol. I, *The Theology of Jewish Christianity*; A. F. J. Klijn and G. J. Reinink, *Patristic Evidence for Jewish–Christian Sects*, 1973; R. Longenecker, *Biblical Exegesis in the Apostolic Period*, 1975; R. Murray, *Symbols of Church and Kingdom*, 1975; M. Simon, *Verus Israel*, ET 1986; G. Strecker, 'On the Problem of Jewish Christianity', Appendix I in W. Bauer, *Orthodoxy and Heresy in Earliest Christianity*, ET 1971, pp. 241–85.

R. P. R. MURRAY

Jewish Exegesis

Within the OT itself, exegetical* considerations sometimes affected the treatment of earlier texts in the later books, e.g. by the Deuteronomist school or by the Chronicler. Such editorial treatment lies outside the scope of the present article (*see* **Inner-Biblical Exegesis**), as do also the exegetical implications of the Greek translation of the Hebrew Bible, which goes back, at least as far as the Pentateuch* is concerned, to the third–second century BC (*see* **Septuagint**).

Two essential points must be understood, if post-biblical address to the Hebrew Bible is to be appreciated, one being programmatic and one historical. 1. The axiom that the Pentateuch (the 'written' Torah) epitomizes the supreme and most comprehensive instance of divine revelation subordinates and refracts exegesis of the remainder of the Bible, in a manner that transcends chronological considerations. 2. The concept of the complementary 'Oral' Torah, explicit within rabbinic* Judaism and to some extent implicit in non-rabbinic movements, means that cumulatively interpretative tradition will sometimes evince incompatibilities. But – at least where practicalities are concerned – it will generally arrive at an official consensus, and may even disavow unpopular decisions as having been 'one-off' rulings. The external counterpart of this approach is the history of editorial compilation of exegetical material prior to the Middle Ages. Orally preserved material is generally left uncollected or uncodified until some external factor, e.g. loss of national independence, or sectarian challenge, renders it desirable or even imperative. Hence the various corpuses may contain material much earlier than the date of editing, its antiquity being sometimes attested from external sources, e.g. the NT or Josephus.*

Major categories. In rabbinic Judaism two major categories are throughout subsumed within Torah ('teaching' rather than 'law') in its plenary sense, even though they are not articulated in the earliest material to be summarized below, and, in the case of non-rabbinic streams (e.g. Qumran; *see* **Dead Sea Scrolls**) are not applicable. The two may overlap, with mutual stimulus to spiritual sensitivity: and, thanks to the vitality of the notion of the Oral Torah, what the modern scholar will classify as eisegesis* rather than exegesis is not felt to be artificially intruded into the significance of the text.

1.' *Aggada* or *haggadah* ('information', 'anecdotage') is concerned with the inculcation of God-awareness into mental attitudes; and although it may condition the approach to law and institutional practice, it is self-substantive. Being largely compiled in the various collections of midrash* ('exposition') between approximately the fifth and tenth centuries, *'aggada* takes the form of moralizing exegesis, sometimes by means of juxtaposing discrete texts; e.g. until leaving the ark (Gen. 8.16) Noah was constantly at prayer, using Ps. 142.8(7). Sometimes, again, by creative elaboration of the narrative; e.g. Abraham,* deprecating thanks for his princely hospitality, would encourage his guests rather to say grace. Or by parable* and anecdote; e.g. a king had a friend who could secure favours for others, but had himself never received nor, indeed, solicited any mark of royal approval until the court pointed this out to the king. Thus Abraham, who procured the healing of Abimelech's temporary impotence (Gen. 20. 17), himself needed treatment; God, prompted by the angels, effects this, and Isaac is born. The fable of the halt directing the blind is applied to the mutual recrimination of soul and body at judgment; God, detecting their collusion, judges them as one. Major theological topics and problems are often dealt with in the *'aggada* by means of anthropomorphic* anecdotage; e.g. God, grieving at mankind's sin before being constrained to cause the flood (Gen. 6.6), himself observed mourning rituals for a week. Clothing profound insights in an unsophisticated form, the *'aggada* constitutes a quarry whence much of the theology of rabbinic Judaism may be constructed. The conviction that scripture contains nothing superfluous may lead to the exploitation of parallelism, or literal treatment of metaphor, in order to fill out the bare biblical narrative with circumstantial detail. Thus, Lamech is stated on the basis of his poem (Gen. 4.23) to have killed both Cain (a 'man') and the boy (a 'child') who allegedly guided him when out hunting, because of his blindness. Despite the relentless disregard of poetical device in the interest of recovering a supposed historical reality, the result can sometimes – despite its prosiness – evince a poetic dimension of its own.

2. *Halakhah* ('procedure': often, by over-simplification, mis-rendered 'law' and equated with the totality of Torah) is concerned to inculcate God-awareness into the implementation of practical matters, whether institutional or routine, and the corollary, self-discipline regarding what is forbidden. Since divinely ordained precept (*miṣwah*) is deemed the pre-eminent expression of revelation, halakhic exegesis of scriptural ordinance, both ritual (sabbath, the tithe-system, etc.) and mundane (law of property, matrimonial causes, etc.) is popularly considered to be primary, aggadic matter being commonly thought of as being supererogatory to essential Judaism. The function of halakhic exegesis is so to handle biblical institutions – especially ones which changed conditions may render problematic – that the resulting decision may, in practice, be socially feasible within the given Jewish situation, ethically tolerable, and logically defensible or acceptable in defiance of logic, in that order of priority. Realistic considerations on the part of jurisprudential leadership led to the evolution of a parallel, topically arranged corpus of this material, culminating in the Mishnah ('repetition', i.e. instruction) *c.* AD 200; and this itself then generated its own exegetical treatment in the two recensions (Palestinian and 'Babylonian') of the Gemara ('completion'), which, with the Mishnah, constitute the Talmud,* in a manner similar to the glossation of Roman law. But earlier Jewish exegetical endeavour must first be sketched out.

The Temple Period. 1. *Sadducees.* The Mishnah and Talmud record controversies between Sadducees and Pharisees,* whose division on party lines is also reflected in the Gospels. The Sadducees, entertaining a static view of pentateuchal inspiration and regarding the 'traditions of the elders' as being without divine sanction, purported to fulfil biblical law *ad litteram*; any supplementary legislation that might be necessary was to be considered purely secular, and enacted without reference to any alleged pointers thereto in the Torah. The Pharisees, conscious that a dynamic approach alone could preserve divinely revealed law, laid the foundations out of which rabbinic Judaism would develop, only to internalize some relics of that same tension after the destruction of the Second Temple spelled the disappearance of the Sadducees. The best known issue between the two concerns the law of retaliation (Ex. 21.24), which the Sadducees insisted should be implemented literally, whereas the Pharisees asserted that 'an eye for an eye' implies not physical retaliation but compensation. Even though the exegetical argument was not spelled out, interpretation is clearly present here.

2. *Qumran.* Although Qumranic exegesis is treated separately, a brief statement is here appropriate to explain its difference from what became mainstream Judaism. The authors of the scrolls, frequently assumed to have emanated from the sect of Essenes, were, like the Sadducees, upholders of the letter, but their thinking is dominated by two considerations: their self-awareness as an isolated and embattled remnant representing true Judaism, all other Jews having been misled by an establishment whose inauthentic calendar rendered nugatory annual public expiation on their purported day of atonement, and the sense of eschatological* immediacy. The sect's literary remains include a significant amount of *pesher** ('interpretation') of many books of the OT – commentaries in which both considerations are the leitmotifs: historical references to ancient Israel's enemies being identified (occasionally even by name) with the sect's contemporary opponents, whilst the suffering righteous in the biblical text are exegetically transmuted into their own heroes. Although Qumranic literature also includes texts such as its *Manual of Discipline*, detailing institutional procedure, it is significant that although these contain biblical allusions they do not claim to deduce their rule exegetically from scripture. The *Temple Scroll* presents its ordinances in the style of the Pentateuch itself, as being divinely commanded. Consequently, to describe such compositions as comprising the Qumranic '*halakhah*', as is sometimes done, is to confound two discrete approaches to institutional matter allegedly of revelational origin.

3. *Emergent Christianity.* Although the hermeneutics* of the early church lie outside the scope of this article, the following observations are pertinent here. The atmosphere of the Gospels is pervaded by familiarity with the institutions of Pharisaic Judaism, but the teaching of Jesus was recognized by his contemporaries as being quite different in style and purpose from that of the early rabbinic schools (Matt. 7.29). Even though it is possible to detect in his language, as reported, some blurred echoes of rabbinic dialectic (e.g. 'you have heard ... but I say', Matt. 5.21ff.), the exegetical address to the OT found in the NT in no way parallels that of the rabbis. In the case of the Pauline corpus (or the Epistle to the Hebrews), this is hardly surprising, since Paul* identifies his Messiah* with (a subsumed and transcended) Torah: so that *miṣwah* 'commandment' – the essential channel of revelation in Judaism – is downgraded, being replaced by *mimēsis*, 'imitation' (of Christ) and *paraenesis*, 'exhortation'. Once it

is assumed that the prophecies of the OT have been fully realized in Jesus, exegesis of the Hebrew Bible ceases to be of paramount importance: the text itself, professedly innocent of any interpretation, stands in a typical (*see* **Typology**) relationship to that of the Gospels.

The Tannaitic period. The age of the 'Teachers' (*tanna'e* in Aramaic), whose halakhic findings were incorporated in the topically arranged Mishnah, begins with Hillel, an older contemporary of Jesus. It is not sharply divided from the period of their predecessors, except by the circumstance that it witnesses the production of running exegetical commentary on the halakhic portions of the Pentateuch (i.e. Ex.12–Deut.) – works which, even when fully formalized, were perhaps at first transmitted orally. In the recorded controversies of Hillel and Shammai and their respective schools of thought, the tension between literalism and creative interpretation, which characterized the Sadducean–Pharisaic opposition, is continued. A spectacular illustration concerns their differing attitudes towards divorce, the Shammaites insisting that the law (Deut. 24.1) envisages it in cases of the wife's infidelity only ('if [the husband] finds in her a matter of [improper] exposure', Hebrew *'erwath dabar*: NEB 'something shameful'). Hillel's school interpreted *'erwah*, 'nakedness' (which is sometimes used metaphorically), as here including 'anything which the husband considers unbecoming', and their ruling would permit (albeit deprecating) cavalier dismissal of the wife by her husband.

This age is important as embracing the evolution of a scheme of halakhic hermeneutics, the Seven Rules for which were established by Hillel and elaborated by Rabbi Ishmael b. Elisha (early second century) into Thirteen Rules. This codification of a formal scheme may have been prompted by familiarity with forensic argument as stereotyped in the Hellenistic and Roman law-courts. Although some of the rules, e.g. that of argument from minor to major premise (*qal wa-ḥomer*), are reminiscent of the universe of discourse within which logic, as known to the Greeks, operates, the two systems serve such different purposes that it is difficult to postulate a Greek academic (as distinct from forensic) influence. The Aristotelian *organon* was designed to promote properly disciplined thinking and, through it, intellectual enrichment. The rabbinic rules were designed to allow room for elaborative interpretation of Pentateuchal texts that involve practical institutions or prohibited matters, but at the same time to exercise a conservative control over innovation. For example, Rule 6, 'a general law limited by a specific application and then treated again in general terms may be interpreted according

to the tenor of the specific limitation only', may be illustrated by its application to Ex. 22,8(9): 'in every case of law-breaking involving an ox, an ass, or a sheep, a garment, *or any lost property* which may be claimed, each party shall bring his case before God; he whom God declares to be in the wrong shall restore two-fold to his neighbour'. Since the items specified are all moveable property, the general extension may not embrace such property as is not moveable.

Alongside this system, the axiom of the literal inspiration of the Pentateuchal text gave rise to two exegetical premises which acted as a check upon each other. The first, associated with Rabbi Akiba (died *c.* 135), insisting that nothing is pleonastic, presses into service 'every jot and tittle', including the occurrence of the untranslateable object-indicator *'eth*, to point towards an extended meaning or reference of the following word. The other principle, associated with the name of Akiba's contemporary Ishmael, the formulator of the Thirteen Rules, resists exorbitant conclusions by flourishing the slogan 'the Torah speaks as if in [normal] human usage'.

The Amoraic period. The two to three centuries following the redaction of the Mishnah (*c.* 200–550) constitute the age of the 'Reporters' (Aramaic, *'amora'e*, 'sayers'), during which the mishnaic text was studied and analysed, and (with a reduced degree of authority) supplemented, in the academies of Palestine, and, more extensively, those of Mesopotamia ('Babylon'). The two resultant recensions of the Talmud then became the object of exegetical scrutiny extending through and beyond the Middle Ages. Although the roots of its subject-matter go back to Pentateuchal institutions, in discussion of which the whole Hebrew Bible is laid under contribution as appropriate, the jurisprudential exegesis of these legal codes emancipates itself into a discipline in its own right, which falls outside our concern here. It is, however, important to appreciate that the exegesis of isolated verses of the Bible occurring *obiter* in the Talmud may sometimes loom large in Jewish tradition, and exercise considerable influence on social-religious attitudes, particularly if the application is linked to some live halakhic issue. A good example is afforded by the construction of Lev. 18.5, '... statutes which, if a man keep, he shall live through them'. The added talmudic comment, '*sc.* and not die through their [observance]', finds in the text a licence to transgress under threat of mortal peril, save in regard to the cardinal sins of idolatry, murder, and the prohibited classes of unchastity (Babylonian Talmud, *Sanhedrin* 74a).

As mentioned above, the Amoraic period saw the beginning of the compilation of non-halakhic exegesis in the earlier midrashic collections, which summarize pulpit homilies or academic addresses, in part anonymously, and sometimes crediting named rabbis constituting a chain of tradition similar to the Muslim *isnad*. Some of these collections, like that styled *Bereshith Rabbah* on Genesis, follow the text through, commenting on almost every verse. Others, e.g. the two *Pesiqta* recensions, follow the lectionary, taking a Pentateuchal or prophetic* reading and commenting on its beginning or main theme, correlating it with appropriate texts from the hagiographa or elsewhere. The aggadic approach, with its free use of imagination and parable, is untrammelled by the halakhic preoccupation with conservatism; and although a looser set of Thirty-Two Rules applicable to aggadic exegesis was formulated and credited to the second-century Rabbi Eliezer b. Jose the Galilean, there is little evidence of these rules being used as a touchstone of exegetical validity. A sound instinct deprecated codification (with consequent official endorsement, and restriction of development) where aesthetic creativity or abstract speculation with possible theological implications were concerned: an instinct which has likewise made subsequent rabbinic Judaism reluctant to promulgate credal statements which distinguished thinkers have privately formulated.

Since these midrashic collections were not edited in accordance with Western literary canons, they often juxtapose heterogeneous matter, so that an item of profound spiritual sensitivity may sometimes jostle with crude imaginative inventiveness, much as might happen in the building-up of a mediaeval Christian mystery-play. This apparent disregard of editorial responsibility may account for the equivocal attitude of Jerome (347(?)–420) towards the midrashic material on which he drew (from oral Jewish sources) so liberally, tending to cite it as 'the Hebrews say' when he entertains or endorses the exegesis concerned, and as 'Jewish fable' when he does not. Jerome was the main source through which echoes of the *'aggada* reached some of the Western church Fathers and their successors, and, through them, exercised an occasional influence upon ecclesiastical iconography.

It was during this period, too, that the Jewish Aramaic versions, or Targums,* as distinct from the Christian *Peshitta* (Syriac* version) were reaching their present form. All targums, however close to the Hebrew they are (and to call some of them 'literal' is to beg the question), involve exegetical decisions, sometimes even where the Hebrew text is perfectly clear. Most noticeable is the policy of palliating anthropomorphism* by paraphrase: God does not 'see', but rather 'it was revealed

before the Lord'. Onqelos' targum is at pains to spell out the halakhic implications of the text as interpreted by the rabbis, so that it came to be reckoned pre-eminently the 'authorized version' of the Pentateuch. Thus, Ex. 23.19, 'thou shalt not seethe a kid in its mother's milk', becomes 'you shall not eat meat with milk'. In general, Onqelos is faithful to Akiban principles (see above), and renders particles, etc. with such care to leave nothing out that his closeness cannot fail to recall the slavishly literal rendering into Greek by Aquila; indeed, their principles (and their names) are so similar that they have sometimes been identified. The targum to the Pentateuch attributed (pseudonymously*) to Jonathan b. Uzziel (first to second century) is in general more concerned with aggadic elaboration than with halakhic matters, but it makes the slave who, volunteering to remain in his master's service after six years, has his ear pierced and then serves him 'for life' (Hebrew *le-'olam*, i.e. in perpetuity, Ex. 21.6), serve rather 'until the jubilee-year', in accordance with halakhic prescription. Where straightforward narrative is concerned, Pseudo-Jonathan resorts to much aggadic embroidery; e.g. the starting-point of Isaac's blindness (Gen. 27.1) was his vision of the throne of glory, upon which he gazed whilst bound by Abraham on the altar. Where prophetic texts or the psalms are concerned, the targumists allowed themselves much homiletic and eschatological scope. The outstanding example is the treatment of the Song of Songs as a full-scale allegory,* worked out in almost symphonic architecture, each verse of the text being 'de-coded' with reference to God's love for Israel, and Israel's sin, penitence, and providential history.

Karaism. The triumphant march of Islam had, by the eighth century, made Arabic the vernacular of Jewish communities stretching from Baghdad to Cordova; and a common opposition to Parseeism in the east, and to Christianity in the west, made some Jews amenable to influence by essentially social trends in the environment which Islam itself might rationalize in theological terms. It is thus possible that the emergence amongst the Arabs of Shi'ism, in opposition to the weight allowed to tradition by the Sunnis, had something to do with the rise within Jewry, in the second half of the eighth century, of Karaism, even though the occasion of its schismatic secession from rabbinism was the failure of 'Anan b. David to secure the office of 'exilarch' in Baghdad. As the designation of themselves by the sect's adherents as *beney* (or *ba'aley*) *miqra'*, or *qara'im*, 'scripturists', indicates, their watch-word denied the validity of talmudic tradition as affording the exegetical machinery to authenticate institutional and other practical aspects of what rabbinism styles the 'oral' Torah. Karaism insisted on exclusive reliance upon the text of the Hebrew Bible itself, the proper method of construing it being the internal correlation of its contents. 'Anan's own motto was 'search thoroughly in the Torah, and do not rely upon my opinion.' Major categories of Karaite exegesis are *hippus* ('searching'), *heqqesh* (or, in Arabic, *qiyas*) ('analogy'), and – although not universally – *hokhmath ha-da'ath*, 'wisdom of knowledge', i.e. reason. The fullest exposition of Karaite hermeneutics was formulated in the twelfth century by Judah b. Elijah Hadassi of Constantinople, who lists 80 rules including the rabbinic thirteen (see above). Karaism was, indeed, more indebted *de facto* to tradition than it was disposed to admit in its repudiation of the rabbinic rationale for that tradition; although its own *regimen* was substantially more burdensome than that of rabbinic Judaism, because of its attachment to literalism.

Karaite biblical exegesis was written for the most part in Arabic. In the tenth century David b. Abraham al-fasi (i.e. of Fez) composed an important biblical lexicon,* which took some philological* account of mishnaic Hebrew. His near contemporary Jepheth ibn 'Ali of Basra translated the entire Hebrew Bible into Arabic and provided it with what became accepted as the standard Karaite commentary.*

Sa'adiah. The rabbanite riposte to Karaism came from Sa'adiah Ga'on b. Joseph (882–942), best known for his philosophical *summa* of Judaism entitled '*amanat wa-*'*i'tiqadat* ('beliefs and convictions'). Sa'adiah, besides producing grammatical works and a study of biblical *hapax legomena* in the light of mishnaic Hebrew, also prepared two Arabic translations of the Hebrew Bible. The first, with commentary, was intended for scholars, and probably covered the whole canon.* The second, called the *Tafsir* ('commentary', cf. *pesher*, above), is a free translation, sometimes paraphrase, intended for the general Jewish public. His approach, which allows scope for the claims of reason, follows the Targum in its concern to eliminate anthropomorphism. The *Tafsir* retained its popularity within Arabic-speaking Jewry right into modern times. Sa'adiah's work elicited the ire of his Karaite contemporary Salmon b. Jeroham, who wrote a series of commentaries designed to controvert it.

Quite apart from inner-Jewish polemic conducted in Arabic, the Muslim cultural milieu afforded much stimulus to biblical exegesis within mainstream rabbinic Judaism; both because Arabic was the channel up which flowed some knowledge of Neo-platonism and of Aristotle, and because of the seriousness of Muslim emphasis on the language of the Qur'an and its grammar, as constituting the purest form of the language, and to pre-Islamic poetry as evincing in its prosody a classical perfection. The impetus which this afforded to Jewish lexicography and Hebrew grammatical studies in Spain, Provence, and southern Italy (with Sicily), where Jews spoke Arabic, was very great, and in their correlation of Aristotle with the Bible the Jewish philosophers frequently apply the exegetical tool to random texts. But before this Sephardic contribution is pursued further, the exegetical achievements of Ashkenazic Jews in northern France must be summarized.

Rashi. Rabbi Solomon b. Isaac, known better acronymically as *RaSHI* (1040–1105), of Troyes and Worms, who glossed the Babylonian Talmud as well as the Hebrew Bible, was conceivably prompted to produce his running commentary by awareness of the availability to Christian clerks of the *Glossa Ordinaria* that consisted of a summary, written in the margin of the text of the Latin Bible, of the comments of the most important of the church Fathers (*see* **Mediaeval Interpretation**). His concern was to produce a popular commentary; and in so far as he sifts the *midrashim*, notes (without always endorsing) the renderings of the Targum, and takes for granted the primacy of the halakhic relevance of the text, Rashi's achievement runs approximately parallel to that of the editors of the *Glossa*. But he also makes his own contribution, which is characterized by its rationalizing approach that will sometimes lead him to reject traditional lore in favour of a worldly-wise appreciation of human nature and inherent probability. This exegetical *Tendenz* Rashi classified as *peshat* ('straightforward', hence realistic, rationally historical), as opposed to *derash* or midrash, i.e. the imaginatively expositional elaboration of the '*aggada*. It is important to appreciate that although the terms *peshat* and *derash* are used in the Talmud to contrast allegedly differing modes of exegetical address to the Bible, they are not clearly differentiated in the way that Rashi and his successors carefully distinguished them. Symptomatic of this approach is Rashi's offering of old French renderings (transliterated into Hebrew characters) for rare Hebrew words, botanical terms, etc., or in order to explain some institution or historical event. Another feature, viz. a concern to refute christological exegesis, is dramatically illustrated by his preamble to his comments on Ps. 2: 'our teachers [*sc.* of the talmudic-midrashic period] expounded [this psalm] with reference to King Messiah, but according to its meaning [*mashma'o*, 'what it gives us to hear', i.e. import] and also by way of rejoinder to the *minim* [sectarians, i.e. Christians], it is proper to explain it with reference to David * himself'.

Rashi's work was immediately hailed, and its succinctness has made it, down to today, the most popular Jewish commentary on the Bible. His successors – notably his grandson Samuel b. Me'ir (*RaSHBaM*), and Joseph 'Bekhor Shor' – continued his methods and sometimes criticized his views. A similar assertiveness of a relative degree of intellectual independence from cumulative tradition, generally accepted *ipso facto* as authoritative, likewise characterized a few contemporary Christian scholars in twelfth-century France who, as the spiritual heirs of Abelard, were themselves immediately stimulated by Hugh, of the Paris abbey of St Victor. The result was to bring them to the Jews, at first for merely oral information; but Hugh's pupil Andrew and Herbert of Bosham (both from England) acquired not only a knowledge of biblical Hebrew, but the ability to read Rashi (whom they style *glossator hebraeus*) for themselves. When Nicholas of Lyra (*c.* 1270–1349) exploited Rashi for his own *Postillae* to the Bible, the church, surmising that the last word had now been said regarding what the Jews (*ex hypothesi* devotees of 'the letter' of scripture) could contribute, read Lyra (whom it dubbed somewhat patronizingly as *doctor planus* or *utilis*), and regarded itself as excused from prosecuting Hebrew studies any further, until the fifteenth-century Renaissance.

Spain and Provence. Like Rashi, the Sephardic exegetes of southern Europe wrote their commentaries in Hebrew. But the impact of Arabic culture on them is well exemplified by the works of Abraham Ibn Ezra of Spain (1089–1164), traveller, mathematician, astronomer, and poet. In his biblical commentaries he sometimes criticizes Rashi, and he is himself not greatly concerned with the halakhic dimension. Sensitive to critical questions prompted by such texts as 'the Canaanite was then in the land' (Gen. 12.6), he will sometimes guardedly allude to the problem; and he followed Moses ibn Gikatilla in recognizing that the book of Isaiah is not a literary unity. The circumspection required in expressing such advanced views is illustrated by the tortuous syntax (here imitated in English) of his discussion of the origin of the rainbow (Gen. 9.12–14): 'did we believe the Greek philosophers that the rainbow is the product of the radiant heat of the sun, one could say that God intensified the sunlight after the flood; and that is the correct way for one who understands [how to view the matter]'. This assertion-through-disavowal is clearly criticized a

century later by Moses b. Naḥman (*RaMBaN*, Naḥmanides) (1194–1270), who, though like Ibn Ezra a rationalist, understood perhaps better than the latter that metaphysical considerations dictate that rational interpretation must be subsumed by, or at any rate be allowed to co-exist with, mysticism.* On the same text Naḥmanides writes: 'we have no option but to believe the view of the Greek philosophers that it is the effect of the sun's brilliance in the moist air, since the same effect can be observed by viewing the sun through a [glass] vessel of water'. (It is noteworthy that just at this period Robert Grosseteste, Bishop of Lincoln, was conducting similar optical experiments.)

The grammatical and exegetical works of the Kimḥi family of Narbonne – David (*RaDaQ*) (1160(?)–1235(?)), his elder brother Joseph, and Moses, their father, all of them doughty proponents of the *peshaṭ* approach – are of abiding importance, David Kimḥi's grammar being used by the Renaissance Hebraists until they produced their own Latin ones, and his commentaries exercising considerable influence on the sixteenth- to seventeenth-century vernacular versions in countries of the reformed churches (see below). His vigour as an exegetical apologist is revealed in his detailed refutation of christological exegesis of Ps. 2.

Levi b. Gershom (*RaLBaG*, Gersonides), also known as maestre Leo de Bagnols (1288–1344), lived in Orange and Avignon, being distinguished as a mathematician, astronomer (he invented the observational instrument known in the west as Jacob's staff, used in navigation), and philosopher. He composed a number of commentaries on Aristotle and Averroes, as well as his own philosophical *summa* of Judaism entitled *sepher milḥamoth Adonai* ('Book of the wars of the Lord'). His biblical commentaries are likewise philosophically slanted, that on Job being the best known. In his pentateuchal commentary he considers the institutional component of Judaism not upon the lines of the traditional Thirteen Rules of halakhic exegesis (see above), but on the basis of nine logical principles.

Mysticism. Mediaeval * Christian exegesis recognized the validity of four (developed out of three) clearly defined senses of scripture, viz. the literal (i.e. historical facts), the allegorical * (pertinent to belief), the moral (relevant to action), and the anagogical (eschatological pointers). Jewish tradition accords primacy to *halakhah*, i.e. what in Christian terms would be labelled the moral sense. Like the Christian scheme, which it may merely have been copying, Judaism enumerated four senses, identifying alongside *peshaṭ* and *derash* (see above) also *remez* ('hint', i.e. pointer) and *sod* ('mystery'), combining them all acronymically as *PaRDeS* ('paradise'). The grounds for suspecting an imitative pattern are that whereas *peshaṭ* is, since Rashi, clearly differentiated from *derash*, the distinction between *derash*, *remez* and *sod* is not worked out with the same intellectual rigour as controls the Christian parallel. It is, however, at any rate feasible to delineate the thrust of Jewish mystical (or rather theosophical) exegesis.

The two classical texts are Ezek. 1, the divine 'chariot-throne' (*merkabah**), and the Song of Songs. Jewish mystical reading of both was already current by the time of Rabbi Akiba (early second century). The targumic paraphrase of the Song of Songs construes it, as we have seen, allegorically of God's love as reciprocated by Israel, and this reading of it in effect dictates the lines of the thirteenth-century *Zohar* ('Book of Splendour'), even though its ground-plan is the conventional form of a commentary on the Pentateuch that adduces other biblical texts at will. The *Zohar* was composed not in Hebrew but in an artificial Aramaic, by Moses de Leon in Spain in the thirteenth century, and it purports to record the discourses of the second-century Rabbi Simeon b. Yoḥai to his intimate circle of fellow mystics. The capacity of the Kabbalah ('tradition', received esoteric lore), as this Sephardic theosophical movement came to be called, to superimpose profound mystical insights on institutional Judaism, is impressively illustrated by the delicacy with which the *Zohar* interprets the 50-day interval between Passover and the first-fruit feast ('Pentecost', Lev. 23.15–16. Num. 28,26), making metaphorical play with the marital self-discipline that is halakhically integrated into the Pentateuchal menstrual law (Lev. 18.19, *Zohar*, Lev. 97a foll.). For devotees of the Kabbalah, the *Zohar* became, alongside the Bible itself and the Talmud, a third fundamental statement of the Jewish endeavour to infuse all aspects of life with spiritual awareness and dedication. Its popularity within the Sephardic communities of the eastern Mediterranean, amongst whom kabbalism was a powerful force, meant that the *Zohar*, when crossed with an intensified eschatological yearning that followed the trauma of the Jewish expulsion from Spain in 1492, became a contributory factor in the enthusiasm engendered by the comet-like career of the pseudo-messiah, Shabethai Ṣebi (1665–66); and the central position which it retained in kabbalism after the *débâcle* meant that it would later contribute to the moulding of Hasidism, the latest manifestation of Jewish mysticism, which emerged in the Ashkenazic milieu of eastern Europe in the eighteenth century (see below).

The Renaissance and Enlightenment. The fifteenth-century revival of learning in Western Europe not only stimulated Christian Hebrew studies and directed attention to the Jewish Bible commentators, but also, when allied to ecclesiastical reform, sometimes permitted Jewish exegesis to influence the vernacular versions of the OT: the rendering of the Hebrew *'elohim*, 'God', by 'judges' at Ex. 21.6 in the King James Version (1611) is a case in point. Jews in Italy – and, to a lesser extent, beyond it – were not isolated from all influences of the new intellectual atmosphere, but its impact on them was mainly observable in literary activity that did not set out to comment directly on the sacred text, even though it might be drawn on profusely for illustration, as it is by, e.g. Yoḥanan Alemanno in his discussion of political philosophy. Nevertheless, the illusory *cordon sanitaire* which the rabbinical establishment assumed that tradition had erected round the Bible was occasionally infiltrated. The extensive biblical commentaries of the Spanish-born Isaac Abravanel (Abarbanel) (1437–1508), which cover the Pentateuch and much besides, are not only substantially influenced by the theological works of Alfonso de Tostado, but they refer to a very wide range both of pagan authors including Aristotle, Plato, Virgil, Seneca, and Pliny, and of the Christian Fathers and their successors, e.g. Thomas Aquinas and Albertus Magnus. Whether these allusions are first-hand or secondary is hardly material; many crypto-Jews educated in Spanish universities were familiar with such sources, and those who, escaping from Spain, reverted to the open practice of Judaism, could not erase them from their cultural background. The eyes of Obadiah Sforno (*c.* 1470–*c.* 1550), who taught Hebrew in Rome to Reuchlin, the founder of German Hebraism, were clearly wide open to intellectual currents and contemporary events. Thus, when he comments that the builders of the tower of Babel (Gen. 11.4) envisaged an idolatrous temple, the height of which would so impress humanity that whoever commanded the city in which it stood would rule the world, he was surely glancing at the plans for the rebuilding of St Peter's by Bramante and Michelangelo under Pope Leo X.

In Germany, the Jewish 'enlightenment'* – a relatively restricted movement, even when it later spread to Russia – had to await the late eighteenth century; itself stimulated by the German *Aufklärung*, it became known (retrospectively) as *Haskalah* ('intelligentsia'). Its father was the philosopher Moses Mendelssohn (1729–86), whose concern to breach the Jewish intellectual ghetto-walls led him with a few collaborators to produce a Bible translation (printed at first in Hebrew characters) in correct high German, with the object of weaning Jewish youth from their mediaeval Judaeo-German that had degenerated into a *patois*. It began to appear in 1783, accompanied by a commentary (styled in Hebrew, *bi'ur*). Although a conservative line was adopted, the fact that the whole enterprise evoked strenuous opposition from the rabbis shows the measure of the difference between the self-contained Ashkenazic Jewish world and the cultural integration of Italian and (in part also) Sephardic Jewry into the spirit of the Renaissance.

Hasidism. The same period witnessed the emergence amongst the Jewish communities of south-eastern Europe, which were as yet unexposed to any enlightening stimulus from the Gentile environment, of a new popular and quasi-mystical movement known nowadays (to those outside its ranks) as Hasidism. This began as a reaction against the formalism of traditional Jewish modes of worship and the premium set by talmudism upon intellectual prowess. Starting in the Ukraine, it recognized as its founder Israel b. Eliezer, better known as the *Ba'al shem ṭob* ('possessor of a fair renown') or *BeSHṬ* (*c.* 1700–60). It spread into Poland, Romania and the Austro-Hungarian empire, to modify the complexion of Ashkenazic Jewish communities in America and elsewhere, after the mass migration westward that began in the 1880s. Its unique feature within Judaism is the central role of the *ṣaddiq* ('[pre-eminently] righteous [leader]'), who exercises a charismatically directive authority over his personal following (*ḥasidim*, 'devotees') in all their concerns, spiritual and material alike. A major channel of his influence was the extended homily, known as '*torah*', which the *ṣaddiq* would deliver, in Judaeo-German, on the weekly scriptural lesson; it would subsequently be translated by a secretary into Hebrew and circulated in manuscript or print. There is no exegetical advance here, although considerable play is made, with a psychological system determined by the circumstance that Hebrew includes several synonyms for *nephesh* ('soul'); and as a source of social history, this literature is of considerable importance. From its beginnings, Hasidism elicited strong opposition from the rabbinic establishment, a prominent leader of which, Elijah b. Solomon of Wilna (the 'Wilna *Ga'on*') (1720–97), left a series of biblical commentaries. Although these are logically articulated and evince great intellectual power, they remain hidebound by traditional terms of reference as these were presupposed by the mediaeval heirs of the rabbis of the Talmud. It is symptomatic that, in a passing reference to the rainbow as the sign of God's covenant, he adds: 'and not as the Greek [natural philosophers] and the [Jewish] commentators who

follow them corruptly aver' (i.e. ibn Ezra and Naḥmanides, see above).

Reform and Counter-reformation. The posthumous influence of Mendelssohn, of *haskalah* attitudes, and of incipient social assimilation of the Jewish middle classes in Germany after Napoleon, combined to produce a religious reform movement emulative of the ecclesiastical modes of the Protestant churches: it introduced organ-music into the 'temple' (the term preferred to 'synagogue'), sermons in German, and the extensive liturgical use of the vernacular rather than Hebrew, which was allowed but token representation. The leading scholar of the movement, Abraham Geiger (1810–74) left a monumental study (*Urschrift*, 1857) of the biblical text and its ancient versions, but rather than engaging in biblical exegesis himself he was concerned to study the history of exegesis in Judaism. A popular translation of the Bible was produced for the reformists by Ludwig Philippsohn (1811–89), but a greater impact was made, nearly three generations later, by that of Franz Rosenzweig and Martin Buber (1925–61), into a German deliberately hebraized in order to challenge the comfortable assumptions bred of familiarity with the established versions. The traditionalist counter-attack in the nineteenth century was mounted in the Hebrew commentaries of Me'ir Löb b. Jehiel Michael (*MaLBiM*) (1809–79), based upon Akiban principles (see above), together with insistence on significance in choice of metaphor in the Bible, and on the grammatical system constructed by him which, he claimed, was pre-supposed by the talmudic sages. Malbim's commentaries won prolonged popular acclamation. The biblical work of the university-trained David Hoffmann (1843–1921), also a leading opponent of reform Judaism, was directed against the Graf-Wellhausen source*-analysis of the Pentateuch and, written in German, was intended for a more sophisticated readership.

The twentieth century. Factors affecting the latest period may be summarized as follows: (a) The pre-eminent political influence between *c.* 1840 and 1948 of the English-speaking Jewish communities; (b) progressive Jewish social integration in the West, and wider Jewish experience of university education in England and America; (c) Hitler's near-extermination of European Jewry; and (d), since 1948, Jewish sovereign statehood and the rapid development of Israeli institutions, with the consequence of enhanced Jewish self-assurance and the (emotionally powerful) illusion as to the identity of the Western thought-categories that are pre-supposed in modern Israeli Hebrew with those implicit in the language of the Bible.

(b) means that serious address to the

Hebrew Bible by Jewish academics will, in principle, be prosecuted on the same premises of a striving for objectivity that underlie the endeavours of their non-Jewish colleagues, so that 'modern Jewish Bible-exegesis' is hardly a meaningful term – even though it may gain a semblance of reality from the conservative approach adopted in nearly all modern Bible-translations produced for a Jewish public. This is well illustrated by the effects of (a). Two popular commentaries have appeared in English, that on the Pentateuch and prophetic lectionary (1929–36) by J. H. Hertz, the British Chief Rabbi, and the Soncino Press series edited by A. Cohen (from 1945) for the complete OT. Both of these digest traditional rabbinic exegesis and, although they purport to take note of modern scholarly opinion, they in effect side-step critical questions, Hertz polemizing vehemently against any source-analysis of the Pentateuch. More recently, *The Torah and Modern Commentary*, edited by W. G. Plaut and others (1981) for the (reform) Union of American Hebrew Congregations, is less inhibited in its use of modern biblical scholarship. The Jewish Publication Society of America, an unaffiliated lay body, had, from 1967, published a new English Bible translation, the editorial committee of which included an orthodox representative alongside a number of conservative and reform scholars; and H. M. Orlinsky's *Notes on the New Translation of the Torah* (1969) cites the latest biblical and oriental scholarship without hesitation. The potential impact of these will be considered after note has been taken of the effect of (c). Not surprisingly, Hitler's massacres – and the relative passivity in face of them of the Gentile world until too late – has at a popular Jewish level reinforced an always active assumption that the driving force behind the (largely German) scholarly criticism of the Hebrew Bible in the nineteenth and twentieth centuries has been antisemitic* prejudice: and this has induced many Jews – including those who have received a high level of Western education – to insist on the sufficiency of the mediaeval Jewish commentators, and to shut their eyes to the sort of chronological* and other problems upon which, in a different context, they would naturally seize. However, this tendency is in part off-set by the effect of (d). Since for those Jews who are intellectually emancipated from scholasticism (not all of whom are entirely secular in outlook), both in Israel and in its Diaspora extension, archaeology* has often either usurped the place of religion or has established itself in a barely subordinate role, the distinguished achievements of Israeli archaeologists and the biblical scholars of the Hebrew University of Jerusalem impart – *de facto* – a greater degree of

popular acceptance to their findings within those Jewish circles where the intellectual attitudes developed by a Western-style education are taken for granted. Significant here, too, is the important contribution of a few Jewish scholars to specifically NT scholarship. The presentation by the media of the results of Near Eastern archaeology, and the discussion of its evidence where it conflicts with the biblical narrative, reach into homes of orthodox and non-orthodox Jews alike, and it is in but a minority of Jewish congregations that the rabbi's veto will ensure that Bible-commentaries like those of Plaut and Orlinsky mentioned above are boycotted. Traditional (i.e. self-styled 'orthodox') rabbinic leadership may, therefore, avoid exposing itself to being flouted, and pragmatically condone the entertainment of critical views by 'lay' Jewish scholars and the exposure to modern biblical scholarship of their congregations, provided that the rabbi is not put into a position of being asked either explicitly to endorse them or to sanction their being taught in his synagogue-classes. It is thus improbable that commentaries on fully 'open' lines intended for a modern Jewish public of moderately intellectual pretensions, comparable to the works mentioned here, will emanate from the orthodox Jewish establishment in the foreseeable future.

See also **Commentary (Old Testament); Law; Rabbi, Rabbinism; Talmud.**

J. Bowker, *The Targums and Rabbinic Literature*, 1969; J. Z. Lauterbach, 'Midrash and Mishnah', *Rabbinic Essays*, 1951, pp. 163–256; R. Loewe, 'The "Plain" Meaning of Scripture in Early Jewish Exegesis' in J. G. Weiss (ed.), *Papers of the Institute of Jewish Studies,* 1, repr. 1989, pp. 140–85; Ch. Pearl, *Rashi,* 1988; G. Vermes. *Scripture and Tradition in Judaism,* 1961.

Articles, with recent bibliographies, on all names and matters mentioned here will be found in the (English) *Encyclopaedia Judaica,* Jerusalem 1972, the index of which (i, 357–8) includes substantial sections dealing with Bible Translations, Exegesis and Study, and Commentators.

RAPHAEL LOEWE

Job

No book in the Bible has been used and abused more freely than Job. Throughout the centuries of the past, but even more since 1950, eisegesis,* as opposed to exegesis,* has celebrated a feast. Curiously enough, this eisegesis has not always been uninformed or wholly separate from the text as translated into Western languages. Indeed, one could claim that Job has inspired a variety of interpretations which related to our pluralistic culture, and one could even support the same.

There are reasons for this unique freedom of interpretation. Above all, the book as it has come down to us raises no historical constraints. We do not know who wrote it and where and when; we cannot even guess the *Sitz im Leben* which could have favoured this production of a prose prologue and epilogue which bracket the major poetical pieces of dialogue and oratory. The connection with known Israelite concerns is conspicuous for its non-existence. Covenant,* law,* kingship,* temple, ritual, messianic* expectation do not figure in the composition. We cannot even tell whether it was Hebraic in origin, or translated from Arabic, how it came to be canonized, whether it was recited in public or only read. Even more obscure remains the purpose of the work. It may be explicated as a metaphysical exercise, a kind of theodicy, or on the contrary as an anti-orthodox cry of despair. It may be viewed as a kind of Matterhorn among the mountains, or as a member of the family of tragedies, such as Oedipus, Prometheus, and Philoctetes.

Not surprisingly the Christian use of Job has been restrained. The NT only refers once (James 5.11) to the 'patience' of Job, a somewhat misleading reference if the whole book is in question. Jesus and his disciples were evidently not interested in this particular scroll, which is in the third part of the OT canon, the Writings.* However, since the text existed in the Greek Septuagint,* and soon in the Latin Vulgate,* it became available to Christians, who could not help identifying the suffering Job with Jesus. A kind of prefiguration was felt rather than proved and the allegorizing of Job became tempting. Dhorme's great commentary is a treasure house, a scholarly display of early and later Christian comments. The most famous of all derives from the *Moralia* of Gregory the Great, begun in the East before AD 600 and finished in the first year of his pontificate. For Gregory the author of Job is the Holy Spirit. He expounds the Word for the edification of his monks. But the words of the text militate against their literal interpretation and demand a typological* understanding within the actual historical context of the preacher's ordeal. Job is a weapon against the evils of the day and an aid to suffering towards perfection. There is hope: for example, the tree of ch. 14 prefigures the cross, and therefore the resurrection.* Job is Christianized and the message is for and about the church. The famous ch. 19 with its 'I know that my Redeemer lives' enters the Christian eschatological* optimism and continues to do so until Handel affirms the belief with the melody in his *Messiah*.

Dhorme traces the influence of Gregory's exegesis down to Thomas Aquinas' *Expositio* and the Catholic scholarship of his own day. Dhorme himself faces the questions of modern criticism as regards language, metre, text, and the versions of the book. He confronts the 'brutal vivisection' of the 'rainbow' Bibles, which present Job as an assemblage of parts, and insists on the unity of the whole work. He concedes that Elihu's speeches may be a supplement though not an interpolation. For Dhorme, the non-Western mode of argument in Job demands an understanding of the 'interior movement' of thought − 'we are not faced by a dialogue of Plato, or a speech of Cicero, or a passage from St Thomas Aquinas'. Some sixty years have passed since Dhorme's commentary first appeared and his influence remains strong. Nevertheless the plea for unity, reinforced by Gordis with his evidence that the 'Elihu chapters are essential to the architecture of the book', is ignored or carries no conviction with the commentators who are more interested in their own thesis than technical and linguistic problems.

Gordis is no fundamentalist* who ignores comparative data. The peoples and cultures bordering on Hebrew life and thought are drawn upon to resolve textual difficulties. But he checks subjective judgments by constant reference to the historical experience of the Jewish people and post-biblical literature. Job is not only superb literature, but, as the Talmud* has it, the 'mashal' or symbol of man's condition in the world. All the allusions, paradoxes, and unconventional expressions reveal God within and beyond reason. The aesthetic grandeur is no end in itself but a means of showing the unity of God in the vast multiplicity of created Being of which man is a part. For Gordis, Job is a vindicated sufferer whose deepest wish has been granted, since 'the beauty of God's world constitutes an anodyne for his pain'. But this is not a pantheistic consolation, rather the I–Thou encounter of redemption.

This theme of vindication (Hebrew *g'l*) provokes endless comment, if only because of the fragile text in ch. 19.25–27, on which critical literature has grown from a snowball to an avalanche. The identity of the vindicator is disputed: is he the Last One who will arise on earth? Will Job see him 'from his flesh' or 'apart from his flesh'? To what temporal dimension does the 'afterwards' refer? The words are proclaimed with real pathos: they are to be 'inscribed on a monument', to be 'hewn in the rock for ever'. Gordis does identify the Redeemer with God: the vision of God comes to Job 'in my very flesh'. Gordis even claims that 'the only element of consensus among moderns, as against older exegetes, is that the passage does *not* refer to resurrection after death'. We are certainly a long way from the triumphant Latin of the Vulgate: *'et in novissimo die surrecturus sum'*, partly because of the erosion of Christian faith. Indeed, by way of counter-attack, agnostic interpreters assail the popular prominence given to this passage as taken out of context.

The humanistic interpreters of Job have no difficulty with the *Goel* or Redeemer. They take the word back to its secular and family root, where it means no more than next-of-kin. Instead of being God, or even a celestial mediator, they take Job's *Goel* to be some hoped-for advocate, or, as we would say, a solicitor to handle his affairs in the case against God. Furthermore, they point to the fact that we never hear any more of this *Goel* in the following chapters. Far from being vindicated or filled with a mystical vision of God, Job continues in the last cycle of speeches with a weary expostulation of depressing monotony. Hope, they say, is squandered, as Job already realized in the magnificent elegy of ch. 14. There may be hope for a tree even after being felled, when it may sprout again under the benign influence of rich water; but the contrast is only too evident: a man does not rise again after being cut down in death. Nature in the hands of God acts out his hostile intent: the very waters which fertilize the roots of the tree and of the vegetation are also the waters which wash away the earth's soil and wear down the stones. God destroys man's hope and does not answer or remember the agonizing cry for help. This radical interpretation may go so far as to explain the enigmatic name 'Iiov' (Job) as being derived from 'O'ev' which signifies enemy. The God who hunts man is the Enemy, and his place cannot be taken by the Satan of chs 1 and 2, who acts merely as an emissary. Job's passionate search for God, his longing to 'find' him, rests upon a false premise.

Clearly this very pessimistic exposition mirrors the horrors of our time, the Kafkaesque universe of hostile bureaucracies which organize imprisonment, torture, and extermination. It is also an exposition which does not even discuss the uniqueness of Job as a legal and moral case, but assumes Job to be Everyman. For scholars trained in anthropology,* Job is typical for a stage in culture. Thus René Girard attaches Job to his major thesis that society requires a victim and that our text reflects the institutionalized murder of the respected leader who becomes the scapegoat. In some detail Girard traces not only the downfall of the former head of the community, but also his own assent to the charges brought against him. Girard cites the show-trials in Stalinist Russia as a threatening contemporary example of political violence and collective hatred. However, the author of Job clearly elects his hero to resist the accepted ritual, for Job does not assent and in a complicated manner regains his freedom. He is not justified by anything but by himself. The divine and the Satanic encumbrances obscure the message of the book as much as the survey of nature's grandeur and the fun of the zoo (chs 38–41).

Gutíerrez melds liberation theology* and the suffering of the innocent, of whom Job is the protagonist. Job the opulent owner of property is nothing, but once an outcast among the poor he is accepted and restored in a true solidarity with the people. Yet Job is not merely a convert to socialism, for he is also raised by God to an eternal dimension of salvation. Indeed, both Girard and Gutíerrez recall Gregory's *Moralia*, for their Job is a pointer to Jesus Christ in his humiliation.

Job is no longer anything like a theodicy if interpreted in terms of *The Triumph of Impotence*, as by Dermot Cox, who even goes so far as to link it with the 'tradition of the absurd'. Camus' *Man in Revolt* and Beckett's *Krapp's Last Tape* may seem to be light-years away from Job, but modern approaches seek to identify our absurd existence with the search after God. This existentialist approach swings back to an individualistic as opposed to a collective interpretation, for the human comedy is played against and not with social organizations. Job's triumphant impotence owes nothing to society, but to his own submission to the world as it really is.

This individualistic interpretation, is not, of course, new. Perhaps the greatest exponent in English is William Blake.* For him, Job's failure to understand is rooted in an infirmity of the imagination which is healed by suffering. The famous illustrations, often reproduced as title pages in commentaries, speak for themselves of an interior pilgrimage, from prosperity through the ordeal to reconciliation. Job and God are ultimately identical, and the dramatic battle is both human and divine. It is astonishing that this great work, published in 1826, did not at first create a whole school of interpretation based upon the central spiritual issue of the transcendent imagination. For Blake, vision is everything, and without seeing, man is dead. This vision is mystical and answers the unanswerable.

Psychologists * rather than theologians have responded in our day to this level of interpretation. For example, Jack Kahn gave us in 1975 his *Job's Illness* which may be said to be a commentary on the book itself and on Blake. Kahn detects the illness as the neurotic pursuit of perfection. The premorbid personality already shows symptoms of what becomes a critical disruption in the patient's organization. The therapeutic situation is shared in its own way by the friends. The price of the release from the obsessional state of fear, the 'inner consummation', is by no means mystical but an acceptance of non-perfection in a maturing self-realization.

Unfortunately, this sane and tentative interpretation is less known than C. G. Jung's far more ambitious *Answer to Job*. Jung wrote as if he were a philosophical theologian, but when criticized for his gnostic speculations, insisted that his insights were psychological. Hence, therapy is also his aim. But his answer is hardly likely to help the suffering and the disturbed, for he erects a quaternity in the Godhead, and this metaphysical edifice with Satan and the Virgin Mary provides an answer to Job which is wholly un-biblical. As a result, God himself has to be prayed for and redeemed by man, but this God is obviously not the God of biblical claims and revelation.*

A life-time is not long enough to plumb the depths of Job, if only because the great gamble, taken up by Pascal and Goethe, continues in the experience of human beings.

See also **Wisdom Literature**.

Francis I. Andersen, *Job*, 1976; E. Dhorme, *A Commentary on the Book of Job*, ET 1967; Robert Gordis, *The Book of Job*, 1978; Nahum G. Glatzer, *The Dimensions of Job*, 1969; Marvin H. Pope, *Job*, 1965; S. L. Terrien, Exegesis in the *Interpreter's Bible*, vol 3, 1954.

ULRICH SIMON

Joel

Like Zephaniah and Obadiah, Joel is a book dominated by the day of Yahweh motif. It has a variable position in the canon: after Hosea and before Amos in the Masoretic text* (MT), but between Micah and Obadiah in the Septuagint* (LXX). The book's chapter divisions are also various: the division of the Vulgate* text of Joel into three chapters by Stephen Langton (*c*. 1205) influenced the chapter division of LXX in the fourteenth century and later printed Hebrew Bibles; subsequent LXX and MT editions reorganized the book into four chapters. English versions follow the earlier chapter division so that ch. 3 is equivalent to MT and LXX 3 and 4 (division at 2.28; 3.1).

A distinctive peculiarity of Joel is its prolific use of other biblical texts (listed in Wolff, pp. 10f.). It is very much a literary work, and seeks to understand and use earlier prophecies as authoritative references. This gives the book a strongly midrashic* shape and reflects the cumulative nature of its creation. It also guarantees it a late date, though the history of recent scholarship on the dating of Joel represents as diverse a view as anything in the prophetic collection. Nothing in the book affords specific information about its setting or date (the reference to 'Greeks' in 3.6 reflects the Second Temple period), so complex interpretative moves are required to give it even an approximate dating. The range of suggested dates extends from the ninth to the second century! Somewhere between 400 and 330 would appear to be favoured by recent work, especially by those who detect a reference to a solar eclipse in 2.31 (dated to *c*. 350). Individual voices suggest specific periods, such as the first decades of the Second Temple (e.g. Ahlström, pp. 109f.).

The literary analysis of Joel may be divided between those who see an essential unity to the book and those who argue for discrete parts in it. Duhm* divided Joel into 1–2, a prophecy of its own time, and 3–4, a synagogue sermon from the Maccabean period's eschatological prose. This two-fold division has been followed, with variable descriptive explanations, by many scholars. More recently the tendency has been to argue for an essential unity to the book (e.g. Childs, Wolff). Such a unity need not be associated with Joel but reflects the final redaction* of the book – like all the books in the prophetic collection Joel is a redactional unity.

The dominant motifs in the book are the day of Yahweh, which may give it some links with Amos in the Hebrew canon, indicating how Amos should be read, and an invasion of locusts. Whether the locusts are to be taken literally or as a metaphor of invading armies or both is an open question and a much debated issue in Joel studies. A crisis, whatever its nature, is interpreted theologically and liturgically so as to rekindle fresh hope in the future (cf. Prinsloo, p. 127). 1–2 are made up of cult* liturgy and lamentation associated with locusts which have destroyed the past and with appeals for repentance, accompanied by assurances that the day of Yahweh is imminent, palpably near. Yahweh's response to Zion's cultic practices will be 'to restore to you the years which the swarming locust has eaten' (2.25) and to flood the land with prosperity (contrast 2.22.24 with Hab. 3.17). There is here a fine example of what theologians love to call 'eschatological'* material, meaning that reality with its nuanced time-space factors will be transformed in the immediate future into all the community's dreams. In 3 (3–4), as prelude to that realization, Yahweh will pour out his spirit on all flesh (cf. Acts 2 for one reinterpretation of that ancient dream) and will then restore the fortunes of Judah and Jerusalem.

The oracles against the nations of Jer. 46–51; Ezek. 29–32 contribute to one dominant tradition complex in Joel, along with 'day of Yahweh' beliefs and the 'enemy from the north' tradition complex of Jer. 4–6; Ezek. 38–39. Joel looks like a midrash or, better still, a mishmash of these tradition complexes, set within a lamentation liturgy and a general cultic setting which argues that 'the right cult is the only foundation for the future of the people' (Ahlström, p. 61). Joel has been identified as a 'literary prophet' producing a 'learned prophecy' (Wolff, p. 11) and associated with an eschatological group constituting a literary opposition to non-eschatological groups in Jerusalem (Plöger, Wolff). Wolff places Joel 'at the threshold between prophetic and apocalyptic* eschatology' (p. 12), but the continuum prophecy-apocalyptic is a much disputed one in recent thought. If a devastating locust attack and drought did disturb the tranquillity of Persian Jerusalem (Wolff), then Joel represents a fairly standard response to the cognitive dissonance* caused by the failure of cultic beliefs in Yahweh's protection. Reinterpretation by means of 'day of Yahweh' expectations and 'oracle against the nations' sought to convince the community that its domain assumptions were still sound.

G. W. Ahlström, *Joel and the Temple Cult of Jerusalem*, 1971; B. S. Childs, *Introduction to the Old Testament as Scripture*, 1979, pp. 385–94; A. S. Kapelrud, *Joel Studies*, 1948; O. Plöger, *Theocracy and Eschatology*, 1968, pp. 96–105; W. S. Prinsloo, *The Theology of the Book of Joel*, 1985; H. W. Wolff, *Joel and Amos*, 1977.

ROBERT P. CARROLL

Johannine Epistles

Although they are in fact anonymous, there is no trace of a stage when these Epistles did not claim to be by 'John', even when the identity of that 'John' and the authenticity of the claim have been disputed. To the modern reader I John stands on its own for its length and for the major theological themes and memorable statements it contains; in content II John has a number of close parallels with I John while it shares with III John a common authorship (the Elder), length and epistolary format. These patterns are reflected throughout the history of interpretation, even in the earliest sources.

I John is attested first (Polycarp), possibly earlier than the Gospel, whose entry into the canon* it may have helped (as it does in the Muratorian Canon). From the second century it is regularly cited as 'the letter of John', the apostle and author of the Gospel. In the Eastern church it is sometimes the sole Catholic Epistle or may be accompanied by I Peter alone or also by James. Besides the theological themes it illustrates, it became a regular source of reference in disputes with or about heresy (esp. I John 2.18f.; 4.1–4; so already Irenaeus*). II John first appears in this context, contributing the measures to be applied against heresy (vv. 10–11), verses cited against Gnostics* (Irenaeus), Arians (Alexander of Alexandria) and others, as well as in the controversy over rebaptism (from AD 256). Thus it is regularly used as an appendix to I John by authors who ignore III John.

The first clear reference to III John is by Origen* (in Eusebius*), recording doubts held by some as to the authenticity of II and III John. Such doubts continue to dominate references to III John even after its acceptance into the canon. Formal recognition is accompanied by practical non-use with few finding much of value in it for homiletic, apologetic or polemical purposes. Thus there is a twofold pattern in the early church, some using I John and its 'shadow', II John, ignoring the third Epistle, others making full use of I John while rejecting, questioning or ignoring both II and III John. The author's self-designation as 'the Elder' could, but did not always, counsel against apostolic authorship, while the questioning of apostolic authorship did not always lead to questioning the letters' authority (e.g. in the *Decretum Damasi* of 382). From the time of Jerome, the identity of 'the Elder' with 'the Elder John' of Papias'* famous reference is developed. Some caution as to the authority of II and III John lay in the inappropriateness of their individual address for 'Catholic Epistles', although the problem was avoided for II John by the still dominant interpretation of 'the Elect Lady' as a/the church.

The same ambivalence is found in the period of the Reformation;* some writers include II and III John in those NT writings of secondary authority (Cajetan; Karlstadt), while others fail to use them (Calvin*). I John suffered none of these troubles; it lent itself to commentary* and citation; its polemical passages were directed against a variety of 'enemies' from Gnostics to Arians and then to 'Papists', while its understanding of God, its concern for love and its dialectic of sinning/not being able to sin, invited doctrinal comment.

In the modern period the Epistles have shared in the wider movements of NT scholarship. The question of the common authorship* of the Gospel and Epistles, debated largely on grounds of language and style since the end of the nineteenth century, has been succeeded by concern for the Epistles' place in the tradition-history* of Johannine theology and in the history and conflicts reflected therein. With minority (but growing) dissent, I John (with II and III) have been placed subsequent to the Gospel, thus giving 'historical' justification for interpreting them in its light, even while recognizing different authorship (which few now would defend as apostolic). Like the Gospel, I John has been mined for sources and for subsequent redaction,* but with little formal consensus.

I and II John have contributed to the tracing of the conflict between orthodoxy and heresy in the early church, with various attempts to identify the opponents. The earlier emphasis on docetism, gnosticism or predominantly Greek modes of thought has more recently been modified by a stress on the Fourth Gospel as providing the background for both I John and its opponents. Moreover, the Qumran literature (*see* **Dead Sea Scrolls**), by showing the presence in a thoroughly Jewish context of so-called 'Hellenistic'* patterns of thought, has led to a new awareness of the Jewish roots of the thought and style of I John.

Debate about authority and ministry within the early church, and recent sociological* approaches to the NT, have given new prominence to III John. The dispute with Diotrephes (9f.) has, since Harnack,* been interpreted as a conflict of styles of ministry and authority, whether or not involving doctrinal issues. The brief, possibly formulaic, references to visits by the Elder and travelling brethren have been taken as primary evidence of an itinerant, 'prophetic' ministry clashing with developing local structures. In the light of the individualism, realized eschatology* and understanding of the Spirit in the Fourth Gospel, this has sometimes become a mirror of modern concern over the relation between the charismatic and institutional in the life of the church.

The Epistles have made a less distinctive contribution to the theology* of the NT, generally being used only to add weight to interpretations of Johannine theology based on the Gospel. In the recent 'history of the community' approach, they have been seen as evidence of the development or hardening of that theology, revealing its potential dilemmas or weaknesses. In the wider area of theology, I John is, as ever, readily cited on a wide number of issues, but the historical context of its thought as one of conflict, which is still the main focus of biblical interpretation, rarely influences its use for theology. Despite their historical interest, II and III John are in practice neglected for theological and liturgical* purposes. With the passing of the impulses that gave value and perhaps canonical status to II (and later III) John, their presence serves mainly to provoke debate about the nature of that canon, and as giving a glimpse into the development of Johannine life and tradition within the early church.

A. E. Brooke, *A Critical and Exegetical Com-*

mentary on the Johannine Epistles, 1912; R. E. Brown, *The Epistles of John,* 1982; J. L. Houlden, *A Commentary on the Johannine Epistles,* 1973; J. M. Lieu, *The Second and Third Epistles of John,* 1986.

JUDITH M. LIEU

John the Baptist

As with other major figures in the Gospels, it is instructive to note that the interpretation of the significance of John the Baptist has marched in step with the approaches taken over the centuries to the elucidation of these documents in general. Thus, over the long period before the rise of historical criticism,* the material was taken at face value and John was seen in part-doctrinal and part-edifying terms as the bridge figure between the old and the new dispensations, the lone prophetic voice pointing to Christ, an example of humble austerity content to direct attention away from himself to Jesus the Saviour. In both art* and spirituality, he was a model for preachers and especially for members of monastic orders who went apart into the 'wilderness' of the monastery to 'point to Jesus'.

With the advent of historical investigation, however, questions of other kinds began to arise. There are three chief areas of investigation. First, who was John and what part did he play on the first-century Jewish scene? Secondly, what was his relation to Jesus? Thirdly, what was the relation of his followers to the movement opening out from the work of Jesus? As, with one exception, the evidence for answering these questions at all directly is contained exclusively in the NT, enquiry has had to tread the delicate path of critical study, with its changing moods and methods.

Thus, in the light of source criticism,* it was possible to see in the Q material, shared by Matthew and Luke and added by those writers to their use of Mark as a source, a picture of John's eschatological* preaching, as partly like that of Jesus in its stern urgency (Matt. 3.7–10/Luke 3.7–9), and yet partly quite different in its asceticism, which contrasted with the world-embracing, even convivial, tone of Jesus' mission (Matt. 11.16–19/Luke 7.31–35). Form criticism* focusses attention on the place of the material about John in the life of the early church (thereby, incidentally, creating a certain scepticism about the historical value of the details of the portrait presented in the Gospels). John seemed to function in various ways as a foil to Jesus, the one who had heralded his approach yet, by his inferiority, had also enhanced Jesus' unique role.

More recently, redaction-critical* work has noted the varying part played by John in the theological presentation of the different Gospels. In Mark, appearing in the very start of the book, he is the arresting prophet of the kingdom,* for whom Elijah is the OT type (cf. Mal. 4.5f.), and who anticipates Jesus' death in his own martyrdom (Mark 6.14–29). Matthew depicts him in part as a 'shadow-in-advance' of Jesus, with the identical message on his lips (Matt. 3.2 = 4.17), yet also, as we have seen, as partly a contrast to the messiah. Luke, in his infancy narrative,* presents John as a relation of Jesus, part of the holy family (Luke 1–2), a matter about which there is no hint elsewhere. If there is a question whether John belongs in the old dispensation or the new, on one side or the other of the crucial frontier, then Luke here places him on the Christian side. But all the same, he is not wholly unequivocal (Luke 16.16; cf. Matt. 11.11).

There is a growing tendency, as one Gospel succeeds another, to enhance Jesus' position in the telling of the crucial story which involved John – the baptism of Jesus at his hands. Mark seems to have seen it as a kind of messianic dedication of Jesus as the one destined to suffer, 1.9–11; cf. 10.38. Matthew, however, discerned a problem: how could the sinless Jesus submit to the baptism of the prophet? So 3.13f. is added to the account: this simply had to happen, in the true fulfilment of God's purpose. Luke's account (3.21f.) minimizes the importance of the baptism itself in favour of emphasis on the pouring of the Spirit on Jesus and his prayer uniting him to God. In John, the baptism itself is actually omitted from the account of John's encounter with Jesus (1.21ff.) and John himself reduced to 'the voice' (v. 23), as if any greater role would raise difficulties by seeming to detract from the status of Jesus. (He even denies being the Elijah figure, 1.21.)

The major question remains. What is the historical truth behind these varied presentations of John? Evidently, early Christian groups, in their different ways, found him both somebody they could not ignore, and also something of a difficulty or even embarrassment, as if he were too similar to Jesus for comfort – that is, for those increasingly sure of the latter's uniqueness.

Here, the one non-NT literary source comes, not very usefully, into play. Josephus * presents John in a way not unlike the general lines of the Gospels' picture, but sees his preaching as quasi-political: it threatens to stir up rebellion. For Josephus, it is this rather than the squalid court scandal known to Mark that leads to his execution by Herod Antipas. Josephus devotes more space to John than to Jesus, but places the two close together in his historical narrative, to that degree confirming the early Christian perception of the relatedness of John and Jesus.

The discovery of the Dead Sea Scrolls * led to a spate of suggestions about the historical reality of that relatedness. The scrolls depicted a stern, apocalyptic,* wilderness group who made use of baptism. The ascetic and eschatological preacher John had been (it was claimed) trained as an Essene before he embarked on his lone mission to Israel, urging renewal and repentance. Jesus (did he also have an Essene phase?) was in reality a fruit of John's mission, a fact that early Christians were at pains to suppress. Hence the constant note in the Gospels that Jesus' dependence on John was simply not true: the 'facts' were quite the opposite.

Sometimes the Gospels do indeed seem to protest too much on this matter; as if the connection of John with Jesus was too well known to be eliminated from the Christian story altogether, yet desperately in need of expressing in such a way that Jesus' uniqueness and superiority were made plain. Did some make higher claims for John than those which the evangelists will allow? See John 1.20f.

More recently it has come to be perceived that another factor lies behind this aspect of the matter. John the Baptist was not quite the lone figure of artists' depictions – or indeed, of much of the Gospels' portrait of him. As the Gospels themselves say, he had disciples (Mark 6.29; Matt. 11.2f.); and as the Acts of the Apostles says (18.24–19.6), he gave rise to a movement which even, surely surprisingly, spread like early Christianity to Ephesus in Asia Minor. (That parallel expansion, of which we have no other evidence, is a matter worth pondering if we seek to build up a picture of the church's early days.) Perhaps, then, it was the existence cheek by jowl of these two communities in certain centres that gave liveliness to the matter of defining the respective roles of the two founders. The Acts passage seeks to do just that: the John movement is an imperfect brand of Christianity – as in Luke 1–2, the mood is firm but irenical. So probably does the Gospel of John, which is full of notes which may be seen as putting John in his place, surely in the face of those who were inclined to do nothing of the sort: 1.6–8,15,30; 3.22–30. All the same, the irenical note remains (5.33–36). It is an olive branch to John's followers, some of whom may even have formed an element in the origins of the church behind the Fourth Gospel (1.35–39). Such a scenario helps to explain the strange two-sidedness of the NT presentation of John the Baptist, though it remains obscure as far as its historical origins are concerned. His problematic character is surely the reason why from the start he was subject to much heavier and more urgent interpretation in the first days than in later centuries, when, relatively smoothly, he was domesticated by the church as St John the Baptist, with his feast days in the calendar and his meed of veneration in the liturgy * and elsewhere. As so often in the sphere of practical piety, the presentation which Luke pioneered became the norm.

See also **Historical Jesus; John, Gospel of; Luke, Gospel of; Mark, Gospel of; Matthew, Gospel of.**

R. E. Brown, *The Community of the Beloved Disciple*, 1979; C. H. Kraeling, *John the Baptist*, 1951; J. A. T. Robinson, *Twelve New Testament Studies*, 1962, chs I–II; C. H. H. Scobie, *John the Baptist*, 1964; J. Steinmann, *John the Baptist and the Desert Tradition*, ET 1958; W. Wink, *John the Baptist in the Gospel Tradition*, 1968.

J. L. HOULDEN

John, Gospel of

If the Johannine Epistles were written after the Gospel, we may see them as the first attempt to interpret it, at least with regard to certain crucial issues. It is possible that the crisis in the Johannine church which the first two Epistles disclose resulted from polarization on questions, notably christology * and eschatology,* which the Gospel had left insufficiently defined, making it possible for people to move in various directions. Had the Messiah * come 'in the flesh' in Jesus or was that 'flesh' only apparent? Was the new age already present or still to come? On both questions, the Gospel could be (and still is) interpreted in either sense. E. Käsemann's *The Testament of Jesus*, 1968, is modern support for the view that the schismatics countered in I John were not wholly wrong to give a docetic turn to the Johannine tradition.

There is every reason to suppose that in the second century such an interpretation of the Gospel became dominant: it was adopted and commented on by Valentinian Gnostics * (Heracleon) and neglected among mainstream Christians until Irenaeus * in the closing quarter of the century. Its absorption into the 'orthodox' fold was largely due to two factors: its attribution by that time to John the apostle, and the ease with which much of its language lent itself to the Platonist expression of Christian belief which was coming to the fore. We now see little reason to think that the Gospel's use of such terms as *logos* * ('word'), *phōs* ('light'), and *alētheia* ('truth') in fact owes much to the religio-philosophical Platonism which was arising about the time of its composition – its background is almost certainly in a style of Judaism – but it was readily adaptable to that setting. From the end of the second century, it played an increasing role in

theological statement and controversy, with opposing groups drawing upon it for arguments and slogans. 'I and the Father are one' (10.30) and 'the Father is greater than I' (14.28) were gifts to opposing sides in the Arian controversy in the fourth century. From Origen * onwards, the Gospel of John was the subject of keen and subtle exegesis, notably in Alexandrian * circles (Origen, Cyril), but also more widely (Augustine,* John Chrysostom, Theodore of Mopsuestia). Already in the late second century, Clement of Alexandria had asserted its superiority as 'the spiritual gospel'.

The aim of this work was to demonstrate the Gospel's conformity to whatever the expositor in question saw as right belief, chiefly in the areas of christology (how exactly were divine and human related in Jesus?) and of Christ's relation to the Father (was he one with him or subordinate to him?). From a modern point of view, all these expositions erred in compelling the Gospel to pronounce on questions and in an idiom which were not those of its origins, and to that extent they were anachronistic. It is not surprising that the statements of the Gospel were rarely such as to produce knock-down arguments. If 10.30 seemed to support the orthodox Nicene Christians of the fourth century, the Arians could claim that it merely implied 'an exact harmony in all words and works' (i.e. not essential being) between Father and Son; and 14.28, so apparently Arian, could be taken by the orthodox to refer simply to Jesus in his incarnate life on earth.

There is no doubt that until relatively recent times the patristic * period was the great period of creative interpretation of the Fourth Gospel. It was both congenial to the contemporary thought-forms and full of material useful in current controversies and theological problems. Indeed, it is interesting to speculate how emerging orthodoxy could have found an appropriate biblical foundation without it.

Though in the modern period the Gospel of John has become again the focus of much interpretative interest, the issues receiving attention and the means by which they have been approached could scarcely be more different. Then, they were chiefly theological; now, they are primarily historical in one form or another. A useful touchstone to illustrate the difference is afforded by attitudes to the difficulty raised through the placing of the cleansing of the Temple by Jesus just before the Passion in the three synoptic accounts and close to the beginning of Jesus' ministry in John. Though the discrepancy was noted in the early centuries, it was seen not as a difficulty but as an opportunity to bring out different religious lessons of symbolic * character. The Gnostic Heracleon saw the elements in the story as allegorical of aspects of the Gnostic story of salvation. Origen, though less exuberantly, also saw it in allegorical* terms, in a variety of ways: it stood for Christ's purging work in his church, or else his triumph over sin on his entry into heaven, or again his work in the human soul. For him, the question of historical veracity (did the incident occur twice, and if not, when did it occur?) is swallowed up by the symbolic meanings.

In the nineteenth century, by contrast, interest came to centre largely on the historical question, and the matter became a glaring instance of the general problem: was John more or less reliable than the other evangelists? Of course different solutions were (and still are) propounded, but overwhelmingly the issue was seen as one of historicity and as contributing to a wider picture of John's value as history. It is noteworthy that while the German tradition of scholarship came early to regard the Johannine placing of the incident as inaccurate, some English scholars* long continued to hold to the full historicity of both placings: F. D. Maurice (1857), B. F. Westcott* (1881), and even R. H. Lightfoot* in earlier work than his commentary (1956) on the Gospel held that there were two cleansings. This example may be taken as symptomatic of the two traditions. Especially in earlier days, English scholarship was reluctant to abandon the historical accuracy of the Gospel of John, just as it had a special fondness for Johannine theology. Indeed, in recent years this flag has been kept flying by C. H. Dodd* (*Historical Tradition in the Fourth Gospel*, 1963) and J. A. T. Robinson (*The Priority of John*, 1985). German scholars, on the other hand, from the time of F. C. Baur and D. F. Strauss* in the first half of the nineteenth century, have been ready to see the Fourth Gospel as distinctly inferior to the other Gospels in its historical testimony and as, in one way or another, 'mythical'* or symbolic in character, with its stories of events largely religious in their significance.

From that base, Johannine scholarship has come to centre on a number of interrelated issues of interpretation:

1. *Authorship.** A great deal of energy was devoted to this subject in the earlier part of the modern period, doubtless because it was so closely bound up with the dominant issue of historicity. The early traditions speak with uncertain voice, and internal considerations, such as the Jewish (or otherwise) character of the style and the circumstantial nature of passages like 20.6f., came to have more weight in persuading scholars like B. F. Westcott that the traditional ascription to John the apostle was correct. Others have given their support, with equal confidence, to other

theories. More recently, interest having shifted away from the question of mere historicity, a more relaxed and candidly sceptical attitude to the matter has become common. A judicious position may be found in a writer like R. E. Brown (*Commentary*, 1966; *The Community of the Beloved Disciple*, 1979), who sees a genuinely Johannine origin to the tradition found in the Fourth Gospel and in the figure of the Beloved Disciple a reference to John's place at the fount of the Johannine community. Associated with this issue is that of the relation between the Gospel and the other Johannine works, the Epistles and the Revelation. Brown and others see this traditional link of authorship as bearing witness to some kind of common debt to Johannine witness and even thought. The guess is even hazarded that of all these works it is the Revelation, with its Semitic style, that is most likely to have close links with the apostle.

2. *Relation to the Synoptic* Gospels.* The many obvious differences and even contradictions between John and the other Gospels not only cast doubt on apostolic authorship (that is, if one takes the others as closer to authenticity); they also raise the question whether he wrote in ignorance of them. There is still every kind of difference of opinion: he knew at least one or two of them, but chose to express himself very differently; he knew only Mark; he knew traditions which they also knew, but only in oral form; he knew them all, but wrote to supplement and correct them. A full-blooded but now unusual version of the last view was put forward by J. A. T. Robinson, 1985. More influential has been the work of P. Gardner-Smith, 1938, in the opposite sense: John wrote independently of the other Gospels. The matter is difficult to resolve partly because of its relation to issue 3.

3. *Mode of composition.* The facts are that (a) the Gospel of John is very different from the rest, and (b) it contains close similarities to them. R. E. Brown and B. Lindars (*Behind the Fourth Gospel*, 1971; *Commentary*, 1972) have tried to hold these together by suggesting some form of development of traditions of both deeds and words of Jesus in the Johannine church from synoptic-type 'kernels'. On this basis, both similarities and differences are explained, though it takes a discussion of issue 4 to tell why the distinctive Johannine method or idiom was adopted. Theories of this type have tended to supersede other accounts of the composition of the Gospel, such as that of R. Bultmann* (*Commentary*, 1941; ET 1971), who envisaged the putting together of sources, one of 'signs' (not unlike stories in the other Gospels) and one of 'discourses' derived from gnostic-type sources and attributed to Jesus,

the two being welded together and supplemented by an 'ecclesiastical redactor'. Many have seen inherent unlikelihood in the process and in the providential matching up of the subject-matter of signs and discourses. Stylometrics have also been used to try and throw light on the formation of the Gospel (G. H. C. MacGregor and A. Q. Morton, *The Structure of the Fourth Gospel*, 1961).

4. *Cultural affinities*. In earlier years, this subject tended to be discussed in terms of 'either Greek or Jewish'. The former view (which could sometimes be in part a legacy from the long tradition of patristic interpretation) has found its most recent advocacy in the still influential *Interpretation of the Fourth Gospel*, 1953, by C. H. Dodd, who saw the Gospel as deliberately making its appeal to cultured inhabitants of a Hellenistic city such as Ephesus. But the balance was tipped in favour of a Jewish background * as determinative by the discovery of the Dead Sea Scrolls * (though there was traditional support for this side too from scholars like Westcott who held to apostolic authorship). There was indeed for a time an outbreak of 'parallelomania', with extravagant claims for similarities between the Scrolls and the Gospel. Nevertheless, it has become evident that the Gospel's background lies in one of the many current styles of partly Hellenized * Judaism. It has close links with Jewish 'wisdom'* theology, notably in the Prologue of the Gospel; it displays Jewish skill (partly akin to that in the Gospel of Matthew and Paul*) in the technical handling of OT texts; it emphasizes Jewish concepts such as messiah, temple, and law, and shows Jesus fulfilling a multiplicity of Jewish strands of argument and imagery. Moreover, it gives every sign of having been written in a milieu where Christian relations with Jews were very much to the fore.

5. *Church setting*. In recent years, several attempts have been made to identify the character and history of the Johannine community.* It is possible to gain some insight into this question through the Johannine Epistles, especially III John, but it has also been approached by way of an extensive (and speculative?) reading between the lines of the Gospel itself. The evangelist himself let his guard slip at one point: in 9.22 he placed in the lifetime of Jesus the expulsion of Christian adherents from the synagogue, which he then, in 16.2, depicted Jesus foretelling for the future. Plainly, this was a situation experienced by the Johannine Christians and read back by the author into the period of Jesus' life to legitimate and explain events and attitudes of his own day. On the basis of ch. 9, J. L. Martyn (*History and Theology in the Fourth Gospel*, 1968) presented a picture of the Johan-

nine church as dominated by relations with neighbouring Jews, to whom they were compelled to explain and justify themselves. More ambitious studies along the same lines, contributing to the widespread 'sociological'* interpretation of NT books, have come subsequently from O. Cullmann (*The Johannine Circle*, 1976), and R. E. Brown, 1979 (see above). The latter presents a full scale picture of the development and composition of the Johannine Church.

6. *Theology*. No interpreter of the Fourth Gospel is likely to forget that it is a theological work. But the intellectual 'location' of its teaching has to be decided after the work on at least some of the issues outlined above has been done. The character of the Gospel's doctrine can only be understood in the light of decisions taken about them. Thus, if the background is Jewish, then the christology may be viewed along lines suggested by P. Borgen ('God's Agent in the Fourth Gospel' in J. Ashton, ed., *The Interpretation of John*, 1986), where Jesus is seen as operating according to well-established Jewish principles of 'agency'; or else by A. E. Harvey who sees Jesus as advocating God's cause, according to models found in the OT (*Jesus on Trial*, 1976). While a work like *The Testament of Jesus* by E. Käsemann (1968) works within parameters firmly established by Bultmann and others (the Gospel is quasi-gnostic and 'naively docetic' in christology), others have moved forward in their demonstration of the Jewish antecedents – and yet the originality – of this book, e.g. M. de Jonge, *Jesus: Stranger from Heaven and Son of God* (1977) and W. A. Meeks, *The Prophet-King: Moses Traditions and Johannine Christology* (1967).

Despite the plethora of interpretative work, the originality of the Gospel of John continues to perplex. It is not just the fragmentary nature of our knowledge of the world in which it was written that hinders identification of its precise origins and character. It is also that it represents a thorough re-working, in the light of reflection on the life of Jesus and relationship with him, of a great number of elements in the (predominantly Jewish) inherited intellectual and religious scene. In many respects it remains a puzzling work. For instance, it is, despite its profundity, not tidy in its structure or 'finished' in its presentation; nor is it clear to what degree it is an individual or a 'community' product. Interpretation remains in flux, not only because evidence is insufficient, and because new ways of enquiry continually arise, but because of the distinctiveness of the Gospel itself.

See also **Johannine Epistles; Patristic Christology.**

In addition to works cited, see: C. K. Barrett, *The Gospel of John and Judaism*, 1975; M. Hengel, *The Johannine Question*, 1990; W. F. Howard, *The Fourth Gospel in Recent Criticism and Interpretation*, 1931, 1955; M. F. Wiles, *The Spiritual Gospel: the Interpretation of the Fourth Gospel in the Early Church*, 1960.

J. L. HOULDEN

Jonah

The claim that 'controversies over the book of Jonah have apparently all but ceased' and that there is 'a remarkable unanimity on the interpretation of the book among OT scholars' (E. M. Good, *Irony in the Old Testament*, 1965) turns out to have been optimistically premature in view of the continuing debate not only about its literary genre* but more especially about its purpose and meaning. As to its genre, the allegorical* interpretation has largely been abandoned as unsatisfactory; the fish, the means of deliverance not punishment, is hardly symbolic of the Babylonian exile, nor is the 'dove' (*yōnāh*) symbolism used distinctively of Israel in the OT (cf. Jer. 48.28; Nahum 2.7). The choice rests, therefore, in the main between the historical and the parabolic interpretations. Neither is without difficulties, the first in the book's apparently legendary* features, the second in that it differs from the generality of parables* both in length and in that Jonah is a named historical figure (II Kings 14.26).

For some, the NT references (Matt. 12.39ff.; 16.4; Luke 11.29ff.) are the deciding factor: 'one cannot reject the historicity of Jonah without also rejecting the authority of Christ' (Gleason Archer, *A Survey of Old Testament Introduction*, 1974), a corollary discounted by others on the grounds that Jesus was simply drawing an illustration from a story familiar to his Jewish audience. The former counter the arguments against its historicity by claiming: 1. historical parallels to the fish episode; 2. the 'three days' journey' (3.3) relates not to some legendary size of Nineveh but to the time required for Jonah's thoroughgoing proclamation; 3. the reference to the king of 'Nineveh' instead of 'Assyria' is comparable to the usage in I Kings 21.1 and II Chron. 24.23; 4. the unhesitating response of king and people to a foreign prophet is explicable in the light of recent disasters which created a climate ripe for repentance (so Gleason Archer). Other features of the narrative, however, which suggest more than simply a historical or biographical concern must not be overlooked. There is a deliberately 'old world' air (Allen) in reminiscences of the flood and Sodom and Gomorrah narratives, and several unmistakable echoes of other prophets (e.g. I Kings 19.4; Joel 2.13f.; Jer. 18.7,8,11).

Whichever stance is taken as to its genre there is little doubt that its significance lies on an altogether deeper level than questions of historicity or zoological exactitude, but its meaning remains elusive and debatable. Is it, indeed, right to look for a single answer, or does deliberate ambiguity lie at its heart (Magonet)? Several other questions remain open. Is the book satirical? Are we to laugh at Jonah or to sympathize with him in his unpalatable task? Is the book intended as commentary* (midrash*), and if so, on which scriptural text? Ex. 34.6 and Jer. 18.8 are among the suggestions. Or does the single other reference to Jonah (II Kings 14.26) hold the clue to the book's purpose? Finally, to what kind of audience does the author address his message? Uncertainty as to the book's date and contemporary situation makes the task more difficult.

The thanksgiving psalm of ch. 2 continues to provoke discussion. One view regards it as inappropriate, a secondary addition which destroys the careful symmetry of the book; another sees in its sustained motif of descent, not now to a ship's hold but to the very roots of the mountains and to the land from which there is no return (v. 6) apart from God's intervention, an essential element in the total impact of the story (Magonet).

There is another question too. Is this the turning point for Jonah at which he commits himself to God, or the height of satire? Taking the second view, Holbert sees here no penitent Jonah confessing his sin, but a hypocrite who, in the very act of thanksgiving, blames God for his plight (v. 3). The one who laments, 'I am cast out from thy presence', is the one whose main objective was to escape that presence. Theology comes easily to Jonah's lips, only to be discounted by his actions (1.9; 2.9; 4.2). In the affirmation, 'Deliverance belongs to Yahweh!', proved by his own miraculous escape yet, when Nineveh is delivered, the reason why he longs to die, lies the ultimate satire. (As Holbert wryly comments, no wonder the big fish throws up!)

But why Jonah? For Holbert the significance lies in Jonah's name, not as representative of Israel, as has traditionally been supposed, but because like Noah's dove (*yōnāh*, Gen. 8.8–12), Jonah, too, can be expected to fulfil his task, and as the 'son of faithfulness' (Amittai) to be obedient. This is where the unexpected happens. God says, Go east: Jonah goes west! God says, Get up and proclaim: Jonah goes down and sleeps! It is left to the ship's captain to reiterate God's call (1.6). Ultimately Jonah remains the one unrepentant figure in the book, cattle included (whether their penitential garb is a humorous touch or akin to attested Persian practice).

Taking hypocrisy on the prophet's part to be the leading theme, Holbert considers the message directed to those who, claiming divine calling, would impose limits on the divine word. These are not only figures of the past: 'their number is legion. For them, and their incessant fulminations, is Jonah written.'

Not all are agreed, however, that abuse of the prophetic calling is the book's main concern. A different approach is proposed by Clements (*VT Supp.* 28, 1975), who argues that its primary purpose is to demonstrate to a demoralized Israel, through the example of Nineveh, the possibility of repentance and a new beginning with God, though, as has been remarked (Emmerson, *ET* 88, 1976), for such a message ch. 3 would have provided an appropriate conclusion. Ch. 4, in its pervasive concern with the prophet's emotions, suggests that the story probes sympathetically the dilemma of a prophet who at personal cost bears Yahweh's word only to find it unfulfilled. To such a one God graciously condescends to justify his ways (4.10f).

Fretheim offers a valuable insight in his suggestion that the question of theodicy is central to the book. However, it is theodicy with a difference, not the problem of innocent suffering but how to square the divine compassion, poured out with such apparent abandon on the wicked, with the demands of justice, the very question posed in Mal. 2.17. Here the significance of the link with II Kings 14.25 is clear, for there God acted to save Israel by virtue of his compassion, not justice. No hint is given of repentance on Israel's part, only of her desperate plight. It is to this that God responds. It is in the light of such unmerited mercy that Israel must regard God's deliverance of *repentant* Nineveh, which is, for Jonah, a northern prophet, the destroyer of his homeland. But the book makes clear that 'God is not programmed to respond in fixed ways to certain patterns of human behaviour', for along with divine compassion goes sovereign freedom. The heathen, unlike Jonah, are aware of this 'divine perhaps' (1.6,14; 3.9). There is no inevitability about God's mercy (4.11). Human co-operation would be irrelevant were it otherwise, and an excuse given 'for the Jonahs of this world to wash their hands of responsibility for the Ninevehs'. Jonah's anger, both when God saves and when he destroys (4.4,9), ultimately questions the justice of God's actions, Jonah sees himself as more just than God. Contrary to the view of many commentators, 4.5 is not misplaced. Jonah's mind is still set on Nineveh's destruction. But for God there is more than justice, and the last verse of the book of Jonah stands in the line of Matt. 20.15, a witness to overflowing divine generosity.

The NT, in contrast, regarded two aspects of the story as of primary significance. Nineveh's response to Jonah's preaching threw into relief the obduracy of Jesus' contemporaries (Matt. 12.41; Luke 11.32), and in authentication of Jesus' words and works the 'sign of Jonah' was adduced (Matt. 12.39f.; cf. 16.4; Luke 11.29f.), left without explanation in Luke but in Matthew explicitly referring to Jonah's miraculous deliverance, symbolic of Christ's burial and resurrection, despite the problematic time reference. A further possible, though far from certain, allusion may occur in I Cor. 15.4. For the church Fathers, on the other hand, Jonah furnished a rich field for Christian exposition, much of it highly allegorical. Jonah was seen not only as a type of Christ in his resurrection, as pictures in the catacombs also testify, but of Israel in its reluctance to admit of Gentile salvation. Augustine found even the worm (4.7) to be symbolic of Christ (cf. Ps. 22.6; *Epistle* 102)! From illustration of the divine will to save (Jerome, *Jonah*) and of the power of prayer (Chrysostom, *On the Incomprehensible Nature of God*, Homily III) to material for controversy with the followers of Pelagius (Jerome, *Dialogue against the Pelagians*), the book of Jonah was pressed into service. Augustine,* finding it a cause of 'jest and much laughter to pagans', vigorously defended its historicity (*Epistle* 102), as had Cyril of Jerusalem earlier in defence of Christ's resurrection* (*Catechesis* XIV).

L. C. Allen, *The Books of Joel, Obadiah, Jonah and Micah*, 1976; T. E. Fretheim, *The Message of Jonah*, 1977; id., 'Jonah and Theodicy', *ZAW* 90, 1978, pp. 227–37; J. C. Holbert, '"Deliverance belongs to Yahweh!": Satire in the Book of Jonah', *JSOT* 21, 1981, pp. 59–81; J. Magonet, *Form and Meaning. Studies in Literary Techniques in the Book of Jonah*, 1976.

GRACE I. EMMERSON

Josephus

The writings of Josephus form one of the most important sources of Jewish history and culture during the Second Temple period (from about 400 BC to AD 100). Although there were apparently other historians who wrote about this time, their writings have not generally survived. Those which have (e.g. I Maccabees) cover only a portion of the period. Thus, Josephus forms an extremely valuable source of information for scholars of both pre-rabbinic Judaism and of the NT and early Christianity. On the other hand, Josephus has his faults and weaknesses (many in common with other Hellenistic* historians), and his information must be evaluated critically.

Josephus was born approximately AD 37.

As a young man in the early 60s, he was sent on a mission to Rome where he met a number of influential individuals surrounding Nero. When the war with Rome broke out in 66, he became a military leader in Galilee. This aspect of his career came to an abrupt end in 67 when he was captured by Vespasian's troops after the siege and fall of Jotapata. Josephus was brought before Vespasian and, according to his own statement and that of Suetonius and Dio Cassius, he predicted that Vespasian would become emperor. This duly happened in 69, and Josephus was released from his bonds. Titus allowed him to be present at the final siege of Jerusalem and even used him to try to persuade the defenders to surrender. Following the fall of Jerusalem in 70, Josephus was taken to Rome, granted citizenship, adopted as a member of the Flavian family (the family of Vespasian and Titus), and given a state pension. He spent the rest of his life in Rome, researching and writing. The last dated event we know of with regard to him is about the year 94 when the *Antiquities* appeared, though he presumably lived some time after that.

The most reliable English translation of his writings is that of Thackeray, et al., in the Loeb Classical Library. However, the translation by William Whiston (made in the eighteenth century) is widely available in second-hand or reprinted editions. Older versions, such as Whiston's, cite Josephus by book, chapter, and section (e.g. 1.3.6 or I iii 6). More recent editions tend to cite by book and paragraph (1.81 or I §81), though the Loeb edition has both divisions in the text. The rest of this article will give both divisions in the citation (e.g., 1.3.6 §81 means Book 1, Chapter 3, Section 36, Paragraph 81).

Josephus' first work, *The War of the Jews* (*War*), was written in the decade after the Jewish revolt. Books 1–6 were completed by about AD 80 since they emphasize Titus who was emperor 79–81. However, there is some evidence that Book 7 was added later, during Domitian's reign (81–96). Book 1 covers from about the time of the Maccabean revolt (167–164 BC) to the end of Herod's reign. Book 2 goes up to the end of AD 66, including the first few months of the Jewish revolt against Rome. Books 3–6 are devoted to a detailed account of the war to the fall of Jerusalem, while Book 7 tells of the aftermath, including the siege of Masada (which did not fall until 73 or 74).

With regard to sources, Josephus seems to have used mainly Nicolaus of Damascus for the early part of the work, to the end of the reign of Herod the Great. Nicolaus was a secretary of Herod who wrote a world history, most of which has been lost, but he was able to make use of his detailed personal knowledge of Herod's court and records. He was thus a valuable source for the Jewish historian. Josephus apparently had no information for the two decades between AD 6 and 26 because he skips over this period. For the most part we do not know his sources for the next few decades, but the events took place shortly before or during his early life, and he could have gained a good deal from oral sources. Much information about the war itself was based on his own experiences, either as a direct participant or by interviewing eye-witnesses, but he would also have used Roman reports. This makes the *War* one of the most data-rich accounts of a military campaign in antiquity. It is also the most straightforward of Josephus' writings and thus generally preferred when there are discrepancies between it and later writings.

The Antiquities of the Jews (*Ant.*) is the most extensive of Josephus' works, completed about AD 94. It begins with Creation* and ends on the brink of the revolt against Rome (overlapping with the *War* for the years from about 175 BC to AD 66). Its main aim seems to be to present the Jews in as favourable a light as possible to Graeco-Roman readers. Books 1–11 are essentially a paraphrase of the OT text, usually (though possibly not always) using the Septuagint* Greek text. Despite his statement that he neither added to nor took from the biblical text (Proem 3 §13), at times he makes some significant alterations. Certain embarrassing episodes are left out (e.g. the Golden Calf), as are some matters of little interest to his presumed Hellenistic audience, and he occasionally adds bits of later midrashic* interpretation (e.g. Moses' marriage to an Ethiopian princess [2.10.1–2 §§238–53]). More significant is the Hellenistic format into which much of the OT material is recast: the patriarchs are modelled on the image of the Hellenistic sage, Israelite laws* are presented as idealistic legislation, and the basic presentation is one to impress those with a Graeco-Roman education and outlook.

Once the biblical narrative books come to an end (about 400 BC), Josephus has extremely little information for the next two and a half centuries. For the Persian period, he has only a few bits of data other than the biblical books of Ezra and Esther (see L. L. Grabbe, 'Josephus and the Reconstruction of the Judean Restoration', *JBL* 106, 1987, pp. 131–46). Indeed, the little information he does have (such as knowledge of the sequence of the first few Persian kings) leads him to give a confusing rearrangement and reinterpretation of the biblical accounts. Similarly, he has little information for the Ptolemaic period beyond a semi-legendary chronicle of the powerful

Tobiad family, though this is important because it played a significant role during this period. Full sources become available only with the Maccabean revolt when he is able to draw on I Maccabees. He reproduces most of I Maccabees though with some differences, most of a minor nature but a few perhaps because of other sources of information.

For the rule of the Hasmonaeans and Herod the Great, Josephus again draws mainly on Nicolaus of Damascus (as in the *War*) but supplements this occasionally with additional sources. When Nicolaus' account ends (about 4 BC), he uses a variety of sources, as in the *War*, many of them not easily identified.

In the early 90s Justus of Tiberias published a history of the Jews (now lost), including an account of the Jewish war with Rome which apparently not only differed from that of Josephus but even criticized him. Josephus responded with a defence in an autobiography (*Life*). Although this work gives a brief résumé of his early life and a few bits of data about events following the fall of Jerusalem, most of it is an account of his activities during his time as commander in Galilee in 66–67. It thus overlaps with a section of the *War* (2.20.3–21.10 §§562–646). In broad outline the story is the same, but the details and especially the emphasis are considerably different. Here he blames Justus and his family for the war, whereas he had not even mentioned them in the *War*. It is clear that the needs of polemic and apologetic have strongly affected his account, though in some cases it seems to provide a correction or supplement to the *War*.

Written after the *Antiquities*, *Against Apion* is a defence of Judaism against the attacks of the Alexandrian writer Apion (who had written around the middle of the first century) and others. It is very useful in seeing the antisemitic* propaganda being put around at the time and the Jewish counter-propaganda against it. It also quotes a number of Jewish and other works now lost (e.g. the Babylonian writer Berossus).

The works of Josephus are so useful that it is easy to forget that they must be approached critically, as any other writings of antiquity. Some questions which should always be asked include the following:

1. What are his sources? Some are obviously more reliable than others, so that his account of some periods (e.g. Hasmonaean rule) is much more trustworthy than that of others (e.g. the Persian period). His source for parts of the war against Rome is his own eye-witness experience, though this needs to be weighed against 3 below.

2. How does his account compare with that of other sources, such as the Graeco-Roman historians and archaeology*?

3. What are his aims or motives? Where does he have a personal interest or bias? As we would expect, the accounts of his own activities in the war with Rome are self-serving to a lesser or greater extent. When he wrote the *War*, one of his aims was to absolve the Romans in general and the Flavians in particular of responsibility for the war, but he also did not want to blame the Jewish people as a whole. Thus, he puts the blame on a few Jewish 'bandits' (revolutionaries) and a few Roman governors – a rather simplistic picture. He claims that the Temple was burned contrary to Titus' intent, whereas a sober consideration of Roman practice, as well as other sources, indicates that Titus himself ordered it.

4. Where there are two accounts of the same episode, how do they compare? The last part of the *Antiquities* (Books 12–20) is parallel to the first part of the *War* (Books 1–2); likewise, the *Life* overlaps the end of Book 2 of the *War*. It is important to notice that the accounts vary considerably from one another in some instances, often because of differing aims of the writer in each case, though sometimes because of different sources.

These points are important because Josephus has sometimes been used, especially by non-specialists, in a 'proof texting'* sort of fashion without recognizing certain genuine historical problems. This does not mean that Josephan specialists will always agree in evaluating his account (contrast the different assessments of Josephus' part in the war in the monographs of T. Rajak and S. J. D. Cohen). But his accounts must always be evaluated by the normal canons of historical criticism* so that his true value can be correctly assessed and appropriated.

From an early time Christians took an interest in Josephus because of the so-called *Testimonium Flavium*, the passage in which Jesus is referred to (*Ant*. 18.3.3 §§63–64): 'About this time there lived Jesus, a wise man, if indeed one ought to call him a man.' This statement is followed by a brief summary of the life, death and resurrection* of Jesus, his role as the fulfilment of prophecy*, and the fact that his followers could still be found. A further passage (*Ant*. 20.9.1 §200) refers to the death of James, the brother of 'the aforementioned Christ'. Although the latter passage is generally accepted as genuine, the former is almost universally agreed to reflect tampering by Christian scribes and thus to be non-original in its present form. A few scholars feel that the entire passage should be excised as inauthentic. More common is the view that Josephus did indeed refer to Jesus but that later Christian scribes made alterations to give a 'christological' interpretation (see E. Schürer, *The*

History of the Jewish People in the Age of Jesus Christ, revised by G. Vermes et al., 1973, vol. 1, pp. 428–41).

The later influence of Josephus has been considerable. The church historian Eusebius* refers to him a great deal and quotes large chunks of material. Both Eastern and Western Christianity followed him in this interest. Josephus disappears from preserved Jewish literature for several centuries but then surfaces again about the tenth century in the Hebrew book known as *Josippon.* This is primarily a translation of a later Latin adaptation of the *War,* with some additions. Josippon became quite influential among Jews of the Middle Ages and was in turn translated into a variety of different languages.

In the eighteenth and nineteenth centuries, Whiston's translation enjoyed a popularity among devout Christians second only to that of the Bible itself, and more recently Josephus has once again been highly esteemed for the light shed by his writings on the Jewish background to Jesus, presenting in some matters (e.g. Jewish 'sects' of the period) a picture rather different from that in the Gospels.

See also **Jewish Background to the New Testament.**

H. W. Attridge, 'Josephus and his Works' in M. E. Stone (ed.), *Jewish Writings of the Second Temple Period,* Compendium Rerum Judaicarum ad Novum Testamentum 2/2, 1984, pp. 185–232; P. Bilde, *Flavius Josephus between Jerusalem and Rome: His Life, his Works, and their Importance, J S P S 2* 1988; S. J. D. Cohen, *Josephus in Galilee and Rome,* 1979; L. H. Feldman, *Josephus and Modern Scholarship (1937–1980),* 1984 (for bibliography); T. Rajak, *Josephus: The Historian and his Society,* 1983.

LESTER L. GRABBE

Joshua

In Jewish tradition Joshua is the faithful servant of Moses,* who became judge of Israel (I Macc. 2.55), worthy to receive from Moses the Torah (Pirke Aboth 1.1). Though the glory of Joshua was inferior to that of Moses ('The countenance of Moses was like that of the sun; the countenance of Joshua was like that of the moon', Baba Bathra 75a), and though he allowed preparations for war to interfere with the study of the Torah, he was, nevertheless, the ideal type of the 'disciple of the wise'. In Christian tradition, the similarity of the names Joshua (Yehoshua) and Jesus (Yeshua) led to the early typological* interpretation of Joshua as a prefiguration of Jesus. Heb. 4.8–9 contrasts the imperfect rest to which Joshua led Israel with the sabbath rest to which Jesus brings his believers. Episodes from the book

of Joshua have been the subject of numerous literary, artistic* and musical* treatments down to the present day. The siege and capture of Jericho have been a popular theme in drama and song, while the crossing of the Jordan, interpreted as foreshadowing the baptism of Jesus, is frequently represented on baptismal fonts.

Since it relates the conquest of Canaan as the fulfilment of the divine promise of land to the patriarchs, the book of Joshua has always been closely associated with the Pentateuch.* The precise definition of that relationship, however, has been problematic, and the interpretation of the book has, therefore, taken different forms in recent critical scholarship.

1. The widely-held view that the conquest story in Josh. 1–12 is a deuteronomistic edition of the old J E narrative, while P is to be found particularly in the detailed settlement description in Josh. 13–21, is rendered doubtful by a number of difficulties: no credible division of J and E sources has emerged; the relationship between the P and D sources in the latter half of Joshua seems to be the reverse of that in the Pentateuch, in that in Joshua D is a framework for P; the nature of the Joshua material is in any case quite unlike that of J, E and P in the Pentateuch.

2. These issues have made more credible the view which, following Noth's basic analysis, has now become dominant, that Joshua is part of the deuteronomistic history* and is independent of the Pentateuch. The narrative of Josh. 1 is the deuteronomistic introduction to the conquest period; the departure speech of Joshua in Josh. 23 concludes it by setting before Israel the condition of life and prosperity in the land: obedience to the law. The deuteronomistic history has incorporated an existing conquest account, comprising aetiological* stories and a few heroic legends.* The account of the division of the land in Josh. 13–22, together with Josh. 24, are, according to Noth, post-deuteronomistic additions. These also, however, incorporate older material, in the former case an old boundary document and a city list from the time of Josiah, in the latter an old covenant* text edited in deuteronomistic style.

Noth's classic treatment has been strengthened and refined, especially in the work of Lohfink and Smend. Lohfink has shown how Deuteronomy and Joshua are inseparably bound on a literary level by those texts relating to the transfer of leadership from Moses to Joshua. Joshua's two-fold task, to conquer the land and to divide it among the tribes, for which he was commissioned by Moses in one action (Deut. 31.7f.), is given divine confirmation in two separate speeches in Deut. 31.23 and Josh. 1.6. This is a deliberate stylistic presentation which closely integrates the two books and the two periods, that of Moses and that of Joshua. An incidental effect of this view is that Josh. 13–22 should be accepted, against Noth, as having formed an original part of the deuteronomistic history, for it is only here that Joshua's fulfilment of the second of his two tasks is related.

In his treatment of the redactional * development of the deuteronomistic history, Smend has shown how secondary additions to this history amount to a consistent and planned editing of the whole. In Joshua this editing may be seen primarily in Josh. 1.7–9a; 13.1b–6; 23. All of these can be shown to be intrusions which stand in some tension with their deuteronomistic context. The first shifts the emphasis away from encouragement in the face of the forthcoming battle to encouragement to obey the law; the second details the land which remains unconquered, in a literary context which is concerned with the division of the whole of the conquered land among the tribes; the third also refers to the peoples who have not yet been conquered by Israel, though Israel's conquest of the land has been successful 'to this day' (Josh. 23.9). Over against the representation of the deuteronomistic historian that the land has been conquered and that Israel now enjoys rest from her enemies (Josh. 21.43–45), the later editing, which is the work of a second deuteronomistic editor, has introduced a conditional note which declares that Israel will enjoy success only if she is obedient to the law.

3. The interpretation of Joshua has generally concentrated on its referential aspect, and so has been concerned with the relationship between the story and that of which it tells. The ultimate purpose of such interpretation has been the reconstruction of Israelite history. * A shift of emphasis towards the interpretation of the text as such is apparent in the study of its deuteronomistic redaction, where the primary focus of attention is the editor and the meaning which he intended to convey. A further step has been taken in those studies which question the criteria * used to distinguish sources or layers and seek to interpret the text as it now stands without regard for editorial intention.

Thus, the tension between complete conquest of the land and partial conquest which will be completed only on condition of obedience to the law, is taken as a characteristic of the text which is decisive for its interpretation: it is a tension between fulfilment and non-fulfilment of the divine promise, in which the non-fulfilment is not a failure on the part of God to aid Israel in its conquest, but a failure on the part of Israel to realize in her life the divine promise which is constantly in force.

The tension is described by Polzin in rather different terms, within a structuralist * study of the deuteronomistic history. Having distinguished reported speech (speeches of God or Moses) from reporting speech (that of the narrator), he has shown that in Deuteronomy the former predominates but in the end gives way to the latter as the ultimately authoritative voice. It is reporting speech which then dominates in Joshua, where the narrator is concerned with the authoritative interpretation and application of the divine word * in Israel's ongoing history. The tension lies between dogmatic insistence on the unconditional nature of the covenant demands, on the one hand, and the necessity for interpretation of the law appropriate to the new situation, on the other. It is reflected in the contrast between the demand utterly to destroy the Canaanites and the story of the sparing of Rahab and the covenant with the Gibeonites. The deuteronomistic account of the occupation of the land is thus a 'hermeneutic * meditation on the word of God'.

4. The effect of such literary * studies on the question of the redactional history of Joshua is an immediate problem which has yet to be resolved. Further in the future, but no less urgent, is the question of the relationship of such literary work to the referential concerns of the exegesis of Joshua. It may be, as Gottwald suggests, that a convergence between them can in time be worked out in terms of understanding both the text and the context from which it emerged and of which it speaks as instances of the activity of 'a constantly structured and structuring human mind'. In the meantime, the story of Joshua is seen in the state of Israel as a paradigm of successful wars waged against powerful enemies, and as such plays a prominent part in Israeli education.

See also **Archaeology, Old Testament.**

R. Alter and F. Kermode, *The Literary Guide to the Bible,* 1987; T. E. Fretheim, *Deuteronomic History,* 1983; N. K. Gottwald, *The Hebrew Bible. A Socio-Literary Introduction,* 1985; A. D. H. Mayes, *The Story of Israel between Settlement and Exile,* 1983; M. Noth, *The Deuteronomistic History,* ET 1981; R. Polzin, *Moses and the Deuteronomist. A Literary Study of the Deuteronomic History,* 1980; *Encyclopedia Judaica,* 1971.

A. D. H. MAYES

Judaizers

The noun is derived from the verb 'judaize', which in turn is technically a transliteration via the Latin of the Greek *ioudaïzein.* In Greek usage the verb meant properly 'to live as a Jew, in accordance with Jewish customs'. It occurs in this sense in Plutarch, Josephus* and elsewhere, including Gal. 2.14 and Ignatius, *Magn.* 10.3. Both noun and verb appear in sixteenth- and seventeenth-century English usage. But, partly no doubt because the biblical reference occurs in a context of compulsion (how can you compel the Gentiles to judaize?), the transitive sense of the verb also makes an appearance, in Milton, for example: 'Error ... in many other Points of Religion had miserably judaiz'd the Church'; 'the judaiz'd Symmachus' (*OED*).

The modern usage, however, dates from F. C. Baur (*see* **Tübingen School**). In his article, 'Die Christuspartei in der korinthischen Gemeinde', 1831, he developed the thesis that Paul* was opposed in Corinth by the judaizing adherents of Peter.* The same judaizing opponents are attacked in both letters to the Corinthians, in Phil. 3.1–2 and particularly in Galatians.* This was a thesis which Baur was to maintain and develop during the middle decades of the nineteenth century – that in apostolic and post-apostolic times the history of Christianity was shaped principally by the opposition between the Paulinists and Petrinists, or judaizers. And thus was established the still dominant meaning of the word: 'Judaizers' as denoting the Jewish-Christian opponents of Paul's Gentile mission, who insisted that all Gentile converts had to be circumcised and to observe the law, in a word, to 'judaize' (Gal. 2.14).

Although Baur's full thesis has not stood the test of time, his interpretation particularly of the polemical thrust of the major Pauline letters has remained influential to the present day. Early on it was qualified by the recognition that his portrayal of early Christianity in terms of a confrontation between two monolithic blocks was too much of an oversimplification. The Jewish Christians* could not be lumped together as a single group opposed to Paul. 'Strict or extreme judaizers' were to be distinguished from 'moderate Jewish Christians', and while the former could be linked to Jerusalem, Peter was to be distinguished from them, with the question whether James should be reckoned a judaizer a subject for some debate. In a similar way Gentile Christianity, the opposite pole from Jewish Christianity, was to be distinguished from Paulinism (see e.g. A. Ritschl and C. Weizsäcker, quoted by Kümmel, pp. 166–7).

Nevertheless Baur's basic claim, that the opposition to Paul during his mission should be designated as 'judaizers', Jewish Christians who insisted that Paul's Gentile converts must be circumcised and become Jews, was widely accepted, and indeed became axiomatic in most of the discussions of the next hundred years. The case in reference to Galatians in particular was generally assumed to be beyond question (see e.g. commentaries* by Lightfoot [1865], Meyer [1873] and Burton [1921]; and introductions* by Zahn [1909] and Moffatt [1911]). Baur's other suggestions of judaizing factions in Corinth and Philippi also met with wide acceptance. With less justification, Rom. 16.17–20 was drawn into the net by some, but the attempt to include the Thessalonian correspondence met with little favour, and J. B. Lightfoot's (*see* **Westcott**) classic discussion of the complexity of the situation addressed at Colossae discouraged simplifying solutions there. The breakdown of Baur's grandiose reconstruction of Christian development across the first two centuries also diminished the appropriateness of the use of 'judaizer' outside the context of Paul's mission and writings, with Ignatius the only significant exception.

This broad consensus has received two major challenges in the twentieth century. At the turn of the century, the rising interest in early Gnosticism* and in the syncretism of Hellenistic* religion drew forth a sequence of attempts to set Paul's correspondence in a different context. For example, W. Lutgert saw Paul's chief opponents at Corinth as spiritual enthusiasts, an early type of gnostic libertines ('the Christ party') and saw them also alongside the judaizing nomists as a second front in Galatians. And W. Schmithals pushed the case further by arguing that in Galatians there are no judaizers in view at all, only Jewish Christian Gnostics, with similar claims for Corinthians and Philippians (*Gnosticism in Corinth* 1956; ET 1971; *Paul and the Gnostics* [1965]; ET 1972).

J. Munck developed the reaction against Baur and the Tübingen school on another front by arguing that there was no judaizing party in Jerusalem and by rejecting the 'pan-judaizer' hypothesis as the background to the Pauline correspondence: Paul's letters were addressed to different situations with different opponents. In the cases where Baur's basic thesis was still largely intact Munck mounted counter-arguments. The judaizing opponents in Galatians are Gentile Christians keen to adopt the practices of the Law. Their objective was thus the same, so that the word 'judaizer' retains the same significance. The point, however, for Munck, is that the compulsion to 'judaize' did not come from Jewish Christianity, which was concerned only for its mission within Israel, but was a Gentile Christian 'heresy' only possible in the Pauline churches. As for the Corinthian church, there were neither factions nor 'judaizers' there, simply a misunderstanding on the part of the Corinthians who regarded Christianity as wisdom. And in Phil 3.2ff. the opponents are not judaizers but Jews.

There would be general agreement that while both Schmithals and Munck have attempted to push the pendulum too far the other way, there does need to be greater recognition of the rich diversity of situations confronting Paul in the three churches on which the 'judaizer' issue has focussed from the first. That Paul confronted some opposition at Corinth seems to be sufficiently clear, but whether it was a united opposition, how the various strands hang together, and whether there was a specifically judaizing element ('the Cephas party'?, the 'false apostles'?), all remain in dispute. So too with Phil. 3, where the resolution of the judaizing and gnosticizing features in the chapter remains similarly unclear. Only in Galatians does the Baur thesis of a Jewish-Christian judaizing opposition remain firmly in place. Indeed, with the current reaction against pan-gnostic hypotheses still strong, and interest in Christianity's Jewish matrix recently renewed, Galatians might still provide a basis for a revived and refined form of the Baur thesis, in which case it would be important that 'judaize' (and 'judaizer') should not be confined to the modern technical sense, to denote a Christian heresy or a predatory form of Jewish Christianity, but should be allowed to re-emerge in its original sense, to denote the attraction which many Gentiles clearly found in the Judaism of the day.

See also **Jewish Christianity; Paul; Tübingen School.**

J. D. G. Dunn, *Jesus, Paul and the Law*, 1990; W. G. Kümmel, *The New Testament. The History of the Investigation of its Problems*, 1973; J. Munck, *Paul and the Salvation of Mankind*, 1959.

JAMES D. G. DUNN

Judges

Of the figures mentioned in the book of Judges, those who have received significant notice in Jewish tradition have been Deborah, Gideon, Jephthah and Samson. Deborah, along with Hannah, is commemorated for having composed praises to God surpassing those written by men, but she is criticized for her haughtiness in sending for Barak rather than going to him (Megillah 14b). Gideon, Jephthah and Samson are considered three of the most questionable characters, but their appearance with Samuel in I Sam. 12.11 indicates for the rabbis* that even 'the most worthless, once he has been appointed a leader of the community, is to be accounted like the mightiest of the mighty' (Rosh Hashanah 25a–b). In the NT not only is Samson one of the heroes of faith (Heb. 11.32), but the story about his birth and devotion to God provided

the language for the accounts of the birth of John the Baptist* (Luke 1.15) and the childhood of Jesus (Luke 2.40) (*see* **Infancy Narratives**). In art* Christian interpretations have been given to these major figures: Jael, from the Deborah episode, represents the virgin and her victory over evil; the angel's appearance to Gideon and his incredulity are, at Chartres, interpreted as a prefiguration of the annunciation; Jephthah's vow and sacrifice of his daughter has been a popular theme in Christian art, writing and music;* Samson, in both the early church and the Middle Ages (*see* **Mediaeval Interpretation**) was seen as a prototype of Jesus, his rending of the lion representing Jesus' victory over Satan. In literature perhaps the most famous treatment is Milton's sympathetic idealization of the blind judge in *Samson Agonistes*.

In modern scholarship, the older critical view, which traced the continuation of pentateuchal* sources throughout Judges, now finds some support only in relation to the proposal that Judges 1 may be the conclusion of one of those old sources. In general, source criticism* of this documentary type has been overtaken by traditio-historical* and redaction-critical* studies on the one hand, and, more recently, by new literary criticism* on the other.

In his seminal study of the deuteronomistic history,* Noth argued that internal structural markers indicated that for the Deuteronomist the period of the judges began with Judg. 2.6ff., and concluded with the speech of Samuel in I Sam. 12 inaugurating the period of the monarchy. In order to describe the period of the judges, the Deuteronomist used and combined two chief sources: on the one hand, an older collection of stories about local tribal heroes; on the other, a list of judges, the so-called 'minor judges', which recorded the occupants of a central judicial office in premonarchic amphictyonic Israel. The Deuteronomist combined these two sources on the basis of the fact that one person, Jephthah, featured in both; and so the list of minor judges now appears, in broken form, on either side of the story of Jephthah as a heroic deliverer (Judg. 10.1–5; 12.7–15).

The list of minor judges had a fundamental influence on the Deuteronomist's conception of the period of the judges: the deliverers were understood as judges (Judg. 2.16,18); the 'all Israel' significance of the judges was carried over to the deliverers, who were now seen as liberators of the whole of Israel from foreign oppression; on the basis of the list of judges, the deliverers also were presented by the Deuteronomist as occupants of a central Israelite office.

The Deuteronomist provided an introduction to his presentation in Judg. 2.6ff., together with a framework for each of the stories of deliverance and a more elaborate introduction to the Jephthah story (Judg. 10.6–16). This was the last such story (except for that about Samuel in I Sam. 7) in the Deuteronomist's account of the period of the judges, for, after incorporating the remainder of the list of judges (Judg. 12.7–15), the Deuteronomist passed on to note the beginning of the Philistine oppression (Judg. 13.1) as background to the story of Samuel. The Samson story (Judg. 13–16) shows no sign of deuteronomistic editing, and it, like the introduction to the book of Judges (Judg. 1.1–2.5) and its concluding stories (Judg. 17–21), is to be taken as a post-deuteronomistic addition.

The most significant recent studies in the tradition-history and redaction-criticism of Judges have been done by Richter, who has uncovered the complexity of the development of the central section of the book by a detailed analysis of the formulaic passages constituting the frameworks to the stories of deliverers. The basic collection comprised stories of Ehud, Deborah–Barak and Gideon–Abimelech. The consistent framework attached to them introduced for the first time a theological and didactic emphasis: it was the sin of the people which made necessary the exploits of the deliverers, who engaged in holy wars of Israel under the leadership of Yahweh.

In a later development the story of Othniel (Judg. 3.7–11) was added as an introduction, giving a typical example of events in the period, and elaborating the theological implications already present in the framework passages of the basic collection. A further development was more extensive. The Jephthah story was added (Judg. 10.6–12.6), with an introduction building on the framework passages to identify Israel's sin as the service of the Baals,, the Ashtaroth and foreign gods, and their cry to Yahweh as an acknowledgment of sin to which Yahweh responded in indignation. This introduction (Judg. 10.6–16) referred not only to Ammonite oppression but also to Philistine domination which formed the background to the Samson story; so this also was brought in at this stage. The Samson story, however, uses formulae which otherwise appear with the minor judges (Judg. 15.20; 16.31), and so it is to this stage that the introduction of the list of minor judges also belongs.

For this complex whole an introduction was composed, and subsequently elaborated, in Judg. 2.11–3.6. Here the Deuteronomist explained Israel's sufferings as Yahweh's punishment for sin. Out of pity for their suffering Yahweh sent judges who saved Israel from their enemies; but Israel did not learn, for on the death of each judge the people reverted to their evil ways and did worse than before.

Studies such as those of Noth and Richter emphasized the development of Judges as a complex process of reinterpretation of older materials. They generally failed, however, to offer interpretations of Judges as a completed and finished whole. A certain impatience with this approach is evident in the work of those who seek an answer to the question of the meaning of the book of Judges as it now confronts us. It is this question which lies behind the recent literary studies of parts of Judges and occasionally of the book as a whole.

Several significant studies of individual stories in Judges, especially those about Ehud, Deborah and Barak, and Samson, have drawn attention to their literary quality, style and structure, and have significantly contributed to the appreciation of them as literature rather than simply as potential sources of information for history. The book as an independent whole has been argued to have a symmetrical structure in which elements in the first half have corresponding elements in the second, a structure designed to highlight the Gideon story, with its presentation of Gideon's lapse into idolatry, as central. On the other hand, Polzin's structuralist *-formalist approach has taken the book as a distinct part of the Deuteronomistic history, in which the Deuteronomist, assuming the role of authoritative interpreter of the word of God */Moses * in Deuteronomy, uses the general theme of Judges, Israel's continued existence despite her apostasy, to illustrate the limitations of any ideology * to explain or predict.

The most recent comprehensive study by Webb has used a musical analogy to argue for unity of plot or theme in the book, which is taken to comprise an overture (Judg. 1.1–3.6), variations (Judg. 3.7–16.31) and a coda (Judg. 17–21). The overture explains Israel's failure fully to possess the land, in fulfilment of the divine promise, as the result of Yahweh's withdrawing his promise because of what happened in the period of the judges: Israel lived among the Canaanites and served their gods. The variations tell of twelve judge-deliverers, presented in a schematic form roughly corresponding to that of the tribes of Israel. 1. The framework passages show some differences, but these reflect the continuous decline of Israel in relation to Yahweh, to her enemies and to her internal stability, a process which reaches its climax in the Samson episode. The coda, which has a structural correspondence with the overture, picks up themes from the variations, in particular the danger posed to Israel by internal division and disintegration. The book of Judges is thus in its finished form a coherent work, the meaning of which is to be determined from an integrated reading of the whole text.

A clear tension currently exists between the synchronic* perspective of new literary studies and the diachronic perspective of other critical approaches. They can be seen to interact fruitfully in some respects, in that a better literary appreciation may in some cases bring about a more refined diachronic view; but the more precise definition of the relationship between the different approaches requires further study.

See also **Joshua**.

See bibliography under Joshua, and: A. D. H. Mayes, *Judges*, 1985; B. G. Webb, *The Book of Judges: An Integrated Reading*, 1987.

A. D. H. MAYES

Kerygma

The Greek word for 'proclamation' or 'announcement' appears eight times in the NT, either in the general sense of 'preaching' (Matt. 12.41 = Luke 11.32) or as shorthand for specifically Christian preaching, a synonym for 'Gospel'* or 'the Word'* (I Cor. 1.21; 2.4; 15.14; Rom. 16.25; II Tim. 4.17; Titus 1.3). In mid-twentieth-century biblical interpretation, however, it has been employed much more extensively in a variety of senses, and has figured as a technical term in debates concerning the nature and content of early Christian faith.

In reaction to the nineteenth-century liberal* 'lives of Jesus' approach (*see* **Historical Jesus**), which tended to make the essence of Christianity dependent upon the outcome of historical research, M. Kähler argued that theology's starting point must be the Christ of faith, i.e. the preached Christ. His position was developed systematically by K. Barth* in what eventually became known as 'kerygmatic theology': the revelation* of the Word of God in Jesus Christ, to which scripture bears witness, is mediated through Christian preaching, independently of questions raised by philosophical theology or the historical criticism* of the Bible.

The pioneers of the form criticism* of the Gospels used the term kerygma to focus attention on the preliterary oral* stage before the production of written texts. They emphasized the importance of preaching as the main setting in which the fragmentary traditions about Jesus were transmitted in the early church. Even if historical reconstruction of the life and teaching of Jesus were theologically desirable, the predominantly kerygmatic interest of the tradition made it practically impossible, for the chronological and biographical details necessary for such a reconstruction had been lost in the processes of transmission.

R. Bultmann* combined the preceding usages of the term. On the basis of evidence from the Pauline epistles, chiefly Paul's* apparent neglect of the historical Jesus and his use of anthropological terms, Bultmann argued that the kerygma should be understood in terms of the activity and effect of preaching rather than of its content: it is the eschatological* offer of salvation addressed to any individual which brings about a new self-understanding in faith. In Bultmannian interpretation, therefore, kerygma may be defined as that pattern of human experience which remains, after the myths* (apocalyptic* and gnostic*) in which early Christian faith was at first expressed have been 'demythologized'* (i.e. translated existentially) into the thought forms of a modern world-view.

In marked contrast to Bultmann, C. H. Dodd* emphasized the content of the kerygma. Apostolic mission preaching consisted of a detailed historical outline of the ministry of Jesus, including his baptism and anointing with the Spirit, his miracles* and teaching, his arrest, trial, crucifixion, burial and resurrection.* Dodd claimed that this outline always remains constant, not only in kerygmatic sections of Paul's epistles (e.g. I Cor. 15.1–7; Rom. 1.1–4) but also in the speeches of the Acts of the Apostles (e.g. Acts 10.37–41; 13.23–32) and in the 'summary passages' which form the allegedly traditional framework of the Gospel of Mark (e.g. Mark 1.14–15; 9.31). Although this basic historical creed* is developed in a variety of ways in the NT in secondary 'teaching' (*didachē*, i.e. preaching to the already converted), it constitutes the unifying core of early Christianity, and indeed of the whole biblical revelation in history.

In short, this comparatively insignificant and innocent term has taken on a great weight of additional meaning, often reflecting polemically polarized positions on hermeneutical* issues. In the debate between the existentialist and salvation-historical* approaches, both sides equally can be accused of indulging in a reductionist and idealized abstraction when they appeal to the kerygma. For both assume from the outset, with the help of this term, the conclusion which itself requires demonstration, namely that there is one 'essential message' of the NT which, negotiating the distance of time and culture without serious loss, can be restated credibly today (*see* **Cultural Relativism**).

Recent scholarship has thus begun to challenge, or even abandon, the use of the term in biblical interpretation. In general, it is less willing to isolate preaching from the other means by which salvation was mediated in early Christianity (i.e. the sacraments and the

social structures of continuing community*
life). In particular, the claimed distinctions
between kerygma on the one hand and history,
myth and *didachē* on the other have been
shown to be without semantic* basis. Furthermore, the emphasis in early Christian
preaching on the present lordship and imminent
return of Christ does not necessarily exclude
historical interest in the earthly Jesus (thus,
Stanton; Roloff). The varied phenomena of
preaching in the early church can be more
helpfully discussed in the terms which the N T
itself prefers, namely prophecy, *paraclēsis* (consolation), *paraēnesis* (exhortation), and *para-
dosis* (tradition) (thus McDonald). And the
varied contents of the N T documents have
even led some to speak of kerygmata in the
plural (thus, Dunn). This is not to say that the
questions to which kerygma responded are
any less important for biblical interpretation,
but that other terminology needs to be developed for handling them.

See also **Eschatology; Kingdom of God.**

R. Bultmann, *Jesus and the Word*, 1935; C. H.
Dodd, *The Apostolic Preaching and its Develop-
ments*, 1936; id., *Gospel and Law*, 1951; J. D.
G. Dunn, *Unity and Diversity in the New
Testament*, 1977; C. F. Evans, 'The Kerygma',
JTS, 7, 1956, pp. 25–41; M. Kähler, *The So-
Called Historical Jesus and the Historic Bib-
lical Christ*, 1964; J. I. H. McDonald,
Kerygma and Didache, 1980; J. Roloff, *Das
Kerygma und der irdische Jesus*, 1970; G. N.
Stanton, *Jesus of Nazareth in New Testament
Preaching*, 1974.

JOHN MUDDIMAN

Kingdom of God

The Synoptic* Gospels are agreed that the
kingdom of God (or kingdom of heaven in
Matthew) was the central theme of Jesus'
teaching. According to Mark 1.15, Jesus proclaimed the imminent arrival of the kingdom,
and summoned his hearers to repent and believe the good news: this brief summary indicates the dual impact of the kingdom, which
brings salvation to those who respond and
judgment to those who do not.

The background of the idea is found in the
OT, for although the actual phrase 'the kingdom of God' is not used there, the kingship of
God is frequently stressed, especially in the
psalms. In the inter-testamental period the
hope grew strong that God would establish
his rule on earth, a hope expressed most
clearly in the apocalyptic* literature. This
cataclysmic event would involve judgment for
the wicked and restoration for the righteous,
who would thereafter enjoy living, in obedience to God, on a renewed earth.

In contrast to the synoptics, the phrase is
rarely used in the Fourth Gospel, but when it
is (3.3,5) it is understood to be synonymous
with 'eternal life' (3.15f.; cf. also Mark 10.23–
30). Underlying this is the assumption that
life in the kingdom is identical with life in the
age to come. In Acts, the kingdom is something which the apostles preach (e.g. 8.12;
19.8); Paul* speaks of 'inheriting' the kingdom (I Cor. 6.9f.; 15.50; Gal. 5.21), yet it
seems to be present also (Rom. 14.17; I Cor.
4.20). Though the phrase itself is little used
outside the synoptics, expectation of God's
coming rule dominates most of the N T.

There is thus an eschatological* tension
running throughout the N T references to the
kingdom: it is both present and future. This
tension focusses on the figure of Jesus himself.
No doubt there was a sense in which the
kingdom was in fact already present (since
God is eternally king) before the time of Jesus,
but of this nothing is said: instead, he proclaims its arrival – something new and significant is taking place or is about to take place.
But does Jesus simply announce the future
coming of the kingdom or does he actually
bring the kingdom? Although most of his
teaching looks forward to its coming (e.g.
Mark 9.1; Matt. 6.10//Luke 11.2), it is clear
that the evangelists* at least believed that the
kingdom had in a sense arrived with Jesus
(e.g. Matt. 12.28//Luke 11.20; Mark 3.27;
Matt. 11.4f.//Luke 7.22; Matt. 11.12f.//Luke
16.16). The question of the presence of the
kingdom is thus inextricably linked with questions about the person and work of Jesus.

All the evangelists include sayings which
refer to the kingdom as something which can
be entered, or as something which belongs to
a particular group of people (e.g. Mark 9.47;
10.14f.; Matt. 5.3,10,20; Luke 18.16f., John
3.5). Although both Mark (4.26,30) and Luke
(13.18,20) each contain two parables specifically about the kingdom, it is Matthew above
all who gives the impression that the parables*
of Jesus were all cast in the form 'The kingdom of heaven is like . . .' (Matt. 13.24,
31,33,44,45,47; 18.23; 20.1; 22.2; 25.1). In
Matthew there is a tendency to identify the
coming kingdom with the kingdom of Christ:
see 13.41–3; 16.28 (cf. Mark 9.1); 20.21 (cf.
Mark 10.37); 25.31–46. This explicit identification of Jesus as the one who rules in God's
kingdom is never made in Mark, but Luke
also implies that there is a kingdom which
belongs to Jesus himself (22.29f.; 23.42).

Traditional Roman Catholic teaching has
identified the kingdom of God with the
church. This goes back to the teaching of
Augustine,* though in fact it was the invisible
body of the elect within the church whom he
identified with the kingdom of God or of
Christ (*City of God*, XX.9). In contrast to the

Catholic view that the ecclesiastical hierarchy represented the power of the kingdom, the Reformers* understood the kingdom to be the spiritual, invisible rule of Christ, exercised in the lives of believers through the preaching of the word and the work of the Holy Spirit.

It was not until the end of the nineteenth century that scholarly interest focussed on the kingdom of God. The first scholar to examine the question of Jesus' own understanding of the idea was Albrecht Ritschl (1822–89), who regarded Jesus primarily as a moral teacher, and thus interpreted the kingdom of God in ethical terms. In proclaiming the kingdom, Jesus set out the ethical demands of God; the establishment of the kingdom inaugurated by Jesus was the goal to which Christians had to strive. Ritschl's interpretation reflects nineteenth-century belief in progress, but from it derives the later Christian political and social idealism which found expression in terms of 'building the kingdom'. In reaction to Ritschl, Johannes Weiss (1863–1914) argued that the background of Jesus' proclamation of the kingdom of God was to be found in Jewish expectation of the future manifestation of the kingly activity of God: the kingdom was not something which could be built or which would arrive gradually, but was expected to burst into history, transforming the world and bringing both renewal and judgment. Jesus expected the kingdom of God in the very near future, and its nearness was the motive for the righteousness which he demanded: his hearers must repent and prepare for its coming, but its arrival depended on God alone (*Jesus' Proclamation of the Kingdom of God*, 1892, ET 1971).

Gustaf Dalman (1855–1941) used his knowledge of Aramaic to demonstrate that the terms 'kingdom of God' and 'kingdom of heaven' were synonymous, and that the term translated 'kingdom', *malkuth*, means 'kingly rule' and refers to sovereignty, not territory. An oriental kingdom was not a constitutionally ordered state, as we understand it; it extended over that area, and embraced those people over which the king was able to establish his rule. On the basis of rabbinic* literature, Dalman argued that the sovereignty of God was understood primarily as eternal, and that individuals could take on themselves 'the yoke of the sovereignty of God'. For Jesus, therefore, the kingdom of God meant the manifestation of divine sovereignty, accepted by men and women through their obedience to God's will (*The Words of Jesus*, 1898, ET 1902). Subsequent scholarship was to question the relevance of this later rabbinic material for our understanding of first-century teaching.

The ideas of Weiss were taken up and de-veloped by Albert Schweitzer* in two books published in 1901 (ET *The Mystery of the Kingdom of God*, 1925) and 1906 (ET The *Quest of the Historical Jesus*, 1910). Tracing the background of Jesus' understanding of the kingdom to apocalyptic literature, Schweitzer interpreted his teaching in terms of 'consistent' or 'thoroughgoing' eschatology. On the basis of Matt. 10.23, he argued that Jesus expected the kingdom to arrive during his ministry; disappointed in his hopes, he attempted to fulfil his messianic vocation by enduring all the final tribulations, thus forcing God to bring in the kingdom. The ethical teaching of Jesus is not to be seen as the new morality which characterizes that kingdom, but as *Interimsethik* – the demands made of those who repent in expectation of the coming kingdom.

The weakness of Schweitzer's approach was the way in which he allowed his theory to predetermine his exegesis; he assumed the existence of a clearly-defined eschatological expectation at the time of Jesus for which there is in fact very little evidence. The strength of his position lay in his attempt to relate Jesus to what he believed to be the contemporary expectation. His work made a lasting impact on scholarship, since it led to the recognition of the kingdom as an eschatological (or 'apocalyptic') event.

Another scholar greatly influenced by Weiss was Rudolf Bultmann,* who also argued that Jesus' teaching must be understood against the background of the eschatological hope found in Jewish apocalyptic. The kingdom does not come gradually, but suddenly, bringing history to an end. Jesus proclaimed its imminent arrival – it was breaking in in his words and deeds, though not yet present; but this future coming determines the present, since the proclamation demands a decision. Because the crisis with which he confronted men and women was expressed by Jesus in terms of contemporary mythology,* Bultmann reinterpreted it in existential terms, and thereby detached it completely from history (*Jesus*, 1926, ET *Jesus and the Word*, 1934). Jesus may have expected the end of history in the imminent future, but his proclamation of the kingdom has become for Bultmann the first-century dress for a twentieth-century summons to decision (*see* **Demythologization**).

In contrast to Bultmann, who denied Jesus any messianic self-consciousness, Rudolf Otto (1869–1937) emphasized the importance of Jesus himself for the kingdom of God, and thus laid more emphasis on the present aspect of the kingdom (*The Kingdom of God and the Son of Man*, 1934, ET 1938). Influenced by the 'History of Religions school,* he argued on the basis of Zoroastrian sources that the kingdom was an other-worldly concept and that genuine eschatology, far from being 'consistent', held together present reality and future hope. Though the Zoroastrian parallels are too late and too distant to be relevant, Otto's insistence on the kingdom as both present and future has proved of lasting value.

The approach of T. W. Manson (1893–1958) to the question, like that of Dalman, was influenced by rabbinic literature (*The Teaching of Jesus*, 1931). The kingdom is primarily a personal relationship, comprising God's claim to rule and man's obedience. Jesus began his ministry by proclaiming the kingdom as future, but later spoke of it as something which could be entered; the turning-point is the episode at Caesarea Philippi, and we may thus conclude that the kingdom comes with the confession of Peter.* The kingdom is manifested in Jesus' own obedience to God's rule and in the recognition of his authority by those who, together with him, make up the community of the elect (referred to, so Manson believed, as 'the Son of man'*), because they acknowledge God as king. The kingdom of God is thus both present and future, and is integrally related to the ethical teaching of Jesus, which is addressed to the community of those who are devoted to God's service. Manson's interpretation was based on the assumption that Mark presents us with a historical outline of Jesus' ministry, and it is vulnerable for that reason. It has also been criticized for relying too heavily on late rabbinic material and ignoring the expectation of the coming kingdom in the form of a decisive eschatological divine intervention which we find in contemporary apocalyptic.

It was C. H. Dodd* who argued for an interpretation most radically opposed to that of Schweitzer. Pointing to passages where Jesus speaks of the kingdom as already present, he argued for what he termed 'realized eschatology' (*The Parables of the Kingdom*, 1935). He took the summary in Mark 1.15 as a statement that the kingdom is already here, explaining the verb *eggizein* as meaning 'to arrive', not 'to draw near'. He interpreted the parables as presenting the same message: the kingdom is here in the ministry of Jesus; the period of growth is over, the eschatological moment has arrived. Jesus' 'apocalyptic' predictions should be understood as symbolic statements about the eternal realities which lie beyond history, not as temporal expectations.

Dodd's work was immensely influential, especially in Great Britain, but he imposed his interpretation on much of the evidence, and ignored the eschatological expectations of first-century Judaism. A corrective to his exclusive emphasis on the present was provided by Joachim Jeremias* in *The Parables of Jesus* (1947;

ET [3] 1972), who rejected Dodd's 'realized eschatology' for what he called 'eschatology in process of realization'. While agreeing with Dodd that the kingdom is present in the ministry of Jesus, he understood Jesus to be pointing forward to a future crisis that will bring both deliverance and destruction. Like Dodd before him, Jeremias attempted to discover the *Sitz im Leben Jesu* of the parables (i.e. their setting in Jesus' life), and distinguished between Jesus' own understanding of them and the interpretation given to them by the early church. Whereas Dodd believed that Jesus' parables were concerned wholly with the present, and were reinterpreted by the church in terms of a future eschatological crisis, Jeremias believed that the shift in emphasis between Jesus and the church was due in part to the delay in the parousia.

W. G. Kümmel's position is in many ways similar to that of Jeremias. Jesus expected the kingdom to come in the near future, indeed in his own generation. Such sayings as Mark 9.1 cannot be explained away, and it has to be recognized that Jesus was mistaken in his expectation. Kümmel agrees with those who had attacked Dodd's interpretation of *eggizein*: the kingdom is drawing near, not already here. Nevertheless, Jesus also spoke of the kingdom as having already begun in his own activity (Matt. 12.28): the future is thus already present. In contrast to those who maintain that the kingdom was for Jesus timeless, and that his proclamation was therefore not concerned with an imminent end, Kümmel insists that he was thinking in temporal terms (*Promise and Fulfilment*, ET 1957).

In the 1960s, a consensus had begun to emerge: although some scholars (especially in Germany) continued to stress the future character of the kingdom, and others (especially in Great Britain) emphasized its present reality, there was a growing recognition that both aspects must be acknowledged. Thus H. Conzelmann, though insisting that the kingdom is future, acknowledged that the 'signs' of the kingdom are already present (*An Outline of the Theology of the New Testament*, ET 1969), while C. H. Dodd modified his earlier position: Jesus' eschatology cannot be described as either totally consistent or fully realized. Above all, there appeared to be a general agreement that the kingdom was 'eschatological' in character: it arrives through the activity of God, and cannot be built by men. But while some understood the kingdom in strictly 'apocalyptic' terms, as a supernatural event, others insisted that it was established in the hearts of men when God's will was obeyed. Among those who have consistently argued against the 'apocalyptic' interpretation of the coming kingdom as a cosmic catastrophe which will bring this world to an end is T. F. Glasson (*The Second Advent*, ³1963; *Jesus and the End of the World*, 1980), who has pointed to the paucity of evidence for this understanding of the kingdom in contemporary Jewish writings. The kingdom comes when everyone recognizes the kingship of God.

An attempt to approach the problem in a new way was made by B. Chilton (*God in Strength*, 1979), who examined references to the kingdom of God in the Targum* of Isaiah, and argued that both there and in the teaching of Jesus it referred to the self-revelation of God, who acts now to save his people but who will be fully revealed in strength in the future. Jesus proclaimed the saving activity of God, not a régime in space or time.

Both Glasson and Chilton express dissatisfaction with the 'eschatological consensus'. So, too, at the end of his life, did Perrin, one of its earlier champions. Turning from historical criticism* to literary criticism,* he argued that understanding of the kingdom had come to an impasse because scholars had failed to realize that it was a 'symbol',* whose function is to evoke a myth – in this case, the myth that God had acted in creation and in history, and would continue to do so. Jesus' parables were metaphorical,* mediating the reality evoked by the symbol to their hearers. Sayings about the kingdom challenged Jesus' hearers to recognize the activity of God and to respond by committing themselves to the claims of God upon them. (*Jesus and the Language of the Kingdom*, 1976). Perrin's interpretation is clearly similar to Bultmann's, but he disagreed with Bultmann in that he denied that Jesus proclaimed the kingdom of God at a definite point in time and expected it to be accompanied by a cosmic catastrophe; it is not only we who understand the kingdom as a symbol, but Jesus himself. Thus for Perrin, as for Glasson and Chilton, the debate about whether the kingdom is to be understood as present or future is a meaningless one.

Perrin is no longer concerned solely with Jesus' own understanding of the kingdom, however, but with hermeneutics,* and with the way in which the symbol of the kingdom functions today. His interpretation is thus open to the accusation that he has read back twentieth-century attitudes into the words of Jesus. Nevertheless, the challenge to the eschatological consensus is a valid one: are Jesus' statements to be understood literally, or do they function at the level of myth and symbol? The insights of literary criticism have been applied to the teaching of the synoptics by R. C. Tannehill (in *The Sword of His Mouth*, 1974), who insists that the sayings are not primarily intended to convey information, but function through their imaginative language. The form of a saying is as important as its content, and Jesus' teaching challenges its readers to respond to the claims of the kingdom.

One scholar who is convinced that the kingdom was for Jesus more than a symbol, and that he must be understood within the expectations of first-century Jewish eschatology, is E. P. Sanders. In *Jesus and Judaism*, 1985, he reminds us of the danger of being influenced by a dislike of first-century Jewish thinking. Unlike many earlier scholars, Sanders recognizes the impossibility of knowing what Jesus said and meant, but does not think that the way out is to be found in ahistorical approaches. While there is no doubt that Jesus proclaimed the kingdom and believed his own career to be closely linked to the kingdom, far too much weight has been placed on Matt. 12.28//Luke 11.20 and Matt. 11.5f., whose meaning and authenticity are not certain. Jesus certainly expected the kingdom to come in the near future, but we cannot be sure that he believed it to be here already. The sayings about the kingdom are diverse, and this suggests that Jesus used the phrase with a wide range of meanings.

Whereas twenty-five years ago a consensus had emerged, there appears now to be only confusion. Nevertheless there is agreement that Jesus proclaimed the kingdom (by which he meant the rule) of God, and demanded a response from his hearers. Attempts to interpret the kingdom as exclusively present or future have foundered. Perhaps this is a warning against imposing modern understandings of time on a culture which did not necessarily share them, and in which future hopes, like past events, could be spoken of as present realities.

See also **Historical Jesus.**

In addition to titles mentioned, see: B. Chilton (ed.), *The Kingdom of God*, 1984; G. E. Ladd, *Jesus and the Kingdom*, 1966.

                                                    MORNA D. HOOKER

Kings

The earliest attempt at interpretation of the books of Kings is to be found in the books of Chronicles (*see* **Inner-Biblical Exegesis**), much of the content of which is best described as exegesis* of material found in Kings. Most scholars believe that we also find such exegesis in the Septuagint.* In both these cases, as in the later work of Ben Sira (Ecclus. 47–49), Josephus* and others (II Bar. 56–74; IV Ezra 7.102–115), there is a very clear sense that the books of Kings form part of a historical work. For biblical interpreters before the modern era, however, information about the past was rarely the most important kind to be gained from books like Kings, and such books were never regarded as 'mere' history. Far more determinative for their interpretation was the general belief that these books were 'prophetic', both in origin (they had been written by prophets*) and in content (they contained divinely inspired, and often esoteric, information of immediate relevance for the present). In the Jewish three-fold division of the canon,* Kings forms part of 'the Prophets'.

They were, therefore, read mainly for information about God – his nature, his realm and his plan for history, specifically with regard to his intervention in the present day – as well as for ethical instruction. Thus to Josephus* (*Antiquities*, 1.14), as to the Chronicler before him, the main lesson to be learned from the historical sources was that men who conform to the will of God prosper and those who do not bring disaster upon themselves. Philo,* too, regarded the biblical text as primarily a witness to mystical, timeless truth. The judgment formulae of the books of Kings, for example, testify to 'souls made immortal by their virtues' (*On the Confusion of Languages*, 149). In the Babylonian Talmud,* the normal use for all non-Pentateuchal scripture is as support for some piece of *halakhah*, as in *Sotah* 46b, where II Kings 2.23–35 is referred to in the context of discussion about the duties of escorts. Little historical sense is displayed in such readings, and what the modern reader would call the 'natural' sense of the text is often completely ignored. Similarly, Jewish and Christian scholars of the Middle Ages (*see* **Mediaeval Interpretation**) often engaged in midrashic,* allegorical* or philosophical exegesis of the Bible (e.g. Bede, *Concerning the Temple*, an allegorical commentary on the construction of Solomon's temple); and where a more literal reading is evident, there is little sense of any historical distance between text and reader which would make problematic the interpretation of the divine will for, or action in, the present. Bede's understanding (in his *Ecclesiastical History*), both of the course of Anglo-Saxon history and of how it should be described in writing, for example, was influenced in a fundamental way by his reading of Samuel–Kings; and these books also played an important part in the formation of political theory, particularly as it related to the rights and duties of kingship,* throughout this period and after it (e.g. Hobbes, *Leviathan*, 2.20 and 3.42; Locke, *First Treatise of Government*, 159–162). Indeed, the influence of Kings (especially I Kings 1) upon the ideology* and language of English, and later United Kingdom, coronation ritual, particularly with regard to the anointing of the ruler, is as evident in the 1953 coronation service for Elizabeth II as it is in the first such service (in AD 973) for Edgar.

Modern interpreters of Kings, while not uninterested in questions about the history of Israel or the later significance of the books, have in general emphasized that it is only when we have attempted to understand the biblical books in their historical context that questions of the relationship between text and history, text and present readership may properly be addressed. More interest has therefore been shown in questions of authorship* and original audience. There has, however, been much diversity of opinion about these matters. Among scholars who have argued that the initial stage in the composition of Kings was pre-deuteronomistic, some (so Budde and Eissfeldt) have held that Kings originally came into being as the concluding part of a great history constructed out of the pentateuchal* sources. The tone of this work was generally regarded as positive, its various parts exuding national optimism and confidence in God's favour upon Israel, albeit tempered with an element of prophetic warning. A quite different view was taken by Jepsen, who considered the first edition of Kings to be part of a priestly cult-history of Israel which was designed to explain within a theological framework the disaster which had befallen Israel, and to encourage its readers to return to God and the temple. More recently, Campbell has suggested that an early 'Prophetic Record', a history of the monarchy from its inauguration to the reign of Jehu, underlies I Samuel 1–II Kings 10.

Among the majority of scholars, who have thought that the books of Kings were from the first a deuteronomistic composition, a similar diversity of opinion exists, which is connected in part with the different analyses offered of the likely date and extent of the first stage of the deuteronomistic history.* Among those who have argued that the first deuteronomistic edition of Kings was composed in pre-exilic times, a wide range of dates has been suggested, Lemaire offering the earliest (around 850 BC) and Clements the latest (during the reign of Zedekiah). Most, however, have accepted a date during or shortly after Josiah's reign. Some have argued for the originally independent composition of Kings (Lohfink, Weippert), although the more generally held view has been that the books were always part of a more extensive deuteronomistic history, whether this covered the whole period from the settlement in the land to the late monarchy (Cross and the majority) or simply the period of the monarchy (Provan).

Interpretation of the purpose of the preexilic Kings naturally depends for its details upon the view taken on such matters, but three broad emphases may be noted in recent publications. Some have laid stress mainly on the likely political function of the books in providing justification for the policies of a reigning monarch; others have emphasized the wider religious significance of the books in terms of an appeal to the people of Israel to repent; while still another view is that the chief use of such material would have been in the education of royal functionaries. What is agreed by most is that the books' message was an optimistic and hopeful one, in contrast to the message of the exilic revision, which is generally held to be one of unrelieved gloom.

This brings us to the view of Noth, that Kings was from the beginning part of an exilic and fundamentally pessimistic work designed simply to tell the story of Israel's downfall. In this opinion he has been followed by many others, although a popular recent view (Dietrich) has been that the books were later transformed by the addition of further redactional* material. To the original history was first joined most of the prophetic material now found in Kings, and then material which stressed the importance of keeping the deuteronomic Law. At this third stage a future hope for Israel, if she is obedient, is clearly envisaged. Others who have held that Kings is an exilic work have argued, however, that such hope was not lacking even in the original edition. Wolff, for example, has contended that in the deuteronomistic history as a whole there is a pattern of repentance and forgiveness which suggests that the author still held out hope for a restoration of God's blessing. Von Rad's view was that there is an unresolved tension between judgment and hope in Kings, and some (such as Childs) follow him in interpreting the latter, at least in part, as messianic hope based on the promise to the house of David of an everlasting dynasty.

See also **Deuteronomistic History; Kingship.**

J. Barton, *Oracles of God: Perceptions of Ancient Prophecy in Israel after the Exile*, 1986; B. S. Childs, *Introduction to the Old Testament as Scripture*, 1979, pp. 281–301; J. McClure, 'Bede's Old Testament Kings' in P. Wormald (ed.), *Ideal and Reality in Frankish and Anglo-Saxon Society,* 1983; J. F. McCurdy, 'Bible Exegesis' in I. Singer (ed.), *The Jewish Encyclopedia*, 1902, vol. 3, pp. 162–78; I. W. Provan, *Hezekiah and the Books of Kings*, BZAW 172, 1988, esp. pp. 1–31; E. C. Ratcliffe, *The Coronation Service of Her Majesty Queen Elizabeth II*, 1953, esp. pp. 1–33, 42–5.

IAIN W. PROVAN

Kingship

1. *The world context of biblical kingship.* Kingship sprang to life in twentieth-century research through new understanding of its importance in Ancient Near Eastern* and other traditional societies. A large part of archaeological* discoveries relates to royal institutions, while study of traditional societies often shows their religion and social life cohering in a system of kingship.

In this context of growing knowledge, scholars began to recognize new facets in the many biblical texts relevant to kingship. But the subject soon appeared quite divisive. At one extreme some were over-hasty in explaining biblical texts through supposed foreign parallels, without due regard to the differences in context or indeed to the problems of understanding the foreign parallels in themselves. At the other extreme some have so disparaged studies in royal ideology* as to betray prejudices born of a modern democratic or theological heritage. It is not easy for those nurtured in today's secular societies to enter sympathetically into the mystical world-view of kingship systems, which in various ways express a community of heaven, people and nature.

Well-established features of kingship outside the Bible include the following: 1. Kingship belongs primarily to heaven. 'King' may be first and foremost the title of a ruling deity, such as the Babylonian creator-god Marduk or the Canaanite El and Baal. Kingship is then given to earth as an extension of the divine order. The human ruler is appointed by the god to be mediator of this single order. Thus he faces subjects and enemies in power, but his god he faces in humble dependence. 2. His mediation of healthful order to nature and society is bound up with his care for the weak. He is often compared to a shepherd cherishing his flock, he is mother and father to his people, defender of widow and orphan. This is royal righteousness, by which alone society and nature can thrive. 3. The great royal ceremonies (enthronement, anniversaries, jubilees) express the derivation of kingship from heaven; they are sacraments whereby the divine relationship is effected, and they naturally form part of the great liturgical events. In Babylon, for example, the king was renewed in office in the preliminary part of the new year festival; there was humiliation and reinstatement – as one text has it, 'The king is removed, the king is established.' In Egypt* enthronement and its renewals were enacted in the ceremonies for the beginning of winter, and here linked to the renewal of cosmic order.

2. *The shape of the subject in the* OT. Important periods preceded and followed the four royal centuries. Only after many generations of clan and tribal life came the first king of all Israel, Saul, about 1020 BC. After his death in battle, his family was supplanted by David.* It was David who took over the Canaanite city of Jerusalem* and some of its royal tradi-

tion. His dynasty lasted till the Babylonian conquest in 586 BC. But only his son Solomon had continued his reign over a great empire and a united people. After Solomon's death in 922 BC the tribes north of Jerusalem had been ruled by other dynasties until the Assyrian conquest in 721 BC. After the monarchy, governors and high priests ruled under the kings of the great foreign empires.

Some scholars have argued that it was only during the monarchy that Israel began to refer to God as 'king' (e.g. Isa. 6.1–5). Earlier allusions to the conception are indeed few and uncertain in date, but one could point to Deut. 33.5, Num. 23.21, and imagery associated with the ark at Shiloh (I Sam. 4.4). The likelihood is that in the tribal period Israel used some monarchical imagery for God and knew of Canaanite 'king' deities. But with Israel's own adoption of kingship, the acquisition of Jerusalem and the building of the temple, a particular complex of ideas about God as king now came into prominence – the Lord as king and creator, high above heavenly beings, the cosmic ocean and all creatures, yet also exercising his reign from his temple on Mount Zion and through the king he installed there.

The beginnings of the monarchy are chronicled with remarkable ambivalence. The compilers of Judges see the previous absence of a king as the cause of unrestrained wickedness (Judg. 17.6 etc.). But in I Sam. 8–12 the view oscillates. Samuel is displeased at the prospect and foretells tyranny; the Lord's own kingship is being rejected (8.6f; 10.17ff; 12.12). But other narratives simply see the institution as the saving act of the Lord mediated through a willing Samuel (9.1–10.16; 11). Scholars have debated whether the unfavourable accounts represent the natural hostility of conservative tribesmen to a drastic change of social order, or whether they express the views of much later times when the royal states had suffered catastrophes that needed explanation. Perhaps both early and late views contribute here. But in any case the stories in the end show that the Lord anoints his chosen king and empowers him by gifts of his spirit.

The final editors of the books of Kings are certainly influenced by the sad end of the royal states. The majority of kings are said to have displeased the Lord, especially in cultic practice (e.g. II Kings 21.11f.; 23.26f.). It is notable, however, that the people's life is still seen to centre on the kings and depend on their righteousness. And the last recorded episode (II Kings 25.27–30) is a hopeful turn which keeps alive the great destiny of David's line pronounced in II Samuel 7.

Some scholars present the prophets as hostile to the monarchy. Hosea (3.3f.; 8.4; 13.11) and Amos (7.9) are shown in conflict with the northern dynasties, Isaiah speaks bluntly to 'the house of David' (7.13), Jeremiah writes off King Jehoiakim and his descendants (22.13f., 30). Second Isaiah is taken to dissolve the ideal of Davidic kingship into a general vocation of all the people (Isa. 55.3–5). This last passage, however, can otherwise be taken to promise the people the blessing of the Davidic hope fulfilled, and none of the other passages amount to a rejection of the Davidic kingship as such. Most of the prophetic books, on the contrary, contain positive statements about it and God's intention to fulfil its destiny beyond the disasters.

Views of kingship as from God are reflected also in Lamentations (4.20), Deuteronomy (17.14–20, rather guarded), and Proverbs (8.15f.; 16.10f. etc.). But the richest source for the ideals of kingship is undoubtedly the psalms. It is the psalms above all which present God as king. In addition to general hymns (e.g. 145), laments (5; 9–10; 74), and Zion songs (48; 84), there are hymns which are wholly dominated by a manifestation of Yahweh as king, as though he has ascended in victory and salvation to commence his reign (47; 93; 97; 99; cf. 29; 95; 96; 98). These pieces (often called 'enthronement psalms') were thrown into prominence by H. Gunkel's great work of psalm classification early this century. He took them to refer to the future and final triumph of God's kingdom, anticipatory songs drawing on the prophets (cf. Isa. 26.1; 42.10f.).

Another interpretation was proposed by S. Mowinckel in a series of *Psalmenstudien* in the 1920s (*see* **Scandinavian Old Testament Scholarship**). He saw them as reflecting the heart of traditional festal celebration, actualizing the primaeval victory over chaos (*see* **Creation Narratives**). All was again made new, and the cry went up, 'Yahweh has become king!' Mowinckel filled out his account of this celebration of God's kingship from other appropriate texts, such as those depicting God's festal procession (24; 68; 132).

Of scholars who did not follow Mowinckel's lead, some maintained the old view that the 'enthronement psalms' depend on Second Iasiah and celebrate events like the return from the Exile. Others came to accept that the proclamation of Yahweh's kingship at Zion's chief festival dates from the early monarchy, but they stopped short of Mowinckel's understanding of the liturgy. Some have stressed the differences within these psalms and so separated them in function and in date. Thus Jeremias takes 93, 97 and 99 as plain homage to the Lord ever king (proclaiming, 'It is Yahweh who is king'); in 47, 95, 96, 98 he acknowledges liturgical re-living, but of historical events.

Gunkel's classification also highlighted nine psalms and parts of two others as connected with ceremonies of the Davidic kings. It came to seem likely that most of these psalms also had a place in the festal celebration of God's kingship. A. R. Johnson's interpretation of such texts was especially striking, with its proposal of a scene of humiliation in the rites showing God's appointment and exaltation of his anointed. The liturgy amounted to a challenging vision of what God would do when the perfect response was given by a son of David.

Breaking over Gunkel's boundaries, some scholars have taken a large number of other psalms featuring a single worshipper to be utterances of the king (e.g. 3, 22, 23, 28, 40, 61, 63, 118, 138). On this basis they bring still more colour and detail to the portrait of the Anointed before his God.

3. *The heart of the subject: the festal revelation.* Amidst many such differences of interpretation, it is reasonably clear that the meaning of OT kingship was expressed above all in the chief festival at Jerusalem during the monarchy. In a series of holy days that were the antecedents of the later days of New Year, Atonement and Tabernacles (1, 10, 15–22 of the autumn month Tishri), the community knew an encounter with God which meant a world made new and gifts of life. In drama and symbol* God was praised as victorious king and creator, master of the rain-sources, supreme in heaven and earth. The encounter centred at Zion, the holy city and temple of Jerusalem. Here was a sacramental form of God's heavenly palace, a manifestation of his throne and presence, a centre from which his healthful rule shone out to all peoples, and to which they all should direct hymns of rejoicing. With the joy came also challenge to be wholly his in trust and obedience. To praise this king of all life was to side with him, replenished and committed.

Within this celebration of God's kingship the vocation of the Davidic ruler was treated. It is widely accepted that in this festal setting he received his first full enthronement and then in subsequent years some form of confirmation or renewal. A series of liturgical episodes showed his being chosen, anointed and granted grace to serve the cause of God's kingdom. Whether or not some symbolic humiliation was involved (after Pss. 18, 101, 118, 144, etc.), the total dependence of the Davidic ruler on God's grace was made clear. The Lord, creator and king of all, invites his chosen one to sit beside him on Mount Zion, a 'priest for ever' and victor over evil. Through him God sends out justice, care and health to nature and society. It is God's laws that he must uphold. He witnesses to the world and preaches of God's sovereignty and faithfulness. To God he turns with all the burdens of his people and prays with peculiar intimacy and acceptance – 'My father, my God and rock of my salvation' etc. Such is the Psalter's ideal of the Davidic ruler – the Lord's Anointed, Chosen, Servant and Son.

4. *Kingship after the monarchy: hope and eschatology.* With the clarification of the royal theology in modern research came the need to re-examine its relation to later Jewish and Christian ideas of God's kingdom in a final age. The way in which the ideas developed from the monarchy through the post-exilic period has been traced in several major studies (Mowinckel, Coppens, Gray, etc.).

In Isaiah 40–55, there is an especially powerful use of royal theology to depict the imminent end of the exile. God is to make procession again into Zion amid the gospel tidings that he is 'become king' (52.7). He will be manifest again as the unique supreme creator, lord of all happenings, shepherd, loving provider. In some way (much disputed) and within this sweep of re-applied kingship themes, the old role of the Davidic son and servant is taken up in the dramatic presentation of a righteous suffering servant.*

Some thirty years later, the prophet Haggai is urging on the restoration of God's royal residence in Jerusalem. He foresees the imminent overthrow of rival kingships and the exaltation of a Davidic heir as the Lord's servant who mediates his supreme authority (Hag. 2.20f.). Promises for the restoration of the dynasty occur widely in other prophetic collections – Isaiah, Jeremiah, Ezekiel, Hosea, Amos, Micah, Zechariah. These bright portraits of a future king represent the old royal ideals projected into the future.

Along with this hope, and generally more pervasive, continues the portrayal of God as king. With the development of apocalyptic* thought, especially from the second century BC, the dynamic aspect of his kingship (his 'becoming king', manifest in new triumph) is linked to the predestined inauguration of a final age, which is to succeed the ages when kingship was allowed to a series of oppressive powers. Whatever is intended by the 'one like a son of man'* in Dan. 7, there is no clear indication here of a Davidic role. Indeed, in a number of other late texts referring to the end-time, the Davidic hope is either unexpressed or overshadowed by the expectation of a figure from the priestly tribe of Levi. It was not extinguished, however. It appears strongly in the Psalms of Solomon, for example, and has a key role in the NT. Thus, six centuries after the removal of the Davidic dynasty, the vision which it kindled blazes afresh, a vision of God's perfected kingship, shining into the world through the service of his Anointed.

See also **David; Deuteronomistic History; Messiah; Psalms**.

_____

J. Coppens, *La relève apocalyptique du messianisme royal: I La royauté*, 1979; J. H. Eaton, *Kingship and the Psalms*, ²1986; J. Gray, *The Biblical Doctrine of the Reign of God*, 1979; Jörg Jeremias, *Das Königtum Gottes in den Psalmen*, 1987; A. R. Johnson, *Sacral Kingship in Ancient Israel*, 1967; S. Mowinckel, *He That Cometh*, 1959.

JOHN EATON

Lamentations

Until relatively recent times, Lamentations has been regarded by most of its interpreters as a prophetic* book. Indeed, it has been understood as the work of that particularly well-known prophet, Jeremiah – a tradition which has very old roots and is reflected throughout the early literature (cf. the Septuagint* of Lam. 1.1, and the Babylonian Talmud,* *Baba Bathra* 15a). That is not to say that there has been no interest in understanding the book in its original historical context. We know of two different historical interpretations of the book dating from the earliest times – that it was Jeremiah's lament over Josiah after his death at Megiddo (II Chron. 35.25, possibly, and the Targum to Lam. 1.18 and 4.20 – a verse interpreted in the same way by Jerome and some mediaeval commentators); and that it was his lament over the destruction of Jerusalem* in the time of Zedekiah (the LXX and other parts of Targum* Lamentations).

For most interpreters, however, Lamentations was much more than simply a lament over past events. Early and mediaeval Christian writers found much in the book which referred to Christ and the church. We may note, among many instances, the possible allusion to Lam. 3.30 in Matt. 5.39, and Clement of Alexandria's use of Lam. 1.1–2, 8 in *Paidagogos* 1.9. Particular interest was shown in Lam. 4.20, with its reference to 'the Lord's anointed' (translated *Christos Kurios* or *Christos Kuriou* in the LXX). This verse appears, for example, in Clement of Alexandria's *Extracts from the Writings of Theodotus* (18.2) as part of the proof that Christ was seen in his descent from heaven by the righteous in paradise; in Tertullian's* *Against Marcion* (3.6) as evidence that Christ spoke in the prophets; in Justin Martyr's *First Apology* (72) as part of the evidence that the cross is a fundamental aspect of human experience; in Irenaeus'* *Demonstration of the Apostolic Preaching* (71) as a prophecy of Christ's suffering; and in the *Apostolic Constitutions* (5.20) in the course of a discussion of the different ways in which the

whole OT speaks of Christ. The link with the Passion in particular became firmly established in the succeeding centuries owing to the use of Lamentations in the *Tenebrae*, the Matins–Lauds services for the last three days of Holy Week. Jerusalem, made desolate by her foes, is variously understood here as the type of the sinful soul, or of the church disfigured by sin, or of the suffering Saviour who took upon himself the sins of the world.

Jewish interpreters, too, regarded Lamentations as pointing beyond its own time. The Targum to Lam. 1.19, for example, sees it as prophesying the destruction of Jerusalem in AD 70. *Lamentations Rabbati*, a rabbinic* midrash* of the fifth to the seventh centuries, understands the book as setting forth the eternal paradigm of Jewish suffering. Jeremiah had prophesied in detail of the various troubles which had fallen upon the Jewish people from his time to that of the reader. A particularly striking consequence of the fact that Lamentations is regarded as prophetic is that it can at the same time be interpreted by the authors of this commentary as God's lament over the suffering which he has inflicted upon his people. The book thus becomes a source of consolation to the reader, since God is viewed as suffering with his people. This attempt to find a more positive message in the book is paralleled, indeed, in other texts from the earlier period of interpretation, and is reflected too in the Jewish liturgical practice of repeating the penultimate verse of the book at the end of its reading so as to close with hope rather than doubt (*Masseket Soferim* 14.2).

Although in the modern period Lamentations is still interpreted by many outside the academic world as 'the words of Jeremiah' (cf. the use of texts from the book by Leonard Bernstein in his 'Jeremiah' Symphony of 1942), and this position has been defended by a few scholars, most have regarded Jeremian authorship as unlikely. There is general agreement that the various chapters, whenever they were combined into one book, do indeed date from Jeremiah's time and are best understood as responses to the specific circumstances surrounding the fall of Jerusalem in 587 BC. There is disagreement, however, as to why they were composed. Brunet and Buccellati have both argued that much of the book is polemical, being directed against the 'pro-Babylonian' party associated with Jeremiah and Gedaliah. Others regard it as theological reflection on the tragedy, while disagreeing as to its theological thrust. Is the tension which Lamentations seeks to resolve that between historical reality and the Deuteronomic faith in a doctrine of retribution and reward (Gottwald) or that between historical reality and

Zion traditions (Albrektson)? Still others (Moore) deny that the author or editor was 'doing' theology at all: his pre-eminent concern was simply to portray the horrifying scope of human suffering during the events of 587, giving artistic expression to his emotions and thereby enabling the nation to grieve. Gwaltney, in fact, suggests that Lamentations was produced for liturgical use at the temple site while the site was being cleared in preparatton for reconstruction. Finally, it has been noted (Cohen) that the connection between text and specific historical event has already been obscured in Lamentations: it contains no chronological data nor any explicit references to the kings of Judah, to Nebuchadnezzar or to Babylon. Perhaps the author himself, like the later rabbis, interpreted the events of 587 paradigmatically, confronting catastrophe as an absolute and lamenting all disasters inflicted by heaven upon a sinful humanity. In all this modern debate, the question of the extent to which Lamentations offers any hope to the reader remains unresolved. Is consolation implicitly present, or does lamentation, in the words of Mintz, express only 'man's struggle to speak in the face of God's silence'?

See also **Jeremiah**.

S. J. D. Cohen, 'The Destruction: From Scripture to Midrash' in *Prooftexts* 2 1982, pp. 18–39; W. C. Gwaltney Jr, 'The Biblical Book of Lamentations in the Context of Near Eastern Lament Literature' in W. W. Hallo, J. C. Moyer and L. G. Perdue (eds), *Scripture in Context II: More Essays on the Comparative Method*, 1983; D. R. Hillers, *Lamentations*, 1972; E. Levine, *The Aramaic Version of Lamentations*, 1976; A. Mintz, 'The Rhetoric of Lamentations and the Representation of Catastrophe' in *Prooftexts* 2, 1982, pp. 1–17; M. S. Moore, 'Human Suffering in Lamentations' in *Revue Biblique* 90, 1983, pp. 534–55.

IAIN W. PROVAN

Law

The process of interpretation of law commences within the Bible itself, even before texts have received a canonized form. The law of the liberation of slaves is applied in the narrative of King Zedekiah (Jer. 34), but in a form of words quite different from (though materially virtually identical to) those used in Ex. 21.2. The law of homicide is also found in a number of versions (Ex. 21.12–14; Deut. 19.4–13; Num. 35.9–34), of which Deuteronomy (at least) is commonly regarded as a reinterpretation (by re-formulation) of the earlier text. The phenomenon of inner biblical exegesis* in the legal context has been closely examined recently by Fishbane.

On a larger level, the laws contained within Deuteronomy are presented as part of a valedictory speech by Moses,* before his death prior to the entry of the Israelites in to the promised land. It is described as *mishneh torah* (Deut. 17.18; cf. Josh. 8.32) – a phrase inadequately translated as a 'copy' of the law (since it is clearly not a literal copy of the earlier Sinaitic revelation) or even as a 'repetition' (if that term implies verbal identity). The literary function of the book of Deuteronomy is, in fact, to provide validation ('recognition', in the semiotic* sense), of the lawgiving at Sinai. Such validation is provided by a process of thematic repetition. That form of literary relationship is different from our normal understanding of 'text' and 'interpretation'.

When the biblical text became canonized, 'interpretation' came to play a central role in the development of the tradition. The earliest clear indication of this process is to be found in the account of the reading of the Law under Ezra (Neh. 8). It should not, however, be assumed that the immediate object of 'interpretation' was application of the laws of the Torah by judges in courts. Interpretation appears to have had, at first, a primarily didactic function. Moreover, the Ezra narrative indicates two distinct processes of teaching, one intended for the people as a whole (8.1–9), the other (8.13ff.) for a more select group. The distinction between popular wisdom* and literary (court) wisdom appears to have been applied to the texts of biblical law from the period of their earliest interpretation. Both in ancient Israel and elsewhere, it is common to find a process of transformation of didactic writing into 'binding' legal text (Jackson, *Am. J. Compar. Law*, 1975).

Before this process came to fruition, the 'application' of law was conceived quite separately from its didactic, or doctrinal function. Application was in the hands of authoritative figures, including kings* and prophets.* They had authority, so it seems, not merely to adjudicate in the light of biblical legal principles (e.g. the prophet Nathan, using Ex. 22.3 as a parable in II Sam. 12), but also to suspend the law as being inappropriate for the needs of the situation in hand (e.g. Elijah in relation to sacrifice on Mount Carmel: I Kings 18.31ff.; cf. *Talmud Yebamoth* 90b; Jackson, 1981). To call that kind of judgment 'interpretation' is to presuppose a status for the legal text which it did not, as yet, possess.

This complex of traditional practices – validation by thematic repetition, verbal interpretation, didactic reformulation, and decision-making loosely guided by legal principles – continued into the Second Temple and early rabbinic periods. The Septuagint* translation of *torah* by *nomos* is sometimes credited with the conversion of Judaism into a legalistic religion, but this may well have done little more than provide a particular form of expression for this same complex of internal practices. The writing of the Aramaic Bible translations (*Targumim**), which closely reflect rabbinic interpretation of the first two centuries, may have been prompted primarily for linguistic reasons, but the practice of verbal interpretation of the biblical legal texts undoubtedly received an impetus thereby.

The literature discovered at Qumran (*see* **Dead Sea Scrolls**) is itself multi-faceted in this respect. On the one hand, the *pesher** form overtly offers a verbal commentary upon canonized biblical texts, but thus far this form is not found in relation to the legal collections of the Pentateuch.* As regards the latter, the practice revealed at Qumran is much closer to Deuteronomy – the reformulation of rules which are taken to repeat the original teachings, albeit in a new form. This reformulation has a sectarian dimension, in the sense that the newly-authorized form is taken to be the particular possession, and obligation, of those who have achieved initiation into the sect. Though direct evidence is lacking, the Qumran community (or communities) was probably not the only such group to have formulated its own rules in this spirit. The Pharisees* may well have had their own such documents, which modern research identifies particularly with the themes of purity and table-fellowship (Neusner, 1971). Some scholars stress the substantive links between the Qumran literature and rabbinic legal exegesis (Schiffman).

The literary connection between the Qumran Rule and the biblical legal collections is perhaps looser than that between Deuteronomy and the 'Book of the Covenant' (Ex. 21–23). Nevertheless, the Qumran texts exhibit strong linguistic and stylistic connections with parts of biblical law, especially some of the so-called priestly sections. The Temple Scroll, in its content, goes beyond the genre* here under discussion. Like the 'Oral Law' of rabbinic tradition, it addresses questions outside the agenda of the biblical legal texts (here, the post-conquest building of the Temple), but nevertheless makes its claim to divine authorship* by having God speak directly in the first person.

Little direct evidence remains of the activity of legal decision-making at Qumran, but some texts associate the Teacher of Righteousness with the biblical figure of the 'prophet like Moses' (Deut. 18.15) and the rule books include provisions concerning evidence which may well indicate a real adjudicatory practice.

The same range of approaches to tradition is encountered in the N T. The antitheses of the Sermon on the Mount* ('You have heard it said ... but I say unto you': see Daube's discussion) evidence the practice of verbal interpretation, but the context is still – very clearly – didactic. At the same time, sectarian rules develop early in the church, as evidenced in some of the Pauline* letters; and decision-making, as reflected in some of the Jesus narratives, is dependent upon the biblical suspensory powers of the 'prophet like Moses' (Jackson, 1981).

With some of the Hellenistic* literature, we can at last identify the motivations of individual authors, a characteristic which it is difficult to ascribe to either the texts of biblical law or the major body of rabbinic legal tradition. Philo,* for example, addresses a Hellenistic philosophical audience. He is most interested in the underlying rationale, and philosophical premises, of the rules of biblical law, rather than the particularities of interpretation (*De specialibus Legibus*). Though he shares elements of his interpretation of specific rules with rabbinic tradition (S. Belkin, *Philo and the Oral Law*, 1940), the overall object and direction of his interpretation is fundamentally different. This is not to say that rabbinic law is concerned merely with particularities, and not with wider philosophical issues. But the mode of philosophical discourse for Philo is that of explicit argument; those of early rabbinics are predominantly formal – notably the choice of material and its literary arrangement, as shown in many of the recent works of Neusner. The view has been expressed that Philo's presentation of biblical law provides evidence of the practice of Jewish courts in Hellenistic Egypt (E. R. Goodenough, *The Jurisprudence of the Jewish Courts in Egypt*, 1929), but this view has not found widespread acceptance.

Goodenough's suggestion does, however, direct our attention to an important question. Jewish courts did function in the Second Temple period, under both Jewish and non-Jewish political sovereignty. What law did they apply? Our clearest evidence, perhaps, comes from the Jewish military settlement at Elephantine in Egypt, at the very beginning of the period. There, we find versions of some rules of biblical law, assimilated with local (non-Jewish) terminology and practice (Yaron). It is not unlikely that such Jewish courts as may have functioned in Egypt in Philo's day would have adopted a similar practice. Such questions equally have to be posed for Palestine, both in the period of Jewish autonomy under the Hasmoneans and later under the Romans.

Some scholars take the view that elements of Mishnaic law (*see* **Talmud**) originated in legal practice under the Hasmoneans (Falk). But the methodological difficulties involved in making such claims prompt scholarly caution.

As regards the Roman period, new evidence will shortly be forthcoming from the archive of Babatha. Interesting light has already been cast upon contemporary practices of marriage and matrimonial property.

A recent study claims that 'in the post-exilic period the entire theological thinking became sapiential' (Schnabel, 1985, p. 5), in that all the different Jewish schools claimed to possess wisdom. This finds its most direct expression in the identification of *torah* with wisdom in Ecclesiasticus (Ben Sira), the work of a priestly scribe in the first quarter of the second century BC. Most likely, it is this same identification which lies behind the place assigned to *logos* * in the opening verses of the Gospel of John.

In rabbinic literature, this correlation of law and wisdom appears most clearly in the fact of the inclusion in the Mishnah of the chapter 'Ethics of the Fathers' (*Pirke Avot*), which contains ethical aphorisms and guidance as to daily conduct. The tractate commences with the classical account of the 'chain of tradition', wherein Moses received *torah* from God, and handed it on to Joshua, Joshua to the elders, etc. We do not have to say, in this context, that the rabbis reinterpreted *torah* as 'wisdom'; it is sufficient to note that for them *torah* contained connotations of wisdom sufficiently strong to make its use in this context unproblematic. But *Avot* is only one small part of the Mishnah. In one sense, the whole of the Mishnah does represent a 'wisdom' conception of *torah*. Though neither the content nor the form of rabbinic literature bears close comparison with 'wisdom' in the OT, the principal function of the Mishnah and its associated literature was originally conceived to be didactic. Only later, recapitulating and reaffirming (if not indeed constituting) the same process in relation to the biblical text, did the Mishnah come to be regarded as a set of binding rules.

Modern research has addressed itself to the development of those rabbinic institutions which made this process possible. After the destruction of Jewish political autonomy in AD 70, the Jewish leadership regrouped around rabbinic scholarly academies, first at Yavne (Jamnia), later at Usha. Any hope of a revival of political autonomy was crushed with the defeat of the Bar Kochba revolt. But the loss of political autonomy did not necessarily entail the destruction of all indigenous legal jurisdiction. Some local (communal, non-rabbinic) Jewish jurisdictions appear to have survived (M. Goodman, *State and Society in Roman Galilee*, 1983). By the end of the second century, however, internal political authority was finding its way into rabbinic hands, in the person of the Patriarch, and eventually (some put it no earlier than the fourth century) this led to the establishment of rabbinic courts, which applied the now-authorized rabbinic interpretation of *torah* as law.

Early rabbinic writings come in two principal literary forms: Mishnah is a free-standing reformulation and restatement of the law (the terminological link with the Bible's own name for Deuteronomy is hardly accidental); and midrash,* which takes the form of a running commentary on the text of the Bible. In the so-called 'halakhic midrashim', originating in the late second or early third century, we have for the first time a systematic verbal commentary upon the texts of biblical law. The rabbinic commentaries are much concerned to show that the texts of biblical law meet the standards to be expected of a divine draftsman, in their consistency and lack of superfluity. But the demonstration of that standard – even in respect of 'legal' texts – is not necessarily for the purpose of application in court. It represents an indirect validation of the authority of the rabbis themselves. For the claim is now made that rabbinic literature embodies a contemporaneous revelation by God to Moses on Sinai, the 'oral' law. This incorporates both Mishnah and midrash. A rabbinic capacity to demonstrate the divinity of the draftsmanship of the written law through midrash may well have been thought necessary to validate rabbinic authority to promulgate new Mishnah.

The content of the Mishnah, and of its supplement, the Tosefta, encompasses all aspects of daily life: agriculture, the festivals, domestic relations, civil law, personal purity – and even the sacrificial system, notwithstanding the destruction of the Temple (Safrai, 1987). This has prompted modern scholars to a variety of interpretations. For some, the presence of rules concerning the Temple indicates that the material (if not the present document in which it appears) originated before AD 70. But it is far from certain that the sacrificial law even claims to describe the practice of the Second Temple. The law of the Mishnah has been persuasively argued to represent a vision of restoration of *first* Temple institutions. That was the form which the eschatological vision of the rabbis took. The discovery of the Temple Scroll perhaps adds weight to this interpretation, since it indicates that this vision of a restored temple existed even in the Second Temple period itself – clear confirmation of the existence of a view that contemporary institutions had become degraded, and were in need of renewal. Not inconsistent with such ideas is Neusner's claim (1981) that the rabbis deliberately created for themselves and their circles a fictional world in which the *halakhah* could continue to exist, excluding all consideration of the political and human tragedies which had so recently torn the Jewish world apart.

A tradition which appears to date from the tannaitic period, and is found at the beginning of the midrash *Sifra* to Leviticus, lists a set of thirteen principles of verbal interpretation of the written law. Smaller selections of these hermeneutic* rules are also ascribed in rabbinic tradition to leading teachers such as Hillel and R. Akiba (L. Jacobs, 'Hermeneutics', *Enc. Jud.,* viii.366–72). The very fact that we find such a systematic collection of rules of interpretation is striking: Roman Law had not yet achieved this form of systematic elaboration. Some of the principles resemble canons of interpretation found in modern systems of law (such as the *eiusdem generis* rule). But this image of scientific interpretation is (then, as now) illusory. Relatively few of these thirteen principles are regularly employed in practice in rabbinic exegesis,* nor are they capable of resolving all possible doubts as to the meaning of the authoritative text. What they attest is the strength of the rabbinic belief in the exceptional character, deriving from divine authorship, of the language of the biblical text.

Rabbinic exegesis also adopts some substantive principles of interpretation, often taken from the biblical text itself (e.g. 'You shall be holy', Lev. 19.2). Interestingly, however, the Decalogue does not appear to have played a privileged part in the interpretative process. One might contrast with this the approach of Philo, who treated the provisions of the Decalogue as categories within which to discuss the detailed provisions of biblical law which follow the Decalogue in the biblical text. But Philo sees the Decalogue as providing 'headings', *kephalaia*, which are not necessarily to be interpreted (despite Philo's attempt to relate biblical law to Greek philosophical tradition) as underlying principles. It is the modern search to ascribe our own forms of rationality to the Bible and early post-biblical literature, which leads us to look for abstract principles, and in their absence to categorize detailed prescriptions as 'casuistry' (Jackson, 1979).

In a sense, all interpretation is apologetic. It is designed to defend a position, by recourse to an earlier text. The particular position to be defended is sometimes quite clear – not least, when we know the audience for whose benefit the interpretation was produced. That is the case, for example, in the account of biblical law provided by Josephus,* designed for his Roman patrons, and with at least half an eye to similarities with Roman law. Rabbinic interpretation may well have had no less political a purpose. Its technicality and detail marked it as the preserve of a scholarly class, and distinguished that scholarly class as spe-cial not only for its knowledge, but (up to the third century at least) for its observance of this particular body of rules. Rabbinic law, like the rule-books of the Second Temple period, was essentially sectarian in origin. But by the third or fourth century AD, it had become accepted as the heritage, and ultimately the obligation, of the large part of the Jewish people. Yet even then, we should hesitate to ascribe to rabbinic law quite the same status as that of modern legislation. The old tradition of suspension of the law by authoritative decision-makers survived, albeit in an attenuated form, in the occasional practice, related in rabbinic literature sometimes without any apparent disapproval, of rabbinic judges deciding actual cases contrary to rabbinic law.

See also **Jewish Exegesis; Rabbi, Rabbinism.**

D. Daube, *The New Testament and Rabbinic Judaism*, 1956; J. D. M. Derrett, *Law in the New Testament*, 1970; Z. W. Falk, *Introduction to Jewish Law of the Second Commonwealth*, 1972–78; M. Fishbane, *Biblical Interpretation in Ancient Israel*, 1985; B. S. Jackson, 'Legalism', *JJS* 30, 1979, pp. 1–22; id., 'Jésus et Moïse: le statut du prophète à l'égard de la Loi', *Revue historique de droit français* 59, 1981, pp. 341–60; J. Neusner, *The Rabbinic Traditions about the Pharisees before 70,* 3 vols., 1971; id., *Judaism, The Evidence of the Mishnah*, 1981; S. Safrai (ed.), *The Literature of the Sages*, 1987; L. H. Schiffman, *The Halakhah at Qumran*, 1975; E. J. Schnabel, *Law and Wisdom from Ben Sira to Paul*, 1985; R. Yaron, *Introduction to the Law of the Aramaic Papyri*, 1961.

BERNARD S. JACKSON

Lectionary

As the name itself implies, a lectionary is a method of selecting passages of scripture for recitation during public worship. Various ways have been employed down the ages. For example, in the early Middle Ages, it was common practice in both East and West to have special Epistle and Gospel-Books (called Epistolaries and Evangelaries) that contained the readings for the eucharist, and nothing else; whereas in contemporary Anglican worship, the lectionary is strictly no more than a table of passages which may be used in conjunction with a full text of the Bible (though the passages for the eucharist on Sundays etc. are often printed out in service books). The two watersheds of the invention of printing and the advent of literacy have affected the way in which the Bible is handled and appropriated during church services.

Early tradition associates three of the Gospels* with particular places, which gave rise to (or arose from?) their popularity in the old Gospel-sequences of those cities; Matthew is connected with Jerusalem, John with Ephesus, and Mark with Alexandria. In the first three centuries, however, before the liturgical year imposed itself on the selection processes of local churches, there is not a great deal of evidence for detailed ways of reading scripture in the liturgy,* although the liturgical material in the Bible clearly had its effect on the eucharist and daily prayer, as witness the widespread use of the psalter as the backbone of the Office, both in monastic and secular communities. The difference between the two (a difference that persists to this day) is that monks and nuns like to employ the whole psalter, whereas people with less time prefer to be more selective.

Already in the time of the NT, however, the Christian Pasch (Easter) emerges as a significant feast, so that by the beginning of the fourth century, Easter is already beginning to develop its own 'cycle', which imposes selection-criteria on surrounding days. Similarly, the Christmas 'cycle', another fourth-century novelty, begins to reflect scripture passages related to the birth and arrival of the messiah.* Such standardization was part and parcel of the structures of church life from the fourth century.

It is easier to select biblical passages for important occasions than to do so for ordinary Sundays. For example, in the diary of Egeria, the nun from France (or Spain) who visited Jerusalem between 381 and 386 and recorded the elaborate liturgical provisions there, we can see a determination to read those parts of the NT that recount the 'events' of Holy Week in a continuous manner, often at the place associated with the particular occurrence. On the other hand, it is not until a few centuries later that the latter part of the Pentecost season gets its lections for use at Mass in the West.

The tension between reading the Bible in course and reading it selectively has never really disappeared. The liturgy has an innate tendency to resist change in its provision for special occasions, which is why, for instance, the Johannine passion narrative* has for centuries been associated with Good Friday, and that from Matthew's Gospel (until recent revisions) with Palm Sunday. What may be good for the conservative faithful may hamstring a preacher who wants some variety. In the mediaeval nocturns, biblical books were read in large chunks, in continuous fashion, to suit the monastic spirituality of the monks who attended; and when the Anglican Reformers* set about their task, a new but equally exacting scheme was invented that once again provided large amounts of scripture, read in course,

and paying no heed to the much shorter scripture lessons at the other mediaeval monastic Offices.

History also reflects some other tendencies. The Fourth Gospel emerges as the favourite, in East and West, for the eucharist, a fact reflected in the mediaeval, Book of Common Prayer and various modern lectionaries. In the past, too, reading all four passion narratives (Mark and Luke on the weekdays of Holy Week) probably echoes the pre-critical desire to harmonize* the Gospels. The OT at the eucharist began to be a bit of a passenger from the fifth century. Passages were selected either to reflect supposed prophecies of Christ's birth or ministry, or to fulfil typological* concerns (Passover at the Easter Vigil); or even to supply material to meet developing trends such as Marian feasts (e.g. portions of Ecclus. 24 for use as a lection at Mass).

A more significant gap in the story is the inevitable delay that exists between the onward march of biblical scholarship and the work of liturgical revisers when they produce new lectionaries. Today, there are two main lection-schemes in the Western churches, apart from the lingering traditions from the Reformation. On the one hand, the lectionary of the British *Joint Liturgical Group* (1967) takes a 'thematic' approach to the use of scripture all through the liturgical year. This has the advantage of allowing each Sunday to stand on its own; it also purports to express some of the insights of the Biblical Theology* movement; and it appears, with minor adaptations, for example, in the Church of England Alternative Service Book (1980), as well as the Methodist Service Book (1975) and the usage of other churches, an ecumenical achievement in itself. It is a two-year cycle and is made up of OT, Epistle and Gospel passages, reflecting the contemporary recovery of the OT at the eucharist. On the other hand, the Roman Catholic *Ordo Lectionum Missae* (1969) is based on the principle of course-reading, with the Fourth Gospel still prominent, but reading the Synoptics* in a three-year scheme. Epistle passages attempt also to go in continuous sequence, with a (not entirely satisfactory) thematic OT series. This has the advantage of letting NT authors speak for themselves; it broadly reflects some of the insights of redaction criticism,* in a conservative manner; and it appears, with adaptations, in many of the lectionaries of the major Protestant churches (Anglican included) in North America and Australia. Not all modern schemes are coloured by such a neo-patristic pattern, however; the new (1985) Danish Lutheran altar book places the Epistle reading at the end of the eucharist, as an exhortation to the community to live out its Christian faith. It is, perhaps, regrettable that the English-speaking world should have to make a choice between two such different lectionaries. The next round of revisions may well produce an improved version acceptable to both Protestants and Roman Catholics.

Meanwhile, three sensitivities need to be borne in mind. First, the growth of feminist* studies means that the way in which women are treated in the Bible needs to be handled with care. Thus, marriage lections (such as Eph. 5.21–6.4) that went without question until relatively recently cannot be used indiscriminately. On the other hand, at Candlemas, there has been a tendency in the West to eliminate Anna from the Gospel narrative (Luke 2.22–40); she is restored in the 1662 Prayer Book but disappears in the 1980 Alternative Service Book. Secondly, concern with the social roots of the biblical books makes readers of this century view communities like the Israelites in exile, Christians at Corinth, and the persecuted faithful depicted in Revelation in a new light. Their 'story' is not just what was said to/about them, but why what was said to/about them came to be written and what meaning it then carried. Thirdly, Christians are much more aware of their antisemitic* past and that makes some people sensitive about NT passages which may be 'heard' in that sense. Every new lectionary solves some problems, but creates many others.

See also **Liturgy, Use of the Bible in.**

C. P. M. Jones, G. Wainwright, E. J. Yarnold (eds), *The Study of Liturgy*, 1978; M. Vasey, *Reading the Bible in Worship*, 1986.

KENNETH STEVENSON

Lectionary Interpretation (New Testament)

The proposal has been made from time to time that the principle on which the episodes in the Gospels* were arranged lay in the liturgical needs of the various early Christian communities* involved in their composition. These communities wished to use at their eucharists or other meetings for worship stories about Jesus or groups of sayings which embodied his teaching. The Gospels were written to supply their need. This means that the biographical appearance of the Gospels is something of a smoke-screen, a device which conceals their real purpose which was to serve as lectionaries.

This suggestion chimes in well with some of the insights of form criticism.* Thus, it confirms that the Gospels are best seen as collections of short sections, each suitable for use on a particular occasion. It confirms too that usefulness in the early churches was the key to

the survival of traditions about Jesus and to the shape in which they survived. However, it narrows that usefulness down to a single aspect: stories were preserved and in due course incorporated in the narrative of the Gospels because of their liturgical serviceability, rather than, for example, for their use in controversy.

The suggestion has interesting implications to intrigue the historian. It means that when scribes* eventually noted in manuscripts* which they were copying (including some of the earliest) the beginnings and endings of sections to be read on successive Sundays or holy days, they were (doubtless in ignorance) reverting to the purpose for which the sections of the Gospels had originally been assembled. It means too that when the churches came to produce books setting out in sequence the Gospel readings for the Sundays and saints' days of the year, taking them from the various Gospels, they were, in a sense, doing again what the evangelists* had done.

There are two main forms of the proposal. Much the more common is the thesis that the early church functioned along the lines of the synagogue and took over many of its institutions. As a religious body, the church had at the centre of its concerns the making of arrangements for worship, and Judaism provided the obvious model. Thus, the Christians surely adopted the main structure of the Jewish calendar, naturally giving to its holy days and seasons new Christian meanings, and the structure of scriptural readings which accompanied it, providing for them Christian parallels in the form of readings from the Gospels, taken in sequence, like synagogue readings from the Law. Such ideas have been put forward by Philip Carrington (1952), Aileen Guilding (with regard to the Gospel of John, 1960), and Michael Goulder (for Matthew, and including a full theory for the composition of Matthew's Gospel by the application of 'midrashic'* methods to Mark, 1974; and also for Mark and Luke, 1978). The last is the fullest and most thorough exponent of the lectionary approach.

The other form of the proposal is that the church itself was much quicker in arriving at its own commemorative liturgical schemes, involving a need for orderly telling of stories about Jesus, than has been recognized. Étienne Trocmé, who had already embraced the unusual hypothesis that the Marcan passion narrative* was a distinct entity, appended subsequently to the original Gospel (Mark 1–13), has suggested (1983) that the passion derived from very early Holy Week observance by the church in Jerusalem. Christians told the relevant stories as they revisited the sacred sites of the final days of Jesus' life.

Thus, the much later devotion of the Stations of the Cross stumbled inadvertently on the practice which in fact gave rise to the passion narrative, in oral and then written form.

It cannot be said that either form of the proposal has won wide support. Attractive and, in a way, commonsensical as they are, especially in the light of the typological* instincts in the early church, they have been found stronger on hypothesis than on firm evidence. The chief difficulties are these:

1. The meagre evidence available for the liturgical practice of the first century tells against rather than for the idea. Admittedly we know little of the worship of congregations outside the Pauline sphere, and things might have been quite different elsewhere, but Paul* is adamant that his Gentile converts renounce Jewish calendrical* arrangements, along with other aspects of the Law (Gal. 4.9–11). Also, even in the middle of the second century, when more fixed arrangements might be expected, Justin seems to envisage rather informal behaviour with regard to the length of readings from both Gospels and Prophets* (I Apol. 67).

2. There is no clear evidence that anything like fixed and universal lectionary schemes for the reading of the Jewish scriptures were in force by this period. While it is probable that certain scriptures had come to be associated with particular times of the year (e.g. Esther with the feast of Purim, and Exodus with Passover), it is far from certain that such associations extended to the provision of either Torah or prophetic readings on the annual or triennial cycles which have been put forward.

3. Recent study of the social* character of the early Christian communities has suggested that, at least as far as Graeco-Roman cities are concerned, their identity may not have been formed by the analogy of the synagogue. Again, whatever may have been true elsewhere in places for which we lack evidence, in cities like Corinth the church approximated to models partly dependent on the Graeco-Roman household and partly on the 'clubs' (*collegia*), then so prevalent as foci of social life. The self-perception of the eschatological* communities of early Christianity may have had little in common with the sober, instructional ethos of synagogue life.

4. The development of redaction criticism,* with its disclosure of pervasive theological themes and patterns in the Gospels, has made it more difficult to see precisely what the evangelists had in mind, if lectionary provision was their primary consideration. While form criticism made the lectionary thesis by no means impossible, in that it presupposed no strong overall theological plan or purpose, the more recent development (and literary criticism* has strengthened the point) has made it problematic. If the evangelist's main aim was to provide a set of readings, designed to be heard at chiefly weekly intervals, what interest can he have had in constructing patterns of cross-references, recurring words and themes, balancing features in different parts of the narrative, and the like, all requiring consecutive reading for their appreciation? While the biographical structure in itself is understandable, and indeed is required by a scheme of reading in sections designed to culminate at Easter, the same cannot be said of the intense detail of structural* features which many critics have discerned. Here we face a conflict of methods, and the method which relies simply on what the text presents is preferable as being less hypothetical.

5. More subjectively, those scrutinizing the parallels of theme and meaning between a given Gospel passage and the readings from Law and Prophets which it is required to match at its place in the alleged lectionary sequence have sometimes found that the 'fit' is less than fully convincing. Yet theories such as those put forward depend for their force on the plausibility of each item in its place.

It is of course demonstrable that in many places, and certainly in the circles from which all the Gospels came, Christian identity and theological understanding were formed largely by reference to the OT scriptures, now seen as fulfilled in and by Jesus. These scriptures provided the essential theological authority and landmark. Clearly, they were the object of intense study and ingenious interpretation. Clearly, too, OT passages have exercised a strong formative influence on the way in which Gospel stories were told. But while it remains possible that, for example, the story of the Feeding of the Five Thousand is designed for telling at (the Christians') Passover (John 6.1–14), as Carrington proposed, or the Sermon on the Mount* for Pentecost, the dominant impression from the early church is that reliance fell on certain stock passages, seen to be of messianic* significance (*see* **Testimonia**); and few indeed may have been the Christian congregations wealthy enough to possess the full range of Jewish scriptures for either liturgical reading or study.

See also **Liturgy, Use of the Bible in.**

P. Carrington, *The Primitive Christian Calendar*, 1952; W. D. Davies 'Reflections on Archbishop Carrington's "The Primitive Christian Calendar"' in W. D. Davies and D. Daube (eds), *The Background of the New Testament and its Eschatology*, 1964; M. D. Goulder, *Midrash and Lection in Matthew*, 1974; id., *The Evangelists' Calendar*, 1978; A. Guilding,

The Fourth Gospel and Jewish Worship, 1960; L. Morris, in R. T. France and D. Wenham (eds.), *Gospel Perspectives*, 3, 1983; J. R. Porter, 'The Pentateuch and the Triennial Lectionary Cycle' in F. F. Bruce (ed.), *Promise and Fulfilment*, 1963 (on Guilding); É. Trocmé *The Passion as Liturgy*, 1983.

J. L. HOULDEN

Legend

The term comes from the Latin *legenda*, that which is to be read. From the thirteenth century A D it came to be applied to the stories of saints, martyrs and confessors of the Christian church. The virtues which were extolled in these stories were meant to act as examples of how others should live their lives. The narrative plot is static, since its main purpose is to highlight particular virtues of the individual hero, rather than to recount a problem and/or conflict which is then resolved. Whereas the legend may have a historical and/or topographical reference, these often become obscured because of a tendency to embroider the story with fictitious elements. In folklore* scholarship, 'legend' is used of a type of prose narrative believed to have originated in oral form. In structure it is similar to myth* and folktale.

The modern study of folk narratives began with the work of J. L. L. and W. C. Grimm. On the basis of the German folk narratives which they collected, they sought to differentiate between the prose narrative types of myth (*Mythus*), legend (*Sage*), and folktale (*Märchen*). The definitions which they gave to these, however, were very general and the distinctions which were made were in terms of content rather than form. One of the significant contributions they made to the discipline of folklore was in arguing that the legend was an originally oral* type of narrative.

This assumption of orality received added support from the work of A. Olrik. Seeking to establish the means of distinguishing oral from written narrative types, Olrik formulated thirteen laws to which he argued that oral narratives conformed. The German term he used for such narratives was *Sagen*. He argued that when narratives conformed to these laws they should be considered as having originated in oral form. What is important to remember is that Olrik's purpose was not to distinguish between the narrative types of myth, legend, and folktale but rather to establish their oral origins.

On the basis of the work of the brothers Grimm and with the added support of Olrik's laws, H. Gunkel, the father of OT form-critical* method, applied their findings to the narratives found in Genesis. Gunkel concluded that the patriarchal narratives had originated as independent oral legends, themselves derived from older folktales which had been collected into legend cycles (*Sagenkranze*), and only subsequently given literary form. The legend was defined as having the following characteristics: 1. a distinct introduction and conclusion; 2. repetitive elements which tended to intensify interest; 3. a small number of characters involved in the plot; 4. only the actions of a few characters in any given scene are recounted because the listener would not be able to cope with a vast diversity; 5. a very clear and simple narrative framework which does not attempt to give prerequisite data; 6. rigid patterning; 7. clear unity of plot; 8. a focussing on one character. It is important to remember that much of the debate surrounding the use of the term legend stems from its form–critical designation as a narrative type which originated in an oral context. Gunkel held to the conviction that legend should be distinguished from history writing. Whereas the legend was most often concerned with family matters and betrayed a certain poetic tone, history related political events which affected the state, and was almost always conveyed in prose.

Gunkel distinguished between Gen. 1–11, which he argued consisted of mythically orientated stories, and Gen. 12–50, which contained individual legends dealing with the lives of the patriarchs. He divided these legends into three categories: 1. historical legends dealing with the migrations of tribes and the various treaties they made; 2. ethnological legends which recount the events of tribes; 3 aetiological* legends which can be categorized as ethnological, etymological, ceremonial and geographical. In addition to these three groups were legends of a mixed character comprising any number of the above types. The legends in Genesis are of a less sophisticated type than those found in the books of Samuel. They reflect a certain artless spontaneity which emerged from the consciousness of primitive man. They are simple and uncomplicated. They are filled with observation and lack reflective thought. On the basis of such an analysis Gunkel considered it possible to reconstruct the primitive form of society together with the mentality of the people who would have created such legends, and suggested that the original setting of these legends was that of the campfire or popular festival when groups of professional story tellers would have practised their art.

G. von Rad, M. Noth, and C. Westermann, while accepting Gunkel's anlysis of the legend's form, relocated its origins in the family. These three scholars were dependent on the work of A. Jolles, who had argued that the earliest form of the legend was the family legend and therefore had its origins in the family circle. It should be noted, however, that the theories of A. Jolles have not found general acceptance amongst folklorists, and therefore caution should be exercised when appealing to his conclusions.

The particular problem of distinguishing legend from myth and folktale has yet to be solved. All three are prose narrative communications which attempt to tell a story. Nevertheless, the meaning of each and the way it is intended to be heard will differ depending on the context. For many contemporary folklorists, it is the aspect of performance which determines a narrative's classification. The attempt to define analytical categories of narrative types which can be applied transculturally is considered by many folklorists to be impossible. Different cultures have their own culturally defined repertoire of narrative types. For these folklorists, therefore, it is the context wherein a narrative is recounted which will determine its narrative category.

More recently, H. Jason has provided the most complete classification of folk narrative types. For Jason all narrative types are realized in one of three modes, i.e., 1. the fabulous, 2. the realistic, 3. the symbolic. The fabulous mode has two forms: the numinous and the marvellous. Legend is one of the narrative types of the numinous. For Jason the fabulous mode is one wherein the narrative recounts human beings confronting the world of the fantastic in which an amorphous power or its agents manipulate the events of the tale.

Jason's classification of folk narratives is extremely helpful, not least because the distinctions she makes between each type are based on form, content and function.

In the area of NT studies M. Dibelius and R. Bultmann,* following Gunkel's lead, attempted to classify the various literary units in the Synoptic* Gospels* according to their form. For Dibelius legends were narratives which recounted the life of a saintly man whose works and their outcome were of particular interest to a specific faith community. They arose in the early church as a result of that community's desire to know more about the life and virtues of Jesus and those men and women who followed him. For Dibelius, whereas the historical element in these legends could not be discounted, the early church's religious interests may nevertheless have led to non-historical accretions. The other narrative forms found in the Gospels were: paradigm, tale, myth, and sayings.

For Bultmann the legend was a religious and edifying story which was not primarily historical even though it may have been based on a historical happening. He therefore combined the categories of legend and historical story into one category, because of his conviction that it was impossible to distinguish between the two. In addition to the historical story and the legend Bultmann isolated the following three major narrative forms found in the Gospels: apophthegms, dominical sayings, and miracle* stories. For both Dibelius and Bultmann it was the church which exercised the greatest influence over the formation and transmission of the Gospel tradition, since it was the early church which formulated the earliest narrative forms.

See also **Aretalogy; Folklore; Saga.**

G. W. Coats (ed.), *Saga, Legend, Tale, Novella, Fable*, 1985; H. Delahaye, *The Legends of the Saints*, 1962; H. Gunkel, *The Legends of Genesis*, 1964; H. Jason, *Ethnopoetry*, 1977; P. G. Kirkpatrick, *The Old Testament and Folklore Study*, 1988; A. Olrik, 'Epic Laws of Folk Narrative' in A. Dundes (ed.), *The Study of Folklore*, 1965, pp. 129–41.

PATRICIA G. KIRKPATRICK

Leviticus

The interpretation of Leviticus produces a strange paradox. On the one hand the book contains some of the most alien and unattractive material in the whole Bible: details concerning long abandoned sacrificial observances; specific requirements relating to hygiene and purity which reflect a way of life very alien to that of most modern readers; detailed ritual requirements which seem totally irrelevant to the way one's life is actually led. On the other hand it is in Leviticus that two of the most important texts for Judaism and Christianity are to be found: the prescriptions for the Day of Atonement (Yom Kippur), which has continued as one of the most sacred days in the Jewish calendar, even if its observance may bear little resemblance to the details set out in Lev. 16; and the command in Lev. 19.18, 'You shall love your neighbour as yourself', identified in the Gospel as one of the two great commands of the Law (Mark 12.31).

The detailed sacrificial commands seem already to have been regarded in the ancient world as something of an embarrassment. In the first century AD Philo,* in *On the Special Laws* and elsewhere, regarded the ritual laws in the Pentateuch* as best interpreted in allegorical* terms (and some other Jewish interpreters moralized them away entirely); an analogous procedure is found in Hebrews where the sacrifices laid down in Leviticus are interpreted as applying to and fulfilled in the perfect sacrifice made by Christ (Heb. 9–10). The requirements of Leviticus have been a sporadic subject of dispute between Jews and Christians in more recent times, but with a certain measure of artificiality, for no suggestion that the sacrificial system should be reinstated has ever gained significant support.

In the present century a major contribution to the understanding of Leviticus has come from anthropologists.* In particular the work of such scholars as Mary Douglas has interpreted the laws of purity in terms of the classification of the world in which Israel lived; 'uncleanness', on such a view, was not related to hygiene, but to inappropriateness. Creatures that did not correspond to the characteristics expected of their class were regarded as an 'abomination'.

Leviticus has also played a prominent part in Pentateuchal criticism. Until fairly recently, the main concern of critical scholarship has been to analyse it from the standpoint of its relationship to the priestly 'source' or P. Since at least the time of Wellhausen, it has been widely accepted that the book forms part of the wider priestly material and that it reached at least its final form, as did P as a whole, in circles of the priesthood at Jerusalem* at some considerable time after the return from exile. Indeed, Leviticus has often been considered as the most characteristic expression of the priestly outlook.

But the question of how Leviticus is to be understood in relation to the priestly strand in the Pentateuch as a whole is a much more complicated one. It had long been recognized that Leviticus could not be a single unitary composition: in particular, the so-called 'Holiness Code', Lev. 17–26, was early singled out as an originally separate entity, not only because of its distinctive language and theology but also because of its content, where the social and ethical* duties of the ordinary Israelite are more prominent than elsewhere in the work. Here, the conclusions of M. Noth – though he was partly anticipated by G. von Rad – have been of decisive importance. It may be said that basically Noth draws a distinction between P and priestly material of a wider nature. For him, P was essentially a narrative work and thus the only part of Leviticus which could genuinely be ascribed to it was chs 8–10, which continue the P narrative from the end of Exodus and are linked with its resumption in Numbers. The rest of the book consists of different blocks of material which have been inserted later into the narrative. They can all be described as 'priestly' in that they are governed by a predominantly cultic* interest, but they differ from P proper in language and in presentation of details of the worship and personnel of the Temple. Hence, Leviticus is the product of a school of Jerusalem priests who, at different periods, collected, re-shaped and finally wrote down a variety of materials which once existed independently.

But what was the origin of these materials and in what form did they reach the priestly school? It was soon observed that the independent blocks attached to the P narrative, such as the sacrificial regulations of Lev. 1–7, the purity laws of Lev. 11–15 and even the 'Holiness Code', were not internally homogeneous but were themselves made up of a variety of traditional elements, not all of which represented the same religious situation and outlook. Scholarship at the end of the nineteenth century and the beginning of the twentieth, in line with Pentateuchal criticism of the period, tended to see the final shape of Leviticus as the result of a process of essentially literary development: the various traditions had assumed a written form before being collected into larger units, which were also themselves documents. Hence very complicated analyses of the book were produced, employing a large number of sigla to indicate the supposed written texts and their subsequent revisions and, on this basis, attempts were made to plot an evolutionary development of priestly theology and practice.

Such an approach is still exemplified by some critics, notably in the large German commentary* on Leviticus by K. Elliger. Increasingly, however, scholars have felt that this kind of treatment is over-complex and unduly atomistic and have preferred to explain Leviticus from the standpoint of the history of traditions,* popularized by Noth and his followers. In this connection, there has been an increasing awareness of the importance in Israelite life of the various great sanctuaries. It is likely that much of the diverse material in Leviticus represents the cultic traditions and liturgical practices of different shrines, which have been brought together, rather than a process of unilinear development. Hence a distinction has to be drawn between the date of the existing form of the book and the date or dates of much of the matter it incorporates. The final redaction of Leviticus is most likely post-exilic, but many of the regulations it contains may well have an oral origin and cannot be dated with any precision: all that can be said is that often they go back a long way and provide evidence for very early aspects of Israel's worship.

As a result, many of the more recent studies of Leviticus have concerned themselves not so much with its possible compositional history but rather with attempts to elucidate the forms and significance of the cultic phenomena it displays, especially what is said about sacrifices. Increasingly, scholars have concentrated on seeking an exegesis* of the book as it now exists rather than on possible earlier stages of its growth, a methodological* approach clearly stated by R. Rendtorff in the first fascicle of his commentary. On the one hand, the laws* in Leviticus have been analysed and arranged according to the methods of form criticism.* On the other, its sacrificial terminology has been the object of intensive study with the aim of discovering the concepts of sacrifice which lie behind it. Here much attention has been paid to later Jewish tradition, as contained particularly in the Mishnah and Talmud,* which is seen as throwing valuable light on the significance and ritual of the various classes of Levitical sacrifice or on the complex problem of the character of the Day of Atonement in Lev. 16.

See also **Anthropology; Pentateuch, Pentateuchal Criticism; Rabbi, Rabbinism.**

N. Kiuchi, *The Purification Offering in the Priestly Literature*, 1987; J. Milgrom, *Cult and Conscience*, 1976; J. Neusner, *The Idea of Purity in Ancient Judaism*, 1973; M. Noth, *Leviticus*, ² 1977; J. R. Porter, *Leviticus*, 1976; G. J. Wenham, *The Book of Leviticus*, 1979.

J. R. PORTER

Lexicons and Concordances

The early part of the sixteenth century was marked by a desire to make the Bible available to people in their own language. William Tyndale translated the Pentateuch* in 1530 and added a short list of 'hard words' and their meanings. So began the making of English biblical dictionaries. Coverdale's version and the Great Bible soon followed and in 1540 a certain Johann Marbeck began to compile an English concordance on the model of those already found in Latin. Since the chapters had not yet been divided into verses the references to words had to be by the chapter number followed by a, b, c, or d according to the position of the word in the chapter. As he neared the completion of his work, Parliament passed the 'Six Articles' by which Henry VIII sought to ensure that although he had replaced the pope as the head of the church, its doctrines and practices should be retained. Unfortunately Marbeck, who was organist and scholar at Windsor and who had sympathies with the continental Reformers,* had copied certain of the works of John Calvin.* For this he was imprisoned and sentenced to death and his concordance was destroyed. His life was spared by the king, and in the reign of Edward VI when the Six Articles had been repealed, he started work again on his concordance which was finally published in 1550. During the next century others followed which included verse numbers. Then in 1737 Alexander Cruden produced a new one based on the King James Version (AV) and this has remained in fairly common use. There followed James Strong's *Exhaustive Concord-* *ance* which also contained a Hebrew and Greek dictionary and Robert Young's *Analytical Concordance.*

The concern for the study of scripture not only in the new English versions but in the original languages may be illustrated by the fact that in 1679 Edward Terrill, an elder of the Broadmead Church in Bristol, made a deed of gift to support a minister at his church who was 'well-skilled in the tongues' of Hebrew and Greek and whose chief task would be to prepare young men for ministry in the Baptist churches of the land. It was further stimulated in the following century by the Enlightenment* in Germany, the Wesleyan revival in England, the evangelical awakening, and in 1804 the founding of the British and Foreign Bible Society. So it is not surprising to find that the need became apparent for dictionaries or lexicons of Hebrew and Hellenistic Greek. Of course there were already classical Greek lexicons, and there were some from Hellenistic Greek to Latin going back to 1619. One of these, compiled by C. L. W. Grimm in 1865, was eventually translated into English by J. H. Thayer in 1886. In 1928 W. Bauer revised a Greek–English lexicon by E. Preuschen which had been published eighteen years earlier. This became the basis for later lexicons by G. Abbot-Smith and by Arndt and Gingrich.

As far as the OT was concerned, W. Gesenius began his influential work on the Hebrew language in Germany early in the nineteenth century. His first Hebrew–German lexicon was published in 1812 and was translated into English by Christopher Leo in 1825. Over the next twenty years Gesenius both revised this and produced new lexicons, so that in 1833 a much superior work was published and its translation into English provided the basis for those still commonly in use by Brown, Driver and Briggs and by Kohler-Baumgartner.

Throughout the years therefore scholars have used lexicons to help them translate the scriptures and also to write commentaries.* For the purpose of this article they can be divided into three groups. First there are the small 'pocket' lexicons which simply give one or at most two or three English equivalents for each Hebrew or Greek word. It has to be said that these are of very limited value since they have no space to examine the various nuances that a word may possess when used in different contexts. Secondly, there are the 'analytical' lexicons which list the Hebrew or Greek words alphabetically in their conjugated forms and which provide the parsing for each word. Again their value is limited, for usually they too give only one or two English equivalents for each root. They can be used to save time working out what root a particular word is derived from but it is then necessary to look up the root in one of the third group.

These are the larger works such as Brown, Driver and Briggs, *Hebrew and English Lexicon*, Kohler-Baumgartner, *Lexicon in Veteris Testamenti Libros*, Abbot Smith, *Manual Greek Lexicon of the New Testament,* Moulton and Milligan, *The Vocabulary of the Greek Testament* and Bauer, Arndt, Gingrich, *A Greek–English Lexicon of the New Testament*. They often give information about similar words in cognate languages, while Arndt and Gingrich make reference to the way a word is used in classical Greek authors, often in non-religious contexts as well as in Christian non-biblical texts. The purpose of these lexicons, therefore, is not simply to provide an English equivalent but to offer as much information as possible about a word and its usage. The translator must then search for an English word or phrase which comes as close as possible to the meaning he believes the original to have in that particular passage. In some cases he will have to be content with an approximation since exact equivalence is often impossible.

There are three notes of warning which must be sounded concerning the use of these major lexicons. First, the view that a word has a certain shade of meaning in a biblical text is simply the opinion of the lexicographer. The wise interpreter will not therefore simply accept this classification without question but will examine personally the various contexts in which a word is used and its different shades of meaning.

Secondly, because some of these major lexicons are rather old, they sometimes use English words which are no longer in common use or are restricted to religious circles. In such cases a further stage is needed to supply or to explain the meaning in contemporary English.

Thirdly, a good deal of scholarly water has flowed under the bridge since they were published. For example, Brown, Driver and Briggs takes no account of the light thrown on the meaning of Hebrew words by the study of Ugaritic* simply because the Ugaritic texts were undiscovered in 1907. Kohler-Baumgartner does, but much more work has been done on Ugaritic since 1953; an updated edition of this lexicon is now almost complete. Abbot Smith makes no reference to papyri written in *koinē* Greek similar to that used in the NT because these have come to light since it was published in 1922. However, the latest English edition of Bauer, Arndt, Gingrich and Danker, 1979, and the more recent sixth German edition (K. and B. Aland, 1988) take these and other developments fully into account.

While the lexicons provide biblical references to every occurrence in scripture of some words, other words occur too frequently for this to be possible. In such cases we may turn to the concordances for help. The Hebrew and Greek concordances list every occurrence of each word or root and some of them include the phrase or sentence in which the word is embedded so that it may readily be seen in context. This means that the interpreter may study fully the significance of these words for which exhaustive references are not given in the lexicons. It also means that one is free to make one's own decisions about the meaning of a word in context without being unduly influenced by the classification found in the lexicon.

Many whose knowledge of Hebrew or Greek is minimal or non-existent will have to rely on concordances to the English Bible. It has to be said that these are often used simply to locate a text the whereabouts of which has been forgotten or never known. This usage should not be despised but they become much more valuable if again they are used to discover and compare the ways a word may be employed by different writers and in different situations.

The multiplicity of English versions has added to the difficulty of using concordances since each translation needs its own. The major ones now have them but it is doubtful whether any has completely replaced Young's *Analytical Concordance*. This is based upon the KJV of 1611 which must therefore be used alongside whatever other version the reader is working from. Its great virtue is that it recognizes that one English word may have been used to translate two or more different words from the original language. Consequently the entry for any word is divided according to the word found in the Hebrew or Greek and this word is printed at the head of each section both in Hebrew or Greek characters and in English transliteration. Even non-specialists can therefore discover not only the sense of a passage but also something of the niceties and nuances of the original. This makes it worthwhile working back through the KJV. For the NT, Clinton Morrison's *Analytical Concordance to the RSV of the NT* (1979) does the same.

The various instruments of study listed above have all been produced manually, and usually over an extended period. The explosion of information technology means that in future the purely mechanical work involved can be done very quickly by computers,* and new lexicons and concordances will no doubt all be produced by this means. The demand upon scholars will be to ensure that an adequate data base is available.

See also **Linguistics; Translations (to the
KJV); Translations (Modern).**

D. R. Jones, 'Aids to the Study of the Bible'
in S. L. Greenslade (ed.), *Cambridge History
of the Bible*, Vol. 3, 1963, pp. 520–30.

HARRY MOWVLEY

Liberalism

Liberalism, in theological thinking as in other
contexts, is not easy to define. The liberal
disposition, it has been said, is 'to release
energy rather than accumulate it, to relax
rather than fortify' (T. S. Eliot). The content
of 'liberal' teaching is determined therefore
more by its starting point than by its end. It
qualifies or moderates a pre-established orthodoxy, and the extent to which it does so
may vary considerably. Thus when applied to
Christianity – a usage of the term comparatively modern – it can embrace a wide range
of attitudes towards received belief and doctrine. Although liberal impulses in religious
thought may be identified in early and mediaeval * Christianity, as a more or less continuous
movement it is traceable back to Renaissance
humanism, the best-known representative of
which is Erasmus* (1466?–1536), for whom
the substance of Christianity lay in the *philosophia Christi*, Christ's own teaching and living
example: hence his desire that the scriptures
should be readily available to all – 'the farmer,
the tailor, the traveller, the Turk'. The humanists' confidence in the spiritual power of
the open Bible interpreted by reason and conscience was later reflected in the Cambridge
Platonists and the subsequent latitudinarian
and rationalizing tendencies of which they
were the precursors. But rationalism as
typified by the English deists* and their followers in Germany (Reimarus,* Semler, Lessing) was prone to find true religion in 'natural' revelation* rather than in the historically-
conditioned mode of it embodied in scripture
and the creeds,* so that its interpretation of
the Bible was apt to be reductionist, albeit
that the preaching of Jesus, if not the miraculous* element in the Gospel* story, was
usually treated with signal respect. Kant's
understanding of Christianity, as expressed in
his *Religion within the Limits of Reason Alone*
(1793), was to all intents a moral symbolism,
the NT being construed in accord with his
own ethical principles. The great defect of all
biblical exegesis* before the nineteenth century was, however, its almost complete lack of
historical perspective. Biblical criticism in any
sense which the modern student finds illuminating, began only with the historical and
philological* scholarship of such men as J. G.
Eichhorn (1752–1827), W. M. L. de Wette*
(1780–1849) and Karl Lachmann (1793–1851).

Liberal theology, when bearing the connotation now generally assigned to it, was mainly
the outcome of the critical approach to historical study first exemplified by J. G. Herder*
(1744–1803). If Christianity were a historical
religion in the special sense that its claims are
based on the veracity of certain uniquely historical events, the relating of these to a scientific investigation of its basic documents will
become a matter of vital importance, since
any account of the historical data which renders their authenticity questionable would
have serious implications for Christian belief
itself, necessitating, it might be, far-reaching
theological reconstruction. But the immediate
attraction of the critical study of the Bible for
an increasing number of Protestant theologians, at first in Germany and then, more
tardily, in English-speaking lands, was the
escape it seemed to offer from the intellectual
and moral difficulties of biblical literalism.*
A scientific history of the biblical literature
would indicate how revelation itself had in
fact been historical, conveyed in the process
of actual events, and not, as in the traditional
teaching, by a verbally inspired oral or written
communication. Moreover, revelation would
be seen to be 'progressive', adapted to its
recipients' developing moral and spiritual insight. Stress fell increasingly upon the human
medium, which a historically grounded exegesis served to highlight, through which this
advancing knowledge of God and his ways
was imparted. While much in the biblical
record could thus be accounted for by the
ignorance and moral immaturity of the biblical authors or their sources, divine truth
might not improperly be described as a distillation from men's religious experience down
the ages – a view which placed Christianity
in intelligible relation with other world-
faiths.

A distinction nevertheless may fairly be
drawn between Protestant liberalism and Liberal Protestantism with a more restricted meaning. 'A moderately orthodox believer,' it has
been said, 'may practise liberalism; he will not
thereby become a Liberal Protestant' (J. Ré-
ville). (Catholicism was little affected by historical criticism until near the close of the nineteenth century. *See* **Catholic Modernism**.) Liberal Protestantism originated in Germany
under the influence of Kant and Schleiermacher, with Albrecht Ritschl (1822–1889) of Göttingen as its great exemplar. The foe of
metaphysics and mysticism in religion, Ritschl
combined Kant's moralism with a positivistic
insistence on the historicity of revelation. The
basis of Christianity, he held, is the historical
Jesus* as portrayed more or less authentically
in the Gospels. Jesus' divinity, on the other
hand, is not a datum of history but a 'value-

judgment' (*Werthurtheil*) of the religious consciousness. Ritschl further maintained that Christianity is unique among religions in that it alone offers redemption in the form of mastery of the natural world through God's personal self-disclosure within it. The ecclesial principle is emphasized – the church as the community of the redeemed is the counterpart of the gospel – but in its historic development Christianity has imbibed foreign elements into its nature, a thesis resumed and elaborated by Ritschl's disciple Adolf Harnack * (1853–1930), whose work is characteristic of liberalism in contrasting a residual 'essence' of Christianity, purely evangelic in substance, with the dogmatic, cultic and institutional articulation of its postbiblical period.

With the early decades of the twentieth century, particularly in face of the Barthian * reaction, liberalism lost ground in Germany, Ernst Troeltsch (1853–1923) being its outstanding survivor, apart from Harnack. But in England, notably among Anglican 'modernists' (Hastings Rashdall, J. F. Bethune-Baker, B. H. Streeter), as also in the USA (whence the names of H. C. King, W. Adams Brown and H. E. Fosdick will be recalled), it remained influential for a generation and more. Indeed neo-orthodoxy, outside conservative evangelical circles, has not sustained momentum, for even in Germany liberalism recovered in mid-century something of its former vigour with the work of Bultmann, whose 'demythologizing' * exegesis proved to be one of the more arresting turns in modern theological thought. But at present liberal religion seems less concerned with biblical interpretation than with relating the faith to current political and social humanism.

See also **Enlightenment.**

Karl Barth, *Protestant Theology in the Nineteenth Century*, 1971; S. L. Greenslade (ed.), *The Cambridge History of the Bible*, vol. 3, 1963, chs 7, 8; W. R. Hutchinson, *The Modernist Impulse in American Protestantism*, 1982; K. S. Latourette, *Christianity in a Revolutionary Age*, vol. 2, 1959, chs 3–5; H. R. Mackintosh, *Types of Modern Theology*, 1937; B. M. G. Reardon, *Religious Thought in the Nineteenth Century*, 1966; id., *Liberal Protestantism*, 1968.

BERNARD M. G. REARDON

Liberation Theology

Liberation theology emerged as a revolutionary theological movement in the 1960s in Latin America. At the Conference of Latin American Bishops held in Medellín, Colombia, in 1968, Christian liberationists stressed that the starting point for theological reflection is the situation of the poor. At subsequent conferences and in a wide variety of studies published in the following decades, liberation theologians have elaborated a number of key motifs that constitute the basis of their religious vision.

The biblical God, they believe, is on the side of those who are down-trodden in society. In the OT, God redeemed the Jews from Egyptian bondage. Similarly, in the NT, Jesus made a personal option for the poor and regarded them as the main recipients of his message. In proclaiming the gospel, the apostles emphasized that the poor should not be ignored. In the light of this biblical inheritance, faith is understood as active – it is verified when informed by love, solidarity, and hunger and thirst for justice. Orthodoxy must be accompanied by orthopraxis. Living the true faith enables the Christian to hear the cry of the oppressed. As in the past, God sides with the exploited against the pharaohs of this world. Through the incarnation, he revealed the divine plan which is to be fulfilled in the course of history. The kingdom of God * is not an otherworldly expectation; it is to be realized in the struggle of those who seek liberation.

In expounding these themes, liberation theologians have appealed to scripture as a basis for their faith. The hermeneutics * of liberation constitutes a new way of reading the Bible. From the pages of the OT and NT, liberation theologians have drawn strength and inspiration in their attempt to create a better society. The parts of the Bible most frequently utilized include the book of Exodus, since it relates the liberation of the ancient Israelites through the intervention of God, and the prophetic * books, used because of their denunciation of injustice and defence of the rights of the impoverished. Further, in the Gospels is found the image of Jesus as liberator who announces the coming of God's kingdom through his liberating activity. The Acts of the Apostles is also seen as portraying the ideal of a free and liberated Christian community. The book of Revelation is understood as describing in symbolic * terms the struggle of the people of God against the monsters of history. Finally, the books of the Maccabees are also drawn on to mobilize those who are committed to an armed uprising against unjust governments.

From God's revelation * in these biblical books, liberationists have formulated themes that speak to the poor. For these writers the poor are not simply downtrodden – they seek fulfilment and spiritual redemption. In this attempt to understand the true meaning of the Christian message, there is a hermeneutical circle,* a dialectical interplay between the poor and the world. For those who engage in this exegetical* quest, God's revelation can emerge only as a message of radical consolation and liberation. This reading of the Bible done from the basis of the poor favours application rather than explanation. Liberation hermeneutics reads scripture as a book of life. Textual meaning is sought only as practical reading; actualization of the divine word is paramount.

Liberation hermeneutics thus attempts to activate the transforming energy of biblical texts. It seeks to find an interpretation that will lead to conversion and revolution. Ideally it is an open and dynamic quest that stresses the social context of the biblical message. It places the Bible in its historic setting to elicit an appropriate religious response in the modern world. In this way, liberating evangelization has become a means of confronting the evil structures of the contemporary world.

Though this biblically-based movement is relatively new, it has had a profound impact on theological reflection throughout the world. In Latin America and the Caribbean it is widespread; in Peru, Chile, Mexico, Brazil and Central America it has become particularly influential. In this connection, the Latin American Confederation of Religious (CLAR) has served as a major arena for the exploration of the ways in which liberation theology can affect religious life. In addition, several scholarly institutes have played an important role in the application of liberationist ideals. The Commission for Studies in Latin American Church History (CEHILA) has undertaken the task of rewriting the history of Latin America and the Caribbean from the standpoint of the poor. The Centre for Biblical Studies (CEBI) supports publications that present the Bible as a force for liberation. The Ecumenical Centre for Service and Evangelization of the People (CESEP) trains individuals from Latin America and the Caribbean in liberating pastoral work.

The central area of concern of liberation theology in Latin America and the Caribbean is the plight of the socio-economically poor and their quest for freedom from oppression. This approach is developed in dialogue with liberation theology in other parts of the world. On the African continent, liberation theologians in Zaire, Tanzania and Ghana have been reflecting on the need for cultural integration of the Christian faith, and their exchanges with Latin American theology have enriched both communities. In South Africa, black liberation theology has become a powerful force for social change. In Asia, liberationists in India, Korea, the Philippines, Sri Lanka and Pakistan have attempted to establish a dialogue between Christianity and other religions to bring about social liberation. By sharing insights and experiences, liberation theologians in these countries have been able to deepen their understanding of the global implications of the liberation perspective.

In the First World, theologians have also become aware of the significance of this new development. Black* liberation theology in the United States is committed to the civil rights movement. In Europe, liberationists are concerned with the responsibilities for Third World deprivation, the problems of the destitute in advanced industrial societies, as well as a variety of ecological issues. In addition, in many countries of the First World, feminist* theology has had an important impact. This theological movement sees women's liberation as an integral part of the struggle to create a better world. Specifically, feminists are concerned about the links between sexual and economic oppression and the sexist elements in traditional religious thought. Thus, in many theological, ecclesial and cultural circles in the First World, liberation theology is having a profound effect on Christian thinking.

Despite the rapid growth and increasing influence of liberation theology worldwide, a number of criticisms have been made of its principles and aims. Some have pointed out that the use of the Bible in liberation theology is selective and often dismissive of biblical scholarship. It is objected that the Bible, and especially the figure of Jesus, is viewed in the light of predetermined models derived from present day needs and situations. The political preoccupation, often strongly Marxist* in tone, of much liberation theology has also been attacked; some opponents maintain that questions relating to oppression and liberation have overshadowed more important spiritual concerns. Liberation theology has been accused of downgrading the value of other theologies and over-emphasizing the socio-economic aspects of evangelical poverty. Yet despite these objections, liberation theology is a powerful force in modern society. It has raised central questions about the role of the church and religious faith in a secular age, placing biblical teaching at the forefront of its activity.

See also **Black Christian Interpretation; Feminist Interpretation; Materialist Interpretation.**

Leonardo and Clodovis Boff, *Introducing Liberation Theology*, 1988; Deane William Ferm, *Profiles in Liberation*, 1988; José Porfirio Miranda, *Marx and the Bible*, 1974; Jon Sobrino, *Christology at the Crossroads*, 1978; Elsa Tamez, *Bible of the Oppressed*, 1982.

DAN COHN-SHERBOK

Lightfoot, R. H.

Robert Henry Lightfoot (1883–1953) was an Anglican clergyman who spent most of his active life teaching N T studies at Oxford, where he was Dean Ireland's Professor of Exegesis of Holy Scripture from 1934 to 1949.

After the First World War he became increasingly dissatisfied with the accounts of the origins and nature of the Synoptic* Gospels* then current in England. A visit to Germany in 1931 to work with Bultmann,* Dibelius and others convinced him that there was a great deal of truth in the insights of the form critics; and in his Bampton Lectures delivered in 1934 (and published the following year) he sought to make form criticism* better known in this country, revealing in the famous last paragraph his conviction that in the upshot comparatively little can now be known about the historical figure of Jesus.*

However, perhaps without his being fully aware of it, his lectures turned out to be far more than just an English account of German form criticism. Influenced by the work of Ernst Lohmeyer* and of the American scholars J. H. Ropes and H. J. Cadbury,* he was led to see the synoptic evangelists as much more than slavish transmitters of pre-existent units of oral tradition.* In their own way they, no less than the fourth evangelist, were theologians, each of them, through his selection, arrangement and editing of his material, giving expression to his peculiar *Tendenz* and presenting a particular picture and understanding of Jesus' work and its meaning. Lightfoot thus anticipated what is now known as redaction criticism.*

If the full extent of his originality has not been recognized, that may partly be due to his extreme diffidence and the very tentative way in which he expressed himself, and also to the fact that the English theological establishment in the mid-1930s was hardly ready for such radical suggestions, especially as Lightfoot, unlike Bultmann, for example, made no recommendations about how the critical position he advocated might be coped with from the point of view of religious faith. There is also the fact that the outbreak of the Second World War prevented wide dissemination of the Bampton Lectures and of the sequel *Locality and Doctrine in the Gospels*. Remaining copies of both had to be pulped during the war and they thus remained largely unknown in postwar Europe and America – Lightfoot's name does not appear, for example, in the index of W. G. Kümmel's influential history of N T studies.

In *The Gospel Message of St Mark* (1950) – a revealing title – he restated his position with regard to the Synoptic Gospels in a perhaps more cogent form; he then turned his attention to the Fourth Gospel on which he wrote an extended commentary, edited posthumously by C. F. Evans and published in 1956. Here there is no mistaking the premiss which underlies the work, and had in fact underlain his interpretation of the other Gospels, namely 'that the key to any particular passage in the book lies in the consideration of the book as a whole or of other sections of it with which the particular passage has affinities'. No doubt because of what by his own high standards was his ignorance of sociological* conditions and non-Christian religions in the first century, he made little attempt to interpret the text on the basis of such external factors. By more recent standards this may seem a weakness, but it meant that he was an early practitioner of the literary-critical* reading of the Gospels now popular in many circles; and in this type of interpretation he showed a degree of sensitivity, good judgment and flair which make his writings still well worthy of study.

R. H. Lightfoot, *History and Interpretation in the Gospels*, 1935; *Locality and Doctrine in the Gospels*, 1938; *The Gospel Message of St Mark*, 1950; *St John's Gospel*, 1956; D. E. Nineham (ed.), *Studies in the Gospels: Essays in Memory of R. H. Lightfoot*, 1955; id., *Theology*, 88, 1985, pp. 97–105.

D. E. NINEHAM

Linguistics

Since the Bible was originally written in three languages, Hebrew, Aramaic (Ezra 4.8–6.22; Dan. 2.4b–7.28), and Greek, and has subsequently been translated, in whole or in part, into most of the 4,000 or so languages of the world, the study of language has always been an integral part of biblical interpretation. Translation* requires a knowledge of two or more languages (cf. Gen. 31.47–8; Neh. 8.8 (?); Ecclus. Prol.; Matt. 27.46), or, as in the case of Jerome who invited Jews to help him with his Latin translation of the Bible (*see* **Vulgate**), reliable informants. Foreign language learning has had a crucial part to play in the study of the Bible. The first Hebrew grammars and dictionaries were composed by Jews for this purpose in the early Middle Ages. For Christians in many parts of the world until modern times, the Bible was in a foreign language which had to be learnt: e.g. Latin in most Catholic countries; Old Church Slavonic in Russia; Ge'ez in Ethiopia. Over the last 200 years the work of missionaries and Bible societies has made a significant contribution to the study of languages, while comparative philology* has had a profound effect on biblical interpretation.

Linguistics as a science is usually said to have begun with the publication in 1916 of Ferdinand de Saussure's *Cours de linguistique générale*. His distinction between diachronic and synchronic approaches is fundamental. It marked a shift from traditional philology, which was predominantly diachronic (= historical) and concerned with ancient written languages, to modern linguistics which had been concerned more with the synchronic description of living spoken languages. The distinction has been particularly helpful in the field of semantics* which had for two centuries been dominated by comparative philology and etymology,* with damaging results for biblical interpretation. Not all the insights of modern linguistics are relevant to the study of the Bible. But the efforts of an increasing number of biblical scholars to bridge the gap between the two disciplines are now proving to be productive.

Fundamental to linguistics, although often difficult for non-linguists to accept, is the distinction between a descriptive and a prescriptive approach to language. Most traditional grammars of English, for example, are prescriptive, and contain rules governing how one ought to write or speak (cf. *It is I*; *Whom did you see?*), however far removed they may be from everyday language. The idea that linguistic data of all kinds, written and spoken, living and dead, regional, idiosyncratic, comic, ritualized, unintelligible, can be studied and described with equal scientific rigour, has had an important effect on biblical research. Variant manuscript* readings, which may be theologically or historically interesting, are examined with the same objectivity as the 'original text'. The ancient versions, especially the Septuagint,* Targum,* Vulgate and Peshitta (*see* **Syriac Tradition**), are now being studied, not only as evidence for the biblical text, but as literature in their own right. How people have understood the text, how it has been used in the history of the church, even what people think the text means, are as legitimate a subject for scientific research as the original author's intention. Even if the word *parthenos*, 'virgin', is not what Isaiah actually said (Isa. 7.14), it is what Greek-speaking Jews believed he said (e.g. Matt. 1.22f.), and for that reason an important part of our data. Prescriptive comments and implied value judgments (e.g. 'late', 'corrupt', 'editorial', 'not original', 'misguided') are not made until the descriptive analysis is complete (*see* **Interpretation, History of**).

One contribution of modern phonetics and grammatical theory to biblical interpretation is in the field of language teaching. For centuries students were taught Hebrew in such a way that they got the idea that it was different from every other natural language, and that the 'Hebrew mind' was reflected in such features as the rarity of adjectives and abstract nouns. Modern approaches to Hebrew have shown that, while the Hebrew Bible is a closed corpus of an arbitrary kind and one that has been heavily influenced by 'unnatural' processes (e.g. scribal* conventions, religious factors), the Hebrew language itself, as documented in ancient extra-biblical texts, including the Dead Sea Scrolls,* and in Mishnaic, Mediaeval and Modern Hebrew, as well as the Hebrew Bible, is much like any other language. Less emphasis on arcane terminology and more use of everyday parallels from familiar languages characterize the modern teaching of Hebrew. The old view that students of the Hebrew Bible ought to learn Ugaritic* or Syriac or Arabic as well to understand it properly, is also less widespread now, and other varieties of Hebrew are recommended instead.

One model of grammatical analysis that can be of value to biblical exegetes is 'generative grammar'. Unlike traditional grammars which deal with 'surface structures' in a language, generative grammar is concerned with the 'deep structures' that underlie languages and the rules according to which surface structures are generated from them. It can be valuable as a method of analysing language, explaining ambiguity and describing meaning. To explain the ambiguity in a noun-phrase like *my salvation*, for example, it is helpful to refer to the two possible sentences underlying it: (a) *I save X* (e.g. Isa. 51.5, where God is speaking) and (b) *X saves me* (e.g. Ps. 89.26 = *Hebr.* 89.27, where David is speaking). Jer. 3.23 contains a more complicated example: *Truly in the Lord our God is the salvation of Israel*. The force of the preposition *in* here can be described by reference to an underlying structure probably containing two sentences: (a) *God saves Israel* and (b) *Israel trusts in the Lord*. In the surface structure, where nouns are used instead of verbs, (a) is said to have been 'rewritten' as *the salvation of Israel* and (b) as *in the Lord*. The association between words for 'trust' and words for 'salvation, help' (cf. Ps. 115.9–11; Isa.30.15) makes this possible even when a word for 'trust, believe, hope, rejoice' or the like, frequently combined with the phrase *in the Lord*, has been deleted.

Another distinction fundamental to modern linguistics is that between syntagmatic and paradigmatic. Syntagmatic relations are relations between words in particular sentences or between sentences in a longer piece of language. They are the subject of syntax,* discourse analysis and text analysis, and must be distinguished from paradigmatic (or associative) relations between words or sentences associated with one another in the language as a whole. They are the subject of lexical or semantic analysis, in which the basic question is, what other associated word or phrase could occur in this slot in the sentence/discourse/text (see **Semantics**).

Some of the most interesting examples of new methods of biblical interpretation have come from the insights of structuralism.* They have reminded us that there is still much to be learnt about larger literary units, chapters and even whole books, which have been neglected in modern times. Traditional grammars, including those of the biblical languages, concentrate almost exclusively on phonology and grammar, the isolated sentence being the largest unit analysed. Syntax has a low priority, and stylistics hardly figures at all. Studies like W. Watson, *Classical Hebrew Poetry. A Guide to its Techniques* (1984) and T. Muraoka, *Emphatic Words and Structures in Biblical Hebrew* (1986) are still rare. The isolation of separate pericopes and literary forms (see **Form Criticism**) has also had the effect of diverting attention from patterns and relationships in larger literary units. But over the last 20 years or so, with the advent of rhetorical criticism,* canonical criticism* and structuralism, there is a new interest in the autonomy of the text as it stands, and the 'final form of the text'. Questions about the theme of the Pentateuch,* the overall structure of the Book of Isaiah or the Book of Job, the autonomy of the Gospel of Mark, and similar topics, are being looked at afresh in the light of new literary and linguistic approaches.

Linguistics owes much to the work of missionaries and Bible societies, not least in the sphere of translation.* Recognition that exact equivalence between source and target languages is impossible, and attempts to define precisely different types of translation according to function or purpose (literary, ritual, social, commercial, etc.), and appropriate methods of achieving this, have produced some interesting results, both theoretical and practical. One topic of interest to biblical scholars is the description and analysis of 'translation languages' such as the Septuagint or the KJV, which contain, for example, 'hebraisms' like 'sons of God' (Gen. 6.2; Job 1.6) and 'Noah walked with God' (Gen. 6.9). What conditions are necessary for a target language to sustain new forms and expressions like these, and what is their lexical status?

Computational linguistics provides techniques for language teaching, text analysis and the compiling of lexicons* and concordances, all of which have been employed by biblical

scholars. There have been attempts to prove the multiple authorship of the book of Isaiah and the Pauline corpus, for example, and several computerized concordances and thesauri have been published. Fully lemmatized computerized* texts of all the relevant literature are not yet generally available (although individual scholars have made their own), and the benefits of this new science for biblical interpretation are only now beginning to be acknowledged.

Socio-linguistics deals with interactions between language and society: how languages reflect social and political conditions, and influence people's attitudes and beliefs. Correct pronunciation can be a matter of life and death (Judg. 12.6). Social class may be marked by language difference (II Kings 18.26f.), as can the written authority of a foreign power (Ezra 4.7). The split between Christians and Jews from the end of the first century AD was sharpened by the linguistic divergence between a Greek Bible and a much shorter Hebrew Bible. Special varieties of religious language are used for preaching, 'tele-evangelism', prayers, speaking with tongues, readings from sacred texts, oaths, exorcisms, and many other ritual purposes. Recent analysis of some of these language varieties (or 'registers') reveals all kinds of subtle but important distinctions which may throw light on the biblical texts themselves as well as on the language of the religious communities for whom they are scripture.

Pragmatics is concerned more specifically with what determines the language people use, and what effect it has on others. Popular beliefs about language provide important insights into social and religious attitudes. The Tower of Babel story about the origin of foreign languages (Gen. 11.1–9) and the Pentecost sequel to it (Acts 2) illustrate how people react with fear and hostility to foreigners (cf. Isa. 33.19). The widespread belief in the power of the word (Gen. 1.4; Ps. 33.6; John 1.3), and in particular that naming gives control (Gen. 32.29; Ex. 20.7), is reflected in the story of Adam* naming the animals in the Garden of Eden (Gen. 2.19f.). The power of modern Bible translators to influence attitudes towards women (see **Feminist Interpretation**), by either perpetuating or avoiding sexist language, is an obvious example (e.g. 'human beings' for 'man' in Gen. 1.26f.). Others are the appalling influence of the passion narrative* on the church's treatment of the Jews, and recent attempts to remove potentially racist language (see **Antisemitism**) from it (e.g. substituting 'the people' for 'the Jews' in John 19.38; 20.19). Heightened awareness of what biblical interpretation involves, in the widest sense of the term and at all levels, is perhaps linguistics' most valuable contribution to the subject.

See also **Etymology; Translation, Problems of.**

D. Crystal, *The Cambridge Encyclopedia of Language*, 1987; R. Kieffer, 'Two types of exegesis with a linguistic basis' in H. Küng, J. Moltmann (eds), *Conflicting Ways of Interpreting the Bible*, 1980, pp. 9–16; J. H. Hospers (ed.), *General Linguistics and the Teaching of Dead Hamito-Semitic Languages*, 1978; J. Lyons, *Languages and Linguistics*, 1981; J. Samarin (ed.), *Language and Religious Practice*, 1976; J. F. A. Sawyer, 'A change of emphasis in the study of the Prophets' in R. Coggins et al. (eds), *Israel's Prophetic Tradition*, 1982, pp. 233–49.

JOHN F. A. SAWYER

Literal Meaning

'Literal' means 'by the letter'. Eustathius, in the fourth century, accused Origen* of interpreting the story of the witch of Endor (I Sam. 28) 'literally', because, by simply taking certain written words at their face value, he assumed that Samuel actually came up from the grave, and then deduced from this the truth of the resurrection.* Such an example indicates some of the pitfalls: concentrating on the 'letter' rather than the context, as Eustathius saw, distorts meaning. Furthermore, if the literal meaning refers to precisely what the words state, then all figurative* language, metaphor,* parable,* and above all irony,* will be misunderstood if it is taken literally.

In the early church, literal interpretation was largely condemned, partly for the reasons already indicated, but also because it encouraged unacceptable approaches to understanding the true meaning of the scriptures. In the first place, literal interpretation was associated with the failure of the Jews to perceive that the scriptures were all about Jesus Christ. Paul* said that there was a veil over their minds, contrasting 'the letter' and 'the spirit'. The law was never meant to be taken 'literally' – rather it had a spiritual meaning. Circumcision of the flesh was replaced by circumcision of the heart. Thus the whole approach in terms of *halakhah* was dismissed as 'literal' and unacceptable since Christ was the 'end' of the law. Ironically, Jewish deducing of *halakhah* from Torah itself often involved symbolic* or allegorical interpretation.*

In the second place, interpretation 'by the letter' led to heresy and absurdities: is God really angry? Scripture contains such impossibilities in order to alert us to the fact that we have to go beyond the letter and search for the spiritual* meaning. 'God is my Rock' cannot mean that I worship the menhir at the bottom of the garden, and it is equally problematic to imagine God in anthropomorphic* terms: surely he does not literally have hands or speak, he is not literally angry, he cannot literally repent or change his mind – for he is invisible, incorporeal, unchangeable and transcendent. So to accuse someone of literal interpretation was often derogatory and polemical.

On the other hand, most of scripture did literally mean what it said: the moral commandments were to be obeyed, and the narratives were about real events. Origen even wondered what happened to the refuse in the Ark with all those creatures there for so many days! The archetypal allegorist could be surprisingly literal in his interpretations.

In fact the use of the term 'literal' often obscures the real issue: namely, what does the text refer to? The early church assumed that for the most part the true reference of the text was to Christ. So in Melito's *Homily on the Pasch*, the story of the exodus refers to the salvation brought about by Christ: only this gives it significance. An interesting development of this is Eusebius'* assumption that the literal meaning of a prophecy is the event it predicted, that is, its fulfilment. The standard account of the Antiochene* reaction against Alexandrian* allegory oversimplifies the issues by suggesting that it was an appeal to the literal or historical meaning: dogmatic, prophetic and typological* interpretations could still thrive in this atmosphere, and it did not produce the kind of interest in history characteristic of modern biblical study. The term 'literal' was and is thoroughly ambiguous.

The inadequacy of the term 'literal' for making meaningful distinctions in the history of exegesis is equalled by its inadequacy for understanding what is going on in modern discussions, especially at the popular level. Those who demand the acceptance of a dogmatic statement that the Bible is literally true, are usually unaware of the complexities and unconscious of their own ambivalent practice. James Barr has pointed out that critics are more literalist than fundamentalists* in that they respect the contradictions in the text, whereas those claiming to honour the literal meaning in fact manipulate the letter of scripture in the interests of consistency. They also accept a large number of dogmatic, prophetic and christological* meanings which are certainly not technically 'literal'. Indeed modern literalists are close to the anti-literalists of the early church in their assumptions.

In fact two developments have tended to shift the application of the word 'literal', turning it for many into a word of approval rather than disapproval. The first of these developments was the Reformation* search for the 'plain meaning' of scripture: if the source of authority was no longer pope, priest or church but *sola scriptura*, then primacy would tend to be given to what the text said. By hindsight we can say that it is not surprising that Protestantism is fissiparous, given the variety of possibilities if the letter of scripture is taken to be prescriptive; but the scripture principle was an important stimulant to the view that primacy must be given to the literal meaning, all the more so in the light of the humanist revival of literary and linguistic* studies in the sixteenth century.

The second development was to some extent fired by the first: namely, the search for the 'original' meaning, and the consequent development of a sense of history, and the importance of the 'history behind the text'. By complex interaction, this essentially Protestant attempt to get back to the Bible, and the challenges to biblical history posed by science and archaeology,* have produced an overriding concern with historicity. When people claim to accept the Bible 'literally', what they think they mean is that they are not prepared to question the truth of the history the Bible purports to tell. This is essentially a reactive conservatism, and not as is often claimed the traditional approach to the Bible. The historicity of the biblical events was never a matter of overt concern as long as it went unchallenged, attention being paid to significance rather than factuality.

Indeed, modern developments have narrowed and impoverished biblical interpretation by making the historical reference the prime concern. The hermeneutical* complexities have been obscured by a simplistic appeal to the 'literal' meaning as if historical reference were the only implication of 'literalism'. Interpretation requires the kind of awareness of the subtleties of language that was the starting point of the anti-literalism of the early church, whatever may be our reservations about the resulting allegorism.

See also **Allegorical Interpretation; Meaning.**

___

James Barr, *Fundamentalism*, [2]1981; Robert M. Grant, *The Letter and the Spirit*, 1957; Robert M. Grant with David Tracy, *A Short History of the Interpretation of the Bible*, 1984.

FRANCES YOUNG

Literary Criticism

The Bible refers to theological, metaphysical, anthropological, ethical and historical issues, but it does so as a collection of literature. It is appropriate, therefore, that some interpreters should study the Bible as literature, and should develop insights and skills in co-operation with literary critics in other fields. Moreover, readers of the Bible are affected unselfconsciously by their experience of other literature, and it is helpful to recognize what kinds of influence are prompting their perceptions of the Bible.

Interpreting the Bible as literature is no new endeavour. R. G. Moulton's *The Literary Study of the Bible* (1895) was published at a time when most biblical scholars were interested in questions of history, reaching behind the texts to their sources, and the events which gave rise to them. (This type of scholarship has often been referred to as 'literary criticism', but is more appropriately described as 'source criticism',* and will not be further discussed here.) Moulton's is a comparative study of literary forms like epic, lyric, rhetoric,* prophecy,* wisdom* and drama, including sections on poetic parallelism, but discussed in terms of a variety of complete poems rather than individual sentences. A greater emphasis on biblical imagery and its influence on English literature is found in a more recent study, *The Bible as Literature* by T. R. Henn (1970). What distinguishes modern criticism from earlier descriptive research, however, is its inquiry into how texts communicate, and what constitutes meaning.*

During the last twenty years, literary criticism has shifted its focus of attention from the author, to the text itself, and thence to the reader. A parallel movement can be traced in the literary criticism of the Bible. The change began because the current explanation of how writings convey meanings to readers was seen to be inadequate. This explanation claimed that the author's intention gives meaning to a text, and that the reader must discover the author's intention to gain understanding. For example, the author of I Sam. 16–31 intended to write a history of David's* rise to power, and the reader must perceive this intention to comprehend the chapters. To read I Sam 16–31 as fiction, then, is to misunderstand the work because it misconstrues the author's intention, which provides its meaning. Although critics argued that the biblical writers took up and ordered older traditions, working as redactors rather than authors, nevertheless redaction criticism* reflects the view that the final redactor/author expresses a theological and pastoral intention in producing a text by editing and re-writing. Studies of the theological intentions of the Yahwist, Deuteronomist, Matthew, Mark, Luke and John proliferated in the 1960s and 1970s.

Attending to the author or redactor is one interesting way of approaching literature. Literary works become facets of the author's biography. The discovery of the part a book plays in the author's life, however, requires information independent of the text itself. For example, the novels of Charles Dickens can form part of Dickens' biography because sufficient evidence exists to write a detailed life of Dickens and to fit the novels into its chronology. Characters and plots can be discussed in the light of Dickens' experiences, and of the interests and intentions Dickens himself expressed in prefaces and other writings. This independent knowledge of the author's circumstances and intentions has been used by critics to discover the meaning of novels. One of the valuable contributions made by this kind of criticism is the elaboration of the historical context in which the author wrote the book.

Nevertheless, even in cases like that of Dickens and his novels, literary critics began to express doubts about defining the meaning of a text through the discovery of the author's intention. Although the author may be assumed to have an intention, or a number of different intentions, in writing a book, he or she may neither be fully aware of those intentions nor fulfil them in the work. It is possible to judge the success of the author's efforts by reading the book, which suggests that it is comprehended independently of the author's claims. In any case, if the text is to communicate, the author is not a free agent, but must write according to some shared linguistic* and literary conventions. Meaning, therefore, is a cultural and social phenomenon, not a matter of individual fiat. And if the meaning can be discovered from the book itself, without recourse to the author's mind, it is because genre* is more important than individual intention. Some literary critics, therefore, abandoned the author's biography in favour of a history of genre. The search for the historical background to a text, which was such a useful feature of the quest for the author's intention, persists in genre criticism, since every instance of a genre needs to be placed socially and culturally, with as much precision as possible (see A. Fowler, *Kinds of Literature*, 1982).

This change brought nothing but gain to biblical scholarship, because no reliable independent evidence exists about the authors or redactors of the Bible, whereas a wealth of non-biblical literature from similar times and places facilitates the definition of genre. The reader of I Sam. 16–31 can construe it as a kind of history, then, in spite of knowing nothing about the author or redactor, by noticing features which belong to that genre rather than to fiction. The identification of a number of genres in biblical literature – myth,* history, legend,* saga,* biography, oracle,* prophecy, apocalyptic,* proverb, hymn* – continues to enliven biblical interpretation.

Another branch of literary criticism which considers fallacious the account of meaning in terms of author's intention, also eschews an interest in history, and with it, the history of genre. Instead, it explores a different account of meaning, which begins with language and ends with literature. An individual word, it is argued, is meaningful only in opposition to its contrary and contradictory. For example, 'male' is opposed to 'female' and to 'non-male'. Hence meaning is given by the structure of the language itself, not by the author's intention, nor by reference to the world. It is the structure of binary opposition which builds meaning in language, and the same is true, so structuralism* asserts, of literature. The meaning of a text is expressed in the binary opposition of its deep structure. Interest is centred, therefore, entirely on this structure rather than on authorship, history or subject matter. All narratives, poems and even shopping lists, exhibit binary oppositions like parallelism, inversion, and equivalence, and these oppositions give the text its meaning. In recent years, scholars have investigated the potential of structuralism for analysing biblical texts. For example, David Jobling probes the myth of the fall in Gen. 2–3 to lay bare its deep structure, which can be described as follows. Woman is the mediating principle between the binary opposites: man and the animals. The myth of the fall functions to avoid censuring God and man for life's difficulties by making their contraries, the serpent and the woman, responsible, but it does so at the cost of attributing to man an unwanted passivity while justifying patriarchal power, a contradiction which the story serves to obscure. (*The Sense of Biblical Narrative*: Structural Analyses in the Hebrew Bible, vol. 2, 1986. See also vol. 1, 1978, or A. M. Johnson [ed.], *The New Testament and Structuralism*, 1976, or volumes of *Semeia* from 1974 onwards.)

Some non-structuralists have judged the results achieved by structuralist interpretations of the Bible to be either banal, in that complicated jargon is used to state the obvious, or bizarre, in that deep structures have nothing to do with the subject of the text. But those who have felt disappointed are urged to turn to the work of a master to appreciate its value. Umberto Eco's sparkling novel, *The Name of the Rose* (ET 1983), painlessly initiates the reader into the subtleties of structuralism by recounting the adventures and conversations of William of Baskerville and his assistant, Adso. The transformation of Sherlock Holmes and Dr Watson into an English Franciscan and a German Benedictine novice, who witness the fulfilment of the book of Revelation's visionary predictions in a fourteenth-century Italian monastery, whose library signifies the known world, boldly demonstrates the 'intertextuality' which characterizes all literature. Although structuralism has no interest in literature's references to the world, it is adept at uncovering the references one text makes to another. In biblical scholarship, the careful definition of sources and forms, originally occasioned by a concern for history, can equally well serve a literary purpose. Each biblical book draws on, develops, inverts and transforms the imagery and structure of other texts. The Gospels,* for example, transform OT narratives about prophets, and invert those about kings. (Jesus is messiah,* but his short life and crucifixion hardly exemplify kingly success as understood in I and II Kings.)

One advantage which structuralism brings to biblical interpretation is that it allows the reader to see the Bible as a whole, rather than as a series of discrete compilations and compositions from different periods of history. This holistic* perspective informs Northrop Frye's reading of the Bible. In *The Great Code* (1982), he discovers the unity which the structure and imagery of the Bible creates through its parallels and inversions. Beginning with the creation* of the world and ending with its final transformation, the Bible tells the story of Adam* and Israel, using the recurring concrete images of city, mountain, river, garden, tree, oil, fountain, bread, wine, bride and sheep, in a dialectical progression of types* and antitypes, paradisal and demonic. The NT with its gospels,* history, epistles* and revelation parallels and foreshortens the OT, with its law, history, writings,* prophets and apocalyptic.* The general form is a series of falls and restorations, misfortunes and misunderstandings leading to disastrous consequences which are reversed to bring about a happy outcome. And this is the form of the whole Bible, from the Fall of Adam to the new Jerusalem.*

Structuralism's deciphering of the text itself, without reference to its authors or history, also throws light on literary technique, on how the structure assembles parts into a meaningful whole. G. Genette's *Narrative Discourse* (ET 1980), for example, plots the ways in which narratives structure time through order, duration and frequency, and determine focus through mood and voice. R. A. Culpepper's *Anatomy of the Fourth Gospel* (1983) uses Genette's network of relations in defining the structure of the Fourth Gospel.

Here the interests of structuralism begin to overlap with those of rhetorical criticism.* Since Wayne Booth's *The Rhetoric of Fiction* (1961) and *The Rhetoric of Irony* (1974), scholars have become interested in the art of persuasion practised in biblical books. A. J. Hauser's study of Gen. 2–3, for example, seeks

to demonstrate how the chapters impress the reader with the shattering effects of the loss of intimacy and the disruption of harmony. This is one area in which biblical scholars can learn not only from the literary criticism of modern works but also from that of ancient texts, since forms of rhetoric have changed over the centuries.

The recognition that literature seeks to persuade readers has led to attempts at describing the sorts of reading skills required by particular texts, and hence the readers implied by their rhetorical strategies. The rhetoric of irony,* for example, requires a reader who is aware of ironic possibilities, and an ironical text inscribes such a reader into its texture. The 'implied reader' is the subject of reader-response criticism.* According to this view, meaning is created by the reader construing the text. The potential of the writing is realized by the reader in making sense of words, phrases, sentences, paragraphs, and eventually the whole complex of the work, forging a comprehensive meaning from the parts. Like structuralism, reader-response criticism treats works holistically, not worrying about the stages of development but about the effects of their final forms. Some reader-response critics emphasize the power of the text to evoke a particular response in the reader, a response which is encoded in the rhetoric, so that the form of the text itself creates its ideal reader. Others emphasize the reader's freedom to make the text conform to desires. W. Iser's *The Act of Reading* (ET 1978) exemplifies the first, and N. Holland's *Five Readers Reading* (1975), the second.

The refreshing vistas reader-response criticism offers interpreters of the Bible are evidenced in a number of studies on sections of the OT. Robert Alter's two books, *The Art of Biblical Narrative* (1981) and *The Art of Biblical Poetry* (1985), and Meir Sternberg's *The Poetics of Biblical Narrative* (1985) bring a new subtlety to the experience of reading the Bible. Sternberg describes how the functional principles of ideology,* historiography and aesthetics are combined in biblical narrative,* in spite of the tensions which exist between them. It is these very strains which force the reader to draw out implications and thereby engage in the drama of reading. Since the narrative provides the nation's sense of identity, however, it must appeal to a wide public. It does this, argues Sternberg, by full proof composition, that is, by presenting a form which can be both overread and underread, but not counterread, because the story-line, word order, and value system are consistently guaranteed by a reliable and omniscient narrator. Nevertheless, the text is sufficiently elliptical to imply more than is stated, so that the reader is repeatedly challenged to discover what lies beyond the explicit.

Reader-response criticism has had little impact so far on NT interpretation, but N. R. Petersen's 'The Reader in the Gospel' (*Neotestamentica* 18, 1984, pp. 38–51) offers a brief examination of the Gospel according to Mark to illustrate the distinction he wishes to make between the readers encoded in the texts themselves, the implied readers, and the actual readers from a later age who are not inscribed in the text, but who are involved in the narrative world of the work.

If questions of reference to anything outside literature are inconspicuous or absent from much modern literary criticism, this is no accident. The focus of interest is upon the details of the literary world created by the text. The underlying assumption is that language and literature tell more about how human beings see things than about the things themselves. Nevertheless, nagging questions about the truth and value of realities envisaged in the Bible, refined as they are by sensitive readings, rightly continue to haunt the reader.

See also **Narrative Criticism; Narrative Theology; Reader-Response Criticism; Rhetorical Criticism.**

R. Alter and F. Kermode (eds), *The Literary Guide to the Bible*, 1987; A. Berlin, *Poetics and Interpretation of Biblical Narrative*, 1983; T. Eagleton, *Literary Theory: an Introduction*, 1983.

MARGARET DAVIES

Liturgy, Use of the Bible in

The Bible is full of liturgical material which has been much quarried for prayers and hymns.* While there may be dispute about just how liturgical were some of these passages in their origin (e.g. Phil. 2.5–11), many of them very probably owe their beginning to early Christian worship (e.g. the *Magnificat* and *Nunc Dimittis* in Luke 1 and 2). The OT contains the obvious corpus of Jewish liturgical hymnody, the Psalter, but there are also such compositions as the canticle of Jonah (Jonah 2) which are rhythmic in style and prayerful in subject-matter. Opinions differ about the extent to which such passages are the work of a specific author or were produced in the corporate setting of worship, Jewish or Christian. For example, the Jewish-style *berakah* ('Blessed be . . .') is the inspiration behind such Epistle* material as Eph. 1.3ff., and I Peter 1.3ff., but whether these passages were in fact prompted by early Christian worship is uncertain. What is certain, however, is that they are related to worship.

When Christian prayers came to be recorded in texts that have come down to us (from the third century onwards the material becomes increasingly reliable), certain tendencies are easily recognizable. Thus, in the eucharistic prayer that is contained in the *Apostolic Tradition* of Hippolytus (*c.* AD 215), the 'word' christology of John mixes with the virgin birth of Matthew and Luke. More noticeable is the self-conscious use of scripture in, for example, the eucharistic prayers attributed to Basil of Caesarea. The early version, used by the Coptic church to this day, alludes biblical passages in its treatment of salvation history,* but the later Byzantine version (used in churches of the Byzantine rite on special occasions) exemplifies a more mannered series of biblical additions that are direct quotations. This proves a liturgical rule of thumb, that such quotations are not a sign of antiquity, but of subsequent editing.

However, nothing could be more influential than the effect of the Bible on the eventual formation of the liturgical calendar, the main structure of which dates from the fourth century. Here too a sense of salvation history was uppermost, especially in the shape of a devout annual following of the career of Christ. It is not surprising that Luke–Acts, with its wealth of biographical detail and datings, compared with the other Gospels,* and its salvation-history character, should have been especially significant in this process. Thus, without Luke–Acts, the relative placing in the year of the following observances would have been impossible: the Presentation of Christ, the Annunciation of the Blessed Virgin Mary, the Nativity of John the Baptist, the Visitation, Ascension Day, Whitsunday. Also, the Feast of the Circumcision of Christ would scarcely have arisen without Luke, though the Epiphany comes from Matthew. Some of these datings depend, of course, on a decision, otherwise determined, about the 'date' of Jesus' birth. All added enormously to the earlier Christian calendar, which centred almost wholly on the Paschal or Easter celebration, with Sunday as its weekly commemoration. It was Luke who, among other influences such as the post-Constantinian sense of Christendom, enabled the church in due course to arrive at a conception of the liturgical year which Gregory Dix (in *The Shape of the Liturgy*, 1945) referred to memorably as 'the sanctification of time'.

Both OT and NT have also been used as sources for Christian hymnody.* The *Gloria in excelsis* takes its inspiration from the angelic hymn in Luke 2.14; several versions are known, but all employ the biblical opening, though the translation of 'men of goodwill'/ 'goodwill towards men' has proved problematical – manuscripts* of Luke's Gospel itself differ. The liturgical year brings with it ample scope for variable chants: for example, the 'Reproaches', sung at the Veneration of the Cross in the Latin liturgy on Good Friday, owe their inspiration to selected passages from Micah 6.3–4; Deut. 8.2,3,7; Isa. 5.4; Jer. 2.21 and Ps. 68.22, and this chant is first found towards the end of the ninth century. More recently, Isaac Watts' hymn, 'When I survey the wondrous cross', written originally as a eucharistic hymn, could be said to be based on the passion narrative* in the Fourth Gospel, with its strong representational piety, set amidst a cosmic drama, into which the believer is drawn.

The Bible has also been used in short passages, often called 'Sentences', as in the beginning of the Book of Common Prayer Morning and Evening Prayer and in the Burial Office (e.g. John 11.25–26, Job 19.25–27, I Tim 6.7, Job 1.21), a liturgical use extended considerably, for example at the eucharist in the Church of England's Alternative Service Book (1980), at the start of the service, as well as after communion, and long traditional as Catholic service chants. This has the advantage of making scripture easily available in smaller units, but it has the disadvantage of taking the material out of its context.

Typology* was a popular theme in the compilation of the patristic and mediaeval* liturgies. Ordination prayers, both Eastern and Western, make frequent reference to Moses* and Aaron, not so much as proof-texts,* but in order to set the new order within the wider context of the old. Sometimes such a use has carried with it a definite hermeneutical* undercurrent, in order to support a particular doctrine. Thus, Mal. 1.11 is a popular text when discussing eucharistic sacrifice; it is used by the early Fathers but also employed at the Council of Trent. It occurs in several eucharistic prayers of eastern provenance, and some of the earlier occurrences remove the reference to the offering of incense, perhaps in order to avoid mention of a liturgical practice not yet accepted by the Christian community at that time. When it appears in the Coptic Church's eucharistic prayer of St Mark, its meaning is clear: Malachi's prophecy of the universal offering of praise is fulfilled in the Christian eucharist. In the Roman Canon (eucharistic prayer 1 in the 1970 Roman Missal), the eucharistic celebration is linked directly with the priestly offerings of Melchisedek, thus supporting a high sacrificial view of the Mass not found in the East, and deliberately eschewed by the Reformers.*

Scripture is also used as a sacramental rationale. Thus, in the mediaeval Sarum rite of baptism (used all over England), the story of Jesus taking children into his arms (Matt. 19.13ff.) is read. It is so closely associated with the action of baptism that it is hard to avoid the conclusion that it was first inserted into the rite (it was not thus used in the earlier tradition) in order to justify the trend away from the baptism of adults and children at the Easter Vigil to baptism of infants only on any occasion. Similarly, the institution narrative of the eucharist (based on I Cor. 11.23ff. or Gospel parallels) is part of nearly every eucharistic prayer; in the West, exaggeration is the order of the day, for the Middle Ages make these words so central that they are isolated within the whole prayer, assuming an importance they never before had. Some of the Reformers read the narrative as a separate 'warrant', before the prayer of thanksgiving could begin.

The motivations behind using the Bible, whether directly or indirectly, for new or revised parts of the liturgy are bound to change as time goes on. Moreover, the influence of scholarship in this process, however delayed, is likely eventually to have its effect. Today's English is more epigrammatic in its style than the sonorous and repetitive periods of the Tudor era, and that seems to make the temptation to compose new prayers incorporating brief biblical phrases out of context at times hard to resist. Among the problems are the use of such passages as John 2.1–11 in connection with marriage: the Cana miracle, strong in Eastern marriage prayers, has tended to be marginal in the West, with its long tradition of seeing marriage juridically. Similarly, there are pitfalls in using biblical symbols* in prayers, because they can become so conceptualized that they lose their resonance, particularly if they are to refer to liturgical ideas (like eucharistic presence) that are controversial. History has one fundamental lesson to teach about using the Bible in composing liturgical material; unless the source itself is abundantly rhythmical and rhetorical in style, it is at its best when indirect and oblique, rather like the nature of biblical truth itself.

See also **Hymnody; Hymns, New Testament.**

T. G. A. Baker, *Questioning Worship*, 1977; J. Daniélou, *The Bible and the Liturgy*, 1960; K. W. Stevenson, *The First Rites: Worship in the Early Church,* 1989.

KENNETH STEVENSON

Logion

The Greek word *logion* (pl. *logia*) is witnessed to from the time of Euripides and Herodotus, signifying an oracle,* 'especially one preserved from antiquity'; that is, a saying or message purporting to come from a deity and mediated by a prophet* or other messenger. It is used exclusively in this sense in the Septuagint,* for divine and not for human sayings. In this way, *logion* is to be distinguished from *logos*,* which occurs much more frequently in the LXX and can be used for both divine and human speech. This distinction between the two terms is true also of the usage of the NT. In the RSV, *logion* is always translated 'oracle', rather than 'saying' or 'word', the usual rendering of *logos*. In Acts 7.38 and Rom. 3.2 it refers to ancient (i.e. in the OT) sayings of God. In Heb. 5.12, the 'first principles of Christ' (6.1) receive special dignity through being described as 'oracles' (*logia*). In I Peter 4.11, the writer asks that believers speak as those who utter 'oracles of God', just as they are to render service 'by the strength that God supplies'.

In the NT, the sayings of Jesus are often described as *logos* (pl. *logoi*), never as *logia*. The latter usage occurs first in the second century. Taking the meaning of the word in a strong sense, then, we may see Jesus' words receiving the new quality of 'oracles of the Lord' in Justin (*Dial.* 18.1) and Irenaeus* (*Adv. haer.* I,8,1): they are already seen as preserved from antiquity (unless, that is, we should take *logia* simply as 'sayings'). Unfortunately, the work of Papias* of Hierapolis (*c.* AD 110), which bore the title 'Expositions of the *logia* of the Lord' (Eusebius,* *Hist. eccl.* III,39,1) has not survived. Papias did not mean by this term only sayings of Jesus – he also included narratives. All the same, the designation by Papias of the Jesus-tradition by the term *logia* gave to it as a whole the special quality of 'oracles preserved from antiquity'.

In the nineteenth century, the title of Papias' work was taken to refer to Q (from German, *Quelle* = source), the collection of Jesus' sayings which was seen as lying behind the Gospels of Matthew and Luke as a second source beside the Gospel of Mark. Also, Papias had written of the Gospel of Matthew, that 'Matthew recorded the oracles (*logia*) in the Hebrew tongue'. It has to be said, however, that this note gives no basis for any particular theory, still less a solution, for the Synoptic Problem.* The symbol Q is wholly neutral in that regard.

Moving on from its use in source criticism,* Bultmann* introduced the term *logion* (German pl. *Logien*) into form criticism* as a technical term. It is evident that for him *logion* was not to be understood in the strong sense of 'oracle', but as it was used in source criticism, i.e. to mean 'saying'; there, Q was defined as a collection not of oracles but of sayings. Bultmann used the term *Logien* for a sub-category of the words of the Lord, alongside prophetic and apocalyptic* sayings, law-sayings and church rules, 'I'-sayings and parables.* By *Logien*, Bultmann designated

those words of the Lord in which Jesus speaks as a 'wisdom*-teacher', a role which, according to Bultmann, does not go back to the historical Jesus.* The term is thus introduced by Bultmann in a sense not covered by ancient usage: *Logien* are simply statements in the Jesus tradition which may be characterized as 'wisdom-sayings'. They are rules for life within this world, or else such rules recalled in question-form, or warnings resulting from them. Both Bultmann and Martin Dibelius apparently avoided using the term *Logienquelle* (sayings source) as a designation for 'the synoptic sayings collection Q', because Q in fact includes other material than sayings alone (e.g. Matt. 8.5–13 = Luke 7.1–10).

The discovery of the Coptic Gospel of Thomas at Nag Hammadi* made it possible to identify the already known Oxyrhynchus Papyri 1, 654 and 655 as fragments of that work. These had already been designated as *logia* of Jesus, but only in the sense of 'sayings'. This led to further use of the word *logion* for the individual sayings of the Gospel of Thomas, in line with the vocabulary of form criticism.

So, in the discussion of this NT material, there is really no difference between *logion* and *logos* as terms for the sayings of Jesus. *Logia* came to be used in this sense, in the context of nineteenth-century source criticism, as a result of its presence in the title of the work of Papias. Bultmann then used it in a very general sense, no longer involving the specialized meaning of 'oracle preserved from antiquity', but now only the general one of 'saying'. It is therefore necessary to distinguish between the sense of the Greek word and its technical application in the sense of 'saying'.

R. Bultmann, *The History of the Synoptic Tradition*, ET 1963, pp. 69ff.; G. Kittel in G. W. Bromiley (ed.), *TDNT*, vol. 4, pp. 137–41.

DIETER LÜHRMANN

Logos

The Greek word *logos* means something spoken, and may cover anything from a word, to a sentence, a story or an argument. In philosophical discourse it was also used for the rational thought or reason existing in the mind before it was spoken. In Stoic philosophy it was used for the rationality or divine order immanent in the universe, and was thus identified with the cosmic deity, the primordial spiritual fire, out of which everything is made.

In the Jewish scriptures, the Word of God* was deeply significant. It was the Word of the Lord that came to the prophets, and in Isa. 55.10f. that Word is depicted as creative. In the creation* story of Gen. 1, God simply spoke and things were called into being: so it became a commonplace that God created *by his Word*.

It is not therefore surprising to find that Greek-speaking Judaism found common links with the philosophical tradition, links which were reinforced by the idea that God's wisdom was involved in creation: i.e. his reason as well as his word. This creative wisdom of God is personified in Prov. 8.22, and that idea is developed further in later wisdom literature* like Ecclus. 24; in the Greek work known as the Wisdom of Solomon, wisdom becomes the all-pervading spirit which penetrates all things and is in the reason of all intelligent beings: she is the breath of the power of God, and a pure emanation of the glory of the Almighty. Stoic language of the immanent divine is married with Jewish awareness of the transcendent Most High God.

In the NT we find the word Logos used in a most striking way in the Prologue to the Gospel of John.* Continuing debate revolves around the question how far this Prologue simply has as its background the idea of the Word of God in the OT, possibly affected by the personification of Wisdom in the wisdom literature; and how far it has been influenced directly or indirectly by the Greek philosophical tradition. An earlier Jewish writer in the same century made a fruitful correlation between philosophy and his religious tradition, namely Philo* of Alexandria. To what extent was the Gospel affected by such developments in Hellenistic* Judaism? To what extent was the Logos envisaged as a pre-existent divine being, and to what extent was the Logos merely a personified attribute of God? The Johannine Prologue is far from clear, but what it seems to be suggesting is that God's meaning and purpose, his creative design, his revealed will, his mind, became embodied in the person of Jesus, and this Logos of God was in a sense God himself, and yet in another sense was with God as the only Son in the bosom of the Father, who alone has seen God and can explain or reveal him.

This notion was to be taken up and developed much more explicitly in the so-called Logos-theology of the Apologists, who in the second century tried to explain Christianity for an uncomprehending public. The Logos, they suggested, was God's Reason, the reason in the mind of God himself. But the transcendent God who is invisible, incorporeal, unchangeable and impassible, when he determined to create a visible, material world, 'spoke forth' his reason, so that the Logos became the 'instrument' through whom he could create and have contact with the creation. So by his Word, God created; and by his Word, he declared his will, spoke through the prophets, and inspired the scriptures. This Logos was also the Reason possessed by all intelligent beings, and Socrates could be claimed

for the Christian tradition as well as the Jewish prophets. Finally this Logos had become incarnate in Jesus Christ, the Son of God, who was the full revelation of God's purpose and will, who demonstrated and taught the moral way of life for all humanity and opened the way to heaven by his death and resurrection.*

The beauty of this position lay in its appeal to the universal reason as the rational order of all creation, and to the common rationality of all humanity, including its moral sense. It was a very profound and subtle marriage of Jewish monotheism and the philosophical tradition. Logos-theology was clearly a development of scriptural ideas within a particular cultural framework. In modern times, the theology of Karl Barth,* focussed as it is on the Word of God, is another kind of development from the same scriptural roots.

See also **John, Gospel of; Patristic Christology.**

L. W. Barnard, *Justin Martyr, his Life and Thought*, 1967; P. Carrington, *Christian Apologetics of the Second Century*, 1921; C. H. Dodd, *The Interpretation of the Fourth Gospel*, 1953; J. N. D. Kelly, *Early Christian Doctrines*, 1960; J. N. Sanders, *The Fourth Gospel in the Early Church*, 1943; M. F. Wiles, *The Spiritual Gospel*, 1960.

FRANCES YOUNG

Lohmeyer, E.

Ernst Lohmeyer was born on 8 July 1890, the son of a pastor in Dorsten in Westphalia. He studied theology, philosophy and oriental languages in Tübingen,* Leipzig and Berlin from 1908 to 1911, and in 1912 received his first higher degree in theology for a thesis, published in the following year, on the idea of covenant* in the NT. From 1913 to 1918 he was occupied in military service. He received his doctorate from Erlangen for a thesis on Anselm of Canterbury's teaching on the will, and this was followed by his Heidelberg 'habilitation' in NT studies in 1918 and then two years later by NT posts at Breslau in Silesia (now Wroclaw in Poland), where, in 1930–1, he was Rector of the University. In 1935, he was disciplined for his opposition to Nazism and transferred to Greifswald in Pomerania. He was engaged in military service again from 1939 to 1943. Having been designated Rector of the University of Greifswald at the end of the war in May 1945, he was removed from office and arrested in February 1946. The Soviet occupation forces condemned him to death in a secret trial and on 19 September 1946 he was executed. His death only became known in 1951 and was confirmed by the Russian Red Cross only in 1957.

Lohmeyer inherited from his teachers,

Adolf Deissmann and Martin Dibelius, an interest in the history of religions* and also in form criticism.* Both concerns come together in his highly influential work, *Kurios Jesus, an Inquiry into Phil. 2.5–11*, 1928, in which he was the first to put forward the thesis, since widely accepted, that in this passage Paul took over an already existing hymn,* whose context in early Christian life (*Sitz im Leben*) was the eucharist and which, when looked at from a 'history of religions' point of view, gave evidence of Iranian influence. Form-critical work was, in the case of Lohmeyer more strongly than with other scholars, bound up with an interest in social history (cf. his *Social Questions in Early Christianity*, 1921). His work in the 'history of religions' area comes into view in various studies, in particular his commentary* on the Revelation of John, 1926.

In his commentaries on Philippians, 1928, Colossians (taken as authentically Pauline) and Philemon, 1930, he interpreted the Pauline letters from a form-critical point of view, in part making use of hypotheses about metrical elements in these texts. In this connection, it is important to note his links with contemporary German lyrical poets (e.g. the Stefan George circle and Jochen Klepper). In *Grundlagen paulinischer Theologie*, 1929, as well as in other essays of that period (collected in *Probleme paulinischer Theologie*, 1954), he put forward his own independent picture of Paul,* including, among other features, the suggestion (now returning to popularity) that the expression *pistis Christou* is to be understood as involving a subjective genitive ('the faith(fulness) of Christ' rather than 'faith in Christ').

The basic thesis of his book *Galiläa und Jerusalem*, 1936, has, with variations, been widely influential in later research, not least in the work of R. H. Lightfoot.* It is that in relation to these two places, we are to distinguish two kinds of early Christianity, not just geographically but also theologically. His commentary on the Gospel of Mark, 1937, as well as the fragments of a commentary on Matthew, 1956, can still be read as a foundation for research into the Synoptic* Gospels,* as can also his exposition of the Lord's Prayer,* 1946.

Lohmeyer's achievement lies in the broad base of his exegetical* work, of which various parts have been proved valid, or at least stimulating for further research. No thorough survey of his work as a whole has so far appeared. Lohmeyer distinguished himself from dialectical theology and especially from the theology of Rudolf Bultmann.* His loyalty lay with German idealistic philosophy, not with the existentialism of Heidegger. (We recall that he had proved himself in philosophy in his second thesis, on Anselm.) Against

Bultmann's theological grounding of Christianity in the Kerygma,* Lohmeyer took his stand on the person of Jesus as the centre of Christianity. The strength of his concern with political and ecclesiastical problems is demonstrated by his interventions both before and after 1933 on behalf of Jewish colleagues and in his strong approval of Martin Buber.

E. Esking, *Glaube und Geschichte in der theologischen Exegese Ernst Lohmeyers*, 1951; W. G. Kümmel, *The New Testament. The History of the Investigation of its Problems*, ET 1973 (see index); W. Schmauch (ed.), *In Memoriam Ernst Lohmeyer*, 1951, pp. 19–21.

DIETER LÜHRMANN

Lord's Prayer

In the accounts of the origins of the Lord's Prayer as found in the earliest texts (the Gospels of Matthew and Luke, and the Didache), at least one or two of the three versions (Luke being much the most distinctive) are already interpretative in character. That is, they develop, with their own purposes in view, earlier texts or perhaps oral* versions.

Thus, on the commonest view of Gospel sources, which places the Prayer in the Q material, it is generally felt that the Lucan version (11.2–4), which is shorter and simpler, is closer to the original teaching of Jesus and that Matthew (6.9–13), which is virtually reproduced in Didache 8, has elaborated Luke's version in characteristically Matthean ways (e.g. adding 'Our' and 'who is in heaven'). Even Luke himself, however, has, on this way of looking at the matter, not left the prayer alone, but probably added to the petition about bread his characteristic term 'each day' (cf. 9.23).

Other accounts of the origins of the Prayer make the point about its interpretative function even more strongly. M. D. Goulder and others have put forward the view that it was in effect composed by Matthew on the basis of suitable material in Mark, notably 11.25 and the Gethsemane story in 14.32–42 (especially v. 36), with the aim of concentrating Jesus' teaching about prayer as it had been disclosed in the earlier Gospel. On this view, Luke, using Matthew as well as Mark, then shortened it, using his own typical forms (e.g. the simple address 'Father', cf. 10.21; 22.42; 23.46). Less dramatically, but no less constructively, the Didache version, predominantly liturgical in aim, added a doxology, a form of which found its way in due course into manuscripts of Matthew and then into more general church usage.

The Didache recommends the use of the Prayer three times each day, probably reflecting early Christian practice of daily prayer, as also the rabbinic* custom in that regard. In the early centuries, its chief use was as a basis for Christian instruction. Manuals by Tertullian,* Origen,* and others expound it, some of them moving some distance from the Prayer's chiefly eschatological* thrust in the setting of the Gospels (especially Matthew) and, on the former view mentioned above, no doubt the teaching of Jesus itself. Cyprian, for example, interprets the 'daily bread' as the eucharist, losing a possible original reference to the 'bread of the coming kingdom',* as does the modern interpretation as referring to daily necessities. Some of this teaching tradition was allied to baptismal catechesis, for in both East and West, the rendition of the Prayer by the candidates is a significant feature of the baptismal process, as witnessed by the classical liturgies.

Different motivations for using the Prayer are apparent in the various liturgies themselves, where it is first attested in the eucharist in the fourth century. In the Roman rite, it has (until recently) almost invariably been introduced at mass, before communion, with words that point to the following of Jesus' teaching.

The Reformers* felt no need either to defend its introduction or to add 'unscriptural' material into its text, though English Puritans often attacked the Prayer's recitation – as 'vain repetition' – as distinct from its use as a model for prayer (Luke 11.1). In the Book of Common Prayer, the Lord's Prayer maintains its traditional position in the Offices (forming a climax of prayer towards the end), but without the doxology. In the communion service, it appears without doxology at the start, but with the doxology immediately after communion; and an analogous position, immediately after the sacramental act, is also found for it at baptism. Lutheran rites, however, tend to place it just before the Institution Narrative at the eucharist, and just before the act of baptism. The other Reformers varied in their view and there are many Free Church congregations where the Prayer naturally comes as a conclusion to the intercessions, not dissimilar to its use in the traditional Western Office.

The Lord's Prayer is known in other forms; for example there are Trope versions of the text in mediaeval books, elaborating on many of the themes of the Prayer. Luther's* 'Vater unser in Himmelreich' (composed in 1539) brings this tradition into a new form of life, in nine rich stanzas, and there are several versions designed for this kind of liturgical usage in today's folk hymnals. They can be popular; they can also be over-interpretative, robbing the original text of its simplicity and directness.

Twentieth-century liturgical revisions have tended to revive the patristic position of the Prayer, and also the tendency to 'introduce' it in a formal manner has been adopted by many Protestant churches, though without the inserted prayer for peace found in the RC mass. With that has also appeared a restlessness about how the Prayer is to be introduced. Many rites repeat the old tradition of 'following Christ's teaching', but alternatives are appearing that pick on certain themes within the Prayer, such as daily bread and kingdom, and these are used both at the eucharist and at the Office. The need to explain the use of such a familiar part of the liturgical repertoire is still alive after so many centuries.

Translation* problems are allied to others. It is hard to get international agreement on 'deliver us from evil' (the 'Evil One'?) and 'lead us not into the time of trial'. The (almost certain) originally eschatological reference to the testing of God's people before the End in the latter clause of the Prayer is not readily picked up in modern use of it, and the familiar notion of 'temptation' has long been the customary interpretation. These difficulties are highlighted by the desire for precision in a modern language, set over against the allusive nature of the original texts. History suggests that variety within the text and variations in liturgical understanding of its function are likely to continue, given the deeply traditional nature of the Prayer.

See also **Liturgy, Use of the Bible in; Sermon on the Mount.**

C. F. Evans, *The Lord's Prayer*, 1963; J. Jeremias, *The Prayers of Jesus*, 1967; E. Lohmeyer, *The Lord's Prayer*, 1965; T. W. Manson, 'The Lord's Prayer', *Bulletin of John Rylands Library*, 1955.

KENNETH STEVENSON

Luke, Gospel of

Justin Martyr used Luke's Gospel, and it may be a source for the Gospel of Thomas. But criticism of it can be said to begin with Marcion,* whose Gospel was Luke, shorn of passages indicating the authority of the OT and the physicality of Jesus' body. Along with the Pauline* letters in his canon, it formed the scriptural base of his radically Gentile Christianity. Marcion's (hostile) insight into the Jewishness of the other Gospels,* and conversely into Luke's difference from them, showed cold critical intuition. Many subsequent critics have shared, rightly or wrongly, his belief in Luke as 'the Gentile Gospel'.

After the formation of the orthodox canon* of scripture Luke had a secure place in the Christian Bible. He did not suffer the neglect accorded to Mark, nor was he as much used as the apostolic Gospels of Matthew and

John, with their obvious appeal to makers of ecclesiastical order and theology. But his first two chapters were deeply influential on the Christian imagination, particularly as a prime source of Christian art.* And his parables* were favourite material for allegorical interpretation.* Origen,* the grand master of this latter exercise, allegorized Luke's birth narrative (*see* **Infancy Narratives**), for example, in terms of the continual descent of angels to declare the timeless birth of Christ (*Homily* XII). Cyril of Alexandria (*Homily* XVIII) retrenched somewhat on this method, allowing literal* reading as well, but the allegorical method rolled on and was famously used by Augustine* in his interpretation of Luke's parable of the Good Samaritan in his second book *Quaestionum Evangeliorum*. The commentators of the Middle Ages (*see* **Mediaeval Interpretation**), such as Thomas Aquinas, anthologized the patristic exegetes.

The New Learning of the Renaissance was not averse to allegorical interpretation (Erasmus* used it) but brought the literal meaning of texts into a new prominence which enabled historical investigation to begin. Calvin,* who commented on Luke within a harmony* of the Gospels (1553), preferred it as a check to uncontrolled speculation. Grotius (d. 1645) virtually ignored patristic exegetes in his notes on the Gospel and set the foundations of grammatical and philological* criticism.

Investigation of Luke's sources begins in eighteenth-century Germany with Lessing, who believed in an Aramaic original, and Herder,* who preferred oral tradition.* Griesbach believed Luke to be an editor of Matthew, a hypothesis which has revived recently. Herder's judgment that Luke's work (including Acts) was 'the first Christian history', as distinct from Mark's collection of stories and Matthew's Jewish argumentation, is the fundamental theme of the more imaginative treatment of Luke as part of the historical development of Christianity. Along with source criticism,* this has become the major way of investigating the Gospel. Herder believed that 'Luke wrote his history like a pure Greek'. In the twentieth century, this view has a competitor in the belief that he wrote his history in a Jewish OT style. Schleiermacher's *Essay on St Luke*, translated into English by Connop Thirlwall in 1825, belongs strictly in the same source-critical tradition. 'He is,' wrote Schleiermacher, 'from beginning to end no more than the compiler and arranger of documents which he found in existence, and which he allowed to pass unaltered through his hands' (p. 313).

In the nineteenth century, the home of the understanding of Luke in terms of Christian history was Tübingen,* and its master F. C. Baur. On sources, Baur followed Griesbach, adding the theory that the Gospel used by Marcion was a source for Luke rather than an adaptation of it, and consequently positing a date in the second half of the second century. But Baur's real and lasting contribution was to see Luke–Acts as part of the politics of Christian history. The two-volume work formed a resolving compromise between Matthew's Jewish particularism and Paul's Gentile universalism. Thus Luke became an indispensable moment in the maturing of catholic Christianity, viewed through Hegelian spectacles. Baur's source theory, particularly concerning Marcion, has not worn well. But while the simplicities of his overall historical reconstruction are not enough any more, his perception of Luke as a reconciling historian, himself addressing a particular and contemporary historical moment, has proved immensely fruitful.

In the second half of the nineteenth century and after Baur, the 'two-source theory' held the field and kept it well into the twentieth. It posits Mark and Q as sources for Luke, Q being a document (mostly) of Jesus' teaching, which Matthew and Luke both used. This pushed the date of Luke to an earlier time than Baur believed likely. This was in line with the pervasive motivation of Gospel studies at this time. Their principal concern was not, as with Baur, the understanding of the development of Christianity, but the recovery of the historical Jesus.* Q played an important part in this. Matthew's account of Jesus' teaching has obvious signs of powerful arrangement in the interests of Christian ecclesiastical order, piety and morality, in the church after Jesus. Luke's, on the other hand, appears to be more diffuse, less tied to church discipline, and more clearly set in Jesus' own ministry. So Luke is often held to retail Q in a purer form than Matthew and, by an unproven but slight projection from that belief, to record the very words of Jesus. This is most noticeable with the parables where the ecclesiastical and eschatological* character of Matthew's compares strongly with the commonplace realism of Luke's. Nobody wanted the Good Samaritan or the Prodigal Son to be by anyone but Jesus. The whole strategy of Gospel criticism in German and English universities, not least Sanday's Oxford Seminar of which Streeter's *The Four Gospels* of 1924 was the grand manifesto, virtually dictated that Luke should be regarded as a dependable source for the life of Jesus with a minimum of ideas of his own and with artlessness being more desirable than the literary skill which Herder had noticed.

This was a precarious position, threatened by any glimpse of Luke's techniques or strategy. It depended on an entirely negative view of Luke as a writer which acquaintance with his work could unsettle. The testing ground for it is the matter in Luke which is found in no other Gospel. It is plentiful and impressive, including his first two chapters, the famous parables already mentioned, and much of the passion narrative.* For Luke to be the literary nonentity hoped for, he has to have used sources here. And for the sources to be convincingly present, incongruity with the rest of the book is required. Such a source was posited by Streeter (op. cit., ch. 8) and Vincent Taylor (*Behind the Third Gospel*, 1926), who called it 'Proto-Luke' (seen as a union of Luke's own matter and his Q material) and held that it was Luke's primary document. He had it before Mark's Gospel came his way. It was earlier than any of the Gospels and so, by implication, highly dependable as a source for Jesus' life. J. M. Creed's still unsurpassed commentary on *The Gospel According to St Luke* (1930) quietly tilted the weight of interpretation to the other end of the scale, presenting Luke's creativity as explaining the material which Streeter and Taylor attributed to Proto-Luke. The passion narrative was the decisive field. Here Creed succeeded, in fine detail and with strong economy of argument, in making out a convincing case for his theory, that 'Luke has himself freely rewritten, rearranged and enlarged St Mark. He may sometimes present independent traditions, but the continuous thread of his narrative appears to be based upon Mark' (p. 262). Creed further noticed that the parables peculiar to Luke both formed a set and deployed themes integral to the Gospel as a whole. And in treating the birth narratives he recalled, with assent, Harnack's* judgment in *Luke the Physician* (ET 1900, p. 217) that 'the Hebraisms, whether adopted or inserted from the Old Testament are *intentional*; the whole style is artificial, and is intended to produce an impression of antiquity – a purpose which has been really fulfilled.' So, while Creed believed in Palestinian sources of some kind (oral, he implies, rather than written) for Luke 1 and 2, he gives grounds and scope for energetic work by Luke himself. His acumen in recovering the pervasive presence of the OT here and elsewhere in the Gospel helped to bring to the fore the indubitable source which Luke used, as distinct from the hypothetical documents which critics pressed upon him: the OT. To confront that was to be in the presence of an early Christian historian working to very different specifications from any modern one.

Contemporaneously the study of Luke as a writer in his own right was given a wealth of resource in the work of H. J. Cadbury.* He had worked with Kirsopp Lake and F. J. Foakes Jackson on the five volumes of *The Beginnings of Christianity*, a huge and definitive investigation of Luke's Acts of the Apostles, which appeared in 1920. His knowledge of Luke's Greek served to unsettle Harnack's view that Luke used specialized medical terminology and so was 'Luke the beloved physician' of Colossians and companion of Paul. Creed followed Cadbury here. In 1927 Cadbury's *The Making of Luke–Acts* came out. It is a rich album of studies of Luke's methods in their historical context, delicately balancing his Jewish and Hellenistic interests, and all presented with lucid urbanity. The book dealt with a very wide range of aspects of Luke's work, from his interest in cities and human character to his historiographical beliefs and techniques. There is a nuanced acceptance of the conventional two-source theory (Mark and Q) (*see* **Synoptic Problem**), but this does not occupy the foreground as consistently as usual, a much fuller context of literary influence, including the OT, Josephus* and Greek literature, being superimposed upon it. Cadbury, however, pays the price of his wealth of reference by a failure to produce a unified appreciation of Luke's strategy out of the bric-à-brac of his tactics.

This came, and came resoundingly, when Hans Conzelmann produced *Die Mitte der Zeit* in 1954 (ET 1960, *The Theology of St Luke*). Following Creed and projecting from him, Conzelmann saw Luke as an energetic, even destructive, editor of Mark, with his own massive ideology* of history as the story of divine salvation* with Jesus at its centre. Before him is the OT history, after him the apostolic history of Acts. Salvation is narrative and Jesus its turning point. Eschatology has receded to a remoter future than the previous evangelists envisaged. It still looms, but its postponement has left room for Luke's spacious historical reflection which Conzelmann sees in terms of a very definite and distinct division into the three eras of salvation. Later writers have had to posit connection as well as separation here, not least where Luke 1 and 2 are concerned. These chapters, which form a bridge between the OT and the time of Jesus, were ignored by Conzelmann, with somewhat distorting effect. Conzelmann's notions of the symbolic* significance of Luke's topography (*see* **Theological Geography**) have also met with suspicion. But none of these detracts from his momentous achievement. Since Conzelmann it is impossible to do justice to Luke's history without continual and detailed attention to the theology which sustains and shapes it. This has been a bitter blow to those hopes of recovering Jesus from an untendentious Luke which motivated so much work from the late nineteenth century onwards. They still go on, but the initiative and the energy are where Cadbury and Conzelmann put them so decisively. Ernst Haenchen's commentary on Acts (ET 1971) is a further powerful boost to the kind of criticism which Baur and his Tübingen colleagues had initiated at the beginning of the nineteenth century. Haenchen showed how powerful theological *Tendenz* had combined with dramatic skills to produce an historical romance or fiction, no more directly dependable for the apostolic age than the Gospel is for Jesus.

This is the point at which to take stock of the major features of the interpretation of Luke which are currently available. The growing emphasis on Luke's creativity has had its effect on the source-critical orthodoxy which hitherto held the field. It allows for increased freedom in Luke's use of Mark, such as Creed had pioneered in his commentary. So while Luke's use of Mark remains as a survivor of that old orthodoxy, the necessity to posit Proto-Luke has gone. The miraculous catch of fish at Luke 5.1–11, for example, can be read as a typically Lucan narrative expansion of Mark 1.16–20. Its symbolic prophecy of the Gentile mission in Acts, Peter's* repentance, and the combination of the wonderful and the workaday are observable Lucan traits. Q has also suffered from the new prominence of Luke himself as a tendentious and resourceful writer. It was a major prop of the Q hypothesis that in Luke Q is preserved in its native simplicity and realism, innocent of the ecclesiastical presuppositions which Matthew imposed on it. When Luke is himself seen as a realist, working to give a more historically plausible and generally acceptable narrative than his predecessors had left him, these features can be attributed to him rather than to his source. This does not demolish Q, but it opens the possibility of his having used Matthew, which is explored by John Drury, *Tradition and Design in Luke's Gospel* (1976) and M. D. Goulder, *Luke: a New Paradigm* (1989). Luke was strong enough to make the necessary changes.

Another argument for Luke as the better retailer of Q was that, whereas in Matthew the Q material is magisterially ordered, in Luke it seems to come higgledy-piggledy between chs 10 and 19. But C. F. Evans in an essay in *Studies in the Gospels* (ed. D. E. Nineham, 1955) discovered a sustained thematic parallelism with Deuteronomy which is a possible control on the Q material – its likelihood being boosted by Luke's large overall debt to Deuteronomy and to Deuteronomic historiography.* This connects with the increasing prominence given in recent criticism to Luke's use of the OT: not simply as a quarry for proof texts but as a source of models and themes for the writing of history.

A major example of this is his treatment of Jesus Christ. It has long been noticed that he has a 'lower' christology* than the other evangelists, and a much lower one than John, with whom he shares some material. This would be congruent with respect for traditional biblical monotheism and providentialism. It surfaces in Luke's portrayal of Jesus as 'a great prophet' (7.16) in the pattern of Elijah. Like Elijah he raises a dead child (7.11–17) and ascends into heaven (Acts 1.9), though unlike Elijah he refuses to call down fire on people (9.51–55). And the apparent incoherence of chs 10 to 19 is considerably reduced by observing the sustained preaching of repentance, the classic prophetic task, which runs through them.

If Jesus is somewhat levelled down by Luke in terms of doctrine and a vertical view of the world's relation to God, in terms of an historical view of the kind propounded by Conzelmann he is axial and central. Either way, there is more room for the apostles and more for them to do than in the other Gospels. They are generously portrayed. In Mark they understand and achieve practically nothing. In Matthew they understand but lack sufficient faith. Luke presents us with the future princes of the church, taken into Jesus' confidence, sharing his work, and given their norms and authority at the Last Supper (22.24–30). Peter is a fallible man, but through the ordeal of failure he will emerge as the support of his brethren (22.31–32). As striking as this, and perhaps more engaging, is the large number of realistically sketched people in Luke's Gospel, but absent from his synoptic colleagues: Martha and Mary, Zacchaeus, the penitent thief and the whole gallery of vivid human beings in the parables peculiar to Luke, from the Prodigal Son and his family to the sharp-practising steward and the indolent judge. Here is the Christian humanism which informs Luke's adaptation of Matthew's long Sermon on the Mount* to a much briefer sermon on philanthropy (Matthew 5–7; Luke 6.20–49). So there we may not be reading Q, but Luke's human abbreviation of Matthew.

Luke's humanism, lower christology, wealth of realistic detail, and historical plausibility have exercised a strong appeal to modern scholars at a level deeper and less conscious than their professional work. This is particularly true of the liberals who, until recently, have tended to dominate the profession. C. H. Dodd,* their most eminent English exemplar, can be said to have worked under the sway of Luke to the extent of trying to maximize the resemblance of the other evangelists to him. Dodd's 'realized eschatology' does not fit Mark or Matthew nearly as well as it does Luke with his constant emphasis on the definitive crises which face people in the present. In his study of the parables, he made the parables of Luke normative as pure parables of Jesus: a preference which seems to have no more objective base than a love of realism and an aversion from allegory and eschatology. This is not at all blameworthy, but rather shows how, beneath the interpretation *of* Luke, interpretation of Jesus and Christianity and the Christian life itself *by* Luke has been constantly at work. In the modern period, Lucan scholarship has certainly been sustained by the pleasure of reading him – noticeably greater than with the other synoptics for the general reader – even when the resulting findings have disappointed hopes of finding historical bedrock or unsettled agreed source theories.

See also **Acts of the Apostles; Gospel.**

In addition to titles mentioned see: P. Esler, *Community and Gospel in Luke–Acts*, 1987; R. Maddox, *The Purpose of Luke–Acts*, 1982.

JOHN DRURY

Luther

As is well known, it is difficult to draw firm lines of demarcation between systematic theology,* preaching and biblical exegesis* in the works of Martin Luther (1483–1546), the great German reformer. In part, this reflects the fact that Luther's reforming theology emerged during a sustained engagement with the exposition of scripture over the period 1513–19. During this period, Luther lectured initially on the Psalter (1513–15), then on Romans (1515–16), Galatians (1516–17) and Hebrews (1517–18), before returning once more to expound the Psalter for a second time in 1519. There is also a suggestion that Luther may have delivered a course of lectures on Genesis during this period, although documentary evidence for this is wanting.

In expounding the Psalter for the first time, Luther distinguishes himself immediately from the mediaeval* exegetical tradition found within the Augustinian Order. Luther makes use of the full range of mediaeval and humanist exegetical tools, and bases himself wherever possible upon the Hebrew original of the Psalter, in order to interpret the text. At this stage, Luther employs two major hermeneutical* schemes: the distinction between the 'life-giving spirit' (*spiritus vivificans*) and the 'killing letter' (*litera occidens*); and the four-fold meaning of scripture, usually designated the *Quadriga*.

Luther draws a distinction between the 'literal'* and 'spiritual'* senses of scripture. It is possible to read the OT at the literal level, as a bare historical narrative, referring to the customs of Near Eastern Semitic tribes; for Luther, however, this is to miss its point. The OT must be read at the spiritual level, through the guidance of the Holy Spirit, as pointing ahead to the life, death and resurrection* of Jesus Christ. This distinction is often expressed in terms of the historical (i.e. literal) and prophetic (i.e. spiritual) sense of scripture. The OT is not merely historical narrative, but prophecy, pointing ahead to the future coming of Jesus Christ. To read scripture at the literal or historical level, failing to discern its spiritual or prophetic sense, is to mistake the shadow for the substance, and the sign (*signum rerum*) for the thing which is signified (*res ipsa*). The OT is the sign, not the thing which is signified. In this sense, therefore, the OT cannot be read without the NT, in that the latter is the thing signified by the former.

Similarly, the OT law may be understood at a purely literal level, as a means of achieving an external visible human righteousness. This, however, is to miss its spiritual meaning, which is to point ahead to the coming of Jesus Christ and his gospel. 'The law, spiritually understood, is the gospel.' Underlying this distinction – also associated with the noted contemporary Tübingen exegete Wendelin Steinbach – is one of Luther's major theological preoccupations, which will feature prominently in his later theology of justification: the conviction that the confusion of law and gospel is the source of most of the errors concerning the Christian faith. 'It is best to distinguish the spirit from the letter in the sacred scriptures, for this is what makes one a theologian indeed.'

Luther also employs the *Quadriga*, or 'four-fold sense of scripture', to draw out the meaning of scripture. In addition to the literal sense, three spiritual senses may be discerned: the allegorical,* tropological or moral, and anagogical senses. It will be clear that Luther is thus able to distinguish eight senses of scripture: the 'literal-historic' and its three spiritual senses, and the 'literal-prophetic' and its three spiritual senses. For Luther, the 'literal-prophetic' sense of scripture refers to the person of Jesus Christ; its allegorical sense to the aid which Jesus Christ brings to the church; its tropological sense to the work which Jesus Christ performs in the individual believer; and the anagogical sense to the eschatological completion of this work. Luther illustrates these eight senses (playfully, it would seem), by considering the meanings of the phrase 'Mount Zion' according to each sense.

Historic	Prophetic
Literal	
The Land of Canaan	The people of Zion
Allegorical	
The synagogue	The church

Tropological	
The righteousness of the law	The righteousness of faith

Anagogical	
Future earthly glory	Future heavenly glory

For Luther, the primary sense of scripture is thus the literal-prophetic sense, pointing to Jesus Christ: 'scripture is the manger in which Christ is laid'.

By 1515, however, we find Luther placing new emphasis upon the importance of the tropological sense. At this point, a major difference between Luther on the one hand, and Erasmus* and Martin Bucer on the other, should be noted. For Erasmus and Bucer, the tropological sense referred to a moral obligation laid upon the believer. It designated the moral deeds which were to be performed by the believer as an expression of his faith. For Luther, however, the tropological sense referred to the work of God in the believer. It designated an act of God in Christ, rather than a human deed in response to that act.

This new emphasis upon the tropological sense of scripture is of importance in relation to Luther's 'theological breakthrough', which seems to date from 1515. Although Luther's breakthrough does not appear to result directly from any new hermeneutical insights, there is every indication that Luther's new emphasis assisted him in this respect. For Luther, the difficulty which required resolution was the phrase 'the righteousness of God'. In a famous autobiographical reflection of 1545, Luther singled out Rom. 1.16–17 as having caused him particular difficulty. In what sense was the revelation of the 'righteousness of God' gospel? How could it be good news for sinners, when it appeared to promise nothing other than their punishment? Taken in its literal sense this phrase seemed to point to God as a stern judge, who would reward individuals according to their merit. However, Luther came to the view that, interpreted tropologically, it represented a righteousness worked within the believer through faith – in other words, something which God himself achieved through Christ within the person of the believer. The precondition for justification was met by God himself. No longer was the 'righteousness of God' to be interpreted as an impartial and impersonal divine attribute, standing over and against the sinner, but as a righteousness whose origin is God and whose recipient is the sinner.

In the 1545 autobiographical fragment, Luther indicates that his new understanding of the 'righteousness of God' arose from a direct engagement with scripture, suggesting that the broad features of Luther's doctrine of justification are to be attributed to a new manner of interpreting the Bible, especially the Pauline* writings. It is, however, difficult to confirm this suggestion on the basis of a study of his exegetical writings of the period 1513–16, and it is possible that the influence of Augustine,* whether direct or indirect, may have assisted his reflections.

The programme of academic reform introduced to the Wittenberg theological faculty in 1518 by Karlstadt and Luther gave scripture an enhanced new status within the theological curriculum. The direct study of scripture in its original languages was seen as central to the early Wittenberg reformation. This reformation, however, was essentially an academic affair at this point: Luther was still no popular reformer. The situation would change suddenly in 1520, with the publication of Luther's reforming pamphlets, of which the most important from the standpoint of biblical interpretation is the *Appeal to the German Nobility.* Luther here calls into question the exclusive right of the pope to interpret scripture, insisting that every believer has this right. All believers, on account of their baptism, possess the right to interpret scripture for themselves. At this point, Luther reflects the exegetical optimism characteristic of the early Reformation – the belief that scripture is sufficiently clear to allow any well-intentioned person to interpret it accurately. The only obstacle in the path of the common believer was a lack of knowledge of the biblical languages. To overcome this difficulty, Luther translated scripture into the language of the people – German. In doing so, he effected a linguistic as much as a theological revolution, establishing his place in the history of German culture as well as in the history of the Christian church.

In dealing with Luther as a biblical interpreter, it is necessary to note that probably his most permanent contribution to the interpretation of scripture was not so much a hermeneutical system, as a biblical translation,* the *German Bible*, which was completed in 1534, and subsequently revised in 1539, 1541 and 1545. This magnificent work, which inspired even Nietzsche to term it 'the best German book', has had an incalculable effect upon popular German biblical interpretation. For this *editio princeps* of the Protestant Bible was no mere translation of scripture: it was in itself an interpretation of scripture, skilfully weaving Luther's leading theological principles into its text so that only those with access to the original could discern their introduction.

In September 1522, the New Testament made its first appearance in German. The

Septembertestament, as it is generally known, was a considerable publishing success. Its interpretation of Paul was, however, open to question. Luther's version of Rom. 3.28, for example, insisted that we are 'justified by faith *alone* (*alleyn durch den glawben*)', introducing a characteristic Lutheran theme into a Pauline passage which did not demand its inclusion. Equally, Luther's dialectic of law and gospel lend him to restrict the theological role of the law in a somewhat un-Pauline sense: Luther's version of Rom. 3.20 states that 'through the law comes *only* knowledge of sin (*durch das gesetz kompt nur erkenntnis der sund*)'. Yet such was the literary impact of Luther's brilliant German style that the subtle twists given to Pauline thought were generally tolerated.

By 1525, however, Luther appears to have retracted his earlier view that anyone could interpret scripture. The rise of the Radical Reformation and the outbreak of the Peasants' Revolt did much to disenchant him concerning the exegetical abilities of German peasants. The view that *Herr Omnes* (Luther's designation of 'Everyman') could interpret scripture increasingly became associated with the Radical Reformation, as Luther came to lay increasing emphasis upon the need for a sound grounding in the three sacred languages (Hebrew, Greek and Latin) as an essential prerequisite for the correct interpretation of scripture. Luther's distancing of himself from the exegetical optimism of the early Reformation finds parallels throughout the Magisterial Reformation – e.g. Zwingli's critique of the radical *Wiedertäufer*. Curiously, a movement which began by suggesting that anyone had the right and ability to interpret scripture finally tended towards the idea of a 'magisterial' interpretation of scripture.

The impact of Luther's biblical interpretation upon subsequent periods, including our own, is considerable. This is perhaps most evident in the case of his interpretation of Paul's concept of 'law', and particularly 'the works of the law'. Intensifying earlier mediaeval approaches to this question, Luther manifests a distinct tendency to identify 'works of the law' with human moral activity in general, with the specific historical context of the Pauline documents being de-emphasized. Thus Bultmann* and Käsemann, to name but two significant twentieth-century exegetes who reflect Luther's approach to Paul, regard belief in 'justification by works of the law' as a general human phenomenon, reflecting a fundamental human desire to be self-sufficient and autonomous. The origins of this interpretation of Paul do not, of course, lie with Luther; they may without difficulty be traced to the *heilsgeschichtlich* exegesis of the Pauline corpus in the Parisian schools of the twelfth century, and the presupposition of an Augustinian theology of grace. Nevertheless, Luther may be regarded as giving a new emphasis to this approach to Paul on account of the centrality of the doctrine of justification by faith alone to his theology and spirituality alike. The understanding of 'justification by faith' to mean 'a rejection of the attempt to earn salvation by one's own moral efforts' is a pervasive feature of the Western theological tradition from Augustine onwards; to designate it 'Lutheran', as if Luther invented the idea, is quite improper. Equally, the use of the epithet 'Reformation' is also problematical: it is evident that other Reformation writers, more familiar with the Jewish background* to the NT (such as Martin Bucer), adopted a significantly different attitude to the role of the law, and the concept of 'justification by faith'. Nevertheless, the new importance attached to the idea by Luther led to this manner of interpreting Paul, without reference to the specificially Jewish context of his polemic, being perceived as one of Luther's more distinctive contributions to the science of biblical interpretation. The long-term importance of the challenge posed to this interpretation, originating with F. C. Baur, but championed in more recent years by writers such as E. P. Sanders, remains to be seen.

See also **Calvin; Reformation.**

Heinz Bluhm, *Martin Luther – Creative Translator*, 1965; id., 'Luther's German Bible' in Peter Newman Brooks (ed.), *Seven-Headed Luther: Essays in Commemoration of a Quincentenary*, 1983, pp. 177–94; Heinrich Bornkamm, *Luther and the Old Testament*, 1969; Gerhard Ebeling, *Luther: An Introduction to His Thought*, 1970; W. J. Kooiman, *Luther and the Bible*, 1961; David C. Steinmetz, *Luther and Staupitz*, 1980, pp. 50–65.

A. E. McGRATH

Lux Mundi

This collection of twelve essays, published in October 1889, marked the acceptance by High Churchmen of evolutionary theory and historical criticism* of the Bible. Most of the authors were products of the Tractarian tradition in Oxford, some were teachers in the university, and the editor, Charles Gore, was Principal of Pusey House. He was later to become Bishop of Worcester, of Birmingham, and then of Oxford.

Gore's essay on 'The Holy Spirit and Inspiration' held that the modern development of historical criticism was reaching results as sure as scientific enquiry, and this affected particularly our understanding of the OT. The inspiration* of the OT writer lay in the fact that he saw the hand of God in history and interpreted his purpose, but it did not guarantee the exact historical truth of that which he recorded. Inspiration excluded conscious deception or pious fraud, but was consistent with an idealizing of history. There was no miraculous communication of facts which would make the recorder independent of the ordinary processes of historical tradition. The OT showed how God had produced an ideal which was realized in the NT, but the 'absolute coincidence of idea and fact is vital in the realization, not in the preparation for it', and this allowed that much in the OT was 'dramatic' (i.e. characters, real or imaginary, were the vehicles for an ideal presentation), while much of the earliest narrative consisted of 'myth'* or allegorical* picture, 'which is the earliest mode in which the mind of man apprehended truth'. 'Are not its earliest narratives, before the call of Abraham, of the nature of myth, in which we cannot distinguish the historical germ, though we do not at all deny that it exists?' Inspiration was, therefore, primarily in the substance of the books of the OT, not in any consideration of the manner in which they came into existence. Since the church had not committed itself to any dogmatic definition of the meaning of inspiration, this altered view was, he believed, perfectly tenable (*Lux Mundi*, pp. 351–8).

Thus, the OT was 'imperfect', showing a low stage of conscience and worship and literary methods which belonged to a rude and undeveloped state of intelligence. Gore amplified these remarks, in response to his critics, in a preface to the tenth edition of *Lux Mundi*, in which he repeated his view that the OT showed a religion in the course of development, an educational process provided by God. The works of Robertson Smith,* S. R. Driver, and German scholars such as König, Riehm, Delitzsch, and Wellhausen, were cited in defence of this position.

Gore recognized that a christological problem was suggested if one assigned a lower status to the OT. Christ saw the OT as inspired and endorsed the Jewish view of their own history. But his teaching did not foreclose certain critical positions as to the character of OT literature. Christ's use of typology* was important in this respect. He saw Jonah's 'resurrection'* as a type of his own resurrection,* but this did not depend on whether it was a historical fact or an allegory. Christ's argument with the Pharisees,* in which he quoted Ps. 110, took the form of a question and was not a positive proposition that David* was the author of the psalm. 'If he had intended to convey instruction to us on critical and literary questions, he would have made his purpose plainer.' The incarnation was the self-emptying of God to reveal himself

under conditions of human nature and from the human point of view. Such a doctrinal perspective excluded a Christ who would possess the correct 'critical' understanding of the OT.

The problem of the unity of the two testaments which the essay raised was answered by Gore along traditional lines. The altered view of the development of OT literature involved no important change in our spiritual use of the OT. As the OT was manifested in the NT, so the NT was latent in the OT. He did not answer so easily the argument that he must allow the same far-reaching historical questions to affect the reliability of the NT. While God's disclosure of himself in the OT was progressive and continuous, the NT revelation* was necessarily 'final and adequate for all ages'. The basic historicity of the Gospel writers was unquestioned. As he said in a later work, 'Mark and Luke have no design except to record things as they happened.' There was a close connection between tradition and the historical reliability of the NT, and the Apostles' and Nicene creeds* found their justification, clause by clause, in the NT. 'If the creeds stand with their historical and doctrinal statements, it must be because the Gospels stand.' In the NT, fact* was of supreme importance: 'the evidence has none of the ambiguity or remoteness which belongs to much of the record of the preparation' (*The New Theology and the Old Religion*, 1907, p. 217; *Lux Mundi*, p. 384).

Lux Mundi, to quote Gore's phrase, was an attempt to prevent an 'unseemly flight from history' on the part of believers, and may thus be compared with *Essays and Reviews** which had a similar aim. It was, however, far more positive in tone than its predecessor, better composed, and more firmly anchored in Christian tradition, with more than 200 patristic references.

The success of *Lux Mundi*, however, in reconciling liberalism* and the Catholic faith was unwelcome to older figures like H. P. Liddon and Archdeacon Denison, who saw it as a betrayal of the Tractarian position. The sharp line drawn by Gore between the OT and the NT was, Liddon thought, indefensible, and raised the gravest problems.

See also **Catholic Modernism; Essays and Reviews.**

J. A. Carpenter, *Gore: A Study in Liberal Catholic Thought*, 1960; R. Morgan (ed.), *The Religion of the Incarnation*, 1989; G. L. Prestige, *The Life of Charles Gore*, 1935; B. M. G. Reardon, *From Coleridge to Gore*, 1971.

IEUAN ELLIS

Magic

The basic premise of magic is that there is a network of forces in and behind the physical universe that can be utilized by knowledgeable persons for benefit to themselves or their clients, or to ward off harm, or to bring harm upon one's enemies. The means of access to these powers include uttering certain words (such as the names of divinities and demons) or the repetition of formulas, or the performance of certain prescribed actions (such as physical contact for transferring good or harmful powers). The benefits include gaining health or a lover, determining the future, or acquiring certain property. The baleful effects include the injury, death or deprivation of one's enemies. Fundamental is the conviction that the correct formula or set of actions can guarantee the desired results.

In the patriarchal narratives, magicians are consulted by Pharaoh to interpret his dreams (Gen. 41.1–8). In Ex. 7–9, Pharaoh engages wise men, sorcerers and physicians to counteract the plagues which Yahweh has sent to force the liberation of Israel. Such magical practices as augury, divination, and sorcery are forbidden in Israel in Lev. 19.26–28 and Deut. 18.10–14. The confrontation between the powers to which the magicians appeal and the purpose of Yahweh for his people becomes explicit in Num. 23.22–23: 'There is no [effective] enchantment against Jacob, no divination against Israel; now it shall be said of Jacob and Israel, "What has God accomplished?"'

In the historical books, Israel is repeatedly enticed into consulting magicians rather than relying on Yahweh (I Sam. 6.28; I Kings 17.21). The prophets* warn against this wicked reliance on magic (Isa. 2–3; Jer. 14.14; 27.9; Ezek. 13.17–18; Mal. 3.1–5). Yet there is evidence of a magical belief in the automatic transmission of power through physical contact in the story in II Kings 13 of the restoration to life of a dead body which came by chance into contact with the bones of Elisha.

The nearest approach to magic as a factor in the Gospels* comes in the accusation brought against Jesus that he can control demons because he is in league with Beelzebub (Mark 3.19–30; Matt 12.22–37; Luke 11.14–23). This narrative embodies the charge that Jesus performs magic through appeal to the name and authority of a prince of demons. In the Q version of this incident, Jesus claims to be performing the exorcisms, not by collusion with the evil powers, but 'by the finger of God' (Luke 11.20), which is precisely the term that is used in Ex. 8.19 to contrast the power of Yahweh and the techniques of the Egyptian magicians. A few of the Gospel narratives report the healing effects of physical contact with Jesus (Mark 5.25–34; 7.31–35), although no importance is attached to the technique or to pronouncing formulae, which are the central features of magical technique.

In Acts there are accounts of punitive miracles and healing by physical contact with objects associated with the apostles. These stories offer the most probable evidence for the influence of magic on the NT: Ananias and Sapphira are struck dead for their greed and deception (4.32–5.11); Peter's shadow effects cures (5.12–16); Herod Agrippa dies a horrible death for his claims of divinity (12.20–23); cloths that had touched the apostles serve as healing devices (19.11). It is significant that these reports appear in a document written in the late first century, at precisely the time that there was a surge of interest in magic among the upper classes and the intelligentsia in Roman society. This phenomenon is evident in literary sources, such as the *Metamorphoses* of Apuleius, where the narrator describes his transmutation into an ass, and the regaining of his human form (111.21–25). The most striking evidence of the popularity of magic in the early centuries of our era, however, is in the Greek Magical Papyri. In them there are lists of deities to whom appeal is made; there are groupings of letters according to geometric patterns or by symbolic numbers (such as 365), extended repetitions of formulas – all of which demonstrate that the essence of magic is technique, by which the desired ends can be guaranteed of achievement. Among the items which are recited in these formulas are biblical names and terms, such as Iao, Adonai, Logos,* Father, Jesus Christ, Holy Spirit. These are intermingled with the names of Greek, Egyptian and Ancient Near Eastern divinities, as well as strings of nonsense syllables and letters. In Origen's* *Against Celsus* he seeks to counter the charge that Jesus and his followers engaged in the practice of magic, which certainly is evident in such post-NT writings as the apocryphal gospels and acts and the Gnostic* writings.

See also **Miracle in the Biblical World.**

Peter Brown, 'Sorcery, Demons and the Rise of Christianity' in *Religion and Society in the Age of St Augustine*, 1972; J. M. Hull, *Hellenistic Magic and the Synoptic Tradition*, 1974; H. C. Kee, *Medicine, Miracle and Magic in New Testament Times*, 1986; id., *Miracle in the Early Christian World*, 1983; Judith Willer, *The Social Determination of Knowledge*, 1971.

HOWARD CLARK KEE

Malachi

In Hebrew 'Malachi' means 'my messenger'. It is possible this is a personal name but it is just as likely that it is a description based on 3.1, 'Behold, I send my messenger . . .' Either the prophet or those who preserved the tradition of his teaching felt that his office was more important than his personal biography.

There has been a general consensus of opinion that the prophet is to be dated between the time of Haggai and Zechariah (520–518 BC) and the coming of Nehemiah to Jerusalem in 445 BC. Virtually unanimous as this belief has been, few of the individual arguments used to support it are impressive. The book is clearly post-exilic since it refers to a 'governor' rather than a 'king' (1.8). Yet although some of the religious abuses attacked by Malachi are those reported as being dealt with by Nehemiah, Nehemiah does nothing about divorce and Malachi makes no mention of sabbath observance. In fact, religious abuses can recur and even major 'reforms' do not usually have permanent effects. All we can say is that the book is alluded to in Ecclesiasticus (Ben Sira, 48.10; 49.10) and so must have been written by the early second century BC.

Malachi speaks of a covenant* with the Levitical priesthood (2.4,8), of marriage as a 'covenant' (2.14), and of God's sending the 'messenger of the covenant' (3.1). This covenant emphasis may explain why some have found strong echoes of the vocabulary of Deuteronomy (so R. L. Smith, *Micah–Malachi*, 1984, p. 300). It may also explain the extraordinary statement of the opening section that God has 'loved Jacob' but 'hated Esau' (Edom). It is such an election of covenant grace which makes Judah especially answerable to God (so Elliger, 1964, pp. 190f.). On the other hand 'Edom' may symbolize 'evil' and the passage be a warning to all (Judaeans included) that God will judge evil wherever he finds it. That seems to be the thrust of the addition in 4.6.

The apparent universalism of 1.11 has led to many interpretations. Traditional Christian interpretation has seen this verse as predicting the Mass (*see* **Liturgy, Use of the Bible in**). Jewish exegetes often argued that it referred to the worship of the Jews of the Diaspora or to Gentile proselytes converted to the Jewish faith. Scholars in the heyday of liberal* theology believed it argued that all religions really worshipped the same God and all worship was equally acceptable to him. An older Christian view, that it expressed an eschatological* hope for the future, has recently found a new champion (B. Glazier McDonald, *Malachi: The Divine Messenger*, 1987, p. 61). Its opening quotation from Ps. 50 may recall the thrust of that psalm that God wants true gratitude and love rather than merely formal outward worship (so Mason, *The Books of Haggai, Zechariah and Malachi*, 1977, pp. 144f.). If 2.16 really does reject divorce in any situation (the Hebrew is not clear), this is a remarkable overturning of the law in Deut. 24.1–4.

One other feature of the book deserves notice. Although its concerns are thoroughly 'theocratic', centring on the temple and its correct ritual worship, on two occasions Malachi meets the discouragement of his hearers with a thoroughgoing eschatological promise of God's coming to deliver them (2.17–3.5; 3.13–4.3). This suggests caution in accepting the conclusions of those who have seen a great gulf between the two streams of theocracy and eschatology in post-exilic Judaism (e.g. O. Plöger, *Theocracy and Eschatology*, 1968, and P. D. Hanson, *The Dawn of Apocalyptic*, 1975).

Two appendices, which have been added to the book (4.4; 4.5f.), come at the end, not only of Malachi and the 'Book of the Twelve' but the whole prophetic section of the Hebrew canon.* Their effect is to link prophecy with *torah* as of equal authority. They also reiterate the promise of Deut. 18.15 that God would raise up another prophet like Moses.* This is now understood as an eschatological promise as it also appears in Ecclus. 48.10 and in the NT (e.g. Mark 6.15; 15.35). Perhaps Elijah is chosen because tradition told how he had not died but had been 'taken up' to heaven (II Kings 2.11).

J. Baldwin, *Haggai, Zechariah, Malachi*, Tyndale Old Testament Commentaries, 1972; R. J. Coggins, *Haggai, Zechariah, Malachi*, Old Testament Guides, 1987.

REX MASON

Manuscripts

A term derived from Latin, meaning something written by hand. In the context of biblical study, it signifies a copy of the whole Bible, or part of it, written by hand: we thus speak of biblical manuscripts (abbreviated MSS), OT MSS, NT MSS, Gospel MSS, and so on. We distinguish not only by content, but by the language of the text used (e.g. Hebrew MSS, Greek MSS), but irrespective of the text, there are many features common to manuscripts of every kind within the biblical field, because of the materials from which they were made and the techniques of the scribes* who wrote upon them. Biblical manuscripts range in date from the third century BC to the eighteenth century AD. Every manuscript has its own interest: as the Cambridge scholar R. P. Casey said, 'a manuscript is something between a gadget and a personality'. But naturally, for the study of the text* of the Bible, the earlier manuscripts are the more important, as reflecting early stages of the evolution of the text; yet a manuscript late in date may sometimes prove to be significant, if it was copied faithfully from an earlier one of valuable type.

Three materials are found used for biblical manuscripts: papyrus, parchment and paper.

Papyrus is a material manufactured in Egypt* and made from reeds. An example is known from around 3,000 BC, and it was in use for about four millennia. It has survived mainly in Egypt where the climate has helped its preservation over many centuries, but it was also used in many other parts of the ancient world. For biblical studies, the relevant period is that of the empires of Alexander and the Romans, that is, for the Greek Bible, both OT and NT (*see* **Septuagint**).

The reeds were separated laterally and the strips so obtained were placed in two layers, in one of which the strips lay vertically, in the other horizontally. The resultant pages were stuck edge to edge into rolls, the writing being written upon the side made of horizontally laid strips. The horizontal lines formed by the natural conformation of the material provided a guide to the scribe for neat and orderly writing. Formerly, in papyrological publications, the side with the horizontal layer was termed the recto, that with the vertical, the verso. This practice (which is inappropriate in a number of ways) has now given way to a description by means of a horizontal right-pointing arrow-shaped mark, or by a similar vertical down-pointing mark of the same shape.

Parchment is made from animal skins, and examples are known from as early as the ninth century BC. In the Greek and Roman world, it was probably not used so much as papyrus while supplies of the latter lasted; but these began to shrink by the fourth century AD and the Arab conquest of Egypt in the early seventh century almost dried up the supply, so that parchment more and more took the place of papyrus. Amongst the Jews, parchment was used for the sacred books. Parchment takes its name from the city of Pergamum in Asia Minor, once an important centre of its manufacture.

The making of paper was a Chinese invention, which passed into the technology of the Arabs in the eighth century and in due course came into the Western world. An instance of its use for a theological document is dateable to about AD 800, but biblical writings on manuscripts partly or wholly of paper are first known in the twelfth century. Paper made in the West, in contrast to Arab manufacture, is characterized by rulings and watermarks.

Manuscripts of the biblical writings are of two forms, the roll and codex. The former term is self-explanatory. Papyrus sheets or portions of parchment were assembled edge to edge to form a roll or scroll. The writing would generally be on only one side (the reference in Rev. 5.1 to a scroll written on the inside and the back is intended to highlight its unusual and remarkable nature). Manuscripts of the Hebrew Bible, and of translations of it

in Aramaic (Targums*) were on scrolls. These were written upon the 'hair side' of the parchment. Books in the Graeco-Roman world are also generally upon rolls, until about the third or fourth century of the Christian era. This is true of most Christian books, except for biblical books. Some liturgical* books, including psalters, continued to be written in roll form, but they are proportionately few. When we speak of manuscripts of the NT and Christian-written manuscripts of the OT, it is of the codex form that we are generally speaking.

The codex derives its name from a Latin word denoting a wooden board: the name of the whole object, a book as we understand the term, is derived then from its covers! Within, the papyrus or parchment is folded and cut to make gatherings, very frequently from four sheets, giving eight leaves or sixteen pages (a quaternion); but other numbers of leaves are known. The codex form is not used for literature before the Christian period, but it is known as a format for notebooks and account books: its adoption for scripture remains a matter of some surprise. It may reflect the social background of the main body of Christians in the early period: literate, but using their literacy in commerce or craftmanship, not in literary sophistication. It would seem to reflect also a deliberate distinction between the church and its Jewish antecedent where scripture was on scrolls.

The papyrus book by its construction presented the guidance which the scribe needed for the neatness of his writing. With parchment it was not so, and ways of ruling the sheets to receive writing were devised. A blunt stylus was used. The sheets of parchment, folded already into their gatherings, were first pricked with holes to guide the ruling of lines, horizontal and vertical. These formed the framework for whatever format the text, and any accompanying material, was to take. In later centuries at least, these frameworks were very complicated and they have formed the basis of analysis of groups of manuscripts and identifications of centres of copy.

Ink on manuscripts is usually a strong black in colour; it was made of soot mingled with gum. In manuscripts from the fourth century onwards, red ink is also found for headings, chapter indexes and lectionary notes written in the margin. It is from this that the term rubric is derived; as also 'red letter day'. A further feature is the provision of illustration, which in Christian manuscripts may take the form of depictions of the life of Jesus or other characters of the biblical story, 'portraits' of the evangelists* (which in fact follow patterns derived from similar 'portraits' of pagan philosophers) or the elaboration of the initial letters of sections of the text, which often extended into the otherwise blank margin. In Jewish manuscripts, on the other hand, illustration is not found, but geometrical elaboration of letters and marginalia can achieve a like richness to that of Christian illumination. Some few Christian manuscripts are known which are clearly de luxe products, probably commissioned for the imperial chapel; these are written on parchment which has been stained purple, and the script itself is executed in ink which is tinctured with gold and silver.

In the period of the earliest manuscripts of both the Hebrew and the Greek Bibles, the scribe worked in a sitting posture with the papyrus or parchment resting upon the knee. We know this from depictions in Egyptian sources, although contemporary Greek or Hebrew evidence is lacking. At the end of a roll of the Iliad of Homer, from the first century AD, however, we have an allusion to the manner of writing. The text concludes with a decorative sign known as the coronis: in a verse, the coronis speaks: 'I am the coronis, guardian of the letters: the pen wrote me, the right hand and the knee.' Some other allusions have also been noted to the posture. It was not until the eighth century that writing desks began to be used; and even so, the practice did not become universal for some centuries. In the excavations at Qumran (*see* **Dead Sea Scrolls**), however, one room has structures made of brick with sloping surfaces, and some inkwells remain with traces of ink in them. It has been considered by most experts that this is the scriptorium or writing room of the community and that many of the manuscripts of that remarkable hoard were written there. Clearly, in that unique community, the practices of writing did not coincide with those customarily found in the world of that day.

Although we may identify different scribes through their style, these remain, for much of the earliest period covered by the production of biblical manuscripts, unknown by name. This contrasts with the much earlier Mesopotamian civilization, where those who wrote down the literature are recorded by name (their work is, of course, on clay tablets). In that culture the scribe was a man of learning and held in high repute, but in the Graeco-Roman culture the scribal function was looked upon with disdain, being the task of slaves. This may be why early Christian manuscripts are anonymous. The social milieu of the early church, in Egypt at any rate, appears to have been that of traders, officials and craftsmen, and early manuscripts have been produced by those with scribal skills, some presumably by professionals employed for the purpose. It is only with the transliteration

from majuscule script to minuscule (probably at the time of the adoption of writing desks) that we begin to find scribal notes at the end of manuscripts of the biblical writings which give the name of the scribe and the date of the writing. This is generally accompanied by a request for prayer. The change has come about since now the scribes are monks and the writing is part of their religious duty. The prayers are for their forgiveness and salvation. They describe themselves with terms of humility, 'the sinful X', 'the lowly Y', and so on. It is interesting that in the field of Syriac *-speaking Christianity, the naming of the scribe and the dating of the manuscript is found at a much earlier date. This suggests that the customs of ancient Mesopotamia survived in the much later Christian setting.

Notes giving the date of writing and the name of the scribe are known as colophons: sometimes we find that they contain information about the scholarly process by which the text copied has been selected and also a record of its antecedents. So we find that particular manuscripts have been copied from ancient exemplars with which they have been carefully compared after the initial copying. The place of preservation or of origin of the exemplar may be recorded and the names of any Christian scholar whose part in the production enhances the accuracy of the text. Pamphilus, a martyr under the third-century emperor Maximin Daia, is known to have written and corrected manuscripts while imprisoned, from such colophons in manuscripts of both the OT and NT. In other colophons we learn of scriptural texts being carefully assembled on critical principles from more ancient manuscripts.

Verses are sometimes found, conventional but nevertheless moving, which record the weariness of the scribe and his delight to see the conclusion of his task and compare him to the sea traveller seeing the harbour, or the prisoner his release. Another common theme is that of the permanence of the achievement which the labour has brought: the hand which wrote this will lie in the grave, but the words will remain for ever. The human labour and longing behind the artefact are thus revealed.

Manuscripts also frequently contain the aids to study and to use in worship which the scholars of the age had made available. Margins will contain cross reference to other parallel passages (in Gospel manuscripts), quotations in the text may be identified, difficult or obscure words or allusions will be explained. In some manuscripts of the Greek OT, there will be critical remarks concerning different recensions, and records of variant readings, going back to the work of the third century Christian scholar Origen.* In Hebrew manuscripts the margins may contain the interpretative and textual notes known as the Masorah (*see* **Masoretic Text.**)

Some Christian biblical manuscripts contain marginal commentaries:* these are often known as catenae or 'chains', since they consist of relatively short excerpts from a number of commentators and homilists.* The careful study of these is proving more and more to be a major advance in the history of the early understanding of scripture and of hermeneutical* method up to the ninth century of the Christian era.

A number of manuscripts are furnished with data known as stichometry. The length of books was measured by a conventional line-length or stichos which was the equivalent to a hexameter verse. Such a measurement given at the close of a work had a dual function. First, since in lists of writings a stichometry was often given, the unabbreviated presentation of the text in the manuscript was guaranteed by the reference to it in the stichometry. Secondly, and very practically, it provided a guide to the payment of the scribe on a piecerate.

Short notices about the origin of scriptural books and, in the case of the Gospels, about their date, may also be found. From time to time an unwary scholar will seize upon such a notice from a single manuscript and base some critical theory upon it. The warning must be given that before such eager use is made of this type of information, it should be traced in the close relatives and ancestors of the manuscript which contains it, and its links with the earliest Christian writers such as Irenaeus* and Eusebius* should be investigated. Rarely, if ever, is independent information of historical value to be found in such sources.

An essential tool for the investigator of manuscripts is the catalogue. These may cover a single library (either all its manuscripts or those in a particular language), a language area represented in many libraries, or the manuscripts in a particular subject area. There are also catalogues of catalogues, very valuable guides into what may seem to the beginner or the visitor a trackless forest of publication and information. Amongst the latter should be mentioned J. D. Pearson, *Oriental Manuscripts in Europe and North America* (1971), and the same compiler's revision of Theodore Bestermann, *A World Bibliography of Oriental Bibliographies* (1975), where not only Hebrew manuscripts can be traced, but also those of the oriental languages of biblical transmission, Syriac, Armenian, Georgian (but with the exclusion of Coptic and Ethiopic). A survey of catalogues of Hebrew biblical manuscripts may be found in Bleddyn J. Roberts, *The Old Testament Text and Versions* (1971), pp. 77–80. The guide to Greek

manuscript catalogues is Marcel Richard, *Répertoire des Bibliothèques et des Catalogues de Manuscrits grecs* (1958, with supplement 1964). The standard list of Greek manuscripts of the NT is by Kurt Aland, *Kurzgefasste Liste der griechischen Handschriften des Neuen Testaments* (1963, with various supplements by the same compiler). The Greek OT was served by Alfred Rahlfs, *Verzeichnis der griechischen Handschriften des Alten Testaments* (1914); it is necessary, however, to know the correspondences of the numbers assigned to manuscripts by Rahlfs with the sigla used in other editions of the Greek OT. A check-list will be found in Sidney Jellicoe, *The Septuagint and Modern Study* (1968), pp. 360–69. Papyrus manuscripts of Jewish and Christian provenance are catalogued by Joseph van Haelst, *Catalogue des papyrus littéraires juifs et chrétiens* (1976). The Dead Sea Scrolls may best be traced in J. A. Fitzmyer's survey of that title (revised, 1977).

The best introduction to manuscript study is by acquaintance with manuscripts themselves, but this does not come the way of everyone. Collections of facsimiles, then, are a good substitute. E. G. Turner, *Greek Manuscripts of the Ancient World* (² 1989), is excellent for papyri. P. Franchi de Cavalieri and Johannes Lietzmann, *Specimina codicum graecorum* (² 1929) and Eugenius Tisserant, *Specimina codicum orientalium* (1914) have splendid plates, but are not limited to biblical manuscripts. W. H. P. Hatch's two collections, *The Principal Uncial Manuscripts of the New Testament* (1939) and *Facsimiles and Descriptions of Minuscule Manuscripts of the New Testament* (1951), have not been surpassed by the more recent *Manuscripts of the Greek Bible* by B. M. Metzger (1981), which has many blemishes. A well-presented introduction is provided by Jack Finegan in *Encountering New Testament Manuscripts* (1975).

See also **Textual Criticism; Writing; Writing Materials.**

C. H. Roberts, *Manuscript, Society and Belief in Early Christian Egypt*, 1979; C. H. Roberts and T. C. Skeat, *The Birth of the Codex*, 1987; E. G. Turner, *Greek Papyri*, ² 1980; E. Würthwein, *The Text of the Old Testament*, revd edn 1979.

J. NEVILLE BIRDSALL

Marcion

Marcion was a Christian leader who was active in Rome in the 140s, when he is alleged to have been repudiated by the church there. He came from Sinope on the Black Sea, and earlier reports suggest he was a high-principled ascetic: his followers rejected marriage, animal flesh and alcoholic drink. Already about 150 Justin reported his teaching had reached 'every race of men', and his churches perhaps posed more of a threat to the emerging Catholic church than the contemporary Gnostics.* Marcionites were numerous in the east, and apparently dominant in Edessa on the Mesopotamian border.

Marcion did not, as is commonly said, reject the OT. He took it literally, and as divine revelation.* The God of the OT plainly held that he was himself the only God, the creator* of the world, and the giver of the Law, who promises judgment through a messiah* and an earthly kingdom. Marcion set out his views in a work called the *Antitheses*, which is unfortunately lost, but scraps of his arguments appear in hostile criticisms of church writers. In it he contrasted the creator with the Unknown God revealed by Jesus. The one is just, fierce, destructive, the other generous, kind and saving. One orders vengeance of eye for eye, the other bids us turn the other cheek. One sends a bear to kill children (I Kings 2.23–24), the other embraces them (Luke 18.15–17). The creator is inconsistent and often changes his mind; he commands the Israelites to rob the Egyptians, contrary to his own law (Ex. 12.35–36; 20.15; interpreting Rom. 2.21). He can be arbitrary, hating Esau for no good reason (Mal. 1.2–3; Rom. 9.13), and hardening hearts so that he can show off his power (Ex. 10.1). He made a world not wholly good, with fierce and unpleasant beasts and insects, and with sex and its lusts. By contrast Jesus' Father is absolutely good: a good tree cannot bring forth evil fruit (Luke 6.43–44), as the creator does. The creator's greatest weakness is ignorance: he believes he is the only God, and tries to force his unfortunate creatures to renounce all others. But it is a lie: there is another, the Unknown God, who intervened to rescue from the creator Enoch and Elijah (both translated to heaven). Finally however the Unknown came down in the form of Jesus to enlighten the creator about his position and to rescue his unfortunate creatures from the world of sin and flesh under condemnation of the Law, and to carry them off into a pure realm of spirit and light.

According to Marcion, Jesus appeared fully adult in the synagogue at Capernaum (Luke 4.31); he could not be contaminated with fleshly procreation and birth. He allowed himself to be called messiah because the Jews expected a saviour of that name. The creator mistook him for his own messiah, who was predicted and was to set up a worldly millennial* kingdom for the Jews. Once Jesus started winning over multitudes from the Law, he plotted to kill him. But Jesus did a bargain (perhaps negotiated by Moses* and Elijah at the transfiguration [Luke 9.28–36]), to buy by his death the creatures of the inferior God; and his death enabled him to go down to the creator's Hades and release the dead of the OT. The destiny of the redeemed is out of this world in the realm of pure spirit. The creator still intends to judge this world through his own messiah in a cruel judgment, and deceived Jesus' chief disciples into thinking that this coming messiah would be Jesus, and that he was still the only God. Hence the NT Gospels* are the result of judaizing the true gospel. Jesus called Paul* to put matters right: his true letters, correctly read, reveal the evil of the creator, the God of this world who blinds the hearts of unbelievers (II Cor. 4.4); they show the corruption of the other apostles by Judaism (Gal. 2.11–13); and they call to renounce the flesh and live in the Spirit, against which Law cannot prevail. But even Paul's letters and the pure Gospel, which is Luke's, had been tampered with and corrupted in the interests of the creator by the false apostles and their churches. So God raised up Marcion to restore the text, and the Marcionites accept as true the Gospel of Luke, with considerable reductions and alterations (it starts with the date at 3.1 and the appearance in the synagogue at 4.31), and an emended collection of Paul's letters (without the Pastoral Epistles*) in which Ephesians appears as 'Laodiceans'. The best reconstruction of Marcion's texts is in Harnack,* summarized in English in Evans, II, pp. 643–6.

Marcion's position is logically prior to the main gnostic systems: he has dislodged the creator in favour of a God beyond, but has not yet explained how the duality came about, a gap his opponents readily exploited. If he was also historically earlier than the usual dating (so Hoffmann), he might have been active before the NT was finished: his 'Laodiceans' could be an earlier version of Ephesians, his Luke a primitive form of that composite Gospel. But while Irenaeus'* assertion that he got his ideas from the gnostic Credo is worthless, Marcion is better seen as a radical biblicist, rejecting both gnostic mythology and the spiritual interpretation of the OT which enabled the church to read in it the saving work of Christ 'according to the scriptures' (I Cor. 15.3–4). In that case he operates on an already existing set of texts, and 'restores' them as God had (he believed) called him to do, by purging all that identified the Unknown God with the creator and lawgiver. His work is often alleged to have provoked the church to define the NT canon;* that may be partly true, but the multiplicity of gnostic and orthodox apocrypha also contributed.

Marcion's system is at its most vulnerable philosophically (as Tertullian* devastatingly points out, following Justin and others): two gods means no God; a God so good that he disapproves of nothing is also unable to approve or justify; we need salvation in the world, not from it. Marcionism also shows the folly of trying to read the Bible theologically without clearly setting out principles of interpretation. In particular, taking the OT literally, without criticism and spiritual insight, leads to the destruction of the NT.

Walter Bauer, *Orthodoxy and Heresy in Earliest Christianity*, 1971; E. C. Blackman, *Marcion and his Influence*, 1948; Ernest Evans (ed.), *Tertullian: Adversus Marcionem*, 1972; Adolf Harnack, *Marcion. Das Evangelium der fremden Gott*, ² 1924; R. Joseph Hoffmann, *Marcion: On the Restitution of Christianity* (AAR 46), 1948; John Knox, *Marcion and the New Testament*, 1942; C. W. Mitchell (ed.), *St Ephraim's Prose Refutations of Mani, Marcion and Bardaisan*, I–II, 1969.

STUART GEORGE HALL

Mark, Gospel of

Few texts can claim to have played such a vital role in the consolidation and subsequent interpretation of the Christian faith as the Gospel of Mark. Its author* is unknown to us, although a tradition dating to the early second century gives his name as Mark, claims that he was the 'interpreter' (*hermēneutēs*) of Peter* himself, and asserts that the work was an accurate report (if not 'in order') of his reminiscences (cited Eusebius,* *Eccl. Hist.* III.39, quoting its ascription by Papias,* bishop of Hieropolis, *c.* AD 140, to a contemporary, 'the Elder'). Subsequent tradition, based on the evidence of Papias, has further identified this Mark with the John Mark of the NT, a figure otherwise associated, for the most part, with Paul.* The internal evidence of the text itself, however, hardly suggests, far less supports, this traditional attribution and, largely for this reason, a majority of scholars nowadays prefer to disregard Papias' testimony.

While the personal identity of the author cannot be established, the value of his (or her?) contribution to the development of Christianity and to a Christian literary tradition can scarcely be doubted. The text he has produced provides us with our earliest written record of the teaching and activity of Jesus as interpreted by a Christian community in the Mediterranean world some forty years or so after his death. Within the relatively brief compass of the sixteen chapters into which it is now divided, the reader is presented with a series of discrete scenes linked with summary passages (e.g. 3.7–12; 6.53–56) which describe the appearance of Jesus as an eschatological* preacher of the gospel (1.1–15), his appoint-

ment and commissioning of disciples (1.16–20; 2.14; 3.13–19; 6.7–13), his activity as a miracle*-worker, healer and exorcist (e.g. 1.21–45; 4.35–5.43; 6.30–52; 7.24–8.26), and his fame as a popular and charismatic teacher 'with authority' (1.21–22). The Marcan Jesus announces, through the didactic medium of the parable* (e.g. 4.1–34), the coming of the kingdom of God* but provokes consternation and controversy on the part of his Jewish kinsfolk, opponents and disciples (cf. 2.1–3.6; 3.20–35; 4.41; 6.1–6; 7.1–23; 8.14–21) with respect to the nature of the authority (*exousia*) which these activities reveal. For the author of Mark, this authority is that of the concealed Son of God whose true significance, to the eyes of faith, is linked with the divine necessity of his redemptive suffering and death.

After the important and carefully constructed central section of the Gospel (8.27–10.52), in which the disciples are further invited (unsuccessfully) to recognize the secret of Jesus' status and identity and are instructed on the nature and cost of the discipleship springing from it, the narrative turns to the passion* and resurrection* of the Son of Man* which has been predicted no less than three times in the central section (8.31; 9.31; 10.33–34). Jesus makes a climactic visit to Jerusalem,* dramatically cleanses the Temple (11.1–25), confronts and bests in argument the Jewish authorities who challenge him (11.27–12.40), and retires after predicting in apocalyptic* terms the signs leading both to the Temple's future destruction and the triumphal coming of the Son of Man (13.1–37). This final part of the Gospel appears from a literary point of view more coherent and presents thereafter, in a relatively continuous narrative, the now familiar account of the Last Supper, the betrayal by Judas, Jesus' anguish in Gethsemane, his arrest, trial and crucifixion (14.1–15.47). The closing section of the book (16.1–8) brings us the first extant narrative account in the developing Christian literary tradition of the empty tomb story (but curiously, according to our best ancient textual witnesses, no post-resurrection appearances by Jesus). Written in a deceptively simple way, and in a less than elegant Greek style, here is a text, nevertheless, which, with stories and scenes like these, has etched its picture of Jesus upon the religious imagination of countless Christian devotees, and one which, at the same time, has played a not inconsiderable role in the academic study of Christian origins.

The value, both academic and religious, of Mark's Gospel has not always been appreciated, as the history of its interpretation* shows. That history might well be summarized as one of longstanding neglect and recent rediscovery. It is now generally recognized that

Mark was used both as a source and as a model by at least two of the other canonical* evangelists. While Matthew and Luke expanded, altered and in various other ways edited Mark, and did so for reasons which can be variously interpreted, the fact itself of such dependence attests, as does the Papias tradition in other respects, the importance of Mark to the earliest Christian communities. Second-century tradition regarded the Gospel of Mark as one of the four pillars of the church (cf. Irenaeus,* *Adversus Haereses*, III, xi, 8) and, in theory at least, it was given equal prominence with Matthew, Luke and John. In practice things were very different and Mark was neglected, in particular in favour of Matthew. Within that same second century, it has been pointed out, Christian writers were reticent when it came to actually quoting from Mark. The first commentary* on the book was not produced until the fifth century, and in canonical lists it never appeared first, thus reflecting the view that the other Gospels, and in particular Matthew, were superior to it. A major reason for this was the common view that Mark was simply an abbreviated version of Matthew. This position, which conflicts with the Papias tradition of Mark's dependence on Peter, was given particular prominence by Augustine* at the beginning of the fifth century. After carefully considering the literary relationship between the Gospels, Augustine's conclusion was that 'Mark follows Matthew closely, and looks as if he were his servant (*pedisequus*) and epitomist (*breviator*)' (*De Consensu Evangelistarum*, I, 2(4)).

To be regarded as a 'pedestrian' abridgment of an apostolic work of greater historical, literary and theological value was not guaranteed to nourish, far less sustain, the reputation of what came to be called 'the second Gospel', and for centuries thereafter Mark lived in the shadow of Matthew and the church's view of Matthean priority. It was not until the latter half of the eighteenth century, with the advent of modern critical scholarship, that the Augustinian view came increasingly to be questioned and with it came a significant reassessment of 'the second Gospel', at least in terms of its historical value. The major factor in this reassessment was the development of what has come to be called the 'Marcan hypothesis'. This view in effect reversed the Augustinian theory of dependence and argued for the priority of Mark's Gospel.

Emerging from a wide field of alternative synoptic source* theories, it is associated with the name of K. Lachmann (1835), who among others laid the groundwork for it, and, later in the nineteenth century, such scholars as C.

G. Wilke, C. H. Weisse and (supremely) H. J. Holtzmann. The effect of a hypothesis that Mark had been used as a source by Matthew and Luke, and not *vice versa*, was dramatic, for it created a whole new interest in this hitherto neglected text. This interest was primarily historical, for if Mark was the earliest Gospel, then, according to a common but not necessarily logical assumption, it was the most historical of the Gospels. The historical value of ancient documents like the Gospels rests not simply in their date of composition or literary relationships but ultimately in the nature and reliability of the sources used and in the treatment accorded to them. When Marcan priority was allied, however, with Papias' claim that the apostle Peter was a major source for Mark, a further stage was reached in the historical revaluation of the Gospel. Within the world of English-speaking* scholarship in particular, there developed the widespread view that Mark represented a fairly simple and substantially objective report of the facts of Jesus' life, teaching and ministry. Such a view, moreover, reinforced a prevailing liberal* theology which was sympathetic to what it considered the 'human' Jesus portrayed in the Gospel. Others, especially in the Germanic tradition, were more sceptical, but, pushing beyond the still widely held postulate that this Gospel represents the earliest literary and narrative form of a tradition (if not a history) about Jesus, attempted to isolate possible further and earlier sources underlying the text upon which the historian could depend.

The course of twentieth-century interpretation of Mark has been one of qualified reaction to the first flush of enthusiasm engendered by this pious and often naive historicism.* Historical optimism has given way to a greater appreciation of the theological and, more recently, literary nature of the work. The first broadside against taking Mark without reservation as a window into the very consciousness of Jesus himself came with the publication of W. Wrede's* *Das Messiasgeheimnis in den Evangelien* at the very beginning of the century (1901) (*see* **Messianic Secret**). Wrede highlighted the distinctive way in which the career of the Marcan Jesus is characterized as one surrounded by secrecy. Mark's presentation, if approached as history, he claimed, is shot through with contradictions, but could be explained in terms of the christological* presuppositions and apologetic motivations of the writer and the tradition in which he stood. Anticipating later developments, Wrede, by illuminating the role of theological hindsight upon a received but developing tradition, in effect exposed the degree to which religious (or 'dogmatic') as well as literary factors were operative in the overall composition of the Gospel.

Further studies, particularly in the inter-war years, came to focus not so much on this overall composition as on the individual units of the tradition about Jesus which the composer of Mark had utilized. Viewing Mark as an editor rather than an author, form critics* like K. L. Schmidt, M. Dibelius and R. Bultmann* drew attention to the artificiality of the putatively historical framework within which Mark had arranged his traditions. They concentrated on the units themselves as a path to understanding the nature and beliefs of the early Christian communities* which had originally created, shaped or transmitted them orally. The tendency to 'fragment' the text exhibited by the form critics, and to deal with its component elements atomistically, was corrected to some extent in the post-war period by the work of redaction critics* like W. Marxsen or N. Perrin. Marxsen in particular emphasized the creative role of the Marcan redactor in bringing into a literary* synthesis what was previously a diverse and fragmented tradition. More recent studies have developed this trend further, by examining the Gospel from the point of view of its literary character and effect, and in the light of its religious message and concerns. In so doing, the literary approach has served to redirect attention to the enduring quality and overall unity of the text but without necessarily prompting a return, at the same time, to the historical questions.

The importance of Mark is clear, as this brief history of its interpretation has shown. From relative obscurity it has become one of the nerve-centres of modern critical study of the NT and primitive Christianity. Its story of Jesus, apparently simple, reveals upon examination a great deal of complexity. It can be investigated at various levels and from various standpoints. When approached by the tools of modern critical scholarship it has much to tell us, whether about Jesus, or the early church or its author. It has also proved amenable to a variety of perspectives other than the historical-critical* method. Many present-day readers may be forgiven for being confused, indeed, by the bewildering array of exegetical* methods which the modern scholar brings to biblical texts. Mark has been no exception, and in fact one allied aspect of its importance over the last one hundred and fifty years has been its own role in the history of biblical interpretation. Very few of the methods developed by biblical scholars have not been applied to Mark, and a number of them have taken Mark as their principal subject. These methods and approaches are treated more fully elsewhere in the dictionary but a brief comment on some of them, with respect to their relation to Mark, should perhaps be given.

Mark's role in the development of historical criticism on the life of Jesus has already been emphasized, although nowadays any approach to Mark as history must take account of the interrelated theological and literary factors which scholarship has highlighted. For those who view the Gospel as a 'scissors-and-paste' collection of early traditions about Jesus, the text has been invaluable. Tradition criticism,* in particular, has often looked to it for what is frequently, though not always, the most primitive recorded version of a story or saying, which the scholar can compare with variations found in other texts, such as the later canonical or apocryphal gospels. Such comparison has provided important insights into the ways traditions develop. The Marcan miracle stories, for example, have provided much grist for the tradition critic's mill.

A basic axiom of all historical criticism is that texts must be placed within their own historical and cultural context if they are to be understood. A biblical text moreover cannot be properly interpreted unless one determines the type of literature it is and what, therefore, its aims and purposes are. The discipline of genre* criticism has concerned itself a great deal with the problem of categorizing the so-called 'gospels' and has benefited from its application to Mark, where the issue of this text's place in the history of ancient literature has been uppermost. In an area where definition is all important and much debated, the earliest 'gospel' has been seen variously as a *nouveau genre* and hence *sui generis*, as a typical Hellenistic biography or 'aretalogy'* (like Philostratus' *Life of Apollonius of Tyana*), or as a literary mutant evolving out of certain partial antecedents (sayings collections, cycles of miracle stories, the apocalypse, martyrologies, etc.), which acted as genre models for its innovative creator. Whatever his literary debt to the contemporary world of Graeco-Roman and Jewish culture (*see* **Jewish Background to the New Testament**), it is clear, nevertheless, that this anonymous creator produced a work, subsequently designated a 'gospel',* which was to become a popular and distinctive type of Christian literature, as evidenced by both its canonical and extra-canonical successors.

Pursuing literary categorization, but more with regard to the individual components of a text than at the level of its overall genre, has been the related method of form criticism (*Formgeschichte*) previously mentioned. Mark has been a prime source for the form critic, standing as it does closest to the oral tradition which produced the stereotypical forms in which the Jesus tradition came to be expressed.

Bultmann, for example, found within Mark a number of these pre-Marcan units or pericopae with their distinctive structure and function. Form criticism highlighted the influence of the practical needs of Christian communities before Mark upon the formation of the Gospel tradition, and in many ways broke the impasse that had been reached by source criticism on the Gospels.

The critical study of the Gospels including Mark had done much to strengthen the discipline of source criticism, a method which was particularly successful in leading to a solution of the Synoptic Problem.* As a result the Gospels had come to be viewed somewhat as scrapbooks, with the role of the evangelists having been to paste together excerpts from the various sources at their disposal. The techniques of source criticism were practised on Mark, to see if even this early text could be considered a compilation of yet more primitive documentary sources. The search has in the end proved unsuccessful, or at least inconclusive, although attempts have been and continue to be made to isolate specific written sources behind the use by Mark of such material as the parables, the miracle and controversy stories, the apocalyptic discourse of ch. 13 and the passion narrative. Form criticism, on the other hand, provided an alternative model to that of the scrapbook, namely that of pearls (the pericopae) on a string (the framework created by the evangelist). In so doing, it enabled the investigation of the Jesus tradition to be carried further back into the oral* period behind Mark without the necessity of establishing prior extensive written sources.

One of the criticisms levelled against form criticism is that it has assigned too creative a role in the formation of gospel tradition to the anonymous community, and not enough either to Jesus himself or to the evangelists. Mention has already been made of the influence of redaction criticism, but its application to Mark has been viewed from the beginning with some scepticism. Form criticism, however, has helped the Marcan redaction critic to identify, though with less precision than with Matthew and Luke, the nature and form of the (oral) sources used by the first evangelist. Indeed, far from being a dubious enterprise, the discipline of redaction criticism has actually developed as a result of being applied to Mark, for the redaction critic has had to broaden the method in order to embrace indicators of the evangelist's literary and theological concerns other than the narrower criteria of source editing (e.g. the nature, arrangement and setting of the material selected, the dominant motifs governing the overall composition, etc.).

In this respect, broader applications of redaction criticism have led to a significant overlap with the techniques of general literary criticism, and it is this approach, perhaps more than any other, which is currently being taken to the Gospel to great effect and which is in turn being enriched by it. Literary criticism has raised a number of general questions about religious texts like Mark, such as the nature of religious language, the role of the religious imagination, the interrelationship of language and theology, and the ways in which theology expresses itself in a variety of forms, the poetics of faith. More specifically, the subjecting of the Gospel to the many methods, techniques and theories of the secular literary critic (e.g. analysis of the style, the point of view of the narrator, the rhetorical* devices used in the composition of the text; examination of the plot, the settings, the characters, etc.) has thrown light upon a number of the traditional questions and issues, as well as opening up fresh avenues of investigation.

Some approaches, while literary in purpose, have retained an interest in the historical dimension. The first-century author and his readership have been a focus for some methods such as rhetorical criticism,* a development of form criticism, which has illumined the structural patterns, rhetorical devices and idioms used by the original author, or certain forms of reader-response* (or audience) criticism, which has investigated the reception of the text by its original readership in the light of their Graeco-Roman or Jewish education. Narrative criticism* has exposed the extent to which Mark's theological intentions have been expressed in a narrative form appropriate to the cultural context. Other approaches have eschewed the notion of 'authorial intention' or, like other forms of reader-response criticism, have emphasized the not insignificant influence of the present-day reader and his community in the interpretative process. Some literary methods like structuralism,* with its complex analysis of the 'deep structures' underlying the text and its abstract investigation of the mechanisms by which texts themselves become meaningful, have even questioned the historical-critical method itself and have attempted to stand outside the historical dimension altogether.

One common denominator in many of these literary approaches is their contribution to a holistic* interpretation of Mark, after a period in which the major emphasis in scholarship has been on the complex traditio-historical process which brought it into being. In turn, they have found this particular Gospel a fruitful subject and one remarkably responsive to their methods.

All the approaches briefly described here have not, of course, exhausted the many that have been or can be applied to Mark. Traditional Christian devotional approaches, which see the text first and foremost as a religious text with a divine message for the contemporary believer, still prevail, and very often, as with fundamentalism,* they are based on the same enduring but naive historicism which is frequently faith's first instinctive response to what is regarded as revelation.* This-worldly questions have also been raised as in the increasingly popular sociological* approach, which seeks to illuminate the social contexts in which the text was generated and has been subsequently used. The Gospel has been interpreted from a Marxist* ideological* standpoint or read through the eyes of the liberation* or feminist* theologian. By continuing to stimulate interest and by showing itself amenable to such a variety of hermeneutical perspectives, the Gospel of Mark demonstrates its essential robustness, both religiously and academically, a robustness which belies its traditional reputation as a text which, from a historical, literary and theological point of view, is simple and unsophisticated.

See also **Gospel.**

E. Best, *Mark. The Gospel as Story*, 1983; H. C. Kee, *Community of the New Age*, 1977; R. P. Martin, *Mark – Evangelist and Theologian*, [2]1979; W. Marxsen, *Mark the Evangelist*, 1969; D. Rhoads and D. Michie, *Mark as Story*, 1982; W. R. Telford (ed.), *The Interpretation of Mark*, 1985.

WILLIAM R. TELFORD

Marxist Interpretation

Marxist analysis has been prominent in theology in the last thirty years, and the treatment of religion has also formed a small but frequently significant component of the work of various thinkers within the Marxist tradition. The important fact to grasp about Marxist interpretation is that religious ideas, their use and development, must be seen as epiphenomena of particular socio-economic formations. They are part of the ideological* level, in which different groups, particularly those who possess economic power, seek to legitimate their position of dominance by political, legal and above all religious means. The North American critic, Frederic Jameson, has stressed that 'the restoration of meaning of the greatest cultural monuments cannot be separated from a passionate and partisan assessment of everything that is oppressive and that knows complicity with privilege and class domination' (*Political Unconscious*. 1981, p. 299). Sometimes a crudely simple relationship is suggested between the economic world and the world of ideas, so that the latter is seen as a mere projection of the competitive interests of the former. Attempts to explain religious belief and its 'parasitic' quality in social terms have not been helped by Marxist use of the image of 'base' (the determinative economic world) and 'superstructure' (the world of ideas). The metaphor* has proved to be unhelpful because it gives the impression that ideas are never influential in determining the form of the base and are always supported by it. Such a view does not do justice to the subtlety of Marx's thought, and more recent treatments of ideology within the Marxist tradition are considerably more sophisticated and nuanced. But however much autonomy is allowed to the realm of ideology in its development and formation, a Marxist interpretation could not fail to allow the socio-economic formation a role as a (if not the) significant determining factor in their evolution (*see* **Sociology and Social Anthropology**).

There are two major strands to Marxist interpretation: the historical studies of religion, particularly the work on Christian origins and the Reformation* period, pioneered by Engels and Kautsky, and the Marxist literary criticism* found in the work of Walter Benjamin. Engels and Kautsky in their studies of early Christianity sought to stress the socio-economic factors which led to its emergence and transformation into an imperial religion. According to Kautsky, Christianity started as a proletarian movement which was an antidote to the decay and oppression of the Roman Empire. In some recent sociological study we find that the move of Christianity from a rural, peasant environment to the urban Hellenistic* world also presumes the determining influence of social formation' on ideas. One of the most influential and consistent applications of Marxist historiography to biblical interpretation is to be found in the work of Norman Gottwald, who explains Israelite origins by the analogy of a peasants' revolt.

Marxist biblical interpretation has concentrated on the socio-economic forces at work, so that individual genius tends to be played down, and the social formation (in particular the role of the development of economic activity) which produced the individual religious figures tends to be stressed. This insight is a necessary corrective to the concentration on individual genius as the locus of divine activity at the expense of the complex totality of particular social formations and movements.

A rather different approach is to be found in the work of the Marxist literary critics. The enormous potential of this method for biblical interpretation may be glimpsed in the work of Walter Benjamin. There is stress on the subversive memory of the tradition, and Benjamin's insistence that every generation has to rescue the tradition from conformity and from the instruments of oppression is a theme which is integral to the prophetic and apocalyptic* horizon of the biblical tradition. In Marxist literary criticism the rescue is effected by attention to the form of a text and its relationship to the mode of production. The conflicts within the text relate to the class struggle in the society at large, but the piece of literature can frequently offer some kind of resolution in the text of what in reality are irreconcilable contradictions in society.

See also **Liberation Theology**; **Materialist Interpretation**.

S. Avineri, *The Social and Political Thought of Karl Marx*, 1968; G. de Ste Croix, *The Class Struggle in the Ancient Greek World*, 1977, esp. pp. 400ff.; T. Eagleton, *Criticism and Ideology*, 1976; N. Gottwald, *The Tribes of Yahweh*, 1979; K. Kautsky, *The Foundations of Christianity*, 1925; G. Lukacs, *History and Class-Consciousness*, 1971; D. McLellan, *Marxism and Religion*, 1987; J. Roberts, *Walter Benjamin*, 1982; R. Williams, *Marxism and Literature*, 1977.

CHRISTOPHER ROWLAND

Masoretic Text

'Masoretes' is a term used to translate *ba'ale hammasoreth* (keepers of the Masoreth): Jewish scholars of the fifth to the tenth centuries A D who devoted themselves to the accurate preservation of the Hebrew Bible, introduced vowel signs into the consonantal text, and surrounded the text with masses of notes, aids to the understanding and protection of the text and known as the Masoreth or (later) Masorah. They operated in Babylonia and Palestine (especially in Tiberias) and, although there were differences of tradition, it was the Tiberian Masoretes whose system of vowel points became standard in the Hebrew Bible. Even in Tiberias there were differences, notably between the ben Asher family and that of ben Naphtali, and it was the ben Asher Masoretic tradition which was given pre-eminence, mainly because both Maimonides and David Kimchi espoused it in mediaeval times. The manuscript which scholars feel best represents this text is the Leningrad Codex B19a, and it is used in *Biblia Hebraica Stuttgartensia*. This Masoretic text has a long history, and its ancestor (minus vocalization and notes) was only one of several versions of the Hebrew Bible present in Qumran (see **Dead Sea Scrolls**). This was the recension which prevailed, and it was handled and transmitted with great care from the second century A D onwards. This care is evident in the numerous notes which began to accumulate and accompany the text's transmission. For example, we occasionally find letters or words with special points over them, indicating reservations on the part of the scribe* on textual* or doctrinal grounds. In addition a number of notes known as *sebirin* appear in the margin, which suggest that a form different from that in the text is to be expected (*sebir* = supposed). For example at Gen. 19.23 the *sebir* on the word אצי indicates that one might have expected to find the feminine form יתאצי here. Another kind of note is the *ketib* (written)/*qere* (read). The written form could not be altered in the text, but the reader is directed to read another form which is written in the margin. In some cases this seems to be a recognition that the form in the text needs correction, while in others it may well represent a variant reading. Above all, the care of the scribes is to be seen in counting the verses, words and even letters of the Hebrew text. Hence they indicate that the ו of גחון ('belly') in Lev. 11.42 is the middle letter of the Torah, and that דרש (a form used to denote emphasis, R S V 'diligently') in Lev. 10.16 is the middle word.

The Masoretes inherited these notes and produced many more, the whole corpus taking the name Masoreth or Masorah (which some say means tradition). In the side margins of the text, notes were added, mostly in Aramaic, identifying *hapax legomena*, noting how often a phrase may occur, drawing attention to peculiarities of spelling etc. Above and below the biblical text were written further notes (known as Masorah Magna) of a fuller nature. Thus while the side margin (known as Masorah Parva) notes at Gen. 1.1 that בראשית ('in the beginning') occurs five times, the Masorah Magna gives the references as Gen. 1.1; Jer. 26.1; 27.1; 28.1; 48.34.

These notes, together with vocalization and punctuation render a text 'Masoretic'. (The student will encounter two spellings of 'Mas-(s)oretic'. The term מסרת Masoreth, found in Ezek. 20.37, has only one 's' but the ס, thought by some to have been pronounced with a sharp 's', is sometimes transliterated 'ss'.)

From what has been said it is perhaps incorrect to speak of *the* Masoretic text. What is usually thus termed is *a* Masoretic text, albeit one which was preferred above others. We should not, however, think of it as the original Hebrew, nor even as necessarily the best in all respects. It is, rather, best viewed as an accepted form of the text and, though accorded a high place in the textual history of the O T, it must take its place with other forms and versions and be rigorously scrutinized.

See also **Textual Criticism (Old Testament)**.

F. M. Cross and S. Talmon (eds), *Qumran and the History of the Biblical Text*, 1975;

C. D. Ginsburg, *Introduction to the Massoretico-Critical Edition of the Hebrew Bible*, 1897, reissued 1966; S. Z. Leiman, *The Canon and Masorah of the Hebrew Bible*, 1974; B. J. Roberts, *The Old Testament Text and Versions*, 1951; E. Würthwein, *The Text of the Old Testament*, 1979.

ROBERT B. SALTERS

Materialist Interpretation

A description of a type of biblical exegesis which has arisen, particularly in Europe, which is related to liberation theology.* In some ways it is an unfortunate title, as the word materialist suggests an excessive dependence on a specific form of historical materialism which is explicitly atheistic. While this interpretative method places the material world and forces of production at the very centre of its interpretation, it is not denying a theistic dimension to the material processes it seeks to expound. An interesting development in some recent liberation exegesis has been the recognition that an approach which is more sensitive to the fabric and detail of the text and the responses it provokes is necessary. Thus in the work of Fernando Belo and Michel Clevenot there is a complicated but fruitful recognition that the NT texts are themselves social products. Materialist interpretation forcibly reminds us that writing is itself part of a process of production in which the product and the producer are themselves parts of complex economic systems. We know little about the production of the original biblical books and the social circumstances of their writers. The material of the text, however, is capable of laying bare some of the secrets of another story to be told, of the writer's world, of oppression and struggles for power, of the suppression of the ideas of the weak and insignificant, and of the dominance of the ideology of the powerful. As monuments to ideological* struggles of the ancient world, the biblical texts can offer the modern reader some glimpse of matters now otherwise lost to our sight. In this the voiceless are given a voice and the social determinants of the producers of ideas, who are involved in the struggle for social and economic power, can be laid bare. Materialist interpretation, drawing upon a long tradition of Marxist* literary criticism, has sought to reconstruct the social formation which gave birth to the biblical texts and, by understanding the economic systems of which they were a part and their place in them, to throw light on ancient struggles and eclipsed movements for change.

While many of the materialist readings have concentrated on the original social formations in which the biblical texts came into being, there has been a growing recognition that a proper materialist exegesis cannot ignore the twin poles of its task. Accordingly, the production of meaning in the modern world, and the location and interests of readers in economic systems which are class-based, are essential components of a materialist reading. In this regard, a proper analysis of the power and influence of those who control the ideology of acceptable readings (e.g. scholars in First World universities and seminaries, and the accepted parameters of taste in learned journals) and a comparison with the character of the biblical exegesis* of those who do not have such economic power offer instructive contrasts. The overwhelming dominance in scriptural study of the quest for the original meaning of the text has coloured the way in which the 'proper' method of reading is outlined. In this respect, the historical method shares with Marxism a common legacy of the Enlightenment.* By contrast, the interpretation of the Bible among the basic ecclesial communities in Latin America and other parts of the Third World reflects different preoccupations, which are curiously more akin to a pre-Enlightenment concern to see the text as a living word, now of immediate application to the realities of oppression and social injustice. For them the Bible is their story, the 'literary memory of the poor' and the outcast.

Carlos Mesters, who has spent all his life working with the poor in both urban and rural areas, never devalues the contribution of the apparently unsophisticated reading. Experience of poverty and oppression is for the liberation exegete as important a 'text' as the text of scripture itself. The poor are blessed because they can read scripture from a perspective different from that of most of the rich and find in it a message which can so easily elude those who are not poor. Yet Mesters himself does not disparage traditional exegetical interest in the original setting and meaning. Indeed, he regards them as an important antidote to the kind of unrestrained fantasy which binds (and limits) the text as firmly to the world of the immediate present context as historical exegesis has bound it to the ancient world. He has spoken in the following way about the use of the Bible by the poor:

> . . . the emphasis is not placed on the text's meaning in itself but rather on the meaning the text has for the people reading it. At the start the people tend to draw any and every sort of meaning, however well or ill founded, from the text . . . the common people are also eliminating the alleged 'neutrality' of scholarly exegesis . . . the common people are putting the Bible in its

proper place, the place where God intended it to be. They are putting it in second place. Life takes first place! In so doing, the people are showing us the enormous importance of the Bible, and at the same time, its relative value – relative to life (in *The Bible and Liberation* ed. Gottwald).

To enable the poor to read the Bible has involved a programme of education in the contents of the biblical material, so that it can be a resource for thousands who are illiterate. In such programmes, full recognition is given to the value of the primary text, i.e. experience of life. Therefore, the poor are shown that they have riches in plenty to equip them for exegesis. This is balanced with the basic need to communicate solid information about the stories within the Bible themselves, of which many remain ignorant.

In that process, the reading of scripture often bypasses the dominant methods of the First World. To those brought up on the historical-critical method* the interpretations can often appear cavalier. They frequently have little regard for the historical circumstances of the text, its writer and its characters. There is often a direct identification of the poor with biblical characters and their circumstances, with little concern for the hermeneutical niceties which are invoked in applying the text to our own circumstances. In their use of scripture the resources of the text are used from their perspective of poverty and oppression, and a variety of meanings is conjured up in a way reminiscent of early Christian and ancient Jewish exegesis.

The biblical text, therefore, is not a strange world which can only come alive by recreating the circumstances of the past. The situation of the people of God reflected in it is their situation, as the material contained in the remarkable collection of *campesino* reflections on the Gospels (*The Gospel in Solentiname*, 1982), edited by the Nicaraguan Minister of Culture, Ernesto Cardenal, indicates. What such biblical interpretation dramatically reminds us is that the pressing question for any critical exegesis must be the rigorous analysis of the complex production of meaning and the contexts in which that takes place and the social and economic interests that interpretation is serving. It has become a commonplace among European and North American exegetical elites that there is an obvious commonsense way of reading texts which seeks to establish as a first priority what the text originally meant. A first step is to recognize that such 'normality' is an ideology promulgated by a powerful interest group which can thereby regulate the canons of the production of meaning. Materialist interpretation will take as its first task the examination of such claims to canonicity and seek to encourage a critical awareness by insisting that at the top of any interpretative agenda issues of social class and economic interest are included as matters of theological concern.

An example of materialist interpretation may be found in the work of Fernando Belo. The sophistication of his interpretative method, influenced as it is by Roland Barthes and Louis Althusser, may seem to make it far removed from the interpretative approach of the poor of Latin America. However, its insights have many affinities with the practice of biblical study in the basic ecclesial communities, particularly its concern to see the text as a subversive story with a ready contemporary application. Belo's reading of Mark exposes the way in which the text is itself a story of radical change, in the first part of the Gospel, particularly the account of Jesus' deeds. This is interrupted by an emerging preoccupation with theological reflection on the significance of Jesus' death. An execution of a subversive messianic* claimant is thus on the way to becoming an unhistorical and otherworldly myth which involves an escape from issues of justice. Jesus' bloody execution by the Romans as a martyr for the kingdom is uprooted from its historical context and made into a timeless abstraction. That process is a product of a situation of political powerlessness, when the living out of a subversive, radical story is compensated for by the construction of theological reflection. That interruption of the subversive story of Jesus is a reflection of the political powerlessness of the first Christians who found no adequate outlet for their messianic enthusiasm. The political structures offered little space for change. Telling the story of Jesus in this form accurately represents the frustration of those who seek to live in the way of the messiah in a hostile environment.

The approach to Mark's Gospel which focusses on the mighty deeds of Jesus in the first part of the narrative, as the primary thrust of the messianic proclamation, contrasts starkly with trends in First World interpretation of Mark. In the latter, there has been an influential view which has regarded the emphasis on the necessity of suffering and the death of Christ in the second half of the Gospel of Mark as a corrective to the optimism and activism which the dynamic account of Jesus' deeds in the first half seems to promote. For the First World exegete, then, it is the idea of the suffering messiah which is primary for the understanding of salvation: believe in this and you will be saved. By contrast, the emphasis on Jesus' *praxis*, with the reflection as a secondary stage (which in fact dilutes the power of the original messianic narrative), corresponds closely to the priorities of the liberation theologians, for whom practical identification with the poor takes precedence over theological reflection. Nowhere are the epistemological undergirdings of the two exegetical worlds better seen than in their approach to Mark's Gospel.

See also **Black Interpretation; Feminist Interpretation; Ideology; Liberation Theology; Marxist Interpretation; Sociology and Social Anthropology.**

F. Belo, *A Materialist Approach to the Gospel of Mark*, 1981; P. Berryman, *Liberation Theology*, 1987; M. Clevenot, *Materialist Approaches to the Bible*, 1985; N. Gottwald (ed.), *The Bible and Liberation*, 1983; C. Myers, *Binding the Strong Man*, 1989.

CHRISTOPHER ROWLAND

Matthew, Gospel of

Matthew may not be the most popular or influential Gospel* today, but it quickly became dominant in the early church. John's Gospel began to rival Matthew in popularity towards the end of the second century, but by then Matthew had played a vital part in creating the climate of ordinary Christianity in most parts of the church. In the early centuries Matthew was cited and commented on more frequently than the other Gospels. With only a very few exceptions, Matthew always heads lists and manuscript* copies of the four Gospels.

It is not hard to find the reasons for its dominance. In the early church there was universal acceptance of the tradition that it had been written by Matthew the apostle, and from at least the third century it was taken as the first Gospel. Matthew's full and carefully ordered collections of the sayings of Jesus in five discourses assisted its widespread acceptance. Today its juxtaposition of Jewish, anti-Jewish (*see* **Antisemitism**) and pro-Gentile traditions fascinates and bewilders many readers, but in the early church its apparently contradictory emphases enabled Matthew to be welcomed both by Jewish Christian* groups (of various kinds) and also by almost the entire Gentile church. K. Stendahl (1968) concludes, surely correctly, that Matthew 'is a witness to a far smoother transition from Judaism to Christianity than we usually suppose. Luke is irenic by effort, as his Acts shows. Matthew is comprehensive by circumstance, and that makes it a rich and wise book.'

The terse comment of Papias* on the origin of Matthew was influential from the middle of the second century until the early decades of this century. About AD 130 Papias stated that 'Matthew put together in the Hebrew language the discourses (*logia**) and each one translated them as best he could.' There is still no agreement on the precise meaning of these words! Did Papias think that Matthew was written in Hebrew or in Aramaic? Or was he referring to Matthew's 'Jewish forms of expression' in his Greek Gospel? Was he referring to Matthew's composition of the five discourses in his Gospel, of Q, or of the whole Gospel? Did Papias mean that the 'discourses' were 'translated' from one language to another, or simply 'interpreted'? A few modern scholars have half-endorsed Papias by holding that at least parts of the Gospel make very good sense as renderings of Aramaic. Papias was apparently unaware of any relationship between the Gospels and Matthew and Mark, treating them as individual works.

Irenaeus* (late second century) probably knew Papias' comment; he certainly accepted this explanation of the origin of Matthew, adding that this Gospel was written for 'preaching among Hebrews'. About AD 170 Tatian composed his important harmony* of the four Gospels. Not surprisingly, he considered that Matthew provided the most reliable historical account of the ministry of Jesus before the passion.*

Although the differences between the Synoptic* Gospels and John were widely appreciated in the early church (and accounted for in a variety of ways), most writers assumed that Matthew's Gospel contained the very words of Jesus. The comments of Clement of Alexandria (early third century) on Matthew's Beatitudes* are a particularly interesting exception. He notes that Matthew has 'added' (presumably to an earlier source) 'in spirit' to the Beatitude about the poor (5.3), and 'for God's righteousness' to the Beatitude concerning those who hunger and thirst (5.6). Clement was probably the first to appreciate that Matthew had modified earlier traditions, so we may consider him to be the first redaction critic!* Most scholars today would accept that his observations on the Beatitudes are correct.

About half of Origen's* commentary* on Matthew (written about AD 250) has survived; it was the most extensive written in the early church. He knows and accepts the tradition that Matthew was written by the apostle in Hebrew 'for the believers from Judaism', but he did not use this view to explain the differences between Matthew and the other Gospels. Origen readily conceded that there are major disagreements between the four Gospels and that it was difficult to accept the literal* meaning of some sayings and stories. At times (and especially in his reply to the shrewd criticisms of the anti-Christian Celsus), he grappled seriously with these problems. More frequently he rejoiced in them because they forced the reader to search for the allegorical* or spiritual* meaning of the text, which he took to be primary.

Origen's distinction between the literal and the spiritual meanings of the text did not win the day. But later writers rarely matched his grasp of the theological and historical difficulties which confront the interpreter of the Gospels. They almost all assumed (without discussion) the traditional view that Matthew the apostle wrote the first Gospel in Hebrew and that he had provided an accurate account of the life and teaching of Jesus.

In both respects Calvin* is a notable partial exception. He claimed that since Matthew cites the Greek translation of the OT (see Septuagint), he cannot have composed his Gospel in Hebrew. He firmly rejected Augustine's* opinion (which he mistakenly attributed to Jerome) that Mark is an abridgment of Matthew and conjectured (cautiously) that Mark had not seen Matthew when he wrote. Calvin did not explore the relationship between Matthew, Mark and Luke closely, but he did insist that it is impossible to expound properly any one of the evangelists without comparing him with the other two. Although Calvin's commentary on his own harmony of the Synoptic Gospels follows Matthew's order very closely, he did not suppose that Matthew had set out a verbatim and chronologically accurate account of the life and teaching of Jesus. In several places Calvin suggested that both Matthew and Luke have rearranged the traditions to suit their own purposes. In his comments on Matt. 23.34 Calvin conceded that Matthew's version of the saying of Jesus is 'defective: its meaning must be supplied from the words of Luke'.

The rise of rigorous historical criticism* in the eighteenth century led to much more thorough investigation of the origins of the Gospels. The traditional view that Matthew was the first Gospel to be written was frequently challenged in the final decades of the eighteenth century, but it was still widely supported in the middle of the nineteenth century. In 1847 F. C. Baur set out his views on the 'tendencies'* of the four evangelists* as part of his bold reconstruction of the development of earliest Christianity. Baur accepted J. J. Griesbach's view (1783) that Matthew (the first Gospel) was used by Luke; Mark used both Matthew and Luke. With the exception of passages which expected an imminent parousia,* Matthew's 'Jewish' Gospel was considered by Baur to be historically reliable.

Just a few years earlier, in 1838, C. G. Wilke and C. H. Weisse had set out (independently) a full and thorough defence of Marcan priority, but their case was accepted only slowly. In 1911 the Pontifical Biblical Commission still echoed the traditional view in its insistence that the apostle Matthew wrote the first Gospel – and not merely a collection of logia. By then (with the notable exception of Theodor Zahn, 1897) most Protestant scholars had accepted Marcan priority.

Abandonment of the traditional view of the origin of Matthew led to a reappraisal of its distinctive features and its setting in early Christianity. Once Marcan priority was accepted, it became impossible to equate the 'Jewishness' of Matthew with an early origin in Palestine and authorship by the apostle. In 1918 B. W. Bacon argued that the evangelist had gathered together teaching material from his sources into five great discourses which correspond to the five books of Moses.* Ten years later von Dobschütz claimed that the evangelist was a converted rabbi who had probably been trained in the school of Johanan ben Zakkai immediately after the fall of Jerusalem in AD 70; Matthew was primarily concerned with catechetical instruction. The structure of Matthew, its overall purpose and its relationship to contemporary Judaism have all been high on the agenda in more recent Matthean scholarship.

The period immediately after 1945 is particularly important for modern interpretation of Matthew. In 1946, G. D. Kilpatrick published a major study of the origins and purposes of Matthew, in some parts of which he anticipated the later development of redaction criticism.* His discussions of Matthean style and of the relationship of the Gospel to Judaism influenced scholarship considerably.

G. Bornkamm's 1948 essay on the stilling of the storm pericope marks the beginning of the thoroughgoing redaction-critical approach which has dominated Matthean scholarship ever since. Bornkamm assumed that Matthew had used Mark's account of the stilling of the storm and paid close attention to the additions, modifications and omissions which the evangelist has made, as well as to the different context in which the pericope has been placed. He concluded that Matthew was not merely handing on the Marcan story but was expounding its theological significance in his own way: Matthew is seen as the first exegete of the Marcan pericope. Matthew's redaction shows 'proof of definite theological intentions' with its references to discipleship and to 'the little ship of the church'.

This brilliant short essay paved the way for numerous studies of Matthew's distinctive theological perspective. The three most influential monographs by W. Trilling (1959), G. Strecker (1962) and R. Hummel (1963) have never been translated into English, but in due course they encouraged many English-speaking scholars to use redaction-critical methods.

It was some time, however, before redaction criticism became the dominant method. Two important books in English adopted other approaches. K. Stendahl (1954) claimed that in Matthew's 'formula' quotations of the OT, the biblical text is treated in somewhat the same manner as in the Habakkuk scroll which had recently been discovered at Qumran. W. D. Davies (1964) cautiously suggested that the Sermon on the Mount* was a kind of Christian counterpart to aspects of the reconstruction of Judaism which took place at Jamnia following the fall of Jerusalem in AD 70.

The translation into English (1968) of J. Rohde's thorough survey of the first phase of redaction-critical work on Matthew stimulated further research from this standpoint. Careful isolation of the evangelist's redaction of his sources has been the basis of numerous expositions of Matthew's christology,* his ecclesiology and the relationship of his community to contemporary Judaism.

One of the fundamental presuppositions of redaction criticism is that individual changes made by the evangelists to their sources form part of a consistent pattern of redaction which reflects the evangelist's purpose and distinctive theological emphasis. But Matthew seems not always to keep to the rules! He frequently includes apparently divergent sayings of Jesus. Two examples are worth noting briefly. In 10.5–6 the disciples are forbidden to go to the Gentiles, but are sent to 'the lost sheep of the house of Israel'. How can this passage be related to the universalist, pro-Gentile and anti-Jewish sayings found throughout the Gospel? Possibly, he sees the former as applying to the period of Jesus' ministry, while 28.19 is meant for the church. Matthew's attitude to the law is equally problematic. While most redaction critics agree that he is generally more conservative than Mark, the evangelist includes disparate or even contradictory statements. M. J. Suggs (1970) echoed the despair of many redaction critics when he concluded that Matthew's presentation of Jesus' attitude to the law makes jugglers of us all!

In recent years some scholars (especially in the USA) have expressed doubts about the validity of the hypothesis that Matthew has used Mark and Q as the basis of his Gospel and reasserted his priority. Some have attempted to set out Matthew's distinctive viewpoint without source-critical* presuppositions. Attention has turned from Matthew's redaction of his sources to his methods of composition – to the overall structure of the Gospel, the structure of individual sections and sub-sections, and the order in which traditions are placed. In his study of Matthew's fourth discourse in ch. 18, for example, W. G.

Thompson (1970) insisted that Matthew must be read 'in terms of Matthew', a method he dubbed 'vertical analysis' in contrast to the 'horizontal analysis' of redaction criticism. This approach has been developed in more recent narrative critical* studies of Matthew, to which we shall turn in a moment.

Over the last ten years or so several attempts have been made to undermine both Marcan priority and the Q hypothesis. Marcan priority has weathered the storm well and remains the basis of virtually all recent Matthean scholarship. Criticism of Q has been more rigorous. M. D. Goulder, for example, claimed in 1974 that apart from a small handful of oral traditions, Mark was Matthew's *only* source. Matthew used midrashic* methods in his very free expansion of Mark for liturgical* purposes. With a wave of the lectionary wand, Q was consigned to oblivion. Goulder's exposition of Matthean style was warmly welcomed, but his midrashic and lectionary theories were severely criticized.

More recently (1989) Goulder has published a thorough defence of the view that Luke has used Matthew and Mark, but not Q. If so, then Luke becomes the very first interpreter of Matthew! It is claimed that, in order to advance his own particular views, Luke has virtually demolished Matthew's carefully constructed discourses and has abandoned Matthew's finely-honed phrases and distinctive vocabulary.

Most scholars still accept that while the Q hypothesis is not without difficulties, they are minimal in comparison with those faced by rival views of Matthew's and Luke's methods. No fewer than three multi-volume commentaries on Matthew are being prepared at present. In their exegesis of Matthew, U. Luz (Vol. 1, 1985), J. Gnilka (2 vols, 1985, 1988), and W. D. Davies and D. C. Allison (Vol. 1, 1988) all accept that Matthew has used both Mark and Q and that redaction criticism remains the most fruitful way of uncovering the evangelist's purposes.

In recent years literary-critical* and sociological* insights have become prominent in interpretation of Matthew, but not as a result of strong convictions that redaction criticism is a misguided method. Some scholars have felt that since that particular seam has, as it were, now been almost fully worked out, methods which have been fruitful in the study of other biblical writings should be explored.

Literary critical studies have taken two forms: structuralism* and narrative criticism. In 1987 D. Patte published a full structuralist commentary. Patte is concerned with the evangelist's faith (or 'system of convictions') rather than with the first-century setting of the Gospel. He works with two basic premises. Since Matthew has set out not only what he wants to say, but also what he does not want to say, attention must be paid to 'narrative oppositions' in the text. In addition, the interpreter must look for the tensions between the readers' 'old knowledge' and the 'new knowledge' the evangelist is seeking to communicate. Patte has lucidly expounded one form of structuralism and shown how it might be used in exegesis.* He does not reject traditional methods – they are in fact used in his notes. But he fails to show how a structuralist approach might be integrated with other methods to provide a fresh 'reading' of the text. This structuralist approach sheds little or no light on exegetical questions which have teased Matthean specialists for decades. More important is its apparent inability to provide a deeper and richer understanding of the text.

Narrative-critical methods which have been fruitful in study of Mark, Luke–Acts, and the Fourth Gospel, have recently been used by R. A. Edwards (1985) and J. D. Kingsbury (1986) in order to elucidate the meaning of Matthew for readers today. Like Patte, these scholars are less interested in the historical context of Matthew than in the ways the text elicits the reader's response.* Matthew is understood to be a 'narrative' comprising a story and its discourse. The 'story' of Matthew is of the life of Jesus of Nazareth from conception and birth to death and resurrection.* The 'discourse' is the language, including the many devices of plot, characterization, rhetoric* and point of view, that are the means by which the story is put across. Kingsbury had earlier written a redaction-critical study of Matthew (1976), concentrating on the structure, christology and eschatology* of the gospel. In his more recent narrative-critical study some of his conclusions are similar, but he does not integrate the two methods.

It is too early to assess the value of narrative criticism for the student of Matthew. Perhaps Matthew is less amenable to this approach than the other Gospels. In the five large discourses the 'story-line' hardly progresses at all. And in the Gospel as a whole there is less development of a story-line or plot than in the other Gospels: as early as ch. 2 the reader is confronted with possible negative and positive responses to the narrator's presentation of the theological significance of Jesus.

As yet, few scholars have applied to Matthew the sociological insights which have been so fruitful in recent studies of John's Gospel, of Acts, and of the Epistles. From this angle it may be possible to explain (in part) why Matthew strengthens considerably his anti-Jewish and apocalyptic* traditions, both of which bewilder and even exasperate the modern reader. Perhaps the anti-Jewish polemic stems from the anger and frustration of the evangelist and of his community at the continuing rejection of their Christian claims and at the continued hostility of Jews towards the new community. It may also represent the community's self-justification for its position as a somewhat beleaguered minority 'sect' cut off from its roots. As elsewhere in contemporary Judaism and early Christianity, perhaps Matthew's apocalyptic traditions are a response to rejection, hostility and a consequent feeling of alienation. The strongly redactional 24.10–12 (for example) may reflect the evangelist's concern to reinforce group solidarity.

See also **Redaction Criticism; Sermon on the Mount; Synoptic Problem.**

Commentaries by F. W. Beare (1981); W. D. Davies and D. C. Allison (1988 chs. 1–7 only); R. H. Gundry (1982); D. Hill (1972); E. Schweizer (1976). See also G. Bornkamm, G. Barth and H. J. Held, *Tradition and Interpretation in Matthew*, ²1982; J. D. Kingsbury, *Matthew: Structure, Christology and Kingdom*, 1975; id., *Matthew as Story*, 1986; J. P. Meier, *The Vision of Matthew: Christ, Church and Morality in the First Gospel*, 1979; P. S. Minear, *Matthew: the Teacher's Gospel*, 1982; G. N. Stanton (ed.), *The Interpretation of Matthew*, 1983.

GRAHAM N. STANTON

Meaning

Philosophers of language note that the general question 'What is meaning?' more readily invites perplexity than concrete enquiries about the meanings of given words or phrases. This is partly because people use the word 'meaning' in a wide variety of ways. Alston and Black list seven important uses, but other scholars distinguish as many as sixteen. Caird warns biblical interpreters against being distracted by certain pseudo-uses of 'meaning'. When someone says that a biblical verse has special 'meaning' for him or her, this may be nothing more than an evaluation ranking its importance. Similarly, the example 'I mean to attend' has more to do with intention than meaning. The notion of meaning as entailment is more complex. Caird follows Barr in warning us that the 'meaning' of faith, for example, in a given passage cannot be said to entail all that later writers or interpreters have themselves experienced about faith. Nevertheless, Schleiermacher's work in hermeneutics* reminds us that certain experiences of life may place us in a position where certain meanings can more readily be perceived and understood.

More positive progress can be achieved by examining major theories of meaning which have influenced ideas, assumptions and practices in biblical interpretation. None of these theories on its own offers a comprehensive account of meaning, but each contributes something to the answering of certain questions about meanings. L. J. Cohen rightly argues in *The Diversity of Meaning* (1966) that progress is made most constructively, not by grading these theories or by selecting some preferred definition of meaning, but by asking what is gained or lost by each main theory of meaning. We shall ask this question in the context of issues in biblical interpretation.

1. The *referential* theory of meaning finds a place in Plato and Augustine.* The meaning of a word lies in the object to which it refers. In Russell, Carnap and early Wittgenstein, this approach was developed to include an account of sentence-meaning. A theory of reference seems to address such a question as 'What does "phylacteries" mean in Matt. 23.5?' In the light of historical research, the meaning of this word can be explained by describing the object to which it refers in first-century Jewish life. Names (e.g. Pilate), many nouns (e.g. cross) and some verbs (e.g. crucify) can be explained on this basis. Statements, according to the logical atomism of Russell and the early Wittgenstein, carry meaning by relating together in a determinate way the objects to which components (or atoms) of the statement refer: 'Pilate released Barabbas . . . delivered Jesus to be crucified'.

This theory anchors language and meaning in the real extra-linguistic world in a stable and determinate way. Meaning is not merely a matter of subjective perception, or even, perhaps, of 'interpretation'. But the theory applies effectively only to a limited segment of language-uses and types of words. It is plausible only as long as we restrict our attention merely to names, to physical objects and to physical acts or processes. (a) Frege pointed out that words which refer to the same referent may bear a different sense. In biblical interpretation 'Jesus' and 'Christ' have different senses but the same reference. (Attempts to modify the theory to meet this difficulty bring new problems.) (b) In his later work Wittgenstein urged that this theory is not only limited to given examples, but also presupposes some prior understanding of forms of life, conventions or social practices. To return to our example, the reference of 'phylacteries' would help if we already knew something about Jewish life. But if we know nothing at all about Jewish thought and religion, to explain the meaning of 'phylacteries' only by describing the object to which it refers would miss the point. (c) The meaning of a sentence or speech-act is not always the same as the sum of the meanings of the component units. In some parts of the NT, it would be impossible without semantic* loss to substitute for 'the twelve' a list of the twelve implied referents.

(d) The referential theory of meaning under-values metaphor.* If meaning is reference to objects, metaphor appears as no more than a secondary or derivative extension of language. The referential theory of meaning offers a tool which is useful in some contexts, but severely limited in others.

2. *Semantic* theories locate meaning in terms of choices within a network of inter-relations and interactions generated within language itself. Where the slogan of one theory is meaning as reference, and of another meaning as use, here it is meaning as choice. The role played by lexicography* and by questions about translation* in biblical interpretation ensures that this approach plays a major part in the ideas and assumptions held by many biblical interpreters.

Choices can be made from a linguistic stock or repertoire of possibilities. The general linguistic storehouse from which choices can be made was carefully distinguished by Saussure from actual specific language-uses by reserving for it the term *la langue*. By contrast, speech, which he called *la parole*, represents the specific operational unit selected and set in action at a given time. Meaning is generated by the relation between the speech-act and two axes of relations in the language-system. One axis of the grid traces contextual or 'syntagmatic' relations between language-units. For example, part of the potential meaning of 'ball' is generated by its syntagmatic relation to 'kick'. The other axis of the language grid exhibits relations of substitution, potential opposition or exclusion. For example, when Mark alludes to the 'green grass', part of the meaning of 'green' is generated by its 'paradigmatic' or contrastive relations with 'yellow' or some other colour. Its choice indicates, 'not red', 'not yellow', but also contextual applicability to 'grass' and to what a bystander could see.

In biblical interpretation the part played by lexicography and by translation encourages an understanding of meaning in intra-linguistic terms, just as historical research points towards its extra-linguistic dimension. The use of smaller dictionaries can seem to support the illusion of wholly intra-linguistic generation of meaning. The meaning of one word may be explained in terms of another, and a chain of synonyms cited which can be virtually circular. Larger dictionaries confirm, however, that all synonyms remain context-dependent, and that idiosyncratic authors or unusual (even unique) situations can call fresh language-uses into play. This brings growth and flexibility into the language-system. Like many systems in the hard sciences, and even more in the social* sciences, language represents an open system, not a mechanical or closed one. In biblical interpretation this has implications for hermeneutics, where the language-choices available in a later era are often not exactly the same in shape and range as those originally available to the author of a text.

Work in the area of semantic theory has been fruitful in biblical interpretation. In *The Semantics of Biblical Language* (1961), James Barr drew heavily on the standard work of Saussure and general linguistics* to indicate a number of fallacies which too often marked work in interpretation. In particular he drew on the contrast between diachronic and synchronic* enquiry, in order to urge that statements about the history of a word were not the same as statements about its meaning. He also attacked the 'illegitimate totality transfer' whereby all the semantic contributions offered in a series of past contexts were lumped together and transferred to a word in a later context as part of its 'meaning'. The 'meaning' of 'church' in Matthew simply cannot include all that it 'means' in certain Pauline* passages.

Another fruitful area has been that of field semantics, which J. F. A. Sawyer applied to Hebrew words for salvation (1972). Utilizing the work of J. Trier, J. Lyons and others, Sawyer showed that the semantic scope of Hebrew words in the field depended decisively on the availability and scope of other near-equivalents, and that the semantic repertoire of Hebrew was not the same in this respect as that of English. One by-product of Sawyer's work is to demonstrate the importance of work on Hebrew and Greek for an understanding of meanings which lie behind English near-equivalents. G. B. Caird took semantic issues further in his book *The Language and Imagery of the Bible* (1980). He drew especially on the semantics of S. Ullmann. The work of E. Guttgemanns is more complex and speculative. While his work embodies some axiomatic principles of semantics, he is also indebted to some structuralist* assumptions which raise doubts and questions.

3. It is doubtful whether much is gained by defining and examining *ideational* theories of meaning as such. These theories locate meaning in the concepts, images, thoughts or ideas which lie behind language. But the only way of approaching or identifying them is through language itself. The well-known 'semantic triangles' of Saussure, Ogden and Richards, and others, derives from Stoic philosophers' contrast between sign, object and idea. John Locke saw language as a system of markers which identify thoughts or ideas. But if these ideas merely represent referents, we have fallen back into a version of the referential theory of meaning. If, on the other hand, 'concepts' represent patterns of language-uses, we have

moved on towards a version of a functional theory.

The interest of this theory of meaning for biblical interpretation probably lies in two specific areas. First, there has often been a tendency among some biblical interpreters to devalue language as inferior to thought. For Herder* and for Romanticism, there was always 'more' meaning behind language than it could convey. But more recent work in the philosophy of language suggests that what lies behind language also lies beyond conceptual thought. Does thought exist independently of language? To claim that thought might not be co-extensive with reality is an entirely different matter. Secondly, this ideational approach would be congenial to approaches in biblical interpretation of a kind which was undertaken in the days of the so-called biblical theology* movement. Writers would trace a 'concept', image, or theme through a succession of varied contexts, and expound its meaning in terms of the distinctive pattern which might emerge. But what is more clearly a matter of 'meaning' is the relation between changing patterns of language-uses and the beliefs, truth-claims, situations and forms of life which these patterns reflect and articulate.

4. *Functional* theories of meaning locate meaning in the particular use which a given linguistic unit has within some specified context, or situation, or pattern of life or action. Language and meaning are seen as part of verbal behaviour. In relatively crude quasi-behaviourist terms, L. Bloomfield, C. Osgood and C. Morris developed semantic theories within the framework of stimulus-response perspectives. With far greater sophistication, the later Wittgenstein argued that 'the *speaking* of language is part of an activity, or of a form of life ... commanding, questioning, recounting, chatting, are as much part of our natural history as walking, eating, drinking, playing ... For a *large* class of cases – though not for all – in which we employ the word "meaning", it can be defined thus: the meaning of a word is its use in the language' (*Philosophical Investigations*, 1967, sects. 23, 25, 43).

Such an approach indirectly vindicates the place traditionally devoted to historical reconstruction as an aid to biblical exegesis.* The meaning of given biblical words and phrases can be determined with accuracy only when the role which they perform within the contextual horizons of the speaker or writer and the addressees is taken into account. Wittgenstein argued the point with a huge range of examples. The meaning of 'exact', for example, will depend on whether the horizons in question are those of the watchmaker, the astronomer, or the travel agent. Difficulties about meaning, he urged, arise when we decontextualize the abstract language-uses from specific surroundings in life, or transplant them from one context to another without noticing the radical consequences which may follow. The problem of re-contextualizing a stretch of language within the framework of a second horizon is the central problem of hermeneutics.

Nevertheless, there are serious difficulties about trying to account for meaning solely in terms of functions or functional equivalents. Bultmann's * bold proposals for a programme of demythologizing * rightly identify the need to distinguish between form and function in biblical language. Kerygmatic * function is not always best served, Bultmann argues, by objectifying, descriptive or mythological * language. Thus, to see language about the last judgment as primarily descriptive in meaning is to risk missing the point that it functions chiefly as a call to present seriousness and accountability. Bultmann's contrast between form and function bears some comparison with Wittgenstein's analogy that to answer questions about meaning is more like explaining the moves of chess pieces than describing their physical properties. Nevertheless, criteria * for functional equivalence are far more complex than Bultmann allows. The descriptive truth-claims about divine judgment are already built into the function of its language as part of the surroundings from which it draws its operational currency. Further, as Wittgenstein himself insists, questions about function answer many, but not all, enquiries about meaning.

5. It is arguable that concessions in the direction of a functional theory give hostages to what Cohen calls *de facto* theories of meaning. It is clear that both in referential and in semantic theories, some controls are imposed which enable an interpreter to say (*de jure*) that a given meaning 'ought' or 'ought not' to be conveyed. But if meaning relates in any sense to use, has not 'meaning' now become simply whatever (*de facto*) is generated in the context of the hearer's situation and perception, in a horizon which is different perhaps from that of a given text? It is to guard against this *de facto* notion that E. D. Hirsch, in his attack on Gadamer, insists that *meaning* is textual-semantic meaning, while *significance* describes its role in the horizon of the hearer.

Such a distinction is both right and wrong. What Hirsch wishes correctly to say is that meaning is generated in accordance with certain conventions (linguistic code), with a particular message in a given context. It is part of the convention on which communication is based that the hearer takes these factors into account. R. Jakobson urged that all communication of meaning between sender and recipient pre-supposes to some degree contact, code,

context and content. But no legal, moral, religious or linguistic 'rule' can prevent the recipient from making some mistake (e.g. misidentifying the linguistic code of apocalyptic * for straight narrative), or from choosing to substitute a different context or code which will change the message. It does not identify the point at issue to speak here only of 'significance', not of 'meaning'. We return to the principle advocated by Cohen. No single theory of meaning is valid for every kind of question. Each offers some contribution within the terms of certain purposes. The key issue is not whether such theories are right or wrong, but what is gained or lost by each particular approach.

See also **Hermeneutics**; **Linguistics**; **Semantics**; **Structuralism**.

W. P. Alston, *Philosophy of Language*, 1964; J. Lyons, *Semantics* (2 vols) 1977; A. C. Thiselton, *The Two Horizons*, 1980.

ANTHONY C. THISELTON

Mediaeval Interpretation

The study of the Bible in the early mediaeval West drew upon a patristic tradition which was predominantly that of the Latin Fathers, above all Augustine * and Gregory the Great. Some influence from the Greeks found its way into Augustine; for example, through Ambrose's use of the Cappadocian Fathers. A little Origen * was known in Rufinus' Latin translation. But broadly speaking there was a substantial separation of the Greek and Latin patristic inheritances until the later mediaeval centuries, when they began to come together again.

This had the effect of throwing great weight on the work of Augustine, and upon Gregory as popularizer of Augustinian principles of exegesis.* Mediaeval library catalogues uniformly show a high proportion of Augustinian texts, after the Bible itself and liturgical books, and Gregory frequently comes next. Augustine explored the Bible's language for Latin-speakers, and here above all he set the lines of mediaeval work. He made use of both the Old Latin and the Vulgate * texts and was aware of differences in wording. But he treated the Latin for purposes of analysis as though it were the actual text of scripture, and for a thousand years the majority of mediaeval scholars did the same: with the result that despite the transformation of biblical studies brought about by work on the Greek and Hebrew texts at the end of the Middle Ages, theological debate still found its natural vehicle in the Latin Bible during the early Reformation * period. This continuing dominance of the Latin is of importance in a number of respects. Attack and defence centred about the Vulgate in a way which unbalanced the picture in the first half of the sixteenth century; longstanding debates about puzzling or theologically challenging phrases in the Latin text were not easily set aside; above all, the long mediaeval tradition of applying the study of grammar, logic and rhetoric* to exegetical problem-solving proved hard to break, and we find Luther* and other Reformers discussing fine points of mediaeval signification-theory, identifying fallacies and noting the names of rhetorical figures in a direct line from Augustine through the mediaeval schools.

Augustine also encouraged the development of the habit within the Western tradition of looking for more than one sense in scripture. Whatever he may have known of the work of Philo* and Origen, the strongest influence on Augustine himself here is likely to have been Ambrose. But he recognized the need for some such understanding through his own reading, where he noted that the apparent contradictions in scripture can be made to disappear if one or both of the passages in question is read figuratively. In his attempt to harmonize* the Gospels,* Augustine inspired a series of mediaeval imitations. He was willing to adopt the rules of interpretation of the Donatist Tyconius, even though the man was a schismatic and a heretic, and we find mediaeval scholars prepared to do the same – Hugh of St Victor, for example, in the early twelfth century. The limitation of Augustine's work on scripture's multiple senses from the point of view of subsequent Western tradition was his failure to set out clearly the quartet of literal* or historical; allegorical;* moral or tropological; and anagogical or prophetic, which Gregory the Great was able to draw from Origen and present as a working system to the mediaeval world. All four are there in Augustine, but he tries out a variety of ways of classifying scripture's senses, though mostly confining himself to the literal and the allegorical. In mediaeval usage the moral sense had a practical place in homiletic,* and here Gregory's *Moralia* on the Book of Job was a strong influence. The anagogical sense was of importance in the prophetic tradition explicated by Joachim of Fiore in the late twelfth century and continuing in the later mediaeval centuries (with a notable offshoot in the 'Antichrist' literature of the dissident movements of the end of the Middle Ages and the early sixteenth centuries).

The allegorical sense could be taken to cover both these two, but in its own right it represented an idea of profound importance for the understanding of the nature of biblical language. Throughout the mediaeval centuries we meet the difficulty that human language is inadequate to express divine reality. God is seen by both Augustine and Gregory the Great as coming to meet us in our limited understanding. Christ himself became 'a little Word' (*verbum abbreviatum*), in which we can read God as he is. Scripture is couched in language which reflects the failings of human insight and which makes allowance for all our frailties. In accordance with this doctrine, scripture's use of figures is seen as a means by which God speaks to us in pictures. But even in its use of words such as 'anger' or 'love' in referring to God, the Bible may be regarded as making a transference of usage from the application of such words in human experience to some sort of figure of divine response to man. This *translatio* is the fundamental principle of allegory as seen by scholars from at least Carolingian times.

The literal sense received a new status from the twelfth century. It had been regarded as fundamental by patristic tradition, but rather in the sense that the rough-cut stones which form the foundation of a building give it a necessary solidity. Some Fathers – especially among the Greeks – held that there was not necessarily any literal sense at all for certain passages. Hugh of St Victor encouraged his pupils to respect this foundation. The airy superstructures of the higher, 'spiritual' senses are, he says, carefully cut to fit into the rough crevices of the foundation, so that the whole meaning of scripture forms a balanced unity. More sophisticated understanding of the behaviour of language on the part of grammarians and logicians now lent new interest to the serious study of the literal sense. It was apparent to Aquinas and his thirteenth century contemporaries that the author's intention was relevant here. Jesus sometimes spoke in parables.* Parables are figures.* It can be argued that these figures constitute a literal sense, because we do not read their figurativeness into them; they are, though technically figures, also the plain sense of the text. Out of this observation came a full debate in the later mediaeval centuries about the role of divine intention and the role of the human author and his intention in writing; the latter was of central importance for the development of the sensitivity to the teaching of Paul* which is a marked feature of early sixteenth-century exegesis, in Erasmus* as in Luther.*

The doctrine of the multiple senses of scripture rests on two principles whose significance for mediaeval exegesis cannot be overemphasized. The first is that all the meanings which can be found in scripture by human ingenuity, and which are consonant with orthodoxy of faith, may be taken to have been put there by God. No human interpreter can think of anything God has not intended. All figurative interpretations are therefore legitimate and helpful, provided they are orthodox. Secondly, it is assumed, with few exceptions, that the text must be made to make sense as it stands. The notion that there may be errors of transmission or translation * is not seriously canvassed until the end of the Middle Ages (although Paris in the thirteenth century saw a thoroughgoing attempt to purge the text of accumulated copyists' errors). This encouraged resort to figurative interpretation where the text was puzzling, rather than to textual criticism.*

These strong main lines of the interpretative tradition running through Augustine and Gregory from the earlier Fathers kept in the forefront of mediaeval exegesis, until at least the thirteenth century, the link with preaching and the liturgy * which had been formative since the earliest Christian period. Late in the Middle Ages, the sacramental aspect of the mass became somewhat divorced in practice from the ministry of the word. In any case, Latin preaching was of little use to the majority of the faithful. It was against this disjunction that the Reformers protested, as they sought to bring the interpretation of the Bible back into its original place in worship through an emphasis on preaching. But mediaeval preaching had, paradoxically, been especially vigorous during the period when it had largely lost its place in the liturgical framework.

Manuals of preaching were produced from the late twelfth century, and in profusion from the middle of the thirteenth century. These – primarily designed for academic use, but carrying over into the training of Dominican and Franciscan preachers who were to go out into parishes and speak to the people in their own tongue – taught a method of expounding a text of scripture. The passage was analysed by examining its key terms, and dividing up their implications into three topics, which were then further subdivided into three and perhaps again into three. With the aid of handbooks of biblical references topically arranged, the preacher could make comparisons with other biblical passages where the term or the topic occurred. Although the more informal and discursive patristic structure of homiletic altered with these manuals for preachers into something much more systematic, they maintained the pattern of serving the ministry of the word which had always been constitutive for exegesis. That remained the case even in the glaring abuses of preaching about indulgences for money about which Luther complains. And the friars did a great deal of good in helping ordinary people to a fuller understanding of their faith, enlivening their discourses with stories and illustrations (for which again handbooks of stock examples were to be had). Where an articulate middle-class laity threatened revolt and laid claim to the right to read the Bible for themselves in the vernacular, as happened from the twelfth century onwards in different parts of Europe (Waldensians in Lyons, Lollards in England, Hussites in Bohemia, for example), the friars were sometimes a valuable point of contact with the *magisterium*; more often perhaps, they failed in this delicate and essential enterprise and were held in contempt by anti-clericalist feeling.

The bread-and-butter task of providing continuous commentary * on the whole Bible was not undertaken seriously until the eleventh and twelfth centuries. The patristic inheritance in the West was patchy here. Some books of the Bible were, and remained, rich in commentaries – notably the Psalms and the Pauline Epistles. To Augustine and Gregory, Jerome's works and the commentaries of Bede, a good deal was added by Carolingian authors by way of the making of selections and compilations of comments attached to specific passages. There grew up a system of glossing the text where such references were added in the margin or between the lines. In the late eleventh century, Anselm and his brother Ralph in the cathedral school at Laon found themselves with able pupils whom they encouraged to write commentaries from these existing resources. The work went on through the twelfth century, and by the end of the century a *Glossa Ordinaria*, a standard gloss, was in existence. It remained standard until the sixteenth century, attracting to itself further concentric rings of commentary. In early printed Bibles, two types are instantly distinguishable: those which retain this Vulgate-based tradition of commentary, and print the *Glossa Ordinaria* and the commentaries which ride piggy-back upon it, and those which give Greek or Hebrew text with a new apparatus of critical material, discussions of the biblical languages, place-names and so on. The apparatus of the *Glossa Ordinaria* proved unsuitable for transfer from the Vulgate for which it was written.

See also **Allegorical Interpretation**; *Biblia Pauperum.*

M. Colish, *The Mirror of Language*, 1967; G. R. Evans, *The Logic and Language of the Bible*, Vol. I: *The Earlier Middle Ages*, 1984; Vol. II: *The Road to Reformation*, 1985; H. de Lubac, *Exégèse Médiévale* (2 vols), 1959; B. Smalley, *The Study of the Bible in the Middle Ages*, [3] 1983.

G. R. EVANS

Merkabah Mysticism

The *merkabah* (Hebrew for chariot) is the short-hand way of referring to the descriptions of the divine throne-chariot mentioned in

Ezekiel's and Isaiah's visions in Ezek. 1 and 10 and Isa. 6. The word is used to describe the vision of Ezekiel* in the Greek version of Ecclus. 49.8. Together with the first chapter of Genesis, these visions became central to early Jewish mystical tradition and are alluded to in the Mishnah (*Hagigah* 2.1, and in more detail in the parallel passages in Tosefta, and the Talmuds*). While Genesis formed the basis of speculation on cosmogony and cosmology, Ezekiel allowed the development of a mystical theosophy which developed into the practice of an ecstatic ascent to heaven to gaze upon the enthroned Deity. Although the rabbinic* accounts tend to present the mystical tradition as if there were two distinct parts, corresponding to the two biblical books, there is a clear overlap. Thus part of the description of the ascent to heaven to see the vision of the *merkabah* involves elaborate descriptions of the various parts of the heavenly world (usually divided into seven) with the multitude of its angelic inhabitants.

When one talks of mysticism* in a Jewish context, there is no question of the mystic being identified with God (although there are remarkable descriptions from time to time of mystics being transformed into angelic beings). Rather, we should understand mysticism as the apprehension of truths beyond the capacity of ordinary reason. As such, *merkabah* mysticism relates very closely to the apocalyptic* tradition of Second Temple Judaism, and may well form the rabbinic continuation of apocalyptic. How early this ecstatic practice began has been the subject of much dispute, though there seem to be indications that already in the period of the Second Temple (i.e. before AD 70), there were a number of teachers practising such heavenly ascents, and this practice was then continued by the first rabbis, even though it became a source of heterodox views, and so necessitated some restriction, as is evidenced in the regulations in the Mishnah concerning the exposition of the first chapters of Genesis and Ezekiel. Paul* seems to stand in this tradition (II Cor. 12.2ff.) and he is an early testimony to the influence of such ideas among the educated elite in Judaism. Other writings such as the Fourth Gospel and the letter to the Hebrews have also been linked with the *merkabah* tradition. The former's concern to locate the revelation of God in Jesus (John 14.9) rather than in heavenly ascents (3.13) answers the mystic's quest to see the enthroned God face to face. The latter's contrast between the earthly and the heavenly shrine, and the ascent of Christ via the cross to enter the heavenly shrine, could owe much to the developed cosmology of the Jewish apocalyptic and mystical tradition (Hofius).

This mystical tradition continued and developed, and there are threads which can be traced into mediaeval Kabbalah and the later influential Hasidic mysticism of recent times (*see* **Jewish Exegesis**). There have been suggestions that there were some links with Gnosticism* (and some elements of the *merkabah* tradition have been found in several early Gnostic works). The indebtedness almost certainly stands on the side of Gnosticism, suggesting that Jewish ideas deriving from groups such as those who practised *merkabah* mysticism may have contributed in some way to the origins of Gnosticism (as has long been suspected). The few hints about *merkabah* mysticism from the early rabbinic sources suggest that we may have a penumbra of eccentric beliefs connected with such mystical practice which may allow us to discern the outlines of a connection between Judaism and emerging Gnosticism as well as nascent Christianity (Segal).

The discovery of the importance of Jewish mysticism has helped to rectify the kind of distortion of Judaism prevalent among Christian scholars which sees it as a religion of works devoid of the spirituality of Christianity. That kind of distortion, which has been the legacy of Lutheran* biblical exegesis,* is not only a travesty of the Jewish attitude to the Torah but also neglectful of that mystical tradition which seems to have been an important component of the leading teachers of Judaism from the first century onwards.

I. Gruenwald, *Apocalyptic and Merkabah Mysticism*, 1978; D. Halperin, *The Faces of the Chariot*, 1988; C. Rowland, *The Open Heaven*, 1982; G. Scholem, *Major Trends in Jewish Mysticism*, 1955; id., *Jewish Gnosticism, Merkabah Mysticism and Talmudic Tradition*, 1965; A. Segal, *Two Powers in Heaven*, 1978; M. Stone, *Scriptures, Sects and Visions*, 1982.
CHRISTOPHER ROWLAND

Messiah

The word is a loose transliteration of the Hebrew word *mashiah* = 'anointed' (from a verb *m–sh–ḥ* = to wipe, anoint). The Greek (Septuagint*) translated this as *christos*, which was taken over into Latin, and became the familiar title applied in Christian tradition to Jesus of Nazareth. Very speedily, it came to be regarded as in effect a personal name for him.

The origin of the messianic hope. In its literal sense the word *mashiah* was applied to the kings* of Israel who were installed to their royal office by a ritual act of anointing (so Saul, I Sam. 10.1; David,* II Sam. 2.4; 5.3; Solomon, I Kings 1. 34,39). This act is presented as the most significant, and most public, of the acts of royal investiture. It is clearly intended as a religious rite, and not solely a legal one, and certainly came to signify an empowering with the gift of God's spirit (cf. Isa. 61.1), thereby endowing the king with wisdom and strength to fulfil the duties of the royal office. Such an action almost certainly came to be adopted into Israel from Egyptian* practice where the Pharaoh's vassal rulers were anointed to office with oil supplied from the Pharaoh himself.

In later post-exilic Judaism, the Aaronic high-priest was also installed to office by an act of ritual anointing (cf. Ex. 29.7), but this must certainly represent a transfer to the high priesthood of a practice which earlier applied exclusively to the kingship. Similarly the idea of a prophetic* anointing to office (I Kings 19.16) would appear to be most plausibly explained as an extension of the royal ritual. This prophetic anointing is then later further emphasized (Isa. 61.1).

Since all Israel's kings were installed to office by the rite of anointing, in a broad sense all such monarchs are messiahs, i.e. anointed ones. However, in Jewish and Christian tradition the term has come to be used in a more restricted sense to refer to the hope of the coming of a divinely appointed deliverer figure. This coming was expected to fulfil many of the functions associated earlier with kingship, and among the Qumran community at least, also many of the functions connected with the priesthood (*see* **Dead Sea Scrolls**). In this case two distinct messiahs were looked for. However, the most central and significant of the qualifications of the messiah was that he would be a descendant of the dynasty of David. The origins of this expectation were centred upon the dynastic prophetic promise set in II Sam. 7.16. Davidic descent came therefore to be recognized as a primary qualification, but the nature of the kingly rule exercised by such a messianic figure came to differ considerably in popular expectation from actual experience of the kingly office. In this way the expected messiah came to acquire many characteristics of the 'ideal' king, and a major feature of his anticipated rule was the freeing of Israel from foreign domination (cf. Isa. 9. 4 [*Heb.* 3]). There grew up in the Judaism of the first century AD, therefore, very politically oriented messianic expectations, as well as more idealist and spiritual ones. There is no clear evidence that, before the rise of Christian claims for the messianic status of Jesus of Nazareth, Jewish hopes envisaged a suffering, or martyred, messiah.

The messianic hope of the Judaism of the late OT and early Christian period remained essentially fluid and only loosely defined. The reason for this lies in the nature of the origin and growth of the hope. Although it centred upon the promise of II Sam. 7.16, it came to be supported and elaborated with the aid of several passages of scripture, chiefly drawn from prophecy (especially the book of Isaiah) and the Psalms. Depending upon which passages were accorded central importance, and how they were interpreted, so the doctrine of the messiah was capable of being formulated in very different ways. Understanding the origin of the Jewish doctrine of the messiah is therefore essentially the pursuit of an understanding of how certain key themes and texts were interpreted during the period when the OT canon* was taking shape in the postexilic era.

Key passages for the rise of messianic expectation. We may group the main texts which have a bearing on the rise and development of Jewish messianic expectation into four main categories. It may be stated at the outset that, in the sense which the word 'messiah' came to acquire by the beginning of the Christian era, none of them expresses such a hope in a rounded and elaborated way. Nevertheless, as the OT literature took shape in the light of the political and religious experience of Judaism, it is plain that certain texts acquired a larger significance than that which they had originally possessed. This process of re-reading and re-interpreting texts was greatly assisted by reading one passage in conjunction with others, thereby building up a more comprehensive picture of their meaning. So far as prophecy was concerned, this larger meaning was controlled by the expectation of the 'fulfilment' to which each such prophecy pointed.

Another general characteristic of the OT messianic hope requires to be kept in mind. The whole of the post-exilic Jewish understanding of prophecy was coloured by an ever-growing and enlarging doctrine of eschatology.* This took on an increasingly transcendental and radical nature, embracing the dissolution of the present social, political, and even physical, world order. In its place there was expected to come a new world order in which Israel's position among the nations of the world would be vindicated, sinners would be punished, and justice and truth prevail. The hope of a coming messiah was essentially part of the content of this hope. It did not itself generate that hope, but simply provided it with one theme showing how victory could be achieved and justice upheld. It is this broader context of eschatological hope that lent to messianic expectations their appeal and that provided the intellectual framework for re-examining and reinterpreting older scriptural passages so as to give them a new messianic significance.

The first group of scriptural passages that relate closely to the messianic hope are those that focus upon the dynastic claims of the Davidic dynasty. The key passage is the prophecy of Nathan to David recorded in II Sam. 7.1–17. This establishes the claim that God has ordained that the Davidic dynasty should rule in perpetuity over Israel (II Sam. 7.16). The entire history of the kingdoms of Israel and Judah which thereafter follows details how this promise took effect. With the break-up of the Davidic–Solomonic kingdom after Solomon's death only Judah remained loyal to the Davidic house. Eventually, after the Babylonian capture of Jerusalem in 587 BC, Zedekiah, the last of the line of Davidic kings, was removed from his throne and taken to Babylon (II Kings. 25.1–7). Nevertheless the historical record of the monarchy ends on a hint of hope for the eventual restoration of the Davidic monarchy (II Kings 25.27–30) through the exiled king Jehoiachin. Further signs of such an expectation are to be seen in the preservation of the list of Jehoiachin's descendants given in I Chron. 3.17–14. This expectation of restoring the monarchy came to be focussed, when the exile ended, upon the figure of Zerubbabel, a grandson of the exiled Jehoiachin (Hagg. 2.23; Zech. 4.9). The eventual fate of Zerubbabel is unclear, but it is evident that neither he, nor his immediate descendants, succeeded in restoring the Davidic family to the throne of a renewed Israel.

The second group of texts that have a bearing on the messianic hope are to be found in a number of royal psalms. These emanated from the period when the Davidic monarchy flourished and they were marked by the richly mythological* and pretentious language that surrounded the institution of kingship in Israel. Among them we should especially note Pss. 2, 18, 20, 45, 72, 89, 110, 132. What is especially striking in such psalms is the remarkably high concept of the person and office of the king which is presented. He is God's 'son' (Ps. 2. 7 [Heb. 6]), the most excellent of men (Ps. 45.2 [Heb.3]), and is destined to achieve great victories and power over the nations (Ps. 110). The roots of this elaborate imagery are to be found in the Ancient Near East* and the notion that the divinely appointed ruler was a channel of divine justice, power and wisdom. It is the psalms which express such a concept of kingship which strengthened the conviction that the anointed ruler was quite distinct from other human beings. This distinctness could be expressed in the idea that the king was God's 'son' (? by adoption, or a process of rebirth. cf. Ps. 110.3).

After the removal of the last of the Davidic kings, it would appear that these royal psalms were retained and used in line with the hope that the Davidic monarchy would eventually be restored to the throne. The expectations that, for a time, surrounded the figure of Zerubbabel almost certainly contributed to this reinterpretation of the royal psalms. However, this hope gradually came to lose all political practicality in the Persian era. We can only assume that, when this happened, these royal psalms which had been retained, came to be understood as a divine assurance that a messianic ruler would eventually be given to Israel. Such a messianic figure, however, became progressively detached from expectations concerning the restoration of Israel's monarchy.

The third group of texts relating to the messianic hope is a series of prophetic passages which have themselves been strongly influenced by the first two. Most to the fore here are Isa. 9. 2–7 (Heb. 1–6), relating to Hezekiah, and Isa. 32. 1–2, relating to Josiah.

The final group of OT texts derives from a slightly later period, when the expectations of reinstating a Davidic ruler after the Babylonian exile had largely faded. They present the expectation of the coming of a new Davidic ruler in the context of a much more radical eschatology. Prominent here are Isa. 11. 6–9 (intended to amplify the promise that precedes it) and Micah 5. 1–6. It was during this period (late Persian and early Hellenistic eras) that the process of reinterpreting the royal psalms in a more radical eschatological sense appears to have emerged. So it came about that, by the close of the OT age, a broadly based expectation that the promise of a coming messiah among the house of David formed an influential, although by no means dominant, element of the many themes that contributed to Jewish eschatological hopes. With no clear definition of the precise status of the person of the messiah, and with considerable hesitancy about the royal office of such a figure, the hope nevertheless expressed many important features. Perhaps three may be especially singled out: it affirmed that the new political order of the 'age to come' would be one of divinely ordained justice and peace. It asserted that the coming of such a new order would be the result of the breaking-in of divine power, setting aside the existing political order. It further drew special attention to the conviction that the messianic age would be one in which the people of God were freed from the scourge of foreign domination.

In the Jewish writings of the intertestamental period we can find three main lines of development. In a whole range of them, often those that express a very far-reaching eschatological hope for the future, the messiah does not appear at all. In others the messiah appears in a rather sporadic way as an established part of the future hope, but not in any very central role. In several writings, however, a messianic-type figure appears, frequently bearing the title 'Son of Man',* where many aspects of the earlier doctrine appear to have been developed and retained. We can, accordingly, make some distinction between the retention of the hope of a national messiah where most of the features of the OT expectation are retained, and the more elaborate expectation of a cosmic messianic deliverer, where many quite new elements appear.

It is particularly noteworthy that the interpretation of the OT presented in the Targums,* especially those to the prophets, develops the expectation of a messiah in a very extensive fashion. In this literature the idea of a coming messiah as a central element of the future hope is introduced into scripture passages where it is not present in the original Hebrew text.

In the early Christian exegesis* of the OT, we find that very much the same process of interpretation is followed. The major difference is in the Christian claim that Jesus of Nazareth was such a messiah and that all such prophecies concerning his coming have now been fulfilled. A major feature of this Christian development of the doctrine was the incorporation of the notion that the messiah must be a suffering figure who would undergo martyrdom (cf. Mark. 8. 31; I Cor. 1. 23). All four of the Christian Gospel* writers express their conviction that Jesus was the messiah expected by the Jews. There are, however, clear indications that the very idea of a messiah figure was being reinterpreted in ways that made it intelligible to a Gentile readership. The messianic claim of Jesus is further supported by Paul's* assertions in his epistles. Where differences emerge between the evangelists* and within early Christian thought, these are to be found in varied evaluations of the significance attaching to the different messianic titles taken over from Judaism. In particular this applies to the concept of the 'Son of God', which has only a limited role to play in the OT and Jewish understanding of the messiah (and indeed has a much wider range of senses), but which has come to take the central position in Christian understanding of the person of Jesus of Nazareth.

The concept of the messiah in Jewish and Christian tradition. So far as the subsequent development of messianic doctrine in Judaism and Christianity is concerned discussion has been heavily affected by polemical interests maintained by the respective religious traditions. In Jewish thought the concept has not figured prominently, being largely overtaken by the idea of the hope of a messianic age. In this the ideas of vindication, justice and freedom from foreign domination have retained a place, without any very strong emphasis being placed upon a central messiah figure. At a more popular level, however, the idea that a particular leader would fulfil the role of a messiah has, from time to time, gained a sporadic measure of local support in Jewish communities. It is noteworthy that, for Jewish thinking, the emergence of Zionism in the late nineteenth century was able to develop and adapt many features of the messianic hope.

In Christian tradition the claim that Jesus of Nazareth was the messiah, and that he fulfilled the prophetic hopes expressed in the OT, has continued to be a central part of Christian interest in that literature. Throughout the Middle Ages, and until the end of the seventeenth century, this was almost entirely dominated by a polemical concern to dismiss Jewish counter-claims relating to the meaning of the prophecies concerning the messiah. With the revival of Hebrew learning in the Christian church during and after the sixteenth century some re-engagement took place with questions relating to the literal meaning of the many prophecies concerning the messiah.

At the beginning of the eighteenth century, encouraged by the arguments of John Locke (1632–1704) that 'Jesus is the messiah' was the most basic of all Christian confessions of faith, interest in the subject re-awakened. Locke's disciple Anthony Collins (1676–1729) put forward strong arguments to show that most of the passages traditionally claimed by Christians as foretellings of the coming of a messiah could not bear such a meaning (*see* **Deists**). This gave rise to the notion, proposed by Thomas Sherlock (1678–1761) and others, that such prophecies could have a double meaning – an original literal* one and a later fuller, or spiritual,* one.

In the nineteenth century, the theology of F. D. E. Schleiermacher (1768–1834) presented a claim that the ascription of messianic titles and status to Jesus had only a marginal relevance for the understanding of his person and work. A far-reaching attempt to counter such a claim was made by E. W. von Hengstenberg (1802–1869) in an influential work which suffered, however, from its unhistorical method of exegesis. Thereafter interest in the nature of Jewish messianic hope waned briefly, until revived yet again through the work of the History of Religions* school of biblical exegesis. This gave rise to a much enriched awareness of the very high concepts of kingship that had prevailed at one time in ancient Israel and the mythological origins of several of its titles and images. From this it became clear that most of the passages in Hebrew psalmody and prophecy which appeared to refer to the messiah had originally been formulated in respect of the kingship.

See also **Christology, New Testament; Historical Jesus; Kingship; Messianic Secret.**

J. Becker, *Messianic Expectation in the Old Testament*, 1980; A. Bentzen, *King and Messiah*, ² 1970; J. Klausner, *The Messianic Idea in Israel*, 1955; L. Landman, *Messianism in the Talmudic Era*, 1979; S. Mowinckel, *He That Cometh*, 1954; G. Scholem, *The Messianic Idea in Judaism*, 1971.

R. E. CLEMENTS

Messianic Secret

Jesus is frequently portrayed in the Gospels, especially in Mark, as trying to maintain an element of secrecy about himself and his work. This feature is usually known today as the 'messianic secret', following the classic study of W. Wrede* (1901).

Prior to Wrede's work, nineteenth-century scholars had read the Gospels, especially Mark, as almost exact transcripts of the life of Jesus. In particular, the secrecy texts in Mark were taken as evidence that Jesus wished to reveal his identity to the disciples only gradually so that they might come to a deeper understanding about him. Such an approach to the Gospels was thrown into question by Wrede's work.

Wrede claimed that the theme of secrecy in Mark is all-pervasive and cannot be explained by theories of development in the disciples' understanding. Wrede referred to a large number of features in Mark as evidence of this theme of secrecy: 1. Jesus regularly commands demons to be silent about his identity (1.25; 1.34; 3.11f.); 2. Jesus orders that his miracles* should not be publicized (1.43f.; 5.43; 7.36); 3. Jesus commands the disciples to be silent (8.30; 9.9); 4. Jesus tries to keep his whereabouts a secret (7.24; 9.30); 5. Jesus gives private instruction to a chosen few (7.17; 10.10); 6. Jesus teaches in parables* in order to hide his meaning (4.11f.); 7. the disciples regularly fail to understand Jesus (6.52; 8.17–21).

Wrede argued that all these features were unhistorical. For example, the secrecy charge in 5.43 was patently absurd, with a girl just restored to life from death and the crowd clamouring at the door. Similarly, the 'parable theory' of 4.11f. could not be traced back to Jesus, since surely Jesus used parables in order to make his message clearer, not to obscure it. Wrede claimed that 9.9 was the key to the secrecy theme. Here a time limit is set: the disciples are to remain silent about what they have seen until after the resurrection.* Wrede argued that this time limit was intended to apply to all the elements of secrecy in Mark: the pre-Easter period was one of secrecy; full revelation occurs after the resurrection.

Wrede argued that the origin of the secret lay in the coming together of two views about Jesus. According to an early view, Jesus only became messiah* at the resurrection; later Christian thought claimed that Jesus' earthly life had also been messianic. So Jesus' earthly life was now described as messianic, but with the proviso that this could only be publicized after the resurrection.

One corollary drawn by Wrede was that, if his reconstruction was right, then the secret could only have arisen when no explicit messianic claims by Jesus were known. Hence Jesus had never claimed to be messiah. This conclusion has often been sharply attacked, and it has often been thought that Wrede's whole thesis could be refuted by pointing to messianic elements in the Gospels which could be traced back to Jesus. This probably misses the point of Wrede's analysis, which attempted to explain the secrecy motifs as they actually appear in Mark.

Wrede's work has been very influential in showing how later Christian tradition may have influenced the Gospel accounts of the life of Jesus. However, his detailed theories about the secret in Mark are no longer accepted by many. Various alternatives have been proposed.

1. *The historical explanation*. Many have argued that much of the secrecy complex isolated by Wrede should be traced back to Jesus and attributed to a variety of motives. Jesus may have wished to reinterpret the term 'messiah' (cf. 8.30); he may have wished to avoid excessive publicity after his miracles; he may have used parables in order to get people to think, etc. It is, however, questionable here whether Wrede's analysis has been met on its own terms, viz. as an analysis of Mark. How do the secrecy charges function within the Gospel, and why do some appear in redactional, rather than traditional, strands of the Gospel (e.g. 1.34; 3.11f.)?

Wrede's claims about the secondary nature of the secrecy elements have always been more readily accepted in German-speaking scholarship. One modification of Wrede's theory which is now almost universally accepted concerns the origin of the secret. Most would argue today that, in so far as the secret is secondary (i.e. not historical), it is to be traced to Mark himself. (Wrede had argued that it was pre-Marcan.) However, this then necessitates a change in the theory of the reason for the secret, for Mark shows no evidence of a non-messianic life of Jesus. Hence, too, Wrede's corollary about the lack of any explicit messianic claims by Jesus may also have to be modified. Several alternative theories have been proposed.

2. *The apologetic explanation*. According to

this theory, the secrecy texts explain the failure of the Jews to respond positively to Jesus (perhaps too the failure of many to respond to the Christian mission in Mark's day). However, whilst this would explain texts such as the parable theory of 4.11f. very well, it encounters difficulties in explaining passages where the secret is broken (1.45; 7.36f.).

3. *The 'epiphanic' explanation.* The points where the secret is broken form the basis for a quite different interpretation. Here, the secrecy texts in Mark are taken as simply literary devices which highlight Jesus' glory. The broken secrecy charges show that Jesus' fame spread irresistibly; the parable theory shows the transcendent revelation* available to the reader. However, this theory also encounters problems in that some secrecy charges are not broken (e.g. 5.43). So too the time limit of 9.9 is not easily explained.

4. *A 'history of revelation' explanation.* Perhaps the most popular explanation today is that the secret represents Mark's understanding of the history of revelation. In particular, the secret is seen as Mark's way, not of imposing messianic belief on un-messianic material (so Wrede), but of controlling the already messianic material to conform to his theology of the cross. The secret is Mark's way of showing that Jesus' true identity can only properly be understood in the light of the cross. Jesus' identity thus cannot be seen by characters in the story prior to the passion;* hence confessions are regularly silenced and the disciples cannot understand. Only as the crucified one is Jesus' identity as 'Son of God' not open to misunderstanding. Hence only as Jesus dies can any human being come to the recognition that Jesus is the Son of God (15.39).

Within this overall explanation there is scope for variation. Some have argued that the secret is a matter of past history alone and that the present era of the church is one of open proclamation. Others would argue for a more 'existential' interpretation: revelation after Easter is a possibility, but only becomes an actuality for the person who is prepared to follow Jesus on the road to the cross as a disciple. In either case, the secret is to be seen as part of Mark's way of pointing to the cross as the definition of Jesus' true identity for the Christian disciple.

Several have tried to be more precise in specifying the christology* which Mark is seeking to control by the secret. Many have seen Mark as opposing a specific christology, usually described as a *theios anēr* christology, i.e. a view of Jesus as primarily the great miracle worker and the bearer of supernatural power. Despite the criticisms which can justly be brought against the use of the term *theios anēr* itself, the theory that Mark is seeking to modify an alternative view of Jesus of this nature, whether by direct opposition or by more gentle incorporation, is attractive.

One part of Wrede's evidence often considered separately concerns the incomprehension of the disciples in Mark. Many have argued that the disciples represent an 'opposition group' in Mark's community* whom Mark seeks to counter by portraying the disciples so harshly. Some have suggested that the disciples may represent the group holding the christology which Mark seeks to oppose. However, this probably makes the evidence in Mark too schematic, and fails to explain adequately the variegated picture of the disciples in Mark since the latter do not appear in a uniformly bad light (cf. 1.16–20; 3.13–19).

Others have suggested that the secret about Jesus' identity is not related to the secrecy charges after the miracles, which can mostly be explained by an 'epiphanic' explanation. So too the parable theory of 4.11f. may be better explained as part of later apologetic and is not necessarily related to the other secrecy elements in Mark.

Wrede's theories have undergone many modifications since they were first proposed in 1901. Probably no one today would agree with Wrede in every respect. The complex of elements he referred to should probably be split up and explained in different ways. Nevertheless, it is widely recognized that Wrede put his finger on elements which occupy a key role in Mark's Gospel. Further, many of these elements are probably due to Mark himself. They are thus not to be traced back to Jesus. They are primarily evidence about Mark and the post-Easter Christian communities; they do not provide evidence about the pre-Easter Jesus. Wrede's work thus anticipates form criticism* and redaction criticism* in pointing to the influence of post-Easter ideas on the account in Mark of the pre-Easter story. Certainly the parts of the secrecy complex in Mark where Jesus' identity is only fully revealed to human characters in the story when Jesus is seen as the crucified one, play a key role in the Gospel. These secrecy texts are thus of vital importance in the understanding of Mark's christology and of his ecclesiology, i.e. in Mark's understanding of who Jesus is and of what it means to be a disciple of Jesus.

See also **Historical Jesus; Mark, Gospel of; Parable; Wrede, W.**

J. D. Kingsbury, *The Christology of Mark's Gospel*, 1983; H. Räisänen, *Das 'Messiasgeheimnis' im Markusevangelium*, 1976; C. M. Tuckett (ed.), *The Messianic Secret*, 1983; W. Wrede, *The Messianic Secret*, 1971.

C. M. TUCKETT

Metaphor

It is doubtful that any one definition could be adequate to the range of linguistic usages we call metaphor. As a working definition we can say that metaphor is that figure of speech* by which, in narrow compass, we speak of one thing in terms which are seen as suggestive of another. For example, Bildad's speech in the book of Job describes the godless man botanically: 'He thrives before the sun,/ and his shoots spread over his garden./ His roots twine about the stoneheap;/ he lives among the rocks' (Job 8. 16–17).

Metaphor is regarded as principal amongst the tropes and frequently distinguished from its close associate, simile. Simile, unlike metaphor, employs directly the language of comparison (e.g. 'they lurk like fowlers lying in wait', Jer. 6.26). Semantically,* however, good metaphor and simile have much in common and neither can be regarded as simply comparison.

Modern studies have demonstrated the inadequacy of holding that metaphor is simply a kind of textual embellishment; rather, something new is said that might be said in no other way. This is most obvious with complex poetic images. Thus, Philip Larkin, speaking of religion as

That vast moth-eaten musical brocade
Created to pretend we never die (*Aubade*)

does more than compare tired religion to old cloth.

Metaphors, unlike similes, have no one distinctive grammatical form but are identified by semantic considerations. Theologians have tended to focus their interest on the 'A is a B' type of metaphor ('God is a rock'), but it is not always the case that metaphor presents two such explicit subjects. Equally metaphorical in their contexts are usages like 'snarling sea' or a 'wicked fist' (Isa. 58.4).

It may be, however, that many striking metaphors suggest a model. This happens in Bildad's speech, already cited, where the godless man is modelled on an invasive plant. Once the model is established, the reader can extend it. Because of their close association with models, metaphors function importantly in the structuring of arguments and perceptions. This is as much the case in theology as it is in natural science or any other area of enquiry.

'Metaphorical' is not strictly speaking the opposite of 'literal'; rather, metaphor is just one of many kinds of non-literal language usages (another is irony,* 'What a good shot!', intending the opposite). Above all, metaphorical and literal are not different degrees of truth; one uses metaphor in speaking of a 'live' electrical wire, but that to which one refers may be real enough.

Context is of the essence in the discernment of metaphor. 'Sapphire eyes' could in one context, as a description of the deep blue of the beloved's eyes, be metaphorical, and in another context, e.g. describing a statue made of precious stones, be literal usage. Apart from context, one has no means of determining a particular predication to be metaphorical, or of rightly interpreting it as such.

Questions about who the audience is affect the identification and construal of metaphor. Some biblical metaphors have complex interpretative contexts, presupposing earlier strata of figurative language, an inner circle of interpreters, or particular social and political circumstances (e.g. Rev. 21.9). Here interpretation of metaphor brings one into wider textual and contextual considerations.

Current interest in the topic of metaphor is considerable and broadly based. Students of biblical interpretation will be interested in works of philosophers, linguists* and literary* critics.

See also **Figures of Speech.**

Kent Bach and Robert M. Harnish, *Linguistic Communication and Speech Acts*, 1982; Christopher Butler, *Interpretation, Deconstruction and Ideology*, 1984; Andrew Ortony, *Metaphor and Thought*, 1979; Paul Ricoeur, *The Rule of Metaphor*, 1978; Janet Martin Soskice, *Metaphor and Religious Language*, 1985.

JANET MARTIN SOSKICE

Metaphysical Poets

The metaphysical poets of the seventeenth century interpret the Bible not only as readers but as writers: besides forming their fundamental beliefs, it shapes their literary strategies. In addition, some of them – notably John Donne (1572–1631) and George Herbert (1593–1633) – engage with the text in their professional capacity as preachers. They are men of learning, with access to the patristic writings and the Kabbalah, mediaeval hermeneutics and Renaissance commentaries, and they are abreast of contemporary controversy. Donne, who converted from Catholicism, records that he had 'survayed and digested the whole body of Divinity, controverted between ours and the Romane Church' (*Selected Prose* ed. Evelyn M. Simpson, Helen Gardner, Timothy Healy, 1967, p. 50). But it is likely that the primary influence on the Anglican Donne, as on Herbert, is the English Reformation* tradition. Consequently they are committed on principle to belief in the unique authority* and authorship of the Bible; its accessibility to all believers; its unity, and the centrality of its literal* sense. Yet because these principles coexist with a lively awareness of its attributes as the supreme literary* text, an analogy and model for other literary texts including their own, an element of paradox creeps in. The Bible is also perceived as difficult enough in places to tax the best intellects, extraordinarily diverse in genres,* and exemplifying all the stylistic resources of poetry. On what level, therefore, is it to be read? How can it be imitated?

Donne and Herbert share the Protestant insistence on 'the literal sense', but this should not be taken over-literally! Donne defines it as authorial intention, 'that which the Holy Ghost doth in that place principally intend', and he criticizes 'the curious refinings of the Allegoricall Fathers' in his early *Essays in Divinity* (ed. Evelyn M. Simpson, 1952, p. 40), just as Herbert in his poem 'Divinitie' criticizes those who 'cut and carve' divinity 'with the edge of wit'. But no poet can disregard the figurative expressiveness of scripture, and Donne discriminates more precisely in a sermon:

> the literall sense is not alwayes that, which the very Letter and Grammr of the place presents, as where it is literally said, *That Christ is a Vine* . . . But the literall sense of every place, is the principall intention of the Holy Ghost, in that place: And his principall intention in many places, is to expresse things by allegories, by figures; so that in many places of Scripture, a figurative sense is the literall sense . . . (*Sermons*, ed. George R. Potter and Evelyn M. Simpson, 1953–62, VI. 62)

A discerning interpreter will therefore apply different methods to Genesis and Revelation.

Donne constantly reveals delight in the style of the scriptures, which he considers the most eloquent of books, and nowhere more so than in his *Devotions* where he speaks not as preacher to congregation but as one poet to another:

> My God, my God, thou art a direct God, may I not say a literal God, a God that wouldst be understood literally and according to the plain sense of all that thou sayest? but thou art also (Lord, I intend it to thy glory, and let no profane misinterpreter abuse it to thy diminution), thou art a figurative, a metaphorical God too; a God in whose words there is such a height of figures, such voyages, such peregrinations to fetch remote and precious metaphors, such extensions, such spreadings, such curtains of allegories, such third heavens of hyperboles, so harmonious elocutions, so retired and so reserved expressions, so commanding persuasions, so persuading com-

mandments . . . as all profane authors seem of the seed of the serpent that creeps, thou art the Dove that flies (*Devotions*, 1959, p. 124, XIX. Expostulation).

The idea of God as poet is traditional, supported by Augustine's* authority; but Donne's God is recognizably a metaphysical poet, as that term later came to be used. The Bible, it follows, may be read as a kind of metaphysical poem, a product of the divine wit of correspondences which also manifests itself in the creation.

This fits in with interpretative methods such as the collation of separate passages. Herbert advises 'a diligent collation of Scripture with Scripture' in his *vademecum* for parsons, *A Priest to the Temple* (ch. IV), and embellishes the advice in 'The H. Scriptures II':

> Oh that I knew how all thy lights combine,
>   And the configurations of their glorie!
> Seeing not onely how each verse doth shine,
> But all the constellations of the storie.
>
> This verse marks that, and both do make a motion
> Unto a third, that ten leaves off doth lie . . .
>   (ll. 1–6)

In his own poems Herbert conflates key biblical passages for mutual illumination in precisely this way. He recalls biblical narrative ('Christmas', 'Easter'), inscribes biblical texts within the very syntax* of his verse ('Coloss. 3.3'), invents parables* ('Redemption'), composes Psalms ('Praise' I, II, and III). (Like others, he particularly values the Psalms of David* as a poetic model.) And the arrangement of his whole collection invites the reader to make interpretative connections: 'this verse marks that'.

According to Augustinian theory, scriptural correspondences function through signs as well as words. Both Donne and Herbert avail themselves of biblical typology.* Donne's use is more limited than Herbert's, but two of his finest divine poems apply typological figures. In 'A Hymne to Christ, at the Authors last going into Germany', he brings together Noah's Ark and the Flood, God's Ark of the church and the sea of Christ's blood, to emblematize his personal voyage (Lewalski). In 'Hymne to God my God, in my sicknesse' he prays that the Adamic* type and antitype may come together in him

> Looke Lord, and finde both *Adams* met in me;
> As the first *Adams* sweat surrounds my face,
> May the last *Adams* blood my soule embrace
>   (ll. 23–5).

Herbert's inspiration is so deeply typological that he unifies his whole structure through a type. The title *The Temple* has a rich multiple sense, spanning past, present and future: it is Solomon's Temple, the Body of Christ, the Church Militant and Triumphant, and above all the individual Christian who is the temple of the Holy Spirit.

This emphasis on the individual has been regarded as the key to the role of typology in Protestant poetry. Neither Donne nor Herbert would separate the theory of biblical interpretation from its human application. If individualism can be taken to excess in how we interpret the Bible – we should not 'rest . . . in our private interpretation of Scripture, without the Church' (Donne, *Sermons*, I. 235) – it answers the question of why we interpret it:

I am commanded *scrutari Scripturas, to search the scriptures*; now, that is not to be able to *repeat* any history of the Bible without booke, it is not to *ruffle* a Bible, and upon any word to turne to the Chapter, and to the verse; but this is *exquisita scrutatio*, the true searching of the Scriptures, to finde all the *histories* to be *examples* to me, all the *prophecies* to induce a Saviour for *me*, all the *Gospell* to apply Christ Jesus to *me* (*Sermons*, III. 367).

Herbert echoes this application in 'The H. Scriptures II': his 'life makes good' Scripture's hidden meanings,

for in ev'ry thing
Thy words do finde me out, & parallels bring,
And in another make me understood
(11.10–12).

That 'other' may be Aaron ('Aaron'), or the Gospel merchant ('The Pearl. Matth. 13'), or the Israelites –

For as the Jews of old by Gods command
  Travell'd, and saw no town:
So now each Christian hath his journeys
  spann'd:
Their storie pennes and sets us down
('The bunch of grapes', 11. 8–11).

Even apart from direct typology, religious metaphysical poetry is saturated with consciousness of biblical precedent and rewriting of biblical discourse. Such poems as Donne's Holy Sonnets and 'Good Friday, 1613. Riding Westward' and Herbert's 'Affliction' poems enact their 'spiritual Conflicts' (Herbert's phrase) in the light of scripture. In a later generation, Henry Vaughan (1621/2–1695) depends still more on the actual scriptural text to mediate and reinterpret experience. Although related models, like the catechism and the liturgy,* can be proposed for this religious verse, its root is in the Bible itself, constantly challenging the interpreter's skills:

We say amisse,
  This or that is:
Thy word is all, if we could spell
(Herbert, 'The Flower', 11.19–21).

See also **Hymnody; Poetry, English**

Chana Bloch, *Spelling the Word: George Herbert and the Bible*, 1985; Helen Gardner (ed.), *John Donne: The Divine Poems,* 1952; Barbara K. Lewalski, *Protestant Poetics and the Seventeenth-Century Religious Lyric*, 1979; Louis L. Martz (ed.), *George Herbert and Henry Vaughan*, 1986; C. A. Patrides (ed.), *The English Poems of George Herbert*, 1974; P. G. Stanwood and Heather Ross Asals (eds), *John Donne and the Theology of Language*, 1986.
                                   CHRISTINE REES

Methodology

Methodology refers to the way or ways which, in a particular field of enquiry, scholars agree to adopt in order to solve problems, resolve disputes and achieve a measure of consensus. More exactly, it refers to the justifications which they offer of such preferred ways. Without broad agreements about methods a discipline will have little cohesion; but equally without a measure of disagreement it will easily become stultified: ways of problem-solving need to be tested and tried and replaced as appropriate.

Talk of methods and methodology is common among biblical scholars. It may refer to a quite broad interpretative strategy; it may equally refer to relatively specific techniques of literary and historical analysis. It suggests a precision about the mode of operation which is beguiling, but rarely achieved, or indeed achievable. Nevertheless, biblical scholars too have tried ways of approaching their texts which, properly understood, form the basis of scholarly debate.

Problems occur for the discipline as a whole at two points: 1. there is insufficient agreement about a broad interpretative strategy, and this makes for considerable mistrust between scholars of different schools; 2. there is disagreement among scholars about the ways in which detailed studies contribute to an overall consensus.

1. There is still a deep division, not always sufficiently acknowledged, between those scholars who adopt a historical and critical approach to the study of the biblical texts, such as would apply to other ancient texts, and others who believe that because of the divinely inspired * and infallible character of the Bible a special way of reading it is required which does justice to its character as scripture. Such views are radically distinct.

The adoption of a historical-critical* approach implies the free use of historical modes of enquiry, i.e. of both the questions and the techniques of historians working in cognate fields. Such ways of working may be adopted in order to establish the original meaning of the texts as opposed to their 'inspired' or 'authorized' interpretations, whether these stem from ecclesiastical institutions or from private individuals. They will also be invaluable to those who wish to set the biblical texts as accurately as possible into their contemporary social, political and religious context, as opposed to seeing them as supernaturally revealed texts, related not to historical, proximate causes, but to their prior, divine cause, the Holy Spirit.

Such historical-critical modes of enquiry are not, however, necessarily opposed to *any* search for the theological meaning of the texts. On the contrary, given the genesis of such texts within a religious community,* there is a strong *prima facie* case that any interpretation which does not pay due attention to their theological sense will be inadequate. The question then is: what counts as due attention? Here it is helpful, as Robert Morgan has argued, to enquire what understanding of religion a particular interpreter may have. Clearly, a great many answers can be given to such a question, but it may be useful to distinguish between those who see religion as one of the ways, individual and communal, in which men and women seek, for good or ill, to come to terms with their environment and structure their lives; and those who see religion as mediating to individuals and communities an experience of the 'living God'. Thus there are important differences among those who agree on adopting a broadly historical approach to the Bible but who differ as to whether the Bible is to be viewed from the standpoint of a humanist or a theist.

In practice, the work of such scholars will overlap to a great extent. The humanist needs to know as clearly as possible how religious beliefs cohere, and how within a given society theological beliefs relate to social attitudes and action. But equally, even those who see the biblical texts as springing from an encounter with the 'living God' need to be aware of and to chart both the historical, social, economic and political contexts of such encounters and the way in which such experience is subsequently embodied in social and communal forms of life.

Within such a broad historical-critical strategy, more specific types of enquiry may be distinguished: religio-historical, sociological,* phenomenological, cultural anthropological,* literary.* Such modes of enquiry have been developed in response to certain specific ques-tions, viz. about the place of the Judaeo-Christian tradition within the development of religious communities and beliefs in the ancient world, or about the ways in which the literary texts of the Bible may be read. Such questions are similar to those posed in other academic disciplines, and there is consequently the opportunity for a considerable measure of cross-fertilization. Such different types of enquiry should in principle be mutually supportive; in practice they are sometimes seen as threatening. Thus it is said that the adoption of a literary approach to the study of the Bible should entail a complete break with the historical-critical search for the original meaning of the text. But such a view does not do justice to the literary history of any text. Those who read and receive the Bible do so, in large part at least, as part of a community with a long and rich history of such reading, which has formed them before they open its pages. In this history the original meaning of such texts in their original setting is by no means insignificant.

2. Basic to all such enquiries are certain techniques for reading the texts themselves. In the first place it is necessary to offer a careful examination of the language and syntax* of the text. Alongside such linguistic study other 'methods' have been developed: text-critical,* source-critical,* form-critical,* tradition-historical* and redaction-critical.* Such methods are concerned with establishing the history of the texts, their underlying sources and traditions, and the ways in which the writers have interacted with those traditions.

Disagreement does exist, however, about the way in which such detailed studies contribute to the achievement of a general scholarly consensus on a particular issue. In the first place, the use of such techniques is not of course restricted to those who are engaged in various forms of historical critical enquiry. Biblicists too, increasingly, make use of such tools, though with a heavy emphasis on linguistic studies. This should not, however, confuse one as to the very different nature of their enterprise. Characteristically, such studies will seek to demonstrate the uniformity and coherence of different biblical texts, and this will often involve considerable virtuosity. Where critical study has carefully distinguished the different beliefs of different strata of tradition and the distinct historical communities represented in the Bible, biblicist studies will strain to accommodate the sense of a particular text to an overall system of belief which, it is believed, is expressed throughout the writings as a whole.

Secondly, the use of words like 'method' in this context seems to invite comparison with scientific methods of measurement and the kind of precision which they may achieve. This in turn may encourage scholars to see the results of detailed linguistic and textual study as hard empirical data on which all subsequent work has to be built. But the analogy can be extremely misleading. There are, for instance, a number of methods for measuring the surface tension of water. None of them is wholly accurate, but they do have definable rules for their execution and the margin of error of each method can be calculated and due allowance made. There is nothing closely analogous to this in biblical studies. To take an example from NT redaction-critical studies: it is true that we can describe certain kinds of procedures which can be followed through with some rigour. We can carefully list agreements and disagreements between the Gospels; we can produce word-statistics, isolate characteristically Lucan usages, favourite titles for Jesus, etc. On this basis we may then begin to build up a picture of Luke's own special theological concerns. But this is not to produce assured results. Rather it is part of what it is to explore a broad hypothesis about the meaning of Luke's texts. Such a hypothesis must indeed find support in the Lucan redaction of his inherited material and can be refuted if such supports are cut. But its general acceptance by scholars will depend on many other issues in NT studies: developments in other areas of synoptic* study, of Pauline* studies, indeed of ancient history in general. In short, such a hypothesis will have to be heard against a background of continuing debate in many areas of cognate study, and its explanatory force in the wider enterprise of drawing a picture of early Christian history will be crucial to its general acceptability.

This might suggest that there is little chance of ever reaching a scholarly consensus, but this is not so. Good hypotheses are good, partly because they are informed by careful study of the texts, partly because of their explanatory power; and they have to be argued out within the community of biblical scholars. Thus, certain 'paradigms', such as the hypothesis of Marcan priority, do come to gain general acceptance within the discipline, because of their ability to provide the most satisfactory explanations of the evidence. Similarly, there may come a time when a particular consensus within the discipline is abandoned, partly because of the intractability of the problems which it causes, partly because a better mode of explanation is offered which resolves many of the problems hitherto encountered. A good example of this is provided by the shift in Johannine studies from the view that John knew and used the Synoptics to the view that he did not. The older view could neither adequately explain the differences between the Synoptics and John on the basis of supposed Johannine characteristics; nor could it offer a satisfactory account of John's purpose in writing the Gospel – was it to supplement or to replace the Synoptics? By contrast, the new view, though it is still the subject of discussion, opened up a fruitful enquiry into the sources peculiar to the Fourth Gospel, which in turn may shed light on the history of the Johannine community. In the end, it is the ability of a hypothesis to make the best sense of scholars' many detailed observations about a text which will enable it to command overall respect.

See also **Authority; Fundamentalism.**

J. Barton, *Reading the Old Testament: Method in Biblical Study*, 1984; R. F. Collins, *Introduction to the New Testament*, 1983; A. H. J. Gunneweg, *Understanding the Old Testament*, 1978; M. Hooker, 'On Using the Wrong Tool' in *Theology*, 75, 1972, pp. 570–81; R. Morgan with J. Barton, *Biblical Interpretation*, 1988; C. Tuckett, *Reading the New Testament: Methods of Interpretation*, 1987; M. Weir, *The Bible from Within: The Method of Total Interpretation*, 1984.

JOHN RICHES

Micah

Micah appears in the prophetic* collection ('the book of the Twelve') as the sixth book in the Masoretic* text, but the third in the Septuagint* (LXX). Its redactional colophon (1.1) attributes it to Micah of Moresheth (cf. Moresheth-gath, 1.14), in the eighth century (virtually the same period as Isa. 1.1). Nothing is known about Micah, though on the strength of Jer. 26.17–18 some have placed him among the city elders of Judah (e.g. Wolff, pp. XV–XVII). 3.12 is referred to in Jer. 26.18 as part of a prophetic narrative (Hillers, pp. 8–9) in which the words of Micah are given significance for the life of Jeremiah. Elements of a *pesher* * commentary on Micah have been found at Qumran (*see* **Dead Sea Scrolls**) as well as fragments of the book, and a long roll of the minor prophets discovered in the caves of Murabba'at includes Micah. According to *The Lives of the Prophets 6*, Micah was murdered by Joram son of King Ahab (cf. 6.16 for the connection!) and a haggada names him as one of the four disciples of Elijah. The formulation of the divine demand for justice in 6.6–8 is among the most famous and oft-quoted pieces in the whole Bible.

The modern study of Micah has produced a very complex redactional* analysis. The growth of the book, the central issue in this study, is 'opaque to the historian's view, its stages and directions more hidden' (Mays, p. 22), and in many ways this illustrates 'the present crisis in exegetical method' (Childs, p. 431). Some individual voices have dissented from this tendency to produce complex redactional analyses of the book: Hillers views Micah from a nativistic perspective and sees him as a prophet of the new age (pp. 4–8). This would make him part of a protest movement of the type described by anthropologists* as 'revitalization movements' or millenarianism,* and Hillers' reading avoids redaction analysis altogether! Beyerlin argues from the cult traditions of the Jerusalem temple and sees Micah as an exponent of the true relationship between the cult traditions and life in Jerusalem. Allowing for a division between chs 1–5 and 6–7, van der Woude also argues for much less complex redaction in the book and treats 1–5 as Micah's arguments against the pseudo-prophets (*VT* 19, 1969, pp. 244–60; 'Three classical prophets' in *Israel's Prophetic Tradition*, 1982, pp. 48–53).

None of these individual arguments is persuasive, and a complex redactional history of the book would appear to be the better explanation for the present state of Micah. The 'historical' Micah has been subsumed under numerous redactions of and additions to the book. This book then reflects on the long history of Yahweh's destruction of Samaria (assuming these references to Samaria refer to the Assyrian period and not the later Samaritan* schism!) and Jerusalem for reasons of corrupt political leadership, and maintains liturgical hopes for Jerusalem's restoration.

The three basic sections of the book are chs 1–3, 4–5, 6–7. The preaching of Micah is to be found in 1–3; salvation oracles in 4–5 attempt to modify the harshness of 1–3; and in 6–7 there is a mixture of critical reflections and cultic psalms. 4.1–4 is very similar to Isa. 2.2–4 and reverses 3.12 or, perhaps, projects a future beyond 3.12. Strong similarities between Isaiah and Micah have been noted: 'Micah is a miniature of the book of Isaiah' (Mays, p. 1); 'Isaiah serves as a commentary* on Micah and *vice versa*' (Childs, p. 438). A common circle of tradents may have worked on both books (cf. Vermeylen, *Du prophète Isaïe à l'apocalyptique* II, 1978, esp. pp. 570–601, 637–9). Similar schemes of organization may be noted between the two traditions in terms of judgment and salvation material. In Micah there is a double two-element eschatological* scheme: 1–3 judgment; 4–5 salvation; 6.1–7.7 judgment; 7.8–20 salvation. Thus the original dominant note of threat (*Drohung*) is tempered by promise (*Verheissung*). Then in 6–7 there is a prophetic dialogue in a time of waiting completed by further promises in the form of psalms (cf. Willi-Plein, pp. 110–14). The exilic editing of Micah shows that the meaning of the catastrophe of 587 as the fulfilment of Micah's message serves the notion of theodicy which justifies Yahweh's destruction of Jerusalem, and this in turn can be used to minister to the survivors of the disaster (cf. Kaiser, p. 237).

The editing of Micah is fundamentally important for understanding the complexities of the redaction of the prophetic books and shows how judgment and promise were the theologoumena of the Second Temple period: judgment reflected the past and salvation the future. In the meantime the warnings of Micah could serve the community in a pastoral role. This judgment-promise alternation is only superficially a dialectical schema. The liturgical shaping of the book served the cult of salvation and therefore had an eschatological (i.e. future) force. Rural protests against urban corruption were subsumed under the larger chauvinism of the Jerusalem temple cult. Ultimately Yahweh's compassion and forgiveness (7.18–20) would turn judgment into salvation and realize the permanent hopes for the community. Only the eschatologized past (7.20) experienced in the future could redeem the appalling present where no trust could be put in neighbour, friend, or family (6.5–6).

B. S. Childs, *Introduction to the Old Testament as Scripture*, 1979, pp. 428–39; D. R. Hillers, *Micah*, 1984; K. Jeppesen, 'New Aspects of Micah Research', *JSOT* 8, 1978, pp. 3–32; O. Kaiser, *Introduction to the Old Testament*, 1975, pp. 226–9; J. L. Mays, *Micah*, 1976; B. Renaud, *La formation du livre de Michée*, 1977; I. Willi-Plein, *Vorformen der Schriftexegese innerhalb des AT*, 1971; H. W. Wolff, *Micah*, ET 1987.

ROBERT P. CARROLL

Midrash

In early Hebrew literature 'midrash' (from the root *darash*, 'to seek', 'inquire into', 'investigate') means: 1. an interpretation of scripture, whether of a single verse (4QFlor 1.14), or of a whole biblical book (cf. Midrash Bere'shit Rabba on Genesis); or more generally, an undefined body of traditional commentary on Torah (CD 20.6; Mishnah Nedarim 4.7); 2. the activity of studying scripture (1QS 8.15; Mishnah Pirqei 'Avot 1.17); hence *bet ha-midrash*, 'house of study' (Ecclus. 51.23), or *midrash* (Babylonian Talmud Menaḥot 44a), for a school in which scripture formed the core curriculum; 3. a legal inquiry or court of inquiry (1QS 6.23; 8.26); 4. a narrative, story or treatise (II Chron. 13.22; 24.27).

Through biblical studies the term 'midrash' entered modern academic vocabulary where it is used to denote early Jewish exegesis* of the Bible as characterized by a certain hermeneutical* approach. In the academic context the scope of the term varies greatly. At its broadest it may be applied to the whole range of early Jewish Bible interpretation as found e.g. in the Septuagint,* Jubilees (*see* **Rewritten Bible**), the Qumran Pesharim* (*see* **Dead Sea Scrolls**), Genesis Apocryphon, Philo,* the N T, Josephus,* the Targumims,* as well as in the classic rabbinic commentaries* such as the Mekhilta deRabbi Ishmael, Sifra, Sifrei and Genesis Rabba. Such a broad usage is problematic since it runs the risk of evacuating the term of any specific meaning and reducing it to jargon. And it is tendentious in that it suggests that the whole diverse range of early Jewish exegetical literature forms a historical and typological continuum – a view that can only be maintained by discounting significant differences of method, content and form. This article restricts 'midrash' to early rabbinic Bible exegesis of the Talmudic* and post-Talmudic periods. Basically it describes midrash from two standpoints, as a process and as an artefact. The former relates to midrash as a distinctive method of interpreting scripture, as a system of hermeneutical rules and techniques. The latter relates to midrash as the concrete end-product of the application of this hermeneutical system, a midrashic text which may range from the exegesis of a single word, phrase or verse of scripture to a whole biblical book.

The texts and their classification. The large body of midrashic literature that survives from Talmudic and early mediaeval times is broadly classified in two ways: 1. as halakhic or aggadic; and 2. as exegetical or homiletic. A halakhic midrash is basically one which comments on the legal portions of the Bible; an aggadic midrash one which comments on the non-legal or narrative portions. An exegetical midrash expounds an extensive, continuous section of the Bible (e.g. a biblical book) verse by verse, often word by word. A homiletic midrash expounds single, discrete verses of the Bible related to a lectionary* cycle. The categories, though widely used, are rather rough and ready, and to some extent cut across each other. Thus in principle a given midrash could be both halakhic and exegetical, both aggadic and homiletic.

The following groups illustrate the main divisions of midrashic literature:

1. *Halakhic midrashim.* This designation applies *par excellence* to the Mekhilta deRabbi Ishmael (on Exodus), Sifra (on Leviticus), and Sifrei (on Numbers and Deuteronomy), which confine themselves largely to the halakhic parts of the Pentateuch.* This group is also sometimes referred to as the Tannaitic Midrashim because the texts quote only Tannaim (i.e. scholars of the period of the Mishnah [first to early third centuries AD]) as authorities. On the basis of their exegetical terminology the halakhic midrashim may be divided into two types: type A, comprising the Mekhilta deR. Ishmael and Sifrei Numbers; type B, Sifra and Sifrei Deuteronomy. D. Hoffmann argued that type A midrashim show a preference for quoting as authoritative pupils R. Ishmael and for employing exegetical methods characteristic of his school, whereas type B tend to cite pupils of Aqiva and to use exegetical methods characteristic of his school. Hence type A can be assigned to the School of Ishmael and type B to the School of Aqiva. It has further been suggested that originally both schools produced a set of four midrashim on the last four books of the Pentateuch, the missing texts surviving now only in fragments. The complete schema is shown below (non-fragmentary texts marked †). The schema in its fully developed form is questionable. In terms of content the corresponding texts of type A and type B display a great deal of overlap, and it is far from certain that the two schools can be sharply differentiated by their exegetical approach. However, that two types do exist seems beyond reasonable doubt. What is in dispute is how to account for the origin of the types.

2. *Exegetical midrashim.* Genesis Rabba is commonly cited as the classic example of an exegetical midrash. It is divided into *parashiyyot* ('sections') which number between 97 and 101, depending on the manuscript.* The basis of these *parashiyyot* remains obscure: they do not correlate in any obvious way with the sections of either the three- or the one-year lectionary cycle. Each *parashah* falls into two parts: it begins with a *petiḥah* or a series of *petiḥot* which have the first verse of the *parashah* as the base-verse; then follows a detailed running commentary on the biblical text. If the second element of each *parashah* were removed, it is arguable that what would be

	TYPE A *School of Ishmael*	TYPE B *School of Aqiva*
EXODUS	†Mekhilta deR. Ishmael	Mekhilta de R. Shim'on ben Yoḥai
LEVITICUS	Fragments (?)	†Sifra
NUMBERS	†Sifrei Numbers	Sifrei Zuta
DEUTERONOMY	Midrash Tannaim	†Sifrei Deuteronomy

left would be a type of homiletic midrash. This observation shows that it is dangerous to make too sharp a distinction between the homiletic and the exegetical midrashim. Another early exegetical midrash is Lamentations Rabba. This opens with a series of 34 *petiḥot* (the vast majority of which have Lam. 1.1 as their base verse), followed by a verse-by-verse commentary on the biblical text.

3. *Homiletic midrashim*. Three types may be distinguished: Type A, Leviticus Rabba. This is divided into 37 *parashiyyot* which appear basically to correlate with the divisions of Leviticus for the triennial pentateuchal lectionary. Only the first verse or verses of the *parashah* is expounded and each *parashah* begins with a *petiḥah* or a series of *petiḥot*. Type B, Pesiqta deRav Kahana and Pesiqta Rabbati. Pesiqta deRav Kahana expounds a series of verses drawn from both the pentateuchal and the Prophetic readings for the festivals and special Sabbaths. It consists of 28 *pisqaot*, each *pisqa* containing a number of *petiḥot* and sayings which combine into a tightly constructed discourse on a single theme. Five of the *pisqaot* are shared with Leviticus Rabba. Pesiqta Rabbati follows a similar pattern to Pesiqta deRav Kahana. However, its *pisqaot*, though topical in content, are less closely argued. Ten *pisqaot* parallel more or less closely material in Pesiqta deRav Kahana. Type C, Tanḥuma-Yelammedenu. The Tanḥuma-Yelammedenu midrashim cover the whole of the Pentateuch, and expound the opening verse or verses of sections for the triennial lectionary cycle. A characteristic pattern is: *Yelammedenu* formula ('May our master instruct us' – *yelammedunu rabbenu*); a series of *petiḥot*; exegesis of the opening verses of the pentateuchal section; messianic* conclusion (*ḥatimah*). There were large numbers of discrete Tanḥuma-Yelammedenu homilies which were combined into different collections.

4. *Anthologies (Yalqutim) and Collected Works*. Large collections of midrashic material were put together in the Middle Ages. Two broad types may be distinguished. Type A deconstructs its sources and reassembles them in the form of a digest arranged according to the verses of the Bible. The two most important examples of this genre are Yalqut Shim'oni (twelfth century), which covers the whole of the Bible, and Midrash ha-Gadol (thirteenth century), which covers the Pentateuch. Type B simply takes a number of texts of widely different date and character and puts them together to form a midrashic collection. Midrash Rabba, which contains the Pentateuch and the Five Megillot (Song of Songs, Ruth, Lamentations, Ecclesiastes, Esther), represents this type. As a collection, Midrash Rabba cannot be earlier

than the date of its latest element (twelfth century). In fact, it may not have been defined as a collection until the first complete printed edition issued in Venice in 1545.

Literary problems.

1. *Sitz im Leben*. The midrashim are 'school' texts, i.e. they represent the deposit of the exegetical traditions that grew up within the rabbinic schools over a considerable period of time. In literary structure they are broadly similar to the Mishnah (*see* **Talmud**), i.e. they are made up of small units of tradition (pericopae) which are more or less self-contained and which may occur in several different works at once. The texts were created by selecting, arranging and redacting pre-existent traditions of widely different date. They do not, therefore, have authors in the sense that Plato was the author of the *Phaedo*. Some do have names attached to them (Rabbi Ishmael, Rav Kahana), but this is a later development and cannot be taken as evidence that these scholars wrote the works. Though individual traditions within the texts are frequently attributed to named authorities, the works as a whole are anonymous, and are composed in a highly uniform 'school' style which makes it difficult to distinguish one from the other. Such distinctions as can be drawn tend to be based on rather external and trivial criteria, e.g. variations in the formulae used to cite scripture. It is difficult to identify any distinctive voice within the tradition, whether in terms of style or content. The contrast between the approaches of Aqiva and Ishmael, which has played a central role in the history of early midrash, does not really stand up to close scrutiny.

The reason the midrashim have this anonymous character is basically ideological.* The *darshanim* saw themselves as engaged in a collective enterprise, as working within a tradition. Their task was to pass on what they received, and to contribute to the development of the oral Torah. This left little scope for individuality or idiosyncrasy. The *darshanim* did not set great store by originality, and if innovation were required it had to be in terms of pre-existent tradition. Nor did they have a strong proprietorial attitude towards their ideas: whatever they contributed to the sum of the tradition became at once public property and could be used freely and adapted by others. The midrashim present themselves as the work not of any one authority, but of all the numerous authorities which they quote. Those authorities stand for the sages to whom was entrusted the oral Torah handed down from Moses.* The authority of the midrashim rests on the implicit claim that behind them stands the collectivity of the sages, and not an individual, however eminent he may be. The primary setting for the midrashim is the *bet ha-midrash*, and their lemmatic form and general style presumably reflects very directly how scripture was discussed within the schools. There is also a secondary setting for midrash in the synagogue (the *bet ha-keneset*). The sermon (*derashah*) was an old-established institution of the synagogue, which was naturally related to the biblical lections. The homiletic midrashim in general, and the *petiḥah* form in particular, appear to reflect synagogue preaching.

2. *Integrity*. If the midrashim are basically collections of school traditions, to what extent can they be distinguished from one another as texts with a definite overall structure and redactional identity? The issues raised are fundamental to the study of midrash. They impinge on how the texts should be edited (e.g. should we try to recover an *Urtext* for any given work?), and on how they should be dated, both absolutely and relative to each other. They also affect how we read the texts, whether atomistically or holistically.* The atomistic approach has tended to predominate: in this, the pericopae are taken as the basic units of sense, whose meaning is to be uncovered by analysing them against the underlying verse or phrase of scripture which they expound. Scripture plays a central role in this kind of reading. The midrashim are seen as collections of individual propositions which on the whole do not add up to a sustained and coherent argument. The larger units within the texts (e.g. chapters, or even the work as a whole) do not mark significant boundaries. As one moves out from the pericopae one does not meet any fundamental lines of demarcation until one comes to the outer limits of the tradition as a whole.

This approach has been strongly challenged by J. Neusner, who has sought to demonstrate that the midrashim are tightly constructed compositions with a well worked out rhetorical* and logical plan and theological programme. They are texts which present coherent and sustained arguments, not merely scrapbooks, or random compilations of episodic materials. They should, consequently, be read holistically: the meaning of any given pericope will have to be determined from the part it plays in the whole; scripture has only a secondary role in midrash, the discourse of the document is primary. Neusner's analysis of Genesis Rabba will serve to illustrate his method. As to its rhetorical plan, he argues that the entire matter of Genesis Rabba can be classified into three main forms: I, the Base Verse-Intersecting Verse Form; II, the Exegetical Form; and III, the Syllogistic Form. (He recognizes the presence of a fourth type – the

Miscellany – which is, apparently, characterized by the absence of form.) These three forms occur in a definite pattern within the midrash, 89% of the *parashiyyot* beginning with Form I, 65% with Form II. As to its theological programme, Neusner argues that Genesis Rabba contains a sustained discourse on the history of Israel and Rome, not political Rome but Christian, messianic Rome. Genesis Rabba constitutes the rabbinic response to the Christianization of the Roman empire in the fourth century. Neusner's analysis raises some fundamental questions, notably how his view of the midrashim as coherent documents can be squared with the fact that textually they are in a state of flux, and that the actual contents of the works vary considerably from manuscript to manuscript. His reply is to argue (a) that he has analysed the text which he has chosen to analyse (usually the standard printed edition) and no other; it remains to be seen whether or not the same conclusions would be reached with other extant forms of the text; and (b) that he deals with such gross traits of the documents that it is unlikely that the manuscript variations will affect the outcome. The latter argument raises a fundamental question: if the same plan and programme hold good for a multiplicity of different text-forms, then are they adequate to establish the kind of authorship and overall structure which Neusner claims for the midrashim?

The most fruitful way to read the midrashim involves a dialectic between the atomistic and the holistic approaches. It is necessary for practical reasons to begin at the level of the pericopae. The meaning of these can be established by analysing them against the scripture that is being exegeted, and by putting them in the context of the history of exegesis of the given biblical verse or phrase. G. Vermes and others have demonstrated how fruitful this tradition-historical* reading of midrash can be. However, the sense of the pericope which emerges from this kind of analysis must remain to some extent provisional. It will be necessary to check whether or not the pericope, whatever its original sense, is adapted or acquires a new sense when seen within the midrash as a whole. The possibility must be left open that the midrash contains larger units of thought which present a sustained and coherent argument. (We may compare the relation between form criticism* and redaction criticism* in the study of the Gospels.)*

3. *Date*. Since the midrashim are composite works the question of dating is acutely problematic. The idea of a 'date' when applied to a midrash can relate to a number of quite different things – the date of the final redaction, when the final form of the text (assuming

there was such a thing) came into existence; the date of a given tradition or pericope within the midrash; or the date at which some of the larger literary structures incorporated in the midrash came into being. There is a broad consensus as to the relative dates of the final forms of the texts. All the texts are post-Mishnaic, and appear to presuppose the Mishnah's programme, and to read Mishnaic halakhah into scripture. The Mishnah is the fundamental generative document of early Judaism, and after its promulgation around AD 210 rabbinic intellectual activity can be regarded as broadly speaking exegetical of Mishnah. The exegesis* had two aspects – to expound the Mishnah itself, and to relate the Mishnah to scripture. The former resulted in the two Talmuds, the latter in the classic midrashim. The earliest of the texts are probably the halakhic midrashim (Mekhilta deRabbi Ishmael, Sifra and Sifrei): they may date from the late fourth or early fifth centuries. Sifra is particularly noteworthy for its typologically primitive character: from time to time it simply juxtaposes Mishnah and scripture. From the fifth century come Genesis Rabba, Leviticus Rabba and Lamentations Rabba. Pesiqta deRav Kahana is from the sixth or early seventh century. To the post-Islamic era (late seventh to end ninth centuries) belong Pesiqta Rabbati and the Tanhuma-Yelammedenu texts. As noted earlier, the Yalqutim come from the high Middle Ages, and Midrash Rabba, as a collection, may be later still. These dates are only very approximate and will be disputed by different scholars. What does tend to be agreed, however, is the relative chronology of the texts.

The dates of the final forms of the midrashim naturally constitute a *terminus ad quem* for the traditions they contain, but the traditions themselves may be very much older. The best way to date the individual traditions is to put them into the context of a tradition history. Having collected all the extant material on a given biblical verse or phrase it is sometimes possible to see how the tradition as a whole has evolved with time: its elements can be arranged in a relative chronology. It may then be possible, using securely dated sources, e.g. Philo, Josephus or the NT, to get an absolute chronological 'fix' on certain stages of the tradition, and thereby arrive at a date, however rough, for the particular element in which one is interested. This methodology, first worked out by Renée Bloch, has been greatly refined by G. Vermes.

Form and style. The fundamental form of midrash is biblical lemma + comment. The lemmata in a midrashic text may constitute a continuous section of scripture, e.g. a biblical book (as in the exegetical midrashim), or they may be a series of discrete and essentially disconnected verses derived from a lectionary (as in the homiletic midrashim). The lemmatic presentation opens up two possibilities, both of which were fully exploited by the *darshanim*: 1. it allows a variety of interpretations to be given for a single biblical element; and 2. it allows an exegetical argument to be explicitly developed. Unlike the Targums, which as translations mirror the form of the original and which consequently can offer effectively only a monovalent reading of scripture, midrash as true commentary can and does offer a polyvalent reading. It is not inevitable that lemmatic commentaries give polyvalent readings, nor that they will develop an explicit exegetical argument. The Qumran pesharim are lemmatic and yet essentially treat scripture as monovalent; moreover they are mantic or oracular in style, not argumentative, and do not make explicit their exegetical reasoning. Lemmatic form offers a variety of options: the particular options taken by the *darshanim* are the result of deliberate choice and reflect their view that scripture is a text rich in meaning* and that its different senses will only emerge through discussion and debate within the guild of the Sages. Both lemma and comment are normally in Hebrew, and if the use of *ve-khulleh* (= etc.) at the end of abbreviated lemmata is ignored, then as a rule lemma and comment are not visually or formally differentiated. The Qumran Pesharim, by way of contrast, quote the biblical text in full, as against its frequent curtailment in midrash, and use the formulae *pesher ha-davar* ('the interpretation of the matter') and *pishro* ('its interpretation') as 'spacers' to demarcate lemma from comment. Despite the lack of formal demarcation there is no real danger of confusing scripture and commentary in midrash. The two are totally separable elements. Midrash does not 'dissolve' scripture in the commentary in the way in which the Book of Jubilees carries Genesis 'in solution'.

The following stylistic features are characteristic of midrashic texts:

1. They quote freely verses of scripture as proof texts,* introduced by standard citation formulae such as *she-ne'emar* ('as it is said').

2. They are fond of stringing together long series of biblical verses. By introducing other verses the *darshanim* demonstrate the fundamental principle of the unity of scripture.

3. They quote named authorities, e.g. Rabbi Ishmael, Rabbi Aqiva, Rabbi Jonathan.

4. They give different and sometimes contradictory interpretations of the same verse, word or phrase, often introduced by the formula *davar 'aḥer* ('another interpretation').

5. They employ *meshalim* ('parables'*), especially to solve theological problems. These

are commonly introduced by the formula, *mashal le-mah ha-davar domeh* ('A parable. To what may the matter be likened?').

Apart from the all pervasive base-form of lemma + comment, the midrashim employ a variety of literary forms and patterns of discourse. A. Goldberg has successfully analysed the structure of a number of these, viz., the Midrash, the Dictum or Logion, the Mashal, the Ma'aseh, the Haggadah, the *Petiḥah* and the Ḥatimah. Of these the *petiḥah* has received most attention. The *petiḥah* is so called because most examples begin with the formula, 'Rabbi X *pataḥ*' (lit. 'opened') – usually translated, 'began his discourse thus'. The distinctive feature of the *petiḥah* is that it plays off two verses against each other: one (the base verse) is from the biblical passage under discussion; the other (the intersecting verse) is from another part of the Bible, and, on the face of it, has nothing to do with the base verse. The aim is to show that there is a connection. The process by which the connection is made is known as *ḥarizah* ('stringing together'). The more elaborate and involved the *ḥarizah*, the more strong and satisfying the *petiḥah*. The *petiḥah* is an effective rhetorical structure whose origin is to be sought in synagogue preaching. It was probably originally a liturgical element used to introduce the reading from scripture: it opened the biblical lection for the day. The preacher began dramatically by announcing a verse remote from the lection and then proceeded to show how it could be keyed into the reading for the day. The audience's attention would be engaged as they waited to see how the connection could be made and which precise verse in the lection was the target. As given in synagogue the intersecting verse would have opened the *petiḥah*, the base verse closed it, and led into the reading from the Bible. However, when the form was transferred from the oral to the written register a number of changes had to be made. The main one was that the readers had to be warned in advance what was the base verse. They lacked the actual setting of the festival or special Sabbath to make that clear. They also had to be told that what was being set before them was a *petiḥah*. So the literary form of the *petiḥah* emerged, viz., base verse + *petiḥah* formula ('Rabbi X *pataḥ*') + intersecting verse + *ḥarizah* + base verse.

Midrash as hermeneutics. It is necessary to distinguish between internal and external description of midrash as a system of hermeneutics, i.e. between description from within rabbinic tradition, in terms of the rabbinic world-view, and description from outside the tradition, from a modern, objective academic standpoint. External description will often present midrash as eisegesis,* as a reading into scripture of ideas that were not originally or historically there. Such descriptions can be implicitly hostile or polemical in purpose, aimed at showing that the *darshanim* were deliberately manipulating scripture. Eisegesis, however, was not admissible from within the tradition: the *darshanim* always imply that they are drawing out meaning latent in scripture, and they developed a doctrine of revelation which allowed them to justify their position. The main elements of that doctrine were as follows:

1. Scripture is divine speech: it originated in the mind of God; the prophets were merely channels through whom the message passed, and contributed nothing of their own to its content (*see* **Inspiration**). Maimonides summed up the position thus: 'We do not know how precisely the Torah reached us, but only that it came to us through Moses who acted like a secretary taking dictation' (*Commentary on Mishnah*, Sanhedrin X; cf. Babylonian Talmud Bava Batra 15a). From this a number of axioms were deduced. The first axiom is that scripture is polyvalent: it is an inexhaustible fountain of truth; in a very real sense all truth is latent in it, waiting to be discovered by the application of the right hermeneutical methods. 'Turn it and turn it again for everything is in it' (Mishnah Pirqei Avot 5:22). The *darshanim* have no concept of the one, true, original sense of scripture. The Torah has 'seventy aspects or faces (*panim*)' (Numbers Rabba 13:15–16) and can be interpreted in different, even contradictory ways. Thus it can be expounded to supply 49 reasons for declaring 'unclean', and 49 for declaring 'clean', yet both views are 'words of the living God'. The *darshanim* are able to accept the notion that scripture may yield contradictory propositions simply because they hold that it is divine speech. The implication is that the contradiction exists only at the level of the human interpreter whose knowledge is limited. But from the standpoint of God, whose knowledge is infinite, the contradiction will somehow disappear.

The second axiom is that scripture is a totally coherent and self-consistent body of truth. This means that what it says in one place may be interpreted in the light of what it says in another. They have no real sense of scripture as evolving, or as historically conditioned. Scripture contains no contradictions, but each of its parts interlock to form a single, harmonious whole. A major aim of the *darshanim* is to draw out the unity of scripture and to resolve apparent contradictions. This principle of the internal consistency of scripture does not conflict with the idea that scripture may generate contradictory propositions.

The *darshanim* admit the possibility of contradiction at the level of interpretation, but not at the level of the actual text of scripture, presumably because they regard the written text as a direct expression of the mind of God. The third axiom is that scripture is inerrant: it can contain no errors of fact. Any that seem to be there are apparent and not real. The fourth axiom is that there is no redundancy in scripture: it is 'all music and no noise'. Everything in scripture, even the spelling of the words as full or defective, or the shape of the letters, is seen as significant. And if scripture repeats itself it is always for a purpose. Repetition may be taken simply as a sign of emphasis, or the repeated word or phrase may be nuanced on each occurrence to yield a slightly different meaning.

2. That scripture is divine speech is only one half of the *darshan*'s doctrine of revelation. The other half is the idea that God gave to Moses on Sinai not only the written Torah, but the Oral Torah as well. The latter, which contains the authoritative interpretation of the former, has been passed down in an unbroken tradition from Moses to the rabbinic schools. The idea of the Oral Torah introduces flexibility into the doctrine of Torah. The written Torah is a closed, canonic* text, fixed and inviolable. The Oral Torah is open-ended, ever developing. It is able to demonstrate the relevance of the written Torah to changing historical circumstances. At the same time the Oral Torah imposes limits on the interpretation. The *darshan* does not stand before the text of scripture with absolute freedom. He must work within the tradition. He is forbidden to disclose in scripture aspects which are not in accordance with *halakhah*. He can only interpret scripture aright if he has studied in the right schools, with the right masters who stand in an unbroken line of tradition going back to Moses himself.

The *darshanim* state some of the general principles which governed their exegesis of scripture in the form of 'tags', e.g. 'Torah speaks in human language' (Babylonian Talmud Berakhot 31b); 'No verse can ever loose its plain sense [*peshat*]' (Babylonian Talmud Shabbat 63a; Sanhedrin 34a); 'There is no "earlier" or "later" in the Torah' (Babylonian Talmud Pesaḥim 6b). They also tried to formulate their specific exegetical techniques. The fruits of these labours are embodied primarily in three lists of hermeneutical norms (*middot*) – the Seven Middot of Hillel (Tosefta Sanhedrin 7:11; Avot deRabbi Nathan A.37; Sifra Introduction), the Thirteen Middot of R. Ishmael (Sifra Introduction; Mekhilta de-Rabbi Shim'on ben Yoḥai to Exod. 21:1), and the Thirty-two Middot of R. Eliezer ben Yose ha-Gelili (Mishnat R. Eliezer I–II; Midrash

ha-Gadol Genesis, Introduction). Hillel's list illustrates the general character of these norms: 1. *Qal va-ḥomer* (inference from a less important case to a more important). 2. *Gezerah shavah* (inference based on the presence in two different laws of a common term). 3. *Binyan 'av mi-katuv 'eḥad u-vinyan 'av mi-shenei khetuvim* (construction of a category on the basis of one text, and construction of a category on the basis of two texts). 4. *Kelal u-ferat* (when a general term is followed by a specific term, the general includes only what is contained in the specific). 5. *Perat u-khelal* (when a specific term is followed by a general term, the general adds to the specific, and everything contained in the general term is included). 6. *Ka-yose' bo be-maqom 'aḥer* (the same interpretation applies in another place). 7. *Davar ha-lamed me-'inyano* (the meaning of a statement may be determined from its context).

The various lists of *middot* are unsatisfactory as a definition of the techniques of midrash. They are often obscure, and the traditional commentaries do not always elucidate them convincingly. They are prescriptive as well as descriptive, and some of them are hard to instantiate from the actual midrashim. They are far from exhaustive: principles recognized within the tradition such as *heqqesh* (argument from analogy), *semukhim* (inference based on the juxtaposition of verses), and *'al tiqrei* (replacing a word with one that sounds similar) are not listed. In fact there are numerous techniques disclosed by modern academic analysis of midrash which do not appear to be formally recognized anywhere in rabbinic hermeneutics. Significantly, the lists of *middot* make a distinction between *aggadah* (non-legal texts) and *halakhah* (legal texts). The Thirty-two are explicitly restricted to the former, the Seven and the Thirteen are implicitly and by tradition applicable to the latter, though they may also be used for *aggadah*. There was a tendency to treat *halakhah* more stringently, and not to depart from the simple sense. Norms such as *gematria* (computation of the numerical value of words or phrases) and *notariqon* (treating words as acronyms) – both found on the List of Thirty-two – were not applied to the elucidation law.

See also **Jewish Exegesis; Talmud.**

A. Goldberg, 'Form-analysis of Midrashic Literature as a Method of Description', *JJS* 37, 1986, pp. 139–52; L. Haas, 'Bibliography on Midrash', in J. Neusner (ed.), *The Study of Ancient Judaism*, I, 1982, pp. 93–106; G. Hartman and S. Budick (eds), *Midrash as Literature*, 1986; J. Heinemann and D. Noy (eds), *Studies in Aggadah and Folk-Literature*, 1971; J. Neusner, *Midrash in Context: Exegesis in Formative Judaism*, 1983; id., *What is Mid-*

rash?, 1987; G. G. Porton, *Understanding Rabbinic Midrash: Texts and Commentary*, 1985; H. L. Strack and G. Stemberger, *Einleitung in Talmud und Midrasch*, [7]1982, pp. 222–322; W. S. Towner, 'Hermeneutical Systems of Hillel and the Tannaim: A Fresh Look' in *Hebrew Union College Annual* 53, 1953, pp. 101–35; G. Vermes, *Scripture and Tradition in Judaism: Haggadic Studies*, revd edn, 1973; id., 'Bible and Midrash: Early Old Testament Exegesis' in Vermes, *Post-Biblical Jewish Studies*, 1975, pp. 59–91.

PHILIP S. ALEXANDER

Millenarianism

Millenarianism is a term that is loosely or strictly used. The looser applications are not necessarily to be discouraged, because they focus attention on the wider relevance of what can be at its narrowest an extreme position. For our purposes millenarianism has two dimensions: one a rather literal view of the future of the world, and the other a sociological* usage widely applied to sects (by extension from the character of early groups dominated by biblical prophecies).

The narrowest definition of millenarianism applies to numerous small sectarian groups through the centuries. These groups are often called 'chiliastic' because of their pre-occupation with the thousand (Greek *chilioi*) years of Christ's reign. They concentrate on the literal realization of the end of the world; biblical prophecies are to be fulfilled within the immediate projection of the group.

But the definition of millenarianism can also be extended to refer to any futurist eschatological* belief that is cast in literal and material terms. This is to generalize from the beliefs of particular chiliastic sects. Such literal readings of apocalyptic* ideas are to be contrasted with other ways of seeing the future: either the allegorizing* of future hope into moral and spiritual truths, or the conviction that a new world had already been realized in the present as a result of the resurrection* of Christ. Taken as one element of doctrine among others, futurist belief is valuable in emphasizing the incompleteness of things as they are. The extremist position emerges when the futurist view takes over the whole. An uncompromisingly literal 'vision' of the biblical future, often coupled with a rigorist view of ethics in face of the last judgment, can dominate people's lives totally and determine the affairs of nations.

The biblical text which set the programme for the millennial kingdom, the reign of Christ with the saints for a thousand years, is Rev. 20.2–7. Although a long period, it is conceived as an interim during which Satan is imprisoned and those who share Christ's resurrection also fulfil a priestly ministry. It resembles an earthly triumph and vindication of the deaths of Christ and the martyrs. The traditional doctrines of Roman Catholicism have regarded it as an error to concentrate on the literal period of one thousand years for this earthly kingdom, rather than to see it as a symbol for the prolonged but indefinite time of the church (between the resurrection of Christ and the last judgment).

This is a small part of the programme of Revelation, and these visions of the end have given rise to much speculative rearrangement. It is not surprising if there is disagreement on the literal nature of the millennium or its relation to the second coming of Christ. For some who closely follow the actual order of Revelation, the second coming (19.11–16) precedes the millennium and these last events are established by divine cataclysm. For others who associate the second coming with the last judgment (20.11–15), the millennium must come first; for them the earthly reign of Christian saints is the climax, and yet the natural outcome, of a gradual but sustained activity of the church in the world. Both of these ways of interpreting Revelation have been widely influential through the centuries. They may be labelled pre-millennialist and post-millennialist respectively. Essentially Christians have taken over the structure of the Jewish dream in Dan. 7, a dream of two ages (this age and the age to come) which fall either side of the coming of a son of man,* and the saints' receiving of the kingdom (Dan. 7.18). So the millennium faces both ways: it is a divine vindication demonstrated on earth, and an earthly anticipation of heavenly conditions. But in Daniel it seems that the kingdom of the saints is God's final word, and not an interim.

Thought on the millennium is inspired, but not confined, by Revelation. To elaborate the picture and apply it to a wide variety of practical circumstances, all kinds of biblical material are employed (as well as related ideas from non-biblical sources such as the Sibylline Oracles). The principal traditions come from Jewish and Christian apocalyptic texts (represented in the canon* by Daniel and Revelation). The prophetic books of the OT contribute visions of a new Eden and paradise regained. The words of Jesus, from such Gospel texts as Mark 9.1, add both authority and a sense of urgency. II Peter 3.8 must also be relevant, if only for the specific reference to 'a thousand years'. In its context this text might be seen as revisionist, offering explanation for the delay in the second coming; but it also shows that (such is the flexibility in Christian interpretation) the doctrine of the second coming is non-falsifiable by anything short of a global catastrophe.

The key figure in and for any millenarian group has been the messianic leader or prophet. He claimed to be the awaited messiah,* often a warlike saviour (in the Sibylline tradition), or the forerunner who prophesied the imminent return of Christ. Usually the prophet claimed to have received a special revelation. He therefore exercised the creative role in the group's expectations, assembling the traditional prophecies and interpreting them to apply to the immediate situation. He was often a priest from a mainstream church, who was overwhelmed by apocalyptic fervour, or who exploited others in his disillusionment with conventional attitudes. Such a charismatic person became the focus for a group of people in high tension or undergoing traumatic change.

An early example of the prophetic figure was Montanus, who was responsible for a revival of apocalyptic ideas in second century Christianity. In AD 156 in Phrygia (Asia Minor) he claimed to be the incarnation of the Holy Spirit who would reveal things to come (John 16.13). Revelation (especially 3.7–13, the letter to Philadelphia) was a major influence on the birth of Montanism in this region. But Montanism did not remain a local cult; it spread widely under the pressures of persecution. It became a threat to established church authorities whose static view was confronted by a prospect of immediate change. The eminent theologian Tertullian* was converted to its apocalyptic literalism and rigorist ethics. He describes a vision of a walled city in the morning sky of Judaea, heralding the descent of the New Jerusalem.*

Jewish and Christian apocalypses use a schematic view of history to calculate the calendar and focus attention on the imminent events of this world's end. In the same spirit later generations (instead of discarding once-failed prophecies) re-use the apocalyptic traditions to provide a once-for-all interpretation of the current crisis. A highly sophisticated example is Joachim of Fiore (1145–1202) who claimed prophetic inspiration in the form of a key to interpret the Bible as a pattern of world history. In a genealogy* as symbolic* and structured as that in Matt. 1.1–17, the generations of the world are grouped in three ages, presided over by the Trinity. After the ages of Law (Father) and Gospel (Son), the world awaits the imminent age of the Spirit. And Benedict and the new monastic orders are 'midwives' for this birth which is expected early in the thirteenth century. With the beginnings of the Franciscan orders, some friars appropriated this prophecy to themselves as 'Spirituals'. Whether for Joachim or the friars, this view of the coming third age was at odds with the received (Augustinian*) tradition that the kingdom of God* is the present church on earth. Resistance to established structures could lead to explicit antinomianism, even the 'sanctification of sin' (e.g. the Brethren of the Free Spirit). The language of the third age long survived, in different if equally revolutionary form: the German 'Third Reich' was set to last for a thousand years.

The revolutionary aspect of millenarianism seems to be its most consistent feature, for groups who are variously motivated to change the world. It can be a social struggle, a peasants' revolt but with cosmic aims. The use of apocalyptic language ensures that the struggle is not for limited objectives, but rather claims 'uniqueness' in the endeavour to transform the world. The upheaval in which the group is engaged is held to be the apocalyptic battle (Armageddon, Rev. 16.16), that is the ultimate purification of society. Clearly this is a mechanism of protest for people unsure of their place in existing society, or with no other means to express grievances. These uprisings are often provoked at a time of national crisis or a terrifying natural disaster (e.g. the Black Death). Or they may be a 'protestant' reaction to the luxury or laxity of the church, and a drive for rigorous asceticism. The long history of millenarian 'happenings' is echoed today in revolutionary movements, especially in the Third World. There the impact of modern colonialism, the culture and 'civilization' of the Western world, is either welcomed as salvation, or (more likely) rejected with every means a primitive (even pre-literate) tribe has to command. Such millennial movements may be expressions of cargo-cults, or rely on trance-inducing drugs, or perhaps relate to vestiges of Judaeo-Christian traditions left by missionaries.

The common feature is a dissatisfaction with the current order of things, which in many cases develops as a result of culture contact. Threatened or tantalized groups seek powerful religious remedies for their helplessness. (Increasing use of apocalyptic rhetoric in modern British socialism suggests a growing consciousness of being disadvantaged or marginalized!) But revolutionary millenarianism is not always a protest of the impoverished and the lower classes. Often the prophetic leader, who creates the group's faith, will come from the educated elite. And some groups, like the Franciscans who were influenced by Joachim, were people from the wealthy classes who voluntarily accepted poverty for the sake of spiritual mysticism.

Edward Irving (1792–1834) was a Church of Scotland minister with a fashionable London congregation. From 1825 he was engrossed in studying the prophecies of Revelation as applied to the years after the French Revolution. (At this time there was an upsurge of literary and artistic interest in the themes of Romantic millenarianism.) Irving preached that the seventh bowl (Rev. 16.17) was about to be poured. The Irvingites are a good example of a middle-class – and more intellectual – involvement in popular millenarian revival. They 'rapidly developed gifts of prophesyings, glossolalia, spiritual healing, automatic writing and telepathy' (Harrison, p. 208). When Irving was expelled from the church, the group met at the Owenite socialist headquarters (clearly the group was no longer acceptable in the eyes of the world!), before they formed the Catholic Apostolic Church.

The complex of millenarian phenomena over the centuries can be explained in various ways. The social reasons of an insecure group on the margins of society, and the historical reasons of a time of crisis (such as the age of Revolution and the Napoleonic Wars), can be supplemented by psychological * explanations. Sectarian movements can have a desperate and paranoid nature: there is a leader who is sure that he is right, offers present religious experiences and promises future bliss; an enemy (society, the Establishment, anyone who does not subscribe to the doctrine as promulgated) who can be labelled as Antichrist; and a group of followers who, because of the circumstances or their own psychology, are so disadvantaged or insecure as to need to be attached to such a leader. There can also be a positive theological explanation of the appeal of millenarian beliefs, in that they analyse the situation in terms of biblical revelation and seem to account for how the world is.

Social anthropological study of modern millenarian groups has shown how resilient they are to the apparent failure of their specific prophecies of the second coming. This 'cognitive dissonance' * which might be expected to lead to the group's disintegration is apparently overcome by a revised message, antinomianism, and increased missionary activity in compensation.

The millenarianism which depends on a certain reading of the Bible might itself be used as an analogy to explain the N T and the rise of Christianity. Thus the wheel has turned full circle in a theory such as Gager's (1975): the early church engaged in vigorous mission, because the belief in Jesus as messiah was disconfirmed by his death and the eschatological hopes of his return were unfulfilled. But the problem is that Gager's analogy is very general, while his millenarian model is based on very precise data. It would be necessary to establish that the early Christians were proletarian poor, that Jesus clearly perceived his fate, and finely calculated the date of his return, for 'cognitive dissonance' to apply. It is not just the mission of Jesus' followers that needs to be explained, but the whole context of

realistic future hope which underlies Christianity and its many millenarian offshoots.

See also **Apocalyptic; Eschatology; Kingdom of God; Revelation, Book of.**

Norman Cohn, *The Pursuit of the Millennium*, 1970; J. G. Gager, *Kingdom and Community: the Social World of Early Christianity*, 1975; J. F. C. Harrison, *The Second Coming: Popular Millenarianism (1780–1850)*, 1979; Marjorie Reeves, *Joachim of Fiore and the Prophetic Future*, 1976; id. and W. Gould, *Joachim of Fiore and the Myth of the Eternal Evangel in the Nineteenth Century*, 1987; Bryan Wilson, *Magic and the Millennium*, 1973.

JOHN M. COURT

Miracle in the Biblical World

For the biblical writers, what the modern world calls 'miracle' is an event in which God acts in a special way, in order to disclose or accomplish his purpose. There is in the scriptures no notion of natural law determining how the universe operates. Hence, although miracle is usually recounted as an extraordinary event, it is never portrayed as a violation of the laws of nature.

Old Testament miracles. There are three major Hebrew words associated with what might be called miracle: *oth* – a sign or indicator, an act of God by which a message is sent to his people or to pagan rulers; *mopeth* – a wonder, an extraordinary event; *pele* – the sovereign act of God.

The *oth* of God may be as basic as those indicators of the divinely established order of the universe, the sun, moon and stars, as signs of the seasons, the days and the years (Gen. 1.14). But the far more frequent use of the term is linked with God's direct actions on behalf of his covenant * people, and especially with the events which promised and then accomplished the deliverance of Israel from bondage in Egypt.* The series of calamities that befell the Egyptians as a vain effort to persuade Pharaoh to set Israel free (Ex. 4.8–30) is intended to convince both Israel and the ruler of Egypt that God has a purpose for the nation. The term *oth* also appears in the recalling of God's acts on behalf of his people (Deut. 26.8). These signs are not self-explanatory, but they have the potential to indicate to the opponents and the members of the covenant people that God has a special plan and purpose which he is at work to fulfil.

The second term, *mopeth*, emphasizes the extraordinary nature of God's acts on behalf of his people. It is used for such events as the turning of Aaron's rod into a serpent (Ex. 17.9–10) and for the later recalling of these amazing events in the liturgical and prophetic * traditions of Israel (Ps. 78.40–55; Jer. 32.17–22).

The third term, *pele*, emphasizes God's sovereignty in performing these and other actions on behalf of his people. The term appears in the historical accounts (Ex. 15.11), in the wisdom* reflection on God's acts (Job 9.10), and in the Psalms, where the history of God's work for his people is celebrated (Ps. 77.11–14). In the Aramaic section of Daniel a term with similar connotations is used, *temah*, with reference to God's interventions to preserve his people from the destructive intentions of their enemies: the young men in the fiery furnace (Dan. 4.2–3) and Daniel in the lion's den (6.27). In both cases, the result of this divine act is the persuasion of the pagan ruler that Yahweh, the God of Israel, is sovereign in the universe.

The accounts of miracles performed by the prophets Elijah and Elisha, which are unique within the OT, are referred to in the Gospel tradition (Luke 4.25–27; cf. I Kings 17.17–24; II Kings 5.8). Elijah calls down fire from God on the altar on Mount Carmel (I Kings 18) and on the two groupings of fifty messengers from King Ahaziah (II Kings 1.10–12). In all these incidents, the effective agent is God himself, as the king's rhetorical question in II Kings 5.7 makes clear: 'Am I God, to kill and to make alive . . .?' Yahweh tells the prophet both what is going to happen, and the specifics of the prophet's role in making it happen (II Kings 8).

Miracle in the later and post-biblical Jewish traditions. In the post-exilic period, healing is at times described as occurring through an intermediary agency: the physician. In contrast to the older OT writings, where physicians are grouped with soothsayers and magicians as charlatans, in Ecclus. 38.1–4 they are said to have been instructed by God and empowered with medicines out of the earth, through which they can effect cures. The physician should seek divine guidance in his God-given responsibility of restoring human beings to health.

In other documents of this period, however, sickness is linked with the demons. When Tobit becomes blind as a result of sparrow droppings that fell on his eyes (Tobit 2.10), the burnt heart, liver and gall of a fish are used to expel demons, including the one that causes his blindness (6.7–16). In the Book of Jubilees, the fallen angels cause suffering and plagues on the earth, for which God alone has the cures (Jub. 10; 48.5–7). In the Dead Sea Scrolls,* the *Genesis Apocryphon* and the *Prayer of Nabonidus* both recount cures of the ailing through the expulsion of demons and the grant of forgiveness of sins. In both cases, the beneficiary is a pagan ruler. In I Enoch 6–11 the present condition of human suffering is the consequence of the presence and activity

of the fallen angels, whose defeat is awaited in the near future. When Daniel is reporting the divine acts of deliverance of the faithful remnant of God's people, he praises God for the signs and wonders which he performs and for his rescue of his people from the powers of evil (Dan. 4.2–3; 6.26–27).

It is in keeping with this point of view, therefore, that in the later apocalyptic* strands of tradition in Isaiah there are promises of God's acts in delivering the righteous from their sufferings and from the power of death (Isa. 26.16–21). Also depicted are the concurrent restoration of the land and the healing of the sick and the handicapped: the lame, the blind, the deaf, the dumb (Isa. 35.1–10). It is God who will accomplish this renewal of the land and his people (Isa. 26.15; 27.1; 35.4).

Miracle in the earlier Jesus tradition. In the so-called Q tradition, it is precisely these texts from the apocalyptic section of Isaiah that are paraphrased by Jesus in response to the question of John the Baptist* whether or not Jesus is 'the One who is to come' (Matt. 11.2–6; Luke 7.18–23). The proof of Jesus' role in the purpose of God is to be inferred from his healing of the blind, the lame, lepers, and the deaf. He adds to this his role as one who preaches good news to the poor – an obvious reference to Isa. 61.1, as Luke 4.16–21 makes explicit. Similarly, in the Q addition to the story of the accusation that Jesus can control demons because he is in league with them (Luke 11.19–20; Matt. 12.27–28; cf. Mark 2.22–27) Jesus declares that his expulsion of the demons is an indication that God's rule is already becoming a reality in the midst of his people. The term 'finger of God' is a direct reference to God's original act through Moses* of deliverance of his covenant people from slavery in Egypt (Ex. 9.18). Now the new covenant people is being freed, not from earthly, but from demonic powers in preparation for the establishment of God's rule over the creation. That New Age has already begun to dawn, as is manifest in the healings and the exorcisms which Jesus performs.

This conviction is shared in our oldest Gospel, Mark, but with elaboration of the theme and increase of the narratives which demonstrate this conviction. Included are not only exorcisms (Mark 1.21–28; 5.1–20; 7.24–30), but also the cure of fever (1.29–31), of leprosy (1.40–45), of epilepsy (9.14–29), of blindness (8.22–26; 10.46–52), and of various ailments (3.1–12; 5.21–43; 6.53–56). In the Marcan accounts of these healings, there are frequent references to the fact that these cures take place among those who by ethnic origin or ritual condition or occupation are excluded from the Jewish people. Examples of those ritually unacceptable are the woman with the bloody flow, the Gerasene demoniac who lives in a tomb, the Syro-Phoenician woman, and the leper. Yet Jesus touches and heals them because of their need and regardless of their ritual condition.

Two types of miracle stories in Mark go beyond the meeting of individual need through healings and exorcisms. The account of Jesus walking on the water and calming the sea (6.45–52) recalls the stories of God's controlling the waters of the Red Sea and the Jordan on behalf of his people Israel, as they made their way from slavery in Egypt to new life in the land of Canaan. The fact that the three Gospel versions of this story (cf. Matt. 14.22–33; John 6.15–21) all link the incident with the second type – feeding the people in the desert – provides the essential clue as to the intention of these narratives. The analogy between Jesus feeding the throng and Moses providing the bread from heaven is obvious in Mark and Matthew, but is made explicit in John's version of this story, to which he appends the discourse on Jesus as the bread of life (John 6.22–65). Further, Mark tells a second version of this story (8.1–10), which takes place in Gentile territory, as contrasted with the Jewish district of Galilee in 6.30–44. What is implied in Mark's reports of these two feeding stories is the two stages of the call to share in the life of God's people: first to Jews and then to Gentiles. The intent of these trans-personal miracle stories is to demonstrate that the promises which God made to Israel are now being fulfilled in a renewed form in the community which Jesus is calling together and for which he is providing the means of common life.

Miracles in the Pauline tradition. Although some scholars have proposed that in II Corinthians Paul* was trying to discredit competitors who were claiming to possess powers superior to those of Paul because they could perform miracles, in fact Paul assigns a high value to miracles and healings. These are among the gifts of the Spirit (*charismata*) which he lists in I Cor. 12.4–11. When he is ranking these roles in I Cor. 12.28, he places the working of miracles and healing just behind the gifts of apostle, prophet and teacher. In writing to the Romans (15.18–20) he notes the importance of signs and wonders performed by him in winning obedience from the Gentiles. He includes no narrative accounts of his signs and wonders or healings, but clearly the ability to perform them was valued highly by him in the fulfilment of his mission to the Gentiles (II Cor.12.12.).

Miracles in Matthew, Luke–Acts and John. As one would expect in documents intended for readers in the wider Graeco-Roman world, Matthew, Luke–Acts and John show the influence of Graeco-Roman culture on their respective narrative styles, and especially on their reports of miracles in connection with the career of Jesus and the apostles.

In Matthew this is especially evident in his unique accounts of the marvels that accompany the birth and death of Jesus. These are precisely the aspects of the careers of the emperors that the Roman historians, Tacitus and Suetonius, depict as accompanied by portents and dreams as manifestations of the divine destiny of these world leaders. Instances of this phenomenon in connection with Jesus' birth (*see* **Infancy Narratives**) include the star that leads the magi to the predestined birthplace of the king (Matt. 2.1–2), the voice from heaven which gives public testimony to Jesus as God's son (Matt. 3.17, in contrast to the private disclosure in Mark 1.11), the instructions given to Joseph and the magi in dreams (Matt. 1.20; 2.12; 2.19–22). Similarly, events linked with his death include the dream of Pilate's wife concerning Jesus' innocence (Matt. 27.19), and the earthquakes which occur at the death and resurrection of Jesus (27.52–53; 28.2) (*see* **Passion Narratives**; **Resurrection Narratives**). These miracles attest the hand of God at work in the coming and the career of Jesus.

Akin to this feature are the miracle stories in Luke which highlight the divine purpose of God at work through Jesus. In keeping with the overarching aim of Luke to show that what God is doing through Jesus is in accord with what happened and was promised in the scriptural traditions of Israel, the miraculous events leading to the birth of John the Baptist closely parallel the features of the stories of the divine preparation for the birth of Samuel, who would anoint David,* God's chosen one, as king of Israel (I Sam. 1–3; Luke 1.5–25, 57–80). Similarly, divine preparations for the birth of Jesus are accomplished through angelic visitors and are in fulfilment of prophetic expectations (Luke 1.26–28; 2.1–20). The aged Simeon and the prophetess, Anna, serve as the oracles of God to depict the special role that Jesus is to fulfil in the purpose of God (Luke 2.25–38).

In his reports of the miracles of Jesus, Luke expands on the Marcan summary of his healings (Mark 1.32–34) to make explicit that Jesus is the Son of God and the messiah* (Luke 4.40–41). He transforms the Marcan story of Jesus' call of the disciples from their roles as fishermen (Mark 1.16–20) into a miracle story for the symbolic portrayal of the divine authority of Jesus and the astonishing results of their mission (Luke 5.1–11). Only in Luke do we have the story of Jesus healing the widow's son, which recalls the miracles reportedly performed by Elijah (I Kings 17.17–24) and Elisha (II Kings 4.32–37). The return of the seventy from their mission, in which they were successful in expelling demons, is interpreted by Jesus in Luke 10.17–20 as an indication of the cosmic triumph over Satan. Similarly, in Luke 17.20–21 there is the claim that the signs which he performs are not merely indicators of a future kingdom,* but evidence of its presence in the midst of his contemporaries. The Lucan interest in the outreach of Jesus to the marginal people and in their response is highlighted in the account of the grateful Samaritan leper who returns to thank Jesus (Luke 17.11–19) and in Jesus' restoration of the severed ear of the slave of the high priest (Luke 22.50–51).

In Acts, the apostles are depicted as working miracles in Jerusalem and as being sought by those in need of healing, as Jesus was (5.12–16; 8.9–13). Some of the stories – such as the healing of the lame man at the Temple gate (Acts 3.1–10) – closely resemble the Gospel accounts. Jesus' role as healer and exorcist is directly recalled (Acts 10.38). Crucial stages in the transformation of the apostles' mission from its initial concentration on Jews to the wider Gentile audience are confirmed by miraculous events. The first of these is the symbolic event of Pentecost, when at the outpouring of the Spirit in fulfilment of prophecy (Joel 2.28–32) there is a miracle of universal understanding of the apostolic message in languages from all over the world (2.5–11). Other symbolic miraculous events, which point to God's protection of the apostles from natural and political dangers, are the stories of the release of Peter* and Paul from prison (Acts 12.1–17; 16.19–39), and the deliverance of the passengers and crew from the storm at sea and Paul from the bite of the viper (27.13–44; 28.1–6).

Distinctive in Acts are two types of miracle story: 1. punitive miracles and 2. those resembling magic.* The former include the death of Ananias and Sapphira for their deceitful violation of the community sharing its resources (Acts 5.1–11), the death of Herod Agrippa (12.20–23) and the contest with the magicians (13.6–12). Bordering on magic are those reports of cures which take place through physical contact with the apostles, rather than through their words and acts linked with the inbreaking of God's rule and the announcement of God's renewal of the creation through Jesus. Two such magic-type accounts are the cures which occur when Peter's shadow falls on the sick (5.12–16) and the use of handkerchiefs and aprons touched by Paul to effect cures (19.11–12). The surge of interest in magic among sophisticated

Romans by the beginning of the second century has clearly had its effect on Luke's account of the activities of the apostles.

In the Gospel of John the miracle stories are not only accounts of the extraordinary powers of Jesus, but also serve as metaphorical* statements about who he is and his unique relationship with God. The stories in most cases sound like those in the other Gospels, but their wider import is made explicit in John's Gospel. In John 5.1–18 the fact that Jesus heals a lame man on the sabbath involves him in violation of the law against work on the sabbath, as is the case in several other Gospel miracle stories, such as Mark 3.1–6 and pars. But in John the issue is Jesus' claim to be son of God and equal with God. Similarly, in the story of the feeding of the five thousand in the other Gospels there is a hint of the eucharistic implications of Jesus' actions ('he took, he blessed, he broke, he gave', Mark 6.41 and pars.). This is echoed in John 6.1–14, but in the discourse which follows (6.22–65) Jesus declares himself to be the bread of life, implying his own heavenly origin and the access to eternal life through him. The story of the man born blind (John 9.1–38) sounds like the other Gospel healing stories, but it leads to a declaration about the sharp separation that is coming between the Jews and those who perceive Jesus to be the light of the world (John 8.12; 9.39–41).

Other miracle stories in John are unique to this Gospel and serve as signs of a larger reality than the incident of divine action that is being described. In John 2, the changing of water into wine points not only to the eucharist but also to the time of fulfilment of God's purpose that lies in the future for God's new people when God's glory is fully manifest in Jesus. In John 11, the raising of Lazarus is a symbol of the eternal life that is available now for those who trust in Jesus as the ground and source of life (John 11.25–26). Like Luke and Matthew, John ends his Gospel with stories of the appearance of the risen Jesus to his followers and his empowering of them for the work that he has commissioned them to do.

In spite of the differences in detail between the miracles of the OT and those of the Gospels, the basic import of these accounts is to demonstrate to the faithful what God is doing on behalf of his people and to accomplish his purpose in the creation.* There is no evidence that the miracles are done to confirm the truth of Jesus' teachings, which is the function miracles serve in the rabbinic* tradition. Nor is Jesus pictured as trying to outdo other miracle-workers or to demolish his opponents, as is the case with some of the miracle stories in the apocryphal NT writings. The two basic connotations of miracle are to be found in both OT and NT: 1. an extraordinary event, 2. performed as a sign to the community* of faith concerning God's purpose for his people.

See also **Miraculous, Interpretation of the.**

H. C. Kee, *Miracle in the Early Christian World*, 1983; C. F. D. Moule (ed.), *Miracles*, 1965; J. W. Rogerson, *Anthropology and the Old Testament*, 1979; Gerd Theissen, *The Miracle Stories in the Early Christian Tradition*, 1983; David L. Tiede, *The Charismatic Figure as Wonder-Worker*, 1972.

HOWARD CLARK KEE

Miraculous, Interpretation of the

Until the Enlightenment,* broadly speaking, people lived in a miraculous world, under God's guiding and intervening hand. It is significant that in the NT the typical words used for what are now seen as events against the laws of nature are 'wonders' (i.e. astonishing occurrences) and 'acts of power' (*see* **Miracle in the Biblical World**). Since then the universe has come to be seen as a closed system governed by observed regularities of cause and effect. Interpretation has consequently been overshadowed by the question of historicity, what actually happened, whereas earlier interpreters, taking that as given, could explore the implications of the stories or look for deeper meanings without worry. More recently, structuralism* and interest in narrative* as such has encouraged a concern for 'what is written' rather than 'what it is written about'.

Pre-Enlightenment

We may distinguish four kinds of interpretation, by no means mutually exclusive, starting within the Bible itself: 1. literal; 2. typological*-eschatological;* 3. parabolic;* 4. allegorical.*

1. *Literal.* Taken at face value, the OT miracle stories illustrate God's character and power, in creating the world (Genesis), and in electing, disciplining and saving his people (Exodus, Judges, Daniel). They glorify God and his agents (the Elijah-Elisha cycle, I Kings 17–II Kings 13). They encourage confident prayer (James 5.17,18) and fidelity under persecution (I Macc. 2.59,60). In Jesus' Nazareth sermon they show God's concern beyond his own people (Luke 4.25–27).

2. *Typological.* Already within the Bible itself people saw such stories as echoed in later events, and as providing a pattern ('type') for God's future action and man's response ('antitype'); for example creation* and exodus stories pointed to God's power to overcome hostile forces and bring his people out of captivity (Isa. 51.9–11). Paul* and Hebrews both take the exodus stories as foreshadowing Christian experience (I Cor. 10.1–11 – these things happened *tupikōs*, by way of example; Heb. 3.16–4.10), and the evangelists* make their miracle stories echo those of the past by using significant words from the scriptural accounts, as with the deaf-mute described as a stammerer (*mogilalos*), a word found only at Mark 7.32 and at Isa. 35.6 (LXX). Paul's raising of Eutychus (Acts 20.10) echoes both Elijah (I Kings 17.21) and Jesus (Mark 5.39; Luke 7.11–17).

A special instance of this kind of interpretation is the eschatological, foreshadowing God's final act of redemption. The exodus stories were retold annually in the Passover Haggadah, prefiguring the messianic* Age. The evangelists, and possibly Jesus himself, interpreted his miracles as fulfilling both the prophecies of Isa.35 and 61 (Matt. 11.2–5; Luke 7.21,22) and the exodus pattern (Luke 9.31).

3. *Parabolic.* Still without questioning their happenedness, it was possible to take the stories as pointing beyond themselves spiritually: the evangelists tell of physical healing or provision in such a way as to point to a spiritual transaction. Just as the rabbis* saw the manna and the water from the rock as pointing to God's Wisdom providing for his people, so Paul and John equated them with Christ (I Cor. 10.4; John 6.31–33). For John, whose key word for miracles is 'signs', the spiritual significance of the healing of the man born blind is explicit (John 9.35ff.). In Mark the context points to the interpretation, as in the account of Jesus opening the disciples' eyes to his status following the healing of the blind man of Bethsaida (Mark 8.22–30), or in the story of the withering of the fig tree, with the cleansing of the temple inserted as a kind of sandwich filling (Mark 11.12–25): in this context the reader is invited to see not just the power of Jesus and the efficacy of prayer, but also God's judgment on Israel's barren religious establishment. In fact the fig-tree raises the possibility of miracle stories arising out of parables (cf. Luke 13.6–9) by way of midrash.*

4. *Allegorical.* Like the parables, the miracle stories could be interpreted allegorically, that is by giving spiritual* meanings to some or all of the details of the story, often without respect to its meaning as a whole. Even if John himself did not take the six water-pots at Cana as standing for the rites of Judaism superseded by the gospel, later interpreters have been in no doubt that their significance was allegorical; for Augustine* they represented the Six Ages of the world. The Jews, pre-eminently Philo,* learnt this method from the Greek grammarians of Alexandria,* as a

means of handling sacred stories which seemed to give an arbitrary or immoral picture of God. Not that Philo or his successors jettisoned the literal sense: they saw it as the outer husk of a spiritual kernel, which was what really mattered. So it was the allegorical method that dominated the patristic and mediaeval * worlds.

Post-Enlightenment

The Protestant Reformers* brought back the primacy of the literal sense of scripture, but for the miracle stories this led to increasing conflict as the regularity of nature became more obvious and the existence of God open to doubt. We may distinguish four further types of interpretation in addition to the straightforwardly literal: 1. naturalistic; 2. mythological;* 3. historical-critical;* 4. structuralist.

1. *Naturalistic.* While orthodox Christians interpreted the miracle stories now not as signs of God's character and power, but as proofs of his existence and of the divinity of Christ (e.g. Paley's *Evidences*, 1794), the unorthodox gave them a naturalistic interpretation: e.g. at the Feeding of the Five Thousand Jesus' example caused the rest to share their food with those who had none; he did not walk on the water but on a log in the water. New medical and psychological knowledge made the healing and exorcism stories no longer necessarily miraculous, in the new sense of miracle, that is, as contrary to natural law.

2. *Mythological.* The sterile deadlock of supernaturalist and reductionist approaches was broken by D. F. Strauss* with his *Life of Jesus* (1835). He demonstrated the bankruptcy of both as applied, for example, to the Feeding, and insisted on the stories' mythical character, meaning by 'myth'* the primitive, imaginative way of interpreting inexplicable events; for example Peter* expressed his mysterious release from prison (Acts 12) through the Jewish belief in angels as ministers of God's providence. Further, recognition of the creative power of biblical types and expectations enables one to see how belief that Jesus was the messiah caused the miracles associated with the messiah to be attributed to him; here is the clue to the Feeding, as John 6.14 indicates: the final redeemer must do all the signs of the first redeemer, Moses,* such as providing bread in the desert.

So the task of the interpreter is not to ask what happened and what it proves, but what the narrators meant by telling such stories; he must learn the biblical language of pictures and stories and translate it into the terms of his own time. This approach could take a weaker or stronger form.

For Feuerbach the stories were projections of the childish imagination which seeks instant fulfilment of its wishes, to be studied for what they reveal about those who tell them, and those who believe them.

But it is possible also to see them as pointing beyond themselves to an explosive capacity in man for transformation. For Ernst Bloch (*The Principle of Hope*, 1986), like Feuerbach an atheist, the stories of Jesus' miracles differed from all others in their eschatological sense, as signs of concrete transformation, the blasting apart of the accustomed *status quo*.

Likewise Bultmann* in his programme of demythologization* found a sophisticated understanding of existence in the stories; for example John, while extravagantly stepping up the miraculous (120 gallons of wine, a man born blind, a corpse four days dead), points beyond it to the new quality of life which Jesus gives.

3. *Historical-critical.* This has been the characteristic modern approach since Strauss and F. C. Baur, who pioneered a thoroughgoing critical study of the Bible, taking seriously its own contexts and thought forms. We may pick out two aspects:

*Form criticism.** The background to Bultmann's interpretative work lies in his study, in *The History of the Synoptic Tradition*, 1963, of the formal characteristics of the miracle stories and their Jewish and pagan parallels. Its main contribution is a negative judgment on their historicity, clearing the way for existential interpretation; but such study may reach more positive conclusions, and in so far as form criticism is concerned with *Sitz im Leben* ('setting in life') it prepares the way for sociological* interpretation of the stories' function, as practised by G. Theissen (see 4 below).

*Redaction criticism.** Shift of attention from the pre-history of the stories to the way they are placed and told within the Gospels has led to better appreciation of the emphases of each evangelist; for example Matthew's drastic abbreviation of some of Mark's stories may be seen to focus attention on the authority of Jesus and the faith of those healed (cf. Matt. 9.18–26 with Mark 5.21–43), and the placing of a story may point to a spiritual interpretation as in the author's intention.

4. *Structuralist.* This term may be used to cover various kinds of interpretation of the unconscious function of a story.

*Literary.** In reaction against concern with the historicity of the stories and their factual implications, one may attend to what is written rather than what it is written about, and to its effect on the reader. For example, Frank Kermode, in *The Genesis of Secrecy*, 1979, finds in Mark's narrative a wealth of conjunctions and oppositions: mystery and stupidity, denial and recognition, silence and proclamation. Attention to these rather than what actually happened may wean us from the urge to rationalize and open us to the stories' inherent power.

*Anthropological.** According to E. R. Leach, sacred texts contain a religious message which is other than that which can be immediately inferred from the manifest sense of the narrative. Analysis of the Feeding stories, for example, in terms of the three-fold pattern of rites of passage, brings out the religious sense of the stories in relation to the central Christian ritual of the eucharist: they show a pattern of (a) 'separation', (b) meal followed by epiphany (the 'marginal' state of holiness,* creative and dangerous), and (c) 'reaggregation' – return to the normal world with renewed potency (Mark 6.30–56).

Sociological. For G. Theissen, miracle stories function as pointers to a new age, a new life-style abandoning traditionally legitimized ways. They relate to the boundary between social worlds, and form-critical study shows a recurrence of boundary-stressing and boundary-crossing motifs, which express both the difficulty and the possibility of breaking out. The NT stories reflect situations of economic and cultural inferiority: demon possession expresses social and political pressure, and stories of exorcism express liberation* – the political angle is hinted at in the story of 'Legion' and his fate (Mark 5.1–20). In other words, the stories tell us not just about the power of Jesus or the theology of the evangelists but about the whole milieu of early Christianity. In addition, they have an expressive power of their own; like the miracles they describe, they are themselves symbolic acts which open up a new way of life (cf. E. Bloch above).

These approaches, while not concerned with exactly what happened, take seriously the forces which were at work then and now, and treat the text of the Bible as alive and creative.

See also **Demythologization; Miracle in the Biblical World.**

R. H. Fuller, *Interpreting the Miracles*, 1963; H. Hendrickx, *The Miracle Stories of the Synoptic Gospels*, 1987; J. M. Hull, *Hellenistic Magic and the Synoptic Tradition*, 1974; E. and M.-L. Keller, *Miracles in Dispute*, 1969; E. Leach and D. A. Laycock, *Structuralist Interpretations of Biblical Myth*, 1983; C. F. D. Moule (ed.), *Miracles*, 1965; G. Theissen, *Miracle Stories of the Early Christian Tradition*, 1983.

JOHN SWEET

Moses

The chief biblical source for the career of Moses runs from the story of his birth in Ex.

2 to the account of his death in Deut. 34. The record thus spanning four books of the Pentateuch* makes Moses the dominant human figure not only in the Pentateuch itself but also in the OT as a whole.

1. In order to evaluate the figure of Moses correctly, the character of this biblical source must be sensitively appreciated. The considerations presented in the article on Exodus, which suggest that it (and, by implication, the following books of the Pentateuch) is primarily a theological statement cast into the form of a linear narrative which exploits lore of many kinds, historical, folk,* institutional, liturgical and legal, are here presupposed. The pentateuchal presentation of the exodus of Israel from Egypt* through to the eve of the settlement of Israel in Canaan is a broadly generalized picture of historical processes taking place in the centuries of transition from the Late Bronze Age to Iron Age I. It is used to explain and justify practices of all kinds which have in origin little or nothing to do with specific historical events, indeed may long antedate or postdate them. It follows that no one individual, not even a Moses, can, historically speaking, have been associated with the inception of all these practices or even with all the historical processes to which they are related in the biblical narrative. For the sake of coherence and accessibility, the biblical narrative focusses them, however, on one figure, for the purpose of communicating not historical truth but, beyond that, theological significance.

The quest for the historical Moses, however well-intentioned, runs, then, counter to the thrust of the biblical source: a preoccupation with the biography of the great man may divert attention from the purpose of the narrative. One may suspect, e.g. that, historically, Moses, like Joshua or Samuel, was a significant local figure, in this case a Levite (was Levi then a secular tribe or a sacral caste?), associated with the Egyptian-threatened semi-nomads, both 'Israelite' and 'Kenite' (and even intermarrying with the latter), of the northern Negev, and functioning especially at Kadesh Barnea (though lack of archaeological evidence there before the tenth century makes that problematical). Under the impetus of the unilinear narrative, he has been extended into an idealized pan-Israelite leader.

Some argue that a religion like Judaism needs such a founder (e.g. R. H. Charles, 'a great religious and moral revelation is not the work of a moral syndicate, but is due to the inspiration of some great outstanding personality', cf. Jesus Christ, Muḥammad). Reconstructions like this, though they have been frequently espoused in whole or in part, remain perforce speculative and leave the reader perplexed as to what is ultimately gained by them. If this is true of attempted historical reconstructions of the life of Moses, whether minimalist like M. Noth's (his identification of the grave tradition behind Deut. 34 as the 'bedrock of a historical reality which is absolutely original' is strangely aberrant) or maximalist as by, e.g. E. Auerbach (*Moses*, 1975), it is still more the case with accounts based on psychoanalysis by S. Freud (*Moses and Monotheism*, 1939) or D. F. Zeligs (*Moses: a Psychodynamic Study*, 1986), or on political science by A. Wildavsky (*The Nursing Father: Moses as a Political Leader*, 1984). Any validity which such essays possess, as some of them indeed recognize, arises not from the recreation of the actual experience of one historical figure, but from the perception of the more all-embracing, fundamentally theological truth focussed on that figure.

2. The figure of Moses provides an example of the presentation of theological truth in concrete terms (cf. J. Neusner: '[the sages] prefer to talk about the acorn and the oak than potentiality and actuality'). Yahweh is the sole agent of deliverance; the entire narrative is an exposition of his Name, i.e. revealed nature, whether in event (Ex. 3.12,14f.; 33.19) or institution (especially Torah, Ex. 20.2; Deut. 5.6; cf. Ex. 34.6f.; Num. 14.18). It is only in his service that the human agent receives any significance, and then it is only reflected. This is dramatically portrayed by a number of incidents, for example:

– Moses' independent attempt, motivated by natural fellow-feeling, to vindicate his people's rights against the Egyptians and among themselves, ends only in humiliating flight (Ex. 2.11ff.);

– it was God who initiated the totally unexpected call at the burning bush (symbol according to, e.g., Philo,* Exodus Rabba and Calvin* of the presence of God [the angel/voice] amid the persecution [the burning] of his people [the bush, a contemptible – and combustible – bramble, according to LXX*], because of which they are not consumed, Ex. 3.1ff.);

– Moses' reluctance to respond, expressed through his four excuses (Ex. 3.11–4.17), is overcome by endowment with undreamed of capabilities, symbolized by the miraculous powers of his transformed staff: what had been his shepherd's staff now becomes God's rod (e.g. Ex. 4.20), with which the plagues are induced, the Red Sea is parted, water is smitten from the rock and Israel is preserved in battle against the Amalekites (Ex. 7–17);

– the focal point of the entire Pentateuch is God's self-revelation at Sinai (Ex. 19.1–Num. 10.10). Its centrality is indicated by the roughly symmetrical disposition of incidents on either side of it (Ex. 15.22–18.27; Num. 10.11–21.35). The supreme moment of this self-revelation is the direct address by God to the people in the Decalogue (Ex. 19f.; Deut. 5). Moses has no mediatorial role at this central point. But the authority of all subsequent revelation,* which is envisaged as the extended secondary exposition of the Decalogue, is indicated by its being communicated to Moses face to face by God in the cloud of glory which shrouds Mt Horeb/Sinai (Ex. 24.12ff.) and which descends to accompany Israel thereafter in the tent of meeting (Ex. 33; cf. 40; also the account of the radiance of Moses' face Ex. 34.29ff.). Moses' mediatorial role is heightened in order to emphasize the significance of what is mediated.

The other elements of Moses' role stem from this central concept that he is the mediator of the law revealed to him directly by God. He is mediator of the covenant (Ex. 24.3–8; 34), and, by virtue of God's direct communication with him, he is portrayed as the prophet* *par excellence* (cf. Deut. 18.15ff.). As intermediary he is uniquely placed to fulfil the role of intercessor (e.g. Ex. 32.30ff.). The priesthood is firmly subservient to him (e.g. Ex.4.16).

But throughout all these activities, it is God's power and purpose which remain supreme, with Moses firmly subordinated (cf. Moses' titles, 'servant of God' [Josh. 1], 'man of God' [Deut. 33.1]). At his death, he is buried by God himself; the site of the grave remains unknown. To turn the tomb of the mediator into a religious fetish or place of pilgrimage would be a mere distraction for a people en route under God towards the eschatological* promised land and, indeed, an infringement of God's sovereignty.

3. The subsequent use of the figure of Moses in the OT is at first sight surprisingly meagre for such an apparently dominant pentateuchal personage, but is consonant with the above view of his subordination to God's purpose. It is also compatible with the view that Moses is, in his present form, largely a Deuteronomic construct (in this regard cf. again Joshua and Samuel). In texts that are probably pre-exilic, he figures only in Hos. 12.13, where he is obliquely referred to as 'prophet'. This may be the growth point for the presentation in the Pentateuch noted above; the affiliation of Hosea to the 'levitical-prophetic opposition party', of which Deuteronomy is a product, has been proposed by H. W. Wolff. In the some 113 occurrences in exilic/post-exilic texts, mostly in the Deuteronomic History* and Chronicles, Moses appears typically in association with the law, now called in convenient shorthand 'the law/book of Moses'. His

role as intercessor is noted in Jer. 15.1 (cf. title of Ps. 90).

4. In post-biblical Judaism the figure of Moses is developed along a number of lines, e.g.:

(a) Moses becomes *Moshe Rabbenu* ('Moses our master/teacher'), understood as responsible not only for the compilation of the written Torah (though not perhaps for Deut. 34), but also for the reception and transmission of the Oral Law.

(b) In Alexandrian apologetics (Philo), Moses' heroic stature was stressed; he was a philosopher-king, who taught the Egyptians the arts of civilization.

(c) In the haggadah there was a similar endeavour to fill out the biblical picture: e.g. Moses ascends into the heavens; at his death God takes his soul with a kiss.

(d) In orthodox observance Moses' role remains firmly subordinated. He is not named in the Passover Haggadah; cf. his omission already in the biblical credo, e.g. Deut. 26.5ff.

5. Many of these emphases from its OT and Jewish background * recur in distinctive form in the NT presentation of Moses. On a crude statistical basis he is the most prominent figure of the OT mentioned in the NT (80 times; the next most significant are Abraham * [73], David * [58] and Elijah [30]).

(a) The frequent use of the post-exilic formulation 'the Law of Moses' presupposes Moses' instrumentality in the revelation of the Written Torah. The divine authority of the Law is, on occasion, acknowledged, either as such (e.g. Matt. 23.2f.; Luke 16.29ff.) or because it is interpreted as predictive of Christ (e.g. Luke 24.27; John 1.45; 5.46; so especially Deut. 18.15,18 in Acts 3.22f.; 7.37). Nonetheless, there is a certain ambivalence towards the Law: elements within it, and not only in the Oral Torah, are portrayed as human constructions (divorce [Mark 10.2–12], circumcision [John 7.22; cf. Acts 15.1–21]).

(b) Legendary * embellishment of the biblical Moses story is retained, e.g. Moses' mastery of Egyptian culture gained at the Pharaonic court (Acts 7.22), the names of two Egyptian magicians who confronted Moses (II Tim. 3.8), the struggle of Satan for the body of the dying Moses (Jude 9).

(c) There is a radical development in the subordination of Moses: he is used typologically * in a sharply contrastive manner to Jesus Christ in God's new act of salvation. The *qal wahomer* argument (*see* **Rabbi**) is in evidence. Examples are:

– Matthew is significantly patterned on the life of Moses (massacre of innocents, flight into Egypt, forty days' temptation, sermon on the mount,* etc.). At the transfiguration (17.1–8) Moses and Elijah, the two figures

associated with the old theophany at Sinai, appear on the new mountain; the voice from the new cloud of theophany designates Jesus not 'prophet', as Moses was, but 'son'.

– In John, Moses' serpent (3.14) and the manna (6.32) are used apologetically. The context of the controversy (Feast of Passover, 6.4) underlines the typology (cf. 5.1; 7.2; 9.14).

– In Acts 7.35ff. Moses is the prototype of the rejected prophet.

– In I Cor. 10.1–13 the pillar of cloud and the crossing of the sea become a type of baptism, while the old covenant * written in stone prefigures the new covenant in the Spirit (II Cor. 3).

– In Hebrews the contrast is between Moses as 'servant of God' and Christ as 'son' (ch. 3; cf. 10.28); Moses receives the *tupos* of the heavenly sanctuary now realized in Christ (8.5).

The epithet 'meek' applied to Moses in Num. 12.3, which at first sight seems so inappropriate, turns out in the end to be wholly apt. Meek, meaning 'submissive' to any human being, whether murderous Egyptian, bullying shepherds, crafty sages, or disdainful emperor-god, Moses emphatically was not. His submissiveness was exclusively towards God (e.g. Ex. 15), under whom he calmly bore the sibling rivalry of his brother and sister and the jealousy of his fellow-tribesmen. He was meek (ʿ*anaw*) in the sense that he shared the indignant outrage of his God who called him at the burning bush to be his agent, redeeming his people from their affliction (ʿ*o ni*), and because in solidarity with his people he shared that affliction. Therein he finds his honour in the gallery of exponents of faith (Heb. 11.23ff.).

See also **Exodus**.

———

M. Buber, *Moses*, 1946; G. W. Coats, *Moses: Heroic Man, Man of God, JSOT*-SS, 57, 1988; J. Jeremias, 'Moses', *TDNT* IV, ET 1967; D. S. Russell, *The OT Pseudepigrapha: Patriarchs and Prophets in Early Judaism*, 1987; D. J. Silver, *Images of Moses*, 1982; R. J. Thompson, *Moses and the Law in a Century of Criticism since Graf*, VT-*S* 19, 1970.

WILLIAM JOHNSTONE

Music, The Bible in

The marriage of music and the Bible has been one of the happiest and most fruitful. The Bible's poetic texts, pithy aphorisms and dramatic situations have inspired composers from earliest times (even if the reference to Jubal in Gen. 4.21 is not to be taken literally!) to the most highly acclaimed modern composers. Yet the union has not been without its difficulties, which largely stem from the inherent power and independence of music. While a theological work may bring intellectual light to a doctrine or an enigmatic passage, music has power to charge from within seemingly obvious texts and colour words and sentiments. For those to whom music speaks, which is apparently almost everybody, some biblical passages are now inseparable from their musical setting. Who can avoid reading such passages as 'Wonderful, Counsellor, the mighty God . . .' (Isa. 9.6), without consciously or unconsciously hearing Handel's *Messiah* (1742)? The understanding of passages has been moulded by the music, though on rational reflection it is not easy to say how. Music's 'meaning' is notoriously elusive but its power to change perceptions remains awkwardly transparent. So awkward, indeed, that the attitude of Christians to it has fluctuated in different ages from the warmly welcoming through the grudgingly tolerant to the violently hostile.

Music might never have been united with biblical texts, since some influential early Christians regarded it as too secular and too associated with the cultures they were trying to break away from; also too enjoyable. On many occasions they would have banned it but for its saturating presence in the Bible. David's* dancing and playing instruments before the Lord (II Sam. 6.3–14), or Solomon's celebrations after seven years of building the Temple (II Chron. 5.12–14) powerfully demonstrated the acceptability, even the desirability, of music in worship for praise and thanksgiving. The singing of psalms came to form the staple diet of private and Temple worship, and many of Jesus' sayings echo them. In Mark's account of the Last Supper, he mentions the participants' singing of the Hallel (Pss. 113–118) after the Passover meal. The expectation of deliverance and of a better world to come so common in the psalms also permeates the earliest NT hymns:* the Magnificat (Luke 1.46ff.), Benedictus (Luke 1.68ff.) and Nunc Dimittis (Luke 2.29ff.), though how much music played a part in the original versions of these is open to question. Paul* confirmed and endorsed the use of psalm-singing and music in public and private worship in his epistles* (Col. 3.16; Eph. 5.19), and in Revelation the elders worship with a 'new song' 'having every one of them harps' (Rev. 5.8–9). Yet, despite all this biblical evidence, some reluctant early Christians claimed liturgical music should be restrained and instruments banned, mirroring the Jewish renunciation of music in exile indicated in Ps. 137.

The attitude of early Christians to music was thankfully not uniform. Many welcomed it, allowing its psychological and cohesive power to permeate worship. Basil the Great (c. 330–c. 379) in his *Exegetic Homilies* wrote:

'The Holy Spirit mingled the delight of melody with doctrine so that by the pleasantness of the sounds we might receive the benefit of the words without perceiving it'; and elsewhere: 'a psalm forms friendships, unites those separated and conciliates enemies. Who can still consider him an enemy with whom he has uttered the same prayer? So psalmody through choral singing brings about a bond which joins people into harmonious unity and produces the greatest blessing, charity.' Basil also commented on the helpfulness of music as a mnemonic: sung texts remained longer with the faithful than those merely said. Similarly, Ambrose of Milan (c. 340?–397) and Hilary of Poitiers (c. 315–367) wrote hymns to inspire the faithful that simply expounded sound doctrines against the inimical teachings of the Arians, whose founder, Arius, had himself used hymns as a propaganda medium.

Augustine's* conversion by Ambrose in Milan profoundly affected his attitude to the use of the arts to enhance worship. He was sensitive to music, but in his *Confessions* also showed a troubled conscience about its use. Music, he said, is sweet when combined with scripture, which it can bring to life; but how can one ensure one is not being lured merely by musical delight, rather than the truth of the words? Could music not obscure rather than illuminate its text? Did it not just make palatable what should be striven for? Would it not be better to forego music, or restrain it so that it was no more elaborate than speech? Eventually he found for music: 'I am inclined to approve the custom of singing in church; by the pleasure of the ear the weaker minds may be raised to a feeling of devotion. Yet whenever . . . I am more moved by the singing than by what is sung, I admit I have sinned grievously, and . . . I should wish rather not to have heard the singing.'

The music by which Augustine was so moved is lost, as musical notation was not invented in the West until the ninth century. So we cannot know how it interpreted or coloured biblical texts, though the fact that it formed a major means of hearing and remembering them for more than the first thousand years of Christendom, and affected their perception, is not open to doubt.

Confronted by their congregations' illiteracy, early religious orders devised vivid means of conveying Christian truths other than reading, such as music and the visual arts.* The story of the passion* and resurrection* provided the basis of one of the earliest dramatic presentations. In the eleventh or twelfth centuries the introit for Easter Day ('Whom do you seek in the tomb?' 'Jesus of Nazareth, who was crucified') acquired additional words and music, and was performed dramatically using local chant repertoire or melodies based on it. From this grew other mediaeval* liturgical dramas, which were performed on major feast days and which instituted a new relationship between biblical stories and music. Noteworthy amongst the earliest dramatizations of the OT in the twelfth and thirteenth centuries were the *Play of Herod* and the *Play of Daniel*.

The passion story proved perennially attractive for dramatization, being central to Christian teaching and full of dramatic incident, pathos and opportunities for psychological exploration. Contemporary with the earliest mediaeval dramas, a practice of dividing the singing of the passion narrative* on Palm Sunday (Matthew) and Good Friday (John) between a narrator (*Evangelista*), Christ (*Vox Christi*) and the crowd (*turba*) emerged. Each part was musically distinct, and each was sung by a different priest. As polyphony (the simultaneous combination of several melodic lines) became established in the liturgy,* it came to be used in the settings of the passion story, with the crowd parts being treated like motets. The earliest surviving example of this is found in a late fifteenth-century manuscript in Modena, almost contemporary with a strikingly beautiful one by Richard Davy in the *Eton Choirbook* (c. 1490). In the sixteenth century, composers such as Palestrina (?1525–1594), Victoria (1548–1611), Lassus (1532–1594) and Byrd (1543–1623) all contributed versions.

Contemporary with these restrained, polyphonic settings, which dramatized rather than interpreted the biblical texts, emerged some more musically elaborate ones, which set the whole text in a motet-style, though the plainsong associated with the original texts was normally preserved in one of the parts (usually the tenor). In these settings composers found more freedom to underline crucial words and used richer harmonies to interpret significant texts. From Italy, these motet-passions spread throughout Europe, particularly to Germany.

Though motet-passions died out in the seventeenth century, their dramatic and expressive presentations paved the way for more operatic types of settings, which included choral and solo parts. These also combined biblical texts with non-biblical interpolations, allowing composers to reflect on the narrative and control the pace of the action as in opera, which, with its sister form, oratorio, provided the initial impetus for the whole genre. Thomas Selle's (1599–1663) *St John Passion* (1643) was the first such passion setting, but its greatest expression was found in the next century in the two Passions of Johann Sebastian Bach (1685–1750), after the biblical texts had been greatly added to by poets such

as Heinrich Brockes (1680–1747). The final version of Bach's *St Matthew Passion* (first version [lost] 1729, current version 1736ff.) is the summa of the genre. Its two ensembles of chorus, soloists and orchestra represent Christ's contemporaries (ensemble one) and Christianity at large (ensemble two). Bach attempted dramatically to illustrate the universal significance of the story. For instance, at the Last Supper, Jesus' prophecy of his forthcoming betrayal by a disciple and each disciple's subsequent inquiry about himself ('Herr, bin ichs') is sung and played by the first choir. The following chorale ('Ich bins, ich sollte büssen', 'Tis I, I should atone') is performed by both first and second ensembles: disciples and Christendom. Judas' betrayal symbolizes Christianity's perpetual betrayal; atonement is needed now as then. Elsewhere, Bach added further layers of interpretation by including French tombeaux (i.e. instrumental pieces commemorating someone's death) for more personal scenes alongside extrovert Italian styles and populist chorales.

Bach's vision of the passion story has not been matched. His own generation preferred the elegant pathos of Carl Heinrich Graun's (1701–1759) *Der Tod Jesu* (1755) or the 46 passions of Georg Philipp Telemann (1681–1767). In the nineteenth century, Louis Spohr's (1784–1859) *Des Heilands letzte Stunden* (1835) began a new line of chromatically sentimental, though occasionally not unmoving, passion oratorios, that were particularly favoured by Victorian England; an example is the perennially popular *Crucifixion* (1887) by John Stainer (1840–1901).

Twentieth-century composers have found in the passion story a mirror of the century's agony. Some have returned to liturgy-inspired restraint, as Hugo Distler (1908–1942) in his *Choralpassion* (1933); or, in an evocative minimalist way, as Arvo Pärt (b. 1935) in his *St John Passion* (1981). Others have explored the dramatic and tragic elements, as Krzysztof Penderecki (b. 1933) in his *St Luke Passion* (1963–5).

Bach's Passions are essentially oratorios. Oratorios originated in the use by the Oratorians (founded in Rome by Philip Neri [1515–1595]) of simple, non-liturgical music to aid spiritual exercises. Music became so important in their meetings that it became ever more elaborate. Eventually a new genre emerged, indebted to opera and cantata, which consisted of dramatic presentations of biblical stories with solos, choruses and other music. Unashamedly vivid, oratorios quickly caught on, finding an early master in Giacomo Carissimi (1605–1674). His larger oratorios use OT texts, treating them like operatic libretti. The portrayal of the storm in *Jonas* or the agony of Jephthah over his daughter's fate in *Jephte* (before 1650) are especially expressive. Their appealing realism set the pattern for Baroque oratorios, which concretized and explored powerful scenes and emotions.

The Baroque oratorio reached its zenith in the English oratorios of George Frideric Handel (1685–1750). They transferred to the imagination what had been portrayed on the stage, and used biblical stories as allegories* of modern life. For instance, *Judas Maccabaeus* (1746), an apocryphal* hero who saved his country from conquest, was identified with the Duke of Cumberland who had driven Bonnie Prince Charlie's Scotsmen back to Culloden in 1745, and, according to London's point of view, saved the day. More personally, Handel was working on his *Jephthah* in 1751 when his sight failed as he reached the chorus 'How dark, O Lord, are thy decrees!' Handel invested his *Jephthah* with more tragic inevitability than Carissimi. Handel's oratorios represent a Georgian vision of the world at a time of relative prosperity. Their darker moments are nearly all private; their public utterances are usually phrased in a generalized language of optimism.

Handel's musical interpretation of the Bible spread in the eighteenth and permeated the nineteenth century, especially in England. Mendelssohn (1809–1847), for instance, despite his rehabilitation of Bach's *St Matthew Passion*, and the obvious acknowledgment of this in the chorales and fugues of his *St Paul* (1836), in his *Elijah* (1846) owed more to Handel than to Bach. But its mood is different, being overall more introverted, its most powerful music focussing on Elijah's doubts. Elijah's circumstances closely mirrored Mendelssohn's own experience, and the work is thinly disguised autobiography; much more so than Handel's *Jephthah*, and more typically of early nineteenth-century composers' approach to biblical texts.

Later in the nineteenth century, oratorios moved from Handel to the more continuous style of Wagner's operas. Good English examples are Elgar's *The Apostles* (1903) and *The Kingdom* (1906), part of an uncompleted NT trilogy. Elgar's interpretation of the NT typically explored 'bad' characters, such as Judas Iscariot, more penetratingly than 'good' characters or scenes. The NT provided him, like others, with a pretext for psychological study rather than traditional theological exposition. This is also true of a musically dissimilar work, Schoenberg's (1874–1951) opera *Moses und Aron* (1930–2). Later, William Walton's (1902–1983) *Belshazzar's Feast* (1930–1) relished the opportunities offered by biblical texts for drama and celebration in a new, less psychologically complicated way.

Benjamin Britten's (1913–1976) opera, *Noye's Fludde* (1957), and church parables are much indebted to mediaeval liturgical drama and have brought fresh insights to musico-biblical interpretation.

Some biblical passages have been set thousands of times; and each setting offers an interpretation. Probably the most set texts are the psalms in the OT and the Magnificat and Nunc Dimittis in the NT, owing to their use in liturgy.

Self-consciously individual interpretations of biblical texts in the main date originally from the late sixteenth century, when the musical interpretation of texts came to be scrutinized by the Reformation* and counter-Reformation. Composers generally felt safer pouring their more expressive ideas into non-dogmatic texts. Palestrina, for instance, whose settings of the Mass established an interpretative norm, tentatively explored more emotive harmonies in motets such as *Super flumina Babylonis* (Ps. 137). His contemporaries went further. The extravagantly poignant settings by Victoria and Gesualdo (1560–1613) of *O vos omnes* (Lam. 1.2) voiced a personal, even public, anguish not unexpected from their strife-ridden, transient world. Similar plangency can be found in some contemporary English anthems, two striking examples being in the settings of David's Lament over Absalom (II Sam. 18.33) by Weelkes (?1575–1623) and Tomkins (1572–1665).

The seventeenth century provided much opportunity for composers to observe grief, carnage and war, which not surprisingly found its way into their biblical settings, armed as they now were with new styles derived from the personalized expressions of opera. Lully's Carissimi-inspired setting of *Psalm 51*, at which the first audience wept in 1664, or Schütz's dramatic account of the conversion of St Paul (*Saul, Saul, was verfolgst du mich?*) (1650) written at the end of the Thirty Years' War, or Henry Purcell's *Jehova, quam multi sunt hostes* (Ps. 3) (*c.* 1680) movingly identified contemporary suffering with biblical. On grander and more optimistic occasions, of course, composers employed other styles, which though musically deft often show merely a well-crafted public face.

The eighteenth century, especially the latter half, expressed personal grief less overtly than the seventeenth century. Comparing Maurice Greene's (1696–1755) wistful *Lord let me know mine end* (Ps. 39) with Purcell's Funeral Music for Queen Mary, or Gluck's setting of Psalm 130 with Schütz's, well illustrates their theologically different understandings of the Bible. Of course, there are exceptions, such as some Bach cantatas, but these exceptions prove the rule.

The nineteenth century elevated the artist, valued personal insights and prized music. The plethora of small-scale and/or liturgical biblical settings stretches from Mendelssohn's austere Berlin Psalm settings (e.g. Ps. 22 [1844]), through Bruckner's intense motets (e.g. *Locus Iste* [1869] and *Os justi* [1879] [Ps. 37]) to the more cloying chromaticism of English anthems, such as Stainer's *I saw the Lord* (Isa. 6), or Franck's (1822–1890) psalm-settings or Verdi's (1813–1901) *Four Sacred Pieces*. Much liturgical music in some measure harked back to older styles. Composers seem to have wanted, through a mixture of old-fashioned counterpoint and modern harmonies, used deliberately evocatively and self-consciously sincerely, to convey a traditionalist Christian view, as contemporary theology was in turmoil. Music seldom voiced doubts, since doubting composers seldom wanted or needed to set biblical passages. An exception was Brahms (1833–1897), who in his *Ein Deutsches Requiem* (1857–68), prompted by his mother's death, wrote an agnostic's meditation on words freely selected from the Bible. Its resigned tone contrasts with the traditional terror of Requiem settings by Verdi and others. Late in life Brahms returned to the Bible in his *Vier ernste Gesänge* (1896), taking passages from Ecclesiastes and I Corinthians for personal appropriateness rather than Christian revelation.

The tendency of many nineteenth-century biblical settings to echo earlier musical styles was enhanced by the rediscovery at the end of the century of plainsong and Renaissance contrapuntal music. Many composers retreated from modernism to deliberate archaism and emotional restraint, perhaps to differentiate religious music and its interpretation from the growing emotionalism of non-religious music.

The twentieth century has been as confusing as the nineteenth. The use of early styles and pseudo-Renaissance counterpoint has often led to an evocative nostalgia in biblical settings. Vaughan Williams' (1872–1958) biblical works, for instance, are more English than Christian; their use of the Bible more literary than theological. The arcane beauty of many of his settings, like the more luxuriant anthems and settings of composers such as Herbert Howells (1892–1983), celebrated more the cathedrals, choirs or occasions for which they were written than any theology.

Stravinsky's (1882–1971) *Symphony of Psalms* (1930), on the other hand, though indebted to Russian orthodox liturgy, is austerely unemotional, and broke new ground in its interpretation of biblical texts, especially in the understated setting of Ps. 150.

The Bible continues to be set by composers and to inspire them, though new translations*

seem to be less favoured than the King James Version or its continental equivalents. Religious music is significantly less important in the output of most composers than secular; and no major recent composers have put their principal ideas exclusively or primarily into religious works or biblical settings.

Finally, it must be noted that in many minds the Bible's primary association with music has not been in elaborate compositions, but in the more functional hymns and psalms of congregational worship. It is not easy to say whether a tune written for a metrical psalm or biblical paraphrase (e.g. *All people that on earth do dwell* [Ps. 100] in the Genevan Psalter [1551] or Luther's *Ein' Feste Burg*) interprets the words, but the long marriage of the words and music has in many cases formed so strong a bond that congregations find them inseparable and they have passed from liturgical function to common heritage.

See also **Hymnody; Hymns, New Testament; Liturgy, Use of the Bible in; Psalms.**

Peter le Huray, *Music and the Reformation in England*, 1967; Carl H. Kraeling, 'Music in the Bible' in *New Oxford History of Music*, vol. 1, ed. Egon Wellesz, 1957; B. Rainbow, *The Choral Revival in the Anglican Church*, 1970; Erik Routley, *Twentieth Century Church Music*, 1964; Basil Smallman, *The Background of Passion Music*, 1957, 1970.

RODERICK SWANSTON

Muslim Interpretation

Within itself, the Qur'ān (or Koran) provides Muslims with a view of the Bible. Mention is made of the 'scrolls' of Abraham* and Moses,* the Tawrah (Torah) of Moses, the Zabūr (usually understood as the Psalms) of David* and the Injīl (Gospel) of Jesus, all conceived as direct revelation* from God to the prophet concerned: 'Surely We sent down the Torah, wherein is guidance and light' (Qur'ān 5.48). 'And We sent, following in their footsteps, Jesus son of Mary, confirming the Torah before him; and We gave to him the Gospel, wherein is guidance and light' (Qur'ān 5.50). Muslim scripture is seen to be a confirmation of these earlier revelations; it also serves to make disputed matters clear: 'We have sent down to thee the Remembrance [i.e. the Qur'ān] that thou mayest make clear to mankind what was sent down to them' (Qur'ān 16.46). Additionally, the Qur'ān serves a correcting function: humans have misinterpreted and tampered with the words of Moses and Jesus especially; people have been 'perverting words from their meanings' (Qur'ān 5.45). The Qur'ān thus presents an uncorrupted version of the word of God.*

The Qur'ān retells stories found in the Bible

in a recognizable form but the accounts are always shorn of their overall biblical narrative context. Frequently the stories are truncated to such an extent that reference to the biblical tradition is necessary in order to make sense of the narrative elements provided in the Qur'ān. Some of the stories are clearly influenced by the exegetical* tradition within Judaism and, to a lesser extent, Christianity. The exact source of the stories – variously suggested to be Arabian Jews or Christians, Samaritans,* remnants of the Qumran community, Jewish–Christian* groups and so forth – remains a matter of debate but a great deal of emphasis in contemporary research falls on the oral* nature of the transmission of the biblical material into the Arabic context in accounting for the form and the content of the narrative.

Scholarship has not, as yet, paid much attention to the actual issue of the interpretation of the Bible from within the Qur'ānic perspective. Of far greater concern up to this point has been the attempt to establish the sources of the basic information itself. A few generalities may be suggested, however. It is clear that the biblical stories are cited not for their narrative or historical significance but for their spiritual and moral guidance, most especially in emphasizing the notion of God's determination of, and involvement in, history. The constant suggestion in the citation of the stories of the prophets of the past, for example (starting with Adam* and mentioning Noah, Isaac, Ishmael, Lot, Aaron, Ezra, Zechariah, John the Baptist* and so on), is that God has sent messengers in the past with his message but the people have rejected both the message and the messengers. As a result, punishment has come down upon each community and God has thereby triumphed in the end. This stylized narrative plot line is illustrated by isolated episodes or single details from the lives of individual prophets, stories which are familiar from the biblical tradition as a whole. Muḥammad's own career is frequently pictured in terms of this plot.

Combined with this constant narrative element in the Qur'ān is a reworking of the Abrahamic tradition in the light of Muḥammad. Abraham* becomes the pivotal figure in the Qur'ānic picture of salvation history, seen as living before the Judaism of Moses* and the Christianity of Jesus. This is the true faith, ḥanīfiyya, which Muḥammad revives in Mecca, where Abraham had established the shrine known as the Kaʿba to the glory of God. The sense in which the Qur'ān 'reworks' this biblical material is limited, however; for the most part, the Qur'ānic position on Abraham is assumed or hinted at, rather than explicitly detailed and demonstrated on the basis of proof texts* or the like.

Because of the truncated and referential style in the Qur'ānic citation of biblical material which presupposed knowledge on the part of its audience of the actual details of the narratives, the emergent Muslim community was faced with the problem of how to understand its own scripture once the original Judaeo-Christian environment was left behind and Islam was established as the religion of the newly formed and widespread Arab empire. On the evidence of extant literary sources, this matter became problematic some 150 years after the death of Muḥammad. At this time, we see the emergence of *tafsīr*: written works providing interpretation of the Qur'ān and thus, given the content of the scriptural text itself, providing a view of Muslim interpretation of the Bible.

One of the earliest such works still extant is that ascribed to Muqātil ibn Sulaymān (d. 767), which clearly displays the way in which biblical materials were interpreted and incorporated into the Muslim tradition in order to complete and supplement the bare bones of the Bible as presented in the Qur'ān. The interpretation of the biblical text is generally left on the level of providing the narrative elements which were needed to embellish the Qur'ān text; certainly the Bible never becomes of relevance to legal issues within the Muslim community itself, nor, generally, for any theological judgments.

Many early Muslim writers, including such people as al-Jāḥiẓ (d. 869) and Ibn Qutayba (d. 889), display a certain measure of acquaintance with the actual text of the Bible itself; modern scholarship has shown a good deal of interest in this aspect of these people's works. One of the purposes of citing the Bible as these authors did seems to have been to provide a check on the more imaginative embellishments which were being made in the interpretation of the Qur'ān in general and which were often claimed to stem from the Bible or Jewish and Christian sources. These exegetical excesses, at times, went to the extent of creating wholly spurious texts going under the name of Tawrah or Zabūr, examples of which still exist.

The tendency to incorporate biblical materials into the Islamic tradition, and to Islamicize them in doing so, sees its ultimate manifestation in the genre of literature known as the *qiṣaṣ al-anbiyā'*, the 'stories of the prophets'. These tales, several of which are available in whole or in part in English translation, display the end result of the exegetical process: a history of the prophets* of the past, recounted in an order which for the most part accepts the biblical chronology,* focussed upon passages of the Qur'ān supplemented by the biblical and most especially biblical-exegetical tradition. Much of this material has become known (pejoratively) as the *isrā'īliyāt*, stories supposedly transmitted in the Islamic world by Jewish (and Christian) converts. Frequently viewed with suspicion by Muslims, the material has provided the basis for the legendary expansion of the picture of the past prophets, but it is always filtered through a Muslim perspective: characteristics of the Islamic conception of prophets, for example their sinlessness, mould every image; the Arabian context becomes the focal point of many stories; the stories themselves must always agree with the Qur'ānic version of the events. Overall, it may be said that the point of all these *qiṣaṣ al-anbiyā'* books is to demonstrate the continuity of the prophets from the time of Adam down to Muḥammad. In the recounting of the lives of the prophets, there is certainly a tendency to avoid any Christian symbolic prefigurements in the events of the 'Old Testament'. Likewise, there is no emphasis on Israel as a land and Judaism's connection to it. The stories are retold, once again, for their value in enhancing the spiritual and moral guidance implicit in the Qur'ān itself. Their function is always to interpret the Qur'ān.

The end result of this writing down of the interpretational process – as embodied in the *tafsīr* works, the spurious Bibles and the *qiṣaṣ al-anbiyā'* genre – was that it was never necessary for Muslims to consult the Bible itself or to write commentaries * upon it, for the necessary material had early on been incorporated into the Muslim exegetical literature.

There was one specific issue, however, which caused the Muslims to look at the Bible itself and provide a more self-conscious biblical interpretation. The Qur'ān suggests that Muḥammad was spoken of in the Bible ('. . . the Messenger, the Prophet of the common folk, whom they find written down with them in the Torah and the Gospel', Qur'ān 7.156). The notion arose in Islam, certainly with some support from the Qur'ān itself, that these references had been removed or hidden by the Jews (rarely are the Christians attacked in this manner): 'Why do you confound the truth with vanity, and conceal the truth and that wittingly?' says Qur'ān 3.64. This alteration of the text of scripture was denoted by the term *taḥrīf*. Despite what would seem to be the consequence of this stance – that there would thus be no references to Muḥammad found in the Bible – Muslims were in fact quick to identify any evidence of 'fulfilment' of earlier scripture that could be proclaimed by the coming of Muḥammad. The stimulus for this was undoubtedly Christian polemical pressure to provide proof of the validity of Islam. The earliest apologetic treatises – which

are some of the earliest pieces of Islamic literature available – speak at some length about the biblical passages which refer to Muḥammad. The most famous of these, *The Book of Religion and Empire* written by ʿAlī al-Ṭabarī probably in the mid-ninth century, details a large number of passages from both Jewish and Christian scriptures which are interpreted in the light of Muḥammad. Prominent passages and ones which recur throughout this type of literature down to the modern day include Gen. 17.20, 'I have heard your prayer for Ishmael. I have blessed him and made him fruitful. I will multiply his descendants; he shall be a father of twelve princes and I will raise a great nation from him.' The 'nation' was, of course, understood to be the Arabs to whom no greater promise God ever made, according to the author; Deut. 18.15, 'The Lord your God will raise up a prophet from among you like myself' and similarly in verse 18, interpreted to be a reference to Muḥammad rather than any of the other prophets or Jesus, none of whom, it is suggested, are actually 'from among you like myself'; Deut. 33.2, with its mention of Mount Paran, identified as 'the land which Ishmael inhabited', frequently further glossed (in the light of the Qur'ān) as Mecca; and John 14.26, 'but your Advocate [Paraclete], the Holy Spirit whom the Father will send in my name, will teach you everything', glossed as Muḥammad, often connected to Qur'ān 61.6 with its reference to Jesus designating 'Aḥmad' as the one to come after him.

This tendency to find Muḥammad in the Bible, despite its rather obvious apologetic nature, remains a popular topic in contemporary Muslim circles. This is evidenced not only by the recent editing of a series of mediaeval texts dealing with the topic but also by works from the Muslim world in Arabic and from elsewhere in, for example, English and French. All are really no more than continuations of mediaeval polemic. A widely circulated pamphlet by the South African Ahmed Deedat entitled *What the Bible says about Muḥammad (Peace be upon him)* uses Deut. 18.18 as its major discussion point: the prophet 'most like' Moses here is Muḥammad, not because of issues of descent as in ʿAlī al-Ṭabarī, but because of such similarities as Moses and Muḥammad having a mother and father and Jesus not; Jesus having a miraculous birth and the other two not; Jesus not marrying as compared to the others, and so on. Emphasis also falls on the latter part of the biblical verse, 'I will put my words into his mouth,' as a reference to the mode of revelation of the Qur'ān to the illiterate Muḥammad.

Another aspect of this polemical debate is found in attacks on the Bible and its veracity.

Ibn Ḥazm (d. 1064), for example, while responding to supposed Jewish attacks on the Qur'ān, retaliates with a collection of attacks on the Bible. Muslim apologists pointed to instances of immorality in the biblical text, logical inconsistencies, absent doctrines (e.g. life after death in the Torah) and anthropomorphisms * as evidence of the corrupt character of the scripture. Many of the characteristics that are seized upon by Ibn Ḥazm are precisely those which Christians especially had cast at Muslims in attacks on the latter's own scripture.

The modern world has produced other areas of thought in which the Bible is contemplated by Muslims; all such situations are tinged by polemic and apologetics. Social organization, family structure and science are some of the issues in which the attitude of the Qur'ān and the Bible are compared. Most famous in this regard is certainly Maurice Bucaille, *The Bible, the Qur'an and Science*. Abū'l-Aʿlā al-Mawdūdī (1903–79), a prominent Pakistani religious and political leader, also uses the text of the Bible in his commentary on the Qur'ān. The purpose is not only to provide explanations of various items in the Muslim scripture but also to illustrate the errors of the Bible and the greater reliability of the Qur'-ānic text; the criterion used to determine this, it is always asserted, is that where the Bible and the Qur'ān agree, the Bible is right; where the two disagree, the Bible is wrong.

One of the few attempts made by a Muslim to write a commentary on the actual text of the Bible itself was that by Sayyid Aḥmad Khān (d. 1898). Called *The Mohomedan Commentary on the Holy Bible*, it was published in 1862 and 1865. Two parts, the first being the 'Preliminary Discourse' (covering the history of the biblical text and questions of dogma) and the second (covering Gen. 1–11) were published in Urdu with English summaries. A portion covering Matt. 1–5 along with a short history of Christianity was apparently prepared at the same time but was not published until 1887 and is available in Urdu only. Aḥmad Khān's general attitude is that the Bible should have a positive role in Muslim life as long as it is read in the light of the Qur'ānic message, so that any distortions which have occurred as a result of Jewish and Christian misinterpretation (the only extent to which he considers *taḥrīf* to have occurred) can be corrected. His work is remarkably free of polemic and is aimed at bringing about a common understanding and inspiration through revealed scripture within the Judaeo-Christian-Muslim tradition.

See also **Other Faiths.**

Translations from the Qur'ān are from A. J. Arberry, *The Koran Interpreted*, 1955.

William M. Brinner, Stephen J. Ricks (eds), *Studies in Islamic and Judaic Traditions*, Brown Judaic Studies 110, 1986; Harry Gaylord Dorman Jr, *Towards understanding Islam*, 1948; Andrew Rippin (ed.), *Approaches to the History of the Interpretation of the Qur'ān*, 1988; Haim Schwarzbaum, *Biblical and extra-biblical legends in Islamic folk-literature*, 1982 (with bibliography); John Wansbrough, *Quranic Studies*, 1977.

The journal *IslamoChristiana* contains a large number of articles and an extensive bibliography on Muslim-Christian relations, covering *inter alia* biblical interpretation.

ANDREW RIPPIN

Mystery Cults

A major chapter in the history of NT interpretation in the nineteenth and twentieth centuries concerns the relationship between early Christianity and the Hellenistic * mystery cults. This has been part of a much larger inquiry into the extent of the indebtedness of the beliefs and practices of the first Christians to their historical and cultural milieu.

Study of the mystery cults was brought into prominence by the so-called History of Religions school * of historiography, which was characterized by an all-inclusive comparative methodology * that sought to explain the beliefs and rituals of one religion by drawing upon analogies or 'parallels' in another. With respect to the comparison of early Christianity and the mysteries, this kind of study was able to take advantage, not only of the well-known literary references to the mysteries in the classical and patristic sources, but also of a massive amount of non-literary information being thrown up by archaeology * and epigraphy.*

Although it is not possible to give a unitary definition or description of the mystery cults, many of them share the following characteristics. 1. They were open only to initiates who had to undergo some form of ritual purification to gain access. The most famous witness is Apuleius' account of his initiation into the Isis cult, in *The Golden Ass*, 11. 2. They involved cultic rites and the sharing of secret, esoteric knowledge which bound initiates together and brought them into communion with a god or goddess. 3. In certain cults, devotees were promised immortality. They also experienced mystical rebirth through ecstatic participation in liturgies and rituals which portrayed the triumphant destiny of their saviour-god, so assuring devotees of escape from the baneful influences of the heavenly powers. 4. Mystery religion was primarily personal religion. Participation was voluntary, access was on an individual (or sometimes familial) basis and membership often involved the observance of ethical obligations. 5. Many of the cults (Isis, Cybele, Mithras, the Cabeiri, for example) were of oriental provenance. Their foundation myths* were indebted to the changing of the seasons and the vegetation cycle. The cults therefore offered a different kind of religious experience from that of more formal, civic religion and co-existed uneasily alongside it.

It was in these oriental mystery cults that many scholars, at the turn of the twentieth century, sought to find the explanation for the evolution of Christianity from a Jewish messianic* sect in Palestine to a Hellenistic religion able subsequently to displace paganism altogether. More specifically, it became common to focus on Paul* as a second founder of Christianity who, under the influence of mystery beliefs about dying-and-rising saviour gods and the practice in the cults of ritual lustrations and sacred meals with the gods, transformed the simple preaching of Jesus the Galilean into a religion on the way towards thorough Hellenization and institutionalization. Most illustrious among the proponents of this kind of interpretation were Richard Reitzenstein (1861–1931), Wilhelm Bousset (1865–1931) and Alfred Loisy (1857–1940).

The debate about the indebtedness or otherwise of early Christianity to pagan religion generally and to the mystery cults in particular has attracted enormous scholarly attention. This is true even of specific aspects of the question, as G. Wagner has shown in his definitive study of history-of-religions 'parallels' to Paul's doctrine of baptism in Rom. 6.1–11, entitled *Pauline Baptism and the Pagan Mysteries* (ET 1967). The range of views extends from those who argue that only a minimum of pagan influence can be detected, to those who argue that the mysteries provide a major clue to the interpretation of the early church's doctrines (notably christology* and soteriology) and rituals (especially baptism and the eucharist). The debate is in progress still. In relation to soteriology, for example, a recent study by A. J. M. Wedderburn (1987) emphasizes how weak is the evidence for the widespread assumption that the rites of the mystery cults involved sharing in the fate of a dying-and-rising deity and, consequently, that the roots of Paul's baptismal theology are to be sought elsewhere.

If nothing else, the vigorous controversies over whether or not early Christianity is best interpreted as one of many ancient oriental mystery religions has sharpened considerably descriptions of Christianity from the historical perspective. The following points are noteworthy.

1. There is much greater caution in the evaluation of historical 'parallels'. Not only is it necessary to draw distinctions within early Christianity and between pre- and post-Constantinian Christianity; it is also necessary to differentiate one mystery cult from another and to take seriously the implications of such variables as the dating of the evidence for the mysteries. It is acknowledged now that very few literary, archaeological* and epigraphic* sources for the mysteries can be dated before the mid-second century AD and that, in the case of certain aspects of ritual (e.g. the efficacy attributed to the *taurobolium* in the cult of Cybele) the influence may have been from Christianity to the mysteries. In any case, it is important, as Adolf Deissmann pointed out, to distinguish parallels of an analogical kind from parallels which are more evidently genealogical, involving dependence or borrowing.

2. The History of Religious school tended to pay insufficient attention to the differences between early Christianity and the mystery cults. For a start, it is debatable whether the category 'religion', defined in terms of cultic worship, is applicable to the gatherings of the Christian believers described in the NT. Related to this is the crucial linguistic observation of A. D. Nock that the common terminology of the mystery religions is conspicuously absent from the NT: 'Any idea that what we call the Christian sacraments were in their origin indebted to pagan mysteries or even to the metaphorical concepts based upon them shatters on the rock of linguistic evidence' (Nock, 1972, II, p. 809). Even the important word *mustērion*, which occurs some twenty-eight times in the NT, has a thoroughly semitic background and requires no elucidation from the pagan cults, as R. E. Brown has shown.

There are other important differences as well. The secrecy laid as an obligation upon members of the mysteries – a secrecy which makes the identification of 'parallels' even more difficult – contrasts with the relative openness of the Christian meetings (cf. I Cor. 14.23–25). The dominance of mythological modes of thought in the cults contrasts with the focus in early Christian faith on its roots in history and in the crucifixion and resurrection* of Jesus of Nazareth in particular. Still further, the syncretistic proclivities of the mystery cults contrast with the particularity and singularity of early Christianity expressed in a sometimes tenacious non-conformity with ancestral custom. The comparative approach has failed often to give sufficient recognition to the *sui generis* aspects of early Christianity, to its almost sectarian resistance to influences from paganism, and to its capacity for innovation within its own boundaries.

3. Where historical dependence is to be sought for the beliefs and practices of the early church, then the overwhelming consensus of more recent scholarship points

towards Judaism in its various forms at the beginning of the Common Era (*see* **Jewish Background to the New Testament**). In confirmation of Albert Schweitzer's* suggestion, the teachings of both Jesus and Paul have been illuminated most strongly against a background in Jewish apocalyptic,* itself rooted in clearly discernible patterns of biblical exegesis. Paul the Hellenizer of the gospel has been replaced by Paul the Christian apocalypticist. The roots of the eucharist are to be sought in Judaism (the Passover being an obvious starting-point), and in the table-fellowship and Last Supper of Jesus, rather than in what little is known about communal meals in the mysteries. Similarly, the antecedents of Christian baptism lie more plausibly in OT flood imagery, Jewish proselyte baptism and the practice of John the Baptist* than in the initiatory rituals of the cults. In general, then, it may be said that the appeal to outsiders of the preaching and common life of the early Christians lay more in what distinguished them from their competitors than in what made them comparable.

R. E. Brown, *The Semitic Background of the Term 'Mystery' in the New Testament*, 1968; J. Ferguson, *The Religions of the Roman Empire*, 1970; B. Metzger, 'Methodology in the Study of the Mystery Religions and Early Christianity' in *Historical and Literary Studies*, 1968, pp. 1–24; A. D. Nock, *Essays on Religion and the Ancient World*, Vols I–II, ed. Zeph Stewart, 1972, esp. chs 5, 17, 47; R. Reitzenstein, *Hellenistic Mystery-Religions: Their Basic Ideas and Significance*, ET 1978; M. Simon, 'The *Religionsgeschichtliche Schule*, Fifty Years Later', *RS* 11, 1975, pp. 135–44; A. J. M. Wedderburn, 'The Soteriology of the Mysteries and Pauline Baptismal Theology', *NT* XXIX, 1987, pp. 53–72.

STEPHEN C. BARTON

Mysticism

Among the earliest uses of the word 'mystical' (*mustikos*), meaning hidden or not to be spoken, from which the term and concept 'mysticism' derives, is that use which applies it to the Bible and its interpretation. The mystical sense of scripture is a hidden or deeper meaning, only open to those who have made progress in their Christian life. It is parallel to the mystical sense of sacramental rites of the church (indeed as the Greek *mustērion* is translated in Latin as *sacramentum*, mystical is the equivalent of sacramental). The sense of 'mystical experience' as a peculiarly intense, individual religious experience (its modern use) is comparatively rare in the early centuries of Christianity, and derivative from the use of 'mystical' applied to scripture and the

liturgy.* So for instance the writings of Denys the Areopagite (the so-called Pseudo-Dionysius) have often been taken as accounts of mystical experience: in reality their constant focus is the deeper meaning of the liturgical rites and of the scriptures that are used in their celebration. 'Mystical experience' here can only mean a deeper grasp of the meaning of scripture and a deeper experience of the liturgy. This 'deeper' experience is an experience that penetrates beyond symbols* and language to become an encounter with the One who speaks in the scriptures, the One who is present in the liturgy, Christ himself.

Central, then, to the use of scripture in the mystical tradition is the conviction that to understand scripture is to come to an encounter with Christ who speaks in the scriptures. In the monastic tradition especially there develops the idea of a slow meditative reading of scripture in which the soul (or the heart) is awakened to God's love for it and its love enkindled by this growing realization. Cassian, and following him Gregory the Great, see the reading of scripture as a way in which God finds a path to the heart of the individual and awakens in it a sense of its sin (compunction) and of his love for it. Cassian sees the psalms as especially apt for this purpose. As this encounter between God and the soul is an encounter of love, mystical writers are fond of exploring their understanding of the soul's search for God (and God's search for the soul) through commenting on the Song of Songs. Later ideas of meditation, seen as a technique whereby the individual, by the use of his imagination, recreates a biblical scene, his place in it and its meaning for him, as a way of arousing his emotion and stirring his will towards the love of God – a technique that reaches its apogee in Ignatius Loyola's *Spiritual Exercises* – these ideas are a development of the monastic 'reading and considering' (*lectio* and *tractatio* or *meditatio*). It is a development, however, that can detach the individual experience of scripture from the liturgy and the life of the church (in a way that *lectio divina* did not), and also leads to other problems.

These problems lie at the root of much Christian mistrust of mysticism as such. The idea of meditation just mentioned suggests a distinction from contemplation: meditation is simply an application of human effort, in contrast to contemplation which is the result of God's action (is 'infused') and is a wordless communion with God in which human activity is suspended. On such a view, scripture seems to be confined to a relatively rudimentary stage of the spiritual life, to be bypassed in the real mystical life, the life of contemplation. These suspicions of mysticism can be generalized: in so far as the mystical tradition in Christianity is deeply indebted to Platonism, must it not inevitably take over the mistrust of Platonism for the particular and contingent? Is it not an attempt to transcend the particular and local in favour of the universal and eternal? Is not the mystic bound to use scripture as no more than a starting-point which he passes beyond, a kind of launching-pad (and indeed is not the historical Incarnate Christ treated in the same way)? Is not the choice of scripture eccentric anyway (the fondness for the Song of Songs)?

These are serious questions, but several points can be made. First, the traditional understanding of the mystical sense of scripture as an *encounter* with the One who speaks there suggests a different estimate of scripture from modern ideas of meditation and contemplation: scripture is not bypassed, it is itself the place of the encounter between the soul and Christ. Further, any tradition of interpretation evolves a 'canon within a canon': it is not clear why the Song of Songs plus the Fourth Gospel is any more (or less) arbitrary than the favoured position Luther* gave to Romans and Galatians. Also, the traditional 'mystical' understanding of scripture (which has never completely died out) is at least not as individualistic as later understandings of meditation seem to be: the One encountered in scripture is the one encountered in the liturgy (compare the idea of the 'two tables' – the altar and the scriptures – found in *The Imitation of Christ* and earlier in David of Augsburg).

In another way the mystical tradition might seem to supplement (or even displace) the Bible, with special visions and revelations, but apart from the fact that such revelations are clad in biblical imagery and thus seem to beg validation from the scriptures, the mystical tradition itself manifests considerable wariness of them and contains decisive assertions of the sufficiency of scripture (see, e.g. John of the Cross, *Ascent*, II.22).

The constant emphasis of the mystical tradition in relation to scripture is that the voice of the One who speaks there needs to be heard personally, and that the heart of the Christian life lies in an encounter with the One thus revealed.

See also **Allegorical Interpretation; Liturgy, Use of the Bible in; Spiritual Meaning.**

H. U. von Balthasar, *Prayer*, 1961; id., *Word and Revelation*, 1964; L. Bouyer, 'Mysterion' and 'Mysticism': an essay on the history of a word' in A. Plé et al., *Mystery and Mysticism*, 1956, pp. 18–32, 119–37; H. de Lubac, *Exégèse Médiévale*, 4 vols, 1959–64, esp. II/2, pp. 487–513; S. Tugwell, *Ways of Imperfection*, 1984, esp. chs 9–11.

ANDREW LOUTH

Myth

Myth is defined in the OED as 'a purely fictitious narrative usually involving supernatural persons, actions, or events, and embodying some popular idea concerning natural or historical phenomena'. This definition is only partially adequate to illustrate the use of the word in biblical interpretation. Indeed it is impossible to define the word satisfactorily, as is shown by the varied attempts at definition in the anthology edited by A. Dundes, *Sacred Narrative: Readings in the Theory of Myth* (1984). However, a brief survey of the ways in which the term has been used can indicate sufficient common ground among scholars to enable some positive points to be made.

The Greek word *muthos*, from which the English 'myth' derives, had a very wide range of meanings, from 'speech' through 'tale', 'story', 'narrative' to 'fiction' (as opposed to historical fact). For the Greek philosophers from the fifth century BC, 'myths' in the sense of stories about the gods created a problem, since there were no fewer than ten ways of explaining them away or re-interpreting them. These included the views that myths were allegorical* descriptions of natural phenomena, or of spiritual virtues; that their sense lay in the etymological meanings of the names of the gods; that they were stories borrowed from non-Greek cultures; that they were developed from stories about great heroes; and finally, that they were the inventions of priests, rulers and lawmakers, and were designed to deceive ordinary people into obedience to certain beliefs or laws. These speculations by Greek philosophers anticipated in a remarkable way the theories regarding myth that have been prevalent from the end of the eighteenth century to the present time.

As far as biblical studies are concerned, the notion of myth was used negatively until the late eighteenth century. Myths were pagan and immoral stories about gods, and had no place in the study of the Bible. However, during the Enlightenment* in Germany the daring suggestion was made in the 1770s that the Bible contained myths. The scholars responsible were J. G. Eichhorn and J. P. Gabler, and their position was that accounts in the Bible of crude supernatural and miraculous* happenings owed their form and content to the fact that their 'authors' were members of the human race in its infancy, who did not understand scientific causality, and who described in terms of the supernatural what enlightened humanity would ascribe to natural causes. ('Authors' is placed in inverted commas, because it was those who experienced the events who explained them in terms of the supernatural, although it was also accepted that stories could be elaborated as they were transmitted orally.*) The aim of Eichhorn and Gabler was to de-supernaturalize the Bible so as to get at the historical truth underlying biblical narratives, and the NT was not exempted from this exercise. A myth, then, was a story involving the supernatural which was the product of the pre-scientific conceptualizing of ancient and oriental humanity. This view was more of a psychological* theory than a formal literary definition of myth.

An opposing view was put forward by De Wette* in 1806–7. He objected to the reduction of religious texts to mere history, and denied that it was possible to recover the historical kernel of biblical narratives. The latter were to be treated rather as an expression of the spirit of the people for whom they were written. De Wette believed that the patriarchal narratives (Gen. 12–50) reflected the spirit and concerns of the period of the early monarchy, but that they also contained intuitions of eternal values. De Wette's stance thus included elements of the symbolic* and social view of myths.

The work of the brothers Wilhelm and Jakob Grimm from the 1830s produced definitions of myth in relation to saga* and folktale which affected biblical interpretation and have commanded respect from folklorists* to the present day. They defined myths as stories about gods, sagas (German *Sagen*, sometimes translated into English as 'legends'*), as stories based upon human persons, localities or events, and folktales (German *Märchen*) as popular stories not tied to specific locations or persons and involving beings such as dwarfs and giants. One result of their work was to lead many scholars to deny that the Bible contained any pure myths, although it was not denied that it might allude to myths or use themes from myths.

In the mid-nineteenth century, the Sanskrit scholar F. Max Müller advocated solar mythology, the view that myths were originally poetic descriptions of phenomena such as the dawn or the setting of the sun. Their original meanings, which had been forgotten, could be recovered by studying the etymology of the names of the gods. This view enjoyed a brief popularity in OT interpretation, and had a lasting legacy in the (probably false) theory that the traditions about Samson in Judg. 13–16 are based upon a solar myth. Müller's theory was displaced by the simpler argument of Andrew Lang, that myths originated when savage peoples personified the forces of nature in terms of their own barbaric ways of life. However, a view of mythology that regarded

myths as accounts of astral phenomena was maintained by the pan-Babylonian school of the late nineteenth century. This school held that Babylonian culture had once covered the whole of the Ancient Near East,* that Hebrew religion was derived from it, and that Babylonian myths, which were greatly influenced by observation of the heavenly bodies, could be detected behind OT narratives.

Out of the pan-Babylonian theories developed one of the most important contributions to the use of myth in biblical interpretation, in the work of H. Gunkel. He accepted the pervasive influence of Babylonian culture in the Ancient Near East, but believed that ancient Israel had re-fashioned Babylonian myths according to its distinctive faith. Behind Gen. 1, Ps. 89, Job 26.13 and Isa. 51.9, Gunkel saw remnants of the myth of the conflict between Marduk and Tiamat which preceded the creation* of the world. His work implied that the OT contained no myths, but that it alluded to them and employed their themes. In the same way, myths could be seen behind the biblical visions of the messiah* and the end of time. Research by NT members of the History of Religions school,* to which Gunkel belonged, explored similarly the mythological background to the NT in the form of saviour myths and myths of the primordial man.

Using some of the same material as Gunkel, a group of British scholars led by S. H. Hooke argued that myth played a central role in OT religion. The so-called 'myth and ritual* school' accepted the widespread view that all myths were originally the spoken accompaniment to rituals. If myths were present in the OT, as Hooke believed, they implied the existence of rituals which were performed annually to ensure prosperity and order during the ensuing year. It was known that the Babylonian creation epic *enuma elish* was recited at the Babylonian new year festival, and it seemed a reasonable assumption that there had been a similar festival in ancient Israel at which the creation story was recited. In some versions of this reconstructed myth-ritual pattern, the king played a central role, and underwent ritual humiliation, death and resurrection* (*see* **Kingship**). The view that myths are necessarily the spoken accompaniment of rituals has now been largely abandoned, and with it the myth and ritual position in OT studies. However, there is no doubt that some myths are associated with rituals, and that some myths enable a society to articulate its shared hopes for the future.

In the 1920s, the philosopher Ernst Cassirer attempted to give a philosophical account of the 'mythopoeic thought' presumed to be characteristic of peoples for whom myths were operative and significant. Cassirer's account was based unfortunately upon unreliable reports of the thought processes of so-called primitive people. However, it led to the introduction in scholarly writing of the concept of 'mythopoeic thought', a state in which the categories of space, time and number lacked the precision of modern thought. In OT studies, mythopoeic thought was attributed to Israel's neighbours, and especially to Canaanite religion. However, the OT did not contain mythopoeic thought because of God's revelation to Israel through historical events.

In the 1940s, myth became the centre of attention in NT studies, when Bultmann's* essay 'The New Testament and Mythology' provoked a long debate which touched upon the most fundamental questions of how an ancient text can be interpreted for today. Bultmann maintained that the world-view of the NT writers was mythological, that is, pre-scientific and partly conditioned by the saviour myths of the Graeco-Roman world. His programme of demythologizing* was an attempt to express in terms consonant with a modern world-view what it was that the NT writers were claiming about the nature of reality.

The past thirty years have seen the structural* and the symbolic study of myths. Lévi-Strauss' structuralist theory regards myths as traditions which try to blur distinctions that are basic to reality but must be overcome if reality is to be coped with. As applied to biblical studies by E. R. Leach, this theory entails that Gen. 1–3 wrestled with the problem that if Eve was created from Adam,* then their sexual union would be incestuous. The serpent 'mediates' this problem and diverts attention away from the implication that the human race is descended from an incestuous relationship. Read from this perspective, many of the OT historical traditions are attempts to overcome the dilemma that Israel must be a 'pure-blooded' nation yet must enter into close relationships with neighbouring peoples. Whatever one makes of the structuralist theory, it has to be admitted that it draws attention to details in the text that might otherwise be ignored, and that narratives such as Gen. 19.30–38 and 38.1–30 and Ruth are concerned with the problems of incest and of 'racial purity'. The symbolic view is maintained in P. Ricoeur's *Philosophie de la Volonté*, under the slogan 'le symbole donne à penser' (the symbol invites thought). It suggests that myths are traditions which hold together in creative tension the paradoxes of human existence. Thus Gen. 2–3 grapples with the questions of human freedom and the power of evil. Adam and Eve choose to disobey God, but in so doing they co-operate with a form of evil independent from themselves. The paradoxes implicit in such stories

invite philosophical reflection on the nature of humanity.

The great diversity of understanding and use of the concept of myth in biblical studies is a warning against over-hasty attempts to define the concept, and to say with confidence 'myth is . . .' However, the following points would probably command a broad consensus:

1. Myths are sacred stories set in a time different from that of the narrator(s), expressing an understanding of reality that justifies some of the institutions of the society of the narrator(s).

2. Some societies are able to enter imaginatively into the situations portrayed by their myths, through the medium of ritual or communal celebrations.

3. Where societies are able to re-enact their myths, and they are not written down, the content of the myths can and does change in order to reflect new economic and political realities. After myths have been written down they are adapted to changing circumstances by means of theological interpretation.

4. As 'rationality' advances in a society the effective link between myths and the understanding of reality is weakened to breaking point, but myths do not disappear. Because they are not born of logic but encapsulate intuitions of reality which, while hardly understood, make it possible for people to transcend their immediate circumstances, myths become a constant source for drama, poetry* and art.*

5. While, in popular use, myths as fictions are opposed to history or art, it is possible for accounts of historical events to function so as to express or reinforce the beliefs or values of a society. The 1988 celebrations of the 400th anniversary of the defeat by England of the Spanish Armada drew attention to the way in which popular versions of this event both glorified English skill and bravery and incorporated the theme of the victory of the small and good over the large and evil. This process can be described as the mythicizing of history.

If these points are taken to the Bible, the following suggestions can be made.

1. Gen. 1–11 contains myths in sense 1 above. They are sacred narratives set in a time different from that of the narrator(s). This is not only indicated by the words 'in those days' in Gen. 6.4 but is implicit throughout the narratives. In the world familiar to the Israelites serpents did not speak, people did not live to be over 900 years old and the human race did not speak one language. The narrative of Gen. 3 states that the world of Adam and Eve after the 'Fall' was different from that before it, while Gen. 6–9 states that the world will not again be covered by a flood. Gen. 1–11 also explains some of the

realities of the Israelites' world, including their affiliation within the family of the human race (Gen. 10.21–31; 11.10–32), and the subordination of the Canaanites to the Israelites (Gen. 9.20–27). What we do not know is whether these myths were communally celebrated by the people. The probable answer is that, in their present form, the narratives in Gen. 1–11 are a theological version of sacrosanct traditions from the standpoint of Israel's distinctive faith. They undoubtedly use some of the themes also present in Sumerian and Babylonian mythology (e.g. the flood). Reference to these myths may be implicit in Isa. 51.9 and elsewhere.

2. The passover and exodus traditions (Ex. 1–15) may well combine elements of points 2 and 5. Grounded in events which are virtually impossible to reconstruct, they have been mythicized in the way in which they describe the rescue of a defenceless and enslaved nation from an oppressor. They were also celebrated communally, although we know nothing about how this was done in the early centuries of Israel's existence. The move in Deut. 16.1–8 to make passover a centralized, national festival may indicate that, by the seventh century, these traditions had ceased to have the immediacy that they once enjoyed.

3. Traditions such as those about the wilderness wanderings (Ex. 16–18; Num. 11–17) are placed in a special time not that of the narrator(s), and contain object lessons about institutions special to Israel, e.g. the sabbath. Also, they explore the themes of God's grace and Israel's disobedience.

4. There may be allusions in the Bible to myths understood as popular stories about the end of the world, the primal man and saviour gods. If so, the prophets and the writers of the NT will have utilized these stories in order to interpret and express their beliefs about God's revelation* to Israel and in the ministry of Jesus.

The term 'myth' is not a biblical one (in the NT the Greek word *muthos* denotes a fable which Christians must not heed, cf. I Tim. 1.4). It is a scholarly, analytical concept employed by various disciplines and it is not special to theology. Its use in biblical studies has often involved the imposition of ideas from other disciplines, e.g. primitive mentality, mythopoeic thought, myth and ritual. This is not necessarily a bad thing if the concepts are well-grounded and do not do violence to the biblical texts, although the history of research indicates that biblical scholars need to be vigilant in the way that they use the term. Its use in biblical studies can be defended on two grounds. Ancient Israel was similar to other nations in possessing sacred narratives, which can be better understood by the comparative study of mythology.

Secondly, because myths have their birth not in logic but in intuitions of transcendence, they are of value to traditions that seek to describe the action of the other-worldly in the present world. However, the term 'myth' must be a servant and not a master. So long as this is understood, biblical interpretation has nothing to fear and much to gain from its application to the text of the Bible.

See also **Bultmann, R., Demythologization; Mystery Cults; Myth and Ritual.**

B. Feldman and R. D. Richardson, *The Rise of Modern Mythology 1680–1860*, 1972; J. W. Rogerson, *Myth in Old Testament Interpretation*, 1974.

J. W. ROGERSON

Myth and Ritual

The expression is taken from the volume of essays *Myth and Ritual*, published in 1933 and edited by S. H. Hooke, who has been described as the founder of the Myth and Ritual school: the theories propounded in that book were developed by the original collaborators and others in subsequent volumes and articles. Hooke himself always denied that such a clearly defined 'school' had ever existed, but it may fairly be claimed that those scholars generally reckoned to belong to it shared the same basic premises, although differing on particular points. The Myth and Ritual movement was an essentially British phenomenon, its original impulse stemming from the work of earlier British anthropologists.* However, its influence on OT scholarship was widespread, particularly in Scandinavia* and the so-called 'Uppsala school', who carried further the theories of Hooke and his colleagues, sometimes to an extent not wholly congenial to them.

What the original British scholars believed they were able to discern was a fundamental pattern underlying all the religions of the Ancient Near East.* This took the form of a complex of rituals, designed to ensure the harmony, prosperity and fertility of nature and the human community, which were accompanied by the recital of myths, myth* being the spoken part of the ritual and embodying the original situation which is seasonally re-enacted in the ritual. This pattern found its supreme expression in a great annual festival, most typically represented by the Babylonian New Year or *akitu* celebration, which was the centre and climax of all the religious activities of the year. Its object was to secure the nation's welfare during the coming twelve months and its essential components were a dramatic enactment of the death and resurrection* of the god, the recitation of the myth of creation,* a ritual combat, symbolizing the victory of the god over his enemies, the sacred marriage and finally a triumphal procession bringing the deity back to his temple to be acclaimed as king. In particular, in this whole pattern the earthly king * played the central role: he was fundamental to the well-being of the community as actually representing the god in the ritual.

As far as biblical studies are concerned, the new contribution of the Myth and Ritual scholars was to claim that such a pattern was also to be found in Israel and indeed that it constituted the 'real' religion of Israel before the exile. This contention received strong support from the Ugaritic * texts, which were only just becoming known at the time when *Myth and Ritual* was published, but in which, in a later work, Hooke was able to find the same pattern as in the rest of the Ancient Near East.

The theories of the original *Myth and Ritual* authors have provoked a great deal of discussion. Criticisms have been made of their understanding of the nature and function of myth and its relation to ritual, of their whole theory of an Ancient Near Eastern religious 'pattern', of their view of Mesopotamian kingship * and of their idea of the diffusion of culture patterns. Detailed consideration of such questions is beyond the scope of this article: suffice it to say that if the authors in question are read carefully, especially in the light of Hooke's retrospective comments in the volume he edited in 1958, these strictures lose much of their force. Attention must rather be concentrated on the permanent value of their contribution to our understanding of Israel's religion.

First, it may fairly be claimed that they demonstrated the extent to which the religiocultural pattern which they discerned in the Ancient Near East could be paralleled in the pre-exilic religion of Israel and the degree to which elements from it were basic to Israel's thought and practice. Certainly, parallels have long been drawn between parts of the OT and various Near Eastern texts. But scholars had tended to view them as somewhat peripheral to the true faith of Israel and to stress the differences rather than the resemblances. The *Myth and Ritual* authors had no doubt that Hebrew religion created a unique scheme from the elements of the Near Eastern pattern but they also held that such elements left an indelible mark on it and retained a continuing vitality within it. In particular, they showed that it is essential for a proper evaluation of Hebrew culture to take seriously all the different levels of religion that existed side by side in Israelite society and that it is inadequate to dismiss some of them as merely 'Canaanite' or 'popular' survivals.

Secondly, their understanding of the relationship between, and the function of, myth and ritual has led to a more positive evaluation of the centrality of ancient Israel's actual worship and a profounder understanding of its character. Such is particularly the case with the Feast of Tabernacles, which the scholars in question viewed as not just a simple harvest festival but as the chief celebration in Israel's calendar, exhibiting many features of the New Year rituals, an approach which many later studies have built on and developed. The influence of worship, as a living reality, could then be recognized as widespread and pervasive: thus the common contrast between priest and prophet had often been too sharply drawn and the close links between prophecy * and cult * were argued, especially in the work of A. R. Johnson, one of the younger *Myth and Ritual* writers.

Thirdly, one of the most striking contributions of the *Myth and Ritual* school was the revolution it brought about in the understanding of Israelite monarchy (*see* **Kingship**). The king was now seen not simply as a secular leader but as a sacral person who functioned as Yahweh's vice-gerent. He was the source of well-being and fertility for the whole nation and hence he had a central role in the cultus; above all, the part he played in the great autumnal festival effected the nation's prosperity for the ensuing year. So, too, the king was the root of the concept of the messiah * and much in apocalyptic * derives from the myth-ritual complex associated with him in that festival. This insight into the real character of Israelite kingship was able to illuminate a whole range of OT passages, especially in the historical books and the psalms,* which hitherto had been generally ignored or misunderstood. It is, perhaps, the *Myth and Ritual* authors' appreciation of Israel's monarchy which has most influenced subsequent scholarship and will remain their most abiding contribution.

See also **Kingship; Psalms; Scandinavian Old Testament Scholarship.**

S. H. Hooke, *The Origins of Early Semitic Ritual*, 1938; id. (ed.), *Myth and Ritual*, 1933; *The Labyrinth*, 1935; *Myth, Ritual and Kingship*, 1958; A. R. Johnson, *Sacral Kingship in Ancient Israel*, ² 1967; J. R. Porter, 'Two Presidents of the Folklore Society: S. H. Hooke and E. O. James', *Folklore*, vol. 88, 1977 ii, pp. 131–45.

J. R. PORTER

Nag Hammadi

Late in 1945 some peasants in upper Egypt found a large jar containing old books. After delays involving peasants, priests, middlemen, blood-feuds, museums, Egyptian revolutions, the Suez war, UNESCO and numerous Egyptian, French, German and American scholars, the contents were gradually made public. The jar had been sealed to preserve twelve papyrus codices (books of modern shape as distinct from scrolls) and part of a thirteenth. Apart from excellent annotated editions and translations into modern languages of individual books, there is a facsimile edition of the original (13 vols, 1972–8), a complete (if uneven) version with informative introduction in *The Nag Hammadi Library in English* (ed. James Robinson et al., 1977–8, hereafter *NHL*), and an edition of most of the texts in Bentley Layton, *The Gnostic Scriptures* (1987). Each codex contained one or (usually) more tractates, i.e. books or documents, which total 52. Scholars have numbered the codices I–XIII, and the tractates in each codex 1–8 (so II,3 is the third tractate in Codex II). The writing is in early forms of Coptic, the Egyptian Christian language. The date of the codices is uncertain, but probably fourth century (Codex VII has re-used papyrus in its binding datable to 333–348). The jar had been hidden near the site of ancient Chenoboskeia, a centre of activity for the monks of Pachomius (c. 290–346). The books have an ascetical, monastic tendency, and it is generally supposed that they were hidden by monks who feared persecution from heresy-hunting agents of such patriarchs of Alexandria as Athanasius (reigned 328–373) or Cyril (412–444). The four tractates from a further codex of similar kind and content (Berlin Gnostic Papyrus = BG 8502) are included in *NHL*. There are some important duplicates among the tractates. Most of the tractates have names in the codices; but sometimes the names are translated differently in different modern books (*The hypostasis of the archons = The reality of the rulers!*). The remainder are usually given descriptive titles by modern scholars, or titles they are known by elsewhere (*Asclepius, The Sentences of Sextus*).

The collection is both Christian and gnostic.* A few tractates are of non-Christian character: VI,5 is a scrap of Plato's *Republic*; VI,6–8 are gnostic works or fragments with Hermes Trismegistus as revealer, two of them known elsewhere among the Hermetic literature; VIII,1 (the longest single tractate) has Zostrianos or Zoroaster, the pre-Christian Persian prophet, as its revealer. Some are gnostic but may lack distinctively Christian features: such as VII,5, *The three steles of Seth* and XI,3, *Allogenes*. Some are claimed as non-Christian Jewish-gnostic, though this is disputed: V,5 *The Apocalypse of Adam*; VII,1 *The Paraphrase of Shem*. But the majority are in the form of Christian apocrypha: they have titles claiming status as gospels about Jesus, as letters of apostles, as revelations to or prayers of Christian figures, or are about Christian subjects like baptism. Most quote the NT, or rely on ideas which are derived from its writings, whether definitely and directly or vaguely and indirectly. It is probably true of each codex and of the whole collection that, however much non-Christian material has been incorporated, the works are envisaged by their compilers as contributing to a particular form of monastic Christianity, partly by way of the interpretation of scripture.

These works are relevant to biblical interpretation in various ways:

1. The alleged works of Jewish Gnosticism (V,5; VII,1 etc.) have been seen as evidence of a pre-Christian Gnosis with a redeemer figure: *The Paraphrase of Shem* is a non-Christian gnostic work which uses and radically transforms OT materials, especially from Genesis. The tractate proclaims a redeemer whose features agree with those features of NT christology* which may very well be pre-Christian in origin. As such *The Paraphrase of Shem* is important for the study of Christian origins, and may contribute significantly to the understanding of the development of christology in the NT (F. Wisse, *NHL*, p. 308). Similarly *The Apocalypse of Adam* has a gnostic redeemer/revealer and an OT history, but no unambiguously Christian words. It is also true that a process of Christianizing less clearly Christian gnostic texts may be observed among the tractates themselves. The *Apocryphon* (= *Secret Book*) *of John* occurs four times, as the first tractate in Codices II, III, and IV, and in BG 8502. It is an early gnostic mythology of 'Barbelo' (already known to Irenaeus*) which may lack direct Christian elements; but the whole has been reworked to present it as a revelation from the ascended Christ to St John. Similarly the dubiously Christian epistle* *Eugnostos the Blessed* (III,3 duplicating V,1) is badly adapted into a question-and-answer session between Jesus and his disciples in *The Sophia of Jesus Christ* (also duplicated, III,4 = BG 8502,3). Such evidence suggests that there was a gnostic myth* of creation, fall and redemption before Christianity. If correct, this is important; it justifies the identification of gnostic ideas and their rebuttal in fundamental aspects of NT doctrine. But the codices are too late for us to be certain that anything in them is free from Christian influence, however remote, and they will hardly support the theory of pre-Christian Gnosticism, unless that is demonstrated from earlier sources.

2. Peculiarly important is *The Gospel of Thomas* (II,2), of which papyrus fragments survive in Greek datable about 200. The composition of the work is usually put about 100. It begins, 'These are the secret sayings which

the living Jesus spoke and which Didymos Judas Thomas wrote down.' It should first be observed that it is thus presented as a typical gnostic revelation – '*secret* sayings of the *living* (i.e. risen) Jesus' – even though many of the sayings are recognizably those of the ministry of Jesus in the Synoptic Gospels; and it is ascribed to 'the Twin' (= Greek *Didymos*, Aramaic *Thomas*) brother of Jesus, the same Judas Thomas who is the hero of the apocryphal *Acts of Thomas*, and of an ascetical variety of East Syrian* Christianity in Edessa (another Nag Hammadi book, *The Book of Thomas the Contender*, is from this tradition). Secondly the gospel is in form a collection of sayings and interrogations of Jesus with minimal narrative setting (as is *The Dialogue of the Saviour*, III,5). It therefore illustrates the form postulated for the hypothetical sayings-source 'Q', widely held to lie behind parts of Matthew and Luke. It cannot possibly be Q itself, but the resemblance has encouraged some to suggest that Q was in some sense 'gnostic'. Thirdly, there are sayings which are parallel to sayings in the Synoptic* Gospels,* especially Matthew and Luke, some of which appear to be in a different and no less primitive form. In saying 47, for instance, Jesus' words about wineskins and patches could possibly be nearer an original from which the longer canonical versions derive (Mark 2.21–22; Matt. 9.16–17; Luke 5.36–39). If so, *Thomas* may be based partly on a source (perhaps a primitive Jewish-Christian* gospel), and some of the sayings *not* paralleled in the Synoptics could have some claim to authenticity as words of Jesus. Because of these possibilities *The Gospel of Thomas* is usually printed in modern Gospel synopses for comparative study. It is in any case certain that some of the sayings are purely gnostic or ascetic/monastic: Mary Magdalene must become a male to enter the kingdom of heaven (saying 114). Others are apparently adapted to a gnostic outlook: 'Give Caesar what belongs to Caesar, give God what belongs to God, and give me what is mine', in saying 100 probably distinguishes Christ from the inferior Creator, who is usually meant by 'God' in gnostic texts; both the saying and the abbreviated narrative before it are probably secondary to the story in Mark 12.13–17 and parallels. All of this requires detailed comparison of a synoptic kind, and judgments about priority vary widely among scholars. It should finally be noted that this gospel was known to the author of the apocryphal *Acts of Thomas* and the late gnostic Mani, and may have influenced some texts in the *Diatessaron* of Tatian. (S. L. Davies has argued that the *Gospel of Thomas* is not gnostic at all, but is wholly prior to the NT Gospels and presents a Wisdom

christology. If he is right, gnostic features were read into the text later, as they were in NT books.)

3. A number of the tractates are clearly Christian and proceed by the quotation and interpretation of biblical texts. *The Exegesis on the Soul* (II,6) illustrates a widespread piece of gnostic spirituality, that the soul is a wayward female until it repents and is reunited to its heavenly male counterpart, when the two become a single (celibate?) life in accordance with Gen. 2.24 ('they shall become one flesh'). The short treatise is full of biblical texts to support the argument, with long quotations from Hosea, Jeremiah and Ezekiel, as well as verses from Genesis, Psalms and NT books. Near the end is a short allegorical* interpretation making the same point from the words of Calypso in Homer's *Odyssey*. *The Gospel of Truth* is not a gospel-history or sayings-collection, but a meditation, probably from the gnostic school of Valentinus, on the joy which knowledge of the truth brings to the chosen vessels, who came to know their want and received knowledge of the Father. But its author begins from biblical elements. Jesus the Christ is the hidden mystery of the Father, whose revelation offends Error, which persecuted him. Nailed to a tree, Jesus became a fruit which gives life to those who eat it. But it is not certain that this means a reversal of the story of Gen. 3, where the tree gives death; it may reflect a gnostic interpretation of it, in which the fruit offered to Eve is the good fruit of knowledge and life denied her by the jealous creator. Allusions and near-quotations from the NT are frequent. Also Valentinian is the *Treatise on Resurrection* (= *The Epistle to Rheginus*), which argues from NT texts (including an interesting allusion to the Marcan account of the Transfiguration, Mark 9.4) that resurrection* in Jesus and in the believer is spiritual, and so the fate of the body is irrelevant compared with the ascent of the intellect. The so-called *Gospel of Philip* is a miscellany of sayings, comments and occasional stories only loosely connected with each other. Only a few sayings are expressly attributed to Jesus or involve incidents affecting him. Biblical events are spiritually interpreted. 'When Eve was in Adam* death did not exist. When she was separated from him (Gen. 2.21–22) death came into being (Gen. 3). If he again becomes complete and attains his former self, death will be no more' (Layton, p. 342; *NHL*, p. 141). Eve's creation and fall are thus an allegory of the fall of the soul into material desire, until it repents and is reunited with its male counterpart. Baptism, chrism and eucharist are also spiritually interpreted, and there is consequently valuable (if disputed) exegesis* of John 6.53 (Layton, p. 333; *NHL*,

pp. 134–5). Jesus' flesh is true (heavenly) flesh, the Word which feeds the soul, and the hearer must rise 'in the flesh' in the sense that his resurrection takes place spiritually in this life. *Melchizedek* (IX,1) turns the OT priest (Gen. 14.18–20) into a prophet* of the coming of Christ, then a model of the baptized praying Gnostic, and finally he himself becomes Jesus Christ the victorious saviour. The Gnosticism involved is of the Sethian variety (see below). This tractate is of interest because of the messianic* view about Melchizedek in Heb. 5.10–7.28 at Qumran (*see* **Dead Sea Scrolls**), and among some second-century non-gnostic Christians (Ps-Tertullian, *Against all Heresies*, 8.24). These and other clearly Christian documents indicate the importance in biblical exegesis of the doctrinal scheme which is brought to scriptural texts: to read Genesis or John as a Valentinian or other Gnostic is to find it substantiating one's views.

4. There are traditions in some tractates about apostles like Peter,* Paul,* Thomas and especially James, which may occasionally go back to early times. But their chief significance is to indicate the course of the person's 'posthumous career'. This may throw light on similar developments within the NT.

5. Finally there is the question how far the general principles of Nag Hammadi religion are biblical. If there is a prevailing form among the varieties at Nag Hammadi, it is 'Sethian Gnosis'. Some tractates are superficially not Christian at all, even if they contain Christian terms such as 'Son of Man'* or 'Saviour'. These are often connected with the figure of Seth, a great heavenly *aeon* whom the third son of Adam and Eve represents. This heavenly saviour-figure repeatedly intervenes to preserve the spiritual seed among mankind, and finally to recover the lost. A good example is the duplicated *Gospel of the Egyptians* (III,2 = IV,2), which tells the story of Great Seth. Sethian Gnosticism may be the early 'classical' form of Gnosticism, or it may be one of several developed varieties. It is compatible with Christianity if Jesus can be made the principal manifestation of Great Seth. This appears to be the case with *Melchizedek*; and one tractate in which Seth is never mentioned and the Saviour is clearly 'Jesus Christ the Son of Man' is entitled in the codex *The Second Treatise of the Great Seth* (VII,2). The Sethian and other gnostic mythologies* involve a fundamental reworking of OT material: the Creator is an inferior and incompetent or hostile being, the temptation of Eve is the offer of true knowledge, and the Creator's claim to uniqueness is unfounded (they often quote 'I am God and there is none beside me' [cf. Isa. 43.11; 44.6] as his ignorant boast). This reworking may have taken place originally among Jewish communities whose religion was threatened by the destruction of the Temple in AD 70 and the secularizing of Jerusalem, communities whose exegesis might alternatively lead them into kinds of Christianity. Whatever the case, they believed that in a new and illuminating way the 'God beyond God', the true pure realm of light unrecognized before, had sent to liberate them from the curse of the false religious Law and from the power of fleshly desire. Their thoughts and books got into the libraries of Christian monks later, and since the codices were rediscovered they have attracted some modern people looking for spiritual illumination. It is questionable however whether such an interpretation can do justice to the earthiness of biblical revelation.

See also **Gnosticism; Spiritual Meaning.**

Stevan L. Davies, *The Gospel of Thomas and Christian Wisdom*, 1983; Charles W. Hedrick and Robert Hodgson, Jr (eds), *Nag Hammadi, Gnosticism and Early Christianity*, 1986; David M. Scholem, *Nag Hammadi Bibliography, 1948–1969*, 1971.

STUART GEORGE HALL

Nahum

Throughout its history, Nahum has been read as proclaiming the righteous divine government of the world, witnessed to by the ultimate overthrow of evil tyrants, while Yahweh appears as a safe refuge in the maelstrom for his trusting people; for such readers, it has been taken to encourage confident hope in the face of contemporary oppressors soon to be overthrown. This is true already for the Qumran *pesher* * 4QpNah (4Q169) (*see* **Dead Sea Scrolls**), which, reading Nahum as a prediction of the final disaster coming on the sect's opponents, identifies the hostile forces mentioned with various contemporary powers (M. P. Horgan, *Pesharim*, 1979, pp. 158–91).

The understanding of Nahum as distant prophetic prediction appears in Tobit 14.4 (Sinaiticus) and in Josephus* (*Ant.* IX, 239–42), where, however, there is the attempt both to locate Nahum historically and, implicitly, to find apologetic value in the fulfilment of his prophecy in the fall of the historical Nineveh. The Targum* explicitly emphasizes God's goodness to Israel (1.7) and looks for the eschatological* destruction of the nations which have ravaged people and temple; the divine favour and judgment in ch. 1 are linked respectively with obedience or disobedience to the Torah. Nahum is here depicted as later than Jonah, after whose mission Nineveh had again fallen into sin. The position of Nahum after Jonah in the Hebrew ordering of the Twelve Minor Prophets probably reflects an earlier expression of the same chronological – and theological? – sequence, and perhaps a suggestion as to their mutual interpretation (in the commonest Septuagintal* order the sequence is immediate).

Of the several patristic commentaries, with characteristic Christian allegorizing,* those of Theodore of Mopsuestia (see **Antiochene Interpretation**) and Jerome offer attempts at 'literal'* readings; Jerome gives also spiritual* interpretation, whereby Nahum is seen as telling of the sure destruction of those who oppose God and reject the safety of the church (cf. J. N. D. Kelly, *Jerome*, 1975, pp. 163–6).

Luther's* *Lectures on Nahum* of 1525 adopt a broadly historical approach in which Nahum, roughly contemporary with Isaiah, is viewed as pointing to the suffering Judah was to experience under Sennacherib, but also to the preservation of a righteous remnant and the destruction of Nineveh: thus Nahum, true to his name, brings 'comfort' to God's beleaguered people, assuring them of the divine victory and of Judah's continued life until Christ's coming. The book thus preaches faith and looks to the gospel. Luther's exegesis* is largely grammatical and historical, and powerfully theological in orientation; so also is Calvin's* characteristically patient and detailed commentary.

With the development of historical criticism* in the nineteenth century, attention was paid, less to the book's long-celebrated aesthetic brilliance than to the precise historical and geographical origin of Nahum's prophecy as offering significant cultural clues to its interpretation. Linguistic links with Isaiah and supposed references to Sennacherib's invasion of Judah (esp. in 1.9ff.) were often taken to suggest a late Hezekianic date, with the positive view of Judah and the antagonism towards Assyria expressive of encouragement to the oppressed people. But the discovery that Thebes (3.8–10) had fallen to the Assyrians in 663 BC naturally led to a lowering of the possible dates for Nahum's work, some arguing for a setting very close to the actual fall of Nineveh (612 BC). It was further widely argued, especially after H. Gunkel (1893), that an acrostic poem could be detected at least partially in ch. 1, and that this was to be regarded as a post-exilic addition expressing an 'eschatological generalizing' of the original poems: it was now open to regard Nahum as composite. And though the book continued to be read by many as testimony to God's just rule of history, interpreters, noting the apparently non-religious character of the poetry in chs 2–3 and Nahum's lack of prophetic criticism of Judah (especially now that he was commonly regarded as Jeremiah's contemporary!), began

to sense in new ways the moral and hermeneutical* questions involved. While some scholars continued to affirm Nahum's expression of ethical-religious values as they attended to these theological-critical issues (e.g. A. F. Kirkpatrick, *The Doctrine of the Prophets*, ³1901, pp. 239–57), others judged Nahum as a nationalistic, optimistic prophet far removed from the epoch-making experience of Yahweh and religious criticism of the great individual prophets – and perhaps as representative of the very 'false prophecy' they condemned.

Such views have retained some influence. Attempts to connect Nahum closely with the Jerusalem cult, to the extent of seeing the book in whole or part as representing actual (new year?) liturgical forms (so especially P. Humbert; more recently J. H. Eaton, *Vision in Worship*, 1981, pp. 14–21) have both sharpened and softened the questions here by suggesting that no simple distinction exists between 'cultic' and other prophecy, and consequently no easy value-judgments are possible.

The presence of some perhaps multi-layered editorial development seems clear; and exegesis must recognize that the textual and redactional histories of the book are inseparably united, so that the history of interpretation of 'Nahum' begins within the book itself. This is true, e.g., of the linking of the (probable) acrostic hymn-element in 1.2–8 (?) with the material that follows, and the likely reshaping of both. Whether or not 'eschatological' or 'mythological'* motifs are found earlier in the book's growth, they seem apparent in its present form, though their precise interpretation remains disputed. We note too not only Nahum's close connections with other 'foreign nation oracles' but also what may be a specific redactional link with those of Isa. 13ff., forged by the first heading *massā' nîneweh* (1.1a) – perhaps a deliberate invitation to interpret Nahum in association with the Isaianic collection, and as sharing the same wider theological patterning.

Recent study has stressed Nahum's connections with the broader oral and literary traditions of OT prophecy (cf. *Israel's Prophetic Tradition* ed. R. J. Coggins, 1982, pp. 79–85), and B. S. Childs maintains that the 'final form' of Nahum bears witness to God's ultimate triumph over all his foes, and that traditional critical assessments miss the authoritative hermeneutical role of this 'canonical* shaping' (*Introduction to the Old Testament as Scripture*, 1979, pp. 440–46). However, Childs' approach cannot carry the theological weight he assigns to it, and the older theological-critical appraisals of Nahum should not simply be disregarded, for they point to the fundamental ambiguity which always attends the interpretation of biblical prophecy: it does not have to be read as 'true', and the interpreter must decide, in dialogue also with his or her own context and experience, whether or how it might come to be received as such. This is also demanded both by critical, intra-biblical comparison of Nahum and Jonah (cf. also Isa. 19.23–25), when the older way (e.g. Luther) of connecting the two prophets with successive stages of God's direct, historical dealing with Nineveh is no longer possible, and by serious theological engagement with the nature of divine involvement in history. To speak of Nahum as pointing to the vindication of God's sovereignty and justice in history may be regarded not as the end, but as the beginning of the interpreter's task.

Commentaries by J. H. Eaton, 1961; R. J. Coggins, 1985; E. Achtemeier, 1986; W. Rudolph, *Kommentar zum Alten Testament* XIII/3, 1975; G. Fohrer, *Introduction to the Old Testament*, E T 1968, pp. 447–51.

EDWARD BALL

Narrative Criticism

Narrative criticism is a method of interpreting biblical narratives with the help of modern and ancient literary theory. It approaches the biblical narrative not as a historical source for something that lies behind the text but as a literary text that may be analysed in literary terms (plot, characterization, point of view in narration, etc.) like other works of literature. Narrative criticism tends to view the narrative as an interactive whole, with harmonies and tensions that develop in the course of narration. It is usually concerned with the possible effects on the reader or hearer of the literary techniques employed in the text. Narrative criticism is sometimes subsumed under the broader label 'literary criticism';* it is applied to both O T and N T, though the examples here are taken from the N T.

The following examples suggest some of the differences between narrative criticism and previous methods in biblical studies:

1. Gaps and repetitions within the narrative. Historical criticism* tends to view gaps and repetitions as indications of a composite narrative, a secondary compilation of earlier sources.* The gaps and repetitions are then used to argue for a particular understanding of these sources. Narrative critics would affirm that gaps and repetitions are very common in narratives and that both may be effective literary techniques. Noting that there are two accounts of Jesus feeding a multitude with the help of the disciples in Mark (6.30–44; 8.1–10), narrative critics will not seek the earliest version in order to account for the develop-

ment of both, but will ask how Jesus and the disciples are being portrayed when the disciples do not understand Jesus' power and intention, even on the second occasion of a feeding. Gaps may be temporary, building suspense for a later revelation,* or permanent, encouraging imaginative exploration of what remains a significant mystery.

2. Development in plot and characterization. If we recognize the significance of narrative, it is not possible to arrive at a biblical writer's view of a subject simply by adding up the relevant references in the text. This additive procedure approaches the text as a compilation, not an ordered narrative. We cannot, for instance, discover the Marcan view of the disciples by simply adding up remarks about them in Mark, some of which are favourable and some unfavourable. Rather, we must be able to recognize the place of these remarks within a developing narrative that moves from a beginning through conflict and crisis to an ending. The placement of particular material within the narrative affects its function. Implications and expectations early in the narrative may, in fact, be reversed at a later point. Therefore, the significance of a narrative scene cannot be judged without understanding its function within the narrative development as a whole.

3. The message of a text. Redaction critics* have sought the theology of a gospel writer as the key to understanding the message that the writer wishes to convey to a particular historical audience. It is not the purpose of narrative criticism, however, to distil a message from the text that can be expressed in a series of theological statements. Indeed, narrative criticism would suggest that such an attempt inevitably reduces the complexity and richness of narrative communication. Instead, one can explore the narrative rhetoric* employed to persuade readers to adopt particular views of the persons and events in the narrative, indirectly influencing readers' views of their own situation. Theological statements may have a place in narrative rhetoric, perhaps in establishing certain norms by which characters' actions may be judged, but much more is involved. Narrative critics would investigate, among other things, the narrator's control of narrative time, including order (the sequence in which events are presented, with previews of later events and reviews of earlier events), duration (the amount of narrative time devoted to particular events, varying between a fully developed scene and a short summary), and frequency (the number of times that an event or type of event is presented). Such investigation can reveal how the narrator evaluates and selectively emphasizes as the story is told. What we perceive in

narrative and how we perceive it are controlled by the narrator (or by the implied author who makes use of the narrator); hence the importance of analysing narrative rhetoric. The resulting 'message' of the narrative cannot be reduced to theological propositions to be accepted by the conscious mind. A narrative's message is the complex reshaping of human life which it may cause through the reader's sensitive involvement. This pertains to attitudes, interpretative images, patterns of action, sympathies, etc. Narrative criticism can approach a narrative as a complex system of influence analysable in literary terms.

Various types of studies in narrative criticism have appeared in recent years. Some are systematic in structure, following an outline dictated by the various aspects of narrative in general, with sustained application, however, to a particular biblical writing. R. Alan Culpepper's *Anatomy of the Fourth Gospel* (1983) and *Mark as Story*, by David Rhoads and Donald Michie (1982), are works of this type. Robert Alter's *The Art of Biblical Narrative* (1981) and Meir Sternberg's *The Poetics of Biblical Narrative* (1985) also follow a topical outline. These two works include extensive discussion of selected OT narratives. Narrative commentaries are also beginning to appear These may follow the order of the biblical narrative from beginning to end or isolate narrative strands (e.g., Jesus' interaction with other important characters) which are considered one by one. Jack Dean Kingsbury's *Matthew as Story* (2nd edn 1988) combines these approaches while Robert Tannehill's study of Luke (*The Narrative Unity of Luke–Acts*, vol. 1, 1986) follows the latter. There are various approaches to narrative in literary studies. It is likely that this variety will increasingly be reflected in biblical narrative criticism. One example of a possible new direction is Richard A. Edwards' short commentary on Matthew (*Matthew's Story of Jesus*, 1985) using 'reader response' criticism,* which follows reading as a temporal process in which a reader repeatedly forms hypotheses and makes judgments, then modifies these as the story continues.

See also **Literary Criticism; Narrative Theology.**

P. Grant, *Reading the New Testament*, 1989; W. A. Kort, *Story, Text and Scripture*, 1988.

                                  ROBERT C. TANNEHILL

Narrative Theology

The name given to various approaches to theology in which stories play a leading role.

Narrative has been a leading feature of Christian theology since its beginnings in the Bible. The stories of scripture, and the tradi-tional Christian overarching story of the world from creation* to eschatological* consummation, have been retold, discussed, interpreted and taken up into doctrine and theology in many ways. They have also been embodied in liturgies,* creeds,* symbols,* artefacts and activities. Since the Enlightenment,* and especially since the nineteenth century, there have been new types of historical and literary scrutiny of these stories as well as accompanying theological efforts to express their meaning and truth in relation to modernity. This is the broad context in which narrative theology needs to be seen.

Narrative theology emerged mainly in North America. Its chief theological precursor there was H. Richard Niebuhr, especially in *The Meaning of Revelation* (1941). He maintained the initiative and involvement of God in history as well as the relative, incomplete nature of all the stories which testify to that. Both stories and general concepts are needed in theology and neither can be reduced to the other. But the fact that our lives are constituted by time (past, present and future) means that narrative is especially appropriate to expressing the revelation of God's grace and glory in contingent existence. Niebuhr was also concerned to do justice both to critical historical research (history as observed) and to our inescapable immersion in our particular individual and communal histories (history as lived), but without claiming that there can be any tension-free integration or any systematic overview of the two.

Since the 1970s narrative theologians have offered various ways of engaging in constructive Christian theology, especially in the aftermath of radical criticism of Christianity in the previous decade. Reasons offered for the attractiveness of narrative have included the following: it is the main genre* of the Bible; it is the underlying structure of the Christian creeds,* baptism and the eucharist; its concreteness and particularity deserve primacy in relation to the more abstract, generalizing approach of much doctrine and theology; more precisely, it gives a proper prominence to people in interaction, to specific contexts and to actions and events, all of which tend to be marginalized or treated too generally and abstractly by traditional theological discourse; it provides a way into doctrine and ethics* which is definite, imaginative and well-suited to the gospel while not claiming an exclusive or imperialistic universality (i.e. the validity of other stories need not be rejected); it is the basic, irreducible way to express human experience and identity; it enables a fresh approach to the relationship of historical fact* to Christian truth; it provides a forum for encounter and discussion, not only between very different types of Christian theology, but also between various religions and cultures (all of which have their stories) and between theology and other disciplines (e.g. literary studies, history, psychology,* anthropology*).

Some key areas to be considered are:

1. *Theology and literature*. Perhaps the most fruitful aspect of narrative theology as it has affected biblical interpretation has been its encouragement of the relationship between theology and literary studies. Most recent schools of literary criticism have been drawn on, leading theology to become involved in debates about 'new criticism', structuralism,* post-structuralism, and various eclectic types of criticism. Besides discussion as to how best to understand the Bible as literature (influential works on that include William Beardslee, *Literary Criticism of the New Testament*, 1969; Northrop Frye, *The Great Code*, 1982; Robert Alter, *The Art of Biblical Narrative*, 1981 and *The Art of Biblical Poetry*, 1985; Robert Alter and Frank Kermode, *The Literary Guide to the Bible*, 1987), a recurrent issue is how literary interpretation can do justice to the historical and theological claims of the Bible.

2. *Genre*. This is a central matter for both literary criticism and narrative theology. It can be crucial for the interpretation of a text whether it is seen as history, myth,* parable* or allegory.* How is genre to be decided? Further, how do various genres, such as poetry, narrative, legal regulation, proverb, prayer and argumentative discourse, relate to each other? On the latter issue, narrative theologians differ considerably among themselves, some giving decisive primacy to narrative as the fundamental and inclusive genre, while others are more pluralist in their claims. Within the broad genre of narrative itself there are further issues. Some, following the literary criticism of Erich Auerbach in *Mimesis: The Representation of Reality in Western Literature* (1957), see 'realistic narrative' as the distinctive biblical form of narration; others make parable, metaphor* or myth their central categories and relate other genres to them. The genres of discursive argument and theory are often criticized for claiming a superior role in theology, imposing criteria* of meaning* and truth which are inappropriate to narrative and other genres. Thus narrative theology, even though it is itself not usually narration but discursive argument, sees itself liberating other genres from oppression by conceptual and theoretical types of theology. A distinction is often made between 'first order' language such as narrative and 'second order', more abstract language, such as that of doctrinal discussion. The latter must be reminded of its dependence on narratives, and the traditional doctrines, from creation to escha-tology, can be seen as corresponding to key events and aspects of the overarching Christian story.

3. *The narrative quality of human experience.* One position on this is that narrative is so fundamental to human experience as to be the basic form of human expression, unavoidable because of the temporal, historical shape of our existence. Our consciousness is inextricable from memory and anticipation, embracing past, present and future. On this account, narrative is like a 'transcendental' category, the inescapable condition for having any human experience at all. Religion, in so far as it connects with what is most fundamental in humanity, is bound to give primacy to story, and Christianity is seen to exemplify this.

An opposing view is sceptical or agnostic about how narrative relates to universal human experience (if, indeed, there is any such reality), and starts with the specific characteristics of Christianity (or any other religion). Christian identity is seen as rendered primarily through particular narratives, above all that of the life, death and resurrection* of Jesus Christ. This story is not an instance of something more general and universal (such as a structure of human experience) but is testimony to a particular person whose universality is, through the resurrection, part of the story itself. The debate between these positions is important for the role of narrative in dialogue between cultures and religions: the first assumes a common basis in human consciousness; the second questions that and stresses specificity and differences.

4. *History, fiction and truth.* Two major types of narrative in our culture are fiction (especially in novels and drama) and history (from academic studies to diaries and journalism). Narrative theology is faced with the question: how does an approach to the Bible and Christian tradition which is literary and has its roots in the study of fiction combine with a theological interest in historical fact? Most agree that truth, including historical truth, can be conveyed in stories which cannot be called history in the modern sense. But there are deep differences over how, for example, theology should be concerned with the 'historical Jesus'.* Should there be a quest for the historical Jesus using historical-critical* methods and an attempt to combine those with literary approaches, as by Edward Schillebeeckx in *Jesus* (1979) and *Christ* (1980)? Is it impossible to combine the two, and, if so, should the theological priority be given to the literary testimony of the Gospels rather than to attempts to get behind them, as Hans Frei argues in *The Identity of Jesus Christ. The hermeneutical bases of dogmatic theology* (1975)? Or should the whole quest for histori-

cal reference beyond language be ruled out, as in John Dominic Crossan's *The Dark Interval. Toward a theology of story* (1988), whose maxim is 'reality is language'? Philosophers who have been especially influential on narrative theologians' approaches to issues of language, reference, truth, fact and fiction have included Ludwig Wittgenstein, Hans-Georg Gadamer, Paul Ricoeur, Jacques Derrida, Alasdair MacIntyre and William Christian.

Other major matters of concern to narrative theologians have included: the authority* of scripture; the literal* or plain sense of scripture; the use of typology* or figuration; the potential of narrative for giving praxis a prominent role in theology; and the relation between shared, communal stories (of Israel, Jesus, the church, other religions, world history) and stories of self (autobiography, biography, conversion). There has also been a variety of proposals, sometimes labelled 'postmodern', which see human reality as constituted by 'texts' (whether written or inscribed in behavioural and social patterns, symbols and other vehicles of meaning), emphasizing the diversity of 'intratextual'* and 'intertextual' worlds which we inhabit and the impossibility of deciding the truth or falsehood of the endless interpretations which are produced. As regards narrative, this has led to a questioning of the usual distinctions between fiction and history, a rejection of the notion of 'correspondence to reality', and suspicion of concepts of causality, objectivity, narrative unity and continuity. So narrative history, in which the historian is now seen to be imaginatively reconstructing the past and imposing some plot on it, is brought nearer to novel-writing, and this encourages the tendency of narrative theology to give priority to the literary rather than the historical study of the Bible.

Narrative is by no means a unified movement and it is not easy (and probably not important) to decide who is or is not a narrative theologian. It has been most enthusiastically embraced as a label at the more popular level of theology, where it is often seen as an attractive way into religion, Christianity or theology, because it resonates with common experience and has considerable educational advantages. In more academic Christian theology, special concern with narrative has been an extension into new literary and philosophical areas of a long-running debate about the Bible and history in relation to Christian faith and practice. Contrasting types of theology have had a major interest in narrative, for example, those who take biblical narrative as offering the key terms in which God and human reality are to be conceived (Karl Barth,* Eberhard Jüngel, Hans Frei,

George Lindbeck, Stanley Hauerwas) over against those who propose a critical correlation between Christian narratives and modernity, or who suggest a revised framework in which Christian narrative can be reinterpreted (Schillebeeckx, David Tracy, Sallie McFague).

Narrative has, like existentialism earlier this century, enabled very different positions (atheist, Christian, Jewish, the latter very prolifically) and disciplines to come into dialogue with one another. The theological interest has both encouraged and also been stimulated by the close attention biblical scholars have been paying to narratives and literary studies. Overall, despite the fact that few theologians would accept 'narrative theologian' as their principal designation, narrative theology has considerably affected the agenda and approaches of theologians and other interpreters of the Bible, to the extent that many of its concerns are normal features of courses and discussions.

See also **Infancy Narratives; Narrative Criticism; Passion Narratives; Resurrection Narratives; Rhetorical Criticism.**

G. Aichele, *The Limits of Story*, 1985; H. Frei, *The Eclipse of Biblical Narrative*, 1974; M. Goldberg, *Theology and Narrative: A Critical Introduction*, 1982; G. Green (ed.), *Scriptural Authority and Narrative Interpretation*, 1987; P. Ricoeur, *Time and Narrative*, 3 vols, 1984 ff.; G. Stroup, *The Promise of Narrative Theology*, 1981; T. R. Wright, *Theology and Literature*, 1988.

DAVID F. FORD

New Hermeneutic

A movement which has arisen out of the work of Ernst Fuchs and Gerhard Ebeling in the decades since the 1950s. Interest in the movement has developed largely in post-Bultmannian circles in Germany and the USA, where further attempts have been made to analyse and explain its rather complex features. Both Fuchs and Ebeling were former students of Bultmann* and owe much to his existential understanding of scripture, but they also differ from his views in important respects. Above all, Fuchs and Ebeling have been concerned with the function of language. Yet, like Bultmann, they approach the question of language and its place in the understanding of human existence primarily as theologians, rather than as philosophers. Their ultimate goal is to express how revelation,* the word of God,* is communicated to the modern hearer. For Ebeling, the question of hermeneutic* forms the focal point of all theological problems. The history of theology and the church is fundamentally the history of the interpretation of scripture. It will become clear, however, that the hermeneutical problem is also the point where theology and philosophy meet.

The importance of 'language' lies in the view of these theologians that language does much more than simply impart information. It actually conveys reality; it is grounded in 'being' and not just in thought. Although there is some debate about actual dependence, one can here find parallels with the ideas of Heidegger and Gadamer. Similar to Heidegger's view is the belief that man is constituted by his relationship to himself, expressed in how he understands himself. This understanding is the key to one's own life and to one's relationship with others, and one gets to this self-understanding by means of language. Language is essential for understanding human existence, and it is active in the sense that it can set events in motion. Language 'makes being into an event', according to Fuchs. Thus one must start from the broad philosophical questions about language and human existence. It is then possible to consider how this applies to the understanding of a text. In this respect, it is argued that the language of a text can lead the hearer to a new horizon of understanding, demanding a decision of the hearer in light of this. It can shatter previously accepted ways of seeing oneself and the world and can become an event that challenges hearers at a deep level to a new understanding of their present existence. When applied to the word of God, the hearer is 'drawn over on to God's side and learns to see everything with God's eyes' (Fuchs). As Ebeling states, the text 'becomes a hermeneutic aid in the understanding of present existence'. When a text does function in this way, it has become for the hearer an authentic 'language-event' (*Sprachereignis*) in the terminology of Fuchs or a 'word-event' (*Wortgeschehen*) in the work of Ebeling.

An important feature of this view of language is the idea of *Einverständnis*, which can be variously translated as 'common understanding' or 'agreement'. Language must originate from shared experience and previous understanding. Such prior agreement is essential for all communication. Yet for Fuchs, this mutual understanding (by which words 'get home' to the hearer) operates at a preconscious level. It is not related so much to cognitive concepts as to one's 'world', that which gives voice to one's 'being' and which also allows others to function and have a place. Authentic language-event is both grounded in and affects this *Einverständnis*.

The New Hermeneutic is 'new' in its approach to the NT not only for its emphasis on the linguistic nature of all human existence, but also for its abandonment of 'rules' of exegesis* and its concern for the rights of the text over against the interpreter. As E. McKnight points out, Bultmann still desired to interpret the text of the NT 'scientifically', although choosing the existential level of questioning. In contrast, Fuchs asserts that the text is not a 'servant that transmits kerygmatic* formulations', but rather the text itself 'interprets' the hearer. The interpreter must not approach the text as an objective outside observer may approach a neutral or passive object. The interpreter must be engaged by the text and 'acted upon'. The process of interpretation is defined not by rules or conventions for working upon a text, but rather is visualized as a fusion of two horizons – that of the modern interpreter and that of the text.

But how does this affect other aspects of the interpreter's work? Certainly one cannot assume faith already on the part of the interpreter, since the text itself is seen as that which calls forth faith. Historical-critical* enquiry still has a place, but not primarily in terms of trying to reach the intentions of the original author. Fuchs describes historical-critical activity as 'striking the text dead'; W. Wink refers to 'distancing'. The point is that critical study may allow the text to be freed from all the accretions and interpretations of the church over the centuries. Every age must be allowed to understand a text in its own way, unaffected by intervening tradition, since modern interpreters are as historically conditioned by their own times as the text was by its time. But this is as far as historical study takes one. The text must then be allowed to engage the interpreter at a 'more than purely cognitive' level. This active role of the text has been demonstrated particularly well for the more poetic sections of the NT, such as the Johannine Prologue, Phil. 2.5–11, or the parables* of Jesus. Studies along these lines include the work of E. Linnemann on parables and that of E. Jüngel on justification by faith in Paul and Jesus. In addition, similarities to this approach may be detected in the works on parables by R. Funk, D. O. Via and J. D. Crossan.

The New Hermeneutic has also had important points of contact with the new quest for the historical Jesus*. Just as authentic language-event is not concerned simply with ideas but 'comes to speech' in actual historical settings, so also Christian faith is viewed as 'actualized' by Jesus of Nazareth. There is a unity between the word and deed in Jesus. The parables of Jesus articulate how Jesus himself reacted to the word of God. This leads to an interest in details of Jesus' life, although his teaching still dominates over his deeds and miracle* stories are considered to have no effective use in leading the hearer to faith as understood in existential terms. Ultimately, faith is viewed as the abandonment of self-assertion in favour of others and as the willingness to remain open to whatever God may require. Historically, this was depicted supremely in the cross of Jesus. The cross itself, not the resurrection* in its own right, is seen as the victory of faith. Interpreting Fuchs, P. Achtemeier declares: 'Faith in the risen Christ therefore means the faith that the historical Jesus was God's word to us, and that that word was present, and is to be believed as present, in the very death of Jesus on the cross.'

Any evaluation of the New Hermeneutic inevitably draws one into wider hermeneutical discussions ranging from Schleiermacher to Dilthey, Heidegger and Gadamer. While many today would accept that language achieves more than merely conveying information, the New Hermeneutic has been pressed to make more precise the relationship between the 'meaning' of a text and its actual 'words'. The rights of the text are clearly defended, but how important are its actual words? How do variations in wording affect the language-events which Fuchs and Ebeling describe? A. Thiselton has also suggested that the view of language in the New Hermeneutic is one-sided in ignoring the value of descriptive or informative language. With reference to the work of J. L. Austin and to Wittgenstein, Thiselton suggests that the performative aspect of language is not undermined by, and may indeed depend upon, certain statements being believed to convey true information. Furthermore, while the subjectivity of the interpreter is clearly involved, there must surely still be some place for propositional concepts so as to safeguard against mere self-delusion. And how does one reconcile Fuchs' belief that it is the word of God that judges the hearer with his view that the hearer himself is the criterion of truth? Thiselton further notes that the New Hermeneutic clearly works better for some parts of the NT than for others, while Achtemeier asks whether in taking the 'historicality of human existence' seriously the New Hermeneutic has adequately answered the question of how modern faith can overcome the distance from NT faith and can claim in any sense to 'interpret' what is found in the NT. On the one hand, scholars such as Thiselton have attempted to modify the theories of Fuchs and Ebeling to avoid the one-sidedness which they detect there. On the other hand, some such as McKnight have preferred to pursue hermeneutical discussion with reference to the new lines of interpretation introduced into biblical studies by structuralism.*

See also **Hermeneutics; Meaning.**

P. J. Achtemeier, *An Introduction to the New*

Hermeneutic, 1969; E. V. McKnight, *Meaning in Texts. The Historical Shaping of Narrative Hermeneutics*, 1978; J. M. Robinson and J. B. Cobb (eds), *The New Hermeneutic*, 1964; A. C. Thiselton, *The Two Horizons*, 1980; id., 'The New Hermeneutic' in I. H. Marshall (ed.), *New Testament Interpretation,* 1977, pp. 308–33.

R. A. PIPER

New Religious Movements

Over one thousand new religions have emerged in the West and Japan since 1945 and an even greater number in Africa. Many of these movements claim to derive from long established religious traditions, and not unexpectedly those that regard themselves as part of the Judaeo-Christian tradition make most use of the Bible. However, new religions of a Buddhist, Hindu and Islamic (*see* **Muslim Interpretation**) kind do not entirely neglect it; and the Rastafarian movement with its decidedly African perspective is biblically centred (see below). While the use made of the Bible is varied, it is resorted to more often than not to support the pronounced millenarian* emphasis found in many of the new Judaeo-Christian derived movements.

This is clear from the use made of the Bible by the Worldwide Church of God, also known as Armstrongism after its late founder, Herbert W. Armstrong, formerly a Baptist pastor in Salem, Missouri; and its offshoot, the Church of God International. The former church has a large following in the United States, is active in Britain and elsewhere in Western Europe, and publishes the *Plain Truth* magazine which has a circulation of several millions.

Its message is essentially millennial and rests on the books of Jeremiah, Ezekiel, Daniel and Revelation. Moreover, the Bible, interpreted literally,* is regarded as the sole authentic source for the understanding of history. For example, Dan. 2 and 7 predict the rise of Nazism; Matt. 24.9, 21–22, we are told, predict the advent of World War Three and the Great Tribulation, involving the annihilation of all life, unless humankind changes its ways.

As the founder of this church expressed it, 'only by UNDERSTANDING (*sic*) Bible prophecies can you know what is now going to happen'. However, this understanding is not open to everyone. Armstrong, citing I Cor. 2.8–9, contends that 'None of the great minds – the most highly educated – the leaders – even the religious leaders' can understand the Bible and the Bible itself explains why, in I Cor. 2.10. This he interprets to mean that God reveals his spiritual truths through the Holy Spirit to those who 'DO (*sic*) keep his commandments', and that excludes all those mentioned above, including the established churches as a whole. The latter are accused, among other things, of neglecting the prophetic element in the Bible and therefore one third of its content.

This apocalyptic,* millenarian thrust and the same selective literalism are found in many other new movements of Christian orientation. The Children of God and/or The Family of Love, founded by the American Moses David in the late 1960s, relying on many of the same biblical sources, also points to the Last Days, the destruction of the present order, and the ushering in of the new age of harmony, bliss and plenty.

Although the interpretation of the Bible is literalist, this does not prevent evolution of doctrine, for it is also highly selective. Moses David's progressive elaboration of the doctrine of salvation is a case in point. He moved from a doctrine of salvation through conformity to the Mosaic Law* to one based on salvation by grace through faith, relegating good works to the periphery.

This movement, furthermore, has made use of the Bible to furnish it with a blue-print for communal life and moral conduct. For instance, the founder has developed a conception of the will and nature of God based on elements of the OT and NT which portray him as sanctioning a wider range of marital and sexual practices than those based on the Mosaic moral code. Again he has had recourse to the Bible, in a clearly selective way, to legitimate his own authority and to counter deviance: the Pauline epistles, esp. I Cor. 8–9 and Gal. 2, are drawn upon to form the basis of an explanation of the corruption of the early churches in terms of their failure to obey Paul;* likewise failure to obey Moses David will lead to the corruption of the Children of God.

Turning to new religions derived from other religious traditions, we find that the Bible is used in a variety of different ways. There are Hindu new movements which have recourse to it to lend support to a number of their religious insights, teachings and practices. The International Society for Krishna Consciousness (ISKCON), better known as Hare Krishna, points to those passages in the Gospels and Epistles which teach the value of asceticism and denounce the worship of Mammon, and thus underpin their own teachings on these matters.

More generally, it is pointed out by this and other movements of Hindu provenance that the notion of the Bible as the efficacious 'Word of God'* is one that is familiar to those Krishna devotees who are versed in the power of spiritual sound.

These movements also consider the biblical notion of faith, for purposes of comparison and contrast with their own ideas of enlightenment. They point out that the Pauline teaching, that we only see in part in this life but will one day fully understand (I Cor. 13.12), is not a distinction that they can accept; for new religions such as the Friends of the Western Buddhist Order (FWBO), full enlightenment can be attained in the here and now.

Eastern movements and Islamic movements have a considerable amount to say about Jesus. Many do not accept that he died on the cross and rose from the dead, or that he is the Son of God, and have recourse to the Gospels to obtain support for these opinions. Jesus, however, is respected and, depending on the movement, is presented as an enlightened guru, an exemplary meditator or a prophet of God for his own time.

A movement that perhaps makes more use of the Bible than any other new movement is the Rastafarian movement, which came into existence in Jamaica in the 1930s and is now to be found in Africa, Europe, and North and South America. This biblically-centred religion looks to the OT and NT not only for many of its beliefs, rituals and customs of dress and hairstyle but also for an explanation and understanding of the history of black people. Moreover, the Bible is used by Rastafarians as a vehicle for the restoration of their dignity and identity as individuals and as a race which was ravaged by slavery.

With the exception of the Rastafarian movement, where everyone is her/his own authority on biblical matters, it is the leader of the movement in question who interprets what the Bible means.

See also **Black Christian Interpretation; Millenarianism.**

P. B. Clarke (ed.), *The New Evangelists. Recruitment, Methods and Aims of New Religious Movements*, 1987; id., *Black Paradise. The Rastafarian Movement*, 1986; T. Robbins, *Cults, Converts and Charisma*, 1988; S. R. Sutherland, L. Houlden, P. B. Clarke and F. E. Hardy (eds), *The World's Religions* (Part Six), 1988; R. Wallis, *The Elementary Forms of the New Religious Life*, 1984.

PETER CLARKE

Numbers

The English title 'Numbers', deriving from the Septuagint,* Vulgate* and Talmud,* refers to the census material which comprises the first four chapters of the book. However, the scope of the work is much more extensive and its title in the Hebrew Bible, 'In the Wilderness', better indicates the nature of its contents which encompass 35 of the 40 years' Wilderness wanderings. Numbers has widely been regarded as one of the most incoherent books in the Bible and the most difficult to interpret as a whole, consisting of a large number of apparently disconnected units, whose relationship to one another is hard to determine. Hence, critical OT scholarship has generally approached the book as being part of a larger work, the Pentateuch* or Tetrateuch, which was only artificially divided into individual books when the entire complex was already complete. It has therefore been mainly analysed according to the various sources which are considered to make up the Pentateuch.

The great majority of scholars are agreed that in its existing form Numbers is a product of priestly circles and reflects the outlook and concerns of those circles: most critics would also hold that it originated in Babylon during the early post-exilic period, although influential voices have recently been raised in favour of a pre-exilic date for all the priestly pentateuchal strands. But in Numbers the priestly contribution consists both of indigenous priestly material and also of a revision of earlier traditions. Hence the book is analysed into two main blocks, P and non-P materials, many of the latter having undergone P revisions.

Specific P materials are in turn to be divided into two groups. There are narrative sections, e.g. chs 31 and 33, which in the view of scholars such as Noth are part of an extended account which represents the original P. There are also a large number of detailed cultic* rites and regulations, which may have been incorporated into the basic narrative, dealing with the Tabernacle, the Levites, sacrifices and the festal calendar,* and atonement ceremonies. In all these, the over-riding concern is the maintenance of the absolute purity of the community and its central sanctuary. Also, clear evidence can be seen of priestly revision of older stories, to orientate them towards particular priestly concerns, most notably in chs 16 and 17, where an original tale of a rebellion against the authority of Moses* has been transformed into an account of a conflict between different groups among the Levites.

The non-priestly material is found most clearly in chs 11–12 and 21–24, but in several other places as well. It is basically narrative and has been discussed from various positions. It may be viewed as 'early historiography' and used to reconstruct a reliable historical picture of the period before the entry into Canaan. From another standpoint, this material has been seen as exhibiting the same phenomena as are found elsewhere in the Pentateuch, a combination of the sources J and E, so that these sections of Numbers originally formed part of an extended JE document. Recent scholars who are primarily concerned with the literary character of the non-P material in Numbers have tended to approach it along one of two lines. There are those who would attribute it to the 'Yahwist', stressing its inner coherence as part of a larger composition, whatever earlier traditions this may have utilized, and as exhibiting the distinctive outlook of the Yahwistic author and redactor. Others look to the individual units of which the material is made up and investigate their traditio-historical* background and development, rather than concerning themselves with the usual Pentateuchal sources. Thus, a number of studies of this kind have been devoted to the Balaam episode in chs 22–24, and the significance in the early sections of Numbers of the theme of Mosaic authority and the challenges to it has been emphasized, with particular reference to chs 11 and 12.

More recently, there has been a tendency to appreciate Numbers not simply as a collection of disparate elements, however important in themselves, or as one component of a larger whole, only to be properly understood in that context, but as an independent work in its own right, using and interpreting older traditions to give expression to its own special interests and purpose. It has been noted that there is evidence of a well-ordered arrangement in the work. The beginning marks a new stage, with the departure into the wilderness from Sinai, which has been the setting of Exodus and Leviticus; and if, as is widely accepted, the account of Moses' death in Deut. 34 originally belonged to the Numbers narrative, the book has a clear conclusion with the demise of its central character. The whole can be seen as directed to the occupation of the Promised Land, structured in three stages: the constitution of the holy community, chs 1–10, the fate of the community as it journeys through the wilderness towards Canaan, chs 11–25, and, after this purgative experience, a new beginning, marked by a fresh census, when the community can make its final preparations for the entry, chs 26–35.

In particular, if the theory that Numbers is a product of those in exile in Babylon who were looking forward to a restoration in their own land is correct, the leading themes of the book can be seen as providing paradigms from the past which could give the exiles encouragement, guidance and warning for their own particular situation. Increasingly, it is recognized that the various writings of the priestly school which can plausibly be assigned to this period do not simply aim to preserve the past but are just as much directed to the present and future. So, in Numbers the Tabernacle is set in the middle of the camp, as the centre of the nation's life and the assurance of God's presence with his people, corresponding to the significance for the community of the restored Temple. But the divine dwelling-place needed to be protected from profanation, such as it had suffered in the past, and here the clear emergence in Numbers for the first time of the Levites as a distinct order within the cultic hierarchy, and its concern to establish their proper position, is highly significant: for it is primarily the Levites' task, through their role as intermediaries, to guard the people at large from profaning the sanctuary's holiness. Again, the dominant theme of Numbers, the journey to the Promised Land, with all its perils and temptations to faithlessness and to turn back to the fleshpots of an alien country, would have a special significance for exiles contemplating the problems of a return to Palestine. These, and other indications in the work, point to a clear underlying structure and purpose behind its apparent surface inchoateness.

See also **Exodus; Moses; Pentateuch, Pentateuchal Criticism.**

J. S. Ackerman, 'Numbers' in R. Alter and F. Kermode (eds), *The Literary Guide to the Bible*, 1987, pp. 78–91; P. J. Budd, *Numbers*, 1984; D. T. Olson, *The Death of the Old and the Birth of the New: The Framework of the Book of Numbers and the Pentateuch*, 1985; G. J. Wenham, *Numbers*, 1982.

J. R. PORTER

Obadiah

Obadiah is the smallest book in the OT. Despite its brevity the book has more than its fair share of interpretative problems and there remains no consensus about its origins, construction, or significance in the prophetic* collection. It consists of an oracle* against Edom (vv. 2–14) and a 'day of Yahweh' proclamation (vv. 15–21), with v. 15 functioning Janus-like for both themes. The common elements in Obadiah and Jer. 49.7–22 complicate its interpretation further by raising questions about literary dependence and common sources for such oracles. The superficial unity of the vision is achieved by the Edom theme appearing in both sections, and the day of Yahweh motif against the nations (vv. 15–16) is used as the occasion for the dispossession of Edom and its neighbouring states.

The older commentaries* linked Obadiah to an occasion of Edomite conflict reflected in II Kings 8.20, though Wellhausen related it to Nabataean attacks on Edom in the first half of the fifth century (cf. Kaiser, p. 270). The modern tendency is to read vv. 11–14 as an allusion to the fall of Jerusalem in 587 and therefore to treat the oracle as exilic, with a post-exilic reference to restoration in vv. 19–21. The name Obadiah, 'servant of Yah',

may be symbolic,* indicating an anonymous devotee of Yahweh (cf. Malachi), with an obvious location in the cult.* Most recent writers prefer to treat the name as a proper one and regard Obadiah as a real person who uttered the vision associated with his name. Some even read the book as the work of an eye-witness to the events of Jerusalem's destruction and Edomite involvement in that catastrophe (e.g. Fohrer, Schmidt). The formal nature of the language and the stereotypical 'oracle against the nations' pattern militate against this understanding of what is essentially anonymous material. The deep hatred of Edom (Esau) displayed in Obadiah is characteristic of the Hebrew Bible (cf. Lam. 4.21; Ps. 137.7; Mal. 1.2–5) and is rationalized by reference to Edomite participation in the Babylonian destruction of Jerusalem. In retaliation for this collaboration with the national enemy Yahweh will annihilate the Edomites and allow the house of Jacob to possess their territory (vv. 18–19). The general hostility to Edom expressed by means of this genre is given a setting in the belief in a day of Yahweh and may well have a cultic location. It has certainly convinced exegetes that Obadiah should be regarded as a cult prophet and that the book is representative of optimistic prophecy (Fohrer).

The theological value of Obadiah is disputed by commentators. For some the last line, 'dominion shall belong to Yahweh', holds the key to understanding the whole book (Watts, p. 66). It exemplifies a prophetic and ritual treatment of the theme of the kingdom of God.* However, v. 21 is better read as an assertion that the kingdom of Esau, i.e. Edom, will belong to Yahweh and be ruled by the people in Jerusalem, thus reinforcing the political hegemony reflected in the 'oracle against the nations' genre. Childs regards Edom in the poem 'as a representative entity, namely, the ungodly power of this world which threatens the people of God' (p. 415). This is an over-reading of the vision, for it is Edom's past which constituted the threat against Zion–Jacob–Joseph–Israel, and now with the day of Yahweh imminent (v. 15a) Zion is secure against Edom. In material of this genre and in conventional day of Yahweh material (how radically different is Amos 5.18–20!) Israel's future is always a positive one and the threat from the nations a transitory one. Obadiah celebrates these themes using a particular Edomite experience as the central motif of a standard generic treatment.

'Obadiah is of little theological interest and its presence in the canon* can easily be explained as a result of the anti-Idumaean polemic which was in full flood at the beginning of the first century AD' (Soggin, p. 399). Such xenophobia with its explicit justification of acquiring neighbouring territory gives Obadiah a permanent value in the canon as a practical programme for political action and may well reflect the real value and function of oracles against the nations in the ancient world of Judaean visionary oracles. Jer. 49.11 hints at a slightly kinder attitude towards Edomites.

The position of Obadiah in the prophetic collection (after Amos in the Masoretic* text but after Joel in the Septuagint*) is usually explained in relation to common emphases on the day of Yahweh motif in Amos 5.18–20 and Joel 2.1–2, 11; 3.14 (Childs, for all his interest in canon as such, studiously refuses to comment on these canonical placings!). More assured is the fact that in both canons the book of Jonah follows Obadiah and subtly undermines its savage xenophobia. In spite of the dubiety of the principle of canonical interpretation of biblical books, the debunking of Obadiah by the book of Jonah through the canonical placement of the two books is a notion worth keeping in mind when reading Obadiah. The theme of repentance is incompatible with the motif of the day of Yahweh – when applied to the nations (cf. Joel 2.12–14; 3)!

B. S. Childs, *Introduction to the Old Testament as Scripture*, 1979, pp. 411–16; G. Fohrer, *Introduction to the Old Testament*, 1970, pp. 438–40; O. Kaiser, *Introduction to the Old Testament*, 1975, pp. 257–60; W. H. Schmidt, *Introduction to the Old Testament*, 1984, pp. 232–3; J. A. Soggin, *Introduction to the Old Testament*, ³1989, pp. 398–400; J. D. W. Watts, *Obadiah*, 1969.

ROBERT P. CARROLL

Oracle

1. In OT form criticism* the term is used to denote the basic units of which prophetic* books are composed. The assumption is usually that individual oracles originated as oral utterances, and that they were linked together into larger collections secondarily, through the work of later editors.

The main types of prophetic oracle are the *Drohwort* or word of threat; the *Scheltwort* or word of condemnation; and the *Mahnwort* or word of exhortation.

A typical threat is Amos 7.8–9: 'Behold, I am setting a plumb line in the midst of my people Israel; I will never again pass by them; the high places of Isaac shall be made desolate, and the sanctuaries of Israel shall be laid waste, and I will rise against the house of Jeroboam with the sword.'

Condemnations usually appear as the explanation for coming disaster in the early prophets: '(their root will be as rottenness, and their blossom go up like dust) for they have rejected the law of the Lord of hosts, and have despised the word of the Holy One of Israel' (Isa. 5.24).

Exhortations do not occur very frequently in the pre-exilic prophets, but become commoner after the exile. A typical post-exilic example is Zech. 8.16: 'These are the things that you shall do: Speak the truth to one another, render in your gates judgments that are true and make for peace, do not devise evil in your hearts against one another, and love no false oath.'

The prophetic books also contain oracles of promise, such as the 'messianic'* predictions of Isa. 9.2–7 (Heb. 1–6) or Jer. 23.5–6: such oracles often begin 'In that day' or 'Behold, the days are coming when . . .' (cf. also Isa. 7.18, 20, 21, 23; 19.16, 18, 19, 23, 24).

One of the characteristic features of the classical prophets is their use of originally non-oracular forms of utterance as a vehicle for their message. Thus many prophetic oracles begin 'Thus says the Lord', a form adopted from the speech of ambassadors in the ancient world (for a secular example cf. II Kings 18.19). Prophets also couch their oracles in the form of a popular song (Isa. 5.1–7), a funeral dirge (Amos 5.2), or a priestly torah (Amos 4.4–5), sometimes with deliberately sarcastic effect. The common form beginning 'Woe to . . .' (cf. Amos 6.1; Isa. 5.8, 11, 18, 20, 21, 22) is also probably derived from funeral laments. In the exilic prophecies of Isa. 40–55 forms borrowed from the liturgical sphere become prevalent, such as the hymn ('Sing to the Lord a new song!' Isa. 42.10, cf. Ps. 96.1; 98.1), the divine self-praise or aretalogy* found in cultic texts in Mesopotamia ('I, I am the Lord, and besides me there is no saviour', Isa. 43.11), and the oracle of assurance ('Fear not, for I am with you', Isa. 43.5). Thus the prophetic books contain oracles whose forms are not prophetic in origin, as well as others that are.

2. The form-critical use of the term 'oracle' is religiously neutral: it does not in itself imply anything about the origin, supernatural or otherwise, of the prophets' utterances. However, the fact that the same term is used of the utterances of certain figures in the classical world, and especially of the famous oracle of Delphi, means that its use tends to suggest some kind of official religious status for the OT prophets. In particular, analogies with Delphi and other ancient cultic centres would imply that prophetic 'oracles' were often the response to questions put by those who consulted the prophets. The narrative books of the OT make it clear that some Israelite prophets did act as consultants. In II Kings 4.23 the question (to the Shunamite woman whose son Elisha will raise to life) 'Why will you go to

him (Elisha) today? It is neither new moon nor sabbath' may imply that it was normal to consult prophets on holy days. Both Isaiah (Isa. 37.1–7) and Jeremiah (Jer. 37.1–10) are consulted by the kings of Judah, and during the exile Ezekiel seems to have received regular deputations of the elders of Israel (Ezek. 14.1).

In this connection it should be noted that most of the longer prophetic books contain oracles against foreign nations: see Isa. 13–23; Jer. 46–51; Ezek. 25–32, 38–39; cf. Amos 1.1–2.5. Some scholars think that such oracles derive from curses which it belonged to the prophetic office to utter against the enemies of Israel. An analogy might be offered by the so-called Execration Texts, used in Egypt in the second millennium BC, in which the enemies of Egypt were solemnly cursed in ordered succession. At the end of this ceremony the tablets on which the curses were written were solemnly smashed, in an act of symbolism* or perhaps of 'sympathetic magic'. If the Israelite prophets did engage in acts of this kind, this would reinforce the case for seeing them as holding an official position at court, part of whose function was to ensure the success of Israel and the downfall of its enemies. On the other hand, there is no clear evidence for cycles of 'oracles against the nations' (as opposed to individual oracles against a particular foe) before Amos, and it may be that the adoption of the execration form is simply another example of borrowing by the prophets from other spheres of activity.

One of the distinctive features of the great classical prophets may have been the fact that they spoke without being consulted, and that they did not occupy official positions at court which would have involved them in partisan political activity. They seem anxious to present their words as the result of direct divine inspiration,* and to deny that they speak from any kind of professional obligation. From this point of view, the word 'oracle' may be somewhat misleading as a description of their utterances, which are seldom either responses to questions posed by others or the expression of official sentiments. It may be best to say that though there probably were prophets in Israel whose function it was to give 'oracles' in something like the Delphic sense – responses to questions (cf. I Sam. 9.6) – or to act as official mouthpieces for curses, the classical prophets do not fit this mould. In that case it might make for clarity to avoid using the term 'oracle' to describe their utterances.

3. According to a popular misunderstanding, the Delphic oracle generally gave riddling or ambiguous answers to the questions posed to it. In fact most of its recorded responses are straightforward enough, but a number of famous ambiguous answers have led to this misconception. The most notable is the 'Croesus' oracle (mentioned by Herodotus), in which the king of Lydia was told that by invading Persia he would destroy 'a great army', and discovered only through bitter experience that the army in question was his own.

This conception of the nature of Greek oracles has led readers of the OT to expect the 'oracles' of the prophets to be dark or obscure. Traditional readings of the prophets as those who foretold the far-distant future, and especially the days of the messiah,* have encouraged a similar supposition. Both in the NT and in the Dead Sea Scrolls* passages from the prophets (and other OT books) are interpreted as messages in code about the time in which the reader is now living. Thus in the epistles of Paul,* and in Hebrews, verses from the psalms are treated as 'oracular' in this sense – predictions whose full meaning was plain only to God when they were written but is now revealed to Christians: Rom. 9.25; I Cor. 10.11; II Cor. 6.2; Heb. 10.5–7.

The Qumran Habakkuk commentary provides many examples of the same tendency, and there some of the places referred to by the prophet are interpreted as cyphers for persons and people of the interpreter's own time: for instance, 'Lebanon' in Hab. 2.17 is explained as referring to the Council of the Qumran community (IQpHab 12).

One way of describing this use of the prophetic and other texts by Christians and Qumran covenanters is to say that they treated scriptural texts as 'oracular'. It may fairly be claimed that one major achievement of critical biblical scholarship has been to show that the words of the prophets were not originally 'oracles' in this sense, but referred to matters of concern to themselves and their contemporaries.

See also **Ancient Near Eastern Interpretation; Logion; Prophets and Prophecy.**

J. Barton, *Oracles of God: Perceptions of Ancient Prophecy in Israel after the Exile*, 1986; J. Fontenrose, *The Delphic Oracle*, 1978; N. K. Gottwald, *All the Kingdoms of the Earth*, 1964; C. Westermann, *Basic Forms of Prophetic Speech*, 1967; R. R. Wilson, *Prophecy and Society in Ancient Israel*, 1980.

JOHN BARTON

Oral Tradition (New Testament)

At the very beginning of modern biblical scholarship (e.g. R. Simon, 1638–1712), scholars were aware of the fact that several books of the Bible originated in oral tradition. But it was the learned philosopher of culture, J. G. von Herder,* who in 1796–97 seriously drew the attention of biblical scholars to the fact that Christianity did not begin with books but with oral preaching. Jesus did not write, and his apostles did not set up a 'Gospel* chancellory' in Jerusalem. The written Gospels are not biographies of Jesus of Nazareth but historical documentation of the oral gospel about Jesus Christ, the messiah* of God, and each one of the evangelists* reproduced in his book, in his own way, important elements of Jesus' preaching and stories about him. Not least thanks to his knowledge of folklore,* Herder made many observations which would not be taken up for proper investigation until the twentieth century. Awareness of oral tradition was to play a role in discussion of the origins of Christianity, the nature of the Gospels and the connection between them, as well as of the question of how the units in the Gospels are to be classified and interpreted.

Individual scholars tried in the nineteenth century to take seriously the insight that the Gospel pericopes (or units) were originally oral traditions, but this insight had no penetrative power because nobody knew of a method for clarification of an oral phase in past time. The debate kept to the written Gospels and their assumed written sources.

At the beginning of the twentieth century, however, great progress had been made within folklore* research (A. Olrik), and these insights also proved to be very fruitful in OT scholarship (H. Gunkel). Inspired by these two disciplines – and by classical scholarship (E. Norden) – some German scholars (K. L. Schmidt, M. Dibelius, R. Bultmann,* and others) made a bold breakthrough into the no-man's-land between the evangelists and Jesus. This happened in the years around 1920. The new programme was given the name *Formgeschichte*, form criticism.*

The form critics stated that the Synoptic* Gospels cannot be classified as literature in the general sense (*Hochliteratur*). The text material that is put together in them belongs to the category of popular 'small-literature' (*Kleinliteratur*): oral texts such as the proverb, the riddle, the folk song, etc. Such texts are not created by individual writers, but grow among the anonymous 'people'. They are formed within contexts where they are needed and used (the *Sitz im Leben* of the texts). Thus the different 'text types' (*Gattungen*) reflect needs and activities vital for the fellowship within which they arise. Inspired by the disciplines just mentioned, the form-critical pioneers developed methods for clarification of the oral stage of the synoptic tradition, and, at the same time, the life of the early Christian communities.* They detached the small units from the framework in which they are placed in the written Gospels, sorted them into different text types (sayings, parables,* miracle* stories, etc.), and tried to determine their primi-

tive form and how they had been altered on their way from their origin down to the collecting, editing and final fixing in writing.

The form critics' theological and historical point of departure was the thesis that Christianity originated with the proclamation that the crucified Jesus was risen. While Dibelius thought that early Christianity had preserved relatively reliable memories from the earthly ministry of Jesus, Bultmann believed that after Easter these memories had been rather freely transformed by the belief in the risen Lord; many synoptic texts were simply fabricated within the Christian community and reflect its needs and attitudes, its creed* and preaching, not the earthly ministry of Jesus. Bultmann thought that the historical Jesus* did not see himself as the messiah and did not preach about himself; his teaching about the kingdom of God* is but an important presupposition for that Christian message ('kerygma'*) which could not be preached until after Easter.

Thus the form critics saw the Synoptic Gospels as expressions of the perfected early Christian message. Their Gospel interpretation is characterized by sensitivity to the prehistory of the texts and to their kerygmatic character, function and meaning. But most of the early form critics had a rather limited interest in the Gospels as totalities; none of the pioneers of form criticism ever wrote a conventional commentary on any of the Synoptic Gospels. This weakness was remedied in the 1950s. Building upon the form-critical basis, many scholars now concentrated on the final stage of the synoptic tradition: the making and content of the finally written Gospels (redaction criticism:* H. Conzelmann, W. Marxsen and others).

A very strong interest in the part played by oral tradition in the Ancient Near East* and Israel arose in Scandinavia* (especially Uppsala) in the 1930s and 1940s. Against the modern Western 'book-view', the orientalist H. S. Nyberg maintained (1935) that many of the books of the OT are based on oral tradition, and moreover that they went on functioning mainly as memorized texts after having been written down. This view was applied, with great energy, to the OT literature in its entirety by I. Engnell. In this milieu, B. Gerhardsson tried to describe the way in which teachers, above all within rabbinic* Judaism in antiquity, formulated, transmitted and commented upon their Oral Torah (*Memory and Manuscript*, 1961). He studied especially the role played by memorization of brief, concentrated texts within the rich and flexible tradition. This comparative study was made in order to elucidate the way in which Jesus and early Christianity created and transmitted their new oral tradition. This work was later carried further by the German scholar, R. Riesner (*Jesus als Lehrer*, 1981), who concentrated on the methods of transmitting texts on a more popular level among the Jews: in homes, elementary schools, and synagogues. This approach is now under debate.

W. H. Kelber's work *The Oral and the Written Gospel* (1983) is the latest attempt so far at incorporating ideas from recent folklore research, in this case carried out by American and English scholars (M. Parry, A. B. Lord). Kelber has also learnt from modern text theorists, intimately linked with this folklore research (W. J. Ong). In this case, scholars have seized on popular epic tradition of a type where narrators draw upon a stock of inherited words, formulas, themes, motives, plots, etc., but present in fact, every single time, a new variation: there is no original or standard text but just an unlimited number of variegated forms of the narrative, each of them influenced by the narrator's actual audience ('composition in transmission'). The writing down of a tradition of this type is a revolution: flexibility becomes firmness, living, audible words become dead, visual, graphical signs, and one of innumerable equal variations suddenly acquires an exceptional position.

In the light of these observations, made in 'oral societies', Kelber draws a sharp division between 'orality' (oral delivery, always flexible) and 'textuality' (written presentation, always firm). In the beginning the Jesus tradition was presented by way of 'composition in transmission'. The writing down of this material meant, according to Kelber, a radical change and a formal break with the oral Jesus tradition. The written Gospel is a direct counter-move against the oral tradition transmitted hitherto, and the evangelist who writes wants to dethrone the authorities of the existing gospel proclamation. Today a new, specific, 'oral hermeneutic'* must be developed, according to Kelber, if the Gospel is to be handled adequately, as it was handled in the beginning.

These ideas have had a considerable response among American scholars. They are, however, open to serious objections. 1. Both oral tradition and written texts may be of numerous different kinds. 2. Orality and literacy (textuality) cannot be put side by side as congruent parallels and contrasted in the way Kelber does: the interrelation between the two is complicated. 3. The folklore parallels Kelber adduces are not adequate. Neither Jesus himself, nor the apostles or teachers of early Christianity, are depicted as popular narrators; moreover, the text material in the Gospel tradition is mostly in the form of very brief units which do not admit the free way of retelling which was typical for the comparative

material adduced by Kelber. They have rather the character of dense teaching material. 4. Jesus and early Christianity did not move within some 'oral society' but in milieux where writing and books had played an important part for many centuries, not least in religious education, and where orality and literacy interacted. On the one hand, the oral Gospel tradition was connected in important ways with the inherited Jewish scriptures, and, on the other hand, the writing down of the Jesus tradition did not mean that oral transmission and exposition of the Jesus traditions suddenly ceased. Preaching and teaching were not immediately replaced by reading. It was not until the middle of the second century that the church found it natural to regard the Gospels as 'holy scriptures' in the same sense as the OT books.

The writing down of the Gospel tradition was, from a historical point of view, inevitable. It was also salutary. In a certain sense, the written Gospel makes the link with the eye-witnesses* who lived within the church during the first Christian decades; when these died, the Gospel tradition was written down (say AD 67–95). These books are, beyond comparison, the most important sources posterity has concerning Jesus and the very first period of the church. They are the foundation documents of the church and its foremost sources of inspiration for its activity. They are also like snapshots from the period of origins, which the church needs as points of reference for its work in later times. Nevertheless, the church started without them.

What was the significance of the fact that basic parts of the Gospel tradition were written down? There were firm texts even during the oral phase (logia,* parables,* narratives, etc.), which were commented upon and applied, but the border-line between text and exposition was not sharp. The texts could themselves be adapted to new problems and situations; normally, only very small alterations were necessary. Some small adaptations of the text of the written Gospels seem to have been possible also during the very first period after their coming into being, but soon the text of the books was immovably fixed. Instead, oral exposition and application became increasingly important. In significant respects, interpreters could follow the principles they had applied to the OT books right from the start. The fact that the written text was not only read but also expounded and applied made it possible to save much of the richness of content, multivalence and flexibility of the oral texts.

In the hermeneutical debate today, there are reasons for thinking once more about the early church Fathers' theme – emphasized even by Luther* – that the gospel is a spoken word (*viva vox*). The double point of departure is that books surely are permitted and important – Jesus and his apostles laid strong stress on the testimonies of the ancient scriptures – but that the gospel was from the beginning a markedly oral word, which should be 'written in the heart' of the listeners in order to create faith within them and govern their attitudes and speech on all issues of life. To achieve this aim, it was vital that the message was living, flexible speech. With regard to the Pauline* letters, it must be remembered that the apostle used to preach and teach orally. He only wrote letters in cases when he could not come himself in person.

Awareness of the fact that the gospel is by nature a spoken word is essential for a sound interpretation of the holy scriptures of the church. It is a guard against the tendency – not uncommon within Protestantism – to think that the church believes in the Bible, not in the triune God, and it counteracts dead ecclesiastical routine, legalism, and rationalistic literalism in interpretation.

See also **Evangelist; Gospel.**

R. Bultmann, *The History of the Synoptic Tradition*, 1963; M. Dibelius, *From Tradition to Gospel*, 1934; B. Gerhardsson, *The Gospel Tradition*, 1986; W. H. Kelber, *The Oral and the Written Gospel*, 1983; B. Reicke, *The Roots of the Synoptic Tradition*, 1986; R. Riesner, *Jesus als Lehrer*, 1981.

BIRGER GERHARDSSON

Origen

Prior to Origen there was much use of scripture and much reference to it, but nothing in the way of formal commentary* or reflection upon how interpretation should take place. Origen was the first great scholar of the Bible, who brought to its interpretation the resources of a Greek literary and philosophical education, as well as sufficient scholarly interest to make enquiries into the original language and into Jewish understanding of those scriptures Christians and Jews had in common. The extent of his contacts with the Jewish community and with Jewish exegetes is far from clear: reasons for thinking it may have been distinctly superficial will emerge below. Nevertheless he was the first to realize that Christian interpretation of the Bible involved 'research' and scholarship, the first to make an attempt at systematizing exegesis,* and the first to outline a 'theory' or 'philosophy' of interpretation. Although much of his output is no longer extant, it is clear that his achievement and subsequent influence were considerable. Later, aspects of his theological position were attacked and eventually in 553 he was condemned as a heretic.

Origen realized that the first prerequisite for reading a text is to get the wording right. Scholars in Alexandria had long since devised a system of signs to indicate different readings (*see* **Alexandrian Interpretation**), and one of the tasks Origen undertook was to create the so-called 'Hexapla', a huge compendium of versions of the OT, suitably marked to show variant readings in the various versions. The versions Origen reproduced are said to have included the Hebrew, a transliteration of the Hebrew into Greek, the Septuagint (LXX),* and the Greek translations by Aquila, Symmachus and Theodotion (though this ancient tradition has been questioned in recent research, and it would appear that the number of columns was not consistently six, as the title suggests). This work was later consulted by Jerome in Caesarea. Origen himself clearly respected the LXX and like his fellow-Christians could regard it as the inspired text; but on occasion he makes it plain that the 'original' should be preferred.

Origen was concerned not simply with questions of wording, but also with questions of meaning.* He wrote commentaries on many of the books of the Bible, and series of homilies* on many more were noted down and published. Despite the loss of the bulk of his writings, a substantial amount of material is available for studying his exegetical techniques and conclusions. One of the most intriguing questions about Origen's exegetical work concerns the relationship between his 'theory' of exegesis and his actual practice in commentaries and homilies.

Origen's theory is set out in his treatise *De Principiis*. Origen takes for granted not only the divine inspiration* of scripture and its unity, but also the fact that the scriptures have not just a meaning that is apparent at first sight, but also another which escapes most people's notice. For the written words are the forms of certain mysteries and the images of divine things; the whole Law is 'spiritual',* So much Origen claims to have received from the teaching of the church, and it is the basis of his understanding of how the scriptures are to be read. The cause of error in interpretation, whether it be the error of failing to see the prophecies fulfilled (the Jews), or thinking the God of creation was imperfect (the Marcionites*), or of attributing to God cruel and unjust actions (simple believers), is failure to understand scripture according to its spiritual meaning, and sticking solely to the letter.

The way to interpret scripture is found in scripture itself: as Proverbs (22.20,21) suggests, scripture is to be portrayed in a threefold manner, so that the simple may be edified by the 'flesh' of scripture, that is its obvious sense, while the more advanced may be edified by the 'soul', and the perfect, the ones with whom the apostle spoke wisdom (I Cor. 2.6,7), may receive edification from the spiritual law, which is a shadow of the good things to come. For as human beings consist of body, and soul, and spirit, so in the same way does scripture. This analogy Origen seems to owe without acknowledgment to the Jewish philosopher, Philo* of Alexandria, who also espoused allegorical interpretation.*

Origen goes on to suggest that while many passages are edificatory for simple believers at the purely 'corporeal' level, this is not always so. Using particularly passages from Paul's* epistles* and the Epistle to the Hebrews, he justifies the view that the Jews served a copy and a shadow of spiritual things, and so the notion that spiritual realities are concealed in the biblical narratives. Because the 'body' of the text makes such good sense, and generally leads to improving ordinary people, the word of God* arranged certain stumbling-blocks and impossibilities to be present in the midst of law and history to provoke investigation. The principal aim of such passages is to indicate the 'spiritual' level, the mystical* meaning interwoven with the history, and they should not be taken literally. Origen even goes so far as to say that since the same Spirit inspired the evangelists and apostles, the same phenomenon can be found in the NT. It is particularly in relation to the Law that he condemns the 'literalism' of Jewish* interpretation and claims that some laws are not only irrational but impossible to keep; but he does not hesitate either to suggest that some sayings of Jesus are impossible to take literally, like smiting the right cheek – everyone smites the left cheek with his right hand! Such things point to the fact that it is the divine intention that we should not receive the letter of scripture alone.

Origen maintains that this does not mean that none of the biblical history is real, or that none of the laws are to be literally obeyed. Far more of the Bible is literally true than not. Nevertheless what is really important is the 'spiritual' sense which is discerned through allegory: for example, the 'corporeal' Israelites are 'types' of 'spiritual' Israelites, and references to Jerusalem* are references to the heavenly city.

Such is Origen's theoretical account of his approach to the interpretation of scripture. It is clear that Jewish interpretation is rejected as literal. Yet in fact Jewish *halakhah* often exploited symbolic* meanings and Origen himself adopts the Jewish practice of finding significance in every little detail of the text, exploiting such details to produce allegories that suit his purpose. Other things are less

clear, the status of the 'literal', for example: Origen gives value to the letter, and yet often rejects it. The ambiguity applies to both literal practice of the Law and literal understanding of historical narrative; in rejecting the Law, he acknowledges that some laws are to be kept, notably those we call 'moral', and in honouring the story, he insists that many narratives are only important for their typological significance, their pointing to Christ.

There is also a certain lack of clarity about the distinction between the 'moral' and 'spiritual' meaning, the meaning for the 'soul' and the meaning for the 'perfect'. The three-fold pattern tends to dissolve into a two-fold pattern. In practice Origen's exegesis is not consistently either two-fold or three-fold. He favours a multiplication of meanings and possibilities, and eschews any criteria* for deciding what is the 'right' meaning. A convincing account of how Origen distinguishes different senses has not really been given: it is generally taken that the meaning for the 'soul' or moral meaning covers those cases where the text is taken to be about general moral principles, the kind of exegesis Origen shares with Philo; and the meaning for the perfect includes all the prophetic,* typological and christological meanings discovered in the text by Christian exegetes. But the more one reads Origen the less confident one becomes that such a distinction really works. It is easier to see how it might in relation to the OT than to the NT, yet the NT also points beyond itself to deeper meanings and deeper realities.

What lies behind Origen's approach to scripture?

1. *Precedents found in scripture itself, and in Christian tradition.* In the seventh Homily on Genesis, Origen finds the precedent for his approach to the story of Sarah and Hagar in Gal. 4.21–24. Hagar, who represents the synagogue, is expelled. A purely historical understanding of this is inadequate. The story refers to the blindness that has come upon Israel until the fullness of the Gentiles has come in (Rom. 11.25). The weaning of Isaac suggests the necessity of leaving milk and moving on to solid food enjoined in I Cor. 3.2 and Heb. 5.12ff. Origen believes that this refers to the necessity of leaving the literal meaning of the Law and discerning its spiritual sense. This is a particularly striking example of how the allegorical approach to the OT was far from arbitrary, drawing its themes and finding its justification by precise cross-reference to other biblical texts. The classic passage for Origen was II Cor. 3.

Much of Origen's allegory in fact integrates long-standing Christian interpretations: e.g. messianic* prophecies and typological parallels found in the Epistle of Barnabas, Melito's

Homily on the Pasch, and Justin's *Dialogue with Trypho*; and spiritualizing interpretations of circumcision, for example, in terms of the circumcision of the heart, or of sacrifice in terms of praise and obedience to the will of God, ideas anticipated in the NT and earlier patristic material. Origen uses some of these traditions to build up consistent symbols: Jerusalem means the heavenly city, and the temple is the type of the body of Christ and of the church. Other consistent identifications are picked up from scriptural metaphors:* 'leaven' means teaching, 'trumpet' means the word. Certainly Origen developed conventional correlations in ways which do not carry the same conviction, but his allegory is not entirely arbitrary, and such precedents were an important source.

2. *The apologetic need to justify the scriptures.* Origen was particularly sensitive to the charge that the scriptures were crude and contained an anthropomorphic* view of God quite unacceptable to the more sophisticated: see his debate with Celsus. He developed a remarkable reply to this, and indeed to the view of the Marcionites* that the God of the OT was an inferior God of Wrath, not the God of Jesus Christ: God in his love for his creatures accommodates himself to the human level. This happened not simply in the incarnation, but in the scriptures; for God adopted human language suitable to his hearers. Just as a father is angry with his child for good disciplinary reasons, and just as a doctor inflicts pain in order to heal, so God appears to be angry and to punish, but it is all for the salvation of his loved ones. There are different levels of meaning in the scriptures because God intends to reach different levels of people and to lead them on to a deeper understanding of his real nature. Hence the need for allegorizing or 'rationalizing' the anthropomorphic language of the Bible.

3. *The intellectual need to make sense of the scriptures.* Origen refused to speculate where the rule of faith passed down in the church had already mapped out Christian understanding. But he believed that many questions remained unanswered, the kind of intellectual questions about 'first principles' debated in the schools, issues like providence, free will, etc., and it was appropriate for a Christian philosopher to try and give a systematic account of 'how things are' which fits with the fundamental truths of the gospel. Although his own exegetical practice is far from systematic, there are ways in which he can clearly be regarded as the first systematic theologian.* His desire to make sense of scripture in terms of the intellectual assumptions of his own day is not to be dismissed as unsatisfactory. The conclusions could hardly remain sound when the intellectual climate changed: but in many ways his endeavour must be regarded as exemplary. Some would say that he 'sold out' on crucial issues, but on other matters he let the Bible modify his philosophy: the God of Jesus Christ was not simply the philosophical first cause, but a God of love.

See also **Alexandrian Interpretation; Allegorical Interpetation; Literal Meaning; Spiritual Meaning.**

H. Crouzel, *Origen*, ET 1989; R. P. C. Hanson, *Allegory and Event,* 1959; H. de Lubac, *Histoire et Esprit*, 1950; Nicholas de Lange, *Origen and the Jews*, 1976; J. W. Trigg, *Origen: the Bible and Philosophy in the Third Century Church*, 1983.

FRANCES YOUNG

Other Faiths

In a real sense the Bible has been a book of many faiths throughout the Christian era. The Hebrew scriptures, from which the Christians' OT is derived, are of course the property of Judaism, and are legitimately interpreted within that community (*see* **Jewish Exegesis**). Both OT and NT are acknowledged by Islam as having a share in that revelation* which was, for Muslims, consummated in the Qur'an (*see* **Muslim Interpretation**). And in the modern period new religious movements* have emerged which also base their traditions at least in part on the Bible – Mormons, Jehovah's Witnesses, Christian Scientists, the Unification Church, and many more. Thus the book we call the Bible is claimed by a surprising diversity of religious traditions – without our even considering whether the very wide divergence of opinion and belief within the broad stream of Christianity does not itself constitute a set of multi-faith interpretations.

These observations should alert us to the fact that the Bible is open to a far wider field of interpretation than its customary restriction to Jewish–Christian scholarly and religious circles would imply. Its place in the gallery of the world's religious texts opens the door to a reciprocity of interpretation at the inter-faith level. Hindus and Buddhists may well find that it speaks to them in ways undreamed of in the Judaeo-Christian tradition; and conversely, the scriptures of other religions form part of the hermeneutical* dialogue by means of which the Bible is appropriated for our own day.

Although these may appear at first sight to be threatening ideas, there is nothing essentially new in them. The Hebrew scriptures are in many ways indebted to the religious and secular texts of the Ancient Near East,* at the level both of controlling ideas and of form and structure. And the NT can hardly be understood without the Hellenistic* religious and cultural milieu which so profoundly interacted with that of the Jewish community to give it its characteristic features of deep continuity with, and yet radical departure from, the Hebrew scriptures.

Jewish and Muslim uses of the Bible are discussed elsewhere in this volume; we shall therefore restrict ourselves to general questions concerning the Bible in relation to other faiths, and to the impact of Hinduism and Buddhism in particular. There is as yet only a very limited number of resource books in this field – to a great extent the ground-breaking work remains to be done. But the recognition that interpretation on a wider basis is required has a long pedigree. Some of those involved in early sixteenth-century missionary work in India and China knew very well that the mere repetition of Western theological formulae and recital of unmediated texts of scripture were unlikely to cut much ice, and embarked on the long process of understanding the religions of their hosts with a view to finding acceptable ways of speaking of their own faith. Notable amongst these are the later Francis Xavier, in his work in Japan; Matteo Ricci in China; and – most dramatic of all – Roberto de Nobili, whose work amongst the Brahmin caste in South India marked a heroic attempt to enter the mind and soul of another faith in order to effect a genuine communication. Vincent Cronin's biography of de Nobili (*A Pearl to India*, 1959) describes both the difficulty and the importance of the enterprise. His comment to the effect that 'the adaptation of Christianity, devoid of unessential trappings, to Eastern customs, imagery and ways of thought, far from being a subject of limited historical interest, can claim to be one of the most urgent needs of our time', has not lost its pertinence. More recently, Klaus Klostermaier's autobiographical study (*Hindu and Christian in Vrindaban*, 1969) conveys powerfully and disturbingly the strangeness of Hindu India and the powerful effect it has on the interpretation of one's own traditions. And the encounter with Buddhism produced a major interpreter in the person of Thomas Merton.

Theoretical theological difficulties often arise when the question of multi-faith readings of scripture is approached. Certain biblical texts are regularly produced as proof that the whole enterprise is misconceived from the start – John 3.16; 14.6; and Acts 4.12 are perhaps the most familiar. It is therefore important to begin by reflecting on these theological problems. To oversimplify the matter, there are essentially three positions: exclusivism, inclusivism, and pluralism. The first effectively sets a fence round the Bible which would rule

out any non-Christian interpretation as inadmissible by definition. The second opens up the possibility that the spirit of Christianity is hidden within other faiths and so suggests a limited freedom of interpretation, though the basic impulse is to reduce or assimilate the other faith to Christianity, rather than to show how a biblical text might be read within Hinduism (for example). Only from the pluralist position is a wholehearted freedom of interpretation possible. These different theological positions are considered in Alan Race's study (*Christians and Religious Pluralism*, 1983); and the recent work of John Hick (e.g. *God and the Universe of Faiths*, 1989) has increasingly been devoted to the pluralist position in the inter-faith debate.

Given the legitimacy of the enterprise, there seem to be three directions in which to proceed: first, to reflect on what the Bible has to say positively about the dialogue between religions; secondly, to allow the fact of that dialogue to become an aspect of the interpretation we engage in as Christians or Jews; and thirdly, to take seriously readings of the Bible by those outside the Judaeo-Christian tradition.

The first of these directions is most commonly encountered, not least because it forms part of the 'exclusivist/inclusivist/pluralist' debate which was referred to above. Kenneth Cracknell (*Towards a New Relationship*, 1986) provides one of the clearest and most accessible treatments of this aspect of the interpretation of scripture, particularly in chs 2 and 3, where he deals with both NT and OT texts. Cracknell's long experience in the field of inter-faith relations, as secretary of the British Council of Churches Committee on Relations with People of Other Faiths, gives his contribution both practical and theoretical force. And he cannot be accused of being narrowly selective; there is scarcely a book of the Bible which is not referred to in the course of his argument.

On similar lines, but emerging from a different experience, is Wesley Ariarajah's 1985 study, *The Bible and People of Other Faiths*, published by the World Council of Churches. Ariarajah, a Methodist minister from Sri Lanka and director of the Dialogue Sub-Unit of the WCC, is familiar with a Hindu and Buddhist context, which he addresses at several points. His book is much slighter than Cracknell's, but is valuable for its distinct perspective.

The second direction follows naturally from the first, with no clear break between the two. To consider the biblical texts in relation to the legitimacy of dialogue is at the same time to begin the task of dialogical interpretation of the text. Thus Ariarajah, discussing the uniqueness of Jesus, draws a comparison with the Buddha (pp. 24f.), and he has sharp things to say (pp. 9f.), in the light of the doctrine of creation, to those who deny that the God of the Christians is also the God of Hindus. In my own study, *Christianity and Other Faiths in Britain* (1985), I have explored the possibility of a kind of dialectic in which the interpretation of texts from the Bible is not exhausted when we have explored the inner-biblical connections, but extends into a debate with non-Christian faiths which in turn feeds back into our understanding of the Bible. Earlier, the implications of a serious dialogue with Judaism are brought to bear on the question of the identity of Jesus and the meaning of his life. This is, of course, a long-standing dialogue and is taken up fully elsewhere. But it is important that the special character of the Jewish-Christian dialogue should not obscure its kinship with the kind of dialectic with which we are here concerned, and its equally profound implications.

Thirdly, we consider the impact of non-Judaeo-Christian modes of thought on the interpretation of scripture. This is a relatively poorly developed topic, not least because the great bulk of work on the scriptures has been carried out in the intellectual West, or under the strong influence of Western scholarly conventions. We have yet to see a Hindu commentary on Genesis or a Buddhist study of the Gospel of John – both of which are potentially intriguing prospects – but with recent emphases on modes of interpretation beyond the limited sphere of historical criticism* the door is now open in principle to such readings. One essay in this direction deserves comment: a study, published by the Bible Reading Fellowship in 1979, of the four Gospels in the context of world religions, by Cecil Hargreaves (*The Gospels in a World Context*). While the four studies are mediated through specific Christian writers, Hargreaves' interest lies in the fact that each of them belongs to or is steeped in a significantly non-Christian milieu.

Mark is read through the thought of Kosuke Koyama, whose background is Japanese Buddhism, and whose writing reflects the traumatic events of both Hiroshima and Vietnam. From this there emerges an emphasis on the slow development of God's dealings with humanity, with an element of surprise – the perception that no human paradigm or set of expectations can ever adequately define the work of God. These connect with the Marcan themes of the hiddenness of the messiah* (*see* **Messianic Secret**) and the slow and patient working out of the plan of salvation.

For insight into Matthew, Hargreaves turns to Kenneth Cragg, a pre-eminent writer in the field of Christian-Muslim relations, 'an inter-

preter of Islam to Christianity ... and of Christianity to Islam' (p. 39). Three themes are singled out: inclusiveness, reflecting both the Matthaean desire to unite Jewish and Gentile insights and the common Christian and Islamic concern that 'God may be all in all' (p. 45); authority and sonship; and law and grace. Hargreaves sums up:

> Looking at the way in which both the author of Matthew and Bishop Cragg ... hold together different insights about power and redemptive weaknesses, authority and sonship, law and grace, obedience and faith, I conclude that both of them may be said to have taken seriously the 'pluralistic' situation of their own day (p. 60).

Luke's Gospel is considered in relation to the work of the Indian Christian thinker, M. M. Thomas. Thomas comes from the state of Kerala in South India, where interestingly it is Marxism* which is the dominant political influence, and where Christian-Marxist dialogue is well established. Thus, though the religious culture of India is Hinduism, what is important in Thomas is this ongoing dialogue. Hargreaves picks up emphases on the importance of history, the humanizing of the world, and the relationship between matter and spirit, as keys to a mutual reading of Thomas and the Gospel of Luke.

Finally, for the Gospel of John, Hargreaves turns to the Cistercian Thomas Merton, whose concerns combined a radical social commitment with a deeply contemplative nature and an interest in oriental mysticism, in particular Buddhism. While it would not be appropriate to read John's Gospel as though it were Buddhist, there are clear parallels which make this association fruitful. But in this case, as in all the examples considered, it must be stressed that what we have done is to suggest a programme of interpretation which is basically still in its infancy.

One genre of resource books which deserves mention in this connection comes from the field of comparative religious studies. I refer to compendia of religious writings arranged thematically. These cannot, of course, replace the direct participation of interpreters who belong to other faiths, but they serve a useful preliminary function in setting out both the similarities and the differences between the Bible and other sacred texts. Two such collections are Mircea Eliade's *From Primitives to Zen* (1967) and Ninian Smart and R. D. Hecht's *Sacred Texts of the World* (1982). The first of these omits all biblical texts – a decision defended in Eliade's preface, but one likely to impair the book for our purposes, though it no doubt made it possible to include a wider selection of less familiar writings from outside the Jewish–Christian world. The second, as well as closing this gap, also refers to new religious movements; a decision which is surely to be applauded. After all, all our faiths were once new religious movements!

ALASTAIR G. HUNTER

Palaeography

The art of deciphering writing* in an ancient document and of dating written documents by their writing. Palaeography is closely allied in subject matter and method to epigraphy,* which is a like art, studying the writing of inscriptions. Traditionally, it has also concerned itself with the material aspects of the hand-written document or manuscripts on which the writing studied is inscribed: such aspects are the substance of which the manuscript is made, how it is prepared, bound, put on sale, and so forth. Recently the study of these matters has tended to be separated from palaeography under the newly coined name of 'codicology', but some attention will be given to them here since the two aspects are interrelated, however difficult it is with the growth of knowledge and technology for one scholar to cover both equally.

Any language which has been committed to writing will provide material for palaeography: it is customary to identify the specific field simply by prefixing the name of the language to the noun. Thus in this article we shall deal with Hebrew and Aramaic palaeography and Greek palaeography, mainly in relation to the manuscript* transmission of the biblical writings and to the decipherment of those manuscripts. We must bear in mind that the Bible has often been translated,* in antiquity as well as more recently, and thus palaeographical skills are called into play in the study of any of the versions which were made before the invention of printing.

There are certain aspects of palaeography common to the two fields of Hebrew/Aramaic and Greek (and indeed any other relevant language). In both, we find scripts used in private or business documents on the one hand, and others, slightly different in detail, used in the reproduction of literature. In the latter case, there is often an archaizing or formalizing factor present, which may lead to difficulty in dating a document if no date is given, while it is upon the former that we rely for knowledge of the basic evolution of the script. So from letters, business correspondence, official material of all kinds we build up a 'typology' or comparative study of the development of the script. In this way, we may date the more formal, even archaizing, hands of scribes* writing literary material, sacred or secular. In both, there are special gifts and skills, for example the reading of palimpsests,

that is, manuscripts which have been twice used, the original writing partially removed. The underwriting, being the older, will often have the greater interest and importance, and skills and technical aids must be developed to read the half-obliterated or destroyed writing. Very similar is the technique of reading manuscripts which have become torn, worn or otherwise fragmented in course of time. Here a precise knowledge of the forms of letters and an ability to recognize even parts of letters is essential. To aid those who practise either of these skills reverse or retrograde dictionaries of the languages concerned have been produced, in which the vocabulary is listed in alphabetical order, but reading the words from the last letter backwards. These are an invaluable tool.

The palaeography of both fields is also closely linked to the history of the language in question. In the case of Hebrew and Aramaic, each newly-discovered manuscript, inscription, or other document of the earliest periods increases our knowledge of the language; and this in its turn not only casts new light upon what is already known but also increases the options for establishing the actual words of further new materials. In the case of the Greek of biblical documents, while there is still some scope for new words to appear or new usage to be discovered which illuminate the biblical text, we may generally say that our knowledge of earlier Greek and its evolution is already large enough to interpret most texts. Where the manuscript discoveries assist is particularly in the orthography or spelling, for here we may perceive the pronunciation of the language at the time of writing of the biblical material, and during its earliest transmission; and we may develop greater understanding of the mistakes which scribes might make because of the similar or identical way in which words of distinct spelling were at that period pronounced.

Hebrew is the language of most of the OT, Aramaic of some parts of Daniel and Ezra, and a few verses elsewhere; but the latter is also of considerable importance as the language of the interpretative translations known as the Targums,* some of which date from before the NT period. These languages are akin, within the North Western Semitic group of languages. Hebrew was the vernacular of the people of Israel, of both the Northern and the Southern kingdoms in the pre-exilic period. After the Babylonian exile of the people of the Southern kingdom, Aramaic became the vernacular, but Hebrew retained a strong position as the language of religion and learning, and, in times of national resurgence, of the state too.

Both languages are found written in an

alphabet, each of the two forms being derived from the Phoenician script. There are Hebrew inscriptions of the tenth century, from Israel, while elsewhere Aramaic is found from the same period. Manuscripts in Aramaic from Jewish sources are known from the middle of the fifth century BC. The discovery of the Dead Sea Scrolls* has increased our resources enormously, with documents as early as the third century BC, many of them biblical or closely linked to biblical themes. Both the Hebrew (palaeo-Hebrew) and the Aramaic alphabets can now be studied in great detail for the period between the third century BC and the second century AD.

These alphabets have 22 signs, representing as many consonantal sounds. At a very early period, however, the practice began of indicating vowels by some of these letters (*aleph* and *he* for long /a/: *yod* for /i/ or /e/: *waw* for /o/ and /u/). It was generally the long forms of the vowels that were thus indicated, but the new materials present some instances of the indication of short vowels too. The indication of vowels by small signs or points above or below the line, which is found not only in Hebrew but in other Semitic languages such as Syriac and Arabic, is a later development, in Hebrew from about the sixth century AD.

There is thus from time to time scope for interpreting a set of signs in several different ways, according to the vocalization, a fact much used in problems of textual criticism* of the OT. Other factors than the purely palaeographical are involved. In the light of wider knowledge, linguistic and textual as well as palaeographical, confidence in emendation based on vowel variation is much more rarely found in recent biblical scholarship.

The Greek alphabet was adapted from the Phoenician and was used in different ways in different parts of the Greek world, as inscriptions show. The form in which it meets us in the palaeography of biblical documents is the Ionic alphabet in which long and short /e/ had been differentiated by the use of the letter *ēta* as a vowel sign (otherwise the 'rough breathing') and long and short /o/ by the use of the divergent forms *o micron* and *o mega*. In manuscripts and other sources from the fifth century BC onwards we find the non-Ionic letters *vau* (F; called *digamma*), *qoppa* (Ϙ) and a sign known only by the Byzantine Greek name of '*sampi*' (= like *pi*: ϡ), used as numerals representing 6, 90 and 900 respectively (such calculations as the 'number of the Beast' in Rev. 13.18 presuppose some such system, or an analogous one in Hebrew). By the use of the alphabet with these supplements, numbers up to 999 can be expressed.

The earliest Greek manuscripts of the Bible are written in uncials, more properly known as majuscules, i.e. 'large letters', corresponding to the upper case in print. Private, commercial and official material was written in a cursive hand, and much of the contribution to lexicography and to our knowledge of the phonology of Greek in the early Christian period comes from the latter class. Round about the ninth century there appears for the Bible and other literature a calligraphic hand based on this cursive, probably imitating the cursive used in the imperial chancery. This script used to be generally called 'cursive', but in the past generation, as a rule 'minuscule' has taken its place.

The transliteration from uncial texts to minuscules could give rise to error when letters of like appearance in Greek uncials could be confused. Minuscule could also give rise to confusion, as for instance through the similarity of minuscule *kappa* and *beta*, *eta* and *nu*. Another source of confusion (more generally to some modern students of manuscripts than to mediaeval scribes!) is the use of combinations of letters written together, called ligatures: a number of spurious variant readings have crept into some recent editions through this instance of ignorance.

A distinctive feature of Christian texts in Greek and some other Christian languages such as Armenian, Georgian, Latin, Coptic, Gothic and Slavonic is the regular abbreviation of names referring to God, Christ, and later to words for the associated notions of heaven, cross and mother. This category of abbreviated words is known as *nomina sacra* (sacred nouns): it appears in the earliest biblical manuscripts known to us, and plausibly goes back into the first century. It may have its origin in the self-differentiation of the early church from the rest of the Jewish community.

In early copies of the OT in Greek (Septuagint*), the unspeakable Name of God is sometimes found not translated, or rendered as *Kurios* (Lord), but written in Hebrew: this was in time not comprehended and the curious 'imitation' in Greek is found, *pi iota pi iota*, reading the Hebrew יהוה (which properly reads from right to left) as if it were Greek letters πιπι read from left to right.

Another feature often encountered in manuscripts must be taken account of by the palaeographer, although it is strictly phonetic rather than graphical in its origin. Official, personal and business documents reveal considerable uncertainty over spelling, especially of certain vowel sounds. There is great confusion between the signs for *ēta*, *iota*, *epsilon-iota*, and, after certain periods of time, *omicron-iota* and *upsilon*. This feature is called 'itacism' (pronounced 'eetasism'), indicating that all these signs, once signifying distinct sounds, had now taken on the single pronunciation proper to *eta* which had itself come to be pronounced as English /*ee*/. A similar confusion is to be seen between *omicron* and *omega*, showing that the differentiation between long and short /*o*/ had disappeared. These factors were already present in the Greek of the first century AD: our pronunciation of the Greek of the NT should be far closer to modern Greek pronunciation than to any approximation to Attic Greek. Such an innovation in our practice would have the advantage, amongst others, of helping the student to understand a number of basic problems of textual criticism more easily. It is often a nice question which grammatical and strictly spelled form to restore from the manuscripts.

See also **Manuscripts; Writings.**

David Diringer, *The Alphabet*, 1948; Jack Finegan, *Light from the Ancient Past*, 1946; L. D. Reynolds and N. G. Wilson, *Scribes and Scholars*, [2]1973; E. G. Turner, *Greek Manuscripts of the Ancient World*, [2]1987.

J. NEVILLE BIRDSALL

Papias

Papias, Bishop of Hierapolis in Phrygia (*c.* 60?–*c.* 130?), is an early but enigmatic source, some of whose statements provide a starting point for commentators* on the Gospels.* Irenaeus* wrote of him as a man associated with Christianity of time past, an *archaios anēr* who had been 'a hearer of John and a companion of Polycarp' (*Adv. Haer.* v. 33, 3f.). Eusebius* was less favourably disposed towards him and suggests (contradicting his *Chronicon*) that he had known only John the Elder (*HE* iii. 39). His Christianity was of that Asia Minor type which would not triumph, associated as it was with the millennialism* of radical Judaism. Indeed Papias looked to the material establishment of Christ's kingdom and to the promise of abundance of food therein (cf. the view of Revelation, of Irenaeus, *Adv. Haer.* v. 34, 2f., and of *Apoc. Baruch.* xli, 29f.). Later Eusebius would dismiss him as an unintelligent chiliast. Papias had received such teachings ('of mythical kind') orally, however, and he believed them to be true to Jesus' own (*Adv. Haer.* v. 33, 3f.; *HE* iii.39).

He was an assiduous collector of traditions, oral* and written, and his stated preference for 'a living voice' has occasioned much scholarly comment. Yet it need not indicate that greater weight was given to oral tradition. He avoided material which he thought was not dominical in origin and like Irenaeus and Clement of Alexandria after him wrote of the 'elders' (*presbuteroi*). These and their followers, who were his sources, had been associated with the apostles. They included John

and Aristion. But despite what Irenaeus wrote, Papias himself is not to be counted among their number.

His work, the *Exposition of the Dominical Sayings* (*Logiōn Kyriakōn Exēgēsis*) has not survived except in fragments in the work of other writers. Eusebius seems to have culled his selection from the extant larger work. It was known to Jerome and he denies having translated it (*Ad Lucinium* Epist. lxxi). Unflattering of Papias as Eusebius was, his choice of quotations from the *Exposition* perhaps represents all that he regarded as sound and not over-imaginative in that work. We know a little of what the original contained. There were miracle* stories and accounts of martyrdoms, that of John the Evangelist, recounted in Book 2, being an example. He preserved accounts of the fates of Judas Iscariot and of the dead who had been raised by Jesus. Justus Barsabbas, who appears in Acts 1.23, is described as being spared death by poison. The *Exposition* contained parable* material too, as well as traditions concerning the millennium and the role of angels in the divine order. Our Phrygian writer had a problem, Eusebius concluded, namely that he failed to interpret allegorically* (*mustikōs*) some of those apostolic traditions he collected. According to Anastasius of Sinai, on the other hand, the Christian interpretation of the early chapters of Genesis in terms of Christ and the church is to be traced back to Papias.

What remains of the witness of Papias is frustrating for interpreters of the Bible. On the one hand he provides a salutary reminder of the debt which we owe to the men and women who transmitted Christian tradition orally. Among them were the daughters of Philip (Acts 21.8ff.), known to Papias in Hierapolis. Moreover Eusebius and others hinted at a wealth of 'legendary'* material compiled by our author which would have been of interest to biblical scholars.

On the other hand what he tells us about canonical Gospels only fuels interest and speculation without providing answers. Notable also is his witness to 'John', whom he credits with having written down the Fourth Gospel at the apostle John's dictation, but it is his claims about Mark and Matthew which are best known.

Mark, he says, was Peter's* *hermēneutēs* ('interpreter'), an ambiguous term. Equally troublesome is his information that what Mark remembered of Peter's evidence he wrote down 'but not in order'. But the claim that Mark's work was carried on while Peter was still in Rome has seemed to support the case for Marcan priority and an early date for the Gospel.

As for Matthew, he compiled the *logia**

('sayings'). The term has been interpreted as indicating the Matthaean Gospel or an element within it such as *testimonia*,* the prophetic oracles or something akin to Q. The latter has seemed more plausible to many writers. Moreover they were compiled in Hebrew (Aramaic?), *Hebraidi dialektō*, and were translated (*hermēneusē*, probably not 'interpret' here) at will. Irenaeus, Jerome and Augustine* echo such belief in a Hebrew original. Not surprisingly a few scholars have taken these statements of Papias as support for theories of a primitive Aramaic *Grundschrift* for Matthew or of the priority of that Gospel. Good commentaries on the Gospels and studies of tradition take account of the evidence of Papias, and some have found good reason to distrust him. It is strange, for example, that he shows no awareness of the close link in content between the Gospels of Mark and Matthew, or of Matthew's dependence on the Greek version of the Jewish scriptures, facts which stare the modern reader in the face.

See also **Evangelist; Mark, Gospel of; Matthew, Gospel of.**

R. P. C. Hanson, *Tradition in the Early Church*, 1962; E. Flesseman van Leer, *Tradition and Scripture in the Early Church*, 1954; J. B. Lightfoot, 'The Fragments of Papias' in *The Apostolic Fathers*, 1889.

CHRISTINE TREVETT

Parable

Modern interpretation of the parables of Jesus in the Gospels usually takes as its starting point Jülicher's two volumes *Die Gleichnisreden Jesu* of 1910. From it descend the two most popular books on the subject, C. H. Dodd's* *The Parables of the Kingdom* (1935) and Joachim Jeremias'* *The Parables of Jesus* (1947, ET 1954). This established tradition is marked positively by a preference for 'realized' (i.e. not futurist) eschatology* and naturalism, negatively by an aversion from allegory.* Jülicher's own starting point is Aristotle who, in *Rhetoric* 2.20, describes parables as indirect ways of proof in oratory. They come in two kinds: historical examples, and fables or allegories such as Plato used. Aristotle decidedly and characteristically prefers the first kind. Aristotle is, however, an inappropriate point of departure for the study of biblical material. The motive for taking him as such could be a desire to dissociate the Gospels* from their Jewish background,* thus enhancing their originality and their aptness to Western humanism – the dethroning of the priority of Matthew's overtly Jewish Gospel, in favour of the alleged Gentile simplicity of Mark, being part of the same tend-

ency. There was opposition to this move at the time: Paul Fiebig had argued for rabbinic* parables as the closest neighbours to Gospel parables in his *Altjüdische Gleichnisse und die Gleichnisse Jesu* of 1904. After the publication of Jülicher's study he returned to the theme in *Die Gleichnisreden Jesu in Lichte der Rabbinischen Gleichnisse des neutestamentlichen Zeitalters* of 1912. In both works Fiebig assembled a formidable array of parallels and similarities, supposing earlier dates for his rabbinic examples than is certain. English readers can find most of them in Feldman's *The Parables and Similes of the Rabbis* of 1927. In any case, Fiebig's work did not enter the mainstream of parable interpretation at the time. This approach has had to wait until the recent tendency to reunite the Gospels with their Jewish matrix exemplified in, for example, M. D. Goulder's *Midrash and Lection in Matthew* of 1968.

Form criticism* provides the setting and choreography for Dodd's and Jeremias' work. Parables respond readily to it, being easily identifiable 'forms' which can be extracted from the Gospel narratives and then analysed as a coherent genre.* This analysis is done according to two criteria. On the one hand, Jesus stands out from Judaism, so what is Jewish in the parables is probably not his. On the other hand, using a powerful rule of Gospel interpretation current since Reimarus* in the eighteenth century, Jesus is distinct from the early Christian church with its known fondness for allegory. So what is appropriate to the early church – eschatology* and church order often being included along with allegory – is probably not Jesus' either. The historical strength of this method, as of form criticism generally, is its insight that the material of the Gospels was not aseptically preserved but used by Christians for the solution of their practical and theological problems. Hence restoration work is needed to reclaim the parables which Jesus spoke. Its weakness is that no parables indubitably by Jesus survive outside the Gospels. There was hope, after the Nag Hammadi* finds, that the Gospel of Thomas included such. But this hope faded with the appreciation of the mainly gnostic* tendencies of that book.

The practical effect, unconscious but determinative, of the absence of the all-important criterion of unassailably Jesus-authored parables was two-fold. First, the criteria* of dissimilarity from Judaism and church had nothing to check them and ran amok, thus advertising their own questionability (why should Jesus have not used parables like a rabbi or like a Christian teacher, since he must have had some things in common with both?). Second, the Jesus whose parables could not be certainly isolated from the Christian Gospels or his Jewish milieu, by being isolated from them nevertheless, became the receptacle of the wishes of the exegetes.* They did not want bald eschatology or allegorical elaboration, so their restored parables of Jesus were marked by concentration to a single point rather than the references to multiple points which mark allegory, and by concern for the present moment as the critical time rather than the future *eschaton* or doomsday. In effect, this meant that the parables found only in Luke's Gospel, particularly in chs 15 and 16, became the standard parables of Jesus; and his versions of parables also found in Mark and Matthew – particularly Matthew – were preferred because of their ostensible setting in the history of Jesus' ministry rather than their Matthaean setting in church life. Above all, it was in Luke's parables that Dodd and Jeremias found the plain naturalism and the integration to a single moral point which they sought.

As a reaction to the historical difficulties which beset this attempt to recover Jesus' parables, American scholars turned to literary* analysis with much lighter historical grounding and an existential rather than naturalist-objective orientation. In the process important discoveries about how the parables work on their readers and hearers were made, e.g. by D. O. Via in *The Parables: their Literary and Existential Dimension* (1967) and J. D. Crossan in *In Parables: the Challenge of the Historical Jesus* (1973) which, despite its brave title, failed to disentangle Jesus from the Christian parable traditions. But without the historical check which earlier interpreters had sought but not found, religious force was accompanied by a certain vertigo and academic despair.

In this brief history of modern parable interpretation there is pathos. In spite of the clear historical hope of recovering Jesus' parables, the hermeneutical* criteria have become all too general and subjective. But there is a set of pieces of the jig-saw which has not usually been deployed, though B. T. D. Smith's *The Parables of the Synoptic Gospels* of 1937 and M. Hermaniuk's *La Parabole Évangélique* of 1947 are among the exceptions. This is the nature and use of parables in the OT. Since the ancient Jewish scriptures were the Bible of Jesus, the first Christian teachers and preachers and the evangelists* themselves, they are obviously an important influence. Above all, they are much to be preferred to Aristotle as a historical starting point. Using them as such could result in a revival or redemption of the historical approach which, if it still cannot recover Jesus' parables in the sense of extracting them from the Gospels, could make sense of the way the parables are used in the Gos-

pels. The best text for such a project is O. Eissfeldt's *Der Maschal im Alten Testament* of 1913. English readers can find a good résumé of the kinds of parable treated there in the early pages of B. T. D. Smith's book. Briefly, *mashal* (parable) in the OT is a much more varied and capacious genre than it is in modern form criticism. And in so far as it coheres to a single integrating form, that form is quite different from the neo-Aristotelian one preferred by form critics. To say what this means in a little detail: the OT *mashal* could be a pithy saying, figurative or not, a taunt, a riddle, a byword, a prophetic oracle* or an allegory. With the passage of time the allegory came to be the most developed and prominent of these. Ezekiel is the culmination of this process. While his book includes most of the kinds of parable mentioned above, it is the allegory, used as a way of understanding the enigmatic historical events in which he lived and suffered, which is foremost. The historical allegory in ch. 17 of his book is his masterpiece in this genre. It is not naturalistic but surreal, its bizarre events are held together by an extremely strong theology of divine providence in history, and it is followed by an interpretation which is indispensably necessary to its explanatory function which would be quite lost without it.

The virtue of reading this chapter of Ezekiel, and above all of adjusting to parable within his strange world at the threshold of apocalyptic,* is evident to a reader who then turns to the crux of Gospel parable-interpretation, Mark 4. As in Ezekiel, the agricultural imagery is not transparent to the naturalistic level, but is a window on to Mark's narrative of Jesus' mission, its enormous failure and eventual success. *Pace* efforts by Dodd and Jeremias to make the sower's purblind carelessness into sensible farming, this is a surreal version of agricultural practice turned to point elsewhere: viz. where its subsequent interpretation points and where in Mark's narrative its gloomy portents are fulfilled (Peter,* as Satan, trying to take away Christ's seminal word 'on the way' at 8.27–33, the rich young man choked by worldly care at 10.17–22). Mark's other big parable is the vineyard at 12.1–12. Here even the sworn enemies of allegory concede that only as an allegory of history is this parable intelligible, which is how Nineham treats it in his commentary.* Beneath the coincidence of form between Ezekiel and Mark there is a deep coincidence in theology. Both compensate for their pessimism about human agency, reflected by their readiness to have animals and plants standing in for people, by an overwhelming belief in divine and supernatural agency. It is in this light (or dark) that Mark 4.11–12 is intelligible as an instance of consistently God-driven historiography. The extremity of it was too much for Matthew and Luke, who soften it, and *a fortiori* for modern exegetes, driving Jeremias into accusing Mark of not knowing what parables were.

Matthew's parables are not so close to Ezekiel's as Mark's, though not as remote from them as Luke's. His neighbours are the rabbis, as Goulder has shown. With them he shares stock images such as the vineyard, the banquet and the king (see Feldman). Above all he uses parables as the rabbis did and as Mark did not: to elucidate and clarify. His allegories – and they are still very much allegories – are transparent, pointing less to historical mystery and more to moral duty. Thus in ch. 13 he adds parables to Mark 4 in which divine judgment at Doomsday sorts out the ambiguities of the present. And in ch. 25 he amplifies Mark 13, which ended with Jesus' mysterious summons 'watch!', with a series of parables which make watching a present duty with eschatological rewards. People, rather than animals and plants, are the figures; but they are not characterized, being simply good or bad, wise or foolish.

Real people, characterized in their vivid ambiguity, enter Christian parabolic tradition with Luke. With him the apocalyptic interpretation recedes (not to disappear, however) and the humane realism of earlier OT narrative found in the stories of Joseph and David* takes over. His most famous parable, the prodigal son in ch. 15, bears many traces of the Joseph story, such as the younger brother in a far country, famine, harlots and the reunion with the father. These are redeployed to make a distinctly Christian story (not a parable on strict OT criteria) about repentance, a major theme of Luke's Gospel which all parables in 15.1–16.31 subserve and illustrate. Matthew's turning of Mark's Gospel towards ethics* is developed in Luke's with realism which is more sophisticated than Matthew's bare dualism.

What has been said above forms an introduction to the development of parables from the OT and through the Christian Gospel tradition. This is an obviously historical kind of interpretation, but quite different from the old quest for the parables of the historical Jesus.* There can be no doubt that these latter were a very important part of this long development. The recovery of them, by new and better historical criteria, is still to be done.

See also **Luke, Gospel of; Mark, Gospel of; Matthew, Gospel of.**

In addition to titles mentioned see J. H. Drury, *The Parables in the Gospels* 1985; J. G. Williams, *Gospel against Parables*, 1985.

JOHN DRURY

Paronomasia

This is a technical term for play on words, a favourite device in the Hebrew Bible but uncommon in the NT (the rare example in Rom. 2.29 is based on the Hebrew of Gen. 29.35; 49.8, where the name Judah [*yehūdā*] and the verb 'to praise' [*hōdā*] are associated through similarity of sound). Recognition of paronomasia is an important aid to interpretation in that it elucidates the connection between otherwise apparently random ideas. Not all examples adduced are, however, equally convincing. In some instances the repetition and rearrangement of consonants may be merely fortuitous.

A notable example of word play which exploits similarity of sound and antithesis of meaning occurs in Isa. 5.7. The following attempts to reproduce the effect in English (from J. Barr, *Comparative Philology and the Text of the Old Testament*, 1968):

> He looked for order (*mishpāt*), what he saw was murder (*mispāḥ*); he looked for right (*tsedāqā*), what he heard was the cry of fright (*tse'āqā*).

A similar device appears in Ps. 96.5 with a play on gods/idols (*'elōhīm/'elīlīm*). In Hab. 2.18 the effect is achieved by alliteration: 'dumb idols' are *'elīlīm 'illemīm*.

Another form of word play depends on variation in vowel pattern. Thus Isaiah exhorts Ahaz, 'Have firm faith (*ta'amīnū*) or you will not stand firm (*tē'āmēnū*)' (Isa. 7.9). Similar association of words through sound rather than meaning accounts for one means of revelatory* experience by prophets.* For Jeremiah, a rod of almond (*shāqēd*) brings the assurance that Yahweh watches (*shōqēd*) over his word (Jer. 1.11f.); for Amos a basket of summer fruit (probably monosyllabic *qaits*) evokes a word of judgment, 'the end (*qēts*) has come upon my people' (Amos 8.2).

Personal and place names are a fruitful source of paronomasia. Ephraim, referring to the northern kingdom, provides a play both on 'heifer' (*pārā*, reinforced in this instance by alliteration on the word 'stubborn': *kepārā sōrērā sārar yisrāēl*; Hos. 4.16) and on 'fruit' (*perī*) in Hos. 9.16 and 14.8. The latter passage is noteworthy for a daring example of word play, for here the reference to 'idols' seems to be picked up in the statement, 'It is I who answer (*'ānītī*) and look after him (*'ashūrennū*)', a play on the names of the Canaanite goddesses Anat and Ashera, perhaps too bold were it not softened by being merely allusive. That Isaac's name (*yitshāq*) is a play on the verb 'to laugh' (*tsāḥaq*) is emphasized more than once (Gen. 18.12ff.; 21.6), and Esau (*'ēsāw*) is named for his hairy appearance (*sē'ār*) at birth (Gen. 25.25). A famous example is the play on Yahweh/*'ehyeh*, 'I will be' (Ex. 3.14f.), and paronomasia is the key, too, to the reversal of the doom-laden name Jezreel ('God sows') to become a word of salvation (Hos. 2.22f., *Heb. 24f.*). The connection is not always made explicit, but Jeremiah's expectation of a coming ruler to be named 'the Lord is our righteousness' (Jer. 23.6) is undoubtedly a deliberate reminiscence of Judah's last, ineffectual king Zedekiah. The several wells dug for Isaac are variously named according to whether or not their possession was disputed (Gen. 26.20ff.). Similarly, in the NT, play is made with the name of Peter (*Petros : petra* = 'rock', Matt. 16.18).

A further type of word play is produced by the use of homonyms, words identical in spelling but dissimilar in meaning. Thus Samson's ditty (Judg. 15.16) plays on *ḥamōr*, meaning both 'ass' and 'heap':

> With the jawbone of an ass, mass upon mass,
> with the jawbone of an ass I slew a thousand men (J. Barr).

So, too, in Eccles. 7.6 *sīr* means both 'thorn' and 'pot' and finds an echo also in the word chosen for 'fool' (*kesīl*). One might also note that by representing 'sound', a purely general word in Hebrew, by the more specific 'crackling', the English well captures the onomatopoeic quality of the original (*keqōl*). A further example occurs in Ps. 137.5, with *shākaḥ* meaning both 'forget' and 'wither', thus resolving what otherwise had seemed a syntactical problem. Less convincing is the view, reflected in NEB, that *kesep* in Isa. 55.1 means both 'food' and 'money'. The result is prosaic in line 2. More likely it is a case of repetition of the astounding offer of purchase without payment! It is likely, however, that Samson's riddle (Judg. 14.18) plays on *'arī* in two senses, 'lion' and 'honey', the latter being later explained by the more familiar word *debash* (J. R. Porter, *JTS* n.s. 13, 1962).

Examples of other more recondite types of word play are also found. A play on reversal of consonants exists in the apparently simple statement, 'Noah (*nḥ*) found favour (*ḥn*) in the eyes of the Lord' (Gen. 6.8), and the device of syllable repetition in Prov. 25.13 where 'harvest' (*qātsīr*) and 'messenger' (*tsīr*) are juxtaposed. Examples of cryptograms are to be found in Jeremiah where, by the use of letters in reverse alphabetical order (a device known as *at'bash*), Sheshak represents Babel (= Babylon: 25.26; 51.41) and *leb qamai* stands for Kasdim (= Chaldeans: 51.1).

See also **Figures of Speech.**

A. Guillaume, 'Paronomasia in the Old Testament', *JSS* 9, 1964.

GRACE I. EMMERSON

Parousia

The belief in the parousia or 'presence' of Christ in glory is firmly rooted in all strands of the NT. It is referred to by the technical Greek term *parousia* (e.g. Matt. 24.3,27,37,39; I Cor. 15.23; I Thess. 2.19; 3.13; 4.15; 5.23; II Thess. 2.1,8,9; James 5.7,8 – this speaks of the parousia of the Lord; II Peter 1.16; 3.4; 3.12 – here the parousia of the day of God; and I John 2.28), though elsewhere the expectation can be referred to without the use of the word (Acts 3.19; Rev. 19.11ff.; I Cor. 15.23ff.; cf. Mark 13.26 and 14.62), or by use of other terms (e.g. *apokalupsis* = 'revelation', 'disclosure', in I Cor. 1.7 and I Peter 1.7). We note that even in those books where the person of Christ does not loom large (like James), the parousia is referred to. The word itself is used also to speak of the 'arrival' of the apostle or his emissary (e.g. I Cor. 16.17; II Cor. 7.6,7; 10.10; Phil. 1.26; 2.12), though even here there may also be analogical links with the parousia doctrine.

The origins of the belief are obscure, though it is possible that there may be some antecedents in Jewish texts like I Enoch 1.9 (which refers to God) and I Enoch 46 (which refers to the Son of Man*). In the NT, the parousia marks the culmination of an eschatological* process set in train by Jesus' proclamation and inauguration of the reign of God (*see* **Kingdom of God**) which was rudely interrupted by his execution. The resurrection* then marks a vindication of God's messiah* and the parousia the final completion of the work he has begun, when he finally puts all his enemies under his feet (I Cor. 15.25ff.).

The absence of Jesus after his crucifixion and the continuing messianic convictions of his followers prompted questions about his presence and the fulfilment of their hopes. That such issues were at some stage being wrestled with in the ancient church can be seen in the way in which the delay of Christ's return and the consequent establishment of God's reign led to some bewilderment (reflected explicitly in II Peter 3.1ff.). In the close link which Paul* offered between the apostolic *parousia*, or presence, and the presence of the messiah, he tempered an exclusively future reference by asserting the eschatological power of the apostolic presence itself. Thus, by means of the presence of the apostle, whether in person, through a co-worker or through letter, the presence of Christ was confronting his congregations (Rom. 15.14ff.; II Cor. 4.14ff.; 5.3ff.; Phil. 2.12).

The theory that the delay of the parousia was of great significance for the development of Christian faith and practice is one which has been extraordinarily influential within biblical exegesis* over the last century or so (Werner). The explicit evidence for the delay of the parousia being a problem within primitive Christianity is not as large as is often suggested, II Peter 3 being in fact rather exceptional. Other passages which are often mentioned (e.g. in Matthew and Luke) have to be set alongside indications which point in the opposite direction. The writings of social* anthropologists on cognitive dissonance* indicate that the non-fulfilment of hope does not as a rule lead to its abandonment or its replacement by something different. The tendency is rather to engage in intensive activity as a compensation. This can perhaps be seen operating in early Christianity in the rise of the missionary enterprise (Gager). Equally, early Christianity may have dealt with non-fulfilment of its grandiose hopes by intensifying those hopes, in the universal perspective of Matthew and Revelation. Also, apocalyptic* passages show an interest in the world above where the reign of God is already acknowledged. Thus, the apocalyptic seer can glimpse the mysteries of eschatology. This preoccupation of the apocalyptic tradition with the heavenly dimension is found, for example, in the identification of the church with Christ in the heavenly places (Eph. 1.21; 3.5ff.).

The pervasiveness of the expectation of the return of Christ to complete the process already begun in his career in Palestine, but cut short by the machinations of his political opponents, confronts the interpreter with a challenge. There is a widespread feeling that a modern person cannot make much of the apocalyptic imagery of the NT. The problem has been dealt with in several ways in modern scholarship. One response is to delve behind the language to ask 'what it really means'. So, for example, Bultmann* argued that the mythology* in the Bible, concerned with protology and eschatology, is so bound up with the culture of the first century that it is impossible for a modern reader to make sense of it as it stands. It becomes necessary to demythologize* it. In other words, one must ask what this language is really about. So the husk of eschatology, found, for example, in the expectation that the Son of Man* would come on the clouds of heaven, has to be removed in order to get at the real meaning of the imagery. It is to be seen as a picturesque statement of the importance of the challenge posed by the gospel, with regard to the ultimate meaning of human existence. Thus the parousia expectation becomes part of a highly symbolic* message addressed to the individual's relationship

with God. In this interpretation, the relationship to history is left behind and the concerns are focussed mainly on the individual's destiny.

Another related way of dealing with the problem posed by the parousia language is to argue that its place in early Christianity marks a significant shift away from the intentions of Jesus (Robinson). It thus becomes evidence of the way in which Jesus' proclamation of the reign of God as present in his ministry became contaminated with Jewish apocalyptic expectation at an early stage. Whereas Jesus did not himself expect to return on the clouds of heaven but to be present with his disciples in the Spirit, the early church understood the parousia language as referring to an actual return in history – a second coming. This kind of approach is typical of much biblical scholarship, which has tended to look for a primitive 'true meaning' of texts which then got lost or covered over by subsequent Christian reflection.

A much more pessimistic view of the cultural conditioning of early Christian discourse is to be found in the views of those who frankly admit that we must resign ourselves to the recognition that we can find little if any present significance in NT eschatological expectation. Early Christian theology was thoroughly permeated with ancient Jewish eschatology, and there remains little alternative for us but to accept the strangeness of the NT world and its irrelevance. That kind of scepticism is understandable. Nevertheless, there is a growing recognition that the eschatological horizon of the NT writers is an important resource for Christian ethics and theology which should not lightly be dismissed: it offers a critical horizon to human existence and demands a subversive and critical process of relativizing every human project and system in the light of the coming reign of God (Ogletree). The point is well made by Theodor Adorno: 'the only philosophy which can be responsibly practised in face of despair is the attempt to contemplate all things as they would present themselves from the standpoint of redemption' (*Minima Moralia*, 1974, p. 267).

The expectation that Christ would return is part of a much larger complex of eschatological beliefs, embracing the resurrection from the dead, the reign of God on earth and the last judgment. In the earliest period, it was closely linked with millenarian* or chiliastic beliefs, so that Christ's return would herald a messianic reign on earth with his saints. The eclipse of millenarian ideas, finally enshrined in Augustine's* enormously influential theology of history in *The City of God*, rendered the parousia hope one that was entirely beyond time and history. That has meant that there has been greater concentration on other aspects of Christ's presence, in which the eschatological orientation ceases to be so prominent. The presence of Jesus in the life of the individual believer, in the eucharistic elements, in the Word of God,* read or preached, are all ways of mediating the presence of one who is at the moment absent. This contrasts with the NT hope, which is generally set in the framework of human and cosmic renewal (e.g. I Cor. 15.20ff.; Rev. 19.11ff.), as it picks up the prophetic promises of the vindication of God's righteousness in human history.

The eclipse of the expectation of the coming of one who would subjugate the earthly principalities and powers and introduce a new order is a mark of the domestication of the faith in the future and the coming of God's kingdom. In one, intense form, this position had already been reached by some Christians by the end of the first century. Whatever hope there may be for the future in the Fourth Gospel, the focus is on Jesus' first coming as the ultimate moment to which the witness of the community and the Spirit-Paraclete both point. Those who love Jesus and keep his commandments are those to whom the incarnate Son of God comes and with whom the Father and the Son make their abode (John 14.21,23). However we interpret the enigmatic reference to the Son of Man and Jacob's ladder in John 1.51, there is the idea of communion between heaven and earth in the now past revelation of glory in Jesus. Also, the presence of the eschatological glory among the disciples who love him has about it a vertical dimension in which the coming Son of Man is not primarily a figure who will appear as a reproach to the nations. It is not a question of 'they shall look upon him whom they pierced' (Rev. 1.9), but 'the world will see me no more but you will see me' (John 14.19).

If Jesus' proclamation of the kingdom marked the moment when God was making all things new, then the parousia hope is the manifestation that the divine purpose has been fulfilled in Christ and God will be all in all. Anything less than this (e.g. speaking of the parousia in other-worldly or transhistorical terms) detracts from the reality of the incarnation itself and the signs of the reign of God already at work in the career of Jesus the messiah. What the symbolism of Christ's return demands is continuity of the life of the future with the contours of Christ's past appearance. The messianic future is, therefore, Jesus-like.

In some contemporary Christian circles, the parousia marks the moment of rescue for the elect. Christ comes to carry them off at the Rapture (I Thess. 4.15), before the ultimate cataclysm engulfs unregenerate humanity. In this version of the parousia hope the well-being of the elect and the return of Christ are separated from the hope for creation as set out in Rom. 8.18ff. In the reading of the parousia material in the NT, the interpretation of the parousia hope must not be separated from the narrative of Jesus' proclamation and inauguration of the reign of God. That means there are few privileges for the elect. Discipleship involves sharing the way of the cross of the Son of Man as he goes up to Jerusalem. Indeed, the emphasis on the cost of discipleship is evident in the immediate context of the parousia hope expressed in Mark 13.26. That is the challenge which faces those who wish to live out the messianic narrative in their own lives. Present-day expectations of the Rapture and salvation from a doom-stricken world on the brink of disaster are but the most recent distortion of the parousia hope. Such assurance for those who are born again is hardly borne out by the disturbing challenge of the eschatological Son of Man of Matt. 25.31ff. In the parable* of the sheep and the goats the achievement of eschatological bliss is based on the uncertain task of recognizing the hidden Christ in the suffering of the present.

Within the NT, the promise of Christ's coming is found in different forms and functions in various ways. In I Thess. 4.13ff., the concern is reassurance. However numerous may have been the words of the Lord known to Paul relating to this future episode, the piece chosen by him is intended to reassure the elect that even those who die before the coming of the messiah will not forfeit the right to share in the privileges of that messianic period. We are told nothing of what will happen after the Rapture; but in I Thess. that is not important, as the point of quoting the word of the Lord is to reassure rather than to provide information. As such, this passage, fragmentary as it is, conveys little of the threat to, and struggle to be undergone by, the disciples of Jesus which we find when we read comparable passages in the wider contexts of Mark 13 and Matt. 24–25. Despite the similar promise to the elect in Mark 13.26, that they will be gathered by the returning Son of Man, deliverance lies on the other side of a period of great tribulation from which they are not exempt and which promises real risks of apostasy (cf. Rom. 8.19ff.). Similarly, in Rev. 19.11ff. the coming of the messiah is a threat even to the elect. In Rev. 1.13ff. the Risen Christ may stand among his churches, but frequently finds himself on the outside knocking at the door (Rev. 3.21) and reproving those who have lost their first love (2.4f). All the inhabitants of the earth run the risk of falling for the illusion of greatness created by the Beast and its agents, and finding that the same apocalyptic light which lights the way to the wedding feast of the elect shines with anger on the wicked.

There is a danger in making too stark a polarization of the ways in which certain ideas function in the NT. But we can properly draw attention to the competing ways in which those documents and ideas are expressed within the ecclesiastical and political struggles of our day.

See also **Apocalyptic; Eschatology; Kingdom of God; Millenarianism; Revelation of John.**

H. W. Bartsch, *Kerygma and Myth*, 1972; O. Cullmann, *Christ and Time*, 1962; R. Funk, in W. R. Farmer, C. F. D. Moule and R. Niebuhr (eds), *Christian History and Interpretation*, 1967; J. G. Gager, *Kingdom and Community*, 1975; A. L. Moore, *The Parousia in the New Testament*, 1966; T. W. Ogletree, *The Use of the Bible in Christian Ethics*, 1983; J. A. T. Robinson, *Jesus and his Coming*, 1957; A. Schweitzer, *The Mysticism of Paul the Apostle*, 1931; M. Werner, *The Formation of Christian Dogma*, 1957.

CHRISTOPHER ROWLAND

Passion Narratives

The term is used to denote those sections of the Gospels* which describe the period leading up to Jesus' death and burial. Usually it refers to: Matt. 26–27; Mark 14–15; Luke 22–23; and John 18–19. This delimitation is supported in part by common sense, and by long custom, especially in the liturgical* practice of the church, where these are the passages traditionally used in the services of Holy Week. However, there are grounds for thinking that the dividing of the Gospels at these points does not in all respects accord with such thinking as the evangelists* may have given to the structure of their works. For example, it may be that Mark thought primarily of a 'Galilee–Jerusalem' division of his Gospel, in which case part two starts at ch. 11. C. H. Dodd*, in *The Interpretation of the Fourth Gospel*, divided John into 'The Book of Signs' and 'The Book of the Passion', beginning the latter at ch. 13. Many have seen sense in this, even though Jesus' entry into Jerusalem, which in the other Gospels may be seen to set in train the passion sequence, occurs at the beginning of ch. 12. There, however, Jesus is still on the public scene, moving within the circle of his followers at 13.1, making this a natural divide.

Moreover, it is only the church calendar,* which perhaps did not elaborate its full scheme of following mimetically the career of Jesus until the fourth century, that leads us to distinguish between the various observances of Holy Week, and in particular to separate Good Friday from Easter Day. The dominant opinion has been that a single paschal celebration was the usual practice in the earlier period and that, whether or not the Gospels had any kind of liturgical custom in mind, they probably thought of the whole passion-resurrection* complex as a single sweep of narrative.* Modern redaction criticism* understands and endorses that perception. However, the idea of the story itself in the earliest form available to us, in Mark, as taking its origin from a step by step following of Jesus through his passion, has received support from É. Trocmé, *The Passion as Liturgy*, 1983, a proposal which, whatever its attraction, has been found speculative, especially as it entails the view that Mark 14–16 was an independent composition. Neither redaction critics nor advocates of a 'narrative' approach to Mark see much reason so to set these chapters off from the rest of the Gospel.

The passion narratives are themselves interpretative in character; they are not simply factual accounts of the last phase of Jesus' life. It has become abundantly clear as a result of the redaction criticism of the period since about 1960 (but see already the writing of R. H. Lightfoot*) that these narratives are acute theological compositions, in each case reflecting the thought of the evangelist in relation to events of the utmost importance to him, and therefore reflecting that thought with special care and strength. The narratives bear this character in two ways: first, in telling the story in such a way as to bring out the meaning of Jesus' death, especially by means of OT quotations and allusions which were seen to throw light on an occurrence at the same time problematic (cf. I Cor. 1.18–24) and stupendous in its implications for the relationship of the human race with God (cf. Rom. 3.21–26; 5.12ff.). The dependence of Mark's (the earliest) narrative on Ps. 22 and on Zechariah is plain. Secondly, the narratives' way of telling their story has been affected both by apologetic* and by religious considerations of their time of writing. Thus, in Mark, Jesus is accused of blasphemy, a charge most unlikely (from our knowledge of the period) to have been levelled against him; rather, he was probably executed, however unjustifiably, for being perceived as a threat to public order. But by the time of Mark's writing, it was unthinkable for Christians, especially in the light of their debates with Jews about Jesus' status, that he had been condemned for other than religious or theological reasons. Their own convictions were read back into the earlier period. In these ways, the narratives of the passion play an important part both in early Christian interpretation of the OT and in the development of Christian identity.

These narratives are, however, as we have them, a creation of the later years of the first century and they are integral parts of greater wholes, the Gospels. Scholars have often suggested ways of discerning behind our present texts earlier versions of 'the passion narrative', the assumption being that the churches possessed such a thing virtually from the start. This may seem the merest common sense, but 1. it is, strictly, pure hypothesis, and 2. redaction criticism has made it harder to trace such versions, the more it has shown the strength of the Marcan, Matthaean, etc. character of the stories we possess. Nevertheless, possible outlines of a 'primitive' passion narrative are put forward, and it is not difficult to see that some items in the story are less integral to the telling and even look like intrusions into the flow of the narrative, e.g. Mark 14.3–9, with v. 2 leading on very happily to v. 10. The fact that precisely such 'intrusions' seem to be particularly powerful in Mark's narrative technique may either confirm such an idea of its origin or persuade us how hard it is to go behind the narrative as we have it, so subtly does it hang together as a whole. As far as there ever having been a truly primitive narrative of the passion is concerned, the evidence is again unclear. On the one hand, Paul,* our only earlier witness, speaks of the fact and the meaning of Jesus' death in formulaic rather than narrative terms (e.g. I Cor. 15.3f.) – unless the statement 'you proclaim the Lord's death' in I Cor. 11.26 should be taken to mean (as has been suggested) 'you read the passion narrative'.

On the other hand, the one piece of narrative found anywhere in Paul's writings (and then only for the accidental reason that it served his admonitory purpose) is the story of the Last Supper (I Cor. 11.23–25), which is told in terms not very (though not insignificantly) different from those used by Mark some years later. This is bound to give pause to anyone inclined to hold that the passion narrative was a late first-century development, perhaps arising out of growing apologetic* or liturgical needs and based as much on OT exegesis* as on genuine tradition or memory.

Those who feel that the curtain of the evangelists' respective theologies is now impenetrable are less optimistic than others about the possibility of using the Gospels to arrive at an understanding of the facts of Jesus' condemnation and death. Whether the others are historians of the period or followers of traditio-historical* method in relation to the Gospels themselves, they are likely to find help in such material as is available concerning relevant aspects of Roman law and administration and concerning Jewish institutions at the time, and especially the high priesthood. E. Rivkin has shown (*What Crucified Jesus?*, 1984) how unlikely it is that what we should recognize as religious motives lay behind Jesus' death. Given our knowledge of the character of Palestinian Judaism, it is unlikely that anything known of Jesus' teaching would have provoked such a reaction. On the other hand, the charismatic character of his mission would have seemed to threaten the uneasy condominium by which the priestly and Roman authorities sought to keep the country in a stable condition. This view, shared by E. P. Sanders, *Jesus and Judaism*, 1985, represents a considerable refinement of a style of analysis put forward by Reimarus* in the eighteenth century and taken up by a succession of scholars (often Jews not unwilling to see the crucifixion as a political and Roman act, by contrast with the tendency of the Gospels, as one succeeds to another, to present it as religious and Jewish) and notably by S. G. F. Brandon. Liberation theologians* have also not been reluctant to see political and even revolutionary motivation as lying behind the conduct of Jesus, thus provoking his arrest. The so-called cleansing of the Temple, as well as the triumphal entry into Jerusalem and the strange saying about swords in Luke 22.38, are taken as pointers to this being the true account, with a subsequently pacific church having largely erased its signs from the story. Painstaking scholarship (E. Bammel and C. F. D. Moule [eds], *Jesus and the Politics of his Day*, 1984) has cast the severest doubt on this version of events. On any showing, however, the modern analyst must always beware of seeing the religion-politics division in modern terms. Even if Jesus was no guerilla fighter, his preaching of the coming new age and the kingdom of God* could not but be seen, if taken at all seriously, as a threat to all existing institutions of government.

Most recent interpretation has, however, concentrated on the features of the narrative as found in each of the Gospels in turn. Thus, Mark's sombre, relentless narrative, with Jesus ever more the silent victim of all men's hostility, cowardice or incomprehension, passively led to his death, after the manner of the image of the lamb in Isa. 53, and with the constant use of the verb *paradidōmi* (= 'hand over', 'betray'), seems to convey a powerful theology of atonement. So meagre is the following story of resurrection that Jesus' death is the heart of the purpose for which he has been sent by God. Matthew's relatively few amendments and additions to Mark's narrative have a significance which is at first sight more apologetic than theological; yet they are typical of Matthew's perception of things as demonstrated throughout his

Gospel: the demonstration that Judas met his deserved fate (27.3ff.), the apocalyptic* import of Jesus (27.50–4), and the inclusion of angels (26.53) and dreams (27.19).

Luke's narrative shows far more divergence from Mark than does Matthew, so much so that many scholars have held that he had an independent passion narrative, into which he incorporated elements of the Marcan story. (This was part of a wider theory of the composition of Luke, that of Proto-Luke, first put forward by B. H. Streeter; see his *The Four Gospels*, 1924.) Plausible as this seems, perhaps especially in the light of Luke's clearly distinct account of the Last Supper, it is now generally held that much of his special and extra material is his own composition, expressing his own theological and religious ideas. Certainly, it is not hard to demonstrate the close conformity of Luke's passion narrative with the rest of Luke–Acts, as a comparison with the story of Stephen's passion in Acts 6–7 quickly shows (the disciple suffers after the manner of his Lord). The words from the cross in Luke (23.34,43,47) all chime in with his picture of Jesus' beneficence and graciousness: he dies the perfect martyr, as devout and as merciful as throughout his life.

John's narrative again seems independent in many respects, not least in its dating of the death of Jesus twenty-four hours earlier than the other Gospels, so that it coincides with the ritual slaughter of the lambs of Passover in the Temple. Opinion divides as to whether this reflects better knowledge (J. A. T. Robinson) or symbolic* considerations and irony* which is thoroughly typical of this evangelist (the true lamb that takes away human sins dies while the outworn ritual proceeds). The much lengthier trial before Pilate, with its subtle discussion of truth and kingship, reflects Johannine themes, as Jesus' final words, 'It is finished', reflect John's doctrine of the cross as the place of glory, exaltation and triumph.

It is salutary to turn back from all this careful theological analysis of the passion narratives to the way they have been interpreted through much the greater part of their history: that is to say, as historical narratives, to be harmonized* at points of difference, with the details of one complementing the others, and as stimulating the Christians' devout identification with Jesus in his suffering (cf. the observance of the 'Three Hours Devotion' from the seventeenth century and the Stations of the Cross from late mediaeval times). They were taken to demonstrate the guilt of all Jews for Jesus' death (the crime of deicide), Matt. 27.25 (*see* **Antisemitism**). Sometimes they gave rise to what we must see as very strange interpretations indeed. Thus, through

much of the Christian period, the reference to two swords in Luke 22.38 was taken to refer to the twin authorities of church and state, the spiritual and secular powers, over both of which (in papal eyes at least) Christ ruled, through the pope his deputy. Suddenly to be led to reflect that such interpretations were long seen by Christian readers as 'the meaning'* of the Lucan text is to realize the great gulf that separates pre- from post-critical interpretation. One can then form a view which method (if either?) leads us closer to the original sense, supposing that that is our aim.

In another vein but again throwing light on the way changes in styles of awareness affect interpretation: we may note that many modern students would feel that the warm devotional atmosphere of J. S. Bach's *St Matthew Passion* is closer to the ethos and outlook of Luke's narrative than to Matthew's (*see* **Music, The Bible in**).

See also **Gospel; Lectionary Interpretation; Resurrection Narratives.**

S. G. F. Brandon, *The Trial of Jesus of Nazareth*, 1968; C. F. Evans, 'The Passion of Christ' in *Explorations in Theology 2*, 1977; H. Hendrickx, *Passion Narratives*, 1984; J. L. Houlden, *Backward into Light*, 1987; W. H. Kelber, *The Passion in Mark*, 1976.

J. L. HOULDEN

Pastoral Care

In Christian pastoral care, the carers work within a framework which has as its basis the belief that the person is made in the image of a God who orders creation* (Gen. 1.27,28); and the outworking of this belief understands pastoral care as involvement in the caring response of God to humanity, humanity to humanity, and humanity to God (Luke 10.27). Pastoral care, then, will understand its work in the context of the whole work of God, and will draw on the Bible as a resource for the practical expression of this acknowledged involvement in the responsiveness of God. This task will involve skill in uncovering what will be the best response for the particular situation.

However, when one turns to the ways in which pastoral care, one of the major activities and concerns of the churches, makes use of the Bible, the situation is curiously unexciting. It seems to be a matter of either the simplistic listing of superficially edifying texts in the manner of Gideon Bibles in hotel rooms or drawing on broad biblical themes which have a bearing on the matter. It is hard to avoid the feeling that the Bible does not feature as a resource in this area at a very profound level and that much of the inspiration comes from secular sources. In this respect, the case of pastoral care may be not untypical of the way in which the Bible is interpreted in relation to many subjects. In that sense, it is far from being insignificant for those interested in the practical impact of biblical interpretation as distinct from its preoccupation with its own internal life, where profundity and sophistication are available in plenty.

Some methods of Christian counselling view the Bible as a text-book of solutions which can be used authoritatively for any problem that may arise in life. For example, faced with anxiety the pastor may direct the client to the following biblical texts: Matt. 8.23–27; II Cor. 4.8,9; Heb. 12.1–3; I Peter 5.10–11; Rom. 8.31–39; Acts 3.1–16. This not only fails to view biblical testimony as a whole and in historical context, but it may also be seen to damage the person by offering a superficial solution, a hasty diagnosis based on a failure to listen, and by failing to open up feelings. Further the pastor is forced into a position of having to provide the correct verse for each succeeding need.

Some writers on pastoral care have placed the use of the Bible in a wider theological context or drawn out significant biblical themes. Thus, Fox explores the scriptures as God's responsiveness to the world made clear in continuous acting through blessing. God blesses people in a privilege of care and love and in this blessing reveals his presence in life and growth. Through our response to this blessing we become most fully human. Blessing is the inner strength of the soul and the happiness it creates.

Virgo suggests that pastoral care is the practical outworking of involvement with the God who blesses. It is a call to work at the interface between blessing and the curse of meaninglessness, loss of value, purposelessness, lack of will, drive and energy, stress, anxiety, aggression. In this context, the Bible is assumed to be already affecting the one who seeks help, who may be seeing it as providing clues to answers, justifying attitudes, or, by contrast, reinforcing inappropriate guilt and fear. The pastor, then, needs to discover by listening why a story, a phrase, an attitude, or an image dominates a person's horizon, and allow this to be a doorway into exploration of the conflicts that are part of pain and growth.

Pattison suggests that the Bible and pastoral care must be related in a way that embodies critical integrity. The starting point is to allow the Bible to shape and form the consciousness and character of people by allowing them to be in a constant dialogue with the text. We are to take the Bible's themes, stories and images, and reflect upon their meaning in the experience of our lives. The Bible contributes to the task of formation and provides a back-ground function with regard to meeting specific pastoral crises or needs. We should always be very careful about laying down the biblical line on any matter in pastoral care. There is no one view or theology in the Bible; pluralism and diversity characterize its message.

Wigglesworth argues that we must be aware of the potential that scripture has in enabling sustaining, reconciling, healing and nurturing to take place. He draws attention to the sense of reassurance mediated by many of the psalms and by Jesus' words and actions as underlying affirmations of forgiveness and love that can mediate healing and reconciliation. These passages can be used in the task of nurturing in community group work, applying such methods as discussion based on particular passages, role-play, simulation games, and psycho-drama. These creative approaches to the Bible allow a freedom to challenge the perceptions of the past and discern the spirit of God in the present, even though, as often practised, they may come close to the simplistic methods outlined earlier.

Matthew Fox, *Original Blessing*, 1983; Stephen Pattison, *A Critique of Pastoral Care*, 1988; Leslie Virgo (ed.), *First Aid in Pastoral Care*, 1987; Hans-Ruedi Weber, *Experiments with Bible Study*, 1981; Chris Wigglesworth, 'Bible: Pastoral Use' in Alisdair Campbell (ed.), *A Dictionary of Pastoral Care*, 1987.

JAMES WELFORD WOODWARD

Pastoral Epistles

Throughout the modern period I and II Timothy and Titus have been known by this collective name; it goes back at least to the eighteenth century. Their history in the early church was mixed: perhaps because they were not known, or not known as Paul's, they are missing from the early papyrus manuscript* P⁴⁶ and Marcion* omits them, more probably because he does not know them than because he objects to them. Indeed, one theory is that they were written in order to reclaim Paul* from the Marcionites. Polycarp appears to quote from them, but Justin Martyr seems not to know of them. By the late second century, however, they are commonly known and regarded as authentic, cf. Irenaeus,* the Muratorian Canon, and Tertullian,* and from that time their place is as assured as that of the other Pauline letters. It was only at the beginning of the nineteenth century that a case was mounted against Pauline authorship.*

The epistles are not rich in theology, being to some extent (supposedly) autobiographical and to a great extent composed of advice on how to live in the church and in the world. Throughout the history of the church, accordingly, although isolated passages have been used theologically, by far their greatest use has been the application of their strongly subordinationist and hierarchical advice on behaviour on the one hand, and the exploitation of their material about the church's structure of ministries on the other hand. It is in the fourth century, with so-called Ambrosiaster, that we first find a full commentary,* not surprisingly giving special emphasis to questions about the organization of the church. Chrysostom, Theodore of Mopsuestia, and Pelagius followed, and in the Middle Ages, Thomas Aquinas. The Reformers* did not exploit the epistles to a very great extent (though Calvin* wrote a commentary on them), presumably because they hardly contain a great deal of grist for Reformation mills; though Anglicans were glad to find in them backing for their retention of the episcopate (I Tim. 3). From the eighteenth, and especially the nineteenth, century onwards, there have been innumerable commentaries, an increasing number of which have taken the author not to be Paul himself.

The behaviour patterns advocated in the epistles are very strongly subjectionist: the church to its tradition, the generality of Christians to bishops and elders (whether these are to be seen as different or the same), of women to men, slaves to masters, and citizens to the state. For many, it is precisely these patterns, so congenial to the church in early and mediaeval times, which cause problems of interpretation in the present day. On the other hand, the letters have been important since the sixteenth century, and especially with the rise of the ecumenical movement in this century, in ecclesiastical discussions about the primitive forms of ministry. Unfortunately, because it is so difficult to know the functions and interrelations of bishops, elders, and deacons in the Pastorals with any precision (and indeed whether these terms are not anachronistic at this early period), it cannot be claimed that studying them has done much to resolve issues, even when it is supposed that early church practice is binding.

On the church's liturgies* and on church orders the influence of the epistles has been considerable. Many phrases from them have passed into prayers, including some in the Book of Common Prayer, especially the Ordinal. If it cannot be demonstrated that the earliest church orders, e.g. the Didache, are directly affected by these letters, the later ones (e.g. the so-called Canons of Hippolytus, *c.* 500) certainly are. This is not surprising if, as is often held, church order material lies behind the Pastorals themselves.

Modern study has tended to be dominated by the question of authorship. This is not an issue unconnected with interpretation, for at important points the way the text is understood depends on a decision about authorship. There are five main groups of arguments leading most critical scholars not to consider Paul to have been the author.

1. The vocabulary and style are, by a wide variety of tests, found not to be consistent with Paul's authorship. The facts are seldom disputed; those who maintain that Paul is the author resort to the theory that he used a secretary (though none is mentioned or implied in any of the Pastorals), or say that a combination of advancing age, different recipients, different circumstances, and different genre* (they are not ostensibly letters to churches) account for the undoubted differences from the undisputed letters.

2. It was for some time held that as the 'false teaching' opposed throughout the epistles shows distinctly gnostic traits, and as Gnosticism* was a second-century heresy, therefore Paul cannot have been the author. This argument is now abandoned, as the beginnings of Gnosticism are widely detected even in Paul's lifetime.

3. It is almost universally agreed that the events described or implied in the Pastorals cannot be fitted into Paul's ministry as it emerges from Acts and from the undisputed letters. Those who maintain Paul's authorship therefore, with few exceptions, propose that he was released from Roman imprisonment and had a further spell of missionary activity in Ephesus (for I and II Timothy) and Crete (for Titus). Thus, if the epistles are authentically Pauline, they are still relatively late.

4. It is argued that the comparatively great emphasis on church structure, with the transmission of authority, and the resting on established tradition, together with a hierarchical ministry, come from an era later than that of Paul himself, in whose time structure was more fluid and reliance was on the Spirit at least as much as on the tradition. It is at this point that interpretation and views of authorship most clearly interact. Those who hold the letters to be post-Pauline tend to stress the difference from Paul, e.g. in seeing in them the beginnings of the monarchical episcopate (cf. the letters of Ignatius of Antioch). Those who think the epistles are Pauline tend, on the one hand to emphasize the signs of emerging structure to be detected in the acknowledged Paulines (e.g. 'bishops and deacons' are greeted in Phil. 1.1), and on the other hand to argue that bishops and elders in the Pastorals are identical, and that they are long before the days of the monarchical bishop.

5. The theological statements of these epistles tend to come in short pieces rather than Paul's use of fuller argumentation, and while those who uphold Pauline authorship

usually see them as implying thoroughly Pauline ideas, others see them as missing the Pauline point (e.g. the treatment of the law in I Tim. 1.8–11, and the treatment of regeneration in Titus 3.4–7). Again, decisions about authorship and decisions about interpretation are difficult to keep separate.

These groups of arguments (or rather, four out of five of them) are widely held to reinforce one another. A case seriously argued is that the author is Luke, because of important affinities between the Pastorals and Acts. Some even take the mid-second-century Polycarp to be the author. It is also still not uncommonly held (following the work of P.N. Harrison in 1921, supplemented and refined in 1964) that the author has worked genuine Pauline fragments into a framework of his own devising, or that the epistles use a variety of sources, including some traditional Pauline material.

One result of the widespread scholarly view that the epistles are pseudonymous * has been that they have been described as lacking in any real theology of their own, being rather a pastiche of traditional materials. Their general aim, it is commonly thought, was to rescue Paul from the heretics of the second century, especially the Gnostics, but possibly even from Marcion. This is why there is almost nothing of theological interest, and 'Paul' has become simply the champion of the *status quo*, whether one looks at doctrine or at social relationships within the limits found acceptable in society at large. 'Paul' does not argue; he simply denounces the false teachers, and commends the tradition handed down. At the same time, the strongly subordinationist ethic,* in family, social, civil and church relationships, reflects the dangers posed by the false teachers with their rejection of commonly accepted patterns of subjection to authority. It is also held to reflect the danger to the infant church of being suspected of subverting the conditions of a secure and settled society, e.g. by ignoring the inferiority of women to men. Thus the letters are seen as an attempt to rescue not simply Paul, but the church itself, and to find for it a way of living safely within the almost universally accepted patterns of life in its contemporary world. So, either the Pastorals can be regarded as capitulation to the norms of secular society, thus regressing from the earliest Christian teaching, or they can be regarded as a reflection of the inevitable process of the church's finding a way of living within the given conditions of its time. Increasingly, for example, commentators are finding it impossible to see the teaching about the inferiority of women in I Tim. 2.8–15 as providing in any direct way a word for the twentieth century (*see* Feminist Interpretation; Women in Early Christian Interpretation); rather, it is seen as conditioned by the particular circumstances of the author, whether Paul or not, and of the congregation addressed.

That, in view of all this, the Pastorals lack a coherent and distinctive theology is not now universally conceded. Thus, the epistles are seen as very much products of the second century, and as using the methods of logic common at that time, a logic that is rhetorical * rather than formal. They do indeed employ traditional materials, joined by catchword linkages, positive statements sometimes being balanced by negative ones, but all is within an overall purpose to promote Christian living within the real world, not by fleeing from it, and to uphold the goodness of God's creation, not fleeing from that either (Karris). Seen thus, it is argued, the Pastorals are not an amalgam of bits and pieces, but have cohesion and a consistent theology of salvation. In this, the device of pseudepigraphy has been seen (Donelson) as central: 'Paul' functions as the paradigm of the true teacher, of whom the present bishops and elders are the equally true successors. To follow Paul may involve rejection, as he was rejected, but it will certainly lead to salvation now (in the form of virtuous living) and hereafter (in eternal life), a salvation which is denied to heretical groups. Thus attacks on false teachers, lists of virtues, and emphasis on valid ministries, all belong together in one matrix concerned primarily with salvation. If the question of authorship has dominated study of these epistles for nearly two centuries, there are signs that attention is being turned rather to their literary character and their own distinctive contribution to the total picture of early Christianity.

See also **Paul; Pseudonymity.**

L. R. Donelson, *Pseudepigraphy and Ethical Argument in the Pastoral Epistles*, 1986; G. D. Fee, *1 and 2 Timothy, Titus*, 1984; A. T. Hanson, *The Pastoral Epistles*, 1982; P. N. Harrison, *The Problem of the Pastoral Epistles*, 1921,² 1964; J. L. Houlden, *The Pastoral Epistles*, 1976; R. J. Karris, *The Pastoral Epistles*, 1979; S. G. Wilson, *Luke and the Pastoral Epistles*, 1979.

J. A. ZIESLER

Patristic Christology

The NT makes a great many diverse statements about the person of Christ, but it never constructs a theory, nor does it try to give the various confessions any coherence. The raw material for affirming both the divinity and the humanity of Christ is there, but it is not developed clearly, and some statements are somewhat ambiguous, pointing to a kind of intermediary figure (*see* **Christology, New Testament**).

It was in the patristic period that attempts were made to clarify these matters, and reach a conclusion about the nature of Christ's person. Reference to the text of the NT was an indispensable element in this process, and debate about the meaning of specific texts had an important role to play in clarifying the mind of the church. But the OT was also of crucial importance. Since Christians held that the whole of the OT was prophetic* of Christ, the patristic picture of his person included many features from key OT passages, and not just the obviously messianic* ones. Passages concerning the pre-existent wisdom* of God were particularly important.

Two early misconceptions seem to be resisted within the NT itself, but remain influential in the earliest non-canonical writings of Christianity. One was the idea that the Christ was a heavenly being and only 'seemed' to be human: Docetism. Sometimes this was coupled with the suggestion that the Christ or the Spirit left Jesus before the passion, and in that sense the suffering of Christ was not 'real'. Ignatius of Antioch insisted that Jesus Christ was of the seed of David,* Mary's son 'who was really born and ate and drank, really persecuted by Pontius Pilate, really crucified and died . . .; who also really rose from the dead, since his Father raised him up, his Father, who will likewise raise us also who believe in him through Jesus Christ . . .' Although it cannot be shown definitively that Ignatius knew the written Gospels,* it is clear that Gospel traditions inform such resistance to Docetism.

The second early misconception seems to be implied by the Epistle to the Hebrews, where the first chapter labours to distinguish Christ from the angels: the angels are merely God's ministers whereas he is Son and Lord. In *The Shepherd of Hermas*, however, he appears as the greatest of the archangels. Such thinking implies the idea of a heavenly court with a hierarchy, and it is hardly surprising that in thinking of Jesus as a supernatural visitant, such a conclusion as to his person and status should have been canvassed.

The need to resist the Docetism of the gnostic* sects meant that from early on the goodness of the material creation and the reality of the flesh of Christ were affirmed. But in the earliest centuries it was not his humanity so much as the question of how he was related to God that was most thoroughly explored. Although the exposition offered by the Apologists owes much to the contemporary intellectual scene, the biblical roots of their Logos* theology should not be underestimated. They were working out a coherent 'theory' which brought together key passages of both OT and NT. Prov. 8.22ff. was taken to

be the words of the pre-existent Christ: he was the wisdom of God, the one through whom God had created (cf. John 1.1–3). God had begotten him before anything else came into being, and he was beside him fitting things together (as the Septuagint* version of v. 30 puts it). So the Word who is God's Son was understood to be the Logos 'spoken forth', God's reason projected forth into speech, so as to become first the instrument of creation, and then of revelation* as the Word of the Lord came to the prophets.

The importance of this development was that God himself was affirmed to be the source of the Logos, and the language which linked the Son with the angels, implying that he belonged to the created order, was left behind. It also had another important consequence: the divine Christ had cosmic and universal significance. Not only did this point the way to future exegesis of the Johannine Prologue, of Col. 1.15ff, Phil. 2.5ff, and Heb. 1.3, but it also allowed the Apologists to claim the best of all human wisdom for Christ. The reason at the heart of the universe was also the reason in the mind of human beings. Christ, as the universal reason, was the fulfilment of all that human moral and intellectual endeavour had been striving for, notably in Greek philosophy.

This kind of thinking shaped the christology of the pre-Nicene period. Christ was regarded as the Word made flesh, the pre-existent Son of God through whom the world was made, now incarnate. Monarchian thinking in both its Adoptionist and Modalist forms seems to have been a monotheistic reaction against this kind of approach: the first suggesting that the one God adopted the human Jesus as his Son, so cutting out any intermediary being like the Logos; the second also excluding the Logos by suggesting that Father, Son and Spirit were different 'modes' of the One God. The christologies of Irenaeus,* Tertullian,* Origen* and Dionysius of Alexandria were developments of Logos theology, in some cases developments informed by resistance to Monarchianism. The Arian heresy was a radical version of Logos theology which rejected the essential link between the Logos as the mind of God himself and the Logos as the instrument of creation generated by the Father.

Throughout the pre-Nicene period it was taken for granted that Prov. 8.22 referred to the generation of the pre-existent Logos, *ektisen* ('created') in v. 22 being interpreted in the light of *gennai* ('generates', 'begets') in v. 25. Arius questioned that interpretation: 'created' meant the Logos was a 'creature'. He was of course the first and greatest of the creatures, the instrument through whom the rest of creation was made. But God being essentially 'ingenerate' (*agennētos*), one begotten (*gennētos*) could not be God in the full sense of the word. Debate about this and other key passages of scripture was at the heart of the Arian controversy, despite the impression given by the apparently philosophical terminology of the discussion. Arius also used Johannine texts like 'My Father is greater than I', together with the many references in the Gospels describing the weakness, ignorance, fallibility, passibility and temptability of Jesus, to demonstrate the fact that the Logos had attributes inappropriate to the truly divine.

The reason why Arius attracted considerable backing among the Eastern bishops was that the assumptions implicit in the accepted Logos theology had shaped their thinking. Everyone had a kind of 'hierarchical' understanding of God's relationship with his creation, with the Logos as a 'second God' mediating between and linking the levels on the ladder of existence. Origen seems to have envisaged this in terms of the Logos being the One-Many or Indefinite Dyad between the ultimate One and the Many of the created order, thus assimilating the Logos-theology even more closely to contemporary Middle Platonic speculations. Eusebius * of Caesarea, the successor to Origen's library and his tradition of scholarship, was more sympathetic to Arius than his opponents, suspecting them of Modalism. Inheriting 'hierarchical' presuppositions from the Origenist tradition, Eusebius could affirm one God and one Lord, and still claim to be defending monotheism.

But if you insist on distinguishing God from his creation, as much in the biblical tradition demands, at what point is the essential distinction to be made? Eusebius failed to discern that what Arius was saying implied this new question, and he is undoubtedly representative of many others. Athanasius rightly discerned the implications: Arius' Logos was not the Logos of God, God's own reason, but a different, separate and creaturely being, cut off from God and therefore unable to communicate him. The 'subordinationist' tendencies of the Logos theology were exposed by this controversy. That the Logos of God was God's Logos, essentially one with him, had to be clarified once and for all. That clarification also drew on scriptural texts, such as the Johannine 'I and the Father are One.' But the clarification laid the anti-Arians open to the charge of Sabellianism, that is, of being in the tradition of the Modalist reaction against Logos theology.

To what extent were Eusebius' suspicions justified that Athanasius, Marcellus and others were Sabellian? Careful study suggests that Marcellus was in fact a conservative Logos-theologian, who insisted that the Logos should not be distinguished from God prior to his generation from the Father for the purposes of creating, communicating and being incarnate. Modalism, on the other hand, had denied the possibility of ever making any distinction: there was one God, known in three different 'modes', or wearing three different masks (*prosōpa*). Tertullian had thrown at them the jibe that they 'crucified the Father', since God himself became the Son, was incarnate, suffered and died. That notion was dead and buried, and the charge was anachronistic. But the charge is another indication of how the Logos theology increasingly failed to cope with the issues. Somehow a way had to be found of saying that it really was God who was revealed in Jesus, it really was God's life and salvation that was imparted to humanity in him, not some 'separated' supernatural but not fully divine being. Since Arius could interpret any formula drawn from the scriptures his way, the Nicene Fathers reluctantly resorted to the non-scriptural *homoousion* ('of one substance') in order to ensure that this point was clear.

In the fourth-century debates, other weaknesses of the Logos theology were exposed. Arius was able to argue that the Logos was creaturely, fallible, etc., because it was assumed that the incarnation meant that the Logos 'became flesh', and therefore anything said about Jesus was actually said about the Logos. So in reply to Arius, the exegesis of Athanasius and others began to insist on a new distinction between things said in the scriptures about the 'flesh' or 'humanity' assumed by the Logos, and things said about the Logos in himself. When Jesus confessed his ignorance of the End, or wept at Lazarus' tomb, or was hungry or thirsty, then these things were not to be attributed to the essentially divine Logos, as Arius assumed, but rather to the flesh he took. Marcellus and Athanasius even took Prov. 8.22 to refer to the incarnation rather than the generation of the pre-existent Logos. This suggestion was a most unfortunate response to Arius, since it precluded a sensible and unified interpretation of the passage as a whole. The scholar Eusebius of Caesarea alone managed to produce a satisfactory and non-Arian exegesis: by showing that *ektisen* does not necessarily mean 'create' in the strict way that Arius was pressing the word. Eusebius was able to interpret the whole passage more traditionally as referring to the Logos being begotten, begotten that is of God himself, as his pre-existent agent of creation.

Athanasius, then, ascribed human weaknesses, including psychological weaknesses, not to the Logos himself, but to the 'flesh' he took, so by implication treating the 'flesh' as full humanity. But his exegesis* is not always very felicitous: he suggests in one passage that Christ imitated our condition. Eustathius of Antioch and Athanasius' fellow-Alexandrian, Didymus the Blind, came up with a better solution: they affirmed the existence of a human soul in Jesus to which weakness, ignorance, emotion, and temptation might be attributed. Previously Origen had used this notion as a metaphysical device: the Logos became incarnate after uniting himself with the one human soul that had not fallen. But with Didymus the human soul takes on another role: it is the human soul that is ignorant, fallible, weak, able to suffer and be tempted. Thus was Arius' exegesis* of the Gospels countered. Towards the end of his life it is possible that Athanasius saw the point of this; certainly he was party to a document opposing the theory of his old friend Apollinarius that the Logos took flesh without a human soul or mind.

Scripture contributed to Arianism; so also, it seems, to Apollinarianism. Did Apollinarius accept a dichotomist (body-soul) view of human nature or a trichotomist (body-soul-spirit/mind) view? Did he in consequence deny that the Christ had a human soul, or a human spirit/mind? The confusion seems to arise because of his propensity to use Pauline* terminology in a somewhat haphazard way. Furthermore, in thinking of the Logos as the soul or mind of the Saviour, who was a unique being uniting God and Man, a mediating being, a hybrid or mixture, Apollinarius seems to have been influenced by Pauline texts: 'Paul calls the last (Adam) life-giving Spirit', he suggests: 'The Christ having God as spirit, that is, mind, together with soul and body, is reasonably called the "man from heaven"'.

However scriptural it might seem, the position of Apollinarius could not be acceptable. Like the Cappadocians, Athanasius saw that 'what is not assumed is not healed'. The incarnation was essential for salvation because the Fall meant that humanity had lost the Logos with which it had been endowed, and as a result was sinking back into the nothingness from which it had been created. What was needed was the re-endowment of humanity with the genuine Logos of God. So 'he became human in order that we might become divine'. Behind that statement lies the very similar affirmation of Irenaeus, 'he became what we are in order that we might become what he is'. For both, the essential humanity of the saviour was as important as his essential divinity.

So the ongoing discussion about how the Logos was related to God eventually led to serious debate about the humanity of Christ. The rejection of docetism had to be refined.

How the essentially divine Logos was to participate in genuine human experience became the issue after Nicaea. The presence of a human soul or mind was settled by the condemnation of Apollinarius; but this did not settle the more difficult question of how divinity and humanity might be related in the one Christ. It is to be observed that much confusion resulted from the application of terms like 'soul' and 'flesh', which in many scriptural contexts signify the self as a whole, to parts of the self, as in Greek usage of the period.

Clearly scriptural interpretation played a central role in patristic discussion from the very beginning, but particularly in the great christological controversy of the early fifth century, scripture comes to centre stage. The resistance to Arius already described produced two distinct christological traditions: that associated with Antioch* emphasized the integrity of each of the natures, and was accused of teaching 'Two Sons', so dividing the Christ, while the Alexandrians* emphasized the one nature of the Logos enfleshed, so being accused of attributing change to the unchangeable Godhead, and confusing the natures like Arius and Apollinarius. These traditions came into direct conflict in the persons of Cyril and Nestorius. The issues concerned the proper exegesis of both the Nicene Creed* and key NT passages.

This is not at first apparent since the controversy was initiated by a dispute over describing Mary as *Theotokos* – mother of God. The problem of speaking about God being born when he was assumed to be changeless, infinite and transcendent would appear to arise not so much from the scriptures as from acceptance of the philosophical concept of God. But one of Nestorius' extant sermons shows that the scriptural contribution was by no means secondary. A key text for him was the statement in the Epistle to the Hebrews about the Saviour being high-priest and apostle. This cannot be said of the Godhead, since a priest acts in relation to God: it must be said of the humanity. Hebrews was in fact a favourite epistle among the Antiochenes. Its emphasis on the saviour's temptation, and on his being the first-born of many brethren, was especially congenial to their position. In the controversial literature, argument also focusses on the proper exegesis of other texts like Phil. 2.5–11 and John 1.14, 'The Word became flesh'; it cannot mean change, and therefore must be understood in terms of 'he took flesh'.

In the course of the controversy, Cyril drew up Twelve Anathemas, to which the Antiochenes reacted very sharply: it is clear from these how central to the controversy was the interpretation of these key texts, along with questions such as what the 'temple of his body' means: John 2.19 was important to the Antiochenes, but played down by the Alexandrians by appeal to I Cor. 3.16–17. Also in the Anathemas the distinction between texts in the Gospels referring to the Godhead and those referring to the 'Man Assumed' is an important issue. Cyril abhorred this practice, but Theodoret was able to quote Cyril's own great predecessor, Athanasius, against him, and Cyril had to admit some distinction. The issue had subtly changed since the time of Arius: the question now was whether these texts were to be referred to one subject or two. For Cyril some things were said of Jesus Christ 'humanly', others 'divinely', but all applied to the one person of the incarnate Logos. For the Antiochenes, the integrity of the immutable God, and the integrity of the humanity which needs salvation, had to be preserved: and so they could speak of the man assumed by the Logos being 'co-worshipped' and 'co-glorified'. Cyril feared the idea of a God-bearing Man, no different from other saints and prophets: scripture texts feature again in this discussion.

The West never experienced such profound turmoil over this issue. The Tome of Pope Leo, setting out the Western view of one Christ in two natures, was among the documents canonized at the Council of Chalcedon (451). The Chalcedonian Definition alludes to scripture only once: 'like us in all things apart from sin'. Leo's Tome, however, constantly appeals to scripture to tell the credal story of one who is God of God, yet becomes Emmanuel, God with us. The trouble with those who are masters of error, Leo suggests, is that they have not gained learning from the holy pages of the OT and NT and submitted to the Gospel teaching. In all their battles, the Fathers were trying to understand the sense of scripture.

See also **Alexandrian Interpretation; Antiochene Interpretation; Hellenism.**

R. A. Greer, *The Captain of our Salvation*, 1973; A. Grillmeier, *Christ in Christian Tradition*, 1965, 1975; J. N. D. Kelly, *Early Christian Doctrines*, 1958; T. E. Pollard, *Johannine Christology and the Early Church*, 1970; R. V. Sellers, *Two Ancient Christologies*, 1940; id., *The Council of Chalcedon*, 1953; Frances Young, *From Nicaea to Chalcedon*, 1983.

FRANCES YOUNG

Paul

In our NT, Paul stands as a dominating figure, yet a controversial one (see, for example, Galatians, II Corinthians, II Peter 3.15–16; even Acts). His version of Christianity was far from universally accepted, especially for its absolving his Gentile converts from the need to keep the Torah. Before long, the wide use made of his writings by Gnostics* and Marcion* made him suspect in 'orthodox' circles. Indeed, although the evidence is not always clear, before the end of the second century there is little sign that post-apostolic Christianity owed much to him. Clement of Rome makes considerable use of I Corinthians, and Ignatius of Antioch quotes him, yet there is astonishing silence about him even in places where he had worked and been influential. Justin Martyr uses Pauline phrases, but never mentions the apostle himself. Irenaeus* (*Adv. Haer.* IV, 41,4) finds it necessary to reclaim him from the 'heretics'. On the other hand, if most scholars are right in thinking that some of the letters (especially I and II Timothy and Titus [*see* **Pastoral Epistles**], but also Ephesians and perhaps Colossians and II Thessalonians) are not by Paul himself but by followers perpetuating his influence and ideas, and in effect being his first interpreters for new situations and needs, then the Pauline movement did flourish in some circles after his death (see also II Peter). Moreover, Acts presents a Paul who has become a legendary figure of the Christian faith, although it is notoriously deficient in conveying his distinctive ideas and appears unaware that he ever wrote a letter. Despite these writings, it seems that for more than a century Pauline influence on wide areas of the church diminished dramatically.

One reason for this diminution is doubtless that at least one of his leading concerns, viz. the relation between Christian faith and Judaism, largely faded away with the establishment of Christianity as a separate faith and a separate community. Another, equally important, is that gnostic Christians like Valentinus made such effective use of his letters to advance their own doctrines. In Romans, for instance, Jews and Gentiles were taken to be symbolic of 'psychic' and 'pneumatic' Christians respectively, and much of the gnostic view of God, the world, and the human condition, was read out of (or into) Paul. Things like dying and rising with Christ, largely ignored by the 'orthodox', were heavily stressed by them, and Rom. 1.21–25 was taken not as an attack on idolatry, but as teaching the folly of worshipping the Demiurge or Creator God, rather than the true God, Christ the Logos.* The suspicion of Paul that all this engendered in anti-gnostic Christians was compounded by the figure of Marcion, who in the mid-second century propounded a radical version of Christianity, based on Paul, which rejected all connection between Christ and the OT, Judaism, the Law, and the Creator God. Only Paul's letters reflected the true gospel of a gracious stranger God who would rescue human beings from this world and this life, but even those letters had been corrupted by Jewish elements. In drawing up a list of books that were authoritative, he included all the Pauline Epistles* except the Pastorals (of which he seems to have had no knowledge), and the Gospel of Luke, all carefully expurgated, and that was all. That Paul survived the embrace of the Gnostics and Marcion suggests that he had already become a sufficiently revered figure, yet for at least 200 years Christian writers were engaged in rescuing Paul from these embraces.

On a quite different front, there were important circles of Jewish Christians, such as those whose piety is preserved in the Pseudo-Clementine writings, who regarded Paul as the arch-enemy of the truth, and attacked him for betraying the Torah. The figure of Simon Magus, who is a major target, is usually believed to be code for the apostle Paul. Similarly the Ebionites rejected him altogether. Of course there were other circles where Paul was venerated, cf. the second-century Acts of Paul which is thoroughly hagiographical, but which also shows little interest in the distinctive ideas of Paul.

From the end of the second century, however, the positions of Paul as an apostle, and of his epistles as fruitful for the life and doctrine of the church, became assured, though it is not until the end of the fourth century that we find a great flowering of commentaries* on the epistles. Then there appeared commentaries, on all or some, by Theodore of Mopsuestia and Chrysostom in the East, and by Victorinus, Jerome, and above all the unknown writer we call Ambrosiaster in the West. The way had been prepared by Irenaeus, Tertullian,* and especially Origen,* but particularly in the case of Ambrosiaster and Theodore, it is now that we meet commentators who decisively influenced subsequent exegesis* for a thousand years and beyond. It is often said, especially from a Lutheran* standpoint, that none of them (except Augustine*) really understood Paul, and it is true that none of them stood within both Judaism and Christianity as Paul did, so that the issues that preoccupied him tended to be ignored or distorted. Nevertheless such a general adverse judgment may mean little more than that the Fathers were not preoccupied with justification by faith (alone) in the same way as Luther was, and a more recent scholarly judgment is that in this they were closer to Paul than some Protestant exegetes have been. Certainly extreme adulation of Paul as an apostle was now common, and the use of his writings in worship can be documented from this time, though it is difficult to know when it began.

Although the Antiochene* tradition was against it, in much work on the Bible,

allegory* (or the finding of spiritual meanings*) was the order of the day. In commenting on the letters of Paul, however, even the Alexandrians,* who had a tradition of allegorizing going back beyond Christianity to Philo,* tended to be concerned much more with straightforward theological teaching. This is true also of the great Ambrosiaster who is sometimes coupled with the Antiochenes by scholars, and whose comments reflect an historical sense as well as much common sense.

Inevitably, because of the controversies that surrounded them, these first great commentators tended to be interested in Paul's support for their christological* positions, and in the process read into Paul much more precision than is really there (*see* **Patristric Christology**). At the same time they are far from treating him simply as a source of such support, just as they are far from ignoring other matters outside the areas of controversy. Perhaps in reaction against Marcion and the Gnostics, they tend to over-simplify Paul's support for the Law, and not to grasp the elusive subtleties of his attitude. Again, in treating faith and works, sometimes the issue is distorted because faith is too narrowly conceived as assent to true beliefs. At times, too, their treatment of Paul's doctrine of man is heavily influenced by a too strict and un-Jewish spiritual/physical dualism. Nonetheless, they continued and advanced a use and understanding of Paul in the church, so that it is quite misleading to suppose that Paul lay undiscovered or misunderstood until the appearance of Augustine.

Augustine was undoubtedly a great and perceptive commentator who was expounding Paul's letters before his controversy with the Pelagians began (as indeed was Pelagius). Yet it was in that controversy that the distinctively Augustinian interpretations were developed which had such a crucial influence on later reading of Paul, and above all on Luther, just as the views – or the supposed views – of Pelagius became abominated. Some time near the end of the fourth century Augustine abandoned a Platonist reading of Paul, characterized by the idea of the spiritual life as an ascent to God. Instead he concentrated much more on the opposition of 'flesh' to 'Spirit', on human universal lostness apart from the unconditioned divine grace to some, on justification by faith understood not as a community issue (how to have both Jews and Gentiles in one church) but as the only way for the individual to be accepted by God. It was with Augustine that justification became seen as the heart of Paul's teaching, and with it self-righteousness as a basic sin.

There is no shortage of commentary on or use of Paul in the Middle Ages. The mainstay of much mediaeval* exegesis was allegorizing, but the Pauline writings give relatively little scope for this. Among the many commentators Peter Abelard is worthy of note, as it was in writing on Romans that he developed his controversial 'subjective' theory of the atonement. The twelfth century also saw the compilation of glosses (marginal and interlinear comments) on the Bible, for which material was drawn from patristic and later sources. The gloss on Paul is among the parts of the *Glossa Ordinaria* thought to have been compiled by Anselm and Ralph of Laon. Peter Lombard's *Glossatura Magna*, much quoted in the thirteenth century, is a compilation of glosses on the psalms and on Paul.

Important elements in Latin theology, from Augustine throughout the mediaeval period, derive from Paul. The doctrines of grace and of original sin are obvious instances, as is the idea that Christ is the head of the church, with the church as his body, an idea much discussed and elaborated in the thirteenth century. For the scholastics Paul was simply 'the apostle' just as Aristotle was 'the philosopher', and their theology was Pauline in the same way as their philosophy was Aristotelian.

Thus Luther and Calvin* were hardly innovators in giving serious attention to Paul. On the contrary, at about the same time thorough commentaries by Catholic scholars were being produced, and when it came to detailed exegesis they and the Reformers' works were not as far apart as might have been expected. Nonetheless the Reformers* made their case almost entirely on the basis of the interpretation of Paul, an interpretation, however, which was highly selective. The eschatological* context and character of Paul's writings were virtually ignored, and justification by faith (alone) was made the centre of Paul, and indeed of Christianity.

Most notably, Luther was indebted to the Fathers, and especially to Augustine, but (perhaps following Nicholas of Lyra) aimed to avoid allegorical exegesis, in favour of a historical approach, and exploited to some extent the new humanist philology.* He, and many Protestant writers after him, saw everything in terms of the basic viewpoint that the gospel was about the unconditioned grace of God to men and women who are otherwise hopelessly enmeshed in sin. Any notion of human effort or merit as contributing in any way to the individual's standing before God was regarded as abominable, and even the most careful Catholic commentators were suspected of such a ('Pelagian') view.

Moreover, it was taken for granted that this was what Paul's letters (especially Galatians and Romans) were about, an assumption which has since had a long history. Luther is

famous for having come to the perception that in Rom. 1.17 'the righteousness of God' is not his own justice in any sense, but rather the status of being right before God which he freely grants to those who have faith. Not all Reformers made the sharp distinction between law and grace that was so crucial for Luther (cf. Bullinger), and although Calvin did not disagree with Luther on the matter, his exegesis is in general much more balanced. To modern eyes, it has stood the test of time much better, despite his preoccupation with and elaboration of a high Augustinian doctrine of predestination.

For two centuries after the Reformation, Protestants tended to use Paul as a source for their own doctrine, much as they criticized the Schoolmen for doing, though with different conclusions. Even after the rise of modern critical study in the eighteenth and especially the nineteenth century, there was a continuation of the Lutheran preoccupation with justification as the centre of Paul (and of Christianity). However, the influence of the Enlightenment* on biblical study led to a greatly increased tendency to be descriptive of Paul's thought: to put him and his ideas into their historical setting and leave dogma to its own devices (though there continued to be scholars who believed that Pauline theology could also be discussed prescriptively, i.e. in its implications for the church of their day). The greatest single revolutionary move was made by F. C. Baur and the Tübingen* school. Baur, partly under the influence of Hegelian philosophy, argued for a fundamental opposition between Jewish Christianity* and Paul's law-free, universal gospel, which dominated the church into the second century. Then a synthesis between the two ('early catholicism'*) was forged, which obscured the original sharp division. Those letters of Paul's which reflect the division are genuine; those which do not reflect it are later and non-authentic. Although Baur's position did not hold the field very long (some simply rejected it, while others carried it further to the point where none of the letters was genuine), his identification of Paul's position in early Christianity is still echoed sometimes today.

Much of the nineteenth- and early twentieth-century work on Paul was preoccupied with him as a Hellenizer* of an originally Jewish movement. For example, it was long held that Paul had two doctrines of redemption, a primitive Jewish-Christian juridical one (justification by faith) which he inherited, and a more Hellenistic one that consisted of transformation from 'flesh' to 'spirit' under the working of the Holy Spirit (cf. H. Lüdemann and others). This was his own contribution. Accordingly, persistent downgrading of the apostle's Jewish roots and of the Jewish character of his thought was predominant. Especially around the turn of the century, the key to Paul was found in the mystery* religions or in Gnosticism (Reitzenstein; Bousset; see **History of Religions School**). So much was this Hellenizing seen to be Paul's role, that there was a major problem in making a convincing connection between him and the historical Jesus.* So Wrede* suspected that Jesus had very little influence on Paul; he was a figure on whom Paul settled an essentially independent story of redemption.

In *The Mysticism of Paul the Apostle*, Albert Schweitzer* reversed the tendency to neglect the Jewishness of Paul. For him, the apostle's basic presuppositions were Jewish-eschatological, in the light of which everything must be seen. Hellenism provided only vocabulary, not ideas. The death and resurrection of Jesus brought in a new age, which will not be fully present until the parousia.* In the brief interim, believers belong to that new age and share in advance in the resurrection,* through the Spirit and the sacraments. Few have followed Schweitzer all the way, but his Jewish-eschatological starting-point has been increasingly accepted (even if, with Bultmann,* it was demythologized* and transmuted into existentialism, and despite Karl Barth,* whose treatment of Romans was so directed to Barth's own time that it often seemed only tenuously linked with Paul's).

In recent years every aspect of the interpretation of Paul has been intensively studied: the chronology* of the letters, their authenticity, the possibility of interpolations within them, their use of already traditional matter, the relation of Paul to Gnosticism, his anthropology, to name only some. The letters have been approached from a structuralist* point of view, and we see the beginning of an approach from literary* theory. W. D. Davies in 1948 demonstrated the fruitfulness of examining Paul against the backdrop of rabbinic* Judaism, and in 1977 E. P. Sanders produced a massive argument against the common presumption that Paul attacked a Judaism that believed the way to acceptance with God was by one's own merit: Paul did not attack Judaism for that, nor was it vulnerable to such an attack. Rather was he concerned to maintain both the universality of Christianity, free from the particular requirements of Judaism, and also the complete adequacy of Christ and faith in him, free from any additional conditions for salvation. The consequences of this argument are still being explored.

The historical realism of Sanders and others has been confirmed in recent years by numerous studies of the social* context in which Paul lived and worked. The effect of such work as that of G. Theissen (*The Social Setting of Pauline Christianity*, 1982), W. A. Meeks (*The First Urban Christians*, 1983), and F. B. Watson (*Paul, Judaism and the Gentiles*, 1986) has been to place Paul even more firmly in his times and to distance him from later religious and doctrinal concerns.

See also **Community; Ethos; Galatians; Romans.**

C. K. Barrett, 'Pauline Controversies in the Post-Pauline Period', *NTS* 20, 1974, pp. 229–45; W. D. Davies, *Paul and Rabbinic Judaism*, 1970; T. H. L. Parker, *Commentaries on the Epistle to the Romans, 1532–1542*, 1986; E. P. Sanders, *Paul and Palestinian Judaism*, 1977; A. Schweitzer, *Paul and his Interpreters*, 1912; M. F. Wiles, *The Divine Apostle*, 1967.

J. A. ZIESLER

Pentateuch, Pentateuchal Criticism

1. *The Pentateuch in the Bible*

The Pentateuch consists of the first five books of the Bible (Genesis to Deuteronomy) which appear in the same order in all standard editions of it, both Jewish and Christian. In the Hebrew canon they constitute the Torah (= 'Direction', 'Instruction') and form the first, and most authoritative, division of the canon.* Jewish tradition has consistently regarded the Pentateuch as a work of law* (Greek *nomos*, cf. Luke 24.44, which could then be applied to the entire OT scriptures; cf. John 10.34). The Christian church has tended to regard it as history as much as law, but the interaction of history and law appears with differing emphases in both Jewish and Christian tradition.

Content. The book of Genesis records the creation* of the world and of humankind, and then follows this (chs 12–50) with an account of the historical adventures of the patriarchal ancestors of Israel. Central to these adventures are stories of their settlement in the land afterwards occupied by Israel as its national heritage. The book of Exodus which follows forms a pivotal axis for the Pentateuch, telling how descendants of the patriarchs, now enslaved in Egypt, were delivered from their slavery under the leadership of Moses. After fleeing from Egypt,* they wander briefly in the wilderness until being led by Moses to the sacred Mount Sinai.

At Mount Sinai the people of Israel is formally constituted as a nation by covenant* with God (Ex. 19) and a charter, or polity, for it is laid down in the form of collections of laws. These laws cover civil issues, moral admonitions and directions, and a large body of cultic rules and instructions for worship. All told they extend from Ex. 20 to Lev. 27, and serve to establish the basis for regarding the entire Pentateuch as a work of Law.

The book of Numbers recounts adventures of Israel experienced during a generation-long period spent in the wilderness, which is then summarized in Deut. 1–3. The remainder of Deuteronomy then consists of a representation of the Law, supported by lengthy admonitory speeches, culminating in a report of Moses' death.

Literary analysis. It will be evident from this summary that the Pentateuch contains a good deal of historical narrative recounting how Israel became a nation. Most of this is contained in Gen. 12–50 and Ex. 1–19. Further narratives concerning Israel's national beginnings appear in the book of Numbers, and the stories of Gen. 1–11, recalling humankind's primaeval origins, focus upon a few major themes with mythological* associations: creation, the great flood and the origin of diverse nations (the Tower of Babel). The whole is held together and given a structure by means of a family genealogy.*

The law sections of the Pentateuch contain civil laws (chiefly Ex. 20.22–23.19), cultic* instructions (chiefly Ex. 25–40; Lev. 1–16) and mixtures of both (especially Lev. 17–26, usually called the Holiness Code). The Law code of Deuteronomy in Deut. 12.1–26.15 is also distinctive, containing a mixture of civil and cultic laws, but now set out as a hortatory speech, or sermon, rather than a Law code proper.

Almost all these diverse literary elements which are now preserved in the Pentateuch can be shown to possess parallels and counterparts in similar types of literature from the Ancient Near East; i.e. myths,* legends,* folktales,* laws, cultic rules, hortatory speeches. Others, such as the series of levitical rulings on cleanness and uncleanness (Lev. 11–15), may be presumed to have possessed such parallels, even though direct examples are lacking. What is striking is the range and comprehensiveness of the contents of the Pentateuch as a whole and the very different types of literature that are to be found in it. This variety first began to be fully recognized and taken into account in the studies of J. D. Michaelis and J. G. Eichhorn in the late eighteenth century. It provided a primary basis for the recognition that a diverse range of sources had been used in its composition. When such sources came to be ascribed to different dates, then a whole new era of pentateuchal criticism emerged.

Theological significance. The religious ideas of the Pentateuch may best be grasped in relation to the specific story, or 'plot', that pertains to each of its major sections. In Genesis this is supremely that of divine promise,

given a central focus in the revelation made to Abraham* (Gen. 12.1–3). The promise is three-fold: that the land to be shown to Abraham will become the territory of his numerous descendants; that they will become a nation; and that they will be a blessing to other nations. This promise then remains an overarching theme for all the stories of the subsequent descendants of Abraham, who are traced, through Isaac and Jacob, into twelve tribes, all descended from sons of Jacob.

While the theme of promise dominates Genesis, it recedes into becoming a relatively minor and superficial theme for the remainder of the Pentateuch, but returns as of major significance in other parts of the OT.

The second major theological theme emerges in Exodus as that of covenant, with which the notion of the divine election of Israel as a nation is inseparably linked. Israel is distinct as a nation from all other nations because it is bound in covenant to God (Ex. 19.1–24.18). The special laws disclosed on Sinai, and the special obligations accepted by Israel, are the outworking of this covenant relationship. So Israel is uniquely obligated to worship only one God, whose name is now revealed as the Lord (Hebrew YHWH). The distinctive nature of the laws, which largely dominate the Pentateuch, is thus explained by reference to this sense of covenant.

The third major theological theme of the Pentateuch is that of holiness. Here many ancient ideas of taboo, sacred space, and a rather mystical understanding of divine power and life are combined to bring a richly comprehensive interpretation of worship and the divine quality of daily living. So the many instructions for worship, cleanness, respect for the orders of kinship and family, avoidance of contact with alien religious institutions, and of any disruption or violation of the divine – holy – order of the world, are comprised under the concept of holiness. This dominates most of Ex. 25–Lev. 27. In Deuteronomy a summarizing amalgam of all three themes – promise, covenant and holiness – appears, making it a convenient reaffirmation of the central message of the four preceding books.

2. *Authorship and the rise of pentateuchal criticism*

Traditional views. Traditional Jewish understanding of the authorship* of the Pentateuch is set out in the Talmud* in *Baba bathra* 14[b], where it is stated: 'Moses* wrote his own book and the section concerning Balaam and Job.' Such a view dominates the Jewish thought of the Talmud, although clearly it cannot have been thought that Moses wrote the account of his own death (Deut. 34.5–12). By the time of Moses Maimonides (1135–

1204), the question of the authority of the Pentateuch had become indissolubly linked with that of Moses' authorship so that he could list as the eighth of the thirteen best principles of Judaism that the Pentateuch derived from Moses. Yet also in the Middle Ages the scholarly Ibn Ezra (1092–1167), in a major commentary* on the Pentateuch, could cast doubt on this question of Mosaic authorship. In the sixteenth century, the Jew Elias Levita could express as an opinion the view that its composition had not been completed until the time of Ezra in the fifth century BC. However, it was not until a century later, with the writings of the celebrated Jewish philosopher B. Spinoza (1632–1677), that the idea that Ezra may have been the true 'author' of the work came to be seriously canvassed. This raised the possibility that much of the content may have originated at a much later time than that of Moses.

Christians were content to accept and maintain this tradition of Mosaic authorship of the Pentateuch, without subjecting it to separate investigation. For them the whole issue of the authority of the Mosaic Law did not devolve upon its time of origin, or its human author, but upon its relationship to the new law revealed in Jesus Christ (cf. especially M. Luther,* *How Christians Should Regard Moses*, 1525; see further H. Bornkamm, *Luther and the Old Testament*, ET 1969, pp. 121–135).

The rise of pentateuchal criticism. A new era, marking the beginning of what we should now call pentateuchal criticism, began in 1753 with the anonymous publication in Brussels of a short tract by the French doctor Jean Astruc (1684–1766). Basing his observations on the use of the divine name in Genesis, he noted the marks of two distinct sources in the book. More fundamentally, however, the whole trend of the French writers of the Enlightenment* was to point in the direction of recognizing that distinct human agencies had contributed to the making of so complex a work as the Pentateuch. When J. D. Michaelis (1717–1791) and J. G. Eichhorn (1752–1827), began to note more precisely the differing literary forms and classes of material in the Pentateuch, the notion of a long and complex literary history began to be widely canvassed. So, for the next three-quarters of a century, a major quest of Christian biblical scholarship was the attempt to trace the literary growth of the Pentateuch (or latterly Hexateuch, in the belief that the book of Joshua shared some common sources with Gen.–Deut.). This culminated in the work of Julius Wellhausen (1848–1918), who published in 1876 essays on the sources of the Hexateuch which argued for four main documents having been combined together. These were subsequently labelled J, E, D and P. These conclusions provided a basis for a major reconstruction of the history of ancient Israel (published initially by Wellhausen in 1878).

The Wellhausen four-source theory, which had been anticipated in part by K. H. Graf, thereafter dominated biblical scholarship for half a century, but gradually fell into disfavour. H. Gunkel (1862–1932), in his Genesis commentary of 1901, whilst still accepting the four-document hypothesis, pointed to the major importance of the short narratives of the book as effectively independent tales. Thereby the so-called sources could be regarded as more akin to edited anthologies of smaller units. H. Gressmann adopted a comparable approach in a study (1913) of the Moses traditions of the book of Exodus. Progressively too, during the twentieth century, the examination of Leviticus found less and less evidence in it of the latest of these documentary sources, P, except as a rather superficial layer of editing. Deuteronomy, which had been ascribed in the four-source hypothesis to a relatively independent D source, came increasingly to be seen as a very distinctive composition with only an indirect link with the remainder of the Pentateuch. By the 1930s, therefore, the established literary account of the origin of the Pentateuch, which had dominated nineteenth-century study of the OT, came increasingly to be questioned.

Jewish scholarship initially remained strongly opposed to this development of pentateuchal criticism among Christian scholars during the nineteenth century, sensing that it sharply conflicted with the eighth of Maimonides' thirteen principles. However, as a critical Jewish historiography of ancient Israel developed during the period (I. M. Jost; H. Graetz), the groundwork for a more sympathetic understanding of pentateuchal criticism emerged. This flourished in the twentieth century, most especially under the leadership of Y. Kaufmann working in Jerusalem, who accepted many of Wellhausen's methods of detailed literary analysis, but differed considerably in his conclusions. These especially related to the dating of the Priestly legislative material (source P), which Kaufmann placed in the late pre-exilic period.

The tradition-historical approach. A major step forward came, in 1938, with the publication by G. von Rad of a study entitled *The Form-Critical Problem of the Hexateuch*, in which fundamental questions regarding the setting and purpose of the supposed J document, the earliest of the major literary sources, were explored. Building on this work, but focussing upon other aspects of the Pentateuch, M. Noth attempted to trace the entire literary history of the Pentateuch from its smaller units to its final form (*A History of Pentateuchal Traditions*, 1948, ET 1972). In this the idea of longer documentary sources played a relatively minor role, since they primarily marked stages of collection and editing by which the various shorter units were brought together. This tradition-historical* approach, therefore, marked something of a return to the 'Fragment-Hypothesis' of the nineteenth century which Wellhausen's documentary thesis had supplanted.

The publication in 1976 of a detailed critique by R. Rendtorff of this tradition-historical method, opened a markedly new era of pentateuchal criticism. His researches challenged the view that it was possible to hold together both tradition-historical and source-critical* analyses. Since the work of Wellhausen, in spite of acceptance that the notion of documentary sources represented a rather modern and 'bookish' approach to solving the problem of the literary origin of the Pentateuch, the conviction had prevailed that it was on the right lines. It needed modification by recognizing that there were many smaller units and compositions which had been incorporated into the whole work at varying stages and that extensive supplementation (especially in Leviticus) had taken place. With the work of Rendtorff, together with that of J. van Seters and T. L. Thompson during the 1970s, the entire thesis associated with the name of Wellhausen and progressively modified by later scholars was put in question.

Two trends in pentateuchal criticism have subsequently become discernible. One, represented by R. N. Whybray, *The Making of the Pentateuch. A Methodological Study* (1987), has sought to work out a radical alternative to the older approaches, building upon the idea of a central core tradition established in the exilic age (cf. similarly J. van Seters). Others have displayed a prudent agnosticism regarding the date of individual parts of the Pentateuch and have urged instead that greater attention should be given to its final form as an integrated and constructed whole. Alongside these approaches, yet others have held firmly to the general features of the Wellhausen hypothesis (cf. W. H. Schmidt, *Introduction to the Old Testament*, 1984).

3. *Other aspects of interpretation*

The interpretation of the Pentateuch in Judaism after the close of the OT canon found in it the key to the survival of the Jewish people after the Roman-Jewish war of AD 66–70. The Torah was the express revelation* of God given to the Jewish people by which they might live before him and avoid further judgments such as had befallen Israel in the past.

The Torah was therefore the foundation of scripture, and the prophets* were seen as the proclaimers of a message concerning the centrality and seriousness of this Law. Two theological factors became inseparably linked with this understanding of Torah. The first was that the eschatological* hope of Israel's achieving greatness at the head of the nations could only be achieved when Israel itself learnt to obey God's law. The second was that, in order to assist such obedience, Israel required to understand fully the requirements of this Law and to 'build a fence around it'. This called for careful systematization of its fundamental demands in the form of a codified series of handbooks defining religious and moral practice (*halakhah*). Such systematization was brought about in the Mishnah (AD 100–300), and then further explored and explained in the Talmud (AD 300–500). So the main line of Jewish interpretation of the Pentateuch for more than a millennium was in essence a process of codification and harmonization to establish a body of instructions and directions for a way of life responsive to God's election of Abraham and his descendants.

Subsequently, in a remarkable era of mediaeval Jewish learning and literary advance, a greater attempt was made to establish the basis of a Jewish philosophy on the teaching of the Torah. The outstanding figure here was Moses Maimonides, who formulated a compact set of teachings and principles which were in accord with the Mosaic revelation of the Pentateuch, thereby condensing the rulings of the Mishnah. By this means a closer ground for comparison and agreement was established between the teaching of the Torah and the classical philosophical tradition of Greece and Rome, as well as with the ideal of the Renaissance.

Early Christian approaches to the study of the Pentateuch focussed upon two assumptions. The first of these, found already in Philo,* was that it was essentially a work of history and that its principal actors and stories served as examples of faith and heroic piety, worthy to be emulated by all Christians (cf. Heb. 11.1–40). A second feature also coloured Christian reading of this literature, and this was to see in the instructions for worship, the building of the tabernacle (Ex. 25–40), and the regulations governing sacrifice (Lev. 1–11), prefigurings of the new order of worship ordained for all humankind through Jesus of Nazareth. So there rapidly grew up a pattern of typological* exegesis in which not only could personalities of the Law be associated with Christian virtues, but also institutions could be seen as partial symbols* of the fuller reality disclosed in the NT. In a larger compass, the whole idea of a Mosaic 'constitution' for Israel could be regarded as a model, or pattern, of a more comprehensive divine world order brought to realization through Jesus Christ.

In the Reformation* the Lutheran tradition found in the Law of the Mosaic order a fundamental disclosure of the divine law which was applicable to all mankind as a law of nature, cf. M. Luther, *The Ten Commandments, Preached to the People of Wittenberg*, 1518; *How Christians Should Regard Moses*, 1525. The Calvinist* tradition, contrastingly, placed great importance upon the historical aspects of the Pentateuch and especially the Abrahamic covenant as a covenant of 'Promise'. This embraced all nations and gave assurance concerning their salvation and the ultimate universality of faith (cf. Gal. 3. 14). Thereby the Pentateuch was seen to possess a prophetic character.

With the eighteenth-century Enlightenment, first in France and later in Germany, greater attention began to be given to the Pentateuch as a source of information about the ancient East, especially Egypt and Mesopotamia. During this period attempts to use the Pentateuch as a source of direct evidence for the age of the world, and of mankind, increasingly gave way, and were ultimately abandoned, in the face of new scientific evidence. This arose particularly from geology, and the recognition emerged by the end of the eighteenth century that parts of the pentateuchal material should properly be classified as myth, comparable to the mythology developed and preserved by other ancient peoples.

By the end of the eighteenth century, scholarship had become fully conscious that the Pentateuch was to be interpreted against the background of the life, and the rise of literature, of the Ancient Near East.* With the Napoleonic commission to examine the ancient monuments of Egypt (1800), and the increase of travel and exploration in the lands of the Bible, the basis for such an examination had begun to emerge.

In the nineteenth century, along with the fresh investigation into questions concerning the authorship of the Pentateuch, the Christian church paid great attention to its value as a historical document concerning the origins of Israel. From the 1830s, the geography of the region of the Bible began to be examined and the customs and culture of the peoples of the area began to be the subject of increasing attention and interest. Milman's *History of the Jews*, Vol. 1, 1829, initially caused offence by seeking, albeit a little superficially, to interpret the pentateuchal story in an oriental context.

By 1870 the first translated parallels to parts of the pentateuchal tradition from ancient Babylon* began to achieve publicity. George Smith lectured on parallels to the flood story in the Babylonian Gilgamesh Epic, and further parallels in the Babylonian creation story (*Enuma Elish*) quickly followed. By the end of the century important legal parallels became available through the translation of the Babylonian law code of Hammurabi. Throughout the first half of the twentieth century attention to the reliability of the pentateuchal historical tradition dominated scholarly interpretation. With a period of thoroughgoing re-evaluation emerging regarding this in the 1970s (J. van Seters and T. L. Thompson), a new attention to a fresh examintion of the narrative* art of the pentateuchal writings became current by 1980 (Northrop Frye; R. Alter; M. Sternberg).

See also **German Old Testament Scholarship; Jewish Exegesis.**

Lloyd R. Bailey, *The Pentateuch*, 1983; J. Estlin Carpenter and G. B. Harford, *The Composition of the Hexateuch*, 2 vols 1902; W. McKane, *Studies in the Patriarchal Narratives*, 1979; M. Noth, *A History of Pentateuchal Traditions*, 1972; R. J. Thompson, *Moses and the Law in a Century of Criticism since Graf*, *VT*-S19, 1970; C. Westermann, *The Promises to the Fathers. Studies in the Patriarchal Narratives*, 1980; R. N. Whybray, *The Making of the Pentateuch. A Methodological Study*, *JSOT*–SS53, 1987.

R. E. CLEMENTS

Pesher

Since the publication in 1950 of the Qumran Habakkuk Commentary (1QpHab), in which the interpretation of each biblical passage is introduced with a formula containing the word *pesher*, the term has come to be widely applied to all forms of scriptural interpretation roughly contemporary with the Qumran community (*see* **Dead Sea Scrolls**). NT scholars have been especially tempted to use it of the use of the OT by the authors of the NT.

More properly, *pesher* is a literary genre,* a sub-genre of pre-rabbinic midrash.* The word midrash is itself used as a technical term in 4QFlor 1.14, introducing a series of biblical quotations, each with *pesher*. As a sub-genre, *pesher* has characteristic form and content. Formally, *pesher* consists of the explicit citation of an extract from scripture which is then given an interpretation. The interpretation is usually introduced by a technical formula containing the word *pesher*, such as, 'the interpretation (*pesher*) of the matter concerns', or 'its interpretation (*pesher*) is'. There is now general agreement that in these formulae the Hebrew term *pesher* (probably a loan-word from Aramaic*) reflects the tradition of the interpretation of dreams and visions attested in Dan. 2, 4, and 5 (cf. Eccles. 8.1; Ben Sira 38.14).

The content of *pesher* is first a scriptural passage that was thought to be prophetic or visionary; for the Qumran community, as for many other contemporary Jews and Jewish Christians, this included not only the prophetic* books, but also visionary passages such as Nathan's oracle (II Sam. 7.5–16) and all the psalms. Secondly, the interpretation describes, albeit in a veiled manner, something relevant to the present experience of those for whom it is intended. Past events, whether real or imagined, are depicted to give the community an identity; thus, Habakkuk (1QpHab) is made to predict what happened to the Teacher of Righteousness. Present circumstances are treated in only the most general terms so that the interpretation remains continuously applicable; so Ps. 37 (4QpPs^a 2.2–5) is made to speak of 'those who return to the Law' and of 'the elect who do God's will'. Future hopes are expressed to give the community a purpose: through its refusal to be led astray it shall be delivered on the day of judgment (4QpNah 3.3–5). Many scholars think that the history of the Qumran community can be reconstructed by identifying the characters referred to cryptically in the interpretations. Such use of the *pesharim* is not altogether appropriate, as the multiplicity of scholarly suggestions shows.

The *pesharim* are of two types. Most are continuous systematic interpretations of one biblical book (e.g. 1QpHab, 1QpMic, 4QpNah); others are thematic, either selecting passages from one book (e.g. 4QpIsa^c) or juxtaposing passages from more than one book (e.g. 4QFlor, 11QMelch), and, in either case, including passages from other biblical books in the interpretation. Some texts (e.g. 4Q*159*, 4Q*177*, 4Q*180*) use the term *pesher* just once or twice, but always introducing the interpretation of an explicit biblical quotation.

The interpretation given to the biblical text is far from arbitrary. Particular exegetical* techniques, especially various kinds of wordplay, are used to link the two: e.g. in 1QpHab 12.15–13.4 'temple' (*hykl*) of Hab. 2.20 is interpreted as 'will destroy' (*yklh*), i.e. the place of God's presence is the place of his judgment. This exegetical method itself has some authority for, when used to convey understandings based on inspired insight (1QpHab 7.4–5), it allows an audience to perceive the aptness of an interpretation. The *pesher* is like some early Christian prophetic interpretation, that is, not only may the prophetic books of the OT furnish the basis for describing events (whether real or imagined, as in Matt. 1–2 or the passion* tradition), but also this identification

was probably ratified by the worshipping congregation to which the early Christian prophet belonged.

See also **Use of the Old Testament in the New Testament.**

———

G. J. Brooke, *Exegesis at Qumran*, 1985; F. F. Bruce, 'Biblical Exposition at Qumran', pp. 77–98 in R. T. France and D. Wenham (eds), *Studies in Midrash and Hagiography*, 1983; M. P. Horgan, *Pesharim: Qumran Interpretations of Biblical Books*, 1979; K. Stendahl, *The School of St Matthew*, ²1968.

GEORGE J. BROOKE

Peter

Until recent times, the references to Peter in the NT have been used by scholars chiefly as data contributing, albeit fragmentarily, to a historical account of Peter's life and a picture of his role in the early church. The story could be completed by the bare reference to his martyrdom in I Clement 5 (*see* **Apostolic Fathers**, and cf. John 21.18f.). It then trailed off into legend* (cf. the late second-century *Acts of Peter*, which presents Peter as an ascetic preacher and miracle*-worker).

However, it has become apparent that, apart from a few rudimentary matters (Peter was an early and leading follower of Jesus, and he was married, I Cor. 9.5; cf. Mark 1.29–31), all we read about Peter in the NT is laden with interpretation. To put it another way, Peter's role in the history of interpretation begins at the beginning. In this way, he is comparable to the historical Jesus* and the other leading characters in early Christianity. The degree and variety of interpretation is indeed a measure of their significance.

Paul,* the earliest witness, provides us with the bare facts referred to above (Gal. 1.18; 2.7–9; I Cor. 15.5). But the picture of Peter which is presented, with regard to the matter which was of greatest importance to Paul, is one-sided. This concerned the admission of Gentile converts to the Christian movement, free of any requirement to adhere to the distinctive practices of Judaism, notably food regulations and table fellowship (the two being closely, though somewhat obscurely, related; cf. J. D. G. Dunn, *JSNT*, 18, 1983). Paul depicts Peter as vacillating and pusillanimous on the subject (Gal. 2.11–14), but we have no means of knowing his own account of it, though it looks as if Peter, in whatever spirit, sided ultimately with the more conservative tendencies of the Jerusalem church.

The Gospels* are more thoroughgoingly interpretative in character, a fact that has been observed in two main ways. Form criticism* seized upon certain common features in stories concerning Peter and discerned variant forms of basic traditions about him. Thus, Mark 1.16–20 was a 'call story' of Peter (and others), and was to be found in other versions (and 'historical' locations) in Luke 5.1–11; John 21.1–14; and, briefly, John 1.40–42. There was also a tradition of the special authorization of Peter, found in Matt. 16.17–19; Luke 22.31f., and a tradition of Peter's confession of Jesus' messiahship* (Mark 8.27–30, with parallels in Matthew and Luke, and John 6.68f.). There was also, though oddly it was unelaborated, a tradition of his reception of a resurrection* appearance (I Cor. 15.5; Luke 24.34).

Redaction criticism,* fortified by narrative criticism,* has proved sceptical about the adequacy of this approach, and, in the end, even indifferent to it. While it is possible to hypothesize about the development of traditions (*see* **History of Tradition**) in the period of oral tradition,* it may be more fruitful to point to the redactional process discernible as one evangelist* takes up and modifies what another has already written.

It is a disappointment to the historian that Mark's depiction of Peter, the earliest in narrative form, gives evidence of heavy interpretation, even though its drift is not wholly clear. Its leading feature is the poor impression it gives of the disciples of Jesus and of Peter in particular, as if to show them as positively inappropriate to be leading followers of Jesus. Though they are undoubtedly his disciples (1.16–20; 3.13–19; 6.7–13) and recipients of his special teaching (4.10–20; 8.34–9.1; 13; 14.22–25), they are nonetheless uncomprehending (6.52; 8.14–21) and ultimately faithless (14.50), though there is a final hint to the contrary (16.7). In all this, Peter is the leader, especially in the denial of Jesus at the passion* (14.54–72). What is to be made of this debilitating picture? Is it 'plain' history, as Papias* said in the second century, depicting the Gospel as virtually Peter's memoirs, conveyed via Mark? Or does it represent a warning about the perils and cost of discipleship? If so, Mark was ready to sacrifice Peter's human reputation for the sake of a spiritual lesson. Or is it a piece of ecclesiastical politics, representing Marcan disapproval of the early leadership (especially perhaps the Jerusalem church), possibly in a Pauline interest (Trocmé)? Much depends on whether one seeks to interpret Mark in a theological or historical light.

These obscurities fade when we turn to Matthew and Luke. Both adjusted Mark to portray Peter much more favourably. The story of the denial is retained (as also in John), but at all other points the interpretation of Peter moves in the direction of making him 'saint' Peter, faithful disciple of Jesus and hero of earliest Christianity. Matthew blunts the dramatic effect of Mark 8.27–33 (Peter's avowal of Jesus followed by his apparent identification as Satan) by inserting the encomium in 16.17–19, which dominates the whole section. It is often taken by scholars expounding Matthew in terms of the evangelist's thought and situation to reflect the leading position of Peter in the history or at any rate the esteem of Matthew's church as it looked back to the first years of the Christian movement. Luke omitted the Satan reference altogether. He also effectively exonerated Peter from responsibility for the denial: Satan (now in his own persona) seduced him into a temporary lapse into cowardice (22.31f.). This Lucan optimism is confirmed in Acts where Peter is the articulate and courageous leader of the church in Jerusalem, who preaches (Acts 2–4) and suffers (5 and 12) like his Lord, and dominates the first half of the book (1–15). Whereas Paul shows Peter dragging his feet with regard to the open admission of Gentiles to the church and as active in the mission at the same time as Paul, Acts shows him as (by heavenly vision) taking the initiative to end the imposition of Jewish food taboos on Gentile converts and as being in effect succeeded by Paul (Acts 13–28). Contrast in early Christian interpretation of Peter is nowhere more striking than here.

In the Gospel of John, the view taken of Peter is complicated by the introduction of the figure of the Beloved Disciple. Peter's importance is accepted, but at several points he is subordinated to the other: the latter is closer to Jesus at the supper (13.23–5), stands at the cross (19.25–7), and reaches the tomb first and 'saw and believed' (20.3–10). R. E. Brown has suggested that these statements need not be seen as raising a historical problem in the life of Jesus. Rather, the roles of the two figures are symbolic,* reflecting the Johannine church's conviction that its mode of discipleship (symbolized in the Beloved Disciple) is closer to the Lord's intentions than that of other apostolic churches (symbolized by Peter and others of the Twelve).

In the subsequent history of interpretation, Peter has, with one resounding exception, not been a major figure, though isolated statements from the letters attributed to him have been prominent as felt appropriate to the needs of controversy or edification (*see* **Peter, First; Peter, Second, and Jude**). In the perspective of the Tübingen school,* he emerged as, with James the brother of Jesus, the leader of Jewish Christianity* in its opposition to Paul's Gentile Christianity. This role was already given to him by second-century anti-Pauline Jewish Christian* writings such as the Preaching of Peter and the Pseudo-Clementine writings (*see* Hennecke, *New Testament*

Apocrypha, 1965, II, pp. 102ff. and 532ff. By contrast, both I and II Peter (taken as pseudonymous) present a *rapprochement* between the two leaders, the former by its teaching, the latter by reference (3.15). All these writings show how important it was soon felt to be to claim Peter's mantle.

The exception concerns the crucial part played by Matt. 16.17–19 in establishing and legitimating the position of the Roman papacy. It did not accomplish its task unaided. In the early mediaeval period, there was the growing part played by possession of a saint's relics in forming belief in his presence and protection. There was also the role of Roman law which made it possible to view a man's successors as identical with himself. But the passage in Matthew provided the vital basis: Peter was the rock on which the whole church was built and he held the power of the keys (interpreted as jurisdiction, ever more potently defined). Especially from the time of Pope Leo the Great (d. 461), but beginning in the early third century, and subsequently with growing audacity, it was possible to see these statements as giving universal pastoral and legal powers in the church to the bishop of Rome, where Peter was believed, from the second century, to have been the first holder of the office. No text of scripture has been more influential in the political, legal, ecclesiastical and religious life of Europe and, in the past century, of the greater part of the world. It is a remarkable result of sayings which many scholars would now see as testifying to the reverence felt for Peter by a Syrian Christian congregation *c.* AD 85. It is noteworthy that in recent years, this text, so long a focus of discord among Christian churches, has seen some convergence of view, as Protestant and Roman Catholic scholars alike have brought modern interpretative methods to its exegesis. The influence of O. Cullmann, who moved out from biblical interpretation into doctrine in his book on Peter, was crucial in this process.

In utter contrast to these matters is the leading role played by Peter in the tradition of Christian piety, as the man whose timid abandonment of Christ was transformed by grace into vigorous mission and ultimate martyrdom (cf. *Quo Vadis?*). Papias' story about the origin of Mark's Gospel whereby Peter himself humbly ensured the preserving of stories rebounding to his discredit, has contributed to this cause (see above); whereas modern scholars see it rather as an early part of the process of claiming Peter's authority, whose outcome has just been described. Peter has thus figured chiefly in two widely separated styles of interpretation, the legal-ecclesiastical and the spiritual. But in a curious way, they combine to make of Peter an epitome of the central Christian paradox of strength through weakness.

P. R. Brown, *The Cult of the Saints*, 1981; R. E. Brown, *The Community of the Beloved Disciple*, 1979; id. et al. (eds), *Peter in the New Testament*, 1933; O. Cullmann, *Peter: Disciple, Apostle, Martyr*, 1953; E. Trocmé, *The Formation of the Gospel According to Mark,* ET 1975; W. Ullmann, 'Leo I and the theme of papal primacy', *JTS*, 11, 1960.

J. L. HOULDEN

Peter, First

I Peter is categorized as a 'general' or 'catholic' epistle because of its address to readers over a large area of northern Asia Minor. It was accepted both early and unreservedly into the canon* of the NT. It is referred to by the author of II Peter (3.1) and quoted, though without attribution, in the Epistle of Polycarp. Although it is absent, surprisingly, from the Muratorian Canon, it was used in the late second century both by the Western writers Irenaeus* and Tertullian* and by Clement of Alexandria. Eusebius* classed it among the undisputed books of the NT. Writers in the Antiochene* tradition worked for longer with a smaller canon, and although John Chrysostom used the epistle, Theodore of Mopsuestia appears not to have done so. It was, however, included in the Syriac* Peshitta translation of *c.* AD 412. Its authority remained unquestioned in the Reformation* period: in his 1522 *Preface to the New Testament*, Martin Luther* singled it out, with the Gospel and First Epistle of John and the epistles of Paul,* as 'the books that show you Christ and teach you all that is necessary and salvatory for you to know, even if you were never to see or hear any other book'.

The popularity of the epistle is easy to understand. Its overall tone is one of warm pastoral care for Christians suffering hardship and expecting worse to come, and it focusses attention on the uncomplaining and redemptive suffering of Christ. It provides one of the clearest presentations in the NT of Christ as the suffering servant* of the prophecies of Isaiah, 2.22–24 containing clear allusions to Isa. 53.5–12. It also provides a clear expression of the ethical* principle of Christian behaviour as an imitation of Christ (2.21; cf. 3.17–18; 4.1–2). In 2.4–5, 9–10 the author explains the character of the church as fulfilling the role of Israel, providing Protestant readers with proof texts* for the notion of the priesthood of all believers. In the Middle Ages, the epistle performed a further important function by providing, in 3.19 and 4.6, proof texts for belief in Christ's 'harrowing of hell', which was a familiar theme in mediaeval art* and drama (though it is not certain that the texts will really bear that interpretation).

The traditional view of the epistle is that it was written by the apostle Peter* from Rome (under the guise of 'Babylon', 5.13) shortly before his martyrdom in AD 64. The address to the 'dispersion' in 1.1 suggest that the readers were Jewish Christians,* in accordance with Peter's brief in Gal. 2.9, though references to their past in 1.18 and 4.3 suggest that Gentile Christians formed at least part of the audience. This traditional view, however, has certain difficulties. The Greek of the epistle is of a literary quality difficult to attribute to the Galilean fisherman, though it is sometimes suggested that the Silvanus of 5.12 may have acted as Peter's secretary or amanuensis. Reference to the possibility of suffering 'as a Christian' (4.16), for the name itself, suggests a situation somewhat later in church history; possibly that described by Pliny during his governorship of Pontus-Bithynia c. AD 112 (*Letters* x.96). Similarities between this epistle and passages in those of Paul have also led some scholars to regard it as derivative and post-Pauline. In F. C. Baur's reconstruction of early Christianity (*see* **Tübingen School**), I Peter is seen as part of the post-apostolic attempt by the Jewish Christian party to seek harmonious relations with the Pauline churches, by presenting Peter in as Pauline terms as possible.

Another way of explaining the similarities between I Peter and the Pauline epistles, developed by P. Carrington (1940) and E. G. Selwyn (1947), is to see them as each drawing upon early common patterns of Christian catechetical instruction, including 'household codes' to govern relationships (I Peter 3.3–7 and 5.1–5, cf. Col. 3.18–4.1). It would, however, still remain uncertain how far such patterns of teaching would have developed in apostolic times.

A further question involved in interpreting I Peter is that of its integrity. Several commentators divide it into two parts: 1.1–2 and 4.12–5.14 being a genuine letter addressed to Christians facing the imminent prospect of persecution and eschatological* judgment; while 1.3–4.11, with its closing doxology, seems to envisage a different situation, where suffering is only a possibility (1.6; 3.13–14), and rules for everyday living are important, and this may have formed a document of a different genre* and function. This central section has an express interest in baptism (3.21), and other baptismal themes appear, such as rebirth (1.3;2.2). Several scholars have followed R. Perdelwitz (1911) and suggested that the document originally had a context in baptism, as a baptismal homily, or even as one version of the baptismal liturgy (H. Pries-

ker, 1951; F. L. Cross, 1954). Links in thought and language with Easter have also been detected, since Easter was traditionally the occasion for Christian baptism. It is not easy to see why one particular sermon or form of the liturgy should have been thus preserved, and perhaps easier to imagine that Christians facing the trial of their faith might be reminded of the occasion when they first undertook it.

In the context of the sociological study of the NT, interest in I Peter has focussed upon the description of the readers as 'aliens and exiles' (2.11). It has been suggested that this was a literal description of a class of persons in the Roman empire from which they had been drawn. More probably, however, it reflects their self-understanding as a community set apart from their surrounding society because of their faith. The sense of not belonging and of being suspect does not, however, result in the creation of sectarian boundaries against the outside world, but instead the author encourages his readers to see their exposed and threatened position positively as an opportunity for presenting their faith to the curious or abusive outsider (2.12,15; 3.15–16). In doing so, he shows a striking confidence in the capaciiy of the outside world to discriminate between good and evil which enables him also to accept its structures of political authority (2.13–14,17). In this respect he provides within the NT a marked contrast to the attitude of the Revelation of John.

See also **Peter, Second, and Jude.**

F. W. Beare, *The First Epistle of Peter*, 1958; John H. Elliott, *A Home for the Homeless*, 1982; J. N. D. Kelly, *The Epistles of Peter and of Jude*, 1969; E. G. Selwyn, *The First Epistle of St Peter*, 1947.

SOPHIE LAWS

Peter, Second, and Jude

II Peter and Jude are classified as 'catholic' or 'general' epistles because of their broad addresses to 'those who have obtained a faith of equal standing' and 'those who are called' respectively (II Peter 1.1; Jude 1); though each seems to envisage a specific community* and situation. They are, with III John, probably the least read of the NT documents, though Jude closes with a magnificent commendation and doxology which is frequently drawn upon in Christian liturgy* (24–25), and II Peter 1.4 has a toe-hold in Christian history as the text read by John Wesley on the morning of his conversion, 24 May 1738.

Considering its brevity and its content, Jude appears surprisingly early in the history of the canon.* It is used both by Tertullian* in the West and by Clement of Alexandria at the end of the second century, and is accepted without qualification in the Muratorian Canon. Doubts appear to have set in later, and Eusebius* classes it among 'disputed' writings. Athanasius, however, retained it in his canon list, and it was eventually admitted to the canon of the Syrian* church with the sixth-century Philoxenian translation. In the fourth century Jerome referred to disputes about its authority because of its use of uncanonical material (Jude 14 quotes I Enoch 1.9, and vv. 6 and 9 allude to the legends of the fall of the angels and of the burial of Moses* as found in Jewish intertestamental literature), and this was among the reasons why Luther* also relegated it to subordinate status in the canon in the Preface to his 1522 translation of the NT.

II Peter, by contrast, appears late and hesitantly. It is referred to in the writings of Origen,* but only in their Latin translation, and Eusebius includes it too among 'disputed' writings. Jerome knows of doubts about its apostolic authority because of its manifest difference in style from I Peter, though he himself suggests that Peter might have used two secretaries. Luther's high regard for I Peter may have led him to allow the second epistle to keep its place on the coat-tails of the first.

There is obviously a close relationship between II Peter and Jude. Virtually the whole of Jude appears as ch. 2 of II Peter, in substance if not in exact wording. Luther believed that the author of Jude had copied II Peter, but the consensus of scholarship since J. D. Michaelis is that dependence is the other way round. Arguments include II Peter's avoidance of Jude's explicit reference to apocryphal material (cf. Jude 9 and II Peter 2.10–11; the quotation from I Enoch is absent from II Peter); the rearrangement in proper historical order of examples of judgment (Jude 5–7, cf. II Peter 2.4–6); and the addition of complementary instances of salvation (II Peter 2.5, 7–8). The question of inter-relationship naturally affects discussion of the epistles' origins. Jude claims authorship* by 'the brother of James' (1), who would therefore also be one of the brothers of Jesus listed in Mark 6.3, and whose grandsons were investigated by the suspicious emperor Domitian (Eusebius, Eccles. Hist. III.20.1–6). Other possible identifications are with the 'Judas (son of) James' who appears in the Lucan lists of Jesus' twelve disciples (Luke 6.16; Acts 1.13); and with Thomas, whose name means 'twin' (John 20.24), and who is called 'Judas Thomas' in the Gospel of Thomas. The epistle's knowledge of Jewish apocryphal material would be consistent with a Palestinian Jewish Christian* author; and it might be argued that so short

and seemingly ephemeral a document would hardly have won early acceptance in the canon unless it was known to have apostolic authorship. However, as Luther noted, the author seems to write of apostles as figures in his own past (17). II Peter makes a more thoroughgoing claim to apostolic authorship. Its opening address includes Peter's* original name 'Simon' (1.1); there is reference to the author's presence at Jesus' transfiguration (1.16–18); to Jesus' prophecy of his death (1.14); to his first letter (3.1); and to his equal status with Paul* (3.15). Hardly anyone would now argue that this authorship is authentic. The epistle's dependence on Jude tells against it, and there is other evidence that it belongs to the post-apostolic period. It is the only document in the NT explicitly to face the problem of the failure of the parousia* hope, that time has gone on and Jesus has not returned (3.3–10). Most scholars regard it as the latest document in the canon, and date it well into the second century AD. The warnings about prophecy (1.20–21) might even indicate a knowledge of the beginnings of Montanism, c. 157. It finds its place among the many pseudonymous* Petrine documents of that period, such as the Gospel and Apocalypse of Peter.

II Peter is, however, of considerable interest in illustrating the emergence of the canon of scripture. The author's omission of Jude's quotation from I Enoch indicates a sense that the boundaries of the OT are fixed, while his juxtaposition of 'the predictions of the holy prophets' with 'the commandment of the Lord and Saviour through your apostles' (3.2) shows the emergence of a distinctively Christian authority alongside the inherited scriptures. His reference to 'all' Paul's letters shows that a Pauline corpus has been collected, and is treated like 'the other scriptures' (3.15–16). He is also clear that the church is the proper context for the interpretation of scripture, both old and new, and that individual or sectarian interpretation is erroneous (1.20–21; 3.15–17).

The epistle of Jude is entirely concerned with false teaching within the readers' community (3–4,12,19). The author denounces rather than describes this teaching, but it appears to include false attitudes to angels or heavenly powers (8), and issues in sexual misconduct (4,7–8). Many scholars see this as, like the false teaching at Colossae, an early form of Gnosticism:* though here the gnostic denigration of the physical body is worked out in indulgence of its lusts as matters indifferent rather than in ascetic repression. Jude's false teachers have been identified as members of the Carpocratian, Cainite or Ophite Gnostic sects, but such precision is unlikely since they still remain within the church. II Peter by contrast seems to adopt some of the language and ideas elsewhere regarded as gnostic. Salvation is through knowledge (1.3); it consists in escape from the defilement of the world (2.4,20); and its goal is union with the divine nature (1.4).

II Peter has been harshly treated in modern, especially German, critical scholarship. Since F. C. Baur, it has been regarded as most clearly representing 'early Catholicism',* because of its attempt to equate Peter and Paul; its appeal to the authority of the church; and its acceptance of the waning of the parousia hope. It is further seen to illustrate the 'Hellenizing'* of Christianity, away from its original and authentic Jewish character, in the adopting of the concepts listed above, and in the characteristic description of Jesus as *sōtēr*, 'saviour' (1.1,11;2.20;3.2,18). It is possible, however, to view it more kindly as an attempt to translate Christian ideas in a context where Jewish terminology is no longer familiar, and thus to maintain the tradition.

See also **Peter, First.**

Tord Fornberg, *An Early Church in a Pluralistic Society*, 1977; Ernst Käsemann, 'An Apologia for Primitive Christian Eschatology' in *Essays on New Testament Themes*, 1964; J. N. D. Kelly, *The Epistles of Peter and of Jude*, 1969; E. M. Sidebottom, *James, Jude, 2 Peter*, 1967.

SOPHIE LAWS

Pharisees and Scribes

Although the identity of the Pharisees and Scribes* and their relation to each other is a matter of debate, the two groups may be combined because of the failure in practice to distinguish between them in much of the history of interpretation. This is a failure found already in Mark and in Matt. 23's polemic against the 'scribes and Pharisees, hypocrites'.

Other than Paul's* description of himself as 'according to the Law a Pharisee' (Phil. 3.5) – a passage of little interest to early interpreters – it is in the Gospels* and Acts that the Pharisees appear, usually as opponents of Jesus, occasionally, in Luke–Acts, as friends. The developing hostility towards the Pharisees which can already be traced from Mark to Matthew and to Luke, and also to John, meant that in the early church they, with the Scribes, are presented as the leaders of the Jewish people and as the prime movers of hostility towards Jesus, even being introduced as responsible for his death despite their absence from the Gospel passion narratives.*

Much patristic interpretation of the Pharisees and Scribes is little more than an exegetical* development of the Gospel material and a microcosm of interpretation of 'the Jews'. They are held responsible for the death of Jesus and the persecution of the church; they perceive only the literal* and not the spiritual* meaning of the Law and scriptures; they introduce and observe human traditions rather than the Law given by God. Yet these charges are developed first not in anti-Jewish (*see* **Antisemitism**) polemic but in defence of the unity of the God of the Old and New Dispensations and of Christian use of the Law – often through allegorical interpretation* – against Marcion* and others who appealed to Jesus' condemnation of the Pharisees in their rejection of the OT (Irenaeus,* Tertullian*). Pharisaic arrogance, greed and self-righteousness are condemned in preaching as much as in polemical contexts, and by failing in 'justification by faith' they could act as a foil for Christian teaching and virtues. As leaders of the Jewish people they could be held responsible for the latter's failure to recognize Jesus or God – in some writers allowing a measure of leniency towards the ordinary people (so later Aquinas). As with the treatment of the Jews, such polemic comes not only in the exegesis of NT passages, but in OT exegesis, especially of prophetic condemnation of Israel, and in a range of homiletic* as well as polemical writings. Almost always the Scribes and Pharisees belong to the time of the early church; if the rabbis* of post-70 Judaism were the heirs of the Pharisees (see below), the church Fathers betray little knowledge of this; there may be a continuity of type, but not of identity.

From Acts or Josephus,* the early interpreters knew of Pharisaic belief in the resurrection* of the dead in contrast to the Sadducees (Acts 23.6–9); although it is mentioned by neither source, they knew too the (possible) derivation of their name from a root meaning 'separated' – 'those who separate themselves' (first perhaps in Origen*); later writers give the alternative 'expounders' (so Calvin*). Independent of the exegetical and polemical tradition is the listing of the Pharisees as one of the parties among the Jews. Not totally dependent on Josephus, they appear as such in Justin and Hegesippus (second century) and in later catalogues of heresies as precursors of Christian heresy. Few further details are given, except in Epiphanius, where ascetical and astrological beliefs possibly drawn from more recent Jewish practice are attributed to them. Epiphanius alone introduces the Scribes as a separate group.

Anti-Pharisaic polemic is often internally directed: literalism in reading the scriptures was the fault not only of Jews and Pharisees but also of some within the church, including but not limited to Jewish Christians* (so

Origen); the pride of the Pharisee in prayer (Luke 18.9–14) and even love of chief seats (Matt. 23.6) could be condemned within the church. 'Whoever so acts to be seen by men is a Scribe and Pharisee' (Jerome). In new contexts new opponents could earn the label: Honorius Augustodensis (twelfth century) saw the Pharisees as clergy and the Sadducees as monks, to the latter's advantage. Calvin applied Matt. 23 to the Papists, hostility against the latter informing the interpretation of the former; some rejected specific application in favour of the charge that anyone 'who is superstitious, ambitious – is a Pharisee and hence a child of eternal hell' (Serarius, see below). Thus the Pharisees acquired any vice to be condemned.

The revival in the West from the thirteenth century of Christian interest in Judaism and of detailed learning in Jewish sources led to new approaches. While in the Patristic period limited use is made of non-biblical Jewish sources, now Targums,* Talmud,* midrashim* and later sources were heavily mined both to convert, by establishing conformity between Jewish teaching and Christian theology, and to vilify. In the wake of the Reformation* this tradition of learning fed into detailed treatises on topics of biblical interest and notes on the NT itself, largely illustrated from Jewish sources. Inevitably Pharisees appear in such treatises, but only rarely as the rigid legalists responsible for a sterile Judaism of some modern discussions. Thus the Jesuit N. Serarius and the Reformed scholars J. Scaliger and J. Drusius engaged in a heated debate about the Jewish sects in a number of substantial works (1603–05), even levelling charges of heresy in the argument as to whether the Pharisees or the Essenes were the Hasidim of I Macc. 2.42; 7.12f. (an issue still, somewhat less heatedly, disputed).

A new development in interpretation came in the nineteenth century, with the search for the piety of Jesus and his teaching of 'Our Father in heaven' being sharply contrasted with Judaism, and with the interest in the sources of Christianity and the conflict with Judaism. The picture of a Judaism characterized by legalism, now in the sense of a rigid adherence to the Law to the exclusion of all else, entailed a new focussing on the Pharisees as the chief proponents of that legalism.

In the 1980s that heritage could still be felt, provoking the charge that ecclesiastical, homiletic and pastoral concerns motivate much study of the Pharisees. The historical-critical* study of the NT and the interest in the person of Jesus have drawn attention to 'Jesus and the Law' and hence to the relation between Jesus and the Pharisees, with the question whether the NT picture of conflict is a retrojection from the life of the early church. For some, Jesus is hardly to be distinguished from the Pharisees in his faithfulness to the Law and its contemporary applicability, differing only in detail – hence the absence of the Pharisees from the passion narratives and a recognition that the points of conflict are largely within the possibilities of halakhic debate. For others, Jesus preached a gospel of grace and acceptance to those excluded by Pharisaic legalism and separatism, provoking a bitter hostility which inevitably led to his death.

Such analysis has demanded conclusions as to the historical identity, development and beliefs of the Pharisees and their significance in first-century Palestinian Judaism, drawing on all the sources which mention them: Josephus, the NT and either those rabbinic traditions referring to 'Pharisees' (*perushim*) or those which reflect pre-AD 70 teaching and conditions. Different pictures are presented by each of these sources according to their divergent interests, audiences and genres.* The different methods of interpretation, the priority given to each source, and the degree of harmonization* attempted have led to comparable divergences in scholarly accounts. While Jewish scholars have justifiably rejected accounts drawn predominantly from NT polemic, they have themselves reached no unanimity as to the origins, development and essential nature of Pharisaism. Josephus suggests an influential, although numerically small, group with an 'accurate' interpretation of the Law and some distinctive beliefs, and with, in origin, a political role and stance; this provides little overlap with the picture drawn from pre-70 rabbinic traditions of a purity sect seeking through their table-fellowship and strict observance of the purity laws the perpetual sanctification of daily life (J. Neusner). Others, also from the rabbinic material but providing a different philosophical and cultural context, have portrayed them as a scholar class devoted to the teaching of the two-fold law and responsible for the internalization and individualization of the relationship with God (E. Rivkin).

The NT has continued to make its contribution, concerning their regard for the Oral Law, their missionary zeal (Matt. 23.15), their presence in the Diaspora (Paul of Tarsus), and their links with and dominance over synagogue Judaism – although, lacking much other support, each of the last three can be hotly contested. Debate about the origins of the conflict between Christianity and Judaism, important since the 1970s, has built on earlier redactional* studies to emphasize that the increasing polemic of the later Gospel traditions is a reflection of the church's conflict with rabbinic Judaism or may be a cover for internal tensions within the church (so of both

Luke and Matt. 23). The former view assumes a continuity between the Pharisees and rabbinic Judaism and the dominance of the latter over a broad area quickly after AD 70, which some scholars would now question on the basis of Jewish sources.

Debates about the historical identity of the Pharisees and about their origins in the Maccabaean period, already an issue in the seventeenth century, have in the past led to the attempt to make them responsible for some of the literature of the period (e.g. Psalms of Solomon). Study of the Dead Sea Scrolls* and other intertestamental literature has extended the awareness of the diversity of Judaism of the period beyond Josephus' three (or four) sects and has inhibited such attempts.

In NT interpretation, the Scribes have been regularly joined with the Pharisees with little attempt to distinguish them, although the term has not acquired the same odium as 'Pharisee'; if distinguished, the Scribes have been seen as a professional grouping whose expertise in the Law would naturally align them with the Pharisees as the party particularly devoted to the Law. Their identity has been discussed more in the study of the development of Judaism from Ezra to the NT period. Despite the absence of the term from Josephus and Philo,* many have seen a continuity from Ezra the Scribe and specialist in the Law to Ben Sira's high regard for the Scribe (38–39) and to the Gospels.

The period after Ezra has been designated the age of the Scribes, with the Scribes as the chief figures in the teaching and interpretation of the Law and hence in the formation of Judaism in this period. The gaps in the evidence allow considerable disagreement as to details of the picture, to the relation with the secular use of the term for public officials and with Wisdom* teachers and traditions, and to the particular contribution and authority of the Scribes in the development of legal precept and practice. The general rabbinic restriction of the term (*soferim*) to either elementary teachers and clerks or 'the words of the scribes' as teaching from the past regarded with particular authority – in the widest sense as the whole Oral Torah – has prompted further disagreement as to their relationship with other groups such as 'Sages' and as to whether they can properly be given a major role as the heirs of Ezra. Thus disputes about 'the Scribes' reflect disputes about the nature and development of Judaism in the Second Temple period.

From the earliest references to them, the Pharisees and Scribes have been presented in Christian tradition as a foil for Christian ideals in polemic against those within as well as those outside the church. This has led to distorted presentations in 'historical accounts', dictionary articles and even in ordinary language (cf. 'Pharisee', OED). In this way interpretation of the Pharisees has both fed and been fed by those anti-Jewish traditions in NT scholarship which have vitiated Christian relations with, and attitudes to, Judaism from early times. Recognition of this in an age more open to dialogue has been joined by an awareness, underlined by Jewish scholars, of the difficulties in using rabbinic material uncritically for pre-70 Judaism and, even more, of seeing that material as representative not just of Pharisaic but even of 'normative' Judaism in the time of Jesus (or after the Exile generally). While awareness of this may lead to greater caution in dogmatic definition, it may be inevitable that the historical obscurity, together with their role in Christian tradition, will continue to render the Pharisees and Scribes subject to the ideological* stances of their interpreters.

See also **Antisemitism; Historical Jesus; Jewish Background to the New Testament.**

G. F. Moore, 'Christian Writers on Judaism', *Harvard Theological Review* 14 (1921) 197–254; J. Neusner, *From Politics to Piety*, 1973; E. Rivkin, *A Hidden Revolution*, 1978; E. P. Sanders, *Jesus and Judaism*, 1985.

JUDITH M. LIEU

Philippians

Until relatively recently, much the greater part of the interpretative attention directed to this letter concentrated on a single passage, 2.5–11. The use made of it is an excellent illustration of the manner in which traditional exegesis,* beginning in the patristic* period, went about its task. It was not a matter of investigating, in a spirit of historical realism, what Paul* intended by the passage, but of seizing upon its terms and expounding them in the light of already formed doctrinal principles. This *a priori* mode of proceeding was wholly characteristic of patristic (and later) interpretation. As the passage was (it is now clear) not written to deal with the issues of the subsequent period, it is not surprising that it was susceptible of a number of interpretations and was a focus of dispute.

It was used to throw light on the following questions, which were central to doctrinal interest at that time:

1. Was Jesus truly human? Those, such as Gnostics* and Marcion,* who held a docetic view of Jesus (i.e. that, being divine, he only seemed to be human), noted that Paul appeared to qualify his statements about Jesus' humanity: he took only the 'form' of a servant and was made only in the 'likeness' of men. Orthodox teachers, however, countered

by pointing out that Paul neatly balanced his statements concerning divinity and humanity and that it was better to see him as speaking plainly of Christ's two natures, with the word 'form' as an equivalent of the now more favoured term 'nature'.

2. Was Christ fully divine? Once again, the word 'form' in 2.6 could be used as grist to either mill: it implied a qualification and therefore a subordination of Christ to the Father, or else it meant his full and total oneness and equality with him. The last three verses of the passage were also taken to be relevant to this question: they seemed to say that there was room for Christ, on his exaltation to heaven, to become greater than he had been before; therefore, he had previously been subordinate to the Father. The orthodox reply to such views was again in terms of Christ's two natures: the passage referred strictly to his human nature and to that alone.

3. How was the incarnation to be understood? As already hinted, it was impossible for thinkers of this period to envisage change of any kind taking place in God. Therefore, if Christ was divine, his incarnation (becoming human) must somehow be explained without the occurrence of change. Paul's verb *kenoō* (v. 7) afforded help with the task, but only when understood in a particular sense. At first sight, it seems to speak of Christ abandoning divinity in becoming human, but, given the assumptions of the time, it was taken quite differently. What was meant was the addition of humanity to a wholly unchanged divinity, in the act of 'humbling himself' (*tapeinōsis*, v. 8). In what then did the renunciation implicit in *kenoō* ('emptied himself' or 'became powerless') consist? It meant that in the taking of human nature (or, as it was often expressed, even by so-called orthodox Fathers, the adding of a body to himself), the Word (*see* Logos) or Son of God suppressed or held in check, by an act of voluntary condescension, the temporarily inappropriate properties of his divine nature. Thus, he expressed a feeling of hunger or admitted to ignorance, not out of true necessity, but out of a fitting accommodation to the human setting to which he had descended. This was seen not as at all bogus, but as a wondrous act of divine identification with the human race, evoking praise and thanksgiving. Phil. 2.5–11 was a key text in the expounding of this doctrine.

In the late nineteenth century, this element in the passage again came to the fore, but in a different sense. It was a time when imagination focussed more vividly on Christ's real humanness, including its mental and psychological* reality, and it came to be felt that there was an uncomfortable element of play-acting in the traditional exposition of his

earthly life. The concept of *kenōsis* came to the rescue. In various 'kenotic theories' of the incarnation, notably that of Charles Gore (but there were earlier Lutheran* proposals along similar lines), it was held that at the point of the incarnation, Christ genuinely renounced divine characteristics such as omniscience and omnipotence, so that his human experience was wholly authentic. This theory, expounded in Gore's *The Incarnation of the Son of God*, 1891, has itself found critics for its unconvincing picture of the identity and continuity of the pre-existent with the incarnate Christ, and in any case, equally with the traditional view, it belongs firmly to the pre-critical era as an exposition of Paul's meaning in Phil. 2.5–11.

In the period of historical criticism,* and especially since the work of E. Lohmeyer,* *Kurios Jesus*, 1928, the passage has continued to receive its full share of attention, but now in a different interest and alongside other historical and exegetical issues seen to be raised by the letter.

In the first half of the nineteenth century, F. C. Baur (*see* **Tübingen School**) already brought Philippians, albeit in a subordinate role, into his account of early Christian development in terms of the power struggle between Paul and Jewish Christians. From a historical-critical point of view, much of the interest of Philippians lies precisely in that secondary role: one may learn much about a writer in turning away from his major works to a composition that seems more relaxed in tone and may therefore reveal much about his everyday outlook. For example, it is in Philippians that we see Paul expressing himself informally and briefly – and in deeply personal terms – concerning his relationship with Christ and the righteousness that comes through faith in him (3.7–9), a theme treated more extensively and formally in Romans. It is much the same with regard to resurrection* and future life: 1.19–26; 3.10–16. These passages are important also for discussion of possible development in Paul's ideas on these subjects from his earlier writings, especially I and II Corinthians.

The following are the leading subjects of interest for interpretation:

1. *Place and time of writing.* That Paul wrote this letter has scarcely been doubted, except by some scholars using computerized* data for style analysis. Along with Colossians, Philemon, and (though its Pauline authorship* is much in doubt) Ephesians, the Letter to the Philippians is ostensibly written from prison, 1.13f.,17 (the 'captivity epistles'). Though this location has usually been seen to imply that the letter was written in Rome during the imprisonment described in Acts 28, this view has not gone without challenge. The

word *praitōrion* (Greek taken over from Latin *praetorium*) has been taken to refer not, as is often suggested, to the 'praetorian guard', but to headquarters buildings of the imperial government, to be found in many cities of the Empire; and the reference to 'those of Caesar's household' in 4.22 may refer not necessarily to members of the palace staff in Rome but to officials in the imperial service, usually freedmen or slaves, operating in many parts of the Empire. So G. S. Duncan (in *St Paul's Ephesian Ministry*, 1929) held that the letter was written during imprisonment in Ephesus (cf. I Cor. 15.32), Lohmeyer placed it in Caesarea (cf. Acts 23.33–26.32), and Corinth has also been suggested (Acts 18.1–8). Naturally, these various suggestions affect the dating: only Rome enables us to see Philippians as reflecting Paul's later thought. Rome remains the most likely hypothesis, but the vagueness of Philippians itself, not only about location but also about the reasons for Paul's imprisonment, may even give rise to doubts about the authenticity of the whole prison scenario and certainly does nothing to help the student of Paul's biography.

2. *The unity of the letter.* If one focusses on the collection of Paul's writings, probably towards the end of the first century, one becomes aware that some at least of the letters in their present form may represent amalgamations of real letters by Paul or even of fragments of letters. Such views have been found especially convincing in the case of the Corinthian correspondence, but they have also won support in the case of Philippians. Thus, F. W. Beare, in his commentary of 1959, suggested a three-fold division, with 3.2–4.1 and 4.10–20 being interpolations into the main letter, but V. P. Furnish found it possible to expound ch. 3 as a sort of extended postscript to the main body of the letter (*NTS*, 10, 1963).

3. *Phil. 2.5–11.* This passage has remained a centre of exegetical interest, as one of the most important christological* passages in the whole of the NT. It raises a galaxy of issues: whether it is to be identified as a unit independent of the rest of the letter, and whether it is correctly or usefully designated as a 'hymn';* then, whether it is by Paul or was taken over by him from existing Christian use; whether it reflects a (hypothetical) gnostic redeemermyth, as the History of Religions school* held, or Jewish wisdom* speculation, as is widely thought, and whether the depiction of Christ is then based on the model of Adam,* perhaps along lines also found in Philo;* then, in the light of that proposal, whether the passage supports the idea of Christ's preexistence, thus witnessing to its presence very early in the church's life, or, apart from vv. 9–11, puts forward a this-worldly account of the drama of Christ, as J.D.G. Dunn has contended (*Christology in the Making*, ²1989). However it is to be interpreted, it is agreed that this passage is an invaluable witness to the rapid development of 'advanced' claims for Jesus and of formulas to express those claims, presumably for use in worship and teaching.

4. *Paul's relations with his churches.* There are hints elsewhere (II Cor. 11.9) that Paul enjoyed a much more agreeable relationship with the church in Philippi than with, for example, that in Corinth. Philippians gives us a close glimpse of that relationship, probably at a considerably later stage. Again, the impression is one of intimacy; yet ch. 4 shows something of that awkwardness about material dependence on others which caused Paul such difficulties in Corinth and which has been the subject of interesting sociological* investigation, for example in R. F. Hock, *The Social Context of Paul's Ministry*, 1980.

5. *The leadership of Paul's churches.* Phil. 1.1 contains a reference, unique in Paul (though taken up by disciples of the next generation, as witnessed in I Timothy and Titus [*see* **Pastoral Epistles**]), to 'bishops' and 'deacons'. Translation using these technical terms, rather than the literal 'overseers' and 'servants', itself begs questions and should now be seen as anachronistic. However, the verse has long been taken as early testimony to the existence of the catholic orders of ministry. More recently, parallels have been found in the types of leaders in the community at Qumran (*see* **Dead Sea Scrolls**) and (more helpfully) in various Greek uses of the terms in question. But the passage does seem to point to the existence of defined officers in the congregation, which tells against some accounts of the amorphous or egalitarian character of Pauline churches.

6. *The opponents.* To take ch. 3 seriously is to realize that the life of the Philippian church was not all sweetness and light. Rather, it was racked with discordant influences. Their precise character is, however, harder to identify, and a multitude of hypotheses has been put forward. While the generally most acceptable view is that the congregation was subject to inroads of a Jewish(–Christian) kind not unlike that which plagued Paul in Corinth, other strands seem also to be present, in particular spiritual enthusiasm and libertinism that tend to attract the adjective 'gnostic' or the more cautious 'gnosticizing'. It may be that Paul's stress in this letter on suffering and death (both his own and that of Christ) was the result not only of his own present predicament but also of his determination to counter euphoric and triumphalist teaching on the part of others.

See also **Christology, New Testament; Patristic Christology.**

J. J. Gunther, *St Paul's Opponents and their Background*, 1973; R. P. Martin, *Carmen Christi*, 1967; id., *Philippians*, 1976; M. F. Wiles, *The Divine Apostle*, 1967.

J. L. HOULDEN

Philo

Philo, philosopher and theologian from the great city of Alexandria (*c.* 25 BC–40 AD), devoted his career almost entirely to the interpretation and application of the Jewish scriptures. Most of what he wrote was about those scriptures and almost everything in them he interpreted allegorically.* Philo did not invent the allegorical method of scriptural exegesis,* but he was certainly one of its most accomplished practitioners. For him the scriptures were the inspired word of God,* incapable of falsehood and addressed to all, both Jews and Gentiles. Careful exposition, however, was required, especially to make the meaning of scripture plain to the non-Jew, and this was applied by him chiefly to the books of the Pentateuch.* The method he used meant that he did not need to take every word of the scriptures literally. The authors of scripture were, in Philo's view, like philosophers recalling, under inspiration, intelligible ideas beyond the world of sense and matter. The Septuagint* (LXX) translators, similarly inspired, produced an infallibly accurate rendering of the Hebrew. Philo's view of the scriptures as impossible without divine inspiration* placed upon him and his fellow exegetes a heavy responsibility to interpret them correctly; but Philo, because he was something of a philosopher himself – the first Jew whom one can call a philosopher in the modern sense – and because the philosophy he embraced was a combination of Platonism and Stoicism, especially the Platonic theory of ideas, was confronted with the task of reconciling Greek philosophy with the religion inherited from his ancestors. The allegorical method of exegesis was a tool that enabled him to derive a multitude of philosophical ideas from the Jewish scriptures without denying his Jewish beliefs.

Philo took over the allegorical method from the earlier Greek writers who had practised it. The LXX itself provided him with encouragement to allegorize by its paraphrases of some of the Hebrew Bible's anthropomorphisms.* Rabbinic exegesis also resorted at times to the allegorical method. Such a departure from the literal* meaning of scripture as Philo allowed himself was possible only because of the generous freedom of exegesis which Judaism permitted. The difference between Philo and the rabbis* was that they perhaps regarded the scriptures with greater awe, while he was prepared to supplement what the text contained from sources far removed from them.

Philo described allegorical exegesis as a 'mystery' into which one must be initiated. Philo the exegete is also Philo the mystic.* So strong was Philo's view that he could accuse those who did not practise allegorical exegesis as guilty of corrupting Judaism into superstition. Judaism, for Philo, was the 'holiest secret', which could be extracted only from the scriptures.

The depths of truth present in the scriptures also required 'scientific skill' for their interpretation. Only by using such skill could a biblically based religion be maintained while a substantial amount of Platonism and Stoicism was retained. In explaining this method of exegesis he uses many of the technical terms used by Greek writers. For example, the early stories of Genesis were not, he believed, mythical* fictions, but *deigmata*, modes of making ideas visual, visible. It is not surprising that Philo's adoption of the allegorical method led him into conflict with those who accepted the literal truth of the scriptures, though he does concede, as has been noted, that the 'simple pious', as well as the philosophically minded, could practise allegorical exegesis. The literalists with whom Philo disagreed no doubt felt that allegorical exegesis involved the introduction into pure Judaism of alien ideas.

Literalists, according to Philo, failed to look for and see what lay beneath the surface of the text, its deeper meaning. The literalists, on the other hand, clearly regarded Philo and his colleagues as patronizing and as guilty of intellectual snobbery, and, more dangerously, as betrayers of the true meaning of the scriptures. The modern battle between those who seek to demythologize* sections of the Bible and those who accept the 'myths' as literally true clearly had its counterpart in Philo's Alexandria.

An example of Philo's exegesis is his treatment of Noah (in the *De agric.*). Philo was unable to accept that the description 'husbandman' (Gen. 9.20ff.), when Noah is said to have been 'the first tiller of the soil', referred solely to agricultural pursuits; and the literalists missed the fact – so Philo thought – that Moses* was not only a 'shepherd' (Ex. 3.9) but also the divine Logos* (*De mut. nom.* 110ff.). Far from merely describing farming activities these words relate, according to Philo, to a philosophical understanding of life involving various organs, the body and its members, and the mind, which may or may not control the body and its impulses. Thus, to be a 'husbandman' means that Noah exercises 'soul-husbandry'; and the life denoted by the word 'shepherd', which Philo invites his readers to live, is the life of the wise man who can control his lusts (*De agric.* 39).

But it is important to note that Philo criticized those who accepted only the allegorical method of exegesis, since it involved 'partial blindness of the soul' (*Quod det. nom.* 227), as, e.g. when the acceptance of the statement in *Qu. in Gen.* 42 that God 'walked' contradicts the truth of God's immobility. Philo accepted both the literal and the allegorical meanings of scripture. To detect an allegorical level of meaning in scripture, as in what Genesis says about the sabbath (see *De opif. mun.* 89ff.), does not mean that its literal meaning should be disregarded, but merely pruned and supplemented. The sabbath is meant to teach man 'the power of the Unoriginate', but all the laws relating to it are still to be obeyed. Philo insists that 'learning' that has grown grey through time 'should not be neglected, despite the existence of a higher wisdom'.

Philo was perhaps driven to practise allegorical exegesis because of his lofty doctrine of God's transcendence. God's word could not be guilty of falsehood or self-contradiction, which taken literally it often was. Allegorical exegesis enabled Philo to remain a Jew both loyal to the nation's scriptures and responsive to the insights of Greek philosophy. Furthermore, the word of God to mankind required skilful exegesis and could not be found to contain anything unworthy, since the scriptures are God's words as well as his Word.

Two of the phrases he uses are important. He refers to the literal meaning of a text as 'what it actually says', whereas the deeper meaning he describes as 'the meaning addressed to the mind'. He contrasts 'the actual words' of a story with its 'spiritual significance', for him the more important.

Though Philo did not discover the allegorical method of exegesis, he did contribute enormously to its enrichment and development. His writings became extremely popular with the Christian church – and were for centuries neglected by Judaism. In the case of some of the Fathers allegory was used to extract philosophical ideas from the biblical texts; later it was used to extract ethical and doctrinal ideas. And just as Philo was not primarily a historian interested in, for example, the life-history of Samuel (but rather in that of which Samuel was the symbol*), so Christian exegetes frequently followed Philo by concentrating on the symbolic meanings of the Bible rather than its historical elements. Philo was one of the ancients who prepared the way for the modern, critical, non-literal understanding of the Bible, even though in the case of his own view not all those adjectives could be applied to what he wrote.

One of the major sources of Philo's exegetical method was his Platonic epistemology (cf. *De somn.* I.185–7, where he refers to the world as 'framed from eternal forms'). God, according to Philo, created first the intelligible world, knowable only by mind, and then the material world; but there is no way, he insisted, of knowing the former through the latter. The literal meaning of scripture Philo compares to the material and visible world, beyond which man must proceed if he is to reach the real world of incorporeal existences. What Moses wrote down, using allegorical language, was what he had seen in visionary form of the incorporeal, the world of essences. The literal meaning of scripture, then, accessible to the superficial reader, corresponds to the world of sense-perception; the truth accessible to allegorical exegesis is the truth about the timeless world of ideas. So to reach the deepest truths of scripture the allegorical method of exegesis is essential.

Another powerful reason for the adoption of the allegorical method by Philo was his deep abhorrence of and antipathy to anthropomorphism.* He quoted Num. 23.19 frequently, interpreting it to mean that God is not to be likened to anything that is sense-perceptible. In *Quod Deus* 62–64 Philo states that the anthropomorphisms of the Jewish scriptures are merely aids to the 'dense and dull', though God is in fact apprehensible, even by the mind, only 'in the fact that he is'. God is absolutely unique and totally dissimilar to any created thing. The allegorical method, however, enabled Philo to avoid the embarrassingly anthropomorphic passages of scripture. But he was able to take such passages seriously even if not literally. God had permitted anthropomorphic language in scripture, in Philo's view, because foolish men had to read it; and, he concluded, even the untruth may benefit the reader if he is incapable of being 'brought to wisdom by truth' (*Quod Deus* 64). Doctors tell untruths to their patients because they cannot understand the full medical truth; anthropomorphisms may evoke piety based on fear (if not on love), but allegorical exegesis reaches to the truth and evokes a piety founded on love.

Bousset demonstrated that the early Christian Fathers knew and were influenced by Philo's writings. Early in the second century, the *Epistle of Barnabas* shows Philo's influence. Later, Origen* closely followed both Philo's Platonism and his allegorical exegesis. Ambrose introduced whole sentences from Philo into his works, with the result that one Jewish writer designated him 'Philo Christianus'. He followed the allegorical method of Philo and Origen, affirming that scripture had a three-fold sense – literal, moral, and mystical (allegorical). He adopted Philo's exegesis of particular passages of scripture, e.g. regarding Noah's ark, as Philo had done, as a prototype of the human body, a unity of many parts. In his *De Noe* he refers to the ark as a figurative description of the body, taking over the details of Philo's exegesis. When he describes scripture as having three levels of meaning, he explicitly describes it as an 'allegory'.

In recent centuries, the interpretation of some books of the NT has involved authors making a considerable number of references to Philo's works. The two most involved are Hebrews and the Fourth Gospel. J. B. Carpzov, in the eighteenth century, attempted in a grand *tour de force* to demonstrate that virtually every verse and almost every word in Hebrews had been influenced by Philo's language and thought. In the twentieth century, this view was given the weighty support of a lengthy two-volume commentary on Hebrews by C. Spicq. His thesis that the author of Hebrews was a 'Philonist converted to Christianity' and that this was responsible for the multitude of Philonisms in Hebrews has more recently been severely questioned and tested by Williamson (1970) and others, though it still has its supporters. S. G. Sowers' work on Philo and Hebrews, with special reference to their hermeneutical methods, seeks to show that the hermeneutics* of Philo exerted some influence over those of Hebrews.

In the case of the Fourth Gospel commentators have tended increasingly to include a section on Philo in the introduction to their commentaries.* C. H. Dodd* has a lengthy section on Philo in his study of the interpretation of the Fourth Gospel (1953). In the realm of NT christology,* J. D. G. Dunn, in his *Christology in the Making* (² 1989), has found Philo's language and ideas, especially on the Logos, to be of great help in explaining the concept of the incarnation of the Logos in John. In P. Borgen's interpretation of John's thought Philo is frequently invoked.

In the most recent period, Jewish scholars (H. A. Wolfson and S. Sandmel) have contributed to the understanding of Philo. Older writers, such as E. R. Goodenough, interpreted Philo's thought as a kind of Hellenistic* mysticism related to the Greek mystery religions.* In the last few years, particularly in North America, editions of several individual treatises of Philo have appeared. In the annual seminar of the *Societas Novi Testamenti Studiorum* a recent session was devoted to a fresh appraisal of eschatology* in Philo (which will almost certainly require a revision of earlier views). Philo studies are increasing and there is hope that problems as yet unsolved may find a solution. It is also possible that the interest in Philo shown by contemporary Jewish scholars may lead to the use of some at least of Philo's ideas and methods in the interpretation of his own scriptures, the scriptures of Judaism.

See also **Alexandrian Interpretation; Allegorical Interpretation; Philosophy; Spiritual Meaning.**

A. W. Argyle, 'Philo the Man and His Work', *ET*, LXXXV, No. 4, Jan. 1974, pp. 115–117; F. C. Copleston. *A History of Philosophy*, Vol. I; 1947; J. Drummond, *Philo Judaeus* (2 vols), 1888; I. Epstein, *Judaism*, 1959; E. R. Goodenough, *By Light, Light*, 1938; S. Sandmel, *Philo of Alexandria: An Introduction*, 1979; R. Williamson, *Jews in the Hellenistic World: Philo*, 1989; H. A. Wolfson, *Philo* (2 vols), 1948.

R. WILLIAMSON

Philology

Philology is here understood in its comparative sense, that is to say, the determination of the meaning of biblical Hebrew words from comparison with extra-biblical Hebrew and languages cognate with Hebrew. These, all Semitic languages, include Akkadian, Arabic, Aramaic, Ethiopic, Phoenician, Syriac,* and Ugaritic.* More recently scholars have turned to the cuneiform tablets of Tell Mardikh (ancient Ebla) in Syria in order to solve problems in biblical Hebrew, but these tablets are as yet too little understood to be used with certainty. More significant, perhaps, may be the tablets found at Meskeneh (ancient Emar), also in Syria, though here too we must wait until they have been studied in more detail.

Why should we have to turn to Hebrew outside the OT or to ancient Semitic languages in order to establish what Hebrew words mean? While a large proportion of Hebrew words is clearly understood there remain some which are not. These include *hapax legomena* (words found only once in the whole of the Hebrew Bible), rare words, anomalous forms or words which tend to be emended away, and some misunderstood terms. While context often helps to determine what a particular Hebrew word means, it remains only a guide and the versions are not always helpful. Another reason is that biblical Hebrew represents only a skewed remnant of a language once much wider in extent. We are dependent on the documents which survived.

How do we know the meanings of Hebrew words in the OT? Largely from Jewish tradition, including the interpretations in the Dead Sea Scrolls,* and of course from the versions (Greek, Aramaic, Syriac, etc.). Extra-biblical Hebrew inscriptions are helpful, but to a limited degree as they are so few. Also significant are semantic* field, the cognate languages and context. In fact a combination of two or more of these factors is required for at least some plausibility when any suggestion concerning the meaning of a Hebrew word (or any proposal concerning grammar and syntax*) is made. In general terms, 'a biblical word may be truly identified with its alleged etymological equivalent in another Semitic language only if the usage of the biblical word in all its contexts can be shown to correspond to the usage of the proposed etymological equivalent in the other Semitic language. If such is the case, then the biblical word may be said to be both semantically and etymologically equivalent to its counterpart in the other Semitic language and the two words may be considered true cognates' (Cohen, *Hapax Legomena*, p. 23). Here only examples which directly affect interpretation will be discussed.

Hapax legomena present a special problem because they each have only a single context which can help determine meaning. Idioms, too, comprise a separate problem and cannot be discussed here in any detail. An example is Hos. 7.9, 'grey hairs are sprinkled upon him'. The expression 'grey hairs' normally has positive connotations (e.g. the wisdom of old age) but here it is negative. In fact it is an idiom used in the Babylonian *Epic of Gilgamesh* to describe mouldy bread and in Hosea forms part of the metaphor* which depicts Ephraim as a 'mouldy cake'.

Philology is not confined to lexical items, however. Grammar and syntax are just as important, for example with reference to prepositions and particles for which several alternative meanings have been proposed. For example, *l*, normally 'to', 'for' in Hebrew, also means 'from' in Ugaritic. Consequently, this other meaning has been proposed in Hebrew as well. However, there is still some controversy over such possible correspondences. Another example is the Phoenician feminine singular ending which looks like the feminine plural ending of Hebrew nouns. It may explain the form of the word for 'crown' in Zech. 6.14, since the agreeing verb is 'it (fem. sing.) shall be' and refers to one of the two 'crowns' mentioned in v. 11: the silver one to go on the high priest's head, the royal crown of gold to be stored in the temple (C. and E. Meyers). Another case of such an apparent plural may be the term for 'Wisdom' in Prov. 1.20.

Some suggestions made on the basis of cognate languages can go astray even if there is a matching context. For example, the affirmation 'He who believes will not be in haste' (Isa. 28.16 RSV) makes little sense in the context of God declaring he is about to lay a massive foundation stone in Zion – imagery for a city he would approve based on principles of justice. In fact, the verb *ḥûš* does not mean 'to hasten' here (though that meaning does occur in Ugaritic in connection with the building of Baal's palace) but 'to shake, waver'. The correct translation, then, is 'Look, I am about to lay in Zion a stone, a massive stone, a cornerstone valuable for a foundation, a foundation which will not shake for the one who trusts.' This is how the Isaiah passage was interpreted in the Qumran scrolls (J. Roberts). Another incorrect suggestion was to see the equivalent of Ugaritic *ktp*, a term for a weapon, in Deut. 33.12 and translate, 'And between his weapons (usually: shoulders) he dwells', on which see below.

In Prov. 30.19 the commonly accepted translation of the last line is 'and the way of a man with a maiden'. This line comes fourth in an enumeration of marvels, all with reference to 'way': an eagle's way in the sky, a serpent's on a rock, a ship's on the sea. However, the word *'lmh* here does not mean 'maiden' or the like, but 'darkness, obscurity' from the Hebrew root *'lm*, 'to conceal'. Corroboration is provided by the Ugaritic cognate (*ǵlm*; Hebrew ' corresponds to Ugaritic *ǵ*). The correct version then is 'the way of a strong man in hidden places (or, in darkness)'. A sexual meaning must therefore be excluded and the whole quatrain refers instead to mysterious methods of travel (G. del Olmo Lete).

Isa. 65.2–4 is a list of abominable practices rejected by Yahweh. V. 4a refers to 'those who sit in graves/ and spend the night *bnṣrym*'. The last cluster could be translated 'in watchtowers', 'in secret places', or even, with a slight change of text, 'between rocks' (as in the LXX*). The Syriac verb *nṣr* 'to shriek, lament,' etc. found also in Akkadian and Ugaritic, suggests that the same verb occurs here, in Hebrew, and the cluster means 'in wailing' (or, 'among the wailers'). The passage does not refer to incubation rites, as some scholars have proposed, but to a funerary cult of the kind well attested in the Ugaritic texts and elsewhere (J. Healey).

It has long been accepted that the sequence *'ly*, which can mean 'upon me' (preposition plus pronominal suffix), is really a divine title. The proposal first made by H. S. Nyberg in 1935 now finds confirmation from Ugaritic, where *'ly*, 'the Most High', is a clear epithet of Baal. In consequence several difficult passages become intelligible. A prime example is Deut. 33.12 which should be translated 'Yahweh's beloved dwells securely/ while the Most High (*'lyw* corrected to *'ly*, cf. LXX *theos*, 'God') surrounds him all day long/ and he dwells between his (Yahweh's) shoulders'. At one stroke several difficulties of grammar and interpretation disappear. The verb 'to surround' no longer appears to have the same preposition in front of it as after; there is no sudden switch of subject from Benjamin to

Yahweh and back to Benjamin; there is no reference to a temple in the last line (as several scholars have thought), since the subject of 'dwells' is not Yahweh but Benjamin (J. Heck). Other passages where *Eli*, 'The Most High' occurs are I Sam. 2.10 and Ps. 7.7,11.

Although II Kings 6.24ff. describes extreme starvation during a siege, it remains beyond belief that 'a quarter of a kab (a dry measure of unknown size) of dove's dung' should be considered edible. In spite of the RSV rendering (contrast NEB) the term is not to be understood literally but denotes a vegetable, the carob seed, for which the descriptive name 'doves' droppings' is known from both Arabic (J. Gray) and Akkadian (M. Held). Such picturesque names for plants are common in Akkadian.

Proposals made within comparative philology for the meanings of Hebrew words, then, need to be based on one or more of the cognate languages and supporting evidence is sometimes provided by the versions, later interpretation such as is found in the Dead Sea Scrolls, and a general awareness of context. (The same applies, of course, to solutions for problems in grammar and syntax.) Not all such proposals stand the test of time; some must be discounted by subsequent epigraphic* finds or by better understanding of the extra-biblical languages from which such proposals derive; others prove to flout phonological correspondences. In general, though, they can serve to better our understanding of the Hebrew text and so merit close scrutiny. Note that all the above, which applies to Hebrew, holds true also of the Aramaic sections of the OT (Daniel, etc.) but the range of comparable languages should then also include Persian and Greek.

See also **Etymology; Semantics**.

J. Barr, *Comparative Philology and the Text of the Old Testament*, 1968; H. R. Cohen, *Biblical Hapax Legomena in the Light of Akkadian and Ugaritic*, 1978; P. C. Craigie, *Psalms 1–50*, 1983; L. L. Grabbe, *Comparative Philology and the Text of Job. A Study in Methodology*, 1977.

WILFRED G. E. WATSON

Philosophy

The problem of the relationship between philosophy and biblical interpretation is anticipated within the Bible itself. In Col. 2.8, 'philosophy' is identified with 'empty deceit', incompatible with faith in Christ, and in I Cor. 1.18ff. a sharp distinction is drawn between 'wisdom' and 'the word of the cross'. The latter passage, like the former, has traditionally been read as an attack on the Greek philosophical tradition, and in the light of

Paul's* assertion that it is 'Greeks' who 'seek wisdom' (I Cor. 1.22) this is probably correct. Paul opposes the view that the Christian gospel requires the philosophical tradition for its interpretation, a standpoint which had perhaps been brought to Corinth by Apollos, the learned Alexandrian Jew. If so, one might see this controversy at Corinth as a paradigm for later controversies about the relationship between philosophy and Christian faith, with (for example) Tertullian,* Luther* and Barth* representing one side of the argument, and Origen,* Aquinas and Bultmann* the other. It would, however, be a mistake to understand the relationship merely in terms of a simple decision for or against philosophy on the part of the theologian and exegete.

The relationship between philosophy and biblical interpretation first became an issue in Alexandrian Judaism. Eusebius* preserves fragments of the work of Aristobulus, dating probably from the mid-second century BC, in which the author rationalizes scriptural anthropomorphisms* and claims that Plato and Pythagoras knew and borrowed from the Law of Moses.* The intention is obviously apologetic. The same concerns, in a more developed form, are also to be found in the voluminous work of Philo* of Alexandria, writing in the first half of the first century AD. Philo uses the Stoic device of allegorical interpretation* to mediate between the Jewish scriptures and Greek philosophy, that is, to discover the true meaning of the former in the doctrines of the latter. For example, the double creation* account in Gen. 1–2 is understood in terms of the Platonic distinction between the ideal and the material worlds. In Gen. 3, Adam,* Eve and the serpent are said to represent Mind, the Senses and Pleasure respectively: Pleasure uses the Senses to seduce Mind away from its true allegiance to the incorporeal world. This philosophical approach to the biblical narratives sometimes leads Philo to oppose those who insist on the importance of the literal,* historical sense. 'It is,' he tells us, 'quite foolish to believe that the world was created in six days' (*Legum Allegoria* 1.2), just as it is absurd to believe in a serpent 'emitting a human voice and using quibbling arguments' (*de agricultura* 96).

Philo's philosophical exegesis* was adapted for Christian use by the two great Alexandrian* theologians of the late second and early third centuries, Clement and Origen. Both shared his emphasis on philosophical studies as an essential preliminary for biblical interpretation, his sensitivity to the problem of anthropomorphisms and apparently incredible statements in the biblical texts, and his use of allegorical interpretation. Origen in particular extends the allegorical method to the interpretation of the Gospels,* and he sees the necessity for this in the 'innumerable' impossibilities he finds in the literal sense. However, the content of Alexandrian Christian allegorical exegesis is no longer supplied purely by philosophy, since it is also deeply influenced by typology,* the correlating of OT texts, events and persons with NT antitypes. Subsequent development of Alexandrian 'spiritual*' exegesis is still more concerned to find a meaning for the biblical texts from within Christian faith, rather than directly from philosophy. Thus the allegorical interpretation practised by Gregory the Great and by Bede, so influential during the mediaeval period, has little to do with philosophical concerns, despite its 'Alexandrian' provenance.

Clement and Origen sought to counter the widespread Christian suspicion of philosophy, exemplified in Tertullian's famous denial that Jerusalem has anything in common with Athens, and in Hippolytus' attempt to blame philosophy for all the errors of the Gnostics.* Like Philo, they had to contend not only with anti-philosophical prejudice from literalists on their own side, but also with attacks on the scriptural tradition from representatives of Hellenistic* philosophy. Origen devotes his most substantial surviving work to refuting one of the most formidable of these attacks, the *Logos Alethes* of Celsus. Celsus, who was familiar at least with the Gospel of Matthew, argued at length that its claims about Jesus – his virgin birth, his Davidic* descent, his foreknowledge of his death, his resurrection* – were incredible. Christians only believe such things, he claims, because they are ignorant and foolish people opposed to education and philosophy. A still more dangerous philosophical opponent of the Bible was Porphyry, the third-century neo-Platonist, who argued that the book of Daniel was composed in the second century BC and is therefore spurious, and that the Gospels and Pauline epistles are full of contradictions.

Within the church, opposition to Alexandrian allegorizing and its philosophical implications is found especially in the Antiochene* exegetical tradition, represented by Lucian of Antioch, Diodore of Tarsus, Theodore of Mopsuestia and John Chrysostom. However, it would be wrong to regard their remarkable stress on the literal, historical sense of scripture as wholly 'anti-philosophical'. A sixth-century textbook on interpretation by Junilius Africanus, which stems from the Antiochene tradition, systematizes Theodore's hermeneutics along Aristotelian lines. Indeed, one might plausibly interpret the entire hermeneutical* controversy between Alexandrians and Antiochenes as a controversy between Platonists and Aristotelians.

The Alexandrian ideal of expertise in classical learning as a prerequisite for the interpreter of scripture was passed on to the early Middle Ages by Augustine* and Jerome. However, biblical interpretation was now dominated by the 'gloss', excerpts from the writings of the Fathers; the aim was to preserve existing interpretations rather than to develop new ways of reading the texts (*see* **Mediaeval Interpretation**). 'Alexandrian' and 'Antiochene' tendencies can still be detected – the former where spiritual meanings (whether 'allegorical', 'tropological' or 'anagogical') are preferred to the literal sense, the latter where the literal sense is made an object of study in its own right, as in the work of Andrew of St Victor (d. 1175). The revival of Aristotelianism tended to support this renewed concern with the literal sense, and, influenced by Maimonides' *Guide of the Perplexed* (1190), William of Auvergne (*c.* 1180–1249) questioned the validity of allegorical interpretation and understood the Mosaic Law in terms of the moral and rational purposes of the lawgiver. Thomas Aquinas rejected this extreme view, but his Aristotelianism nevertheless led him to emphasize that spiritual senses must be founded on the literal and that the literal alone can be made the basis for theological argumentation.

Renewed interest in the relationship between theology and philosophy in the thirteenth century was accompanied by a degree of separation between theology and exegesis. One result of this was that the biblical texts could be studied in the light of the new scientific interests stimulated by the rediscovery of Aristotle. For example, the Oxford theologian Simon of Hinton (*fl.* 1250) discusses the meaning of the *zizania* in the parable* of the wheat and the tares, and, in opposition to his patristic authorities, identifies it with 'darnel'. He asks how Jonah was able to survive in the belly of the great fish, withstanding the fish's *virtus digestiva*. Such botanical and zoological questions indicate that rational, scientific curiosity could now be a motive in the study of scripture.

Luther's* theological revolution is marked by the strongest possible repudiation of the Aristotelian tradition in theology, and its replacement by christocentric exegesis. Radicalizing his own Ockhamist tradition, Luther thus separates theology and philosophy, and as a consequence contributes to the emancipation of philosophy from theology. In the seventeenth century, after the disillusioning experience of religious conflict centred on biblical interpretation, this possibility of an autonomous philosophy ('reason') interpreting the Bible on its own terms gradually took shape. In its more radical form, this autonomous philosophy directly questioned the credentials of the alleged biblical revelation.* In its more cautious form, it sought to reinterpret scripture within its own frame of reference.

Spinoza's *Tractatus theologico-politicus* (1670) belongs to the former category. The Jews, Spinoza tells us, do not acknowledge secondary causes, and ascribe all events to God. This is so even in the Bible, and accounts of supposed revelations and miracles* are therefore inaccurate. The purpose of the biblical authors was not to convince the reason of the educated but to move the uneducated to devotion in the most effective possible way. In this way, the old argument which explains anthropomorphisms as divine accommodations to human weakness is radicalized. For those able to live by reason, the Bible is therefore of little value, and it is to be interpreted on a purely historical level. This may well produce startling results; for example, Moses* was not the author of the Pentateuch,* and the other historical books indicate that they were written long after the event (probably by Ezra).

John Locke discusses biblical and theological matters in a more cautious vein but with equally radical implications (*see* **Enlightenment**). In the *Essay Concerning Human Understanding* (1690), he argues that the meaning of the biblical texts is obscure, owing to the gulf between our own language and culture and theirs (3.9). In particular, according to *The Reasonableness of Christianity* (1695), we can no longer accept the timeless validity of the Pauline letters, since they were written in response to particular circumstances. In the posthumous *Paraphrases and Notes on the Epistles of St Paul* (1705–7), Locke seeks to reconstruct those historical circumstances and to make them (rather than Protestant dogma) the interpretative key. Underlying this emphasis on the importance of the historical context may have been the same motivation as Spinoza's: to establish the autonomy of philosophy by refusing to allow the biblical texts any fundamental significance outside the historical circumstances in which they originated. However, the Gospels and Acts retain their significance, for it is in them that the essence of Christianity – belief in Jesus as the messiah* – is to be found.

An approach to biblical interpretation of a less historical and more strictly philosophical kind is to be found in Kant's *Religion Within the Limits of Reason Alone* (1793). For Kant, historical knowledge without any bearing on morality is of no interest, and he therefore demythologizes* biblical doctrine to expose what he takes to be its essential moral content. Thus, God's eternal Son is humanity in its complete moral perfection, an archetypal idea existing in our reason independent of any empirical exemplar. The founding of the kingdom of God* on earth is the victory of the good over the evil principle. This apparently ahistorical exegesis was later to influence the much more historically-conscious theology and exegesis of Ritschl.

Hegel is equally uninterested in 'purely historical' exegesis. He finds in the NT story of the God who became man and who surrendered his life on the cross the disclosure and paradigm of absolute Spirit, which particularizes itself by taking limited form and then allows its particularity to be abolished and absorbed as it comes to consciousness of its own universality. Christianity is thus the absolute and universal religion. This philosophy of religion is at the same time a philosophy of history; Hegel sees history not as a mere chronicle of facts and persons but as the process in which Spirit unfolds itself. This understanding of history as process proved fruitful in F. C. Baur's work on early Christian history, despite the fact that many of his historical conclusions proved to be incorrect. In D. F. Strauss'* *Life of Jesus Critically Examined* (1835), Hegel's interpretation of the Christian 'myth' is invoked in order to show that the essential truth of Christianity may be maintained even when exegesis has shown the Gospel texts to be largely unhistorical. However, the substance of Strauss' exegesis is not significantly affected by Hegel.

Reacting against Hegel's grand synthesis of philosophy, theology and history, Kierkegaard attacked the Hegelian idea of history as a rational process and of Christianity as a phenomenon of world history. There is an 'infinite qualitative difference' between God and the world; the incarnation is the divine 'incognito', a 'paradox' which can only evoke 'offence', and faith is a 'miracle'. The accuracy or otherwise of the historical accounts written by contemporaries is thus of no importance, since the essential fact is not 'historical' in the normal sense of the word. This reinterpretation of Pauline and Lutheran themes played an important part in the theological exegesis of 'dialectical theology', most notably in the commentaries by Karl Barth on Romans ([2]1922) and by Rudolf Bultmann on John (1941).

However, a still more important philosophical influence on Bultmann was Martin Heidegger. In his book, *Being and Time* (1927), Heidegger sought to analyse the structure of human being-in-the-world. He distinguishes between the 'fallenness' of inauthentic existence, characterized by an involvement in the world which is an evasion of care, finitude and death, and the authentic existence in which one freely recognizes and accepts these realities. Heidegger sees the possibility of a transition from the one to the other in the 'call' of conscience, the result of which is a new understanding of oneself. Bultmann argues that this analysis is also implied in the NT (especially in Paul and John). The one significant difference is that there the actual transition to authentic existence only occurs through a divine act – the cross of Christ proclaimed in the kerygma* – and not by means of an immanent anthropological possibility. Bultmann understands Heidegger's view of the attainment of authentic existence as another form of 'salvation by works', but he nevertheless relies heavily on Heidegger's analysis to provide the framework and the justification for his programme of 'demythologizing' or existentialist interpretation. As in the case of Strauss, philosophy leads to an understanding of the essence of Christianity which permits or perhaps requires a radical historical criticism* of the biblical texts.

Biblical interpretation is also affected by recent developments within philosophical hermeneutics. Hans-Georg Gadamer attacks the Enlightenment's myth of the detached, objective observer, and appeals for a new recognition of the linguistic and cultural traditions within which we are inescapably embedded. This makes possible authentic 'conversation' with the classic texts we inherit, which has as its goal the 'fusing' of the two 'horizons' (the text's and our own), rather than the alienation produced by purely historical interpretation. Paul Ricoeur shares many of Gadamer's concerns, but has been more directly involved in questions of biblical interpretation. He argues that myth* is a problem for us not because it is a primitive world-view that we have outgrown (as in Bultmann's demythologizing) but because of our own linguistic impoverishment. Poetic language, including myth, can restore to us the true participation in existence from which it springs. This, he thinks, is one way of understanding the biblical category of 'revelation'.

The influence of philosophy on biblical interpretation has tended to be tangential, and resources for interpretation have generally been drawn either from within the Christian tradition or (since the Enlightenment) from the methods of secular historiography and textual scholarship. The present situation is marked by widespread scepticism about the ability of historical-critical scholarship to do full justice to the biblical texts, and increased awareness of the insights provided by the philosophical tradition might help to clarify this issue.

See also **Deism; Enlightenment; Hermeneutics; Meaning; Mediaeval Interpretation.**

The Cambridge History of the Bible (3 vols), 1963–70; H. Frei, *The Eclipse of Biblical Nar-* *rative*, 1974; K. Froehlich (ed.), *Biblical Interpretation in the Early Church*, 1984; R. M. Grant, *A Short History of the Interpretation of the Bible*, [2] 1984; B. Smalley, *The Study of the Bible in the Middle Ages*, [3] 1983; A. C. Thiselton, *The Two Horizons*, 1980.

FRANCIS WATSON

Poetry, English

It is almost universally acknowledged that the Bible is the most important single source of English literature. While it could justifiably be maintained that until the nineteenth century classical culture – the myths,* legends* and history of ancient Greece and Rome – furnished English poets with as much material for their verse as the Bible, there was no single source from which this material was chosen, so that the exact location of a classical story or allusion is often difficult to trace. From the very beginnings of English poetry, however, the Bible was known and treated as a single source. It had helped to shape the culture of Western Europe long before English emerged as a recognizable language and, despite the fact that it is in itself composed of various kinds of documents, it was, quite simply, the central book of English culture for over a thousand years, transmitted and received as a unity. This does not mean that it was known in its entirety or that its text was handled directly throughout this period, but even before the Reformation* when it moved to occupy an even more important position in life and worship, a large part of its enormous bulk had been incorporated into the liturgy* and was thereby conveyed to the people, or at any rate to those capable of understanding Latin. After the invention of printing and the appearance of translations (from the middle of the fifteenth century) it could be, and increasingly was, read in private more than any other book. So deep has been its penetration that it is impossible to conceive of the formation of the English poetic tradition apart from its influence; impossible to plot the development of English diction without taking into account the impact of the King James Version (1611); and impossible to imagine any poet in any period whose writing could be said to be entirely unaffected by the Bible. These facts put a comprehensive survey of the use of the Bible in English poetry beyond the scope of a brief article: the map will have to be drawn on the largest scale with only the most obvious landmarks indicated. For the easier reading of this map an interpretative key is provided by C. S. Lewis who drew attention to the difference between a 'source' and an 'influence': 'A source gives us things to write about; an influence prompts us to write in a certain way . . . If these terms are accepted we can distinguish the Bible as a source for English literature from the Bible as a literary influence' ('The Literary Impact of the Authorized Version', 1950). Before its translation the Bible can scarcely be called an influence at all: the vocabulary and rhythms of Old and Middle English were quite different from those of the Latin Bible, yet it was quarried extensively by poets as a source for stories, quotations and allusions. By contrast, in the centuries after the Reformation it was used less and less as a source but it was powerful as an influence: the vocabulary and syntax* of the Authorized Version can be seen to be affecting poetic diction in what must often have been a quite unconscious way.

1300–1600. The choice of this starting-date is not arbitrary: the fourteenth century saw the emergence of a language which an intelligent reader in the late twentieth century can recognize as English and read without recourse to a translation. It is also the century of some of the finest English poetry. To a large extent the Bible was mediated, even to the literate and educated, by the liturgy of the church; principally the mass with its Propers, Epistles and Gospels, but also the Breviary with its Psalms, Lessons and Responsories. Furthermore, biblical stories figured prominently in preaching and instruction, often (e.g. in the nativity story) supplemented by apocryphal material of great antiquity. This fact accounts for the kind of biblical material to be found in the poetry of the fourteenth and fifteenth centuries; it is, normally, the more picturesque historical narratives of the OT, the Psalms, the visionary books of Daniel and Revelation, the Song of Solomon and, of course, the four Gospels* (*see* **Biblia Pauperum**).

Many of the anonymous and untitled lyrics and ballads of this era are directly connected to the celebration of the seasons of the church's calendar. A theme, e.g. the nativity, the crucifixion, the resurrection,* is taken up and embroidered. Some have the narrative form of ballads ('The Cherry-tree Carol', 'Who is this that cometh from Edom', 'When that my swete sone/Was thirty winter old'); others are delicate, almost private devotional lyrics ('I saw a fair maiden', 'I saw him with flesh all be-spred'). Many of the loveliest reflect the strength of the cult of the Blessed Virgin Mary and are only tangentially connected to the biblical texts ('Adam lay ibounden', 'I sing of a maiden that is makeles'). It is not surprising to find in this context many echoes of the biblical book the Song of Songs The best-known poet of this period is Geoffrey Chaucer (1343?–1400) and one of the loveliest poems is a hymn in honour of the Virgin, the famous A B C. But biblical allusions

are to be found in his even more famous work *The Canterbury Tales*: The Man of Lawes Tale refers to the stories of Daniel, Jonah, Judith and the exodus; the Song of Songs appears again in The Merchant's Tale; and his long poem *The Parliament of Fowles* has as its background the mediaeval Hexaemeron, a commentary* on the six days of creation* as described in the first chapter of Genesis. The anonymous dream poem *The Pearl* (1350–1380) takes for granted a capacity on the part of the reader to recognize the biblical allusions: to Matthew's parables* of the pearl without price and the vineyard, Paul's* teaching on the body of Christ, and the symbolism* of the book of Revelation; they are an integral part of the poem's imagery and message. *Piers Plowman* (William Langland, 1330?–1420?) is saturated in biblical material: passages often read like poetic sermons expounding biblical teaching (poverty, humility) and the text in all its redactions is larded with quotations from the Latin Bible. However, it is unlikely that many of the quotations which the author has inserted into his text came directly from the text of the Vulgate;* they seem to have been drawn from liturgical sources, most particularly the Breviary, but also the Missal.

From the middle of the fifteenth century onwards, as the ideas of the Renaissance thinkers of France and Italy gained a greater hold on the literary imaginations of English writers, the Bible's importance as a source for poetic subjects and literary allusion began to decline. Classical and mythological motifs took the place that was once occupied by biblical stories and images. Even the greatest poets of this period, William Dunbar (1460–1520?) and Edmund Spenser (1552?–1599), and for that matter William Shakespeare, seem for the purposes of their poetry to have moved away from, if not consciously abandoned, a book which had been of central significance to most of their predecessors. A revival of interest in the Bible as both source and influence was to come at the beginning of the seventeenth century in poetry that was to be given the name 'metaphysical' *.

1600–1800. At the beginning of this period stands the work of those poets who have come to be recognized as some of the most original poetic geniuses in English literature: John Donne (1572–1631), George Herbert (1593–1633), Abraham Cowley (1618–1667), Andrew Marvell (1621–1678), Henry Vaughan (1622–1695); contemporary with them and very different from them, John Milton (1608–1675). It would be no exaggeration to say that a failure on the part of the reader to grasp the significance of the biblical material in the poetry of the 'metaphysicals' – especially Donne and Herbert – results not merely in an inadequate response to the subtlety and richness of the poetry, but sometimes in total incomprehension. The long sequence by Donne, *Holy Sonnets*, begins with six sonnets on incidents in the life of Jesus from nativity to ascension, and the whole sequence employs the biblical imagery of the Lamb, the Temple, the Bride, the Dove, the Blood of Christ, Satan, the Sabbath. In his tribute to Sir Philip Sydney's translation of the psalms there are pointed references to Moses,* Miriam, David* and John the Baptist.* Donne wrote an English 'version' of Jeremiah's Lamentations and the intensely moving 'Hymne to God, my God, in my sickness' is given an epic depth in its allusions to Jerusalem* and Calvary, Japhet, Ham and Shem, Adam* and Christ. In the poetry of George Herbert, the biblical material is even more prevalent and, if anything, even more deftly used. Sometimes there is a complete paraphrase of a biblical text as in 'The God of love my shepherd is' (Ps. 23); sometimes there is an obvious and direct use of biblical imagery as in 'The Bunch of Grapes' (Noah, Canaan, Red Sea, grapes, blood) or 'Decay' (Jacob, Gideon, Moses, Miriam, Lot) or 'The Sacrifice' (Aaron); sometimes the references are so subtly and fleetingly woven into the verse that the echoes, though heard, go unremarked unless they are consciously being sought as in 'The Priesthood' or 'Prayer' (I). Perhaps there is no one whose poetry has been so enriched by the Bible or who has used its material so extensively and to such profound effect. Not even Milton could match Herbert for subtlety and complexity; but then Milton's intention was to write a different kind of poetry, though he too, like his contemporaries, produced biblical paraphrases of psalms. His deliberate choice of classical models for the forms of his most ambitious works, *Paradise Lost, Paradise Regained* and *Samson Agonistes*, to some degree dictated the ways in which he handled biblical material. They are epic representations of biblical narratives, at times relying heavily upon the original, at other moments departing radically, and with superb imagining (as in Satan's hymn to light in *Paradise Lost*), from the usually spare biblical account. But Milton could also adopt a more allusive way with biblical imagery and phrases: the 'Ode on the Morning of Christ's Nativity' is an extraordinary amalgam of material drawn from Genesis, Job, the Psalms, Revelation and numerous classical myths. His more intimate, personal, interior poems show a spirituality nourished by the Bible, e.g. 'The Passion' or the sonnet 'On his Blindness'.

Milton is the last of the major English poets to have allowed the Bible to be a determining force in the creation of his own poetic imagination; and after his death English literature (with one exception) had to wait for two and a half centuries before its texts were to be used with a facility that could equal the poets of the seventeenth century. From the end of the seventeenth century to our own era the use of the Bible directly, unaffectedly and openly passed into the hands of minor, and specifically devotional, poets. One of the most important of these was Isaac Watts (1674–1748), a poet whose gift was the simple, elegant religious lyric. In 1719 he published a selection of metrical psalms, and throughout the rest of his life he produced poems that were rooted in the Calvinist tradition of sobriety, all of which carry strong biblical allusions: 'We are a garden walled around', 'There is a land of pure delight', 'When I survey the wondrous Cross'. The popularity of Watts was exceeded only by that of Charles Wesley (1707–1788) who published over six thousand verses, most of which touch upon biblical stories or contain biblical references. The major poets of the late seventeenth century and early eighteenth century, John Dryden (1631–1700) and Alexander Pope (1688–1744) eschewed the Bible as a primary source for poetry. They reflected the changing values of English society: a turning away from the fervour of religious idealism (though neither was irreligious) and the passionate public debate about dogma and morals. Both were more interested in the possibility of classical mythology as a source for poetry; but Dryden did put the Bible to peculiar use in *Absalom and Achitophel* (1681). In this long satirical poem characters from the OT appear as allegorical* representations of well-known public personalities and the whole biblical story becomes an allegory of his own contemporary England.

Towards the end of the eighteenth century there appeared one of the most controversial figures in the history of English literature, and one who was, perhaps, as steeped in the Bible as Herbert or Milton: William Blake* (1751–1827). He is a poet for whom the Bible was not only a source but also an influence: the vocabulary and cadences of his texts repeat and echo those of the King James Version. But what one notices is the startling originality of the biblical imagery. The famous protest against rationalism, 'Mock on, Mock on, Voltaire, Rousseau' ends with a brilliant image of the exodus: and the metaphor* of the Lamb of God informs the whole sequence of *Songs of Innocence* (1789). The *Prophetic Books* (1797–1804) are apocalyptic* visions, often biblical in origin, and weave the rich symbol of Jerusalem into their private mythology. Much of Blake's work remains unfathomable, but the audacity with which he incorporated biblical material was equalled by no one until the twentieth century when T. S. Eliot wrote *The Waste Land*.

1800–1950. The Romantic era presents us with a picture in which the major poets show little interest in using the Bible as a source and whose poetic style, whether it is the plain, direct manner of William Wordsworth in the *Lyrical Ballads* (1798–1802) or the luxuriant verse of John Keats' 'Endymion' (1818), owes little to the King James Version. It must be remembered, however, that all of these poets wrote at a time in which references to the Bible could be made easily and naturally. England was still assumed to be a Christian country in which the Bible would have an important place in education. Keats' passing reference to 'Ruth amid the alien corn' in his *Ode to a Nightingale* would not have required a footnote to explain it. And the situation had not radically changed by the time their younger contemporaries started publishing their work. Alfred, Lord Tennyson (1809–1892), Robert Browning (1812–1889) and Matthew Arnold (1822–1888) would all have been nourished on the Bible and all made use of it to a greater or less extent. What we do notice in all of them is a typical Victorian scepticism, even in those who seem to be believers. Tennyson's best poems have only the faintest echo of a biblical sensibility, though *In Memoriam* contains a section of four stanzas which vividly tell the story of the raising of Lazarus. There was a sad rejection of religion, and thus of the Bible as a religious book, by Arnold, though a love of its literature remained, and the imagery of the shepherd, the Sea of Galilee and the City of God can all be found in the melancholy 'Rugby Chapel'. Browning used the Bible much more extensively: he not only quoted the words of the King James Version but created some of his most famous quasi-dramatic poems out of biblical themes. 'A Death in the Desert' (a fantasy about John the Evangelist) and 'Saul' are the best examples, and the satirical 'Holy Cross Day' is packed with biblical allusion.

As the century grew older the mood of scepticism deepened, though a knowledge of the Bible could still be expected. Arthur Hugh Clough (1819–1861) depended upon this knowledge for his mocking 24-line poem 'The Latest Decalogue'; and A. E. Housman (1859–1936) conveyed his bleak pessimism in a lyrical verse that occasionally, ironically, recalled biblical themes. 'Easter Hymn', for example, is a meditation on the death of Christ, and 'When Israel out of Egypt came' takes the ideas of Israelite election and the Promised Land as starting points for personal reflection on Fate.

The First World War stimulated some poetry which, in accordance with one aspect of the mood of that period of highly wrought emotion, turned to the Bible for material. One of the most moving poems, 'The Parable of the Old Man and the Young' by Wilfred Owen, takes its place in a tradition of exegesis* reaching back, in both Jewish and Christian circles, to the start of the Christian era, and in Judaism perhaps even earlier. It retells the story of the near-sacrifice of Isaac recounted in Gen. 22 (*see* **Aqedah**), but gives it a wholly new twist: the angel tells Abraham* not to slay his son, but to 'offer the Ram of Pride' instead.

But the old man would not so, but slew his son,
And half the seed of Europe, one by one.

There are only two other major modern poets who incorporate biblical material into their work with a facility that is the equal of the mediaeval poets and those of the early seventeenth century: D. H. Lawrence (1885–1930) and T. S. Eliot (1888–1965). Lawrence's attitude to Christianity was ambiguous: he rejected much that was conventionally Christian, yet he raised religious issues and used religious language again and again in both his prose and his poetry. Only a few examples may be cited: the sequence of poems on the four evangelists,* 'Almond Blossom', a relatively early poem at the centre of which is a daring conceit which involves the almond tree, the tree of the cross and the garden of Gethsemane, many of the verses in *Pansies, More Pansies* and *Late Poems*. Sometimes the poetry is a passionate protest against a biblical concept, as in 'Shedding of Blood', 'Lucifer', 'Commandments' and 'Love Thy Neighbour'; at other times it is an equally passionate attempt to wrest a new and personal meaning out of a biblical text: 'The Hands of God', 'Abysmal Immortality' and, most remarkable of all, 'Lord's Prayer',* in which the original text is 'broken' so that its phrases can be woven into a complex pattern of religious invocation and nature imagery. And mention must be made of one of his most famous poems, 'Song of a Man who has come through', a tender and courageous lyric which makes its impact only when the reader recognizes the allusion to the angels of Gen. 18.

Only three years separate the birth dates of D. H. Lawrence and T. S. Eliot, yet the contrast between the two men, both as human beings and as creative artists, could hardly be more pronounced. Lawrence was raised in a mining community with a strong Nonconformist tradition; Eliot came from a highly-educated, sophisticated Unitarian family. To Lawrence the Bible retained much of its traditional power; its teachings might be denounced and rejected but it still occupied a place of central significance in what was perceived to be English culture. To Eliot, before 1927, it was simply one of the many documents that had been inherited as part of Western European culture, a 'book' which could be used as one used any other. The early poems contain only passing references to biblical material: the story of Lazarus in 'The Love Song of J. Alfred Prufrock', a passage from Revelation in 'Aunt Helen', the betrayal of Jesus Christ in 'Gerontion'; and 'The Hippopotamus' has an epigraph that is taken from the fourth chapter of the Epistle to the Colossians. Then in 1922 Eliot's most original creation appeared, *The Waste Land*; and in this extraordinary mosaic of allusion and quotation, the biblical references acquired far greater significance. They are not more obvious in the texture of the verse, but they are used to more telling effect: Ezekiel and Ecclesiastes in Part I, Psalm 137 in Part III, and Luke's Gospel in Part V. A few years later specific biblical stories became the subject of entire poems, 'The Journey of the Magi' and 'A Song for Simeon'. Even a poem with a political subject, 'Difficulties of a Statesman', has a repeated biblical phrase (Isa. 40.6) as a refrain. 'Ash Wednesday' is rich in biblical imagery: Part II contains allusions to I Kings, Ezekiel, Ecclesiastes and the Song of Songs; Part V begins with a pattern of puns on 'word', 'Word' and 'world'. It was to be expected that the choruses from his 'pageant' *The Rock* would contain much biblical material, and that its imagery would be, on the whole, disappointingly conventional. In what is, perhaps, Eliot's greatest achievement, *Four Quartets*, biblical material is used sparingly: there is a brief reminder of Eccles. 3 at the beginning of 'East Coker', and the fourth section of that same Quartet is constructed on the stories of the fall of Adam and the death of Christ; but the Bible is a submerged force in the poetry; there is only the sense of it being present as one of the foundations of the Christian faith which is at the centre of this poem's vision.

See also **Hymnody; Metaphysical Poets; Translations (to the KJV)**.

D. Davie, *A Gathered Church*, 1978; A. Fowler, *A History of English Literature*, 1987; D. C. Fowler, *The Bible in Middle English Literature*, 1984; T. R. Henn, *The Bible as Literature*, 1970; C. S. Lewis, 'The Literary Impact of the Authorized Version' in *They Asked for a Paper*, 1956; P. Levi, Introduction to *The Penguin Book of English Christian Verse*, 1984.

BRIAN HORNE

Poetry, Hebrew

In some translations* of the Bible and even in some printed editions of the Hebrew text there is no indication that much of the OT is in verse. While the Psalms have always been considered to be poetry, as has Proverbs, it is now evident that nearly all the prophetic* books are also in verse. This includes most of Isaiah, large sections of Jeremiah and Ezekiel, almost all of Hosea, and so on. Whether or not the non-narrative parts of the OT (that is, excluding the Pentateuch,* Joshua to Kings, Chronicles, Ezra–Nehemiah and Esther) are verse has been a matter of debate since at least the first century BC. Now that our models are not classical Greek and Latin verse but the poetic traditions of the Ancient Near East* the debate, in essence, has been resolved. Hebrew poetry is very like the poetry of ancient Syria (written in Ugaritic* on clay tablets dating to approximately the fourteenth century BC) and not unlike Assyrian and Babylonian verse. The surprising aspect of the OT now is why the narrative sections are not in verse; the bulk of Ugaritic literature, for instance, is narrative verse.

Scholars have isolated several fragments of poetry in the prose books (e.g. Ex. 16.12; Num. 14.2) and there are also complete poems (Gen. 49; Deut. 32 and 33; Judg. 5; etc.). Generally speaking, however, the division between books in verse and books in prose is clear, even allowing for the short passages identified as verse. It follows, therefore, that passages and books in verse cannot be properly understood if they are read simply as prose. 'In interpreting the prophetic texts we need to make allowance for the prophets' use of exalted and poetic language ... and their use of symbols,* metaphors* and ambiguous diction' (J. Lindblom, *Prophecy in Ancient Israel*, 1962, p. 363). In other words, too literal* an interpretation is misguided; poetry must be read and understood on its own terms.

Here only a brief indication can be given of how recognizing poetic devices and techniques can lead to correct interpretation. Special attention will be paid to recent developments, some still controversial, since they are not all included in the available textbooks. Awareness of such devices, techniques and structural* patterns, many of which have come to light from comparison with Ancient Near Eastern verse, is significant, but always within the overall evaluation of a poem or segment of verse. While it is now accepted that parallelism is fundamental to Hebrew poetry, the usual classification of parallelism as synonymous, antithetic or synthetic is far from accurate or complete. Here some additional comments will be made on parallelism and other topics and several texts will be discussed by way of illustration.

It is now evident that often synonymous

parallelism between consecutive lines in a couplet is really parallelism of greater precision: the B-line specifies the A-line in some way. In Job 7.13 the second line 'My bed will ease my complaint' is narrower in meaning than the first: 'If I say "My couch will comfort me"'. Similarly, Ezek. 6.6; Ps. 34.13; etc. In such cases the poet is not merely repeating himself in different words but correcting his focus.

In some parallel word-pairs, such as the numerical pairings 'seven'//'eight', the focus is on only one of these numbers. In Job 5.19, 'He will deliver you from six troubles/in seven, there shall no evil touch you', 'seven' symbolizes any kind of trouble and the accompanying 'six' is unimportant. The same applies to 'mother' in Prov. 4.3 where matching 'father' (in the first line) is the really significant term.

Another type of parallelism explains the difficult verse Job 38.30. If the final verbs are understood as interchanged then the couplet makes sense: 'Like a stone the waters become hidden/and the surface of the deep is frozen' (contrast RSV). First water freezes, then the surface is obscured from view. This kind of switch, called metathetic parallelism, also explains Ps. 35.7; Mic. 2.1; Isa. 17.5; etc.

Besides antithetic parallelism (e.g. Prov. 12.10), antithesis is also effective on a large scale. Judg. 5.2–31, which at first reading appears to be an impressionistic composition, is in reality a carefully structured series of antitheses (powerful God/miserable people; the willing and unwilling tribes; curse and blessing; and the final contrast: Jael victorious/ Sisera's mother vainly awaiting victory), closed by a summary couplet in antithetic parallelism: 'So perish all your enemies, O Yahweh/but may your friends be like the emergence of the sun at its strongest.' See also Jer. 10.2–16 and Ps. 73.

A recent advance in techniques of interpretation is the discovery of word-pairs common to the OT and to Ancient Near Eastern literature. One such is 'to recover'//'to get up' in Hos. 6.2. There it refers neither to covenant* renewal nor to resurrection* but to healing, since the same word pair in Babylonian also denotes healing.

Some poems are set out as acrostics, each of the 22 lines or sets of lines beginning with a different letter of the alphabet. One purpose of such poems was to include everything 'from aleph to tau' (the first and final letters of the Hebrew alphabet). This is particularly evident in Ps. 119 where the psalmist is demonstrating how he observes God's law in everything he does, in every way and at all times. Another purpose may have been to impose some sort of order on seemingly disparate elements. An additional implication is that acrostic poems (Pss. 9–10; 25; 34; Lam. 1–4; etc.) should be interpreted as complete units and not as mere compilations.

In chiasmus a sequence (A B C . . .) is followed by the same sequence in reverse (. . . C B A) focussing attention on the central element. For example, chiastic patterning shows the core of Ps. 26 to be vv. 6–8 which describe the officiant 'going round' Yahweh's altar, which in turn provides the setting (the temple) and the genre* (private prayer). Also, it is at the centre of his chiastic prologue (Job 32.6– 10) that Elihu makes the crucial observation that wisdom comes from inspiration and is not merely the concomitant of age.

In one form of word-play the same word is repeated, the second time with a different meaning, e.g. Job 11.7 'Can you understand (mṣ) the designs of God/or can you attain (mṣ) the perfection of Shadday?' The second line goes beyond the first: Job cannot even grasp the divine plan let alone reach divine perfection. Elsewhere, repetition is not simply monotonous, but highlights the key word of a poem, for instance, 'land' in Jer. 2.6–7.

Nahum 2.14, 'I will burn your chariots in smoke/and the sword will devour your "young lions"', comes in the context of war, and so a literal meaning for 'young lions' must be excluded. The expression is metaphorical for 'warriors' (cf. 2.3). The same applies to 'the beast of the reeds' and 'the herd of bulls with the calves of the peoples' (Ps. 68.31 EVV 30), which evidently refer to Israel's enemies. 'Woe to . . . the notable men at the head of the nations . . . they shall now be at the head of those going into exile' (Amos 6.1–7). The ironic* aspect of the mock-lamentation – those first in rank will be the first to go into exile – is reinforced by the mention of 'the first-class perfumes' (v. 6) which they used.

Form cannot be dissociated from content, as these examples show, and appreciation of poetic technique can provide crucial clues to the correct interpretation of passages in verse.

See also **Paranomasia; Ugarit.**

L. Alonso Schökel, *A Manual of Hebrew Poetics*, 1988; R. Alter, *The Art of Biblical Poetry*, 1985; A. Berlin, *The Dynamics of Biblical Parallelism*, 1985; E. R. Follis (ed.), *Directions in Biblical Hebrew Poetry*, 1987; J. L. Kugel, *The Idea of Biblical Poetry. Parallelism and Its History*, 1981; W. G. E. Watson, *Classical Hebrew Poetry: A Guide to its Techniques*, ² 1986.

WILFRED G. E. WATSON

Proof Texts

Throughout the history of the church the Bible has been quoted as the primary authority in connection with doctrine, ethics* and spirituality. It is common to make a statement and then adduce a text of scripture in support of it. Thus in the fourth-century Arian controversy on the divinity of Christ, John 14.28, 'The Father is greater than I', was a key text. So also modern discussions among Christians about marriage after divorce constantly refer to the sayings attributed to Jesus in Matt. 5.32 and Mark 10.2–12. Within the NT itself, Paul* quotes Deut. 25.4 in I Cor. 9.9, 'You shall not muzzle an ox when it is treading out the grain,' as authority for the recognized practice of paying expenses to preachers on mission (cf. I Tim. 5.18).

Proof texts are distinguished from *testimonia** in that the latter belong to a scriptural argument in which OT prophecies* are claimed to be fulfilled in Jesus and his saving work. Proof texts do not necessarily entail this idea of fulfilment, but are chosen because they are felt to be relevant to the matter under consideration. Paul's choice of Deut. 25.4 hardly seems relevant to his purpose, but he explains that, in including it in the Law, God must have intended it to be understood metaphorically.* Thus the text is taken out of context and applied arbitrarily to an issue which is not covered in the OT laws. It is obvious that such use of scripture is open to abuse.

The basis of this use of scripture is the authority* of the Bible. The process of canonization* of the Hebrew scriptures had already advanced sufficiently to make the Law central to Jewish self-definition and normative for Jewish life. A similar process took place in the formation of the NT, making the OT and the NT together normative for Christians. One result of canonization was a high view of the inspiration* of scripture. This gave it an oracular* quality as the Word of God* himself. The early Fathers, especially in the Alexandrian* school of exegesis,* held that all scripture has a divine or spiritual* meaning, even if the surface meaning appears incomprehensible or unworthy. Following Jewish traditions in Alexandria they used allegorical* exegesis to obtain the spiritual meaning. Paul's use of Deut. 25.4 is in line with this tradition.

Christian use of proof texts is comparable to rabbinic* practice with regard to law. In the Mishnah and the Talmud* the laws of the Pentateuch* are cited as precedents for halakhic rulings on matters which are not covered by the Law itself. Various principles of interpretation were developed, whereby a ruling might be deduced from a text. A well-known example is *qal wa-ḥomer* (light and heavy), i.e. the *a fortiori* argument, often employed in the NT (e.g. John 10.34–36). Guide lines for Christians were provided by the *Rules of Tyconius* (AD 382). By modern standards these methods often do not pay sufficient attention to the meaning of the text in its context.

Contextual understanding was hindered by the assumption, universal in the patristic period and the Middle Ages, that scripture and the church's tradition of faith and practice are always in agreement when rightly understood. In the West, the Reformation* raised the authority of scripture to a new eminence by making it the sole source of divine knowledge, leading to ideas of infallibility and verbal* inerrancy. The Reformation churches sought to rebuild church life in conformity with the NT, and so took seriously the literal meaning* of scripture. The endless controversies and splitting of sects which that entailed can be attributed at least partly to the impossibility of reaching agreement on the interpretation of crucial but highly disputed texts. This is reflected in the vernacular translations* of the Bible at this time. Thus in the KJV *presbuteros* in the NT is rendered not 'priest' but 'elder' to exclude the mediaeval interpretation.* When the Bible is very highly valued as the inspired Word of God, people easily deceive themselves into thinking that they have divine warrant for what are really arbitrarily chosen interpretations based on a sectarian position.

Modern scholarship has questioned the concepts of infallibility and verbal inerrancy at the same time as seeking to maintain the authority of the Bible as the collection of books which are central and normative for Christian self-understanding. As such the Bible remains a primary reference-point and source of proof texts. But these must be chosen responsibly, with care to determine the meaning of the text and to respect the context. Many false applications of scripture in the past were due to ignorance. Today as a result of critical scholarship there is less excuse for this. Appeals to the teaching of Jesus or of Paul can be made on an informed basis. The limits of the application of scripture can and should be recognized. Jesus' teaching on divorce has to be seen in the light of the broader scope of his teachings in the context of Jewish discussion of the question in the NT era. To take a single text out of his teaching on the subject and to apply it to the current situation without more ado is an illegitimate procedure. Paul's use of Deut. 25.4 to warrant payment of missionaries can be recognized as a telling metaphor, but it has no probative force because it rests on dubious exegesis: 'Is it for oxen that God is concerned? Does he not speak entirely for our sake?' (I Cor. 9.9f.). Animal lovers are unlikely to accept Paul's presupposition, which in any case involves rejection of the literal sense.

D. H. Kelsey, *The Uses of Scripture in Recent Theology*, 1975; D. E. Nineham, *The Use and Abuse of the Bible*, 1976; B. Vawter, *Biblical Inspiration*, 1972.

BARNABAS LINDARS, SSF

Prophets and Prophecy

1. *Traditional interpretations.* Before the rise of biblical criticism,* the prophets of the OT were evaluated very differently in Jewish and in Christian tradition. Jewish assessment of the prophets was closely linked to an understanding of scripture in which the Torah was central, so that the prophetic books were important chiefly for their value as commentary* on Torah (*see* **Pentateuch**). The prophets were felt to provide guidance in interpreting the ethical* injunctions of the legal system. A prophet was thus traditionally seen as having the same function as a rabbi,* though it was recognized that the degree of divine inspiration possessed by the biblical prophets was greater than that of later teachers. In Christianity the reading of the prophetic books, from the NT onwards, was deeply influenced by the Christian 'argument from prophecy'. In this, the predictive powers of the prophets were highlighted. They were believed to have foreseen the events of the age of salvation, and especially the coming of the messiah,* which Christians believed had now arrived with the birth, death, and resurrection* of Jesus Christ. Accordingly Christians came to value the prophetic portions of the OT above the other parts, but in the process to read them quite differently from Jews. So great was the shift that Christians came to read much of the Torah itself in prophetic terms.

Both readings of the prophets, the ethical and the eschatological,* have genuine roots in the prophetic books themselves. They are found in combination, for example, at the end of the last of the minor prophets, in Mal. 4.4–6 (Hebrew 3.22–24). This passage admonishes the reader to obey the law, and looks forward to the return of Elijah at the end-time, but expects his role at that time to be one of moral exhortation: 'Remember the law of my servant Moses, the statutes and ordinances that I commanded him at Horeb for all Israel. Behold, I will send you Elijah the prophet before the great and terrible day of the Lord comes. And he will turn the hearts of fathers to their children and the hearts of children to their fathers, lest I come and smite the land with a curse.'

A simple reading of the prophetic books, along with the stories of prophetic activity in the historical books, shows that those who compiled the OT thought of prophets as charged with both types of message. In the books of Samuel and Kings, as well as in the (largely deuteronomistic*) narrative sections of Isaiah and Jeremiah, prophecy is presented as an institution which existed in Israel from the time of Moses* onwards. Men and women were inspired by the Spirit of Yahweh to utter reliable predictions of future events, and to exhort and warn the people to repent and remain loyal to him. The 'classical' prophets (i.e. those who have left books bearing their names) are conceived by the editors of the OT after the same model, as bearers of a tradition that goes back to Moses himself. Prophets are seen as people raised up by God to monitor his people's progress (or decline) in obedience, and to strive to keep the nation on the course originally intended by him for its good. Many of them are presented as state officials (for example, Huldah in II Kings 22.14–20), though others (such as Elijah) are clearly seen to have opposed the king. Their importance in the history of Israel is emphasized even more in the writings of the Chronicler than in the Deuteronomistic History; and Ben Sira includes them as major characters in his list of the great heroes of Israel (Ecclus. 44–49).

2. *Critical evaluation.* A major shift in the understanding of biblical prophecy came through the work of Julius Wellhausen (1844–1918) and Bernhard Duhm* (1847–1928). Against the traditional Christian understanding of the prophets as those who predicted the messianic age, Wellhausen and Duhm saw them as concerned with the needs of their immediate contemporaries. The future into which the prophets looked was not the distant future, but the very near future – the future that would arise directly from Yahweh's reaction to the people's present sins. There was no concern to deny in principle that prophets could have delivered a message about more remote times; but on the basis of an exact study of the books of the classical prophets, it was suggested that their words made far more sense if seen as directed to contemporary society. This resulted in some redatings of prophetic collections, most obviously the (now widely accepted) proposal that Isa. 40–66 could not be the work of the eighth-century prophet Isaiah, but must come from a prophet living no earlier than the Babylonian Exile of the sixth century. But it also directed attention to the moral content of the prophets' message, which Christian exegesis,* in its concern with messianic prediction, had somewhat neglected.

Wellhausen remained convinced that the prophets' moral teaching was logically secondary to their predictions of immediate doom on the nation. Having become convinced that Yahweh was about to intervene in judgment, the prophets sought to justify this foreboding by looking to the sins of the people as its sufficient cause. Duhm was more inclined to see the moral condemnation of Israel as equally primary in the prophets' thinking, and from him derives a tradition in OT scholarship of seeing the prophets more as moral and political analysts of society than as clairvoyants. In some ways this has meant a return to something nearer the traditional Jewish reading of the prophets, but with the difference that Duhm and those who followed him did not see the prophets' moral teaching as deriving from Israel's legal traditions. The keynote of the great prophets' message, on his view, was not moral teaching so much as moral outrage. This made the prophets far more uncomfortable figures than the designation of them as 'teachers of Torah' would imply, and the conventional Jewish reading began to look like a domestication of them.

For both Duhm and Wellhausen, the prophets did not merely hand on an existing moral tradition, but were in many ways the founders of the high ethical monotheism which would come to characterize Judaism and thence Christianity. Their conviction that the God of Israel was about to intervene decisively in history to punish his sinful people made them sensitive, as no one in Israel before had been, to the moral obligations incumbent on the chosen people of God. It is from them that the moral teaching eventually codified in short summaries such as the Ten Commandments (and in due time in the Pentateuch* as a whole) ultimately derived. This impression was greatly strengthened by Wellhausen's demonstration that the Priestly (P) material in the Pentateuch, containing much of Israel's distinctive ethical code, was in any case later than the work of the eighth- and seventhcentury prophets.

Through the work of Wellhausen and Duhm there arose an image of the prophets of Israel no longer as cogs in a machine – transmitters of a tradition they neither founded nor transformed – but as highly individual and creative figures, radically changing the whole religious landscape of their day. Through them the religion of Israel developed into 'ethical monotheism', and was changed from a 'natural' bond between Yahweh and his people into a contractual relationship which depended on unswerving obedience to the Law. Wellhausen saw this as a deeply ambiguous development. The prophets' greatness was to introduce a high ethical idealism into Israel which the earthier tradition of preexilic times had not known; yet their pathos was that they sowed the seeds of moralism which would eventually grow into the religion of the Pharisees,* which he viewed as an artificial and obsessive legalism rightly condemned by Jesus.

But OT scholars in general did not share this ambivalence, and in the early years of the twentieth century the central and beneficial importance of the prophets in the growth of Israel's faith was taken for granted. Among

the effects of this high view of the great 'classical' prophets of the eighth and seventh centuries (Amos, Hosea, Isaiah, Micah, and Jeremiah) was a certain coolness towards both their predecessors – the prophets of court and sanctuary whose deeds are recorded in Samuel and Kings – and their successors, exilic and post-exilic figures such as Ezekiel, Haggai, Zechariah, and Joel, who seemed in many ways a throwback to a more primitive model of prophecy, preachers of 'smooth things' to a complacent people.

There was also a consequence in the literary sphere: since what mattered was the original prophets as people, rather than the literary works which bore their name, much importance was attributed to recovering their original message by 'deleting' from the books all later additions by disciples of the prophets or scribal* editors of their works. Whereas in the study of other OT books, such as the Pentateuch or the wisdom* literature, equal weight was given to all strata of whatever date, in the study of the prophetic collections there was a tendency to dismiss as of small account anything that could be shown to postdate the prophet whose name the book bore – except where (as in the case of Isa. 40–66) it was possible to detect a second or third equally impressive prophetic genius behind the additional material. The criticism sometimes levelled nowadays at scholarship of the early twentieth century, that it was too concerned for the 'original' core of OT books and dismissive of secondary material, is valid chiefly as a comment on the study of the prophetic literature. It may be fair to see a link with the Romantic ideal of the lone poetic genius, and some have thought that Wellhausen and Duhm were excessively influenced by this model.

3. *Some issues in modern study.* Modern biblical scholarship has never reversed the trend begun by Wellhausen and Duhm of seeing the prophets as central to the development of Israel's life and theology. Nevertheless, scarcely one stone remains on another of the edifice they constructed. This can be illustrated by examining a number of issues that have occupied scholars during the twentieth century.

Through the work of Hermann Gunkel (1862–1932) form criticism* came to be applied to the oracles* of the classical prophets. Form criticism does not in itself represent a challenge to the startling uniqueness attributed to the prophets by Wellhausen and Duhm; but its concentration on the typical and conventional in prophetic utterance has tended to encourage a view of the classical prophets as part of a larger tradition, using forms of speech that were already established before the eighth century and which, there

fore, they shared with the 'institutional' prophets who worked at cultic* centres or were
employed by kings.* The contrast between
institutional and 'independent' prophets,
which was important in early critical studies
of the prophets, has become blurred in the
wake of form-critical approaches. Whereas in
the late nineteenth century it was held that
prophets such as Elijah or Amos were so
remarkable and unusual that they could share
the name 'prophet' with state clairvoyants
only by straining language to the limits, form
critics have tended to see the difference as at
most one of degree. Between the wars, some
scholars were so impressed by the use made
by the classical prophets of cultic forms of
speech, that they argued for seeing them as
actual cultic officials. More recently it has
been pointed out that the classical prophets
do in general use forms of speech borrowed
from non-prophetic spheres – Amos, for example, uses the lament (5.2), Isaiah the popular song (5.1–7) – but this is a literary device,
rather than an indication that they themselves
belonged to the sphere in question. Nevertheless, form-critical research has severely
reduced the impression of the classical prophets as wholly original geniuses which prevailed at the beginning of this century.

For Wellhausen, as we have seen, the prophets were the fountain-head of Israel's ethical
tradition. But in the years that followed the
work done by Martin Noth and Gerhard von
Rad on the religious life of early Israel, it
came to be thought that many of their ethical
ideas, especially that of the covenant* between
Israel and Yahweh, were far older than the
eighth century, and genuinely went back to
the earliest years of the Israelite nation. According to Noth's theory, Israel under the
judges had been an 'amphictyony' or league
of twelve tribes, whose common bond was the
covenant with its ethical stipulations. Of this
covenant the prophets were the guardians and
transmitters, not the inventors. Prophecy as
an office whose function was to maintain the
covenant of Yahweh with his people accordingly went back, if not indeed to Moses, then
at least to the time before Saul. This necessarily reduced the impression of originality in the
great classical prophets, who now once more
seemed to be links in a chain not of their own
making. It is only in the last decade or so,
when the theory of an amphictyony has been
widely abandoned, that scholars have again
begun to stress the creative influence of the
classical prophets, and to ask whether Wellhausen and Duhm may not in this respect
have been right after all.

The impression that the classical prophets
enjoyed a direct experience of divine inspiration unlike anyone before or since has had

to be modified in the light of comparative
studies of both ancient and modern societies,
which have shown that 'ecstatic' experience is
a common phenomenon and does not of itself
argue for the uniqueness of the Hebrew prophets. At the same time, biblical scholars have
been concerned to examine in more detail
possible ways in which the OT prophets are
distinctive, and have produced some sophisticated theories to distinguish genuinely prophetic 'ecstasy' from that of mystics, dervishes,
and shamans in other religious systems. The
fact that unusual psychic states such as seem
to characterize the 'institutional' prophets of
the books of Kings recur in Ezekiel and in
some apocalyptic* writings has led many, however, to feel that the intervening classical prophets probably also belong in reality to the
same world of experience, rather than being
so radically distinctive as on Duhm's model.

Comparative study of other Ancient Near
Eastern* cultures has also been important
in attempting to identify the social location
of the great prophets. Nineteenth-century
scholars tended to speak as though they belonged to no definable social category, but
were wholly unique, 'outsiders' to every kind
of institution; but modern sociological* theory
finds the idea of someone with no social location or role hard to accept, and has encouraged biblical scholars to discover what
roles may have been available in ancient societies that could offer analogies to the Hebrew
prophets. Texts from Mari in particular have
revealed that court prophets were a common
phenomenon in the ancient world, and that
prophets who uttered an uncompromising and
unwelcome message of impending judgment
were not necessarily so unparalleled as older
scholars supposed.

Finally, the idea that prophecy declined
sharply after the Exile, as part of the steady
slide into legalism that was supposed to have
characterized the religion of the post-exilic
age, has also been radically revised. For one
thing, this is now recognized to be a travesty
of the character of Second Temple Judaism;
for another, it is not clear that prophecy
changed in any particularly important way,
though it came to use different modes of expression over the course of time. One of the
most striking changes in the scholarly climate
in recent years has been the fresh appreciation
of apocalyptic, and with this a willingness to
recognize that the apocalyptists can be seen as
true heirs of the classical prophets. Their style
and their historical context are vastly different, but in their concern to speak to their
contemporaries of God's imminent intervention in human affairs they and the prophets
are at one. Influential interpretations of apocalyptic present it as a radical reaction to the

religious 'establishment' of its day, just as the prophetic movement had been a reaction against the pretensions of the pre-exilic kings. Even if Judaism did have strains of thought that can be called 'legalistic', in apocalyptic it also possessed a strong protest movement against any attempt to quench the Spirit; and so the classical prophets were not without true heirs in the post-exilic age.

Thus the late nineteenth-century consensus about prophecy has broken up in subsequent years. Most scholars would now agree that it was too simple, though it transformed OT studies, especially by its stress on the originality of the classical prophets and their priority to the Torah. The prophets have remained a subject of primary interest, especially to Christian OT scholars.

In recent years the trend towards readings of the 'final form' of the OT text has led to attempts to interpret the prophetic books as they stand, rather than looking behind them for the personalities and theology of the original prophets themselves. Thus there has been an interest, for the first time since the rise of biblical criticism, in the book of Isaiah as a whole, ignoring (though not denying the validity of) the division into three sections which had been normal in critical scholarship. Some scholars are even beginning to be interested in larger collections, such as the Book of the Twelve (treated as a single work in the Hebrew Bible), or in the Prophets as a whole. Such developments have been encouraged by the growth of canonical criticism,* which is interested in the shaping effect of the canonizing process on older biblical materials.

See also **Ethics (Old Testament); German Old Testament Scholarship.**

J. Blenkinsopp, *A History of Prophecy in Israel. From the Settlement in the Land to the Hellenistic Period,* 1984; R. E. Clements, *Prophecy and Tradition,* 1975; id., 'Patterns in the Prophetic Canon' in G. W. Coats and B. O. Long (eds), *Canon and Authority,* 1977, pp. 42–55; J. Lindblom, *Prophecy in Ancient Israel,* 1962; E. W. Nicholson, *God and his People,* 1986; C. Westermann, *Basic Forms of Prophetic Speech,* 1967; R. R. Wilson, *Prophecy and Society in Ancient Israel,* 1980.

JOHN BARTON

Proverbs

The earliest and most important literary deposit of Israelite wisdom, Proverbs consists of several collections of sayings (chs 1–9; 10–22.16; 22.17–24.22; 24.23–34; 25–29; 30; 31.1–9; 31.10–31) compiled at different times before they were gradually brought together to form the book. Its composition was probably not completed until the post-exilic period. The attribution of the book to Solomon (1.1) reflects more royal patronage of wisdom, together with the growing tradition of Solomon as the wise man *par excellence*, and less actual authorship. In its final form, Proverbs presents itself as an educational programme designed to teach young men how to live wisely (1.2–6). It contains three main kinds of material: short proverbial sayings (chiefly in chs 10–31); longer discourses in which a 'father' (teacher) gives instructions to his 'son' (pupil) (chs 1–9; 22.17–24.22); and speeches by personified Wisdom (1.20–33; 8.1–9.6).

During the nineteenth century, Proverbs was commonly viewed as a kind of philosophical piety applying the moral principles of Israel's religion to everyday life. Towards the end of the century, in the wake of Wellhausen's theory of Israel's religious development, it came to be interpreted by some scholars more particularly as an application of the moral principles proclaimed by the great prophets. This appeared to account for the mundane character of the sayings in chs 10–31 set beside the strongly religious tone of chs 1–9, and for the emphasis on divine retribution. It also gave clear definition to the place of Proverbs within Israel's religious development. However, closer study of the literary forms employed by Proverbs and the discovery of similar wisdom* literature from Egypt* and Mesopotamia soon made it necessary to reassess such views of Proverbs. Most notable was the discovery of the Egyptian *Instruction of Amenemopet,* whose thirty chapters of moral instructions were adapted, in part, by an Israelite sage to produce the 'thirty' sayings in 22.17–24.22. It thus became clear that the beginnings of Israel's wisdom pre-dated the prophets,* and that it had its own distinctive character and its own specific setting within early Israelite life and society as part of a wider, international pursuit of wisdom. The main problems in the interpretation of the book came to centre on the questions concerning the setting and character of the wisdom it represents.

The question of the original setting of wisdom has been widely debated. Some scholars have emphasized the book's many parallels in form and content with Egyptian school texts used for the education of royal princes and state officials, and have argued that Israelite wisdom literature had its origins in court schools established during the early monarchic period to meet the demands for a well-trained administration. Other have emphasized the book's connections with the ethos of early Israelite law, and believe that the wisdom literature originated within the sphere of the ancient Israelite family and clan. It seems best to allow for a variety of sources and settings for wisdom literature within Israelite life. R. E. Murphy points to three possible settings: the family or tribe, the court school, and the post-exilic scribal* school. To these R. B. Y. Scott adds three other possible sources for wisdom sayings: proverbial folk wisdom, the advice of elders and counsellors, and the intellectual curiosity or moral concern of individuals.

The character of wisdom in Proverbs has proved to be equally debatable. Although there is general agreement that early Israelite wisdom is best represented by the proverbial sayings in chs 10–31, and that it derives from observation of and reflection upon the world around and human life, different views are held concerning the goal of this experiential wisdom and its relation to the religious elements found most especially in chs 1–9.

Zimmerli believes that wisdom had its centre of gravity in man and his well-being. Its central question was: 'what is good for man?' The answer wisdom gave carried no authority beyond its power to persuade: its admonitions did not command, but advised; leaving man free to ponder and decide. What commended them was their clear statement of the consequences of either following or ignoring their counsel as proven by experience. Not only mundane matters, but also religion was evaluated from this standpoint. Consequently, religious values such as fear of the Lord and trusting in God were recommended to man on the basis of the benefit they bring him, without appeal to divine authority; while by rewarding the righteous and punishing the wicked God simply did what the wise expected him to do from their observation of experience. In Zimmerli's view, therefore, the wisdom of Proverbs is utilitarian and non-authoritarian in character. From this single standpoint the book represents a total disposition towards life which embraces equally the religious and the mundane. At a later stage, the wise found legitimation for this approach to life in the doctrine of creation, with man authorized by God to 'go out' and master the world and human life (Gen. 1.28).

McKane is in basic agreement with Zimmerli's characterization of Israel's mundane wisdom as man-centred and utilitarian, though he prefers to lay greater stress on the personal authority of the wisdom teacher. However, he does not think that the mundane and the religious elements in Proverbs can be embraced within a single system of wisdom. He therefore draws a sharp distinction between an old mundane wisdom and a later theological wisdom of an entirely different kind. Israel's mundane wisdom was indebted to foreign (chiefly Egyptian) models, and took the form of a rigorous intellectual discipline designed to teach the skills required for successful living. The intellectual values and procedural skills it inculcated paid scant regard to moral or religious considerations. Its ethos was therefore quite alien to Israel's religious faith. Nevertheless, in the course of time, and chiefly under prophetic criticism of their self-sufficiency, the wise came to terms with religious faith and brought their wisdom into relation with it. This resulted in a radical re-interpretation of old wisdom and its language, so that it ceased to be an intellectual discipline and became a discipline in religious piety inculcating reverence for and submission to God. McKane holds that this process of reinterpretation is particularly evident in chs 1–9, but that many proverbial sayings in chs 10–31 also represent a religious reinterpretation of the old wisdom.

Many scholars reject the view that Israel's early wisdom was entirely mundane and utilitarian, and alien to Israel's religious faith. Of importance here has been the contention that underlying Israel's wisdom is a concept of 'order' discernible both in the natural world and in human society – a concept for which support has been found in the significance of *maat*, 'right', 'order', in Egyptian wisdom texts. Thus von Rad argues that the goal of Israel's empirical wisdom was to discover the laws of this 'world order' for human life and society so that human beings could live their lives in harmony with it. An essential aspect of the order was the intimate connection between good and evil deeds and their beneficial or harmful consequences. By living in conformity with the order, its beneficial potential for the individual and society could be realized, and its harmful potential could be avoided. Von Rad further argues that within Israel this order was viewed as being established by God at creation for man's blessing, and as dependent upon him for its stability. This imparted a profound religious dimension to Israel's pursuit of wisdom. On the one hand, wisdom's experiential basis presupposed the reliability of the order for human life, and therefore presupposed knowledge and faith in God. On the other, it was also concerned to recognize its own limits and to identify those areas of life which belong to God alone, which made trusting in God an essential component of wisdom. It is therefore wrong to set up a polarity between a mundane and utilitarian wisdom and religious faith. Rather, the religious elements in Proverbs must be seen as making explicit what had always been implicit in Israelite wisdom from earliest times.

A prominent feature of Proverbs is the (female) figure of Wisdom who addresses mankind in 1.20–33 and 8.1–9.6. Scholars have differently assessed the origin and significance of this enigmatic figure. Some think that it has a mythological* origin. Christa Kayatz notes that in Egypt *maat* was not only the term for 'world order', but was also the personal name of a goddess, and she points to some striking parallels between the goddess Maat and the figure of Wisdom in Proverbs. Without necessarily denying some such mythological influence in the portrayal of Wisdom, others believe that it originated within Israelite wisdom circles as a personification. While Whybray believes that it is a personification of divine wisdom developed to overcome the gap between a basically mundane wisdom tradition and Israel's religion, von Rad suggests that it represents the orderliness implanted by God in the world at creation, placed mysteriously beyond the reach of man (Job 28), but which beckons man to live in conformity with it. In later Judaism the figure of Wisdom was identified with the Law of Moses* (Ecclus. 24) or with the Spirit of God (Wisdom 7). The NT and early Christian writers identified Wisdom with Christ, and drew upon the language of 8.22–31 to express the pre-existence and cosmic significance of Christ (*See* **Patristic Christology**).

See also **Wisdom Literature.**

Joseph Blenkinsopp, *Wisdom and Law in the Old Testament,* 1983; James L. Crenshaw (ed.), *Studies in Ancient Israelite Wisdom,* 1976; id., *Old Testament Wisdom: An Introduction,* 1981; John G. Gammie et al. (eds), *Israelite Wisdom,* 1978; William McKane, *Proverbs,* 1970; Gerhard von Rad, *Wisdom in Israel,* 1972.

KENNETH T. AITKEN

Psalms

The Psalter has been extensively used in both public worship (*see* **Liturgy, Use of the Bible in**) and private devotion within the Jewish and Christian traditions. The Hebrew Psalter bears the title Book of Praises (*sēper tᵉhillîm*), a name which indicates the overall tone of much of its contents, although the 150 poems exhibit considerable variety. Tradition attributes the Psalter to David,* though only 72 psalms are specifically attributed to him by name (3–9, 11–32, 34–41, 51–65, 68–70, 86, 101, 103, 108–110, 122, 124, 131, 138–145); coincidentally, there is a comment appended to Ps. 72 that 'The prayers of David, the son of Jesse, are ended', though the psalm itself is ascribed to Solomon. This note implies that at some stage it belonged to a collection of psalms which contained no more attributed to David, and is one of the clues to the commonly held view that the present book of psalms is an anthology of a number of smaller collections and single songs. Other clues include the presence of doublets (e.g. Pss. 14 and 53), the predominance of 'the LORD' (representing the name Yahweh) or 'God' in different sections, and the presence or absence of titles. Some of the smaller collections may have originated from or been preserved by guilds of temple singers (e.g. those associated with Asaph and the sons of Korah). It is no longer possible with any certainty to reconstruct the various stages in the compilation of the Psalter. It clearly contains songs from the pre-exilic period (notably psalms associated with the king*) and from the exilic and post-exilic period (e.g. Ps. 137), and the compilation into the 150 songs of the Hebrew Psalter must have been completed before the translation of the Hebrew Bible into Greek, because the Septuagint* (LXX) includes a Ps. 151 whose title describes it as being 'outside the number'. (A Hebrew version of this psalm has been found at Qumran: *see* **Dead Sea Scrolls**.)

The beginnings of the process of interpreting the psalms can perhaps be seen within the Psalter itself. For example, the last two verses of Ps. 51 may have been added at a time later than the composition of the remainder of the psalm, perhaps to modify the impression that God required only 'spiritual' sacrifices; the addition, which appears to contradict the preceding verses, may have been made during or immediately after the exile, when the rebuilding of Jerusalem* and the re-establishment of the temple cult* with its 'right' sacrifices was an issue of great importance. The retention in the post-exilic period of a number of psalms which relate to the king or to the Davidic dynasty (e.g. Pss. 2, 18, 20, 21, 45, 72, 110, 132) may be due to the fact that they came to be re-interpreted as pertaining to the messianic* hopes associated with a future ideal descendant of David.

Another form of interpretation within the Psalter is perhaps to be seen in the psalm titles, and, in particular in those which link a psalm to an event in the life of David. These are 13 in number in the Hebrew Bible (Pss. 3, 7, 18, 30, 34, 51, 52, 54, 56, 57, 59, 60, 63), and the number is expanded in the LXX. This may represent the beginning of a traditional type of Jewish interpretation which sought to understand many of the psalms by relating them to a context in David's life. It has even been suggested that, in view of the fact that David's song in II Sam. 22.1–51 and Hezekiah's 'writing' in Isa. 38.9–20 have historical titles, some of the titles could have been attached to the psalms before their incorporation into the Psalter. The historical notes tend to follow a fairly stereotyped form and depend on material within the Books of Samuel. It appears that an attempt has been made to find an episode in David's life which was similar to the circumstances envisaged within the particular psalm. The intention was perhaps to imply that the words of David's response to a situation in his life might suitably be appropriated by an individual as a response to a similar circumstance. The titles have been described as 'midrashic',* but it is perhaps safer to note the more cautious words of B. S. Childs that perhaps '. . . one can recognize analogies in an exegetical method of inner-biblical* interpretation which later developed into full-blown midrash'.

From Qumran comes a very fragmentary document, 4QFlorilegium (4Q174), which contains a section on Pss. 1 and 2 which is headed 'midrash'. The psalms are 'explained' with the help of quotations from the prophetic* literature, and the writer seeks to demonstrate that these psalms refer to the Qumran community, whose members have not walked 'in the counsel of the wicked', and who are the remnant which will survive the times of trial and testing. To distinguish this very particular type of interpretation from rabbinic* midrash, it has been suggested that it should be defined as 'Qumran midrash' (Brooke). Mention should also be made of manuscripts 4Q171 and 4Q173, which preserve quotations from Pss. 37 (primarily), 45 and 127, and interpretations which relate them to the life of the community, taking them to refer to difficulties and opposition which members of the sect have faced or will face, and sometimes specifically to the conflict between the 'Teacher of Righteousness' and the 'Wicked Priest'.

It is in the *Midrash Tehillim* (Midrash on Psalms) that the full development of the midrashic method can be seen. This is a haggadic midrash on the psalms which covers most of the Psalter; there are some omissions in certain manuscripts and printed editions, but the only psalms definitely lacking a midrash are Pss. 123 and 131. It is thought that the period of writing covered several centuries, and that the midrash on Pss. 119–150 is perhaps later than the preceding sections and may date from the thirteenth century. Sometimes the midrash on a psalm will involve a series of homiletical* notes on virtually every word of the text, but usually the notes will only be on selected verses or perhaps the first and last verses. The usual method adopted is that a quotation from the psalm is discussed in the light of a related biblical passage, which is also quoted; then a number of interpretations of the related passage are given, the last of which is intended to shed special light on or clarification of the words originally quoted from the psalm. Although this type of interpretation does sometimes exhibit an interest in the meaning of the words used and their literal* interpretation, the primary interest is

homiletical. In no sense was this an attempt to alter the original or natural meaning of a psalm. Rather, the rabbis believed that scripture was capable of a variety of meanings, and their eisegesis* and exegesis* reflect this view.

Before leaving examples of Jewish* interpretation of the psalms, mention should be made of the Aramaic Targum* of the Psalter; in written form this may date from the ninth century, but its origins lie much earlier in the oral form of the Targum. It was not merely a translation, but an expanded paraphrase containing explanatory material.

In the NT it is made clear that it was believed that the divine promises to David had been fulfilled in Jesus (cf. Acts 13.34 which quotes Isa. 55.3). Thus, passages in the Psalter which had appeared to refer to David or which had come to have a messianic interpretation were taken to refer to Jesus Christ. This can be seen particularly clearly in Peter's* sermon on the day of Pentecost, where the writer of Acts presents Peter as quoting the LXX version of Ps. 16.8–11 and arguing that the verses could not refer to David because his body did 'see corruption' and his soul did descend to Hades; the only person to whom the words could apply was Jesus, who must therefore be the messiah (Acts 2.22ff.). (It is noteworthy that a statement in *Midrash Tehillim* on Ps. 16.9 suggests that a messianic interpretation was held by some, although the concluding comment on the verse is that it 'proves that neither corruption nor worms had power over David's flesh'.) The argument in Acts was supported by quoting Ps. 110.1, which could not refer to David since he did not ascend to the heavens, but which, it was claimed, had been fulfilled by Jesus.

That Ps. 110.1 was interpreted messianically is shown in Mark 12.35–37 (cf. Matt. 22.41–46; Luke 20.41–44). Here the belief that the messiah was son of David is challenged because David (the presumed author* of the psalm) addresses him as 'my Lord'. The evangelists* no doubt intended to imply that the verse referred to Jesus, as is the case in Heb. 1.13, where the verse is used to clinch an argument for Jesus' superiority over any angel; no angel had ever been addressed in such terms, and it is clearly implied that they are appropriate only to Jesus. Elsewhere the NT writers interpret verses from the psalms as applicable to Jesus, or as being prophetic of events which they record. For example, in the story of the temptation, Ps. 91.11–12 is taken to refer to the Son of God and so to be appropriate to the devil's challenge to Jesus (Matt. 4.5–7; Luke 4.9–12). Jesus is presented as relating Ps. 118.22–23 to himself (Matt.

21.42; Mark 12.10–11, Luke 20.17). In Acts 1.16–20, the fate of Judas is presented as fulfilling two statements in the Psalter (Pss. 69.25; 109.8).

Ongoing Christian interpretation of the Psalter tended to use the psalms as though they related to the Christian church; this is the case with Augustine * (d.430) in his *Enarrationes in psalmos*, and with Cassiodorus (d. 583) in his *Expositio psalmorum*. Such views continued into the mediaeval period. Hugo Cardinalis (d. 1263) in his comment on the title of Ps. 79 (in *Biblia latina cum postilla*) interprets the name Asaph as meaning 'congregation' and goes on to note that this is none other than the church, the congregation of the faithful. Faber Stapulensis (d. 1536) could refer, in his *Quincuplex Psalterium*, to Zion as the *ecclesia fidelium*, which he understood to be the gradually increasing number of people who have come to profess their faith in God. The psalms were not only related to the church. For example, Nicholas of Lyra (d. 1340), in common with longstanding Jewish practice, applies some of the psalms to the faithful individual. In a tradition which went back to Justin in the second century, mediaeval Christian commentators on the psalms found them fruitful soil for engaging in arguments against Jews and the synagogue, particularly over whether passages taken to relate to the Messiah indicated that he had come or not, and whether statements about the people of God should be understood as referring to the synagogue or the church.

For Martin Luther * it seemed entirely natural to interpret the Psalter as though it related to the individual Christian, or the church. Thus in Ps. 27.5 the 'tabernacle' is taken to be the church, the body of Christ, and in Ps. 37 the references to those who will 'inherit the earth' (RSV 'possess the land') are interpreted as an allusion to true Christians. In Ps. 45, the ointment made from the various spices mentioned is understood as referring to the grace which is spread among all the faithful of Christ.

An important aspect of Christian appropriation and interpretation of the Psalter can be seen in the prominence of the psalms in the hymnody* of the church. The psalms themselves have been sung from early times as part of the liturgy, and many Christian hymn books have contained a selection of psalms. The beginnings of English hymnody are to be found in the preparation of metrical versions of the psalms, and metrical psalms and paraphrases of psalms continue to figure prominently in hymn books. Frequently these will be psalms in praise of God and his attributes, such as Ps. 100 paraphrased in the form 'All people that on earth do dwell'. A recent major Christian hymn book, *Hymns and Psalms*

(1983), contains over 50 hymns (out of a total of 823) which are paraphrases of, metrical versions of, or based on, psalms or sections of psalms, in addition to a large number of hymns which make allusions to verses from the Psalter; it also contains a selection of over 50 psalms for congregational use, printed after the other hymns.

Especially popular have been various versions of Ps. 23, doubtless because of its association with the idea of Jesus as the 'Good Shepherd'. Here again we are introduced to the fact that, just as some Christian commentators have seen fit to interpret the psalms from a Christian perspective, so too Christian hymn writers have taken psalms and given them a Christian and often christological * interpretation. The intention is made clear, for example, in the full title of a collection of hymns by Isaac Watts (1674–1748): *The Psalms of David, imitated in the language of the New Testament, and applied to the Christian State and Worship*. In his preface to this work, Watts indicates that his purpose is '. . . to accommodate the Book of Psalms to Christian Worship . . . to divest David and Asaph of every other Character but that of a Psalmist and a Saint, and to make them always speak the Common Sense and Language of a Christian'. This process may involve the taking of a psalm originally referring to the Israelite king, which would have come to be interpreted messianically, and moving to a Christian understanding. So, for example, Watts' hymn 'Jesus shall reign where'er the sun doth his successive journeys run' is based on part of Ps. 72 (vv. 5–19), originally a great prayer for the Israelite monarch; and his hymn 'This is the day the Lord has made' is based on Ps. 118.24–26 which Watts understood as a prophecy of Christ. Similarly, Charles Wesley (1707–88) takes part of Ps. 45, a wedding hymn for an Israelite king, and transforms it into a song of praise to Christ in his hymn 'My heart is full of Christ, and longs its glorious matter to declare!' Wesley's 'Rejoice, the Lord is King!' begins with a paraphrase of the opening words of Ps. 97, then moves into an adaptation of the Christian creed.* Although many such adaptations of psalms date from the eighteenth and nineteenth centuries, the tradition has continued, as is witnessed by hymns of Timothy Dudley-Smith (b. 1926), 'Sing a new song to the Lord' (based on Ps. 98), 'Timeless love! We sing the story' (based on Ps. 89. 1–18), and his paraphrase of Ps. 148, 'Praise the Lord of heaven', though in these examples the psalms are not explicitly Christianized.

It is of course not only by Christian hymn writers and relatively early commentators that psalms have been given a christological interpretation. For example, the introductory notes to the book of Psalms in the *New Scofield Reference Bible,* published in 1967, state, 'The Psalms include a vast body of Messianic prophecy: relative to Christ's suffering (22; 69), Christ as king (2; 21; 45; 72), in His second advent (50; 97; 98), and, fundamentally, the brief 110th Psalm, depicting Christ as the Son of God and Priest after the order of Melchizedek . . .'

When critical scholarship began to be applied to the Psalter, and ideas such as Davidic authorship were largely rejected, the tendency to approach the psalms historically continued, with attempts to relate particular psalms to an appropriate context in Israel's history. Two major approaches have dominated the study of the Psalter in the twentieth century. The first is associated particularly with the German scholar Hermann Gunkel, who used a form-critical* approach; he attempted to classify the psalms into various 'types' (*Gattungen*) on the basis of their literary form, and sought to find the original setting (*Sitz im Leben*) of these 'types' in ancient Israelite religion. He identified five major 'types': hymns (*Hymnen*), national or community laments (*Klagelieder des Volkes*), individual laments (*Klagelieder des Einzelnen*), individual thanksgivings (*Danklieder des Einzelnen*), and royal psalms (*Königpsalmen*). Some of these major 'types' were thought to contain subsidiary 'types'; the hymns included a number of songs of Zion (*Zionslieder*), and enthronement psalms (*Thronbesteigungslieder*). Various minor 'types' were also recognized, including wisdom* poems (*Weisheitsdichtungen*), national or community thanksgivings (*Danklieder des Volkes*), pilgrimage songs (*Wallfahrtslieder*) and Torah-liturgies (*Thoraliturgien*). Since not all psalms could be assigned to one of these 'types', it was necessary also to speak of mixed poems (*Mischungen*).

The second major twentieth-century approach is associated with the Norwegian scholar Sigmund Mowinckel, who followed the approach of Gunkel, but with the significant development that he believed the vast majority of psalms to have originated within the cult* (*see* **Scandinavian Old Testament Scholarship**). On this assumption he sought to reconstruct features of the worship of the Jerusalem temple in the pre-exilic period, making use not only of indications which he found within the Psalter itself, but also of information about the religious practices and festivals of neighbouring peoples. Perhaps the most noteworthy illustration of his contribution is to be seen in his reconstruction of an annual enthronement festival, which he believed to be the original setting of the so-called enthrone-

ment psalms. He suggested that this was a feature of the New Year rituals, and was an annual celebration of God's kingship, based on the ceremonies which would accompany the accession of an earthly monarch, analogous to the ceremonial enthronement of the patron-deity of Babylon, Marduk, at the Babylonian *akitu* festival held at the New Year.

The form-critical and cultic approaches to the interpretation of psalms have been highly influential on subsequent studies. Commentators continue to relate psalms to particular categories, although the 'types' suggested by Gunkel are frequently modified. Few would question the view that the soil from which many psalms grew was the cult, but the hypothesis of an enthronement festival has by no means been universally accepted, and there have been some rather extreme manifestations of the cultic approach which need to be treated with considerable caution. There has been an increasing realization that these approaches, though important, are somewhat limited, and an over-rigid application of this type of interpretation can result in something which is of little more than antiquarian interest in view of its heavy concentration on the original setting of a psalm. Psalm interpretation must reflect not only these questions of origins, but the ongoing interpretation and re-interpretation within the Jewish and Christian traditions which has enabled the Psalter to be a valuable devotional aid throughout the ages. This is summed up by some words of Luther about the psalms in his second preface to the German Psalter. 'The very best thing is that they speak such words about God and to God.'

See also **Cultic Interpretation; Hymnody; Jewish Exegesis.**

W. G. Braude, *The Midrash on Psalms* (2 vols), 1959; G. J. Brooke, *Exegesis at Qumran: 4Q Florilegium in its Jewish Context,* 1985; B. S. Childs, 'Psalm Titles and Midrashic Exegesis', *JSS* XVI, 1971, pp. 137–150; S. H. Hendrix, *Ecclesia in Via: Ecclesiological Developments in the Medieval Psalms Exegesis and the* Dictata Super Psalterium *(1513–1515) of Martin Luther,* 1974; S. Mowinckel, *The Psalms in Israel's Worship* (2 vols), 1962.

A. H. W. CURTIS

Pseudepigrapha

'Pseudepigrapha' is a convenient, but imprecise, term that has been used in the modern period to refer to a group of writings of Jewish origin that date from the third century BC to the second century AD. Strictly speaking the term ought to be reserved for those writings, such as the Ethiopic Book of Enoch, that make the false claim that they were written by some worthy figure from Israel's past. But the term is also used for writings from the same period, such as Joseph and Aseneth or Pseudo-Philo's Book of Biblical Antiquities, that contain narratives about Israel's heroes of the past. And the term has also been used more loosely still to include other Jewish writings from the same period that do not fit into either of the above categories, such as the Sibylline Oracles (where the direct link with the OT is limited) or the Letter of Aristeas (which purports to be a narrative about contemporary events and does not strictly belong here). Because of the imprecise way in which the term is used, there is no universal agreement as to which writings belong in the category of the pseudepigrapha, as may be readily seen from a comparison of the contents of two recently published English translations of these works, the one (*The Apocryphal Old Testament* ed. H. F. D. Sparks, 1984) being perhaps unduly restricted in its choice, the other (*The Old Testament Pseudepigrapha* ed. J. H. Charlesworth, 2 vols, 1983, 1985) containing works that do not properly belong in this category.

The following may, however, be regarded as the most important of the pseudepigrapha: Pseudo-Philo's Book of Biblical Antiquities, the Life of Adam and Eve, the Ethiopic Book of Enoch (I Enoch), the Slavonic Book of Enoch (II Enoch), the Sibylline Oracles, the Apocalypse of Abraham, the Testament of Abraham, the Testaments of the Twelve Patriarchs, Joseph and Aseneth, Jubilees, the Testament (Assumption) of Moses, the Psalms of Solomon, the Lives of the Prophets, the Ascension of Isaiah, the Paraleipomena of Jeremiah, the Syriac Apocalypse of Baruch (II Baruch), and the Testament of Job. Many of these writings may well at first have been accorded some kind of scriptural authority, but they were ultimately excluded from both the Hebrew Bible and the Greek version of the OT (*see* **Septuagint**), that is – to express it in different terms – from the OT and the Apocrypha;* and some can be identified with non-canonical writings that are mentioned in lists of canonical and non-canonical books that ultimately derive from the first half of the fifth century AD (see below). But the pseudepigrapha obviously have close links with the later books of the OT and the books of the Apocrypha, and they have to be studied alongside these writings. They also have to be studied alongside other Jewish writings from the same period with which they have affinities: the corpus of Qumran writings (*see* **Dead Sea Scrolls**), the Letter of Aristeas, the fragments of the Hellenistic*-Jewish authors, and the works of Philo* and Josephus,* as well as the NT writings and – from a slightly later period – the rabbinic* literature.

The precise motives which led to the composition of the pseudepigrapha will have varied considerably from case to case, but what can be said of virtually all of these writings is that their authors, in a somewhat similar way to the authors of a number of OT writings, attempted to respond to new circumstances by reflecting upon Israel's past traditions. The majority of the pseudepigrapha certainly draw heavily upon the OT, whose traditions they frequently elaborate and expand, and in a broad sense they can be regarded as interpretative writings. This can be seen most obviously in the case of writings such as Jubilees and Pseudo-Philo's Book of Biblical Antiquities, which retell the biblical narrative as a means of propounding new theological ideas (*see* **Rewritten Bible**); or in the case of a writing like the Testaments of the Twelve Patriarchs, where the narrative sections draw their inspiration from the narratives in Genesis concerning the twelve sons of Jacob. But it can also be seen in the case of writings like I Enoch, whose first section (chs 1–36) is built up on the basis of a wide range of OT traditions. More generally it may be observed that the literary genres* used in the pseudepigrapha (e.g. accounts of visions and of journeys through the heavens, psalms, testaments) represent a continuation of literary genres used in the OT.

Fragments of some of these writings were found at Qumran: these include fragments in Aramaic of all sections of I Enoch except the Parables (chs 37–71), fragments in Hebrew of Jubilees, and fragments of an Aramaic work that lies behind the Greek Testament of Levi. For our present purposes those of Enoch and Jubilees are particularly important because they indicate that some kind of status was accorded to both these writings within the Qumran community. But apart from this we have virtually no information about the reception given to the writings of the pseudepigrapha within the Jewish circles for which they were composed. It does appear, however, that from the early second century AD onwards the pseudepigraphical writings fell out of favour in Jewish circles and no longer circulated amongst Jews. According to a saying of Akiba preserved in Mishnah (*see* **Talmud**) Sanhedrin X.1, those who read 'the outside books' have no share in the world to come. The meaning of the expression 'the outside books' is disputed, but it probably does include within its scope what we know as the apocrypha and pseudepigrapha, and the passage is indicative of the attitude of rabbinic Judaism towards these writings.

Two factors appear to have been at work here. Inasmuch as the pseudepigrapha were sectarian in character, or even simply not part of the pharisaic*-rabbinic heritage, they would have been regarded with suspicion by rabbinic Judaism. But it was perhaps even more because the pseudepigrapha were taken over by the Christian church and became Christian writings that they were rejected by rabbinic Judaism. The rejection of the pseudepigrapha may be seen as part of the process of Jewish self-definition and is no doubt to be linked to the fixing of the canon* of the Hebrew Bible, which, in comparison with the Greek version of the OT, contains a restricted number of writings. In a broader context it is no doubt also to be related to the establishment of an authoritative text of the Hebrew Bible (*see* **Masoretic Text**). Be that as it may, the pseudepigrapha only survived because they were taken over and copied by Christians, exactly as is the case for the Apocrypha or the works of Philo and Josephus. The one exception to this is Ecclesiasticus in the Apocrypha, which, although regarded as one of 'the outside books' (see above), did survive for a time in Jewish circles.

Some of the pseudepigrapha appear to have been composed in Greek (e.g. Joseph and Aseneth, the Testament of Job), others, as the Qumran discoveries have demonstrated for the greater part of I Enoch and for Jubilees, in Aramaic or Hebrew. It seems clear, however, that all the writings whose language of composition was Aramaic or Hebrew were at some stage translated into Greek, and it was in Greek that the pseudepigrapha were taken over and used by the early church along with the Greek version of the OT. The fate of these writings within the early church varied. Some continued to circulate in their original Jewish form, as for example Jubilees and the Testament of Job. Other writings were, however, subjected to editing of various kinds. For example, the Life of Jeremiah (cf. v. 8–10) has been recast by a Christian editor, and a Christian ending (9.10–32) has been added to the Paraleipomena of Jeremiah. In two cases in particular, the Ascension of Isaiah and the Testaments of the Twelve Patriarchs, the process of Christian editing has been taken to considerable lengths.

In the former an original Jewish work, the Martyrdom of Isaiah, consisting of the basic material in 1.1–3.12 + 5.1–16, has been combined with two Christian writings, an account of a vision seen by Isaiah (3.13–4.22) and a work known as the Vision of Isaiah (chs 6–11), to form the present (Christian) Ascension of Isaiah, The Jewish material has itself been subject to Christian editing (e.g. in 1.2b–6a,7,13), and it cannot simply be assumed that what remains after the obviously Christian passages have been removed constitutes the original Jewish Martyrdom of Isaiah.

So far as the Testaments are concerned, there has been considerable debate as to whether this is a Jewish work with a limited number of identifiable Christian interpolations, or a Christian work which makes use of extensive Jewish traditions including probably a Jewish Testaments of the Twelve Patriarchs. But there is no question but that the work is Christian in its present form, and it is very doubtful whether it is possible to recover a Jewish version of the Testaments by the removal of Christian 'interpolations'.

These examples illustrate that the church not only appropriated the pseudepigrapha, but also in some cases had no hesitation in totally recasting them to suit its own purposes. By way of contrast, reference may also be made to the Ethiopic Book of Enoch. We do not know the precise stages by which the Enochic materials discovered at Qumran were transformed into the book as it now exists in the Ethiopic version, in which the Parables (chs 37–71) and the astronomical section (chs 72–82) have been inserted into what is now an Enochic pentateuch. As we have already noted, the Parables are the only part of the present book of Enoch of which no trace was found at Qumran, but the view, recently revived by J. T. Milik, that the Parables are a Christian composition has received little support. It is possible, if not probable, that Christians were involved in the editorial process which led to the composition of the present book, but if they were, they have left virtually no trace of their activity.

The pseudepigrapha were known to the early Fathers, and they quote from or allude to many of them, but at times with recognition of their ambiguous status. Thus, for example, Origen* refers to Testament of Reuben 2–3, but notes that the Testaments of the Twelve Patriarchs do not belong in the canon, and Jerome similarly refers to Testament of Naphtali 2.8, but notes that the 'book of the Patriarchs' belongs among the apocryphal books, i.e. among the pseudepigrapha. The NT Epistle of Jude (see vv. 14–15) cites I Enoch 1.9. Among the Fathers, the Epistle of Barnabas gives summary quotations of I Enoch 89.56 and 91.13, which the author introduces with the formulas 'For scripture says' and 'For it is written', and Clement of Alexandria gives free quotations from or alludes to several passages in Enoch. But Origen (*Contra Celsum*, 5,54) notes that the Book of Enoch is not recognized as 'divine' in the church, and Jerome regards Enoch, like the Testaments of the Twelve Patriarchs, as belonging among the apocryphal books. (For details of the quotations from and allusions to the pseudepigrapha in the Fathers, see the works by Schürer [vols III.1 and 2] and Denis in the bibliography.) The Apostolic Constitutions, from the fourth or fifth century, condemn the writings of Moses,* Enoch, Adam,* Isaiah, David,* Elijah, and the Three Patriarchs as 'pernicious and enemies of the truth', while the anonymous 'List of Sixty Books and those which are outside' gives a similar list of some fourteen 'apocryphal' books. The 'List of Sixty Books' and several other comparable lists of canonical and non-canonical books have been thought to go back to a common ancestor dating from the period between 400 and 450.

It was no doubt because of uncertainty about their status that several of the pseudepigrapha appear to have fallen out of favour in the following period and to have all but disappeared. Some works, it is true, continued to be copied in Greek. Thus, for example, we possess four manuscripts of the Testament of Job that range in date from the eleventh to the sixteenth century. The Psalms of Solomon were sometimes copied in manuscripts of the Septuagint and in total eleven Greek manuscripts are known, dating from the tenth to the sixteenth century. Again, the large number of Greek manuscripts and the numerous versions both of the Testaments of the Twelve Patriarchs and of Joseph and Aseneth attest to the popularity of these two works. In contrast other writings among the pseudepigrapha appear to have fallen out of circulation and to have survived only because they had been translated from Greek into various daughter versions: Latin, Old Church Slavonic, Armenian, Coptic, Syriac* and Ethiopic. Thus it is only in Ethiopic that complete versions of I Enoch, Jubilees, and the Ascension of Isaiah have survived. Until quite recently our knowledge of the greater part of II Baruch was dependent on the evidence of a single Syriac manuscript from the sixth or seventh century. II Enoch and the Apocalypse of Abraham have survived only in Old Slavonic. Pseudo-Philo's Book of Biblical Antiquities is preserved only in Latin, while for the Testament (Assumption) of Moses we are dependent on the evidence of a single sixth-century Latin palimpsest. The range of the manuscript* and versional evidence suggests that it was particularly in the West that the pseudepigrapha fell out of favour, but that in the Eastern churches they were regarded more highly, and indeed both I Enoch and Jubilees form part of the canon of the Ethiopian church.

Revival of interest in the pseudepigrapha in the modern period coincided with the emergence and growth of the scientific study of biblical literature in general. Early evidence of this revival can be found in the work of J. A. Fabricius. In his *Codex Pseudepigraphicus Veteris Testamenti* (2 vols, 1713, 1723), Fabricius published an annotated collection of

the pseudepigrapha on the basis of the evidence available at the time from Greek and Latin sources, whether in the form of complete texts (as, for example, in the case of the Greek version of the Testaments of the Twelve Patriarchs), or in the form of the extracts and allusions that were preserved in the writings of the Fathers and in other writings (as, for example, in the case of the Book of Enoch). However, a much more significant turning-point occurred in the early nineteenth century as the writings of the pseudepigrapha that had effectively been 'lost' began to be discovered and published. The first of these writings was the Ethiopic version of the Ascension of Isaiah, of which an edition with a translation was published by R. Laurence in 1819. This was soon followed by a translation (1821) and edition (1838) by Laurence of the Ethiopic Book of Enoch, which until that time had been known only from the quotations and allusions in the Fathers and the brief fragments preserved by the chronographer Syncellus. Editions and translations of other 'lost' pseudepigrapha followed in the succeeding decades.

The publication of this new material stimulated a considerable scholarly interest in the pseudepigrapha and led to the publication during the nineteenth century of a substantial volume of secondary literature that was concerned with the origin and interpretation of these writings. But it is important to observe that the scholars who carried out this research were for the most part Christian, and that the pseudepigrapha were to a great extent regarded as important because they provided information about the religious milieu in which Christianity had its origins. Thus, to mention just one illustration of this point, it is significant that E. Schürer's magisterial treatment of the history, institutions and literature of the Jews in the period with which we are concerned was originally entitled *Lehrbuch der Neutestamentliche Zeitgeschichte* (*Manual of the History of New Testament Times*). In later editions this was changed to *Geschichte des jüdischen Volkes im Zeitalter Jesu Christi*, and it was as *A History of the Jewish People in the Time of Jesus Christ* that the work was first published in English (5 vols, 1885–91).

Nineteenth-century research on the pseudepigrapha reached its culmination in the publication in the early twentieth century of two important collections of these writings, the first in volume 2 of *Die Apokryphen und Pseudepigraphen des Alten Testaments* ed. E. Kautzsch (1900), the second in volume 2 of *The Apocrypha and Pseudepigrapha of the Old Testament* ed. R. H. Charles (1913). Both works contain a fairly limited selection of writings in comparison with the number that are now classified as 'pseudepigrapha', but they summarized and brought to some kind of conclusion the work that had been done on the pseudepigrapha up to that time. The volume edited by Charles acquired a particular authority. He had himself published editions and translations of, and commentaries* on, several of the writings included in his collection, and the authority of the volume was such that for some considerable time after its publication little new research was undertaken on the pseudepigrapha. The pseudepigrapha were of course still referred to, but largely as providing antecedents or illustrations of ideas found in the NT.

This situation lasted until the period after the Second World War, when, partly stimulated by the discovery of the Qumran scrolls, there began a revival of interest in the pseudepigrapha which has continued with ever-increasing vigour until the present. An early indication of the revival may be discerned in the publication in 1953 of M. de Jonge's dissertation, *The Testaments of the Twelve Patriarchs: A Study of their Text, Composition and Origin*, in which he argued that the Testaments had to be regarded as a Christian composition, and not as a Jewish work interpolated by a Christian; the debate sparked off by de Jonge's arguments still continues. However, the real revival of interest in the pseudepigrapha began slightly later. It has been marked by the publication of new editions and translations of the texts, in many cases on the basis of a wider and a better range of manuscript evidence than was available in the nineteenth century; by the publication of new commentaries and introductions, and of new collections of the pseudepigrapha in modern translations, in English (the volumes edited by Sparks and Charlesworth mentioned above), German, French, and several other modern languages; by the publication of new periodicals that are concerned with the pseudepigrapha, the *Journal for the Study of Judaism*, which began to appear in 1970, and the very recently established *Journal for the Study of the Pseudepigrapha*; and by the setting up of two seminars that have the pseudepigrapha as a primary interest, the one under the auspices of the Studiorum Novi Testamenti Societas, the other under the auspices of the Society of Biblical Literature. Three things deserve to be said here about this modern revival of interest in the pseudepigrapha.

First, although the pseudepigrapha are obviously of importance for the interpretation of the NT writings, the concern now is much more with the pseudepigrapha in their own right as evidence for the Judaism of the age in which they were composed. Secondly, it is recognized that from a scholarly point of view the distinctions between the pseudepigrapha and other contemporary corpora of Jewish writings are to some extent artificial, and that the pseudepigrapha have to be handled alongside these other groups of writings. This approach is reflected, for example, in the volume edited by M. E. Stone, *Jewish Writings of the Second Temple Period* (1984), in which writings from the OT, the Apocrypha, and the pseudepigrapha, the writings of Josephus and Philo, Qumran texts, and other contemporary Jewish writings are all treated side by side. Finally, the pseudepigrapha have been seen to be important because they demonstrate that Judaism in the period from the third century BC to the second century AD had a much more variegated character than was at one time assumed. It is certainly misleading to think of Judaism as stratified into the three religious groups mentioned by Josephus: Pharisees, Sadducees, and Essenes. Rather the pseudepigrapha, along with the other writings just mentioned, provide evidence of a wide range of religious beliefs and attitudes in this period.

See also **Jewish Background to the New Testament; Jewish Exegesis.**

In addition to titles mentioned in the text, see A.-M. Denis, *Introduction aux pseudépigraphes grecs d'Ancien Testament*, 1970; M. de Jonge (ed.), *Outside the Old Testament*, 1985; G. W. E. Nickelsburg, *Jewish Literature between the Bible and the Mishnah*, 1981; E. Schürer, *The History of the Jewish People in the Age of Jesus Christ (175 BC–AD 135)*, rev. and ed. by G. Vermes, F. Millar, and M. Goodman, 4 vols 1973–1987.

MICHAEL A. KNIBB

Pseudonymity

Pseudonymity is writing under a false or assumed name, and resulting texts are pseudepigrapha.* Such writings were an accepted literary form in the ancient world, but because the reasons for pseudonymity are not perfectly understood, these texts raise for the biblical scholar questions concerning authenticity, canonical status (*see* **Canon**), and forgery. Old and New Testaments pose separate but related problems. The encyclical *Divino afflante Spiritu* (30 September 1943) suggests that Roman Catholic commentators could admit pseudonymity for both, although in practice they do not often find it necessary for the NT. Evangelical commentators usually take a firmer line: documents which claim to be something they are not can no longer carry full weight as canonical scripture.

Greek literature affords several examples of pseudonymity: the Epic Cycle and other hexameter poems were once ascribed to Homer; short pieces by members of the Academy bore the name of Plato; and rhetorical* exercises in a particular style could be attributed to the actual person imitated. Pseudonymity became forgery with the development of the great libraries of the Ptolemies, for example when good prices were paid for works by great authors. The practice of attributing similar works to a well-known ancient worthy accounts for one of the types of pseudonymity found in the OT. All laws were attributed to Moses,* with the result that four centuries of royal lawgiving have been eclipsed. Psalms were attributed to David,* even though many were clearly from a later period. Wisdom* was attributed to Solomon the wise king: Proverbs, Ecclesiastes, the Song of Songs and, in the Apocrypha,* the Wisdom of Solomon are all pseudonymous. Another possibility is that works of Law were deemed to be in the spirit of Moses, works of Wisdom in the spirit of Solomon, and so forth; in an age when individual authorship* was not important, such anonymity is not hard to understand. It resembles the ancient Chinese practice of 'sheltering' under the name of an ancient. Writings were regarded as the recording of tradition to save it from oblivion, and thus even new ideas were presented as ancient, often from ritual self-effacement.

The prophetic* writings present a particular problem; here there are several texts which have been inserted into, or added wholesale to, older material. Isaiah has many such insertions; the whole of chs 40–66 is regarded as two or more additions to the work of an eighth-century prophet. Strictly speaking such additions are pseudonymous, even though they may have originated in attempts to explain the original text, to make it relevant to a new situation, or to add to it in the spirit of the original prophet. There may have been an Isaiah school of disciples who perpetuated the characteristic teaching of their founder. Similar additions were made to Zechariah. All the prophetic books have been 'edited' to some degree, but since the editors do not actually acknowledge their work, this too is pseudonymity. Ancient authors such as Josephus* (in the first century AD) were not aware that this had happened; he could state categorically that nobody had added, removed or altered a single word of the holy books* (*Against Apion* 1.42).

Late post-exilic prophecy operated under different conditions; in this period the Law had become the dominant factor in religious life, and prophecy was regarded by many as either a thing of the past, or as the art of interpreting existing prophetic writings in accordance with the Law. When inspired* writings were thought to be something from the past (even though there was not any idea of a canon as such until much later), pseudonymity had yet another role. New teachings had to be given the semblance of ancient lore, and thus there were works attributed to Moses (Jubilees, the Temple Scroll); to Ezra (IV Ezra); to Isaiah (the Ascension of Isaiah); to Abraham* (the Apocalypse of Abraham, the Testament of Abraham); to Enoch (I and II Enoch); and to many others. Some, such as Jubilees, were reworkings of a biblical text (Genesis) (*see* **Rewritten Bible**). Some, such as the Apocalypse of Abraham, were expansions of one part of a text (Gen. 15) and were akin to interpretations of it. Some, such as I Enoch, were the supposed records of ancient revelations destined for fulfilment in the present time.

The belief that all true revelation* was ancient was not confined to Judaism; the Babylonians, according to Berossus, believed that all knowledge had been revealed to the ante-diluvian sages, even if all such knowledge had not yet been rediscovered; many Neo-pythagorean treatises were attributed to early Pythagoreans; and the Sibylline oracles were attributed to a daughter of Noah (Sib. 3.823). The last two pre-Christian centuries were enthusiastic for ancient prophecies, and pseudonymous writers obliged.

There are several theories as to why writers identified themselves with ancient figures. They were trying to gain a hearing for a new point of view, and could only do so by claiming that it was the true tradition. Or they exemplified the Hebrew idea of a corporate personality and identified closely with the figure in whose name they spoke; this theory has recently fallen out of favour. Or they exemplified the related idea of a dual personality, like that of a prophet who saw in his visions a character and knew this to be another aspect of himself; he then identified with that character and spoke as from him. Or, since many pseudonymous writings are polemical and warn of future (i.e. present!) apostasy, they may have been expressing an excluded point of view. This need not have been an innovation, but simply a view recently excluded as a result of the religious ferments which characterized the history of the Second Temple period when the Law, and one particular interpretation of it, became increasingly dominant. This aspect of pseudonymity is closely bound up with the questions of 'orthodoxy' and authority;* where there was no exclusion process and no urge to power, it would not have been necessary.

Pseudonymous writing in the NT is more hotly debated: some scholars say that there are no pseudonymous writings; others list Matthew, Mark, Luke–Acts, John, Ephesians, the Pastoral Epistles,* James, I and II Peter and

Jude – i.e. almost everything except Paul's*
authentic letters. Many of these writings are
epistles,* and those who hold that there are
no pseudonymous writings point out that
there are very few pseudonymous Jewish
epistles; the Letter of Jeremiah and the Letter
of Aristeas are the best examples. The NT
Apocrypha also include only six: the Letters
of Christ and Abgarus, the Letter of Lentulus,
the Epistle to the Laodiceans, the Correspondence of Paul and Seneca, and the Epistle of
the Apostles. M. R. James (*The Apocryphal
New Testament*, 1924) suggests that epistles
were too difficult to forge.

The early church was aware of forgeries
and did not tolerate them. The story of the
Asian presbyter who composed the Acts of
Paul, was convicted of forgery and removed
from office (Tertullian,* *De Baptismo*, 17),
shows that even by the middle of the second
century the church treated detected pseudepigraphy as forgery. The Muratorian Canon
lists the scriptures acknowledged by the
Roman church, and rejects epistles to the Laodiceans and Alexandrians because they were
forged in Paul's name to suit the Marcionite* heresy. Any pseudepigrapha which were
received within the church must have been
accepted very early, when their true character
was not known. Yet this would have been in
the period when their supposed authors were
still alive or recently remembered, a most difficult time to perpetuate a forgery. Less
weighty arguments suggest that anyone who
could pen the noble sentiments of Ephesians
or the Pastorals' emphasis on the truth would
have found it impossible to be a deceiver.
'Pro-Pauline' scholars argue that a truly professional forger would have made the letters
more Pauline than they are, and would have
left no incongruities; the very un-Pauline
idioms are proof that they are genuine.

Those who argue for pseudonymity emphasize that writing in the name of one's master or
mentor was a relatively common practice, and
would not have been thought forgery. Thus
Ephesians could have been an encyclical in
Paul's name, perhaps composed as an introduction to the collection of his letters. Anything so saturated with Pauline phrases and
ideas could not have been claimed by its true
author since he would have been accused of
plagiarism. This resembles the 'school of disciples' explanation for some OT pseudonymity.
Another possibility is that it was convention
for authors to put words into the mouths of
their characters. Just as the speeches in Acts
are not eye-witness accounts, but what Luke
thought would have been appropriate on those
occasions, so too Pauline letters might have
been composed in what the author considered
an appropriate style. When the infant church

was threatened by teachers of new doctrines,
it was necessary to re-emphasize what were
seen as the original teachings, and this was
done in the name of the apostles. The Pastoral
Epistles, II Peter and Jude probably originated
thus. On the other hand, the teachers of new
doctrines were also claiming apostolic authority: the Gospel of Philip was forged by
fourth-century Gnostics,* according to Epiphanius (*Heresy* xxvi.13); the Gospel of Peter
was condemned by Serapion Bishop of Antioch about AD 190 (Eusebius,* *History* vi.12).

Another aspect of NT pseudonymity concerns prophecy, inspired utterance and visions.
Whereas the OT prophetic pseudepigrapha
could have been explained on the grounds
that the voice of prophecy was believed to be
silent and therefore all new revelations had to
be 'ancient', one of the fundamental beliefs of
the early church was that the gift of prophecy
had returned to them. This is the basis of
Peter's* Pentecost sermon (Acts 2.17ff.).
There should have been no need for pseudonymous prophecy. Some Christian prophets are
known by name: Agabus (Acts 11.28) and
Hermas (*The Shepherd*) did not need pseud-
onyms. But John of Ephesus, even though
writing under his own name, claimed to be
the amanuensis of Jesus himself (Rev. 1.1–
2.11), and Paul claimed something very similar
when he said that his gospel was a direct
revelation from Jesus (Gal. 1.12). If this was
possible, then early Christian prophecy in the
name of Jesus could have infiltrated the Gospels* too, providing additional sayings attributed to Jesus, for example in the Son of Man*
sayings, and the discourses of the Fourth Gospel.

Several pre-Christian pseudonymous 'prophecies' attributed to ancient figures were
modified for Christian purposes; the Ascension of Isaiah and I (Ethiopic) and II (Slavonic) Enoch are the earliest examples, possibly
from the end of the first century. Others were
composed in the name of Christian figures:
the Apocalypse of Peter was accepted as
canonical by some churches. Apocalypses of
Paul, of Thomas, of the Virgin, of Stephen
and many others are known to have existed,
though not all have survived. There are many
pseudonymous writings from the first few centuries of the church: gospels; works prescrib-
ing liturgy and church order, many attributed
to Jesus or the apostles; the Clementine
Homilies and *Recognitions*; the treatises in mystical* theology ascribed to Paul's Athenian
convert Dionysius the Areopagite; and a huge
number of apocalypses* attributed to ancient
worthies.

The claim to authenticity was important,
and the pseudepigrapha in the early church
may be vestiges of a power struggle between
ideas which only the wisdom of hindsight has

enabled us to distinguish as orthodoxy and heresy. Many are of Gnostic provenance and express or assert Gnostic teaching.

See also **Authorship.**

J. Barton, *Oracles of God,* 1986, pp. 61–2, 210–13; J. H. Charlesworth, *The Old Testament Pseudepigrapha,* 2 vols, 1983, 1985; E. J. Goodspeed, *New Chapters in New Testament Study,* 1937, pp. 169ff. (a radical statement); D. Guthrie, *New Testament Introduction. The Pauline Epistles,* 1961, Appendix C; E. Hennecke, *New Testament Apocrypha,* 1963, 1965; C. Rowland, *The Open Heaven,* 1982, pp. 61ff., 240ff., and bibliography on p. 460 n. 24.

MARGARET BARKER

Psychological Interpretation

'Psychology of religion' textbooks, reviewing psychological investigations of contemporary religious belief, behaviour and experience, altogether omit the work of biblical scholars seeking to use psychological insights in interpreting scripture. Consequently the instances of psychological interpretation remain rather scattered and inaccessible to the student. Nevertheless, for as long as both academic psychology and critical biblical studies have been actively pursued (i.e. for at least the whole of this century), there has been a strand in biblical interpretation which has sought to appropriate psychological theories and concepts, though limited largely to those which have become known by way of the 'psychology of religion'.

In the early part of this century, 'psychological' approaches to the text were far from being the systematic application of well articulated psychological theories which is now being pursued. Rather, they viewed, for example, the *personality* of Job, the *consciousness* of Jesus, the *conversion* of Paul,* as (essentially abnormal) phenomena requiring (and legitimating) *ad hoc* psychoanalytic explanations. While freely speculating about these 'inner lives', scholars rarely reflected at all critically upon their own implicit psychological assumptions. It was assumed not only that the biblical text provided reliable information about psychological characteristics, but that one could go beyond the text and, using modern categories, infer psychological causes. Much of this naive 'psychologism' was as arbitrarily selective, speculative and scientifically suspect as the contemporary psychology it sought to apply. The discipline of psychology, seeking to establish its academic respectability as a science, was itself having to explicate criteria* for the validity of its theories and methods.

With the development of scientific methodology in psychology, and the critical stance towards the 'historical Jesus'* approach, enthusiasm for psychological interpretation dwindled. As mainstream scientific psychology, and the growing popularity of behaviourism increasingly marginalized Freud and Jung, and psychology no longer concerned itself with religion in the same way, so biblical scholars remained unaware of the new directions psychologists were pursuing. What little psychological interpretation of the Bible continued during the 1950s and 60s derived almost exclusively from the Freudian and Jungian schools, and this approach survives today, encouraged perhaps by its increasingly fruitful application in pastoral* theology and counselling. Much psychoanalytic interpretation of the Bible proceeds these days (e.g. Rubenstein, Theissen) with a more sophisticated awareness of the problems of reductionism and of cultural* distance, but perhaps with a less than full appreciation of the psychological critique to be made of psychoanalysis.

Since the 1970s, in line with theologians' broad appreciation of anti-positivist and anti-reductionist trends in modern social sciences, biblical scholarship has recognized that modern psychology offers new insights beyond psychoanalysis and behaviourism. Indeed, it has been via the hermeneutical* appropriation of sociology* and structuralism* in biblical studies (rather than through the psychology of religion) that modern psychological theories and concepts come these days to be seen as legitimate interpretative tools. It has perhaps required a certain disillusionment with the historical-critical method,* and the recognition of the impasse to which our awareness of cultural distance has brought us, for the way to be opened for such new approaches. Perhaps even more than the anthropologists* and the sociologists, psychologists have sought for their own purposes to ask, as self-critically as possible, whether their findings identify universal and fundamental properties of human behaviour rather than merely culturally relative* ephemera. If the psychologist succeeds in discerning non-obvious and enduring aspects of our common humanity, then should not these enable new insights into the biblical text in spite of the cultural-historical divide?

So it is that biblical scholars have begun to make use of insights drawn from across the wide range of cognitive, social, clinical and developmental aspects of modern empirical psychology. We may note, as actual examples, the psychology of memory in understanding the transmission of oral tradition;* the social psychology of roles, identity, and conflict in the formation and maintenance of distinct social groups; the psychology of cognitive development to identify pre-logical characteristics of some biblical conceptualizations; clinical perspectives on ecstatic utterance, on psychotherapeutic healing through preaching and touch, and on biblical 'leprosy' as a psychosomatic disorder.

One modern social psychological theory still attracting quite sustained attention in biblical interpretation is L. Festinger's theory of cognitive dissonance,* which explains how individuals and groups in complex cognitive environments restructure their beliefs and behaviour in order to maintain cognitive consistency and equilibrium. Gager uses the theory to explain how apparently disconfirmatory events (the death of Jesus and the delay of the parousia*) led not to the dissolution but to the strengthening of the earliest Christian communities.* Since the theory also predicts an intensification of post-decisional contrast between a chosen and a rejected alternative, Gager has also applied it to understanding Paul's view of the Law. The same theory has been used in a more detailed study by Carroll to understand certain social and cognitive characteristics of prophecy* and of the communities that evolved around the prophets. Carroll stresses that 'dissonance gives rise to hermeneutic', in the sense that new or revised hermeneutics evolve to reduce cognitive dissonance.

The rationale for the hermeneutical appropriation of modern psychological theory is that, after rigorous empirical testing, psychology can yield non-obvious and counterintuitive insights into such fundamental aspects of individual and social behaviour that one would expect them to throw new light on the biblical text. Alas, after years of such rigorous testing, cognitive dissonance has proved to be a less ubiquitous and more complex phenomenon than it once promised to be. Regrettably, while social psychology has moved on from cognitive dissonance theory, biblical scholars have shown limited awareness of the extensive modifications and elaborations that have superseded Festinger's original formulation after thirty years of further research. The biblical scholar faces considerable difficulty keeping abreast of changes in such a rapidly developing discipline as psychology. It may well be asked whether this very rate of conceptual growth does not altogether negate the claim that the findings of psychology are of such universality as to be of use in biblical interpretation. Some theories and findings are no doubt more robust than others. Perhaps the identification of well-established empirical patterns may, whilst having limited explanatory power, yield more appropriate hermeneutical tools than theories and abstractions which attempt to explain too much.

By far the most ambitious effort in recent psychological interpretation of the Bible has been the work of Gerd Theissen on psychological aspects of Pauline theology. Theissen attempts the 'hermeneutical integration' of three widely divergent paradigms in psychology – psychoanalysis, learning theory, and cognitive psychology – and abstracts from each of these in offering new insights into various aspects of Pauline texts, including the phenomena of glossolalia, Paul's understanding of the unconscious, of wisdom, of the Law, of sin, and of Christ. For all the new insights presented in this scholarly and wideranging appropriation of psychological theories and concepts, the 'hermeneutical integration' project remains highly suspect from a psychological point of view. While Theissen is not alone among biblical scholars in preferring to employ psychological concepts pragmatically, eclectically and piecemeal as 'heuristic devices', few psychologists would approve of Theissen's somewhat arbitrary integration and application of only those concepts which suit his immediate purposes without regard to the inherent contradictions between the theoretical paradigms from which those concepts properly derive.

Finally, mention must briefly be made of the developmental psychologist Jean Piaget. Much structuralist interpretation of the Bible (e.g. E. Leach, P. Ricoeur) appeals for psychological validation of presumed 'structures' to Freud (and occasionally to Chomsky). However, Piaget is seen by a significant number of structuralists (e.g. Polzin) as providing a bridge between a totally synchronic* structuralist approach and the historical approach, because of Piaget's concern with the genetic transformations of thought which are a consequence of the essentially synchronic relations between and within the cognitive structures themselves.

In view of these developments and in spite of these difficulties, the psychological interpretation of the Bible promises to be an increasingly fruitful line of inquiry, not only as biblical scholars become better acquainted with the vast corpus of existing psychological theory and research, but also as psychology and theology continue to grow as partners in dialogue.

See also **Anthropology; Sociology and Social Anthropology.**

R. P. Carroll, *When Prophecy Failed*, 1978; J. G. Gager, *Kingdom and Community*, 1975; R. M. Polzin, *Biblical Structuralism*, 1977; R. L. Rubenstein, *My Brother Paul*, 1972; G. Theissen, *Psychological Aspects of Pauline Theology*, ET 1987; W. Wink, *The Bible in Human Transformation*, 1973.

DAVID K. MIELL

Rabbi, Rabbinism

The term *rav* ('great one', 'master', 'chief') is used in the Hebrew Bible to denote someone holding a position of power and authority over others within a group (e.g. Jer. 39.9: *rav ha-tabbaḥim* = 'chief of the guardsmen'). The head of a school could appropriately be designated a *rav* (Mishnah Pirqei Avot 1.6, 16), and so could respectfully be addressed by his pupils as *rabbi* ('my master'). From this usage the custom arose of addressing any respected sage as *rabbi* (probably with the nuance of 'my *teacher*'). Note its application to John the Baptist* (John 3.26) and to Jesus (Mark 9.5) in the NT. Within the Pharisaic movement the title began to be regularly applied to the Torah scholars only in the generation after Hillel (died early first century AD). Strictly speaking, only those who had received ordination (*semikhah*) could bear the title, and since ordination could not be performed outside the Land of Israel, the Torah scholars of Babylonia were addressed simply as *rav*. An augmented form of *rav* – *rabban* ('master') – was used as a distinctive honorific for the heads of the House of Hillel (e.g. Rabban Gamaliel). They also bore the title *nasi'* ('prince' or 'patriarch') (e.g. Rabbi Judah ha-Nasi', the redactor of the Mishnah). In the Mishnah (*see* **Talmud**) the commonest term for the collectivity of the scholars is *ha-ḥakhamim* ('the sages'). Later rabbinic texts refer to *rabbanan* ('our masters') or, sometimes, to *rabbotenu* ('our rabbis').

History of the rabbinate. One of the most significant developments in Judaism in the Second Temple period was the growing authority in religious matters of the scribes* (*soferim*). Scribes had been a part of Israelite society at least from the time of David.* They formed a class of professional administrators who helped run the state. Their training was in the international wisdom* traditions of the Ancient Near East,* which laid down how the sage and the king* should behave, and how government was to be carried on efficiently. In the Second Temple period, a consensus emerged that prophecy* had come to an end: God could no longer be expected to speak directly to his people through the medium of the prophetic voice. And so a process was set in train to collect and to canonize the prophetic writings as a body of revealed truth. The scribes made themselves the masters of this national, sacred literature, and it was on this expertise that they based their claim to religious authority. That authority was in principle absolute. Since the sacred writings contained the divine laws* for the ordering of the temple and the running of

the state, the scribe as the expert exponent of those laws could claim authority over both priest and king: he could tell both how they ought to conduct their affairs if they were to conform to the divine will. The emergence of the scribes marks an attempt by academics and administrators to seize power in Israel, to subordinate to themselves the charismatic authority of the prophet and the hereditary authority of the priest and the king.

All the major parties and movements in late Second Temple Judaism were to a degree scribal in character, and sought to validate their position from the sacred writings. But the influence of scribalism on the Pharisees* was especially profound (cf. Josephus, *War*, II, 162–66). And it was circles of Pharisees who laid the foundations of rabbinic Judaism after the destruction of the Temple in AD 70. Later rabbinic tradition was to pay particular tribute to the work of Yohanan ben Zakkai and the academy which he established at Yavneh (=Jamnia) in this process. Though the Pharisees may have wielded real political power under the Hasmonaeans, notably under Alexander (76–67 BC) (Josephus, *Ant.* XIII, 408f.), there is no evidence that they did so in the period just before the war against Rome of AD 66–74, despite claims to the contrary. The surviving traditions suggest that they were largely concerned with Sabbath and food laws, and with questions of ritual purity, and not with the substantive issues of administering a community. Some of them appear to have banded together into 'fellowships' (*ḥavurot*) whose aim was to observe strictly the laws of tithing and to prepare and eat their everyday food in conditions of ritual purity. A rather similar picture emerges after AD 70. The surviving traditions show the rabbis actually adjudicating essentially parochial religious cases concerned with such matters as ritual purity, tithes, Sabbath, idolatry, vows and fasts, not major cases of criminal or civil law. It is very probable that the rabbis and their followers remained a sect within Judaism down to the end of the second century AD. They appear to have been largely artisans and consequently their social status would not have been high, or their political influence great. There was a powerful ideal among the scholars that they should not take payment for teaching Torah: they should support themselves with a secular occupation (Mishnah Pirqei Avot 2.2). Given that their group was not wealthy, and that patronage was very uncertain, they were to some extent making a virtue out of necessity. Running through early rabbinic writings is a strain of bitter invective against the *'ammei ha-'areṣ* (literally, 'peoples of the land'), a term used for those who did not scrupulously observe rabbinic law (*halakhah*). These were probably the wealthier landowning classes who actually controlled the Jewish communities and who opposed the rabbis' attempts to usurp their power.

Towards the end of the second century the situation began to change. A turning point probably came with Judah the Patriarch, who by all accounts was a wealthy man of considerable political influence. The change is reflected in the history of rabbinic ordination. According to a tradition in the Palestinian Talmud (Sanhedrin 1.2) the scholars originally ordained their own pupils; later the approval of a *bet din* (a rabbinic court) was required; finally, ordination could only take place with the approval of the Nasi'. The picture emerges of an increasingly centralized bureaucracy (cf. Palestinian Talmud Yevamot 12.6; Ḥagigah 1.7). In the third century, polemic against the *'ammei ha-'areṣ* dies down and we find the rabbis functioning as judges (*dayyanim*) in a well-regulated system of Jewish courts spread through the Jewish towns and villages of Palestine, supervised by the Nasi', who was recognized by the Romans as the political head of the Jewish community. They adjudicate cases involving property, bailments, torts, damages, contracts, wills, marriage and divorce, and questions of personal status, all largely according to rabbinic *halakhah* as contained in the Mishnah. We begin to hear for the first time of money being paid for the teaching of the Mishnah (Palestinian Talmud Nedarim 4.3).

Though rabbinism has experienced many vicissitudes over the centuries, the rabbis have never entirely lost the standing within the Jewish communities which they gained in the third and fourth centuries. Rabbinism was carried to Babylonia by Babylonian scholars such as Abba Arikha, known simply in the sources as Rav, who had studied with Judah ha-Nasi' in Palestine. Rav founded the great rabbinical academy at Sura on the Euphrates in *c.* 219. In the fourth and fifth centuries the Babylonian scholars, like their Palestinian contemporaries, staffed the community courts. In Babylonia they were supervised by the Exilarch (*resh galuta*), the counterpart of the Patriarch in Palestine. Rabbinic authority reached a peak in the ninth to eleventh centuries, when the *ge'onim*, the heads of the great Babylonian rabbinic schools of Sura and Pumbeditha, exercised spiritual hegemony over most of world Jewry, and were applied to for legal rulings (*responsa*) from as far away as Spain and Tunis.

In the nineteenth and twentieth centuries rabbinism has had to face the challenge of secularism. It has also had to face the fact that, in the modern, centralized bureaucratic state, Jews, like other minorities, have lost much of their communal autonomy. Matters which before the French Revolution would have been left to community courts are now judged by the secular courts of the state. This has robbed the rabbinate of one of its traditional power bases. The institution of the rabbinate continues to show signs of vitality and has demonstrated an ability to adapt to meet the challenge of modernity. In the state of Israel it has reverted very much to the role it played in Palestine in the third and fourth centuries. There the rabbinic courts are an official part of the legal system and under the Rabbinical Courts Jurisdiction Law (1953) they are charged with applying to Jews in matters of personal status the age-old rabbinic *halakhah*.

The ideology of the rabbinate. The rabbis developed a powerful ideology to support their claim to legislate for all Israel in law, doctrine and morals. The classic statement of that ideology is found in the Talmuds. It has three main elements.

The first of these is the assertion that Moses* received the Torah on Sinai in two forms, one written (*Torah she-bikhtav*), the other oral (*Torah she-be'al peh*). The latter, which supplemented and interpreted the former, had been passed down through a secure line of tradents to the rabbis themselves (Mishnah Pirqei Avot 1.1–18; 2.8), and it was in virtue of their possession of that Oral Torah that they maintained the correctness of their understanding of scripture and of God's will against that of other Jews, of Christians and of Gnostics* (Pesiqta Rabbati 5.1). At first sight, some formulations of the doctrine of Oral Torah seem to imply that the content of the tradition went *in toto* back to Moses on Sinai (e.g. Babylonian Talmud Berakhot 5a). In more nuanced contexts, however, it becomes clear that the rabbis actually held that the content of the Oral Torah only emerged with time. This view amounted to a doctrine of continuous revelation.* It was through the activities of the sages in their schools, as they analysed and discussed the Law, that the Torah unfolded in all its fullness. Neither miracles nor even a voice from heaven had any probative force in determining what was Torah – only the majority decision of the scholars (Babylonian Talmud Bava Meṣi'a 59a–b). The rabbis were thus continuing the work of Moses (cf. Matt. 23.2, 'sitting in Moses' seat'), and if Moses himself were to return to earth and visit the schools he would be unable to follow the legal discussion, so far had the law developed since his day (Babylonian Talmud Menaḥot 29b). Categorizing the traditions of the rabbinic schools as 'Torah' put those traditions on a par with the written text of scripture (cf. Palestinian Talmud Sanhedrin 10.1). The 'holy spirit' (*ruaḥ ha-qodesh*) which had inspired the earlier prophets, was still at work in Israel, no longer in individuals but in the collectivity of the Sages (Babylonian Talmud Bava Batra 12a; cf. Seder 'Olam Rabba 30). Paradoxically the rabbis could assert the superiority of the sage to the prophet, and of Mishnah to scripture (Palestinian Talmud Horayot 3.5). Rabbinic ordination by the laying on of hands (*semikhah*) must originally have been an attempt to symbolize the sacramental transfer of the spirit of Moses from one authority to another. Though the ending of this practice, possibly in the fourth century, created a theological problem for some rabbinic authorities, in fact little emphasis has traditionally been placed on legitimating rabbinic Judaism through *semikhah*. Continuity has been traced primarily through the verbal traditions of the schools.

In keeping with their doctrine of Oral Torah, the rabbis 'rabbinized' scripture and sacred history. Through a highly developed system of Bible interpretation they attempted to show that their ideas could be found in scripture. Furthermore, they represented the heroes of the Bible, King David and above all Moses, anachronistically as studying Torah in a rabbinic fashion. They even pictured the patriarchs of pre-Mosaic times as attending 'rabbinic' schools. This appeal to the Bible was necessary to validate their position, and to commend it to Jews in general, since the sacred scriptures were the one source of authority universally respected in Judaism. The rabbis also created the myth that there was a rabbinic academy in heaven (*yeshivah shelema'alah*) in which God himself studied Torah like the sages (Babylonian Talmud Bava Meṣi'a 86a; Gittin 68a). From a modern perspective this seems a blatant case of projecting rabbinic institutions into the heavenly, ideal world. The rabbis, however, saw it quite differently. They regarded the academy on earth as an image of the academy above, and legitimated their activities by claiming to be engaged in an *imitatio dei*.

The second major element in the ideology* of the rabbinate was the claim that the rabbi not only possessed Oral Torah, but was in himself an embodiment of the Torah. Great stress was placed on doing, as well as on knowing (Mishnah Pirqei Avot 1.17; 3.10). Thus one discovered Torah not only from what a master said but also from what he did, and the actions and behaviour of a competent scholar could minister as precedent (*ma'aseh*) in legal argument. The identification of the rabbi with his Torah is symbolically expressed in a number of Talmudic sayings by physically comparing the sage to a scroll of the Law (e.g. Palestinian Talmud Mo'ed Qaton 3.1,7).

It was on the basis of their incarnation of Torah that the rabbis claimed extreme respect not only from their disciples but also from the community at large: they should be honoured in the way in which the sacred scriptures were honoured. They exemplified the Torah, and holiness could be attained by imitating them, as they imitated God. This applied to the community at large, but *a fortiori* to the disciples of the sages, who were expected not only to hear the sage's teaching but to minister to him and to observe his every deed. The teacher was owed more respect and service than a father, for a father only brought one into this world, whereas the teacher brought one into the world to come (cf. Palestinian Talmud Bava Meṣi'a 2.11).

The third major element in the ideology of the rabbinate was the belief that the rabbis had a religious duty to spread Torah and to bring all Israel under the yoke of the kingdom* of heaven (Mishnah Pirqei Avot 1.12). Given the nature of Torah as God's will for Israel, the 'missionary' imperative arose inevitably. The rabbis saw the 'rabbinization' of Israel as their goal: the supreme ideal was that all Israel should become rabbis and that the distinction between them and the rest of the community should disappear. Those who could not achieve the supreme ideal could at least become disciples of the sages. The major instrument of this programme of rabbinization was study of the Torah, which became the paramount religious rite, of greater importance than prayer and other forms of worship: when one studied, the Shekhinah* was present (Mishnah Pirqei Avot 3.6). Such study ideally was not on one's own, but with a master, or a fellow student (*ḥaver*) (Mishnah Pirqei Avot 1.6,16). Study of the Torah led to holiness, to conformity with the will of God. Increasingly, from the third century onwards, the rabbis were to claim that it did more than this; it led to salvation: if all Jews were to keep the Torah, the messiah* would come and Israel would be delivered from foreign domination (Palestinian Talmud Ta'anit 1.1). This doctrine gave concrete meaning to Torah-observance, and shrewdly linked acceptance of the sage and his discipline with Jewish political aspirations. Torah-study was defined as a salvific act which atoned for the sins of Israel and hastened the redemption.

The rabbinic school. Though the rabbis claimed the right to control the synagogues (cf. Palestinian Talmud Megillah 3.3), they were accorded no special privileges or role in the synagogue or in the actual performance of its liturgy. The synagogue is a pre-rabbinic institution, which for most of its existence has been run by people who have not been rabbis. The distinctive and central rabbinic institution was the rabbinic school (*yeshivah*). This was the power-house of rabbinism, which generated rabbis and sent them out with their distinctive message into the community. It was a positive duty for every established scholar to make many disciples. In the Talmudic era there were numerous schools differing in size and in prestige. The basic pattern was very simple: rows of students (*talmidei ḥakhamim*) sat before the sage, probably, at least in the most primitive establishments, on the ground at his feet, with the sage raised on a dais or chair. One's progress in study could be gauged from the row in which one sat: the nearer the front, the further one had advanced (cf. Babylonian Talmud Menaḥot 29b). The content of the curriculum consisted largely of Oral Torah, from *c.* 200 onwards of Mishnah. Great stress was placed on orality: it was forbidden to produce written texts of the oral law in class, or to take notes. Much effort was expended on learning off by rote the traditions, which were formulated so as to assist memorization. The student also listened from time to time to discourses by the teacher on some theme of law. As he progressed he would have increasingly been expected to engage in dialectic and debate with his teacher, to question him and argue with him, and he might be called upon, from time to time, himself to deliver a discourse (Avot deRabbi Natan A.6). Each school appears to have built up its own body of traditions, its Mishnah, which underwent constant reformulation and expansion. It is these traditions that form the bedrock of classic rabbinic literature (Mishnah, Tosefta, the two Talmuds and the midrashim). All the classic rabbinic texts are school-texts which digest the discussions of the schools extending over many generations.

The Yeshivah was more than a law-school: it had also something of the character of a monastery. It was a religious community devoted to the rituals of the study of Torah. There is some evidence to suggest that students remained celibate while they attended the school. All aspects of the school's life – the relationship between master and pupil, between pupil and pupil, the manner in which communal meals were eaten, grace recited and the legal debates conducted, the way one walked, talked and relieved oneself – were governed by elaborate codes of etiquette which were seen as distinctively rabbinic. When the scholar left the school, he continued to observe these codes, which functioned socially to set him apart from other men. It is not clear whether the rabbis also adopted a distinctive 'clerical' dress, but they certainly observed some form of dress-code, which involved covering the head (Babylonian Talmud Qiddushin 31a; cf. Qiddushin 8a).

After leaving the school, the student might return from time to time for further periods of intensive study of the law. The schools were largely supported by charitable donations, though part of the 'patriarchal tax' in the fourth century may have gone towards their upkeep. The rabbis went out collecting donations for the schools, and stories were told of how heaven prospered those who subscribed (Palestinian Talmud Horayot 3.4).

The rabbi in society. The rabbi is a complex figure of authority who has played and still plays diverse roles within Jewish society. This complexity may be illustrated from the Palestinian Talmud. There the rabbi is depicted as a judge (*dayyan*) applying in the community courts rabbinic *halakhah*. His position as an authorized judicial authority formed the basis of his power within the community. But he also aspired to a more general role as a religious leader directing all aspects of religious life and general behaviour. He advised on social and commercial contacts with the local Gentiles (whose idolatrous practices caused many problems); he supervised communal funds, particularly charitable monies; he ruled on the disposal of synagogue property, on synagogue decoration, and on the conduct of services; he claimed to be able to annul vows. In some cases his opinion was directly sought; in others he himself took the initiative and tried to impose his views. He used preaching in synagogue as a way of giving spiritual direction to his community (Palestinian Talmud Sotah 1.4). He was also widely seen as a charismatic figure, a holy man with supernatural powers who was able to avert disasters such as fires and epidemics (Palestinian Talmud Nedarim 4.9; Ta'anit 3.4), to protect towns from attack (Palestinian Talmud Ta'anit 3.8), and to bring rain in time of drought (Palestinian Talmud Ta'anit 3.4). Even these magical* powers were usually related to his central function as a Torah-expert. In some cases it is implied that the magic depends on the sage's piety: his keeping of the Torah gains him merit with God, who in effect performs the miracles* on his behalf. Sometimes, however, a more subtle argument is used, linked to the doctrine of the cosmic Torah. Torah is seen as in some sense the instrument by which God created the world. Through his knowledge of Torah the rabbi has access to the laws of creation, and is able through this knowledge to affect the physical world.

The rabbis wielded considerable judicial, civic and spiritual power in the Palestinian Jewish communities of the third and fourth centuries. They were able to effect the transfer of property (including real estate), to intervene in personal affairs, and to impose penalties through fines (Palestinian Talmud Avodah Zarah 1.6) and floggings (Palestinian Talmud Qiddushin 4.4). Their authority was based in part on the power of the Patriarch, who was backed by Rome, and who, if need arose, could send his personal retainers to compel compliance (Palestinian Talmud Ketubot 9.2; Ta'anit 3.1; Horayot 3.1). The threat of violence from the rabbi's disciples, who seem to have been ready physically to defend his honour (cf. Palestinian Talmud Sotah 1.4), may have been sufficient on some occasions to inspire obedience. The rabbi could also use the power of excommunication (*ḥerem*), though this could only be effective if the community at large co-operated (Palestinian Talmud Mo'ed Qaton 3.1). Finally, he could in his capacity as a holy man with access to supernatural power pronounce a curse on those who did not do his will (Palestinian Talmud Bava Meṣi'a 4.2). But there were limits to the rabbis' power, and they were well aware of it. The rabbi is frequently exhorted in moral tales to behave with humility and circumspection (e.g. Palestinian Talmud Sotah 1.4). The rabbis show a marked respect for local custom (*minhag*) even when it does not strictly conform to rabbinic practice (Palestinian Talmud Beṣah 1.9; Ta'anit 1.6; 3.11). And they take care not to antagonize the 'great ones of the generation' (*gedolei ha-dor*), i.e. the powerful non-rabbinic families and individuals in the community (Palestinian Talmud Qiddushin 4.1). In the last analysis they could not have achieved their position in society by relying solely on the Patriarch's retainers. They must have achieved it essentially by gaining the respect and trust of the majority of Jews, who must broadly have subscribed to the rabbinic world-view.

The three classic roles of the rabbi depicted in the Palestinian Talmud – judge, spiritual leader and magician – have remained remarkably constant down to modern times, though one role may be stressed more than another, depending on the time, the place and the person. There are still rabbinical figures in the Hasidic and ultra-traditional movements who continue to fulfil all three rabbinic roles, including that of holy man and magician. Perhaps the most radical challenge to the rabbi's traditional roles occurred among Reform Jews who, as a result of emancipation, became acutely aware of the ways of the dominant non-Jewish culture. In nineteenth-century Reform, a new type of rabbi emerges who is in many ways comparable to the Protestant minister of religion. He is attached to a congregation and in effect exercises a 'cure of souls': he plays a leading role in synagogue worship, officiates at weddings, bar mitzvahs and funerals; he undertakes a wide range of pastoral duties, and generally ministers to the spiritual needs of his flock. The question has arisen in recent years as to whether or not a woman can perform the functions of a rabbi: Reform, Reconstructionist and Conservative Judaism have all argued that she can and so have ordained women rabbis. Since the rabbi's authority is based on expertise in the Torah, in principle there would appear to be no objection. Traditionalists, however, have strongly opposed this development: they argue that it is contrary to *halakhah* for women to hold public office. There is no obligation on a woman to study and teach Torah, and her juridical powers are limited because she is not qualified to act as a witness. The main objection, however, is that ordination of women is contrary to custom and tradition and runs counter to, among other things, the traditional separation of men and women in the synagogue. Some rabbinic authorities have tried to stress the differences between the new type of rabbi and the older traditional rabbinate. The 'new' rabbis have sometimes been issued after training not with a rabbinical diploma but with a minister's diploma, and have been called not 'rabbi' but 'reverend', or some other such title. However, common parlance among Jews ignores these niceties; the ministers are usually referred to as 'rabbis', and the distinction now appears generally to have been abandoned – with some justification, for even in the case of the most modern rabbi his (or her) authority is still, when all is said and done, based on a claim to expertise in the Torah.

Rabbinism. 'Rabbinism' is today used mainly by academic historians of religion as a convenient term for 'the teachings and traditions of the rabbis'. It is arguable that the rabbinic world-view developed in the Talmudic period has predominated in Judaism from the third century AD down to the present day. It has, indeed, been powerfully challenged. For example, Qaraism, which emerged in the seventh century in Persia, rejected rabbinic Oral Torah contained in the Talmud and midrash, and claimed to go back to scripture as its sole source of authority. And Hasidism, which arose in the Ukraine in the eighteenth century, also challenged the rabbis by giving allegiance to a new type of charismatic leader (the *ṣaddiq*) whose authority did not rest on his mastery of *halakhah*. Both these movements gained numerically significant followings, but rabbinism successfully fought them off. Rabbinic scholars such as Saadia Gaon (882–942) developed a highly effective anti-Qaraite polemic. And, after a period of bitter conflict, rabbinism reached in the nineteenth century a *modus vivendi* with Hasidism, largely due to the increasing 'rabbinization' of Hasidism. Most Jews have acknowledged in principle the spiritual leadership of the rabbis, and have regarded the classic texts of rabbinism (the Talmuds and the great mediaeval rabbinic law codes such as the Shulhan 'Arukh) as authoritative for the definition of Judaism. Through all the changes of history, from late antiquity to the present, the Torah-expert – the rabbi – has remained the major figure of religious authority in Judaism. It is, therefore, historically justifiable to see rabbinic Judaism as 'normative', or even 'orthodox' Judaism, a view which rabbinism itself has naturally been eager to promote. However, two points should be borne in mind. First, the rabbis have always been an intellectual elite within Judaism: a small band of scholars who have offered spiritual guidance to all Israel. They have never dominated the Jewish communities to the degree that they would like, or to the degree that they often claim. Their power has always been limited within the community: many of those who have acknowledged their authority in principle have failed to follow fully the rabbinic way of life, and the rabbis have seldom been in a position to compel compliance with their views (even when they wanted to). Secondly, the Torah in which the rabbi is an expert has changed over the years, and varies substantially from group to group. Oral Torah is by definition an open-ended, constantly evolving tradition. There has always been a tendency to identify it with all that was taught and studied in the schools. And it is open to dispute what belongs to Torah and how the fundamental tenets of rabbinism and the earlier stages of the tradition are to be interpreted. As a result rabbinism is not monolithic but embraces within itself divergent trends, movements and parties, some of which even refuse to recognize the positions adopted by other parties as legitimate forms of Judaism.

See also **Jewish Exegesis.**

S. W. Baron, *The Jewish Community: Its History and Structure to the American Revolution*, 1942, vol. II, pp. 66–200; L. Finkelstein, *Jewish Self-Government in the Middle Ages*, 1942; M. Goodman, *State and Society in Roman Galilee, AD 132–212*, 1983, pp. 93–174; J. Neusner, *Judaism in Society: The Evidence of the Yerushalmi*, 1983, pp. 113–254; id., *School, Court, Public Administration: Judaism and its Institutions in Talmudic Babylonia*, 1987; E. Schürer, *The History of the Jewish People in the Age of Jesus Christ*, vol. II, revd G. Vermes, F. Millar and M. Black, 1979, pp. 323–403; E. E. Urbach, *The Sages: Their Concepts and Beliefs*, 1987; 'The Making of American Rabbis', *Encyclopaedia Judaica Yearbook 1983/5*, 1985, pp. 84–105.

PHILIP S. ALEXANDER

Reader-Response Criticism

Reading is a dangerous activity. It can change our perspective, stir our emotions, and provoke us to action. In other words, reading elicits a response in the reader. This happens because the reception of literature is not passive but active and constructive. We try to make sense of the text. The text itself is impotent until we realize its potential meaning, and while we are engaged with it, we may be influenced by our interpretation.

Recently, some literary critics have turned their attention away from the author and towards the reader who comprehends the text, who deciphers words and sentences, relates parts to the whole, selects and organizes, anticipates and modifies expectations, and creates meaning. Reading is a co-operative endeavour. Through its literary conventions and strategies, the text presents a puzzle, which the reader must solve to gain understanding. The reader is drawn into the adventure not only by what the text spells out but also by what it withholds. To understand literature, the reader must begin to fill in the gaps, to infer what is not given, at least provisionally, until what is unclear at first is clarified by what follows. This creation of meaning * may change the reader in the process, because literature in the Bible does not simply tell us about the spirit of a past age or its social conditions, but allows us to experience them.

Consider a short example from the Acts of the Apostles, the story of Ananias (5.1–6). After noting that believers in Jesus Christ formed in Jerusalem a community * which held everything in common, the narrative illustrates the manner in which this happened by the example of Barnabas, who sold a field, brought the money and laid it at the apostles' feet (4.32–37). 'But a man named Ananias with his wife Sapphira sold a piece of property, and with his wife's knowledge, he kept back some of the proceeds, and brought only a part and laid it at the apostles' feet. But Peter said, "Ananias, why has Satan filled your heart to lie to the Holy Spirit and to keep back part of the proceeds of the land? While it remained unsold, did it not remain your own? And after it was sold, was it not at your disposal? How is it that you have contrived this deed in your heart? You have not lied to men but to God." When Ananias heard these words, he fell down and died. And great fear came upon all who heard it. The young men rose and wrapped him up and carried him out and buried him.'

The introductory 'but' in the English translation * alerts the reader to the possibility of construing what follows as a counter-example to that of Barnabas, but the Greek *de* is ambiguous. It could mean 'and', suggesting merely a second example. Ananias and Sapphira have not appeared in the story before, so the reader knows nothing of their characters. Moreover, there is no hint in the first sentence that they conspire to act dishonestly. It is possible, therefore, to place Ananias and Sapphira on a par with Barnabas, their story being told to explain that some members of the community were able to give more than others and were free to make their own decisions. Indeed, Peter's question in v. 4 confirms the possibility of this interpretation.

When Peter is introduced into the story, in v. 3, he is already known to the reader as a spokesman and leader of the apostles. Nevertheless, his question occasions surprises. First of all, it is couched in theological terms, implying that Satan can corrupt a man's heart. Secondly, the question incorporates an accusation of lying, and again in theological terms: not lying to the apostles but lying to the Holy Spirit. These particular theological expressions are already familiar to the reader, and their application to this case encourages a connexion with the general theological structure of the book. But why is the accusation made? How did Peter discover a motive so private that even the reader's knowledge of what took place before Ananias met Peter has not made it clear? The reader is nevertheless inclined to accept Peter's interpretation because he has been portrayed as a reliable character. On this basis, the action of Ananias must be re-interpreted by supplying information: Ananias presented the money as if it was the whole amount, in order to appear more generous than he was. The question still remains, however. How did Peter recognize the dishonesty? The reader is left to ponder whether Peter noticed something shifty in Ananias' behaviour, received a revelation from God which is not recounted, or could read other men's thoughts.

The conclusion to the story also leaves open a number of possibilities. Who are the 'all who heard it' who were afraid? Were they afraid of God's wrath or of sudden death? Did their fear affect their behaviour? Who are the 'young men' and why was it their role to wrap, remove and bury the corpse? They perform a similar service in v. 10, but are never mentioned again in the book. The reader who comes to Acts after enjoying novels by Dickens will be astonished that many of the minor characters in Acts appear only once, within episodes, and play no further part in the plot.

Other questions arise too. When did the young men bury the corpse—immediately or after some time? The reader has to continue reading before discovering that they must have done so quickly, because the corpse had disappeared when Sapphira arrived three hours later. Further, was it customary to bury corpses, and, if so, where were they buried in Jerusalem and what arrangements had to be made? Was it usual to bury a man without consulting his wife?

Noticing both what information is supplied and what is withheld helps to bring the narrative into focus. The ambiguous opening sentence gives Peter's question an awesome force. The theological references show that theology, not psychology, is central to the story. Ananias' feelings, whether of shame or consternation, go without mention, allowing only a theological explanation of his death as God's judgment, in spite of the fact that the text does not state boldly: God struck Ananias dead as a punishment for his dishonesty. The fearful reaction of those who heard encourages the reader to respond likewise, and the burial is mentioned to confirm the fact of death. What is completely lacking in this story, and in most biblical narratives, is any description of details in the setting. Nor are we told how old the characters are, or how they looked. The reader is left to fill in these gaps in order to make the story more concrete. The omission of such details highlights the significance of theology so that the reader is not distracted by irrelevances.

It was suggested earlier that the involvement of the reader in actively making sense of these sentences, forming and revising hypotheses, has an effect. The effect is structured by the form of the text, which suggests a response of awe and fear. The 'implied reader', that is, the reader encoded by the text's strategies, should make that response. But actual readers may react differently. A modern reader could respond with moral outrage or theological disapproval.

Because reception theory (as a school of German literary criticism is called) or reader-response criticism (the name given to the work of a group of literary critics in North America*) is based on gestalt psychology,* it expects the reader to form the text into a coherent whole. For example, it expects the reader to discover an overall theological pattern in Acts, into which to fit the story of Ananias. But it recognizes that different readers will create different unities. Two reasonable assumptions are made: that texts are open to more than one meaning and that readers may be more competent at construing some kinds of texts than others. The reader who fails to recognize irony,* for example, will miss one of the dimensions in the account of Jesus' ministry given by the Fourth Gospel, but may recognize other strategies. This kind of competence can be learned, moreover, and critics like Wolfgang Iser not only explore the varieties of response required by the different conventions of narratives but, in so doing, teach new skills. Nevertheless, it soon becomes clear that Iser's ideal reader is a person of liberal persuasion, receptive to the influences of profoundly new human insights. Other critics are less sanguine about the openness of individuals. The Freudian critic Norman Holland, for example, pictures the reader constrained by psychological needs which the text is forced to meet. He accounts for different interpretations of the same text among people of similar background and experience by suggesting that 'the individual can accept the literary work only to the extent he exactly recreates with it a verbal form of his particular pattern of defence mechanisms' (see his essay in Tompkins, 1980). Perhaps more important for religious texts is the reader's membership of a particular religious institution, which predisposes to one interpretation rather than another. At the very least, however, the text can make the reader conscious of the presuppositions brought to it.

See also **Genre; Literary Criticism; Narrative Criticism; Rhetorical Criticism.**

R. C. Holub, *Reception Theory: A Critical Introduction*, 1984; W. Iser, *The Act of Reading*, ET 1978; M. Sternberg, *The Poetics of Biblical Narrative*, 1985; J. P. Tompkins (ed.), *Reader-Response Criticism*, 1980.

MARGARET DAVIES

Redaction Criticism

That aspect of biblical study which tries to discover the ideas of the author of a text. The term is used particularly in relation to the books of the Bible which purport to recount the events of history. In contrast to an approach which is interested in discovering historical information about the events described, redaction criticism is concerned with discovering information about the author from the way in which the story is told.

As a discipline within NT study, redaction criticism is often thought of as applying primarily to study of the Synoptic Gospels* and, as such, as being the successor of form criticism.* In fact, redaction criticism, in the broad sense of identifying the concerns of an author, is as old as the *Tendenzkritik* (*see* **Tendency Criticism**) of the Tübingen school's* work on the Gospels. But certainly the discipline has in some shape or form dominated Gospel studies ever since the 1950s.

In relation to the Synoptic Gospels, redaction criticism is concerned to discover the contributions which the evangelists* themselves have made to the Gospel tradition. Form criticism had analysed the way in which

the stories about Jesus had circulated within the Christian church prior to their inclusion in the present Gospels. Many form critics had a relatively low opinion of the work of the evangelists themselves. The latter were regarded as simply 'editors', 'scissors-and-paste' collectors of the material who put the story together in a relatively simple way. This view of the evangelists changed in the 1950s with a number of significant studies devoted to the work of evangelists, e.g. G. Bornkamm on Matthew, W. Marxsen on Mark, and H. Conzelmann on Luke. In these studies, attention was focussed on the ways in which each evangelist had imposed his own ideas on the material which he had available. As a result, the three evangelists emerged much more as creative theologians in their own right, rather than just as editors of the material.

The method employed, especially in earlier studies of redaction criticism of the Gospels, was to look at the way in which one evangelist had altered his tradition. Such alteration and changes to a tradition are usually known as 'redaction' of the tradition: hence the name of the discipline. This procedure is easy to adopt in the case of Matthew and Luke, provided one assumes that Mark's Gospel was used by both these evangelists as a source (*see* **Synoptic Problem**). Since we have Matthew's and Luke's source independently available to us, we can compare the wording of each of these Gospels with that of Mark to see how the later evangelists have redacted their source.

For example, Luke changes Mark's form of the words of Jesus' reply to the High Priest at the Sanhedrin trial quite significantly. In Mark 14.62, Jesus tells the High Priest 'You will see the Son of man sitting at the right hand of Power and coming with the clouds of heaven.' Luke 22.69 has 'From now on the Son of man will be seated at the right hand of the power of God.' All ideas of a universally visible event ('you will see') of the Son of man* 'coming on the clouds' disappear in the Lucan version, so that in Luke the prediction refers only to the immediate session of the risen Jesus in heaven. This may indicate a certain tendency by Luke to play down some aspects of eschatology* in his tradition and to place all weight on the ascension of Jesus.

A redaction-critical approach outside passages where Matthew and Luke have used Mark is inevitably more complex since we do not have the evangelists' sources directly available. However, such an approach is not impossible. In the case of the so-called 'Q' material, it is sometimes possible to be reasonably confident about the wording of the Q source and hence to see how Matthew/Luke have modified that source. For example, it is probable that the so-called 'doom oracle' in Matt.

23.34/Luke 11.49 is more original in its Lucan version in that it is in the form of a saying of 'the Wisdom of God'. Matthew's version has the saying as one of Jesus himself and this may reveal a facet of Matthew's christology:* Jesus for Matthew takes the place of divine Wisdom.

In the case of Mark, the situation is harder since we do not have independent access to Mark's sources at all (assuming Marcan priority). However, many have argued that Mark's own contributions and concerns can be identified in his Gospel, e.g. in the 'seam' passages linking the individual stories together, in some of the general summaries which Mark periodically gives (e.g. 3.11f.), and in some common features which recur at significant points throughout the Gospel. Above all, many have argued that features in Mark associated with the messianic secret* are due to Mark's own redactional activity and reveal his own ideas.

The contribution of the evangelists is shown not only by the small details where they change the wording of their sources. It can also be seen by the way in which the whole story is arranged. Matthew rearranges his sources to bring together a whole block of ethical* teaching in the Sermon on the Mount* (Matt. 5–7), followed by a series of miracle* stories (Matt. 8–9), perhaps to show Jesus as messiah* in both word and deed. Luke brings forward the story of the rejection of Jesus in Nazareth to act as a programmatic summary of the whole story to follow in Luke–Acts (Luke 4.16–30). Mark's arrangement too is often significant, e.g. when he 'sandwiches' one story in the middle of another. For example, the story of the 'cleansing' of the temple is sandwiched between the two halves of the story of the cursing of the fig tree (Mark 11.12–20), perhaps to show that Jesus' action in the temple is really to be regarded as a final rejection, or 'cursing', of the temple.

Early redaction-critical studies of the Gospels concentrated almost exclusively on the changes which one author had made to his sources.* It is now recognized that such a procedure may lead to a somewhat distorted picture of a writer's theology. For a writer's decision to include a tradition,* perhaps unaltered, may be seen in just as positive terms as actually changing a tradition. A writer may decide to preserve a tradition unaltered precisely because he agrees with it very strongly. Hence in more recent Gospel study there has been a strong trend to take seriously the whole of an evangelist's work as potentially contributing to an understanding of his theology. Clearly alterations to the tradition will be significant in this respect, but the tradition which is preserved cannot be written off as 'merely' tradition. Thus many today would adopt a more 'literary'* approach to the Gospels, looking at each as a literary whole in its own right and seeking to illuminate the theology of the author as much from the work as a whole, its structure* and inner connections, as from an analysis of the ways in which sources and traditions have been changed by the evangelist.

If redaction criticism is regarded not only as an analysis of the detailed changes made to a source by a writer, but as the attempt to discover the theology of the author of a text, then it goes wider than the study of the Synoptic Gospels alone, and can be regarded as the approach which governs almost all study of John's Gospel and also of all the epistles* of the NT. In the case of the epistles, critical study has always sought to discover the ideas of the author of the epistle concerned. So too with the Fourth Gospel, most scholars today would argue that the work is primarily a source for the ideas and the theology of its author rather than a source of information about the events which it describes. Hence most modern critical study of John's Gospel is concerned with the thought of the evangelist himself.

At times redaction criticism in the narrower sense, i.e. analysis of the way in which prior traditions have been redacted by the author of a text, can be applied to these documents as well. We do not have Paul's* or John's sources directly to hand, but, for example, several traditional elements in Paul's letters have been identified (cf. Rom. 1.3f.; 3.25f.; Phil. 2.5–11), and Paul's modifications of his tradition can sometimes be pin-pointed. For example, in Rom. 1.3f., Paul may have added the words 'concerning his Son' and 'in power' to the mini-creed he seems to cite in order to avoid the possible implication that Jesus only became Son of God at the resurrection.* Paul's redaction of his tradition thus enables us to have insight into an aspect of his christology.

The precise identification of John's sources is more problematic. However, many have argued that John used a source for his miracle stories (the so-called 'Signs' source) and that in doing so he tried to shift the accent away from the miracles themselves in order to focus on the supreme importance of the person of Jesus alone for Christian faith (cf. the discourses which often follow, and 'interpret', the miracles). In this way too John's 'redaction' of his tradition can tell us something about his theology.

Redaction criticism has dominated modern Gospel study over the last forty years. In a sense, it has dominated study of Paul and

John ever since the rise of critical scholarship. Redaction criticism has successfully shown how the authors of the books of the Bible have made significant contributions to their texts. Especially in the historical books of the Bible, redaction criticism has shown how each author has imposed his own ideas on the story by shaping his account in the way he has. As such, redaction criticism has made us aware of the individuality of each author. It has given us insight into the rich variety within the Bible, and it has made us aware of the complex problems involved in rediscovering the events described in any historical book of the Bible. Above all, it has shown us that the biblical authors were religiously sensitive people, struggling with their traditions and seeking to apply their traditions to their own day in changing situations.

See also **Luke, Gospel of; Mark, Gospel of; Matthew, Gospel of; Tradition, History of.**

N. Perrin, *What is Redaction Criticism?*, 1970; N. R. Petersen, *Literary Criticism for New Testament Critics*, 1978; J. Rohde, *Rediscovering the Teaching of the Evangelists*, 1968; C. M. Tuckett, *Reading the New Testament*, 1987.

C. M. TUCKETT

Reformation

The centrality of the Bible to the Reformation of the sixteenth century is sufficiently well known to require no further documentation. The principle *sola scriptura* soon became established as fundamental to both the Swiss and German reformations. Not only did this phrase refer to a new emphasis upon the theological priority of scripture; it also included a new understanding of what scripture actually was. Two major points of difference between the Reformers and their Catholic opponents may be noted: first, the former excluded from 'scripture' the apocryphal* works included in the Vulgate;* second, the Reformers insisted that 'scripture' designated canonical* works in their original languages, and not in their Vulgate translation.

The new textual,* philological* and hermeneutical* tools of the European Renaissance placed at the disposal of the sixteenth-century Reformers a formidable armoury with which to challenge the prevailing interpretations of scripture. The implicit assumption of much mediaeval* theology (that 'scripture' could be identified with the Vulgate text) was discredited through the new interest in philology and the desire to return *ad fontes*, to the original sources of Christian faith rather than their inadequate Latin translations.

The importance of this point in relation to biblical interpretation will be obvious. Thus the reference to the sacrament of penance which appeared to be implied by the Vulgate translation of Matt. 4.17 ('do penance') was eliminated, in favour of a reference to the inward psychological attitude of repentance. The Vulgate reference to marriage as a *sacramentum* was eliminated, in favour of its being a *musterion*. The Vulgate suggestion that Mary was 'full of grace' (Luke 1.28) was dismissed: Mary was simply 'highly favoured'. Major shifts in interpretation of scripture thus took place simply on account of the programmatic return to scripture in its original languages. No new hermeneutical presuppositions attended these alterations: these new interpretations rested solely upon the rejection of the Vulgate translation in favour of the text in its original languages. The rise of the new biblical scholarship, of course, also resulted in alterations to the text of scripture itself (such as the elimination of I John 5.7, now seen as a later insertion): none of these, however, seem to have been of major importance to biblical interpretation at the time.

The importance of humanism in connection with the methods of biblical interpretation employed by the Reformers cannot be overemphasized. It was the humanists who made scripture generally available in its original texts, and who made accessible the philological skills required for their translation.* It must, of course, be emphasized that in the sixteenth century the term 'humanist' did not possess the secular overtones now associated with it. The long-held assumption that Renaissance humanists propounded a secular view of the world has now been successfully challenged, opening the way to a new appraisal of the religious thought of humanism. That religious thought is closely linked with the exegesis* of scripture, as Erasmus'* *Enchiridion* (1503) made clear.

The approach to scripture exemplified in the writings of the Swiss humanists Vadianus and Xylotectus, and derivatively in those of Zwingli, should be noted: scripture is regarded as a textual framework which is capable of mediating an experience. With the use of the appropriate textual, literary and philological tools, the first-century experience to which the NT bears witness may be recaptured. The theme of *Christianismus renascens*, characteristic of Swiss humanism and the early Swiss Reformation, is based upon the belief that humanist textual methods hold the key to the contemporary encounter with the risen Christ within the church. Perhaps unsurprisingly, it was also the humanists who made available one of the most important hermeneutical schemes for the interpretation of scripture.

Zwingli's approach to biblical interpretation in the period 1515–20 is basically Erasmian. Expressing a marked preference for Origen's* allegorical* method of exegesis, Zwingli developed a dialectical approach to the 'word' and the 'sense' of scripture. The literal* words of scripture may not adequately convey its meaning. At points, Zwingli grounds this distinction in II Cor. 3.6, 'the letter kills, but the Spirit gives life'. Thus in Gen. 22, Zwingli suggests that Abraham* should be understood to represent God if the spiritual* meaning of the text is to be discerned, whereas the true meaning of the episode in the following chapter (Gen. 23) can only be grasped if Abraham represents faithful believers. It seems, in fact, that Zwingli's approach to the OT at this point is probably better regarded as typological,* rather than allegorical. Although this might seem to render the literal sense of scripture superfluous, Zwingli nevertheless insisted that it had a crucial role to play: without the literal sense, people could interpret scripture in whatever manner they pleased (a criticism which, it need hardly be added, was brought against Zwingli himself). The literal sense is thus viewed as a safeguard against radical interpretations.

Later, however, Zwingli came to place increasing emphasis upon the literal, or 'natural', sense of scripture. In part, this development may also be put down to Erasmus' influence: following his editorial work leading to the publication of the first printed Greek NT text, the *Novum Instrumentum omne* (1516), Erasmus had come to regard the literal sense as having priority over the non-literal, or 'spiritual', senses. This shift is marked by the development by Zwingli of a preference for Jerome over Origen among the church Fathers, reflecting the former's giving of priority to the natural sense of scripture, and his emphasis upon the importance of scholarship in its interpretation.

This new appreciation of the importance of the literal sense of scripture is particularly clear in the case of Zwingli's OT commentaries* of the mid-1520s, as the conflict with the Anabaptists became of especial significance. We now find him following the later Erasmus, and insisting upon an adequate knowledge of the Hebrew and Septuagint* text of the OT as an essential prerequisite for its interpretation. To illustrate this point, Zwingli uses the analogy of a horse and its reins. The horse (the spiritual sense) and the reins (the literal sense) are joined together in the act of drawing something. The reins do not draw without the horse, nor the horse without the reins. Yet the reins act to keep the horse on the track.

Martin Bucer, while drawing upon Erasmus' hermeneutical insights, modified them significantly. For Bucer, the allegorical interpretation is to be rejected totally, in that it allows human ideas to be imposed upon scripture. It allows virtually any interpretation to be read into a passage. Erasmus (here followed by Zwingli) treated the 'letter' of scripture as the husk or outward form of a passage, and the 'spirit' as its kernel or inward meaning. For Bucer, the 'letter' is to be understood as referring to scripture when read apart from the life-giving power of the Holy Spirit. The historical sense of a passage is fundamental, and through judicious use of Greek, Hebrew and Aramaic and the guidance of the Holy Spirit, the believer may expect to be led to find the relevance of the passage to him.

At this point, a convergence between Erasmus and Bucer is obvious. Both place emphasis upon the tropological, or moral, sense of scripture. In other words, scripture is understood to be orientated towards the practical questions of human existence. It is *lex Christi*, defining the contours of the believer's existence. Through the guidance and inspiration of the Holy Spirit, the believer is empowered to fulfil the demands of the new obedience of the gospel. In interpreting OT and NT alike as law, Bucer echoes Erasmus' *philosophia Christi*. A decisive break with this moralist exegesis of scripture was only finally achieved within the Reformed church through the contribution of John Calvin.*

The Reformed approach to biblical interpretation underwent significant development through his contribution, which relates primarily to the popular dissemination of his particular understanding of scripture, rather than the method of scriptural exegesis which he himself employed. Calvin fashioned biblical commentaries* into a sophisticated means of propagating the ideas of the Genevan Reformation, capable of breaking down national and cultural barriers. His highly influential *Institutio Christianae religionis*, particularly in its 1559 edition, made available a comprehensive authority for the interpretation of biblical *loci*. As Calvin stated his intention in the preface to the 1541 French edition of this work, it 'could be like a key and an entrance to give access to Holy Scripture to all the children of God, in order that they might really understand it'. A similar function was served by Luther's* German translation of the Bible, which intermingled translation and creative interpretation.

In contrast to Zwingli and Bucer, whose background was Renaissance humanism, Luther developed within a framework dominated by scholastic theology. While he was familiar with many of the ideas and methods of humanism, Luther remained hostile to its general ethos. His reforming theology arose within the context of biblical exposition during the period 1513–17. Initially in the course of his first lectures on the Psalter (the

Dictata super Psalterium of 1513–15), and subsequently during his lectures on Romans (1515–16) and Galatians (1516–17), Luther wrestled with the theological questions which dominated his personal agenda – questions of justification, judgment and grace. In wrestling with the biblical texts, and creatively employing them as a mirror in which his own personal theological preoccupations were reflected, Luther came to link the origins of his reforming theology with the interpretation of scripture. This sharply distinguished Luther from Zwingli, for example. Although some scholars have suggested that Luther's theological breakthrough of 1515 is linked with the development of a new hermeneutic, the evidence for this suggestion is wanting. Luther's new hermeneutical insights appear to have developed alongside his new theology, the two mutually reinforcing each other.

Luther initially employs the standard scholastic hermeneutical device of the *Quadriga*, or 'four-fold sense of scripture', in his exposition of the Psalter. He has little initial use for the anagogical sense of scripture, but makes extensive use of the literal, allegorical, and especially the tropological or moral sense. Drawing on the hermeneutical insights of Lefèvre d'Étaples, rather than those of Erasmus, Luther argues that the 'killing letter of scripture' must be distinguished from the 'life-giving Spirit'. Indeed, at one point he suggests that it is precisely the ability to discern spirit and letter which makes a theologian. In O T interpretation Luther thus draws a distinction, following Lefèvre, between the 'literal-historic sense' and the 'literal-prophetic sense'. The former is the historical sense of the O T, understood as a narrative concerning the nation of Israel, whereas the latter is the same text viewed as a prophecy of the life, death and resurrection* of Jesus Christ. By employing this distinction, Luther is enabled to adopt a christological approach to the O T, particularly the Psalter, consolidating and developing the exegetical insights of Augustine.* Indeed, scripture possesses authority for Luther precisely in so far as it centres upon Jesus Christ.

It was, of course, for this reason that Luther questioned the authority of the Epistle of James: reference to Jesus Christ was conspicuously absent. Luther's criterion of canonicity in the early 1520s can be summarized in the slogan *treibt es Christum oder nicht?* The German verb *treiben* appears to have conveyed two senses – 'impel' and 'direct'. If a writing does not direct its reader towards Christ, its canonicity may be called into question. This criterion* naturally underscores the importance of a christological approach to the O T: if the O T cannot be interpreted in such a manner that it directs the reader towards

Christ, its authority* must be called into question. Luther's christological exegesis of the O T undergirds his defence of its continued authority within the Christian church.

Luther's hermeneutical insights, however, appear to have been of minor importance in relation to the origins and development of the Reformation in general, whatever their importance to his personal theological development may have been. The Lutheran Reformation as a whole is perhaps better regarded as a recovery of Augustine, and his particular method of interpreting scripture, rather than as a recovery of scripture itself. Furthermore, there were serious disagreements within the early Lutheran Reformation concerning the manner in which scripture was to be interpreted. Thus Andreas Bodenstein von Karlstadt, Luther's colleague at Wittenberg in the later 1510s, argued that the literal sense of scripture was of fundamental importance (where Luther placed the emphasis upon the tropological sense), and that scripture was to be interpreted in the same manner as a human will or last testament.

A final point should be made. The phrase *sola scriptura* is often misunderstood to imply that the Reformers interpreted scripture as individuals, apart from the tradition of the church. It is certainly true to state that the Radical Reformation, or 'Anabaptists', elevated private judgment above that of the church. It is this section of the Reformation which retained the radical sense of the phrase *sola scriptura*, i.e. by scripture alone, as interpreted by the enlightened pious believer, through the guidance of the Holy Spirit. In the case of the Magisterial Reformation (what one might call the official, mainstream movement), especially in the case of Luther, the corporate judgment of the church was regarded as an essential element in the interpretation of scripture. The Reformers felt at liberty to diverge from traditional interpretation only when obliged to do so by the latest philological or textual advances. Thus Melanchthon felt able to correct Augustine on points of interpretation, where philological techniques suggested that it was proper to do so – but the essential framework of his thought was accepted as reliable. For example, Melanchthon argued that, in relation to Augustine's doctrine of grace, his deficient knowledge of both Greek and Hebrew led him to misunderstand what the verb *iustificare*, 'to justify', meant. Augustine understood it to mean 'make righteous', where the Hebrew was, according to Melanchthon, more accurately translated as 'declare righteous'.

Nevertheless, the overall structure of Augustine's theology of grace was accepted as correct by Melanchthon. The strongly conservative views of the Reformers in relation to their christology and views on the Trinity further reflect their conviction that the early church had interpreted scripture correctly on these points; their hostile attitudes to mediaeval views on the sacraments and Mariology equally reflected their view that these departures from the consensus of the early church could not be justified on the basis of the new scientific approach to scripture which was now developing. The *sola scriptura* principle, as used by the magisterial Reformers, actually amounts to a programme of returning to the interpretation of scripture associated with the early church.

See also **Calvin; Luther; Mediaeval Interpretation.**

Jerry H. Bentley, *Humanists and Holy Writ*, 1984; Alister E. McGrath, *The Intellectual Origins of the European Reformation*, 1987, pp. 122–74; id., *Reformation Thought: An Introduction*, 1988, pp. 95–116; W. P. Stephens, *The Holy Spirit in the Theology of Martin Bucer*, 1970, pp. 129–55; id., *The Theology of Huldrych Zwingli*, 1986, pp. 51–79.

A. E. MCGRATH

Reimarus, H. S.

Hermann Samuel Reimarus (1694–1768) was from 1728 Professor of Hebrew and Oriental languages at the Academic Gymnasium in Hamburg, where he lectured also on philosophy, mathematics, and natural sciences. He wrote an orthodox defence of OT prophecy* against Spinoza, Grotius, and the deists* (1731), edited Dio Cassius (1751–2), and published a theological bestseller defending natural religion against atheism (1754), a major work of philosophy (1756), and a classic on animal psychology (1760).

But this Enlightenment* man, a public supporter of Wolff's Christian synthesis of revelation and reason, was in the 1730s also persuaded by the criticisms of orthodoxy found in Pierre Bayle's *Dictionnaire* and in the writings of Toland, Collins, Woolston, Tindal and Morgan in England. Over some thirty years he penned his *Apologie, oder Schützschrift für die vernünftigen Verehrer Gottes*, completing it in 1767, but prudently showed it only to a few trusted friends who like him were 'rational worshippers of God', practising the virtue and love of humanity which Christ preached, i.e. deists. He considered his society not yet ready for the truth about the Bible and revealed religion.

In 1774–8, Lessing published from his librarian's position at Wolfenbüttel seven *Fragments* of an early (around 1750) draft, concealing Reimarus' authorship. He added some comments of his own, arguing that the falsifica-

tion of the biblical history did not undermine Christian truth, which is Spirit, not letter. Protestant orthodoxy responded, led by Pastor Goeze of Hamburg, and censorship cut short the controversy. Though the complete manuscript was not published till 1972 (2 vols, Frankfurt), Lessing's *Fragments of an Unknown Author* (Reimarus' son disclosed his identity in 1814) contain the gist. They were badly excerpted for English translation by Voysey in 1879 (reprinted 1962), but the last and most important two, 'On the Resurrection Narratives*' and 'On the Intention of Jesus and his Disciples', were in 1970 edited by C. H. Talbert for L. E. Keck's *Lives of Jesus* series.

The complete *Apologie*, divided into Part 1, a defence of deists and a thorough analysis of the OT (878 pp.), and Part 2 on the NT (475 pp.), synthesizes the deists' rationalist criticisms of the biblical history and morality, while seeking to preserve a moral and rational kernel. This separation of wheat from chaff was not difficult in the OT, and Reimarus represents no great advance on men like Morgan (*The Moral Philosopher*, 1737). His most remarkable achievement, anticipating two centuries of life of Jesus research, stemmed from his puzzlement about the contradictory viewpoints contained within the Gospels.* His seminal insight was that these contain not only some authentic teaching of Jesus but also (superimposed on this) a very different system, which other writings show to be that of the apostles. Even Jesus himself is for Reimarus an ambiguous figure, preaching an enlightened morality but also presenting himself (not without trickery) as the Jewish messiah* who would liberate Israel. But criticism of Jesus is muted; the apostles are the real crooks.

Impressed by Luke 24.21, convinced that the disciples could not totally have misunderstood Jesus, and recognizing that if he did not reinterpret the coming 'Kingdom of God'* Jesus must have expected to be understood in the current Jewish sense, Reimarus reconstructed a credible human picture of Jesus. When he called himself Son of God, that Jewish phrase meant messiah, not a divine being. But the Gospels project a different picture of a spiritual messiah who would be killed, would rise, and would shortly reappear on the clouds. As these two messianic theories are contradictory, they cannot both go back to Jesus, and Reimarus attributes the latter, which corresponds to subsequent Christian preaching, to the apostles themselves. Huddled together behind closed doors after the crucifixion they rewrote the Jesus script in a way that would preserve their own cosy clerical positions. They stole the body and claimed that Jesus had been raised by God and had appeared to them. They rewrote his teaching to make him prophesy his death, resurrection* and coming in glory to judge the world, thus terrorizing people to join their movement. And they twisted some OT prophecies into support for their claims. The fraud was successful, but is now discredited by a more rational approach to miracle* stories, a more responsible exegesis of the OT, and the non-arrival of the parousia.*

The hinge of this reconstruction of Christian origins is the bold hypothesis that the resurrection was a fraud. Reimarus provides arguments against its factuality. The accounts of the appearances are hopelessly contradictory, and also suspect because limited to insiders. Most interestingly, Matthew's story of the guard at the tomb is adjudged a legend designed to answer the claim that the body had been stolen. Assuming apostolic authorship of this Matthean fiction, Reimarus not unnaturally deduced that the accusation itself provided the best explanation of what had actually happened. Once the movement was launched, it is not hard to see why such a convenient religion of forgiveness and grace obtained by someone else's suffering had proved so successful.

Many, including Semler, responded to the *Fragments*, accepting the rationalist's ground of a non-supernatural account of Christian origins. But it was not until Strauss* (1835) that the suggestion of different layers in the Gospels made real progress. Freed from eighteenth-century ideas of clerical fraud and from pre-critical assumptions about the apostolic authorship of Matthew and John, Reimarus' discovery in the Gospels of a tension, perhaps even contradiction, between Jesus' intentions and the subsequent system of Christian belief became a fundamental issue for nineteenth- and twentieth-century theology and criticism. Albert Schweitzer* celebrated him for a different reason – for seeing the importance of eschatology* in the Gospels. But the *Apologie*, perhaps rightly, attributes the apocalyptic* Son of man* theory to the apostles, not to Jesus. So it was not Schweitzer, but the history of traditions* approach of Wrede,* that in 1901 silently signalled the partial vindication of Reimarus.

See also **Enlightenment; Historical Jesus.**

In addition to the *Apologie*, Reimarus' other important writings have recently been republished: *Vindicatio dictorum Veteris Testamenti in Novo allegatorum* (1731) ed. P. Stemmer, 1983; *Allgemeine Betrachtung über die Triebe der Tiere* (1760) ed. J. von Kempski, 2 vols, 1982; *Die vornehmsten Wahrheiten der natürlichen Religion* (1754) ed. G. Gawlick, 1985; *Die Vernunftlehre* (1756), ed. F. Lötzsch,

1979. See also G. Pons, *Gotthold Ephraïm Lessing et le christianisme*, 1964; A. Schweitzer, *The Quest of the Historical Jesus*, ET 1910; P. Stemmer, *Weissagung und Kritik*, 1983.

ROBERT MORGAN

Resurrection

The language of resurrection, a latecomer in Judaism, was interpretative from the first. It expressed God's unlimited capacity to achieve his purposes for the world. Those who had forfeited life through loyalty to him and his kingdom* he would raise from death to participate in the life of that kingdom (Dan. 12.2; II Macc. 7). It was thus theocentric language: the subject of the verb 'to raise' is God, and 'he was raised' means 'God raised him'. It was also eschatological* language. Along with other eschatological concepts such as the judgment, the gathering of the elect, etc., it referred to God's ultimate actions in bringing his creation to its consummation. There was no fixed orthodoxy about this in Judaism, nor a single understanding of resurrection. It might be of the righteous only, of righteous and unrighteous to life and condemnation respectively; to earth, to a transformed earth, or to paradise; in a physical body, a transfigured body, or without a body. Approximations were also made to the Greek philosophical concept of an immortal soul in a mortal body, generally in a hybrid form that men would 'put on' immortality (Wisd. 3.1ff.; IV Macc. 14–18; cf. Josephus,* *War*, 2.162ff. on the Pharisees*).

To affirm the resurrection of Jesus as 'according to the scriptures' was thus to interpret whatever was to be understood by 'Jesus' as the medium through which God, in pursuit of his purposes in and towards Israel, had initiated the eschatological era. The expected general resurrection had been anticipated in a single figure – cf. I Cor. 15.20, Christ 'the first fruits of those who have fallen asleep'. This brought about a certain fission and reaction in the constituents of Jewish eschatology, which were to be profoundly creative for Christian thought about God, the world, and human existence. Thus God is known as creator in raising Jesus (Rom. 4.16–24), through a supreme exercise of his power (Eph. 1.15–23). He thus effected the overthrow of the enemies of life (I Cor. 15.20–28), to appropriate which is to receive salvation, i.e. present and future deliverance from all hostile powers (Rom. 8.33–39; 10.9; II Cor. 1.9–11). As God's counter to the operation of sin in the death of Jesus the resurrection spelt the annulment of sin and a right relation with God (justification) and righteousness (I Thess. 1.9f.; Rom. 4.16–25; 6.1–23). As counter to death it meant rebirth to an existence orientated towards God, and already possessing eternal qualities

(I Peter 1.3–9; Col. 3.1–4), or to life in the Spirit, which is a pledge and foretaste of redemption and heavenly glory (John 20.19–23; Acts 2.29–33; Rom. 8.9–25).

What occurred is not described. Empty tomb and appearances presuppose its having taken place. It is improperly called 'miracle',* which would denote resuscitation to further life in the world (cf. Lazarus, and contrast Rom. 6.9). It is rather a primal act of God, unimaginable and indescribable, like the creation,* with which it is sometimes compared. Interconnected, but difficult to trace, are 1. the conviction that by resurrection Jesus is not simply the first of God's elect, but their present and future Lord, in the position of God towards them, and ultimately to the universe (Rom. 10.9; 14.9); 2. the relation to resurrection of the companion (alternative?) concept of exaltation, which goes more naturally with lordship (Phil. 2.5–11; Hebrews; the Johannine writings); and 3. the erroneous but potent belief in an imminent return (parousia *) of the risen (exalted) Lord to complete what had been initiated (I Cor. 16.22; Rev. 22.20).

In subsequent Christian thought, the resurrection of Jesus becomes by comparison somewhat inert. In the creeds* it occupies a single clause in a sequence of clauses, and without special emphasis; 'according to the scriptures' tends now to refer to its basis in the NT text. Easter as a focal point in the liturgical* year informed the worship of the Eastern churches with its emphasis on heavenly glory, but not that of the West (it has a bare mention in the canon of the Roman mass, and none at all in the communion service in the Book of Common Prayer).

The ferment on the subject in the second and third centuries was over the resurrection of believers, of which that of Jesus was a guarantee and model rather than a cause. Its corporeal nature in the Gospel resurrection narratives* was appealed to against the docetism of Gnostics,* whose gospels tended to begin from the risen Lord, sometimes described in terms of light symbolism,* giving esoteric teaching on an angelic existence to chosen disciples. Irenaeus* and Tertullian* treated it more profoundly by setting it in the context of the scriptural doctrines of the creation of man in the image of God, and of the incarnation as the perfection of that image, with which it was congruous in its conjunction of flesh and spirit, with the transformation of the first by the second (only occasionally is this note heard again, cf. Aquinas, *ST* 3a, Q.53, art. 3).

Its theocentric force was further weakened in the orthodoxy which emerged from the christological* and trinitarian discussions of the fourth and fifth centuries. For there the dominant theological category was not eschatology but incarnation, and resurrection no longer conveyed the relationship between God and Jesus, but was internal to the Son of God, the operation of the divine incorruptible nature of the incarnate Logos* upon his human and mortal nature. The seeds of this could be found in John's Gospel, where the interaction between Father and Son was expressed in other terms than resurrection, and where the earthly Jesus proclaims himself to be 'the resurrection', and secures it both for himself and for others (John 11.25; 2.19; 6.39).

In Reformation* theology the resurrection was seen primarily, if not exclusively, as the divine attestation of the sacrificial and uniquely atoning character of the cross. The insights of Luther* and Calvin* that it was also evidence of the availability of the new life itself were hardly retained. In theologies such as those of Schleiermacher, Ritschl, etc., which located the core of Christianity in the spirit and teaching of the historical Jesus,* it was completely marginalized.

The recovery of its centrality through historical criticism,* which also brought to light the diversity of the NT traditions about it, and in 'biblical theology',* which sought a synthetic view, has inevitably issued in acute debate, since resurrection involves a unique combination of the historical and the non-historical, of fact* and symbol. Some have approached it as an 'event', to be established by the kind of investigation proper to the historical. Thus for B. F. Westcott* (*The Gospel of the Resurrection*, 1866) it was 'the central point of history, primarily of religious history, and then of civil history, of which it is the soul'. For W. Pannenberg (*Jesus – God and Man*, 1968) it was a public event: the appearances were 'objective visions', and the apocalyptic* view of history, to which it belongs, is indispensable for Christian faith. These, however, have found it difficult to do justice to its theological and transcendent significance, and to avoid presenting it in naturalistic terms as resuscitation.

Others have approached the resurrection as transcendent and salvatory, but have found it difficult to accommodate the historical element. Thus for R. Bultmann* the language of resurrection is mythological,* and refers, not to an objective occurrence, but to the emergence of the faith of the disciples in the efficacy of the cross. It must be translated into language which performs the same function now. K. Barth,* in reaction from the subjectivity of this, abandoned a previous position, that Jesus' resurrection was a symbol of the transcendent ground of his life and death, for a more objective, but also ambiguous position, that it constituted a 'second' or 'further' or 'higher' history of Jesus, which, however, had the character of 'legend'* and 'saga',* and was somehow immune from historical enquiry.

Debate continues over these and similar issues with respect to the interpretation of the biblical texts and the relation in them of event and symbol. It may be seen in the form of dialogue (e.g. between D. Cupitt and C. F. D. Moule in *Explorations in Theology 6*, 1979, pp. 27ff. and between G. W. H. Lampe and D. M. MacKinnon in *The Resurrection. A Dialogue arising from Broadcasts*, 1966), and within individual treatments of the subject (e.g. W. Marxsen, *The Resurrection of Jesus of Nazareth*, 1970; W. Schillebeeckx, *Jesus: an Experiment in Christology*, 1979). A further question is whether the NT proclamation of the lordship of the risen (exalted) Christ can be validly restated 1. as for the salvation of mankind, in face of modern pluralism in religion (*see* **Other Faiths**), and 2. as cosmic rule over the universe, in face of modern cosmologies (cf. the writings of Teilhard de Chardin).

The resurrection 'of the dead' (sc. believers; so the NT, but in the creeds 'the resurrection of the body' or 'of the flesh') first appears as auxiliary to the primary eschatological tenet, in its Christian form, of the union of the community of the elect with the risen and exalted Lord at his parousia to share his unique status and rule until the final consummation. For the living, this would mean metamorphosis, and the open 'bodily' manifestation of their present hidden participation in his glory through the Spirit; for the dead 'in Christ' it meant resurrection (I Thess. 4.13–17; I Cor. 15.12–56; II Cor. 4.16–5.10; Phil. 3.20–21).

Subsequent thought involved the systematic application of such texts individually and together, and their appropriation in the light of current anthropologies and cosmologies. On the one hand present experience of the risen life consequent upon God's victory over sin in Christ could be stressed to the point of rendering future resurrection secondary or otiose, as in the heresy condemned in II Tim. 2.17f., and in the teaching of some Gnostics that baptism initiated into immortality. The effect was comparable when the belief pronounced by Justin (*Dial.* 80), Irenaeus and Tertullian to be error eventually became orthodox, viz. that some, variously described as 'the saints' and 'the souls of the righteous' (cf. Heb. 12.23), passed directly at death to the vision of God. In millenarian* thought, these were the martyrs sharing through a 'first' resurrection a thousand years interregnum of Christ (Rev. 20.1–6), a doctrine which was dominant in the second and third centuries,

and which, though repudiated, has continued to have a sectarian history.

On the other hand, attention could be focussed on the interim period. Interpretation here postulated some form of hybrid of resurrection and immortality. There was a disjunction of body, which corrupted, and soul, which maintained an independent existence, either in 'sleep' (i.e. insensibility, a view encouraged by I Cor. 15.20 and I Thess. 4.13) to be awakened for resurrection with the body (so Luther), or in a sensible and expectant state, cf. Luke 23.43 and Phil. 1.23 (so Calvin). Hence the amalgam in e.g. the Westminster Confession: at death bodies corrupt, souls return to God; those of the righteous see God and wait for the redemption of their bodies, those of the wicked are cast into hell; at the last day those alive are changed, the dead are raised with their selfsame bodies, though with different qualities, to be united with their souls. The concept of purgatory, arising in mediaeval times, invests the interim state with spiritual content as making possible the soul's amelioration through suffering.

The disjunction also affected understanding of the resurrection of the body (flesh). In Semitic thought 'body' could be an inclusive term for the form of the self or person as a psycho-somatic (flesh-spirit, body-soul) creation: cf. I Cor. 15.35–54, 'with what body . . .?', and 'spiritual body' as the glorified existence of flesh and blood. The resurrection of the body, often affirmed against conceptions of redemption as the deliverance of the soul from encumbering matter for its ascent to the divine, could stand anthropologically as an imaginative symbol of an ultimate perfection of the whole human person, and cosmologically of a divine recreation of the universe (Rev. 21.1f.). When the body is conceived of in the Greek and more usual manner as a separable and corruptible component in man as a body-soul entity, its resurrection inevitably gave rise to fantasy (e.g. however dispersed it has become, the original physical body will be reconstituted by God, with whom 'nothing is impossible'), and to literalism, perhaps aided by one description of the (temporary) risen body of Jesus as 'flesh and bones' (Luke 24.39). In modern statements of the Christian hope immortality has become dominant. For the language of resurrection to have force requires attention to its symbolical character, as also to that of associated ideas such as the world as 'creation', 'mankind' as a totality, and 'the human person'.

See also **Apocalyptic; Eschatology; Resurrection Narratives.**

Peter Carnley, *The Structure of Resurrection Belief*, 1987; Lloyd Geering, *Resurrection: A*

Symbol of Hope, 1971; W. Künneth, *The Theology of the Resurrection*, 1965; C. F. D. Moule (ed.), *The Significance of the Resurrection for Faith in Jesus Christ*, 1968; Pheme Perkins, *Resurrection: New Testament Witness and Contemporary Reflection*, 1984.

C. F. EVANS

Resurrection Narratives

Each of the four Gospels* contains a narrative of women coming to the tomb on the morning of the first day of the week and finding it empty; but even in this they disagree on details, and after this they diverge from one another considerably. In Matthew, the women run to tell the disciples what the angel told them and meet Jesus who repeats the message; there is then an account of how the guards at the tomb were bribed by the Jewish authorities to say that the disciples had stolen the body; finally the eleven go to Galilee and are commissioned by the risen Jesus. In Mark, the women say nothing to anyone, but there follows in 16.9–20 (a passage which is not present in some manuscripts*) a summary of appearances of Jesus to Mary Magdalene, to two disciples walking into the country and to the eleven; and the passage ends with an account of the ascension. (Another ending, shorter than 16.9–20, is found in one old Latin translation after 16.8 as the conclusion of the Gospel; and in some manuscripts the Gospel ends with both this shorter ending and 16.9–20.) In Luke, the women go to report the resurrection* to the apostles, not to send them to Galilee, and they are not believed (Luke 24.12 describing Peter's* visit to the tomb is omitted in some texts); the story continues with the walk to Emmaus, the return of the two disciples to Jerusalem, the report of the appearance to Peter, the appearance of Jesus to the disciples and his departure from them on the Mount of Olives, all apparently on Easter Day. In John, Peter and the disciple whom Jesus loved run to the tomb, and the latter believes; then there is the appearance in the evening to all the disciples, except Thomas; the appearance to Thomas follows a week later and seems to lead into the conclusion of the book, but then there is a further account of the miraculous catch of fish, in Galilee, and the meal and conversation that follow it. To add to the confusion, there is also a list of appearances in I Cor. 15.5–8 which says nothing about appearances to women, or about the places in which the appearances occurred, whether Galilee or Jerusalem.

Set out in this way, the material is not only diverse but also contradictory. In the early church, attempts were made (e.g. by Augustine* of Hippo) to show that the apparent contradictions could be resolved, but some of these attempts, while ingenious, were far-fetched and seem to most present-day readers highly implausible, though those who started, or still start, from the view that scripture could not contradict itself, would not find them so.

H. S. Reimarus* pointed out the problems contained in the four Gospel accounts and in their relationship with one another. He drew particular attention to the fact that none of the other three refer to Matthew's story of the guard at the tomb who saw the angel, and that it is never mentioned in Acts or elsewhere; and he listed ten major contradictions between the four accounts. Much of Reimarus' argument was repeated by D. F. Strauss* in his *Life of Jesus Critically Examined* (1835–6: ET 1846); but he also made the interesting and prophetic observation that whereas harmonizing the four accounts into one continuous story produces a narrative that is restless and repetitive (*see* **Harmony**), what we should do is consider each evangelist* on his own: 'we then obtain from each a quiet picture with simple dignified features' (ET p. 713). Strauss had foreseen a major part of the solution to the problem: Gospels and Gospel-narratives were never intended to be read alongside one another, but each was designed to be read on its own; they were intended to supplant, not to supplement, each other.

Before this could be developed and made clear, however, certain basic principles had to be established. One of these was the literary relationship between the first three Gospels. Reimarus' discussion had started with Matthew and he took that Gospel as the norm with which to compare and contrast the others; but when it was suggested (e.g. by K. Lachmann, in 1835) that Mark was the earliest Gospel and thus that both Matthew and Luke had used Mark 16.1–8, Matthew's narrative could then be seen as the elaboration of a simpler and shorter story, for apologetic* and other purposes; and Luke's narrative similarly as another adaptation of Mark made so as to prepare the way for the story of the ascension, and the account of the church in Jerusalem, Samaria, and all the way to Rome, as we find it in his second volume, the Acts of the Apostles.

This then raised the question, to what extent did the later evangelists have traditions (unused by Mark) which preserved historical reminiscences of the appearances of Jesus to the women and to the disciples on Easter Day and the days that followed? While it might be thought that Matthew had least claim to have had access to such traditions (he was apparently dependent on Mark for very nearly all his narrative, as distinct from sayings, between the baptism of Jesus and the finding of the empty tomb; and what he had not received from Mark often has very little value in respect of historicity), Luke, it was thought, might have had access to independent reliable traditions (e.g. the walk to Emmaus and the appearance to Peter), and John too. C. H. Dodd* (1884–1973) applied the methods of form criticism* to the resurrection narratives in all four Gospels, and argued that they were 'ostensible records of things that happened' and merited the same degree of critical consideration as the narratives in the earlier parts of the Gospels.

Another issue that needed to be settled before further progress could be made concerned the final chapter of Mark. J. Wellhausen (1844–1918) at the beginning of the twentieth century, and J. M. Creed and R. H. Lightfoot* in the 1930s, argued not only that the longer ending (16.9–20) was an addition to Mark 1.1–16.8 made by another writer, but also that Mark intended to conclude his book at 16.8, the point where we are told that the women said nothing to anybody because they were afraid; that is to say, there never was a lost ending of Mark's Gospel: 1.1–16.8 was the complete book, as the author envisaged it. A strong reason for thinking that this was so was that it was manifestly difficult to see how any further paragraph could have followed 16.1–8: if the women must tell the disciples to go to Galilee; and if that was where Jesus would be seen, and nowhere else; and if the women said nothing – how could the story continue? Neither Matthew, nor Luke, nor the author of the longer ending, nor the author of the shorter could solve this problem without either revising what Mark had written (so Matthew and Luke) or creating a hiatus between 16.8 and what immediately followed (so the authors of the two endings). It is thus far more common now than it was forty years ago to think that Mark meant to finish where two of the old uncial manuscripts and some of the old translations and quotations say that he finished, with the failure, fear and silence of the women. If this is what happened, it would explain another problem: why did Mark end in this way? If he was the first to write an account of the finding of the empty tomb (and, so far as we know, he was), the silence of the women would provide an answer to the question, why has no one ever heard this story before?

There is a further point about the end of Mark's Gospel that can be dealt with here: how did Mark understand the words of the young man in the tomb, 'There you will see him, as he said to you'? The usual view is that this is a promise of a resurrection appearance to the disciples in Galilee, and certainly Matthew understood it so; but if the reference is

not to Mark 14.28 but to 13.26 (cf. 14.62; these are the only places in Mark where the future tense of the verb 'to see' is used), then the promise looks forward, not to a resurrection appearance, but to the coming of the Son of Man* in glory to gather the elect into the kingdom of God.*

Matthew's decision to produce a revised and enlarged version of Mark will have been determined in part at least by his sense that Mark's conclusion was inadequate; the last words of Jesus in the earlier Gospel will have been, 'My God, my God, why have you forsaken me?' Matthew changes this by introducing a short final speech of Jesus that is more in accordance with his understanding of the Christian faith and more appropriate in his view to the needs of the church. The speech begins, 'All authority is given to me in heaven and on earth', and in it Jesus goes on to tell the eleven that they are to make disciples of the Gentiles, to baptize them and to teach them the commands of Jesus who promises to be with them till the end of the age. Matthew's story of the earthquake, the guard at the tomb and the angel who rolled back the stone makes the resurrection of Jesus into a public event which has to be concealed by the Jewish authorities, and in this way, as in other matters before this, Matthew aggravates the guilt of the Jews. Reimarus was surely right to draw attention to the unlikeliness that this was historical.

Once we have seen how Matthew rewrites Mark's resurrection narrative to meet the needs of his situation, it is possible to apply the same method to Luke and John, and to read their conclusions as the appropriate endings to their books. Luke, for example, is preparing for his second volume; he emphasizes the physical nature of the resurrection body (which will be taken up to heaven on the fortieth day after the resurrection), the command to preach repentance and remission of sins (a Lucan theme), and the doctrine that the suffering, death and resurrection of Jesus had been foretold by Moses* and the prophets* in the OT; moreover, the apostles are to wait in Jerusalem for the gift of the Spirit which will transform them into witnesses. These themes are so strong in Luke–Acts that it becomes less and less necessary to call in the help of a hypothesis of sources and traditions used by Luke to supplement Mark, other than the tradition which was also known to Paul* that the first appearance of Jesus was to Peter (I Cor. 15.5).

Similarly, the resurrection narratives in John's Gospel are full of the theology that is peculiar to that book; and here much will depend on what position is adopted on the question of the historicity of the traditions used by John. At the present time, two dia-metrically opposed points of view have their advocates: that John is closer to the events he describes than the other evangelists; and, on the other side, that in John narrative is created by faith and is used in the service of faith.

There can be no doubt that the Christian movement began with the conviction that Jesus had been raised from the dead and was exalted to God's right hand; this faith was responsible for the writing of resurrection nar-ratives. It is an extraordinary but indisputable fact that the four Gospels diverge from one another so widely both in their beginnings and in their endings. The best explanation of this now seems to be that the evangelists did not understand themselves primarily as re-porters of events, but as tellers of stories through which the gospel can be heard.

See also John, Gospel of; Luke, Gospel of; Mark, Gospel of; Matthew, Gospel of.

C. F. Evans, *Resurrection and the New Testa-ment*, 1970; R. H. Fuller, *The Formation of the Resurrection Narratives*, 1972; J. L. Houl-den, *Backward into Light*, 1987; R. H. Light-foot, *Locality and Doctrine in the Gospels*, 1938; W. Marxsen, *The Resurrection of Jesus of Nazareth*, 1970; N. Perrin, *The Resurrection according to Matthew, Mark, and Luke*, 1977; H. S. Reimarus, *Fragments* (ed. C. H. Talbert), 1970.

J. C. FENTON

Revelation

The disclosure of what was up to that point hidden or unknown. The term as normally used implies full clarity: a secret plan is shared in its entirety, one's present mood is displayed unmistakably. Something or some one can be said to be 'partially' revealed, but that would seem to mean either that a distinct part is fully seen or known, or some aspect of an otherwise indistinct whole is fully seen or known (perhaps a precise character trait of a person, or the clear outline of a ship). The term is current in journalism and literary criticism,* used of suc-cessful communication: 'startling revelations', 'careful revelations of character', and so on.

'Reveal' and 'revelation' have become im-portant words in Christian theology since the early eighteenth century; for some theologians and interpreters of the Bible, they have become the dominant motif. The scriptures are designated 'revealed truth', or (more recently) 'the self-revelation of God' (or 'the record of' such self-revelation). The life of Israel to the first century, the life and death and resurrection* of Jesus, the life of the first Christians are a drama whose whole point lies in successful communication being achieved through the resultant transcript, 'the scriptures'.

Some of the advantages and disadvantages of this interpretative model are now to be discussed. That it can be shown to be a relative newcomer to theology and biblical interpreta-tion is in itself no disqualification. It might be all the better for it, unless we take a view of biblical authority* that insists that the canoni-cal* documents be interpreted solely in their own terms, however translated.*

It is still worth pointing out, though, that it is not at all a major interpretative model used in many, if any, of the writings themselves. Hebrew and Greek words that may sensibly be translated by 'reveal' etc. are used inci-dentally of God communicating particular messages, disclosing plans, and so on (Isa. 22.14; Dan. 2.28; I Cor. 14.30); of resurrection appearances; and of the expected final 'revela-tion' of Jesus in glory. But at no point is it said, certainly not in so many words, that things happened in order to reveal 'truths about God', still less 'as God's self-revelation' (Barr, Downing; and one may note the ab-sence of 'revelation' as in any way a major theme in J. D. G. Dunn, *Unity and Diversity in the New Testament*, [2]1990).

The Fourth Gospel comes closest to deploy-ing a communication model in its interpret-ative narrative, with its frequent use of 'know-ing', 'believing', 'truth', etc. (John 14.7; 17.3). Even so, there are at important points qualifi-cations that suggest that for the time being believers are being prepared for such know-ledge rather than already provided with it (14.9; 16.31); and this seems to be clearly asserted at I John 3.2. Paul* presses the point even more explicitly at I Cor. 13.12: 'Now we see puzzling reflections in a mirror, only then shall we see face to face: now our knowledge is partial, then shall we know fully, as we are fully known'; and we may compare also Paul's unease with any claim to 'know' God at I Cor. 8.1–3, and his use of 'reflection' language at II Cor. 3.18–4.6 (where NEB introduces the word 'revelation' without any warrant in the Greek). For Paul, we are being changed into the image of Christ, who is the image of God. When the change has happened, we shall enjoy a full awareness of God, a full relationship with him. But for now we have only the puzzling clues of our present experience to reflect on.

Early biblical interpretation proceeds along these lines (soon with help from Philo* and the Platonic tradition). In our present finite and sinful state we are quite incapable of knowing God, of receiving any 'self-revela-tion'. The scriptures help us towards saying less inappropriate things about God, but human language is as inadequate as human minds and hearts. Christian tradition and com-munity allow us to be where God can best change us for results that are necessarily as yet unknown to us. On this view the scriptures focus our attention on God become human, so that we may eventually 'become divine'.

The preferred interpretative models implicit in the scriptural writings are those of education, the enabling of personal growth, social reform, political change. In the elaboration of such models there is often a subordinate strand of preliminary communication involved, people are told what they need to know at a particular stage, and these discrete communications may be said to be revealed (e.g. Phil. 3.15). But anything that can be called 'revelation', in any grand sense of God's primary intention, lies ahead. Something properly called 'revelation' may be the point and purpose of it all, but is not at all the present reality.

If this conclusion is accepted (and no more than an indication of the evidence can be displayed here), it is necessary to consider the effect of using as an interpretative model one that seems to run counter to the explicit and implicit convictions of most or all of the texts in hand. It could seem rather as if we were to use the model of the romance to interpret a history of the First World War, or the model of farce to interpret *Oedipus at Colonos*. We need to check both what the model seems to imply, and the extent to which it fits or forces the texts to be interpreted.

We see a parent feeding a small child, playing, talking sometimes in adult language, sometimes echoing the child's own vocabulary, washing, dressing, cooking, cleaning, listening to music; or a grown person doing all this for a senile parent. It makes sense to us to see it all as purposive activity, as caring, loving, and so on (even when some or much of it seems routine, automatic, or instinctive). It may seem to 'reveal' something of or about the carer. But to ask, 'What is she or he trying to say in all this, what is all this meant to communicate?' is to ask the wrong question. The activity may (with the child, at least) incidentally convey the message that the parent loves the child, and the parent may hope that it will (even if he or she is a consummate actor, and doing it all only in response to social pressure). The care may very well be the necessary and sufficient cause of the child ultimately being capable of and in fact attaining to a true awareness of her or his parent. But to interpret the activity as primarily and initially communication is to suggest charade, pretence: it was being done to make a point, to make an impression, to appear caring; for show, even.

It may well be better to stay with those early theologians, such as Paul or Philo, who saw God as preparing us for awareness of

himself, rather than talk of a revelation already achieved. At least, however, we must check carefully before using 'revelation' as our model in interpretation, to see how happily the texts in question respond to it; and to determine whether it has in fact the kinds of disadvantage that have just been suggested.

There are further implications for any use of the term in our own interpretation of the canonical texts, singly or together. 'Reveal' and 'revelation' in their ordinary literal use tell of making seen, not just making visible. Things are not 'revealed' if no one (not even an ideal reader) 'sees' them. In its common metaphorical* use, as already pointed out, 'to reveal' is to make known, not just 'knowable'. And in both cases, as also already indicated, clarity and certainty are implied, so that even if what is revealed, clearly seen, is enigmatic, it is clearly seen in all its puzzling character. To claim, then, that the Jewish or Christian scriptures convey revealed truths seems to entail a claim that clear and definite information has been received. At the very least, it would seem unnecessary to produce this *Dictionary of Biblical Interpretation* in all its complexity and diversity, if such clear and definite information already stood in the canonical texts.

On the same basis, to say that (in scripture, in this instance) I have received a revelation entails an exclusive claim, repudiating all other interpretations. It is, of course, always open for an individual or a cohesive group to assert that through their (inspired) interpretation God's truth is revealed, knowable and known; and that all competitors are more or less importantly wrong. While the rest of us remain unpersuaded, we are in effect insisting there is no such revelation to us, and we do not see that interpretation as valid knowledge. The scriptures in fact remain open to varied interpretations, and no one of them is so clearly and persuasively right as to warrant the claim to be the revealed truth. Talk of 'revelation' does not fit comfortably with our common experience of biblical interpretation.

In this present century, there has been an unease with talk of 'propositional revelation', the revealing of truths about God and the universe, and a preference (noted already) for seeing the biblical transcription of events and reflection as 'God's self-revelation'. Such claims are even harder to justify in themselves (as well as being even further from the overt intent of the biblical writers). While people continue to make very different assertions about the character and will of God, it is very difficult to justify a claim to have been accorded a full knowledge of him. Our differing interpretations of the biblical 'vehicle' of this supposed self-disclosure continue to belie any such claim for it. And when the possibility of in any sense 'seeing' God is broached by the biblical writers, it seems clear that the seer must be appropriately changed for the encounter and will be still more changed to be like God by it. Evidence for such godlikeness is even harder to come by.

A number of writers (more often dogmatic or philosophical theologians, these days, than biblical scholars) continue to attempt to justify a modified, carefully qualified use of 'reveal' and 'revelation' in the exposition of Christian faith, and so in the interpretation of scripture. The words do conveniently emphasize 'givenness', 'grace', divine initiative, and so on. So, taking note of some of the difficulties outlined here, the words are qualified by terms like 'partial', 'gradual', 'mysterious' (even 'veiled'!). There is no reason why a convenient word should not be given a modified use, with care, full notice, and consistency. However, it must be insisted again that if something or someone is said to be 'partially' revealed, then at least those 'parts' must be clearly seen and/or known; if we are told there has been a gradual revealing, then we have a right to expect that what has so far emerged is seen and/or known. And all this remains just as hard to justify in practice.

If someone gives an important place to 'reveal' and 'revelation' in their biblical interpretation, the reader is advised at the very least to look for an explanation of how the words are intended, what sort of qualifications are suggested, how consistently they are maintained; and so examine to what extent the terms are used to justify an otherwise unsupported claim to clarity, certainty, and the right to discount others' argued conclusions. It remains very odd to use a word that for most people means 'made clear' for material where clarity is so hard to achieve.

J. Barr, 'Revelation' in *Hastings Dictionary of the Bible*, ²1963; F. G. Downing, *Has Christianity a Revelation?*, 1964; id., 'Revelation, Disagreement and Obscurity' in *Religious Studies*, 1986; A. Dulles, *Models of Revelation*, 1983; P. Helm, *The Divine Revelation*, 1982; J. K. Kuntz, *The Self-Revelation of God*, 1964.

F. GERALD DOWNING

Revelation of John

A book whose business is 'revelation'* has revealed little of the circumstances which produced it. But it has generated a wide variety of interpretation and application, bearing scant relation to its origins. Largely the work of a single author, named John, but probably not otherwise identifiable, Revelation comes from a situation of actual (or threatened) persecution of Christians by the local Roman imperial authorities in Asia Minor towards the end of the first century. While there are connecting links in theological imagery with the Gospel and epistles of the Johannine corpus, there are also major differences in language and ethos,* which preserve a sense of distance.

Revelation is correctly classified as an apocalyptic* work, and sometimes referred to as 'the Apocalypse'. While there are several other examples of apocalyptic traditions within the NT, Revelation is the only work where the whole structure is apocalyptic. Six aspects of the definition of apocalyptic are important as exemplified in Revelation:

1. Essentially revelatory, within a framework of narrative.

2. Unlike a prophetic* oracle,* the revelation is imparted through an other-worldly mediator (e.g. the risen Christ, or angels) to a human recipient (John).

3. What is disclosed is transcendent: those realities, stored up in a heavenly repository, which have a direct bearing on human events.

4. Either these transcendent realities are temporal, concerned with linear history, ultimately envisaging an eschatological* salvation,

5. Or they are in the spatial dimension, concerned with a supernatural world, and symbolize* a relationship between the macrocosm and local happenings in the microcosm.

6. Such visionary perspectives originated in a situation of crisis, to exhort and console 'the righteous'. Subsequently, in less stressful circumstances, a work of this type is used in other ways, e.g. to inculcate morality.

The renewed emphasis on Revelation as apocalyptic, properly understood, is a fruit of modern critical scholarship. Earlier scholars in the modern period had sought to make Revelation acceptable by selective presentation. To concentrate on the letters to the seven churches (Rev. 2–3) and their environments in Asia Minor, as did Sir W. M. Ramsay, might allow the Graeco-Roman world to regain ascendancy over Jewish corrupting influences. Equally, to speak of Revelation as Christian 'prophecy' rather than 'apocalyptic' was to reassert the main emphasis of Protestantism in polemic against the shadowy world of sects and cults. But such selectivity is unbalanced and inaccurate. Only with the 'rediscovery of apocalyptic' (e.g. K. Koch, 1972) did German-speaking scholars come to share with their English counterparts a general appreciation of its relevance as a significantly radical strand of Judaism, feeding into Christian thought. The bizarre world of Revelation might still be dismissed by some as the delusion of a sick nature, but, with new literary* and historical understanding it would at least be appreciated that the apocalyptist had been made sick by the evil realities which he was forced to suffer. Revelation belongs to the literature of protest and religious revolt. Or at least that is the emphasis which speaks to our time.

Such historical understanding of the circumstances which produced Revelation is not quite unique to modern scholars. But in earlier centuries there was a more general and didactic historical perspective; to say 'these are the lessons of history' still offered a variety of options for interpreting this work. 'Historical' is too loose a word; it was defined in five ways:

1. History of world epochs: just as Daniel speaks of four world empires, so Revelation provides the structure for seven periods, or three ages, of world history. The interpreter so calculates the sequence to arrive at his own day and identify the Beast (Antichrist) as e.g. Napoleon or Hitler.

2. History of the church or Christendom, a particular application favoured by mediaeval* commentators.* So the church suffers a sequence of conflicts (against Jews, Romans, Arians, Saracens and the degenerate Holy Roman Empire) until redeemed by the rise of the new religious orders (e.g. the Friars). Later, in Reformation* polemic, Antichrist is identified with either Luther* or the Pope.

3. The climax of history in the millennium, a literal reading of Revelation focussing on 20.1–6 which prophesies a reign of Christ for a thousand years, between the 'first resurrection' and 'the second death' or final judgment. This eschatological view appealed particularly to early commentators, generations living an appropriate mathematical interval after the NT, and a multitude of chiliastic sects. (*See* **Millenarianism**.)

4. History as a number of cycles, recapitulated in Revelation, which is not therefore a consecutive account. The sequences of seven seals, trumpets and bowls replay the same facts in different forms. This emphasizes the totality of evil come to judgment, as summed up in 666, the number of the Beast (Rev. 13.18).

5. The contemporary history of the time when the book was written. This 'modern' method arose when much knowledge of the circumstances had long been lost; its motivation when it first appeared in the sixteenth and seventeenth centuries was largely reaction against the construction of fantastic schemes of world history. New sources of information (archaeology* and comparisons with classical history) enabled Ramsay's study of the seven letters and S. Giet's (1957) comparison with the Jewish War. Sometimes, with limited knowledge, historical parallels have been identified too easily.

Methods of interpretation are like changes of fashion, and are usually thought mutually exclusive. Even more so, the historical interpretations seemed incompatible with other options: an allegorical* reading, literary reconstruction, or the 'comparative religion' approach. The principle of allegory was defined by Origen's* 'levels' of meaning; for him the sealed book (Rev. 5.1) is scripture, to be decoded in terms of religious experience or pilgrimage to the heavenly Jerusalem.* Classic literary criticism was preoccupied with identifying separate visions, distinct sources, or editorial corruption, all of which jeopardized the unity of the work and the consistency of its interpretation. Nevertheless, light has been cast on John's uniquely barbarous Greek (e.g. G. Mussies, 1971). Comparative studies of religion, perhaps motivated to diminish the Jewishness of Revelation, investigated parallels with Egyptian, Greek and Babylonian myths* and astrology, in search of 'borrowings'. The image of the woman and the dragon (Rev. 12), studied by the History of Religions school,* had a mythological pedigree and has been 'baptized' as a symbol of the gospel message.

Few books have experienced such great oscillations in interpretation as has Revelation over the centuries. But the major traditions of exegesis* in the past – often highly polemical and polarized – are being superseded as independent instruments by changing attitudes and some new methods* within the last twenty years. Some attitudes are corrections of older prejudices, and there is an encouraging pluralism in method, with possibilities of synthesis.

Partly the change is in the intellectual climate, with a growing sense of the relevance of themes handled by Revelation. The book which used to be regarded as a script for a horror film is now applicable to a Marxist*/Socialist view of the twentieth century. 'We have been taught by the experience of our century to live in the expectation of apocalypse' (E. J. Hobsbawm). 'All the big things, just now, are against us, but within what is not only a very powerful but also an exceptionally unstable social and cultural order there are forces moving of which nobody can predict the outcome' (Raymond Williams). Since the bombing of Hiroshima, the nuclear threat has been dominant, and visualized in terms such as Rev. 16.17–21.

The Christian Apocalypse consoles those who glimpse what hell can be, and encourages those who would build a new Jerusalem. Sects have in the past built Jerusalem to Revelation's ground plan. What is different now is the scale of the threat and the wider recognition of society's vulnerability. Like the placards proclaiming the end of the world, the text of Revelation is taken literally, especially by influential fundamentalist* groups in the United States of America. And in the fight against apartheid in South Africa, Archbishop Desmond Tutu has testified to the power of the vision of Rev. 7.9–12 to uphold him. Such readings of the text (by literal* or allegorical means) are analysing world conditions by reference to scripture, not prophesying directly from scripture like a confident mediaeval* exegete. As with nuclear apocalyptic, comparisons may be simplistic and mistake the broadly similar theme for the exactly identical situation; but the text is a relevant handling of issues, not an esoteric code.

Alongside these changed attitudes are new methods of interpretation:

1. Literary criticism has been rejuvenated by computer* technology, e.g. identifying Rev. 12 as the only wildly discrepant source material; and making a grammatical analysis of the Greek of Revelation, to facilitate statistical comparisons within the Johannine writings and between John and Paul.*

2. Sociological* methods have been employed to interpret data on the community* which produced Revelation. The model is a sectarian group marginalized by the attitudes of society. It is under severe stress, not necessarily overt physical persecution, but certainly ostracism and social contempt. The group feels threatened and insecure and also must contend with religious stress (not only externally enforced emperor worship with economic sanctions for nonconformists, but also internal conflicts symbolized by the Nicolaitans [2.6,15] and the synagogue of Satan [2.9]).

3. The various schools of literary structuralism* seek to explain the symbolic universe constructed in this book (a response to the social world of a group on the margins). If sociology builds on the contemporary-historical approach, then structuralism suggests taking another look at theories of recapitulation (see the fourth definition of 'historical' above). For the order of Revelation is not chronological, but theologically conceived. The combination of linear narrative, repetitions and hymnic* celebrations deliberately sets up structural tensions, and the shape of the work has been likened to a conic spiral.

The contrast between the old and new approaches is most marked as Revelation is applied to Christian preaching. Not so long ago typical selections were the seven letters and the comforting passages used at funerals. Now the focus is on political and social threat and the themes of justice, judgment and vengeance. The book is a study of power, raising ethical* questions about the responses to power at a crisis. Revelation functions as a warning to the complacent within society, or has a cathartic effect on the community by arousing intense feelings of inflammatory aggressiveness. Or it is a moral lesson on the victim's desire for vengeance. To decide which function is most appropriate may require more evidence about the situation in John's community than can be derived from the symbolism of Revelation.

Some refuse to see the book as relative to any one particular situation, but rather as valid for all times. As allegorical exegesis emphasizes the moment of interpretation as much as, or more than, the moment of writing, so a modern hermeneutic* theory insists that the meaning of a work is primarily what it means to the reader.* There is a heady sense of freedom about such interpretation. But the contributions of the author and of his situation to the meaning of the book must surely be significant.

Revelation is a relevant text (and not only for Third World liberation*). But the intoxication of a theme like justice and judgment should not blind one to the balance of other issues in the book. Literature rich in imagery and symbolism deserves to be studied as a work of art, in the light of the great works of art* (e.g. paintings) which it has inspired. But the vision of an alternative world in Revelation derives power from the contrast with the socio-political realities which produced it. For literary tensions and theological dialectic to be fully understood, historical questions must remain part of the interpreter's task. To appreciate the apocalyptic traditions which feed into the book, and the theological, sectarian and monastic traditions which are fed by it, Revelation's place in the story must be identified. The 'new look' of Revelation produced by structural and sociological analyses is welcome, precisely because it contributes to a fuller reading of the book and of the circumstances which produced it. The real need is for a total view, to interrelate methods and results and demonstrate the contribution of Revelation to the Christian tradition.

See also **Apocalyptic; Blake, W.; Eschatology; Jerusalem.**

G. B. Caird, *The Revelation of St John the Divine*, 1966; A. Y. Collins, *Crisis and Catharsis: the Power of the Apocalypse*, 1984; J. M. Court, *Myth and History in the Book of Revelation*, 1979; A. M. Farrer, *A Rebirth of Images*, 1949; E. S. Fiorenza, *The Book of Revelation: Justice and Judgement*, 1985; F. Kermode, *The Sense of an Ending: Studies in the Theory of Fiction*, 1967; J. Sweet, *Revelation*, 1979.

JOHN M. COURT

Rewritten Bible

A term coined in recent years to describe a series of post-biblical Jewish writings which, by re-presenting and re-drafting original books of scripture, seek to interpret and expound those books for particular purposes. The authors/compilers of such rewritten texts present their work as if they were biblical books, and thereby seem to have claimed for them an authority* approaching, if not actually equal to, that of scripture itself. The beginnings of the rewritten Bible may be discerned within the canon* of the Hebrew scriptures. Thus Deuteronomy redrafts older forms of law* in the light of changed social and religious conditions (cf. e.g. Deut. 15.12–18 with Ex. 21.2–6, and Deut. 16.1–8 with Ex. 12.1–18). Modern scholarship has shown how prophetic* oracles* were modified or supplemented by those who transmitted them; and the books of Chronicles constitute a major attempt to re-present the history of the Judaean monarchy related in Samuel–Kings from one particularly influential religious and political standpoint of Second Temple times.

The Chronicler's work is instructive as providing examples of principles and practices which informed the authors of rewritten biblical books. With Samuel–Kings as his main source, the Chronicler regularly omits material which does not suit his purpose. He also supplements the given biblical material with narratives drawn from other, sometimes named, literary works, or from oral tradition.* He then sets about removing inconsistencies from the stories of Samuel–Kings; he eliminates contradictions; and he bowdlerizes material which may discredit or tarnish the reputations of great national figures like David* and Solomon. Even the crass behaviour of the politically inept Rehoboam is partly explained away, to enhance the standing of the Davidic house (II Chron. 13.4–7).

Examples of rewritten history in poetic form are not uncommon: Pss. 78, 105, and 106, amongst others, apply to sections of Israel's history* the same sorts of principles discerned in the Chronicler's work, with clear theological and homiletic* objectives in mind. Although not poetic, passages from the NT such as Acts 7.1–53 and Heb. 11 testify to the enduring appeal of this method of scriptural elaboration, even outside Jewish communities.

Amongst the earliest post-biblical literature, the Wisdom of Jesus ben Sira (Ecclesiasticus) (early second century BC) recounts the praises of Israel's past heroes by a deft rewriting of biblical material (chs 44–49). Selected characters are singled out and treated in such a way as to highlight fundamental concerns in Ben Sira's thought, like the various covenants* (44.18,20,22; 45.24f.); the dignity of the priesthood (45.6–24); the mysterious nature of prophecy* (46.1; 49.8–10); and the rewards of piety and the fear of God (45.1–5,

23–24; 46.11; 49.1–3). In a similar way, the Wisdom of Solomon (c. 50 BC) retells parts of the patriarchal story to demonstrate the operation of Wisdom and its consequent benefits in the lives of Israel's ancestors (chs 10–19).

Pride of place in the rewritten Bible belongs, however, to the Book of Jubilees (mid(?)–late second century BC), which gives a sustained re-working of Gen. 1.1 to Ex. 12.51. Not unjustly described by R. H. Charles as primitive history rewritten from the standpoint of Law, Jubilees proceeds, in the manner of the Chronicler, to omit material (e.g. Abraham's* dealings with Abimelech king of Gerar; Jacob's blessing of Ephraim and Manasseh), and to supplement the Genesis stories with material as diverse as a testament of Noah (Jub. 7.34–39), Abraham's polemic against idolatry (12.1–8,12–14) and Jacob's wars against the Amorites and Edomites (34; 38). There is a pronounced tendency to present the patriarchs as pious men who kept the Law, especially the regulations for worship, before it was promulgated at Sinai; and biblical narratives which do not redound to their honour are often restructured. Thus the sexual misdemeanours of Reuben (33.1–20) and Judah (41) are carefully edited and explained.

All this rewriting, however, is undertaken in an attempt to convince the author's contemporaries of the necessity of obeying the Law as he himself understands and interprets it. The pious deeds and words of the patriarchs are models for the author's own deeply Hellenized* generation to emulate. Thus contemporary breaches of the Law like nudity and attempts to obliterate the marks of circumcision are roundly condemned (3.31; 15.33–34), as are neglect and abuse of sabbath and festivals (6.17–19; 23.19), and failure to abide by the 364-day solar calendar,* which alone Jubilees considers authentic (6.32–38). Indeed, chronology* is a major preoccupation of Jubilees, which seeks to date exactly the activities of the patriarchs, often with reference to annual festivals. To indicate its authority, Jubilees is presented as an angelic revelation to Moses* on Sinai, imparting knowledge of heavenly mysteries and of world history, which is divided into neat periods of weeks of years and jubilees. Thus the future is 'predicted', and second century Jews are urged to accept and obey the commandments.

Closely related to Jubilees is the Genesis Apocryphon from Qumran Cave 1 (see **Dead Sea Scrolls**), dating most probably from the early first century BC. Like Jubilees, this work is concerned to provide answers to questions raised by the biblical text itself. For example, Gen. 12.11–12 has Abraham predict that the Egyptians will kill him because of Sarah his wife. How could he have known this? The

Genesis Apocryphon answers by relating a dream which came to Abraham on his entry into Egypt, symbolically foretelling what the Egyptians were likely to do (1QapGen col. xix, lines 14–19). Once again there is a concern to specify chronology (e.g. col. xix, line 9; xxi, line 5; xxii, lines 27–29), to supply narrative details missing from the Bible (e.g. the name of Noah's mother and the circumstances of his birth, col. ii, lines 3–18; the site of Noah's vineyard, col. xxi, line 13; the name of the Pharaoh who took Sarah and the nature of the plague which afflicted him, col. xx, lines 14–21); and to depict the patriarchs as pious men (col. xxi, lines 1–3).

The desire to fill gaps in the biblical record is very marked in the writings under consideration, and particularly in the great Temple Scroll from Qumran Cave 11, which probably dates from a time before 125 BC. Much of it gives orders for building the Temple and organizing its service after the conquest of the land of Israel, matters not touched by the Bible. Laws from different parts of the Pentateuch * relating to sacrifice and festivals are brought together and harmonized; and the whole work is presented as a divine speech, in the first person, uttered to Moses after the events of Ex. 34. For the Qumran sect, it appears almost certainly to have possessed the same kind of authority as the Pentateuch; and it is a key witness to the very high esteem in which the rewritten Bible could be held by certain Jewish groups.

While the Temple Scroll seems to have been confined to sectarian use, the Book of Biblical Antiquities enjoyed a wider currency. This work, wrongly attributed to Philo,* is almost certainly to be dated to the first century AD, and probably pre-dates the fall of the Temple in 70, although this last point is disputed. It rewrites the biblical history from Adam * to the rise of David, the period which had not been treated by the Chronicler. Although it has been suggested that the book was written with some overall polemical purpose in mind (e.g. as an anti-Samaritan * tract), most recent scholarship tends to view it as the product of mainstream Palestinian Jewish synagogue piety. It proceeds very much in the manner of Jubilees and the Genesis Apocryphon, and is valuable as a source which confirms the great antiquity of certain traditions found later in rabbinic * literature. Two examples must suffice. We read that the Flood did not cover the land of Israel (7.4; cf. Babylonian Talmud * Zebachim 113a); and that Phinehas the priest is identified with Elijah (48.1; cf. Targum * Pseudo-Jonathan on Ex. 4.13; 6.18; 40.10; Deut. 30.4; Pirqe de R. Eliezer 29,47).

Like Jubilees, the Book of Biblical Antiquities detests idolatry, and urges Israel to avoid sexual involvement with Gentiles. Israel's unique position in the world is much stressed: God, who alone is light, has given his Law, which is light, to Israel alone. The Law is eternal, and demands Israel's purity: she is God's vine, which cannot be destroyed. If she were destroyed, God would have no one left to praise him; thus specially composed psalms are a feature of this book, being put in the mouths of its heroes. The book holds out the hope of resurrection * to eternal bliss of the righteous dead, consigning sinners to everlasting torment; and it is tireless in its exhortations to Israel to remain faithful to the Law and its commandments, so that the promised rewards may be theirs on the last day.

Other inter-testamental writings, such as I Enoch 6–11, the Life of Adam and Eve, and the Ascension of Isaiah may also be considered as rewritten Bible; to these may be added the Book of Noah, Testament of Kohath, Testament of Amram, and Samuel Apocryphon, all of which are extant in more or less fragmentary manuscripts discovered at Qumran. These supplement the Bible's information about the lives and actions, not only of famous characters, but also of those who are little known. Thus Amram, the father of Moses, is credited with a number of predictive visions; and Kohath, father of Amram and Levi's son, gives a Testament in first-person form. Such writings also attest the long history of pious and scholarly reflection on biblical narratives and personalities which led to the development of rich and complex pre-rabbinic * haggadah.

In the last decade of the first century AD, Flavius Josephus * published his Jewish Antiquities. His work must be included as an example of rewritten Bible, since large parts of it exhibit traits similar to those which are typical of such works as Jubilees. Although he promises his readers that he will relate the precise record of the Bible without additions or omissions (Ant. 1.17), he actually embellishes his account, most often with material found also in other Jewish sources; and he omits embarrassing details. So, for example, he identifies Mount Moriah, the place where Abraham bound Isaac in sacrifice, as the Temple Mount in Jerusalem (Ant. I.224–226), a tradition found also among the rabbis; and he entirely omits the episode of the golden calf, thereby drawing the sting from the story just as Targum Neofiti (on Ex. 32) neutralizes the narrative by leaving parts of it untranslated.

Finally, the Targums themselves fall into the category of rewritten Bible in so far as they interweave with their rendering of the biblical text into Aramaic explanatory comments and edifying homiletic material. Designed to give the meaning of the text to attenders of school and synagogue, they have a partly didactic purpose, and are concerned to remove inconsistencies and contradictions in the text, to amplify it where necessary, and to emphasize its continuing relevance to Israel despite changes in Jewish society over the centuries. Thus they share many traditions with other works described here, and like the Book of Biblical Antiquities, demonstrate the widespread knowledge and popular character of much of the rewritten Bible.

See also **Midrash; Pseudepigrapha; Rabbi, Rabbinism.**

R. T. France, 'Jewish Historiography, Midrash and the Gospels' in *Gospel Perspectives*, vol. 3, 1983, pp. 99–127; G. W. E. Nickelsburg, 'The Bible Rewritten and Expanded' in M. E. Stone (ed.), *Jewish Writings of the Second Temple Period*, 1984, pp. 89–156; D. Patte, *Early Jewish Hermeneutic in Palestine*, 1975; E. Schürer, *The History of the Jewish People in the Age of Jesus Christ*, vol. 3.1, rev. and ed. G. Vermes, F. Millar and M. Goodman, 1986, pp. 308–41; G. Vermes, 'Bible and Midrash' in *Cambridge History of the Bible*, vol. 1, 1970, pp. 199–231; id., *Scripture and Tradition in Judaism*, [2] 1973.

C. T. R. HAYWARD

Rhetoric

The character and influence of rhetoric in ancient society has to be appreciated before the critical methods based upon it can be properly understood. The classical world was fascinated by the power of speech, and its educational system was founded upon analysis of language and communication. The effective public speaker was the person who could sway assemblies and acquire power. In the Hellenistic and Roman period the principal practical application of rhetoric was in the law courts, and despite its decline in the political sphere, speech-making remained the path to high reputation, and continued to be central to the educational process.

Training for effective communication began in the elementary school where the basic literary skills were imparted by the *grammaticus*, along with practical analysis of classic literary texts, so as to read them aloud with maximum effect. To do this it was necessary to construe sentences written without word division or punctuation, even to settle between different wordings in different manuscripts;* to explain archaic words and obsolete grammatical forms; to distinguish proper linguistic usage, while noting the characteristic usages of the classical author being studied; to identify and note the use of figures of speech,* the meaning and effects of metaphor,* allegory,* irony,* etc.; to study metre and the rhythm not only

of poetry but of good prose; to examine the construction of effective sentences and the overall structure of powerful speeches; to enter into the spirit of the text by spelling out its context and allusions; to identify the intention and argument of the text; to discern the moral qualities communicated by its content and form.

All this activity in the grammatical schools was the precursor of the techniques used in biblical exegesis.* But its primary purpose was to create an appreciation of the communication-skills of the great literary masters, so that the pupil could go on to the rhetorician to learn how to master the techniques for himself. Rhetorical handbooks show how very sophisticated and detailed the analysis had become, developing a complex battery of technical terms. The pupil was trained to be highly self-conscious in matters of aim and content, structure and style, suiting his compositions to different situations, learning the art of persuasion – the techniques of creating conviction and eliciting emotional response.

If we are to understand ancient texts, we need to hear them as their original hearers would have done. Someone trained in formal analysis hears a classical symphony differently from the innocent listener; someone whose ears were tuned by the all-pervasive presence of rhetoric in Graeco-Roman society would hear biblical texts in a way lost to us unless we become rhetorically self-conscious. The first essential point to grasp is that texts were not private communications to be read in silence, but the spoken word recorded. So an ancient work should be read linearly, as if we were hearing the content unfolding as it was recited or read aloud. The meaning is related to the kind of effect the author intended to produce on the listener.

The pioneering work in this field tackled the epistles* of Paul.* In the ancient world there was a tradition of literary letter-writing exploiting rhetorical techniques and showing off the skill of the writer. But since A. Deissmann's *Light from the Ancient East*, it had been generally assumed that Paul's letters were not like those: rather they were like the personal and business letters discovered in papyri from Egypt. But letter-writing in all cultures follows conventions. Paul has his conventions, some of which are illuminated by the papyri, but not all. Beginning with H. D. Betz on Galatians, scholars, particularly in North America,* have begun to discover that the structures of speeches recommended in the rhetorical handbooks throw considerable light on several of Paul's letters. Paul also uses stock images, figures of speech, and techniques like irony, understatement, the rhetorical question, etc. He is clearly aiming to have an effect on his hearers, and though not conforming to the 'sublime' style of high rhetoric, his language has a rhetoric of its own. To recognize this is to gain insight into the function and intention of Paul's writing.

There are those who greet this kind of approach with scepticism: Paul had no rhetorical education as far as we can make out, and he says he is a 'layman in speech'. How much more when we turn to the Gospels!* But this is to miss an important point. Quintilian, an educationalist of the first century whose works are one of our principal sources for understanding rhetoric, points out that what the Greeks and Romans analysed so self-consciously, the barbarians did instinctively. There are fundamental 'laws of rhetoric' which are transcultural. Molière's character M. Jourdain had been speaking prose for forty years without realizing it: similarly Paul and Jesus could be skilled rhetoricians unconsciously and without formal training. There is an important analogy in structuralism:* just as the 'deep structures' are there in the text or the narrative, even if unrecognized until the structuralist critic begins to analyse them and bring them to the reader's attention, so with rhetoric. Add to this the characteristic rhetoric of Jewish speech, and the process is clearly justifiable. Here more recent work turns to earlier studies of chiasm and parable* to illuminate the communication techniques of both Jesus and the evangelists.* Some work has also been done in OT studies on the rhetoric of prophecy.

Matthew and Luke certainly have their own rhetoric, and in the case of Paul there are undoubtedly historical grounds for taking his use of rhetoric seriously. Paul came from the Diaspora and was clearly at home in Greek urban society, even if he did go to study at the feet of Gamaliel in Jerusalem. There is evidence that Palestinian rabbis* approved of Greek education, and indeed that Palestine was far from immune from the influence of Hellenization. Paul is no Demosthenes, but he himself says that his letters were powerful, no doubt especially when read aloud by someone who could do justice to their rhetoric.

See also **Hellenism; Hellenistic Writers; Rhetorical Criticism.**

H. D. Betz, *Galatians*, 1979; Amos Wilder, *The Language of the Gospel: Early Christian Rhetoric*, 1964; Frances Young and David F. Ford, *Meaning and Truth in 2 Corinthians*, 1987.

FRANCES YOUNG

Rhetorical Criticism

While rhetorical criticism is 'an approach of eminent lineage' (Muilenburg, 1969), its

impact upon modern exegesis* and biblical interpretation was not particularly evident until the second half of the twentieth century. The change may be ascribed partly to a growing concern with language and communication in the biblical field, and partly to developments within the study of rhetoric.* When the latter succeeded in breaking out of the traditional straitjacket which bound it to matters of style, ornamentation and rhetorical figures and defined rhetoric as 'that quality of discourse by which a speaker or writer seeks to accomplish his purposes' (Kennedy, 1984), a much more dynamic understanding of rhetoric was made available to the biblical interpreter.

J. Muilenburg pointed OT studies in the direction of rhetorical criticism which, he believed, could reveal the texture and fabric of the writer's thought: 'not only what it is that he thinks but as he thinks it'. He proposed to reach out beyond form criticism* to the individual text as rhetorical unit and to examine both its structure* and the configuration of its component parts. That his initiative was timely and productive is well illustrated by the Muilenburg Festschrift (*Rhetorical Criticism* ed. Jackson and Kessler, 1974), yet there remained an acknowledged need (in Kessler's phrase) 'to develop and refine rhetorical methods of literary criticism'.* and also a proclivity to reduce rhetoric to stylistics. The same is true of other OT studies. Even the lively work of R. Alter (*The Art of Biblical Narrative*, 1981) falls within the broad category of literary rather than rhetorical criticism (but cf. Clines, 1982).

In NT studies, A. N. Wilder's work on *Early Christian Rhetoric* (1964) was an important marker in so far as it raised basic questions about the whole phenomenon of language, speech, communication and rhetoric in the context of the rise of Christianity. His identification and exploration of genres* such as dialogue and story, parable* and poem, indicated directions for future research. As literary interest quickened, works on style and textual structure became a veritable growth industry in NT criticism, but they tended to represent a fragmented or 'restrained' view of rhetoric. Of greater significance, perhaps, was the development of a socio*-rhetorical approach to interpretation (cf. V. Robbins, *Jesus the Teacher*, 1984), but this effectively confined interpretation to the realm of social history. H. D. Betz and W. Wuellner based their more comprehensive approaches on a revised classical tradition of rhetoric (cf. Kennedy, 1984).

Kennedy's methodology entails a number of interrelated stages:

1. *Determination of the rhetorical unit to be studied.* While it may be large or small (cf. pericope, speech, parable, epistle*), each unit

has an identifiable opening and closure, connected by some action or argument. Smaller units interrelate with the larger to form a strong overall unity, as is well illustrated by I Corinthians.

2. *Examination of the rhetorical situation and problem.* Every unit (large or small) has its own rhetorical situation. This term denotes the rhetorical occasion or exigency which has prompted the author's or speaker's response and includes the rhetorical problem to be overcome (cf. E. S. Fiorenza, 1987). In tracing the interaction between speaker and audience, one notes how the sympathies of the audience are engaged (*ethos*), the appeals to emotion (*pathos*), and the use of logical argument (*logos*). The genre of the argument may also be important. The three traditional types are judicial (or 'forensic': designed to elicit judgment), deliberative (or 'symbouleutic': aiming at effecting decision), and epideictic (fostering assent to, or dissent from, a particular stance); but mixed types are also possible. Kennedy illustrates the importance of genre from H. D. Betz's treatment of Galatians (1979). On the basis of the earlier chapters, Betz took the argument to be judicial or forensic, whereas linear reading and holistic* assessment (see below) suggest that the letter employs deliberative rhetoric. It is not essentially a defence of Paul but a setting forth of the gospel and Christian praxis in order to bring the Galatians to decision about their belief and life-style for the future. It is, of course, possible for deliberative or epideictic genres to include apologetic concerns. W. Wuellner finds an 'epideictic apology' in I Cor. 9.

3. *Consideration of the rhetorical arrangement of the text.* Rhetorical invention produces the arrangement (*dispositio*) of the text: the identification of the parts and their deployment for rhetorical effect. Rhetorical structure is a dynamic strategy developed in relation to the rhetorical situation, rather than a skeletal analysis or architectonic sketch. It also reveals much about the intended or implied audience.

4. *Analysis of the devices of style.* The arrangement of the material entails the employment of rhetorical figures and stylistic devices to accomplish the rhetorical purpose. However, over-emphasis on this aspect alone leads to what Wuellner has called 'the Babylonian captivity of rhetoric reduced to stylistics'. Style and content cohere and work together in the interests of the author's purpose.

5. *Review of whole unit as a response to the rhetorical situation.* Since the impact of an oral text is cumulative, it is important to follow it through to the end as in linear reading. The whole is greater than the sum of its parts. We should then ask: How successful has the author been in responding through this unit as a whole to the rhetorical problem? What impact would the unit have on the rhetorical situation? What is its impact on the modern reader?

How are we to assess the importance of rhetorical criticism for biblical interpretation? Its contribution is many-sided. At a time when literary criticism has challenged facile assumptions about the author's purpose, rhetorical criticism provides access to the purposive and persuasive nature of the author's utterance. It can open up the rhetorical vision in given texts and so fire the reader's imagination and elicit response. It transcends the atomism and antiquarianism of many types of criticism, combines close reading with holistic perspective, and follows the dynamics of the text through to encounter, transformation and renewed practice.

Readers, ancient and modern, are essential participants in the process described by rhetorical criticism, and their involvement entails their 'whole being' in its cognitive, affective and conative aspects. In view of the fact that rhetoric can be used for propaganda purposes, one of their tasks (as Fiorenza has emphasized) is to make an ethical evaluation of it. The impact of the text, however, may create new political and personal initiatives, as in liberation* and feminist* interpretations. Phyllis Trible (*God and the Rhetoric of Sexuality*, 1978), for example, uses rhetorical criticism as her 'methodological clue' in her feminist hermeneutics.* In homiletics,* there is the closest relationship between rhetoric and preaching, not simply as a speech act but as the communication of the power of the gospel (cf. Keck, 1983). Rhetorical criticism stands in close relation both to narrative theology* and to *praxis*. Indeed, it may be that the concerns of a previous generation with 'Word'* and 'kerygma'* (cf. McDonald, *Kerygma and Didache*, 1980) are now beginning to receive expression in appropriately dynamic terms through rhetorical criticism, but much work remains to be done on its development and application.

See also **Holistic Interpretation; Metaphor; Reader-Response Criticism.**

D. J. A. Clines et al. (eds), *Art and Meaning*, 1982; E. S. Fiorenza, 'Rhetorical Situation and Historical Reconstruction in I Corinthians', *NTS*, 33, 1987, pp. 386–403; L. E. Keck, 'Toward a Theology of Rhetoric/Preaching' in D. S. Browning (ed.), *Practical Theology*, 1983, pp. 126–47; G. A. Kennedy, *New Testament Interpretation through Rhetorical Criticism*, 1984; J. Muilenburg, 'Form Criticism and Beyond', *JBL*, 88, 1969, pp. 1–18; W. Wuellner, 'Where is Rhetorical Criticism Taking Us?', *CBQ*, 49, 1987, pp. 448–63.

J. I. H. MCDONALD

Romans

As well as having a decisive influence on such luminaries as Augustine,* Aquinas, Luther,* Melanchthon, Calvin,* Barth* and Bultmann,* Romans has played a major part in theological controversy, church history and Christian piety from before Augustine to our own day. The chief phases of the history of its interpretation are: the patristic period and especially the Pelagian controversy; the mediaeval* period; the Reformation;* and the nineteenth and twentieth centuries.

Patristic period. The most notable commentaries* are those of Origen* and Chrysostom in the East and Ambrosiaster and Pelagius in the West. Augustine's early *Expositions* of parts of the epistle* are unremarkable, but his use of the epistle in the Pelagian controversy set the agenda for subsequent debate. The need to refute Marcion,* the Gnostics* and other heretics dominated patristic interpretation before Augustine; hence the insistence of orthodox interpreters on free will, the integrity of human nature and the harmony of gospel and law, often to the point of blurring if not obliterating the bold contrasts of Paul's* thought in Romans.

In his commentary on Romans (*c.* 406), Pelagius did little more than accentuate the concerns of other commentators (though it must also be said that he lacked an adequate theology of the atonement and of the Holy Spirit). Although moralistic in character and not intentionally controversial, his commentary already implied the positions which were to prove so provocative to Augustine: sin comes from people's free imitation of Adam* and can be overcome by imitating Jesus; the grace of Christ is essentially a heightening of the divine imperative summoning people to make use of their creaturely capacity to obey; justification is through resolute moral endeavour. Against all this Augustine in his anti-Pelagian writings (411–427; e.g. *On the Spirit and the Letter*, 412), in which he made extensive use of Romans, insisted relentlessly on the absolute necessity of grace (the transforming and energizing power of the Spirit) for justification.

Central to Augustine's rebuttal of 'Pelagianism' and crucial for the epistle's subsequent interpretation are the following points: 1. The 'works of law' which Paul says can never justify mean moral actions in general without the grace of Christ, not Jewish practices as Pelagius and others maintained. 2. The 'righteousness of God' (Rom. 1.17 etc.) is not an attribute of God but the gift he confers in making people righteous. 3. Rom. 5.12 now became the key text for Augustine's doctrine of original sin: all individuals (infants included) were co-involved in Adam's sin. As is well known, Augustine's exegesis of this verse largely depended on the Latin translation *in quo* ('in whom') of the Greek *eph'hōi* ('in that', 'because') and on the omission in his manuscripts* of the second mention of 'death', with the result that 'sin' became the subject of 'spread': sin spread to all (by 'generation', not by 'imitation'). 4. Rom. 7.14–25, which before the controversy Augustine had understood to be referring to humanity without Christ, he now applied to the Christian to deprive Pelagius of the opportunity of applying the positive elements in the passage (esp v. 22) to unredeemed humanity. To do this, Augustine was obliged to water down Paul's negative statements: the apostle is describing not the bondage of sin but the bother of concupiscence; and he laments not that he cannot do good (*facere*) but that he cannot do it perfectly (*perficere*). 5. During this period Augustine came to express more boldly his teaching on predestination. It does not depend on God's advance knowledge of people's merits as Pelagius and others maintained in their interpretation of Rom. 9.10ff., nor even on his advance knowledge of the 'merit of faith' as Augustine had supposed in 394 in his remarks on the same passage; it depends rather on God's 'most hidden judgment' whereby he graciously chooses whom he will deliver from the mass of fallen humanity. Everything is pure gift (I Cor. 4.7).

Augustine's interpretation of Romans, implicitly canonized at the Councils of Carthage (418) and Orange (529), was to dominate Western (though not Eastern) exegesis* and theology for centuries to come, in spite of many distortions to his thought.

Mediaeval period. The mediaeval period recast Augustine's interpretation in its own image and likeness. Under Aristotelian influence Paul's teaching on justification was reinterpreted in terms of the scholastic doctrine of grace as 'something added to nature'. Divine *charis* became 'infused grace'. Although the best of the scholastics preserved the theocentric character of Paul's thought, the overwhelming tendency was to shift attention away from the God who 'justifies the impious' to the psychology of justification and the human contribution to its process, with the attendant danger of 'separating the gift from the Giver'. This led to a preoccupation with merit. In a debased scholasticism, as exemplified in the nominalist school of Ockham which gave Luther his early theological formation, such concerns encouraged the 'Pelagianism' which Luther was to regard as the antithesis of the gospel: 'I lost Christ there but now I have found him again in Paul.'

Reformation. Luther discovered in Romans

both a personal liberation and a colossal scriptural protest against what he saw as the trivializing theology and piety of contemporary Catholicism. The epistle was 'the gospel in its purest expression': here at last was a 'gracious God', one who imputed righteousness to the sinner out of sheer grace and on the sole basis of faith apart from any 'work'. The believer, while remaining intrinsically sinful, is justified by a righteousness which belongs to another. The object of Paul's polemic in Romans is self-righteousness, the deadliest enemy of the gospel and the besetting sin, Luther believed, of both Judaism and Catholicism: 'The sum and substance of this epistle is . . . to destroy all wisdom and righteousness of the flesh . . . and to implant, establish and make large the reality of sin, however unconscious we may be of its existence' (on Rom. 1.1). Luther's commentary on the epistle, the fruit of lectures delivered in 1515–1516, dates from the time before his break with Rome; it nevertheless contains the substance of his later teaching. The doctrine of justification which he believed he found in the epistle was to become the organizing principle of his theology and a new basis for Christian piety and church order.

On the following points in particular Luther's exegesis was to prove decisive for him and the tradition he founded: 1. The 'righteousness of God'. In the *Preface to his Latin Works* (1545) he recalls how in his youth, 'through the customary teaching of all the doctors', he had been taught to understand the righteousness of God as a punitive righteousness, a notion which made him 'hate the righteousness of God' and 'rage with a wildly aroused and disturbed conscience'. His discovery that God's righteousness was God's gift 'straightaway made me feel as though reborn and as though I had entered through open gates to paradise itself'. Later he was thrilled to find that Augustine (*On the Spirit and the Letter*) agreed with him on the righteousness of God, 'though he did not clearly explain about imputation'. This remark was surely made with tongue in cheek, or it betrays a profound misinterpretation of Augustine, whose understanding of justification is thoroughly incompatible with the notion of imputation. Luther's use of this (Ockhamist) concept signals a completely new beginning in the interpretation of Romans. 2. Luther explains imputation in his comments on Rom. 4, but it is clear that its exegetical basis lies in Rom. 7.14–25. His scholia on this passage are devoted almost entirely to showing (through a rehearsal of Augustine's anti-Pelagian arguments) that Paul with his talk about bondage to sin is speaking in his own name as a Christian. Luther adopts Augustine's (revised) inter-

pretation that 'sin' in this passage means 'concupiscence' but makes a crucial move beyond it when he defines concupiscence as the radical sin (of self-seeking) which remains in the justified. If Rom. 7.14–25 is indeed speaking of Christian experience it affords a firm scriptural basis for the classic Lutheran formula *simul justus et peccator* (which in fact makes its earliest appearance in Luther's commentary on Rom. 4.7), and for the characteristically Lutheran pessimism about human nature (for if the Christian's situation is so gloomy, what must be said about mankind without grace?). The far-reaching influence of Romans on Luther's anthropology can be seen in his *On the Bondage of the Will* (1525), his classic answer to Erasmus* and the humanists. 3. Worthy of mention is Rom. 13.1–7, which has proved even more chameleon-like in the history of interpretation than Rom. 7.14–25. Here it should be enough to note its influence on Luther's 'two kingdom' theory and his teaching on Christian social ethics. Christians are 'subject to no one but God' in the spiritual sphere; in the temporal sphere they make themselves subject to all earthly powers, out of love.

A mere mention must suffice here of the epistle's decisive influence on Melanchthon's *Loci Communes* (1521) and on the second edition (1539) of Calvin's *Institutes*. This contains the classic Calvinist doctrine of 'double predestination' elaborated on the basis of Rom. 8.29 and Augustine's 'hidden judgment of God'.

Mention must also be made of the part played by Romans in the Evangelical Revival of the eighteenth century onwards, beginning with John Wesley's Aldersgate Street experience when he 'felt his heart strangely warmed' on hearing a reading of Luther's preface to the Epistle. The revivalist interpretation did much to soften the harsher antinomies of Lutheran and Calvinist orthodoxy. It is significant that Wesley, like the German pietists, rejected Luther's 'Christian' interpretation of Rom. 7.14ff., and looked rather to chs 8 and 12ff. for the epistle's central message to Christians.

Nineteenth and twentieth centuries. The possibility of a completely new approach to Romans came with historical criticism,* which sought to explain the epistle on its own terms rather than in the light of Augustinian and Protestant polemics. Foundational was the attempt in the mid-1800s of F. C. Baur to explain it as a protest against Jewish particularism (thus shifting the focus of attention on to chs 9–11 and away from the 'dogmatic' chs 1–8, which Baur saw as merely preparatory to the main theme). The historical approach to Romans was here to stay. In fact, however, its effects on the interpretation of Romans, at least until recently, have proved far less decisive than in most other areas of NT studies, partly because it has not come up with any generally acceptable reconstruction of the epistle's historical background and partly because traditional dogmatic concerns have not failed to reassert themselves, often with an impressive array of historical learning.

Startling among the reactions against historical criticism was Karl Barth's passionately anti-liberal* Epistle to the Romans (1919). Claiming to presuppose but in fact largely bypassing the findings of historical criticism, Barth appealed 'through and beyond history' to the 'spirit of the Bible, which is the Eternal Spirit'. Thus he sought to make the 'mighty voice of Paul' speak its timeless message (actually the message of a renewed Protestant orthodoxy in the harsh accents of dialectical theology) to the people of his day. His most novel move was to turn Paul's critique of the 'wisdom and righteousness of the flesh' against the entire culture, religion and society of the nineteenth and early twentieth centuries. Curious are: his extension of Paul's tirade in Rom. 1–2 to the concept of 'religion' in liberal theology; his application of Rom. 7.7–13 to romanticism and of Rom. 7.14–25 to pietism; and his identification of Israel in Rom. 9–11 with the Christian church. Variously described as 'an act of violence' on the text and 'the most important theological work written in the twentieth century', Barth's commentary, while finding few takers for its anti-critical stance, in fact gave a powerful boost to the renewed quest of a religiously relevant interpretation of Romans in the decades that followed.

The chief trends in interpretation in the last sixty years may be outlined as follows. 1. Interpreters have generally sought to co-ordinate dogmatic concerns with historical enquiry. Enormously influential in earlier decades was Bultmann, who wedded existentialism with Gnosticism to produce a Lutheran Paul in thoroughly modern dress. Still in the Lutheran tradition, and intent on reaffirming Paul's soli Deo gloria against Bultmann's human-centred existentialism, E. Käsemann has more recently appealed to Paul's Jewish background* to elaborate an interpretation of the epistle centred on the supposed apocalyptic* understanding of the righteousness of God as divine power salvifically reordering creation under the creator's dominion. His majestic commentary remains the most influential among modern theological treatments of Romans. 2. Catholic scholars too have contributed effectively to the exegetical and theological discussion of the epistle. Chief among them are French and German exegetes (e.g. Cerfaux, Lyonnet, Kuss, Kertelge). 3.

There has been a significant rapprochement between Catholics and Protestants over traditional doctrinal differences, as can be seen, for example, in the ecumenically sensitive commentaries of the Catholic Kuss and the Lutheran Wilckens, the interconfessional Traduction Oecuménique de la Bible and, in the Anglican-Roman Catholic context, the recent ARCIC document on justification. 4. The nature and function of the Epistle have recently been the subject of a vigorous and productive debate: was it intended as a 'timeless' summary of Paul's theology, or is it (like the rest of his epistles) tied to a particular situation (the 'Romans Debate')? Many imaginative attempts have been made to correlate the Epistle's contents with theories about a concrete situation in the Roman community or a particular juncture in Paul's relations with Jerusalem (e.g. Klein, Jervell, Minear, Donfried and those who attempt to apply to Paul the general patterns of the sociology* of religion). 5. The delayed impact of Baur, already discernible on one side of the 'Romans Debate', has been most evident in the rigorously historical and avowedly anti-dogmatic approach of some recent influential studies of Paul and of Romans in particular. Notable among the exponents of this approach is Krister Stendahl, who in some important essays in the early 1960s reminded the scholarly world that Paul's concern was not the Augustinian-Lutheran problematic of the 'introspective conscience' but the practical and theological questions arising from the inclusion of the Gentiles in the church and the coexistence of church and synagogue in God's plan of salvation (for Stendahl, as for Baur, the Epistle's centre of gravity is located in chs 9–11).

The most radical and most influential representatives of this approach to Romans are Sanders and Räisänen. Sanders in particular has argued that the Lutheran view of Judaism as the prototype of the Catholicism Luther hated is a gross misconstrual. Both of these scholars have done much to rescue Paul from Protestant dogmatics in order to replace him in his true historical perspective. In so doing, however, they have revealed a new and unflattering picture of Paul as one who first decided on a priori grounds that Judaism was not the way and then proceeded to invent not very good arguments against it. An example: the classic ch. 7 of Romans, so long the crux of doctrinal disputes over the Epistle, turns out to be the product of Paul's 'tortured thinking' (Sanders) or his 'secondary rationalization' (Räisänen). A constructive intention of this approach is to remove the obstacles traditionally posed by Paul to Christian-Jewish relations. As a radical challenge to the Lutheran approach to Paul, it still awaits an effective answer.

Karl P. Donfried (ed.), *The Romans Debate*, 1977; John D. Godsey, 'The Interpretation of Romans in the History of the Christian Faith', *Interpretation* XXXIV, 1980, pp. 3–16; Robert Jewett, 'Major Impulses in the Theological Interpretation of Romans since Barth', *Interpretation* XXXIV, 1980, pp. 17–31; Douglas Moo, 'Paul and the Law in the Last Ten Years', *SJT*, 40, 1987, pp. 287–307; Wilhelm Pauck (ed.), *Luther: Lectures on Romans*, 1961; James M. Robinson (ed.), *The Beginnings of Dialectic Theology*, vol. I, 1968; Krister Stendahl, *Paul Among Jews and Gentiles*, 1977; Maurice F. Wiles, *The Divine Apostle*, 1967.

T. J. DEIDUN

Ruth

How the book of Ruth is interpreted has been largely determined by what view is taken of its date, unity and purpose. Although some conservative critics would still claim that it is a trustworthy record of a historical episode in the period of the judges, the majority consider it as a 'novelle' or short story: it is worth noting that in the Hebrew Bible the book is not linked with Judges but occurs as an independent work in the third section of the canon,* the Writings.*

A common approach to Ruth in the earlier part of this century was to see it as a conscious protest against Ezra's policy on mixed marriages and thus to date it around the period of his activity. The author's purpose was to present his Moabite heroine as a devout adherent of Yahweh, who was welcomed into the chosen people and who, moreover, became the ancestress of Israel's greatest king. This opinion, however, is now increasingly rejected. It has been pointed out that there is no clear evidence of a polemic in the book, such as might be expected were that the writer's primary purpose. Claims that the language of the work is late are difficult to substantiate and if, as many scholars would hold, the Davidic* genealogy* in 4.18–22 is a later addition, no great stress is placed on Ruth herself as the ancestress. Further, the same arguments used to show that the work is an attack on Ezra's exclusive policy can be adduced for the view that it defends that policy: Ruth is depicted as the ideal proselyte and a sign of Israel's mission to convert the Gentiles to Judaism. The only reference to Ruth in the NT is genealogical (Matt. 1.5), and its point seems to be a drawing of attention to 1. the Gentile status of the women in Christ's ancestry and 2. the irregular character of their alleged sexual and marital status – as also in the case of Mary (*see* **Infancy Narratives**).

Those who reject the idea of deliberate pol-

emic generally understand the book in one of two ways. On the one hand, a theological interpretation has been proposed: the work displays the hidden causality of Yahweh in the direction of human affairs, perhaps specifically to provide the divinely chosen ancestor of the royal line. Ruth can thus be compared with the Joseph story and the so-called 'Succession Narrative' of II Sam. 9–20, which are similar examples of the working of hidden divine providence; this comparison would suggest a setting for the book in learned circles during the period of the monarchy. However, the theological thrust of the work can be easily exaggerated. It is noteworthy that in only two instances is Yahweh seen as intervening to set events in motion and these occur only towards the beginning, 1.6, and the end, 4.13.

On the other hand, there have always been those who have viewed Ruth as essentially a folk-tale (*see* **Folklore**), a view fully developed most recently by J. M. Sasson. The carefully worked out artistic structure of the work had been discussed by various commentators,* but Sasson anchors all its features in the typical pattern of a folk-tale, by means of a detailed comparison between the successive phases of the biblical narrative and the folkloristic 'functions' discovered by V. Propp in his famous *Morphology of the Folktale*. Ruth, then, as is characteristic of folklore, would mirror certain concerns of the culture which gave rise to it, not least dynastic ones, which Sasson finds to be present throughout and not just in the closing verses. All this, however, does not mean that the work had an oral prototype, originating among the general populace: rather, its polished style and rich vocabulary point to an educated circle working with a folk-tale model sometime during the period of the monarchy. Here is a fresh approach to Ruth, which points the way to further investigations of the nature of this much discussed work.

E. F. Campbell, *Ruth*, 1975; R. M. Hals, *The Theology of the Book of Ruth*, 1968; J. M. Sasson, *Ruth*, 1979.

J. R. PORTER

Sachkritik

The word has been translated 'content criticism', 'material criticism of the content', 'critical study of the content', 'critical interpretation' and 'theological criticism' (as well as, wrongly, 'objective criticism'). The *Sache*, 'content' or 'subject-matter', about which it 'makes a judgment' is theological: the gospel, or revelatory event of God being proclaimed and acknowledged in Christ. But what the word means is not criticism of the gospel (which would be blasphemous) but criticism of particular theological formulations in the light of this non-objectifiable gospel. It thus gives a neo-Kantian edge to Luther's* (and Paul's*) distinction between the 'living voice of the gospel', i.e. the Spirit or living Christ, and the letter of scripture or tradition. The latter is necessary for proclaiming Christ and making revelation* and faith possible, but must not be identified with the gospel itself, and can even be criticized in the light of it.

This anti-biblicist dialectic between scripture and the gospel was characteristic of Luther's 'theology of the Word'.* It found sharp expression in his willingness if necessary to 'urge Christ against scripture' (WA 39/1, p. 47) and in his theological criticism of the Epistle of James in the September Testament of 1522. Liberal* Protestantism preserved an echo of this 'self-criticism of the canon* through the instrumentality of believing enquirers' (Dorner), but the word owes its prominence in twentieth-century NT theology* almost entirely to Rudolf Bultmann's* qualified reception of Karl Barth's* Epistle to the Romans (1919), and the revival of a neo-Reformation* theological interpretation of scripture by these two theologians.

Bultmann welcomed Barth's concern for the theological subject-matter of scripture (Sach-exegese), but followed Luther in reserving the right to criticize the biblical writers' fallible human formulations. Barth saw the danger of subjectivism inherent in any such appeal to a criterion which was not objectively available. Bultmann argued correctly that even Barth engaged in such discrimination, but his own practice of combining a pre-understanding of the subject-matter with theological criticism of what disagreed with this justified Barth's unease.

Bultmann later tried to strengthen his position by appealing to the general theory of interpretation developed by Schleiermacher and Dilthey. We always understand the part (a particular part of a text) in the light of the whole, and vice versa. Bultmann went on to distinguish between 'what is said' in the text and 'what was meant' by the author, and to correct the former in the light of the latter. Behind this stands Schleiermacher's presumption that the interpreter can understand an author better than he understood himself. It is true that interpreters do occasionally venture such corrections, based on their understanding of the whole text or the author's whole work. But this is at best a supporting argument, and masks what is really going on. In the Sachkritik of Bultmann and his school (e.g. Käsemann) the real criterion* is not their historical conclusions about the ancient authors, but their own theological convictions,

which are only partly informed by historical exegesis.* The hermeneutical circle* is always in danger of becoming vicious, unless theological interpretation is balanced by a more purely historical exegesis or is open to persuasion by alternative theological proposals.

The theological problem highlighted by the controversy over Sachkritik concerns the authority for a believer's understanding of the gospel, and the difficulty of finding a path between the liberals' subjectivism and the conservatives' biblical or ecclesiastical authoritarianism or absolutism. What is the precise relationship between tradition (particularly scripture) and experience in determining the truth of the gospel? Can this question be answered in advance, or is it settled in particular cases by the community faithfully attending to scripture and expecting guidance of the Spirit? This is a central problem for any Christian theological interpretation of scripture.

Like any other interpretation, a critical theological one (i.e. one that disagrees with the biblical text in the light of the interpreter's present and provisional understanding of the gospel) can only ever be the tentative proposal of a fallible and historically conditioned interpreter at a particular time and place. It is only a contribution to the church's on-going engagement with its scripture. It is not a method but an act of interpretation, seeking to persuade others of its truth. The only way to prevent this necessary but dangerous procedure from undermining its own basis by eroding the authority* of scripture is by insisting that any criticized texts remain on the church's agenda, to be considered afresh by future interpreters.

B. Ehler, Die Herrschaft des Gekreuzigten, 1986; R. Morgan, The Nature of New Testament Theology, 1973.

ROBERT MORGAN

Saga

This Old Norse/Icelandic word (sagn in Norwegian) is used of narrative, story, history. The term is normally applied to mediaeval prose narratives of Norwegian and Icelandic origins, which can be categorized in terms of their subject matter as: 1. lives of Icelandic bishops; 2. biographies of Norwegian kings; 3. stories of early and notable Icelanders; 4. stories of legendary heroes; 5. stories relating events in the lives of a prominent Icelandic family during the twelfth and thirteenth centuries.

There are certain stereotypical themes and episodes which are common to all sagas. Frequently these are formed and developed in a symmetrical fashion which results in various stylized patterns. These sagas seek to relate the history of a particular group and therefore they are firmly rooted in the real world and not the world of fantasy or myth.* The history they recount has, however, been embellished by legends, anecdotes, and tales.

Scholars are divided in their assessment of the possible oral origins of the saga. Until more complete criteria* are established for determining such origins, however, great caution should be exercised before ascribing them to earlier oral tradition.*

The most recent application of the term saga to OT narratives can be found in the work of G. W. Coats, who argues that the saga has a multi-episodic structure comprised of 'Tales, Reports, Legends, Anecdotes, Hymns, and various other smaller pieces'. Whereas its main concern is with the real world, saga can nevertheless incorporate fables and myths. The world of fantasy which is described by these genres* is transformed into a representation of the real world.

Given the complex nature of saga, Coats argues that the term 'saga cycle' should no longer be used. For Coats 'saga cycle' does not indicate the level of cohesion which is present in the saga, and instead he emphasizes the redactional work of the collector of original independent sagas.

For Coats three types of saga are found in the OT: 1. the primaeval saga; 2. the family saga; 3. the heroic saga. In all three instances Coats is convinced that the saga is the product of the storyteller who would have functioned within the social structures of ancient Israel in an official capacity. Whereas the saga no doubt was used for purposes of entertainment, it also served to preserve familial and state traditions and could therefore be used as a tool of legitimation and/or moral teaching.

The choice of the term saga to translate the German Sage has unfortunately led in the past to a confusion between the categories of saga and legend.* Folklorists have, however, consistently translated Sage as legend. Since biblical form critics* originally borrowed the term from the field of folklore* studies, it would seem wholly reasonable to suggest that in the interests of clarity, such a practice should be adopted by biblical scholars.

G. W. Coats (ed.), Saga, Legend, Tale, Novella, Fable, 1985; H. Jason, Ethnopoetry, 1977; P. G. Kirkpatrick, The Old Testament and Folklore Study, 1988; F. J. Oinas (ed.), Heroic Epic and Saga, 1978.

PATRICIA G. KIRKPATRICK

Salvation History

The expression translates the German Heilsgeschichte, introduced into biblical study by J. C. K. von Hofmann and the Erlangen School, a conservative wing of nineteenth-century Lutheran* thought. In his key work, Weissagung und Erfüllung (2 vols, 1841–44), von Hofmann sought to base the unity of the scriptures as a whole, and of the OT and NT, each in itself, on their being the proclamation of a divinely-achieved process of redemption in history with Christ at the centre, to be understood and personally appropriated by faith. His approach thus combined three features of biblical faith which have led to his ideas being taken up by three different schools of theology. His emphasis on the actual events of the history of Israel* and the life of Christ, forming a purposeful sequence leading from Old Testament to New, appears in the work of scholars such as G. E. Wright (God Who Acts, 1952), O. Cullmann (Salvation in History, ET 1967) and G. E. Ladd (A Theology of the New Testament, 1974). They stress the factuality of God's acts in history by which human redemption was achieved, particularly major 'acts of God' such as the exodus* and the resurrection.*

Cullmann's work, in particular, was written in polemical dialogue with that of R. Bultmann,* who took up a second aspect of von Hofmann's approach in his contributions to Essays on Old Testament Interpretation/Hermeneutics (ed. C. Westermann, ET 1963) and The Old Testament and Christian Faith (ed. B. W. Anderson, 1964). For Bultmann the important element in von Hofmann's approach was his stress on the individual's personal appropriation of the salvation events. Salvation history is our ever-repeated personal journey from the pre-Christian time of promise or law to the Christian experience of fulfilment or gospel.

A third appropriation of the model appears in G. von Rad's Old Testament Theology (ET 1962–64). Von Rad's stress on salvation history relates more to von Hofmann's understanding of the Bible as the history of the proclamation (see Kerygma) of salvation. Von Rad was aware as von Hofmann was not of the difficulty of establishing what events lie behind the biblical story: his theology was a study of what Israel said about Yahweh's deeds rather than a study of the significance of the deeds themselves. More recent interest in the OT story as narrative could also be seen to link with the feature of von Hofmann taken up by von Rad.

The taking up of the model by such different theological schools has generated confusion. Scholars who wanted to stress the factuality of the redemption events have suspected others who talked in terms of salvation history lest they were using the expression in the second or third sense. Scholars who emphasized the necessity of personal faith were sometimes hostile towards any stress on factual events, seeing this as rationalist and doubting whether history could really bring salvation. Scholars who gave themselves to the study of OT tradition* history and doubted whether one can identify historical events behind it were in turn wary of the stress on factual acts of God, on the grounds of its being unreflectively supranaturalist and/or uncritical in its approach to the Bible. From other perspectives, the stress on salvation history was faulted for oversimplifying the nature of scripture (which has other themes than this one), for falsifying the nature of Israel's distinctiveness in relation to other peoples (who also portrayed their gods as acting in history), for understating the significance of word in relation to event in biblical faith, and for working with a Pickwickian understanding of 'acts of God' and/or an idiosyncratic definition of 'history' and/or a different conception of history from the Bible's own. This has led to widespread belief that it is 'time to say goodbye to *Heilsgeschichte*' (J. L. McKenzie, *A Theology of the Old Testament*, 1974, p. 325, following F. Hesse, *Abschied von der Heilsgeschichte*, 1971). This may be an overreaction, given that the model does hold together three important features of biblical faith which need to be prevented from flying apart.

See also **Biblical Theology; Theology (New Testament); Theology (Old Testament); Word of God.**

J. Goldingay, *Approaches to Old Testament Interpretation*, 1981; A. H. J. Gunneweg, *Understanding the Old Testament*, 1978; Henning Graf Reventlow, *Problems of Old Testament Theology*, 1985.

JOHN GOLDINGAY

Samaritans

The Samaritans offer a unique example of the survival of a small (fewer than 1,000 people) religious community from biblical times to the present day, when some continue to live at their traditional site near the sacred Mount Gerizim, and others near Tel Aviv in modern Israel. They regard themselves as the true heirs of the traditions of the Hebrew Bible, and at many periods of their history they have been in conflict with the Jews, for whom Jerusalem* and Mount Zion rather than Schechem and Mount Gerizim have been the true holy places. Their own form of the Torah, their own cultic practice, and their own distinctive tradition of biblical interpretation assure them of an important place when different ways of understanding holy writings are being considered.

They regard as scripture only the Pentateuch,* and the scroll of the Pentateuch preserved in their community is their most treasured possession. It is known as the Abisha scroll, and popular tradition maintains that this Abisha was the great-grandson of Aaron and that the scroll dates back to the time when the Israelites first entered the promised land; modern scholarly opinion is agreed that it is in fact mediaeval. Most of its differences from the standard Hebrew (Masoretic*) text, calculated to number more than 6,000, are only matters of spelling, but at Deut. 27.4 the Samaritan reading of Gerizim rather than Ebal has often been preferred. In other respects the Samaritan Pentateuch, which probably reached substantially its present form around the turn of the eras, is important for text-critical* study because of the tendency it shares with some of the Dead Sea Scrolls* to offer a more expanded form than the received Hebrew text.

Within Samaritan cultic* practice most attention has been given to the Passover, at which lambs are slaughtered according to the ritual requirements laid down in Ex. 12; this ceremony is carried out on Mount Gerizim, and thus offers a closer approximation to the actual carrying out of the biblical injunctions concerning sacrifice than any other modern religious ceremony. The various upheavals of Samaritan history should, however, make us chary of any claim to continuity from biblical times to the present day; many of the details of contemporary practice arise from study of the biblical text rather than from a continuous living tradition handed down through the centuries.

When we turn to consider the Samaritans' own tradition of biblical interpretation, some attention must first be given to their history, not only as an aid to understanding but also as an example of the strength of ideological* attacks within the biblical text itself. The Samaritans claim that the division between themselves and their southern neighbours took place at the time of Eli (I Sam. 1); of this there is no trace in the biblical record. The OT view in its final form associates the Samaritan 'schism' with the fall of the northern kingdom (II Kings 17), but this is equally unhistorical, and represents anti-Samaritan polemic at a later date in the Jerusalem community. Not until the last centuries BC can a distinctive group which can plausibly be described as Samaritan be identified (Ecclus. 50.26 is the first clear reference).

Indeed, the word 'schism' may be a somewhat misleading one to describe the rift that developed, in so far as such a word implies a sudden dramatic division; rather, the state of hostility between the two communities was a matter of gradual development. At John 4.9 the traditional rendering 'Jews have no dealings with Samaritans' (RSV) may be better understood with NEB as 'Jews and Samaritans do not use vessels in common'; other NT references to the Samaritans could be taken as implying either their inclusion within Israel or their distance from it. Thus in Luke 17.11–19 the presence of a Samaritan among the group of ten lepers might suggest inclusion, but in the dénouement of the story Jesus describes him as a foreigner. The various references to the Samaritans in Acts have similarly received different interpretations. A mediaeval Samaritan tradition claimed that Stephen was a Samaritan, and a few modern scholars have accepted this; note the favourable references to Shechem and the denigration of Jerusalem in his speech (Acts 7.16,47–50). More recent controversy has been caused by the suggestion made by M. D. Goulder in *The Myth of God Incarnate* (1977) that the idea of incarnation found its way into Christian thought from Samaritan sources, with Simon Magus, referred to in Acts 8, playing a significant part.

Samaritan biblical exegesis* has been the subject of increasing scholarly interest in recent decades. Two forms may briefly be noted here. First, there are numerous Samaritan 'chronicles', which elaborate upon and interpret the community's traditions. Since there is no agreement on the dates of these chronicles which have continued to be elaborated over centuries, it is difficult to be sure whether they retain genuine ancient traditions. Secondly, a distinctive exegetical tradition developed, showing considerable similarities to rabbinic* scholarship; its most distinguished product was the fourth-century work *Memar Marqah*, with elaborate commentary* on parts of the Pentateuch (though the unity and date of this work have recently been challenged). At least down to the Muslim period many of the characteristic features of Jewish biblical interpretation have their Samaritan counterparts; their subsequent history has been chequered, but there was at least one period of resurgence: the fourteenth century, which saw the production of their great Torah scroll, of much liturgical material, and of the historical writings of Abul Fath, to whom we owe much of our knowledge of earlier Samaritan tradition.

R. J. Coggins, *Samaritans and Jews*, 1975; A. D. Crown (ed.), *The Samaritans*, 1989; S. Lowy, *The Principles of Samaritan Biblical Exegesis*, 1977; J. Montgomery, *The Samaritans*, 1907 (reprinted 1968); R. Pummer, *The Samaritans*, 1987.

R. J. COGGINS

Samuel

The prophet Samuel features in only the first

third of the two books that bear his name and for this reason alone cannot be regarded as their author. Significantly, in the Greek Septuagint* version the books form a quartet with I and II Kings,* being designated as the first and second of the 'Books of Kingdoms'. Later tradition, mindful of Samuel's reputation as 'an accurate prophet' (Ecclus. 46.15; cf. I Sam. 3.19–4.1; 9.6), could on occasion attribute the two books to the prophet himself (TB Baba Bathra 14b–15a). Josephus,* with the improbable assistance of I Sam. 10.25, even contrived to make Samuel into a Nostradamus figure who 'wrote down for them what would come to pass, read it in the hearing of the king, and laid up the book in the tabernacle of God, to be a witness to future generations of what he had foretold' (*Ant.* 6.66). Modern scholarship, on the other hand, has tended to reduce Samuel's significance to that of a minor judge, exercising influence in a restricted tribal area. A more favourable estimation of the Samuel tradition is represented by, for example, W. F. Albright in *Samuel and the Beginnings of the Prophetic Movement*, 1961.

The complete absence of Samuel from I Sam. 4–6 has been one factor in the recognition of this section (occasionally with II Sam. 6) as an originally independent account of the 'ark of God', composed as early as the tenth century and, according to L. Rost, intended for the edification of festal pilgrims coming to David's* new political and religious capital in Jerusalem.* The loss of the ark in the Babylonian destruction of Jerusalem in 587 BC encouraged a somewhat different reading of its significance; how much the liability of its loss could be turned into a theological asset is evident from Jer. 3.16f.

As much as anything, Samuel functions as 'king-maker' in I Samuel (chs 8–12; 16), though he is portrayed as a stern opponent of the innovation of monarchy (*see* **Kingship**). That he is the mouthpiece of the Deuteronomistic* editor responsible for the composition of I Sam. 8–12, as also of the larger framework within which I and II Samuel are set, seems very likely, the misgivings of a number of scholars notwithstanding. The possibility of tension between such an interpretation of the section and the apparent acceptance of monarchy as a natural development in Deut. 17.14–20 has been noted by a number of scholars who prefer not to see the Samuel passages as opposed to monarchy in principle. The mediaeval Jewish scholar Maimonides (*see* **Jewish Exegesis**), in grappling with this same issue, claims that the people's fault lay only in the spirit in which they brought their request to Samuel (*Code*, 14). The pros and cons of the démarche were argued again in the sixteenth century when the Protestant reformers* attempted to define the proper relationship between the church and the temporal powers. Philip Melanchthon expressed a widely-held view that the magistracy as the guarantor of social order, represented in the biblical period by the institution of the monarchy, made for better conditions than the hand-to-mouth alternative of the 'charismatic' leadership of the period of the judges. At this time, even Samuel's negative depiction of kingly ways in I Sam. 8.11–18 was not necessarily read as condemnatory of such rule. A little later King James I of England could reportedly declare that the section outlined 'what Subjects ought with patience to bear at their Sovereign's hand'.

The fact that Saul, Israel's first king,* was not conspicuously successful in establishing his kingdom colours most of the account of his reign in I Sam. 9–31, where indeed, from ch. 16, his involvement in the narrative is subservient to the theme of David's progress to the throne. The Chronicler has very little to say of his reign, telescoping the passing of the house of Saul into the single, tragic day at Gilboa and attributing his failure to disobedience, notably in his resorting to the medium of Endor for guidance (I Chron. 10.1–14). In the rabbinic* literature, as in much recent writing on Saul, he is viewed more sympathetically and, for example, his sparing of the Amalekites (I Sam. 15) is attributed to noble motives (TB *Yoma* 22b; *Berakoth* 12b). Modern explanations of the 'tragic' aspects of the Saul narrative tend to see him as a man perhaps 'more sinned against than sinning', someone who had the misfortune to encounter 'the dark side of God' (cf. D. M. Gunn).

The uniqueness of David and, by implication, of Davidic rule finds its clearest ideological* expression in II Sam. 7, which records a dynastic oracle associated with the prophet* Nathan. This oracle sets forth the terms of the 'everlasting covenant'* (cf. II Sam. 23.5) by which God was believed to have guaranteed the security of the Davidic line in perpetuity. The failure of all but a couple of David's successors to live up to expectation did not mean the end of the dynastic hope. Instead, the hiatus between performance and expectation contributed to the emergence of a 'Davidic' messianic* hope which was not tied to the reigning monarchs in Jerusalem. The messianism of Judaism in the late Second Temple period (e.g. Pss. of Solomon 17) and christological* formulations in the NT (e.g. Heb. 1.5) are both extensions of the OT idea.

That part of II Samuel which describes the reign of David (II Sam. 9–20; plus I Kings 1–2) became widely known as 'The Succession Narrative' after the publication of Rost's 1926

study. Its preoccupation with domestic aspects of the reign, and not least the failings and feuds of the royal family, rendered much of it unsuitable to the Chronicler's purpose of idealizing David as, with Solomon, a twin pillar of the kingdom of Israel. Such material was simply omitted. In the NT, which is as firmly attached to its version of Davidic kingship, one important episode in David's career is even, in a manner of speaking, rewritten when, in Matthew's account of Palm Sunday, the 'Son of David' makes his entry into Jerusalem riding upon a donkey and, as if in repudiation of the violent ways of the original David, receives the blind and the lame in the temple and heals them (Matt. 21.14; cf. II Sam. 5.6–8).

There is much evidence of narrative skill on the part of the author(s) of Samuel, and the books have deservedly featured in a large number of studies of OT narrative* style (e.g. the writings of J. P. Fokkelman, M. Garsiel, D. M. Gunn, P. D. Miscall, W. L. Humphreys), as also in studies written from a structuralist* point of view (e.g. D. Jobling, C. Conroy).

See also **David.**

———

D. M. Gunn, *The Story of King David, JSOT-SS* 6, 1978; id., *The Fate of King Saul, JSOT-SS* 14, 1980; B. Halpern, *The Constitution of the Monarchy in Israel*, 1981; A. M. Hershman (tr.), *The Code of Maimonides, Bk 14. The Book of Judges*, reissued 1963, esp. pp. 205–43; P. D. Miscall, *I Samuel. A Literary Reading*, 1986; L. Rost, *The Succession to the Throne of David*, ET 1982.

R. P. GORDON

Scandinavian Old Testament Scholarship

When the critical movement in biblical study first made an impact on Scandinavian OT scholarship, the dominant influence, as in several other countries, came from Germany, and those who sought to communicate the new theories did not develop a distinctive line of their own. This state of affairs continued until the 1920s, when there were on the one hand independent developments in Scandinavia and on the other hand an interplay of influences between Germany, Denmark, and Norway, which later stimulated new developments in Swedish OT scholarship. The work of the Danish anthropologist V. Grønbech influenced both the Danish Semitist J. Pedersen and the Norwegian OT scholar S. Mowinckel, whose studies on the psalms also received a powerful stimulus from the pioneering work of the German H. Gunkel.

Pedersen's magisterial work, *Israel: Its Life and Culture, I–II; III–IV*, contains first an account of the ancient Israelite conception of man, both as an individual and as a member of a community,* and second an exposition of the nature of 'holiness', of sacred persons, places, and objects, and of the ritual acts and sacred seasons by which the holiness of the community might be renewed. Though his presentation of these themes has been subjected to criticism in some quarters, his work has had a profound and continuing influence on much subsequent work on the OT. In Scandinavia, Mowinckel freely admitted his debt to him, and at a later date the members of the so-called 'Uppsala School' claimed Pedersen as one of the sources of their inspiration.

Mowinckel's work spans a wide range of OT subjects; but it is his contributions to the study of the psalms that contain his most distinctive achievements and that have most powerfully influenced subsequent Scandinavian research. The starting point of his approach to the psalms was Gunkel's system of literary classification of the psalms into types; but he went far beyond Gunkel in applying a cult*-functional and cult-historical interpretation. He held that the psalms were composed for and used in the Israelite cult and were for the most part not (with the exception of the royal psalms), as Gunkel maintained, later non-cultic compositions based on cultic models. The most influential of the hypotheses which Mowinckel presented in a series of monographs (*Psalmenstudien I–VI*) in the 1920s was that of the annual celebration in pre-exilic Israel of a New Year festival, the climax of which was the ritual enthronement of Yahweh, who triumphed over the power of chaos and ensured the security, stability, and fertility of the natural order and of the life of the community for the coming year. Mowinckel's reconstruction of this festival was based on the analogy of the Babylonian *akitu* festival: his interpretation of it was influenced by the idea, previously put forward by Grønbech, of the cult as creative drama, bringing into effect that which it presented in word and action. In the ritual of the autumnal festival a vital role was performed by the king.* This was an item which Mowinckel and others, notably the Uppsala School, were later to elaborate.

Mowinckel further argued in the second part of the monograph that at a later date the several elements in the festival provided the pattern for the eschatological* hopes in post-exilic Israel, which looked forward to the final vanquishing of the powers of chaos, the overthrow of Israel's enemies, and the renewal of land, people, and monarchy. What had been experienced in the cult was now projected into the future. The Day of Yahweh on which his enthronement was enacted became the final

Day, a day of both judgment and deliverance. The correspondence between present cultic experience in the autumnal New Year festival, as delineated in the first part of *Psalmenstudien II,* and the various elements in the post-exilic future and eschatological hope is striking; but it must be emphasized that on Mowinckel's view the eschatological hope owed its content to the autumnal New Year festival with its enthronement ritual, but owed its origin not to the cult but to a particular historical situation, 'the breaking down of the national existence of the Covenant* people. It grew out of the depths of the Yahwistic religion.' This part of Mowinckel's argument was expanded and extended in a detailed examination of the development of the messianic* hope and of eschatology, *Han som kommer* (1951), ET *He That Cometh* (1956), in which he reconsidered the pre-exilic ideal of kingship,* the emergence and development of the future hope and the place in it of a royal figure, the concept of the Servant* of the Lord (discarding the autobiographical view which he had advanced in 1921) and its relationship to the prophetic* rather than the kingly ideal, the character of the eschatology of later Judaism, the national messiah, and the Son of Man.* He both expanded and made more precise views which he had previously stated, and also criticized some of the arguments of members of the 'Uppsala School'.

In *Psalmenstudien III* Mowinckel carried his cultic interpretation of the psalms further. Gunkel had drawn attention to the presence, particularly in the royal psalms, of passages which in form and content resemble prophetic oracles.* In the main he attributed this resemblance to reciprocal literary influence between the canonical* prophets and the psalms. Mowinckel argued that these oracular passages were the utterances of cultic prophets who were members of the sanctuary staff and who delivered their oracles in the ritual of the autumnal New Year festival, in occasional acts of communal worship, in rituals involving the king, and in those involving private individuals, as reflected particularly in the laments of the individual. The hypothesis of such participation in the cult by prophets led not unnaturally to the conclusion that some parts of the canonical prophetic literature are liturgical in character and perhaps in origin.

The first of Mowinckel's *Psalmenstudien* was devoted to a much debated problem in the interpretation of the laments of the individual. Who were the 'enemies' and 'evildoers' (doers of '*awen*') to whom reference is made in some of these psalms? Mowinckel argued that the Hebrew word '*awen* meant supernatural or magical* power and that the enemies referred to as 'workers of '*awen*' used powerful spells to bring illness on the pious sufferers. The laments were used as a means of counteracting the spells. Mowinckel's view was criticized by various scholars and on various grounds. These need not be enumerated here, since Mowinckel later modified his position, having been persuaded by some of the arguments of his own disciple H. Birkeland who, in a dissertation on the enemies of the individual in the psalms, argued that all or nearly all individual psalms are royal psalms and that the enemies (workers of *'awen*) are foreign nations and their leaders who, by military attacks and also by potent words, sought to weaken the king (or in the later period some other leader) and the nation.

In 1951 Mowinckel published a comprehensive work on the Psalms entitled *Offersang og Sangoffer* (*Song of Sacrifice and Sacrifice of Song*) which appeared in English in 1962 as *The Psalms in Israel's Worship*, the text having been revised and one chapter omitted. This book sums up the entire range of Mowinckel's contributions to the study of the psalms over a period of four decades.

Mowinckel's contributions to OT research covered a remarkably wide range: Ezra–Nehemiah, the problem of the Pentateuch,* the Prophets,* the Decalogue, and, at the very end of his life, two major historical studies, one on Palestine before Israel, the other (posthumously published) on the origin and earliest history of Israel*; but his work on the psalms is his most substantial and creative achievement.

Both Mowinckel and Pedersen influenced the group of Swedish scholars known as 'the Uppsala School'. The label is in some ways an unsatisfactory one. It came to be applied to a group of scholars at Uppsala: H. S. Nyberg, G. Widengren, I. Engnell, A. Haldar, and some others who, while not in agreement on some points, adopted on the whole a common approach to some OT problems and a common type of solution. We may therefore think of the Uppsala School as a distinctive but not wholly coherent group within a larger Scandinavian School, which included the Danes, A. Bentzen and F. F. Hvidberg and Mowinckel's successor, A. S. Kapelrud. In Uppsala two lines of thought which had been started elsewhere in Scandinavia were developed, extended, and in some instances carried to extremes. One was concerned with the formation and transmission of OT literature, especially the Pentateuch and the Prophets. The other was concerned with the character of the religion of Israel, and in particular the nature of the cult and the part played in it by the king. On this latter point Nyberg did not share the views of his younger colleagues.

In the early 1930s Pedersen had indicated

that he rejected the generally accepted documentary hypothesis of the composition of the Pentateuch, dismissed the precise delimitation and relative dating of the sources (all of which he asserted contained both pre-exilic and post-exilic elements) and claimed that Ex. 1–15, which he held to be a cult legend* of the Passover, was the central element in the Pentateuch. In 1945 the Uppsala scholar I. Engnell produced the first volume of what he called a traditio-historical* introduction to the OT (*Gamla Testamentet: En traditionshistorisk inledning*, I), in which he launched a vigorous attack on the criteria* commonly used by literary critics* in the identification and dating of documentary sources. In his treatment of the Pentateuch he held, like M. Noth (of whose use of literary critical methods he nevertheless disapproved), that Genesis–Numbers, which he called 'the P-work', should be regarded as separate from the Deuteronomic History* (Deuteronomy–II Kings). The narrative portions in the P-work may be presumed to be derived in the main from oral tradition* and not from continuous documents such as the literary critics hold J and E to have been. The supremely important section in these narratives is Ex. 1–15, a paschal legend which has been 'deculticized' and historicized. The legal portions of the P-work were given written form at an early stage. P is 'simply the last transmitter and editor of the "P-work" or "Tetrateuch"' and has 'set his theological stamp on the whole work'. The Deuteronomic History is a compilation made shortly after the exile, consisting of legal material from different periods, edited to maintain cultic centralization, followed by traditional narrative material. In the work of the Chronicler, Engnell admitted that a considerable amount had been derived from documentary sources referred to in the context of the work. His emphasis on the formative influence of oral tradition did not lead him to deny the incorporation of written documents in the OT books; but he poured scorn on the methods used by the literary critics. He held that various types of material had been preserved and transmitted orally by circles or schools of traditionists: the wisdom literature* by the scribes* and the 'wise', the psalms by priests and Temple-singers, the laws by priests, and the prophetic oracles and narratives by the communities of the prophets' disciples.

This strong emphasis on the importance and trustworthiness of oral tradition is one of the distinctive characteristics of the Uppsala School. A decade earlier, an older Uppsala scholar, H. S. Nyberg, had maintained in the preface to a textual study of Hosea that the Hebrew text of the OT is dependent on a trustworthy oral tradition, and that the OT in its written form is for the most part a creation of the post-exilic Jewish community. In the pre-exilic age, saga,* legend, law, and prophecy had been transmitted mainly orally. Though the process of oral transmission was reliable, yet in it the material was adapted and expanded. Nyberg's view was carried further by H. Birkeland in a study of the composition of the prophetical books. He adduced parallels from Islamic traditions and early Arabic poetry, and maintained that in Israel the prophetic material was not only transmitted, adapted and expanded but also arranged in complexes by the circles of prophetic disciples who preserved their masters' teaching.

The latter point had already been made by Mowinckel in a short work on Isaiah's disciples (1926). In it he argued that they had preserved the teaching of Isaiah and in successive generations were responsible for the transmission of much post-Isaianic, pre-exilic material (Micah, Zephaniah, Nahum, Habakkuk, and the Song of Moses). In subsequent publications Mowinckel developed his hypothesis, emphasizing further the role of the circles of disciples in selecting and arranging the oracles and adding new prophetic sayings which, though they originated in the prophetic community, were regarded as sayings of the master himself. The committing of the prophetic material to writing took place at a late stage, except in a few instances when it seemed important to record in writing that a particular oracle or group of oracles had been uttered by the prophet in a particular situation (Isa. 8.1f.; 30.8; Jer. 36).

In spite of Engnell's emphasis on the importance of oral tradition, he held that not all literary types were transmitted by the same process. In the prophetic literature he distinguished between two types: 1. the liturgy type (e.g. Joel, Nahum, Habakkuk, and Deutero-Isaiah), which were the work of individual prophets and were probably in written form from the outset; and 2. a type consisting of prophetic oracles and traditions about the prophet, collected and transmitted by circles of disciples (e.g. Amos, Hosea, Isa. 1–39, Jeremiah). To the latter type, Engnell applied the Arabic term *diwan*. It is to be noted, however, that the claims made by Engnell and others for the place of oral tradition in the formation of the prophetic literature, and the alleged supporting evidence from Arabic literature, were contested by G. Widengren in his monograph, *Literary and Psychological Aspects of the Hebrew Prophets* (1948). On this subject Uppsala did not speak with one voice.

The views of the Uppsala School on the religion of ancient Israel were influenced by several factors. The rejection of the Graf-Wellhausen theory of the composition of the Pentateuch, and in particular the alleged dating of the documents, led to the abandonment of the view of the development of Israelite religion which these documents had been alleged to demonstrate: a development from a pre-prophetic stage to prophetic religion and then to a legal stage, or again from polydemonism and polytheism through henotheism to monotheism. The rejection of an evolutionist view of religious development was strengthened by the theory (based on the work of N. Söderblom, H. S. Nyberg, G. Widengren, and others) that belief in a 'high god' was a very early form of monotheism and that polytheism arose when features and functions of the high god were separated from him and hypostatized. He then became an 'otiose deity' (*deus otiosus*) until he was 'activated' in the experience of a religious leader of prophetic type. Yahweh was a form of the old west-Semitic high god El, who had become otiose but was activated in the experience of Moses.* After the entry of Israel into Canaan, Yahweh became fused with the Canaanite El, and in particular with the Jerusalemite El Elyon, and the Israelite religion was so transformed that it became a variant form of Canaanite religion. There are questionable features in this line of argument. The equation of belief in a high god with monotheism is of doubtful validity; and Israelite religion was not assimilated to Canaanite religion to the extent suggested, though it was undoubtedly influenced by it.

The religious life of Israel in Canaan was understood by the Uppsala School in ways which reflect the influence of Pedersen and Mowinckel. The influence of the English Myth and Ritual school, with their view of a myth and ritual* pattern common to the whole of the Ancient Near East,* was also important. A new factor was the discovery and deciphering of the important religious texts from Ras Shamra (ancient Ugarit*) in north Syria. When Mowinckel advanced his hypothesis on the nature of the Israelite New Year festival, some of his critics objected that the *akitu* festival which he had used as an analogy belonged to a milieu too far removed from Palestine to provide a convincing parallel. This argument, however, could not be used against the alleged parallels in the Ugaritic texts – a point which has been strongly made by Mowinckel's successor, A. S. Kapelrud.

Much discussion centred on the status and functions of the king, the character of divine or sacral kingship. Engnell discussed this in considerable detail in his *Studies in Divine Kingship in the Ancient Near East* (1943, [2] 1967), in which, however, he did not deal fully with the OT evidence. His view, as expressed elsewhere, was that the king was regarded as the son of the deity and also as the embodiment of the community and the guarantor of its well-being. In the annual festival, he atoned for the sins of the people; but he also triumphed over the powers of chaos in the ritual drama. He was identical with both the creator high god and the dying and rising vegetation god. The view that Israelite religion was assimilated to Canaanite belief and practice to such a degree met with criticism. It was not acceptable to Mowinckel, who had emphasized the importance for Israel of the historical traditions and of the renewal of the covenant in the festival. Some years previously Pedersen had maintained that the idea of a dying and rising vegetation god was irreconcilable with the nature of Yahweh. A. Bentzen of Copenhagen also laid emphasis on the importance for the Israelite cult of the historical traditions, and argued that prior to the idea of the divine king is the concept of the primal man from which are derived the functions of the king, the priest, and the prophet.

In spite of the sometimes considerable differences of view between the scholars hitherto mentioned, they were the formative influences in a distinctively Scandinavian group, who may be said to have formed a school. One member of the group who maintained a moderate stance throughout is H. Ringgren, Engnell's successor. His first major work, *Word and Wisdom: Studies in the Hypostatization of Divine Qualities and Functions in the Ancient Near East* (1947), demonstrates the development from monotheism to polytheism. Of his many other works, his *Israelite Religion* (1966) is a valuable survey, particularly of the pre-exilic period.

Much important biblical work was produced in the Scandinavian countries during the above period which would not be classed as Scandinavian in the narrower sense presupposed by this article. The omission of reference to them does not imply any adverse reflection on their importance. One exception may be made, J. Lindblom's magisterial work on prophecy in Israel (1934), which appeared in English in a completely revised form as *Prophecy in Ancient Israel* (1962), does not bear the stamp of any school. Its discussion of the prophets and mysticism is of particular value and interest and reflects Lindblom's indebtedness to two great Swedish historians of religion, N. Söderblom and T. Andrae. It was to his interest in the Swedish St Bridget that he owed the stimulus to investigate the revelatory experiences of the prophets.

See also **Kingship; Oral Tradition (New Testament); Psalms.**

———

A. Bentzen, *King and Messiah*, ² 1970; I. Engnell, *Critical Essays on the Old Testament*, 1970.

G. W. ANDERSON

Schweitzer, A.

Albert Schweitzer (1875–1965) was a Protestant scholar born in Alsace-Lorraine and is sometimes described as French, though he was in fact German. A many-sided genius, he obtained doctorates in philosophy, theology and music before he was thirty, and later added a doctorate in medicine. As an organist he was an outstanding exponent of Bach, whose organ works he helped to edit and on whom he wrote an important monograph. In 1913 he effectively put an end to an already distinguished academic career when he went out to Lambaréné in French Equatorial Africa to found a hospital and carry on missionary work. After being interned by the French in the First World War, he returned to Lambaréné in 1924, rebuilt his hospital on a larger scale, and continued working there for the rest of his life. In 1953 he received the Nobel Peace Prize for the previous year.

In his biblical work, which, though idiosyncratic, has been very influential, he concerned himself almost enirely with the Gospels* and the Pauline* epistles.* His thinking was informed throughout by 'thorough-going eschatology'* (*Konsequenteschatologie*), i.e. the thesis that primitive Christianity was conditioned throughout, in one way or another, by the conviction that the parousia* and the end of the world were coming in the more or less immediate future.

He first became widely known in 1906 as a result of the appearance of his book *Von Reimarus* zu Wrede* (ET *The Quest of the Historical Jesus,* 1910, which has unfortunately never been revised to take account of the large amounts of new material added in later editions of the original, published under the title *Geschichte der Leben-Jesu-Forschung*, from 1912 onwards) in which he reviewed over two hundred lives of Jesus (mostly German) produced in the previous century and a half. He concluded that the evidence is in fact insufficient to permit the reconstruction of the figure of Jesus on the scale attempted, especially as nineteenth-century scholars had sought to trace the inner development of Jesus' life and thought. Schweitzer attributed the great variety in the pictures put forward to the fact that they had been arrived at quite largely by (unconsciously) reading back the authors' own presuppositions into the life and teaching of Jesus, a procedure which had the incidental effect of making him seem more modern and more immediately attractive to the nineteenth century than the genuinely historical Jesus could possibly have been.

The logic of this might have seemed to be that no account of Jesus is possible, but at the end of the book Schweitzer outlined an account similar to one he had already put forward in earlier books (most notably in *Das Messianitäts und Leidensgeheimnis*, 1901; ET *The Mystery of the Kingdom of God*, 1914). According to this, Jesus became convinced that the inbreaking of the reign of God, understood more or less as in some strains of contemporary Judaism, would take place in his own lifetime and that he would then be revealed as the Son of Man,* the ruler of it. He kept secret his status as messiah-*elect, but when the kingdom* failed to come, concluding that he was called upon to spare his followers the great tribulation expected to precede the end by taking it upon himself, he decided to put the matter to the test and go up to Jerusalem to confront the authorities. 'Jesus . . . lays hold of the wheel of the world to set it moving on that last revolution which is to bring all ordinary history to a close. It refuses to turn, and He throws Himself upon it. Then it does turn; and crushes Him' (*Quest*, p. 369; typical of Schweitzer's lively style).

Jesus' teaching, since it was put forward from that perspective, must be regarded as an *Interimsethik*, i.e. 'a morality for the time being', the short time, that is, before the arrival of the kingdom. This accounts for much of its character, e.g. its attitude towards evil and aggression (cf. Matt. 5.39), and its disregard of social and political questions (e.g. Mark 12.17; Luke 12.14).

The feeding of the multitude is understood from the same perspective as a non-miraculous cult-meal at which Jesus, without revealing the secret* of his status as messiah-elect, distributed sacred food to those he expected to be joining him soon at the messianic banquet, as an earnest of their participation in it. The Last Supper had a similar significance, though by then Jesus had disclosed his secret to the disciples.

Schweitzer claimed two merits, among others, for this interpretation. It allowed Jesus to remain a man of his own day and culture, and, as such, 'a stranger and an enigma to our time . . . who will not allow himself to be modernized as an historical figure. He refuses to be detached from his own time.'

Secondly, he held that this interpretation makes possible the acceptance of the synoptic* accounts in something much more like their present form, without the need to postulate large numbers of redactions,* later accretions and the like, as contemporary scholars tended to do. The Sermon on the Mount* and the commission of the Twelve, for example, could be accepted, for the most part, as having been delivered in approximately their present form. In this last Schweitzer has not on the whole been followed, and he has

often been criticized for placing too much weight on certain isolated texts, e.g. a dubious verse such as Matt. 10.23.

Schweitzer always insisted that a reconstruction of historical events should be accepted only if it makes good sense of the events that came after. He therefore set himself to show that Pauline theology was a natural upshot of the Gospel events as he reconstructed them. He began in 1911 with a survey of modern Pauline interpretation, parallel to the *Quest*, *Die Geschichte der paulinischen Forschung* (ET *Paul and his Interpreters*, 1912). The First World War and its aftermath then intervened, and it was not till 1930 that he published *Die Mystik des Apostels Paulus* (ET 1931, under the perhaps misleading title *The Mysticism of Paul the Apostle*; it is not altogether clear what *Mystik* means in this context). In it he argued that the epistles had been anachronistically and misleadingly interpreted, under Lutheran* influence, and that in fact eschatology* was the key to Paul's, no less than to Jesus', thought. He saw Paul as 'a powerful elemental thinker, despite the rabbinic* method of arguing which remains here and there', who was determined to make coherent sense of Christ, and life in him, in a way that church leaders before him had not been able to do. They had recognized in the death of Jesus a sacrifice for the expiation of sin, but Paul went much further; he saw in the death and resurrection* of Jesus (whom he regarded not as God but as a heavenly being), a great cosmic event through which not only was Jesus himself raised from the dead to a new condition of existence, but the dominion of the angelic beings, and therewith the natural world, were brought to an end. By virtue of a union with the risen Christ, which is both mystical and natural, those who are fore-ordained to be 'the companions of the Messiah' can begin to enter here and now into his post-resurrection mode of being; the forces which, working in him, effected his death and resurrection, begin to work the same effect in them, from the time of their incorporation in him – according to Schweitzer, the phrase 'in Christ' is the key to Paul's thought. Those who are in Christ wear the appearance of natural men only as a sort of veil, and that veil will soon be thrown off. Paul expected the end-time to come very soon, as Jesus had done, but he worked with a different strand of Jewish eschatological thought and his expectation was different; note the absence of Son of Man terminology from his epistles. According to the strand of thought with which he worked, the General Resurrection, and with it the last judgment and the onset of eternity, would be preceded by a supernatural but transitory kingdom of the messiah. In this kingdom, Paul believed, those who were now 'in Christ' would fully share with him the mode of existence on which he entered at his resurrection; meanwhile all other human beings would await the General Resurrection in the grave.

The means of unification with Christ were the sacraments of baptism and eucharist, which Paul interpreted in a fully realistic sense, though neither in his understanding of them nor in anything else was he influenced by Hellenistic* religion. (Schweitzer believed the History of Religions school* had been responsible for much misunderstanding.) Christians were not bound by the OT Law, which was for 'natural' man, but the spirit of Jesus, in which they had become participators, compelled them to behave as those who had ceased to belong to this world, and whose lives were the expression of love.

From this perspective, justification by faith alone, which had since Luther been regarded as the linchpin of Paul's thought, is seen as relatively peripheral – 'only a subsidiary crater which has formed within the rim of the main crater', i.e. the mystical doctrine of redemption through being 'in Christ'. Paul put forward the doctrine of justification in the course of his struggle against Jewish Christianity,* with its insistence on the abiding validity of the OT Law. He insisted, per contra, that Christians are free from the Law, which cannot be the basis of salvation for them, but he had no intention of depreciating the vital importance of good works as such.

In the penultimate chapter of the book Schweitzer glances at the development of post-Pauline Christianity as exemplified by Ignatius (see Apostolic Fathers), Justin and the author of the Fourth Gospel, which he dates to the early second century. In the thinking of these writers eschatological expectation, while still present, has lost its dominating force, and the Hellenization of Christianity which Paul had made possible, without in any way promoting it, sets in in earnest. The essential thing about Jesus is now seen as the becoming-one in him of spirit and flesh; and this same becoming-one of spirit and matter in the eucharist is the means by which redemption is conveyed and appropriated. Since such an interpretation could not be found in the synoptic tradition, the assumption had to be that that tradition was incomplete, and the author of the Fourth Gospel undertook to complete it, allegedly from the evidence of a specially loved disciple who remembered and understood mysterious hints of Jesus which the other disciples had not understood and therefore failed to pass on. Schweitzer's few pages on the Fourth Gospel certainly deserve notice, and it is to be regretted that he never had opportunity to expand them.

Schweitzer's colourful career and personality, and his philosophy of reverence for life, caught the public imagination throughout Europe and the Western world, and his works were translated into the major European languages. This gave extended currency and added authority to what he wrote. That eschatology was central to NT thought was not something he had recognized for himself; he derived it from a short but seminal book by Johannes Weiss published in 1892, Jesus' Proclamation of the Kingdom of God (ET 1971). What Schweitzer did was to work the idea out much more fully, to express it in his own vivid and memorable way (even if his appreciation of the matter was less delicate), and to lend it the weight of his reputation.

The result has been an undoubted revolution in NT interpretation. Even those who believe that Schweitzer overstated his case and that there is no single key to the understanding of the NT, have had to acknowledge that expectation of an early end was a constitutive element in all primitive Christian thinking.

In his account of it Schweitzer showed flair and a keen eye for significant trends, but perhaps less readiness to attend patiently to exegetical* detail, for which indeed his career left him little opportunity. As a result the general thrust of his contentions has been more influential than his interpretations of individual passages. Also, although he was fully aware of the cultural-relativist* problem to which his conclusions gave rise (e.g. 'Jesus' religion of love appeared as part of a world-view which expected a speedy end of the world. Clothed in the ideas in which he announced it, we cannot make it our own; we must reclothe it in those of our modern world-view'), he has had more influence through stimulating others (e.g. Bultmann*) to grapple with it than he has through any solution of his own. His own proposals, expressed rather rhetorically, and never very systematically worked out, are not altogether clear. Those interested should consult his philosophical and general theological writings. For him the essence of the matter was that the real subject of Jesus' teaching was love. His real followers are not those who hold any particular view of his person, but those who surrender their wills to him and allow themselves to be taken possession of by the love he taught, and to express it in the circumstances of their culture, however different from his. It is in doing this, as he put it in the famous last paragraph of the Quest, that 'as an ineffable mystery, they shall learn in their own experience who he is'.

See also Apocalyptic; Historical Jesus; Kingdom of God.

D. E. Nineham, 'Schweitzer Revisited' in Ex-

plorations in Theology 1, 1977, pp. 112–33; Albert Schweitzer, *My Life and Thought*, 1933.

D. E. NINEHAM

Scribes

The profession of a scribe does not at first sight seem to be a controversial one, yet it is remarkable how many of the biblical references to scribes are hostile. In the Gospels* they are regularly grouped with the Pharisees* and pictured in unflattering terms as enemies of Jesus. Much earlier than that Jeremiah regards the scribes as perverters of the tradition, whose 'false pen' has made the Torah into a lie (Jer. 8.8). In fact our knowledge of the precise role of scribes, and of the part they had in transmitting the sacred traditions of the people, is very limited.

Scribes are mentioned as part of the staff of the royal court from the time of David* on (II Sam. 8.17; RSV 'secretary'); no doubt in a period of limited literacy this was an appointment demanding special skills, and the books of Samuel and Kings contain intermittent references to such scribes. But from approximately the time of the exile the term is applied to people whose role, so far as we can reconstruct it, was more concerned with the handing down of sacred traditions than with official business. Thus Baruch is said to have had an important part in the development of the Jeremiah tradition and he is described as a scribe (Jer. 36.32); his older contemporary Shaphan was prominent in the discovery of the 'book of the Law' which according to II Kings 22–23 led to a major religious reform under Josiah.

In each of these cases it is difficult to know whether these were professional scribes whose role is placed in a religious context because of the particular historical circumstances of their time, or whether scribes were coming to be seen as specifically religious figures whose importance was in ensuring that sacred traditions were handed down accurately. The same ambiguity applies to the figure of Ezra, who is called a 'scribe' (Ezra 7.6): some interpreters have taken this to be a reference to his role in the Persian royal service, as seems to be implied in the official status he bore; others have seen him as one of those responsible for transmitting the sacred Torah, as is suggested by his role in Neh. 8.

Two particular theories have been important in recent treatments of possible scribal activity in the OT period. There has been much discussion as to the possible authors of Deuteronomy, and Weinfeld has proposed that the scribes are the group most likely to have been involved. He has stressed the links between Deuteronomy and the wisdom writings (and it may be significant that in Jer. 8.8 the possession of wisdom* is said to have been

one of the claims of the scribes), and has noted also the way in which Deuteronomy represents a gathering together of earlier traditions – again a role which fits well with that of the scribes. His theory remains an attractive possibility, but not one which can readily be proved.

The other recent theory regarding the role of scribes is that of Lang, who regards them as 'charismatic' figures in the sense in which that term is used by anthropologists:* men of authority in the religious community, intellectuals who have access to the kind of knowledge which gives power within a religious group. Lang understands the role of Ezra in this way, and also draws extensively on the evidence provided by Ecclesiasticus, written probably around 200 BC, which has an extensive section (38.24–39.11) in praise of scribes, comparing them and their value for society very favourably with those engaged in manual trades. It is probably legitimate to see here the forerunners of the scribes mentioned in the Gospels – those whose role was the preservation and proper interpretation of the sacred traditions, especially the Torah.

Lang describes the scribes of Ecclesiasticus as the 'honourable idlers' of society, and his whole essay is a very interesting sketch of how the role of prophets* in Israelite society might have passed to scribes. But the evidence is too slight to build any firm conclusions upon it. We know of the importance of scribal activity from the remarkably careful way in which the traditions of ancient Israel have been handed down to us, but of the mechanics of the process our ignorance must remain considerable.

See also **Ancient Near Eastern Interpretation; Pharisees and Scribes; Writing and Transmitting Texts.**

M. Fishbane, *Biblical Interpretation in Ancient Israel*, 1985, esp. pp. 23–88; B. Lang, 'From Prophet to Scribe' in *Monotheism and the Prophetic Minority*, 1983; E. Lipiński, 'Royal and State Scribes in Ancient Jerusalem', *VTS*, 40, 1988, pp. 157–64; M. Weinfeld, *Deuteronomy and the Deuteronomic School*, 1972.

R. J. COGGINS

Semantics

The science of the meaning of words. Although the term itself was not much used in biblical interpretation before the publication of James Barr's *The Semantics of Biblical Language* (1961), the application of scientific methods to the task of understanding the meaning of the Bible was not unknown before then. Dictionary definitions of biblical terms and minute, often quite sophisticated semantic discussions can be found in the work of biblical scholars of the past such as Jerome and

Rashi. Questions like, Why does the author use this word here and not another? and, How has a word's meaning changed from its original meaning to how it is understood now? are semantic questions central to all biblical interpretation. Twentieth-century semantics has heightened biblical scholars' awareness of the problems involved, and provides some new methods and terminology.

First, there is the distinction between synchronic* and diachronic semantics. Synchronic semantics is concerned with describing the meaning of a word as it is used in a particular context. Diachronic (or historical) semantics is concerned with the history of words, changes in meaning,* etymologies,* etc. Biblical interpretation is primarily synchronic. Questions about the etymology of words, their relation to words in other languages, what they 'originally' meant, and the like, however interesting, are usually irrelevant and misleading. What each word or phrase means in its context is the ultimate goal of the interpreter, and the first step in semantic description is therefore to define that context.

The immediate linguistic environment limits the meaning of words which have various different meanings or associations. In Job 19.25–27 (cf. Ps. 17.15; Isa. 53.11) an accumulation of words associated with life and death influences the meaning of other terms in the immediate linguistic context and explains the traditional eschatological* interpretation (KJV). Its meaning in the wider literary context of the Book of Job (cf. 14.7–17) is quite different (NEB). The literary context of a word like *elohim* may help to determine whether it means 'God', as in most biblical contexts, or 'of supernatural proportions', as in the storytelling style of the book of Jonah (3.3, 'an exceedingly great city').

The situational context of a word or passage is also important. Texts regularly recited and continually interpreted and reinterpreted are said to be 'contextualized' in many different situations, from their original context in the Ancient Near East,* where they were first uttered or written down, to modern times. The original context of a passage like Ps. 127 with its title, referring to Solomon, is not the same as the original context of the psalm without its title. In the first case, v. 2 refers to Solomon's dream at Gibeon (I Kings 3.4–15; II Sam. 12.25); in the second, the reference to 'sleep' is obscure (as in NEB, which omits all psalm titles). Similarly, the original context of what Amos actually said is not the same as the original context of the Book of Amos. Both contextualizations are interesting and can be investigated with equal objectivity and scientific rigour, as can later stages in the process, provided the context is clearly defined.

A word can also be studied against the background of its 'associative field'. The theory of semantic fields is one of the most productive insights of modern linguistics.* A semantic field contains words and phrases associated with one another at the level of meaning, and vocabulary can be arranged in fields as well as in alphabetical order (cf. Roget's *Thesaurus*). This provides a useful means of identifying subtle semantic distinctions between synonyms, without translating them into another language where associations and distinctions may be quite different. Semantic studies of colour terms, terms for prayer, words for help, save, etc., and many other 'fields', which leave etymology and translation to the end, can achieve a new degree of subtlety. Commentaries on the biblical text may in future lay greater emphasis on questions like, Why does the author use this word here and not one of the other words associated with it? or, What are the special associations and nuances of this word as opposed to its closest synonyms?

The main goal of semantics is to define terms as delicately as possible and establish precise distinctions or oppositions between associated words. Even an everyday Hebrew word like *dam*, 'blood', means something different, at this level of subtlety, from its Greek or English equivalent. In biblical Hebrew it never has the positive, homely sense of 'kinship' (as in 'blood brothers'), for which the words *basar*, 'flesh' and *'esem*, 'bone' are used (Gen. 2.23–24). The Greek word *kephalē* is not associated with authority to the same extent as English 'head' or Hebrew *roš*, and often suggests 'the most precious, dearest' (?Eph. 5.23). Distinctions may be due partly to historical factors. For example, Hebrew *pardes*, a loan word borrowed from Persian, may in some contexts (e.g. Eccl. 2.5) have distinctly exotic overtones, as opposed to the more ordinary Hebrew word for 'garden', *gan*. *Barzel*, 'iron', another loan-word, similarly carries with it foreign, perhaps aggressive associations in phrases like 'iron yoke' (Isa. 9.4 = Heb. 9.3) and 'iron chariots' (Judg. 4.3; cf. Amos 1.3), which other metals do not have.

The distinction between transparent and opaque words is a helpful one. Words like 'folktale' and 'hedge sparrow' are said to be 'transparent' because they are composed of elements that can be understood independently, as opposed to 'opaque' synonyms such as 'myth'* and 'dunnock' which are not. Gen. 1.26 contains a Hebrew word-pair of this kind: *selem*, 'image', is more opaque than *demut*, 'likeness', a noun formed from a familiar verb meaning 'to resemble'. It seems likely that the word-structure of Hebrew and its consonantal script give many words in Hebrew a special type of transparency which cannot be represented in translation but is exploited by authors.

The notion of semantic range is also useful, especially as between words in one language and their nearest equivalents in another. The semantic range of Hebrew *šalom*, for example, is very different from that of 'peace', its commonest English equivalent. *Šalom* is associated with words for health, abundance, etc. rather than rest, tranquillity, and opposed to words for illness, poverty, etc. rather than war. Distinctions and nuances have to be worked out within Hebrew: translation* is the last and crudest stage in the process of defining meaning. Thus a monolingual dictionary of Hebrew like that of A. E. Shoshan (1971) contains semantic data of a very much higher order of subtlety than Brown, Driver and Briggs or Koehler-Baumgartner (*see* **Lexicons and Concordances**).

See also **Meaning; Semiotics.**

A. Brenner, *Colour Terms in the Old Testament*, 1982; J. Lyons, *Language, Meaning and Context*, 1981; J. F. A. Sawyer, *Semantics in Biblical Research*, 1972; M. Silva, *Biblical Words and their Meanings*, 1983; A. C. Thiselton, 'Semantics and New Testament Interpretation' in I. H. Marshall (ed.), *New Testament Interpretation*, 1977, pp. 75–104; S. Ullmann, *Semantics*, 1962.

JOHN F. A. SAWYER

Semiotics

A word derived ultimately from the Greek *sēmeiotikos*, meaning 'an observer and interpreter of signs'. The object of semiotic analysis is therefore anything that can be regarded as a sign, and a sign is 'a reality perceivable by sense perception that has a relationship with another reality which the first reality is meant to evoke' (Jan Mukarovsky). Examples of signs commonly given in classical antiquity are: smoke as a sign of fire, clouds as a sign of an approaching storm at sea, a flushed complexion as a sign of fever. Each of these observable realities (smoke, clouds, flushed complexion) has a relationship with another reality (fire, storm, fever) which it evokes.

In recent times such studies of signs have become exceedingly technical. Until this century, the discussion of signs was always ancillary to some other philosophical or psychological enterprise. Aristotle, Hippocrates, Parmenides, Cicero, Quintilian, Augustine* (and others) all wrote about signs but always in the context of larger philosophical issues. However, with the work of the American philosopher Charles Sanders Peirce (who referred to his work as 'semeiotics') and the Swiss linguist Ferdinand de Saussure (who referred to his

work as 'semiology'), semiotics has become a discipline in its own right, with the result that there is now an established Congress of the International Association for Semiotic Studies.

C. S. Peirce (1839–1914) is regarded as the American founder of semiotics. He proposed a complex classification of signs based on the difference between *signans* and *signatum*, or *signifier* and *signified*. In Peirce's system, a sign is something which stands for something else (the sign's *object*), which stands for something to someone (its *interpretant*), and which stands for something to somebody in some respect (its *ground*). From here Peirce argued that there are ten trichotomies by which signs can be classified, yielding a possible 59,049 classes of sign. Even though Peirce reduced these to 66 classes, the complexity of Peirce's system and the plethora of neologisms which accompanied it make it extremely difficult to follow and to use.

The semiology of Ferdinand de Saussure was developed in a course of lectures on general linguistics* which he delivered at the University of Geneva between 1906 and 1911. Saussure argued that human beings are animals who devise and invest in language. They construct signs with which to speak, and these signs are made up of concept and sound-image, or *signified* and *signifier*. The phonemes C-A-T, for example, constitute a *signifier* whose *signified* we recognize (by registering its difference from all similar signifiers, such as R-A-T) to be a furry quadruped which goes 'miaow'. There is no necessary connection between this *signifier* and its *signified*. In fact, the relationship is entirely arbitrary and is established through social convention. To put it another way, there is nothing intrinsically feline in the phonemes C-A-T.

Mentioning the name of Saussure may lead us to regard semiotics as synonymous with structuralism,* but in reality semiotics should be seen as a distinct though related discipline. Structuralism is a method of enquiry which aims to discover the basic and universal mental operations ('deep structures') which generate literary texts, games of football, fashion garments and so on. Semiotics is more a field of enquiry encompassing things which can ordinarily be regarded as signs. Some of these have been identified by Umberto Eco in his *Theory of Semiotics* (1976). Amongst others, he lists animal behaviour, olfactory signs, tactile communication, medical symptoms, musical codes, written language, codes of taste. What is distinctive about semiotic studies is the fact that they all analyse the life of signs within society, whether those signs are poems, advertisements or bird calls.

It is clear from this that semiotics is about verbal and non-verbal communication. In the eyes of the semiotician, we transmit messages to one another through language, posture, gesture, hairstyle, perfume, clothing, accent, social context, and so on. When driving in cars we communicate with other drivers not only through what we say and through the gestures we make, but also through traffic signals, indicator lights, horns and so on. In our social behaviour, we are relentless communicators, whether that communication is implicit or explicit. As Roman Jakobson has written: 'Every message is made of signs; correspondingly, the science of signs termed *semiotic* deals with those general principles which underlie the structure of all signs whatever.' More precisely, semiotics 'seeks to identify the conventions and operations by which any signifying practice (such as literature) produces its observable effects of meaning' (Jonathan Culler).

Like structuralism, semiotics has moved into the area of literary criticism,* and it is here that the discipline becomes most relevant to the area of biblical interpretation. Semioticians look at literary texts as signifiers and their chief aim is to discover the operations and conventions by which the reader understands what is signified. Yury Lotman's *Analysis of the Poetic Text* (1972) is a good example of this because it examines poetic texts as signifiers made up of patterns of sound and rhythm, and then looks at the conventions which enable them to communicate meaning to the reader. In Lotman's work (as in semiotic analyses of literature in general), we are no longer confronted by descriptions of imagery, structure, tone and other qualities within the literary text – as in the era of what I. A. Richards called 'practical criticism' and others 'literary criticism'. We are now confronted by a highly technical explanation of the distinctive ways in which poems generate significance for each reader. Thus the emphasis in semiotic analysis of literature is no longer upon the literary text but upon the reader and upon intelligibility.

Semiotic analysis of literature is consequently a theory of reading which focusses upon the conventions by which the work produces its meanings. An example of such an approach in biblical studies can be found in Susan Wittig's 'Theory of Multiple Meanings' (*Semeia* 9, 1977), an essay which examines how the parables* encourage such a wealth of different interpretations (in this sense it is comparable to Lotman's approach to poetry). Wittig's emphasis is not on the surface structure of the parables, nor on their author's manipulation of the surface components of style and narrative detail. That would be 'aesthetic criticism'. Instead, she tries to explain how the parables in the Synoptic* Gospels* have yielded multiple, often apparently contradictory meanings. Wittig's solution is that parables are signs and that every sign consists of a linguistic signifier (Sr) and its conceptual signified (Sd), and these together denote or designate a referent. However, the parables also have a second-order relationship between signifier and signified which is connotative rather than denotative. At this level, significance is unstated and has to be created, under certain constraints, by the reader. It is precisely because this second-order relationship between signifier and signified has no dependable meaning that the parables elicit multiple meanings.

We can see from Wittig's essay that semiotic analysis of the Bible has something to offer in the area of reader-response* because it helps to explain why we come up with the readings which we do. Throughout Wittig's essay, the emphasis is not upon the author or the text but on the reader, and indeed the essay moves into the area of reader-response and reception-theory towards its conclusion with quotations from Wolfgang Iser's phenomenological explanations of the reading act. This concentration on the reader is an important characteristic of semiotic analysis of literature. Jonathan Culler actually calls semiotics 'a theory of reading', and has suggested to semioticians that they should align themselves with Hans Robert Jauss' *Rezeptionsästhetik*, because Jauss' desire to replace the traditional approach to literature with an aesthetics of reception and impact is really semiotic in character. It is interesting to note, in this respect, that Gary Phillips' essay, 'Creating a Reader in John 6' (*Semeia* 26, 1983), combines reception-theory and semiotics without apologizing for the fusion of the two disciplines.

A second area where semiotics might also be fruitful is in our attempts to discover how biblical narratives* (and indeed other genres*) might have been understood by their first readers. This is because, as Jan Mukarovsky has often insisted, a sign is really an intermediary among members of a community.* Biblical narrative is a social sign system and therefore our interpretation of it partly involves discovering those social conventions by which meaning was generated for its first readers. Looking at biblical narrative as a social sign-system might well be the logical sequel to form criticism,* since it could provide a more scientific account of the community dimension reflected in the language of biblical narratives.

This last judgment will encourage readers of Erhardt Güttgemanns to ask whether there is any similarity between the semiotic analysis of biblical texts and the post-form-critical programme developed by this influential German scholar. Güttgemanns developed a method of biblical interpretation in the 1970s which he called 'generative poetics', a term derived from Noam Chomsky's linguistics. What Güttgemanns was mainly concerned with at this stage was the discovery of the grammatical rules (what Saussure called *langue* and Chomsky *competence*) by which gospel narratives were constructed. The goal, as he put it, was 'to learn how Gospel narrative is "made"', to gain 'a narrative competence' which would enable us to narrate today stories about God. Güttgemanns attempted to do this by finding the grammatical structures from which the Gospel writers produced their significatory effects. In this sense, Güttgemanns' method was broadly speaking semiotic. Where he differs from the kind of semiotic approach delineated above is in his belief that synoptic 'signs' do not become significant through a shared, conventional interpretation of them in the earliest Christian communities, but rather through atemporal structures which we can still use today. Meaning, for Güttgemanns, is not conventional but ontological.

What criticisms, finally, can be levelled against semiotics? On the negative side, some have asked the following questions: is it really possible to grasp, classify and catalogue the effects of signification which one wishes to account for? Can signification ever be mastered by a coherent and comprehensive theory? What sense is given to the word 'meaning'* by semioticians, and is that sense consistent and valid? In what sense is a literary text a signifier? Is it a signifier *in toto*, or is it composed of many different, interrelated signifiers? On the positive side, some have praised semiotics for introducing methodological clarity into the area of literary interpretation. Others have praised semioticians for the way in which they have made explicit the implicit knowledge which enables people within social groups to understand each other's acts of communication. There are as many cautious criticisms as enthusiastic accolades. Ultimately, semiotics will make a contribution to biblical interpretation because it will help us to understand how and why we interpret biblical texts, and it will help us to discover those community conventions with which the first biblical writers and readers were operating.

See also **Meaning; Semantics, Structuralism.**

D. S. Clarke, *Principles of Semiotics*, 1987; J. Culler, *The Pursuit of Signs*, 1981; E. Güttgemanns, *Studia Linguistica Neotestamentica*, 1971; Y. Lotman, *The Structure of the Artistic Text*, 1977; Jan Mukarovsky, *Aesthetic Function*, 1970; id., *Art as Semiotic Fact*, 1978.

MARK W. G. STIBBE

Semitisms

Greek words, phrases, or syntactical* phenomena that stand out because of a relation to a Semitic background that may be held to account for their unusual character.

Semitisms are important in the NT in general, and in the Gospels* and Acts in particular, because all 27 books have come to us originally written only in Greek. It is, moreover, Greek with varying degrees of Semitic interference, and the kinds of Semitisms have to be sorted out.

In general, the Semitic interference reflects the Palestinian Jewish* matrix of Christianity itself. It bears in an important way on the stages of the Gospel tradition and is intimately related to the quest for the historical Jesus.* What he actually did and said comes to us filtered not only through the preaching and teaching of his followers who carried his Aramaic-formulated message into the Hellenistic* world of the eastern Mediterranean, but also through the writings of Greek-speaking evangelists* who culled, synthesized and explicated that preaching and teaching, thus adapting his message further to their own Hellenistic literary ends. None of the evangelists is likely to have composed his Gospel on Palestinian soil, and yet Semitisms shine through the Greek texts of each of their Gospels. This phenomenon is more pronounced in Mark and John, but is not lacking in Matthew, Luke, or Acts.

In speaking of a Semitism, one has to be precise in the use of the term, since it is often employed loosely. Thus, it is sometimes used for a 'Septuagintism'. Luke, who among the evangelists writes the best Greek, not only imitates the style of the Greek OT, but often uses specific phrases from it. For instance, instead of the dative of indirect object with *legein*, 'say to', he often writes *legein pros* (with the accusative; 1.13; 4.21; 5.22). This construction is found abundantly in the Septuagint* (e.g. Gen. 19.5; Ex. 7.1, 8; Dan. 3.36; 6.5). There it is a Semitism, reflecting either Hebrew *'āmar lĕ-* or *'el* or Aramaic *'āmar lĕ-*. But it is a Septuagintism when Luke or some other NT author writes *legein pros*. Similarly, a Septuagintism is used when Mark writes *apokritheis eipen*, 'answering, he said' (6.37; 10.3). Commentators have related this expression to Hebrew *wayya'an . . . wayyō'mer*, 'he answered . . . and said'. But this Hebrew expression often becomes in the Septuagint a participle and a finite verb, *apokritheis eipen* (e.g. Gen. 18.27; 27.37,39). Such a Septuagintal construction Mark and other evangelists imitate.

Properly, 'Semitism' is restricted to those words, phrases, or syntactical phenomena in NT Greek which reflect a Hebrew or Aramaic background that cannot be further specified. Thus, in John 12.36 the phrase 'sons of light' occurs. Found neither in the OT nor in rabbinic* literature, it has often been labelled a Semitism because of the introductory 'sons of . . .' Both the Aramaic and the Hebrew counterpart of the phrase, however, have turned up in the Palestinian Jewish texts of Qumran (*see* **Dead Sea Scrolls**): Aramaic *běnê něhôrā'* (4Q'Amram*ᵇ* 3.1) and Hebrew *běnê 'ôr* (1QS 1.9). The result is that one cannot tell whether the interference in the Johannine Greek phrase is Aramaic or Hebrew; so recourse is had to the generic 'Semitism'. But if the interference can be identified as Aramaic or Hebrew, then 'Aramaism'* or 'Hebraism' is used instead. In many cases this specification can be established.

One can show that Aramaic phraseology underlies expressions such as, 'he will be great and will be hailed as Son of the Most High . . . he will be called Son of God' (Luke 1.32,35), because the exact Aramaic equivalents of these clauses appear in 4Q*246* 1.7–9; 2.1 (see *NTS* 20, 1973–74, p. 393). Such evidence raises a problem for those who claim that Luke had Hebraic sources for his infancy narrative.* Again, Aramaisms are clear in such Greek words as *abba* (Mark 14.36; Gal. 4.6; = Aramaic *'abbā'*, 'Father'), *gabbatha* (John 19.13; = *gabbětā'*, 'ridge'), *maranatha* (I Cor. 16.22; = *māránā' tā'*, 'Our Lord, come!') or in Graecized names like *Kēphas* (Gal. 1.18; = *Kēpā'*, 'Rock') or *Barabbas* (Mark 15.7; = *bar 'abbā'*, 'son of Abba' [or 'the Father']).

Hebraisms in NT Greek are less frequently found, and they too have to be scrutinized more carefully than they have been in the past, since many of them are Septuagintisms (e.g. the periphrastic *kai ēn* ('and it was') + a participle: Gen. 4.17; Judg. 16.21; II Kings 6.26; Isa. 10.20; Dan. 1.16). One construction often called a Hebraism is *kai egeneto/egeneto de*, followed by a temporal clause, 'and it happened, while . . ., that . . .'. But in reality there are three forms of this construction, one found in Hellenistic Greek papyri, one used in the Septuagint, and one possibly a Hebraism. 1. *Egeneto de* + an infinitive (with a subject accusative): *kai egeneto auton en tois sabbasin paraporeuesthai dia tōn sporimōn*, 'he happened one sabbath to be making his way along grainfields' (Mark 2.23). This construction is found in Greek papyri and is an extension of the more usual *sunebē* with an infinitive (see Acts 21.35). See further Luke 3.21; 6.6,12. 2. *Egeneto de* + a finite verb (indicative) without an intervening conjunction: *kai egeneto en ekeinais tais hēmerais ēlthen Iēsous apo Nazaret*, 'in those days Jesus happened to come from Nazareth' (Mark 1.9). This construction is often found in the Septuagint (Gen. 4.3; 8.6; 11.2), where it translates Hebrew *wayyěhî . . . wě-* (+ a finite verb) with-

out the intervening conjunction. See further Mark 4.4; Luke 1.8,23,41,59. 3. *Egeneto de* + *kai* + a finite verb (indicative): *egeneto de en tō ton ochlon epikeisthai autō . . ., kai autos ēn hestōs . . . kai eiden*, 'and it happened, while the crowd was pressing about him . . . and he was standing . . ., that he saw' (Luke 5.1). In this case, the construction is found in the Septuagint (Gen. 4.8; I Sam. 24.17; II Kings 19.1), where it is, however, a literal translation of the Hebrew *wayyěhî . . . wě-* (with a second conjunction rendered by *kai*).

Some commentators on the NT appeal to such Semitisms in their interpretation because they consider them a promising way of coming closer to the words of the historical Jesus.

See also **Jewish Background to the New Testament.**

K. Beyer, *Semitische Syntax im Neuen Testament*, ² 1968; M. Black, *An Aramaic Approach to the Gospels and Acts*, ³ 1967; J. A. Fitzmyer, *A Wandering Aramean*, 1979; D. Hill, *Greek Words and Hebrew Meanings*, 1967; E. C. Maloney, *Semitic Interference in Marcan Syntax*, 1981; G. Schwarz, *Und Jesus sprach: Untersuchungen zur aramäischen Urgestalt der Worte Jesu*, ² 1987; M. Wilcox, *The Semitisms of Acts*, 1965.

JOSEPH A. FITZMYER, S.J.

Sensus Plenior

This expression (literally, 'fuller meaning') was first used in 1925 by A. Fernández and achieved a relatively wide currency in Roman Catholic theology in the four decades leading up to the promulgation of the constitution *Dei Verbum* at Vatican II in 1965. It is defended in Vol. I of *Mysterium Salutis* (1965) by Herbert Haag, who speaks of a growing consensus among Catholic theologians. But since the theory of the *sensus plenior* was the product of a particular constellation of theological factors, it has receded from the centre of theological interest in the very different situation after Vatican II.

Negatively, the anti-Modernist (*see* **Catholic Modernism**) decrees of Pius X (1903–1914) and the statements of the Biblical Commission which he set up directed theological enquiry away from a close consideration of the original intentions of the writers of the biblical texts. Positively, the *sensus plenior* theory was generated by the theological convictions of the unity of the whole of scripture and of its christological and ecclesiological reference points. Since God is author of the Bible, God has put in the words of the authors of the OT books a deeper meaning unknown (or at least not fully known) to the human authors, but in harmony with their own intentions, in such a way that the messianic* interpretation in the NT and in Christian tradition is authentic exegesis* of the OT texts, not the introduction of concerns foreign to the authors. This idea is meant to safeguard the NT and Christian interpretation from the charge of imposing arbitrarily a finality ('Whatever was written in former days was written for our instruction', Rom. 15.4), and thus a whole interpretative theological structure (OT as preparation, NT as fulfilment), on OT texts that have a finality and theology of their own, which ought to be primary for exegesis.

Since this theory is derived from theological principles, in keeping with a general trend in Roman Catholic theology at that period to proceed by deduction from *a priori* postulates, its acceptance depends on the acceptance of those principles; it cannot be assessed solely by means of exegesis of the OT texts taken by themselves. It is this fact that has caused the *sensus plenior* to lose its importance in contemporary Catholic theology, where exegesis begins with the OT texts in their historically conditioned individuality and pays attention to the theology expressed in these texts as itself the due object of our theological interest, without rushing to level down the theological differences by subordinating the OT christologically and ecclesiologically to the NT. An academically neutral exegesis is reluctant to speak so readily about what God intended the authors of the OT texts to say; and in the *de facto* separation of exegesis and dogmatics as autonomous disciplines in Catholic theology, theories like the *sensus plenior* which concern both disciplines at once are not likely to find persons sufficiently competent in both to be able to discuss and defend them.

See also **Christian Interpretation of the Old Testament; Mysticism; Typology; Use of the Old Testament in the New Testament.**

Raymond Brown, *The Sensus Plenior of Sacred Scripture*, [2] 1960.

BRIAN MCNEIL

Septuagint

1. *As interpretation of scripture.* Our earliest Greek translation* of the scriptures, by its very nature also a work of interpretation, the Septuagint (LXX) contains much material of an exegetical* nature distinct from the Massoretic text* of the Hebrew Bible (MT). This has not yet been systematically studied, so any picture is necessarily provisional. The major work this century has been the critical editing of the text, but with this now well under way there is new impetus to study translational policies and procedures (S. Brock, J. de Waard and others). Scholars are less ready to attribute 'mistakes' in the LXX to the translators' incompetence or to a different Hebrew

Vorlage (although this may sometimes be the case), but recognize the creative processes at work. Even the most literal of translators were forced by ambiguities or difficulties in the text to make choices, and these often reveal their concerns and the kind of common knowledge they could draw on.

We assume that their attitude to the sacred text included a belief in its relevance to their own time (cf. the Prologue to Ecclus.) and even that it was actually speaking about that time (cf. some of the material found in the exegetical Dead Sea Scrolls* texts). A translation may thus also be a 're-reading' of the parent text in the light of the convictions, needs and prejudices of the community* from which it emerges. There is ample evidence to show that unacceptable features in the Hebrew text were altered to suit contemporary theological ideas, cultic* requirements, etc. (e.g. the regularizing of the sabbath reference in Gen. 2.2a by a substitution of 'sixth' for 'seventh'; prohibitions against Greek cults added to Deut. 23.18; Solomon standing where liturgically permitted and not encroaching on the High Priest's area, III Reigns [I Kings] 3.15; and many others). This kind of readjustment was achieved by various methods: additions to or omissions from the text; the flexibility given by unpointed Hebrew; supposed etymologies;* altering the order of consonants in a word; and many other exegetical ploys of a type already found in the OT (e.g. the updating of Jer. 25.11 in Dan. 9.2,24), the NT (e.g. the significance attached in Gal. 3.16 to the singular noun in Gen. 12.7), and the earliest rabbinic* sources. In identifying this material our methodological* departure point is comparison with the MT. Leaving aside the question of the relationship between the two texts, such comparison is the simplest way of showing up the distinctive character of the Greek. Even if differences may sometimes be attributed to another *Vorlage* (whose readings the translator was evidently happy to accept), the fact remains that the LXX is our witness to interpretations different from those in the MT.

Work on the LXX as exegesis has until now been very scattered. Findings have to be extracted from other material, such as the studies accompanying the Göttingen editions of the text. There have, however, been some works which deal specifically with interpretation. Examples of studies of entire books are G. Gerleman on Job, Chronicles and Proverbs, and I. L. Seeligmann on Isaiah. These draw attention to tendencies in these mainly freer-style translations, either to adapt to the outlook of a readership at home in Hellenistic* culture (Job, Proverbs) or to relate the text to contemporary issues (Isaiah). M. Harl's edition of Genesis includes exegetical comment on passages differing from MT. Examples of studies of major sections are P. Grelot on the Servant Songs* in Isaiah (*Les Poèmes du Serviteur*, 1981) and J. W. Wevers on a portion of III Reigns. ('Exegetical Principles underlying the Septuagint Text of I Kings ii 12 – xxi 43', *OTS* 8, 1950, pp. 300–322), Grelot shows how (a) the 'servant' is nearly always identified collectively as Israel; (b) the eschatological* nature of salvation is emphasized; and (c) there is a heightening of religious nationalism. Wevers identifies exegetical principles at work, which include: rationalizing and harmonizing;* improving the image of the Davidic* line, especially Solomon; denigrating the Northern Kingdom; hostility to pagan practices and attention to cultic propriety; concern for divine transcendence.

Examples of studies of smaller sections are J. F. A. Sawyer on Isa. 19.18 ('"Blessed be my People Egypt" [Isaiah 19.25]', in *A Word in Season* ed. James D. Martin and Philip R. Davies, 1986) and Amos 3.12, ('"Those Priests in Damascus"', *ASTI* VIII, 1970–71, pp. 123–30) and J. Lust on Ezek. 21.30– 32 and 28.11–19. ('Messianism and Septuagint', *VT-S* 36, 1985, pp. 186–90). Both scholars show how partisan a translation may be. Isa. 19.18 may contain an approving reference to the Oniad temple at Leontopolis; Amos 3.12 may, with its reference to 'priests in Damascus', contain a polemical reference to Qumran-like dissidents; the two Ezekiel passages may contain quite strong veiled criticism of the Hasmonean high-priestly dynasty. In all these cases, although interpretation is tentative, it looks as if difficulties of one kind or another in the text have led the translator to renderings which reflect his own and his community's current concerns.

A few examples taken from LXX Amos will illustrate some of the difficulties, or opportunities, encountered by one translator, and the exegetical implications of his solutions. In 1.6,9, the word construed by MT to mean 'whole' (RSV) is taken by LXX as the name Solomon (the difference arises from the pointing of the Hebrew): a hint perhaps of a historicizing tendency in this translator and of the popularity of Solomonic traditions in the latter part of the second century BC. Decisions about pointing also lie behind the appearance of Gog in 7.1 (one of the earliest sources for the development of the eschatological Gog tradition outside the OT, cf. Num. 24.7 LXX) and in 4.13, where there is also a question of word-division. Here the translator found a messianic* reference: 'I (am he who) . . . proclaim(s) to men his anointed, *christon autou*.'

Other examples where pointing has affected translation, producing an eschatological effect,

occur at 1.14; 8.8; 9.5. In 3.12 a Hebrew word for 'couch' (correctly translated in 6.4) has either not been recognized or has been deemed unintelligible in its context. Its resemblance to the Greek for 'priest', in either spelling or sound or both, has led to an audacious transliteration and to the polemical threat already mentioned. In several places, decisions concerning moods and tenses may reveal an interpretative stance, e.g. 4.4f., where past indicatives for the cultic 'sins' at Bethel etc. (MT has imperatives) perhaps indicate aversion to perpetuating an apparent command to participate in the condemned northern cult (cf. III Reigns 16.32f.). In 7.14 the Hebrew nominal clause ('Not a prophet I') has forced the translator to make a choice. He has opted for a past tense ('I *was* not a prophet . . .') and so for an interpretation of what the ambiguous statement means (cf. Isa. 7.14 LXX). In 9.12 there seems to have been a deft reworking of the text to produce a universalistic rather than a nationalistic prediction, which then shares the outlook of passages like Zech. 14.16ff.; Isa. 19.19ff.

Examples could be multiplied throughout the LXX, but until there are complete commentaries on the various books, bringing out their interpretative contributions and any overall tendency in their cultural and historical settings within mainly Diaspora Judaism of the third to first centuries BC, conclusions must remain fragmentary and tentative. It is better to avoid generalizations, since books, or even sections within books, vary considerably in their outlook. It has been shown, for instance, that the avoidance of anthropomorphisms* is by no means consistent; nor is there a systematic heightening of eschatological interest, let alone a more generalized trend towards a developed royal messianism,* as has sometimes been claimed.

2. *As interpreted in the early church*. In assessing how distinctive features in the LXX affected early Christian exegesis, it must be borne in mind that, with time, the books of the LXX were treated as a unified, authoritative and inspired corpus, which existed primarily to bear prophetic* witness to Christ; interpretation was carried out according to various guiding (and often overlapping) principles: allegorical,* historical and especially typological;* and the ultimate touchstone for truth was the NT: all other texts must be shown to be in line with this (e.g. the universal preference for the NT variant 'beyond Babylon' in Amos 5.27 LXX as quoted in Acts 7.43). These factors result in a certain flattening of contours, as individual passages are read in these wider interpretative frameworks, especially when it comes to the full-scale commentaries* (e.g. the patristic writers understand Isa. 19.25 in a universalistic sense,

whereas the focus of the LXX seems to be more restrictive; identification of Jesus with the Suffering Servant overlays the collective interpretation of the LXX). There are, however, many places where the distinctive readings of the LXX have made their mark. A few examples follow.

(a) In the NT: the universalistic outlook of Amos 9.12 LXX has helped the author of Acts 15.17 to underline the importance of the Gentile mission in a way the MT could not have done. So too the future indicatives in Isa. 6.9 (MT has imperatives) enable the prophecy to be applied to the conversion of the Gentiles in Acts 28.26 (cf. Zech. 13.7 LXX in Matt. 26.31). In Matt. 13.14, however, the fulfilment of this prophecy consists in the unbelief of the crowds; and Hab. 1.5 LXX, quoted in Acts 13.41, provides a convenient warning to the unconverted ('scoffers'), where MT has a less threatening 'among the nations'.

(b) In Christian-Jewish controversy: differences between LXX and Hebrew are used polemically, with each side accusing the other of tampering with the sacred text, as in the famous argument over 'from the tree' added to (?), removed from (?) Ps. 95(96).10. In Isa. 7.14, translational variants (*parthenos*/*neanis* for the neutral Hebrew *'almah*) in the LXX and in the Greek version being used by the Jews, are given theological weight. The Christian interpretation of a reference to the virgin birth was of course strengthened by the LXX's choice of a future tense here. Gen. 31.13 (where *theos* occurs twice) was used to prove the presence of the Second Person of the Trinity in the OT (this text had already been used by Philo* about the Logos*).

(c) In inner-Christian controversy: one of the proof texts* which played a major part in the Arian controversy was Prov. 8.22 LXX because of its unambiguous 'creation' verb (*ektise*; MT has a verb less common in creation contexts) (*see* **Patristic Christology**). In the later controversy over the status of the Holy Spirit, Amos 4.13 played a similar role, being used as a proof text by both sides. Here the apparent reference to Christ led to the words 'creating the wind' (= 'spirit') (*ktizōn pneuma*) earlier in the verse being given a trinitarian sense. Some shrewd exegetical arguments were developed, especially by Athanasius, until the usefulness of the text was undermined by the dawning realization that there was no reference to Christ in the Hebrew.

(d) In homiletic and exegetical works: there is as yet little detailed study as to how the LXX influenced patristic exegesis, although the *Bible d'Alexandrie* project in France is a step in this direction for the Pentateuch.* There is a lack of critical editions for many exegetical works, and of commentaries on them; there is

further the problem of sorting out the text-types being used, in view of the various recensions of the LXX (but cf. the work done by N. Fernández Marcos and others in Spain on the Antiochian* text of Theodoret of Cyrrhus). Scattered references to patristic use of the LXX need to be brought together and evaluated. (From over a century ago, for instance, useful examples abound in W. R. Churton's *Influence of the Septuagint*, 1861, and F. W. Farrar's *History of Interpretation*, 1886, though both works are heavily apologetic in approach.)

Keeping these difficulties in mind we may look at some examples: (i) In LXX Job, the character of Job himself is more submissive than in MT. This was largely responsible for the picture of Job as the patient sufferer, the prototype martyr, which so impressed the early church (cf. James 5.11; I Clement 17; Tertullian,* *De Patientia* 14). But the LXX is not entirely consistent: Theodore of Mopsuestia had such difficulty with passages where Job curses or complains that he considered the book to have been written by a pagan who put inappropriate words into the mouth of the historical character. Pagan authorship was further proved by Job's youngest daughter being called 'Horn of Amaltheia' (Job 42.14); the elegant rendering from Greek mythology* by the cultured translator of LXX Job proved too shocking for the Christian commentator! (In fact, mythological references are handled variously, cf. Jerome on Amos 5.8.) The LXX tends to avoid translating Hebrew *ṣur* literally as 'rock' when it occurs as a divine title, with the result that it is virtually unknown in this sense to the Greek and Latin Fathers, e.g. in Ps-Basil's commentary on Isaiah, which has a section dealing with the different scriptural uses of 'rock'. (ii) Recensional activity soon led to the 'correction' of Amos 3.12. The word *hiereis* ('priests') was, however, always retained, though shifted to the beginning of v. 13. There were then varied explanations of their identity in the commentaries. (iii) Jerome's work may be singled out, since his exegetical commentaries (produced between AD 381 and 420) mark the point, in the Latin church, when the Hebrew text is brought back into full view. (The Greek Fathers of this period from which come most of the extant complete commentaries, even when aware of the parent text, are hardly able to handle the comparisons, see e.g. Cyril of Alexandria on Amos 3.9.) Jerome's method includes a detailed comparison between Greek and Hebrew texts, with preference now given, controversially, to the latter, where the two diverged. He is aware of the effect of different readings on interpretation and offers explanations, including the suggestion that the

LXX translators sometimes made deliberate changes for theological reasons (see e.g. his Preface to the Pentateuch). But far from ignoring the LXX exegetically in places where he has rejected its readings as erroneous, he employs a 'two-tier' exegesis: the Hebrew provides him with the literal or historical sense, the LXX with a spiritual* or allegorical one (often put to polemical use); e.g. on Amos 1.3; 2.8; 4.13. Occasionally he even uses the LXX for his 'historical' exposition, despite having demonstrated the text to be mistaken, e.g. on Amos 2.7. The influence of the time-honoured traditional text has clearly remained irresistible, and in this way some at least of the special material of the LXX could be absorbed into the traditions of the Western church. But by and large the exegetical resources of this very early version of the Bible still await rediscovery, although of course they have never ceased to animate the liturgical life of the Greek-speaking churches.

See also **Textual Criticism (New Testament); Textual Criticism (Old Testament); Translation, Problems of.**

P. R. Ackroyd and C. F. Evans (eds), *The Cambridge History of the Bible,* vol. 1, 1970, ch. 5; G. Gerleman, *Studies in the Septuagint,* I: *The Book of Job,* II: *Chronicles,* 1946; III: *Proverbs,* 1956; D. W. Gooding, *Relics of Ancient Exegesis: a Study of the Miscellanies in 3 Reigns 2,* 1976; M. Harl, *La Bible d'Alexandrie: I, La Genèse,* 1986; I. L. Seeligmann, *The Septuagint Version of Isaiah: a Discussion of its Problems,* 1948; E. Tov, article on 'Septuagint' in *IDB*-SV, 1976, pp. 810–11.

JENNIFER DINES, CSA

Sermon on the Mount

'The history of the church is the history of its interpretation of scripture.' G. Ebeling's dictum certainly applies to the Sermon on the Mount, for no other short section of the Bible has been more prominent in theological discussion and controversy. Throughout the history of the church the Sermon on the Mount has been understood as a compendium of Christian ethical* teaching. Many writers have made even more extravagant claims. John Donne, for example, claimed in 1629 that 'all the articles of our religion, all the canons of our church, all the injunctions of our princes, all the homilies of our fathers, all the body of divinity, is in these three chapters, in this one Sermon on the Mount'.

Augustine* seems to have been the first to use the term. His important commentary on Matt. 5–7, *De Sermone Domini in monte,* was probably written between 392 and 396. In spite of his influence, the term did not gain wide currency until the sixteenth century.

Since the beginning of the twentieth century most writers have accepted that the evangelist* Matthew compiled the Sermon from various sources: Jesus did not 'preach' Matt. 5–7 as a sermon. But even in recent decades many have paid only lip-service to the fact that the Sermon is the first of the evangelist's five discourses. The Sermon is often taken without further ado to be a summary of the ethical teaching of Jesus. As we shall see, it is important to distinguish between two ways of approaching the Sermon. On the one hand it is a composition of the evangelist Matthew which contains some of his own distinctive emphases. On the other hand, behind these three chapters of Matthew are some sayings of Jesus which can be appreciated fully only when they are set alongside other sayings which probably go back to Jesus himself.

Interpretation of the Sermon has been dominated by five overlapping sets of questions. 1. Does Jesus simply interpret or clarify the law of Moses,* or does he present on a 'new Sinai' a 'new law' for a 'new people'? Matt. 5.17 is often taken as the preface to the central section of the Sermon which runs from 5.17 to 7.12. But this verse bristles with difficulties. Matthew's Jesus clearly rejects any suggestion that his coming overturns the 'law and the prophets', but what is meant by 'fulfilling' them? Does Jesus set forth the real intention of the law? Or does he confirm or establish the law? The latter suggestion is often supported by linguistic* arguments based on the force of the Aramaic word which Jesus may have used, and by an appeal to 5.18 and 19. These two verses seem to underline the continuing importance of the law: 'not a letter, not a stroke will disappear from the law' (NEB). In the next section of the Sermon (5.21–48), however, Jesus seems to contrast his teaching with that of Moses. Six quotations of the law are followed by the solemn phrase 'but I say to you'. In some cases Jesus seems to strengthen the teaching of the law (5.22; 28,34); in others, he seems to overturn the teaching of Moses (5.39,44 and perhaps 32).

2. What is the relationship between Matt. 5–7 and Paul's* gospel of grace? Is the Sermon (as 'law') intended to make the reader or listener aware of his need of 'grace'? Or does the Sermon presuppose forgiveness and acceptance of the sinner and therefore set out demands for true discipleship? We shall return to these questions in our discussion of Luther's* interpretation of the Sermon.

3. To whom is the Sermon addressed? To men and women in general, or to those committed to the way of Jesus? The text itself is ambiguous at this point. The introduction and conclusion (5.1 and 7.28) imply that the Sermon was addressed to the crowds, but 5.2

notes that 'when the disciples had gathered around him Jesus began to address them'. While many parts of the Sermon seem to set out an 'ethic of Christian discipleship', the final verses of the whole Gospel imply that the teaching of Jesus is to be part of the message taken to 'all nations' (28.18–20).

4. Is the Sermon a *code* of ethics to be followed in every detail? Or does it set out principles or attitudes on which conduct is to be based? Are all parts of the Sermon to be interpreted literally? Or do some sayings (such as 5.22,39,43) contain hyperbole? Many writers have urged that the harsh demands of the Sermon can be understood and obeyed only if they are taken to portray 'the attitude of heart' appropriate for a 'member of the kingdom'.*

5. To what extent are individual sayings dominated by the expectation (either of Jesus or of Matthew) of the approach of the end-times (i.e. eschatology*)? For example, does Jesus commend a casual attitude to food and clothing in 6.25ff. because of the approach of the end-times, or simply because this is the right attitude regardless of when the end-times come? Several writers have urged that each petition of the Lord's Prayer* (6.9–13) is to be interpreted eschatologically. On this approach, the 'bread petition' is understood as a request for the 'bread of heaven' – a partial anticipation of the 'feast of heaven'; 'lead us not into temptation' concerns the time of testing expected in the end-times, not everyday temptations.

The modern interpreter of the Sermon will quickly find that the interpretation of individual sayings or groups of sayings will be determined by the answers to all these questions. Some of them have been more prominent than others in different periods of church history.

The first commentary on the Sermon was probably written by Origen* in the middle of the third century, but only a short fragment of it has survived. The two most important expositions of the Sermon in the early church were written by Chrysostom and Augustine at the end of the fourth century. They both taught that the Sermon was the perfect pattern for the life of all Christians. In his homilies* on the Sermon Chrysostom attacks the heretical views of Gnostics* and Manicheans. He rejects their view that the body is evil and the mind and spirit are good; 5.29 teaches that it is the 'evil mind' which is accursed, not bodily organs such as the eye and hand. Chrysostom also refutes 'those heretics who say that the old covenant* is of the devil'; the sayings of Jesus do not repeal the old law, they 'draw out and fill up its commands'.

Augustine also grappled with the relationship of the Sermon to the law of Moses.

The Manichean Faustus had claimed that 5.17 was a saying neither of Jesus nor of Matthew; someone else had written it under Matthew's name! In his *Reply to Faustus* Augustine stresses the continuity of the 'old law' and the 'new' more strongly than was usually the case in the early church. In his own exposition of the Sermon, however, he emphasizes sharp discontinuity by distinguishing between the 'lesser precepts given by God through his holy prophets and servants to a people who still needed to be bound by fear' and 'the greater precepts given through his Son to a people now ready to be freed by love'. Augustine is not the only interpreter to have interpreted 5.17–48 in different ways either in different contexts or at different points in his life!

In the thirteenth century, Thomas Aquinas also stressed the discontinuity between the old law ('the law of bondage') and the new law ('the law of liberty'), but without conceding that the latter contradicts or abrogates the former. He used the analogy of the tree (the new law) which is in a sense contained in the seed. Aquinas also introduced a distinction which was to become very influential in Catholic thought. In addition to the commandments of the new law which are necessary in order to gain salvation, there are also optional counsels which 'render the gaining of eternal bliss more assured and expeditious'. The latter are intended for those who strive for perfection; they are based on poverty, chastity and obedience and are therefore primarily for those who join the religious life. This distinction is hardly hinted at in interpretation of the Sermon in the early church, though it may be implied by Matt. 19.11–12.

Luther, Zwingli and Calvin* wrote extensively on the Sermon. They all insisted that Matt. 5–7 represents the true interpretation of the law of Moses which had been obscured in Judaism and whose ceremonial aspects had been wholly transformed in Christian life and worship. On the whole they emphasized the continuity between the 'law of Christ' and the 'law of Moses' more than their Catholic opponents. They rejected the use made of the Sermon by radical Anabaptist groups who claimed that the ethical teaching of Christ was a clear development beyond the law of Moses. Anabaptists claimed that the Sermon should be interpreted literally and that Christians should therefore never use violence (Matt. 5.39), never swear oaths (5.34), and never hold office as a judge or ruler (7.1). Their literal interpretation of the Sermon led them to opt out of secular government completely.

In a series of sermons on Matt. 5–7 (and in other writings) Luther developed his well-known doctrine of the two realms, the secular and the spiritual. The Christian lives in both spheres. In the spiritual sphere the Christian must obey all the commands of the Sermon; in the secular, natural law or 'common sense' prevail. In his remarks on Matt. 5.38–42 Luther claimed that most interpreters failed to distinguish properly between the kingdom of Christ and the kingdom of the world. In these verses 'Christ is not tampering with the responsibility and authority of the government, but he is teaching his individual Christians how to live personally, apart from their official position and authority . . . A Christian person should not resist any evil; but within the limits of his office, a secular person should oppose every evil.' For Luther a 'secular person' included Christians participating in the secular realm.

Luther also discussed the Sermon in terms of 'law' and 'gospel'. In some of his writings he emphasized that the Sermon is the 'law of Christ' that makes people aware of the gospel of God's grace through Christ: 'we are not able properly to fulfil one tittle out of our own strength . . . but must always crawl to Christ'. But in other passages Luther insists that the Sermon is not just the accusing law that points to sin: it is also 'gospel'. This is especially true of the Beatitudes* (5.3–12). Christ 'does not press but in a friendly way entices and speaks: "Blessed are the poor."'

By referring to the Sermon both as 'law' and as 'gospel', Luther confused his later followers. Many Lutherans have stressed that the Sermon is the law that awakens knowledge of sin. But some (notably J. Jeremias,* 1961) have claimed that the demands of Jesus in the Sermon are preceded by 'gospel', i.e. by his proclamation of the kingdom and by his encouragement to his disciples to share his own sense of sonship.

Calvin emphasized the continuity of the Sermon with the law of Moses. In his comments on Matt. 5.21, for example, he insisted that 'we must not imagine Christ to be a new legislator, who adds anything to the eternal righteousness of his Father. We must listen to him as a faithful expounder . . .'

Calvin partially anticipated eighteenth- and nineteenth-century discussion of the sources of the Sermon in his recognition that Matt. 5–7 is 'a brief summary of the doctrine of Christ . . . collected out of his many and various discourses'.

All the various approaches which we have just sketched can be found in modern discussion of the Sermon. Twentieth-century scholarship, however, has added two new issues: the extent to which the Sermon reflects the views of Jesus (or of Matthew) concerning the end-times (eschatology) and the extent to which Matthew the evangelist has shaped the traditions he has incorporated into chs 5–7.

In 1892 Johannes Weiss published a short but influential discussion of Jesus' proclamation of the kingdom of God. Jesus expected that the kingdom would shortly be ushered in through a cataclysmic divine intervention. In 1902 Albert Schweitzer* developed this approach even more vigorously. Both writers believed that the ethical teaching of Jesus was intended as a preparation for the short period before the end ('interim ethics'). Thus most of the issues with which earlier interpreters of the Sermon had grappled were declared to be irrelevant.

Weiss and Schweitzer raised in an acute form the relationship between the ethical teaching of Jesus and his proclamation of the coming kingdom. Discussion of this issue has to range far beyond Matt. 5–7 and consider all the relevant sayings of Jesus.

In 1902 B. W. Bacon published one of the first discussions of the Sermon in English which attempted to reconstruct its earliest attainable form. He concluded that in the original form of the Sermon Jesus spoke as a prophetic interpreter of a new law; Jesus did not lay down rules, but opened up principles. These conclusions were hardly novel, but in his isolation of the 'intrusive additions' of Matthew Bacon paved the way for later redaction-critical studies. Bacon claimed that Matthew has supplied 'neo-legalistic touches' in verses such as 5.16 ('good works'); 5.18–19; 5.32 (the 'exception' to no divorce); 7.12b. The original Sermon of Jesus is not legislative (as Matthew seems to have regarded it) but prophetic.*

Since 1945 interpretation of the Sermon and of Matthew's Gospel as a whole has been dominated by redaction criticism.* This approach underlines the extent to which the evangelist himself is responsible for chs 5–7. In the last few years fresh approaches to the interpretation of the Sermon have drawn on structuralism* (A. Kodjak and D. Patte), literary criticism* (J. D. Kingsbury and R. A. Edwards), and even political theology (S. Van Tilborg). But for the foreseeable future, discussion of Matthew's intentions in chs 5–7 is likely to be based on redaction criticism.

Several scholars, notably M. D. Goulder, have attacked the Q hypothesis (*see* **Synoptic Problem**) which has been almost axiomatic for nearly all recent interpreters of the Sermon. But most scholars are not convinced by attempts to argue that Luke has radically reinterpreted Matthew's Sermon (seen by Goulder as the evangelist's* own work) by preserving only a much truncated version of it (Luke 6.20–49), and by placing other parts of Matt. 5–7 in quite different contexts.

On the more widely accepted view, Matthew has expanded considerably the earlier version of the Sermon in Q by including in his first discourse other Q traditions and also further oral traditions* to which he had access. Redaction criticism has confirmed that Matthew is more than a compiler. In all his five discourses the evangelist has rearranged and reinterpreted the sayings on which he drew. He often elucidates them with extra phrases or even (on occasion) with whole verses which he himself has composed. The following may be noted as examples: 5.10,13a,14a,16,20; 6.10b and c, 13b; 7.12c,19,20,21. In many places Matthew's own distinctive vocabulary and emphases are evident. For example, the five important references to 'righteousness' (5.6,10,20; 6.1,33) are all redactional additions made by the evangelist himself.

In recent years several proposals concerning the structure of the Sermon have been made. Some have suggested that the Beatitudes are a 'table of contents' for the whole Sermon. U. Luz (1985) has claimed that the Sermon has been built symmetrically around its centrepiece, the Lord's Prayer, 6.7–15. The first section, 5.3–16, corresponds to the last section, 7.13–27; the second section, 5.17–20, to 7.12; 5.21–48 to 6.19–7.11 (these two passages are identical in length); and 6.1–6 corresponds to 6.16–18. Although the theory is not completely convincing (the correspondence between 5.21–48 and 6.19–7.11 is forced), there is little doubt that Matthew intends 5.17–20 to introduce the central section of the Sermon and 7.12 to conclude it: both passages concern fulfilment of the law and the prophets.

The first half of the Sermon is carefully structured: 5.1–16; 17–20; 21–48; 6.1–18. But what about the second half? 6.19 to 7.11 seems to be a rag-bag of sayings, only some of which are loosely related to others. G. Bornkamm (1978) has offered a novel solution: this part of the Sermon is a 'commentary' on the Lord's Prayer. 6.19–24 expounds the first three petitions of the Lord's Prayer, 6.9–10; 6.25–34 then works out the implications of the bread petition, 6.11; 7.1–5 is an exposition of the forgiveness petition, and 7.6 takes up the theme of 6.13. Bornkamm's ingenious explanation has not convinced other scholars, but he has shown just how strongly the whole section 6.5 to 7.11 is dominated by the prayer theme.

Some of the themes Matthew emphasizes in the first of his five discourses are also prominent elsewhere in the Gospel. For example, in 5.20, one of the key verses which Matthew himself has almost certainly composed, disciples are told that their ethical conduct must exceed that of the scribes and Pharisees;* in 5.48, a related verse, they are told to be perfect or whole-hearted. In 6.1–18 their conduct is contrasted starkly with that of the 'hypocrites'

(6.2,5,16) whom the reader naturally assumes to be none other than the scribes and Pharisees of 5.20. These same points are developed in ch. 23. The crowds and disciples are urged not to follow the example of the scribes and Pharisees (23.2–3) who are then referred to explicitly as 'hypocrites' six times. There is even some verbal correspondence between 6.1, 5 and 16 on the one hand, and 23.5 and 28 on the other. Both in chs 5 and 6 of the Sermon, and in ch. 23 the evangelist uses the scribes and Pharisees as a foil: disciples are called to 'superior' ethical conduct.

For Matthew, the Sermon is but one part of his attempt to set out the significance of the story and teaching of Jesus for the life of his own community.* In the Sermon and in the Gospel as a whole, grace and demand are linked inextricably. The Jesus of the Sermon is the Son of God through whom God is acting for mankind: it is his demanding teaching which is to be central in the life of the community and in its discipling of the nations.

See also **Beatitudes; Ethics (New Testament); Historical Jesus; Matthew, Gospel of.**

H. D. Betz, *Essays on the Sermon on the Mount*, 1985; R. A. Guelich, *The Sermon on the Mount: a Foundation for Understanding*, 1982; H. Hendrickx, *The Sermon on the Mount*, 1984; W. S. Kissinger, *The Sermon on the Mount: a History of Interpretation and Bibliography*, 1975; J. Lambrecht, *The Sermon on the Mount*, 1985; H. K. McArthur, *Understanding the Sermon on the Mount*, 1960; G. Strecker, *The Sermon on the Mount: an Exegetical Commentary*, 1988.

GRAHAM N. STANTON

Servant Songs

The phrase is a partial translation of the German *Ebed-Jahwe-Lieder* ('Songs of the Servant of Yahweh'), a title given by B. Duhm* in his commentary on the book of Isaiah (1892) to a group of passages in the second half of the book: 42.1–4; 49.1–6; 50.4–9; 52.13–53.12. (It should be noted that the phrase 'servant of Yahweh' itself does not occur in them: the phrases used are 'my servant' and 'his servant'.) Duhm's singling out of these passages as distinct from the rest of the book does not, however, rest on the occurrence of the word 'servant': the word occurs frequently elsewhere in the surrounding chapters, where it refers to the people of Israel as a whole in its relationship to Yahweh. Moreover, in one of the four passages (50.4–9) it does not occur at all. Duhm's hypothesis depends on the contents of these passages: on what they say about the figure depicted there. Despite the reference to Israel in 49.3, Duhm believed that they can only refer to a real individual. They must then belong to a distinct group of poems, perhaps originally more extensive, which describe the experiences of a faithful servant of Yahweh who had been chosen by him for a special mission and who had suffered and died, but who was expected to be vindicated after his death and triumphantly restored to life. These poems were originally unconnected with the rest of the material in the surrounding chapters. They were composed at a later date and had been subsequently inserted into it piecemeal. The 'servant' whom they portray was an otherwise unknown teacher of the Law who had died of leprosy.

Although it was not until 1892 that these poems were formally differentiated from their contexts and treated as a coherent group, the figure which they portray had evoked the special interest of commentators from very early times. The earliest interpretation of them is possibly to be found in the book of Isaiah itself, in the verses which immediately follow the first three: 42.5ff.; 49.7ff.; 50.10ff. Interpretations of the figure are also perhaps to be found in other OT texts such as Zech. 9.9; 12.10 and Dan. 12.3. In the NT the figure is interpreted christologically:* Acts 8.26–35 contains a specific exegesis* of Isa. 53.7–8, and there are echoes of a similar interpretation in Mark 10.45 and elsewhere.

During the history of both Jewish and Christian interpretation, the identity of the Servant has been very differently assessed. Since until recent times no idea of a separate group of 'Servant Songs' existed, it was possible to interpret the four passages individually in different ways. The references to Yahweh's servant in the first two did not appear to be different in kind from those in the rest of the book, especially in view of 49.3, where the phrase 'my servant, Israel' seems to preclude any interpretation other than a collective one. 50.4–9, where the word 'servant' does not occur, could similarly be held to refer to Israel. Throughout the history of interpretation, including the most recent period, it is ch. 53, with its detailed account of a sinless, persecuted man and its apparent reference to his suffering and death on behalf of others and his expected restoration to life, which was seen to have particular theological importance and to present special problems of interpretation.

Early Jewish exegesis* was varied. The identification of the Servant with Israel – represented, for example, by the Septuagint,* which reads 'my servant Jacob ... my chosen one, Israel' in 42.1 – was evidently thought by some exegetes to be unsatisfactory, because in ch. 53 the Servant is represented as guiltless. Consequently the figure was sometimes seen as a type of righteous persons in general, or

identified with particular individuals such as Moses.* More commonly, as, for example, in the Targum* of Jonathan, in ch. 53 the Servant is the messiah* who will inaugurate the kingdom of God.* This interpretation, however, raised a number of difficulties, especially that it implied a suffering and dying messiah. Later Jewish exegesis, for example that of the great mediaeval exegetes Rashi, Ibn Ezra and David Kimchi, tended more and more to interpret the poems collectively, perhaps in reaction to Christian exegesis. The view that the Servant is the people of Israel remained the standard Jewish interpretation until modern times. In contrast, the standard Christian view was that the Servant in these poems, especially in ch. 53, is the messiah: they predict the mission, life, sufferings and resurrection* of Jesus Christ.

The modern era of critical interpretation of these passages was signalled by the rejection by a number of Christian scholars towards the end of the eighteenth century of the ascription of the whole of the book of Isaiah to the eighth-century prophet. This accorded with the growing new perception of prophecy in relation to its historical setting rather than as part of a collection of authoritative scriptures. Those who accepted the notion of an exilic 'Deutero-Isaiah' as the author of chs 40–66 (subsequently modified by Duhm, who postulated a separate and later authorship for chs 56–66) began to interpret the chapters in a new way: no longer as the visionary predictions of a remote new age, but as the utterances of a sixth-century prophet addressed to the immediate situation of a community living in exile. Other interpretations of the Servant of Yahweh than the messianic one now became possible. Although the messianic theory still remained an option, though not necessarily with specific reference to Jesus, the prophet could equally have had in mind a figure from the past history of Israel, or a contemporary person, or a new Jewish leader shortly to appear on the scene. Variations of the collective theory also came under consideration. The new freedom to investigate the problem in all possible ways led in the nineteenth century to a plethora of alternative theories.

Duhm's commentary was epoch-making in that he defined quite precisely four passages in Deutero-Isaiah which formed a distinct group, and in which the figure of the Servant of Yahweh was sharply distinguished from that of the servant-Israel of the other chapters. In other respects his views had little following: neither his identification of the Servant as a leprous law-teacher, nor his judgment that the Songs are the work of a poet of later date whose theology is distinct from that of Deutero-Isaiah, was widely accepted. But his hypothesis of a sharply defined corpus of distinct 'Servant Songs' has been the inescapable starting-point of all subsequent discussion. The majority of later scholars – apart from those who have maintained the total identification of the Servant with Israel throughout the book and so questioned the existence of a separate group of 'Servant Songs' altogether – have accepted Duhm's delimitation of the Songs without argument. Of those who have disagreed, few have wished to reduce either their number or their compass: rather, they have tended to extend the first three beyond the limits postulated by Duhm, or to add new items to the collection, such as 50.10–11 or 61.1ff. In general, discussion has been mainly concerned with the problem of the Servant's identity and with the relationship of the Songs to their contexts in the body of the book.

No useful purpose would be served by a chronological survey of the history of the exegesis of the Servant Songs since Duhm. Widely divergent theories of the identity of the Servant have been held simultaneously throughout the period, some interpreters hesitating between the various possibilities: E. Sellin, for example, produced a series of works in which he identified the Servant in turn with Zerubbabel, Jehoiachin and Moses. A brief account of the main theories which have been proposed and of the objections which have been made to them will best illuminate the question.

From earliest times the main exegetical division has been between corporate, or collective, theories and individual ones. One of the advantages of the traditional corporate theory is its simplicity: the Servant of Yahweh is identical with the people of Israel – or, at least, with the body of exiles, whom Deutero-Isaiah addressed as Israel or Jacob – throughout the corpus of prophecies. This title is not confined to Isa. 40–55 but is applied to Israel elsewhere in the OT. The theory has strong support in the Songs themselves in 49.3, where, as elsewhere in Deutero-Isaiah, the double phrase 'my servant, Israel' occurs. In spite of this, serious objections have been raised against this identification. The Servant in the Songs is depicted as faithful and sinless, whereas elsewhere in Deutero-Isaiah, as in other prophetical books, Israel is condemned as faithless and sinful and as deserving its fate. Further, in 49.5–6 the Servant appears to be set apart from the nation: he is given a mission to bring the nation back to Yahweh. Attempts to circumvent these difficulties have been made by introducing qualifications and nuances: by identifying the Servant of the Songs with an 'ideal' Israel, with a faithful group within Israel, or the like; but there is no textual evidence to support such views, some of which seem oversubtle.

Theories which identify the Servant with a historical individual necessarily regard the word 'Israel' in 49.3 as a gloss. Since an identical gloss is actually found in the Septuagint text of 42.1, this possibility can by no means be ruled out. The Servant has been identified with Moses, Hezekiah, Isaiah, Jeremiah, Jehoiachin, Zerubbabel and other oustanding figures of Israel's past or of the exilic period. These identifications have been widely rejected on the grounds that what is known of these individuals does not fit sufficiently closely with what is said about the Servant in the Songs. Moreover, if the usual interpretation of ch. 53 is maintained, it would be necessary to suppose that the person in question, if already dead, was expected to be restored to life, a belief not usually thought to be as old as the sixth century BC. The same may be said of the view, recently put forward by a number of scholars, that the Servant of the Songs is the prophet 'Deutero-Isaiah' himself. However, the view that 53.8–12 does in fact speak of death and subsequent restoration to life has recently been challenged.

Several scholars have argued for a mythological* interpretation of the Servant: that is, that the poems use the mythology of a Near Eastern dying and rising god as a symbol* either of Israel's 'death and resurrection' (i.e. exile and restoration) or of the redemptive work of a quasi-messianic figure. However, some important features of the Songs, especially the vicarious suffering which is usually held to be a feature of ch. 53, can hardly be reconciled with the myths in question. Moreover, specialists in Near Eastern religions now regard the supposed evidence for such a myth as dubious. The likelihood of the myth's being known to Deutero-Isaiah and the plausibility of its influence on him have also been seriously questioned, and this type of theory appears to have been abandoned.

The messianic interpretation in its purely christological form – that is, the view that the primary function of the poems is to predict in some detail the life, atoning death and resurrection* of Jesus Christ from a standpoint several centuries earlier – depends on a view of the nature of scripture and of prophecy* which since the eighteenth century has been largely rejected by critical scholars. It must, however, be distinguished from 'messianic' theories expressed in purely OT terms, according to which the Servant is a wholly future figure comparable with, though probably distinct from, the future Davidic* king of other exilic and post-exilic prophecy.

The variety of interpretations of the figure of the Servant is so great that many have had to be omitted from this account. It should, however, be noted that according to some scholars the search for the precise identity of the Servant is misconceived: the figure is a composite one in which, for example, individual traits, prophetic, royal and priestly, have been fitted together to create a mysterious but imprecise image of a future Servant who is and yet is not the Israel of history, but who in some way embodies Deutero-Isaiah's confident message of imminent national redemption. It has been questioned whether the original recipients of this message would have been capable of decoding it; nevertheless, the fact that these poems have given rise to so many theologically and religiously significant interpretations should warn the exegete of the danger of too readily accepting oversimple solutions to the problem.

See also **Isaiah.**

J. Lindblom, *The Servant Songs in Deutero-Isaiah*, 1951; T. N. D. Mettinger, *A Farewell to the Servant Songs*, 1983; C. R. North, *The Servant Songs in Deutero-Isaiah*, 1948; H. M. Orlinsky and N. H. Snaith, *Studies in the Second Part of the Book of Isaiah*, ²1977; R. N. Whybray, *The Second Isaiah*, 1983.

R. N. WHYBRAY

Shekhinah

A central theological term in Judaism, used to denote God's 'abiding', 'indwelling', or 'presence' in the world. Though the term itself first appears in the Targums * and in early rabbinic * literature, the ideas associated with it (at least in classic rabbinic sources) are for the most part already found in the Bible. It does not mark a radical new theological development, but rather the drawing together of several different strands of biblical thinking.

The term is in origin exegetical,* being derived from certain verses (mostly in the P source in the Pentateuch*) where the verb *shakhan*, 'to dwell', occurs with God as subject. The P source describes God's presence among his people as an 'abiding' or 'indwelling'. In most cases the usage relates specifically to the divine presence in the sanctuary – the Tabernacle (= *ha-mishkan*, 'the dwelling-place [of God]' in P), or the Temple: e.g. Ex. 29.44f., 'I will sanctify the tent of meeting . . . and I will dwell (*ve-shakhanti*) among the children of Israel and I will be their God'. 'Shekhinah', a *nomen actionis* like *'akhilah* ('eating'), *shemirah* ('keeping') and *behirah* ('choosing'), originally denoted God's act of dwelling, or being present in the Tabernacle/Temple as described in Ex. 29.44f. and parallels. This primitive sense is reflected in the Targums which use *shekhinah* simply to paraphrase the verb *shakhan*: e.g. Targum Onqelos to Ex. 29.44f., 'I will sanctify the tent of meeting . . . and I will cause my Shekhinah

to reside among the children of Israel, and I will be their God.' This sort of paraphrase is typical of targumic style, so it is possible that the Aramaic translators actually coined the technical usage of the term. The rabbis frequently associate the Shekhinah with the sanctuary. The Tabernacle/Temple is referred to as 'the camp of the Shekhinah' (Tosefta Kelim, Bava Qamma 1.12) or 'the house of the Shekhinah' (Sifrei Zuta, Naso' 5.2). They often speak of the 'splendour' (*ziv*) or 'brightness' (*ma'or*) of the Shekhinah (e.g. Mekhilta de-Rabbi Ishmael, Ba-ḥodesh 5; Sifrei Numbers §41), and generally associate it with images of light. Behind this lies ultimately Temple symbolism: the visible sign of God's presence in the Tabernacle/Temple was the luminous cloud of glory which filled the sanctuary (Ex. 40.34–8; Num. 9.15–22; I Kings 8.11). The Shekhinah is closely related to the concept of the glory of God: it is, in effect, the divine glory as it manifested itself in the sanctuary. Exegetically the connection between the cloud of glory and the Shekhinah is easily made through Ex. 40.35, which states that the cloud 'abode' (*shakhan*) on the tent of meeting.

God's abiding with his people is the culmination of the covenant * between him and Israel: it is, therefore, a positive good which brings all manner of blessing. The term 'Shekhinah' does not simply state the objective fact that God is there, but that his presence is subjectively perceived by people: he is there for communion and blessing. Hence sin drives away the Shekhinah, whereas Torah-observance brings it near (cf. Isa. 59.2 with Sifrei Deuteronomy §173): 'Whoever is humble will cause the Shekhinah to dwell on earth [cf. Isa. 57.15] . . . but whoever is haughty brings about the defilement of the earth and the departure of the Shekhinah' (Mekhilta de-Rabbi Ishmael, Ba-ḥodesh 6; cf. Mishnah Pirqei 'Avot 3.2,6). The nearness and distance of the Shekhinah are sometimes represented graphically in concrete, spatial terms. Genesis Rabba 19.7 describes how the Shekhinah was driven up to the seventh heaven by successive sinful generations after the fall of Adam,* only to be brought back again to earth by successive righteous generations culminating with Moses.* In similar language, 'Avot de-Rabbi Nathan, A 34, describes the gradual departure of the Shekhinah from the Temple: it lingers near the Temple for a while hoping that Israel will repent, but finally withdraws to heaven. In these traditions there seems to be no hint of a generalized immanence of God in the world. The Shekhinah is God's numinous presence at a particular locality, as perceived by the righteous.

In keeping with the primitive sense of the

term some authorities assert that the She-khinah did not reside on earth till the Tabernacle was built (Tanḥuma, Naso' 16; Numbers Rabba 12.5). Others, however, speak of the Shekhinah in the context of theophanies prior to, or outside, the Tabernacle/Temple, e.g. Sinai (Targum Onqelos to Ex. 34.6; Exodus Rabba 3.1; Tanḥuma, Ki Tissa' 33) and the burning bush (Pesiqta de-Rav Kahana 1.2). An analogy may be implied: God was present in these places and on these occasions in the manner in which he was present in the sanctuary. This idea gives added force to the statement, 'If two sit together and occupy themselves with words of Torah, the Shekhinah abides in their midst' (Mishnah Pirqei 'Avot 3.2). The suggestion is that there is no need of a Temple to experience communion with God: God is with the righteous everywhere. There was speculation as to what happened to the Shekhinah when the first Temple was destroyed: according to some it returned to heaven (Pesiqta de-Rav Kahana 13.11; Lamentations Rabba, Proem 24; cf. Hos. 5.15); according to others (cf. Ezek. 11.23 and 43.2) it went into exile with the people. It travelled with them, as it had in the wilderness before they entered the Land (Mekhilta de-Rabbi Ishmael, Jethro 1), and remained in their midst even though they had no Temple (Mekhilta de-Rabbi Ishmael, Pisḥa 12,14; Sifrei Numbers §84; Babylonian Talmud* Megillah 29a). This line of thought leads inevitably to de-emphasizing the Temple as the exclusive locus of the divine presence. Some went so far as to claim that the Shekhinah was never present in the second Temple, or only intermittently, though others, apparently reacting to this view, insisted that not only was it present while that Temple stood, but even after the Temple's destruction it was still to be found there (Exodus Rabba 2.2; Midrash Psalms 11.3).

The concept of the Shekhinah as a localized numinous presence which can be experienced in different places leads to obvious theological difficulties. Babylonian Talmud* Sanhedrin 39a raises one of these: if the Shekhinah abides with any company of Jews who study Torah (cf. Mishnah Pirqei 'Avot 3.2,6), is there a plurality of Shekhinahs? The issue is serious, for if there is a multiplicity of divine presences, might there not be a multiplicity of gods? The doctrine of the Shekhinah could be pushed in the direction of paganism. Building on the biblical doctrine of a pervasive divine immanence in the world (cf. Jer. 23.24; Zech. 4.10; Ps. 139.7–10), the rabbis asserted that the Shekhinah, wherever experienced, is the presence of the one God who fills the world. There is no place in the world devoid of the Shekhinah (Pesiqta de-Rav Kahana 1.2); the

manifestation of the Shekhinah at one locality does not involve its diminution elsewhere (Canticles Rabba III 10 §1). They used various images to represent their understanding of the relationship between the generalized and localized presence of God. It is like a sea rising to fill a cave (Canticles Rabba III 10 §1), or the rays of the sun shining on a multiplicity of individuals at once (Babylonian Talmud Sanhedrin 39a). In one tradition the localized presence is depicted as a 'contraction' or 'concentration' (ṣimṣum) of the generalized presence (Pesiqta de-Rav Kahana 1.3; Genesis Rabba 4.4). None of these images or similes is, perhaps, of much use at a philosophical level, but they show that the rabbis were aware that there was a problem, and made some efforts to address it.

The second major theological problem is the relationship of the Shekhinah to God. This question arises even at the most primitive levels of the tradition. When Targum Onqelos paraphrases the biblical 'I [God] will dwell among the children of Israel' by 'I will cause my Shekhinah to reside among the children of Israel', some sort of distinction is certainly being drawn at a linguistic* level between God and the Shekhinah. The Targumic language reflects a linguistic distinction already found in the Bible, for Deuteronomy replaces the idea of God 'dwelling' in the sanctuary with the idea of him 'causing his name to dwell there' (Deut. 12.11; 14.23). What is the precise nature of this distinction between God and the Shekhinah? The issue has been much debated down to modern times. Saadia (*Beliefs and Opinions*, II 10) and Maimonides (*Guide of the Perplexed*, I 21) took the view that the Shekhinah is ontologically distinct from God, an entity which he created to mediate between himself and the world. Naḥmanides (*Commentary*, Gen. 46.1) attacked this position, arguing (correctly) that classic rabbinic sources clearly represent the Shekhinah as divine, as in some sense equivalent to God, and that this fact is clearly expressed in certain liturgical usages. He appears to see Shekhinah as simply a title for God. This line of thought has been taken up strongly by a number of modern writers, who maintain that what we have (certainly in the Targumic Shekhinah texts) is essentially a linguistic phenomenon, merely reverential language intended to avoid anthropomorphism.* A third position, favoured by certain Christian scholars, is to see the Shekhinah as a divine hypostasis, i.e. an aspect of the deity accorded a quasi-independent identity within the godhead. There is probably no single view which will apply in all contexts, simply because there is no unified doctrine of the Shekhinah, but rather a continuously developing tradition of theological speculation. All three views involve to some extent the application of alien categories to the rabbinic texts, and are marked by apologetic overtones. The first two are concerned to defend a certain view of the unity of God; the third appears at times to be prompted by the desire to find within Judaism forerunners or analogues to the Trinity.

There can be little doubt that in certain contexts the idea of the Shekhinah implies a dichotomy or bi-polarity within God. In two of these contexts the nature of that dichotomy is reasonably clear. 1. The Shekhinah occurs in contexts concerned with prophecy* or revelation.* When the prophets have a vision of God, what they are said to see is the Shekhinah (Deuteronomy Rabba 11.3). When they receive a verbal communication from God, it is the Shekhinah which communicates with them (Mekhilta de-Rabbi Ishmael, Pisḥa 1). The Shekhinah becomes in effect identified with the 'holy spirit' (ruaḥ ha-qodesh). Here the Shekhinah designates the revealed aspect of God, in contrast to his hidden aspect which is beyond all human comprehension. 2. According to one tradition 'primarily the Shekhinah dwells among the inhabitants of the earth' (Pesiqta de-Rav Kahana 1.1; Genesis Rabba 19.7), as opposed to being in heaven. Implied here is a dichotomy between God as immanent and God as transcendent: the Shekhinah represents God as immanent, and so strictly speaking is not appropriate to God in heaven. Certain texts do, of course, speak of the Shekhinah in heaven, but they are using the term in its other sense to denote the revealed aspect of God. The Shekhinah is the manifestation of God on the Throne of Glory (see **Merkabah Mysticism**) – it is the form of the glory – as perceived by the souls of the righteous (Babylonian Talmud Bava Batra 10a; Berakhot 17a), by the angels (Exodus Rabba 23.4) and by mystics who ascend to heaven (III Enoch 1.6; 18.19). The immanence/transcendence dichotomy rests on the dichotomy between earth and heaven: immanence belongs to earth, transcendence to heaven. The revealed/concealed dichotomy, however, applies both to earth and to heaven. In the early mystical texts (the so-called Heikhalot literature) the tendency emerges to restate the revealed/concealed dichotomy on the heavenly plane as an immanence/transcendence dichotomy. This may be seen in the speculations about the heavens above the seventh from which God descends to sit upon the Throne of Glory (III Enoch 48A.1; Massekhet Heikhalot 7).

The rich and suggestive rabbinic traditions on the Shekhinah were further developed in the Middle Ages, most notably by the Kabbalists. In the Kabbalah the Shekhinah unquestionably becomes a divine hypostasis which, as a result of Israel's sin or a primordial 'fall', goes into exile from the rest of the godhead. The Kabbalists were particularly taken with the thought that the Shekhinah accompanies Israel in exile, and they developed the notion that the Shekhinah suffers with Israel in exile. They also used the fact that 'Shekhinah' is grammatically feminine in Hebrew to introduce the idea that there is a feminine aspect to God. The Shekhinah is the Matrona, the Princess, the Queen, and the final reunification of God is portrayed, sometimes with explicit sexual imagery, as a sacred marriage (Zohar, 'Aḥarei Mot, III 77b).

See also **Jewish Exegesis.**

I. Abelson, *The Immanence of God in Rabbinical Literature*, 1912; A. Chester, *Divine Revelation and Divine Titles in the Pentateuchal Targumim*, 1986, pp. 313–22; R. Patai, *The Hebrew Goddess*, 1967, pp. 137–56; G. Scholem, *On the Kabbalah and Its Symbolism*, 1969; E. E. Urbach, *The Sages: Their Concepts and Beliefs*, 1987, pp. 37–65.

PHILIP S. ALEXANDER

Smith, W. Robertson

Arguably the greatest, certainly the most brilliant and original, of modern British OT and Semitic scholars, William Robertson Smith (1846–1894) was educated at home, at Aberdeen University, and at New College, Edinburgh, where his prodigious learning and abilities were already becoming apparent. The son of a Free Church of Scotland minister, he was appointed Professor of Hebrew and OT at the Church's Aberdeen college in 1870, in the same year being ordained.

Visits to Germany in 1867 and 1869 drew him into close contact with the thought of R. Rothe and of A. Ritschl (and, behind these, Schleiermacher's wrestling with the theological significance of Kant's epistemology) which profoundly influenced his own views. This influence (along with that of his great Edinburgh teacher, A. B. Davidson) is visible in student papers and professorial lectures (*Lectures and Essays*, 1912, pp. 97ff.) which display a passionate commitment, never relinquished, to marry living evangelical faith to historical criticism,* and which thus adumbrate themes crucial to Smith's later work: the personal and historical character of revelation* as rooted in living relationship with God, and the Bible as a record thereof rather than the infallible communication of doctrine; the consequent theological necessity of historical treatment of scripture to allow the modern to hear as did the original listeners, and to show the unfolding progress of revelation within 'the organic unity of all history' (p.

164), with Israelite prophecy* as of central importance, historical and religious, in the process leading to Christ; and the inability of criticism to detract from the fundamental, experienced reality of the believer's faith-relationship with God in Christ, with its priority over explicative theology (pp. 134–6, 222ff.): 'the church is not redeemed by its theology; it theologizes because it is redeemed' (p. 155). Smith saw the possibility of applying rigorous historical criticism, still virtually unknown or rejected as subversive of faith within most British churches, as the vital and providential tool in liberating a renewed sense of the historical-experiential nature of God's involvement with humanity as the real subject-matter of the Bible and for the mediating of which – seen in the light of the culmination of the process in encounter with Christ – it chiefly exists.

The protracted series of ecclesiastical hearings after the appearance of Smith's article 'Bible' (1875) and others in the *Encyclopaedia Britannica* (cf. A. L. Drummond, J. Bulloch, *The Church in Late Victorian Scotland 1874–1900*, 1978, pp. 40–78), which led to his dismissal from his chair in May 1881, engendered some of his finest work: apart from Smith's *Answer to the Form of Libel . . .* and *Additional Answer . . .* (both 1878), themselves eloquently stating the case for a critical view of the Pentateuch* while both denying the rationalistic nature and affirming the positive religious value of such investigation, there came *The Old Testament in the Jewish Church* (1881, ²1892) and *The Prophets of Israel* (1882, repr. 1895). These works, based on public lecture courses, state with a clarity and elegance never excelled in Britain, and with an influence perhaps rivalled only by S. R. Driver's *Introduction*, the reasons for adopting a nontraditional view of the OT close to that espoused by Smith's friend Wellhausen – and that, for Smith, within evangelical faith (cf. J. Rogerson, *Old Testament Criticism in the Nineteenth Century*, 1984, pp. 275–81).

In *OTJC* Smith argued again for the coherence of his position with the Reformers'* theological apprehension of the Bible as a living means of grace. He stressed the need for historical criticism to make scripture more real by its sketching of a 'living and consistent picture of the Old Dispensation', in that exegesis* so determined draws us to the 'human side' of God's converse with people: such interpretation thus allows us entry into 'the drama of Revelation' and points us to the inner work of the Holy Spirit. Then, after chapters analysing how the history of the OT text* and canon,* and of the Psalter, itself suggests the necessity of criticism, Smith moved to argue fervently for the reversal of the traditional

order Law-Prophets, and constructively to outline the positive significance of the shift which now gave historical (and theological) priority over the levitical legislation to the great prophets.*

This stress on the towering primacy of prophecy within the consistently unfolding divine disclosure exposed by criticism was developed in greater detail in *Prophets*. This was not the first British attempt at critical study of prophecy, but it was easily the most coherently persuasive and influential, linked as it was to a Wellhausenian reconstruction of Israel's religious history. Smith contends for the necessity of seeing the prophet as addressing his contemporaries in specific historical circumstances and plays down traditional 'predictive' understandings. The vivid analysis of the greatness of the eighth-century prophets is linked closely with their preceding the full Pentateuchal law and with their radical difference from the religion Israel shared with its Semitic environment. Prophecy is thus seen by Smith as history-related, as moral, personal, and rational: the great prophets are the crucial exemplars of that intimate experience of God which is seen as underlying the OT and as constituting its essential and normative organic relationship with NT religion (cf. Smith's preface to the ET of Wellhausen's *Prolegomena*, 1885, pp. viif.).

Before his early death Smith served as editor of the *Encyclopaedia Britannica*, as Reader and later Professor of Arabic at Cambridge, and as university librarian. This period saw the studies which mark out Smith as a pioneer in sociology* of religion: *Kinship and Marriage in Early Arabia* (1885) and *Lectures on the Religion of the Semites* (1889, ²1892, ³1927). Smith's emphasis on the social character of ancient Semitic religion, perhaps not unrelated to his much earlier Ritschlian stress on the social nature of faith and the church as redeemed community;* his argument for the priority of ritual over myth,* and the central importance of sacrifice as expressing the communion between the clan and its god, in relation to social organization – these views proved influential even where quite major aspects of his work (e.g. his use of theories of totemism, the postulated primacy of sacrifice as communion) came eventually to be rejected (cf. J. Rogerson, in *ET* XC, 1978/9, pp. 228–33).

Smith is here still quite evidently concerned to vindicate on a broader cultural canvas a generally Wellhausenian view of Israel's religious development, in seeing the full levitical system of P, focussed on sin and expiation, as late; though his social emphasis differentiates his position from Wellhausen's romanticist delineation of the 'naturalness' and 'spontaneity' of early religion. The argument for communion with the deity as primary in primitive Israelite (Semitic) religion, and as providing a thread of continuity through all the later changes, especially those due to prophecy, by which 'spiritual truth' was freed from the 'husk of material embodiment' (*RS*, p. 439), clearly carries theological value-judgments also, and returns full circle to Smith's earlier critical and theological emphases. For the postulated continuity opens out into that faith-communion with God, seen in scripture in fullest measure when it is cracked open by critical study, which Smith wished to commend.

Behind any particular criticism – say, of Smith's views of progressive revelation, his idealism, his (perhaps) too great emphasis on prophecy and ambiguous views of the relation of creative individuals to the community (though see W. McKane in *ZAW* XCIV, 1982, pp. 251–66) – his work, itself seen as an organic whole, raises questions still crucial for biblical interpretation. Smith was not simply attempting to unite his critical views with accepted Protestant 'orthodoxy': rather, he sought the establishing of what he regarded as a truly Reformed view of faith and scripture, by using historical criticism as a vehicle for theological criticism of 'the tradition' and implicitly of the Bible itself. And for all his quite deliberate and oft-criticized exclusion of ancient Mesopotamian material from consideration, Smith's magisterial exploration of the wider Semitic context and relatedness of Israel's religion, and his preliminary attention to their theological significance in terms of the nature and scope of divine engagement with humanity, with its bearing on biblical study and vice versa, remain relevant. His work makes clear that no simple causal relating or 'objective' separating of criticism and theology is possible. Evaluation of that work will be connected to the interpreter's own stance; how far necessarily and unavoidably is a question to which Smith's own achievement directs us.

T. O. Beidelman, *W. Robertson Smith and the Sociological Study of Religion*, 1974; J. S. Black and G. Chrystal, *The Life of William Robertson Smith*, 1912; R. A. Riesen, *Criticism and Faith in Late Victorian Scotland*, 1985.

EDWARD BALL

Sociology and Social Anthropology

It is sometimes difficult to distinguish between sociology and social anthropology. One way to describe the difference is to say that anthropology* deals with 'primitive' societies, while sociologists are mainly concerned wth the institutions of more 'advanced' nations. This is only partially true. The anthropologist Lucy Mair classifies social anthropology as a branch of sociology. She admits that anthropologists are largely concerned with 'peoples of simple technology', but sees the essential difference either in theory (anthropologists observe the totality of relationships between people within a social unit, whereas sociologists study specific institutions), or in technique (anthropologists go and live among the people they are studying rather than using techniques such as questionnaires). In British usage social anthropology is distinguished from ethnology, which is interested primarily in the past history of peoples without written records, and is thus closely related to archaeology.*

Until recently NT scholars were chiefly concerned with text,* exegesis* and theology, although most were classicists and related NT society to their knowledge of the Graeco-Roman world, while those working in the OT field were mainly influenced by evolutionary ideas of religion stemming from the early anthropologists, particularly James Frazer. Max Weber seems to have had less influence, despite his major work on ancient Israel. Today biblical scholars are more sensitive to current sociological and anthropological theory and apply the theory with more sophistication.

Before leaving questions of definition, it should be noted that the early anthropologists were keenly interested in folk-lore,* a subject which was also of interest to OT scholars such as Gunkel, and again it took a long time for clear distinctions to be made between the different disciplines.

With a few important exceptions, OT scholars have drawn their main inspiration from anthropology, while it is sociological theory that has been chiefly applied to the NT, so that it is convenient to treat the two Testaments separately.

J. W. Rogerson (*Anthropology and the Old Testament*, 1978) is critical of OT specialists, pointing out that few had any training in anthropology (a rare exception was S. H. Hooke) and so they made judgments about Israelite religion and social institutions on the basis of anthropological assumptions that were often outdated. He adds that it needs to be recognized that nineteenth-century OT study was pursued in the light of ideas that were widely accepted among the intelligentsia, and credit should perhaps be given to the early scholars for seeing the value of anthropological discovery, even if those observations and theories have subsequently been shown to be faulty.

The reason for utilizing both anthropology and sociology in the study of the Bible is much the same now as it was then. The biblical texts form only part of the literature of Israel and early Christianity and were collected into the canon for reasons of religion rather than a desire to conserve the history of the people or the early church. Modern scholars wish to learn about features of that society and culture which can only be glimpsed in fragmentary form in the texts that have survived. Sociological theory is seized upon as perhaps offering a way to fill the gaps in knowledge or to suggest fresh interpretations of the material which the Bible presents. It is here that the greatest danger of misunderstanding arises.

Broadly two approaches can be seen. The one adopted by the majority of the earlier scholars was to assume an evolutionary development of society and religion. Thus religion was supposed to have developed along a common pattern, from animism to monotheism by way of polydemonism and polytheism, and present-day 'primitive' societies were held up as examples of earlier stages in the process. A particularly striking example of the way this was done is *Hebrew Religion* by Oesterley and Robinson, in which isolated features in OT narratives are picked out as evidence of the earlier levels of 'semitic religion'. The widespread interpretation of sacrifice by means of totemism is another instance of this method of elucidating the biblical texts.

Later scholars have been more circumspect, although the same readiness to apply a theory directly to the biblical material often survives. OT specialists are now more aware of the difficulties involved in utilizing anthropological field studies: the differences between societies, the need to follow the most recent anthropological studies and not to work on the basis of outdated theory, and the very fragmentary nature of the biblical sources which allows too great scope for theorizing.

Undoubtedly the value of the contribution of anthropology to OT research has been very great. Many scholars have acknowledged their indebtedness to the work of anthropologists as inspiring them to look at the texts with fresh eyes: J. Pedersen from Grøbech, H. Wheeler Robinson and Aubrey R. Johnson from L. Lévy-Bruhl are obvious examples, though Johnson rejected the accusation that he imported Lévy-Bruhl's theories into the OT. But equally it has to be admitted that the influence of anthropology has also been baleful. Two instances have already been given: the belief in the universal evolution of religion and the alleged presence of totemism. It also needs to be remembered that many of the early anthropologists and sociologists were atheists. Frazer's *Golden Bough* and *Folk-Lore in the Old Testament* were deliberate attempts to show the falsehood of Christianity by im-

plication: if it was so similar to these uncouth rites and beliefs it could not be true. Only W. Robertson Smith,* among the circle of early anthropologists, retained his firm Christian faith up to his death, despite his treatment by the Free Church of Scotland. (There have been later Christian anthropologists, Evans-Pritchard being the most notable.) It is curious, therefore, that the early theories were accepted so uncritically by OT scholars, though this may be seen as evidence of their openness to what was regarded as the truth.

W. Robertson Smith's *The Religion of the Semites* (1889) is one of the most notable of the nineteenth-century works that made great use of the anthropological knowledge of the time. Evolutionary ideas, a wide reliance upon totemism, and the belief in original matrilineal clans are marks of the period of its origin. Robertson Smith's ideas had a wide influence, not only in biblical studies but also on Durkheim and Freud, although Evans-Pritchard says of his theory of sacrifice: 'Bluntly, all Robertson Smith really does is to guess about a period of Semitic history about which we know almost nothing.' The emphasis upon the very earliest periods of Semitic religion is also characteristic of the times.

Other ideas derived from anthropology which have been extremely influential and which have been criticized in recent years are 'corporate personality' (the idea that the ancient Israelites, as a 'primitive' people, made little distinction between the individual and the group and moved easily from the one to the other), and nomadism or 'semi-nomadism'. Corporate personality has been attacked from both a legal perspective and because of its reliance upon a supposed 'primitive mentality'. The social structures of ancient Israel and the other peoples of the Ancient Near East* are now seen to be far more complex than a simplistic transition from nomadic to settled ways of life suggested.

More recently the structuralist* theories of C. Lévi-Strauss have been more influential. Although he has not himself made a study of the OT, his analysis of myths* has been taken up by OT specialists. More directly Mary Douglas has applied broadly structuralist analyses to the OT lists of clean and unclean animals in Lev. 11 and Deut. 14, and her theory that unclean animals are those which are not 'proper' animals since they do not fit into the schema of Gen. 1 has been generally accepted with favour. Thus the lists are not completely arbitrary and meaningless, nor even prohibitions against foreign influence, but find their meaning in the holiness of God and a liturgical way of recognizing and worshipping him in his purity and oneness.

A feature of Mary Douglas' work which

has not been utilized as fully as it might is her discussion of the relation between primitive ideas of contagion and ethics, no doubt because her illustrations are taken from the Nuer and Bemba peoples of Africa and she does not refer to the OT in this section of her book *Purity and Danger* (1966). It would be valuable to see this worked out in relation to the way what to us are quite distinct ritual and moral laws are placed together in the law codes of the OT with no apparent attempt to distinguish between them. Mary Douglas suggests that two separate systems operate, contagion and ethical wrong-doing, and that there are ways in which the pollution system might buttress the moral code, although it rarely does because of the ambiguities of ethics. Moreover, since pollutions are more easily cancelled than moral defects, the pollution system can assist reconciliation between aggrieved parties.

Another professional anthropologist who wrote extensively on OT themes was Edmund Leach. His main work was on biblical myths, which he analyses from a structuralist perspective, holding that it is a mistake to look for history in the Bible and seeking rather to decode the text. OT scholars have criticized details of his handling of the material, and since structuralism itself is now being severely criticized, it may be questioned whether this approach is more than a passing phase in biblical interpetation. In one of his most recent writings Leach attempted to apply the theory of *rites de passage* to a number of biblical texts, including the baptism of Jesus and the call of the first apostles in Mark, the story of Moses* in Ex. 2–4, and the concept of the wilderness.

Finally, attempts to apply sociological theories to the OT must be considered. Here Max Weber's *Ancient Judaism* is outstanding. Weber's learning was prodigious. In his day he was fully abreast of current biblical study, and although there have been great advances in knowledge and research since his time, his mastery of the material remains impressive. In some ways it is a curious work. Intended as part of his comparative studies of the origins and development of capitalism that also included work on China and India, there is little explicit theory in the book, and it reads much like a history of Israelite social institutions. Its influence on OT studies has been less than might have been expected, although he introduced 'charismatic' into the vocabulary of biblical scholars. It must be doubted whether there is sufficient evidence ever to carry through Weber's project of tracing the interaction between society and ideas by means of historical studies.

In *When Prophecy Failed* (1979) Robert P. Carroll used the theory of 'cognitive dissonance',* proposed by Leon Festinger and others, to examine the problem of OT prophecies which were not fulfilled. Festinger himself saw the failure of the parousia* in the NT as a major instance of cognitive dissonance, but held that the evidence was too ambiguous to make an analysis possible. Carroll has detected in the prophetic books the responses which Festinger proposed, and offers a wide-ranging analysis, particularly of the reinterpretation of prophecy* in response to the failure of expectations.

Even more ambitious is Norman K. Gottwald's attempt in *The Tribes of Yahweh* (1979) to apply sociological and anthropological models to the early history of Israel.* His main theory of the occupation of Canaan, the 'peasant revolt' hypothesis, is questionable, but the wide-ranging discussion contains sociological interpretations of many subjects along the way, such as clan and tribe, city, nomadism, leadership, kinship systems, law,* ideology,* economic organization. Archaeological* discoveries are impressively combined with sociological theory and a study of biblical writings, yet doubt must remain as to the feasibility of any attempt to reconstruct historical events by utilizing sociological models in this way. Where contemporary written sources are lacking it is hazardous to assume that societies had to develop along particular lines drawn from sociological theory.

In the area of the NT two approaches need to be separated, although their proponents frequently appear unaware of precisely what they are attempting. Some scholars have applied particular theories to NT situations in much the same way as Carroll did in the OT. On the other hand there have been those who follow in the tradition of the older scholars who interpreted the early church from their knowledge of the surrounding Graeco-Roman society, examining the social structures of the communities* of the NT and the pressures exerted upon them. A subgroup of this second type utilizes explicit sociological concepts such as 'sect', 'millenarian* cult', 'class', 'role', and 'charismatic authority'. Both approaches have expanded into a massive literature and it is possible only to point to the main trends.

Research into the social history of the early church has produced the more solid and in many ways more satisfactory results. As early as 1908 Adolf Deissmann wrote *Licht vom Osten* (ET *Light from the Ancient East*, 1910, ²1927) and this led to a series of German and English studies of the social world of the first Christians, among which the work of Shirley J. Case and Frederick Grant is notable. In more recent years a series of massively documented studies by Martin Hengel has followed similar lines, Hengel himself being particularly interested in problems of Jesus and the Zealot movement and relations of power in N T times. Work by Abraham Malherbe and Robert Grant can also be included under this head. Several of these scholars utilize sociological concepts and theory, particularly that of Max Weber, whose breadth of understanding makes his writings particularly amenable to research in N T society.

One of the most important books within this category is Wayne A. Meeks' *The First Urban Christians* (1983). Its value lies both in the picture of 'The Social World of St Paul* which is presented, and in the careful way in which Meeks uses sociological ideas. Thus he is unwilling to transfer terms like 'middle class' directly to the first century, but rather examines ways in which stratification can be measured, correctly restricts 'social class' to distinctions derived from economic factors, and picks up the concept of 'status' from the work of Lipset. Throughout the whole book general studies of the Graeco-Roman world form the basis of the interpretation of the first Christian communities.

Turning to studies which attempt to apply specific sociological theories to N T issues, the most significant of the earlier works is John G. Gager's *Kingdom and Community* (1975). Gager utilizes theories of millenarian movements, cognitive dissonance, and the functions of social conflict. In his discussion of cognitive dissonance he modifies Festinger's original theory, partly in the light of other sociological studies, and applies it to conversion, and in particular to Paul's conversion. His main aim is to explain the missionary activity of early Christianity and its polemic against Judaism and paganism. Other chapters in the book belong more correctly to the social history category, although the influence of Weber is pervasive throughout.

A second major writer in this area is Gerd Theissen, who combines sociological insights with psychological theory. Thus in *The First Followers of Jesus* (1978; US title *The Sociology of Early Palestinian Christianity*) he not only picks up theoretical concepts from sociologists, in particular from Weber, but also leans heavily upon Freudian psychology. In a later book, *Psychological Aspects of Pauline Theology* (1987), he applies psychological theories to a number of texts from Paul's letters.

Beside these studies of the social setting and character of the early Christian communities there have been attempts to examine the thought of the N T writings by applying the sociology of knowledge, the theory that human perception and interpretation are dependent upon social factors. Meeks contributed an important article, 'The Man from Heaven in Johannine Sectarianism', in which he rejects Bultmann's* theory of a Gnostic* myth and attempts to relate the Johannine language about Jesus to the Johannine community* which had been expelled from the synagogue and needed a new 'symbolic universe' to give it legitimacy. Thus he is concerned with the social function of theology. Philip Esler attempts a similar exercise in his examination of the Lucan writings, in a book which is notable for the very valuable discussion of the application of the social sciences to the N T (*Community and Gospel in Luke–Acts*, 1987).

Finally mention must be made of avowedly Marxist* interpretations of the Bible. The first major attempt to interpret the rise of Christianity entirely from a Marxist perspective was Karl Kautsky's *Foundations of Christianity* (1925). Milan Machovec recognizes that this is a Marxist classic, but has considerable reservations about the way the methodology is applied. His own work (*A Marxist Looks at Jesus*, ET 1976) is one of the most important recent studies of the life of Jesus. Marxist interpretation is a component of liberation theology,* although it would be wrong to regard liberation theology as simply Marxist. An example of such writings is George V. Pixley's *God's Kingdom* (1981), in which he interprets the kingdom in both Testaments in economic terms, the Jesus movement being one of several responses to the oppression of the peasants in Palestine in the first century. In a sense we are all Marxists today, for we are aware as never before of the economic basis of social movements and intellectual thought, even though we may adopt a more Weberian approach to the relation between ideas and society.

It is unquestionable that the application of anthropological and sociological theory has played a highly significant part in the development of biblical studies. Hardly any work in the O T field is uninfluenced by such assumptions, even where they have remained unacknowledged and perhaps unrecognized. Within N T scholarship it has also been of considerable importance, although not perhaps to the same extent until very recently, despite a general awareness of the social background to the early church and more direct studies of that background in the first half of the present century. What is apparent in the last twenty or thirty years is a greater self-consciousness about what is being attempted and the adoption of a more critical stance.

The following criticisms have been made:

1. There is the charge of reductionism. If sociological explanations of the rise and development of Christianity and Christian doctrine can be given, it is easy to conclude that

this is the total cause of the movement and its 'truth' may seem to be in jeopardy. Most biblical scholars accept this and guard against it.

2. The paucity and fragmentary nature of the evidence within the canonical writings and the difficulty in relating extra-canonical material to the biblical sources mean that it is impossible to test the anthropological or sociological theories for validity. This makes all historical study suspect, but applies particularly where sociological theories are assumed to be true and are then used to fill in gaps within the biblical evidence.

3. Much theory is special to the society for which it is propounded. The same is true of sociological models. Care must therefore be taken to avoid a simple transfer of theory or models that have been devised within the setting of modern society to biblical societies. General theory may escape this limitation, but it suffers from the high level of abstraction at which it operates.

4. There is a danger of producing circular arguments. The texts are used to construct the society in which they were created, and then that reconstruction provides the basis for an interpretation of the texts. Most scholars are aware of this danger, but few completely avoid it.

5. There is always a time gap between scholarly disciplines. Thus there is the danger that biblical scholars will be working with outmoded or discredited anthropological or sociological theory. (It should be remembered, of course, that this works in reverse. The published papers from a conference which aimed at combining biblical, theological and anthropological approaches to the study of sacrifice reveal that some of the biblical scholars knew more about anthropology than the anthropologists did about recent biblical research.)

Of these 2. is the most dangerous and the most intractable. All the other difficulties can be overcome with sufficient caution, but there is no escape from the limits presented by the biblical evidence and there is an all too ready encouragement to turn to anthropology or sociology to supply a means of filling out the picture. Empirical testing of the theories or models is impossible. It is of the utmost importance, therefore, to search out every bit of evidence from the ancient world and the surrounding cultures before assuming that theories derived from the social sciences can supply what is lacking. Even the comparative method upon which Weber laid so great store is a very imperfect instrument for sorting out truth from falsehood. How great this danger is can be seen from the fact that it is commonly the periods of Israelite history for which there is the least firm historical evidence

that are subjected to sociological or anthropological analysis.

See also **Community; Ethos.**

CYRIL S. RODD

Son of Man

Son of Man is a frequent and familiar phrase in the Gospels.* To most people it represents Jesus in his humanity, sharing in the hardships and sorrows of the human lot. But the phrase also occurs in sayings of Jesus which refer to his future glory, and from this point of view it is natural to take it to mean his glorified humanity. These general impressions, however, do not find confirmation from close study of the actual use of the phrase. Difficult problems emerge, which have exercised the minds of scholars for the past century, and still no agreed solution has been reached.

Behind the usage in the Gospels there is the use of 'son of man' in Hebrew and Aramaic, and this will be investigated first. The data include the influential vision of Dan. 7.13f, in which 'one like a son of man' is brought before the Ancient of Days and receives royal dominion. Later references to this vision identify this figure with the messiah.* It has thus been conjectured that 'the Son of Man' was a recognized title of the messiah in NT times which Jesus adopted to make a messianic claim, though other evidence suggests that he did not openly claim to be the messiah.

One solution to this problem is that when Jesus spoke of the future Son of Man (e.g. Matt. 25.31) he was not referring to his own destiny but to the messiah as one other than himself. On this view sayings of Jesus in which the Son of Man functions as a self-reference are inauthentic, or result from adaptation within the Christian community.

The self-reference sayings can be classified under two headings: present sayings, in which Jesus refers to himself in relation to his public ministry (e.g. Matt. 8.20), and passion* sayings, in which he predicts his crucifixion and resurrection* (e.g. Mark 8.31). In some of these at least 'son of man' functions according to Aramaic idiom, so that it is difficult to argue that none is authentic. Indeed some scholars hold that these sayings preserve the true tradition of Jesus' use of 'son of man', and that the 'future' sayings are products of the Christian community* in the light of the proclamation of the resurrection and exaltation of Jesus as messiah in heaven. On this view there can be no suggestion that the 'future' sayings refer to someone other than Jesus.

Many scholars attempt to retain an authentic nucleus of all three classes of 'Son of Man' sayings. The 'future' sayings thus attest Jesus' understanding of his own destiny, which is also implicit in a different way in the 'present' and 'passion' sayings. This is at first sight the most attractive solution, but it will be shown below to encounter serious difficulties.

One difficulty is that, if Jesus used 'Son of Man' as a messianic title, it is astonishing to find that with one exception (Acts 7.56) it is never used as such in the NT other than in sayings of Jesus (or references to them). It has been suggested that its use as a title rapidly ceased after the church expanded into the Gentile world, because it was not meaningful outside Judaism. On the other hand it is claimed that it has left a trace in Paul's* Adam* typology* (Rom. 5.12–21; I Cor. 15.21f, 46–47). This observation generally forms part of a larger theory that behind the vision of Dan. 7.13f. and later allusions to it there was a myth,* derived from Zoroastrian influence of the primal man who holds the destiny of all mankind. In any case the question remains why, if some classes of Son of Man sayings are not authentic, the phrase was introduced into sayings attributed to Jesus at a time when it was dropping out of use in general because it was felt to be incomprehensible.

*The Old Testament and pseudepigrapha.** In the OT the usual Hebrew phrase for son of man is *ben adam*. In the Aramaic portions of the OT the singular *bar enash* occurs once only (Dan. 7.13) and the plural twice. Basically the phrase in both languages is a typical Semitic locution denoting a member of a class, i.e. a human being (Num. 23.19). The plural denotes human beings without regard to gender (Gen. 11.5). The singular is often collective, referring to humanity in general (Ps. 8.4).

There is a notable use in Ezekiel, where 'Son of Man' is a designation of the prophet, always in address by God himself (93 times). This has been thought to imply a special meaning whereby God characterizes Ezekiel as a spokesman to the people or as a representative of the people. However, in the Hebrew sections of Daniel there is an exactly parallel usage in 8.17, where Daniel is addressed by an angel as 'Son of Man'. In both cases it is simply the address of a heavenly being to an earthly being, the opposite of the address 'Lord'. The suggestion of a special meaning arises from misunderstanding of the function of the phrase in Ezekiel.

In Dan. 7.13 (Aramaic) the phrase is 'one like a son of man', and it is not clear whether this means a symbolic* man, like the symbolic beasts representing the nations in the earlier part of the vision, or an angel in human form. The latter is supported by Dan. 8.15 (Hebrew) where one like 'the appearance of a man' is the angel Gabriel. If an angel is intended, it would probably be Michael, who represents the Jews in the heavenly court (12.1). There may

be a reflection of ancient Canaanite mythology in which the young warrior-god Baal gains power from the aged father-god El, but if so, this has been transmuted into new categories of thought concerning the heavenly world. As the text stands the Son of Man certainly represents the loyal Jews in the crisis of the Maccabean revolt. If he is not an angel, he might be intended to be a symbolic figure representing them collectively, and this is suggested by 7.18, 27, where the people receive the kingdom.* Alternatively he might be the future messiah as their leader.

There are only a few references to the Daniel vision in the intertestamental literature, but the Son of Man figure is clearly understood as the messiah. The vision is taken as the model for the setting up of the celestial kingdom in the Similitudes of Enoch (I Enoch 37–71), which is a special development of the Enoch literature, perhaps written in the second half of the first century AD. In 46.1 Enoch sees God 'and with him another, whose face had the appearance of a man', and thereafter he is referred to as 'that Son of Man', and clearly identified with the messiah or 'Chosen One'. The vision of Dan. 7.13 is also the basis of two visions in II (4) Esdras, composed around the end of the first century AD. II Esd. 11–12 is a development of the description of the beasts in Dan. 7.1–12, and the messiah (represented as a lion) performs the judgment on them. Then II Esd. 13 is concerned with 'the figure of a man', who is identified with the messiah and has the same function. It is also noteworthy that R. Akiba (d. AD 135) is recorded as claiming that the plural 'thrones' in Dan. 7.9 means one for God and one for David,* i.e. the messiah (b. *Hagigah* 14 a).

From these references it has been generally supposed in modern scholarship that Son of Man was used as a title for the celestial messiah in apocalyptic* circles in the time of Christ. This is disputed, however, on linguistic grounds. In I Enoch 46–71, which survives only in Ethiopic, it is probable that the original, presumably Aramaic, text had son of man, but it is usually in the form 'that son of man', i.e. the man of the vision of ch. 46. This differs from the clearly titular form of 'the Chosen One', and reflects the tendency in Aramaic to use son of man generally as 'a man'. In II Esd. 13 the Latin version (derived from a lost Greek version) does not use son of man, and it is probable that the original Hebrew simply had *adam* in spite of the use of son of man in the Syriac* version, which develops further the Aramaic usage. In both cases it has been suggested that the designation is due to Christian influence, perhaps based on the usage in Matthew. If so, it would make I Enoch and II Esdras irrelevant to consideration of the Jewish background* to Son of Man.

The Bible does not speak of a celestial messiah as opposed to the earthly messiah, but in these and other apocalyptic books the idea of the messiah is transferred from the notion of the coming earthly ruler to that of a heavenly agent in the divine judgment (cf. II Esd. 12.31–34; 13.32–38). Some scholars have suggested that this form of messianism is derived from a myth of the primal man who is to appear at the end of the age, derived from Zoroastrian influence, which has left traces in Paul's Adam typology (see above). On this view the Son of Man belongs to an esoteric brand of Judaism which existed alongside the popular ideas of the Davidic messiah, and was available to the church in its task of understanding the significance of Jesus. Theories of this kind are highly speculative. Even if such a myth was current among some Jews in NT times, it still has to be demonstrated that it was sufficiently popular to be known to Jesus' audience. Moreover it depends on the claim that the phrase 'Son of Man' was a current title for this mythological figure, and would be recognized as such when Jesus used it.

Jesus and the Son of Man. To determine the significance of Jesus' use of 'Son of Man' two fundamental points must be borne in mind. First, the 'Son of Man' functions as a self-reference in the majority of sayings, and is probably intended to do so in them all. Second, Jesus never explains the phrase, and it must be assumed that its meaning was available to his hearers from normal currency.

The use of 'Son of Man' as a self-reference is most easily explained from Aramaic usage, in which 'son of man' commonly means just 'a man'. By using it instead of the first person the speaker can refer to himself in an oblique or ironical manner. This is characteristic of the 'present' sayings. Significantly, several of them touch on the identity of Jesus, e.g. Matt. 11.19 = Luke 7.34, where Jesus compares the reception accorded to John the Baptist,* popularly regarded as a prophet,* with the reception accorded to himself. If the 'passion' sayings have an authentic nucleus, Jesus is likely to have preferred this oblique way of speaking to express his awareness of the danger to his life: one must face the possibility of death (cf. Mark 8.31). Many people sense a difficulty here, because Jesus never says 'a son of man' but always 'the Son of Man' (John 5.27 is only an apparent exception). The difficulty can be resolved by observing the idiomatic usage of the article in Aramaic, though it is claimed that in fact the two forms were used without strict discrimination. A further problem is that this attractive explanation of the

'present' and 'passion' sayings cannot be applied to the 'future' sayings, which presuppose the identification of the Son of Man with the figure of Dan. 7.13.

Some scholars have suggested that Jesus adopted the son of man from Ezekiel as a title for himself in his prophetic and representative role. But it has been shown above that this view depends on a misunderstanding of the usage in Ezekiel. Moreover son of man is far too common a phrase in Aramaic for Jesus' hearers to have picked up the allusion, if this is what he intended.

The theory that the 'Son of Man' is a messianic title in the sayings of Jesus rests on the supposition that it was already current in this sense, either as a result of the influence of Dan. 7.13 or from wider use as suggested above. If so, it would have been possible for Jesus to use it in reference to the messiah as someone other than himself. This could be the case in many of the 'future' sayings (e.g. Mark 13.26). It has been supported from Luke 12.8f., where Jesus speaks in the first person of his present position ('everyone who acknowledges me before men'), but changes to Son of Man when referring to the future ('the Son of Man also will acknowledge before the angels of God'). A probably independent version of the same saying in Mark 8.38 adds detail from Daniel 7 in the second part. But the parallel in Matt. 10.32f. maintains the first person in both parts of the saying. However the use of Son of Man for an oblique self-reference suggests that the original intention was more subtle and ironical: 'Every one who acknowledges me before men, *someone* will acknowledge before the angels of God', i.e. he will have an advocate at the divine tribunal, not so much the person of Jesus (though that is not excluded) but the fact that his response to Jesus now will itself be decisive then. If this is the correct interpretation of the saying, it does not require either the theory that the Son of Man was a current title of the messiah or the claim that Jesus used it in reference to an apocalyptic figure other than himself.

The Danielic features found in many of the 'future' sayings lie behind what is probably the most widely held view, that the consistent use of 'Son of Man' in the Jesus tradition is in all cases a direct reference to the figure in Dan. 7.13. This would be comparable to the references to 'that Son of Man,' in I Enoch 46–71. On this view, whenever Jesus used the phrase he was referring to himself as the one destined to fulfil this future role. There are, however, serious difficulties in this position. It means that every Son of Man saying involves a messianic claim, which runs counter to the evidence that Jesus was extremely reticent about his personal position. This remains true, even if it is held that his audience was aware of a distinction between the earthly messiah, which Jesus did not claim to be, and the celestial messiah of the future. But it is really very doubtful if the Son of Man phrase could be interpreted in this way by his listeners unless Jesus also mentioned other Danielic features, because *bar enasha* is too common in Aramaic to suggest this on its own. This also makes it difficult to accommodate the 'present' and 'passion' sayings under this heading without importing further considerations. In the 'present' sayings it is suggested that Jesus used the 'Son of Man' to emphasize his mere humanity or his solidarity with humanity in view of the representative position of the Son of Man in Dan. 7 as leader of the loyal Jews. In the 'passion' predictions it is suggested that, though the description in Daniel does not mention the suffering of the Son of Man, his position as representative of the suffering Jews could be taken to imply this, so that suffering was regarded by Jesus as part of the destiny of the Son of Man.

In the present state of research there are two main positions, and neither has yet emerged as the victor in the debate. There are those who regard the reference to Dan. 7.13 as primary. This position does not necessarily entail the wider speculations about the mythological background, or the view that the Son of Man was not Jesus himself. But it has its own difficulties, and makes the loss of the title from the rest of the NT hard to explain. The second main position starts from the Aramaic usage of Son of Man, which makes a reasonable interpretation of the 'present' and 'passion' sayings possible, but creates difficulties for the 'future' sayings. On this view these sayings are best attributed to the use of the sayings of Jesus for christology, in which the Son of Man phrase, already established as a style-feature of Jesus, is correlated with Dan. 7.13 to produce new sayings which support the proclamation of Jesus as the risen and glorified messiah. This does not require the use of Son of Man as a messianic title outside the sayings tradition.

The New Testament and Apostolic Fathers. Whichever of these two positions is adopted, very few scholars maintain that all the Son of Man sayings in the Gospels are authentic. On the other hand, some have denied that any are authentic. This is unlikely, because the frequency of Son of Man sayings in the Gospels and their absence from the rest of the NT indicates that the use of Son of Man as a self-reference was recognized as a striking and unusual style-feature of Jesus' diction. This explains the development of Son of Man exclusively in the sayings tradition. The creation of Son of Man sayings tends to reflect develop-

ments of christology* which are expressed without the Son of Man designation outside the Gospels. From this point of view, each of the four evangelists* has his own special emphasis, whether we think of him as creating fresh sayings by expansion of the tradition or as making a selection from traditional sources. Matthew multiplies Son of Man sayings in relation to judgment scenes. It is notable that in Matt. 16.28 he substitutes 'Son of Man' for 'kingdom of God' in Mark 9.1. Mark has a series of 'future' sayings based on Daniel to express the authority of Jesus (Mark 8.38; 13.26; 14.62). Luke's special sayings convey the humanity of Jesus and suggest his future position as advocate in the judgment (Luke 18.8; 19.10; 21.36; Acts 7.56). John has a theological use, based primarily on the tradition of the 'passion' sayings. 'Son of Man' is his designation for Jesus as one whose actions on earth reveal the truth of his heavenly glory, especially the cross (John 1.51; 3.14; 8.28; 12.34).

John shows that, when attention is drawn to the issue of Jesus' humanity and divinity, Son of Man tends to be taken as a way of referring to his humanity. The only other occurrences of Son of Man in the NT are neutral. Heb. 2.6 quotes Ps. 8.5, where Son of Man is collective, and applies it to Jesus in his humanity. Dan. 7.13 is referred to in descriptions of the glorified Christ in Rev. 1.13; 14.14, but in both cases the reference is to one like a human being, as in the original text, and the phrase does not function as a messianic title.

In the early Christian literature the reference is always to the humanity of Jesus. Ignatius, *Eph.* 20.2, refers to him as 'the Son of Man and Son of God' in a credal* passage. Barnabas 12.10, in a different kind of context, speaks of him as 'not a [mere] Son of Man but Son of God'. In the Gospel of Thomas Son of Man occurs only in a close parallel to Matt. 8.20, one of the 'present' sayings (logion 86). It is left to later theology to combine the present and future aspects in the idea of the glorified humanity of Jesus God and man.

See also **Apocalyptic; Christology, New Testament; Daniel; Kingdom of God.**

P. M. Casey, *Son of Man*, 1979; A. J. B. Higgins, *The Son of Man in the Teaching of Jesus*, 1980; M. D. Hooker, *The Son of Man in Mark*, 1967; B. Lindars, *Jesus Son of Man*, 1983; N. Perrin, *A Modern Pilgrimage in New Testament Christology*, 1974; H. E. Tödt, *The Son of Man in the Synoptic Tradition*, 1965.

BARNABAS LINDARS, SSF

Song of Songs

If this series of love poems appeared in any other ancient or modern publication, it would be hailed as a masterpiece without raising further problems. However, the exegesis* of them can never be divorced from the scriptural context. The poems seem to be secular and belong to the world of human emotions, but they have reached us in many translations only because they are found in the scroll of the Writings* in the OT. Hence these love lyrics answer to many different claims, both secular and sacred. The contemporary approach is in danger of neglecting the revelatory* and transcendent substance which Rabbi Akiba stressed by stating 'the whole world is not worth the day on which the Song of Songs was given to Israel ... the Song of Songs is the Holy of Holies'.

Taken at this mystical* level of interpretation the Song is 'given' and not contrived. It is uttered by 'The King whose is the Peace' (Solomon) on behalf of the whole creation through Israel, communicating in words the gestures of inexpressible Love. The lovers' bodies give voice to, and thereby sight of, the intense devotion which enables human beings to attain to an eternal felicity. Death and the underworld are confronted and vanquished by the Lord's flash of fire which no flood can extinguish. This cosmic element (8.6f.) pertains to the most intimate and personal drama of courtship with its changing fortunes of losing, seeking and finding the beloved. God does not, and need not, figure in these verses, for here is not a presentation of a pagan marriage, but rather the immanent presence of the transcendental Beauty and Perfection. Bride and bridegroom articulate a spiritual dialectic which is seen to become seminal and authoritative in Jewish and Christian literature. Far from interpreting the erotic glory in an enfeebled allegory,* the genius of mankind evokes metaphors* and symbols* which extend the understanding of Love in terms of darkness, wonder, and fulfilling union. The aim of mystical exegetes is to enter the garden, to pluck the myrrh, to eat the honey, to eat and to drink, to be drunk with love.

European poetry responds to, develops, and even parodies the Song in form and in content. Monologues, dialogues and choruses set a pattern, as now printed in the Jerusalem Bible with a bold lack of authority. The contexts, themes and motifs reappear whenever poets imagine the countryside with its cultivated fields and vineyards as well as its untamed wildness. The city streets are watched by guards and peopled with women, the daughters of Jerusalem. Animals and birds, shrubs, flowers and herbs, can be identified; the reader may note new dictionary entries from Israeli scholarship. But the major themes remain constant, such as self-discovery in longing, through passionate desire, and the huge scale

of love from mating to the final consummation and peace.

Goethe may speak for all major poets when he declares the Song to be the measure of perfection (to Eckermann on 18 January 1825). He characterized the Song as the most tender and inimitable expression of passionate yet graceful love. More particularly, the force of metaphor and analogy has left a lasting legacy for love lyricism. Love itself cannot be portrayed or defined; hence our praises and plaints depend upon comparisons. Dawn, sun, stars, the moon as well as the dove and the lotus flowers, the heaped grain, the gazelles, belong to the tradition of ambiguous and evocative images which go beyond merely illustrating the power and the beauty of the giving and receiving of love. The absence of structured progress or plotting, and the freedom of the composition, constitute no liability but rather an asset to contemporary exegesis. For example, the enigmatic 'Catch the little foxes' poem can be taken out of the context (2.15) or may be connected with the pair of lovers, whose bed is mentioned before. These spoilers of the vineyard may echo the lines of Theocritus ('A plague on the foxes') or hallucinogenic mushrooms (Robert Graves in 1960). But equally well, the Jewish allegorists may detect here reference to the Amalekites or later enemies of Israel, while Christian interpreters condemn violations of monastic rules and offences against the Lord of the vineyard. Herder* cited the unhappy consequences of illicit love, while most moderns refer to traces of a fertility rite.

In his outstanding commentary,* Pope does full justice to the varieties and ambiguities which the text evokes. He gives a systematic survey throughout, beginning with the rabbinical* and midrashic* renderings and additions, followed by Christian patristic and mediaeval* (St Bernard and others) voices and modern comparative data. For example, the famous 'I am black and beautiful' (1.5) opens a huge perspective of hermeneutical* complexities. Not only is there the question of affirmation or antithesis ('black and/but beautiful'), noted by all translators,* but a look at all the black goddesses of Europe and Asia. In this connection Pope also makes us realize the amazing silence about the Song in the NT and the gradual appropriation of the girl as the Lady who soon becomes either the Virgin Mother of God or the Una Sancta Ecclesia. Landy in his remarkably original work takes the reader into the whole paradox of Paradise with its relationship of the lovers and the enigma of beauty. He deals with this 'mosaic of fragmented stories' not only in a historical framework but with Jungian and other categories of understanding.

The hermeneutical problem inescapably raises a host of post-structural* possibilities. One may proceed as if the text, and the text alone, hit our eyes and ears, irrespective of background material and possibly linking exclusively with our own world of passion, concubinage, pornography, disenchantment, in short with the erotic and sexual revolution of a post-biblical age. Or one may once again soberly re-examine the cultural background to the Song, even if its dating and exact locality remain uncertain. Love songs from ancient Egypt, Syria and Mesopotamia and cultic* texts which celebrate the sacred marriage as well as the ordinary *wasf* (Arabic love songs in praise of bride and groom) still remain a potent weapon in the kind of biblical criticism* common since the turn of this century. But archaeology* is not enough in itself, though the finds in the museums cannot be ignored in elucidating the text.

The major thrust of these poems in the moral and the theological sense is often ignored. It is generally held that they are not concerned with monogamous marriage and life-long fidelity. Yet the plea 'Set me as a seal upon thine heart' (8.6) at least raises the question of abiding love, and therefore the painful issue of the tragic slipping away of passionate belonging through death or sin. The Song simply does not contrast Eros and Agape and challenges the exegete to distinguish between appearance and reality. The drama of Romeo and Juliet takes up the theme which may, but need not, end in the blackness of Troilus and Cressida. It is at this highest level that the Song must be understood and interpreted.

See also **Mediaeval Interpretation; Mysticism; Poetry, Hebrew.**

Marcia Falk, *Love Lyrics from the Bible*, 1982; Francis Landy, *Paradoxes of Paradise*, 1983; Marvin H. Pope, *Song of Songs*, 1977.

ULRICH SIMON

Soteriology

Soteriology is concerned with understanding salvation. Christian thinking about this subject has always had a close relationship with biblical exegesis,* since the biblical tradition is the primary source of such ideas. This is not to say that non-biblical aspirations have not contributed; indeed they often have, but usually as a means of interpreting biblical ideas.

To save is to rescue. So the question underlying soteriology is: what do we need to be rescued from? Stories from the OT imply a number of 'this-worldly' answers: the Israelites were saved from slavery in Egypt;* then the people needed salvation from sickness, from their enemies, from death. Within Christian tradition these ideas became symbolic* of the

need for a more spiritual salvation. We need salvation from slavery to the powers of evil, from the devil and his angels, from the sickness of sin and ignorance, and from eternal death, or eternal punishment. The Promised Land was projected into the heavens.

This development was undoubtedly provoked by Christian reflection on the life, death and resurrection* of Jesus. In the earliest Christian writings outside the NT, Jesus is presented as the teacher who communicates the way of life, and the characteristics of this way are contrasted with those of the way of death. Martyrs wanted to follow him through death to life. The eucharist was the 'medicine of immortality' (Ignatius). Salvation was focussed on the future, but depended upon how one lived in the here and now, and on one's response to the saving work of Christ.

The patristic literature shows how these basic ideas were expressed in a very rich language drawn from the Bible: Origen,* Athanasius, Gregory of Nazianzus and many others provide examples of how the 'names of Jesus' were collected from all over the scriptures, the OT as well as the NT, since prophetically,* if not actually, all scripture spoke of Christ. Christ is Wisdom, Word, Life, Truth, Son of God, Sun of Righteousness, Saviour, Propitiation, Light of the World, First-born of the Dead, Shepherd, Physician, Healer, Redemption, Resurrection, the Way, the Truth and the Life, Door, Messiah,* Lord, King, Vine, Bread of Life, First, Last, Living One, Alpha and Omega, Beginning and End, Lion of Judah, Jacob/Israel, Rod, Flower, Stone, a Chosen Shaft, Sword, Servant of God, Lamb of God, Paraclete, Power of God, Sanctification, High-Priest, Pearl, Earth, Salt, Worm, Mustard-seed.

These 'names' were given soteriological exegeses:

He is called Salt because he has drawn near to our body corrupted by sin and has removed from us the stench of idol-worship and has prepared our souls with sweet savour by the faith of the worship of God.

He is called Worm because he said 'I am a worm and not a man'. By the brightness of the Godhead, as a hook in a worm, thus he hid his own Godhead in his body and cast it into the nether-regions of the world and drew it up like a good fisherman; about whom he says 'He took the dragon with a hook and put a bridle in his mouth and a spike through his nose', that is the devil he took and whose wiles he broke, about whom the Psalmist David bears witness 'Thou hast broken the heads of the dragon' (from a Georgian work clearly dependent on a long popular tradition in the East, translated and included by J. N. Birdsall in *New Testament Textual Criticism*, ed. E. J. Epp and G. D. Fee, 1981).

Such brief selections are sufficient to give the flavour of a use of the Bible which clearly spanned both popular preaching and more sophisticated thinking. These examples also draw attention to some of the main soteriological themes in the patristic period: the need for revelation* and illumination to meet ignorance, idolatry and false religion; the need for expiation of sin and teaching to further a moral way of life; and the need to deal with the supernatural powers who have caused the deception and corruption of humanity. To these should be added the need for immortality and an end to death. Indeed, the horror of death and of the physical corruption accompanying it was peculiarly intense at this period.

Among more philosophical thinkers, this wealth of imagery often served an underlying 'theory' concerning the plight of humanity. For Origen, God's eternal spiritual creation had suffered from a devastating fall; the material world was the providential answer, a school to win back fallen souls. The Saviour was part of that educative process. But he was more than that. The many titles were important because the one Christ was a 'multitude of goods', uniting in himself the multiplicity of creation and the unity of God like the One-Many of Middle Platonism, providing the link in the chain of being, restoring the union of the transcendent God with his marred creation in the mediating 'second God'. Salvation meant the restoration of pristine perfection.

For Athanasius, the problem was envisaged rather differently. God had called his creation into being out of nothing through his Logos* (Word/Reason); he had made humanity in his own image, and endowed this creature alone of all creatures with his own Logos, so imparting the divine life and reason to the human race. Adam* had disobeyed; so he had lost the Logos. Humanity was therefore drifting back into the nothingness from which it had been created. God could not compromise his integrity; neither could he let his most wonderful creation be destroyed. So the incarnation alone could resolve the problem: only thus could humanity be re-endowed with the Logos.

So the Saviour became the archetype of a new perfect humanity. He was absolute Wisdom, very Word, absolute Light, absolute Truth, absolute Justice, absolute Virtue, absolute Holiness, absolute Life, and absolutely Son of God. Human beings become wise, rational, illumined, true, just, good, holy, living, and sons of God by participation in this absolute. Through his condescension to created beings to give them knowledge, he becomes Door, Shepherd and Way, King, Guide and Saviour, Life-giver, Light and universal Providence. 'He became human, that we might become divine.'

In both these cases, Platonic ideas undoubtedly contributed to the underlying theory of salvation. But the details and the language were drawn from scripture, often by exploiting figurative expressions to provide symbolic presentations of the saving work of Christ. Allegory* and typology* contributed much. This mode of thought continued to shape the Christian tradition as it was expressed in liturgy* and hymns,* in preaching and in mystery-plays. It was in the Middle Ages in the Western church that this wealth of ideas was constrained into two competing doctrines of atonement.

The two mediaeval* theories which came to dominate discussion were those of Anselm and Abelard. The Anselmian theory has become identified with conservative doctrine, both Catholic and evangelical, the latter somewhat ironically since Anselm himself barely refers to the scriptures. By a process of logic he argued that justice requires that sin be punished. Before God could forgive, the demands of justice had to be met, and God's honour satisfied. The satisfaction had to be commensurate with the sin. But nothing within the power of human beings could make up for their sin, given that all good works were a matter of obligation anyway. The debt could only be paid by God, yet humanity owed it. So only the God-Man could pay it. He suffered the punishment due, thus making forgiveness possible. The theory depends on logic, and also on mediaeval assumptions concerning honour. Scripture certainly does not spell it out in these terms.

Nevertheless apologists for this doctrine have built up a scriptural basis for it. Pauline* language about justice and justification might indeed seem to support it, especially when it is taken in a Roman legal framework and associated with cultic* language suggesting that God needs to be propitiated by the sacrificial blood of Christ so that his wrath against sin might be turned aside (cf. Rom. 3.25). This supposedly more scriptural form of the doctrine, however, has been subjected to considerable criticism, especially among 'liberals',* in the nineteenth and twentieth centuries. It is regarded as the product of confusion between civil and criminal law procedures, as damaging to trinitarian theology, and as objectionable on moral grounds: justice is simply not served by punishing an innocent person in place of a criminal. Above all, it is taken to be contrary to the scriptural revelation of God's mercy and love in Jesus Christ.

Liberals have taken up the other mediaeval

view, that of Abelard. For Abelard the cross was a demonstration of the sheer love and grace of God – this was the length that God would go to communicate that love. The effect of response to this love was repentance. Redemption consisted in the love which this response produced in human beings, freeing them from slavery to sin and bringing them to the true liberty of sons of God. The idea that God could require the blood of an innocent victim as a ransom-price was totally abhorrent to Abelard. Many scriptural texts (e.g. John 15.13) have been exploited in support of this view: but opponents suggest that it is too subjective: it takes away the cruciality of the cross.

The polarization produced by these two competing doctrines was modified by the work of Gustaf Aulen, *Christus Victor* (1931). He pointed to what he called the 'classic' theory of atonement, in the patristic writings and indeed in Luther.* This theory focussed upon the cross as victory over the powers of evil. The ransom was offered to the devil. Salvation was an act of God, not an act directed at him.

Aulen would resolve the very varied and diverse language of the Fathers into this single basic conception. There is much to support this view, and other scholars have suggested that the idea of such a cosmic conflict is fundamental to the NT. If it seems crude and mythological* (and we should not overlook the fact that Anselm developed his view as an explicit rejection of this idea, in view of the problems both moral and philosophical which it presented), it has won a hearing in the twentieth century because it can be understood to represent symbolically the modern experience of being caught up in dire events and processes beyond human control, what has been called the 'total nexus of evil' in the world – the social, psychological, political and economic forces that bind us. It promises salvation on the grounds that Christ confronted all this on the cross and broke it, proclaiming liberty to the captives (Luke 4.18). The problem with this approach is its 'dualism', though Aulen seeks to show that it was never an 'ultimate dualism'.

Clearly all three approaches have their limitations as 'global' theories. More recent writings have sought to do justice to the evident variety within the tradition, each approach contributing some insight into the human predicament from which Christ has freed humanity. The result is not a doctrine or theory, but a series of parables, pictures or stories which capture the experience of salvation. One suspects that this retreat from any attempt to provide a rationale is perhaps truer to the diversity of the early church, and the lack of systematic reflection in scripture. Whether it is ultimately satisfactory is another question,

but it may be that the world of the imagination is more appropriate for understanding soteriology than the imposition of strict logic or the search for a coherent philosophy.

Certainly the most recent reaction has been to stress *praxis*: salvation is liberation,* liberation from the forces of economic and political oppression manifest in so many parts of the world. Salvation is apprehended not so much through reflection as through action, which is to bring freedom and peace. Once again the Bible has fuelled this perception, though contemporary frameworks of thought like Marxism* have affected the way the scriptures are read.

Salvation is bound to be seen in different terms depending upon the needs of the time; scripture has proved a rich treasure of language in which to express these varied needs and responses. It could also provide a necessary critique of fashionable solutions to the needs of humanity.

See also **Liberation Theology; Patristic Christology; Systematic Theology.**

Gustaf Aulen, *Christus Victor*, 1931; F. W. Dillistone, *The Christian Understanding of Atonement*, 1968; R. Leivestad, *Christ the Conqueror*, 1954; H. Rashdall, *The Idea of Atonement in Christian Theology*, 1919.

FRANCES YOUNG

Source Criticism (New Testament)

As its name suggests, 'source criticism' is concerned with discovering the sources which an author has used in producing his work. Every writer brings a certain background of thought and ideas to the production of a text. But at times, one author may take over a previous source and incorporate it into a new work.

Within NT study, one particular problem of source criticism concerns the nature and identity of the sources of the Synoptic Gospels. This problem is usually known as the 'Synoptic Problem'* and will not be discussed in detail here. But this is only one of several problems of source criticism in the NT and in the Bible as a whole. These problems may be divided into two classes. One concerns the problems of the precise relationship between two (or more) extant texts. Sometimes, two texts are so close to each other in their wording that one suspects that one text has been used by the author of the other as a source. This is the case with the Synoptic Gospels: the agreement (in order and wording) between the Synoptic Gospels has led to the widely held view that one Gospel, Mark, has been used by the other two evangelists,* Matthew and Luke, as a source. There are similar problems elsewhere in the NT. For example, the relationship between Colossians and Ephesians, or between II Peter and Jude, seems so close that it looks as if the author of one text has used the other as a source. Today, the almost unanimous view is that Ephesians has used Colossians, and that II Peter has used Jude.

The main kind of argument used in such source-critical problems is to try to see which way round a change in the tradition* is most likely to have occurred. Clearly a text and its source do not agree precisely. Someone must have changed a source slightly. Hence, given two versions, A and B, one must ask whether A is more likely to have been changed to B or B to A. For example, Col. 2.7 speaks of Christians being 'rooted and builded up' in Christ; Eph. 2.20 speaks of the church 'built upon the foundation of the apostles and prophets'. The phraseology in Ephesians is often held to imply a later date, with its stress on the importance of the apostolic foundation of the church, and hence to be more likely to be secondary to the parallel version in Colossians.

A rather different kind of source-critical problem is raised in cases where the alleged source is no longer extant. Sometimes a writer appears to be reproducing an earlier tradition, but that tradition is no longer available to us independently. For example, it is widely assumed that several hymn*-like sections in some of the epistles* (cf. Phil. 2.5–11; Col. 1.15–20) may be quotations of earlier traditions. Other instances of the same phenomenon may occur in creed*-like summaries such as Rom. 1.3f. or Rom. 3.24–26. At times too the debt to earlier traditions is quite explicit, as when Paul* cites what he says is traditional teaching, in I Cor. 11.23–25 (on the eucharist) or I Cor. 15.3ff. (on the resurrection*).

Other 'sources' may be of rather greater extent than these (relatively) small units. For example, Luke may have used extensive source material in his account of the history of the early church in Acts. How much of this lay in a single connected source is not clear, but it may be that Luke had some tradition about the places visited by the Christian mission (cf. Acts 14.24–26, where a series of place names is given, though with no information about what happened at each place). The so-called 'we' passages in Acts (those passages where the narrative slips into the first-person plural, e.g. Acts 16.10–17) may also indicate that Luke has used a source, possibly an eye-witness* account, for those parts of his narrative. (The significance of these passages is much debated. They may reflect the fact that Luke himself was an eye-witness of the events concerned, so that the 'source' is simply Luke's own memory. On the other hand, the use of the first person may be a stylistic device to add vividness to the narrative.)

The problem of sources in John's Gospel is also relevant here. John has evidently used source materials in writing his Gospel. (Cf. the overlaps with the Synoptic Gospels: either John has used the Synoptic Gospels themselves, or he has used traditions which were also used by the Synoptic evangelists. Either way John has used sources.) The precise extent of John's sources is not certain. Majority opinion today is still in favour of the theory that John did not use the Synoptics directly but had access to Synoptic traditions at an earlier stage than that of the finished Synoptic Gospels. The existence of other sources in John is less certain. John may have used a source for his miracle* stories, the so-called 'Signs' source. This may be indicated by the numbering of the first two miracles in John (cf. 2.11; 4.54). However, other alleged sources in John (cf. Bultmann's* theory that John used a source for his discourses) are less probable.

A problem which can also be regarded as 'source-critical', though in a slightly different way, concerns possible later additions to a text. For example, John 21 is widely regarded as a secondary appendix to an earlier form of the Gospel which finished at ch. 20. Moreover, the slightly different vocabulary used in John 21 suggests that this chapter has been written by someone other than the author of the rest of the Gospel. A similar phenomenon may occur sometimes in the NT epistles. II Cor. 6.14–7.1 has often been thought to be a non-Pauline insertion into Paul's original letter. The two verses in I Cor. 14.34f., which say that women should keep silent in church, have also been suspected of being a post-Pauline gloss. These instances are slightly different from the kind of 'sources' previously discussed in that they are possible elements which have not been incorporated into the text by the person usually regarded as 'the author'* of the text. (Clearly this may create problems in discussing who 'the author' of, say, the Fourth Gospel was: is he to be regarded as the author of chs 1–20, or as the person responsible for the finished form of the text as it has come down to us, i.e. as chs 1–21?) However, the phenomenon of such additions to a text can still be included within the broad rubric of 'source criticism' in that one is seeking to determine the potentially different origins of different parts of the text.

The criteria* used to isolate sources within a text can vary. At times, the existence of a source is suspected because a passage uses words or phrases that are unusual or uncharacteristic of the writer of the rest of the text. Phil. 2.5–11 uses words and ideas (e.g. Christ being in the 'form' of God) which are rare elsewhere in Paul. At times too a writer seems to correct what he has just said, suggesting that a tradition is being used and corrected. For example, John 4.1 suggests that Jesus baptized people, but then 4.2 instantly 'corrects' this impression. At other times, what is said in a text seems so tangential and almost irrelevant to the writer's concern that one suspects that source material is being reproduced. As we have already seen, this might apply to some of the place names given in the itinerary in Acts.

The value of source criticism is that it enables us to delineate the history of the tradition with far greater accuracy. This can help in a number of different ways. In terms of the tradition/source itself, source criticism enables us to get behind the writer of a given text to an earlier stage of history. The identification of pre-Pauline fragments, for example, enables us to see the way in which Christian thought was developing in the period prior to Paul.

The identification of a source also enables us to pin-point more precisely the way in which the source has been used, and perhaps modified, by the author of the text in which the source appears (*see* **Redaction Criticism**). Some words of caution are, however, necessary. The fact that some words in a text can be ascribed to a 'source' does not necessarily mean that the source has nothing to contribute to the author's own theology. It may at times be the case that an author adopts a source in order deliberately to correct it. However, at other times a source may be adopted because the author agrees with it whole-heartedly.

A comment should also be made about source criticism applied to historical works. Clearly, a proper source-critical analysis is essential in evaluating the historical value of any given text. If one's primary aim is to discover something about the historical events described in a work, then a thorough knowledge of the sources used by the writer is essential. However, one cannot assume that simply by isolating an earlier source, we have *ipso facto* recovered a source which is historically more reliable. In the case of the Gospels, modern study has emphasized more and more the theological contribution which the evangelists themselves have made to the tradition. Thus the identification of Mark as the (probable) source of Matthew and Luke does not solve all historical problems at a stroke. We cannot assume that Mark, simply by virtue of being the source of Matthew and Luke, gives us a straight transcript of history. Mark's account is dominated by his own ideas, just as much as Matthew's is (e.g. by the messianic secret*). So too recent study of the second source probably used by Matthew and Luke,

usually known as Q, has shown that Q has its own theological slant as well. An earlier source may be more reliable than a later source, but it may also be just as dominated by secondary ideas. Similarly Luke's possible sources in Acts are not necessarily reliable in absolute terms. So too the existence of even a possible eye-witness* account in Acts (cf. the 'we' passages) cannot be taken as *ipso facto* an indicator of the absolute reliability of the account concerned. Eye-witnesses are not always reliable; equally, non-eye-witnesses are not necessarily unreliable. Each case must be examined on its own merits.

In isolating the different strata which make up any biblical text, source criticism thus makes an important contribution at a number of levels. Above all it illuminates the living process by which the final form of the text as it appears in our Bibles was originally put together. It thus contributes to our understanding of the history which leads up to the texts we have and enables us to see more of the religious faith and commitment of the people who lie behind the written word.

See also **Synoptic Problem.**

W. A. Beardslee, *Literary Criticism of the New Testament*, 1971; C. M. Tuckett, *Reading the New Testament: Methods of Interpretation*, 1987.

C. M. TUCKETT

Spiritual Meaning

To speak of the 'spiritual meaning' of scripture is to draw a contrast with the 'literal meaning'.* The roots of the terminology lie in II Cor. 3 where Paul* contrasts the letter of the Law with the covenant* in the Spirit, suggesting that there is a veil over the minds of those who read the scriptures until they 'turn to the Lord'. Certainly Paul never meant to contrast the OT and the NT, which at that stage did not even exist; nor did he mean to contrast 'literal' and 'spiritual' readings of the Law. But that was what he was taken to mean by the third century.

Once the contrast was explicitly drawn, the 'spiritual meaning' was taken to include all the prophetic* and typological* meanings traditional in Christian apologetic.* Jesus was the fulfilment of the Law and the Prophets. Key messianic* texts were applied to him. Eschatological* typology which expected the 're-play' of the exodus at the coming of the kingdom* was adapted to fit, the Passover lamb foreshadowing the Lamb who takes away the sin of the world by dying on the cross, the escape from Egypt* foreshadowing our escape from slavery to the devil and his angels. Circumcision of the flesh was replaced by circumcision of the heart, and literal sacrifices in a literal temple were replaced by spiritual sacrifices in a spiritual temple, the church, the Body of Christ.

The process of understanding the Jewish scriptures in this way began in the NT, was developed in the preaching and apologetic of the second century, and was inherited by the first self-conscious exegete, Origen.* He it was who developed the theory that impossibilities in the 'letter' of scripture were deliberately placed there to stimulate the reader into exploring its spiritual meaning. He was the first to produce running commentaries* on the bulk of the OT, showing how spiritual meanings could be discerned everywhere. He developed the idea of the spiritual meaning consistently, using allegory* as well as typology to produce relevant applications of the text which went far beyond its literal sense or obvious reference. He anticipated what became the 'mystical'* understanding of scripture, discerning in the sacred text the journey of the soul back to contemplation of God. But to the extent that he focussed on the christological sense of the OT, his work had long been anticipated, the pre-existent Christ having already been discerned everywhere in the Jewish scriptures. This Christian interpretation had already been opposed to the literalism of Jewish interpretation in such works as the *Epistle of Barnabas* and Justin's *Dialogue with Trypho.*

Origen's legacy was a divergence of exegetical* traditions in the Eastern church. Some embraced the allegorical method with enthusiasm, and contributed to its further development and systematization; others reacted against it. It is important to observe, however, that the Antiochene* reaction did not on the whole abandon the traditional prophetic and typological understanding: Theodoret spoke of *theōria* ('contemplation') and in fact not only adopted all the traditional 'types', but also followed Origen in seeing the Song of Songs as referring to the marriage between Christ and his church. The spiritual meaning was still important as differentiating Christian interpretation from Jewish – indeed, one charge levelled against the earlier extreme Antiochene Theodore of Mopsuestia was that of reverting to Jewish understanding. Those involved in the Origenist controversies may have accused Origen of excessive allegorization, but they did not abandon the notion that scripture had more than one sense. Indeed, despite his opposition to Origen and his scepticism about his own early over-enthusiasm for allegory, Jerome remained deeply indebted to Didymus the Blind, an Origenist exegete, and Jerome's commentaries ensured that the mediaeval* West received the legacy of a tradition that sought spiritual meaning in reading scripture.

In fact the picture of two competing traditions can be misleading. Many of the most influential patristic writers cannot be categorized in these terms: people like the Cappadocians, or indeed Augustine,* have sometimes puzzled students of exegetical* method, since they seem to oscillate from one tradition to another. The fact is that all the exegetes of the patristic church were influenced by the educational system of the ancient world. Education was traditionally based upon literature. Literature was a prized possession, a distillation of ancient wisdom, treated with enormous respect. It had been recognized long since that the 'letter' of the text was only the starting-point of interpretation: sorting out the proper reading and the correct grammar, the meanings of archaic terms and the references to ancient myths, was only preliminary to discerning the 'moral' or 'spiritual' meaning. When Basil advised young Christians to study literature as valuable preparation for scriptural exegesis, but to distinguish between what was appropriate and useful and what was harmful, he was simply Christianizing a long-standing educational maxim. Everyone in the ancient world agreed that interpretation involved going beyond the letter, and everyone used some degree of allegory to distil out of texts the deeper meanings that they sought.

The more philosophical,* the more allegorical: so Gregory of Nyssa sees scripture, especially the life of Moses,* as a great parable of the ascent of the soul to knowledge of God. He set the precedent for the 'mystical' exegesis of one like Dionysius the Areopagite, who like Jerome had a profound influence on the exegesis of the mediaeval West. This kind of influence led to the theory of the four-fold sense of scripture: literal, figurative, moral and anagogical. It was the last which represented the 'mystical' or 'spiritual' aspect of the text. Aquinas represents something of a reaction against these views, though they continued to affect preaching and devotion right up to the time of the Reformation* and beyond.

Since the Reformation and the rise of biblical criticism,* the notion that scripture might have more than one meaning has largely fallen into abeyance, though never entirely in Catholic circles. Many of the 'spiritual' meanings in the tradition have survived in popular Christianity, despite the scholarly preoccupation with the 'original' meaning. The signs are that current movements reacting against the historico-critical* approach, such as canon criticism,* structuralism,* etc., will give 'spiritual meaning' a new respectability.

See also **Christian Interpretation of the Old Testament.**

J. Daniélou, *From Shadows to Reality*, 1960;

R. M. Grant, *The Letter and the Spirit*, 1957; R. P. C. Hanson, *Allegory and Event*, 1959; G. W. H. Lampe and K. J. Woollcombe, *Essays in Typology*, 1957; A. Louth, *Discerning the Mystery*, 1983.

FRANCES YOUNG

Strauss, D. F.

In 1835, at the age of 27, David Friedrich Strauss (1808–74) was dismissed from his tutorship at the Tübingen Stift (theological college) for publishing the book which finally compelled European Protestantism to face the questions raised by the historical criticism* of the Gospels. *The Life of Jesus Critically Examined* (ET by George Eliot, 1846; latest ed. P. C. Hodgson, 1972) contributed to the reputation for critical radicalism which Tübingen owes especially to F. C. Baur and his school. Though a pupil of Baur at school and university, Strauss can scarcely be included in the Tübingen school* of his teacher because this epoch-making book preceded Baur's Gospel criticism and lacked its distinctive characteristics: a methodical historical investigation of the Gospel sources themselves, and the attempt to interpret the development of early Christianity theologically as the divine Spirit moving dialectically through history. In the same way, Strauss' critical demolition of the history of doctrine, *Die christliche Glaubenslehre* (1840–1), both preceded and stopped short of Baur's more constructive Hegelian interpretation. Like earlier rationalists, such as Reimarus,* on whom in 1862 he published a monograph (part ET 1970), Strauss challenged the historicity of the Gospels by pointing to contradictions between the four accounts, and by denying outright any possibility of supernatural or miraculous events. Influenced by the 'mythical school' of C. G. Heyne, he considered the Gospels' fabulous or 'mythical'* material, the product of early Christian consciousness, often modelled on OT prototypes, notably the Elijah and Elisha cycles. Unlike his successors, he considered this mythical material more significant for religion than the historical. The truth of the Gospels' picture of the 'God-man' was to be found by translating the pre-scientific representation (*Vorstellung*) into the Hegelian concept (*Begriff*) of the unity of the divine and the human, and applying this idea not to Christ but to the human race.

These speculative proposals found no support, and the chief importance of *The Life of Jesus* was that it provided the decisive impulse for subsequent study of the 'historical Jesus'.* Contrary to the then still prevailing views of Schleiermacher, and anticipating the more methodical research of Baur (1844 and 1847), Strauss judged the Synoptic* record more reliable than the Johannine, wavering only briefly in the third (1838) edition.

Despite the negative impression created by an account that systematically destroyed the historical credibility of much of the Gospel record, Strauss' conclusions do not today seem unduly sceptical, however briefly he expressed them. In 1864, following Renan's successful *Vie de Jésus* (1863), he unfolded his positive conclusions in his *Leben Jesu für das deutsche Volk*, 1864, ET *A New Life of Jesus*, 1865. His literary skills are also evident in a biography of Ulrich von Hutten (1857), in six lectures on Voltaire (1870), and in many other historical and political writings. In the historical study of the Gospels, however, he was stronger in criticism than construction. When Schleiermacher's 1832 lectures on *The Life of Jesus* appeared posthumously in 1864 (ET 1975), Strauss published a brilliant critique under the significant title *The Christ of Faith and the Jesus of History* (1865, ET 1977). But his last testament, *The Old Faith and the New* (1872, ET 1874), is a dismal warning of what can happen to theology without belief in God.

See also **Enlightenment; Historical Jesus; Myth.**

The *Streitschriften* by which Strauss defended his *Life of Jesus* against various critics are now partly translated by M. C. Massey, *In Defense of my Life of Jesus*, 1983; H. Frei, *The Eclipse of Biblical Narrative*, 1974; H. Harris, *David Friedrich Strauss and his Theology*, 1973; L. Keck, Introduction to *The Christ of Faith and the Jesus of History*, 1977; N. Smart et al. (eds), *Nineteenth-Century Religious Thought in the West* Vol. 1, 1985.

ROBERT MORGAN

Structuralism

In the context of biblical interpretation, structuralism has contributed most significantly to our understanding of biblical narrative* (though some scholars have attempted structural analyses of Paul's* letters). General structural analysis of narrative derives ultimately from Ferdinand de Saussure's pioneering work in the area of linguistics* at the turn of this century. Saussurian linguistics was innovative because it questioned the presuppositions behind previous linguistic philosophies. The general philosophical perspective which Saussure inherited was one in which the world was seen to consist of independently existing objects which are clearly visible and easily classifiable. People began to see, however, 1. that it is impossible to perceive individual entities with complete objectivity, 2. that there is a relationship and not a detachment between the observer and the observed, and 3. that the world is made up of relationships rather than things. It is this emphasis on 'relationships' which marks the great change in perception at the beginning of the century and forms the basis of all structuralist thinking. The new perception recognized that 'the full significance of any entity or experience cannot be perceived unless and until it is integrated into the structure of which it forms a part' (Terence Hawkes).

Fredric Jameson has described structuralism as 'an explicit search for the permanent structures of the mind itself, the organizational categories and forms through which the mind is able to experience the world'. This emphasis upon permanent structures is first evident in Saussure's complex linguistic theory. His *Course in General Linguistics* (1915) presented the argument that language should be studied not only in terms of its individual parts, and not only diachronically, but also in terms of the relationship between those parts, and synchronically.* In short, he proposed that a language should be studied as 'a *Gestalteinheit*, a unified "field", a self-sufficient system, as we actually experience it NOW' (Hawkes). Previous linguistic philosophies had been too preoccupied with the historical development of language (the diachronic emphasis). Saussure insisted that language is a system which is complete at every moment, no matter what developments take place. This system Saussure called 'langue', a concept which he distinguished from 'parole'. Langue signifies the abstract set of rules, the permanent structures, the grammar of language. A parole is the individual, concrete speech-utterance which we make in obedience to that grammar. Langue is like the rules of chess; a parole is like an individual chess move.

Structuralism began with Saussure's attempt to discover and describe the permanent, deep structures of language. It was the Russian folklorist* Vladimir Propp who first applied a broadly-speaking structuralist approach to narratives. In his *Morphology of the Folktale* (1928), Propp endeavoured to establish a scientific explanation of the way Russian fairy-tales are composed. For Propp, the highest goal of any science is to discover laws, and this was precisely his aim in the more limited area of the fairy-tale genre.* The very word 'morphology' denoted this since it referred to a branch of the natural sciences whose aim was to provide a holistic* description of the overarching scheme that embraces all nature. On the ground that the realms of nature and of man share common laws, Propp tried to find the overarching scheme that embraces all fairy tales. After close inspection of 100 such tales, Propp began to notice that there were significant constants or fundamental invari-

ants in them. Underneath the multiplicity, there seemed to be a unity which could be determined logically. For example, in one story, a king gives an eagle to a hero and the eagle carries the hero away to another kingdom. In another story, a princess gives a hero a ring from which some men magically appear in order to whisk him away to another place. In both stories, though the characters have different names, the same action is performed, namely, a gift causing a transfer.

What is the permanent structure behind the narrative genre known as the Russian fairy tale? Propp reckoned that he had found a deep structure or grammar of possible relationships which all fairy tales obey. This structure was composed of a limited number of possible 'actions' which the characters of the stories perform (e.g. the giving of a gift effecting the transfer of a protagonist). These actions Propp called 'functions' and their principal characteristic was simply that they did not change. Whilst the names of the characters in the above illustration seem variable (a king and a hero//a princess and a hero), the actual function is essentially the same. As Claude Bremond has put it, 'the invariant is the function that a particular event, by its very happening, fulfils in the course of the narrative. The variable is the concrete manifestation chosen for the production and circumstances of this event. What counts therefore is to know what a character does and what function it fulfils.' Propp discovered these invariable functions through a specific comparative analysis of the material and through the abstraction of a logical structure from many cases. The permanent or 'monotypical' structure which Propp inferred from his research turned out to be a kind of Russian alphabet of 31 possible functions which involved 7 types of characters.

The second seminal application of a structuralist approach to a narrative genre was made by Claude Lévi-Strauss, who used Saussure's linguistic system in his study of myths.* Lévi-Strauss firmly believed that the rules which govern myths and the rules which govern language emerge from identical unconscious structures. For Lévi-Strauss, the unconscious structure behind myth is the tendency to think in oppositions and the tendency to resolve such oppositions. This stress on 'unconscious mental structures' means that Lévi-Strauss' analyses are not characterized by a careful concern for surface stories, however interesting these may be in themselves. Nor do they exhibit any central interest in the characters and their actions in terms of their psychological depth and verisimilitude. Lévi-Strauss is interested in the permanent structure (the langue, one might say) behind mythical

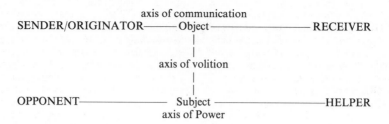

Fig. 1

stories. This langue is established through the discovery of recurrent combinations of constant features or 'mythemes'. These combinations obey the rules of a kind of transcendental grammar, a universal 'mythologic' which is manifested in the resolution of things existing in binary opposition. When reading Lévi-Strauss, one therefore finds a concentrated preoccupation with the degree of mediation between certain universal contrasts, such as Immortal/Mortal, Male/Female, Parent/Child, and so on.

The systems developed by Propp and Lévi-Strauss must be fully appreciated if we are to understand the many examples of structural analysis we find in biblical studies. To put it into the language of structuralism, we shall not be able to comprehend the individual paroles (examples of structural analysis) unless we have penetrated their langue (the methodological systems from which they ultimately derive). As far as biblical narrative is concerned, most examples of structural exegesis resemble either Propp's or Lévi-Strauss' method. They are concerned either with plot functions or with the resolution of binary oppositions. A word of qualification needs to be added here, however. It is really more accurate to say that the structural analysis which derives from Propp's 'morphology' sometimes resembles A. J. Greimas' adaptation of Propp's system. Greimas came up with a model which he regarded as the permanent structure behind *all* narratives (see fig. 1).

The diagram reveals six different character poles of narrative (subject, object, sender, receiver, helper and opponent) and three functional axes (communication, power and volition). A story is usually begun when a sender

tells a receiver to undertake some task. The volitional axis represents this quest, the power axis represents the struggle involved in its execution. Thus, a story in which a king sends a prince to find his daughter, and in which the prince is waylaid by bandits before being helped by a magic horse to his prize, would be schematized by Greimas as in fig. 2.

The first experiments in biblical structural analysis were carried out on Genesis, perhaps because it was felt that this, of all the books of the Bible, most closely resembles the genres of fairy tale and myth. One of the first scholars to use the method deriving from Propp and Greimas was the French structuralist, Roland Barthes. His essay entitled 'The Struggle with the Angel' (1971) was to become one of the most celebrated examples of structuralist literary criticism. Barthes' earlier essay, 'An Introduction to the Structural Analysis of Narratives', had asserted that all narratives obey a fundamental narrative grammar. Just as sentences obey a system of rules, so do narratives, because 'a narrative is a long sentence'. Behind and within the great variety of narratives in the world, there is 'an atemporal logic lying behind the temporality of narrative'. In 'The Struggle with the Angel', Barthes attempted to test the implications of this grammatical approach in the context of biblical narrative.

In the second part of his essay, Barthes subjects the narrative to the kinds of approach established by Propp. The story itself is about Jacob's struggle with a man or an angel who turns out, at the moment of the dénouement, to be God. Barthes begins by defining the actants (characters) in the tale in terms of their functions. As far as Barthes is concerned, they are stock items from the world of folk-

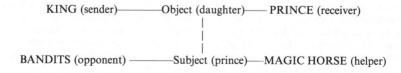

Fig. 2

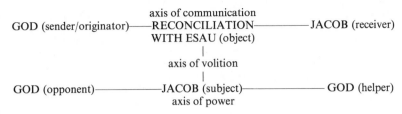

Fig 3.

tale plots. Jacob is the hero who is on a quest, one of the commonest of all folk-tale plots. God stands behind the events of the story as the 'sender' or 'originator' of this quest. The man with whom Jacob wrestles is his 'opponent', since he is the one who waylays the hero and tries to prevent him from accomplishing his mission. Barthes argues that, at the moment of the struggle, a number of narrative developments are possible. The originator (God) could step in and help the hero defeat his opponent. A magical helper could appear to transport Jacob away. But what actually occurs is in effect quite peculiar and unexpected. At the moment of discovery, Jacob recognizes that his opponent is none other than God himself. In narratological terms, the receiver realizes that the sender and the opponent and the helper are all one and the same. It is God who sends Jacob down the axis of volition, and it is God who meets Jacob on the axis of power. In Greimas' diagrammatical terms, the story looks like fig. 3:

The diagram accentuates the surprise factor here. As Barthes proposes, 'that the sender be the opponent is very rare'; it is bound to surprise. In fact, there is only one kind of narrative which can present this paradoxical form: narratives relating an act of blackmail; and it is this that makes the reader recognize how audacious the tale is, both structurally and theologically. Structurally, it seems to break a rule of folk-tale grammar. Theologically, having the same supernatural protagonist as both the originator and the opponent implies the kind of radical monotheism which will not permit the existence of an opposing spiritual power. In short, Barthes' structural analysis reveals how and why Gen. 32.22–32 is a tale of the unexpected.

Whilst Roland Barthes was one of the first to apply the method deriving from Propp and Greimas to biblical narrative, Edmund Leach was one of the first to apply the method deriving from Lévi-Strauss. In *Genesis as Myth* (1969), Leach used Lévi-Strauss' structural analysis of myth in order to highlight the permanent mythical structures behind Genesis. Leach agreed with Lévi-Strauss that myth is constantly setting up opposing cate-

gories. Myth has a binary structure; it 'first discriminates between gods and men, and then becomes preoccupied with the relations and intermediaries which link men and gods together'. 'In every myth system,' Leach continues, 'we will find a persistent sequence of binary discriminations as between human/superhuman, mortal/immortal, male/female, legitimate/illegitimate, good/bad ... followed by a "mediation" of the paired categories thus distinguished.' Right the way through Genesis, Leach claims, we are presented with common opposites: Heaven/Earth, Light/Darkness, Man/Garden, Tree of Life/Tree of Death, Unity (Eden)/Duality (outside Eden), Gardener (Cain)/Herdsman (Abel), and so on. As Leach concludes, 'every myth is one of a complex' and 'any pattern which occurs in one myth will recur, in the same or other variations, in other parts of the complex'. There is a structure which is common to all variations and that structure lies behind and within Genesis. Genesis, like all other myths, is an observable phenomenon expressive of unobservable realities – namely the permanent structures of myth.

What summary statement can be made about the distinctive approach of structural exegetes* to biblical narrative? The following points are relevant: 1. structuralism in general and structural analysis in particular are both concerned with the discovery and description of transindividual, permanent structures; 2. the permanent structure in mythical narrative is the mind's innate tendency to mediate opposites (Lévi-Strauss); 3. the permanent structure in fairy-tales and other narrative genres is a grammar of limited actants and functions (Propp and Greimas); 4. structural analysis of biblical narrative will most commonly follow either Lévi-Strauss' binary approach, or the more 'functional/actantial' procedure reminiscent of Propp and Greimas; 5. structural analysis alone can elicit the kinds of insights about which Barthes and Leach have written; 6. structural analysis of biblical narrative is now an important methodology for the holistic appreciation of the final form of a text.

What are the limitations and strengths in

these structural approaches to scriptural narratives? There are five major weaknesses in the method which require urgent attention by structuralists. First, structural analysis of the Bible has a very ambiguous and sometimes even antagonistic attitude towards historical criticism.* It has tended completely to ignore the historical or diachronic aspect of biblical narratives. In its emphasis upon the final form, it suppresses all consideration of pre-textual transmission. In its post-structuralist suspicions concerning the relationship between signifier and signified, it has neglected the referential dimension of historical narratives. Structuralists need to ask with integrity how appropriate a method evolving out of the study of myths and fairy tales is in the context of historical narratives such as the Gospels.* This question has become even more urgent in the light of deconstructionist theories of the relationship between text and reality.

Secondly, there is an arbitrariness and subjectivity about some structural classifications. Part of the structural exegete's procedure involves the identification and naming of binary oppositions and/or basic genre components. Yet it is precisely in this very act of labelling that structural analysis sometimes falls apart. For example, when Edmund Leach proposes that Orpheus rescues Eurydice from Hades by means of music, but loses her because of silence, it seems that the desire for a binary opposition has suppressed the obvious explanation. Orpheus quite plainly loses Eurydice because he turns round. The process of event-labelling in structural analysis requires greater methodological rigour than it has so far received. In this respect structural analysis of biblical narrative is subject to the same criticisms as the kind of architectural analysis practised by C. H. Talbert and others (which also takes liberties with the labels or summary statements it places over various narrative pericopes).

Thirdly, structural exegetes have not recognized the limitations of the interpretative models which they employ. For example, Greimas' actantial model for the interpretation of *all* narratives has not been as versatile as its discoverer wished. Whilst it works very well in the context of smaller and simpler narrative units, such as folk-tales or myths, its usefulness in longer and more complex narratives is highly questionable. Thus, when Daniel and Aline Patte try to use it in their structural analysis of the Marcan passion narrative,* they find it impossible to fit the whole of Mark 14–16 on to one semiotic* square. Instead, they are reduced to applying it to much smaller narrative units, with the result that their book becomes an almost indecipherable plethora of actantial diagrams. This over-ambitious exploitation of narrative models inevitably gives structuralism a bad name because its highly technical, mathematical appearance makes it unreadable.

Fourthly, Terry Eagleton has demonstrated that structural analysis undermines the details of narrative, especially characters. He invents a story about a boy who runs away from home and falls into a pit. The father comes after him, peers into the pit but cannot see him. At that moment, the sun rises to a point directly overhead and illuminates the pit's depths with its rays, allowing the father to rescue his boy and effect a joyous reconciliation. Eagleton points out that a structural analysis of a story like this is bound to change it into a series of binary oppositions (low versus high, for example). The problem with such a procedure is that one 'could replace father and son, pit and sun, with entirely different elements – mother and daughter, bird and mole – and still have the same story. As long as the structure of relations between the units is preserved, it does not matter which items you select.' Structural analysis tends to obscure the importance of narrative characters and actions by reducing them to abstract items on a quasi-mathematical grid.

Fifthly, structural analysis of narrative at best ignores and at worst obliterates the figure of the author.* Roland Barthes' celebrated essay entitled 'The Death of the Author' (1968) typifies this anti-authorial stance within structuralism. It needs to be recognized that the whole structural approach to narrative really depends on the notion that it is deep structures and not we ourselves that generate meaning.* And yet, is this not after all a form of linguistic totalitarianism? Jean-Marie Domenach writes that this sort of linguistic philosophy ends up with the following scenario: 'I don't think, I am thought; I don't speak, I am spoken; I don't deal with something, I am dealt with.' This is unacceptable because 'The system, a thinking that is cold, impersonal, erected at the expense of all subjectivity, individual or collective, negates at last the very possibility of a subject capable of expression and independent action.' It is questionable whether NT structuralists can really subscribe to such a view in the light of redaction critics' insistence that one cannot avoid questions of theological motivation and authorial intention in any narrative criticism* of the Bible.

In spite of its methodological weaknesses, structural analysis is capable of providing insights into biblical narrative which no other method could supply. This is evident especially in essays like Roland Barthes' 'Struggle with the Angel', which helps to explain how and why we experience a powerful sense of disorientation in reading the tale – a disorientation not unlike discovering that the detective is really the murderer. As Tony Thiselton has put it, 'it is possible to use structural methods without necessarily subscribing fully to structuralism as an ideology'. Of the Lévi-Straussian method, Thiselton writes that 'without question the human mind does rely on the use of semantic* opposition, and meaning can be fruitfully analysed in terms of the structural relations between semantic components at various levels, from that of the word to that of the narrative, or even that of a whole biblical book'. Of the method deriving from Propp and Greimas, he writes: 'Even if the "narrative grammar" of Greimas sometimes seems forced in its application to biblical texts, this and other structural models help us to see the familiar texts in a fresh light and from a fresh vantage-point.' These judgments are sound and should encourage exegetes to consider structural analysis as a legitimate tool for biblical interpretation. Just as learning English involves mastering a linguistic system of norms and rules, so appreciating biblical narrative must involve for us the mastering of that narrative system which governed its composition.

See also **Anthropology; Hermenentics; Holistic Interpretation; Narrative Criticism; Reader-Response Criticism; Semiotics; Synchronic Exegesis.**

Roland Barthes, *Image, Music, Text: Essays Selected and Translated by Stephen Heath*, 1977; Terence Hawkes, *Structuralism and Semiotics*, 1977; Elizabeth Malbon, *Narrative Space and Mythic Meaning in Mark*, 1986; Daniel Patte, *Paul's Faith and the Power of the Gospel*, 1983; id., *The Gospel According to Matthew: A Structural Commentary on Matthew's Faith*, 1987; Vladimir Propp, 'Structure and History in the Study of the Fairy-Tale', *Semeia* 10, 1978.

MARK W. G. STIBBE

Symbol

In its native Greek, the word *sumbolon* meant the token or insignia whereby someone or something was identified, their place in the world fixed. Such badges are close to words and interchangeable with them. So words, and the forms in which they are arranged and work, are symbols. They are not the things themselves but the means or media whereby those things are got into patterns which make more or less coherent sense to people. The American poet Wallace Stevens said that we do not live in the world but in a picture of it, voicing a radical apprehension of the symbolic nature of all the thinking and doing whereby we get to grips with our world. This difference between things and how we deal with them has preoccupied philosophers,* at least since Kant.

Biblical interpretation has played a strong part in bringing this state of affairs to the surface of consciousness. The Bible has been an integral and major part of the symbolic structuring of Western societies. It has been *the* book, used for oaths, haruspication and as a gift on solemn occasions. Its patterns of time, politics, ethics* and theology have been enormously influential. Its symbols, and itself as a symbol, have been normative. Even in the late 1980s the leaders of the British government and opposition fought for possession of it. So the story of how it came to be consciously recognized as symbolic is momentous in modern Western history.

To live among symbols and to recognize them as such are two very different things. The first is unavoidable and allows no human exceptions. The second is optional and rarer. To recognize as such the symbols whereby one lives requires the occupation of an intellectual standpoint somewhere outside the symbolic system itself. It was never difficult for a prophet* to notice the symbolic nature of a cult* which did nothing to promote his own moral concerns. Likewise to regard other people's religions as symbolic, even in the stultified form of idolatry, was an easy way of making sense of them if their abolition was impracticable. But to recognize one's own cherished religion as symbolic is an intellectual and moral feat of another order, and requires extra resources.

Before it can happen, a base outside the symbolic system has to be constructed: a platform from which that system can be viewed. The opposite of symbol, which is by nature equivocal and Janus-faced, is fact,* which is believed to be simple and univocal. (This may emerge to be symbolic too in the end, but that does not matter for the present because it temporarily provides an extra-mural position vis-à-vis the prevailing system of symbols.) It was the empirical and experimental search for facts, in nature and in history, which gave seventeenth-century biblical critics this all-important base of operations. In France, Richard Simon gave cogent historical reasons for the contradictions, gaps and errors in the OT text by reconstructing the conditions of writing in ancient Israel. In England John Locke restored Paul's* letters to their particular historical contexts and by means of historical inquiry represented the teaching of Jesus as based on only one simple doctrine, his own messiahship.*

Neither Simon nor Locke cared for symbols. They were pioneers of that quest for historical facts which is still so powerful in biblical studies because it is its charter of freedom from the symbolic system of the church's orthodoxy. Within their set of mind, the identification of any major part of the Bible's structure as symbolic was a negative achievement and not nourishing of belief. When Locke's friend and successor Anthony Collins exposed the freely allegorical* methods of interpretation which allowed Christian writers like Matthew to fulfil OT prophecies by NT occurrences – in other words, unearthed the highly symbolic nature of early Christian exegesis* and its indifference to facts – his work was neither kindly meant nor kindly taken. A sincere and honest Newtonian Christian, like Collins' opponent Whiston, stood foursquare by the literal fulfilment of prophecies as the bedrock of faith.

Positive and sympathetic study of biblical symbolism required a further movement of the mind. To stand outside biblical symbolism was not enough. It was necessary also to appreciate and value it as something of deep human importance and not antique absurdity. This was done for the OT in the remarkable 'Lectures on the Sacred Poetry of the Hebrews' given by Robert Lowth in Oxford from 1741. He proclaimed that the symbolic and figurative utterances of prophets and psalmists had religious value superior to that of abstract and unambiguous assertions, because they were the product of feelings profounder than thought. Religion and poetic symbolism were united in the primal depths of human nature. Lowth's protest vindicated the role of symbolic imagining in the Bible. His influence was wide and affected poets such as Smart and Blake* as well as German OT scholarship* in its brilliant phase from Michaelis onwards. He became Bishop of London. But this did not signal the church's espousal of his insight. In the next generation even Coleridge's* high doctrine of symbols and his enthusiastic application of it to the Bible in *Confessions of an Inquiring Spirit* (1840) failed to carry beyond a few of the Anglican intelligentsia.

There was starker confrontation in Germany. The whole issue of symbolism becomes most explosive when the genre* of 'myth'* is raised. In myths, symbols are sustained within a narrative.* If that narrative is believed to be a record of historical fact substantiating fundamental beliefs, then the suggestion that it is nothing of the sort can only lead to trouble. Strauss'* *Life of Jesus Critically Examined* (1835) presented mythic exegesis of the NT Gospels as the only alternative to reading them as narratives, either of impossible and unconnected supernatural facts, or of natural facts (thunderstorms etc.) invariably misunderstood. The abrasive boldness of Strauss' style gave his opponents a pretext for evading the hectoring cogency of his case, and his theological career petered out in revisions.

In the century and a half since Strauss, symbolic biblical interpretation has been resisted by most Christian exegetes in favour of a Lockean quest for factual bedrock. Rudolf Bultmann,* who went no farther than Strauss and did so much more considerately, was too radical for most of his colleagues in Europe. Austin Farrer's brilliant work on biblical symbolism, both exegetical and theoretical, was marginalized as eccentric. However, decisive changes in this state of affairs will occur if the present influx of ideas from anthropology* and literary criticism* is kept up or increased. Practitioners of these disciplines are used to making sense of, and giving value to, symbolic systems which they do not themselves inhabit or accord the allegiance of faith to. They seek to describe, rather than to threaten or defend. They use both Lockean empiricism and Lowthian sympathy on a wide range of societies and texts, and contribute in their turn to the post-modern apprehension of the inescapability of symbols and symbolic structures. Examples are Frank Kermode's literary inquiry into eschatological* symbols in *The Sense of an Ending* and Edmund Leach's application of anthropological studies of kinship and rites of passage to biblical texts in *Structuralist Interpretations of Biblical Myth* (1983).

Practically every kind of symbol is exemplified in the Bible. We have already touched on myths. Both time and space are, as ever in human affairs, symbolically ordered. The priestly seven-day week is embedded in the myth of creation* in Gen. 1, as is the symbolic structuring of space as the roofed house of the world, lit and furnished and set between waters. The Bible is exceptional in its epic historical sweep from creation to doomsday. This vast tract of time is marshalled and articulated by another symbolic structure which we have noticed, the rhythm of prophecies made and fulfilled which sustains the work of the deuteronomistic historians* of the OT and the two books by Luke in the NT, not excepting Paul's historical scheme and the other Gospels. Within this, typology* is a major way of symbolically connecting important figures to one another. The depictions of Jesus in the NT all draw on OT types: priests, prophets and patriarchs, not least Moses* the promulgator of the old covenant* as Jesus is of the new. Symbols are particularly prominent in rites and ceremonies. They therefore dominate the two biblical books which are most concerned with cult, Leviticus and the Epistle to the Hebrews. A function of cult is to correct the muddle of life as it is lived by a clear presentation of life as it ought to be lived. To this end audible, visual, touchable and even eatable symbols are clearly presented. The symbolic world is called in to redress the moral imbalance of the ordinary. Hence symbols are also particularly prominent in times of stress and deracination. The prophecies which Ezekiel made in Babylonian exile and which the Christian John made in exile on Patmos (Revelation) are among the richest and heaviest stores of symbols in the biblical canon.* But these should not blind the reader to the prevalence of symbols in less anxious times when the ordinary way of things was not so disjointed from faith. In Ps. 104 the natural world, as it is, is eloquent of divine providence and symbolically transparent. Ordinary birds and beasts are there as much tokens of God's rule as the grotesque hybrid creatures which appear in the visions of Daniel.

See also **Allegory; Figures of Speech; Typology.**

A. M. Farrer, *The Glass of Vision*, 1948; E. R. Goodenough, *Jewish Symbols in the Greco-Roman World*, 1953; Edmund Leach and D. Alan Aycock, *Structuralist Interpretations of Biblical Myth*, 1983.

                                JOHN DRURY

Synchronic Exegesis

In modern biblical studies, synchronic exegesis is an approach which focusses attention both on texts as totalities and also on the interaction of interpreters with the texts they are studying. These two features are discussed below. To begin with, it may be helpful to distinguish synchronic exegesis from approaches which find the key to interpretation in diachronic terms, i.e. in the historical antecedents of the text.

Although examples of synchronic exegesis are found in many different ages (like horizontal branches from a diachronic trunk), the diachronic approach has so dominated critical scholarship that the term 'literary criticism' * acquired a different meaning in the biblical field from that current in general literary studies. Traditio-historical * criticism was preoccupied with the search for sources,* forms * and redactional * elements, the identification of author,* date and place of writing and, even more dubiously, the author's intention in writing – in blissful ignorance, apparently, of the 'intentionalist fallacy'. Hence the influence of synchronic linguistics * (cf. Saussure), which studied language as a living whole at a particular time, and of the synchronic approach to texts adopted by Jacobson and the Czechoslovakian structuralists,* for example, was slow to permeate the world of biblical scholarship. Within the last twenty years the process has been assisted, however, by demands for a new approach which sprang both

from dissatisfaction with the results of obsessive allegiance to diachrony – 'historical biblical criticism * is bankrupt' (Wink) – and from the perception of a modern cultural * change which points strongly towards the adoption of a holistic* paradigm in place of the subject-object underlying diachronic approaches.

The first consequence was to move the focus of interpretation from the author to the text. Synchronic exegesis evinces 'a primary exegetical respect for the final literary work itself and a productive concentration upon interpreting that work in its own terms' (R. M. Frye). It gives full expression to the hermeneutical * principle that the part is to be related to the whole and the whole to the part (*see* **Hermeneutic Circle**). It resists the atomizing of the text, insists on the integrity of the whole text, and respects its genre* (e.g. narrative,* poetry *).

The second move, implicit in the first, was to focus on the interaction of reader and text: i.e. as in structuralism, account is taken of the creative and structuring activity of human beings. The reader thus engages with the world of the text in such a way that the text can address issues in the world of the reader. In this way, the material is understood as live communication, as rhetorical * discourse, as invitation to change one's understanding of oneself, one's world and one's actions, through imaginative participation in the world that is opened out in front of the text.

Synchronic exegesis is often sharply distinguished from diachronic and dogmatic approaches: the former focussing on 'the world behind the text' (e.g. sources) and the latter on 'the world in the way of the text' (e.g. doctrine). Yet synchronic and diachronic approaches are not incompatible. The synchronic approach relies on sound textual scholarship. The structural method of Jacobson, Lévi-Strauss, Barthes and others did not rule out referential and historical dimensions of the text. Diachrony exists in synchrony. Texts may convey a 'history-likeness', which is misleading only when modern interpreters take the basic meaning to reside in 'ostensive reference to historical events' (Poland). When the diachronic is allowed to usurp the primacy of the synchronic, the wholeness of the text is put in jeopardy.

Dogmatic presuppositions also can disable the reading of the text. It is often suggested that synchronic exegesis may appeal to readers in a variety of contexts, not least those outside the community of faith. The basic point, however, is that the text is read in a particular context, which may or may not be a context of faith. In any case, doctrinal or other philosophical presuppositions should not be allowed to get in the way of engagement with the text itself.

Synchronic exegesis is found today in rhetorical criticism,* narrative theology,* the application of reader-response* theory to exegesis,* and the new literary approaches to biblical study. Not surprisingly, since the holistic approach assists the interaction of the text and the socio*-political realities of the interpreter's context, synchronic exegesis is also evident in modern liberation* and political theology.

See also **Holistic Interpretation; Narrative Criticism.**

Hans Frei, *The Eclipse of Biblical Narrative*, 1974; Edgar V. McKnight, *Meaning in Texts*, 1978; Lynn M. Poland, *Literary Criticism and Biblical Hermeneutics*, 1985; George W. Stroup, *The Promise of Narrative Theology*, 1981; Walter Wink, *The Bible in Human Transformation*, 1973.

J. I. H. MCDONALD

Synopsis

The synopsis has proved to be an important tool for both Gospel* and textual* criticism, and the increasing variety of modern synopses has been accompanied by some debate about the form and purpose of such works. Synopses most commonly juxtapose corresponding texts from the three 'Synoptic' Gospels and sometimes also from the Fourth Gospel (and indeed other sources), so that each page is divided into three or four columns to permit easy comparison of the parallel Gospel accounts. The precise ways in which such parallels are defined and divided, however, may vary considerably. Synopses should also probably be distinguished from Gospel 'harmonies'.* Harmonies, which were common in the centuries before modern biblical criticism,* sought to weave the various canonical Gospel accounts into a single chronological sequence, and attempted thereby to resolve apparent contradictions or discrepancies amongst the accounts. Synopses, on the other hand, have tended to be more concerned with enabling comparisons of texts for textual and source-,* form-* or redaction*-critical purposes than with producing a single compatible unity from the different accounts.

The history of identifying Gospel parallels can be traced back to the early Christian centuries. Eusebius* of Caesarea devised a system of section numbers for indicating parallel accounts without actually disturbing the scriptural text. By the end of the eighteenth century Fabricius recorded that he was familiar with almost 150 concordances* and harmonies, although most of these were still concerned to demonstrate the agreement of the Gospel testimony or to present a consistent description of the historical chain of events behind the Gospels, sometimes even designating the year, month and day for the various events in Jesus' ministry.

A critical turning point was reached with the synopsis of J. J. Griesbach, first published in 1776 and followed by later editions. Griesbach's synopsis differed from previous work both in its purpose and form. His synopsis was designed to complement his lectures in which the individual method and sources of each Gospel writer were analysed. There was no attempt to reconcile differences in the Gospel accounts. Thus he left the order of each Gospel relatively intact, except where relevant parallels required that he disturb the sequence. Even then, references to parallels were often just noted rather than the full text being displayed. Parallels to the Fourth Gospel were restricted, but an extensive textual apparatus was published. His synopsis did not openly reflect his own theory of synoptic relationships, however, and indeed it was criticized by H. L. Planck (1809) for being concerned mainly to aid interpretation of the Gospels and not being sufficiently orientated on questions of Gospel relationships.

Griesbach's work stimulated the production of many new critical synopses. Some were concerned with text-critical questions, giving increased attention to the textual apparatus, finding in the Gospel texts evidence of later scribal harmonizations and tracing the wording of texts through the apocryphal and patristic literature. The works by Tischendorf (1851) and A. Wright (1896, 1903) were significant in this respect. But this concern with the history of the text is not wholly separable from the Synoptic Problem* itself, as Wright demonstrated, and synopses began increasingly to be used to demonstrate particular theories of source relationships. Early critical synopses which sought to illustrate Marcan priority or the Two Source theory include the works of J. Gehringer (1842), W. G. Rushbrooke (1880), J. Weiss (1913), Burton and Goodspeed (1920), and notably the first edition of A. Huck (1892), which was published initially to supplement Holtzmann's commentary* on the Synoptic Gospels. This aim was abandoned, however, by Huck's third edition of 1906. The synopses of B. Solages (1959) and R. Morgenthaler (1957) introduced statistical analyses into their consideration of the text. Morgenthaler's 'synopsis' is striking in that it supports a modified Two Source theory by examining the frequency of words in the text rather than simply by presenting the Gospel texts themselves in parallel. A multiple-source theory of synoptic relationships is set out in the synopsis of P. Benoit and M. Boismard (1969), and the recent synopses of J. B. Orchard (1982, 1983) openly support the neo-Griesbach or 'Two Gospel' hypothesis.

Synopsis construction has not only been influenced by source criticism of the Gospels, but also by form-critical considerations. To facilitate form-critical analyses, W. E. Bundy's synopsis (1932) attempted to divide the Gospel texts into units which reflected the primitive units of tradition from which he believed the Gospels were composed. This resulted in about 470 pericopes. Interestingly, K. Aland's important synopsis (first edition 1963) depicts 367 units, inclusive of some Johannine sections, while the recent Huck-Greeven synopsis (1981) lists 275. Clearly the division of the text into units is an editorial decision which may depend on many factors, and it is not always clear whether the divisions in synopses of recent decades are consciously intended to correspond to units of pre-Gospel, oral traditions.*

Literary* and redaction criticism of the Gospels, however, have been less well served by recent synopsis construction. To some extent, these interests may come into conflict with form-critical interests. The need to depict the narrative units in the mind of each evangelist* places importance on preserving the integrity of each Gospel in the synopsis' presentation. Division into form-critical units will not necessarily reflect any given evangelist's plan of arrangement. Yet R. W. Funk (1985) has constructed two volumes of *Gospel Parallels* which attempt to show the structure of the Gospel narratives themselves, presenting each Gospel 'in its own narrative integrity', dividing according to its own narrative markers, with parallel passages noted as appropriate.

It will be obvious that the theory of synopsis construction is becoming an area of growing interest, although the discussion has in fact been remarkably limited thus far. In articles in 1980 and 1985 D. L. Dungan has raised questions about how far modern synopses should seek to be multi-purpose tools and how far any synopsis can in fact be neutral regarding source-critical hypotheses. With respect to the first question, he suggests that future synopses should limit themselves to specific purposes – text-critical study, study of pre-Gospel oral traditions, or study of the literary composition of the Gospels – and not seek to cover all these sometimes conflicting aims. Secondly, he takes issue with those, such as H. Greeven, who argue that synopses can and should be neutral with respect to source theories, aloof from efforts to prove a particular theory of synoptic source relationships. Modern synopses may claim to be objective by presenting the text of each Gospel in its consecutive order and by repeating Gospel sections out of order as often as necessary to show parallels with other Gospels, but Dungan claims that no synopsis can actually be 'objective' in this way. By its selection of

the text, its division into sections and its ordering of them, every synopsis, he argues, is influenced by the source-critical assumptions of its editors. In Dungan's view, future synopses should show greater frankness about these assumptions and be openly committed to a particular source theory from the outset. Such views are not yet widely accepted, but these issues will undoubtedly have to be considered in future synopsis construction.

See also **Gospel; Source Criticism (New Testament).**

D. L. Dungan, 'Theory of Synopsis Construction' in *Biblica* 61, 1980, pp. 305–29; id., 'Synopses of the Future' in *Biblica* 66, 1985, pp. 457–92; H. Greeven, 'The Gospel Synopsis from 1776 to the Present Day' in B. Orchard and T. R. W. Longstaff (eds), *J. J. Griesbach: Synoptic and Text-Critical Studies, 1776–1976,* 1978, pp. 22–49.

R. A. PIPER

Synoptic Problem

The three 'Synoptic' Gospels, Matthew, Mark and Luke, are very closely related to one another: all agree extensively in the order of the events they describe, and there is a high measure of verbal agreement between them in the stories they have in common. Some sort of literary relationship between them seems necessary to explain these facts. Determining just what that relationship might be is known today as the Synoptic Problem.

The most widely accepted solution to the Synoptic Problem is the so-called Two Source theory. This theory claims that Mark's Gospel was used as a source* by Matthew and Luke; further, Matthew and Luke had access to other common source material, usually called Q, which accounts for the extensive agreement of these two Gospels outside their Marcan material. There are thus two basic sources, Mark and Q.

The Two Source theory has been widely accepted ever since the mid-nineteenth century and was popularized in English-speaking scholarship by the work of B. H. Streeter in 1924. Recently, however, there has been a strong upsurge of support for an older critical theory, viz. that of J. J. Griesbach, who argued that Matthew's Gospel was written first; Luke then used Matthew; Mark's Gospel was then written third conflating the accounts of both Matthew and Luke. Today this theory is vigorously supported in the work of W. R. Farmer and others. Different solutions to the problem have also been proposed. Some have maintained a belief in Marcan priority but have questioned the Q theory, arguing that Luke knew Matthew and that the Matthew–Luke agreements are to be explained in this way.

(So Farrer, Goulder.) Others have proposed extremely complex theories of prior stages in the tradition with links between these stages to explain the agreements between the Gospels (e.g. Boisard).

The revival of the Griesbach hypothesis has led to a critical re-evaluation of some of the arguments used to support the Two Source theory, and it is now recognized that some of the arguments used by Streeter and others in the past to support the theory of Marcan priority are not as conclusive as was sometimes thought. Many of Streeter's original arguments may have to be modified. Nevertheless, majority opinion today is still in favour of some form of the Two Source theory as the most satisfactory (or least problematic) solution to the Synoptic Problem. In particular some of Streeter's more formal arguments can be supplemented and strengthened by appealing to redactional* considerations, i.e. by considering in which direction the tradition is most likely to have developed.

For example, Streeter appealed to the phenomenon of common content as supporting the theory of Marcan priority: practically all of Mark appears in either Matthew or Luke, and often in both. In itself this fact shows nothing. Yet when one considers the actual contents of the Gospels, and considers the various theories proposed, the argument for Marcan priority can be strengthened. The Matthean and Lucan parallels to Mark are usually shorter, and Matthew and Luke both contain a lot more material. According to the theory of Marcan priority, Matthew and Luke abbreviated Mark in order to make space for further material which was available to them. This appears to many to be a plausible redactional procedure. By contrast, the Griesbach hypothesis must assert that Mark omitted large portions of Matthew and Luke but also expanded the material he did retain quite considerably. Such a redactional procedure seems rather less plausible.

Streeter also appealed to the fact that Matthew and Luke hardly ever agree against Mark in wording or order. (There are, however, some notable exceptions to this 'rule' in relation to the detailed wording within pericopes: cf. below on the 'minor agreements'.) It has been pointed out by many that if one deduces from this that Mark was the common source used by Matthew and Luke, one is guilty of a logical fallacy, the so-called 'Lachmann fallacy': the facts can be explained by any theory where Mark is in a 'medial' position in the 'tree' of relationships between the Gospels. However, once again a concrete approach can be more helpful. Take, for example, the phenomenon of order. On the theory of Marcan priority, Matthew and Luke rarely change Mark's order; and in each case a plausible reason in terms of Matthew's or Luke's redaction can be given. (E.g. Matthew collects together a series of miracle* stories in chs 8–9 as part of his schematic ordering, and hence changes Mark's order slightly; Luke brings forward the rejection story to Luke 4.16–30 so that it acts as a programmatic summary of the whole story to follow in Luke–Acts.) The reverse changes as postulated by the Griesbach hypothesis seem hard to envisage. Mark must have oscillated back and forth between his sources with no clear reason for doing so. Further, he must have taken some care to avoid the Sermon on the Mount* (Matt. 5–7, with Lucan parallel). Why should he have done this? The fact that no good reason seems available thus leads many to maintain the theory of Marcan priority.

Study of the detailed wording in the Gospels often leads to the same conclusion. For example, the words of Peter's* confession at Caesarea Philippi are in Mark 8.29, 'You are the Christ'; in Matt. 16.16, 'You are the Christ, the Son of the Living God'. If Mark's Gospel were prior, Matthew's version can be seen as a natural expansion of the shorter text, adding a term ('Son of God') which is clearly important for Matthew's christology.* If Matthew were written first, then Mark must have deleted this reference to Jesus as Son of God. Given Mark's clear interest in the idea of Jesus as God's Son (cf. Mark 1.1; 1.11; 9.7; 15.39) it seems highly unlikely that Mark would omit such a reference from a source if it were available to him.

The theory about the existence of Q is slightly different in that one is postulating the existence of a source which is no longer extant to explain the agreements between Matthew and Luke. For the most part, arguments for the existence of Q are in the form of negative arguments against the view that the Matthew–Luke agreements could be explained by the theory of one evangelist* directly using the work of the other. (Almost always this is in the form of Luke using Matthew.) Against such a view one can refer to the fact that Luke never seems to be aware of Matthew's larger additions to Mark in Marcan material (e.g. Matt. 16.17–19). Further, many would argue that neither Matthew nor Luke consistently gives the more original form of the tradition in passages where they are parallel: sometimes Matthew seems to be more original, sometimes Luke (e.g. Luke's shorter version of the Lord's Prayer* in 11.2–4 is widely regarded as more original than Matthew's). These considerations make it most likely that Matthew and Luke depend on common source materials. Whether Q ever formed a unified source, or whether Q represents an amorphous mass of otherwise unrelated materials, is a further, logically separable, problem. However, many studies have recently tried to analyse the Q material from the point of view of redaction criticism, seeking to identify its particular theological characteristics. In so far as they are successful, these studies might suggest that Q formed a unified source at some stage in the tradition. However, in terms of the Synoptic Problem itself, the question of the unity of the Q material can perhaps be regarded as a subsidiary issue. The main point is that the Matthew–Luke agreements are not easily to be explained by direct dependence of one evangelist on the work of the other.

The theory of Marcan priority has always encountered difficulties, especially in relation to the so-called 'minor agreements'. These are passages where, contrary to the usual pattern, Matthew and Luke do agree against Mark. According to the theory of Marcan priority, one would not expect Matthew and Luke to change their Marcan source in exactly the same way if they are working independently of each other. Instances where this occurs thus constitute an anomaly for the theory of Marcan priority. A few such agreements would not be unexpected, but the number which in fact occur seems to many rather high for comfort. A variety of explanations has been proposed. Some agreements, chiefly of a stylistic kind, may be due to independent redaction by Matthew and Luke. Others may in fact disappear if one follows the reading of different manuscripts * of the text. Each case must be adjudged on its own merits, but probably the best explanation, on the theory of Marcan priority, is that they are due to independent redaction of Mark by Matthew and Luke.

Although these texts often form the basis of arguments of those who want to question the theory of Marcan priority (as also of those who, denying Q, claim that Luke used both Mark and Matthew), it is by no means clear that these texts can be explained any better by other source hypotheses. For example, the Griesbach hypothesis has to explain these texts as due to Mark's editorial changes of the common witness of his two alleged sources. But whilst this can explain some of the minor agreements, it cannot explain all of them. These texts thus constitute an anomaly for almost any solution to the Synoptic Problem, certainly for any simple solution.

In the past, scholars have thought that the prime relevance of the Synoptic Problem is in relation to rediscovering the history described in the Gospels. In one way this is perfectly valid. The more original form of any saying of Jesus will be found in Mark or Q, rather than in Matthew's or Luke's modifications of those sources. However, one must not proceed

too far too fast. The fact that Mark and Q are earlier than Matthew and Luke does not mean that we can read Mark and Q as simple transcripts of the life of Jesus without more ado. Mark and Q take us back to the 50s or 60s of the first century, but this is still at least 20 years after the death of Jesus. In order to use our sources to get back to Jesus, we have to use the insights of form criticism * as well as be aware of the possible theological nature of the basic sources Mark and Q themselves.

Perhaps more important than historical considerations is the way in which the Synoptic Problem lies at the basis of all modern redaction criticism of the Gospels. By isolating the sources used by each Gospel writer, we can have insight into the way in which each writer has used his tradition. Given the dominant position occupied by redaction criticism in contemporary Gospel study, it is extremely important that the basis for such redaction-critical work, i.e. one's solution to the Synoptic Problem, be soundly based. Hence the importance of modern developments which have questioned the Two Source Theory. A different solution to the Synoptic Problem might have very great repercussions in relation to results claimed at the level of redaction criticism.

See also **Source Criticism; Synopsis.**

A. J. Bellinzoni (ed.), *The Two-Source Hypothesis: A Critical Appraisal*, 1985; W. R. Farmer, *The Synoptic Problem*, 1964; J. A. Fitzmyer, 'The Priority of Mark and the "Q" Source in Luke', *Jesus and Man's Hope* I, 1970, pp. 131–170; M. D. Goulder, *Luke: a New Paradigm*, 1989; B. H. Streeter, *The Four Gospels*, 1924; C. M. Tuckett, *The Revival of the Griesbach Hypothesis*, 1983.

C. M. TUCKETT

Syntax

Differences of interpretation arise in many instances not from textual * problems or words of uncertain or ambiguous meaning, but from a different assessment of the structure of a sentence and of the function and interrelationship of words within it. As far as Hebrew is concerned, its structure appears deceptively simple. Its clauses are linked mainly by co-ordination, rendered literally in English by a series of 'ands' (parataxis) rather than by a variety of subordinate clauses introduced by such words as 'when', 'as', 'though' (hypotaxis). Nevertheless their precise relationship is sometimes difficult to determine. An immediate example of a choice of possible relationships occurs in Gen. 1.1. This may be taken as an independent sentence expressing an absolute beginning, God alone being pre-existent. However, it is more attractive grammatically to see it as part of the overall structure of vv. 1–3 with the meaning 'when God began to create' (*bᵉrēshīt* as construct before the verb; cf. Hos. 1.2), with v. 2 as a circumstantial clause and v. 3 the main clause announcing the first creative fiat, a structure parallel to the beginning of the second creation* story (2.4b–7). The NEB, taking v. 2 as the main clause, has Genesis open on a strangely negative note, less in keeping, too, with word order and verb tense.

Ambiguity attaches also to the structure of Ex. 6.3, a passage of fundamental importance for the development of Israelite religion, and generally translated with two parallel clauses: 'I appeared to Abraham,* to Isaac and to Jacob as El Shaddai, but *by* my name Yahweh I did not make myself known to them', a rendering which conceals the awkward fact that the preposition 'by' is not in the text. As part of the larger structure of vv. 2–4 the intended parallel may be not between El Shaddai and Yahweh but between 'I am Yahweh' (v. 2) and 'and my name is Yahweh' (v. 3) (Andersen). V. 3b may then be linked with v. 4 as a rhetorical question expecting the answer 'yes', of which there are numerous examples similarly unmarked by an interrogative particle. In view of other explanations proposed for the absence of a preposition before 'my name' (*shᵉmī*), the matter cannot be resolved on grammatical grounds alone but wider considerations of context must be taken into account, a salutary reminder that it is not always a matter of unambiguous syntax clarifying interpretation but of context and appropriate meaning being decisive.

The question of the relationship of clauses may also arise from difficulty in determining the precise function of particles. Thus *hēn* and *hinnē*, frequently translated as 'behold!', may on occasion function also as conjunctions meaning 'if' or 'when' (cf. Lev. 13.5; Josh. 2.18). The problem lies in determining their function in specific instances. New insights do not always resolve difficulties; rather, they open up fresh possibilities. Thus in the famous crux in Isa. 7.14 the possibility exists that *hinnē* may function not as the interjection 'behold!' but as a conjunction introducing a conditional clause; 'if a young woman, who is now pregnant, bear a son, she will call his name Immanuel' (Kaiser's translation, *Isaiah 1–12*, ET ² 1983), thus focussing attention not on the proclamation of a birth but on the significance of the name. A similar approach has been suggested in Isa. 32.1–3. If the initial word *hēn* is understood not as an interjection but as a conjunction, 'when a king reigns in righteousness and the rulers rule with justice', the main clause is the question, 'will not the eyes of the seeing see?' (identical in structure

to Ex. 8.26 [*Heb.* 22]), giving an excellent parallel to the following clause and avoiding the common emendation of *shā'āh*, 'see' to *shā'a'*, 'be blind' (Labuschagne). A textual difficulty is thus resolved. There are, however, consequences for interpretation since the passage is not then strictly a messianic* prophecy* but a portrait of ideal kingship.*

It is clear that in assessing the function of a particle the question of its relationship to the clause in which it stands is fundamental. Does it relate to the clause as a whole or qualify a particular word within it? This is well illustrated in the divergent translations of Isa. 45.14. If the particle *'ak* is held to function on clause level it carries an emphatic sense, 'Surely God is with you' (NEB, NIV); if it relates to the prepositional phrase it has a restrictive sense, 'God is with you only' (RSV, JB. See Andersen). Here word order is not decisive and broader considerations of meaning* are involved. The same two possibilities exist also in Ps. 23.6. A similar question arises in Gen. 18.20 with the particle *kī*. It may be taken on clause level as a conjunction meaning 'because' (so RSV) or, more likely in view of its position in Hebrew, as qualifying the following adjective in an elative sense, giving the meaning 'exceedingly great, utterly grievous' (cf. NEB, JB).

Likewise the precise function of prepositions is notoriously difficult to determine. The preposition *min*, for example, may indicate comparison, 'knowledge of God rather than burnt offerings' (Hos. 6.6, RSV) or negation, 'not whole-offerings but the knowledge of God' (NEB), a matter of considerable importance for the prophet's attitude to sacrifice. The issue turns on more than syntax and must be resolved on the basis of the prophet's thought in general. It is similar ambiguity as to the function of the preposition which allows the translation of Job 19.26 as 'from my flesh' (RSV) or 'without my flesh' (RSVmg). The possibility that the preposition *lᵉ* has an emphatic sense accounts for the significant difference in Ps. 89.18 between 'Yahweh truly is our king' (cf. NEB) and 'our king belongs to Yahweh' (cf. RSV). For an entirely different reason a syntactical problem of considerable exegetical* importance occurs in Lev. 19.18: is the familiar prepositional phrase 'as yourself' adverbial, that is, 'You shall love your neighbour as you love yourself', or adjectival, 'your neighbour who is as yourself', that is, in this context (cf. v. 18a) an Israelite, hence the reference to non-Israelites in v. 33. The former is clearly the meaning in the NT (Mark 12.31), but the latter arguably in the OT (Muraoka, *JSS* 23, 1978).

To what extent Hebrew usage may be elucidated from Ugaritic* is a matter of some debate. Thus there is no consensus of opinion whether enclitic -*m* exists in Hebrew. This suffix of uncertain vocalization appears a number of times in the Ugaritic texts, though its significance is not clear. Some have espoused its presence in Hebrew with vigour, believing that the Massoretes* failed to recognize it and thus vocalized it wrongly; others are sceptical of its very existence in Hebrew. Certainly its acceptance would solve a number of problems, though they are in general capable of other explanations. An interesting example occurs in Ps. 29.6 where recognition of enclitic -*m* in place of the pronominal suffix, 'he makes them skip like a calf' (KJV), produces the excellent parallelism, 'he makes Lebanon skip like a calf, and Sirion like a young wild ox'. Andersen and Freedman, *Hosea*, 1985, have posited 'an unassailable example' where MT has the strange juxtaposition 'bulls our lips' in Hos. 14.2 (*Heb.* 3); enclitic -*m* here produces the usual translation 'the fruit of our lips', though a redivision of the consonants is equally possible (NEB).

Attention has also been drawn to expression of simultaneous action by the following sequence: imperfect consecutive verb, followed by noun or pronoun subject, preceding a perfect tense. The dramatic effect of I Kings 1.41 is then recognized: at the proclamation of Solomon as king, Adonijah and his guests 'heard and stopped feasting', simultaneous not consecutive action as in RSV and NEB (Sutcliffe, *JSS* 3, 1958). The same grammatical structure giving dramatic impact occurs in Ex. 9.23. Context must, however, be the guide in the decision between this and similarly structured circumstantial clauses.

Discussion of the syntax of NT Greek is beset by the problem of its relationship to classical Greek on the one hand and to contemporary secular Greek on the other. There is further complication in the undoubted Semitic influence on it, whether mediated through the Septuagint* or more directly from the use of Semitic sources (*see* **Semitisms**). To distinguish between these, however, is not easy. The Semitic quality of Luke's infancy narratives* and of Acts 1–15 has suggested that Hebrew and Aramaic sources respectively may lie behind them. Others are less confident that a Semitic quality in the Greek indicates that the writer is drawing on a Semitic source. It may be that Luke adapts 'his style and syntax to suit the nature of his narrative' (Turner, *NTS*, 20, 1974). The peculiar features of the Greek of Revelation, particularly in its neglect of strict agreement in gender and case, are found also in *koine* and later Greek, but it is likely that a conscious striving after a Semitic quality is operative, perhaps for reasons of piety (S. Thompson, *The Apocalypse and Semitic Syntax*, 1985).

The unique character of NT Greek must not, therefore, be underestimated, but this of itself presents problems for interpretation. One such is the famous crux of Mark 4.12. Does it express the purpose of parables,* their result, or the reason for their use? Each view has advocates. The problem is the conjunction *hina*; is it 'in order that' or 'so that' or 'because'? Cranfield (*St Mark*, 1966) takes it unambiguously as in classical Greek to indicate purpose (a final clause), interpreting the saying, difficult though it is, with reference to the veiled nature of the revelation* which creates 'a separation between faith and unbelief'; though he relieves the harshness of the verse by taking *mēpote* (v. 12b) as 'unless' or 'perhaps', the former on the supposition that Aramaic underlies it, the latter a usage found in earlier Greek, thus allowing for God's saving purpose. If, however, the rigorous standards of classical Greek are abandoned, the second possibility ('so that') may be preferred as more appropriate to NT thought, being explained as a 'Semitic blurring of purpose and result' (Moule). This seems clearly the case in John 9.2: 'who sinned ... with the result that (*hina* for the more usual *hōste*) this man was born blind?' The third suggestion depends on the possibility that in *koine* Greek *hina* may sometimes mean 'because' (cf. Rev. 14.13 for a possible example). Thus interpretation varies according to the view taken of the relationship of NT language to either classical or *koine* Greek, and of the extent of Aramaic influence.

The logical connection of a conjunction is also sometimes ambiguous and may depend on the context for clarification. Thus in Luke 7.47 love is not the ground of forgiveness but its proof, as v. 47b makes clear, despite the order of the Greek. A related question of the relationship of words is at issue in the ambiguity of I Cor. 15.19. By its position in the sentence the word 'only' (*monon*) seems to refer to the verb: 'we have only hoped (and nothing more)' (cf. NEBmg). However, the positive content given to 'hope' in the NT suggests that the word order is loose and 'only' refers to 'in this life'.

Problems of interpretation arise in some instances from the use or non-use of the definite article. The use of one article to govern two nouns 'God and saviour' (Titus 2.13; II Peter 1.1) suggests that Jesus is here explicitly called God, a usage rare in the NT but in all probability the intended meaning. Yet comparison with Acts 15.22 (one article with two personal names) and examples in the *koine* show that the issue is not beyond doubt, hence RSVmg and NEBmg. The same question arises in Eph. 2.20; are 'the apostles and prophets' one group, or is this a reference to 'the apostles and the (OT) prophets', though only one definite article occurs? It is for a similar reason that ambiguity attaches to the centurion's confession in Matt. 27.54, 'a son' or 'the son of God', the latter supported by the 'rule' that predicate nouns preceding the verb usually lack the article. The uncertainty is, however, reflected in both RSV and NEB footnotes with their contrasting decisions.

Whilst due weight must be given to the various functions of prepositions, overtranslation must be avoided. In some NT writers, though not usually in Paul,* there is a blurring of the distinction between *en* (usually 'in') and *eis* ('into'). Thus the Son is 'in (*eis* not *en*) the Father's bosom' (John 1.18), but there is 'nothing very profound here concerning mutual motion between Father and Son' (Turner). In the distinctively Christian formulation 'in the Lord', however, the primary force of the preposition *en* must be noted. To translate Col. 3.20 as 'pleasing to the Lord' is inadequate, for *en Kuriō* signifies a mystical relationship of the Christian with Christ. Meaning must therefore be determined 'from theology and biblical syntax, and not from comparative syntax' (Turner). Of considerable importance exegetically is the significance of the dative in Rom. 8.16: does the Spirit witness with, or to, our spirit that we are God's children? Despite the general consensus of modern English versions in favour of the former, it is arguable that the latter is to be preferred (cf. Vulgate *), for the divinely given assurance 'from outside and beyond ourselves' is the warrant for calling God 'Father' (Cranfield, *Romans*, 1975).

In general, the Greek case system precludes ambiguity in the relationship of nouns and qualifying adjectives or participles. John 1.9 is a famous exception. It may refer to the incarnation, the light coming into the world (RSV, NEB), or to the enlightenment of every man as he comes into the world (NEBmg). The matter turns on whether the participle 'coming' (*erchomenon*) agrees with 'light' or with 'man'. The former is generally preferred, but its resolution, as in many other instances, requires careful balancing of extra-biblical parallels on the one hand and context on the other.

See also **Philology; Translation, Problems of.**

F. I. Andersen, *The Sentence in Biblical Hebrew*, 1974; J. K. Elliott (ed.), *Studies in New Testament Language and Text*, 1976; C. J. Labuschagne et al., *Syntax and Meaning. Studies in Hebrew Syntax and Biblical Exegesis*, OTS 18, 1973; C. F. D. Moule, *An Idiom-Book of New Testament Greek*, 1968; N. Turner, *A Grammar of New Testament Greek Syntax*, Vol. III, 1963.

GRACE I. EMMERSON

Syriac Tradition

The origins of Syriac Christianity are very obscure and it is not until the fourth century that literature becomes plentiful. In the earliest period the Judaic element seems to have been strong, and there are some links with the Targum* tradition. The Syriac church became divided ecclesiastically as a result of the christological* controversies of the fifth-sixth centuries into two main traditions: 1. East Syrian, represented by the Church of the East (misleadingly named Nestorian); and 2. West Syrian, represented predominantly by the Syrian Orthodox Church (misleadingly named Monophysite), but also by the Maronite Church.

The most productive period of Syriac exegetical* tradition can be divided into two parts: fourth to seventh centuries (the more creative), and seventh to thirteenth centuries. The biblical text in general use was the Peshitta (OT translated from Hebrew, NT from Greek), though later writers also make some use of other versions, notably the Syrohexapla (translated from Origen's* revised Septuagint* text, with some marginal readings from Aquila, Symmachus and Theodotion) and the Harklean NT, both very literal translations from Greek produced in Alexandria *c.* 615.

Biblical exegesis can take many forms. From the earlier period there are commentaries* on individual books (notably Ephrem, d. 373, on Genesis, Exodus, the Diatessaron [i.e. Tatian's 'harmony'* of the Gospels*], Acts, and Epistles*), homilies* on specific passages in prose or verse (the latter notably by Narsai, d. *c.* 500, and Jacob of Serugh, d. 521), lyric or narrative poems on biblical persons or topics (Ephrem, or attributed to Ephrem), and 'rewritten Bible',* represented by the Cave of Treasures (*c.* sixth century). Under Arab rule, from the seventh century onwards, exegetical works become more learned and encyclopaedic in character. Commentaries often cover the entire Bible, notably Isho'dad of Merv (ninth century) in the East Syrian tradition, and Dionysius bar Salibi (d. 1171) and Barhebraeus (d. 1286) in the West Syrian. Those on the Hexaemeron (the six days of creation*), by Jacob of Edessa (d. 708), Moshe bar Kepha (d. 903) and by Barhebraeus (incorporated into a larger theological work), serve as repositories of much scientific knowledge. Other genres* include scholia (Jacob of Edessa; Theodore bar Koni, eighth/ninth century), questions and answers (Isho'barnun, ninth century), exegetical homilies (especially Moshe bar Kepha), catenae (notably that of the monk Severus, ninth century), and an extensive East Syrian commentary on the lectionary,* the *Gannat Bussāmē*, probably of the thirteenth century.

Earlier writers, such as Aphrahat and Ephrem in the fourth century, were aware of many haggadic traditions, and indeed the haggadic process can be said to have continued for a while in Christianized form. Already in Ephrem's commentaries the distinction is made between 'factual' (or literal*) and 'spiritual'* interpretation, though in practice commentaries of all periods employ a mixture of approaches. Ephrem and other poets like Narsai and Jacob of Serugh make extensive and creative use of typology* and symbolism:* symbols (*rāzē*, literally 'mysteries') lie hidden in both scripture and nature, visible only to the eye of faith; they serve as pointers to the 'hidden power' or spiritual meaning within the text, offering the reader a subjective experience of an objective spiritual reality. Typology and symbolism also serve to provide interconnections between the OT and the NT, the Bible and the sacraments, this world and the heavenly.

From the fifth century onwards, the influence of Greek authors, especially those writing in the Antiochene* exegetical tradition, becomes strong. Through the Persian school in Edessa, closed in 489, and its successor in Nisibis (in the Persian Empire) the influence of Theodore of Mopsuestia dominates exegesis in the church of the East. Thus an interest in historical interpretation, and a hostility to allegorical,* is widespread, intermingled with 'spiritual interpretation'; characteristic of this is the interpretation of Daniel, correctly seen as referring to the Seleucid period, in the later East Syrian commentaries (and indeed already in Aphrahat's *Demonstration* 5). Since some important West Syrian exegetes, notably Jacob of Serugh and Philoxenus, studied at the Persian school, some influence of Theodore can also be found in Syrian Orthodox exegetical tradition, alongside that of John Chrysostom, Athanasius, the Cappadocians, and Cyril of Alexandria, many of whose exegetical works were translated into Syriac in the fifth and sixth centuries. In the case of Philoxenus, above all, commentary becomes the vehicle for christological discussion.

Distinctive to the earlier Syriac tradition is the large amount of exegesis in poetic form. Both Narsai and Jacob of Serugh have cycles on the six days of creation (verse treatment of this theme is still found in the tenth-century East Syrian Emmanuel bar Shahhārē). Lively narrative poems, sometimes semi-dramatic in character, on biblical persons or themes are especially common from the fourth to sixth centuries, e.g. on the Sacrifice of Isaac (*see* **Aqeda**), a cycle of twelve books on Joseph (Balai, fifth century), the repentance of Nin-eveh (Ephrem), the Sinful Woman of Luke 7 (attributed to Ephrem), etc.

In the early Arab period two outstanding exegetes in the Syrian Orthodox tradition were Jacob of Edessa and Moshe bar Kēphā; the former was exceptional both for his critical sense and for his knowledge of Hebrew (probably modest), as well as Greek, while the latter is remarkable for his detailed and extensive coverage of the biblical text. Subsequent commentaries in both East and West Syrian tradition often have the character of compendia of earlier opinions.

For biblical chronography,* Syriac writers were largely dependent on Julius Africanus, Eusebius,* Annianus and Pandorus.

The influence of Ephrem and probably of other Syriac sources can be discerned on the sixth-century Byzantine poet Romanos, and Ephrem's Commentary on Genesis is quoted by the ninth-century George Synkellos. Behind Junilius Afer's Latin introduction to biblical studies (sixth century) lies the influence of Paul of Nisibis and (presumably) the school of Nisibis. Commentaries by, or attributed to, Ephrem were translated into Armenian at an early date, and some of them survive only in that language. At a much later date the Syriac commentary tradition exerted a strong influence on the mediaeval exegetical traditions of the Coptic and Ethiopian Orthodox Churches through Arabic translations of (lost) Syriac commentaries by Ibn at-Taiyib (d. 1048) and others.

See also **Jewish Christianity.**

J. C. McCullough, 'Early Syriac Commentaries on the New Testament', *Near East School of Theology Theological Review 5*, 1982, pp. 14–33, 79–126; L. van Rompay, *Le Commentaire sur Genèse–Exode*, 1986.

S. P. BROCK

Systematic Theology

The aim of systematic theology is the truthful invocation of God for and in each age. It operates at the interface of received truth and current means of establishing truth. Its particular mark, therefore, is the intensity of its attempts to establish a truthful understanding of God from within the conditions of each time and place, if necessary by reconstructing them. For the fulfilment of this aim, at least in Christianity, a proper understanding of scripture in its own terms is necessary, but not sufficient. The 'truth' of scripture needs to be 'concentrated' in terms which render it credible and useful for the present time.

Throughout the history of Christianity, the scriptures and doctrine or systematic theology have each normally enjoyed a position which is to some extent independent of the other, while also enhancing the other. The acknowledgment of their independence is important, for it recognizes, on the one hand, the unique position which is accorded to 'Holy Scripture' in Christian faith, and, on the other hand, the necessity of some 'rule of faith' of the sort with which systematic theology is concerned. At the same time, each is seen to rely on the other, the use of scripture (as well as scripture itself) drawing on conceptions of what is 'normal' for Christian faith, and doctrine or systematic theology requiring recourse to scripture for the origin and beginning of Christian faith. While, therefore, the ongoing life of Christianity through the centuries has been coterminous with its use of the Bible, Christianity has also sought to consolidate the central features of the Bible and the purity of Christian faith itself by various doctrinal or systematic means. The two, scripture and systematic theology, are mutually supportive, each 'conserving' the other.

Within this mutual support, there has been a complex interrelation between the use of the Bible and systematic theology. At times, each has sought to domesticate the other for its own purposes, with the result that it has ceased to benefit by it. Two examples will show such domestication. First, it is possible for biblical interpretation to be 'inflated' in such a way as to displace systematic theology. For example, pre-eighteenth-century notions of the Bible encouraged a realistic reading in which it was seen as literal history containing the story of the whole world, including the world of the modern reader; correspondingly, the task of biblical interpretation was to show the reader how his/her own history was provided there. In this view, the place of doctrine or systematic theology was sharply limited to an architectonic one, that of structuring the presentation; its independent value was subsumed within its function in biblical interpretation. The effect was to allow systematic theology only to reinforce a particular kind of biblical interpretation. Secondly, it is possible for systematic theology to be 'inflated' in such a way as to displace biblical interpretation. For example, doctrinal theologies conceived under the influence of modern rationalism, or later reactions to it, employed notions of idea and event which indicated the nature of God's presence in the world in such a way as to reduce the historical concreteness of the central events of Christianity to that of a guarantee of rationality (Descartes), guiding symbols* (Kant) or transcendent experience (Schleiermacher, Tillich). In such views, the Bible was reduced to its ideational content, thereby losing its concrete historical value. The two examples show how the position of either the Bible or systematic theology may be compromised by overextending the sphere of the other, permitting it only to reinforce. The effect is to confine the one or the other in an unquestioned naivete.

A more fruitful practice, which can be seen to operate in much systematic theological use of the Bible, as well as much biblical interpretation, is to allow biblical interpretation and systematic theology to question and confirm each other. This, which might be called a hypothetico-hermeneutic method, allows for the use of systematic hypotheses (whose concern is the establishment of the truth of Christianity today) in the interpretation of biblical material, the one focussing the other, while the actual interpretation of biblical material by the systematic hypothesis improves the hypothesis and confirms it as Christian. This allows for a fruitful contact of the biblical text with the present day. The two disciplines, biblical interpretation and systematic theology, remain independent but have a mutually liberating effect.

This relatively simple issue, of the independence and mutual dependence of the use of the Bible and systematic means of grasping what is normal to Christian faith, has been overtaken in modern times by the many ways by which both the Bible and systematics have been opened up. The advent of the natural sciences and modern theories of rationality, of history and historical criticism,* of literary studies, textuality and textual studies, of the social sciences and modern understanding of society: all have provided important new – and apparently inexhaustible – avenues in both biblical and systematic study. Each form of study now appears as an indefinitely rich field of inquiry. As a result, both biblical interpretation and systematic theology now appear more as 'clusters' constituted by many 'trajectories' of inquiry, than as unified disciplines. For example, systematic theology now attempts to form hypotheses aesthetically, doctrinally, socially and ethically. And each of these is not simply applied to the Bible, as if alien to it, but as an attempt to illuminate the Bible from within and to allow the Bible to correct and enlarge the hypothesis.

Because the goals of the study of the Bible and systematic theology are still often conceived rather simplistically, this new richness sometimes seems to lose, rather than enhance, the meaning and authority of the biblical text or systematic theology. But it may instead produce a far more subtle form of realism, one combined with many of the features of modern-day idealism and particularism, in which both Bible and systematic theology are seen to point to God's work in the world in a fashion which is more realistic, particular, dense and interrelated.

See also **Authority; Hermeneutics; New Testament Theology.**

H. Frei, *The Eclipse of Biblical Narrative*, 1974; D. Kelsey, *The Uses of Scripture in Recent Theology*, 1975; G. A. Lindbeck, *The Nature of Doctrine*, 1984; B. Lonergan, *Method in Theology*, 1972; D. Ritschl, *The Logic of Theology*, 1986.

DANIEL W. HARDY

Talmud

The Talmud comprises Mishnah and Gemara. The Mishnah is a code of Jewish law,* arranged by topic in 63 tractates and compiled around AD 200. As it includes anecdotes and minority views, it might better be termed a digest of the discussion which had spanned perhaps four centuries and aimed to codify the law. The Mishnah was studied in the academies of the Holy Land and of Mesopotamia ('Babylon'), and these discussions (as now redacted) are called Gemara. The discussion often moves far from the Mishnah, and sometimes includes independent exegesis of scriptural passages. The Palestinian Gemara was compiled at the end of the fourth century AD and the Babylonian at the end of the fifth. The Babylonian is much the more voluminous, running to some six thousand pages, and enjoys greater authority. Either Gemara, when combined with the Mishnah, is called Talmud. (Originally, however, the discussion on the Mishnah was called not Gemara but Talmud, which term did not then include the Mishnah itself.) About three-quarters of the verses in the Pentateuch* and about one-quarter of the verses in the rest of the Hebrew Bible, receive an interpretation somewhere in these writings. In the broader sense that it aims to explain and complete scripture, this whole literature is one of biblical interpretation.

The Mishnah attempts to work out scripture's laws in the detail needed for implementation with special attention to marginal cases. For example, Lev. 23.42 enjoins Israel to dwell in outdoor booths on the Feast of Tabernacles, but the Mishnah's tractate (Sukkah) fixes minimum and maximum heights for the booth, specifies the material and density of its covering, and discusses whether the latter may be laid over gaps in a house roof, whether one may eat with most of one's body inside the booth but the table indoors, how heavily it must rain before the commandment lapses, and so on. Again, the injunction in Deut. 22.1–3 to return a lost object to the owner is supplemented in the Mishnah (B.M. 1–2). The finder may keep anything of which ownership could never be proved (e.g. scattered coins); pigeons tied together behind a fence are not lost and should be left alone; while waiting for the owner to come forward, the finder of lost birds should not supply fodder indefinitely but sell them and eventually return the proceeds; and so on.

Insight into biblical laws was further deepened through consideration of more complex cases. Thus if a husband died without issue, Deut. 25.5 requires his brother to marry the widow or to release her; but the Mishnah's tractate Yebamot discusses many more complex cases, e.g. if two brothers marry two sisters and one brother dies childless, the surviving brother must not marry (and no question arises of releasing) his wife's sister (Lev. 18.18), and is equally exempt regarding any co-wife of the deceased (Yeb. 1.1). Again, Num. 27.8 laid down the order of heirs (son, daughter, brothers, uncles), but the Mishnah (B.B. 8.2) goes on to rule that the surviving issue of a deceased son ranks as the son (and so for other relatives), and that the father (whom scripture had not mentioned) takes precedence over all.

The Mishnah also resolves conflicts between biblical laws. For example, from the different tithe laws in Num. 18.21 and Deut. 14.22 the obligation of two tithes is inferred: the first for the Levites, the second in some years to be given to the poor and in others to be consumed on pilgrimage to Jerusalem. Again, the Mishnah (Men. 7.6) reconciled Ex. 12.5 (which restricts the Passover sacrifice to 'sheep or goats') with Deut. 16.2 (which adds 'cattle'). Deuteronomy is held not to permit cattle as the Passover sacrifice; cattle are mentioned to show that just as the Passover sacrifice must be brought from what is not already consecrated (e.g. as Second Tithe), so too must any sacrifice that a man might be obliged to offer (e.g. as a promised thank-offering), even one of cattle.

The Mishnah does not always keep scripture so closely in view. While some tractates for the most part fill out an already copious scriptural source (e.g. Yoma adds to Lev. 16 such details as the High Priest's preparations and confessions), others rest on a narrower base. The Pentateuch forbids work on the Sabbath but offers few examples (e.g. agriculture [Ex. 34.21], kindling [35.3]); it fell to the Mishnah, in tractates Shabbat and Erubin, to define and discuss the types of forbidden labour. The fasts at times of national emergency, regulated in the tractate Taanit, are not enjoined in the Torah (i.e. Pentateuch) at all, but mentioned elsewhere in scripture (e.g. Joel 1.14). Many laws of the Mishnah have no direct connection with scripture, e.g. those of property and commerce in Baba Batra, which presuppose an economy more developed than biblical Israel knew.

The Mishnah may offer a radical interpretation. So Hebrew *qinne'* at Num 5.14, which literally means 'be jealous', is interpreted as 'warn', so that a husband could not subject his wife to the ordeal of bitter water unless she had disregarded an earlier witnessed warning not to go in secret with some specific man (Sotah 1.1). Similarly Sanh. 8 restricts the application of the law of Deut. 21.18–21 to a son who stole from home and consumed elsewhere huge quantities of meat and wine. These laws, like those explicit in scripture, are delimited through marginal cases: thus, if someone outside held an object and put his hand indoors, where another man took it, neither infringed the Sabbath, as neither executed the complete act of carrying from domain to domain, one of the forbidden types of labour.

Scripture is often interpreted in accordance with the Mishnah's aim of a system that would permeate everyday life. Thus the injunction to speak, at home and on the way and on lying down and rising, 'the words that I command you today' (Deut. 6.6–7) might have been understood to enjoin meditating continually on the pentateuchal laws in general. Instead the Mishnah infers that the paragraph Deut. 6.4–9, beginning *Shema* ('Hear'), is to be recited every evening and morning. Again, 'Be fruitful and multiply' (Gen. 9.1) was viewed as a commandment which could be fulfilled (on one view) through one son and one daughter, since 'male and female he created them' (Yeb. 6.6). To prevent inadvertent trespass, the Mishnah enacted additional measures, building a 'fence around the Torah' (Ab. 1.1); for example, tools of forbidden work could not even be moved on the Sabbath (Shab. 17.4). How far the system was implemented is another matter; for example, the statement that 'the king can neither judge nor be judged' (Sanh. 2.2) bears little relation to the conduct of Herod!

Scriptural verses are explicitly interpreted in the Mishnah in many ways. Sometimes a straightforward inference is drawn. Thus, as an example of an accidental slayer, who had to flee to a city of refuge, Deut. 19.5 describes one whose axe-head came away and struck his fellow as they cut trees in the forest. The Mishnah (Makk. 2.2) therefore restricts the law to deaths occurring somewhere like a forest where slayer and victim were equally entitled to be; it excludes death on the property of the slayer (who had faced an intruder and was not to be punished with exile) or of the victim (in which case exile is too lenient a sentence and the slayer must instead remain to face the dead man's relatives). Sometimes the interpretation runs against the natural flow of the sentence. Thus Lev. 16.30 was explained: 'from all your sins before the Lord – you shall become clean', i.e. the Day of Atonement does not atone for transgressions against an unreconciled fellow-man (Yoma 8.9). Again the words of Deut. 22.2 ('until your brother searches it out') are reinterpreted: 'until one searches out your brother regarding it', i.e. the veracity of the claimant of lost property should be tested (B.M. 2.7).

Formal exegetical* rules are sometimes applied. One is the *qal wa-ḥomer* ('from minor to major') argument; e.g. as the priest was entitled to the hides of burnt-offerings (Lev. 7.8), though he received no flesh, he is entitled to the hides of sin- and guilt-offerings, of which he eats the flesh (Zeb. 12.3). Another is the *gezerah shavah*, i.e. analogy from identical wording; thus the declaration over first-fruits (Deut. 26.5) must be recited in Hebrew, as it is introduced by the same verbs ('answer and say') as the curses recited by the Levites when the Israelites first entered Canaan (Deut. 27.14). Different rabbis* may offer rival interpretations; one held that the phrase 'when you lie down and rise up' (Deut. 6.7) determined the posture in which one said the Shema, while another argued that it indicated the time alone, and that the phrase 'when you go on the way' showed that one could say the Shema in any way, i.e. posture (Ber. 1.3). Occasionally a lengthy passage receives comment as in halakhic midrash.* Thus Sotah 8 comments phrase by phrase on Deut. 20.2–9; while Deuteronomy exempts from war one who had just built a house, the Mishnah adds one who had just bought or inherited or been given a house; while Deuteronomy calls for captains at the vanguard, the Mishnah requires them at the rear also, to catch deserters; and so on.

Sometimes moral rather than legal lessons are drawn. One who needs charity but refuses to accept it will ultimately prosper, for 'blessed is the man who trusts in the Lord' (Peah 8.9, citing Jer. 17.7). God spared the people of Nineveh not because of their sackcloth and fasting, but because of 'their works, that they turned from their evil way' (Taan. 2.1, citing Jonah 3.10). The same phrase ('a fire-offering, an odour of sweet saviour') is used of cattle, birds and meal (Lev. 1.9, 17; 2.9), to show that sincerity, not lavishness, renders a sacrifice acceptable. Taan. 4.8 attests the interpretation of Song of Songs as an allegory of God's love for Israel. The insistence that Abraham* was not to be called 'perfect' (Gen. 17.1) until his circumcision (Ned. 3.11), and that he kept the whole Torah (Qid. 4.14, citing Gen. 26.5), may be aimed against Paul's* representation of Abraham's faith while uncircumcised (Gen. 15.6) as a model of righteousness without the law (Rom. 4.11).

Whether for economy, or because it did not rest on scripture alone, the Mishnah does not usually state its scriptural basis. To identify the latter is a primary aim of the Gemara. Thus the 39 types of labour forbidden on the Sabbath are said (Shab. 49b) to be those involved in building the Tabernacle, the account of which (Ex. 35.4ff.) immediately follows the Sabbath law of vv. 1–3. In fact, however, these prohibitions must rest to some degree on tradition, rather than rabbinic deduction from the scriptural juxtaposition, because the act discussed at greatest length in the tractates Shabbat and Erubin, namely carrying from one domain to another on the Sabbath, is already forbidden in the later biblical books (Jer. 17.21; Neh. 13.19). Even where the Mishnah contradicts scripture, the Gemara finds biblical support. The Mishnah had permitted the Court to cancel the vow of one who had not appreciated at the outset what hardship his vow might entail; and the Gemara adduces Num. 30.3: '"he may not annul his word" – but others may annul it for him' (Hag. 10a). The scriptural passage adduced in the Talmud is often paralleled in works of halakhic midrash.

Many false starts may precede the discovery of satisfactory biblical support for the Mishnah. For example, immediately after the laws of Passover, scripture commands a sheaf of new grain to be offered on 'the morrow of the Sabbath' (Lev. 23.11), before which date new grain may not be eaten; thereafter fifty days are counted, the last being the feast of Pentecost. The Sadducees took 'Sabbath' to mean whichever day of Passover fell on a Sabbath, while the rabbis intepreted it as 'feast-day', i.e. the first day of Passover. The rabbis argue for their interpretation in Men. 65ab. Arguments from scripture are advanced and refuted, until an analogy is accepted from the two loaves of Pentecost (Lev. 23.16f.); just as these are offered on a feast-day, so too should the sheaf be offered on (or at the conclusion of) a feast-day, namely the first day of Passover.

The Palestinian Gemara is less punctilious than the Babylonian. For example, the Mishnah (Qid. 2.1) allows both bride and groom to appoint an agent to act on their behalf in effecting the marriage. The Palestinian Gemara finds adequate scriptural basis for agency in the law that each Israelite take and slaughter the Passover sacrifice (Ex. 12.3–6); for men in fact formed companies, each with a single victim taken and slaughtered on behalf of them all. The Babylonian Gemara, however, objects that it is in the nature of sacrificial ritual to be performed by agents of the sacrificer, i.e. by priests; therefore no analogy for agency may be brought from sacrifice

to secular life. Instead, the Gemara cites the law that a divorcee may not after a second marriage remarry her first husband (Deut. 24.1–4). As the word we-šilḥah, 'and he sends her away', which appears twice (vv. 1, 3), may (after slight changes) be instead rendered 'and he (or she) sends', the Gemara deduces that both husband and wife may appoint agents in divorce. The mention of both divorce and marriage in a single verse ('and she goes out . . . and remarries', v. 2) authorizes the extension of the principle of agency from divorce to marriage, so that the Mishnah is finally justified through scripture.

However, the Gemara's discussion of the Mishnah ranges well beyond the search for biblical sources. Every clause is analysed as closely as the Midrash analyses scripture: each term is defined, the purpose of apparent redundancy is explored, and contradictions with another statement of the Mishnah or with a Baraita (i.e. a rabbinic tradition considered as ancient as the Mishnah but not included in it) are reconciled. Further questions are asked. Some elucidate the Mishnah; some explore conflicts of principles. The range of discussion in the Gemara is wide. Thus the arrangement whereby every member of a company of drivers contributes to finance replacement of any ass that any may lose (B.K. 116b) amounts to mutual insurance; the debate as to whether throwing an object between two points in a single domain over a projection belonging to another constitutes carrying from domain to domain (Shab. 4ab, citing 11.1) entails the concept of air space. The many cases considered, however far-fetched at times, sharpen the definition of the principles which underlie the law. These principles often unite seemingly different topics. One such principle, for example, is that where the facts or the law are in doubt, the status obtaining before the doubt arose is presumed. Thus a priest's wife, who is entitled to eat heave-offering throughout her husband's life, may eat it in his absence in the presumption that he remains alive.

Where the Mishnah gives no ruling, the Gemara sometimes appeals directly to scripture. Thus Ezek. 46.6, which prescribes six lambs and one bullock for the New Moon offering, does not contradict the seven lambs and two bullocks specified at Num. 28.11; rather, it teaches that failing seven lambs, one may offer six, or however many can be found (Men. 45a). The principle that scripture contains nothing redundant is often applied. Thus at Ex. 21.19, on compensation for battery ('only, he shall pay for his lost time and his cure'), the particle raq, 'only', is said to indicate an exclusion, namely that of complications due to the victim's disregard for medical advice (B.K. 85a).

A category of biblical interpretation rare in the Mishnah (on account of the Mishnah's reluctance to quote scripture) but common in the Gemara, particularly the Babylonian, is the homiletic (*haggadah*). While the content of this material (often paralleled in haggadic Midrash) is too varied for summary here, it is worth tracing a spectrum, ranging from explanations of difficulties in scripture to lessons attached to biblical verses in defiance of context.

As an example of the former type, Meg. 13b explains how Jacob failed to notice on his wedding night that his bride was not Rachel but Leah: Jacob and Rachel, anticipating Laban's deception, had agreed secret signals, but to save Leah from embarrassment Rachel disclosed these to her. Furthermore, the Oral Torah, believed to have been in force since the revelation at Sinai, had to be fitted in with the biblical narrative. Thus Joab's murder of Amasa is ascribed to a difference in interpretation of Josh. 1.18: 'whoever disobeys your command shall be put to death; only be strong.' Amasa had failed to carry out David's* command to call up the men of Judah within three days (II Sam. 20.5), and therefore, on Joab's reading of Josh. 1.18, deserved death. Amasa, however, deduced from the particle 'only' that an exception existed, namely if one was studying Torah; and he had happened to find the men of Judah beginning the study of a tractate (Sanh. 49a).

In the middle of the spectrum we find interpretations which aim primarily to draw a moral lesson but still respect the context. The commandment to 'walk after the Lord' (Deut. 13.5) means following in his ways, by clothing the naked (Gen. 3.21), visiting the sick (Gen. 18.1 – Abraham was recovering from circumcision), comforting mourners (Gen. 25.11) and burying the dead (Deut. 34.6) (Sotah 14a). Again, Ex. 14.20 describes how the Israelite and Egyptian camps 'did not approach one to the other' the night before the Egyptians perished in the Red Sea. Now the only biblical passage where the phrase 'one to the other' (*zeh el zeh*) recurs is Isa. 6.3, where the seraphim called 'one to the other' to praise God. Hence the Gemara deduces that that night God silenced his angels: 'My creatures are drowning in the sea, and would you utter song?' (Meg. 10b).

An example of an interpretation that disregards context occurs in Qid. 40b, where Job 8.7 ('however small your beginning, your end will be great') is taken to mean that God punishes the righteous in this world for their few sins, so that on death they may enter Paradise forthwith. The context of course shows that the speaker (Bildad) had this world alone in mind, and his words are in any case declared false at Job 42.7; yet for the Gemara

the verse can be interpreted as a self-contained unit. Several biblical verses may be combined in this way. For example, in Nid. 30b, R. Simlai taught that a human being's happiest days are those in the mother's womb. His first proof text is Job's cry (29.1): 'Oh that I were as in months past, as in the days when God preserved me'; only before birth do the days run into months but not years. Job's further reference to 'when the secret of God was upon my tabernacle' (v. 4b) implied, for R. Simlai, that a human being is then taught the whole Torah. Prov. 4.4 ('And he taught me: Let your heart retain my words; keep my commandments and live') is then cited to confirm that the child is taught the commandments before entering this world. Yet, R. Simlai continues, at its birth an angel strikes it on the mouth so that it forgets the whole Torah, for 'sin crouches at the entrance' (Gen. 4.7). Many more verses are cited, and once again, the contradictions posed by the context are ignored; the demonstration that 'our birth is but a sleep and a forgetting' rests on the verses in themselves.

The Mishnah was believed to rest not on the written Torah alone, but also on the Oral Torah (as well as a number of enactments by men who claimed the authority vested in the priests and judges at Deut. 19.8–13 to innovate law). The Oral Torah began in explanation of the written Torah, expository methods and supplementary rules all revealed together with the written Torah to Moses at Sinai, and was enriched by new insights discovered by successive generations through application of the proper expository methods to this growing tradition (Ab. 1.1–6). Modern scholarship would agree that some of the pentateuchal laws must have been accompanied by tacit explanation from the first (e.g. the Pentateuch never specifies the marriage ceremony, nor the sense of 'chastise' at Deut. 22.18), and that the adoption of the complete Pentateuch must have produced oral commentary to harmonize conflicting laws. However, whereas the traditional view is that the laws of the Oral Torah arose through a process of discovery of what had always been implicit in the revelation at Sinai, modern scholarship instead considers that sometimes the rabbis first invented new measures to adapt to external conditions and then looked for justification in the existing body of Torah. Thus a shift from agriculture to urban commerce may have led the rabbis to interpret 'Sabbath' (Lev. 23.15) as the first day of Passover, making Pentecost the fixed anniversary of the revelation at Sinai (Ex. 19.1), rather than an agricultural feast as in scripture.

Attacks on the authority of the Oral Torah, by the Sadducees (Josephus *Ant.* 13.10.6) and others (Mark 7.5–8), increased the need for scriptural proof, however indirect. Thus the identification of 'tree of glory' (Lev. 23.40) as the citron, once accepted as an oral explanation revealed together with the text, was now derived from the text: Hebrew *hadar* ('glory') was re-interpreted as *ha-dar* ('which endures'), indicating a tree bearing fruit all year round, i.e. the citron (Suk 35a).

In this space the barest outline has been attempted, not least because biblical interpretation is not always explicit. For example, Ber. 29b records a prayer of R. Eliezer (*c*. AD 100) which is often compared with Matt. 6.10: 'Do thy will in heaven above, and grant gratification (Heb: *naḥat ruaḥ*) to them that fear thee below, and do that which is good in thy eyes.' Although no biblical background is mentioned, the prayer seems to be an interpretation of Ps. 145.19b: 'He performs the *raṣon* of them that fear him.' The Hebrew *raṣon* here is usually translated 'will'; but in the Bible it more often means 'goodwill', which sense is exploited in the prayer so as to avoid the paradox that God performs the will of human beings. The prayer affirms that to them that fear him, God grants 'goodwill, gratification'; but the will he performs is his own.

The Talmud's tradition of biblical interpretation continues to the present day in response to legal questions. For example, does the injunction to raise up the fallen beast of one's brother (Deut. 22.4), or even of one's foe (Ex. 23.5), require one to help a stranded motorist? The answer depends on the purpose of the biblical laws: the obligation applies if that purpose was to help the owner, but not if the purpose was solely to prevent the animal's suffering. Unfortunately, the rabbis of the Talmud are divided on whether the avoidance of animal suffering is a biblical or rabbinic law. However, the alternate descriptions of the owner as brother or foe imply some, if not exclusive, concern with him; whence the decision that the biblical injunctions indeed extend to the stranded motorist. For determining law, the Talmud has remained authoritative; beyond that, however, later generations of rabbis felt increasingly free to interpret scripture directly.

See also **Jewish Exegesis; Law; Rabbi, Rabbinism.**

A. Cohen, *Everyman's Talmud*, 1932; H. Danby, *The Mishnah*, 1933 (whose abbr. for titles of tractates I have followed); L. Jacobs, *The Talmudic Argument*, 1984; J. Neusner, *Method and Meaning in Ancient Judaism: Second Series*, Brown Judaic Studies XV, 1981; D. Weiss Halivni, *Midrash, Mishnah and Gemara*, 1986.

                                        M. P. WEITZMAN

Targum

An Aramaic word meaning 'translation', used specifically of the various Aramaic versions of biblical books which were made in the early centuries of the Common Era. All translation* necessarily involves a degree of interpretation; but the Aramaic Targums are remarkable in that they combine translation and interpretation of the original texts in such a way that their renderings often resemble Rewritten Bible.* Thus paraphrases of verses, some quite lengthy, and the insertion of material known from other traditional sources, are common features of these versions.

The Targum was essentially a popular medium, which strove to make available the meaning of the scriptures to ordinary Jews whose normal daily language was Aramaic and who knew little or no Hebrew. Targum found its home in the synagogue, where it had an honoured place in the liturgy as translation of the sacred Hebrew Bible, and in the schoolhouse (*Beth ha-Midrash*) where, as in the synagogue, it served to instruct ordinary Jews in observance of the commandments and fidelity to the Torah. The centrality of the Torah in the life of the Jewish community and of the individual devout Jew required that clear knowledge of authorized practices and beliefs be readily available; and the Targum was one of the most influential means of exhortation and dissemination of *halakhah* and *haggadah*. We see this illustrated quite clearly, for example, in Targum Onqelos' interpretation of the command not to seethe a kid in its mother's milk (Ex. 23.19; 24.26) as referring to the well-known prohibition against consuming meat and milk products together.

As translations of the scriptures, the Targums have always provided valuable material for textual criticism* of the Hebrew Bible, and their explanations of rare or difficult Hebrew words and expressions have assisted generations of commentators.* Where these explanations coincide with material found in the Septuagint,* Vulgate,* Syriac,* or other ancient versions of the Bible, it is sometimes possible to discern relics of an ancient exegetical* tradition, or of a Hebrew text available to the translators which may have differed from the Masoretic text.* Yet study of the Targums has wider significance, as scholars have acknowledged their importance in the history of Jewish* biblical exegesis* and in the development of rabbinic* Judaism. Study of the Targums in their own right, and assessment of their potential value for NT scholarship, have thus been particular features of much recent research.

Targums are extant for all the biblical books except Daniel, Ezra and Nehemiah. Given

Targum's purpose, and its setting in synagogue and school-house, it is not surprising to find that the Pentateuch* has three almost complete Targums. According to Jewish tradition, Targum is as old as the days of Ezra, who, according to Neh. 8 read the Torah to the assembled crowds while the Levites gave its interpretation, that is, its Targum (Babylonian Talmud *Megillah* 3a). Indeed, the growing importance of the Aramaic language then among the Jews, which is attested by the use of Aramaic in portions of the book of Ezra itself, would suggest that oral renderings into Aramaic of parts of the Bible might well have been given in early Second Temple times.

The three complete Targums of the Pentateuch known to us, however, are certainly later than Ezra's time. Targum Onqelos is the 'official' Targum recognized by the rabbinic authorities; originating in the land of Israel, it was carefully worked over by the Babylonian scholars, and bears the distinctive marks of the academies of the Eastern scholars. The Palestinian Targums are represented by Targum Neofiti, the discovery of which revitalized modern scholarly work on the Targums, and by the First Jerusalem Targum (Targum Jerushalmi I), sometimes called Targum Pseudo-Jonathan. This Targum includes long paraphrastic sections, and shows signs of internal consistency and unity which have led some scholars to conclude that it is the product of a literary process, and not the outcome of repetition of oral exegesis in synagogue worship. It seems to share with late rabbinic texts such as the *Pirke de Rabbi Eliezer* a number of peculiar traditions, and the date of its final redaction must lie somewhere in the Islamic period, since the wives of Mohammed are named at Gen. 21.21. All this, however, is not to say that every one of its traditions is of such late date, as we shall see presently.

The Palestinian Targums include more exegesis and paraphrase than Onqelos, whose interpretations can be restricted to the deliberate choice of individual words used to convey, often by implication, a larger interpretative tradition of a particular verse of scripture assumed by Onqelos, but found fully only in other Targums. In certain passages, notably poetic ones, Onqelos expounds verses every bit as fully as the Palestinian Targums.

To this last category belong also the Fragmentary Targums, consisting now of single words, now of extended interpretations of one or more verses, surviving in different manuscripts:* a critical edition of these important texts has recently been prepared by M. L. Klein. The Cairo Genizah* has also yielded fragmentary MSS of Palestinian Targums the publication of which by Paul Kahle in 1930

heralded a new wave of interest in Targumic studies.

All these Targums are related to one another, often sharing the same language, expressions, exegeses and haggadic additions. But the precise nature of their relationship has been hotly debated. Some scholars argue that the apparently simpler and more direct Onqelos is an old Targum on which the later, more elaborate Palestinian Targums are based. The oldest Targum MSS known to us are fragments of Targum of Leviticus and of Job found in the Qumran Caves (*see* **Dead Sea Scrolls**), and these seem to translate the original Hebrew in a mostly plain and straightforward 'literal' manner of the kind associated with Targum Onqelos. Others, however, claim that Onqelos represents an expurgated and abbreviated version of Palestinian Targum material produced under the careful eye of rabbinic authority. Arguments from the language, exegetical traditions, and life-setting of the several Targums are marshalled on behalf of both schools of thought; and, while current scholarly opinion seems to favour the priority of Onqelos over the Palestinian Targums, the case for the opposite point of view cannot be lightly dismissed.

The Targums of the Prophets are traditionally ascribed to the first century AD sage Jonathan ben Uzziel. The Aramaic of these Targums is similar to that of Onqelos; however, they include much more exegesis and extended comment than the latter. The language of the Targum of the Former Prophets, the subject of recent careful examination, is of such uniformity and consistency that it may be possible, given our increased knowledge of the growth and development of the Aramaic language, to date it with some precision to the period immediately preceding the Second Revolt against Rome, which ended in AD 135. The Latter Prophets have Targums which are more paraphrastic in approach, using a language less unified than that found in the Targum of the Former Prophets; possibly they date, in their present form, from a later period.

Critical printed editions are available of all the Targums discussed up to this point; but this is not the case with the Targums of the Writings.* Targums of individual books (e.g. Song of Songs and I and II Chronicles) have received some critical study, but a great deal remains to be done. Furthermore, the character of the Targums of the various Writings varies greatly, from the sometimes quite plain and 'literal' translation of the Psalms to the highly complex and extended paraphrases of Song of Songs. Two Targums of quite different kinds exist for the book of Esther; and the very close similarities between the Targum of

Proverbs and the Syriac version of that book may indicate that it originated in a milieu quite different from that of other Targums.

All the extant Targums are concerned to convey the meaning of the sacred text to the ordinary, possibly unlettered, layman. This is not to say, however, that the men responsible for the Targums were themselves uneducated. On the contrary, they seem to have been familiar with the learned exegesis of their times, so much so that a subtle and significant relationship between the Targums and the rabbinic midrashim * is unmistakable. This may clearly be seen, for instance, by comparing the Palestinian Targums of Ex. 15 with the commentary of the *Mekhilta de Rabbi Ishmael* on the same text. On the other hand, the Targums, particularly those of the Pentateuch, include items of traditional exegesis known to us from pre-rabbinic works. Thus, for example, the Book of Jubilees (second century BC) sets Abraham's * sacrifice of Isaac at Passover time, in common with the Pentateuchal Targums; over against this, the general corpus of rabbinic tradition associates the sacrifice with New Year's Day. It is evident that the traditions enshrined in the written Targums are not all of the same date, and it is clear that the Targumic traditions themselves evolved, perhaps quite slowly, over a considerable period of time.

Dating the various Targums, and the traditions which they contain, is therefore a complex and difficult business which finds expression in the large number of scholarly monographs devoted in recent years to the Targumic treatment of individual biblical words, ideas and theological themes. Once again, it is the Pentateuchal Targums which attract most attention, and it is perhaps not surprising that different scholars can offer quite different estimates of dates for the traditions which they study. Nevertheless, there is a growing body of evidence which suggests that a substantial proportion of traditions in the Pentateuchal Targums stands at a point in time mid-way between the pre-rabbinic writings and the developed rabbinic midrashim. Of particular importance here is the witness of Christian church Fathers like Justin Martyr and Jerome, who often refer to Jewish exegesis of their own days which is very similar to Targumic material. Some traditions are possibly much older, being rooted in the pre-Christian period: here one may cite the Targum Yerushalmi I (Pseudo-Jonathan) of Deut. 33.11 with its most probable (though still disputed) reference to the High Priest John Hyrcanus I, 135–105 BC. The linguistic argument for the dating of the Targum of the Former Prophets has already been noted; and there are signs that by the end of the fourth century AD the

Latter Prophets, too, possessed Targums not unlike those extant today. Suggestions of dates for individual Targums of the Writings have also proposed, although there is some agreement that these Targums are in general later than the others. Even so, the discovery of fragments of a Targum of Job among the Qumran documents demonstrates the very high antiquity of Targum to this particular book, whose Hebrew is especially difficult; and the reference to a written Targum of Job in Babylonian Talmud *Shabbat* 115a, sometimes regarded as non-historical, may, therefore, reflect some genuine memory of written Targums of the Writings in the first century AD.

The dating of the Targums and their traditions directly concerns the relationship between themselves and the NT. Obviously, if a particular Targumic tradition may confidently be dated to the period before AD 70, there is a possibility that it may have been known to Jesus, the early church, or the evangelists,* and that it may therefore be used to expound NT texts which seem to have knowledge of it. The use of Targumic texts to throw light on NT subject matter is as popular in some quarters as it is unacceptable in others, and is the subject of continuing debate. While extravagant claims that Targumic material alone might provide the key to the meanings of NT texts must surely be rejected, it cannot be denied that the Targums have as important a contribution to make to NT study as the rest of rabbinic literature; and their essentially popular character can give profound insights into the religious life of ordinary Jews in the land of Israel which are not so easily obtainable from other sources.

See also **Jewish Exegesis; Midrash; Talmud.**

The Aramaic Bible, 1987 ff., includes ET of all extant Targums; J. Bowker, *The Targums and Rabbinic Literature*, 1969; P. Churgin, *Targum Jonathan to the Prophets*, 1983; M. McNamara, *The New Testament and the Palestinian Targum to the Pentateuch*, 1966; L. Smolar and M. Aberbach, *Studies in Targum Jonathan to the Prophets*, 1983; G. Vermes, *Scripture and Tradition in Judaism*, 2 1973.

C. T. R. HAYWARD

Tendency Criticism

Tendenzkritik was F. C. Baur's label (*see* **Tübingen School**) for the literary * and historical-critical * method by which he analysed the literature of early Christianity. Whereas Strauss * asked directly about the history of Jesus, Baur applied what he had learned from the Roman historian B. G. Niebuhr: that historical research must begin with a critical evaluation of the sources themselves. He therefore looked in each document for the author's 'tendency', 'motive', or 'standpoint'; and since this is most clearly profiled in the Fourth Gospel, he began his Gospel criticism and was most successful there, in 1844. In 1846 he continued with an investigation of Luke, and in *Kritische Untersuchungen über die kanonischen Evangelien* (1847), included an introductory discussion of his method. Baur had already applied his method successfully to the Pastoral Epistles* (1835), identifying an anti-Gnostic* tendency and dating them late, and to Acts (1845), as reconciling the Gentile and Jewish-Christian parties.

This investigation of each document's aim, and each author's purpose, is now as uncontroversial as the historical criticism of which it forms an indispensable part. But it was initially opposed because it undermined the theological unity of the NT and the historicity of the Gospels* and Acts. Increased knowledge of the second and third phases of the development of the church was considered poor compensation for that loss.

Baur's approach set the historical understanding of early Christianity on a secure basis, but his application of his own principles was defective and led to some mistaken conclusions. Critical historians place each source in a larger historical context constructed on a basis of their understanding of all the available sources. But Baur's expectations were inflated by his idealist belief in the rational course of intellectual history, and in the rational historian's ability to detect this. It soon became clear, also, that his understanding of the whole development gave too much weight to the conflict between Jewish and Gentile Christian standpoints in the Pauline mission, and their gradual reconciliation in the emergent Catholic church. Placing the NT documents in their supposed historical contexts on the basis of their stance on this single issue of the Jewish law provided a series of interesting theses and partial truths about Paul* and Acts, but led to distortion when applied across the whole range of early Christian literature. Corrections were introduced by those who saw the development differently. Baur's liberal* Protestant successors accepted but reapplied his method, paying attention to other factors in the development, including non-theological factors. Differences in eschatology,* Hellenistic* influences, proto-gnostic tendencies in Corinth, differences of literary form and authorial capacity are also relevant to the historical understanding of this literature. The limitations of Baur's method and the error of some of his conclusions became especially clear as his successors took seriously the literary arguments for the priority of Mark, and later accepted the authenticity of seven Ignatian epistles (*see* **Apostolic Fathers**).

But those who corrected Baur did so largely by pursuing his methods on a wider front. In that respect 'tendency criticism' remains fundamental to the historical study of the NT, especially to historically oriented accounts of NT theology. Combined with source criticism* and later with history of traditions* research, it points to redaction criticism,* without losing sight of the larger historical map of early Christianity. Nothing in this method is tied to the metaphysics through which Baur himself interpreted the meaning of the history he reconstructed, and those who seized on the label to suggest that his work was tendentious themselves exhibited the pejorative sense of the word. In responding to the spirit of his age and engaging in conscientious historical criticism, reconstruction, and interpretation ('speculation'), Baur saw himself as carrying through without fear or favour the Christian theologian's absolute commitment to truth.

J.-C. Emmelius, *Tendenzkritik und Formengeschichte*, 1975; P. C. Hodgson, *The Formation of Historical Theology*, 1966.

ROBERT MORGAN

Tertullian

Tertullian was the first Latin theologian we know of, writing between 190 and 220 in Roman Africa (roughly modern Tunisia). He was born perhaps about 160. Well educated in rhetoric* and strongly influenced by Stoic philosophy* (though he repudiates philosophy as inimical to the gospel), he writes with force and intelligence. The belief of Jerome that he was a lawyer is widely held, but now rejected by the best authorities.

Tertullian probably had available an Old Latin version of the scriptures, perhaps made in his lifetime from the Greek Bible of OT and NT (*see* **Septuagint**); though some hold that he worked direct from the Greek, translating his quotations. He regards the Greek as authoritative. Alluding to Gen. 2.7, for instance, he argues that man's soul is not God's Spirit (*spiritus*) but God's breath (*afflatus*): 'We must hold what the Greek scripture says, using the word "breath" and not "spirit". Some, when translating from the Greek, fail to observe the difference' (*Adv. Marc.* 2.9). On John 1.1–2, aware of the ambiguity of the Greek, he recommends the rendering of *logos* * as 'reason' (*ratio*) rather than the usual 'word' (*sermo*) (*Adv. Prax.* 5). His Bible included the regular canon * of the NT; but he is notable for condemning the popular *Acts of Paul and Thecla* on the grounds that it was written recently, and while in his youth (*De paenitentia*) he advocated principles present in *The Shepherd of Hermas*, as a Montanist he repudiated it by name (*De pudicitia*) as non-apostolic and encouraging adultery.

Tertullian's overriding passion is obedience to God's Word.* Many of his works are on conduct: prayer, dress, baptism, discipline, marriage, fasting. God has revealed his Law (*lex*), a term he uses for scripture as a whole. It is to be obeyed and believed, its offer of forgiveness accepted. He moved during his writing career from the more moderate traditionalist body of Christians to the Montanists. These revivalists from Phrygia had instituted a more rigorous code (on fasting, marriage, and above all against lapses into idolatry or adultery), which they based on the new dispensation of the Paraclete superseding the concessions allowed by Jesus and Paul* (interpreting John 16.12–13). Tertullian is not a mere graceless legalist who argues for earning merit and penal satisfaction, as many moderns allege. But morality prevails: behaviour must follow scriptural precepts. Must even little girls be veiled in church? The matter is determined by scripture, nature and discipline: scripture prescribes it, nature (rational observation of human nature) confirms it, discipline (the strict life) requires it. He has adapted a triad familiar in philosophical writers like Aristotle and Cicero (nature, custom, reason), but gives the Bible priority. In this case Christ is the truth, not the custom of the church: his Montanism has prevailed over the doctrine of tradition (*De virginibus velandis*).

Tertullian wrote vigorous polemical works against heretics, especially Valentinians (*see* **Gnosticism**) and Marcion.* Here he found his opponents working from the same biblical books, but deriving from them very different doctrines. His retort is that the truth is established in the churches founded by apostles, who gave the gospel complete and uncorrupted. The church possesses the scriptures, and the heretics coming later than the orthodox apostolic community have no right to trespass (*Praescr.* 21.6). The Spirit lives in the church to preserve its truth, which is universal, unanimous and original. Therefore, interpretation must be tested (as in Irenaeus*) by the rule of faith – a sort of summary of doctrine based on God the Creator, the saving incarnation and passion of Christ, the Spirit present in the church, and the coming judgment (*Praescr.* 13.1–6). In his later years, Tertullian lessened his emphasis on tradition, and relied increasingly on the direct inspiration of prophets in the church to direct and interpret.

Tertullian particularly needed such an exegetical* principle for the OT. He was proud of the prophetic* scriptures, and invited a heathen governor to read them (*Apol.* 18). Taken literally the OT might lead to Judaism or Marcionism; the wrong allegorizing* critique produced Gnostic mythologies.* Rightly understood in accordance with the Rule, it speaks of one Creator, his Christ and his Spirit. Many of the proof texts* he uses are familiar (Psalms like 45[44] and 110[109] are quarries for christology*); but whereas earlier writers cite briefly as if from a collection of *Testimonia*,* Tertullian often quotes a longer extract. He is apparently using a Bible and not merely a testimony-book.

In his book against Marcion, Tertullian argues in great detail, first that Marcion is wrong in principle about a second God beyond the Creator; secondly that the features of the Creator, the God of the law and prophets, are compatible with the one revealed in Jesus Christ; and thirdly that the scriptures which Marcion does accept as true revelation of the saving God (most of Luke and the Pauline letters) fit or require belief in the Creator God of the OT. He spends three entire books expounding Luke and Paul; unfortunately in much of them he is saying what he thinks a Marcionite would be obliged to say, and then ridiculing it; he does not report as much true Marcionite exegesis* as some commentators suppose. But despite the polemics, these books contain much positive exegesis, and constitute the earliest NT commentary* apart from Heracleon on John. Here and elsewhere Tertullian has interesting insights into the interpretation of Jesus' parables.* In *De pudicitia* 8–9 he concedes that there are many interpretations in circulation of the parables in Luke 15, but he is suspicious of the elaborate allegorizing of details: it is idle to try to identify the meaning of the ten coins or the hundred sheep, and such discussions distract from the message of the parable, which is simple, direct and usually practical.

See also **Patristic Christology.**

ETs of Tertullian's writings are included in the *Ante-Nicene Fathers* series ed. A. Roberts and J. Donaldson, Vols III and IV; see also T. D. Barnes, *Tertullian*, 1971; G. L. Bray, *Holiness and the Will of God*, 1979; H. von Campenhausen, *The Fathers of the Latin Church,* 1964; J. Daniélou, *The Origins of Latin Christianity*, 1977.

STUART GEORGE HALL

Testimonia

Testimonia, or testimonies, form a particular class of OT quotations in the NT and early Christian literature (*see* **Use of the Old Testament in the New Testament**). They are texts chosen to support the claim of the earliest Christian preaching that the OT prophecies* concerning the messiah* and the End Time have begun to be fulfilled in Jesus and in the events in which he was the chief figure. These prophecies appear in current Jewish expectations of a divine act of deliverance. Many of the relevant texts are alluded to in the Dead Sea Scrolls,* the apocalyptic* literature, the *Psalms of Solomon* and other writings. The Targums* also preserve interpretations of the prophetic books which reflect these expectations.

The apostolic preaching continued the proclamation (*see* **Kerygma**) of Jesus himself that 'The time is fulfilled and the kingdom of God is at hand' (Mark 1.15), but the need for testimonies arose from the specific claim that Jesus is the messiah. This was asserted on the basis of the resurrection,* using Ps. 2.7 (Acts 13.33; Heb. 1.5; 5.5), Ps. 110.1 (Mark 12.36; Acts 2.43f.; Heb. 1.13), and Ps. 118.22 (Mark 12, 10; I Peter 2.7). However, it was necessary to show that Jesus had the proper qualifications for messiahship. The most damaging objection was his death as a failed messianic claimant. It is in this connection that the function of testimonies is most clearly seen. For it has to be shown from scripture that the suffering of the messiah is included in the plan of God which the scripture foreshows. The chief source of testimonies for this purpose is the prophecy of the Suffering Servant* in Isa. 53, which is quoted and alluded to throughout the NT, and is probably the primary reference in I Cor. 15.3. Further texts dealing with this issue are Zech. 12.10 (John 19.37) and 13.7 (Mark 14.27 and parallels) and Pss. 22 (Mark 15.24,34 pars.) and 69 (Mark 15.23,36 pars.; John 2.17; Rom. 11.9f.). A related issue was the credibility of the claims made about Jesus in the light of the treachery of Judas Iscariot. The embarrassment which this caused is reflected in the number of testimonies used in this connection from the same range of scriptures (Zech. 11.13; Pss. 41, 69 and 109).

The messiahship of Jesus was also supported from the Davidic* prophecies, notably II Sam. 7.14 (Heb. 1.5); Amos 9.11f. (Acts 15.16f.); Isa. 55.3 (Acts 13.34). The infancy narratives* naturally incorporate messianic texts, e.g. Isa. 7.14 (Matt. 1.23); Micah 5.2 (Matt. 2.6, cf. John 7.42). Moreover, the relationship between John the Baptist* and Jesus had to be sorted out. This was done with the aid of Isa. 40.3 (Mark 1.3 pars.) and Mal. 3.1 (Matt. 11.3 pars.). The claim that Jesus had inaugurated the new covenant* appears in the tradition of the eucharistic words (Mark 14.24; I Cor. 11.25), and Jer. 31.31–34 is quoted in full in Heb. 8.8–12. A special problem was posed by the failure of the apostles to win acceptance of the gospel message among many of the Jews. This also must be shown to be allowed for in scripture. Foundation texts are Isa. 6.9f. (cf. Matt. 13.14f. pars.; John 12.40; Acts 28.26f.) and the 'stone' testimonies Isa. 8.14 and 28.16 (conflated in Rom. 9.33; separately in I Peter 2.6,8).

The testimonies which were most widely used must have been selected very early, before any of the NT books were written. This is supported by their text-form, which often follows the Masoretic* text (MT)* rather than the Septuagint* (LXX), and which may be repeated in more than one book. Thus the text of Zech. 12.10 agrees with Theodotion (= MT) against LXX in both John 19.37 and Rev. 1.7 (cf. also Matt. 24.30). In Matt. 8.17 there is a more literal translation of Isa. 53.4 than the interpretative LXX version. Matthew and John both use a fulfilment formula to introduce testimonies for theological comment on items in the Gospel tradition (e.g. Matt. 1.22; John 19.36). These often rank as the most primitive testimonies and continue their original function in the apostolic preaching.

The above facts have suggested that the earliest Christian writing might have been a testimony book, providing a collection of such texts for use in debate with Jewish opponents. Such books are known from later church Fathers, e.g. Cyprian's three books of *Testimonia* (= *Ad Quirinum*, AD 248) and the *Divine Institutes* IV of Lactantius (AD 308), and can be traced back through Justin's *Dialogue with Trypho* (AD 155) and the *Epistle of Barnabas* (soon after AD 100). The suggestion that such a book existed in the primitive church, first put forward by J. Rendel Harris in 1916, appeared to receive confirmation from the discovery of 4Q *Testimonia* among the Dead Sea Scrolls. This is a single sheet containing four messianic texts. But it is not clear that it was compiled for use in debate, and the title *Testimonia* given by its modern editor is tendentious and misleading. The NT facts have a better explanation in the theory of a growing oral tradition,* which accounts for the differences as well as the similarities in quotations of the same text.

The growth of a tradition also explains two other features. First there is the clustering of related texts around a foundation text, which may not be quoted, but can be deduced. Examples include the 'blindness' testimonies (Deut. 29.3; Isa. 29.10; Ps. 69.22f in Rom. 11.8–10, all dependent on Isa. 6.9f, not quoted) and the 'exaltation' testimonies (Ps. 8.4–6 in I Cor. 15.27; Eph. 1.22; Heb. 2.6–8, dependent on Ps. 110.1). Secondly the wide currency of some of these texts made them a ready resource for secondary applications. Thus Isa. 53.1, which belongs to the prophecy of the Suffering Servant, is applied to the problem of unbelief in John 12.38; Rom. 10.16. The same prophecy is used to express the moral example of the suffering of Jesus in I Peter 2.21–25. They thus cease to be *testimonia* in the strict sense and function rather as proof texts.*

C. H. Dodd, *According to the Scriptures*, 1952; J. R. Harris, *Testimonies* I and II, 1916–20; B. Lindars, *New Testament Apologetic*, 1961.

BARNABAS LINDARS, SSF

Tetragrammaton

This term (Greek, 'four letters') refers to the name of the God of Israel, YHWH. Because of a taboo on its pronunciation dating from post-exilic times, in the Masoretic text* the consonants are supplied with vowel-points directing the reader to say $^{a}d\bar{o}n\bar{a}y$, 'my LORD' (the first vowel is, however, changed from an 'a' to a *shewa* [a very short, indistinct, vowel sound], lest the unwary reader should try to utter the word as written and get too close to the actual pronunciation). The hybrid $y^{e}h\bar{o}w\bar{a}h$, 'Jehovah', compounded of the consonants of the Name with the vowels written in the text, dates from the sixteenth century, and is found in some translations* of the Bible (e.g. occasionally in KJV, as at Ex. 6.3). In the Greek OT (LXX,* Aquila, etc.), it seems that the Tetragrammaton was often written in Old Hebrew letters, but pronounced as *Kurios* (= 'Lord'). It is disputed whether YHWH is the original form, or some such shorter version (e.g. *Yāh, Yahû* or $Y^{e}h\hat{o}$) as is found in personal names and in $Hall^{e}l\hat{u}y\bar{a}h$, but the weight of the evidence favours the originality of the longer form (as in, e.g. the occurrence in the ninth-century BC Mesha stele). Its original vocalization is most likely to have been *Yahwē* or *Yahwǣ* (the second 'h' was not a consonant but a *mater lectionis*, that is, a guide to vocalization).

The Name has the appearance of deriving from the archaic verbal root *hwy*, which in the OT normally means 'to become' (Aramaic?) or to 'fall' (Hebrew) but has been also taken in connection with 'YHWH' to mean 'blow', 'be passionate' or 'be' (the senses 'blow', 'fall' and 'be passionate' are possessed by the Arabic root *hawā*; the meaning 'to be' is suggested by Ex. 3.14 and perhaps Hos. 1.9, on which see below, and by the Amorite verb *hwy*, 'to be'). Most scholars take the verb as equivalent to *hāyāh*, 'to be', which would make the name mean 'he who is' (a pre-biblical *qal* perfect-present aspect of *hwy*) or perhaps 'he who brings to be' (the causative form of the verb, which, however, does not occur in Hebrew, though it does in Aramaic and Syriac*), i.e. the creator. The full name may originally have been *Yahwe-el* (God, i.e. El, creates; the [human] name *Yahwi-ilā* has been found in discoveries at Mari).

That the worship of a God YHWH antedates Moses* is probable; but the history of Yahwism in pre-Mosaic times cannot be re-

constructed. An Amorite origin is possible. There are, however, OT poetic texts speaking of YHWH as coming from the south: from Paran (Deut. 33.2; Hab. 3.3), Seir (Deut. 33.2; Judg. 5.5), Sinai (Deut. 33.2) and Teman (Hab. 3.3). Further, Ex. 3 speaks of Moses first worshipping YHWH in Midian and Ex. 18 has been taken by some as evidence that the Midianites worshipped YHWH.

Two OT texts play upon what they take to be the meaning of the name:

1. In Ex. 3.14, when Moses asks God's name, he is told $^{e}hyeh$ $^{a}\check{s}er$ $^{e}hyeh$ (probably 'I am/shall be who/what I am/shall be'; though some scholars have construed the verb as an archaic third person form and/or have looked for a causative meaning); he is instructed to tell the Hebrews that $^{e}hyeh$ ('I am'?) has sent him. Rashi (eleventh century) took $^{e}hyeh$ to mean 'I shall be with you [in your sufferings]', and some modern commentators agree (this interpretation fits Hos. 1.9 quite well; see below). Nachmanides (fourteenth century) thought the term denoted God's unity ('I am he who [alone] is'); this monotheistic interpretation has some modern sponsors, but it would probably require a late date for the text (which, admittedly, has been suspected of being a secondary insertion into its present context). Obadiah ben Jacob Sforno (sixteenth century) took the text to be speaking of YHWH as eternal. Philo* and Christian commentators of Hellenistic* outlook found in it the idea of God as pure being. The expression has also been taken to indicate 'I shall be efficacious' (cf. Ex. Rabbah III.6: R. Abba b. Mammel), 'I am because I am', or 'I am what I will be (= show myself to be)'.

Some scholars, noting God's refusal to tell Jacob his name at Gen. 32.29 and the parallel in form between Ex. 3.14 and 33.19 (where God before proclaiming the Name declares 'I will be gracious to whom I will be gracious, and will show mercy on whom I will show mercy'; cf. 34.6), argue that the force of $^{e}hyeh$ $^{a}\check{s}er$ $^{e}hyeh$ is a divine refusal to give his name (this is implausible, for the extant text, at least: he gives it in v. 15!) or at least to limit his freedom by any precise self-definition.

2. In Hos. 1.9, MT has '"You are not my people and I am not to you"' (. . .w^{e} $\bar{a}n\bar{o}ki$ $l\bar{o}$' $^{e}hyeh$ $l\bar{a}kem$). RSV and NEB have 'I am not your God', following some miniscule MSS of the LXX, but MT may well have the original reading. The real force of this, it has been suggested, is 'I am not your "I am"', or 'I shall not be with you' with a reference to the perceived meaning of the Name.

The Name does not occur with equal regularity in all parts of the OT. Within the Pentateuch,* the variation has until recently been widely explained in terms of the use of

Yahwistic and non-Yahwistic sources, but today few would rely on this criterion for source-critical analysis, at least without corroboration from other directions; the situation is complicated by the fact that the terms for the deity may well have undergone changes at the hands of early redactors. In some parts of the OT (e.g. Esther and Pss. 42–83, the 'Elohistic Psalter'), use of the Name has been either avoided or eliminated, presumably because of the taboo. Where YHWH and alternative designations (Elohim, El, Eloah, etc.) occur side by side, it is unclear whether there is theological significance in the choice of terms, or whether it is a matter of (conscious or unconscious) 'elegant variation': sometimes, as in Job, one finds that non-Israelites are not credited with the use of the Name; in other cases it is possible to argue that YHWH means specifically the God of Israel whereas the other terms speak more generally of God *qua* deity; but often, as in Jonah 4.1–11 and Num. 23.8, there appears to be no reason for the variety of usage.

B. S. Childs, *Exodus*, 1974; D. N. Freedman, M. P. O'Connor, 'YHWH', *TDOT* 5, 1986, pp. 500–21; J. P. Hyatt, *Exodus*, 1971; W. H. Schmidt, *The Faith of the Old Testament*, 1983, ch. I; R. de Vaux, *The Early History of Israel*, 1978, vol. 1, ch. 12; W. Zimmerli, *Old Testament Theology in Outline*, 1978, ch. 1.

B. P. ROBINSON

Text of the Bible

Text is a technical term meaning the wording of a book, textual criticism* the study of the changes which that wording has undergone in the course of its transmission. The Bible in all its component parts, in many cases after a period of oral* transmission, has, until the invention of printing, been handed down in manuscript.* Our knowledge of the text is derived from a number of sources.

The original text is the text in the language of its composition as written. In the case of the OT, this is mainly in Hebrew with a few sections in Aramaic. In the case of the so-called Apocrypha,* the language of composition has sometimes been lost, or only recently come to light. Within the church the transmission has been in Greek. The NT's components were composed in Greek. Any Aramaic antecedents were presumably during the oral stage. All copies of these originals will not necessarily have the same wording: there will be found differences great and small, and the manuscripts which contain the text of the original will be found, as a rule, to group themselves according to the presence in them of certain sets of differences, or variant readings as these are called.

Our knowledge of the text is provided by two other sources as well. The use made of the text by leaders and teachers within the Jewish and the Christian communities,* especially in early days near to the time of composition or to the earliest stages of the transmission, is a source of great importance. By examining the variant readings latent or patent in quotations we may often date and localize the configurations of variant readings. Both Greek and Hebrew parts of the Bible were translated: the Hebrew into Greek from the third century BC, the Greek NT, in certain cases in the second century of the Christian era, into Latin and Syriac* and other oriental languages of Christendom. The notion of the translation of such extensive documents was otherwise unknown: its origin lies in the religious needs of an alien people who have lost the mother tongue in which their scripture was originally written. It has been pointed out that it is not the host group who require the translation* or provide the translator: it is the deracinated group to whom the scripture belongs who need to understand it.

Until the discoveries by the Dead Sea, there was a great contrast between the apparently uniform Hebrew text and the sometimes widely divergent text of the Greek translation. The library at Qumran, however, has shown that already before the Christian era and the end of the Second Jewish Commonwealth in AD 70 there was divergence of a marked kind in Hebrew manuscripts. This divergence, now observable and capable of being linked with the data of the Greek, has given rise to the hypothesis of three divergent local texts in a period of time which stretches back as far as the fifth century BC. Others would see the divergence and number of identifiable forms as greater still. The previously known uniform text has the name of Masoretic* text, from the work of the scholars who provided guidance about vocalization, word division, accent and so on, expressed in a marginal apparatus known as the Masora, and those who assembled it are called Masoretes. The basis of their work was an earlier text which can be localized in Palestine. After the destruction of Jerusalem* in AD 70, the Jewish religion became deliberately more unitary, and the critical work which led to the uniformity of the text is one aspect of this.

The Greek translation is known by the name Septuagint* (Latin *Septuaginta*, LXX, = seventy), from the legend found in the pseudepigraphical* Letter of Aristeas, which ascribes the translation to a group of seventy Palestinian rabbis* working at the behest of Ptolemy II, King of Egypt, for inclusion in the library of Alexandria just founded by him. This document is now widely seen as a tendentious fiction, part of a debate about the textual reliability of the Greek by comparison with the Palestinian Hebrew text. We can now see that Hebrew texts in fact existed from which many of the divergences may be explained: but these would mostly be those current in Egypt.

In the course of the early Christian centuries, it became clear that a certain amount of argument for the Christian faith on the basis of fulfilment of scripture was based upon the divergent Septuagint text. This led to significant developments in the Jewish settings where a tendency to translation of greater accuracy by comparison with the Hebrew was developed further in order to provide a Greek text which could be used in controversy to confute the Christian arguments. The names of Theodotion and Aquila are known from tradition as representatives of this kind of translation of greater conformity, Aquila's being so closely literal, and consequently un-Greek, that it was practically incomprehensible. There was also a third, Symmachus, a Jewish Christian,* whose translation was related to his own theology and inherited traditions. It is now seen from the new materials which have come to light that there were also forerunners of these. We see their impact on Christian argument in the works of Justin Martyr.

Another major aspect of this work, namely the Christian attempt to come to terms with more accurate information on the biblical text, was seen in the massive text-critical work of Origen,* known as the Hexapla (or 'six-fold') from its presentation of data in six columns. These are said to have set out the Hebrew, a transliteration of that, Aquila's text, Symmachus', the Septuagint, and the text of Theodotion; additionally, three other versions discovered by Origen are to be found in the case of certain books. Into the Septuagint text Origen introduced diacritical signs, which indicated material which the Septuagint had but the Hebrew did not, and material missing from the LXX, which was supplied by using the version of Theodotion. In the third century, a further Christian recension was made in Antioch,* traditionally ascribed to Lucian the martyr. This came to exercise a wide influence. Amongst the Jews, however, the LXX came to be treated as a Christian book.

There were other translations from the Hebrew text. In Palestine, since the exile, while Hebrew was known and used in worship and scholarship, Aramaic had become the vernacular; a series of interpretative renderings into Aramaic appeared over the centuries, some of which remained in Jewish use; others disappeared until rediscovered at Qumran (see **Dead Sea Scrolls**). These are known as Targums.* The Samaritans* also, in schism from

the Jews, retained the Pentateuch,* written in the palaeo-Hebrew script. Although related to the Masoretic text, it has distinct readings, sometimes in common with the LXX. The version in Syriac* or Eastern Aramaic is a Christian translation known as the Peshitta: in the various parts of the OT it has a very varied text, sometimes showing affinity with the Hebrew, sometimes with the Targums, sometimes translated from or influenced by the LXX.

The LXX was the base for most Christian translations of the OT. These were made, as the church expanded and need was felt, in Latin, Coptic, Ethiopic or its ancient form Ge'ez, Armenian and Georgian. The Latin of the second century is termed the Old Latin, since at length (c. 400) a new translation from Hebrew was undertaken by the Christian scholar Jerome. His translation is known as the Vulgate.* All these translations have complex histories of transmission, and of correction to more accurate standards, sometimes by contact with the Greek, sometimes from other contacts, e.g. Ethiopic from Coptic, or Georgian, late in its history, from a Slavonic version.

The NT was composed in Greek, in the first century of the Christian era. At a very early period we find variations of text arising. There is a continuing debate how we should analyse the groupings of manuscripts and other witnesses, and how we should establish the nature of the original text. Most of the languages and nations represented in the translation of the OT are to be found in the history of NT translation, with some additions, especially the Gothic, which contains, from the OT, only a meagre part of Nehemiah, whereas both the four Gospels* and the Pauline* epistles* are known. Different versions ally themselves with different strata of the Greek text; but the process of revision can lead to situations where readings related to one Greek stratum overlie others related to another, to which an earlier stage of the version is related.

Each and every version has its own history, and its study can be an end in itself, related to the cultural, religious and political history of the people who spoke the language into which it had been made. It is frequently the case that the Bible was the first work of literature in a given language, and so will have considerable importance and interest to the historians of the language and the comparative philologist.* Their research in its turn can cast light upon the Greek text from which the translation was made, through their understanding of the nature of the language. Not every language possesses the same linguistic equipment; thus, except in rare cases of very literal translation (which have occurred in the sphere of the NT as well as in the OT), it is impossible to deduce the Greek text from the evidence of the versions.

The use of quotations too is a complex art. The text of the works of the author who quotes must first have been established. There was a frequent tendency on the part of scribes* to emend biblical quotations to agree with the standard text of their own day, and so to obscure what is, for us, a very important aspect of the data (this has even happened in the present century through over-zealous but uninformed editorial work!). Often, for this reason, we must seek the text known to the author in his comments and asides, or, if he is a commentator* or homilist,* not in the text at the head of his disquisition, but in the catchwords with which he refers to his text and introduces his comment. If we are dealing with poetic adaptations of biblical material, we have further problems since the demands of metre and the traditional imagery of the language in question may by coincidence give rise to features which could be interpreted as derived from variants of the text of the model. The study of the second-century Gospel harmony* known as the Diatessaron has been bedevilled by problems of this category and the subsequent debate.

Handing down a biblical text, whether in its original tongue or by translating it into another, is an act of interpretation. Many parts of the OT were already old when they were written down, and their meaning had become obscure. The Greek of the Septuagint too sometimes had meaning only by reference to an unknown Hebrew. NT Greek, too often spoken of as simple, is in fact highly complex: as a linguistic phenomenon it is like an escarpment where a geological fault shows itself, the strata revealed lying above each other. The language is first-century Hellenistic Greek, in a vernacular form (related to the language of books dealing with technical subjects), but it is dealing with deep matters, and thus philosophical terminology creeps in. Some NT authors have literary pretensions, but others none. Some material was uttered at first in Aramaic, and this has left its imprint, while the LXX style is sometimes adopted, or phrases from it, since it is sacred history that is being written and a sacred style must be assumed. All these factors lend themselves to interpretation of various kinds, or to alteration, the object of which is to make comprehensible the obscurities in the present form of the text.

Thus, both the perusal of variant readings and the study of renderings in the various translations can illuminate the meaning of the text, or the interpretation placed upon it in a certain place or time. In John 4.9 the phrase 'Jews do not use the same vessels as Samaritans' is absent in some witnesses. It seems to be a gloss inserted to enable those who do not know the custom to appreciate the woman's surprise at Jesus' request for a drink from her. In the same Gospel, in ch. 5, the lame man complains that he cannot get into the pool when the 'water is disturbed' (v. 7). In some manuscripts there is no prior explanation for this, but in others the explanation is given in words which form the end of v. 3 and the whole of v. 4 in older translations. This explanation is a gloss, not an original part of the text. If we compare the Matthean genealogy* of Jesus with the OT kings to whom it alludes, we find in Matt. 1.8 that three generations are missed out. Some witnesses have put them in!

Punctuation can make a difference to sense. In John there are several examples where early translations make it plain that they are punctuating, either in line with certain groups of manuscript witnesses in Greek, or sometimes without any Greek support but interpreting nevertheless a Greek text. John 1.3 concludes with a Greek phrase which can either go with what precedes as a relative clause, to read 'there was not anything made that was made', which is the easier linkage, or stand with what follows, as a phrase 'hanging in the air', giving a rendering (rather literally) 'in what was made, in it he was life', as many early Christian writers in both Greek and Latin understood it.

Difficulties observed are sometimes simplified. In Mark 7.31, Jesus is depicted as journeying, by an almost impossible detour, 'from the regions of Tyre through Sidon to the sea of Galilee'. Most of the early witness attests this: but it has already been simplified in a third-century papyrus to give, 'he came from the regions of Tyre and Sidon', removing the crucial preposition. The cause for divorce in Deut. 24.1 is an obscure phrase literally meaning 'a nakedness of a thing'. We know that in the debates of the early rabbinical schools the influential Shammai took this to mean unchastity, as if he turned the phrase around to read 'a thing of nakedness'. The phrase in Matt. 5.32, 'a word of fornication', i.e. 'a matter of fornication', using the Greek *logos* (word) to render Hebrew *dabar* ('word' or 'thing') is similar and shows Jesus to follow the strict interpretation, presumably by the same exegetical means (cf. Matt. 19.9).

Harmonization is an interpretative feature found in many places. As the Bible comes to be treated as a single canonical* entity, differing accounts, ostensibly of the same events but presented in distinct ways, with items of one account lacking in another, come to be harmonized. There are many instances in the Gospels: in the passion* and resurrection* narratives there are several well known examples. The new Qumran finds extend the examples to cover, for instance, the account of Hezekiah's illness and the healing work of the prophet Isaiah. Different accounts in Isaiah 38, II Kings 20 and II Chron. 32, although distinct in previously known sources, are found with elements of harmonization in manuscripts of the Dead Sea.

Specifically doctrinal changes are to be found. The phrase 'the Spirit was not yet' in John 7.39 was changed to 'the Spirit was not yet given' or 'was not yet upon them', avoiding an implication of the non-existence, at that stage, of the Holy Spirit. In Heb. 2.9, Jesus dying 'apart from God', has become Jesus dying 'by the grace of God', by the simple change of Greek *chōris* to *chariti*. In I Cor. 8.6, the reference to God and Jesus Christ is 'completed' in a number of manuscripts and other witnesses by 'and one Holy Spirit, in whom are all things and we in him'. In I Cor. 15.51, changing views and emphases about the last things have led to change in the text. 'We shall not all sleep, but we shall all be changed' appears to coincide with primitive Christian eschatology:* 'we shall all sleep, but not all shall be changed' seems to echo more pessimism about the majority of humankind for whom resurrection leads to judgment. A variation runs 'We shall all rise but we shall not all be changed.' The earliest papyrus apparently combines primitive eschatology with pessimism: 'We shall not all sleep nor shall we all be changed.' As it is almost alone in this reading, it may be due to error and not to be taken on a par with the others.

The text of the Bible then reveals the transmitters of the ancient books, both in Israel and in the church, introducing interpretative change. Theologically, this might raise a problem: it is not only those whose views of scripture might be described as 'strict inspirational'* who prefer a single text. We may find it fruitful to look on scripture, not only as containing a divine message, but also, in its variant textual data as well as in other ways, displaying the hermeneutical* wrestlings of those who received the message. We can learn both from their insights and from their false steps, deepening our understanding by the views of other ages, and avoiding pitfalls into which they could stumble. Close attention to the text provides a rich experience from which the private reader, the expositor and the scholar can continually derive benefits of understanding, from all levels of the text, and a sense of community with many generations.

See also **Manuscripts; Syntax; Textual Criticism; Translation, Problems of.**

————

J. N. Birdsall, 'The NT Text' in *The Cam-*

bridge History of the Bible, Vol. I, ed. P. R. Ackroyd and C. F. Evans, 1970, pp. 308–377; id., 'Texts: 6. The NT.' *The Illustrated Bible Dictionary* ed. J. D. Douglas, 1980, pp. 1546–52; F. M. Cross and Shermaryahu Talmon (eds.), *Qumran and the History of the Biblical Text*, 1975; Sidney Jellicoe (ed.) *Studies in the Septuagint: Origins, Recensions and Interpretation*, 1974; B. M. Metzger, *The Text of the New Testament*, [2] 1968.

J. NEVILLE BIRDSALL

Textual Criticism (New Testament)

No literature is ever transmitted without variation of its text creeping in. This is so even in literature written since the invention of printing: but the variation is inevitably of greater proportions in earlier literature which has been handed down in manuscripts.* Variations will arise which are purely accidental – mis-spellings, omissions, repetitions, the writing of a word similar to the right one, but misheard (if dictation was being used) or misread (if the scribe* was reading his exemplar). In a popular text, widely used for whatever reason, variations will also arise which are intentional in origin: the text of the exemplar appeared obscure, or did not concur with other information, or if it carried any kind of authority, seemed out of line with received concepts, practices or opinions. The NT from the beginning was a collection of documents, most of which circulated widely almost from the first; there were then many copies and many opportunities for error and intentional change.

This circumstance and its effect are shown in the present situation. There are in existence over 5360 Greek manuscripts containing part or all of the writings of the NT. In working back towards the origins, we must also take into account the ancient translations* (or versions) and the quotations made from scripture, at least in the writers of the first five centuries. We find that the present number of variations has been calculated as a quarter of a million. These are by no means of equal significance: they range from the presence or absence of twelve or so verses to grammatical and orthographical changes. Critical editions of the last hundred years, by a recent calculation, have about 62.9% of the text in common; but between the influential text of Westcott* and Hort (1881) and the text of the majority of (mostly mediaeval) Greek manuscripts (which there is an attempt to revive) there are about 10,000 variations (between the modern critical editions the number is almost 3,700).

Lying behind this scale of variation is first of all the history of the individual books. These were not written in order to be part of a fixed list of authoritative writings: indeed the notion of an authoritative list or canon* of books took three or four centuries to establish itself. Gospels,* letters (*see* **Epistle**), the Acts, the Apocalypse or Revelation, all had distinct histories. The Gospels circulated independently, and, although there was use of (and interaction with) other Gospels, the notion of a four-fold gospel took about a century to grow. Once the four-fold Gospel was treated as a unity, there was harmonization,* not only in verbal details but in theological expression as well. There was also some accretion of material which had circulated in the oral tradition.* Acts was written as the second part of a work of which the Gospel of Luke was the first, but may sometimes have had a separate circulation: by the mid-third century, however, we find a manuscript containing the four Gospels and Acts. The striking textual differences within Acts have been variously explained. Some would trace them back to the author himself, either in successive editions or in the influence of additional notes, inserted posthumously. Some consider one form of text to be produced from the other by redaction, some for theological and social reasons, some for literary reasons. The case of the Pauline* epistles is yet more complex. The letters were occasional and written to different churches. They would lie for some time in the records of the individual church. Churches may have exchanged letters and several different collections would have been made, and at length a consolidated recension have emerged, or else a single act of collection may have been made. Letters may have deteriorated before these acts were done and copying would increase the problem (there are certainly some cases of corruption which can be traced to before the end of the first century). In two cases, namely Romans and Ephesians, the omission of 'Rome' or 'Ephesus' in some manuscripts suggests that a universal circulation may have been intended, or have taken place very early, as well as the original sending to a single church. For all these reasons, and for the additional reason that Paul's thought is difficult and his style terse and obscure, there was much occasion for corruption. None of the Catholic epistles claiming authorship by apostles appears to have circulated as widely as Paul's: this may account for their relatively more stable text. By the time the canon of the NT was fixed in the fourth century, they were part of it. The Revelation of John had a very varied and even turbulent history of circulation, which affected its text. It was viewed with great suspicion in the East but known and used early in the West: when we analyse the support for the variations of its text, we find that this falls into a pattern quite distinct from that for any other part of the NT, and in the comparison of variation in modern editions and other texts, the incidence of variation is far higher.

There was for some time after the epoch-making edition of Westcott and Hort (1881) confidence that the original text could be established and that a history of textual corruption and preservation could be elucidated which would justify the text as established. These two scholars, who worked almost thirty years at their task, seem to have set out to establish the original Greek text, judging at first on grounds of transcriptional probability (that is, how scribes were likely to have erred) and intrinsic probability (that is, what is most likely to be original in the light of the style of the individual writers and other factors). They accepted a scheme which had been before scholars for a hundred years: the evidence for the text of the NT could be divided into three main groups of witnesses, which in the work of Westcott and Hort were called the Syrian text, the Western text and the Neutral text. There was a fourth text known as the Alexandrian text, but it was an 'outlyer' of the Neutral text and played no central role in their understanding of the history. This understanding sees the development of the text as a kind of dialectic (one might suspect the influence of Hegel, but there is no overt trace of knowledge or approval of that philosopher in their work or letters).

The Neutral text, of which they approved on the grounds of transcriptional and intrinsic probability, was, in all but one feature, that attested by two great fourth-century manuscripts which had come to light in the nineteenth century, namely Codex Vaticanus and Codex Sinaiticus, the text of which was also to be found in Origen,* the Alexandrian Christian scholar of the third century. Westcott and Hort acknowledged that, so far as attestation went, the witness of the second century went not with that text but with the text they called Western. Its second-century attestation was to a large degree in the works of patristic writers, but they believed that the Old Latin version, which also attested it, was a second-century translation. Their main Greek evidence in manuscript was, however, the Graeco-Latin bilingual named Codex Bezae, which they believed to be from the sixth century, but nevertheless considered an unmixed example of a second-century text. Despite this dating, they believed on intrinsic grounds that this text was a corruption of the original preserved in the Neutral text of the great codices and Origen, its corruption being due to the licence allowed themselves by the churchmen of those days in their treatment of sacred texts. These two texts, however, were attested by only very few of the manuscripts of the Greek NT. In the majority, Westcott and Hort discerned a text which they observed (fairly accurately) to be first known in the quotations made by the late fourth-century preacher and patriarch, John Chrysostom. That text, therefore, in their analysis, was a conflate text derived from the others, as a number of actual conflations in the text, especially of the Gospels, was used to demonstrate. Thus, this text of the majority of manuscripts, which had been enshrined in the first and subsequent printed editions of the NT since the sixteenth century, was deposed by them from its status of presenting the original text. Their approach was termed a genealogical method: the three texts were interrelated as original, corruption and conflation. There was, however, one curious feature in the resultant text: a number of shorter readings (or omissions) in the Western text were accepted as original. Now one of the main features of that text was its propensity to expand. When it was the Neutral text which showed expansion, this was so out of character that the Western text was taken to give the original at those points. Westcott and Hort could not, however, bring themselves to call these extraneous elements in the Neutral text interpolations and coined the involuted phrase 'Western non-interpolations' to describe them. These longer readings were mainly in the text of the Gospel of Luke (e.g. 22.19b–20).

With hindsight, we may perceive that the scheme began to break down under the scrutiny of experts already within the next generation. A number of factors led to this. Over a period of about fifty years, it became clear that Codex Bezae could not be taken to be a pure representative of a second-century text: even if a Western text had existed at that early date, it was rather to be seen in the Old Latin and in some other evidence. The clearly demarcated tripartite division of the attestation of the Greek text contained in their description by Westcott and Hort held the seeds of its own disintegration: the anomalous 'Alexandrian' text, and the phenomenon of the Western non-interpolations were the most outstanding marks of this. Scholars of the generation after Hort, such as Rendel Harris, K. Lake and F. C. Burkitt, began to take an interest in the text of a number of families of manuscripts, often of late date of writing, but textually akin to some works of Origen (whose text therefore, as they perceived it, fluctuated in its type) and Eusebius.* Several Old Latin and Old Syriac* manuscripts were either discovered or came to be better known through new editions, and their joint testimony was often contrary to the two manuscripts on which Westcott and Hort had relied. To take account of the new evidence, B. H. Streeter and Lake evolved a theory of 'local texts' according to which each important centre of early Christianity sponsored a particular type of text, each of which had some links with the original. This was an interesting and imaginative theory as a historical reconstruction of the evolution of the situation which confronts us in the various sources of attestation. But no one devised a means of relating it to a process of determining the original text, and it thus became too often a kind of criticism by majority vote, at best of the ancient witnesses or centres of sponsorship, at worst of the members of a modern editorial panel.

It was from the base of Burkitt's regard for the united witness of the Old Latin and the Old Syriac to readings which had a claim to originality that the work of G. D. Kilpatrick arose. He devoted a major part of his research to the investigation of possible criteria* by which it may be determined whether a reading is original. The method used by him is known as rational criticism: its essential principle, long known in the classical field, where an outstanding practitioner was the Latinist A. E. Housman, is that the 'original reading is that which explains the origin of the other readings'. The Dominican scholar M.-J. Lagrange applied it to the NT. Following these examples, Kilpatrick suggested a number of criteria, and others have elaborated them. We may find the explanation of variation in palaeographical* factors, where one combination of letters was mistaken for another, or where there were mistakes of omission through similarity in the end or beginning or phrases; in linguistic factors, where similar or identical pronunciation led to confusion; in correction of the harshness of an original phrase, perhaps because it had been woodenly translated from Aramaic oral tradition, later to be accommodated to a more sophisticated sense of Greek style; or there may be found cases where the original terminology of the NT writings in technical matters, such as weights and measures, coinage, official titles and topography, was inaccurate and has lent itself to correction. One factor which in his view was deeply influential was the 'Atticizing' movement amongst Greek critics of the second century, who sought to bring literary language back from closeness to the contemporary vernacular to conformity with the standards of classical Attic literature. Where variants are found in the NT, they may not infrequently be explained by the difference between Attic and Hellenistic* forms, which can be illustrated from the handbooks and lexica of the Atticists. In such cases, the original will be the Hellenistic form, the correction the Atticizing form.

A parallel approach is marked by the work of Günther Zuntz, a classical philologist,* who utilizes rational criticism but starts his investigation (limited to the Pauline Epistles) from the earliest known papyrus manuscript. By that critical method, he demonstrates where this third-century papyrus (the Chester Beatty papyrus of the Epistles, listed as P46) has preserved a text which we may judge original and where it has a corrupt text. In the wake of this study, he is able to bring into the discussion the later manuscripts and versions and to show their relation, first to the oldest extant witness and then to the original text. Of particular interest is his discernment of a scholarly tradition within the early church, especially in Alexandria and perhaps also in Caesarea, which succeeded in preserving early material. This does not mean that only those texts of the NT which we can demonstrate to have come through these centres contain ancient material; but it does indicate that there were those who were aware of the problems of transmission and applied their skills to preserve the text.

Such a combination of judgment of readings with knowledge of documents would seem to be the way forward. We must use as a primary source the early papyri; but we must also extrapolate from quotations and allusions in early Christian writings, and must not neglect the early versions. We should also work back upstream from later materials. All kinds of tests and safeguards must be devised to avoid treating what is late as early. This is the documentary side of our criticism. On the other hand, we must judge what is original and bring readings which pass our scrutiny into consideration along with the knowledge which the documentary evidence gives. We find that we cannot rely on any one form of text, preserved in certain groups of witnesses: original readings will be found in many different texts. In many cases the original was soon supplanted by forms which had suffered corruption in a number of ways. In the earliest strata we may perceive three chief factors of change. First, the influence of the living oral tradition, which we know from a mid-second-century writer like Papias* still throve in his day: in this way, for instance, the story of the woman taken in adultery was gradually assimilated into the written Gospels, as part of John (at 7.53) or Luke (at 21.38). A second factor which often led to the obliteration of original features was the process of the defence and definition of the faith. To this may be ascribed the textual variation which we find in the Cry of Jubilation (Matt. 11.25–27//Luke 10.21–22) or in the variation of number and reference (to Jesus or to believers) in John 1.13. If the traits in the text of Acts in Codex Bezae which have been deemed anti-Jewish are not original, they will spring from controversy with the Jews in the second and subsequent centuries.

A third factor was the role of scholarship, which was not always detrimental in effect. When we examine, with Zuntz, such a text as that of P46, which he considers to be a product of Christian scholarship, we find that frequently it is the scholar's sense of niceties which has preserved the original pithy text; or in the Gospel papyrus P75, we find that the tendency to Atticize has been on the whole withstood. On the other hand, such a conjecture as that of Origen, that 'Bethabara' should stand at John 1.28, entered the manuscripts of the Gospel within a century.

Zuntz, on grounds of internal criticism, takes scholarly activity in the church back as far as AD 100. Recent palaeographical study by C. H. Roberts and T. C. Skeat can list fourteen second-century Christian papyri. They bear marks of the social* background of their users: they are tradesmen or minor officials, whose books have been account books and official documents. All the same, these papyri carry some signs of greater literacy such as aids to both public reading and private understanding. But shortly there appear manuscripts written by experienced scribes. It is against this background that we should understand the textual situation of the early and mid-second century. Christians were concerned about their special books; and thus it is no surprise if scholarly care of the text appeared as early as Zuntz thinks. This did not, however, lead to uniformity, but to the complex textual situation which in fact meets us. To such an early point have our data now led us, that we may envisage a future when textual criticism will have to operate against the background of a first-century context and to be far more closely interwoven with other forms of criticism than has generally been the case hitherto.

See also **Manuscripts; Text of the Bible.**

———

See bibliography for previous article, and G. Zuntz, *The Text of the Epistles*, 1953.
J. NEVILLE BIRDSALL

Textual Criticism (Old Testament)

The majority of scholars of the OT text would recognize various stages in the development of the text of our Hebrew Bible. The first stage consists of the oral or written 'texts' or 'sources' embedded in our text, and recoverable by means of source criticism. The second stage involves the earliest form or forms of the text, which may be detected by means of analysis of various textual evidence. This is the earliest text witnessed to either directly or indirectly. The third stage is the consonantal text established *c.* AD 100 by the Jewish authorities, while the fourth is the text known as the Masoretic text* dating from the ninth-tenth centuries AD.

There are those who say that it is this 'final' form of the text which should be the basis for translation and study, and which should be recognized as the authentic Hebrew text, but when they begin to investigate or to translate they find that they often reach an impasse; the text is incomprehensible as it stands and is in need of correction or adjustment. At this point textual criticism begins, and the translator or interpreter has to begin to ask what the correct or best reading is, and why.

When it is realized that not a single sentence in the Hebrew Bible is extant in an original manuscript,* and that the earliest manuscripts at our disposal are removed from the original authors, in some cases, by hundreds of years, one of the questions that immediately arises is that of the reliability of the text that we do have. Anyone who has been obliged to copy a lengthy piece of writing knows how easy it is to make a mistake, however slight, and how difficult it is to copy the entire passage accurately. It is, therefore, understandable that mistakes have crept into the text of the Hebrew Bible over the years just as they have done in the transmission of any ancient literature. It is true that biblical books will have been thought of as sacred and that transmission of such texts may have been undertaken with great care, but even in such circumstances mistakes will occur if only because the concentration of scribes* is never constant, however well intentioned they may be. And if we allow that these texts were transmitted before they were generally regarded as holy writ, or before the text was standardized, we must admit of the possibility that alterations to them may have been deliberate and that care in copying may not have extended to word for word transmission.

If we allow that the afore-mentioned stage two is the text that we are trying to recover and establish, what means are there at our disposal for this task? Most of the Hebrew evidence is Masoretic, i.e. comparatively late, and is quite different from the NT MSS in being very uniform in character. All Hebrew MSS comprising the whole of the OT in fact represent this tradition. On the other hand the discovery of Hebrew MSS at Qumran (*see* **Dead Sea Scrolls**) has brought to light Hebrew texts which, although they do not by any means cover the whole OT, being mainly fragmentary, are the most ancient Hebrew texts we have. These discoveries show us a period when there were quite a number of variations in the textual tradition lying alongside one another, a time when there may not have been much interest in uniformity. At least three types of text existed at Qumran: a Palestinian type related to the Samaritan* Pentateuch* and characterized by frequent explanatory notes and glosses; another expansionist type which seems to have been the one that for the most part underlies the Septuagint;* and a third type which is the prototype of the text which we have in our Hebrew Bibles. The Samaritan Pentateuch is a Hebrew text dating back to about the fourth century BC, the period of the division between the Samaritans and the Jerusalem community. Then there is the Septuagint version of the OT – a Greek translation begun in the third century BC, which will have been made from Hebrew texts which predate Qumran; and other Greek translations by Aquila, Symmachus and Theodotion from the second and third centuries AD; the Latin (Vulgate*), the Syriac* (Peshitta), made from Hebrew texts which follow the 'fixing' of the consonantal text (stage three) but which pre-date the period of the Masoretes – all these are not just part of the history of translation but witness indirectly to the OT text and offer valuable evidence for the textual critic. Finally, quotations from the OT by the early church Fathers and in the Talmud* may also be of value in determining the 'original', since they too pre-date the Masoretes.

The move to establish a single text (stage three) was probably taken in conjunction with the movement to complete the Jewish canon. After the 'Council of Jamnia' (*c.* AD 100) there was pressure in rabbinic* Judaism to regard certain books only, and a particular form of the text of those books, as sacred. We should not assume that the ancestor of our Hebrew text existed without variant readings or that all was plain sailing. We can see from Aquila, Theodotion and Symmachus that the Hebrew which they rendered was roughly, but not exactly, the text as we know it. Nevertheless, extreme care and reverence characterized the next centuries as the scribes sought to copy the ancient texts faithfully.

In the light of these circumstances textual critics must proceed cautiously. It will often be difficult to identify an addition or an interpolation as such. They may find that a difficult Hebrew text cannot be elucidated by appealing to the ancient versions and all the aids at their disposal, because corruption is deep and real. However, although the restoration of the original may seem a long way off and may be ultimately impossible, they can, by probing here and nibbling there, especially in areas where scribes often commit mistakes, make steady progress toward their goal.

Textual critics are aware that in Hebrew, certain letters are easily confused, and could easily have been ambiguously formed in a manuscript, giving rise to accidental error. They are also aware that the script which appears in Hebrew Bibles (the so-called square script) is not the one which was used in ancient times, and that letters in that ancient script (the so-called Phoenician script) could also be confused. An example where confusion has taken place is at II Kings 16.6 where the unvocalized text read: 'At that time Rezin, king of Aram, restored Elath to Aram, and he drove the Judahites out of Elath, and the Aramaeans came to Elath and have dwelt there to this day.' Anyone knowing the geography and history of the Ancient Near East will spot a problem here. Elath had been formerly in the territory of Edom, not in Aram, and II Kings 14 informs us that Judah had, earlier, captured Elath from Edom. What had happened was that a scribe had misread a ד as a ר (these letters may be confused in both scripts). Subsequent to this another scribe identified the king of Aram as Rezin (mentioned in verse 5) and added the name. Verse 6 should read: 'At that time the king of Edom restored Elath to Edom, and he drove the Judahites out of Elath, and the Edomites came to Elath and have dwelt there to this day.'

There is some dispute among scholars as to whether the writers of the OT text practised *scriptio continua*, or whether word-division was the order of the day (*see* **Writing and Transmitting Texts**). It now seems likely that, for the most part, the ancient writers/scribes did practise word-division, but were not altogether consistent. A recognition of this by the Masoretes is implied in the *Qere* to I Sam.9.1 and to Ps.123.4.

An example where a scribe has made a mistake of this kind is to be found in Amos 6.12 where the rhetorical questions are asked: 'Do horses run over rocks? Does one plough with oxen?' In the context one expects in each case a question which invites the answer 'No', but the second line does not fit. If, however, we were to divide בבקרים into בבקר ים the line may be translated: 'Does one plough the sea with oxen?' This makes better sense and is surely the original reading.

In a separate article on the Masoretic Text reference is made to the system of vowel signs which were added to the consonantal text. While the system was the creation of the Masoretes, the vocalization itself was not. In this too they were transmitters, handing down the traditional pronunciation of the Hebrew text; but by the same token their tradition was not infallible.

An example of where they may have got it wrong is at Isa. 7.11 where we have העמק שאלה או הגבה למעלה literally, 'ask, making it deep or making it high above'. Even without consulting the Versions we might have conjectured that the vocalization should be שאֹלה, 'to She'ol', to balance למעלה; and such conjecture is supported by Aquila, Theodotion and Symmachus together with the Peshitta, the Targum* and the Vulgate. Hence RSV 'let it be as deep as She'ol'.

In any textual transmission the accidental transposition of letters is a common error. At Ps. 49.12 the MT is literally 'their inward part their houses for ever'. Clearly, there is something wrong here, and we may solve the problem if we examine the Septuagint. There the rendering is: 'And *their graves* are their houses for ever', which, if we translate back into Hebrew, is *qibram* instead of *qirbam*; that is to say the ר and the ב have been accidentally transposed in the MT, thereby producing nonsense.

There may be many abbreviations embedded in the text which have been misunderstood by readers and interpreters down the centuries. It has been suggested that the MT of Esth. 6.1 נדדה שנת המלך conceals the abbreviation ה for יהוה and should read נדד ה 'Yahweh made the king's sleep to flee'. This is suggested by the Septuagint rendering.

Confusion of words which sound alike may occur when copying under dictation, but it may also occur in conventional scribal activity. The scribe carries a phrase or a half line in his head and misrepresents it by confusing two words of similar sound. This seems to have happened at Ps. 100.3 הוא עשנו ולא אנחנו 'he has made us and not we ourselves'. This is the reading behind many of the ancient Versions; but the *Qere* suggests ולֹו for ולֹא, giving the sense 'He has made us and we are his!' This is the reading of many Hebrew MSS and Aquila, and is followed by RSV, JB and NEB.

One does not have to be a text critic to recognize that dittography and haplography are common scribal errors. Dittography (mistaken duplication of a letter, word or phrase) is the cause of the corruption at II Kings 18.17 where the repetition of 'Jerusalem' in that verse has caused the scribe to repeat 'and they went up and came'. This is a fairly straightforward instance and in fact its identification is helped by the absence of the words in the Septuagint. Cases of haplography (the mistake of writing once what should have been written twice) are frequent; one example will suffice. At Gen. 4.8 we read: 'And Cain said to Abel his brother, and when they were in the field . . .' Clearly, something is missing here. The Samaritan Pentateuch and the Septuagint reveal what has happened: 'And Cain said to Abel his brother: "Let us go into the field", and when they were in the field . . .' The scribe's eye jumped from the first occurrence of the word 'field' to the second, causing him to omit the words in between.

Up to now we have, for the most part, assumed that errors have crept into the text inadvertently in the course of copying; but we have to allow for the possibility that copyists occasionally altered or emended the text they were copying, either because they found it unintelligible or because they found it offensive in some way. Here we are on difficult ground, for the identification of this category is not easy. It may be that if the change is the addition of a word or a phrase to a poetic line, we may be able to ascertain that it is an explanatory gloss, but our knowledge of Hebrew metre is so patchy that we often cannot be certain. In fact we are told of some of these alterations in rabbinic commentaries and in the work of the Masoretes themselves. The *tiqqune hassopherim*, 'the corrections of the scribes', are emendations which mostly involve attempts to avoid anthropomorphisms* and anthropopathisms in the text, or constructions which might be interpreted blasphemously. For example, at Hab. 1.12 we read: 'Are you not my God from of old, O Yahweh, the Holy One; we shall not die.' It is alleged that scribes changed the final verbal form from second person singular = you shall not die (cf. NEB, JB). The reason for this would be to remove any possible suggestion that Yahweh might be subject to death. Some of these alleged 'corrections' are questioned by scholars, and we should note that in the example given the RSV translators follow MT.

There are a number of places where we might have expected a 'correction' to have been recorded, and where indeed an adjustment has taken place. For example at Deut. 32.8ff. we read that God 'laid down the boundaries of every people according to the number of Israelites'. A Qumran fragment has בני אלהים ('sons of God') instead of Israelites, a reading which is presupposed by Septuagint, Vulgate and Symmachus. אלהים, translated 'God', is plural in form, and seems to have been suppressed in favour of ישראל because of its possible polytheistic implications.

We should not imagine that the task of the textual critic is unrelated to other disciplines, and attention should be given to the textual criticism of classical and other ancient texts. A great deal must still be done on the Judaean desert texts, some of which have still to be published, and on the relationship between our MT and the earliest forms of the ancient Versions. It may be that there is nothing new under the sun, but sometimes things which are very old still need to be detected.

See also **Masoretic Text; Text of the Bible.**

F. M. Cross and S. Talmon (eds), *Qumran and the History of the Biblical Text*, 1975; R. W. Klein, *Textual Criticism of the Old Testament*, 1974; L. D. Reynolds and N. G. Wilson, *Scribes and Scholars: A Guide to the Transmission of Greek and Latin Literature*, ²1974; B. J. Roberts, *The Old Testament Text and Versions*, 1951; J. Weingreen, *Introduction to the Critical Study of the Text of the Hebrew Bible*, 1982; E. Würthwein, *The Text of the Old Testament: An Introduction to the Biblia Hebraica*, ²1979.

ROBERT B. SALTERS

Theological Geography

It is widely accepted that many statements in the Bible which appear at first sight to be historical are in fact primarily theological. This is not necessarily to say that they have no historical interest, but rather that the historical interest is subservient to the theological. This may also be the case with a variety of statements which seem to be 'geographical' but which on closer inspection are found to have a theological significance. These statements may occur in descriptions of past events or in a context which seeks to describe a permanent reality, but sometimes they may have a future reference.

The Israelites shared with other peoples of the Ancient Near East* a concern to know where it was possible to have access to the presence of their deity. In the stories about the journeyings of the early ancestors of Israel, the Patriarchs are recorded as having visited various places where altars or stones are set up in recognition of the fact that God had somehow made himself known in that location (e.g. Gen. 12.1–9; 13.14–18; 22.9–14; 28.10–22). This does not mean that those who preserved these traditions had no geographical interest, but that their primary concern was with the presence of their God in their midst.

Other 'journey' stories may have a theological significance. Attempts to reconstruct the route taken by the Israelites when they made their exodus* from Egypt,* wandered in the wilderness, and eventually entered the Promised Land, are fraught with difficulties, and it is noteworthy that many maps which seek to trace the route have question-marks beside many, and sometimes almost all, of the place-names indicated. There are hints within the account of the journey that some of the places visited were thought to have a special significance. The name Marah is associated with a Hebrew root *mrr* meaning 'bitter' (Ex. 15.22–25); the names Massah and Meribah are associated with the Hebrew words *massāh* ('trial, test') and *mᵉrîḇāh* ('contention, quarrel')

(Ex. 17.7). These aetiological* elements may be an indication that the significance of the story lies not so much in the route travelled as in what it says about the relationship between God and his people.

At the beginning and end of the account of the journey from Egypt to the Promised Land are stories of a divine intervention to enable the Israelites to cross a stretch of water, first the 'Reed Sea' (Ex. 14.10–31), and subsequently the River Jordan (Josh. 3.7–17). The significance of these traditions may be much more than to account for how two particular obstacles were overcome, and lie in the claims they make about the power of Israel's God, Yahweh, to control and divide the waters. The recollection of such demonstrations of divine power would be important in combating the claims of the Canaanite god Baal who was believed to have shown his control over the waters by defeating and slaying Yam (the personification of the seas and rivers), and perhaps also of the Babylonian patron-deity Marduk who had slain Tiamat (the personification of the salt water). Here again the primary significance of the stories is theological.

A 'journey' story of a very different nature is that of the progress of Jesus and his disciples from Galilee to Jerusalem.* It has been suggested that there are theologico-geographical considerations in the composition of Luke's Gospel. Particularly relevant in the present context is the view that the presentation of the ministry of Jesus as a journey is an important aspect of the understanding of Christianity as a 'way' which emerges from Luke's Gospel and Acts. On a number of occasions Christianity is referred to as 'the Way' (Acts 9.2; 19.9,23; 24.14,22).

Here it may be noted that significance has been seen in Luke's location of the activity of John the Baptist* by the Jordan outside Judaea and Galilee, and so outside the areas of Jesus' ministry. Was this an indication that John belonged to a different dispensation from that which had been inaugurated by Jesus? Davies has argued that a contrary indication is to be seen in the Fourth Gospel, where John 10.40–42 attaches the activity of Jesus geographically to that of John the Baptist not just to reflect a historical reality but in order to stress a theological relationship between John and Jesus.

A much more complex issue is the extent to which geographical details in the presentation of the life of Jesus have been affected by the desire of the Gospel writers to stress that Jesus was the messiah* and therefore fulfilled certain messianic expectations. It was necessary, for example, to emphasize that Jesus the Galilean had in fact been born in Bethlehem where it had been foretold that the messiah would

be born (Micah 5.2), and that he had been taken down to Egypt so that the words of Hos. 11.1 (which had apparently come to be regarded messianically) might be fulfilled (see **Infancy Narratives**).

It is not only in geographical statements about the location of important events or spheres of activity that theological significance is to be seen. Indeed it is perhaps even more prominent in certain statements about the land of Israel in general, and the city of Jerusalem in particular. For example, utopian descriptions of the extent of the land such as that recorded as part of the covenant* between Yahweh and Abraham* ('To your descendants I give this land, from the river of Egypt to the great river, the river Euphrates', Gen. 15.18b) may have more to say about the theological idea of a Promised Land than about the area of territory ever actually occupied by the Israelites. The accounts in the first half of the book of Joshua of the successive victories of the Israelite armies under Joshua's leadership culminating in the taking of the whole land and its allotment among the tribes is doubtless more a statement about the power of the God in whose name and with whose aid the victories had been won, and about the fact that the land was believed to be in a real sense Yahweh's land because he had been instrumental in its acquisition, than a description of historical events; the fact that the archaeological* evidence for a conquest has increasingly come to be regarded as very flimsy may support such an interpretation of these traditions. It is also appropriate to note that the land of Israel was believed to be the object of Yahweh's special care, as demonstrated by his watering of it by the rains, in contrast to the situation in Egypt where hard work was involved in the irrigation of the soil (Deut. 11.10–12).

There are hints in the biblical narrative at a belief that the land of Israel, and more specifically the city of Jerusalem, was the very centre or navel of the earth. In Ezek. 38.12 the Israelites are described as those who 'dwell at the centre (ṭabbûr) of the earth'; in the Septuagint* ṭabbûr is translated omphalos 'navel'. The word is also used in Judg. 9.37 in association with Shechem, but here it may simply mean 'height'. It has been suggested that this word could be connected with the name of Mount Tabor and imply a belief that this conspicuous dome-shaped hill was the omphalos, but it is not certain that the words are associated. In Ezek. 5.5 it is Jerusalem which is described as having been set 'in the midst (RSV 'centre') of the nations', and it is clear that the idea of Jerusalem being at the centre of the earth, or the 'navel', persisted (cf. Jubilees 8.12,19; Josephus,* *Jewish War*

III.3.5). It is not possible here to discuss the extent to which the whole complex of ideas which came to be related to the earth-navel myth elsewhere (e.g. at Delphi) became attached to Jerusalem.

That Mount Zion came to have something of the significance of the holy or cosmic mountain in other Ancient Near Eastern traditions is rather clearer, though it is again necessary to be wary of assuming that all features of such traditions came to be attached to Jerusalem. In Ps. 48.1–3, Zion is described as 'the city of our God', 'his holy mountain', 'a beautiful height', 'the joy of the whole earth', 'the recesses of Zaphon', 'the city of the great king'. It is noteworthy that here Zion is associated with Zaphon (*spn*), the abode of Baal according to the Ugaritic* texts, which may be a clue that some of the 'holy mountain' motifs which came to be attached to Zion may be of Canaanite origin. Other features frequently held to be part of a Zion tradition include the idea that it was the source of the river of Paradise (Ps. 46.4; cf. Ezek. 28.13ff. where a link seems to be made between God's holy mountain and the Garden of Eden), or that it was the scene of Yahweh's defeat of the waters of chaos (Ps. 46.2–3) and of the earthly kings and peoples (Ps. 46.6; 48.4–6; 76.3,5–6). So a relatively small hill is presented as a very special place where God has chosen to dwell.

When statements about the future are considered, an even more surprising situation emerges. This little hill 'shall be established as the highest of the mountains, and shall be raised above the hills' (Isa. 2.2; cf. Micah 4.1). The rest of the land will be levelled into a plain leaving Jerusalem 'aloft upon its site' (Zech. 14.10). In Isa. 4.5–6 it seems to be envisaged that a protective canopy will be over the whole of Zion. It is difficult to date such passages, but the thoughts which they express go considerably beyond the mere hopes for a Jerusalem restored after destruction. However, at the end of the book of Ezekiel (chs 47–48) are details of a future complete reorganization of the land in which the tribes are allocated successive strips of territory from Dan in the north to Gad in the south. Between the territories of Judah and Benjamin, the Jerusalem Temple lies within an area which is set apart as the 'holy portion'. From below the threshold of the Temple rises a river whose waters flow down to the Dead Sea giving it life. Clearly such statements are not topographical, but theological claims about the God who dwells in Zion.

The concept of a new Jerusalem is to be found in the NT, where the city is a heavenly city (cf. Gal. 4.26; Heb. 12 .22) and something which will be achieved in the future (Heb.

13.14). It is most fully developed in Rev. 21–22 where the writer describes, as part of his vision of a new heaven and a new earth, 'the holy city, new Jerusalem, coming down out of heaven from God' (21.2). This city had no temple 'for its temple is the Lord God the Almighty and the Lamb' (21.22), but the 'water of life' flowed from the throne of God and of the Lamb (22.1). In the new heaven and earth there was no more sea (21.1) – perhaps a final theological statement that the age-old threat of chaos would be removed completely.

See also **Aetiology; Babylon; Jerusalem.**

R. E. Clements, *God and Temple*, 1965; R. J. Clifford, *The Cosmic Mountain in Canaan and the Old Testament*, 1972; W. D. Davies, *The Gospel and the Land*, 1974; D. E. Gowan, *Eschatology in the Old Testament*, 1986.
                                    A. H. W. CURTIS

Theology (New Testament)

NT theology is the child of both modern biblical scholarship and Christian theology. It stems from a period and place in which the relationship of the two parent disciplines was institutionally still close but methodologically* already full of tension: from nineteenth-century German Protestant faculties which were training clergy to think and preach theologically from an authoritative scripture, but whose standards of truth were dictated by critical reason, not drawn from an authoritative tradition.

It attained the dignity of a sub-discipline because teaching in those universities was a by-product of research, and lecture series found their most enduring monuments in large textbooks or 'handbooks'. But in reality it is less a hybrid sub-discipline than one of the fields in which the forces of faith and reason meet. It is Christian theology engaging with an area of modern knowledge that is of central importance for its own identity, and biblical studies wrestling with its material's own definition of its subject-matter.

More important than the now outgrown compendium format are the aims and ingredients of an activity which a secular biblical scholarship can ignore, but which remains indispensable for any modern Christian theology that depends heavily on scripture. Its theological character accounts for its currently precarious position, its critical edge blunted by neo-conservatism, and its religious aims despised by an aggressively secular minority in the media and academy. It is the fruit of interaction between its now independent parent disciplines, and is threatened where the distinct identities of both are lost by their being melted in hermeneutical* fusion, or where their relationship falls prey to the deep hostility which still exists between traditional Christianity and modern rationalism.

This modern, Janus-like, discipline is usually dated from J. P. Gabler's *Oratio* or lecture 'On the proper distinction between biblical and dogmatic theology and the specific objectives of each' (1787, ET *SJT* 33, 1980), even though the first to separate the Testaments in carrying out Gabler's programme was G. L. Bauer (OT 1796, NT 1800–2). Gabler is celebrated because his 'proper distinction' helped to liberate biblical scholarship from the shackles of doctrinal theology, allowing it to develop as an independent discipline. The ideas of the NT could now be considered in their own terms, with reference to particular authors and contexts, not drawn upon at will to provide proof texts* for different parts of the Christian doctrinal system.

Gabler himself, however, was not so much concerned with the integrity of biblical scholarship as with the Christian theological use of scripture, and despite the shift of some of the best modern scholarship away from explicitly theological locations (seminaries, cathedrals, and Christian faculties) this interest has usually provided its hidden agenda. The general truth and authority* of the NT have been taken for granted and the contemporary task seen as identifying and communicating its theological content. What that is, however, and how it is to be communicated, are not self-evident, and are in fact hotly contested.

Gabler was a theological rationalist, and could not identify the whole Bible with revelation.* He tried to sift what was true and valid. This may or may not have been a blind alley, but it rightly suggests that a NT theology which aims to articulate or to help to clarify Christian faith, i.e. which aims to be Christian theology, is likely to hinge on its view of revelation, just as all pre-critical theological uses of the Bible had done. The revolutionary impact of critical thinking on Western theology destroyed the earlier identification of the Bible with revelation, but did not make this category any less essential to Christian faith and theology.

When the historical paradigm began to dominate NT scholarship in the 1830s (*see* **Tübingen School**), it dovetailed with a German idealist view of revelation as God perceived in the historical process. A 'purely historical' history of dogma, of which NT theology was the first part, could on this presupposition still speak of God. The history was done with integrity, but it also served the theological purpose of making the biblical talk of God intelligible in the modern world.

But around 1850 the ebbing tide of Hegelian metaphysics left this elegant synthesis like a beached whale, to be picked apart by a positivistic historiography. The liberal* Protestants' corrections to F. C. Baur's historical constructions were reinforced by distaste for his metaphysics, and by conservative opposition to both his consistently historical method and his radical conclusions. In this climate only conservative scholars (e.g. B. Weiss, 1868), whose own theological views matched their cautious historical judgments, could claim that their NT theologies were theological, not merely historical, a situation again prevalent in Europe a century later. The great liberal scholar H. J. Holtzmann could publish his outstanding compendium (1896–7) as a 'textbook of NT theology', but the historical orientation so far outweighed any theological aims as to make it an easy target for Wrede's* attack.

Wrede's complaint, in *The Task and Methods of New Testament Theology So-called* (1897, ET 1973), was that Holtzmann was not consistent in his historical presentation, but still residually influenced by theological interests and assumptions. Wrede, however, revealed his own assumptions when he sought to abolish the misleading label NT theology (so-called) and replace it with 'the history of early Christian religion and theology'. This consistent historical scholar, perhaps led astray by the ambiguity of his word 'task', but true to what he and his contemporaries were actually trying to do, had in the name of historical integrity discounted the theological interests which have normally informed the discipline. He supposed that the consistent application of historical methods, in itself legitimate, implied – or should imply – a purely historical aim or task. Underlying this conviction was the historicist assumption that only history, not theology, was academically respectable or *wissenschaftlich*. If theology was concerned to make truth-claims, it had better turn itself into history.

The classic exponent of this view was Overbeck, who drew the consequences and abandoned Christian faith. NT scholars who remained Christians, on the other hand, were left the task of re-uniting their faith and their historical research in a new model of NT theology. The social, intellectual and artistic upheavals of the 1920s included a new theological movement led by Karl Barth.* Rudolf Bultmann* joined it and built a new synthesis out of Wrede's history of traditions* research, the early Barth's (and Luther's*) kerygmatic* theology, Herrmann's theology, Dilthey's existentialist historiography, and Heidegger's phenomenology. Like its predecessors, it hinged on a particular view of revelation. It made room for historical research, while evacuating it of the theological significance which it had

had for the idealist synthesis and for the romantic theologies of later liberal Protestantism.

Bultmann's synthesis, like Baur's, succumbed to new historical knowledge and the
changing philosophical climate, but it contained the seeds of new developments. What
these will be is only now emerging. Despite
some impatience with the narrow vision of
some historical scholarship, it seems inconceivable that any intellectually responsible theology should wish to lose the gains of the past
200 years. It is, however, another question
whether the historical paradigm of Baur and
Holtzmann can again become the bearer of a
theological vision. If Overbeck and Wrede
were right to separate history and theology,
then Troeltsch was chasing a chimera in fusing
them, and Barth was right to point theology
in a different direction. Bultmann's emphasis
(following Barth's *Romans*) on theological interpretation of the NT invites translation from
its residually historical into its implicitly literary frame of reference.

It is their failure to break new theological
ground, and elucidate the biblical writers' talk
of God, which is disappointing in the more
recent textbooks. Conzelmann's *Outline* (1967,
ET 1968) continues Bultmann's hermeneutics,
offering only historical modifications. Whether historical accounts of the proclamation
of Jesus, sifted out of the Gospels,* can be
reckoned within the genre,* or whether this
should be restricted to interpretations of the
canonical* documents, is still disputed. If the
latter, Jeremias'* so-called *New Testament
Theology* (1971) is excluded. L. Goppelt (Vol.
1, 1975, ET 1981, Vol. 2, ed. J. Roloff, 1976, ET
1982) finds an alternative to Bultmann's existential interpretation in the salvation-history*
perspective pioneered by Hofmann in the nineteenth century. The biblicist handbooks of
G. E. Ladd (1974) and D. Guthrie (1981), and
the doctrinally arranged work of the Roman
Catholic K. H. Schelkle (1968–74, ET 1971–8)
are serviceable, but offer nothing new, and
the more critical works of W. G. Kümmel
(1968, ET 1973) and E. Lohse (1974) are rather
slight. J. D. G. Dunn, *Unity and Diversity in
the New Testament* (²1990), is a valuable historical overview.

All these recent textbooks have their merits,
but only L. T. Johnson, *The Writings of the
New Testament: An Interpretation* (1986), assists a new theological interpretation of the
texts, corresponding to contemporary understandings of religion and revelation. Creative
developments of NT theology can be found in
monographs and articles, but most textbooks
report on the human historical contents of the
NT without showing how this reflects what
Christians consider its divine content. For NT
theology to be more than mere repetition, or a

historical reconstruction of the emergence of
the contents of these 27 books, a view of
revelation, or theory licensing the modern interpreter to speak of God, is needed.

Over the past 200 years, two alternative
partners have always been on offer to literary
and historical biblical scholarship, producing
two types of NT theology: an authoritative
dogmatic system, and a rational theory of
religion, whether developed by philosophical*
rationalism, the speculative philosophy of history, phenomenology, or the social sciences
(*see* **Sociology and Social Anthropology**). Only
the last of these partners is compatible with a
free biblical scholarship, leading to a critical
NT theology. And only the social sciences are
today providing plausible (i.e. empirically
tested) theories of religion compatible with its
truth or claims to revelation. The future shape
of critical NT theology will therefore be found
here.

The important questions for NT theology
concern its shape or form, because this implies
a proposal about how the documents may be
read as mediating their presumed theological
content, the revelation of God in Christ. The
historical and exegetical contents of the work
are drawn from the deep well of biblical scholarship and include whatever in that well is
deemed necessary or useful for understanding
Christian faith.

See also **Biblical Theology; Revelation;**
Sachkritik; **Systematic Theology; Theology
(Old Testament).**

H. Boers, *What is New Testament Theology?*,
1979; W. G. Kümmel, *The New Testament.
The History of the Investigation of its Prob-
lems*, 1973; O. Merk, *Biblische Theologie des
Neuen Testaments in ihrer Anfangszeit*, 1972;
R. Morgan, *The Nature of New Testament
Theology*, 1973; G. Strecker (ed.), *Das Prob-
lem der Theologie des Neuen Testaments*, 1975.

ROBERT MORGAN

Theology (Old Testament)

The beginnings of OT theology are usually
traced back to J. P. Gabler's inaugural lecture
'On the proper distinction between biblical
and dogmatic theology' at the University of
Altdorf in 1787 (ET *SJT* 33, 1980). The two
centuries which have since passed have seen
the publishing of many volumes in which OT
theology at least formed a part, beginning
with that of G. L. Bauer (1796, ET 1838);
countless other works have also considered
aspects of the significance of the OT within
Christianity, which has been a subject of
Christian thinking from its beginnings (see H.
Graf Reventlow, *Problems of Old Testament
Theology* and *Problems of Biblical Theology*,
ET 1985, 1986; J. H. Hayes and F. D. Prussner,

Old Testament Theology, 1985). Yet these two hundred years have seen no progress towards agreement regarding the aim and method of OT theology.

The fundamental reason for this lies in an inherent tension between the concept 'theology' and the entity Christians know as 'the Old Testament'. Theology is a reflective, analytic, abstract discipline which seeks to formulate a carefully conceptualized account of ultimate truths regarding God and his relationship with the world in the light of the ways of thought which characterize the academic thinking of the day. 'The Old Testament', however, is a collection of pre-Christian stories, laws,* prayers and praises, proverbs, poems, oracles,* and visions, the work of many groups and individuals over many centuries, addressing many contexts and pursuing many aims. It is more symbolic* than conceptual, intuitive than reflective, concrete than abstract, holistic* than analytic, instinctive than disciplined, contextual than timelessly universal, concerned with obedience, worship, and faithfulness rather than ideas in themselves.

Inferring that justice cannot be done simultaneously to the nature of the OT and to the concerns of theology, a number of scholars have separated the two ventures. Thus H. Schultz, author of one of the first independent OT theologies (i.e. ones which did not lead into a NT theology) (1869, ET 1892), in later editions of his work devoted one volume to the development of theological and ethical* ideas in Israel against the background of Israelite history* and religion and a second to the ideas of the OT examined systematically. During the nineteenth century, scholarship focussed increasingly on the former set of questions and the latter concerns came to be neglected until the beginning of the Barthian* era and the revival of theological interest in the OT in Germany after the 1914–18 war. Then in a famous article in *Zeitschrift für die alttestamentliche Wissenschaft* (44, 1926) O. Eissfeldt specifically argued for the separation of historical-critical* study of Israel's religion with its objective, historical approach from the writing of OT theology with its requirement of the commitment of faith. The two-part approach was taken up again by E. Sellin (1933) and O. Procksch (a work completed during the 1939–45 war but published only in 1950).

Generally, however, OT theologians have resisted such a bifurcation of interests and have sought to combine them by 'bending' the OT to make it more theological and/or 'bending' the concept of theology to assimilate it more to the nature of the OT.

Both aspects of this bending are already apparent in Gabler. He advocated a biblical theology* which began by being historical and descriptive rather than timeless and prescriptive, yet which then went on to eliminate ideas limited by time and place. His aim was to systematize the normative, unchanging truth of the Bible so as to be able to hand this over to the dogmaticians to express it in terms appropriate to the day. Inevitably the decisions involved in this process would reflect contemporary philosophies such as romanticism, rationalism, Hegelianism and idealism, as well as the consistent concerns of the OT itself. Even when fulfilling its descriptive task, OT theology was unconsciously shaped by categories from elsewhere.

A different form of the bending of the OT to theology is the traditional structuring of OT theology by means of categories from Christian systematic theology* such as God, man, salvation, and eschatology,* by writers such as Bauer, Sellin, and L. Köhler (1936; ET 1957). Recent writers have generally structured their work by means of categories which they see as more reflective of the OT's own underlying concerns. Most famously, W. Eichrodt (1933–39; ET 1961–67) took the motif of the covenant* relationship between Yahweh and Israel as the broad framework for his presentation, though (like Bauer) he combined that with a historical approach to many themes treated within this framework. T. C. Vriezen made the communion between Yahweh and Israel the framework for the revised edition of his work (1966; ET 1970). Many other writers have begun from some aspect of the person or activity of God himself or from some aspect of his relationship with humanity such as his presence (S. Terrien, 1978) or his promise (W. C. Kaiser, 1978). Others have been content to examine what they see as key OT themes, without claiming that these comprise a system (e.g. J. L. McKenzie, 1974).

Eichrodt described his method as a cross-section approach, while J. Bright (*The Authority of the Old Testament*, 1967) called it an attempt to identify the OT's underlying concerns: the latter expression makes particularly clear that part of the bending involved in such treatments is that they are not handling the text itself but something they believe lies beneath it.

Writers such as Eichrodt declare that they aim both to do justice to the OT's own concerns and to demonstrate their points of connection with the NT. In practice their works, like the OT theologies that more explicitly follow categories adopted from Christian theology, can be seen with hindsight to assimilate the OT to Christian theological concerns in their value judgments and in the way they understand the OT's priorities. Litmus tests for this process are the way OT theologians handle the themes of the land and the cult,* two prominent theological themes within the OT. The former is ignored by most OT theologies (even recently by B. S. Childs, 1985). The latter is not ignored but treated with a negative slant which derives from Protestant theological convictions rather than from the OT (see e.g. Köhler). But some more recent works have made some progress in their treatment of such OT themes (e.g. W. Zimmerli, 1972, ET 1978; C. Westermann, 1978, ET 1982; E. A. Martens, 1981).

Eichrodt's programmatic statements, paralleled in Procksch and Vriezen and given more emphasis by G. A. F. Knight (1959), might make one expect more by way of explicit Christian bending of the OT than in fact appears in their work. It is actually no more marked than that in many writers who do not acknowledge such an aim. Indeed, such bending is generally less evident in actual OT theologies than it is in some other works concerned with the theological significance of the OT for Christians, which rework a number of traditional ways of establishing connections between the OT and the NT (see A. H. J. Gunneweg, *Understanding the Old Testament*, ET 1978; J. Goldingay, *Approaches to Old Testament Interpretation*, 1981). Thus (among writers accessible in English) W. Vischer uses typology* to establish links between OT characters and Christ as he expounds *The Witness of the Old Testament to Christ* (1934–42, ET of Vol. 1, 1949); cf K. Barth's theological use of the OT (e.g. the treatment of Job in *Church Dogmatics* IV 3 i, 1961). W. Zimmerli in *Essays on Old Testament Interpretation/Hermeneutics* (ed. C. Westermann, 1963) sees the OT as embodying a hope and promise that are fulfilled in the Christian gospel. Bright pictures the OT as Act I to the NT's Act II in the story of salvation. R. Bultmann* (see discussion in *The Old Testament and Christian Faith* ed. B. W. Anderson, 1964) emphasizes the disjunction between OT and NT by means of the Lutheran* antithesis between law (the OT) and gospel (the NT). In itself the very title 'the Old Testament' of course already expresses a theological judgment which does not emerge from the OT – nor for that matter directly from the NT.

As we have noted, the converse bending of theology to do justice to the nature of the OT appears in the nineteenth-century stress on a historical approach to the OT. The early decades of this century saw continuing development of the study of ancient Israel against the background of religions and ways of thought characteristic of contemporary or parallel societies. An implication of such study is that Israel's religious ideas or theology can

hardly be appreciated apart from their context in Israel's religious and social life, though in the process of the bending of the OT to the nature of theology (and given German scholarship's generally negative stance in relation to 'religion') this implication has often not been perceived (see R. E. Clements, *Old Testament Theology*, 1978).

After the approaches with less emphasis on history which characterized the period between the wars, G. von Rad (1957–60, ET 1962–65) reasserted the significance of history and powerfully advocated its specifically theological significance. In contrast to the cross-section approaches von Rad also encouraged a further bending of theology in order to do justice to the OT through his stress on the diversity of the OT expressions of faith rather than the oneness of an alleged underlying theology. That has been a key awareness of scholarship over recent decades (see P. D. Hanson, *The Diversity of Scripture*, 1982).

Discussion of von Rad's work stressed the difficulty of his theological stress on history, given his minimal evaluation of the actual historical value of the material from Israel's early period with its theologically foundational importance. Arguably the real subject of von Rad's theological work was the development of Israel's traditions, not Israel's actual history. This tradition history* became the explicit object of the OT theological enterprise in the work of H. Gese, though his stress on the significance of the last form of the tradition which subsumes all the others undermines the significance of earlier parts of the OT (see e.g. *Essays on Biblical Theology*, 1981; and more generally *Tradition and Theology in the Old Testament* ed. D. A. Knight, 1977). The bending of theology to the actual form of the OT is taken further in the concern with the theological significance of the final, canonical* form of the OT text which appears in different ways in the work of B. S. Childs (*Introduction to the Old Testament as Scripture*, 1979) and J. A. Sanders (*From Sacred Story to Sacred Text*, 1987; and more generally *Canon and Authority* ed. G. W. Coats and B. O. Long, 1977).

In this context we may also note that some of the most significant OT theological work of the century has appeared in OT commentaries.* Among writers in English one should mention Childs' *Exodus*, 1974, and works by W. Brueggemann on Genesis and Psalms; but a theological interest is more characteristic of German commentators such as von Rad, Westermann, Zimmerli, A. Weiser, H. W. Hertzberg, H. W. Wolff, H.-J. Kraus and H. Wildberger in the series *Das Alte Testament Deutsch* and *Biblischer Kommentar: Altes Testament*; translations have been published in the

Old Testament Library, the Hermeneia series, and separately. In a commentary, theology has a particularly clear opportunity to follow the OT itself rather than reflecting alien concerns, though the explicit theological work in such commentaries may nevertheless assimilate the text's interests to those of Christian faith by the techniques which we have noted above.

In explicit attack on such OT interpretation which subordinates the OT to the NT, the importance of the theological message of the OT in its own right was asserted by A. A. van Ruler (*The Christian Church and the Old Testament*, 1966; see also K. H. Miskotte, *When the Gods are Silent*, 1967). As we have noted, substantial specific areas of OT thinking have been missed in much OT theology. Von Rad's stress on the OT's concern with Israel's history obscured for scholarship its equally explicit concern with the world, with nature, and with human experience, though von Rad took up these themes in his *Wisdom in Israel*, 1972, virtually a third volume to his *Theology* (see further J. Goldingay, *Theological Diversity and the Authority of the Old Testament*, 1987, ch. 7; Reventlow, *Problems of Old Testament Theology*, ch. 5). This theme features in several of the 'Overtures to Biblical Theology' series such as W. Brueggemann's *The Land* (1978) – noted above as a topic characteristically avoided by Christian OT theology.

A paradoxical aspect of the study of OT theology surfaces here. In an important article on biblical theology in *The Interpreter's Dictionary of the Bible*, 1962, K. Stendahl argued, like Gabler, for a descriptive approach, a study of OT and NT in their own right independently of a desire to discover what they have to say prescriptively. There is a sense in which this bends theology to the OT, but because the nature of theology is to formulate what we may or should believe, not merely to analyse what people have believed, Stendahl advocated this approach out of a concern to do justice to the text itself and to avoid bending it to our agenda. But like Gabler he risks a hermeneutical* naivety that fails to recognize how we all see only in part; we have prejudices which both facilitate and limit our seeing, even when we are overtly seeking to understand something for its own sake and not in order to get answers to our questions. All the more will this be the case with OT theology (as history since Gabler shows), which though formally descriptive is ultimately designed to point to what should be believed, and which often has a specific hidden agenda of which even its author may be hardly aware. So the descriptive approach may miss theological aspects of the OT such as its this-worldly and human concerns, which an overt concern with the present-day message of the

OT brings into clearer focus. Liberation* and feminist* approaches to the OT illustrate this point. Another way of perceiving more of the theological potential of the OT lies in studying the work of writers of different backgrounds and faith commitments. For Christians, this will mean especially Jewish writers (see e.g. J. D. Levenson, *Sinai and Zion*, 1985).

While it is disappointing that two centuries of study have not yielded an agreed methodology* for OT theology, it is gratifying that the period has yielded a rich corpus of illuminating works which often complement each other by bringing out various aspects of the diverse richness of the OT itself as well as by being critically corrective of each other.

See also **Biblical Theology; Systematic Theology; Theology (New Testament).**

JOHN GOLDINGAY

Theophany

The term is derived from the two Greek words, *theos*, 'a god', and *phainō*, 'appear, show oneself, make manifest'. The basic meaning of 'theophany', therefore, could be given as an 'appearance of God to man'. On this definition, it could be argued that, strictly speaking, there are no theophanies in the Bible; the God of Israel was an invisible God, and, further, it was believed that humans could not see God and live (cf. Ex. 33.20). Passages which seem to refer to 'seeing' God must be understood as describing visions, or else some quite out of the ordinary experience. However, if 'theophany' is defined as a '(self) manifestation of God', it becomes possible to interpret as theophanic biblical passages which refer to a variety of phenomena which are taken to indicate the presence or coming of God.

It could be argued that it would be more appropriate to use the term 'epiphany' to describe some of these manifestations. Westermann has suggested that it is appropriate to speak of a 'theophany' when God appears in order to reveal himself and communicate with the people via a mediator (e.g. Ex. 19 and 34), whereas an 'epiphany' is when God appears in order to aid his people (e.g. Judg. 5). However, the term 'theophany' is frequently used to refer to the latter type of appearance, and 'helping intervention' has been suggested as a primary feature of theophany.

Phenomena associated with the presence or coming of God may be visible or audible. God's presence may be indicated by fire, smoke or cloud (e.g. Ex. 13.21; 19.18; 24.17); a term associated with God's presence particularly in the Priestly material is 'glory', which has even been taken to be the earthly manifestation of God himself (Morgenstern). The coming of God is often associated with the phenomena of the powers of nature – perhaps those of volcano or earthquake, but, in particular, those of the storm, and considerable attention has recently been paid to the possible origins of such a concept in Canaanite thought about the storm-god Baal (Cross, Miller). Another visible manifestation of God may be noted in the enigmatic figure of the 'angel/messenger (mal'āk) of Yahweh' (e.g. Gen. 16.7ff.; Judg. 2.1ff.; 13.2ff.); whereas this figure sometimes seems to be quite distinct from God, at other times the 'angel' seems to be God himself.

The attempt to categorize theophany stories is fraught with difficulties, not least because some seem to fall into more than one category. A helpful starting point may be Jeremias' differentiation between manifestations of God in the powers of nature, in which he appears as the divine warrior striking fear into his enemies, and manifestations which are primarily demonstrations of favour to individuals; the latter group can be further divided into legitimations of a special person or place which are really aetiologies,* and cultic* theophanies which take place under circumstances which can be repeated. The very ancient Song of Deborah preserves an example of the 'divine warrior' type of theophany, which contains the basic elements of Yahweh coming from his abode, accompanied by the phenomena of the storm, and with attendant upheaval in nature (Judg. 5.4–5); in other passages, such ideas as the defeat of the forces of chaos or earthly enemies, and/or that of Yahweh as divine king are associated (e.g. Pss. 18.15; 46.6; 97; Hab. 3.3–15). Ex. 19.16–25 provides the outstanding example of a theophany which is a demonstration of favour to an individual; although the rest of the people observe the phenomena at a distance, it is Moses* whom Yahweh meets on Mt Sinai and for whose significance the story provides legitimation. Within this episode there are elements which seem to owe their origins to the cult, e.g. the preparatory consecration and purification, the sounding of the trumpet, and perhaps the presence of fire and smoke; this implies that there were cultic contexts in which Yahweh was believed to 'appear'.

It is far from easy to distinguish between theophanies and visions. For example, how should the experience of Isaiah at his call (Isa. 6.1ff.) be understood? Even where the situation is clear, as in Jacob's dream at Bethel (Gen. 28.10–22), it is difficult to avoid seeing similarities with the type of theophany which legitimates a cult centre or special person. Nor is it easy to tell whether a theophany description is based on the recollection of some event or circumstance, however embellished, or whether it is a purely artificial literary creation.

Various explanations are offered to account for those special occasions when God was believed to have appeared to a human being. After Moses' second encounter with Yahweh on Mt Sinai, it is revealed that his face shone so that he had to wear a veil when speaking to the people (Ex. 34.29–35). In Ex. 33.17–23, when Moses asks to be shown Yahweh's glory, the statement that 'man shall not see me and live' (v. 20) is followed by a description of how Moses was hidden in a cleft of the rock and sheltered by Yahweh's hand while he passed by so that Moses was only able to see his back. Probably dependent upon this tradition is I Kings 19.9–12, but here Yahweh is not present in such phenomena as wind, earthquake and fire, but in the voice; perhaps this is to be seen as polemic against the type of theophanic thought which was derived from Canaanite notions, and a defence of God's self-revelation via the spoken word.*

Examples have been given from the OT because, in the NT, it is stressed that God's self-revelation is in Jesus, and it is probably inappropriate to use the term 'theophany' to refer to the concept of incarnation (but see John 1.18). However, there are NT passages reminiscent of the theophany language of the OT, for example, the description of the divine manifestation with flames of fire and the sound of wind at Pentecost (Acts 2.2–3), the light from heaven at the conversion of Saul (Acts 9.3), and, in particular, some of the descriptions of the Second Coming (e.g. Matt. 24.30; 26.64; Mark 13.24–26).

See also **Parousia; Revelation; Shekhinah.**

F. M. Cross, *Canaanite Myth and Hebrew Epic*, 1973; E. Jacob, *Theology of the Old Testament*, 1958; J. Jeremias, *Theophanie*, 1965; T. N. D. Mettinger, *The Dethronement of Sabaoth*, 1982; P. D. Miller, *The Divine Warrior in Early Israel*, 1973; C. Westermann, *The Praise of God in the Psalms*, 1966.

A. H. W. CURTIS

Thessalonians

The two epistles* of Paul* to the church at Thessalonica have seen neither the same range of extensive theological debate nor the same prolonged contentious interpretation within the history of scholarship as other parts of the Pauline corpus. The main contribution of I and II Thessalonians (hereafter I and II) to the area of hermeneutical* discussion has been restricted to one or two peripheral matters not really central to the major concerns and issues which gave rise to the letters themselves. Nevertheless, questions concerning the precise literary relationship between the two epistles; the possibility of eschatological* and christological* development in Paul's thought as traced through the letters; the meaning of the 'man of sin' or 'lawlessness' described in II Thess. 2.3 and the meaning of the 'restrainer' (*katechōn* in Greek) in II Thess. 2.6–7, have all been focal points for scholarly discussion.

It is generally agreed that I is the earliest of Paul's epistles and its authenticity is not in serious doubt today, although F. C. Baur did question this in the last century. However, II has been the subject of a continuing debate as to its authenticity, with the major concern being how it relates to I in terms of contents, vocabulary, style and form. A. von Harnack* went so far as to explain the difference in tone between the two epistles as being due to the fact that I was directed to a Gentile group within the church at Thessalonica while II was directed to a Jewish group. In any event, some literary dependence between the two letters seems highly probable, at the very least on a form-critical* level.

Marcion* included II in his Pauline collection and it appears in all subsequent canonical listings. The first to cast doubt on its authenticity was J. E. Christian Schmidt in 1798, who based his contention mostly on a comparison of the eschatological material of the letter with that contained in I. This point of comparison has remained the dominant area of discussion to the present day. The decision one makes about the compatibility of the eschatological teaching of the two Thessalonian epistles is usually directly related to conclusions about the authenticity of II.

Closely connected with this is the question of the respective dating of the two epistles. Is the eschatological teaching contained within them so incompatible that the traditional understanding of close chronological connection, a gap of as little as a couple of months, is made highly unlikely? Given the occasional nature of the correspondence, this judgment appears hasty. Scholars point out that we may in fact have two genuine letters of Paul in which he responds pastorally to the eschatological issues being raised by the church at Thessalonica, taking care, in I, to emphasize the nearness of the parousia* of Christ and then countering, in II, with a correction to an over-enthusiastic interpretation of his teaching by the Thessalonians. It is thus not impossible to take both epistles as genuine and to see them as coming from the pen of the apostle within a short time of each other.

Some scholars have suggested that II was written before I. Hugo Grotius first suggested this in 1641 and it has found some modern adherents, notably T. W. Manson. Central to this proposal is the idea that many of the eschatological tensions between the two epistles are more readily resolved in this way. All the same, most scholars now accept that the canonical order was also the chronological one.

Some interpreters (such as W. Schmithals) have explored the possibility of both I and II being composite documents, each made up of two or more shorter letters. However, this approach has not been widely accepted and most interpreters today accept the integrity of both I and II even if they are not agreed on the matter of the apostolic authorship* of the latter.

The question of deutero-Pauline interpolations into the text of I has also been a major concern of Pauline interpreters since the days of F. C. Baur. The curious passage 2.13–16 is one example which provides material to support such a suggestion, with scholars exploring how it compares with Paul's teaching about the Jewish nation in Rom. 9–11.

The identity of 'the man of lawlessness' (II Thess. 2.3) and the meaning of 'the restrainer' (II Thess. 2.6–7) have engendered considerable scholarly debate. Some have sought to interpret the former in the light of prevailing Antichrist mythologies* of the day (F. H. Kern suggested an association with the later 'Nero Redivivus' myth, an interpretation which of necessity presupposes non-Pauline authorship of II); while various suggestions have been put forward for the latter, including God himself, the Roman empire, the church, and the unfulfilled gospel mission to the world. The debate about the meaning of 'the restrainer' is due in part to the fact that it is ambiguous in Greek and occurs as both a neuter participle in v. 6 and a masculine one in v. 7. Both concepts, that of 'the man of lawlessness' and 'the restrainer', are probably derived from a generalized Jewish eschatological background with which the author (whether he be Paul or not) was well acquainted. We should perhaps look to the 'abomination of desolation' reference in Mark 13.14 and, ultimately, to the Antiochus Epiphanes episode in Jewish history (as channelled through the Caligula incident in AD 41?) for the basis of a proper interpretation.

———

Ernest Best, *The First and Second Epistles to the Thessalonians*, 1972; Raymond F. Collins, *Studies on the First Letter to the Thessalonians*, 1984; C. H. Giblin, *The Threat to Faith*, 1967; A. J. Malherbe, *Paul and the Thessalonians*, 1987; C. L. Mearns, 'Early Eschatological Development in Paul: the Evidence of I & II Thessalonians', *NTS* 27, 1980–81. pp. 137–57.

L. KREITZER

Torrey, C. C.

Charles Cutler Torrey (1863–1956) was Professor of Semitic Languages at Andover from

1892 and at Yale from 1900 until 1932. A founder-member and director of the American School of Oriental Research in Jerusalem, he made important archaeological* finds in Palestine. An eminent biblical and Arabic scholar, he is remembered for the brilliance of his teaching and the versatility of his activities outside scholarship.

He wrote on a wide range of topics: the biblical prophets, especially Jeremiah, Second Isaiah and Ezekiel; the Ezra-Nehemiah-Chronicles collection; the apocryphal* and pseudepigraphal* literature; the Aramaic background of the Gospels* and Acts; and Islamic mysticism. He had completed a study of the Book of Revelation by the time of his death, and he also did notable work in epigraphy,* especially seals and coins.

President of the Society of Biblical Literature in 1915, he was long remembered for his lively and combative style, especially in his clashes over the Aramaic* origins of some of the NT writings. Equally contentious was his main contribution to biblical scholarship, in the area of prophetic studies and the Ezra-Nehemiah material, in particular his claim that the 'Exile' and its concomitant 'Restoration' was a fiction created by the Chronicler as part of his propaganda against the Samaritans.* It was typical of Torrey's brilliant reading of texts; it was also typical that this view was rejected by most scholars of his time and since (cf. the 1970 edition of Pseudo-Ezekiel). Yet much may be said for his claim, and the notions 'Exile' and 'Restoration' need to be rethought in current biblical scholarship. What also needs to be given more serious consideration is his argument that the books of Jeremiah, Second Isaiah and Ezekiel belong to a 'sacred library of the prophets' formed in the third century BC (The Second Isaiah, pp. 98–104). Recent work on Jeremiah (e.g. Carroll, Jeremiah, 1986) may well be heading in Torrey's direction, especially in terms of the claim that there is 'only an imaginary connection with the seventh century BC' (JBL 56, p. 216) in the book of Jeremiah. Opposition to his radical re-reading of Ezekiel as a response to Alexander's conquest of the East, and hence as a pseudepigraph of the third century BC, is as strong now as it was during Torrey's lifetime and recent commentaries* on Ezekiel (e.g. Brownlee, Greenberg) show no signs of deviating from conventional opinion on the matter. Torrey's opinions have proved to be too specific, though the arguments have considerable force, to be persuasive in modern scholarship. In Ezra studies his dismissal of much of Ezra-Nehemiah as unhistorical remains a starting point for any serious discussion of that Second Temple literature. Garbini's recent rejection of the historicity of Ezra (History and Ideology in Ancient Israel, 1988, pp. 151–69, 204–9) suggests that Torrey's position may yet be taken up by serious scholars working on the Second Temple period.

Torrey remains one of the outstanding scholars of the past century of biblical scholarship. Although few of his innovative readings of the prophetic texts have had the impact they deserved, his day may yet come when scholars finally do the rethinking of the prophets which those biblical books now need. Part of the failure of Torrey to reshape biblical studies in recent decades is no doubt due to the subsequent domination of American biblical scholarship by his implacable opponent W. F. Albright. Once that stranglehold on American scholarship has disappeared Torrey's star should rise to its rightful place in the scholarly firmament.

E. W. Saunders, Searching the Scriptures: a History of the Society of Biblical Literature, 1982.

ROBERT P. CARROLL

Tradition, History of

The terms 'history of tradition', 'tradition history' and 'tradition criticism' (Traditionsgeschichte, Überlieferungsgeschichte) refer to an approach to texts which seeks to ascertain the history of the motifs, themes, or other constituent parts of the text, before they came to be fixed in their final forms. (The two German terms, though apparently very similar in meaning, have in practice been understood quite differently: Traditionsgeschichte has been used of the work of those Scandinavian* scholars who have emphasized the extended oral stages in the tradition process; Überlieferungsgeschichte of the work of German* scholars who have given greater emphasis to literary tradition.) Secondarily, it attempts to shed light on the communities* which created, fostered and passed on the units of tradition. Its basic presupposition is that social* and religious reality is formed by tradition. The religious beliefs and practices of a community are not created in a vacuum, nor by isolated, gifted individuals, but are passed on in the life of a community. The process of collecting, criticizing, interpreting, and adding to the inheritance of the past goes on, consciously or unconsciously, as the community maintains its existence or adapts to new circumstances.

Within biblical studies this approach arose out of dissatisfaction with literary and source criticism,* particularly in the field of pentateuchal* studies. Reacting against J. Wellhausen's source criticism which regarded the Pentateuch as a collection of written sources of varying antiquity, H. Gunkel investigated the influence of pre-literary, oral traditions* on the formation of the canonical* texts. In order to do this he investigated the forms of OT literature and their 'setting in life', and thus made the decisive contribution to the related method of form criticism.* Similarly, by enquiring into the history of the transmission of OT forms and literature, he anticipated, to a limited extent, what has come to be called redaction criticism.* As he carried out his form and tradition criticism as part of his wider study of Israelite religion in the light of comparable material from other regions of the Near East (the history-of-religions* approach), his work contains all the main impulses for historical interpretation. At the same time, because Gunkel and those who have followed him combined these methods, the term 'history of tradition' is used in a variety of ways, or even as a synonym for historical interpretation (*see* **Historical-Critical Method**). Thus, K. Koch's useful, introductory, study of form and tradition criticism appeared in German under the title *What is Form Criticism? New Paths in Biblical Exegesis* and in English as *The Growth of Biblical Tradition. The Form-Critical Method'*. Koch cautions against the use of the term 'history of tradition' on the grounds that it is too vague. Here it will be used in two ways: firstly, as one of the different methods used in historical interpretation; secondly, with reference to those attempts which make the history-of-traditions approach the dominant method for historical interpretation, usually because of dissatisfaction with the use of form criticism.

With regard to method, tradition criticism focusses on both the characteristic content of material and on the process of transmission. Whereas form criticism starts by analysing form, tradition criticism begins by enquiring into the identity and significance of recurring motifs or units of traditions. These units of tradition can be a single word or phrase (e.g. the kingdom of God*), a concept (the delay of the parousia*), a general theme (eschatology*), or a combination of motifs characteristically found together. The method proceeds by the comparison of examples within the same 'tradition field', and then attempts to construct the history of the tradition in question. At the same time the process of transmission is studied. The attempt is made to identify the groups (e.g. priestly circles, prophetic* or wisdom* schools) which collected, shaped and passed on the biblical material before it reached its final form. In addition, the method should also pay attention to the manner in which material was passed on, respecting the differences between the dynamics of oral and written traditions.

It has also proved fruitful to attempt to localize traditions in geographical or institutional terms. Thus, traditions have been connected with a particular religious site, or with settlements which took on religious and political significance (in this respect Jerusalem* features in the study of both Testaments). S. Mowinckel emphasized the importance of the institutions of kingship* and temple for the shaping of Israelite traditions. In general, the enquiry into the social, political and religious dynamics which effected the process of tradition is closely related to the attempt to determine the 'setting in life' of literary units in form-critical investigations.

For Gunkel, the hypothesis of the influence of oral tradition freed the critic from the need to date a document or tradition to its earliest discernible source. Instead, units of tradition, originally preserved orally and now embedded in later texts, can be reconstructed and studied as sources for the earlier period to which they relate. However, Gunkel did not investigate in detail the differences between the dynamics of oral and pre-canonical written traditions, and his work called forth a vigorous reaction, particularly from Scandinavian scholars.

In the meantime the importance of Gunkel's work was not lost on German scholarship. In particular, M. Noth and G. von Rad carried forward his concerns, but, in contrast to the Scandinavian school, with far greater emphasis on written traditions and in conjunction with older source-critical hypotheses. Enquiring into the early oral period, which he held to be the creative phase for the formation of the Pentateuch, Noth argued that the core of Israelite tradition is to be found in a series of themes, which now follow each other in a continuous narrative: the promise to the patriarchs, the guidance out of Egypt, the revelation at Sinai, the guidance in the wilderness, the guidance into the arable land (so B. W. Anderson, in his helpful introduction to Noth's monograph). The individual themes go back to the experience or knowledge of individual tribes or earlier configurations of tribes, and their present arrangement was fixed in the oral period. In this pre-literary stage, the originally discrete themes were welded together into a 'short historical credo' (von Rad's description of Deut. 26.5–9) which was transmitted in the cult.* Here Yahweh's great acts in history, the source of Israel's identity, were celebrated. The 'sources' (in this case of the Pentateuch, though the same methods were increasingly applied to other parts of the OT and NT) were no longer regarded as the products of individuals but as the deposits of communities* and groups.

While the term 'history of tradition' has not been so prominent within NT study, the same issues have arisen in the discussion of form criticism. Bultmann* categorizes the material of the Gospel tradition according to its literary form and then investigates the history of the individual units and their setting in the communal life of the early church. Bultmann's radical scepticism on the question of the authenticity of much of the material brought forth a (belated) Scandinavian response which emphasized the importance and reliability of oral tradition in the formation of the Gospels. Contemporary NT historical scholarship in general has continued to use the combination of form and tradition criticism while acknowledging the existence of methodological* problems with this approach and while coming to less radical solutions than those put forward by Bultmann.

A new challenge has, however, been thrown down by W. Kelber's application to the NT of insights from recent studies of oral cultures. While lip-service has been paid to the distinction between oral and written language, there has been no real appreciation of the fundamental differences between these two modes of communication. In contrast to Bultmann's view that the written Gospel was the inevitable end-product of an evolving tradition, and to Gerhardsson's faith in the reliability of oral traditions, Kelber posits that the act of writing a Gospel brings to an end an era of fluid oral tradition which follows its own rules. Indeed he finds evidence, within Mark, of hostility to the key institutions of oral culture, the family and prophets.

The Gospel traditions have provided an obvious but not the only field for the application of the history-of-traditions approach to the NT. Another important area has been the study of liturgical or credal* traditions within the Epistles.* In the case of pre-Pauline traditions this has had the added incentive of allowing scholars to push back into the critical but obscure period between Jesus and Paul.* (The study of pre-Pauline tradition has the added attraction of not being dependent on Acts, which itself has to be assessed for historical reliability and read in the light of its author's own interests.) Thus I Cor. 11.23–25 and 15.3–5, which Paul explicitly acknowledges as being traditional, give rare, if brief, insights into the beliefs of the pre-Pauline church on the subjects of the eucharist and the resurrection.* By extension, literary and theological analyses have suggested (with a fair degree of probability) the presence of christological*–soteriological* traditions in Rom. 1.2-4; 3.24–26; Phil. 2.6–11, etc. In turn, Paul's use and understanding of, and modifications to, these traditions can also be studied. Given the existence of deutero-Pauline epistles this allows a relatively long and unbroken line of tradition to be studied.

The history-of-traditions approach to the

Bible is not without its problems in the contemporary debate about interpretation. Its own methodology gives rise to the problem of multiple, increasingly unverifiable, hypotheses. The biblical material has been divided up into ever smaller units which are ascribed to an ever increasing number of communities, circles, and authors.* The proliferation of equally plausible hypotheses to account for any one unit of tradition highlights the inevitably hypothetical nature of its methodology: the more sophisticated the method becomes, the more it depends on scholarly hypothesis. Secondly, with the end of the dominance of kerygmatic* theology in biblical studies, the method has lost a powerful ally which gave it a theological rationale. By tracing the kerygmatic intention of the various levels of the tradition, the method yielded theological, as well as historical, results. In an earlier period, which sought theological inspiration in the original, pure, forms of belief, the method promised to deliver the faith of the Bible unencumbered by later accretions or interpretations. In fact it can only yield insights into the probabilities of the historical processes which created the biblical traditions. Today, while the method continues to be widely used as one of the family of methods which are the basis of historical interpretation, its importance for the wider question of biblical interpretation is under attack from literary, structuralist,* and canonical* approaches, all of which, like the church, are primarily concerned with the final state of the text.

See also **Biblical Criticism; Form Criticism; Oral Tradition.**

E. Boring, *Sayings of the Risen Christ: Christian Prophecy in the Synoptic Tradition*, 1982; D. R. Catchpole, 'Tradition History' in I. H. Marshall (ed.), *New Testament Interpretation. Essays on Principles and Methods,* ³1985; B. Gerhardsson, *The Origins of the Gospel Traditions*, 1979; W. H. Kelber, *The Oral and the Written Gospel*, 1983; M. Noth, *A History of Pentateuchal Traditions*, 1948, ET 1972; G. von Rad, *The Problem of the Hexateuch and Other Essays,* ET 1966; W. R. Rast, *Tradition History and the Old Testament*, 1972.

DAVID V. WAY

Trajectory

The concept of 'trajectories' was applied to biblical criticism in a volume of essays by James M. Robinson and Helmut Koester entitled *Trajectories through Early Christianity* (1971, but drawing on earlier essays). It was conceived as an attempt to alter the way in which NT scholarship approached its critical tasks. By using the analogy of 'trajectory', they proposed a restructuring of historical, literary and theological discussions of the NT and its environment, away from older fixed categories – Judaism and Hellenism, or orthodoxy and heresy – and towards the idea of tracing lines of development. This was a powerful articulation of a concept that had begun to be recognized much earlier, as for example in W. Bauer's *Orthodoxy and Heresy in Earliest Christianity* (1934).

On the one hand, Robinson argues that the previous two centuries of biblical scholarship demonstrated an excessive concern for treating the NT documents as fixed points or discrete entities for study, rather than emphasizing the developments within which they played a part. It is not that there was no awareness at all of development or movement, but rather that the movement itself was seldom the focal point for the study. Even where the historical relativity of early Christian thought was accepted and where general trends were noticed, *religionsgeschichtliche* studies (*see* **History of Religions School**) into background and environment were still largely used as if they presented a static, monolithic backdrop for the various NT writings. On the other hand, Robinson observes that a different danger has arisen since the discovery of the Dead Sea Scrolls* and Nag Hammadi* documents. These discoveries challenged many previously held 'uniform' categories such as 'Palestinian Judaism' or 'Hellenistic Judaism' and brought a new sense of the diversity of these settings to the fore. But this has often led scholars to avoid any generalizations at all. The newly-discovered texts are cited, he claims, in a disorganized way without proposing any relationships between the traditions.

In contrast, the identification of trajectories is an attempt to look for and trace relationships or trends wherever they may be found. Lines of unity are sought within the recognized diversity of the period. Variant traditions within the broad streams or movements are also as important as the broad streams themselves. There is no single trajectory. There are many, and the interplay between them is of considerable significance in understanding the period. So, the historical relativity of the NT period is accepted, and its diversity accepted. But most importantly, early Christianity must be understood primarily in terms of the various tendencies at work at the time, the interplay between such tendencies and the departures that are sometimes found from the general trends.

This approach can be applied to historical questions, theological concepts or even literary genres,* as the various essays by Robinson and Koester demonstrate. For example, the question of the relationship of the kerygma* to the historical Jesus* can be analysed in terms of distinct but interconnecting 'movements' whose trajectories, variations and interactions can be traced within the diversity of early Christianity. Or, the genre of Q may be treated as part of a trajectory. Rather than fixing on isolated hints that Q might be of one or another literary genre or citing a few parallels to other early sayings collections, Robinson seeks to trace a genre which he describes as *logoi sophōn* (sayings of the wise), beginning with Jewish wisdom* literature through Q itself and on to Gnostic* works including the Gospel of Thomas. On this basis he also conjectures that the disappearance of Q may have been due to unacceptable gnosticizing overtones that became attached to such collections. His work on the genre of Q has recently been taken several steps further by J. Kloppenborg (*The Formation of Q*, 1987), who has surveyed a wide variety of genres of sayings collections in antiquity and located Q within that context. Ideally, the field for these trajectories must be extended as far as possible within the ancient world. It is important to note, however, that the relationships which are traced are not necessarily viewed as direct causal ones, indicating the actual dependence of one work upon another. Rather the relationships simply show how movements can successively come to expression.

The consequences of this approach are far-reaching and go well beyond rejecting the traditional, unyielding theological classifications that had arisen in NT scholarship. It becomes clear that NT writings and ideas are not to be separated by appeal to 'canonicity'* from other literature, but rather must be seen as part of a wider history of tradition* in the early Christian era. As Koester points out, there is also no inherent reason why such trajectories should be limited to the NT or early Christian era. They may be applied to the whole history of the Christian proclamation up to today, shedding light on our own world and existence.

While the aims of this approach to biblical criticism* have been widely applauded, there are some difficulties to be faced. Firstly, although the fragmentary nature of our early sources might seem to frustrate ambitions to trace clear lines of development, the sheer enormity of the task is probably a greater obstacle. The information that one needs to assimilate in order to trace trajectories throughout the thought of the ancient world at large, and the knowledge of various social conditions and regional variations that is required, set a task that one can only hope to begin to unravel. When one allows for interacting, overarching and variant trajectories, one again faces the sheer complexity of the endeavour. Secondly, the metaphor of 'trajectory' itself has limitations. Robinson was aware that the term 'trajectory' may imply a kind of initial simplicity and determinism at the point of departure, which runs counter to his belief that movements undergo modifications, interact with other movements and even show evidence of 'conflicting directionalities'. Robinson himself at times uses other metaphors,* such as 'streams' or 'trends'. Without completely abandoning the analogy of trajectory, J. D. G. Dunn (*Unity and Diversity in the New Testament*, ²1990) suggests a preference for the terms 'unity' and 'diversity' to express the sketching of relationships and variations in early Christianity. Others prefer to refer to 'crystallizations' or 'lines of development' (cf. *Entwicklungslinien* in the German edition of Robinson and Koester's work). Finally, N. Perrin ('Unravelling the Tangled Skein', *Interpretation*, 26, 1972) asked whether the emphasis on trajectory, even with the qualifications above, does not imply a certain inevitability about the appearance of individual documents or ideas. With respect to the 'gospel' genre, he questioned whether this approach did not tend to treat the evangelists* (and especially Mark) in the older form-critical* way, as reaching the point that they did because of certain compelling forces in the tradition. This may do less than full justice to the newer redaction-critical* appreciation of the evangelists' creativity and individual historical circumstances. Such warnings, however, have seldom sought to undermine the theory as a whole. The concept of trajectory has largely been accepted as an aid towards a dynamic and process-oriented approach to NT problems.

See also **Genre; Logion; Tradition, History of.**

R. A. PIPER

Translation, Problems of

A simple contrast is often drawn in popular thought between translation and paraphrase, as if the former were an almost mechanical activity with no trace of interpretation and free of subjectivity. Although the distinction is, broadly speaking, a valid one, it is not always easy in specific instances to define the dividing line, for in any translation, especially of such ancient texts as the OT and NT, interpretation is a necessary part of the task and difference of opinion is unavoidable. Thus, quite apart from difficulties presented by obscure or unintelligible texts which, in theory at least, may be solved by advances in knowledge whether of language or of cultural background, there are problems, some ultimately insuperable, inherent in the process of translating, however competent and unbiased the translators. This is not to suggest, however, as

has sometimes been done, that in the case of the OT the grammatical structure of the original language is such as to reflect theological reality in a unique way (see Barr's criticism of this view in *The Semantics of Biblical Language*, 1961). Rather the problems arise in the transfer from one language to another, as the preface to Ecclesiasticus recognized already in the second century BC. Nevertheless, translation is not an impossible task, as the Bible's continuing challenge to individual and society testifies.

From the outset two fundamental decisions influence the character of a translation: the first, its proposed use and intended readership (is dignity or simplicity to be its priority?); the second, the translators' understanding of the nature of their task and the extent of their freedom to modernize and explain. Thus, far from being merely a copy of the original in another language, a translation inevitably takes on a life and purpose of its own. Yet, these considerations apart, the problems involved and questions of interpretation to be faced are complex even in the most literal of translations, for there is no possibility of mechanical transfer from one language to another. Words in different languages are rarely precise equivalents. Their meanings overlap rather than coincide, and the more abstract a term the more difficult it is to find a corresponding expression in another language which carries similar connotations. Thus it is not only rare and unfamiliar words which present problems for the translator.

Gen. 1.2 provides an apt illustration of the difficulty. Does it refer to 'the Spirit of God' and thus to the beginning of creative activity, or to 'a mighty wind' (NEB, understanding the word 'God' as the equivalent of our superlative, a use well attested in Hebrew), an aspect of pre-creation chaos? Either meaning is appropriate to the context and the decision must rest ultimately with the translators. Similarly Ps. 16.3 has the familiar word 'holy ones', but are these 'saints' (RSV) or 'gods whom earth holds sacred' (NEB)? On this decision turns the sense of the rest of the verse, whether it is praise or judgment (the latter requiring some small emendation). The Hebrew is awkward and the decision not an easy one.

A common word with a range of connotations is *ba'al*, used not only as the name of a Canaanite god, but also with the meanings 'lord, owner, husband'. To suppose that each occurrence of the word has an identical connotation is misleading. Clearly the same English word cannot represent it in Ex. 21.28 as in Prov. 31.11! In general the context determines the particular connotation, but this is not always so, and here interpretation is unavoid-

able. The new covenant* promise in Jer.
31.32, where the cognate verb (*bā'alti*) occurs,
illustrates the problem. Does it speak here of
a husband's love rejected (RSV) or of a
master's authority repudiated (JB)? The
latter's rendering, 'so I had to show them who
was master', carries a judgmental note not
present in RSV. Thus more than a simple
choice of words is involved; questions of meaning are at issue. The same verb occurs in Jer.
3.14, and here RSV makes the reverse decision
('I am your master'), doubtless considering a
reference to 'husband' inappropriate since the
nation is addressed as 'faithless children'. NIV,
however, translates as 'husband' here also,
easing the difficulty by using the expression
'faithless people'. Thus RSV has allowed the
word 'children/sons' to influence the translation of the verb, whereas NIV has made its
understanding of the verb's connotation the
deciding factor. Both versions retain as far as
possible the form of the original. Nevertheless
the necessity of interpretation and consequent
difference of meaning between them is clear.

Difficulty is also caused by words of uncertain meaning, a problem particularly acute in
the OT in the absence of contemporary
Hebrew material to throw light on the meaning. The extent to which other Semitic languages may provide elucidation is a matter of
some disagreement among scholars. An interesting example of this philological* approach
occurs in Song of Songs 3.10, where Solomon's palanquin is variously described as
'lovingly wrought within' (RSV), or, assuming
the existence of a rare homonym of the familiar word 'love' ('*ahabāh*), 'its lining was of
leather' (NEB), a meaning well suited to the
context, and drawing on the evidence of Ugaritic* and Arabic. The latter meaning may
occur also in Hos. 11.4 (so 'reins of hide', NEB
margin). The decision of the translators has
here gone in favour of the traditional rendering. Similarly in Isa. 53.3 the contrast between
'acquainted with grief' (RSV) and 'humbled
by suffering' (NEB) arises from the possibility
that *yāda'* 'to know' has a less familiar homonym 'to bring low', recovered from the usage
of cognate languages and solving a problem
in the Hebrew text. The adoption of this meaning in Judg. 16.9 clarifies the sense (cf. NEB
with RSV's insertion of 'the secret of'), and in
Prov. 14.33 removes the need to suppose the
text defective (so RSV). Either way the translator is involved in the process of interpretation.

Despite new insights and possibilities of
meaning such as these, there is, nevertheless,
some inevitable loss in translation. Alliteration, onomatopoeia and play on words (*see*
Paronomasia) can rarely be adequately reproduced, nor can the acrostic form of several

psalms (e.g. especially Ps. 119), and of Lam.
1–4 and Prov. 31.10ff. The exigencies of language require the representation of two Greek
verbs 'to love' (*philein* and *agapān*) by one in
English (John 21.15ff.) and of a single noun
(*pneuma*) by both 'wind' and 'spirit' (John
3.6,8); in the one instance the interplay of
words is lost, in the other the point of association is obscured. Similarly Ezek. 37 plays on
the various connotations of the Hebrew *rūaḥ*
'breath, spirit, wind', a feature impossible to
capture in translation. Again, the translator
must unfortunately choose between 'save' and
'heal' for *sōzō*, e.g. Mark 10.52, and constantly between 'sir' and 'lord' for *kurie* in
addresses to Jesus, the former implying a
natural or historical reading of the text, the
latter seeing it as written with religious meaning to the fore.

Other problems arise from the different
grammatical structure of languages. Not only
are Hebrew tenses problematic, especially in
poetry (*see* **Poetry, Hebrew**); so, too, is the
Hebrew verbless clause. Amos 7.14 is a
famous crux. Is he disclaiming identification
with professional prophets* ('I am not a prophet') or affirming that by divine call he
became one ('I was not a prophet')? Scholarly
opinion is divided, but the passage is significant for Amos' attitude towards those who
are called *nābī'*.

Modern English, with its loss of the 'thou'
form, blurs the distinction which exists in both
Greek and Hebrew between second person
singular and plural. This does not often
present a problem, though occasionally it
obscures significant features of the original,
as, for example, in John 3.11 where the sudden
change to the plural may reflect the later
situation of church and synagogue. Particularly striking in this respect is the abrupt introduction of the singular in Gen. 18.3 (despite
NEB's rendering), a hint perhaps, as is evident
later in the narrative, of Yahweh's mysterious
presence in one, or all, of Abraham's* guests.

A second category of problems relates to
the translators' view of their task. In transferring from ancient to modern language how
far are they to move from the idiom of the
original? Its historical and cultural features
must be fairly represented, but is God to
remain 'the horn of my salvation' (Ps. 18.2
RSV)? Here approaches differ, from provision
of an explanatory note that 'horn' symbolizes
strength (JB), interpretation as a geographical
configuration, hence 'my mountain refuge'
(NEB), to the prosaic 'he defends and keeps
me safe' (TEV). The matter becomes still more
serious in deciding whether to retain or interpret theological terms. A case in point is the
expression 'the flesh' in Rom. 8.3–4, rendered
literally in RSV and variously elsewhere as

'lower nature' (NEB), 'sinful nature' (NIV) and 'human nature' (TEV), which last attracted some adverse response, well illustrating the extent to which interpretation enters when once the translator moves from the original form of expression, misleading though that may be in modern English. Likewise, controversy has arisen in the past over the appropriate translation of *hilastērion*, 'propitiation' or 'expiation' (Rom. 3.25). On such theological grounds translations have been approved or rejected. TEV, avoiding theological terms in the interests of simplicity, has 'the means by which people's sins are forgiven'. The meaning of 'jealous' when applied to God, as it frequently is in the OT, requires explanation for the modern reader. Again translators are divided as to whether this is properly their task. With considerable freedom and admirable clarity TEV opts for interpretation in Zech. 8.2: 'I have longed to help Jerusalem because of my deep love for her people, a love which has made me angry with her enemies' (cf. RSV 'jealous with great jealousy, jealous with great wrath').

An associated problem concerns the freedom of the translator to add explanatory notes in the interests of clarity. Thus in Song of Songs several modern versions insert, albeit marginally, an indication of the various speakers, either specifically 'bride, bridegroom, companions' (NEB) or in more general terms 'beloved, lover, friends' (NIV), leaving open the debated question whether it is a marriage song. TEV goes further in this direction in Isa. 52–3, introducing into the text 'the Lord says' (52.13; 53.10), 'the people reply' (53.1), clearly interpretation but undoubtedly clarifying the meaning. Into the same category falls the matter of marking direct speech where in the original it is unmarked and its limits uncertain, as in John 3.10ff. where Jesus' words may extend to v. 15 (RSV) or to v. 21 (NEB). Similarly in Isa. 40, NEB and others understand vv. 6b–8 to enshrine the prophet's message; RSV leaves the question open. It is, however, arguable that v. 8 contains the message, the prophet's despondency being expressed in the previous lines. The fact that the treatment of Jer. 4.22 shows the opposite tendency, with NEB leaving it unmarked, RSV and others indicating it to be the Lord's word, illustrates the extent to which questions of interpretation are constantly involved.

More fundamental, however, than any of these is the question of what is to be translated, a problem relating to the OT by virtue of its special characteristics (*see* **Textual Criticism**). The NT with its multiplicity of manuscripts* is in an entirely different situation. To what extent is the translator free to emend the Hebrew Masoretic text,* not only in extreme cases where the text appears untranslatable, but according to his own judgment of what is logical and appropriate? Isa. 62.5 illustrates the problem: 'your sons shall marry you', a strange figure even though used metaphorically of Jerusalem.* Those more conservative towards the text (RSV, NIV) retain it unchanged; others (NEB, JB) by a simple change of one vowel point produce a reference to the one who built her. But is it a textual corruption or in its unexpectedness a powerful metaphor?* Two other figurative passages illustrate a similar dilemma. Does Hos. 11 contain two images, a toddler (v. 3) and an animal (v. 4), or only the former (so NEB with slight emendation)? Is Wisdom in Prov. 8.30 personified as male ('a master workman' RSV), or, as elsewhere in Proverbs, as female ('his darling' NEB)? The word is a notable crux and some scholars would revocalize. There is always the possibility, however, that further insights will prove an emendation incorporated into a translation to be both unnecessary and mistaken. Such is the case in Ps. 51.8 where RSV 'fill me with joy and gladness' (based on the change of a single consonant) obscures the allusion to the giving of a divine oracle* in worship (MT has 'make me hear' rather than 'fill me with') as is apparent elsewhere in the psalms. In NEB we have an example of a still more comprehensive attempt to recover an elusive 'original' behind the traditional text. On these grounds the psalm titles are omitted, not only as obscure but as undoubtedly secondary, yet thereby evidence of the earliest interpretation of the psalms is lost to the reader; decisions are made as to what is or is not authentic (Hos. 1.7 appears in a footnote; Hag. 2.5a is omitted with no footnote to the effect in some editions) and there is occasional rearrangement of the text. Thus Job 41.1–6 is transposed to follow 39.30, and Isa. 5.24–25 to follow 10.4 by virtue of a common refrain. Such decisions are not taken lightly. Nevertheless, it is in these areas that translators differ in their estimate of the nature of their task and their justifiable freedom to depart from the text as transmitted. Special problems arise in translating the psalms owing to their continual use and reinterpretation during centuries of church and synagogue worship. Is the translator's primary concern to be their original setting in ancient Israel (so NEB), or is he to take cognizance of a wider perspective? (See Rogerson and McKay, *Psalms*, 1977.) Translation, especially of the Bible, is a risk. Interpretation is inescapable and there is an element of the subjective, but under God it opens to many the inexhaustible riches of Holy Scripture.

See also Etymology; Linguistics; Meaning; Semantics; Translations, Modern; Vulgate.

Ll. R. Bailey, *The Word of God: A Guide to English Versions of the Bible*, 1982; J. Barr, *Comparative Philology and the Text of the Old Testament*, 1968; F. F. Bruce, *The English Bible*, 1970; C. H. Dodd, *Introduction to the NEB New Testament*, 1961; G. R. Driver, *Introduction to the NEB Old Testament*, 1970; E. A. Nida, *Toward a Science of Translating*, 1964.

GRACE I. EMMERSON

Translations (to the KJV)

The origins of the English version of the Bible are to be found in the centuries immediately following the arrival of Augustine at Canterbury in AD 597. The revival of Christianity, stimulated by missionaries from Rome and Ireland, led to a desire for a greater understanding of God's Word.* The earliest attempts at providing a vernacular version are linked with the names of Caedmon, Bede, Egbert and Aelfric. Although these individuals translated only parts of the Bible, notably the Psalms and the Gospels,* they prepared the way for the eventual appearance of a complete translation.

The Wycliffe Bible (c. 1384). It was not until the end of the fourteenth century that the Bible in its entirety was translated into English. This epoch-making version is traditionally associated with John Wycliffe, 'the last of the Schoolmen and the first of the Reformers.* As part of his programme for the renewal of the church, Wycliffe claimed that every person should have the opportunity to know God's law as laid down in the Bible. This meant that the scriptures had to be made accessible to all in their native tongue.

Scholars distinguish two versions of the Bible attributed to Wycliffe. The first appeared c. 1384, while the second, a revision of the first, is dated c. 1395, some ten years after Wycliffe's death. It cannot be stated with certainty that Wycliffe was responsible for translating any part of the original work himself. But whether he was personally involved as a translator or not, the version qualified to be called Wycliffe's Bible since it was inspired by him and executed under his guidance. Nicholas of Hereford was responsible for a substantial part of the OT, and John Purvey, another of Wycliffe's ardent supporters, undertook the revision.

Wycliffe's text was the Vulgate,* the authoritative version of the scriptures in his day. Even if he had wanted to by-pass this in favour of the original texts, he could not have done so, since neither he nor his colleagues had any appreciable knowledge of Greek and Hebrew. The 1384 version is a word-for-word translation of the Latin, with no attempt made to render the phrases and constructions into English idiom. This method reflects the belief, current during the Middle Ages, that a translation had to be absolutely literal if it was to preserve the sacred quality of the original. But the result was a stilted and unnatural rendering which must have been of limited use for those less learned clerics whom it was meant to benefit. It was only with Purvey's revision that the first English Bible became worthy of the name.

Wycliffe's followers greeted the new translation with open arms. Since they believed that the sole authority* in religious matters was the Bible, they insisted on every man's right to read and interpret it for himself. This belief, which went hand in hand with an open anti-clericalism, was propagated enthusiastically by unlicensed preachers. The ecclesiastical authorities were incensed by such heretical teachings, and as a result, Archbishop Arundel called the Convocation of Oxford in 1407 to combat 'the unfruitful doctrines of the Lollards', the nickname given to Wycliffe's supporters. To remedy the 'danger and loss' suffered by the church at the hands of the itinerant preachers, the Archbishop proposed thirteen constitutions, the most important of which was the one which forbade the translation of the scriptures into English. Though he was closing the door after the horse had bolted, Arundel did instigate a vigorous campaign against Wycliffe's Bible in an attempt to stamp out heresy. In 1415, at the Council of Constance, the wider church joined in the condemnation of Lollardy, especially the demand to have the scriptures in the vernacular. A few years later Wycliffe's bones were disinterred and burnt.

The work of Tyndale (1526-34). Despite its importance in the annals of the English Bible, Wycliffe's version was essentially a translation of a translation. It was William Tyndale, during the second decade of the sixteenth century, who first attempted to make an English translation directly from the Hebrew and Greek. Faced by hostility to his plans to provide his fellow-countrymen with the Bible in their own language, Tyndale left his native land in 1524 never to return. It was on the continent that he produced his English version of the NT in 1526, the Pentateuch* in 1530 and the Book of Jonah in 1531. He issued a revised edition of the NT and Genesis in 1534, but his translation of Joshua to II Chronicles was only in manuscript at the time of his martyrdom in 1536. The vernacular Bible was still proscribed in England when his NT was smuggled into the country soon after its publication at Worms. Two copies of this first edition are still extant, one at the Baptist

College in Bristol and the other in the library of St Paul's Cathedral.

Tyndale's translation is significant in that it was the basis of all later official versions, and justly merits the 'chief place of honour' in the lineage of the English Bible. The translator's reputation as a scholar rests on two qualities, namely his sense of judgment in literary matters and his proficiency in the original languages. Though in many places it is no more than a literal rendering of the Hebrew or Greek, Tyndale's version has the merit of being simple and flexible. The narrative portions of the OT especially testify to his skill in recreating a particular scene without resorting to obscure and unsuitable vocabulary. A great many of his words and phrases have, through the KJV, become the stock in trade of English-speaking Christians. In the past, Tyndale's competence as a linguist was questioned. It was felt that he was largely dependent on the versions of Luther* and Pagninus and that his knowledge of Hebrew and Greek did not amount to very much. But recent and more thorough research has led scholars to a different conclusion. It is now believed that although he consulted contemporary translations into other languages, he was also perfectly capable of handling the original.

Coverdale's Bible (1535). It is ironic that within eight years of the public condemnation of Tyndale's NT, the Convocation of Canterbury was petitioning the Crown for an official English version of the scriptures. The request was granted, and the task of producing it was given to Archbishop Thomas Cranmer. But Cranmer failed to find suitable scholars in England to do the work, with the result that the first complete Bible to appear in English was that of Miles Coverdale. It is probable that Coverdale, who was at the time on the continent, had already prepared a substantial part of his version. If not, then he must have worked quickly and diligently as soon as he heard of the king's approval for the venture, for on 4 October 1535 'Coverdale's Bible' was printed, probably in Cologne.

On his own admission, Coverdale knew no Hebrew and had only a smattering of Greek. The 'five sundry interpreters' on whom he claims to have relied have been identified as Jerome, Tyndale, Pagninus, Luther and the group of Zurich divines led by Zwingli. C. S. Lewis describes him as being a 'translator whose choice of rendering came nearest to being determined by taste'. In other words, since he had no knowledge of the original languages, he had to choose between his 'sundry interpreters'. In this he was guided by his own judgment, which, fortunately, was sound.

Perhaps the most important characteristic of Coverdale's Bible is its rendering of Hebrew poetry.* Two hundred years before Robert Lowth's analysis of the parallelism of meaning which is fundamental to Hebrew verse, Coverdale had appreciated and reproduced the pattern of the original. It is not for nothing that his version of the psalms was included in the Book of Common Prayer.

Matthew's Bible (1537). Within two years of the appearance of Coverdale's Bible another version, which claimed to have been 'truly and purely translated into English by Thomas Matthew', was printed at Antwerp. The translator was in reality John Rogers, a Cambridge graduate who had gone to Antwerp in 1534 as chaplain to the English community. There he became friendly with Tyndale and Coverdale, and under their guidance trained as a translator. Essentially, however, Rogers was an editor, for his version contained little that was original. He was heavily dependent on the existing translations of Tyndale and Coverdale, and on the French version of Robert Olivetan published in 1535. It was Olivetan's Bible which Rogers used as the source of many of his marginal notes and as the basis of his revision of the earlier translations. The new Bible was greeted enthusiastically by Cranmer and Cromwell, and submitted to the king for his approval. This was given, together with the express command that it should be 'openly laid forth in every parish church'.

Matthew's Bible had been in print for only a few months when it was revised by Richard Taverner, a protégé of Cromwell and a competent Greek scholar. The only notable feature of Taverner's Bible was the revision of the NT, but its influence is to be found in the Douai Bible and in the KJV.

The Great Bible (1539). With the appearance of Matthew's Bible in 1537 there were two versions of the scriptures in English published 'with the king's most gracious licence'. For different reasons both were unsatisfactory. Coverdale's version was based on other translations and not on the original languages, while that of Rogers was doctrinally suspect and therefore unacceptable to many because of its propensity to endorse the Reformers in its marginal notes. Accordingly, Thomas Cromwell invited Coverdale to prepare yet another edition. Coverdale complied and in 1539 produced the Great Bible, which he claimed had been 'truly translated after the verity of the Hebrew and Greek by the diligent study of diverse excellent learned men expert in the aforesaid tongues'. In order to please conservative clerics, all marginal notes and explanations were omitted, much to Coverdale's disappointment. In 1540 a second edition was issued bearing on its title page the words 'This is the Bible appointed to the use of the churches'. Thus, the Great Bible was the first 'authorized' version of the scriptures. It got its name because of its size: $16\frac{1}{2} \times 11$ inches, printed in heavy Gothic type.

Although Coverdale states in his preface that he translated from the original languages, it is doubtful whether he knew any more Hebrew in 1539 than he did four years previously. But he did have one invaluable aid which was not available to him when he produced his first Bible, namely the Hebrew–Latin version of Sebastian Muenster with its copious explanatory notes on difficult and obscure words. Many examples can be found of the way in which he altered his 1535 translation as a result of consulting Muenster. It is at this stage that traditional Jewish renderings, accepted and preserved by Muenster, found a permanent place in the English Bible.

The Geneva Bible (1560).   The translation of 1560, in marked contrast to its predecessors, was the product of a team of scholars, some of whom had a more than adequate knowledge of Hebrew and Greek. There is nothing in the Bible itself to indicate who the translators were, but it is believed that the leading light was William Whittingham, John Knox's successor as pastor of the English church in Geneva. The completed work was dedicated to Queen Elizabeth I and published at the expense of the Marian exiles resident in Geneva. It was not printed in England until 1576, after Archbishop Parker's death.

The Geneva Bible has several noteworthy features. It was the first version to be divided into verses. Earlier translations indicated separate sections by inserting A, B, C and D in the margin, but in this Bible each verse became an independent paragraph. Roman rather than Gothic type was used for the first time, and words in italics were inserted to make the translation more readable. But the most significant feature of all is the marginal notes which provide a valuable insight into the method adopted by the translators. Sometimes they offer a literal rendering of the Hebrew or Greek original; at other times they contain explanations of the text or an alternative translation. They have an unmistakably Calvinistic ring to them, a fact which suggests that John Calvin * exerted considerable influence on the translators, and even advised them with regard to difficult passages.

The Bible of the Marian exiles enjoyed great popularity in England. This was Shakespeare's version, and it was upon this that the translators of the KJV based their version half a century later. The use of 'breeches' to describe Adam * and Eve's clothing in Gen. 3.7 led to its being given the nickname 'Breeches Bible', though the word itself had already been used in the Wycliffe version.

The Bishops' Bible (1568).   The enthusiasm with which the Geneva Bible was received in Elizabethan England had two important consequences. It undermined the authority of the Great Bible and led Archbishop Matthew Parker to commission yet another revision. In spite of its excellent qualities, the translation of the Genevan divines was not acceptable in some circles. The Protestant bias of its annotations was keenly felt, and it was regarded by many as 'an instrument of Puritan propaganda'. Though Parker himself was not averse to the Geneva version, it was clear, from the opposition of the Catholic party, that it would never be appointed to be read in churches. The Archbishop, therefore, at the instigation of Richard Cox, the Bishop of Ely, launched a new version. He assigned various parts of the Bible to different translators, most of them his fellow bishops, and provided them with instructions on how to proceed. Although the avowed purpose of this version was to be a more faithful representation of the original than the Great Bible had been, Coverdale's efforts were not to be despised. The translators were 'to follow the common English translation used in churches and not to recede from it but where it varies manifestly from the Hebrew or Greek original'. An attempt was also made to win the support of the Catholic party. The revisers were instructed 'to make no bitter notes on the text, or yet to set down any determination in places of controversy'. Thus the marked Protestant tone of the Geneva Bible was excluded.

Despite its declared intention of following the original more closely, the linguistic ability of those responsible for the Bishops' Bible is not immediately apparent. Much of the version is a collation of previous translations, with but little attention paid to the original Greek and Hebrew. In no way could its scholarship be compared to that of the Geneva Bible. But despite its shortcomings, it became the second authorized English Bible and was printed for the last time in 1602. In its presentation and format it represented the best in early English printing.

The Rheims-Douai Bible (1582–1610).   The proliferation of Protestant Bibles led the Catholics to make their own translation. The NT was printed at Rheims in 1582 after four years' work by Gregory Martin, William Allen and Richard Bristow, all of whom were members of the exiled Catholic community living in Flanders. The OT appeared almost thirty years later in 1610 and was published at Douai. The preface ascribes the delay in completing the work to 'the poor estate in banishment' of the translators. This was undoubtedly the case, but the work was also hindered by the lack of competent Catholic scholars who could cope with Greek and Hebrew.

Though based on Jerome's Vulgate, which was considered to have preserved the meaning of the original far better than Greek and Hebrew manuscripts marred by centuries of scribal error, the Catholic Bible did take cognizance of the original texts. Like the Geneva version, it was well-annotated throughout. Many of the notes make doctrinal points in a polemical fashion by referring to the early Fathers and contemporary commentators. Occasionally Greek and Hebrew words are printed in the margin, thus giving the educated reader an opportunity of assessing the merits of the translation by bringing to his notice the literal meaning* of the text. But at the same time, the allegorical* significance of a word or phrase is frequently emphasized.

Although the use of the Rheims-Douai version was limited to Catholic circles, it did not go unnoticed by the translators of the KJV; there is evidence to suggest that its rendering of the NT had considerable influence on them.

The King James Version (1611). With the King James Version or, as it is called in Britain, the Authorized Version, we come to a work of real scholarship. The task of translating was undertaken by a group of linguists and theologians, both clerical and lay, who were divided into six companies. Although King James I approved of the venture in 1604, the groups were not convened for consultation until 1607; for the first three years each translator worked independently. Strictly speaking those responsible were to do no more than revise the existing official version, as the rules published for their guidance indicate. 'The ordinary Bible read in the Church, commonly called the Bishops' Bible, to be followed, and as little altered as the truth of the original will admit . . . These translations to be used when they agree better with the text than the Bishops' Bible: Tindale's, Matthew's, Coverdale's, Whitchurch's (i.e. the 1549 edition of the Great Bible), Geneva.' That the translators believed that they had done just this is clear from the preface: 'Truly we never thought to make a new translation, nor yet to make of a bad one a good one, but to make a good one better, or out of many good ones one principal good one.'

The need for a new Bible was felt for two reasons. First because of the mounting criticism against the Bishops' Bible. Many were only too aware of the shortcomings of the version currently 'appointed for use in churches' and were clamouring for a new one. Secondly because of the lack of uniformity occasioned by the existence of several translations. While the Bishops' Bible was used in public worship, the Geneva version was read in private. The Great Bible had been printed

as recently as 1569, albeit for the last time, and Tyndale's Testament had appeared once again in 1566. There were, therefore, several versions of the English scriptures to choose from, and it is to James I's credit that uniformity was attained by means of a translation which was not revised until 1881.

See also **Translations (Modern).**

C. C. Butterworth, *Literary Lineage of the English Bible*, 1941; G. Hammond, *The Making of the English Bible*, 1982; G. Lloyd Jones, *The Discovery of Hebrew in Tudor England*, 1983; B. F. Westcott, *A General View of the History of the English Bible*, [5] 1905.

                                        G. LLOYD JONES

Translations (Modern)

1. *Linguistic principles.* The period since the first publication of the Authorized Version, especially the twentieth century, has been marked by increasingly detailed study of what language is and how it functions; the nature of meaning,* understanding and interpretation; and how human beings communicate. Much of this research has been applied to the translation of the scriptures. Conversely, such theoretical reflection on the translation of the Bible, the most frequently translated book in the world, has influenced developments in general linguistics,* translation theory, hermeneutics,* and the philosophy of language.

This research has resulted in a growing consensus, though not universal agreement, that the central function of language is the communication of meaning; that the analysis and transfer of meaning from one language to another is thus the central task of the translator: and that this principle should be applied to the translation of the Bible as of other writings.

The translation of the Bible may be seen as the third of five principal stages in the transfer of the message of the biblical writers from their original setting to a situation in a different time, place and/or culture. Presupposed in the translation process are textual criticism,* the comparative study of the original manuscripts;* and exegesis,* the determination of the original meaning of the biblical texts. Normally dependent on translation are the formulation of a biblical basis for systematic theology;* and the application of the biblical message to the situation of groups and individuals other than the original addressees. The stages are parts of a single process, which may conveniently be called interpretation; yet it is essential to maintain the distinction between them. In particular, the translator, while using the language of his or her own time and people, must preserve the cultural* distance and strangeness of the biblical texts; (s)he must also beware of pressing the meaning of individual texts into a mould determined by general doctrinal convictions (see section 3 below).

The view of language and translation outlined above has four corollaries which are important for the practice of Bible translation. First, the transfer of meaning can best be achieved by analysing the meaning of the original text as a whole, including the structure of whole discourses. Secondly, it will normally be necessary, in order faithfully to reproduce meaning, to exercise responsible freedom in the choice of lexical items, syntactic* structures, figures of speech,* etc. in the receptor language. Thirdly, the translator will need to determine as precisely as possible the linguistic competence and relevant knowledge of intended readers of the translation. Fourthly, a modern translation of an ancient text like the Bible will almost always need to include introductions,* notes, glossaries, and other reader's helps required to convey information available to the original receptors, but not to the intended readers of the translation.

The following technical terms are used to distinguish various types of translation: dynamic equivalence translation (also known as functional equivalence translation and meaning-for-meaning translation) is contrasted with formal correspondence translation (also known as word-for-word translation); and common language translation, intended for a broad range of readers of average education, is contrasted with literary language translation. The term 'paraphrase' is avoided in discussion of translation; it is best reserved for the restatement of a text in the same language. Such terms as 'liberal', 'evangelical' and 'conservative' are also often confusing when used to describe translations of scripture: it is quite possible, for example, for a conservative evaluation of the Masoretic* text to be combined with a liberal* theology, or for a 'rigid evangelical position' in theology to be expressed in a free translation, as in *The Living Bible*.

2. *Historical development.* Limitations of space preclude a complete survey of modern Bible translation throughout the world: between 1800 and 1987, the number of languages into which at least one book of the Bible had been translated rose from 66 to 1,907, largely through the efforts of the Bible Societies (British and Foreign Bible Society 1804, United Bible Societies 1946) and later of other specialized agencies such as the Wycliffe Bible Translators/Summer Institute of Linguistics (1934). What follows is concerned primarily with the English Bible, a restriction justified to some extent by the enormous range of scripture publications in English (A. S. Herbert, *Histor-*

ical Catalogue of printed editions of the English Bible 1525–1961, 1968, listed 2,524 items), and by the fact that these include examples of each of the types of translation mentioned above.

The translators of the K J V, like Luther* and other influential translators of the Reformation* period, had realized that strict formal correspondence translation was neither possible nor desirable: the genius of each language must be respected, and its resources used as naturally as possible. This principle, however, was sometimes in tension with the view, still expressed today, that biblical language as language, irrespective of the message it transmitted, was somehow unique. The preface to the Geneva Bible, for example, stated that the translators had often 'reserved [i.e. kept] the Hebrew phrases notwithstanding that they may seem somewhat hard in their ears that are not well practised and also delight in the sweet sounding phrases of the holy Scriptures' – a sentence which is perhaps as unclear in its logic as in its syntax.

The Geneva Bible was regularly reprinted until 1644, and again in 1776; its notes were printed (e.g. in 1649 and 1672) with the K J V text. Roman Catholics used the Douay Bible, first published complete in 1610 (N T Rheims 1582), reprinted abroad until 1635, and from 1750 in R. Challoner's revision, often reprinted; the Rheims N T was several times printed in England, with anti-Catholic notes by W. Fulke (1589) and others. The tradition of metrical psalms, initiated by Thomas Sternhold *c.* 1548, was continued by John Hopkins (1562) and Henry Ainsworth (1612), and remained particularly strong in Scotland (Sir William Alexander (?) 1631; Francis Rous 1650).

With these exceptions, the K J V overcame initial opposition to become, a generation after its first appearance, the English Bible *par excellence.* Successive corrected editions were published at Cambridge in 1629, 1639 and 1762. Selections, mainly from the O T of the Geneva Bible, appeared in 1643 under the title *The Souldiers Pocket Bible*; this was lightly revised in 1693, using the K J V. John Canne produced in 1647 an edition of the Bible containing a full apparatus of references, and also variant readings and renderings. The chronology* of James Ussher (1581–1656) was incorporated in editions from 1701.

Other translations tended to be for use in private Bible study. The translations themselves fell into two main categories: 'paraphrases' or expanded translations, such as those by Henry Hammond (N T 1653 with extensive notes, reprinted until 1845) and Philip Doddridge (N T 1765, extracted from his commentary* published 1739–45), and revised; and literal translations, such as the Quaker Anthony Purver's 'new and literal translation' of the Bible (1764).

The English biblical tradition did not become isolated from continental influence. The text and notes of the Dutch States-General Version of 1637 were translated into English and published in 1657; notes are enclosed in brackets and incorporated in the text. An attempt to replace the obsolete Rheims NT was made by Cornelius Nary in 1719; his translation, though based on the Latin, included notes which made frequent reference to the Greek. A plan to publish an English version of the French translation of the NT by de Beausobre and Lenfant did not go beyond Matthew (1726). This was, however, remarkable for its notes and long introduction, and reprinted as late as 1819. It initiated a period of renewed activity in translation and annotation of the NT.

Several revisions of the KJV appeared in the nineteenth century. Baptist versions were also published, notably by the American Bible Union (NT 1864); and John Nelson Darby, one of the founders of the Plymouth Brethren, published his translation of the NT in parts from c. 1859, and in one volume, revised, in 1871(?). Tischendorf's own translation of his Greek NT appeared in 1869, and was followed by other translations of it, often in fresher style, by Samuel Davidson (1875) and George R. Noyes (1878). These led to the production, in 1877, of the Revised English Bible, by F. W. Gotch and others, intended to correct 'indisputable' errors in the KJV, and to incorporate emendations to the NT text. More important was the Revised Version, commissioned in 1870 by the Convocation of Canterbury; the NT was published in 1881, the OT in 1885, and the Apocrypha in 1895, with an American recension in 1900–1. It was conservative both textually (changes from the KJV supported by less than two-thirds of the revisers were printed in the margin) and linguistically, making a systematic attempt at formal correspondence. It did not supersede the KJV (the 1611 edition of which was reprinted in 1909), but was itself largely superseded by the Revised Standard Version (NT 1946, OT 1952), a less rigidly formal correspondence translation in the same tradition.

The twentieth century has seen a multiplication of new translations, including Robert G. Moulton's Modern Reader's Bible (1895–1905, reprinted); The Twentieth Century New Testament (1898–1902), based like the Revised Version NT on Westcott and Hort's Greek text; Frank Schell Ballantine's The American Bible (NT 1902); Ferrar Fenton's The Bible in Modern English (Bible 1903); The Historical New Testament (1901) and A New Translation in Modern Speech (NT 1913, OT 1924, both by James Moffatt); The New Testament

in Modern Speech by Robert F. Weymouth (1903); the Roman Catholic Westminster Version, published in portions from 1913; The Holy Scriptures according to the Masoretic Text (Jewish Publication Society of America, 1917); The New Testament. An American Translation by Edgar J. Goodspeed (1923; corresponding OT by J. M. Powis Smith and others 1931; Apocrypha 1939); the Concordant Version (NT 1919–26); with an interlinear literal translation, and an idiomatic translation on the opposite page; a translation 'into very simple English' (Luke 1933, NT 'in plain English' 1952) by C. Kingsley Williams, a British missionary in Ghana; not to be confused with The New Testament. A Translation in the Language of the People, by the American Baptist Charles B. Williams (1937); the version in Basic English (NT 1941, Bible 1949); the Roman Catholic Confraternity Version (NT 1941, OT 1952), a revision of Douay-Challoner, superseded from 1970 by the New American Bible, translated from the original texts (revised NT 1986); the translations by the Roman Catholic Ronald A. Knox (Bible abridged and rearranged 1936; The New Testament in English 1945, corresponding OT 1949); the Berkeley (California) Version by the Dutch-born Gerrit Verkuyl (NT 1945, Bible 1959); J. B. Phillips' influential translation in dynamic-equivalent literary, but fully contemporary language (Epistles 1947, NT 1958, revised 1972; Four Prophets 1963); the Jehovah's Witnesses' New World Translation (NT 1950, OT 1960); Hugh J. Schonfield's Authentic New Testament (1955), superseded in 1985 by his Original New Testament; and The Amplified New Testament (1958), edited by Francis E. Siewert.

The New English Bible (NT 1961, OT 1970) is a British interdenominational translation in literary language; a revision under the title Revised English Bible appeared in 1989. Other widely used current versions include the bestselling Good News Bible (GNB), also known as Today's English Version (TEV) (NT by Robert G. Bratcher 1966, Bible 1976), the first consistently dynamic-equivalent English translation in common language; the Roman Catholic Jerusalem Bible (1966), translated from the original texts, and its successor the New Jerusalem Bible (1985); the New International Version (NIV), by a large group of translators 'united in their commitment to the authority and infallibility of the Bible as God's word in written form' (NT 1973, Bible 1978). The Anchor Bible, a commentary series by Roman Catholic, Protestant and Jewish scholars, including a new translation, has been in progress since 1964.

Mention should also be made of The Living Bible by Kenneth N. Taylor (NT 1967, Bible

1971), described as a 'paraphrase', and not based directly on the original texts; and conservative revisions in the KJV tradition, including the New American Standard Bible (1960) and the Revised King James Version/Revised Authorized Version (NT 1979, Bible 1982), the NT of which is based on the Majority Text.

3. *Theological implications.* The Bible in its original languages has rarely if ever dominated the Christian tradition in the sense in which the Hebrew Bible has dominated Judaism, or the original text of the Quran has dominated Islam. In other words, Christians have generally been committed to the translation of their foundational documents, ever since the words of Jesus were translated from Aramaic to Greek, and early Christians became active in the transmission of the Septuagint.* Where, at times, Christians have refused to make the scriptures generally available in the language of the people, their refusal has often been based on appeal to the authority of a translation, such as the Vulgate* or the Church Slavonic or Coptic scriptures (*see* **Holy Book**). The linguistic principles outlined in section 1 thus generally enable churches and other Christian groups to express more completely a central element of their faith, namely that God wills to reveal himself to human beings in human language, and thus in the plurality of human languages. There are, however, translations which have attempted to reproduce (especially) Hebrew idiom at the expense of the receptor language, as in the literal translations mentioned in section 2; an influential example is the German translation of the OT by the Jews M. Buber and F. Rosenzweig (1925–9).

In practice, this conviction has been subject to various constraints, some of which may be identified as theological, though in other cases the operative factor may be nothing more than an unreflective view of language (see section 1). The conservative evangelical view that the scriptures are infallible 'as originally given' in practice leaves wide scope for textual criticism and dynamic equivalent translation, as the example of the NIV shows. In fact, however, this view is sometimes associated with a preference for the Textus Receptus or Majority Text (as in the Revised King James/Revised Authorized Version), and more often with a tendency towards formal correspondence translation (as for example in the New American Standard Bible).

A high view of the authority of scripture more often leads to attempts to eliminate from a translation apparent errors or inconsistencies, as for example where The Living Bible has 'fourteen of the generations' for 'all the generations . . . were fourteen generations' in Matt. 1.17. Even the GNB, in later editions,

has at Heb. 11.9 '[Abraham] lived in tents, as did Isaac and Jacob' for '. . . with Isaac and Jacob', to avoid a chronological difficulty.

The problem is particularly serious in passages of the OT which are quoted or alluded to in the NT, or which are traditionally held to be fulfilled in Christ. For example, translations of Gen. 3.15 tend to retain a singular translation 'seed', followed by singular pronouns, in order to leave open the possibility of a reference to Christ (cf. Gal. 3.16 with Gen. 12.7), whereas a fully dynamic equivalent translation would probably render the Hebrew generic singular by a plural (the GNB has 'offspring' followed by a plural pronoun). The translation of *'almah* in Isa. 7.14 (NIV and many others) as 'virgin' rather than 'young woman' (GNB) appears to be influenced by the quotation of the Septuagint in Matt. 1.23.

More easily identifiable are translations of particular terms in texts which reflect the interests of denominational or other groups; for example, the use of 'immerse' rather than 'baptize' in Baptist translations, and of 'Jehovah' in the New World Translation of the Jehovah's Witnesses. Each such option must be assessed on its exegetical merits. The movement for the use of inclusive rather than sexist language has challenged translators to eliminate exclusive male reference where it is not in the text; but the transculturation which would be involved in referring, for example, to God as 'parent' or 'Father-and-Mother' in biblical texts is to be resisted.

See also **Translation, Problems of; Translations (to the KJV).**

On linguistic principles: M. L. Larson, *Meaning-Based Translation*, 1984; E. A. Nida and C. R. Taber, *The Theory and Practice of Translation*, 1969; J. de Waard and E. A. Nida, *From One Language to Another*, 1986; on Bible translations generally: B. F. Grimes (ed.), *Ethnologue*, [10]1984; E. A. Nida (ed.), *The Book of a Thousand Tongues*, [2]1972; on the English Bible: F. F. Bruce, *History of the Bible in English*, [3]1979.   PAUL ELLINGWORTH

Tübingen School

In sharp contrast to the 'old' supernaturalist school of G. C. Storr and E. G. Bengel, who combined Kant's critical philosophy with biblicism in a conservative apologetics, and to the Roman Catholic Tübingen School of the 1820s led by J. S. Drey, J. A. Moehler, and J. Kuhn, the phrase normally refers to Ferdinand Christian Baur (1792–1860) and his followers.

Baur combined a radical historical criticism* of the NT and subsequent Christian tradition with a reconstruction which highlighted its conflicts and their resolution. This 'Tübingen' reconstruction of early Christian history as a sharp opposition between Jewish (Petrine) and Gentile (Pauline) parties gradually flattening out into reconciliation in the catholic church of the late second century was introduced in 'Die Christuspartei in der korinthischen Gemeinde, der Gegensatz des petrinischen und paulinischen Christenthums in der ältesten Kirche, der Apostel Petrus in Rom' (1831). The foundation-stone was an analysis of the divisions at Corinth disclosed at I Cor. 1.12. In 1835 Baur progressed by establishing the late date and non-Pauline authorship of the Pastoral Epistles.* The coping-stone of his outline reconstruction was reached in 1845 with the argument, based on its apparent theological 'tendency',* that Acts is historically unreliable, stemming from the Gentile Christian side at an advanced stage of the opposing parties' mutual accommodation. This fine discussion of the value of Acts as a source forms Part I of Baur's classic monograph on *Paul** (ET 1873). Part II also investigates which material is relevant for a truly historical account and judges only the four major epistles (Romans, I and II Corinthians and Galatians) certainly authentic. These then (Part III) provide the raw material for Baur's account of the apostle's theology.

The early date of the other epistles is cautiously questioned and they are placed later along the Gentile Christian line of development. In *The Church History of the First Three Centuries* (1853, ET 1878–9), the picture is complete, with all the NT and other early writings placed on this bi-linear model of the development according to their Jewish or Gentile Christian provenance and their stage in the process of reconciliation. Thus Luke and Marcion* plainly represent Pauline universalism, the Apocalypse Jewish Christian* particularism. Matthew, Hebrews and I Peter reflect the gradual softening of Jewish Christian opposition to Gentile Christianity.

Together with his accounts of Paul and Acts, the greatest triumph of Baur's analysis of the NT writings is his account in 1844 (untranslated) of the Fourth Gospel as a theological rather than a historical document. But his *Kritische Untersuchungen über die kanonischen Evangelien* (1847), which sums up his Gospel criticism, reveals a fatal flaw in his application of 'tendency criticism', though not in the method itself.

Writing before Holtzmann established the Two Source hypothesis (*see* **Synoptic Problem**) in 1863, Baur (like Strauss*) adhered to the priority of Matthew and placed Mark late in the development. His attempt to justify this almost certainly mistaken conclusion by Mark's indistinct theological tendency shows

the limitations of Baur's 'single issue' approach to early Christian history and his comparative neglect of literary arguments. An account of the development must consider other factors too. Subsequent liberal* scholarship discovered a more complex picture and that made possible the correction of Baur's late dating of the Gospels.* Even greater diversity in primitive Christianity meant that different viewpoints need not be strung out on one of only two trajectories* or lines of development.

This revision of Baur's chronology was clearly necessary when Zahn and J. B. Lightfoot (*see* **Westcott, Lightfoot and Hort**) demonstrated the authenticity and early second-century dating of seven Ignatian epistles (*see* **Apostolic Fathers**). It did not, however, prove Baur mistaken in his judgments about the historicity of the Gospels, especially the Fourth Gospel, as the conservatives hoped. But it did imply that the historical development was less tidy than Baur thought, and this cast doubt on a modern idealist theology which depended on the historian being able to discern the meaning of history in the patterns of its development. This was the 'Hegelianism' of which Baur was unjustly accused. There is no evidence that he imposed on the texts an *a priori* pattern of thesis and antithesis leading to a synthesis, which then becomes a new thesis. Much as he later learned from Hegel about historical development and its presumed theological meaning, conflict in the early churches is a matter of historical fact. Baur's eye for it was perhaps sharpened before he read Hegel by his own historical experience of theological oppositions, especially between Protestantism and Catholicism on which he wrote in 1833 to refute J. A. Moehler. But he was a philosophical* theologian, influenced by Schelling and Schleiermacher and specializing in the history of religions, before becoming a NT critic. He thus looked for meaning in the history he was reconstructing, and was helped by modern German idealist philosophy as early as 1824, in *Symbolik und Mythologie*. Hegelian influence is not apparent until 1835, in *Die christliche Gnosis*, and is very strong in his interpretations of the development of Christian doctrines (1837 to 1847), and of Pauline theology (1845). Only here, in his idealist interpretation of Paul's view of Spirit, can Baur be said to have been led astray by Hegel – as he was by Kant in viewing Jesus as preaching ethical idealism under a cloak of Jewish messianism.*

These modernizations were not the reason why Baur was hated and his pupils' careers destroyed. The Tübingen construction was bitterly opposed by more conservative churchmen because it denied their view of the NT canon's* theological unity, disputed the apostolic authorship* of almost all its writings, and abandoned the supernaturalist account of the origins of Christianity. To see the Fourth Gospel as the crown of NT theology, rather than as historical fact, seemed to remove the foundations of the doctrine of the incarnation. The 'Johannine question' was the rock of offence on which this pious Christian theologian was labelled 'pagan Baur'. The struggle against the Tübingen school was essentially a struggle against radical historical criticism, and the 'Hegelian' label merely a stick with which to beat it. That is why Baur was so sensitive to criticism from within the school and so determined in answering Hase (1855) and Uhlhorn (1858) from outside it. Less radical scholars were compromising with ecclesiastical orthodoxy instead of standing fearlessly for the historical truth on which alone a modern theology could be based, and the basic principles by which this was reached, above all the rejection of absolute causality or divine interventionism. If the school's results prove mistaken (Baur wrote), its axioms are not refuted but must be carried out more strictly, and the future would vindicate this stand.

In view of the different relationships of various pupils and followers to the master, the 'school' is not easily defined. Though inextricably associated with Baur and Tübingen, D. F. Strauss* is better considered separately, since his epoch-making *Life of Jesus* (1835) precedes Baur's Gospel criticism and lacks some of the characteristic marks of the school. The two main figures are Eduard Zeller (1814–1908), the friend and pupil of Strauss, and Baur's son-in-law; and Albert Schwegler (1819–57) who died at 37. Zeller first edited the school's vital organ, the *Theologische Jahrbücher* (1842–57), produced its standard commentary on Acts (1854, ET 1875–6), and became its first chronicler (1860) and defender (1861). The large work on *Das Nachapostolische Zeitalter* (1846), which Schwegler wrote after his youthful work on Montanism (1841), is the most sharply profiled product of the school. Both these scholars were driven out of theology by hostility to their radical criticism, and achieved eminence in other fields, Zeller in philosophy and Schwegler in Roman literature and history. The brilliant K. H. Planck (1819–80), who wrote on Ebionism (1843) and opened up the 'Jesus and Judaism' theme (1847), and also K. H. Köstlin (1819–94), who wrote on Johannine theology (1843) and the Synoptics (1853), were denied theological careers.

These six central figures were, like Baur's successor Carl Weizsäcker (1822–99) and his last outstanding disciple, Otto Pfleiderer (1839–1908), natives of Württemberg, educated in the church seminaries. Three

'foreigners' from North Germany are also to be included in the school, giving it a looser sense. Albrecht Ritschl (1822–89) spent a semester in Tübingen in 1845–6 and his monograph (1846) suggesting that Marcion's Luke is older than canonical Luke gained Baur's approval. But his review (1847) of Baur's *Paul* was critical, and his great book *Die Entstehung der altkatholischen Kirche* (1850) was extremely critical of Schwegler. The second edition (1857), following a breakdown in his personal relationship with Baur, was a wholesale rejection of the Tübingen construction, and Ritschl is seen as 'the apostate' of the school. His defence of the miraculous* (1861) confirmed his intention to accommodate historical criticism to ecclesiastical orthodoxy and was answered by Zeller (1861–2).

Adolf Hilgenfeld (1823–1907), by contrast, was its staunchest defender, though accepting the Pauline authorship of I Thessalonians and Philemon. His journal, *Die Zeitschrift für wissenschaftliche Theologie* (1857–1914), was the closest to a continuation of the *Theologische Jahrbücher*. His work on Johannine theology (1849), seeing it as dependent on Gnosticism,* placed him in the Tübingen camp and wrecked his career (an outstanding scholar, he became a full professor at Jena only at the age of 67). But he never met Baur and belongs to the Tübingen school according to the spirit, not the flesh, through his letters and general agreement with its approach.

Gustav Volkmar (1809–93) was a student in Marburg and (expelled from Hesse for political reasons) from 1853 lecturer and professor at Zurich. In 1850 he persuaded Ritschl to abandon the improbable thesis about canonical Luke, and later (1870), in a book which anticipated Wrede's* theory of the messianic secret,* joined Ritschl (1851) and Köstlin (1853) in recognizing the priority of Mark. With Köstlin and Volkmar, tendency* criticism was being supplemented by the literary criticism* which had been making progress since 1838 (Wilke and Weisse) and peaked in 1863 (Holtzmann). But the Tübingen School is a landmark on account of Baur's historical reconstruction of early Christianity, and when the Hegelian dressing faded in the 1850s it remained a symbol of the uncompromising search for the historical truth about Christianity, claiming the loyalty of an Overbeck (1837–1905) who had no interest in Baur's theological interpretation of the history. The school has been attacked and misrepresented from Hengstenberg (1836) and Ewald (1848) to Stephen Neill (1964) and Horton Harris (1973 and 1975). It was also justly criticized and corrected by E. Reuss (1842, 1852) and later liberals, especially the History of Religions school.* But Baur's historical methods have survived his conclusions, and elements of his construction remained visible throughout the period of 150 years, during which the historical-critical paradigm in NT studies retained its hegemony, largely unchallenged by other methods.

See also **Tendency Criticism; Theology (New Testament).**

H. Harris, *The Tübingen School*, 1975; P. C. Hodgson, *The Formation of Historical Theology*, 1966; W. G. Kümmel, *The New Testament. The History of the Investigation of its Problems*, ET 1972; O. Pfleiderer, *The Development of Theology in Germany since Kant*, 1893; N. Smart et al. (eds), *Nineteenth Century Religious Thought in the West*, Vol. I, 1985.

ROBERT MORGAN

Typology

The first example of typological exegesis,* which became standard in the whole patristic* period, is in Paul's* 'Adam'* christology:* Adam is the 'type (*tupos*) of the one to come' (Rom. 5.14). Typology is distinct from the allegorical* interpretation of the OT which claims that the 'real' meaning of the OT text is something with no continuity with the historical intention of its writer (cf. e.g. Philo,* the Qumran *pesher* * on Hab., and Paul's exegesis of Deut. 25.4 at I Cor. 9.8–10). Typology argues for a continuity in God's plan such that the OT is a true 'prefiguration' (Melito, *Paschal Homily*, 19.5) of what God would do in the NT. To the OT 'type' corresponds the NT 'antitype' (the word is first used at I Peter 3.21). Thus, in the Epistle of Barnabas (12.2–7), the Spirit leads Moses* to set up the bronze serpent in the wilderness (Num. 21) 'in order that he should make a type of the cross and of the one who was to suffer'.

The writers of the second century who develop systematic typological exegesis, Barnabas, Justin, Melito and Irenaeus,* always do so in a polemical context. The primary concern of all is to argue for the unity of the two Testaments: for the first three, against the Jews who reject the NT; for Irenaeus, against the Gnostics* who reject the OT. All assert that the OT is fulfilled in Jesus. The typological argument goes beyond the argument from fulfilled prophecy* that can be seen in Justin's *Dialogue* with the Jew Trypho: Justin argues that the Jews are wrong to understand Ps. 110 of King Hezekiah and Ps. 72 of King Solomon, because the things described in these psalms never happened to those OT kings, but only to Jesus (*Dial.* 33–34); but Trypho repeatedly declares that even if the messianic* interpretation of the OT is accepted, he is not convinced that it can be shown that these prophecies were fulfilled in Jesus. Justin tries to bring more convincing evidence by moving to the deeper theological level of the typological coherence willed by God between the OT and Jesus. God's commands to Moses about eating the paschal lamb were given with a view to the suffering of Jesus on the cross (*Dial.* 40); the offering of fine flour was a type of the eucharist, and bodily circumcision a type of the 'true' Christian circumcision (41); the 'horns of the unicorn' (Deut. 33.17 LXX) are a type of the cross, as is Moses' stretching out his hands in prayer (Ex. 17; *Dial.* 90–91); and all 'wood' in the OT can be seen as a symbol of the cross (86): 'In short, I can prove that they were types and symbols and statements of what would happen to Christ, of those who were known beforehand to be his believers, and of the things Christ himself would do' (42).

Although Trypho remained unconvinced, Justin had developed an exegetical tool that led to the theology of the two Testaments in Melito's Homily and Irenaeus' *Adversus Haereses* (c. 190). The central concept for Irenaeus is the recapitulation in Jesus of the whole of the old covenant:* the Logos* 'had formed beforehand for himself the future dispensation of the human race' in such a way that an antithesis of type/antitype exists between Adam and Jesus, Eve and Mary (III, 22). This argument works in both directions: the necessity for Jesus to recapitulate the OT means (against the docetics and gnostics) that he must have had a true body and a truly human life (e.g. V, 14), and also gives the OT itself a positive value as preparation, in the divine pedagogy, for the full revelation in Jesus (against those who argued that it was simply superseded by the NT, or even – like Marcion* – that it was the work of a god other than the God of the NT). 'The treasure hidden in the scriptures is Christ, since he was pointed out by means of types and parables' (v. 26). The same arguments are used, in the same polemical context against Jews and Gnostics, by Aphrahat and Ephrem in fourth-century Syria (*see* **Jewish Christianity; Syriac Tradition**).

The typological interpretation of the OT loses its directly polemical thrust when it is applied, in keeping with I Peter 3.21, to the sacraments of the Christian life and to the church. The exegetical strategy is the same: Tertullian* sees in Eve, born of the sleeping Adam, a type of the church, born of Jesus while he slept in death on the cross (*De Anima* 43), and sees in the crossing of the Red Sea and the drowning of Pharaoh a type of baptism in which the Christian is freed and the devil's power destroyed (*De Baptismo* 9). The typological interpretation of the OT is prominent in fourth-century baptismal catecheses (cf. Cyril of Jerusalem, Ambrose of Milan) and inspires both liturgical* rites and church architecture after the peace of Constantine. It also guides the choices of biblical texts in the lectionaries* for worship (this is still true at the present day, e.g. in the choice by the Roman Catholic lectionary of 1969 of Ex. 14 for the Easter Vigil). Typology is therefore not only a 'learned' exegesis but also a 'popular' interpretative framework.

The word 'type' is also used in contexts where it is not a strictly typological exegesis but the allegorization of an OT text that is being carried out, e.g. at I Cor. 10.11. When Paul says that 'these things happened as types for us', the word is not used in the technical sense of Rom. 5.14, but indicates only significant patterns which are found in the OT and in the life of believers. The same is true of the allusion to 'Jannes and Jambres' at II Tim. 3.8. This allegorical use of the OT in parenesis is very common in inter-testamental literature and the NT, and finds its highest patristic expression in Gregory of Nyssa's *Life of Moses*. But even where the word 'type' occurs, the theology of salvation-history* underlying genuine typological exegesis is missing.

Typology provided the patristic and mediaeval* periods with a universally accepted key to reading the OT in the light of Jesus. It remains a significant key for understanding much in Christian liturgy and symbolism* (e.g. the ark used as a symbol by the World Council of Churches: Noah's ark is a type of the church in the eyes of the Fathers; cf. Cyril of Jerusalem, *Procatechesis* 14). Even though the centrality in exegetical and theological concern of the OT read in its own right has displaced the questions to which typology gave an answer, it nevertheless enjoyed something of a renaissance in the middle years of this century. Several scholars who were committed to the historical-critical method* nevertheless found it appropriate to turn to typology in their development of a biblical theology.* Thus, on the NT side, W. G. Kümmel worked out a pattern of promise and fulfilment, and L. Goppelt produced a major study, entitled simply *Typos*, on the correspondences between OT and NT. Among OT scholars, G. von Rad ended his presentation of OT theology* by suggesting typological patterns which reached their fruition in the NT. Austin Farrer was a biblical scholar who fitted into no particular school, but his brilliant reading of the Gospels* and of Revelation could also be described as typological. While the last generation has seen less work of this kind, it may well be that the wider use of literary critical* methods may bring about a revival of typology in some form.

See also **Allegorical Interpretation; Symbol**.

———

Jean Daniélou, *The Bible and the Liturgy*, 1956; id., *From Shadows to Reality*, 1960; A. M. Farrer, *The Glass of Vision*, 1948; G. W. H. Lampe and K. J. Woollcombe, *Essays on Typology*, 1957; Robert Murray, *Symbols of Church and Kingdom*, 1975.

BRIAN MCNEIL

Ugarit

The ancient city of Ugarit (modern Ras Shamra), the discovery of which followed an initial chance find in 1928, is a short distance from the north Syrian coast near modern Latakia. Excavation has led to the recovery of hundreds of texts, some quite long, in a previously unknown language closely related to Hebrew (though written in a cuneiform script), as well as many texts in Akkadian and Hurrian. The texts date approximately to the fourteenth and thirteenth centuries BC. As a result of the discovery of the 'Ugaritic' texts, Ugarit has had a major impact on biblical studies, not so much in directly archaeological* and historical matters, but rather through the significance of the texts on the one hand for the language and poetic (*see* **Poetry, Hebrew**) tradition of the OT, and on the other for the study of Ancient Near Eastern* religion. The importance of the texts for the study of the OT, despite their early date and their place of origin, arises from what may be called the 'Canaanite' connection, since the Ugaritic texts provide us with uniquely valuable information on the language, poetry and religion of ancient Canaan.

From the beginning, however, caution is needed, since the question may legitimately be asked whether the Ugaritic texts are truly Canaanite. The term 'Canaanite' is a slightly odd one, since Semitists generally use this term for first millennium BC languages like Phoenician and Hebrew, and in fact the ancient Ugaritians do not seem to have called themselves Canaanites. Also there were many outside influences at Ugarit, most notably the strong Hurrian influence, which might have rendered Ugarit atypical of Syria-Palestine. From comparative evidence, however, scholars are inclined to regard Ugarit as fairly representative of the Canaanite culture of ancient Syria-Palestine, though it is still necessary to keep in mind the possibility of considerable variation over such a wide geographical and chronological span.

Language and poetry. From the earliest stages of the study of the Ugaritic texts the close language link with Hebrew was recognized. Such difficulties as there are in upholding this close linkage are resolved diachronically, i.e. differences can be explained on the basis that Ugaritic is several hundred years older than the Hebrew we know. The result of this close link has been the use of Ugaritic to solve problems of the Hebrew Bible. This is undoubtedly legitimate in principle and productive in practice. Indeed, reliance on other Semitic languages has always been inevitable in the study of the rather limited corpus of biblical Hebrew, which contains hundreds of words which occur only once. At the same time it is important not to get carried away: Ugaritic is not Hebrew and even where the meaning of a word or grammatical form is certain in Ugaritic, this does not guarantee that an etymologically* related form in Hebrew has the same meaning there. Account must be taken of the context. Nor is the Ugaritic itself always clear. Though 'Ugaritic Studies' now stands largely on its own feet as an independent scholarly discipline, many texts are still very obscure and their interpretation must rely on extra-Ugaritic sources.

However, there are numerous well-established examples of lexical and grammatical illumination of the OT from Ugaritic. In Prov. 26.23 the obscurity of the Hebrew text has been resolved by the recognition of the fact that a Hebrew scribe* has at some stage corrupted a word corresponding to Ugaritic *spsg*, meaning 'white glaze'. The comparison is with 'glaze covering an earthen vessel', a translation already guessed at in the RSV. The existence of this vocable was unknown until it was found in Ugarit. Another Ugaritic word, *tpt*, corresponds etymologically to Hebrew *šōpēṭ*, traditionally translated 'judge' (as in the title of the Book of Judges). However, the wider use of the term in Ugaritic for 'ruler' confirms the suspicion that 'judge' is not always the right English translation of the Hebrew word. Again Amos' profession in Amos 1.1 is described as that of *nōqēd*, which translators found difficult to explain. It now appears that the equivalent term in Ugaritic referred to a type of sheep or wool merchant of some standing in society, occasionally to an official temple shepherd. Finally, apart from meaning 'to' the Ugaritic equivalent of Hebrew *lᵉ* can be used as a vocative particle translatable as 'O', as in 'O, Lord'. This has been detected as a possible meaning of the Hebrew word, for example in Ps. 73.1, where the translation 'good, O Israel, is God to the upright' is better than 'good to Israel is God to the upright' (see RSV footnote).

At a different level, that of poetic style, the Ugaritic texts have proved enormously illuminating by setting the long-known biblical poetry of the Psalms and other OT books in the context of the Canaanite poetic tradition. The result has been a series of new studies of the poetry of the OT, the analysis of its techniques and the understanding of its subtleties. European poetry is characterized, at least in the popular mind, by rhyme and metre. Canaanite and Hebrew poetry* makes elaborate use of other techniques, like balanced repetition, the matching of pairs of words which have been fixed as pairs by tradition, chiasm, etc. Ps. 29 provides an excellent example of a piece of Hebrew poetry which might even have been Canaanite in origin, perhaps dedicated to Baal. It is certainly under strong Canaanite influence with regard to both poetry and theological imagery. As a striking example of similarity of poetic style the following Ugaritic and Hebrew passages are commonly cited:

> 'Now your enemies, O Baal,
> now your enemies you must smite,
> now you must vanquish your foes'
> (*Baal* 2 iv 8–9).

and

> 'For behold your enemies, O Lord,
> for behold your enemies shall perish,
> all evildoers shall be scattered'
> (Ps. 92.9).

Religion. Our knowledge of Ugaritic religion is based on the religious texts, mythological* and non-mythological, and to a limited extent on iconography, religious architecture, etc. It should be noted that we can detect differences of emphasis between mythological texts, which reflect an older and more theoretical theology, perhaps in part superseded, and texts of the regular cult,* such as offering lists, which sometimes give prominence to gods who have little role in the extant myths. A third aspect is revealed by popular religion known from personal names, which in ancient Canaan as in ancient Israel carry religious meaning, and from evidence of 'superstitious' practices (which may have been limited to the private sphere and may, as in ancient Israel, have been looked upon unfavourably by the priests in the temples). There seem to have been two major temples at Ugarit. Iconographic evidence of statuary suggests that one was probably dedicated to Baal. The other might have been dedicated to El or Dagan. All three of these deities are known to us from the OT, as is also the Canaanite goddess Aṯirat/Asherah, the consort of El. An important group of mythological texts, which were probably recited in the context of an elaborate New Year ritual, tells the story of Baal's victories over the Sea and Death and his being established as a major power in heaven. El by contrast seems to have been passé, a wise judge but rather inactive. In his battle with Death, Baal descends temporarily into the underworld and it may be noted that the dead, particularly the dead kings, who are called *rp'um* (a title related to the Hebrew title of the dead, $r^e p \bar{a}' \bar{\imath} m$), had a prominent role in Ugaritic religion at both the official and popular levels.

All of this information is important in the context of the development of Israelite religion, which drew on Canaanite sources for much cultic and theological terminology, e.g. terms for different types of sacrifice, personnel and liturgical installation, and even more important concepts like that of God as the source of agricultural fertility. Other Canaanite mythological themes found their way into the biblical picture of God as the thunderer (Ps. 29), the president of the divine assembly on the sacred mountain in the far north (e.g. Job 1–2; Ps. 48.3), and the vanquisher of the sea monster (Isa. 27.1).

The biblical polemic against Canaanite religious practices is well known. The wrath of the prophets* focussed especially on the fertility cult and particularly cultic 'prostitution' and necromancy. If Ugaritic gives us a fair picture of Canaanite religion, it was a good deal more sophisticated and much less concerned with sexual rituals and consultation of the dead than the prophets imply. Cultic 'prostitution' (the quotation marks are intended to remind the reader to set aside the moral issue) is not certainly evidenced at Ugarit, though the sexual activities of deities are sometimes celebrated, while the consultation of the dead is unknown, despite the importance of the cult of the dead. We may assume that the prophets were picking on individual aspects of Canaanite ritual which they found particularly objectionable, or which were, perhaps, particularly seductive and might lead the Israelites to abandon the worship of Yahweh. Fertility rites and necromancy may have been important in popular belief even if they had little role in 'official' Canaanite religion. It should not be forgotten also that the actual situation in ancient Israel at the level of popular religion was much more syncretistic than the biblical ideal suggests and this sometimes infected the cult. Apart from ancient evidence for this (e.g. the fact that foreign gods were from time to time worshipped even in the Temple, II Kings 16.10–13; 21.3; 23.4), it may also be noted that there is much evidence of Canaanite popular theology being passed on in oral tradition* to re-emerge in the poetry of the later biblical books, the intertestamental literature and the NT. Daniel is the hero of a Ugaritic legend who reappears at a later stage as a model of virtue in the Book of Daniel (see Ezek. 14.14,20; 28.3). Much of the apocalyptic* imagery of the conflict with the dragon/Satan, etc. reflects the ancient traditions found at Ugarit of the cosmic conflict between Baal and the sea monster, the power of chaos (Isa. 27.1; cf. also Rev. 12.3ff.).

Caution is clearly needed in the application of information derived from Ugarit to the solution of problems in the OT and the clarification of the cultural background. Culturally the Israelites took an enormous amount from the environment they entered when they settled in Palestine – a range of inherited cultural baggage ranging from the Hebrew language (a Canaanite dialect) to ways of talking about God. Until the Ugaritic texts were found, the Canaanite background of the OT was virtually unknown (apart from what the OT tells us) and much comparative importance was given to Assyrian and Babylonian tradition. This led earlier in this century to a tendency among some scholars which was condemned as pan-Babylonianism. In a sense Ugarit has supplanted Mesopotamia as the source to which we should look for the background to Israelite ideas and practices. At the same time, finds of copies of Mesopotamian texts like the *Epic of Gilgamesh* at Ugarit and in Palestine confirm the strong influence of Mesopotamian culture in the West. There are many different influences in the background to the OT and it is necessary to beware of slipping into pan-Ugaritism.

See also **Archaeology (Old Testament)**.

A. Caquot and M. Sznycer, *Ugaritic Religion* (Iconography of Religions XV, 8), 1980; P. C. Craigie, *Ugarit and the Old Testament*, 1983; A. Curtis, *Ugarit: Ras Shamra*, 1985; J. C. L. Gibson, *Canaanite Myths and Legends*, 1978; J. Gray, *The Legacy of Canaan: The Ras Shamra Texts and their Relevance to the Old Testament*, *V T*–S 5, [2] 1965.

JOHN F. HEALEY

Use of the Old Testament in the New Testament

Christianity began as a movement within Judaism, for which the Hebrew scriptures were normative and central. Hence these books are constantly quoted or referred to in the early Christian writings. The OT is the chief resource for rulings and illustrations in ethical* discourse. Its theology is the foundation on which Christianity builds. The Christian concepts of God, salvation, sin and forgiveness, the Spirit, the messiah,* all have their starting points in the 'OT'.

For obvious reasons the concept of 'OT' did not arise until the Christian writings began to be formed into a new canon* of sacred books. But the way was prepared by the argument of Paul* in II Cor. 3 that Christians are 'ministers of a new covenant'* (KJV 'testament', v. 6), which completely changes the interpretation 'when they read the old covenant' (KJV 'testament', v. 14). The old covenant here means the Sinai covenant, to which all the legislation in the Pentateuch* is attached. It is 'the Law', and this is the designation of the Pentateuch as the primary scripture of Israel. By extension it comes to embrace the whole of the Hebrew canon (cf. John 10.34). Christians claimed that, through Jesus, God had at last brought in the era of the new covenant prophesied in Jer. 31.31–34. Thus the new situation changed the point of reference. Prophecies* concerning the future were now seen to be in process of fulfilment (Mark 1.15) and to some extent already fulfilled in the person of Jesus, especially in his death and resurrection* (Luke 24.25–27). There is thus a change in the understanding of future elements in the OT. But this also changes the value placed on its record of the past. The exodus from Egypt* and the Sinai covenant cease to be the primary grounds for faith in Yahweh as a God of redemption and are relativized as pointers towards the final act of redemption through Christ (Rev. 5.9f.). Similarly the Law takes second place. It is no longer the complete revelation* of God, the final expression of the divine Wisdom and the means of spiritual life (John 1.14–18; II Cor. 3.4–9). The response to God is measured not by deeds of the Law but by faith in Christ as God's gift (Rom. 3.21–26; 5.1–5; 12.1f.).

The Christian interpretation of the OT was unique in its time because of the central position of Jesus. But it belongs to a wider tendency in contemporary Judaism, without which it would be inexplicable. This has two sides to it. The Dead Sea Scrolls* and apocalyptic* literature already give evidence of a vivid expectation that the eschatological* prophecies are on the brink of fulfilment. The Qumran sect regards itself as the nucleus of the people of the new covenant (CD 6.19; 8.21). The obscure prophecy of Habakkuk is interpreted as an encoded forecast of events in the history of the sect itself (1QpHab). OT quotations, which are applied to Jesus and the church in the NT, are found already in the scrolls applied to the sect. Secondly the Law was subject to a variety of interpretations. The Qumran sect had its own tradition of interpretation derived from the Teacher of Righteousness. 11Q *Temple* is a complete rewriting of much of the Law (*see* **Rewritten Bible**). Among the Pharisees* the rival schools of Hillel and Shammai show that there was scope for difference of opinion on the interpretation of many specific issues of the Law. The disputes between Jesus and the scribes and Pharisees in the Gospels* fall within this wider discussion. Subsequently the church's proclamation of Jesus as messiah and Lord added a new criterion to the interpretation of the Law.

Jesus and the scriptures. These two facets

of biblical interpretation appear in the teaching of Jesus. The emphasis on the kingdom of God* in his preaching reflects the contemporary eschatological expectations and has a scriptural basis. In particular the concept of 'gospel' (*euangelion*, Mark 1.15) as the message of salvation suggests the influence of Isa. 40.9. This text also forms a bridge between the traditions of John the Baptist* (Mark 1.3) and the preaching of Jesus. When Jesus says that some 'will not taste death before they see the kingdom of God come with power' (Mark 9.1), his words reflect the Targum* of Isa. 40.9–10, in which the coming of God is expressed in terms of the manifestation of the kingdom of God. The Beatitudes* (Matt. 5.3–12; Luke 6.20–3) allude to Isa. 61.1–2 and certain psalms, applied to the situation of coming salvation.

Jesus' attitude to the Law is not to deny it but to radicalize it, so as to face people with the ethical* demands of the coming of God. The 'antitheses' of the Sermon on the Mount* (Matt. 5.21–48; cf. Luke 6.27–36) contrast the moral requirements of the Law with the sterner challenge of the imminent confrontation with God. In debate with the scribes* Jesus defends his disapproval of divorce by going behind the law of Deut. 24.1ff. to the intention of God in creation (Mark 10.2–9). The controversy on purity (Mark 7.1–20) takes up the prophetic protest (Isa. 29.3) to insist that what counts is purity of heart before God. Finally the love command (Mark 12.29–31) brings together Deut. 6.4f. and Lev. 19.18, and its influence has penetrated all strands of the NT.

The influence of the scriptures on Jesus' self-understanding is more difficult to assess. The divine words at his baptism by John (Mark 1.11) appear to be a combination of Ps. 2.7 and Isa. 42.1. The provenance of this tradition is doubtful, because these are testimonies of the early church. But the second concerns the Servant* of the Lord, which could have helped to form Jesus' sense of vocation. If so, this would be likely to be an important factor in his acceptance of the necessity of suffering, following the example of the Servant in Isa. 53 (cf. Mark 8.31; 10.45; 14.24). It is disputed whether he was directly influenced by this prophecy, though it was certainly applied to him after the resurrection* from the earliest days. A further question is whether Jesus' self-designation 'son of man'* carries with it a messianic sense derived from scripture (Dan. 7.13).

Proof texts and testimonia. Jesus' teaching includes appeal to particular passages of scripture, and where these are isolated from their context to make a debating point they can be referred to as proof texts.* Nearly all the NT writers similarly draw proof texts from the

OT, because it is normative for moral and religious discourse. It is the authority accepted by both writers and readers. This usage is not merely a matter of citing texts, but also includes allusions to OT examples, e.g. I John 3.12. In I Tim. 2.12–15 a restrictive attitude to women is supported by appeal to the story of Adam* and Eve. A positive appreciation of the marriage relationship is argued on the basis of the same story in Eph. 5.28–33. Many more instances could be cited from all parts of the NT.

Proof texts of this kind should be distinguished from the OT *testimonia*,* which are concerned with the fulfilment of prophecy. The church's proclamation that Jesus is the risen and exalted messiah carried with it the claim that in him the messianic prophecies have been fulfilled. This has its basis in Jesus' preaching of the kingdom of God, but it now includes direct application to him of particular prophecies. Very quickly a few classic texts were established as central to the Christian proclamation, e.g. Ps. 110.1 (cf. Acts 2.34–6). The use of this text is fundamental, because it provided the means of expressing the theology of the heavenly lordship of Jesus as the exalted messiah, who is reserved in heaven for the completion of God's plan at the coming judgment. Other messianic texts, e.g. Ps. 2.7 (Acts 13.33; Heb. 1.5; 5.5), could be similarly interpreted. Thus in the course of the earliest Christian preaching more and more messianic or otherwise relevant texts were exploited as testimonies to the gospel message, and the concept of Jesus as the heavenly messiah absorbed more and more facets of the contemporary eschatological expectations. In this way the use of testimonies helped to lay the foundation of a distinctively Christian theology.

Old Testament themes. All four evangelists* have written their Gospels in the light of this scriptural theology. Besides using testimonies for theological comment (e.g. Matt. 1.23; John 12.38), they include many scriptural quotations and allusions which reflect the apostolic kerygma* and its developments. Thus the infancy narratives* of Matthew and Luke are composed in such a way as to show Jesus as the messiah and the fulfilment of the expectations of Israel. This is done not only by the use of a wealth of OT quotations and allusions, but also by the genre* of the narratives themselves. Thus in Luke 1 the annunciation story of John the Baptist is modelled on that of Samson (Judg. 13) and the Magnificat is modelled on Hannah's song (I Sam. 2.1–10). The genealogies* in Matt. 1.2–17 and Luke 3.23–38 point to Jesus as the heir of messianic expectation. The prologue of John 1.1–18 is modelled on such Wisdom passages as Prov. 8.22–31 and

Ecclus. 24, and uses the creation narrative* of Gen. 1 to point to Jesus as the incarnation of the Word of God (*see* **Logos**). So again all four Gospels indicate the function of John the Baptist as forerunner of the messiah by referring to Isa. 40.3 and Mal. 3.1. The identity of Jesus is specified further at a climactic moment in the story of the Transfiguration (Mark 9.2–8 and its Synoptic* parallels), in which Moses and Elijah appear with Jesus in a setting with impressive OT overtones. Thus by means of OT allusion a theological statement about Jesus is made in the form of a story. At another crucial moment Jesus' entry into Jerusalem and cleansing of the temple (Mark 11.1–17 pars.) are linked with OT prophecy. There are important scriptural allusions in the eucharistic words of Jesus at the Last Supper (Mark 14.24 pars). The story of the crucifixion (*see* **Passion Narratives**) has clearly been composed with an eye to proving that the death of the messiah is not contrary to the plan of God as revealed in scripture. So particular details are linked to Pss. 22 (Matt. 27.35, 46 pars.) and 69 (Matt. 27.34, 48 pars.).

Stories and parables* in the Synoptic Gospels often show the influence of OT parallels (compare II Kings 4.42–4 with the feeding of the multitudes in Mark 6 and 8, pars.). The question then arises whether some of them have been evolved entirely out of the OT, either by the evangelist* or in the underlying tradition. However, there is no case where this can be proved. Modern approaches such as structural* analysis suggest that the OT parallels belong to the writer's mental stock and form part of the materials used in the composition, but do not necessarily imply a deliberate intention to invent a story on the basis of the OT. In any case the historical value of stories in the life of Jesus cannot be decided on the basis of observation of OT influences on their literary form.

In Acts the stories of the Ascension (1.6–11) and Pentecost (2.1–13) make use of OT models and references to express the theological significance of these events in dramatic form. Several of the speeches in Acts are built on the traditional apostolic kerygma, using OT testimonies (2.14–36; 13.16–41). The speech of Stephen (7.2–53) is a sustained reappraisal of the OT history from a Christian standpoint, which may have been adapted from a written source.

The theme of the Law is specially prominent in Paul and John. Paul in Galatians and Romans argues against the Judaizers* that the plan of God to include the Gentiles in the church without circumcision or other obligations of the Law can be deduced from scripture itself. Justification by faith is proved from Hab. 2.4 (Gal. 3.11; Rom. 1.17). Abraham* is cited as the model of faith (Gal. 3; Rom. 4). As the confession of faith consists in acknowledging the lordship of Jesus, in whom God's plan of salvation has been accomplished, Jesus replaces the Law as the focus of relationship with God. This can also be seen in the Gospel of John, in which the discourses, or disputes, of Jesus with the Jewish authorities are so constructed as to present Jesus as the Son of God over against a Jewish concept of revelation* through the Law (cf. John 1.14–18). A striking example of this is the discourse on the bread of life in John 6, where Jesus is presented as the true bread from heaven by contrast with the manna in the wilderness (Ex. 16). The argument requires that the manna be understood as a symbol* of the revelation of God in the Law, which Jesus supersedes (cf. 6.46). Similar symbolic use of the manna tradition is known from Jewish sources.

The Wisdom* tradition of the OT provided the church with another scriptural basis for the development of christology.* Starting in Paul's observation that the Wisdom of God is expressed in the Christ-event (I Cor. 1–3), it opened up a cosmic interpretation of Jesus as the one in whom the divine Wisdom resides (Col. 1.15–20; Heb. 1.1–3) and culminated in the idea of Jesus as the Word of God incarnate (John 1.14). A contrast is implied here with the notion that God's Wisdom has found her predestined expression in the Law (Ecclus. 24.23).

The sacrificial death of Jesus was also expounded with the aid of OT allusions. The use of Isa. 53 goes back to the earliest period (I Cor. 15.3). Further details were based on the Passover sacrifice (John 1.29; 19.36; I Cor. 5.7; Rev. 5.6). There is a special development in Hebrews, in which the writer shows how the death of Jesus fulfils all the requirements for an atoning sacrifice: Jesus is qualified to offer it as a high priest, his death includes the essentials of the ceremonial of the Day of Atonement, and it has the effect of inaugurating the new covenant (when God 'will remember their sins no more', Jer. 31.34), comparable to the sacrifice of the Sinai covenant (Ex. 24). That Hebrews is building creatively on traditional scriptures is evident from its brilliant exploitation of priesthood 'after the order of Melchizedek' (Ps. 110.4), which is a previously unused facet of the messianic Ps. 110. The OT is used as the standard of what makes an atoning sacrifice, and Jesus is shown as carrying it through to its eschatological fulfilment.

References to the future employ expressions and images from the OT in line with the contemporary apocalyptic and eschatological literature. The picture of the portents which herald the End Time in the Little Apocalypse (Mark 13 pars.) and Revelation is made up of a wealth of OT allusions. The prophecy of Isaiah especially is exploited for expressions of salvation.

Exegetical techniques. Typology* is frequent in the NT because of the prophetic character ascribed to the OT in general. There is a classic example in I Cor. 10.1–11, ending with the statement that the events of the exodus 'were written down for our instruction, upon whom the end of the ages has come'. Allegory* is less common, but Paul gives a fine example along the lines of Jewish midrash* in his interpretation of Sarah and Hagar (Gen. 21) in Gal. 3.21–31. In Rom. 10.6–8 he reproduces Deut. 30.12–14 with explanatory glosses in midrashic style. Another rabbinic* technique occurs in Gal. 3.16, where Paul seizes on the singular *sperma* ('offspring') for application to Christ, though the context in Gen. 12.7 requires a collective sense. Also in such passages as Rom. 9.25–29; 10.18–21; 15.9–12 there are examples of *ḥaraz* (texts strung together like a string of pearls) and *gezera shawa* (catchword connections). A rabbinic style of argument from scripture can be seen in John 10.34–36. The influence of interpretation of the Targums has been noted above.

This brief survey shows how the books of the NT are the work of writers who for the most part are thoroughly familiar with the OT and with the ways in which it was used and expounded in contemporary Judaism. The OT is the primary influence on their thought and expression as they confront the implications of the act of God in Christ which crowns their religious inheritance.

F. F. Bruce, *This is That*, 1968; D. A. Carson and H. G. M. Williamson (eds), *It is Written: Scripture Citing Scripture*, 1988; E. E. Ellis, *Paul's Use of the Old Testament*, 1957; R. T. France, *Jesus and the Old Testament*, 1971; L. Goppelt, *Typos: The Typological Interpretation of the Old Testament in the New*, 1982; A. T. Hanson, *The Living Oracles of God*, 1983; R. V. G. Tasker, *The Old Testament in the New Testament*, [2]1954.

BARNABAS LINDARS, SSF

Verbal Inspiration

The theory that the divine inspiration* which Christians attribute to scripture has determined the exact wording of the biblical text. It is thus to be distinguished from theories which locate the supernatural element in scripture in the events to which the biblical books bear witness (a common theory among adherents of the so-called 'biblical theology* movement' of the 1950s and 1960s) or in God's choice of writers whose minds he could inspire but who then wrote freely out of this inspiration.

In the twentieth century, belief in verbal inspiration has usually been the hallmark of evangelical Christianity, and especially of conservative evangelicalism. As developed especially by B. B. Warfield (1851–1921) in his *The Inspiration and Authority of the Bible* (reissued ² 1951), a theory of verbal inspiration was seen as the only sufficient safeguard of the full ('plenary') inspiration of the biblical books, and any other theory was taken to concede too much to the human element in their production. Such a concept of verbal inspiration goes back, however, to post-Reformation Protestant orthodoxy. In thinking out the implications of the Reformers'* *sola scriptura* principle, Protestant theologians saw it as essential to claim that each and every word in scripture was fully inspired by God. Quenstedt, for example, dismissed the theory of 'content inspiration' (as it would come to be called in nineteenth-century Catholicism) and any theory that would attribute inspiration only to the minds and thoughts of the sacred writers, and stressed instead that it is the very words of the Bible that are God-given: 'The Holy Spirit not only inspired in the prophets and apostles the content and sense contained in scripture, or the meaning of the words, so that they might of their own free will clothe and furnish these thoughts with their own style and words, but the Holy Spirit actually supplied, inspired and dictated the very words and each and every term individually' (*Theologia didacticopolemica*, 1685, 1.72; quoted in J. K. S. Reid, *The Authority of Scripture,* 1957, p. 85). In the case of the O T, this inspiration was held to apply not only to the consonantal Hebrew text, but also to the vowel points which were added many centuries later. In this, Protestant theories approached closely to traditional Jewish ways of understanding scripture, as a sacred text whose smallest details were divinely given.

Although the Bible moved into the centre of interest for Protestants after the Reformation, traditional Catholic theories about scripture had in any case also generally supposed that divine inspiration extended to the precise wording of the text. Much biblical exegesis* from the patristic age, indeed from N T times onward, makes sense only on the assumption that God had inspired the verbal details of the text. For example, in Gal. 3.16 Paul* notes that in Gen. 12.7 God makes promises to Abraham's* 'seed' (singular), not 'seeds' (plural), and argues that this wording was chosen to indicate that the promises would be fulfilled in one person (Jesus). Very much patristic exegesis similarly involves pressing the precise verbal form of the text in this way – as indeed does much Jewish* rabbinic* interpretation. It can reasonably be said that

verbal inspiration in some form has been the majority opinion about the nature of scripture throughout most of Christian history.

As the quotation from Quenstedt makes clear, however, traditional thinking about verbal inspiration tended to equate it with a theory of the divine dictation of scripture. Thus Jowett in his famous essay 'On the Interpretation of Scripture' (*Essays and Reviews,** 1860) distinguished 'verbal organic inspiration by which the inspired person is the passive utterer of a Divine Word' from 'an inspiration which acts through the character of the sacred writer'. In this contrast, verbal inspiration is taken to imply that the writer was merely a channel through which divine inspiration flowed, and contributed nothing to the finished text of scripture 'except tongue and pen' (Quenstedt, op. cit., 1.72).

Modern theories of verbal inspiration, however, have generally rejected the idea of dictation. On the Protestant side, this can be seen in the 'Princeton theology' developed by Charles Hodge (1797–1878), B. B. Warfield, and A. A. Hodge (1823–86). They stressed that the Holy Spirit did not do any violence to the individuality of the biblical writers. Though the words of scripture derive from God, they do not do so because he simply dictated them to the biblical authors as to an amanuensis: their exact form is the product of the differing temperaments, styles and intellectual equipment of the separate authors. This helps to explain why it is that the Bible is not marked by a 'house style', but is a library of books whose individual character is very diverse. 'Dictation' is felt by most modern evangelicals to suggest a purely mechanical process which fails to do justice to this perceived diversity.

A similar subtlety can be found in the Catholic version of the verbal inspiration theory, pioneered by such scholars as Marie-Joseph Lagrange in the 1890s. Lagrange wished to defend verbal inspiration against the theory, common among Catholic theologians since the 1840s, of 'content inspiration', and he had immediately to face the question whether this did not reduce the sacred writers to mere instruments, 'pens writing under dictation'. 'On the contrary, says Lagrange, his view stands between the two extremes. According to one system, that of dictation, the entire book is deposited ready-made in the mind of the human writer. Another system locates God's whole influence in the writer's will: he chose out those men whose ideas he wanted passed on to us. The first theory was devised by the Protestants in their first biblical fervour; it deprives man of any meaningful authorship.* The second, held by modern Protestants, makes the Bible no more God's than any other book' (J. T. Burtchaell, *Catholic Theories of Biblical Inspiration since 1810*, 1969, p. 134). Lagrange tried to steer a middle course, by arguing that God as the ultimate author of scripture none the less respected the human intellects of the writers who were his agents, so that they freely wrote words which perfectly expressed the truths he wished to be communicated through them. 'His thesis was that not only were the biblical thoughts of divine origination as well as human, but that biblical ideas were humanly conceived and organized, albeit under divine supervision' (ibid., p. 139). It is probable that most theologians, Catholic or Protestant, who believe in verbal inspiration would subscribe to some such formula as this, to express their sense that the very words of the Bible are God-given while at the same time distancing themselves from the older 'dictation' model.

It remains probable, though, that this understandable desire to allow a genuine place for the human authors actually amounts to a watering-down of the classic doctrine of inspiration. Verbal inspiration is meant to stress that the words of scripture are divine and not human words; and a dictation model may be a more secure way of assuring this point than the more subtle theory developed by Lagrange or by evangelical apologists. If a dictation theory is to be rejected, it may be more consistent to say that the Bible is not verbally inspired, and to find some other way of safeguarding its character as divine revelation.* James Barr has argued (*Fundamentalism*, ²1981, p. 289) that the issue at stake in questions about verbal inspiration is whether or not the Bible is correctly seen as 'part of a movement of true doctrine from God to man' which 'does not emerge from the community; rather it is directed towards the community and transmitted to the community by people like prophets and apostles who are authoritative didactic functionaries'. If this is the correct way of understanding the Bible, then to say that its words were 'dictated by God' may indeed exceed our evidence about the exact mode of its communication, but it is not seriously misleading; and it does not seem to matter very much whether or not we say that the verbal inspiration of scripture implies such a dictation.

If, however, we believe that the Bible is more properly seen as the product of the human community (in Israel and in the early church) which was in touch with God but which thought out its religious ideas through the normal operations of the human mind, then the expression 'verbal inspiration' is really no less misleading than 'dictation' to describe this process. The alleged distinction between dictation and verbal inspiration un-

helpfully fudges this more important question, and can be a means by which people believe they are maintaining a traditional, 'high' doctrine of scriptural inspiration when in fact they have abandoned it in favour of a more 'liberal' one. If one really holds that scripture is a form of divine communication to man, it is not clear why one should be unwilling to regard it as dictated by God.

On the other hand, if Christians are to call the Bible 'inspired' at all, it is hard to see how the phrase 'verbal inspiration' can be avoided. Most alternative theories of scriptural inspiration are not really theories about scriptural inspiration at all, but about the inspiration of the writers, the community from which the Bible came, the events which the Bible records and on which it comments, or the religion to which the Bible bears witness.

This is particularly clear in the case of the theory, popular in the biblical theology movement since the 1950s, that 'inspiration' inheres in the 'salvation history'* recorded in the Bible – such as the exodus* or the resurrection* – rather than in the words of scripture about these events. If these events can be considered inspired 'in themselves', that is, even apart from the interpretation placed on them in the text of scripture, then surely it would be better not to call this theory a theory of scriptural inspiration at all; for its subject is not scripture, but events which occurred, and were in principle capable of mediating knowledge of God, before and apart from their being recorded by the biblical writers.

Again, it may be said that what is inspired is the whole history of religious thought in Israel and in the early church which led to the existence of the Bible; but if so, then this is more accurately expressed by saying that this history of thought rather than the Bible is inspired, not by calling the theory a theory of biblical inspiration. So long as we are talking about the inspiration of scripture, it is hard to see how we can avoid calling the inspiration verbal, since the Bible, being a book or collection of books, is composed of words. There is a considerable paradox in saying that a book is divinely inspired while denying that the inspiration extends to the words which comprise it.

Even the theory that it is not the words but the content of the Bible that are inspired is difficult in the light of the recognition, in modern linguistic* study, that the content of a text cannot be separated from the words through which that content is expressed. If the words were different, the content or 'message' would necessarily be different, too.

Thus, if we are to continue to speak of the inspiration of the Bible, and to mean this literally rather than as a shorthand for the inspiration of some other phenomenon (events, ideas, or writers), then there is every reason to retain the expression 'verbal inspiration'.

An important assumption in evangelical discussion of verbal inspiration has been that it necessarily implies the inerrancy of the inspired words. By inspiring the exact words of the Bible, that is to say, God guarantees their accuracy. Most Christians who are committed to verbal inspiration probably feel that it is more or less equivalent to the doctrine of the inerrancy of scripture. However, it is possible to believe that God inspired Israel and the church to produce precisely these books and to canonize them as Holy Scripture without also holding that they are perfect, free from error, and infallible on all matters of fact and doctrine.

The possibility of 'inspiration without inerrancy' (Burtchaell, op. cit., pp. 164–229) was especially canvassed by a number of liberal and Modernist* Catholics at the beginning of this century, especially (in England) by Baron Friedrich von Hügel, and (in France) by Alfred Loisy. They argued that the inspiration of scripture implied its sufficiency in matters of faith and morals, not its perfection; and that each biblical book, being a work of its own time, was necessarily affected by errors of fact and opinion – a perfect book that was valid in every respect for every period of history being, in fact, a complete impossibility. To claim that only a perfect book could be divinely inspired would be, in effect, to claim that God never could inspire a book at all, for God cannot do what is inherently impossible. Nevertheless, it is by God's providence that the church has the Bible, and it provides all the guidance that is needed on all essential matters of the faith; and this sufficiency can properly be called its 'inspiration'. Furthermore, since (as argued above) the inspiration of a book is necessarily a verbal inspiration, there is no reason why we should not call scripture verbally inspired, while yet affirming that it contains errors.

This strain of thought did not develop further in Catholicism, being prematurely arrested by the proscription of Modernism in 1907, but it has some analogies with liberal* Protestant theories of scriptural inspiration such as that of C. H. Dodd* (in The Authority of the Bible, 1928). For such a theory, as James Barr puts it, 'inspiration as a power influencing the writing down of the text, far from being the most important aspect, is a very unimportant one, though not therefore to be neglected. The real lively centre of the process is the fact that God was with his people in ancient Israel and in the early church' (Fundamentalism, p. 288). Nevertheless, on such a view it would still be proper to say that scripture, and not just the tradition process, was inspired, and 'verbally' inspired at that; for it was at least partly through the existence of these particular books that God chose to be with his people, and it is only through reading and studying these books that modern Christians can come to understand and enter into that relationship with God in which their forbears stood.

Thus a theory of verbal inspiration might be defended, without the need to include the note of infallibility or inerrancy which evangelical writers generally assume to be part of any such theory. There is a persuasive account of a non-inerrantist theory of inspiration in W. J. Abraham, The Divine Inspiration of Holy Scripture, 1981. For most theologians today, however, the ideas of verbal inspiration and of scriptural inerrancy are probably so closely connected that it does not seem worthwhile to attempt to separate them; and consequently few scholars of a 'liberal' stamp are prepared to use the category of verbal inspiration at all.

See also **Authority of Scripture; Fundamentalism; Inspiration; Sensus Plenior.**

J. Barr, The Bible in the Modern World, 1973; J. Barton, People of the Book?, 1988.

JOHN BARTON

Vulgate

This article does not repeat the mass of generally available data about the Latin translations* of the Bible, viz. 1. those versions that preceded the work of Jerome (sometimes called Old Latin, =OL); 2. Jerome's own work on the biblical text, extending from c. 383 to c. 405 and summarily called 'the Vulgate' (= VG), a singular noun that, like OL, implies a unity that never was; 3. the story of subsequent corruption; 4. the work of revision that is now recorded in the Oxford, Rome (unfinished) and Stuttgart editions.

Like all notable literary phenomena (in the religious field compare Septuagint,* Luther's* German Bible, KJV) VG was both an expression of the author's (authors') understanding, interpretation and modification of what he (they) had received, and also a stimulus to further interpretation (and therefore misinterpretation) by those who inherited it. It represented a judgment upon earlier work, from what required fresh translation (Hebrew OT), to what required close revision (Gospels*), to what required much slighter revision (rest of NT), to what merited little or none (OT Apocrypha*), and this judgment was expressed in the use of Hebrew and Greek MSS and in their translation into a purer and more accurate Latinity. But once launched, VG assumed a life of its own and made its own contribution to the unceasing task of biblical interpretation, where even its corruptions might be made the base or justification of certain features in mediaeval* theology.

Jerome's text and language. Jerome introduced into his revision of OL Gospels some renderings unique to himself. At Matt. 6.11 he understood the very difficult Greek *epiousion* to mean not 'daily' (so OL) but, to judge from his commentary* on the passage, 'outstanding' or 'eschatological' or 'spiritual' (*supersubstantialis*), though he kept 'daily' for the same word in the Lucan parallel at 11.3. At John 10.16 he replaced OL's 'flock' with 'fold'. While this could be put down to a high doctrine of the church (and, no doubt, its presence in VG entrenched such a doctrine in later times), yet his commentary on Ezek. 46.21f. and the incidental way in which John 10.16 is quoted there lead one to assume that he found it in his Greek text. But as far as our current knowledge goes, it lacks any other support, and at least twice elsewhere Jerome quotes the verse with 'flock'. From VG it made its way into the KJV.

Yet often he does not follow the Greek. At Matt. 27.8 he reads 'Acheldemach' (following OL but against Greek); at 27.55 'seeing' is omitted after 'afar off' (against Greek and some OL); at Mark 6.27 'having left' is omitted before 'he beheaded' (against Greek and most OL); at 10.43 the second 'amongst you' is omitted (against Greek and most OL). At Luke 9.44 'in your hearts' replaces 'in your ears' (with almost no Greek and little OL support); at 22.55 VG reads 'Peter was in their midst' (against Greek and most OL); at 22.61 and 70 'to him' and 'to them' are not taken up into VG, though both are found in most Greek and OL MSS; at John 7.25 'Jerusalem' replaces 'Jerusalemites' (against Greek and some OL); at 8.37 'sons' replaces 'seed' (against Greek and OL); at 21.16 'lambs' replace 'sheep' (against Greek and OL).

Yet it is important to stress again 'as far as our current knowledge goes' because it is quite clear that Jerome had access to Greek MSS that are no longer extant. I have already noted John 10.16, but more telling are the words that Jerome said he found 'chiefly in Greek MSS' after Mark 16.14 (the passage is too long to quote – it is part of the so-called Freer Logion). This had only Jerome's support until the publication of the logion in the Washington MS of the Gospels (W) in 1908 and 1912.

Moving from issues of text and language to theology proper, as one might expect, the person and work of Jesus Christ explain a number of emphases and modifications where on the basis of the Hebrew one would not expect them. At Gen. 49.10 'Shiloh' is translated 'he who is to be sent' (against OL); at

Isa. 7.14, following LXX, we have 'virgin'; at 16.1 the lamb is not sent to the lord of the land but is the lord of the land; at 45.8 the abstract nouns 'righteousness' (once) and 'salvation' are personalized and understood prophetically of Jesus Christ: 'righteous' and 'saviour'; similarly at 62.1f. 'righteousness' (twice), 'salvation' and 'glory' become 'righteous', 'saviour' and 'glorious'. At Jer. 23.6; 33.16, we have a similar phenomenon: 'righteousness' becomes 'righteous', and at Hab. 3.18 'the God of my salvation' is rendered 'God my Jesus'.

Unlike Jerome, later VG MSS and early printed editions kept the future tenses of most OL renderings at Matt. 26.28, Mark 14.24, Luke 22.20 (the interpretative glosses – 'which shall be poured' – over the cup and wine) and at I Cor. 11.24 (where the gloss – 'which shall be given' – is over the bread), although the Greek originals have present participles passive. A recent critic, J. N. Suggit, sees in the futures an attempt to historicize the events to which the wine and bread point, i.e. Good Friday, and so a withdrawal from the attempt of the evangelists* to include the post-Easter Christian readers in the current celebration of the eucharist, an attempt also to be found in the Jews' celebration of the Passover. At the end of his article Suggit asks: 'Was the lack of a present participle in Latin a contributory factor to the Reformation?*'

If Hab. 3.18 can speak of 'God my Jesus' it will be no surprise if later forms of VG can introduce a reference to the Trinity in the so-called Comma Joanneum, inserted into I John 5.7f. As is well known, this passage about the three heavenly witnesses became a bone of contention between Erasmus* and his critics, since it was the major proof text* for that doctrine in contemporary Bibles and was being attacked by humanists as spurious.

If one reason for the insertion of the Comma is to assert and defend the divinity of the Spirit, one may see the same motive at work in the adoption by later forms of VG of OL's additions, at John 3.6. After 'what is born from Spirit is spirit' was read 'because the Spirit is God', which itself was sometimes supplemented by 'and born of God'. Similarly, at Phil. 3.3 Augustine* shows his knowledge of Latin MSS that read 'God the Spirit' rather than 'Spirit of God' or 'God by the Spirit'.

Proceeding from christology* and pneumatology, we overhear the views of Jerome and his successors about women* and Jews. Jane Barr has shown how Jerome's translation of Genesis was made to reflect both his general anti-feminist* stance and his appreciation of women. Here are some examples of the former: at 38.24 he shows his distaste for the physical signs of pregnancy by translating the

Hebrew 'lo she is pregnant' as 'her belly is swelling for all to see'; in the story of the attempted seduction of Joseph by Potiphar's wife (39.6ff.), the Hebrew in v. 8 'he refused' becomes 'absolutely rejecting the wicked deed', which in v. 10 becomes a 'debauchery' with which she 'pesters' him. Verse 13 speaks of her being 'turned down' by Joseph (very proper!) and v. 19 speaks of Potiphar's too ready acceptance of his wife's version of events. Finally at 3.16 the monk does not like the idea that a woman's sexual appetite is part of the divine judgment and so in a sense natural. Now it is woman's subjection to man (in general) which is the result of Eve's disobedience. In none of these instances is there any Hebrew or OL support. Barr might have added the gratuitous clause at 38.5: after Shuah had borne three sons, Jerome says: 'she stopped bearing further'. Evidently enough was enough! At I Cor. 9.5 most Greek MSS read 'sister as woman/wife'. The Greek *gunē* is ambiguous (as Tertullian,* Jerome and Augustine recognized) but the clear implication is that most apostles were married. This phrase was also known to Jerome in the easier plural form, 'sisters as women/wives', but rejected by him in favour of 'women' (as in some OL). The possibility of 'wives' was excluded apparently because he understood 'sisters' literally and not as a reference to Christian women, and 'sisters' then became redundant before 'women'. However, the earliest state of VG still has 'sister as woman', with OL, but some later states have 'woman as sister' or even 'girl as sister', the latter two presumably meaning 'woman'/'girl' in a non-conjugal role, perhaps as attendants similar to those who ministered to Jesus and the apostles (Luke 8.2f.). In this way it was possible to uphold apostolic (and so clerical) celibacy and the practice of *virgines subintroductae* (i.e. women living with men in celibacy).

We may here refer to two texts that figured prominently in later Mariological debate. At Gen. 3.15 it is not clear what Jerome read, whether *ipse* ('it', the 'seed' of v. 14) or *ipsa/illa* ('she', Eve). Both were known in OL. Scholars of the calibre of de Bruyne, Burkitt and Stummer believed he wrote the former; the Rome and Stuttgart editions read the latter. What is clear is that it was 'she' that achieved very wide acceptance in the Western church and, however it was understood originally, its application (first in the seventh century by Isidore of Seville?) to the new Eve and her Son helped to buttress and promote Marian devotion and discussion. Another famous Marian text is Luke 1.28 where 'full of grace' (some OL endorsed by Jerome), hardly the best translation of the Greek 'favoured', contributed considerably to early and mediaeval* appreciations of Mary.

It may be possible to gauge the stance of the Latin Bible towards the Jews from each of its three forms. The OL translation of Ecclus. is presented to us in two forms, an African translation without chs 44–50 (the praise of the Jewish fathers) and a later European form with them. It has been suggested that the omission in the earlier form is deliberate and that the translator found chs 44—50 inappropriate in a Christian Bible. As for Jerome himself, at Judith 8.24f. he gratuitously adds to the report of Jewish disaffection in the wilderness sentences from I Cor. 10.9f, about the annihilation of those guilty of it. Finally at Dan. 9.26 some VG MSS and early editions reshape and supplement the phrase 'and it will not be his' to read 'he will have no people who will deny him'. This has been introduced from Jerome's commentary on Daniel. The anti-Jewish thrust of these variously contrived modifications is clear (*see* **Antisemitism**).

As for moral theology, one of the OL and VG expressions most strenuously debated in the Renaissance and Reformation was *paenitentiam agite* at Matt. 4.17 as a translation of Greek *metanoeite*, 'repent'. In mediaeval theology *paenitentia* became the technical word for the elaborate penitential system, and its use in current Bibles not only strengthened its hold but also encouraged readers, or hearers, to assume and believe that the system they knew in church was part of the original teaching of Jesus. Erasmus engaged in the debate and finally translated the Greek with a Latin word meaning 'come to your senses', as Lactantius and more recently Valla had done before him, but VG never.

Allied with penance is prayer for the dead. At two places this doctrine has left its mark on VG. At II Macc. 12.39–46, the classical passage, the Greek has been modified in a number of ways in order to give clearer expression to it. In v. 42 the last reference to 'sin' is rendered 'sins' in late forms of VG (as does codex Alexandrinus in LXX); 'sin' in v. 43 becomes 'sins of the dead' in these same forms; in vv. 45f. Jerome himself has reconstructed the Greek (as had Lucian of Antioch before him) by detaching 'a holy and wholesome thought' from what precedes (v. 45 in VG) and making it describe what follows (v. 46b in VG); but restructuring continues in that it is no longer Judas' sacrifice for the dead that is a 'holy and wholesome thought' but his praying for the dead. Though Jerome himself preserves the historical link with Judas, later forms of VG remove the sentiment from the particular to the general by, as earlier, making 'sin' in v. 46 plural and by reading the present tense 'may be loosed' for the imperfect 'might be loosed'. Again the historical becomes contemporary. Luther and Eck argued about this passage in 1519 in the controversy over purgatory.

The second example is even more interesting if more violent. Printed as an appendix to VG and translated in the RSV Common Bible is II (IV) Esd. In 7.102–105 Ezra is informed in his third vision that intercession for sinners on the day of judgment will not be permitted. It is frequently and probably correctly said that it was this prohibition of prayer for the dead which led to the mutilation of a MS which contained it. A folium (containing seventy verses) was cut out of the MS, and since this MS was the one from which nearly all our Latin MSS of II (IV) Esd. were copied and the earliest Latin Bibles printed, it was not until 1875 that its contents became generally known. Since, II (IV) Esd. survived only on the fringe of the Latin Bible (Jerome repudiated it violently precisely because it rejected prayers for the dead) it was felt that more extreme measures could be taken with the offending passage – the knife! – even though more than sixty other verses had to suffer as well. (On the other hand the book was not so unimportant that a chance to insert a christological clarification was ignored: at 7.28 'my son the Messiah' was replaced by 'my son Jesus'. However, the christological insertion at 12.32, found in slightly differing forms in the oriental versions, is not found in VG.)

A notorious example of the influence of a misunderstanding or corruption in Jerome's work on later theology may be found in his commentary on Ezek. 1.7. Though this is not strictly relevant in an article on VG it does illustrate the impact of Jerome upon posterity. In the comment he uses the Greek word for conscience (*suneidēsin*). But 400 years later the German churchman and scholar Hrabanus Maurus in his commentary on Ezek. quotes Jerome as reading *suntērēsin*, not only a corruption but a nonsense. Yet such was the respect in which Jerome was held that in the form *sundērēsis* it became the name for an important doctrine in moral theology. If that is some measure of the hypnotic effect of Jerome's non-biblical activity, there will be no surprise when we turn to contemplate the impact of VG, warts and all, upon Western Christianity, an impact so far-reaching that, ironically, it could hold back for a time the protagonists of an OT in Hebrew, a NT in Greek and Bibles in the vernacular, to the understanding of which Jerome himself gave a great part of his life.

See also **Text of the Bible; Translation, Problems of; Translations (to the KJV).**

The Cambridge History of the Bible, Vols I & II, 1969–70; Jane Barr, 'The Vulgate Genesis and St Jerome's attitude to Women' *Studia Patristica*, vol. 17, 1982, pp. 268–73; J. L. North, '*akedia* and *akedian* in the Greek and Latin Biblical Tradition' *Studia Evangelica*, vol. 6, 1973, pp. 387–93; V. Reichmann and S. P. Brock in *Theologische Realenzyklopädie*, vol. 6, 1980, pp. 172–81.

J. L. NORTH

Westcott, Lightfoot and Hort

Brooke Foss Westcott (1825–1901), Joseph Barber Lightfoot (1828–1889) and Fenton John Anthony Hort (1828–1892) are sometimes referred to as the 'Cambridge Triumvirate'. All became Fellows of Trinity and Professors of Divinity. Westcott succeeded Lightfoot as Bishop of Durham. Westcott and Hort's Greek text, the fruit of nearly thirty years' collaboration, was a landmark in the history of textual criticism.* Published in 1881, five days before the Revised Version of the NT, the text had been at the disposal of the Revision Company, of which all three were members. Together they planned a series of commentaries* on the entire NT. The plan was only partly fulfilled: Westcott completed commentaries on John, the Johannine Epistles and Hebrews, and Lightfoot on Galatians, Philippians, Colossians and Philemon; Hort, however, produced nothing of his share in his lifetime, owing to his extreme fastidiousness, though posthumous fragments appeared on James, I Peter and Revelation.

Westcott shared a theological kinship with F. D. Maurice, whose writings he apparently refrained from reading in order to preserve his own originality. The titles of certain of his books (for example, *Christus Consummator* and *The Incarnation and Common Life*) evince his characteristic emphasis that in Christ the life of the whole of humanity is taken into God. His exegetical work is marked by a scrupulous attention to detail. In the preface to his commentary on the Johannine epistles he took up Jowett's call in *Essays and Reviews*★ to interpret the Bible 'like any other book' and applied it in a sense of his own – that 'the minutest points of language, construction, order' must not be neglected. Jowett had warned of the danger of 'making words mean too much', and at times Westcott was guilty of excessive subtlety. But the many word-studies scattered throughout the commentaries remain valuable, not least because they contain a wealth of patristic material, 'which we are unlikely to quarry for ourselves' (C. K. Barrett). Hoskyns,* in his survey of work on John's Gospel, gives an important place to Westcott, paying tribute to his 'theological concentration'. But this goes hand in hand with the assumption that the Johannine account is substantially accurate. No sharp distinction must be made between John and the

Synoptics.* For Westcott, John's dogmas are 'concrete facts' and the synoptic narratives are 'implicit dogmas'; 'in both cases the exactness of historical truth is paramount'.

Lightfoot was a historian and linguist rather than a theologian. His aim was to establish the facts of early Christian history. He contested the results of F. C. Baur and his disciples in the Tübingen School,* who dated most of the NT writings in the second century. Lightfoot's commentaries are notable for their terseness and lucidity. The comment on Gal. 3.20 is typical: 'The number of interpretations of this passage is said to mount up to 250 or 300. Many of these arise out of an error as to the mediator, many more disregard the context, and not a few are quite arbitrary. Without attempting to discuss others which are not open to any of these objections, I shall give that which appears to me the most probable.' There are also some lengthy 'dissertations', the most famous being 'The Christian Ministry' in the commentary on Philippians. Here Lightfoot argued that 'bishop' and 'presbyter' were originally synonymous and that 'the episcopate was formed not out of the apostolic order by localization but out of the presbyteral by elevation'. Lightfoot is remembered now even more for his work on the Apostolic Fathers* – Clement of Rome, Ignatius and Polycarp.

Notwithstanding his exiguous output, Hort is being increasingly recognized as the most important of the three. His letters reveal him to have been a more daring thinker than his colleagues. He wrote to Westcott (10 March 1860): 'Have you read Darwin? . . . In spite of difficulties, I am inclined to think it unanswerable.' He almost withdrew from the joint venture because Westcott and Lightfoot seemed to him to be making *a priori* assumptions about the infallibility of the NT and thereby fettering freedom of criticism. His profoundest thought is to be found in *The Way, the Truth, the Life* (the Hulsean Lectures for 1871), a theological meditation on John 14.6. Lecture two on 'I am . . . the Truth' is particularly penetrating: 'truth is never that which we choose to believe, but always that which we are under a necessity to believe' and 'no truth can be alien to Him who is the Truth'. In a letter written while the Hulseans were being prepared Hort said (8 November 1871): 'I have not merely a keen interest in criticism, physical science, and philosophy, but a conviction that their vigorous and independent progress is to be desired for the sake of mankind, even when for the time they seem to be acting to the injury of faith.' Unfortunately, for all the boldness of his thinking, Hort did not declare himself in print. He declined an invitation to be a contributor to *Essays and Reviews*,

though he sympathized privately with the aims of the essayists; and even *The Way, the Truth, the Life* was not published until after his death. William Sanday, who considered him to be 'our greatest English theologian of the century', regretted his silence and likened him to Achilles in his tent.

The background against which Westcott, Lightfoot and Hort did their work was the consternation occasioned by the publication in 1860 of *Essays and Reviews*. Westcott, in a letter to Hort (6 August 1860), felt the need 'to show that there is a mean between *Essays and Reviews* and Traditionalism', and the three did indeed restore a measure of confidence to the faithful. It would be a mistake, however, to claim too much for them. Their critical scholarship looks in retrospect generally conservative and defensive. Westcott and Lightfoot in particular reached reassuring conclusions. Yet perhaps, as Henry Chadwick has suggested, it was this very fact which 'enabled them to do much to make the church safe for critical methods in theological study'.

See also **English Interpretation.**

C. K. Barrett, *Westcott as Commentator*, 1959; H. Chadwick, *The Vindication of Christianity in Westcott's Thought*, 1961; A. F. Hort (ed.), *Life and Letters of Fenton John Anthony Hort*, 2 vols, 1896; W. F. Howard, *The Romance of New Testament Scholarship*, 1949; S. Neill and N. T. Wright, *The Interpretation of the New Testament 1861–1961*, 1988; E. G. Rupp, *Hort and the Cambridge Tradition*, 1970.

BRIAN G. POWLEY

Wisdom Literature

A term used by modern scholars to describe the books of Job, Proverbs and Ecclesiastes, together with a few so-called 'wisdom psalms'. In the Apocrypha,* Ecclesiasticus (Ben Sirach), the Wisdom of Solomon and Tobit are also included within this category.

Although the term itself is a modern one, several of these books were early designated 'books of wisdom', as in titles such as 'The Wisdom of Jesus Son of Sirach' and 'The Wisdom of Solomon'. In the Roman Missal the readings from certain books were introduced by the heading 'Lectio Libri Sapientiae'. Such usages reflect an early recognition that they belong to a distinct category among the books of the OT: their special function, as the frequent occurrence of the words 'wisdom' and 'wise' indicates, was instruction – to communicate the contents of the divine wisdom which had been revealed to the wise men of past ages. For Christians, the ultimate source and authority for this teaching was Christ himself, who is 'the wisdom of God' (I Cor.

1.24) and the Holy Spirit, the 'spirit of wisdom and understanding' (Isa. 11.2).

Until modern times, in both Jewish* and Christian exegesis,* 'the wisdom books were, then, generally used as a source of moral and religious instruction. Proverbs and Ecclesiastes were attributed to Solomon, the archetypal 'wise man', on the basis of Prov. 1.1 and Eccles. 1.1. In the case of Job, the Babylonian Talmud* asserted that it was written by Moses,* but this opinion was not universally accepted by the rabbinical* writers. The question whether Job himself was an historical character or a fictitious one was also a matter of debate.

Modern critical scholarship, on the other hand, tended from the first to favour a late date for the wisdom books. It was argued that their moral and religious precepts presuppose the teaching of the prophets* and that the 'wise men' to whom large sections of them are attributed in the texts themselves were in fact 'scribes* of the Law'* concerned to systematize and develop the traditional teaching of previous ages in accordance with their own understanding of religion as obedience to the Law.

The understanding of OT literature was put on an entirely new basis with the discovery, from the nineteenth century onwards, of the previously unknown extensive literature of the peoples of the Ancient Near East.* In the field of wisdom literature as in other fields, it became clear for the first time that Israel was neither unique nor a pioneer. From the beginning of the twentieth century literary works from Egypt* and Mesopotamia became available for study which clearly belonged both in form and content to the same literary types as the OT wisdom books, and which were in most cases very much older, some of them dating back to the third millennium BC. That these similarities were not due to chance became clear when in the 1920s Erman and others showed that a section of the Book of Proverbs was based directly on an Egyptian work, the *Instruction of Amen-em-opet*. Admittedly such direct literary dependence proved, as far as could be seen from the limited amount of non-Israelite material available, to be an exception. However, it was now beyond dispute that the OT wisdom books were not simply the product of the native Israelite genius but were part of a much wider literary tradition which, as latecomers in the cultural history of the Ancient Near East, the Israelites had inherited rather than initiated.

The existence of this comparative material now made it possible to make plausible inferences about the milieu in which the OT wisdom books might have been produced. They themselves provide scant information about their provenance; but the corresponding Egyptian and Mesopotamian works are far more informative: there could be no doubt that they were composed by a class of professional scribes, and in particular of scribes attached to the royal court, a class of civil servants administering national policy. It was also clear that many of these works, especially the Egyptian so-called 'Instructions', were written as textbooks for use in schools for the training of scribal apprentices who would form the succeeding generation of royal officials.

Here, it was concluded, was the clue to the identity of the Israelite 'wise men': they were members of a similar class of royal scribes at the Israelite court (such as the 'men of Hezekiah' in Prov. 25.1) who maintained a 'wisdom school' corresponding to foreign models, and who composed 'wisdom literature' to be used in the instruction given there. This theory became very widely accepted, especially through the influence of G. von Rad, who argued very convincingly that it was during the reign of Solomon that these institutions first came into being in Israel as part of a large-scale imitation of Egyptian political and cultural models which brought the nation for the first time into the mainstream of the cultural world of the great empires.

This theory of the origin of Israelite wisdom literature was most clearly applicable to the Book of Proverbs, which contains material especially relating to the king* and to the life of the court. Ecclesiastes, on the other hand, was generally recognized to be a late post-exilic work which could have had no connection with a royal court, and such a connection was also lacking in the case of Job. But it was postulated that the scribal profession and scribal education, though they had originated in court circles, had become diversified: even in pre-exilic times not all scribes were royal scribes, and various kinds of 'wisdom school' came into existence besides that of the court. Such schools continued to flourish during and after the Exile, and it was in connection with them that the later wisdom books were written. These later scribes were the forerunners of such men as Ben Sirach, who as a 'scribe' and master of a 'school' in the second century BC composed the book of Ecclesiasticus, in which the ancient literary wisdom tradition was combined with the study of the Law and the Prophets. In this way a 'history' of Israelite wisdom literature covering almost a thousand years was reconstructed.

The view that Israelite wisdom literature originated in the circles of royal scribes who were state officials and who were dependent on foreign, pagan models had important consequences for the interpretation of the earlier wisdom literature such as Prov. 10–29. Early

Israelite wisdom was held to be an essentially pagan phenomenon, the possession of a small upper class whose way of life had little to do with traditional Yahwism, and was in fact basically non-religious. Such 'wisdom', it was believed, is reflected in the accounts of political and court life in the reigns of David * and Solomon, where it was a recipe for the attainment of political or private ends which took no account of religious scruples or moral considerations (see, e.g., II Sam. 13.3; I Kings 2.6). This so-called 'old wisdom' was, however, subsequently brought into conformity with the religious and ethical * traditions of Israel under the influence of the teaching of the prophets (McKane).

These views have subsequently been challenged, especially on two counts. Firstly, it is now recognized that Egyptian (and Mesopotamian) wisdom literature is far from being amoral or non-religious. The twin concepts of *maat*, the 'world order' to which everything must conform and which contains a strong moral element, and of the gods as seeing and judging human conduct, are fundamental to its teaching. If early Israelite wisdom literature was based on Egyptian models, this is a significant fact, which must be taken into account in any assessment which may be made of it. Secondly, it has been argued that foreign influence on it was less extensive than had been supposed: a native 'wisdom' tradition existed in Israel long before the time of the monarchy, and has left a definite mark on the literature.

The character of this native Israelite wisdom has been the object of considerable research in the last twenty-five years. It is undisputed that most if not all societies have their own stocks of popular lore or 'wisdom', particularly in the form of short proverbs, and Israel was no exception to this. In the narrative and prophetical books of the OT there are a number of such 'popular' sayings (e.g. I Kings 20.11; II Kings 14.9; Ezek. 16.44). It is true that these differ from the sayings in the Book of Proverbs in that they are very brief and lack the poetical form of the latter, though it has been argued (but denied by others) that some of the sayings in Proverbs may be elaborations of such brief 'popular' sayings.

The fact that only a few of the sayings in Proverbs refer to the specific concerns of kings, courtiers and politicians, while agricultural and pastoral matters and family, community and personal relationships are the subjects of a large proportion of them, has raised the question whether the activity of the scribes who actually wrote down the Book of Proverbs may have been to a large extent editorial: in other words, whether in addition to sayings which they composed themselves they may have drawn on a large stock of orally * preserved material which antedated the foundation of the monarchy. Since this material differed in form from the 'popular' proverbs found elsewhere in the OT, the question was then posed whether some other form of traditional wisdom may have existed in that early period apart from the merely 'popular' saying.

This question was answered in the affirmative by J.-P. Audet (1960) and E. Gerstenberger (1965), followed by other scholars. They argued that there was a connection between the origins of Israelite wisdom and of Israelite law. Gerstenberger used the term *Sippenweisheit* ('clan wisdom') to denote a kind of code of behaviour which he supposed to have been developed in patriarchal society to regulate the relationships between members of Israelite or proto-Israelite clans before the development of formal law-codes governing the whole nation, and which was still in use in monarchical times. From this, he maintained, there developed, side by side, both the law-codes and the wisdom collections.

Although it has been objected that Gerstenberger's theory is purely speculative and presupposes more knowledge of the social structure of pre-monarchical Israel than we actually possess, some support has recently been given to it from the study of the 'oral literature' of modern pre-literate societies. Anthropologists * have compiled large collections of 'oral literature', especially from Africa, in the form of proverbs, and have shown that these proverbs are not 'popular' in the modern sense of that term, but are forms of 'wisdom' which are regarded by those peoples as authoritative guides to social and personal behaviour and may have binding force. Both in thematic range and in form, including poetical parallelism, many of these are astonishingly similar to the sayings in Proverbs.

In summary one may say that although no consensus has so far been reached about the origin and history of Israelite wisdom literature, it is now widely recognized that more than one influence was at work. On the one hand, it is clear that to a large extent it stands within the cultural tradition of the Ancient Near East and, more specifically, shares the purpose and methods of the scribal education which was at first restricted to the training of civil servants but which, even in Egypt, later became more widely available. On the other hand, it is equally clear that the Israelite authors were not content simply to borrow this ready-made foreign literary culture but, probably from the first, gave it a distinctively Israelite flavour, drawing on earlier native wisdom preserved in oral form and also accommodating it to the specific religious notions of Israel, to create a distinctively Israelite product.

So far in this article the appropriateness of the term 'wisdom literature' as an all-embracing term covering the books of Job, Proverbs and Ecclesiastes has not been examined. In fact some recent studies of the individual books suggest that it may be somewhat misleading in that it tends to conceal very real differences between them.

Form-critical* studies have emphasized that these books do not constitute a distinct literary genre:* on the contrary, each comprises a number of different genres, some of which are not distinctive 'wisdom genres' but occur in other OT books, e.g. the lament, the disputation, the hymn, narrative prose. The same is true of 'wisdom themes'. Further, the concept of a continuous 'wisdom tradition' linking these three books together in a historical progression is now seen to rest on shaky foundations. There is no certainty that the pre-exilic 'wise men' of Prov. 10–29 and the 'wise' author of the Hellenistic* book of Ecclesiastes have much more in common with one another than the name: the intervening centuries are a complete blank as far as evidence of a 'history of wisdom literature' is concerned. Again with regard to the Book of Job, many recent interpreters have been extremely cautious about including it among the 'wisdom books' at all, since it makes no claim to be the work of a 'wise man', and has, on the other hand, many affinities with quite different types of literature. Thus although all three books undoubtedly have much in common in theme and to some extent in form, it may well be that a better understanding of them will be gained by interpreting each on its own terms and in relation to the OT and to Israelite religious teaching as a whole than by treating them all simply as examples of a unique category, 'wisdom literature'.

See also **Proverbs**.

J. Blenkinsopp, *Wisdom and Law in the Old Testament*, 1983; J. L. Crenshaw, *Old Testament Wisdom. An Introduction*, 1982; id. (ed.), *Studies in Ancient Israelite Wisdom*, 1976; W. McKane, *Prophets and Wise Men*, 1965; G. von Rad, *Wisdom in Israel*, 1972; R. N. Whybray, *The Intellectual Tradition in the Old Testament*, 1974.

R. N. WHYBRAY

Women in Early Christian Interpretation

Seen from a modern perspective, Christian discourse has always had a gender problem. The Word was made flesh in Christ, yet Christ himself was male. The range of problems that arises from these fundamentals includes some of the most central and controversial issues in current debate. Not only is there the problem of finding a role for women in Christianity which can be reconciled with the male gender of Christ and with the idea of man, but not woman, as having been made in the image of God, but also that presented by the inescapable fact that the texts of early Christianity are written by men and represent a male-centred textuality.

Feminist* theology is of its very nature concerned with questions of texts and their interpretation. It has indeed consciously borrowed the techniques of hermeneutics* and applied them to the NT and later writings. Nevertheless, the abundant modern literature has tended to focus either on the actual role of women in the early church (especially as reflected in Acts) or on the supposedly misogynistic tone of Christian writers, especially from the second century on. Paul's* attitude towards women has been a natural starting point, whether to be contrasted with the more sympathetic attitudes attributed to Jesus in the Gospels* or with the far more openly hostile opinions of later writers from Tertullian* to Jerome and on into the mediaeval* period. It is equally important to note, however, that despite attempts to claim female authorship for certain works, the discourse of the early church is nonetheless a male discourse; the texts were written by men in the context of a society in which on the whole education and in particular literary production were male prerogatives. It is doubtful even in principle how far historical fact about women in early Christianity can be derived from such material. Recent work on later periods concerning male and female language suggests that the gender of the writer is likely to be a strongly determining factor in the linguistic practice observed, and thus in the attitudes expressed. It is likely that not only Christian thinking about God but also Christian thinking about women has been deeply influenced by its evolution within a context of male textuality.

In response to this recognition, some feminist theologians confront the problem of maintaining historical objectivity by adopting a stance of avowed engagement, and seeking to get beyond the apparent misogynism of the texts by reclaiming a more positive female meaning through feminist hermeneutics, a procedure for which they find support in current debates within historical study in general. In particular, when the very possibility of historical 'fact'* is challenged by structuralist* and other approaches, and when history itself has been declared to be no more than a species of rhetoric,* the well-known repertoire of NT passages relating to the 'position of women' is no longer seen as offering a series of discrete sets of historical data but itself becomes available for reinterpretation in terms of textuality.

Thus the famous saying of Paul to the Galatians that 'there is neither male nor female, neither bond nor free, for you are all one in Christ Jesus' (Gal. 3.28) has in the past often been made the foundation for the argument that Christianity revolutionized attitudes to women in the early Roman empire; the women named in Acts and in Romans are taken to exemplify this new status. To take another example, the tone of a number of the apocryphal acts of the apostles (especially the *Acts of Paul and Thecla*) has been interpreted as indicating the actual prominence of female ascetics, and even of communities* of virgins and widows, in the church of the day. But recent scholarship increasingly emphasizes Paul's debt to prevailing rhetorical convention and the extent to which an individual verse must be interpreted in its textual and rhetorical context. He was not advocating practical equality for women any more than emancipation of slaves; similarly, the 'household codes' (e.g. Col. 3.18–4.1) in which an increasingly hierarchical social order is envisaged, with women's place defined in relation to the male-centred family, follow a pattern that can also be found in pagan moral literature. As for the apocryphal acts, their qualities as examples of narrative fiction have long been well recognized, and they provide ample material for literary analysis in terms of modern theory. The further fact that pagan critics of Christianity such as Celsus made its supposed appeal to women part of their attack has also led many scholars to an overestimation of the prominence of women, through failure to observe the extent to which the topic of women in male-dominated writing of all periods is associated with the realm of all that is regarded as worthless or undesirable.

All the same, the NT clearly does offer indications about women in the early church that are at once important and problematic. Not surprisingly in this male textual environment, the number of references is not great. There are perhaps more than might be found in most pagan texts of the period. Thus the degree of attention given to women in the Gospels, though not in fact amounting to a great deal (the absence of Mary from so much of the Gospel narratives has always proved an embarrassment to Christian interpreters), is nevertheless perhaps more than might have been expected. But it is important to see both these and the relevant passages of Acts and in the Epistles* in textual as well as historical terms.

It will be found that the women in the Gospel narratives often serve as a counterpoint to the theme of the disciples. Whereas the latter often fail to understand Jesus' meaning, and are not present at the last, the women often possess true faith and real, because silent, understanding. Rarely do the women indulge in the vain questions of the disciples: a woman's role in male discourse is to be silent, but whereas that is more usually the silence of male disregard, here, paradoxically, it is the silence of wisdom (Luke 10.38–42). This too inspires an explanation in terms of textuality: Jesus speaks in parables,* which the disciples often do not understand, but it is equally a paradox that women – who should keep silence – possess real wisdom, the wisdom that cannot be expressed. In Pauline terms, the role here given to women is part of the foolishness of man that is the wisdom of God. Thus such questions as whether or not Jesus was in any sense a feminist seem not merely out of place in themselves, but also an inadequate response to the complications of the texts in gender terms.

Nevertheless, if it was to be man's role to speak the word, what of woman? If the new order that was preached was an order of reversal, in which woman as a category played an integral role, the next stage, by which the early millennialism* was softened into something more socially respectable, would also necessarily be reflected in its sayings about women. Paul's saying to the Galatians, qualified by his strictures on the women at Corinth, and by the passages in which women are seen as occupying a fixed and secondary place in the divine and natural hierarchy, finds a still clearer and more ominous commentary in the later NT texts. Thus at I Cor. 7 Paul emphasizes the duty of wives to their husbands, while at I Cor. 11.2ff (thought by some not to be Pauline) the head-covering enjoined on women in church is set within the context of their position as secondary to men (I Cor. 11.3, cf. 8–9, 'the man is not of the woman but the woman of the man'). Women (or perhaps 'wives') are not to speak in church (I Cor. 14.34); thus if women represent the 'foolish' and the foolish are chosen by God (I Cor. 1.27), nevertheless their new freedom is to have well-defined limits. At Eph. 5.24 we read that wives must be subject to their husbands in everything (cf. Col. 3.18–19; Tit. 2.5), and in I Tim. 5.6 that women who live in pleasure are dead while they live. The indications in Acts of active participation in church life by women (Prisca, Mary, Apphia; cf. Nympha, Col. 4.15; Junia, Rom. 16.7; and especially Phoebe, called *diakonos*, Rom. 16.1) are thus to be read in the context of a discourse which allocated a place for woman defined by reference to man, in terms familiar in contemporary and earlier pagan male texts from Aristotle to Plutarch. To argue that the 'household codes' represent a patriarchal reaction to the early leadership of women within house churches is tempting and may be partly true, in the sense that a desire to impose acceptable social norms is indeed perceptible in the late first- and second-century writings; it depends, however, on a view of earliest Christianity as egalitarian which understandably relies on Gal. 3.28 and gives insufficient weight to the textual complexities in gender terms of the Gospels and the Pauline writings. This is the danger of a 'feminist critical hermeneutics' which for reasons of present-day concern explicitly seeks to 'remember' or recapture a positive role and image for women in earliest Christianity. A sense of the actual 'position of women', whether in the Gospels or in the other NT writings, must be founded not simply (as so often) on somewhat over-simplified assumptions about their role in contemporary society, which is only partially recoverable by historians through sheer lack of the quantity of evidence that would be needed for an understanding of women's roles in all the very varied surroundings of the early Christian communities; it also requires a literary* analysis of the language practice of the texts themselves. There are those who may feel that, like the 'quest for the historical Jesus',* the search should simply be abandoned; more optimistically, however, it could be argued that recent work in literary theory and gender discourse in other, mainly modern, periods offers more hope of an advance in this area than perhaps at any previous time.

See also **Feminist Interpretation.**

Adela Yarbro Collins (ed.), *Feminist Perspectives on Biblical Scholarship*, 1985; Elisabeth Schüssler Fiorenza, *In Memory of Her*, 1984; Sandra M. Gilbert and Susan Gubar, *No Man's Land. The Place of the Woman Writer in the Twentieth Century, 1. The War of the Words*, 1988, ch. 5; Susanne Heine, *Women and Early Christianity*, 1987; Rosemary R. Ruether and Eleanor McLaughlin (eds), *Women of Spirit*, 1979.

AVERIL CAMERON

Word of God

1. *OT usage*

A useful but generalized way of referring to a small family of expressions and situations in the Hebrew scriptures. Normally construed with the divine name *yhwh* rather than 'God', the commonest relevant Hebrew verbs and nouns are *'mr* (with *'mrh*), *dbr*, *n'm*, and (noun only) *ph/py*. The verbs of 'saying' and 'speaking' have to be mentioned in even a brief account of the related nouns, because 1. talk of God 'saying' occurs so many hundreds of times from the command bringing light into

being (Gen. 1.3), and 2. in several and possibly many cases 'speaking' verbs may have been edited into 'word' nouns at an advanced stage of the production of these writings. In Hebrew, unlike English, this can be achieved in most cases editorially without alteration of the consonantal text.

dbr yhwh (c. 240 ×), regularly rendered 'the word of the Lord', and the still commoner *n'm yhwh* (c. 355×), sometimes rendered 'speech/oracle of the Lord', sometimes 'says the Lord', belong overwhelmingly to the prophetic* literature. The nouns *'mrh* (mostly [c. 30×] of God's word or command) and *'mr* (more commonly of human talking [c. 10× of God]) are found almost exclusively in Pss., Job, and Prov.

The Pentateuch* is almost innocent of these less precise nouns. *dbr yhwh* occurs only in Gen. 15.1,4; Ex. 9.20f.; Num. 15.31; and (?) Deut. 5.5. *n'm yhwh* is used in Gen. 22.16; Num. 14.28 and 7× in Num. 24 in connection with Balaam. *'mr* is found twice in the same chapter, while *'mrh* is paired with 'covenant'* in the poetic Deut. 33.9. However, probably in its later strata, it does use a number of phrases involving *py yhwh*, literally 'Yahweh's mouth', but often rendered his 'command' (Ex. 1×; Lev. 1×; Num. 19×; Deut. 5×). In fact the Pentateuch prefers more precise terms to describe God's purpose for mortals, such as *bryt* (covenant), *mṣwt* (commands), *qwl* (voice), *twrh* (instruction). It also talks very commonly of Yahweh 'speaking' (*dbr*) to individuals – especially to Moses:* Ex. 37×; Lev. 46×; Num. 65×; Deut. 32×; but also (in Gen.) to Noah (1×), Abraham*(8×), Hagar (1×), and Jacob (4×). In most cases within Gen., this divine address refers to the solemn oath to Abraham; in 35.13–15 it underlines the importance of Bethel where the terms of this covenant were repeated to Jacob.

Yahweh's *dbr* (both verb and noun) is used in a similarly focussed way in the narratives of the Former Prophets and Chronicles. The term clusters in the account of Nathan's oracle concerning the houses of David* and Yahweh (II Sam. 7 = I Chron. 17) and the related report of the dedication of Solomon's temple (I Kings 8 = II Chron. 6). Fundamental dynastic issues in Judah are also involved in two further single occurrences which Kings and Chron. share: the revolt of Jeroboam and the warning to the wicked Manasseh, to which II Chron. 23.3 adds the restoration after (queen) Athaliah's usurpation. The final narrative they share, about Jehoshaphat, Micaiah, and common action with Israel in Transjordan, talks of Yahweh speaking – but by Micaiah, rather than to anyone. Similarly most episodes of the unhappy story of (northern) Israel are told (in Kings alone –

Chronicles mentions the north only incidentally), as happening 'according to the word of Yahweh which he spoke by agency of so-and-so (the prophet)'. Finally, *dbr* and also *py yhwh* are used to give authority to a whole miscellany of separate instructions in later editorial interruptions and supplements to the narrative of Joshua, and very occasionally in Samuel and Kings. These varied situations and expressions within Deuteronomy–Kings represent the basis on which scholarly consensus holds that the (so-called) Deuteronomistic History* has at its core a theology of the word of God operative in history. The case is cumulative, yet its foundation may be rather narrow.

It is in the Latter Prophets that the relevant phrases are most at home. *n'm yhwh* is the commonest overall, and its occurrences cluster in Jeremiah, Ezekiel, Amos, and Haggai. Normally it is appended to an individual saying; and even when within, it hardly seems integral to what is said. More than one third of its many occurrences in the Hebrew book of Jeremiah do not appear in the shorter LXX.* How many more, in Jeremiah and elsewhere, also represent late affirmations by the receiving community rather than elements integral to the primitive text, and how often the formula is an editorial device to urge the divine authority of an addition to the text, are matters open to discussion. The sole exception is Isa. 1.24, where its use is introductory, and offers a link with the few cases of *n'm* found outside the Latter Prophets. Some of these, against the traditional Hebrew vocalization but with the LXX throughout the Bible, suggest that *n'm* may often be better treated as a verb.

The Hebrew idioms including *dbr yhwh* ('word of the Lord') also deserve scrutiny. It has already been noted how commonly the Pentateuch reports *wydbr yhwh 'l* [*mšh*] ('and Yahweh spoke to [Moses]'). The fact that this apparently straightforward language is used in only three passages in all the rest of the scriptures demands explanation. In Josh. 20.1 the Mosaic formula is exceptionally but understandably extended to Joshua. The two instances of *wydbr yhwh 'l* in Chron. may offer a clue, for each appears in modified form in Sam.–Kings: in place of 'and Y. spoke to Manasseh' (II, 33.10) II Kings 21.10 reports 'and Y. spoke by his servants the prophets', while in place of the simple 'and Y. spoke to Gad' (I, 21.9) II Sam. 24.11 offers *wdbr yhwh hyh 'l gd hnby'*, 'now the word of the Lord – it came to Gad the prophet'. Both are apparently theological corrections within the text of the Former Prophets in the light of Num. 12.6–8. The evidence we have noted of correction, together with this need to enshrine within Torah itself the distinction between Moses and prophets, entitle us to ask how many of the more than a hundred instances of 'the word of the Lord came to so-and-so' (an odder expression in Hebrew than translations suggest) originally read 'the Lord said to so-and-so'. They may also explain why later tradition preferred to read *n'm* as a noun rather than a verb. The less malleable language of poetry offers little control here. God's *'mrh* or *'mr* is integral to several poetic contexts. Yet the prevalence of *'mrh* in Ps. 119 (19x, elsewhere 18x) may suggest that these nouns too were mostly used in later verse.

All of these expressions draw attention to the fact and not the manner of divine address to intermediaries and representatives. The mystery of the 'how' is most strikingly evoked in Job 4.12–16, within the Bible's most relentless scrutiny of the inadequacy of words. Essentially this OT 'word of God' language notes the imparting of God's decrees, the unveiling of his will; it does not describe mutual divine–human verbal communion.

In later Second Temple Judaism, together with the NT, we see categories from the prophetic literature being generalized to refer to other parts of the scriptures. When all the sacred texts become 'prophetic', then 'prophetic' comes to mean simply 'inspired' or 'authoritative'. In translating these Hebrew scriptures LXX uses, apparently indifferently, the more restricted (and accurate?) *rēma* (word/saying) and the more open *logos* (which also encompasses thought/reasoning).

GRAEME AULD

2. *Subsequent interpretation*

The first section of this article was concerned with the very frequent biblical, and especially OT, usage wherein God is himself pictured as speaking, either directly or through a human intermediary. Sometimes the NT writers echo this usage, referring to the whole body of OT scripture as 'the word of God' as in Mark 7.13, or to 'the word' coming to a prophet, as in the case of John the Baptist* (Luke 3.2). But the NT also testifies to developments in the use of the expression 'the word of God' (or 'of the Lord'). For Mark, notably in the interpretation of the parable* of the sower (4.14–20), 'the word' is virtually synonymous with 'the gospel', that is, the message which Jesus brings. In his parallel Luke expressly says 'the seed is the word of God' (8.11). This usage, extended to signify the message about Jesus, is very common in Acts (11.1; 12.24).

More audaciously, and perhaps reflecting Jewish personification of the word of God (cf. Isa. 55.9–11; Wisdom of Sol. 9.1; 18.14–16; Philo*), the Gospel of John identifies Jesus himself as God's eternal and pre-existent word (*see* **Logos**), though the writer of I John 1.1–4 leaves it unclear whether he maintains this idea or draws back to mean God's message encountered in and through Jesus. The author of Revelation regarded 'the Word of God' as a title for Jesus (19.13). In patristic* theology the Johannine idea of Jesus as God's word was immensely fruitful, thanks largely to the wide range of senses and associations which the term had in the Greek world.

The idea of the whole Bible as 'the word of God' also remained central, and it is scarcely possible to over-estimate the degree to which it was taken as 'sheer words', the very utterance of God. This usage was not without its problems. Sometimes the apparent meaning of the word of God in the Bible was unacceptable, and had to be refined by allegorical* or typological* interpretation; sometimes it was inadequate to the complexities of new situations, as in the controversies surrounding the formation of creeds,* when no purely scriptural expression proved appropriate to express the relation between Jesus and God the Father. There was much anxiety over the introduction into doctrinal statements of non-scriptural terms.

In later centuries, however, the description of the Bible as 'word of God' seems not to have been a matter of controversy. Even at the Reformation,* though there were many disputes concerning the proper understanding of scripture, these arose more because of a concern for the appropriate understanding of the Word of God than because such a description was itself at issue. On the Catholic side scripture could be buttressed by tradition; among Protestants there developed the tradition of a 'canon within the canon' – certain parts of the Bible which were felt particularly to enshrine the Word of God, which had come in effect to mean 'the Christian message'.

Only since the seventeenth century, with the increasing practice of examining and criticizing the Bible in the same way as any other book, has the term itself come to be regarded as problematic. There are, indeed, survivals of pre-critical usage, for example in the liturgy,* both Catholic and Protestant. Thus, the Church of England Alternative Service Book of 1980 has the reader of OT lesson and epistle end with 'This is the word of the Lord', without any indication of the difficulties which might be raised by such an expression; and this practice is found in other liturgies similarly.

Much more controversy has been caused by the demand of some Protestant scholars that the Bible must be understood as the Word of God so as to ensure due respect for its authority.* Probably the fullest and most systematic defence of this viewpoint was put forward by the Princeton scholar of the late nineteenth century, B. B. Warfield. For him 'whatever the Bible may be found to say, that is the Word of God'. There was, that is to say, no limitation to contexts in which God was represented as speaking; and it was primarily through the Bible that the modern believer might obtain access to the word, and therefore the demands, of God. Such a view of the Bible as 'God's word written' naturally carries with it the correlates of inerrancy and infallibility, and is often accompanied by the conviction that it is possible to deduce from the Bible a series of doctrinal propositions, relating to such matters as a substitutionary view of the atonement. This kind of approach, though often dismissed in academic theological circles, is probably very widely held, and the growth of fundamentalist* groups in recent years suggests that it is not a phenomenon that will soon disappear.

Other scholars have held more subtly expressed views of the meaning of 'Word of God'. Barth,* for example, saw the Bible as Word of God in so far as it is a witness to Jesus as God's word, though at times he expressed himself more forcefully: 'We have no reason for not taking the concept "Word of God" in its primary and literal sense. "God's word" means God speaks. "Speaks" is not a symbol' (*CD*, I.1, p. 150). Elsewhere, however, in a famous passage he said that 'God may speak to us through Russian Communism or a flute concerto, a blossoming shrub or a dead dog' – surely a much more symbolic* understanding of God's word.

In the biblical theology* movement God's action in history was often described in terms of his word. (Thus, for example, Eichrodt in his influential *Theology of the Old Testament*.) For the most part, however, attempts to find an understanding of the expression along these lines have been abandoned, and the use of such phrases as 'God's word written' is a clear demarcation between fundamentalists and other Christians. Those who find such an expression unacceptable face the continuing problem of the sense in which they would wish to regard the Bible as in any sense distinctive, beyond being a mere memorial of what the Christian (and Jewish) traditions have believed in the past. Symbolic understandings may no doubt have their part to play, but it is not easy to see how such an understanding can carry the significance that a wide range of Christian tradition has wished to grant to the biblical material.

See also **Authority; Biblical Theology; Inspiration; Oracle; Revelation; Verbal Inspiration.**

A. G. Auld, 'Word of God and Word of Man' in L. M. Eslinger and G. Taylor (eds), *Ascribe to the Lord*, 1988; J. Barr, *Escaping from Fundamentalism*, 1984; J. Barton, *People of the Book?*, 1988; B. S. Childs, *Old Testament Theology in a Canonical Context*, 1985, pp. 133–44; D. H. Kelsey, *The Uses of Scripture in Recent Theology*, 1975; J. Muddiman, *The Bible, Fountain and Well of Truth*, 1983.

R. J. COGGINS

Wrede, W.

William Wrede was born on 10 May 1859, the son of a pastor, in Bücken near Hanover. From 1877 to 1881 he studied theology in Leipzig and Göttingen. After a period of theological college work in Loccum and Göttingen and in the parish ministry, he took his higher degree at Göttingen in 1891 with a thesis on I Clement. He became professor of NT at Breslau in Silesia (now Wroclaw in Poland) from 1893 and died there after a long illness on 23 November 1906. In his time as a student in Leipzig he encountered von Harnack* and in Göttingen Albrecht Ritschl. But he was particularly influenced by a group of roughly contemporary young scholars who came together in Göttingen about 1890 and described themselves as the 'History of Religions school'.* Apart from Wrede, they were Wilhelm Bornemann, Wilhelm Bousset, Albert Eichhorn, Hermann Gunkel, Heinrich Hackmann, Wilhelm Heitmüller, Rudolf Otto, Alfred Rahlfs, Ernst Troeltsch and Johannes Weiss. What they had in common was the idea of producing a thoroughgoing, 'history of religions' understanding of Christianity. That meant on the one hand a historical description of religion rather than a definition in terms of doctrinal concepts; on the other hand, a concern with historical development rather than a static doctrinal view of Christianity. They also had in common the impulse to work not only within the university but also among educated lay people in the church.

Wrede's contribution to the common programme appeared in a set of projects, all produced in sketch-form at the time. Later, however, directly or indirectly, their significance was recognized. Thus, his concise study 'On the task and method of so-called New Testament theology',* 1897, provides to this day the structure for the class of books labelled 'Theology of the NT'. In place of the traditional construction of such works by way of theological concepts, Wrede proposed a scheme in which the development from Jesus through the Palestinian and Hellenistic* primitive church, by way of Paul* and John, led to the emergence of 'the early church'. Wrede himself did not follow up his own suggestion, but it is found in all subsequent books on the 'theology of the NT', in the first place that of Bultmann.*

Wrede's book *Das Messiasgeheimnis in den Evangelien*, 1901 (ET *The Messianic Secret*,* 1971) also remains influential to the present day. In origin, this book is indebted to the historical investigation of Jesus' life as it had been carried out in the nineteenth century. Its effect, however, was to counter the then prevailing source criticism,* which took the view that according to the Synoptic* Gospels* the historical Jesus understood himself as messiah.* According to Wrede, the relevant texts in the Gospels were first formulated in the early Christian church, with a view to legitimating the confession of Jesus as messiah historically as Jesus' own claim. This view was adopted above all in the study of Mark's Gospel and prepared the way for redaction-critical* work.

Wrede's book on Paul, 1904, was written for the wider public of the educated laity. It depicts Paul in the religio-historical setting of syncretistic Judaism. However, it also makes possible the bridging of the gap between religious and dogmatic perspectives on the one hand and historical-theological perspectives on the other. Wrede suggests that for Paul 'theology' is not merely a matter of dogmatic instruction; for example, he understands Paul's teaching on justification as simply polemical – it was developed in the face of Judaism and Jewish Christianity.*

The fact that Wrede's somewhat sparse surviving work remains influential to the present day is the result above all of its acceptance in the theology of Rudolf Bultmann.* The latter's grounding of Christianity in the kerygma* and not in the historical Jesus turned the negative of Wrede's 'messianic secret' into a positive factor. The same was true of Bultmann's decisive representation of Paul as a theologian, not simply a religious 'thinker'. Wrede's work, however, retains its own value, independently of its adoption by Bultmann.

See also **Messianic Secret.**

H. Boers, *What is New Testament Theology?*, 1979, pp. 39–66; W. G. Kümmel, *The New Testament. The History of the Investigation of its Problems*, ET 1973 (see index); G. Lüdemann and M. Schröder, *Die Religionsgeschichtliche Schule in Göttingen*, 1987.

DIETER LÜHRMANN

Writing Materials (Old Testament)

Papyrus. When the Egyptians* began to write, shortly before 3000 BC, stimulated by the invention of writing in Babylonia, they did not make clay tablets from the Nile mud for their writing surfaces, but invented a form of paper made from the papyrus reed growing in the river. The oldest papyrus roll known was found in a First Dynasty tomb (*c.* 3000 B C), where it was left blank for the owner's use in the next world. Sheets of papyrus were made up to 19 inches high and up to 16.5 inches wide. Twenty sheets pasted together side by side made a standard roll, the horizontal fibres of the papyrus being on the inside, the primary writing surface. A roll 19.5 feet long could easily be grasped in the hand. Scrolls were cut in half horizontally, giving a height of 6–8 inches for most purposes. The amount of writing a scroll could contain depended on the scribe's handwriting and arrangement. Extra sheets could be added if the normal twenty gave too short a scroll. The longest papyrus extant is the Great Harris Papyrus of the twelfth century B C, which is 135 feet long.

Israelite scribes,* heavily influenced by Egyptian habits inherited from the Canaanites, wrote with ink on papyrus, the lines running from right to left down the page. Reference in the O T to books should, therefore, be understood as meaning scrolls (e.g. Deut. 28.61; I Kings 11.41). This is clearly seen in the account of king Jehoiakim cutting Jeremiah's scroll to pieces, column by column, as it was read to him (Jer. 36.20ff.). Physical circumstances prevent the survival of papyrus manuscripts* from ancient Israel and Judah, so that recovery of a scroll from the time of the monarchy is unlikely. (One small papyrus sheet of that time was discovered in the unusually arid conditions of a cave near the Dead Sea. It bears traces of an epistle which was mostly washed away so that the papyrus could be re-used for noting the issue of flour to various individuals.) Indisputable evidence that administrative, economic or legal deeds or letters were written on papyrus comes from the hundreds of clay sealings found at Samaria, Jerusalem, Lachish, and other sites. On the front they carry the imprints of seals, on the back imprints made by the fibres of the folded and tied papyrus sheets they secured. Papyrus had to be imported from Egypt and so was not very cheap. Like the Egyptians, Israelite scribes picked up potsherds to use as 'scrap paper' and to carry short, ephemeral messages. These ostraca have often lasted to the present day, several hundred being known, although many are illegible because the ink has been partly rubbed or washed away. The number and distribution of these ostraca in seventh century B C Judah point to a widespread knowledge of writing and reading; there can have been few places without a man who could read and write, even in military outposts.

The predominance of ostraca among ancient Hebrew documents should not lead to a minimizing of the use of papyrus, nor should their almost exclusively mundane content lead to the supposition that Israelite scribes did not write or copy works of literature. A peculiar discovery at Tell Deir Alla in the Jordan valley, possibly biblical Succoth, gives an illustration of what they may have done. Lying face down in the soil were fragments of plaster fallen from the wall of a building which the excavator judged to be a shrine. When lifted, the face of the plaster was seen to have lines of writing on it. Carefully pieced together, the plaster revealed a column of writing with the left and top margins ruled, and the opening words written in red. This text, which relates a story about the seer Balaam, was clearly copied from a book, and the writing on the plaster reproduces a column of a scroll. The script is Aramaic, the language a local dialect, the date about 700 B C.

An analogy from a later date strengthens the argument that papyrus scrolls existed in ancient Israel. At Elephantine in Upper Egypt (by ancient Syene, modern Aswan), where there was a prosperous settlement of Egyptians, Jews and Arameans in the fifth century B C, a quantity of ostraca was found. Written in Aramaic, they bear ephemeral messages, accounts and short memoranda comparable with the older Hebrew ones. Beside these ostraca, the dry soil had preserved scores of papyrus documents. They record sales of property, lawsuits, wills, marriage and divorce agreements, letters – including some to and from the Persian king and his officials – and longer memoranda and accounts. Legal deeds and letters were folded, tied with thread, and secured with a small lump of clay to take a seal's imprint. The Elephantine archives exemplify the use of papyrus for day-to-day business and administration. They also yielded some fragmentary papyrus scrolls containing literary works. These were evidently products of the same scribes in the same community. The most interesting is 'The Words of Ahiqar', a collection of proverbs introduced by a narrative about Ahiqar, an adviser to Sennacherib and Esarhaddon. Versions of this composition circulated widely, the best known being contained in the apocryphal Book of Tobit. Only parts of the Elephantine scroll remain, from 15 or more columns of writing filling 11 sheets of a papyrus roll.

Other scrolls held stories too poorly preserved for understanding. One scroll contained a copy of Darius I's triumphal proclamation known from the trilingual version carved on the cliff at Behistun. This scroll had 11 columns of 17 or 18 lines each, spread over 24 sheets of papyrus, with two of the columns on the back of the scroll. Altogether it was about 8.2 feet long. These papyri from Elephantine happen to preserve the oldest West Semitic book scrolls known at present. They exemplify the style of book current in Ezra's day (cf. Neh. 8), but there can be little doubt that they reflect a form current long before. Indeed, they are a transposition into Aramaic of the common Egyptian book form. Their presence in the Elephantine archives, which may be considered similar to ancient Hebrew archives in other ways, supports the assumption that the Hebrew scribes not only drew up legal documents and wrote letters on papyrus, but that they also wrote and copied books on to papyrus scrolls.

Leather. As well as papyrus, Egyptian scribes used leather scrolls, especially for taking notes in such places as law-courts, for diaries of military campaigns, or for daily accounts. After the information had been transcribed at a central office, the ink could be sponged off and the leather used again. Elsewhere in the Near East leather scrolls are not attested until the sixth century B C. From the fifth century B C come the earliest West Semitic documents on leather, the letters of Arsham, Persian governor of Egypt, sent from Babylonia to his officials in Egypt. There is no reason to think that papyrus was less durable or suitable for book scrolls than leather. It is as strong, smooth and flexible when fresh or kept on a bookshelf; the fragile appearance of papyri in modern collections is the result of the dehydration that has preserved them.

Pen and ink. Egyptian scribes wrote with a reed cut to a point and softened by chewing, and Hebrew ostraca often have strokes showing the fibres of the pen. Ink was made from soot formed into small hard cakes. For headings, instructions to the reader and opening words, red ink was used, the earliest rubrication. Wooden palettes with sunken areas for ink cakes and holders for reed pens exist in Egypt from as early as the Third Dynasty (c. 2600 BC). Already in the First Dynasty the scribe's essential tools, his writing palette and pens, gave the hieroglyphic sign for 'scribe'.

Writing boards. Further away from Egypt papyrus was costly, so scribes wrote cuneiform and other scripts on boards covered with wax. Babylonian texts refer to them from slightly before 2000 BC onwards (Akkadian *lē'um*). One wooden pair, their wax lost from the inner sunken surfaces, has been found in a Late Bronze Age shipwreck at Kaş off the Turkish coast, and fragments of others lay in a well at Nimrud, south of Nineveh. Luxury versions in ivory, made about 700 BC, were found in the same Assyrian well. The twelve ivory boards, originally hinged together, had some pieces of wax still in position, bearing lines of minute cuneiform characters. These boards once carried a divinatory composition

some 6,000 lines long. No one has yet found writing-boards bearing West Semitic texts, but stone reliefs from Syria illustrate their use for Aramaic, and the Bible refers to them in Judah (Isa. 30.8; Hab. 2.2; Hebrew *luaḥ*). Writing could be added at any time on the wax surface, and as easily erased. Babylonian scribes wrote accounts, omens, chronicles, and literature on these tablets, and Hebrew scribes may have done the same. However, papyrus seems to have been their normal material for making books.

The written text. Putting pen to paper, the Hebrew scribe wrote a cursive hand in which each letter was separate. In the Old Hebrew script a small point stood between each word as a divider, a practice inherited from the Canaanite alphabet of the Late Bronze Age, and continued by scribes writing this script in the second and first centuries B C, as the Dead Sea Scrolls* reveal. The Samaritans* maintain it still. In Old Aramaic the majority of inscriptions on stone have no word division, but Aramaic papyrus and leather manuscripts of the Persian period and later regularly have a space after each word. Jewish scribes adopted this custom when they transferred to the Aramaic 'square script' in exilic times, as the Dead Sea Scrolls, again, show. The overwhelming evidence for word division in the scribal traditions which produced the copies of the books of the O T makes proposals for re-dividing the letters of the Hebrew text to reconstruct the sense implausible. The supposition that Hebrew was written continuously, as Greek was, is denied by the facts. A few examples of wrong division can be accepted as normal scribal errors (e.g. Amos 6.12 reading *bbqrym* as *bbqr ym*, see RSV, NEB). Where the Septuagint* has been taken to reflect a continuously written Hebrew text, careless or deliberate misreading may be suspected, or perhaps an unconscious treatment of the Hebrew as if it were Greek by Greek-educated Jews.

Ends of sentences were not marked. In Aramaic and square Hebrew manuscripts from the fifth century B C and later, larger sense units were distinguished by leaving the remainder of the closing line blank. Shorter sense units, such as the proverbs of Ahiqar, were sometimes separated by a sign like an *aleph*.

Capacity of scrolls. Scrolls did not have title pages, although a sheet or column was left empty at the beginning to avoid damage to the start of the text. Occasionally the title would be added at the end of the work. In theory scrolls could reach any length, as Egyptian examples already cited show. Among the Dead Sea Scrolls, the Temple Scroll and the Isaiah A Scroll are the longest, 28.7 feet and 24 feet respectively. The former contained nineteen leather sheets sewn together, with sixty-six columns of writing, the latter ten sheets with fifty-four columns. The Isaiah Scroll is 10.25 inches high. Greek literary papyri from the beginning of the era include one 35 feet long, holding books 21–23 of Homer's *Iliad*, others of 19 or 20 feet. It is estimated that Matthew, Luke or Acts would need a scroll 32–35 feet long. A codex in Berlin contains Gen. 1–38.5 and it is suggested that was the extent of a scroll from which it was copied. These figures, and other calculations, demonstrate that even the longest of the OT books in Hebrew and Greek – Isaiah, Deuteronomy, the Twelve Minor Prophets – could each fit on a single long scroll. A complete OT in the first century would have needed a series of papyrus or leather scrolls. We know from the Dead Sea Scrolls that both materials were acceptable for holding books of scripture at that period.

See also **Manuscripts; Writing and Transmitting Texts.**

Jaroslav Černý, *Paper and Books in Ancient Egypt*, 1952; Alan R. Millard, '"Scriptio Continua" in Early Hebrew: Ancient Practice or Modern Surmise?', *JSS* XV, 1970, pp. 2–15; Donald J. Wiseman, 'Books in the Ancient Near East and in the Old Testament', *Cambridge History of the Bible* I, 1970, pp. 30–47.

                                        A. R. MILLARD

Writing and Transmitting Texts

By the time of David * and Solomon writing had been used in the Near East for over two thousand years. From Sumer the idea of writing spread up the Euphrates through Syria and on to Egypt * before 3000 BC. While the Egyptian scripts, the formal hieroglyphic and the cursive hieratic, were tied closely to the Egyptian language, speakers of several different languages adopted the Sumerian cuneiform writing system in a principally syllabic form. Among them were the Semitic Babylonians, then Hurrians, Elamites, Hittites, Canaanites and Urartians. Cuneiform reached its apogee during the second millennium BC as the means of communication for diplomacy and trade throughout the Fertile Crescent. Rulers of Canaanite cities wrote to the Pharaoh, their overlord, in Babylonian, and he replied in kind. The ruins of the 'heretic pharaoh' Akhenaten's short-lived capital at El-Amarna yielded letters from this correspondence. With them were relics of the scribes' * education in the form of Babylonian works of literature used as exercises in writing and language, lists of Sumerian and Babylonian words, and a 'dictionary' of Egyptian words with their Babylonian equivalents.

The training of scribes in cuneiform followed a similar pattern everywhere, and some of the text-books were universal, so that incomplete copies found in Babylonia can be restored from duplicates found in north Syria. Evidence of a scribal school was uncovered in the ruins of Late Bronze Age Aphek (Ras el-'Ain) in Canaan, with a Sumerian–Akkadian–Canaanite word-list.

Babylonian influence from the north brought the traditions of cuneiform writing into Canaan; Egyptian influence and military conquest brought the hieroglyphic and hieratic scripts from the south-west. Local princes at Byblos aped the fashions of Egypt in the monuments they had erected during the eighteenth century BC. Official buildings of the Late Bronze Age at Beth-Shan, Jaffa and Megiddo had entrances graced with hieroglyphic inscriptions, and the ubiquitous scarab often carried the hieroglyphs of a royal name. In fact, during the second millennium BC the Egyptian scripts had a higher profile in Canaan than the Babylonian. Only the perishable quality of the normal Egyptian writing material, papyrus, as opposed to the more durable clay tablets, distorts the picture. Officials of the pharaonic administration used the hieratic script as freely in Canaan as they did in Egypt. Ink-written tax receipts on potsherds from Lachish and Tell esh-Shari'a are the meagre remnants of their labours.

Familiarity with these two major scripts and, probably, dissatisfaction with their complicated systems, stimulated the invention of several alternatives in the second millennium BC. Best known are the Hittite hieroglyphs, the Byblos syllabary, and the Cretan scripts which culminated in 'Linear B'. One other arose at this time eclipsing all others, the alphabet. By 1000 BC the letters of the alphabet had become fairly stable in shape and stance. It was the ideal writing system for the newly emergent states of the Early Iron Age, the Aramaean and Phoenician, the Israelite, Ammonite, Edomite and Moabite kingdoms; the cuneiform and Egyptian systems were no longer used there.

Writing in Ancient Israel and adjacent states. Discoveries of Hebrew texts on stone, metal, and pottery suffice to prove that writing was widely known in the days of the kings, even if the number who could actually read and write was small. Inscriptions on stone range from the record of the digging of the Siloam Tunnel, engraved on the rock by artificial light, in a fine cursive hand, shortly before 700 BC, to notices scratched on tomb walls which are almost illegible (although one, at Khirbet el-Qom, is noteworthy as it may mention YHWH and his Asherah). Small fragments from Jerusalem * and Samaria point to the former existence of other texts on stone slabs, perhaps comparable with the Moabite Stone from Dibon. Numerous ostraca demonstrate clerical abilities in accountancy and letter writing while inscribed seal-stones and their imprints on clay sealings show that hundreds of men accepted the use of signets which bore only their names as their signs of authority or ownership. Most writing was done on papyrus or on waxed tablets, which are lost to us (*see* **Writing Materials**).

A similar situation prevailed in adjacent realms. More royal inscriptions on stone survive, perhaps by accident, some of a few lines, some of dozens (e.g. the Moabite Stone, *c.* 840 B C, the stele of Zakkur of Hamath, *c.* 780 B C, texts of the kings of Byblos, tenth century B C). On the other hand, fewer ostraca and seals have come to light. However, the range and variety of writing on metal, ivory, stone and pottery exhibit an equal readiness to use the alphabet. Carvings from Aramaean and Assyrian palaces which depict scribes with writing boards and papyrus scrolls illustrate what has been lost.

While the engravers of the longer texts, notably the Aramaic treaties from Sefire, may have worked from drafts on papyrus or waxed tablets, these are all unique texts, not intended for later reproduction.

Copying and transmitting texts. Texts that may be termed 'traditional', composed in one generation and copied over many, are all but non-existent in manuscripts* of the Israelite monarchy period in the Levant. A tomb in the Hinnom Valley contained two tiny silver sheets incised with forms of the Priestly Blessing from Numbers 6, in Hebrew script of about 600 B C. Made as amulets, they attest the copying of sacred formulae in Judah. Another religious text is the inscribed plaster from Tell Deir Alla, a century earlier, almost certainly copied from a scroll written in a local dialect. A lower level of copying appears on jars from a caravanserai in north-eastern Sinai, Kuntillet 'Ajrud. Various graffiti include alphabets and the opening phrases of a letter, exercises, it may be, of an apprentice about 800 B C. (Other texts from the site have religious importance.)

Examples of copyists' work from the pre-exilic period are readily available only from Mesopotamia and Egypt. Although these cultures used different languages and scripts, there is no reason why basic scribal attitudes should have varied.

Accurate copying was a major aim in training scribes. Faulty copies could be misleading or dangerous then as now; a word omitted may upset the sense. Reproducing older texts was one means of inculcating accuracy, and to that exercise are owed many surviving Sumerian and Babylonian literary works. Scribes knew their fallibility, so they devised conventions to overcome it. In cuneiform texts every tenth line of a long composition might be marked, the number of lines noted column by column, the total given at the end, to guard against omission or repetition. A colophon at the end may give the title or first line of the work, the number of lines and tablets, the name of the copyist and sometimes of one who collated the text, and the date. When a work was copied from small tablets on to a large one, the points where the exemplars ended might be noted. If a copyist could fit two short lines of his exemplar into one on his tablet, he might mark the division with a colon. The effects of this care are evident when manuscripts of the same work prepared over many centuries are compared. Scribes copied Hammurabi's 'Laws' for a thousand years after they were issued, with only minor variations. A Sumerian poem survives in 54 manuscripts, none complete, copied between 1800 and 500 B C. In its 207 lines the modern editor has noted 64 variants, of which only 12 alter the sense of a line, but not of the whole text. Copyists in Babylonia and in Egypt might note where their exemplars were defective by the words 'broken' or 'missing' without trying to complete the texts. Mistakes were corrected by obliterating and writing over, or, in Egypt, by writing above the line.

Editors and revisers. Besides texts copied over centuries with little variation are others which were changed extensively. Manuscripts* of the Babylonian Epic of Gilgamesh written a millennium apart present the same composition, yet sections of the earlier copies do not stand in the later, and vice versa. Speeches are attributed to different characters, some of the sentiments altered, lines of poetry frequently expanded in the later version. Modern scholars ascribe the re-casting of material five centuries old to a scribe working late in the second millennium B C whom later colophons name. Some other literary compositions suffered similar revision, some underwent smaller changes, some endured unchanged. Royal 'annals' of Sennacherib and Ashurbanipal (seventh century B C), preserved in numerous versions produced at intervals during their reigns, allow recensional variations to be observed in detail. Earlier campaign reports were compressed or even omitted as later ones were added, two incidents relating to one person might be joined, although other events occurred between them, and the role of the king could be increased. The resulting compositions, however, were acknowledged as fresh ones by their dated colophons. It is important to notice that these extensive changes were deliberate, creating new texts which were then copied. It is even more important to realize that it is only when two copies of different periods or recensions are available that the changes can be seen. They do not fall into predictable patterns.

Biblical scholars frequently invoke the work of glossators to account for explanatory or seemingly redundant phrases (e.g. 'Bela, that is Zoar', Gen. 14.12). Such glosses were awkward to add to old clay tablets, and they are rare in Egyptian papyri. Contrariwise, they do occur in original, unique documents where they are part of the author's, or first scribe's, composition, plainly not added later (the 'Canaanite' glosses in the El-Amarna Letters are well-known examples). Babylonian scribes separated these words from the main text by a stroke. Similarly, scribes of the seventh and sixth centuries BC took care to avoid received texts being confused with their commentaries* and interpretations, even when copied on to the same tablet, and to note variant readings in their exemplars, marking them 'alternatively'.

The biblical text. The oldest biblical manuscripts, the Dead Sea Scrolls* (second century BC to first century AD), exemplify all the common copyists' errors and attempts at correction. Where words or sentences are written between lines and down the margin, a later copyist might introduce them into his text at the wrong point. The Scrolls attract especial attention for their variations from the later, standard text, the Masoretic.* Many are minor variants of types usual in the transmission of traditional compositions. Some are certainly interpretative, implying that the copyists had a freedom not apparent in the ancient manuscripts described above. Available publications show that each biblical manuscript is unique in this respect, indicating that these are not to be treated as straightforward copies but as individual products based on a recognized text.

Occasionally the work of the Hebrew copyist can be checked on small points. The transmission of foreign personal names in the Bible is notable. Here the copyists win respect for preserving Assyrian and Persian forms, meaningless to them, in consonantal shapes accurately reflecting their proper pronunciation.

Jer. 36, describing the secretary writing the scroll at the prophet's dictation, is the most explicit account of a book being written. Cuneiform tablets also witness the immediate recording and transmission to the palace of oracles concerning the king (cf. Amos 7.10ff.), and some Assyrian tablets are collections of several oracles,* each with its speaker's name attached. Even if most people learnt from oral instruction, writing was available and used throughout Israel's history, and so could provide authoritative sources. A survey of surviving documents from all over the Ancient Near East* demonstrates that scribes copied literature almost continuously. There is no support for the supposition, associated with the Scandinavian* 'Oral Tradition' school, that literature was only put into writing at moments of crisis such as the Babylonian attacks on Judah.

Ancient examples of literary works copied and transmitted deserve more attention from biblical scholars than they have received, for they supply the only objective comparisons for reconstructing the processes of Hebrew book production in OT times.

See also **Ancient Near Eastern World; Writing Materials.**

John C. L. Gibson, *Textbook of Syrian Semitic Inscriptions* I–III, 1971–82; Alan R. Millard, 'In Praise of Ancient Scribes', *The Biblical Archaeologist* XLV, 1982, pp. 143–53; Jeffrey H. Tigay, *The Evolution of the Gilgamesh Epic*, 1982.

A. R. MILLARD

Writings

The Hebrew Bible is divided into three sections: the Torah (Law) (Genesis-Deuteronomy), which is the core and the most revered part of the tradition in Judaism; the Prophets (Joshua-II Kings and Isaiah-Malachi), primarily understood as commenting upon the Torah; and the Writings. This title is a literal translation of its Hebrew name *Kethubim*; the description *Hagiographa* (Greek, 'holy writings') is also sometimes found.

This collection is much more heterogeneous than the others, both in form and subject-matter; its order varies somewhat in different manuscripts,* but the Psalms are almost always found first. There follow Proverbs and Job, then the five *Megilloth* or Festal Scrolls, which came to be interpreted in the context of different Jewish festivals from the early Middle Ages onwards: Song of Songs (Passover), Ruth (Pentecost), Lamentations (the 9th of Ab, when Jerusalem was destroyed), Ecclesiastes (Tabernacles), and Esther (Purim). Finally come Daniel, Ezra–Nehemiah (regarded as one work until the Middle Ages) and the books of Chronicles.

A few points are worthy of note with regard to the way in which the works which comprise the Writings have been understood. The reference to 'the Law, the Prophets and the Psalms' at Luke 24.44 has sometimes been taken as implying the existence of a collection of Writings referred to only by their first work. Again it is striking that Daniel is included here rather than among the Prophets, as understood by much Christian tradition (Matt. 24.15) and perhaps also at Qumran (*see* **Dead Sea Scrolls**). Finally, the placing of

Ezra–Nehemiah before Chronicles has evoked much discussion, particularly because the closing words of Chronicles are the opening words of Ezra; it might be that Ezra–Nehemiah came to be included in the canon first because there was no parallel elsewhere to the events there described, but if this is so it is difficult to perceive a reason for the later addition of Chronicles.

Much attention has been given to the date of the completion of the canon* of the OT, but a new dimension has been added to the argument in recent years by the suggestion made by Barton that there was no discernible separate category known as the Writings in the early years of our era. The expression 'the Law and the Prophets' is found on several occasions in the NT (e.g. Matt. 22.40), and it has commonly been held that this implied either an imprecise manner of description or that the third part of the OT did not reach its final form until the Synod of Jamnia at the end of the first century AD. But there are also references which seem to include passages from the Writings within the Prophets (e.g. Acts 2.30, where David,* envisaged as the author of Ps. 16, is described as a prophet) and it may well be that a three-fold grouping was not formally established until a later period. This point is of some importance in interpretation, for some writers (e.g. Beckwith) have claimed that the three-fold division was in fact established much earlier than the deliberations at Jamnia, and that a three-fold canon forms part of the background against which the NT took shape.

See also **Canon.**

J. Barton, *Oracles of God*, 1986; id., '"The Law and the Prophets": Who are the Prophets?', *OTS* 23, 1984, pp. 1–18; R. T. Beckwith, *The Old Testament Canon of the New Testament Church*, 1985; K. Koch, 'Is Daniel also among the Prophets?' in J. L. Mays and P. J. Achtemeier (eds), *Interpreting the Prophets*, 1987, pp. 237–48.

R. J. COGGINS

Zechariah

The observations on the change in critical attention to and appreciation of the post-exilic prophets made in the article on Haggai* apply here. Zechariah also fits into the same historical context as Haggai, the two prophets being contemporaries according to the dates given in the books. The core of Zechariah's message is contained in eight 'visions of the night' together with accompanying oracles* found in chs 1–8 of the book. While many details of the visions are obscure their general message is clear. They assure the people of Judah, with many echoes of the words of Ezekiel, that God is about to return to his people, to over-throw their oppressors, bring back their exiles, cleanse the community and dwell in their midst in Jerusalem, granting the prosperity of a new age. Most critical interest has centred on the form of the visions, their relation to the oracles and the 'genre'* of chs 1–8, whether it be 'prophecy'* or some early form of 'apocalyptic'.*

Pre-exilic prophets had received 'visions' but it is in Ezek. 40–48 that we encounter visions so mysterious as to need detailed heavenly explanation. Later, Daniel speaks of 'visions of the night' (7.2) which need an angelic interpreter. This has led some to argue that the book of Zechariah approaches 'apocalyptic'. G. von Rad detected another element of apocalyptic in the visions in that they see events on earth as projections of what is happening in the heavenly realms. However, 'apocalyptic' is a slippery word, and others have suggested that one influence is Ezekiel's picture of the prophet as 'watchman' and the soteriological* theme of deliverance coming in the morning. Others have found closer affinities between Zechariah and the pre-exilic prophets. P. D. Hanson (*The Dawn of Apocalyptic*, 1975), far from finding Zechariah as in any way an 'apocalyptic' prophet, saw him, with Ezekiel, as standing in a theocratic tradition whose main interest was the re-establishment of the temple and Zadokite priesthood. His view of God's action was based therefore very much within this world's history, far removed from the 'other-worldly' hopes of apocalyptic.

The most detailed study of the oracles accompanying the visions is that by A. Petitjean (1969). Petersen (1985) believes that the oracles are an early form of exegesis* of the visions, while C. L. and E. M. Meyers (1987) see the hand of Zechariah more directly in their composition.

There is no clear source, like the 'editorial framework' in the book of Haggai which can clearly be seen to be secondary, but some believe that the vision in ch. 3 is later (it is distinguished from the others by form-critical* features), with the prominence it gives to Joshua and the priestly line. These seem to assume earlier royal functions and either to guarantee or to be themselves the 'branch' of messianic* hope now no longer identified with Zerubbabel (cf. 6.9–14). Zerubbabel (the governor) is described only as temple builder in an oracle which is clearly inserted into its present context (4.6b–10a). The opening section of 1.1–6 is somewhat akin to the description of the response to Haggai's preaching (1.12–14) and has led C. L. and E. M. Meyers to the conclusion that Haggai and Zech. 1–8 belong closely together. Others have noted the close parallel to the words attributed to Hezekiah by the Chronicler (II Chron. 30.6–9). This, together with teaching on the nature of true fasting in 7.4–7; 8.18f. (cf. Isa. 58.1–14), the catechetical-like summaries of the ethical* teachings of the pre-exilic prophets (7.8–14; 8.14–16), echoes of earlier oracles of Zechariah (8.1–3,7; cf. 1.14; 1.10; 2.6f.) and Haggai (8.9–13; cf. Hagg. 2.4; 2.15–19), together with re-affirmation of his more 'universalistic' outlook (8.20–23; cf. 2.10), has led them to deduce that these represent 'exposition' of Zechariah's and Haggai's prophecy in the circles which handed down the prophetic teaching in the Second Temple period. C. L. and E. M. Meyers are the latest of those who have argued that all this suggests that Haggai and Zech. 1–8 have been compiled as one work, either by Zechariah or by someone close to his time and outlook.

The belief that chs 9–14 of the book are from another and later author is as old as the seventeenth century AD and today may be said to be a commonplace in OT scholarship. They contain nothing akin to the oracles of chs 1–8, nothing of the building of the temple, no reference to the historical period of Darius I and only in 11.4–17 does the prophet speak in the first person. I have elsewhere suggested that there is a certain continuity between the two parts of the book (arguments summarized in Mason, 1977, pp. 78f.), just as some scholars have seen continuity between 'First' and 'Second' Isaiah. This later material may have emerged from those circles which preserved and passed on the Zechariah tradition, and this would account for the two sections being combined in one book.

The chapters present us with a wide variety of prophetic material of an extremely difficult nature which, not surprisingly, has yielded a great number of differing interpretations. They consist of a number of eschatological* oracles in 9.1–11.3 (omitting 10.1–3a), which include an advance of God on Jerusalem* whose traditional enemies he slays (9.1–8); the coming to Zion of the 'king' (9.9f.) and a number of detached oracles taking up earlier prophetic themes of hope (9.10–11.3). Indeed much of the material in chs 9–14 echoes and evokes earlier prophetic literature. Another section (12.1–13.6) envisages a siege against Jerusalem which God defeats, and this leads to a general repentance by all sections of the community from the Davidic house down leading to a divine cleansing. An even starker picture is painted in ch. 14 of the ordeals which must precede final deliverance, with God himself bringing the nations against Jerusalem. Only when half the citizens have been taken into exile will God appear on the Mount of Olives (as Ezekiel had predicted, Ezek. 43.1–4; cf. 11.25). Then God will reign as universal king, Jerusalem will be elevated, its enemies destroyed and all peoples who are left (even Egypt) will come annually to celebrate the Feast of Tabernacles in a purified Jerusalem. Interspersed are several 'controversy' passages which in various ways attack false leaders of the community as 'shepherds' in the manner of Jeremiah and Ezekiel (10.1–3a; 11.4–17; 13.7–9).

Early Christian exegesis built on the NT allusions to these chapters in the Gospels,* where such passages as 9.9f., 11.12f., and 13.7 are seen as predictions of events in the life, suffering and death of Jesus, to interpret them as 'messianic prophecies'. With the rise of historical criticism,* which sought the literal* meaning of the text in its original historical context, that option was no longer open. Since then, critical discussion has centred on, first, the unity of chs 9–14. Some have seen a tightly-knit chiastic pattern to the chapters which they thus saw as a close literary unity. Others have said resignedly that we have here only 'a loose collection of eschatological oracles'. Many have argued that the new heading 'An oracle' at 12.1 (it occurs also at 9.1 and Mal. 1.1), together with a more 'apocalyptic' outlook means that chs 12–14 are later than chs 9–11, and some therefore speak of a 'Trito-Zechariah'. The occurrence in both sections of the controversy passages and a continuing dependence on earlier biblical material have led some to reject this. A second issue for interpretation has been the attempt to date the material on the basis of supposed historical allusions to be found in it. The supposed military campaign featured in 9.1–8, the references to the 'Greeks' in 9.13 and to the 'three shepherds' slain in one month (11.8) have been used in this way. Results have varied so widely, however, as to cast doubts on the legitimacy of the method. Others believe we often have here 'symbolic'* allusions comparable to the description of Rome as 'Babylon'* in Rev. 14.8, a 'typical' enemy of God's people from the past. It is argued that we have also deliberate 'exegesis'* of earlier biblical material, relating it to the time of the writer or the community from which these chapters come.

Some scholars have interpreted much in these chapters cultically,* believing that behind much of the language and symbolism lie echoes of the 'Enthronement Festival' which some have argued took place in the temple of pre-exilic Jerusalem and was associated with the Feast of Tabernacles (or 'Booths') in the autumn (e.g. 14.16). This involved the king* as representative of God and the community in ritual combat with and victory over the forces of darkness (e.g. 9.1–10), celebrated and affirmed the kingship of God over the forces of chaos as at Creation* (e.g. 14.9) and secured again for another year the vital gift of rain (14.17). Again, it has been suggested that the only way to see these chapters as a thematic unity is to take them as the work of a prophetic group in the Zechariah tradition who became increasingly at odds with the official Judaism of their time and who see the future in increasingly stark and 'other-worldly' terms. It has to be confessed, however, that the interpretation of these chapters must always remain tentative.

P. R. Ackroyd, *Exile and Restoration*, 1968; J. Baldwin, *Haggai, Zechariah, Malachi*, 1972; R. J. Coggins, *Haggai, Zechariah, Malachi*, 1987; R. A. Mason, *The Books of Haggai, Zechariah, and Malachi*, 1977; R. L. Smith, *Micah – Malachi*, 1984.

REX MASON

Zephaniah

Since the rise of critical study, Zephaniah has received far less attention than many prophets,* but, as with other prophetic collections, increasing regard has recently been paid to the early stages of interpretation embodied in the redactional shaping of the book itself. This has come to be viewed more positively than by earlier scholars who were interested only in seeking 'authentic' prophetic words. The relating of prophecies of divine judgment to those of future salvation, and the varying ways in which their eschatological* import came to be grasped, appear particularly significant, especially given Zephaniah's awe-inspiring focus on the coming 'Day of Yahweh'.

Outside the book itself, interpretation of Zephaniah perhaps begins with the striking 'exegetical-homiletical embellishment' (M. Fishbane) and reapplication of elements of 3.1–8 in Ezek. 22.23–31, and with the use of 1.18 in Ezek. 7.19, probably editorial, but a pointer to Ezekiel's own reception of the motif of the approaching day of Yahweh's wrath from Zephaniah and elsewhere. The Qumran (*see* **Dead Sea Scrolls**) commentaries* (fragments 1Q15, 4Q170) presumably offered eschatological interpretation in relation to contemporary events, and the *Apocalypse of Zephaniah* (first century BC or AD?) understands the prophet himself as an apocalyptic* visionary, a seer of heavenly glory and of the final punishment of sinners. In the NT, use of phrases or motifs in contexts simultaneously eschatological and christological* occurs at Rev. 6.17 (probably Zeph. 1.14, 18; and Zeph. 3.8 in Rev. 14.5?) and Matt. 13.41, while the quotation in John 12.15 seems to correlate and unify the salvation oracles of Zeph. 3.16 and Zech. 9.9 in application to Jesus' entry into Jerusalem, and perhaps to point to him as 'the king of Israel' of Zeph. 3.15 (cf. John 12.13).

There are several patristic commentaries, of which the most notable and extensive are those by the Antiochene* Theodore of Mopsuestia, Theodoret, Cyril of Alexandria, and Jerome. These in various ways and proportions offer 'Christianizing' interpretation alongside attempts at broadly literal*–historical reading. With them may be set Augustine's* finding reference to Jesus' resurrection* in the divine 'rising' of 3.8 and his understanding of 3.9–12 in terms of the Jewish remnant who have believed in Christ (*City of God* XVIII, 33). The mediaeval Christian hymn* *Dies irae*, many times translated, drew inspiration from Zeph. 1.14ff., which it interprets apocalyptically as describing the last judgment.

Luther* found in Zephaniah both direct announcement of the forthcoming Babylonian exile and the promise of restoration for the remnant of returnees. He understands 3.1–5 to be speaking of the continuing sinfulness of the restored community; but Zephaniah's eye is fixed ultimately on the gathering of a new people (3.12ff.) in the coming kingdom of Christ, of which Luther finds here the clearest prophecies in all the minor prophets. The idolatry of Zephaniah's day, and the humiliating circumstances of true believers, are made the basis for comment on Luther's own time. This interpretation coheres well with Luther's overall view of prophecy. Calvin,* as usual, attends carefully to the exegetical* problems, and finds that in his own dark age Zephaniah brought a message of hope for the church – that is, for God's faithful people of all times. This highly sensitive theological interpretation is much concerned to show how the change of addressees gives a key to its understanding: the promises are granted to the faithful remnant only, to comfort them in the suffering they too must share.

Most nineteenth-century historical-critical* studies of Zephaniah accepted that the prophet had worked in Josiah's reign (1.1) immediately preceding the reformation of 621 BC (perhaps influencing and supporting it), and often found the contemporary impulse for his work in the supposed Scythian invasion of Palestine; this latter view, expressed for example by H. Ewald, continued to have supporters into the twentieth century (cf. H. H. Rowley, *Men of God*, 1963, pp. 146–8), but the evidence for such an 'invasion' and the linking of Zephaniah with it is now commonly regarded as very problematic.

With the growing stress on the prophets as addressing their contemporary situation with the threat of judgment and the demands of Yahweh's ethical will, Zephaniah was perhaps somewhat neglected. E. B. Pusey's commentary (1860) is concerned to rebut the Scythian hypothesis and find direct supernatural prediction of judgment at the hands of Babylon, and presents very direct Christian spiritualizing throughout. With this may be contrasted F. D. Maurice's moving interpretation of the preacher of righteousness and pointer to the universal scope of God's kingdom of peace. In Germany, a series of scholars (notably B. Stade, F. Schwally, K. Marti) came to argue for more thoroughgoing critical analyses which, while differing in detail, commonly saw large parts of the foreign nation oracles in 2.4–15, and the bulk of ch. 3 as secondary, post-exilic additions. British interpreters remained more cautious: A. B. Davidson (1896) and S. R. Driver (1906) in their commentaries were broadly committed to the unity of the book, apart from possible small additions in chs 2 and 3. G. A. Smith's widely-used study (1898), with its eloquent exposition and moral application, was a little less conservative.

Though most scholars have certainly come to see elements of the material as later than Zephaniah's own time, the increasing emphasis on sympathetic and careful attention to the work as a theological whole, in which the processes of interpretation are already woven into its redactional formation and texture, may point us towards more critical and fruitful engagement with it. Most have continued to adhere to a pre-621 date for Zephaniah's preaching (contrast J. P. Hyatt), and consideration has more recently been given to its possible social location and role in respect of contending factions in Jerusalem in the late Assyrian period (R. R. Wilson); the view that Zephaniah may himself have prophesied in quite direct connection with the temple cult* and the New Year festival (J. H. Eaton, A. S. Kapelrud) remains, however, very uncertain. But we must also consider the socio-religious role of the book itself, as a written work within a developing corpus of authoritative prophetic scripture in the exilic and post-exilic Jewish communities. Major attempts at philological* elucidation of the book (L. Sabottka, 1972) and form-structural analysis (H. Irsigler, 1977) have met only a limited reception. The detailed redactional study by G. Krinetzki (1977) essays a fairly precise historical locating of the many smaller units he detects, and discerns two significant redactional levels. Along with W. Rudolph's characteristically solid and cautious commentary, this may form a useful basis for further work. We may consider e.g. the role of the superscription; the character and origin of the 'eschatological' language; and the significance of the 'remnant'. Links between Zephaniah and earlier prophets, especially Amos and Isaiah, have often been noted, and sometimes made the basis for disparaging comments about his lack of 'originality'. But investigation of the precise scope and nature of such 'links' may well provide clues to interpretation. It is perhaps doubtful whether squeezing the book into a 'three-part eschatological structure' (as e.g. G. Fohrer, O. Kaiser) can do justice to the complex redactional patterning of the material, yet we may certainly seek an approach which is concerned to interpret the work as a literary whole, paying heed to the features which give it coherence. When we seek to take into account the profound theological issues and affirmations embodied in it, it is salutary to ask whether we (whoever 'we' are!) do in fact know how to read such a prophetic book.

Commentaries by J. H. Eaton (Torch, 1961), E. Achtemeier (Interpretation, 1986), K. Elliger (Das Alte Testament Deutsch, ⁶1967), W. Rudolph (Kommentar zum Alten Testament XIII/3, 1975). B. S. Childs, *Introduction to the Old Testament as Scripture*, 1979, pp. 457–62.

EDWARD BALL

SELECT INDEX

Neither this nor the following index of biblical references makes any claim to exhaustive coverage. Their purpose is to offer the reader guidance where information about important individuals and topics not covered in the body of the book may be found, and where particular biblical passages receive significant discussion.

INDEX OF BIBLICAL REFERENCES

References are not normally made to passages from a biblical book cited in the article on that book.